SHERIFF COURT PRACTICE

SHERIFF COURT PRACTICE

by

I. D. Macphail, Q.C., M.A., LL.B., LL.D.
Sheriff of Lothian and Borders at Edinburgh

SECOND EDITION
Volume 1

Edited by

C. G. B. Nicholson, Q.C., M.A., LL.B.
Sheriff Principal of Lothian and Borders

and

A. L. Stewart, Q.C., B.A., LL.B.
Sheriff of Tayside, Central and Fife at Dundee

with contributions by

P. R. BEAUMONT, LL.B., LL.M.
Professor of European Union and Private International Law, University of Aberdeen

M. G. CLARKE, Q.C., M.A., LL.B. (Hons)
Advocate

J. M. S. HORSBURGH, Q.C., M.A., LL.B.
Sheriff of Lothian and Borders at Edinburgh

A. LOTHIAN, M.A., LL.B.
Sheriff of Lothian and Borders at Edinburgh

P. G. B. MCNEILL, Q.C., M.A., LL.B., Ph.D.
Formerly Sheriff of Lothian and Borders at Edinburgh

G. MAHER, LL.B., B.LITT.
Professor of Law, University of Strathclyde

N. M. P. MORRISON, Q.C.
Sheriff of Lothian and Borders at Edinburgh

D. J. RISK, Q.C., M.A., LL.B.
Sheriff Principal of Grampian, Highland and Islands

J. M. SCOTT, M.A. (Cantab)
Advocate

D. B. SMITH, M.A., LL.B.
Sheriff of North Strathclyde at Kilmarnock

C. N. STODDART, LL.B., LL.M. (McGill), Ph.D., S.S.C.
Sheriff of Lothian and Borders at Edinburgh

A. B. WILKINSON, Q.C., M.A., LL.B.
Sheriff of Lothian and Borders at Edinburgh

Published under the auspices of
SCOTTISH UNIVERSITIES LAW INSTITUTE LTD

EDINBURGH
W. GREEN
1998

First published 1988
Second edition 1998
Reprinted 1999
Reprinted 2001
Reprinted 2003

Published in 1998 by W. Green & Son Limited of
21 Alva Street,
Edinburgh, EH2 4PS

Typeset by Hewertext Composition Services
Edinburgh

Printed in Great Britain by Bookcraft, Bath

No natural forests were destroyed to make this product; only farmed timber was used and replanted

A CIP catalogue record of this book is available from the British Library

ISBN 0 414 01218 6

PREFACE TO SECOND EDITION

When the first edition of Sheriff Macphail's scholarly work on Sheriff Court Practice was published in 1988 it filled an immense gap in Scottish legal literature since, as he observes in the Preface to that edition, some 40 years had by then passed since the publication of Sheriff Dobie's work on the same subject. Almost at once "Macphail", as the book quickly came to be known, became a standard text in advocates' and solicitors' libraries, in the sheriff courts, in the Court of Session, and even on occasions in the House of Lords; and it was regarded, rightly, as an authoritative and reliable source of information and guidance on most matters relating to civil practice and procedure in the sheriff courts.

However, in the 10 years which have elapsed since the publication of that first edition substantial changes both in substantive law and in the day-to-day practice of the courts have taken place with the consequence that a growing need was seen for a new, updated, edition of "Macphail". Sheriff Macphail himself did not feel disposed once again to take on the immense task of preparing such a large volume for publication, and instead the Scottish Universities Law Institute invited a number of contributors to undertake the revision of one or more chapters each. At the same time Sheriff Principal Nicholson was invited to assume the general editorship of the new edition. Some time thereafter, and at Sheriff Principal Nicholson's request, Sheriff A. L. Stewart, Q.C. was invited to become joint general editor.

Thereafter, some of the contributors who had originally been approached found themselves unable to undertake the commitment, and had to withdraw. In due course they were replaced by others including, in some instances, ourselves. A full list of those who did contribute to this second edition is to be found on the title page of this work. We are most grateful for all of the work done by the contributors. We as editors accept full responsibility for all that appears in this second edition, and we simply express the hope that it will enjoy the same high reputation as Sheriff Macphail's own first edition.

This new edition closely follows the arrangement, and titles, of chapters in the first edition. However, there are now three wholly new chapters and, as is explained below, there are two other chapters which have yet to appear in a second volume. The new chapters are on the subjects of fatal accident inquiries (Sheriff C. N. Stoddart), adoption (Mrs J. M. Scott), and the enforcement of judgments (Professor G. Maher). Although all of these subjects are dealt with in other books, the view was taken that the usefulness of this book would be enhanced if they were also to be covered in it. We are particularly grateful to the contributors who prepared those new chapters.

The chapters which will appear in a separate second volume will deal mainly with the subjects of summary causes and small claims. The first edition contains a section dealing with summary causes, but gives no guidance in relation to small claims on account of the fact that they had not been introduced by the date when that edition was published. During the period when the second edition was being prepared we were advised by the Sheriff Court Rules Council that new, revised, rules for both summary causes and small claims were being drafted; and in that situation it was our hope, and expectation, that the second edition would, in the light of the new rules, incorporate fully up-to-date chapters dealing with the procedures in both of these classes of action. In fact, however, the promulgation of these new rules has been much delayed, and it is now unlikely that they will appear until some time in 1999. In that situation a decision was taken, by Greens and by us as editors, that publication of the bulk of the new edition should not be held up in order to await the new summary cause and small claim rules. Consequently, the present volume does not deal with those matters, and a second volume, which will deal with them, will be published as soon as possible after the new rules have come into existence. We should add, however, that that second volume will include a consolidated index and tables so that users of the two volumes need only refer to a single index or table. We should also, perhaps, add that in the circumstances it would be advisable that copies of the first edition should not be discarded at this stage: that edition contains material relating to summary causes which will still be relevant until Volume 2 of this edition is published.

Since it may be some months before Volume 2 of this edition is published, and since there may be further developments of the law during that time in respect of subjects covered in Volume 1, it is hoped that Volume 2 may also contain a chapter designed to update the material in Volume 1.

In the course of preparing this new edition we have received considerable help from a number of people. We have already mentioned the great assistance given by the main contributors. In addition, however, Alan Delaney, Craig Watson, and Derek Young all undertook helpful research in connection with particular chapters, and in some instances they were able to guide contributors in the intricacies of word-processing systems. Their willing assistance is much appreciated.

We are also most grateful to Professor W. W. McBryde and Professor George Gretton who, as successive Directors of the Scottish Universities Law Institute, supported and encouraged the preparation of the new edition at all times. And, finally, of course, we are grateful to all at W. Green & Son Ltd who guided and assisted us in the course of our work. In that regard particular mention must be made of Elanor Bower who kept us on the right track in the early stages of the project; of Karen Taylor, her successor as commissioning editor, who constantly found ways to lessen our burden, and who contrived to keep our spirits high even when the work appeared most daunting; of Heather Palomino who gave us expert help and advice in the latter stages of editing the text; and of Noel Keenan who guided us with an expert hand through the more technical aspects of preparing the new edition. Our grateful thanks are also due to Chantal Hamill who undertook the preparation of the index. It was a great relief to us to be able to leave that task in such capable hands.

In this edition we have endeavoured to state the law as at September 30, 1998, but later developments have been noted where it has been practical to do so.

GORDON NICHOLSON
ALASTAIR STEWART

PREFACE TO FIRST EDITION

FORTY years have passed since the publication of Sheriff W. Jardine Dobie's *Sheriff Court Practice*. During that time there have been so many changes in the practice and procedure of the sheriff court that it would scarcely be possible to prepare a new edition of Sheriff Dobie's work without rewriting the text so extensively that most of the original would disappear. It was therefore decided that it would be appropriate to prepare an entirely new book.

This work is in no sense a revision of Sheriff Dobie's book, nor is it based upon it; but "Dobie" is so familiar to Scottish courts and practitioners that it seems desirable to explain the extent to which the present volume differs from it in scope. This book, unlike Sheriff Dobie's, is not a comprehensive guide to all the forms of civil proceedings which are competent in the sheriff court. In some areas, namely adoption of children, bankruptcy, commissary proceedings and company law and practice, the practitioner is already well provided with modern textbooks. In others, new procedural rules will soon be promulgated: the forthcoming rules on diligence would supersede any account of the subject in this book very shortly after its publication; and it is also too early to anticipate the introduction of small claims procedure. Nor does this book attempt to expound the law of civil remedies, which has already been fully examined in Professor Walker's volume on that subject in the Scottish Universities Law Institute series, or the substantive law relative to particular procedural rules, on which much guidance is available elsewhere. In the field of family proceedings, for example, Dr. Clive's work in this series has been so well supplemented by a number of excellent monographs on recent legislation that it would be otiose for this book to venture beyond an exposition of the relevant rules of procedure.

This volume, accordingly, is not an exhaustive treatise but a general textbook. It attempts to explain the modern statutory rules of procedure and the principles and practices which regulate the conduct of all forms of civil proceedings in the sheriff court other than those already mentioned as the subjects of specialist works or forthcoming rules. I have tried to state the law in the light of the sources available to me on May 1, 1987.

The longest chapters in the book, and two of the most useful, are those on summary cause procedure by Sheriff A. L. Stewart and on miscellaneous statutory powers and duties by Mrs. Elizabeth R. Colwell Wilson. I supplied each of these contributors with the relevant part of my card index, various other materials and a scheme of the proposed chapter. Mrs. Colwell Wilson was also able to use materials which were most generously made available by Mr. C. M. G. Himsworth of the Department of Constitutional and Administrative Law of Edinburgh University. These materials had been compiled and analysed by Mr. Himsworth with the assistance of Mr. Neil Farrell, LL.B. Both Sheriff Stewart and Mrs. Colwell Wilson, however, undertook much further research and considerably improved the original schemes, making creative contributions which fully justify the appearance of their names on the title page. I am most grateful to them both.

I am also indebted to The Hon. Lord Dunpark and Professor W. A. Wilson, the President and Director of the Scottish Universities Law Institute, for their support throughout the writing of the book, and to the members of the

Institute's advisory committee. The committee's chairman, Sir John Dick, M.C., Q.C., LL.D., read the entire book in draft, as did Sheriff Principal P. I. Caplan, Q.C. Members of the staff of Scottish Courts Administration read Chapters 1, 3 and 6, and Professor Robert Black read Chapter 3. All made valuable comments, and I offer them my sincerest thanks. It is with particular pleasure that I thank Sir John Dick, who has influenced my professional life at many points. I alone am responsible for the errors which remain in the text.

I am also grateful to the many people who willingly responded to my requests for information. Among them are Professor A. E. Anton; Sheriff Principal S. E. Bell, Q.C.; Professor Black; Mr. W. Bryden, S.S.C.; The Hon. Lord Coulsfield; Sheriff G. L. Cox; Dr. A. G. Coyle, Governor of H.M. Prison, Greenock; Mr. P. B. Cullen, Advocate, Clerk of Faculty; Mr. I. Dean, Crown Agent; Mr. P. Feeney, Secretary to the Sheriff Court Rules Council; Mr. H. S. Foley, Deputy Principal Clerk (Administration) and Keeper of the Rolls of the Court of Session; Sheriff Principal M. G. Gillies, T.D., Q.C.; Sheriff A. C. Horsfall; Sir Jack I. H. Jacob, Q.C., LL.D.; Mr. H. R. M. Macdonald, Advocate; Sheriff R. G. McEwan, Q.C.; Mr. C. McLay, Regional Sheriff Clerk of Glasgow and Strathkelvin; Mr. A. A. McMillan, when Solicitor to the Secretary of State for Scotland; Dr. A. L. Murray, Keeper of the Records of Scotland; Sheriff Principal Sir Frederick O'Brien, Q.C.; Mr. F. G. N. Rennie, Principal Sheriff Clerk Depute, Glasgow; Mr. W. Russell, Keeper of the Registers of Scotland; Miss Linda Ruxton, Solicitor; Sheriff D. B. Smith; Mr. G. W. Waddell, Assistant Sheriff Clerk, Paisley; Mr. E. H. Weir, W.S., Auditor of the Court of Session; and Mr. D. N. Yule, Solicitor.

My wife Rosslyn compiled the tables of cases, statutes and rules. Mrs. Colwell Wilson helped with the statutes. Mr. K. G. McGregor, S.S.C., prepared the index. The publishers, W. Green & Son Ltd., and the printers, the Oxford University Press, discharged with skill and care the task of converting a combination of word-processor print-outs and typescripts into a handsome book.

It would have been impossible for me to complete this work without the help of my wife. She devoted hundreds of hours of her time to the book, not only in preparing the tables and in assembling, copying and proof-reading the text, but in providing me with all the conditions necessary for a prolonged period of intensive work. With remarkable forbearance our children bore the loss of many leisure hours when they might reasonably have expected to be in my company. In recognition of the burdens which this task has imposed on them, I dedicate this book to my family.

I. D. MACPHAIL

Edinburgh
September 14, 1987

CONTENTS

PART V — MISCELLANEOUS POWERS AND DUTIES

PART VI — ENFORCEMENT OF JUDGMENTS

TABLE OF CASES

TABLE OF STATUTES

TABLE OF STATUTORY INSTRUMENTS

TABLE OF ORDINARY CAUSE RULES

TABLE OF SUMMARY CAUSE RULES

TABLE OF SUMMARY APPLICATIONS RULES

TABLE OF RULES OF THE COURT OF SESSION

TABLE OF ABBREVIATIONS

(other than standard law reports)

Alexander's Abridgment	W. Alexander, *Abridgment of the Acts of Sederunt of the Lords of Council and Session*, Edinburgh, 1838; *Supplement*, Edinburgh, 1843.
Anton with Beaumont	A. E. Anton with P. R. Beaumont, *Private International Law*, 2nd ed., Edinburgh, 1990
Anton and Beaumont	A. E. Anton and P. R. Beaumont, *Civil Jurisdiction in Scotland*, 2nd ed., Edinburgh, 1995.
Bell, *Arbitration*	J. M. Bell, *Law of Arbitration in Scotland*, 2nd ed., Edinburgh, 1877.
Bell, *Comm.*	G. J. Bell, *Commentaries on the Law of Scotland and the Principles of Mercantile Jurisprudence*, 7th ed. by John McLaren, 2 vols, Edinburgh, 1870.
Bell, *Dict.*	W. Bell, *Dictionary and Digest of the Law of Scotland*, 7th ed. by G. Watson, Edinburgh, 1890.
Bell, *Prin.*	G. J. Bell, *Principles of the Law of Scotland*, 10th ed. by W. Guthrie, Edinburgh, 1899.
Bennett	S. A. Bennett, *Divorce in the Sheriff Court*, 5th ed., Edinburgh 1997.
Burn-Murdoch	H. Burn-Murdoch, *Interdict in the Law of Scotland*, Glasgow, 1933.
C.A.S.	Codifying Act of Sederunt, 1913.
Clive	E. M. Clive, *The Law of Husband and Wife in Scotland*, 4th ed., Edinburgh, 1997.
Currie	J. G. Currie, *Confirmation of Executors in Scotland*, 8th ed., by E. M. Scobbie, Edinburgh 1995.
Dicey and Morris	A. V. Dicey, *The Conflict of Laws*, 12th ed., under the general editorship of L. Collins, London, 1993.
Dickson	W. G. Dickson, *The Law of Evidence in Scotland*, 3rd ed. by P. J. Hamilton Grierson, 2 vols, Edinburgh, 1887.
Dobie	W. J. Dobie, *Law Practice of the Sheriff Courts in Scotland*, Edinburgh and Glasgow, 1948.
Dobie, *Styles*	W. J. Dobie, *Styles for Use in the Sheriff Courts in Scotland*, Edinburgh, 1891.
Dove Wilson	J. Dove Wilson, *The Practice of the Sheriff Courts of Scotland in Civil Cases,* 4th ed. by J.C. Dove Wilson, Edinburgh, 1891.
Encyclopaedia	*Encyclopaedia of the Laws of Scotland*, 18 vols, Edinburgh, 1926–52.
Encyclopaedia of Styles	*Encyclopaedia of Scottish Legal Styles*, 10 vols, Edinburgh, 1935–1940.

Ersk.	John Erskine of Carnock, *An Institute of the Law of Scotland*, 8th ed. by J. B. Nicholson, 2 vols, Edinburgh, 1871.
Fyfe	T. A. Fyfe, *The Law and Practice of the Sheriff Courts of Scotland*, Edinburgh and Glasgow, 1913.
Gill	B. Gill, *The Law of Agricultural Holdings in Scotland*, 3rd ed., Edinburgh, 1997.
Gloag	W. M. Gloag, *Law of Contract*, 2nd ed., Edinburgh, 1929.
Gloag & Henderson	W. M. Gloag and R. C. Henderson, *Introduction to the Law of Scotland*, 10th ed. by W. A. Wilson, A. Forten, Lord Rodgers, A. Paton, L. Dunlop, P. Hood and A. R. W. Young, Edinburgh, 1995.
Goudy	H. Goudy, *Law of Bankruptcy in Scotland*, 4th ed., Edinburgh, 1914.
Graham Stewart	J. Graham Stewart, *Law of Diligence*, Edinburgh, 1898.
Grant	*The Sheriff Court*, Report by Committee appointed by the Secretary of State for Scotland (Chairman: The Rt. Hon. Lord Grant, T.D.), Cmnd. 3248, Edinburgh, 1967.
Gretton	"Diligence and Enforcement of Judgments: Diligence" in *Stair Memorial Encyclopaedia of the Laws of Scotland,* Edinburgh, vol. 8.
Grieve	*Administration of Sheriffdoms*, Report by Committee appointed by the Secretary of State for Scotland (Chairman: The Hon. Lord Grieve, V.R.D.), Cmnd. 8548, Edinburgh, 1982.
Guild, *Arbitration*	D. A. Guild, *The Law of Arbitration in Scotland*, Edinburgh 1936.
Guthrie, *Sel. Ca.*	*Selected Cases Decided in the Sheriff Courts of Scotland*, collected by W. Guthrie, 2 vols, Edinburgh, 1879, 1894.
Halliday	J. M. Halliday, *Conveyancing Law and Practice*, 2nd ed. by I. J. S. Talman, 2 vols., Edinburgh, 1996 and 1997.
Halsbury	*Halsbury's Laws of England*, 4th ed., 56 vols, London, and subsequently updated.
Hume, *Lectures*	Baron David Hume, *Lectures on the Law of Scotland, 1786–1822*, ed. by G. C. H. Paton, 6 vols (Stair Soc. 5, 13, 15, 17, 18, 19), Edinburgh, 1939–58.
Innes of Learney	Sir Thomas Innes of Learney, *Scotts Heraldry*, 2nd ed., Edinburgh, 1956.
J.L.S.	*Journal of the Law Society of Scotland.*
J.R.	*Juridical Review.*
Kearney	B. Kearney, *An Introduction to Ordinary Civil Procedure in the Sheriff Court*, Edinburgh, 1982.
Lees, *Interlocutors*	J. M. Lees, *Notes on the Structure of Interlocutors in the Sheriff Court*, 2nd ed., Edinburgh and Glasgow, 1915.
Lees, *Pleading*	J. M. Lees, *A Handbook of Written and Oral Pleading in the Sheriff Court*, 2nd ed., Edinburgh and Glasgow, 1920.
Lewis	W. J. Lewis, *Sheriff Court Practice*, 8th ed., Edinburgh, 1939.

Lewis, *Evidence*	W. J. Lewis, *A Manual of the Law of Evidence in Scotland*, Edinburgh, 1925.
McBryde & Dowie	W. W. McBryde and N. J. Dowie, *Petition Procedure in the Court of Session*, 2nd ed., Edinburgh, 1988.
Macdonald	H. R. M. Macdonald, *A Guide to the Family Law (Scotland) Act 1985*, Bicester, 1986.
McGlashan	J. McGlashan, *Practical Notes on the Jurisdiction and Forms of Process in Civil Cases of the Sheriff Courts of Scotland*, 3rd ed. by H. Barclay, 1854.
Mackay, *Manual*	Ae. J. G. Mackay, *Manual of Practice in the Court of Session*, Edinburgh, 1893.
Mackay, *Practice*	Ae. J. G. Mackay, *The Practice of the Court of Session*, 2 vols, Edinburgh, 1877–79.
McKechnie Report	*Report of the Committee on Diligence* (Chairman: Sheriff H. McKechnie, Q.C., LL.D.), Cmnd. 456, Edinburgh, 1958.
Maclaren	J. A. Maclaren, *Court of Session Practice*, Edinburgh, 1916.
Maclaren, *Expenses*	J. A. Maclaren, *Expenses in the Supreme and Sheriff Courts of Scotland*, Edinburgh, 1912.
McLaren, *Wills and Succession*	John (The Hon. Lord) McLaren, *Law of Wills and Succession*, 3rd ed., Edinburgh, 1894; *Supplement* by D. O. Dykes, Edinburgh, 1934.
McNeill, *Adoption*	P. G. B. McNeill, *Adoption of Children in Scotland*, 3rd ed., Edinburgh, 1998.
Macphail, *Evidence*	I. D. Macphail, *Evidence*, Edinburgh, 1987.
Maher & Cusine	*Law and Practice of Diligence*, Edinburgh, 1990.
Maxwell	D. Maxwell, *The Practice of the Court of Session*, Edinburgh, 1980.
Maxwell Report	*Report of the Scottish Committee on Jurisdiction and Enforcement* (Chairman: The Hon. Lord Maxwell), Edinburgh, 1980.
Miller, *Partnership*	J. B. Miller, *The Law of Partnership in Scotland*, 2nd ed. by G. Brough, Edinburgh, 1994.
Nichols	D. I. Nichols, *The Family Law (Scotland) Act 1985*, 2nd ed., Edinburgh, 1991.
Nichols & Meston	D. I. Nichols and M. C. Meston, *The Matrimonial Homes (Family Protection) (Scotland) Act 1981*, 2nd ed., Edinburgh, 1986.
Nicholson, *Sentencing*	C. G. B. Nicholson, *Sentencing Law and Practice in Scotland*, 2nd ed., Edinburgh, 1992.
O.C.R.	Ordinary Case Rules, contained in the Sheriff Courts (Scotland) Act 1907, Sched. 1, as substituted by S.I. 1993 No. 1956 and subsequently amended as indicated in *Parliament House Book* updated to August 21, 1998.
Palmer	Palmer's *Company Law*, 23rd ed., London, 1982.
Paton & Cameron	G. C. H. Paton and J. G. S. Cameron, *The Law of Landlord and Tenant in Scotland*, Edinburgh, 1967.
R.C.S.	Rules of the Court of Session, contained in the Act of Sederunt (Rules of the Court of Session) (S.I. 1994 No. 1443) and subsequently amended as indicated in *Parliament House Book* updated to 1998.

Renton & Brown	Renton & Brown's *Criminal Procedure according to the Law of Scotland*, 6th ed. by G. H. Gordon and C. H. W. Gane, Edinburgh, 1996, and subsequently updated.
Scolag	*Scolag: The Bulletin of the Scottish Legal Action Group.*
S.C.R.	Summary Cause Rules, contained in the Act of Sederunt (Summary Cause Rules) 1976 (S.I. 1976 No. 476) and subsequently amended as indicated in *Parliament House Book* updated to August 21, 1998.
Scot. Law. Com.	Scottish Law Commission.
Sellar, *Forms*	G. Sellar, *Forms for Sheriffs and Sheriff-Clerks*, Glasgow, 1881.
Stair	James, Viscount of Stair, *The Institutions of the Law of Scotland*, 2nd ed., 1693, reprinted, ed. D. M. Walker, Edinburgh and Glasgow, 1981.
Stair Memorial Encyclopaedia	*The Laws of Scotland*, 25 vols, Edinburgh, and subsequently updated.
Stewart	W. S. Stewart, *Scottish Contemporary Judicial Dictionary*, Edinburgh, 1995.
Stoddart	C. N. Stoddart, *The Law and Practice of Legal Aid in Scotland*, 4th ed., Edinburgh, 1996.
Thomson	J. M. Thomson, *Family Law in Scotland*, 3rd ed., Edinburgh, 1996.
Thomson & Middleton	G. R. Thomson and J. T. Middleton, *Manual of Court of Session Procedure*, Edinburgh, 1937.
Trayner	J. Trayner, *Latin Maxims and Phrases*, 4th ed., Edinburgh, 1894.
Walker, *Civil Remedies*	D.M. Walker, *The Law of Civil Remedies in Scotland*, Edinburgh, 1975.
Walker, *Contracts*	D. M. Walker, *The Law of Contracts and Related Obligations in Scotland*, 3rd ed., London, 1995.
Walker, *Delict*	D. M. Walker, *The Law of Delict in Scotland*, 2nd ed., Edinburgh, 1981.
Walker, *Digest*	N. M. L. Walker, *Digest of Sheriff Court Practice in Scotland*, Edinburgh, 1932.
Walker, *Judicial Factors*	N. M. L. Walker, *Judicial Factors*, Edinburgh, 1974.
Walker, *Prescription*	D. M. Walker, *The Law of Prescription and Limitation of Actions in Scotland*, 5th ed., Edinburgh, 1996.
Walker, *Prin.*	D. M. Walker, *Principles of Scottish Private Law*, 4th ed., 4 vols, Oxford, 1988.
Walkers, *Evidence*	A. G. Walker and N. M. L. Walker, *The Law of Evidence in Scotland*, Edinburgh and Glasgow, 1964.
Wallace	W. Wallace, *The Practice of the Sheriff Court of Scotland*, Edinburgh, 1909.
Wilson, *Debt*	W. A. Wilson, *The Scottish Law of Debt*, 2nd ed., Edinburgh, 1991.
Wilson & Duncan	W. A. Wilson and A. G. M. Duncan, *Trusts, Trustees and Executors*, 2nd ed., Edinburgh, 1995.

Wilton	G. W. Wilton, *Company Law and Practice in Scotland*, Edinburgh and London, 1912.

STATUTES

1907 Act	Sheriff Courts (Scotland) Act 1907.
1971 Act	Sheriff Courts (Scotland) Act 1971.
CJJ Act	Civil Jurisdiction and Judgments Act 1982.

PART I

CONSTITUTION AND JURISDICTION

Chapter 1

THE CONSTITUTION OF THE COURT

The court

The main civil courts in the modern Scottish judicial system are the Court of Session and the sheriff court. Jurisdiction to decide civil causes in Scotland is concentrated in these courts, subject to the reservation of particular matters to special courts and tribunals. The Court of Session is the supreme, central court, subject only to such review as may be competent by the House of Lords, while the sheriff court is the local court. Although inferior in status to the Court of Session, to which certain appeals may be taken, the sheriff court exercises a wide jurisdiction and disposes of the main bulk of civil litigation in Scotland. The sheriff court is of ancient origin,[1] and its jurisdiction and procedure in civil matters have been regulated by a number of statutes, those now of the greatest practical significance being the Sheriff Courts (Scotland) Acts of 1907 and 1971.[2] The 1907 Act, as amended, continues to regulate the jurisdiction and ordinary procedure of the court, while the 1971 Act makes provision for the administration of the sheriff courts, the introduction of a summary cause procedure for actions under a prescribed sum in value, and the regulation by the Court of Session of the rules of procedure in all civil proceedings. **1.01**

The distinctive characteristics of the modern sheriff courts are these. "Their jurisdiction in many branches of the law, and especially in regard to the ordinary transactions between man and man, is co-extensive with that of the Supreme Court. Their proceedings [in ordinary causes] are conducted by regular pleadings in as formal a manner; their procedure is regulated by statute, and by the rules prescribed by the supreme Courts."[3] Their judges are experienced lawyers. While in ordinary causes their procedure is similar to that of the Court of Session, in summary causes and summary applications it is intended to be in general simple, expeditious and inexpensive. The courts are readily accessible to most citizens, there being a court in almost every large centre of population and in several of the smaller towns. The sheriff courts therefore seek to fulfil an important social duty: "if the quality of a country's laws may best be assessed by considering the pronouncements of the highest tribunals, the quality of a country's justice is most frequently tested in those lower courts which handle the great bulk of civil and criminal business."[4] **1.02**

---

[1] For the history of the sheriff court see *Introduction to Scottish Legal History* (Stair Society, 1958), Vol. 20., Chaps. 25, 26, 32; D. M. Walker, *A Legal History of Scotland*; *Stair Memorial Encyclopaedia*, Vol. 6, "Courts and Competency".

[2] These Acts are hereafter referred to as "the 1907 Act" and "the 1971 Act".

[3] *Hamilton v. Anderson* (1856) 18 D. 1003, *per* L.J.-C. Hope at 1018; approved (1858) 3 Macq. 363, *per* Lord Cranworth at 379; *cit. Macleod v. Spiers* (1884) 5 Coup. 387, *per* Lord Adam at 393. While the procedure of the sheriff court is regulated by statute and act of sederunt, it is not wholly derived therefrom: there are many common law rules and practices.

[4] T.B. Smith, "Legal Imperialism and Legal Parochialism", 1965 J.R. 39 at 44.

The sheriffdoms

1.03 For the purpose of the administration of justice in the sheriff courts, Scotland is divided into sheriffdoms. The Secretary of State may by order alter the boundaries of sheriffdoms, form new sheriffdoms or provide for the abolition of sheriffdoms existing at the time of the making of the order.[5] The sheriffdoms which exist today came into being in 1975 by virtue of the Sheriffdoms Reorganisation Order 1974,[6] which abolished the 12 sheriffdoms then existing in Scotland and divided the country into six new sheriffdoms comprising areas described by reference to the local government areas under the Local Government (Scotland) Act 1973. These sheriffdoms are: Grampian, Highland and Islands; Tayside, Central and Fife; Lothian and Borders; Glasgow and Strathkelvin; North Strathclyde; and South Strathclyde, Dumfries and Galloway.

1.04 Each sheriffdom other than Glasgow and Strathkelvin is divided into a number of sheriff court districts, in each of which is situated a town where the sheriff court is held. There are at present 49 districts. The Secretary of State may by order alter the boundaries of sheriff court districts, form new districts or provide for the abolition of districts existing at the time of the making of the order, and he may also provide that sheriff courts shall be held, or shall cease to be held, at any place.[7] The modern pattern of sheriff court districts has its origins in the Sheriff Court Districts Reorganisation Order 1975,[8] which abolished the sheriff court districts then existing, provided for the division of five of the six sheriffdoms into new sheriff court districts and specified the places in each district where sheriff courts were to be held. That order has been amended from time to time.[9] The boundaries of the sheriff court districts in most cases correspond to the boundaries of districts and islands areas as those were defined under the Local Government (Scotland) Act 1973 but subsequent adjustments[10] include those made to take account of the reorganisation of local government under the Local Government etc. (Scotland) Act 1994.[11]

1.05 In any enactment passed or made before the commencement of the 1971 Act, for any reference to a county, where it appears in relation to a sheriff or a sheriff-substitute or in any similar context, there must, unless the contrary intention appears, be substituted a reference to a sheriffdom.[12] In any enactment passed before, or during the same session as, the Local Government (Scotland) Act 1973, and in any instrument made before that Act under any enactment, any reference to a sheriff clerk of a county, however expressed, must be construed as a reference to the sheriff clerk of the sheriff court district concerned.[13]

---

[5] 1971 Act, s. 2(1).

[6] S.I. 1974 No. 2087. These descriptions are still in use despite the reorganisation of local government under the Local Government etc. (Scotland) Act 1994.

[7] 1971 Act, s. 3(2).

[8] S.I. 1975 No. 637.

[9] By S.I.s 1975 No. 1539; 1977 No. 672; 1983 No. 1028; 1996 No. 1005; 1996 No. 2192.

[10] S.I.s 1996 Nos. 1005 and 2192, *supra.*

[11] See Charles McCaffray, *Greens Guide to Sheriff Court Districts in Scotland* (2nd ed., 1992); Ann Paton, *Map of Sheriffdoms and Sheriff Court Districts in Scotland,* (2nd ed., 1980).

[12] 1971 Act, Sched. 1, para. 1.

[13] Local Government (Scotland) Act 1973, Sched. 27, Pt 1, para. 1 (1), (3).

The judiciary

The judges of each sheriffdom are ordinarily the sheriff principal and several sheriffs. Temporary sheriffs principal, "floating" sheriffs, temporary sheriffs and honorary sheriffs may also be appointed. The offices of sheriff principal, sheriff and honorary sheriff were formerly known as sheriff, sheriff-substitute and honorary sheriff-substitute, and were given their present names by section 4 of the 1971 Act. Any enactment or other document in force or having effect at the commencement of the 1971 Act which refers to those offices by their previous names is to be construed accordingly.[14] In Acts passed and in subordinate legislation made after 1889 the word "sheriff", in relation to Scotland, includes sheriff principal, unless the contrary intention appears.[15] **1.06**

The sheriff principal[16]

The right of appointing to the office of sheriff principal is vested in Her Majesty, and is exercised on the recommendation of the Secretary of State for Scotland.[17] By convention the Secretary of State is advised by the Lord Advocate, who selects and nominates the person to be appointed.[18] He must be, and have been for at least 10 years, an advocate or a solicitor.[19] There is no statutory requirement that any part of the qualifying period should have been spent in private practice. In modern times those appointed as sheriffs principal have been Queen's Counsel or have had judicial experience, usually as sheriffs. The appointment may be full-time or part-time, but in practice all those made since the reorganisation of the sheriffdoms in 1975 have been full-time appointments. As soon as may be after his acceptance of office a sheriff principal takes the oath of allegiance and judicial oath, normally before the Lord President of the Court of Session.[20] **1.07**

A full-time sheriff principal may not engage, whether directly or indirectly, in any private practice or business, or be in partnership with or employed by, or act as agent for, any person so engaged.[21] The Secretary of State may require him to reside ordinarily at such place as the Secretary of State may specify,[22] and may approve leave of absence (other than leave granted on account of ill health) which, unless the Secretary of State for special reasons otherwise permits, may not exceed seven weeks in any year.[23] A part-time sheriff principal is forbidden, so long as he holds office as such, to advise, or act as an advocate in any court, in any cause civil or criminal arising within or coming from his sheriffdom.[24] Every sheriff principal is excluded from membership of **1.08**

---

14 1971 Act, s. 4(2).

15 Interpretation Act 1978, ss. 5, 22, 23; Sched. 1; Sched. 2, Pt I, para. 4(1)(a), Pt II, para. 6; *Hardy v. Robinson*, 1985 S.L.T. (Sh. Ct.) 40.

16 The tenure of sheriffs principal and sheriffs is the subject of an unpublished paper by Sheriff P. G. B. McNeill, "The Independence of the Shrieval Judiciary".

17 1907 Act, s. 11.

18 Grant Report, para. 368. It is understood that Scottish Courts Administration (see para. 1.46) are involved before the Lord Advocate decides on nomination.

19 1971 Act, s. 5(1).

20 Promissory Oaths Acts—1868, s. 6 and Sched., Pt II; 1871, s. 2 (all as amended).

21 1971 Act, s. 6(1), as amended by the Law Reform (Miscellaneous Provisions) (Scotland) Act 1985, s. 20, Sched. 4.

22 1971 Act, s. 13(1).

23 *ibid.* s. 13(2).

24 *ibid.* s. 6(3).

the House of Commons[25] and from jury service.[26] If appointed before March 31, 1995[27] he may remain in office until the end of the completed year of service in the course of which he attains the age of 72 years.[28] Subject to certain transitional provisions[29] for persons who held a relevant office[30] immediately before March 31, 1995, a sheriff principal appointed after that date must retire on the day on which he attains the age of 70.[31] The Secretary of State may, however, if he considers it desirable in the public interest, authorise the continuation of a sheriff principal in office after his compulsory retirement date for a period or periods each not exceeding one year and not extending beyond the day on which he attains the age of 75.[32] A sheriff principal may, in any event, continue to deal with cases pending at the date of his retirement in which proceedings are uncompleted.[33] The salaries of sheriffs principal are determined by the Treasury and are charged upon and payable out of the Consolidated Fund.[34] On a report from the Lord President of the Court of Session and the Lord Justice-Clerk the Secretary of State may make an order by statutory instrument, subject to annulment by either House of Parliament, removing a sheriff principal from office on the ground of unfitness by reason of inability, neglect of duty or misbehaviour.[35]

1.09 The sheriff principal may be authorised to act in another sheriffdom in two situations. (1) Where a vacancy occurs in the office of sheriff principal of any sheriffdom the Secretary of State may, if it appears to him expedient to do so in order to avoid delay in the administration of justice in that sheriffdom, authorise the sheriff principal of any other sheriffdom to perform the duties of sheriff principal in the first-mentioned sheriffdom, in addition to his own duties, until the Secretary of State otherwise decides. (2) Where the sheriff principal of any sheriffdom is unable to perform, or rules that he is precluded from performing, all of, or some part of, his duties as sheriff principal, the Secretary of State may authorise the sheriff principal of any sheriffdom to perform the duties of sheriff principal, or as the case may be that part of those duties, in the first-mentioned sheriffdom, in addition to his own duties, until the Secretary of State otherwise decides.[36]

---

[25] House of Commons Disqualification Act 1975, s. 1(1)(a), and Sched. 1, Pt I.

[26] Law Reform (Miscellaneous Provisions) (Scotland) Act 1980, s. 1(1)(d), and Sched. 1, Pt I, Group A. They remain ineligible for 10 years after ceasing to hold office: Group A, para. (g).

[27] The commencement date of the Judicial Pensions and Retirement Act 1993 (S.I. 1995 No. 631).

[28] Sheriffs' Pensions (Scotland) Act 1961, s. 6(1).

[29] 1993 Act, s. 26(11), Sched. 7.

[30] *ibid.* s. 26(1), Sched. 5.

[31] *ibid.* s. 26(1); 1971 Act, s. 5A as inserted by 1993 Act, Sched. 6, para. 10.

[32] *ibid.* s. 26(5).

[33] *ibid.* s. 27.

[34] 1907 Act, s. 14. As to travelling allowances, see 1971 Act, s. 19. As to pensions, see Sheriffs' Pensions (Scotland) Act 1961; Judicial Pensions Act 1981, ss. 6, 16–29; Judicial Pensions and Retirement Act 1993, ss. 1–13, 16–20, 22–24, 28–31.

[35] 1971 Act, s. 12, which also applies to sheriffs. Two sheriffs have been thereby removed from office: see Sheriff (Removal from Office) Order 1977 (S.I. 1977 No. 2046); H.C. Deb., Vol. 939, cols 922–925, Vol. 940, cols 93–94, 245, 397–398, 1288–1332; and Sheriff (Removal from Office) Order 1992 (S.I. 1992 No. 1677); *Stewart v. Secretary of State for Scotland*, 1995 S.L.T. 895; 1996 S.L.T. 1203.

[36] 1971 Act, s. 10(1), (1A), substituted by Law Reform (Miscellaneous Provisions) (Scotland) Act 1980, s. 10(a).

In the same two situations the Secretary of State may instead appoint a temporary sheriff principal.[37] A temporary sheriff principal must have been legally qualified for at least 10 years,[38] and may be a sheriff.[39] It is possible for a temporary sheriff principal to be appointed under section 11(1A) of the 1971 Act only for the purpose of hearing appeals, while the sheriff principal of another sheriffdom carries out the other duties of the office by virtue of an authorisation made under section 10.[40] **1.10**

The functions of the sheriff principal are judicial, administrative and ceremonial. The judicial powers of the sheriff principal and the sheriff are the same, unless otherwise provided expressly or by implication.[41] There is, however, a right of appeal to the sheriff principal from most decisions of the sheriff in civil matters,[42] and in practice the sheriff principal's main judicial duty in civil matters is the hearing of appeals in such cases.[43] **1.11**

The sheriff principal's administrative responsibilities as head of the courts of his sheriffdom are considered below.[44] In addition to these, the sheriff principal appoints honorary sheriffs,[45] sheriff court auditors,[46] sheriff officers[47] and valuation appeal panels.[48] He maintains lists of potential jurors,[49] and exercises a number of other administrative or executive functions either because they are confided to him by statute[50] or because, although they are not legally reserved to either the sheriff principal or the sheriff, he deems it appropriate to exercise them himself. He may hold other appointments *ex officio*,[51] and may be appointed to perform additional duties.[52] Each sheriff principal is a Commissioner of Northern Lighthouses,[53] and the Sheriff Principal of Lothian and Borders **1.12**

---

[37] 1971 Act, s. 11(1)–(1B), substituted by Law Reform (Miscellaneous Provisions) (Scotland) Act 1980, s. 10(b).

[38] 1971 Act, s. 11(3)(a).

[39] *ibid.* s. 11(7).

[40] 1980 S.L.T. (News) 258; 1981 S.L.T. (News) 23, 193.

[41] *Fleming v. Dickson* (1862) 1 M. 188; *Glasgow Corporation v. Glasgow Churches Council*, 1944 S.C. 97, *per* L.J.-C. Cooper at 127–128.

[42] On appeals to the sheriff principal see paras 18.06 to 18.90; on judicial precedent see para. 18.08.

[43] The sheriff principal may dispose of civil business at first instance with the parties' express agreement (*Dixon Street Motors v. Associated Rentals Ltd*, 1980 S.L.T. (Sh. Ct.) 46), but this course would appear to be exceptional and is not recommended: any appeal would have to be heard either by the Court of Session or by another, or a temporary, sheriff principal appointed in terms of s. 10(1A) or s. 11(1A) of the 1971 Act.

[44] See para. 1.47.

[45] para. 1.17.

[46] para. 1.26.

[47] para 1.27.

[48] Local Government etc. (Scotland) Act 1994, s. 29(2), (7).

[49] Jurors (Scotland) Act 1825, s. 3, as amended by Law Reform (Miscellaneous Provisions) (Scotland) Act 1985, s. 23(1); A.A. (Circuits) 1985 (S.I. 1985 No. 1534), para. 3(1).

[50] *e.g.* the chairman of any independent schools tribunal is a sheriff principal (Education (Scotland) Act 1980, s. 100(1), Sched. 2, para. 4).

[51] Each sheriff principal is *ex officio* a general commissioner for income tax: Taxes Management Act 1970, s. 2(4).

[52] In 1977 a public local inquiry into circumstances surrounding the escape of two patients from the State Hospital Carstairs, was conducted by a sheriff principal with assessors under the Mental Health (Scotland) Act 1960, s. 108, and the Local Government (Scotland) Act 1973, s. 210: see Report (H.M.S.O., 1977), and now the Mental Health (Scotland) Act 1984, s. 123.

[53] Merchant Shipping Act 1995, s. 193(1), Sched. 8, para. 1(2).

is the Sheriff of Chancery.[54] Each sheriff principal also undertakes ceremonial duties in connection with Royal and other official visits to his sheriffdom.

1.13 In the discharge of his duties the sheriff principal is protected by the law of contempt,[55] by the common law crime of slandering judges[56] and by immunity from suit in respect of acts done in his judicial capacity.[57]

The sheriff

1.14 Sheriffs are appointed in the same manner as sheriffs principal,[58] except that the sheriffs principal are consulted before the Lord Advocate decides on a nomination.[59] A sheriff, unlike a sheriff principal, is not required by statute to take the oath of allegiance and judicial oath after accepting office,[60] but in practice he takes them before his sheriff principal. The provisions as to qualification for office, salary, retirement, suspension and removal from office[61] are the same as for sheriffs principal.[62] The post is full-time, and the disqualifications applicable to full-time sheriffs principal[63] also apply to sheriffs.

1.15 On the appointment of a sheriff the Secretary of State gives him a direction designating the sheriff court district or districts in which he is to perform his duties,[64] and thereafter he may give him further such directions.[65] The sheriff principal may give him instructions of an administrative nature,[66] and may instruct him to act temporarily in a different district of the sheriffdom where there is a vacancy, or a sheriff is unable to perform his duties, or for any other reason it appears to the sheriff principal expedient so to do in order to avoid delay in the administration of justice in the sheriffdom.[67] The Secretary of State may in similar circumstances direct him to act temporarily in another sheriffdom[68];

---

54 Succession (Scotland) Act 1964, s. 35; Sheriff of Chancery (Transfer of Jurisdiction) Order 1971 (S.I. 1971 No. 743); see, generally, *Stair Memorial Encyclopaedia*, Vol. 6, para. 1031.

55 See para. 2.18; G.H. Gordon, *Criminal Law of Scotland* (2nd ed.), pp. 1088–1089.

56 *ibid.* pp. 1089–1090.

57 J. D. B. Mitchell, *Constitutional Law* (2nd ed.), pp. 262–263; Walker, *Delict* (2nd ed.), pp. 101–106, 801–802, 875; *Harvey v. Dyce* (1876) 4 R. 265; *Russell v. Dickson*, 1997 G.W.D. 22-1058.

58 See para. 1.07.

59 *Administration of Sheriffdoms* (hereafter "the Grieve Report") (Cmnd 8548, 1982), para. 46. It is understood that, as in the appointment of a sheriff principal, Scottish Courts Administration (see para. 1.46) are also involved. See n. 18, *supra.*

60 Promissory Oaths Act 1868, s. 6 and Sched., Pt II.

61 Two sheriffs have been removed from office in terms of the 1971 Act, s. 12: see n. 35, *supra.*

62 See paras. 1.07, 1.08. The pension rights of sheriffs principal differed from those of sheriffs under previous legislation but come within the same scheme of the Judicial Pensions and Retirement Act 1993 where that is applicable. As to travelling allowances for sheriffs, see Judicial Offices (Salaries, etc.) Act 1952, s. 3.

63 See para. 1.08. A sheriff may be appointed as a member of the Scottish Law Commission (Law Commissions Act 1965, s. 2, as amended by Law Reform (Miscellaneous Provisions) (Scotland) Act 1985, Sched. 4), or as Director of Scottish Courts Administration (1971 Act, s. 8). In practice a sheriff is included among the members of the Parole Board for Scotland (Prisoners and Criminal Proceedings (Scotland) Act 1993, s. 20, Sched. 2).

64 1971 Act, s. 14(3)(a).

65 *ibid.* s. 14(3)(b).

66 *ibid.* s. 15(2).

67 *ibid.* s. 16(1)(b).

and may also transfer him to another sheriffdom, after consultation with the Lord President of the Court of Session, for the purposes of securing the efficient organisation and administration of the sheriff courts.[69] The Secretary of State may require any sheriff to reside ordinarily at such place as the Secretary of State may specify.[70] The sheriff principal may approve leave of absence which, other than leave granted on account of ill health, may not exceed seven weeks per year unless otherwise permitted for special reasons by the Secretary of State.[71]

The sheriff normally acts as judge of first instance in civil and criminal matters, and exercises a very wide jurisdiction. Unless the power of the sheriff to act in place of the sheriff principal is excluded, expressly or by implication, the sheriff may discharge and exercise all the duties of the sheriff principal,[72] and in the discharge of his duties he is protected to the same extent as the sheriff principal.[73] By virtue of his appointment as sheriff he is entitled to exercise the jurisdiction and powers attaching to the office of sheriff not only in the sheriff court district or districts designated in any direction given to him by the Secretary of State, but in all parts of the sheriffdom for which he is appointed.[74] In the discharge of his duties a sheriff is protected in the same way as a sheriff principal.[75] **1.16**

The term "floating sheriff", which has no statutory sanction, is applied to a sheriff who, although appointed for administrative purposes to hold the office of sheriff for a particular sheriffdom, is empowered to act elsewhere. When an advocate is appointed as a floating, temporary or honorary sheriff he is empowered to act in all the sheriff court districts of Scotland, but when a solicitor is appointed he is not empowered to act in a district in which he has practised and appeared regularly in court. Floating sheriffs sit in different courts, as directed by the Secretary of State acting through Scottish Courts Administration, when a resident sheriff is ill or otherwise unable to perform his duties, or when a vacancy occurs, or when for any reason it appears expedient to do so in order to avoid delay in the administration of justice.[76] In similar circumstances the Secretary of State may appoint a temporary sheriff,[77] who must have been legally qualified for at least five years.[78] Floating and temporary sheriffs sometimes sit in courts where a sheriff is regularly required but the appointment of a full-time resident sheriff is not justified or for reasons of financial constraint is considered impracticable. A temporary sheriff, unlike a permanent sheriff, whether resident or floating, holds a commission for a fixed period. The sheriff principal may appoint such persons as he thinks proper to hold the **1.17**

---

[68] 1971 Act, s. 10(2). Alternatively, the Secretary of State may appoint him to act as a temporary sheriff in the other sheriffdom under s. 11(2). Both courses were adopted in 1981 when Glasgow sheriffs whose court had been affected by industrial action by certain court staff volunteered to sit in other courts.

[69] *ibid.* s. 14(4).

[70] *ibid.* s. 14(2).

[71] *ibid.* s. 16(2).

[72] *Fleming v. Dickson* (1862) 1 M. 188; *Glasgow Corporation v. Glasgow Churches Council*, 1944 S.C. 97, *per* L.J.-C. Cooper at 127–128.

[73] See para. 1.13.

[74] 1971 Act, s. 7. See para. 2.03. He is *ex officio* a general commissioner for income tax for any division wholly or partly within his district: Taxes Management Act 1970, s. 2(4).

[75] See para. 1.13.

[76] 1971 Act, s. 10(2). As to Scottish Courts Administration see para. 1.46.

[77] *ibid.* s. 11(2).

[78] *ibid.* s. 11(3)(b).

office of honorary sheriff within the sheriffdom during his pleasure.[79] An honorary sheriff sits by arrangement with the sheriff clerk acting on behalf of the sheriff principal, and need not be legally qualified: if he is, he is not precluded from practice,[80] but he may not try a case in which he is personally interested.[81] The sheriff clerk is not considered eligible for appointment as an honorary sheriff.[82] Floating,[83] temporary[84] and honorary[85] sheriffs are entitled to exercise the jurisdiction and powers attaching to the office of sheriff in the sheriffdom in which they sit, but in practice the duties of honorary sheriffs, who are unpaid, are often confined to business which is formal or of minor importance.

1.18 The dignity of the office of sheriff principal is recognised by the Royal Warrant of March 9, 1905 regulating the order of precedence in Scotland. By that warrant a sheriff principal in his own sheriffdom ranks next after the Royal Family, the Lord High Commissioner to the General Assembly of the Church of Scotland, and a Lord Lieutenant in his own territory.[86] Outwith their sheriffdoms, sheriffs principal have a general precedence immediately after the Lord Lyon King of Arms and before knights bachelor, while sheriffs rank immediately after knights bachelor.[87]

1.19 All judges of the sheriff court are addressed in court as "My Lord" or "My Lady". Off the bench, sheriffs principal should be addressed as "Sheriff Principal" and sheriffs as "Sheriff". Those who are Queen's Counsel wear the court dress appropriate to that rank. Others wear the court dress of junior counsel, except that the tie is replaced by the linen fall worn by Queen's Counsel. Honorary sheriffs normally wear a bar gown.

The officials

The sheriff clerk

1.20 The office of sheriff clerk is of ancient origin. His whole powers and duties are nowhere authoritatively defined, but it appears to be generally accepted that as clerk to the sheriff court his powers and duties are to act as clerk in every matter in which the sheriff principal and the sheriff have jurisdiction.[88] He acts either personally or through duly authorised members of his staff, and in the rules of court "sheriff clerk" includes "sheriff clerk depute" unless the context otherwise requires.[89] In any enactment passed before, or during the same session as, the

---

[79] 1907 Act, s. 17.

[80] *Henderson v. Warden* (1845) 17 Sc.Jur. 271.

[81] *Encyclopaedia of the Laws of Scotland* (2nd ed.), Vol. 13, "Sheriff" by Sheriff (later Lord) Wark, at p. 526.

[82] *ibid.* p. 527. See *Stewart v. Lord Advocate* (1857) 2 Irv. 614.

[83] 1971 Act, s. 10(3).

[84] *ibid.* s. 11(6).

[85] 1907 Act, s. 17.

[86] For the territories of Lord-Lieutenants see Lord-Lieutenants Order 1975 (S.I. 1975 No. 428), made under the Local Government (Scotland) Act 1973, s. 205(3) and (7).

[87] The order of seniority of the sheriffs at Glasgow is, subject to any special directions which may be given by the Secretary of State, according to the dates of their respective appointments to Glasgow: Sheriff Courts (Lanarkshire) Order 1954 (S.I. 1954 No. 712), para. 11.

[88] Lord Wark, n. 81 *supra*, p. 527.

[89] 1907 Act, s. 3(f); A.S. (Summary Cause Rules, Sheriff Court) 1976 (S.I. 1976 No. 476), para. 2(2). Other enactments and instruments may prescribe different interpretations, *e.g.* Sheriff Court Fees Order 1985 (S.I. 1985 No. 827), para. 2(1).

Local Government (Scotland) Act 1973, and in any instrument made before that Act under any enactment, any reference to a sheriff clerk of a county, however expressed, must be construed as a reference to the sheriff clerk of the sheriff court district concerned.[90]

The appointment and conditions of service of sheriff clerks are mainly governed by the Sheriff Courts and Legal Officers (Scotland) Act 1927 which requires that there should be a sheriff clerk for each sheriffdom. Where, however, the divisions of sheriff court districts or other circumstances render it expedient, a sheriff clerk may be appointed for an area other than a sheriffdom whether situated entirely within one sheriffdom or not. The power of appointing and dismissing sheriff clerks is vested in the Secretary of State for Scotland, but apart from normal retiral or resignation a sheriff clerk can be removed from office only upon a report by the Lord President of the Court of Session and the Lord Justice-Clerk.[91] The Secretary of State also appoints and dismisses sheriff clerk deputes, clerks and other assistants,[92] and may transfer a sheriff clerk from one district to another where in his opinion the transfer is for the purpose of securing efficient organisation and administration.[93] All sheriff clerks and their substitutes hold full-time appointments, and consequently are deemed for all purposes to be employed in the civil service of the State,[94] and may not engage in private legal practice.[95] A clerk should not officiate in a cause in which he is personally interested.[96] There is no statutory qualification for the office of sheriff clerk, but in practice members of the sheriff clerks branch of the Scottish Court Service are thoroughly trained. The office of Sheriff Clerk of Edinburgh is united with that of Sheriff Clerk of Chancery.[97] **1.21**

Many of the duties of the sheriff clerk in relation to civil proceedings are prescribed by rules of court. Thus, the Ordinary Cause Rules prescribe certain of his duties in relation to citation[98]; reponing[99]; fixing a date for an options hearing[1]; the receipt of notices of intention to defend[2]; the custody of the process[3] and certain other documents[4]; the issuing of warrants for[5] and precepts of[6] arrestment and of extract decrees[7] and interlocutors[8]; the certifying of interlocutors for various purposes[9]; **1.22**

---

90 Local Government (Scotland) Act 1973, Sched. 27, Pt I, para. 1(1), (3).
91 Sheriff Courts and Legal Officers (Scotland) Act 1927, s. 1.
92 *ibid.* ss. 2, 5.
93 *ibid.* s. 1(4), added by the Law Reform (Miscellaneous Provisions) (Scotland) Act 1985, s. 47.
94 *ibid.* s. 6, as amended by Superannuation Act 1972, Sched. 6.
95 *ibid.* s. 3.
96 *Manson v. Smith* (1871) 9 M. 492; *Macbeth v. Innes* (1873) 11 M. 404.
97 Union of Offices (Sheriff Courts and Legal Officers (Scotland) Act 1927) Order 1974 (S.I. 1974 No. 599).
98 1907 Act, Sched. 1, substituted by A.S. (Ordinary Cause Rules 1993) (S.I. 1993 No. 1956), and hereafter referred to as "OCR", rr. 5.1(1); 5.6(2), (4).
99 OCR, r. 8.1(1).
1 OCR, r. 9.2(1), (2).
2 OCR, r. 9.1(1).
3 OCR, r. 12. 2.
4 OCR, r. 28.3(1), Form G11 (3).
5 OCR, r. 5.1.
6 OCR, r. 3.5(2).
7 OCR, rr. 30.1; 30.2; 30.3; 30.4; 30.5.
8 OCR, r. 12.2(5), (6).
9 OCR, *e.g.* r. 28.9(3).

appeals[10]; taxation of expenses[11]; actions for sequestration for rent[12]; actions of multiplepoinding[13]; the disposal of money payable to persons under legal disability[14]; and references to the Court of Justice of the European Communities.[15] The Summary Cause Rules likewise impose a variety of duties on the sheriff clerk[16]; the Judicial Factors Rules 1992 prescribe his functions in relation to applications for the appointment of factors and guardians[17]; and numerous other statutes and Acts of Sederunt[18] require him to undertake many important responsibilities.

1.23 Fees are payable to the sheriff clerk in respect of sheriff court proceedings, and are specified by the Secretary of State.[19] It is doubtful whether the sheriff clerk is required to do any act (including the acceptance of any writ) in connection with the matter without payment of the appropriate fee.[20] In many courts the sheriff clerk will not accept a writ unless the appropriate fee is paid. In some courts the sheriff clerk may be prepared to accept a writ without payment of the fee, mark it as having been "tendered" (not "lodged") and draw the non-payment to the attention of the sheriff, but it is thought that that practice is liable to lead to confusion and should be avoided. No procedure can follow on a writ for which the appropriate fee has not been paid.[21]

1.24 The sheriff clerk also discharges a number of important functions which do not appear from the rules of court, the table of fees or other provisions. Either personally or through his staff, he scrutinises initial writs and other pleadings and documents when lodged to ensure that they are *ex facie* appropriate to the jurisdiction of the court, timeously lodged and in proper form, and advises the sheriff if in any respect they do not appear to conform to the practice and procedure of the court; attends the court while it is sitting; prepares the court rolls and formal interlocutors; and keeps the court books, the commissary seal and the sheriff court seal. The latter may be used to seal extract decrees, extracts of documents registered in the books of the sheriff court, commissions of honorary sheriffs and of sheriff officers, and other documents. The sheriff clerk's specialised

---

[10] OCR, rr. 31.4(8); 31.5(1).

[11] OCR, r. 32.3(1).

[12] OCR, r. 34.3(2).

[13] OCR, r. 35.9.

[14] OCR, rr. 36.15(8); 36.17.

[15] OCR, rr. 38.3 (2), (3), (5); 38.5 (1).

[16] A.S. (Summary Cause Rules, Sheriff Court) 1976 (S.I. 1976 No. 476), Sched. as amended (hereafter referred to as "SCR"), rr. 16, 19, 24, 24A, 25, 26, 28, 36, 38(4), 40(2), 45, 46, 47, 48, 51, 52, 61, 63, 68A, 73(3), 74(3), 75, 76, 81, 83(4), 85A(7), 86, 88(1), 88(3), 88(4), 88(5), 88(6), 89, 92(2) and (3), 93, 96, 97. The foregoing rules are likely to be replaced by new rules in the near future: see Vol. 2 of this work.

[17] A.S. (Judicial Factors Rules) 1992 (S.I. 1992 No. 272), rr. 6(3), 7(2), 8, 11(2), 14, 19(5), 19(6), 20(2), Sched.

[18] Some of these are noticed elsewhere in this book; others, relative to bankruptcy and liquidation proceedings, and commissary practice, are outside its scope, as are his functions in relation to criminal procedure.

[19] Courts of Law Fees (Scotland) Act 1895, s. 2, substituted by the Divorce Jurisdiction, Court Fees and Legal Aid (Scotland) Act 1983, s. 4. See the Sheriff Court Fees Order 1985 (S.I. 1985 No. 827); Sheriff Court Fees Amendment (No. 2) Order 1993 (S.I. 1993 No. 2957).

[20] The terms of the A.S. (Fees for Sheriff Court) 1982 (S.I. 1982 No. 652), para. 2(2), which provided that he was not required to act, were revoked by the A.S. (Fees for Sheriff Court) 1984 (S.I. 1984 No. 233), and not repeated in subsequent sheriff court fees orders. The current order is the Sheriff Court Fees Order 1985 (S.I. 1985 No. 827), as amended by the Sheriff Court Fees Amendment (No. 2) Order 1993 (S.I. 1993 No. 2957).

[21] *Muir v. Muir*, 1994 S.C.L.R. 182.

knowledge of practice and procedure is available to the sheriff[22] as well as to solicitors and party litigants, and in practice the efficient running of the court depends very much on the helpfulness and expertise of the sheriff clerk and his staff. The sheriff clerk is not, however, required to act as agent for party litigants or for solicitors who do not practise in the district, or to keep them advised of the progress of cases depending in the court: such persons are required to appear in court, or to make their inquiries at the sheriff clerk's office, either personally or through a local solicitor.[23] In the course of his administrative duties the sheriff clerk manages the office facilities which are required for the administration of the court,[24] and acts as accommodation officer and incident control officer with responsibility for the day-to-day maintenance and security of the sheriff court house. Some sheriff clerks are responsible both for their own courts and for small neighbouring courts staffed by sheriff clerk deputes: for example, the sheriff clerk at Greenock is responsible for the courts at Dunoon and Rothesay.

The post of regional sheriff clerk was introduced in 1986, after con- **1.25** sideration of certain recommendations in the Grieve Report as to administrative support for sheriffs principal.[25] A regional sheriff clerk was appointed for each sheriffdom and located at the court used by the sheriff principal as a base court,[26] the post of regional sheriff clerk being combined with that of sheriff clerk at the base court save in Edinburgh and Glasgow. The office was created with two objectives in view: to ensure that the staff and financial resources provided to the courts within the sheriffdom were used economically and efficiently, and to provide appropriate administrative support for the sheriff principal. The regional sheriff clerk accordingly discharges many administrative responsibilities including the management of staff; the co-ordination and allocation of manpower, finance other resources; the provision of advice and direction to sheriff clerks on administrative and policy matters, and of advice to the sheriff principal, the Scottish Courts Administration, and the Scottish Courts Service on such matters; and the collection of the information which the sheriff principal requires to plan and co-ordinate the work of his courts. He assists the sheriff principal in arranging for the assistance of temporary sheriffs, and in the appointment and regulation of sheriff officers. The title "regional sheriff clerk" is perhaps something of a misnomer for this important administrative officer. The office is not mentioned in any enactment, and thus the regional sheriff clerk has no statutory functions as such. Where he is the sheriff clerk at the base court, he discharges the statutory and other duties relative to litigation which attach to the office of sheriff clerk at that court, but he does not and cannot have any such duties in any of the other courts of the sheriffdom, where they remain exclusively the responsibility of the sheriff clerk of each particular court. He does, however, exercise substantial control and influence in administrative matters, without encroaching on the statutory

---

22 *Furnheim v. Watson*, 1946 S.L.T. 297, *per* L.J.-C. Cooper at 301.

23 *Miller v. Chapelside Chemical Co.* (1887) 3 Sh.Ct.Rep. 83 at 88.

24 Grant Report, paras 8, 9, 413–424.

25 Grieve Report, paras 24–27, 49(7). The report did not favour the introduction of regional sheriff clerks (para. 26).

26 In the sheriffdoms of Grampian, Highland and Islands and of South Strathclyde, Dumfries and Galloway the regional sheriff clerk is located at a different court from the regional procurator fiscal.

responsibilities of the sheriff principal. Under a pilot scheme introduced in 1997 an area director, who is also the deputy chief executive of the Scottish Court Service, has been appointed for the area comprising the sheriffdoms of Glasgow and Strathkelvin, North Strathclyde, and South Strathclyde, Dumfries and Galloway, which are linked for this purpose. It is understood that if this scheme proves successful two further area directors will be appointed, one for the sheriffdoms of Lothian and Borders and of Tayside, Central and Fife and the other for the sheriffdom of Grampian, Highland and Islands, and that the post of regional sheriff clerk will become obsolete. Area directors will fulfil the functions previously fulfilled by regional sheriff clerks but in a manner more closely integrated into the general management structure of the Scottish Court Service.

The auditor[27]

1.26 The auditor of each sheriff court is appointed by the sheriff principal, and holds office during his pleasure. There is no statutory qualification for the office, but the holder requires an intimate knowledge of the working of the sheriff court and of the various rates at which professional fees may properly be charged. The sheriff clerk or one of his deputes is frequently appointed.[28] The auditor is primarily concerned with the taxation of judicial accounts, which are solicitors' accounts of expenses in litigations in which the sheriff has made an award of expenses. Taxation involves a critical scrutiny of the accounts and the disallowing of items considered to be unnecessary or excessive.[29] The auditor's fees for this service are fixed by statutory instrument[30] and, where he is a sheriff clerk, pass to the Exchequer. The auditor may also tax extra-judicial accounts, such as solicitor's business accounts, and retain any fees which he receives for such work. The fees charged for such extra-judicial audits are not regulated by Act of Sederunt, but it is understood that in practice they are in general based on a standard percentage of the amount due to the solicitor in the audited account.

Sheriff officers[31]

1.27 Sheriff officers are employed by litigants in civil actions to carry out certain steps of procedure, including the personal service of writs[32] and the execution of warrants and decrees. Although they are employed and paid by the litigants instructing them,[33] they are officers of the sheriff court, appointed by the sheriff principal.[34] The appointment has been said to be a discretionary act of administration by the sheriff principal, and not subject to appeal or review. In considering an application for appointment, the sheriff principal has regard to the necessity for securing the proper administration of justice,[35] and may

---

[27] Grant report, paras 434–437.

[28] The sheriff clerk does not hold the office in Aberdeen, Edinburgh or Glasgow.

[29] See Chap. 19.

[30] Sheriff Court Fees Order 1985 (S.I. 1985 No. 827), Sched., Pt IV, para. 34, substituted by the Sheriff Court Fees Amendment (No. 2) Order 1993 (S.I. 1993 No. 2957).

[31] Maher and Cusine, *The Law and Practice of Diligence* (1990), Chap. 14.

[32] See Chap. 6.

[33] A table of fees is prescribed by Act of Sederunt: A.S. (Fees of Sheriff Officers) (S.I. 1994 No. 392).

[34] *Stewart v. Reid*, 1934 S.C. 69, *per* L.P. Clyde at 72, Lord Sands at 75, Lord Blackburn at 76. An officer may hold commissions from more than one sheriff principal.

[35] *Stewart, supra*, Lords Blackburn and Morison at 76.

take into account such matters as an applicant's business interest in debt-collecting.[36] He may also consider whether there is a need for an additional sheriff officer in the district applied for, whether the introduction of a new sheriff officer will seriously prejudice existing sheriff officers who have served the district well and whether the applicant will be in a position to offer the level of service which the sheriff principal is entitled to expect.[37] It is not, however, for the sheriff principal to inhibit competition among sheriff officers.[38] Applicants are examined as to the law and practice applicable to the office, and must find caution for the due performance of their duties. Their organisation, training, qualifications, functions, conduct, discipline and keeping of records and accounts are regulated by statute and Act of Sederunt.[39] In addition to his disciplinary powers, the sheriff principal has powers of inspection and of investigation of complaints.[40] It has been said that sheriff officers hold office during the pleasure of the sheriff principal[41] but their removal on the ground of misconduct is now subject to procedures under which appeal lies from the sheriff principal's decision to the Court of Session.[42] As an officer of court, a sheriff officer may not act in a case in which he is personally interested and if he does so the service of any charge or the execution of any diligence or warrant is void.[43]

There was formerly some doubt as to the extent to which messengers-at-arms might act in sheriff court proceedings.[44] It appeared clear that while they might not act in relation to summary causes,[45] they might execute diligence in ordinary causes.[46] The Debtors (Scotland) Act 1987 provides, however, that a messenger-at-arms shall not be authorised by his commission to execute a warrant granted by a sheriff or sheriff clerk.[47] A messenger-at-arms unless he also holds a relevant commission as a sheriff officer is therefore excluded from executing citation or diligence in connection with sheriff court proceedings. **1.28**

The procurator fiscal

The right of appointing to the office of procurator fiscal is vested in the Lord Advocate,[48] who may issue instructions to procurators fiscal for the purpose of securing the speedy and efficient disposal of business in the **1.29**

---

[36] *Lewis, Petr*, 1963 S.L.T. (Sh. Ct.) 6.

[37] *Macpherson, Petr*, 1989 S.L.T. (Sh. Ct.) 53 at 55 C–D; *cf. Wardell, Petr*, 1993 S.C.L.R. 398.

[38] *Macpherson* at 55E.

[39] Debtors (Scotland) Act 1987, ss. 75, 76, 78–86; A.S. (Messengers-at-Arms and Sheriff Officers Rules) 1991 (S.I. 1991 No. 1397). The Advisory Council on Messengers-at-Arms and Sheriff Officers keeps all matters relating to officers of court under review and advises on the making of Acts of Sederunt (1987 Act, s. 76).

[40] *ibid.* ss. 78, 79.

[41] *Stewart v. Reid, supra, per* Lord Morison at 76–77; *Lewis, Petr*, 1963 S.L.T. (Sh. Ct.) 6.

[42] Debtors (Scotland) Act 1987, ss. 80(6), 82.

[43] *ibid.* s. 83. The prohibition extends to interests of members of the officer's family and of business associates and interest is widely defined. For the law prior to the 1987 Act, see *McLachlan v. Black* (1822) 1 S. 217 (N. E. 206); *Dalgliesh v. Scott* (1822) 1 S. 506 (N.E. 469); *John Temple Ltd v. Logan*, 1973 S.L.T. (Sh. Ct.) 41; *Lawrence Jack Collections v. Hamilton*, 1976 S.L.T. (Sh. Ct.) 18; *British Relay Ltd v. Keay*, 1976 S.L.T. (Sh. Ct.) 23.

[44] The principal authorities are cited in *Thornton*, 1967 S.L.T. (Sh. Ct.) 71.

[45] SCR 6(4). *Cf.* T.C. Gray, "The Summary Cause Rules", 1977 S.L.T. (News) 129 at p. 132.

[46] Sheriff Courts (Scotland) Extracts Act 1892, s. 8.

[47] s. 77(2).

[48] Sheriff Courts and Legal Officers (Scotland) Act 1927, s. 1(2).

sheriff courts.[49] Neither the sheriff principal nor the sheriff is empowered to give the procurator fiscal any instructions in the performance of his duties, nor may the Court of Session order him to perform any tasks in relation to civil causes, and he is not required to grant his aid in the execution of a civil warrant.[50]

1.30 Although the procurator fiscal is mainly concerned with criminal matters, he has certain duties in the sheriff's civil court. He presents evidence in inquiries held under the Fatal Accidents and Sudden Deaths Inquiries (Scotland) Act 1976, and his concurrence is requisite in proceedings for breach of interdict,[51] for contravention of lawburrows,[52] and for breach of sequestration for rent where penal consequences are sought.[53] Where a person has been arrested for breach of a matrimonial interdict to which a power of arrest has been attached, the facts are reported to the procurator fiscal, who may then proceed not in the civil but in the criminal court: he may either take criminal proceedings or present a petition to the sheriff sitting as a court of summary criminal jurisdiction.[54]

1.31 The procurator fiscal may appear as a party in civil proceedings; he may be sued as such in the civil court,[55] although he enjoys a large measure of immunity from liability[56]; in certain civil proceedings he may be called as defender for the public interest, or the proceedings may be intimated to him in order that he may appear or be represented, if so advised, in the public interest[57]; and he may appear as pursuer in an action of multiplepoinding brought to resolve competing claims to the ownership of a production in a criminal cause which is in his hands, and may be exonered, discharged and found entitled to expenses on consignation or deposit of the fund *in medio*. In such cases he observes the rules of practice and procedure in the civil court in the same way as any other litigant. A depute may act on his behalf.[58] Government departments which are not represented by the Solicitor to the Secretary of State or other permanent legal adviser in Scotland are represented not by the procurator fiscal, but by solicitors in practice who are nominated by the Lord Advocate.

Audience and right to practise

1.32 Limitation of the categories of persons whom courts are prepared to hear as advocates for parties to proceedings before them is a feature of all developed systems for the administration of justice.[59] In ordinary causes in the sheriff court the only persons who are permitted to appear and conduct cases are members of the Faculty of Advocates,[60] solicitors and parties who are natural persons. The latter, when conducting their own

---

49 Sheriff Courts and Legal Officers (Scotland) Act 1927, s. 8(1); 1971 Act, s. 20.

50 *Caldwell v. Caldwell*, 1983 S.L.T. 610.

51 See para. 21.96.

52 See para. 24.05.

53 See para. 23.22.

54 Matrimonial Homes (Family Protection) (Scotland) Act 1981, ss. 16, 17.

55 *Hester v. MacDonald*, 1961 S.C. 370.

56 Walker, *Delict* (2nd ed.), pp. 444, 448, 873–874.

57 *Evans v. McIntyre*, Aberdeen Sh. Ct, March 17, 1980, unreported (action for interdict of disposal of dead body intimated to procurator fiscal of district where body lying).

58 *Carmichael v. Wingate*, 1990 S.L.T. (Sh. Ct.) 64.

59 *Abse v. Smith* [1986] Q.B. 536.

60 For the rules as to the appearance of counsel in civil proceedings in the sheriff court see paras 12.21 to 12.26.

causes, are known as party litigants.[61] Firms,[62] companies[63] and other artificial entities[64] must always be represented by solicitors or counsel.[65] The object of the rule is to secure that the court will be served by lawyers who observe the rules of their profession, who are subject to a disciplinary code, and who are familiar with the methods and scope of advocacy which are followed in presenting cases in court.[66] Special rules are applicable to representation in summary causes,[67] in proceedings under the Debtors (Scotland) Act 1987[68] and in inquiries under the Fatal Accidents and Sudden Deaths Inquiry (Scotland) Act 1976.[69]

A person may practise as a solicitor[70] in any court in Scotland if he has **1.33** been admitted as a solicitor, his name is on the roll of solicitors kept by the Council of the Law Society of Scotland and, unless he is or acts under the direction of a person authorised to act as a solicitor to a public department without admission, he has in force a practising certificate.[71] The Council annually sends to each sheriff clerk a list of all solicitors holding current practising certificates.[72] Solicitors who appear professionally at the bar of all courts in open session are expected to wear gowns.

Regulation of procedure

The civil procedure of the sheriff court is regulated by statute, by Act of **1.34** Sederunt, by such orders and directions as each sheriff principal may give for the courts of his sheriffdom, and by the practice of the court.

The principal statutes are the Acts of 1907 and 1971, as amended. The **1.35** 1907 Act by its First Schedule enacted Rules for Regulating Procedure in the Ordinary Court. These have now been replaced by the Ordinary Cause Rules 1993, but by virtue of section 39 of the 1907 Act the latter rules are to be construed and have effect as part of the Act. While several other provisions of the 1907 Act have also been repealed, it continues to regulate a number of important matters regarding the appointment of sheriffs principal and sheriffs, jurisdiction, removings, summary removings, summary applications, appeals and fees. The 1971 Act, which had its origin in

---

[61] For the rules as to party litigants see paras 4.118 to 4.121.

[62] *Macbeth & Maclagan v. Macmillan*, 1914 S.C.(J.) 165.

[63] *Equity and Law Life Assurance Society v. Tritonia Ltd*, 1943 S.C. (H.L.) 88; *Thomson Ship Cranes Ltd, The Scotsman*, Dec. 9, 1971. A limited company is not a party litigant and cannot be represented by a director: *Bargeport Ltd v. Adam*, Sh.Pr. Dick, Glasgow Sh. Ct, Feb. 15, 1985, unreported. The course adopted in *Road Transport Industry Training Board v. John Duncan Removals Ltd*, 1975 S.L.T. (Sh. Ct.) 2, is not consistent with these authorities.

[64] *Scottish Gas Board v. Alexander*, 1963 S.L.T. (Sh. Ct.) 27.

[65] The practice in ordinary causes follows that of the House of Lords (*Equity and Law Life Assurance Society*, *supra*, n. 56) and the Court of Session (*Gordon v. Nakeski-Cumming*, 1924 S.C. 939, at 941, 942; *Thomson Ship Cranes Ltd*, *supra*, n. 63; *Rush v. Fife R.C.*, 1984 S.L.T. 391), except that the right of audience is extended to solicitors.

[66] *Equity and Law Life Assurance Society*, *supra*, at 90.

[67] SCR, r. 17. See Vol. 2 of this work.

[68] OCR, r. 1.3; A.S. Proceedings in the Sheriff Court under the Debtors (Scotland) Act 1987, 1988 (S.I. 1988 No. 2013).

[69] Fatal Accidents and Sudden Deaths Inquiry Procedure (Scotland) Rules 1977 (S.I. 1977 No. 191), r. 7. See Chap. 27.

[70] On the solicitor's duties to the court, see R. M. Webster and J. H. Webster, *Professional Ethics and Practice for Scottish Solicitors* (3rd ed., 1996), Chap. 3.

[71] Solicitors (Scotland) Act 1980, ss. 4, 24 and 25. For the categories of solicitors required to take out practising certificates see (1993) 38 J.L.S. 130.

[72] Solicitors (Scotland) Act 1980, s. 20(1)(b).

the Grant Report, is the principal statute concerning the constitution, organisation and administration of the sheriff courts, and the provision and maintenance of court houses, buildings and offices. In the field of civil jurisdiction, procedure and appeals it makes provision for an upper limit to the privative jurisdiction of the sheriff court; establishes summary cause procedure and enacts certain rules as to procedure and appeals therein, and as to the remitting of cases to the Court of Session; and replaces earlier provisions as to the regulation by the Court of Session of the rules of procedure in the sheriff court.

1.36 By section 32 of the 1971 Act the Court of Session is empowered to regulate and prescribe by Act of Sederunt the procedure and practice to be followed in any civil proceedings in the sheriff court. By virtue of the power so conferred the court has substituted the current Ordinary Cause Rules for the First Schedule to the Act of 1907,[73] has enacted the Summary Cause Rules[74] and has made provision for a wide variety of other matters,[75] including emergencies created by industrial action.[76] Many other enactments empower the court to regulate sheriff court procedure in particular statutory proceedings,[77] or to enact rules in regard to numerous other subjects.[78] The court may also in exceptional circumstances regulate procedure in particular cases in the sheriff court in the exercise of its *nobile officium.*[79]

1.37 Before making an Act of Sederunt under section 32 the court is obliged to consult the Sheriff Court Rules Council and take its views into consideration, unless the proposed Act of Sederunt embodies draft rules submitted by the Council. The Sheriff Court Rules Council consists of 16 members,[80] one of whom is appointed by the Secretary of State and two, having a knowledge of the working procedure and practices of the civil courts, a knowledge of consumer affairs and an awareness of the interests of litigants, by the Lord President of the Court of Session after consultation with the Secretary of State. The remainder, who are appointed by the Lord President after consultation with such persons as may appear to him appropriate, are: two sheriffs principal, one of whom is chairman; three sheriffs; one advocate; five solicitors; and two whole-time sheriff clerks. The secretary to the Council is appointed by the Secretary of State,[81] and is in practice a member of the Scottish Court Service who has

---

[73] A.S. (Sheriff Court Ordinary Course Rules) 1993 (S.I. 1993 No. 1956).

[74] A.S. (SCR, Sheriff Court) 1976 (S.I. 1976 No. 476).

[75] *e.g.* A.S. (Statutory Appeals) 1981 (S.I. 1981 No. 1591).

[76] A.S. (Emergency Powers in the Sheriff Court) 1972 (S.I. 1972 No. 220); A.S. (Suspension of Business) 1979 (S.I. 1979 No. 226). On the question whether the latter was *intra vires* see R. M. White, "Courting Disaster", 1979 S.L.T. (News) 197 at pp. 199–200.

[77] *e.g.* Licensing (Scotland) Act 1976, s. 39(9): A.S. (Appeals under the Licensing (Scotland) Act 1976) 1977 (S.I. 1977 No. 1622).

[78] *e.g.* Administration of Justice (Scotland) Act 1972, s. 4: A.S. (Interest in Sheriff Court Decrees and Extracts) 1975 (S.I. 1975 No. 948), as amended by S.I.s 1983 No. 409; 1985 No. 1179; 1993 No. 769. The court also regulates the places where commissary business may be conducted in the commissariat of each sheriffdom: Sheriff Courts (Scotland) Act 1876, s. 54; A.S. (Commissary Business) 1975 (S.I. 1975 No. 539), as amended by S.I.s 1978 No. 1509; 1979 No. 1415; 1984 No. 969; 1986 No. 267.

[79] *Manson v. British Gas Corporation*, 1982 S.L.T. 77.

[80] 1971 Act, s. 33 as amended by the Law Reform (Miscellaneous Provisions) (Scotland) Act 1985, Sched. 2, para. 13 and Law Reform (Miscellaneous Provisions) (Scotland) Act 1990, Sched. 8, para. 26.

[81] *ibid.* s. 33(4).

held a commission as a sheriff clerk and is seconded to Scottish Courts Administration. The Council's duties are to keep under review the procedure and practice followed in civil proceedings in the sheriff court and to prepare and submit to the Court of Session draft rules of procedure such as the court have power to make by Act of Sederunt under section 32.[82]

The sheriff principal is empowered both by the 1971 Act and by the common law to issue orders and directions for the administration and procedural regulation of the court. Section 15(1) of the 1971 Act imposes on the sheriff principal a duty to secure the speedy and efficient disposal of business in the sheriff courts of his sheriffdom, and section 15(2) empowers him to give such instructions of an administrative nature as appear to him to be necessary or expedient. Section 16 confers on him functions with respect to the duties and leave of absence of sheriffs, and section 17 empowers him to fix the sittings and business of the sheriff courts in his sheriffdom and their sessions for the disposal of civil business.[83] The sheriff principal also has powers at common law to regulate the practice and procedure of the courts of his sheriffdom.[84] The orders, directions and instructions which the sheriff principal is empowered to give may take the form of orders, acts of court or practice notes, depending on the custom and practice of the sheriffdom.[85] A distinction which is sometimes made is that orders and acts of court are promulgated to regulate administrative matters while practice notes deal with the conduct of litigation. Thus, orders and acts of court may deal with such administrative matters as the fixing of sittings, sessions and court holidays,[86] the administration of commissary business,[87] arrangements for registering deeds in the court books of the sheriffdom[88] and the establishment of sheriff court advisory committees,[89] while practice notes prescribe rules relative to practice and procedure and regulate the conduct of practitioners in relation to litigation. In some sheriffdoms, however, the latter matters are regulated by act of court. **1.38**

The sheriff principal may regulate the procedure of the courts of his sheriffdom by issuing orders and directions in the exercise of the powers conferred by section 15(2) of the 1971 Act and his common law powers.[90] Acts of court and practice notes regulate a wide variety of matters of practice and procedure including appeals,[91] extracts,[92] diligence[93] and **1.39**

---

[82] 1971 Act, s. 34.

[83] See paras. 5.11 to 5.15.

[84] Directions by the Lord Justice-General or Lord President as to the suspension of criminal sittings or civil business in the event of industrial action may be varied or revoked, with his Lordship's concurrence, by a sheriff principal in respect of his sheriffdom: A.A. (Suspension of Sittings, etc.) 1979 (S.I. 1979 No. 232), para. 2 (4); A.S. (Suspension of Business) 1979 (S.I. 1979 No. 226), para. 2(4).

[85] *United Dominions Trust v. Stark*, 1981 S.L.T. (Sh. Ct.) 58 at 60.

[86] 1971 Act, s. 17; Criminal Procedure (Scotland) Act 1995, s. 8.

[87] North Strathclyde Act of Court (Consolidation etc.) 1992, ss. 3.01 to 3.05. All acts of court and practice notes issued by sheriffs principal are to be found in Vol. I of the *Parliament House Book*.

[88] *ibid.* s. 3.06.

[89] South Strathclyde, Dumfries and Galloway Act of Court 1993, No. 1; Glasgow and Strathkelvin Act of Court 1982, No. 1. See para. 1.47.

[90] See, for example, preamble to Glasgow Sheriff Court Practice Notes.

[91] See Glasgow Sheriff Court Practice Notes, *supra.*

[92] *ibid.*

[93] *ibid.*

decrees for payment in foreign currency,[94] and they may supplement the provisions of Acts of Sederunt.[95] The sheriff principal may not, however, issue orders or directions which purport to create substantive law or to amend or alter the law as laid down by Parliament, Act of Sederunt or authoritative decision,[96] or to restrict the sheriffs' powers to decide questions of law which are *primo loco* within their jurisdiction.[97]

1.40 It is submitted that an act of court or practice note which is *intra vires* of the sheriff principal has the force of law within the sheriffdom. In so far as it is issued by virtue of section 15(2) of the 1971 Act it must be observed by the sheriffs and by any officer or servant engaged in the administration of the sheriff courts in the sheriffdom.[98] It has been doubted whether a sheriff was empowered to ignore a practice note issued in pursuance of the sheriff principal's common-law powers.[99] It is submitted that such a practice note has the force of law within the sheriffdom since it derives its authority from the inherent jurisdiction of the court to make and enforce rules of practice.[1] In certain circumstances, at least, the reduction of a decree may be warranted by a failure to follow such a practice note,[2] or even by a failure to follow the ordinary practice of the court which is not expressed in a practice note.[3] It is also submitted that a failure to observe the terms of any act of court or practice note may be taken into account in determining liability for payment of any relevant expenses.

1.41 As well as orders and directions, the sheriff principal may issue informal recommendations for the assistance of practitioners in their conduct of litigation.[4]

1.42 "Practice in the course of litigation is due to two distinct causes—one the written rules, and the other the accepted and traditional practice of the courts."[5] "The practice of the courts" is difficult to define or to ascertain, but perhaps it may be defined as a course of proceedings which has been followed over a period of time throughout the sheriff court system by successive sheriffs,[6] and may be ascertained by a sheriff by reference to his own experience.[7] A rule of practice may, however, be modified by innovation combined with persistence of practice until, through lapse of

---

[94] Lothian and Borders Act of Court (Consolidation etc.) 1990, No. 1, s. 14; South Strathclyde, Dumfries and Galloway Act of Court 1981, No. 4.

[95] North Strathclyde Act of Court (Consolidation etc.) 1992, s. 1.19 makes provision for reduction in solicitors' fees in a summary cause action of delivery where the value of the article is not specified: not provided for in the A.S. (Fees of Solicitors in the Sheriff Court) 1986, Sched., para. 14(f) (now revoked) nor in the current A.S. (Fees of Solicitors in the Sheriff Court) (Amendment and Further Provisions) 1993 (S.I. 1993 No. 3080), Sched. 1, General Regulations, reg. 14(f).

[96] *United Dominions Trust v. Stark*, 1981 S.L.T. (Sh. Ct.) 58; and see para. 21.74.

[97] *McCulloch v. McLaughlin*, 1930 J.C. 8.

[98] 1971 Act, s. 15(2).

[99] *Mitchell Construction Co. (Scotland) Ltd v. Brands Transport and Demolition Ltd*, 1975 S.L.T. (Notes) 58.

[1] See paras 2.07, 2.08.

[2] *Mitchell Construction Co. (Scotland) Ltd, supra.*

[3] *Brennan v. Central SMT Co.*, 1947 S.N. 7 (not fully reported on this point, 1947 S.L.T. (Notes) 4).

[4] See Glasgow Sheriff Court Practice Notes, Appendix, (1982).

[5] *Park v. Wilsons and Clyde Coal Co.*, 1929 S.C. (H.L.) 38, *per* Lord Buckmaster at 50.

[6] Sir Jack I. H. Jacob, "Practice and Procedure", *Halsbury's Laws of England* (4th ed.), Vol. 37, para. 15.

[7] *Drummond's Trs v. Peel's Trs*, 1929 S.C. 484, *per* Lord Anderson at 509.

time, a new rule has been evolved; and a sheriff may depart from the practice of the courts if in any case he thinks that the peculiar exigencies of the case demand in the interests of justice that it should not be obeyed.[8] It is thought that a distinction should be drawn between practices which are regularly followed in all sheriff courts, and practices peculiar to individual courts. A sheriff would not readily depart from any of the former, while the latter may be changed at any time by the sheriff principal or by the sheriff or sheriffs in post at the particular court provided that reasonable notice is given to practitioners. A sheriff's unheralded and unexplained departure from the ordinary practice of his local court may amount to such failure in the due observance of the judicial administration of justice as to warrant reduction of a decree.[9]

Rules of principle apply equally to the Court of Session and to the sheriff court. It is therefore submitted that where any lacuna appears in the rules of procedure laid down for the sheriff court by statute, by Act of Sederunt or by the sheriff principal and where sheriff court practice offers no precedent, a sheriff may properly resort for guidance to the general principles of Scottish civil procedure which may be discerned in the practice of the Court of Session.[10] It has been said that there is truly one system of civil procedure in the Scottish courts, and that it is erroneous to conceive of the Court of Session and the sheriff courts as administering entirely separate codes of procedure.[11] **1.43**

Administration[12]

The present scheme for the administration of the sheriff courts was promulgated in Part I of the 1971 Act, which was inspired by the Grant Committee's recognition of a need for authoritative direction of court business both at the centre and at local level.[13] At the centre the Act makes the Secretary of State responsible for undertaking the general direction of the work of the courts, while at local level it confers on the sheriff principal certain powers in relation to the courts in his sheriffdom. Throughout, the statutory provisions emphasise the necessity for efficient organisation and administration, and the avoidance of delay in the administration of justice.[14] **1.44**

By section 1 of the Act the Secretary of State is made responsible for securing the efficient organisation and administration of the sheriff courts. For the purpose of securing that objective and, in particular, the speedy and efficient disposal of business, he may give to sheriff court judges and administrative staff such directions of an administrative nature as appear to him to be necessary or expedient.[15] He is also required to undertake various duties including the designation of sheriffdoms[16] and sheriff court districts,[17] the appointment of sheriffs principal,[18] sheriffs[19] **1.45**

---

8 *Park v. Wilsons and Clyde Coal Co., supra.*
9 *Brennan, supra.*
10 *McKidd v. Manson* (1882) 9 R. 790 at 791: *Banque Indo Suez v. Maritime Co. Overseas Inc.*, 1985 S.L.T 117.
11 Lewis, p. 2.
12 See *Administration of Sheriffdoms* (Cmnd 8548, 1982).
13 Grant Report, rec. 90, paras 325–334.
14 1971 Act, ss. 1, 9, 10(1), 11(1), 15(1), 16(1), 18, 20.
15 *ibid.* s. 9.
16 See para. 1.03.
17 See para. 1.04.
18 See paras 1.07 to 1.10.
19 See para. 1.14.

and court staff,[20] and the exercise of final disciplinary powers.[21] He is also empowered to regulate court fees.[22]

1.46 In practice the functions of the Secretary of State are normally discharged through Scottish Courts Administration (SCA), which came into being in 1971 as part of the Scottish Office. The Transfer of Functions (Secretary of State and Lord Advocate) Order 1972,[23] which came into effect in 1973, and a concurrent reallocation of legal functions in Scotland between those ministers which was made by administrative arrangement, left unaffected the Secretary of State's responsibilities in relation to the sheriff courts under the 1971 Act,[24] but since the functions transferred to the Lord Advocate are discharged on his behalf by SCA, it is answerable to both ministers and is no longer held to be part of the Scottish Office. In practice, however, all the members of the staff of SCA, apart from those seconded from the Scottish Court Service, are "on loan" from the Scottish Office. The Director of SCA may be, but need not be and has not since 1978 been, a sheriff principal or sheriff.[25] In 1995 the Scottish Court Service was established within SCA as an executive agency with its own chief executive. Its responsibilities include the provision of staff, court buildings and associated services for the sheriff courts.

1.47 As an administrative officer the sheriff principal is empowered at common law to exercise a general supervision over the work of the sheriffs in his sheriffdom, and he is available for consultation by them on matters affecting the conduct of business in their courts. Further administrative functions are conferred by the Act of 1971, which imposes on the sheriff principal a duty to secure the speedy and efficient disposal of business in the sheriff courts of his sheriffdom, enables him to give such instructions of an administrative nature as appear to him to be necessary or expedient, and requires the sheriffs and any officer or servant engaged in the administration of the sheriff courts in the sheriffdom to give effect to these instructions.[26] Subject to any direction of an administrative nature given by the Secretary of State, the sheriff principal may provide for the division of business between himself and the sheriffs and for the distribution of business among the sheriffs.[27] He may also make special provision of a temporary nature for the disposal of business by himself or by any of the sheriffs in the event of a vacancy in the office of sheriff, or a sheriff's inability to perform his duties, or where it appears to him expedient so to do in order to avoid delay in the administration of justice in the sheriffdom.[28] He may also approve leave of absence for the sheriffs.[29] He prescribes the sittings and business of the sheriff courts in the sheriffdom, and their sessions for civil business.[30] In some sheriff court districts Sheriff Court Advisory Committees have been set up to advise the

---

[20] See para. 1.21.
[21] See paras. 1.08, 1.14, 1.21.
[22] Courts of Law Fees (Scotland) Act 1895, s. 2, substituted by the Divorce Jurisdiction, Court Fees and Legal Aid (Scotland) Act 1983, s. 4.
[23] S.I. 1972 No. 2002.
[24] 1973 S.L.T. (News) 11.
[25] 1971 Act, s. 8. The first two Directors were sheriffs: see Grieve Report, App. E.
[26] 1971 Act, s. 15.
[27] *ibid.* s. 16(1)(a).
[28] *ibid.* s. 16(1)(b).
[29] *ibid.* s. 16(2).
[30] *ibid.* s. 17. See paras 5.11 to 5.15.

sheriff principal on matters affecting the work of the court and the convenience of the users of the court. In some sheriffdoms a committee of sheriff clerks has been constituted which may make recommendations to the sheriff principal with a view to achieving reasonable uniformity in administration and practice throughout the courts of the sheriffdom.

The Secretary of State may himself rescind or exercise any of the functions conferred on the sheriff principal by sections 15 to 17 of the 1971 Act if he considers that a sheriff principal's exercise of them, or failure to exercise them, is prejudicial to the speedy and efficient disposal of business in the sheriff courts of that sheriffdom or to the efficient organisation or administration of the sheriff courts generally, or is otherwise against the interests of the public.[31] **1.48**

All sheriff court houses[32] together with certain rights, liabilities and obligations attaching to them are vested in the Secretary of State,[33] and the responsibility for the provision and maintenance of court houses and other accommodation rests with him.[34] Buildings belonging to local or other public authorities may be used as court houses in order to avoid delay in the administration of justice.[35] **1.49**

Statistics relating to the civil business of the sheriff courts are included in the Civil Judicial Statistics Scotland which are prepared by Scottish Courts Administration and published annually by The Stationery Office. A code for the preservation or disposal of sheriff court records is prescribed by the Preservation of Sheriff Court Records Regulations 1969.[36] The sheriff court records of the sheriff court district of Linlithgow are selected for preservation with a view to preserving a representative sample of records relating to the development of sheriff court procedure and administration.[37] **1.50**

---

[31] 1971 Act, s. 18.

[32] Many sheriff court houses are described in *Historic Buildings at Work* (Scottish Civic Trust and Property Services Agency, Dept of the Environment, 1983).

[33] 1971 Act, s. 23; Sheriff Courts (Scotland) Act 1971 (Transfer Date) Order 1973 (S.I. 1973 No. 277); Sheriff Court Houses (Transfer) (Scotland) Regulations 1973 (S.I. 1973 No. 402). The Secretary of State for the Environment was designed in the 1971 Act (s. 23(7)) as the minister in whom buildings vested. It is understood that that was done for purposes of conveyancing of buildings and interests in buildings from the bodies in which they had previously been vested. The designation of a particular Secretary of State is otherwise unnecessary. All responsibilities in relation to buildings were exercised on behalf of the Secretary of State for the Environment until they were assumed by the Scottish Courts Administration. They are now exercised by the Property and Services Unit of the Scottish Court Service on behalf of the Secretary of State for Scotland.

[34] 1971 Act, s. 24. See Grieve Report, para. 45.

[35] 1971 Act, s. 25.

[36] S.I. 1969 No. 1756.

[37] *ibid.* reg. 5, Sched. 1.

Chapter 2

JURISDICTION: SUBJECT-MATTER, REMEDIES, EXCLUSION

I. General

Definition[1]

The "jurisdiction" of a validly constituted court connotes the limits which are imposed upon its power to try a cause and pronounce therein valid and enforceable decrees, by reference to three considerations: (1) the subject-matter of the cause, in that the court must have power to deal with it; (2) the remedy which is sought or the application which is made, in that the court must have power to grant it and the proceedings must conform to the practice and procedure of the court as to the way in which it will exercise its power to do so; and (3) the persons convened as defenders or the conduct or property in respect of which the remedy is desired or the application is made, in that the court must in general have authority over such persons or conduct or property. The term "jurisdiction" also embraces the court's right or duty to decline in certain circumstances to exercise the power which it otherwise possesses to try the cause. The expressions "territorial jurisdiction" and "the inherent jurisdiction of the court" also require explanation and are considered in the following paragraphs. Thereafter the jurisdiction of the sheriff court is considered as regards the subject-matter with which it may deal and the forms of remedy or application which it may grant, and the circumstances in which the jurisdiction of the court is excluded where its exercise would otherwise be competent. The subject of jurisdiction over persons, conduct and property is to a large extent dominated by the provisions of thc Civil Jurisdiction and Judgments Act 1982, which is separately considered in the next chapter. In this chapter the subject is noticed when proceedings outside the scope of the Act are examined. 2.01

Territorial jurisdiction

The expression "territorial jurisdiction" signifies the territory over which a court's power to try causes and pronounce judgment extends. The territorial jurisdiction of a sheriff court in civil causes extends, in general, only over its own sheriffdom. It includes, however, all navigable rivers, ports, harbours, creeks, shores and anchoring grounds in or adjoining the sheriffdom; and where sheriffdoms are separated by a river, firth or estuary, the sheriffs on either side have concurrent jurisdictions over the intervening space occupied by water.[2] In seaboard territories the 2.02

---

[1] See Maclaren, p. 33, Thomson and Middleton, p. 22; Maxwell, pp. 77–80; *Carthwaite v. Carthwaite* [1964] P. 356, *per* Diplock L.J. at 387.

[2] 1907 Act, s. 4. S. 4 applies in relation to hovercraft as it applies in relation to ships: Hovercraft Act 1968, s. 2(1).

jurisdiction of the sheriff extends, at common law, over the waters within three miles of the shore, and *inter fauces terrae*.[3] By statute it extends over all persons engaged in catching, curing and dealing in fish in all the lochs, bays and arms of the sea and within 10 miles of the coast[4]; and it includes power to hold inquiries into shipping casualties and other such events not necessarily occurring within the waters of the sheriffdom.[5] Under section 23 of the Oil and Gas (Enterprise) Act 1982, orders may be made conferring jurisdiction on the sheriff court in, for example, fatal accident inquiries. No current orders do so. The jurisdiction of the sheriff court relative to the air space over the sheriffdom appears to extend to such a height as to enable the court to entertain actions which may otherwise competently be brought in respect of rights in the air space[6] and damage caused by aircraft.[7] Jurisdiction in actions of damages in respect of carriage by air is conferred by the Carriage by Air Act 1961.[8]

2.03 The sheriff principal and sheriffs of a sheriffdom have jurisdiction in all parts of the sheriffdom.[9] A sheriff exercises that jurisdiction when on an instruction of the sheriff principal given under section 16(1)(b) of the 1971 Act he sits temporarily in a different district of the sheriffdom from that designated by the Secretary of State in terms of section 14(3) of that Act as the district in which he is to perform his duties. A sheriff may also exercise that jurisdiction without instruction under section 16(1)(b) by dealing in his designated court with a cause which might competently have been brought in another court of the sheriffdom: he is entitled to exercise a discretion whether to instruct the issue of a warrant for the citation to the court of a defender more suitably amenable to another court of the sheriffdom.[10] He may also deal in his designated court with a case which is in dependence, or which it is intended should depend, in another court of the sheriffdom, as where an order is desired when the latter court is closed for a local holiday or no professionally-qualified sheriff is available there and it is considered that the matter cannot appropriately be disposed of by an honorary sheriff. In such a case the sheriff sits in his designated court as a sheriff of the other court, and any court fees payable should be paid to the sheriff clerk at the designated court and remitted by him to the sheriff clerk at the other court.[11] It is thought that any interlocutor thus

---

[3] Stair, II, ii, 5; Ersk., II, ii, 6; Bell, *Prin.*, s. 639; *Macleod v. Dobson* (1900) 16 Sh.Ct.Rep. 33, 104; *Mortensen v. Peters* (1906) 5 Adam 121. The island of Rockall is in the sheriff court district of Stornoway: Island of Rockall Act 1972, s. 1, as amended by Local Government (Scotland) Act 1973, s. 214, Sched. 27, Pt II, para. 202; Western Isles Islands Area (Electoral Arrangements) Order (S.I. 1992 No. 3323); Sheriffdoms (Alteration of Boundaries) Order (S.I. 1996 No. 1006); Sheriff Court Districts (Alteration of Boundaries) Order 1996 (S.I. 1996 No. 1005) as amended by S.I. 1996 No. 2192. See J. J. Rankin, "Life on Rockall", 1985 S.L.T. (News) 321.

[4] Herring Fishery (Scotland) Act 1808, s. 60 (unaffected by the Fishery Limits Act 1964, ss. 1, 3 and Sched.); *Macpherson v. Ellen* (1914) 30 Sh.Ct.Rep. 206.

[5] See Chap. 26.

[6] *Halkerston v. Wedderburn* (1781) Mor. 10493; *Miln v. Mudie* (1828) 6 S. 967; *Hazle v. Turner* (1840) 2 D. 886; *Glasgow City and District Ry v. MacBrayne* (1883) 10 R. 894; *Brown v. Lee Constructions Ltd*, 1977 S.L.T. (Notes) 61. *Cf. Bernstein v. Skyviews & General Ltd* [1978] Q.B. 479.

[7] Civil Aviation Act 1982, s. 76; *Bernstein, supra*; *Steel-Maitland v. British Airways Board*, 1981 S.L.T. 110.

[8] See para. 2.77.

[9] 1907 Act, ss. 4, 3(a); 1971 Act, s. 7 and Interpretation Act 1978, ss. 5, 22; Sched. 1; Sched. 2, Pt 1, para. 4(1)(a); *Spence v. Davie*, 1993 S.L.T. 217 at 219.

[10] See para. 6.02.

[11] *Simpson v. Bruce*, 1984 S.L.T. (Sh. Ct.) 38.

pronounced in an ordinary cause should be entered in the books of the other court, and its date deemed to be that upon which it is so entered.[12]

Irrespective of the ambit of his territorial jurisdiction the sheriff may in certain circumstances transfer a cause to another court[13]; and interlocutors pronounced by the sheriff are valid throughout Scotland and may be enforceable furth of Scotland. The sheriff may interdict the commission of an act outside his territorial jurisdiction if the defender is domiciled within it.[14] In an action in which he would have jurisdiction to make an order under Part I of the Family Law Act 1986, or in any proceedings in which it would be competent for him to grant an interdict prohibiting the removal of a child from his jurisdiction, he may grant interdict or interim interdict prohibiting the removal of a child from the United Kingdom or any part of the United Kingdom or out of the control of the person in whose care the child is.[15] **2.04**

Inherent jurisdiction

Definition

The inherent jurisdiction of a court of law enables it to do whatever is necessary to discharge all of its responsibilities.[16] Erskine sums it up as follows: "In all grants of jurisdiction, whether civil or criminal, supreme or inferior, every power is understood to be conferred without which the jurisdiction cannot be explicated . . . [E]very judge, however limited his jurisdiction may be, is vested with all the powers necessary either for supporting his jurisdiction and maintaining the authority of the court, or for the execution of his decrees."[17] A similar understanding exists in England enabling a court to enforce its rules of practice and to suppress any abuses of its process and to defeat any attempted thwarting of its process.[18] The inherent jurisdiction of a court accordingly appears to be derived from its nature as a court of law, and to be exercisable provided that it does not contravene any statutory provision, rule of court or authoritative decision.[19] **2.05**

The inherent jurisdiction of the sheriff court may be exercised by various methods, principally (a) by the regulation of its practice and proceedings, (b) by the noticing of matters which are *pars judicis*, and (c) by the punishment of contempt of court. **2.06**

Regulation of practice and proceedings

The inherent jurisdiction of a court includes power to make and enforce rules of practice.[20] In the sheriff court, in areas of practice which are not **2.07**

---

[12] OCR, r. 12.2(1),(5).

[13] OCR, r. 26.1; SCR, r. 22; see paras 13.51 to 13.56; and see Vol. 2 of this work.

[14] Civil Jurisdiction and Judgments Act 1982, Sched. 8, rr. 1 and 2(10); see para. 3.104. For the earlier law see *Allen & Leslie (International) Ltd v. Wagley*, 1976 S.L.T. (Sh. Ct.) 12; *McKenna v. McKenna*, 1984 S.L.T. (Sh. Ct.) 92; Duncan and Dykes, *Principles of Civil Jurisdiction*, pp. 123, 126–127, 350; *contra, Calder Chemicals Ltd v. Brunton*, 1984 S.L.T. (Sh. Ct.) 96; Burn-Murdoch, *Interdict*, pp. 23–24; Lewis, pp. 26–27.

[15] Family Law Act 1986, s. 35 (3) as amended by the Children (Scotland) Act 1995, Sched. 4.

[16] See *Hall v. Associated Newspapers Ltd*, 1979 J.C. 1 at 9.

[17] Ersk., I, ii, 8.

[18] *Connelly v. DPP* [1964] A.C. 1254, *per* Lord Morris of Borth-y-Gest at 1301.

[19] See Sir Jack I. H. Jacob, "The Inherent Jurisdiction of the Court" (1970) 23 *Current Legal Problems* 23, reprinted in Jacob, *The Reform of Civil Procedural Law* (1982), p. 221.

[20] *Connelly, supra, per* Lord Morris of Borth-y-Gest at 1301, Lord Devlin at 1347; *Abse v. Smith* [1986] Q.B. 536.

governed by statute, Act of Sederunt or authoritative decision that power is exercised by the sheriff principal, who has been empowered from time immemorial to make directions for the regulation of the practice and proceedings of the court.[21] From the court's inherent jurisdiction is also derived the sheriff's power to regulate questions of procedure in any cause that comes before him, as by ordering that the court will sit in private,[22] dealing with a variety of incidental applications,[23] deleting scandalous and irrelevant averments from the pleadings,[24] granting or withholding interim protective or remedial orders[25] and making awards of expenses.[26] While the circumstances and the manner in which these powers may be exercised by the sheriff are in many cases regulated by statutory provisions, Acts of Sederunt or authoritative decisions, in cases where no such rules apply it may be necessary for the sheriff to draw upon the inherent jurisdiction of the court and make such orders as may be necessary for the ends of justice.[27] Such orders should not contravene the rules or prejudice a party who has in good faith relied on them. It appears, however, that the sheriff court does not possess an inherent protective jurisdiction in the matter of children such as the Court of Session possesses and may exercise where the interests of justice or of the child so require.[28]

2.08 Under the inherent jurisdiction of the court the sheriff has power to compel observance of the orders of the court since he is "vested with all the powers necessary . . . for supporting his jurisdiction and maintaining the authority of the court",[29] and thus may "take effective action to vindicate its authority and preserve the due and impartial administration of justice".[30] The consequences of failure to implement an order of the court are largely provided for by rule 16.2 of the Ordinary Cause Rules, which regulates the sheriff's power to grant decree by default in ordinary causes,[31] and by the dispensing power (now termed "Relief from compliance with rules") conferred in relation to both ordinary[32] and summary[33] causes. Otherwise, however, as in cases of breach of interdict,[34] any failure or refusal to obey or comply with an order of the court may be

---

[21] See paras 1.38 to 1.41.
[22] See paras 5.19 to 5.25.
[23] See Chaps 12, 13 to 25.
[24] See para. 10.60.
[25] See Chap. 11.
[26] See Chap. 19.
[27] *High-Flex (Scotland) Ltd v. Kentallen Mechanical Services Co.*, 1977 S.L.T. (Sh. Ct.) 91 at 94.
[28] Thus at common law the Court of Session, but not the sheriff court, may grant authority for the taking and testing of blood samples from a child, as in *Docherty v. McClynn*, 1983 S.L.T. 645: see L.P. Emslie at 648, Lord Cameron at 650. In *Clark, Petr*, April 26, 1984 (unreported: see Macphail, *Evidence*, para. S13.03C) on an unopposed petition by a pursuer in a sheriff court action of affiliation and aliment, the First Division granted authority for the taking and testing of a blood sample from the child. It is thought that if the court had considered that the sheriff could competently have granted such authority, the petition would have been dismissed as unnecessary. Under s. 6 of the Law Reform (Parent and Child) (Scotland) Act 1986 the Court of Session or the sheriff may consent to the taking of a blood sample from a child.
[29] Ersk., I, ii, 8.
[30] *H.M. Advocate v. Airs*, 1975 J.C. 64 at 69.
[31] See paras 14.02 to 14.14.
[32] OCR, r. 2.1. See paras 5.93 to 5.97.
[33] S.I. 1976 No. 476, para. 5.
[34] *Stark's Trs v. Duncan* (1906) 8 F. 429; *Johnson v. Grant*, 1923 S.C. 789.

dealt with under the inherent jurisdiction of the court. In certain circumstances such failure may be dealt with as a contempt of court.[35]

Matters which are pars judicis

Under the inherent jurisdiction of the court to preserve the due administration of justice the sheriff is empowered to take notice of certain matters whether or not they have been urged upon him by any of the parties to the action. It is submitted that such matters include any aspect of the litigation which may cause prejudice to a specific public interest, such as the public interest in the regular conduct of litigation, or to the interests of third parties not called in the action, or which may require the court to exceed its proper powers; but that they do not include objections based on rules conceived only for the benefit of a party to the action. "Parties to litigation are free to waive many advantages designed for their benefit, be they evidential or procedural, and indeed they may have perfectly sound reasons, tactical or otherwise, for doing so."[36] It is thought, accordingly, that where a party waives such an advantage, as by failing to state a plea or objection, and does not thereby infringe any public interest or public policy or the interests of any party not called, it is not for the sheriff to take exception.[37] **2.09**

In certain cases this aspect of the inherent jurisdiction of the court has been supplemented by important statutory provisions. The various matters which are *pars judicis*, whether at common law or by statute, are classified in the following paragraphs by reference to the subject-matter of the cause, the form of the remedy sought and the conformity of the proceedings to the practice and procedure of the court, and the persons convened as defenders. **2.10**

(1) Subject-matter. As to the subject-matter of the cause, it is *pars judicis* to notice whether it is within the jurisdiction of the court, to raise the question of jurisdiction before entering upon the merits of the cause and to take exception if the subject-matter is outwith its jurisdiction, as where it is within the privative jurisdiction of another court,[38] or where the issues raised are directed to be determined by arbitration in terms of an imperative statutory provision.[39] The court is bound to notice the rules as to exclusive jurisdiction in the Civil Jurisdiction and Judgments Act 1982, which confer exclusive jurisdiction on the courts of Contracting States or of parts of the United Kingdom in certain proceedings concerned with immoveable property, companies and other entities, public registers and the enforcement of judgments. Where a Scottish court, including a sheriff court, is seised of a claim which is principally concerned with a matter over which another court has exclusive jurisdiction, it must declare of its own motion that it has **2.11**

---

[35] See paras 2.18 to 2.25.

[36] *McFadyen v. Wilson*, Sh. Pr. Caplan, Kilmarnock Sh. Ct, Jan. 20, 1984, unreported.

[37] *Hill v. Black*, 1914 S.C. 913; *Reid v. Tudhope*, 1986 S.L.T. 136; and see the discussion of the maxim *Quilibet potest renuntiare juri pro se introducto* in *Thomson v. Stirling D.C.*, 1985 S.L.T. (Lands Tr.) 4.

[38] *Connell v. Ferguson* (1857) 19 D. 482, *per* Lord Deas at 486, 487; *Beattie & Son v. Pratt* (1880) 7 R. 1171, *per* Lord Ormidale at 1173, 1174; *Walls' Trs v. Drynan* (1888) 15 R. 359, *per* L.P. Inglis at 363: *MacDougall v. Chitnavis*, 1937 S.C. 390, *per* L.P. Normand at 401; *AB v. CD*, 1957 S.C. 415 at 419.

[39] *Taylor v. Brick*, 1982 S.L.T. 25; see para. 2.102.

no jurisdiction.[40] Further, where in any case a court has no jurisdiction which is compatible with the 1982 Act, and the defender does not enter an appearance, the court must declare of its own motion that it has no jurisdiction.[41] The Ordinary and Summary Cause Rules accordingly provide that in an undefended action the sheriff must not grant decree unless it appears *ex facie* of the initial writ or summons that a ground of jurisdiction exists under the 1982 Act.[42]

2.12 "It is probably now established as a general rule, both in Scotland and England, that it is the duty of the court to take cognisance of the illegality of any claim, even although no plea to that effect is put forward, if the illegality appears on the face of the contract. If it depends on surrounding circumstances it must be pleaded."[43] It is also *pars judicis* to take notice of any objection arising under the rule "*Ex turpi causa non oritur actio*"[44] and to dismiss any action raised for payment of money due *ob turpem causam* whether the defender has appeared to plead that defence or not.[45] If the court becomes aware that the contract on which a party is suing is one that this country has accepted in an international obligation to treat as unenforceable, the court must take the point itself and refuse to lend its aid to enforce the contract.[46] In a cause based on contract it is also competent for the court to take notice of the absence of any contract between the parties and dismiss the action.[47] Where it is contended that the dispute between the parties to an action falls to be referred to arbitration in terms of an arbitration clause in the contract between them, the court is entitled and bound to see that there is a real question between them of a kind which the contract appropriates to the determination of arbiters.[48] It is said to be also *pars judicis* to take a plea of prescription, since the right founded on no longer exists and a decree in the pursuer's favour would be a legal nullity.[49] In an action for aliment in which the court has jurisdiction,[50] the court may award less than the amount claimed even if the claim is undisputed.[51]

2.13 While the court must exercise its jurisdiction in all matters competently before it,[52] in defended actions it will usually exercise it in the decision of live, practical questions only and will decline, although perhaps less

---

[40] Civil Jurisdiction and Judgments Act 1982, Sched. 8, r. 7; see para. 3.113.

[41] *ibid.* Sched. 8, r. 8. See para. 3.113.

[42] OCR, r. 7.2(1); SCR, r. 55(5).

[43] Gloag, *Contract*, p. 549, citing *Hamilton v. McLaughlan* (1908) 16 S.L.T. 341; *Scott v. Brown* [1892] 2 Q.B. 724; *Gedge v. Royal Exchange Assurance Corporation* [1900] 2 Q.B. 214; *North-Western Salt Co. v. Electrolytic Alkali Co.* [1914] A.C. 461; *Rawlings v. General Trading Co.* [1921] 1 K.B. 635. See also *Re Robinson* [1912] 1 Ch. 717; *Montefiore v. Mendav Motor Components Ltd* [1918] 2 K.B. 241; *Lipton v. Powell* [1921] 2 K.B. 51.

[44] *Bile Bean Manufacturing Co. v. Davidson* (1906) 8 F. 1181.

[45] Trayner, p. 438. *Cf. United Dominion Trust Ltd v. McDowell*, 1984 S.L.T. (Sh. Ct.) 10 at 15.

[46] *United City Merchants Ltd v. Royal Bank of Canada* [1983] 1 A.C. 168. See Anton with Beaumont, p. 374.

[47] *Mathieson Gee (Ayrshire) Ltd v. Quigley*, 1952 S.C. (H.L.) 38. In such a case the question at issue is hypothetical: see para. 2.13.

[48] *Woods v. Co-operative Insurance Society*, 1924 S.C. 692, *per* L.P. Clyde at 698; *Albyn Housing Society Ltd v. Taylor Woodrow Homes Ltd*, 1985 S.L.T. 309.

[49] Walker, *Prescription and Limitation of Actions*, p. 4; see para. 2.114.

[50] See para. 2.63.

[51] Family Law (Scotland) Act 1985, s. 3(1)(d).

[52] *Gow's Trs v. Mealls* (1875) 2 R. 729.

readily than formerly,[53] to entertain questions which are hypothetical or premature,[54] or which have been superseded by events, unless some useful purpose will be served such as the clarification of the law for the future.[55] It will also decline to entertain questions which have not been argued.[56]

(2) Form. As to the form of the remedy sought and the conformity of the proceedings to the practice and procedure of the court, it is *pars judicis* to notice questions of competency notwithstanding the absence of a plea[57] and to dismiss an action as incompetent in respect of the form of action adopted,[58] or in respect of the remedy craved,[59] or in respect of the procedure followed as where all parties whose appearance or failure to appear is necessary to have the question at issue effectively decided have not been called.[60] It is also *pars judicis* to notice that the citation of an absent defender has been irregular.[61] Where in an action to which the Civil Jurisdiction and Judgments Act 1982 applies the defender is domiciled in another part of the United Kingdom or in a Contracting State which is not a party to the 1965 Hague Convention on the Service Abroad of Judicial and Extrajudicial Documents in Civil or Commercial Matters, and does not appear, the court may not grant decree until it has been shown that the defender has been able to receive the initial writ in sufficient time to enable him to arrange for his defence, or that all necessary steps have been taken to that end. Where he is domiciled in a Contracting State which is a party to the 1965 Hague Convention, and does not appear, the court may not pronounce decree until it is established that the initial writ was duly served or delivered to him or to his residence in sufficient time to enable him to defend, unless certain conditions are fulfilled.[62] **2.14**

It is also *pars judicis* to notice and order the deletion from the pleadings of any averment which is scandalous and irrelevant.[63] The court will not, however, dismiss an action *ex proprio motu* on the ground of irrelevancy,[64] **2.15**

---

[53] *MacIntyre v. Cleveland Petroleum Co. Ltd*, 1967 S.L.T. 95 at 100.

[54] *Connell v. Ferguson* (1857) 19 D. 482, *per* Lord Deas at 486–487; *Harvey v. Harvey's Trs* (1860) 22 D. 1310; *Glasgow Navigation Co. Ltd v. Iron Ore Co. Ltd*, 1910 S.C. (H.L.) 63; *Macnaughton v. Macnaughton's Trs*, 1953 S.C. 387; *Bailey's Trs v. Bailey*, 1954 S.L.T. 282; *Unigate Food Ltd v. Scottish Milk Marketing Board*, 1975 S.C. (H.L.) 75, *per* Lord Fraser of Tullybelton at 110; *Annandale and Eskdale D.C. v. North West Water Authority*, 1979 S.L.T. 266 at 268–269; *N. v. Hutcheson* (1979) 39 SCOLAG 188; *cf. Att.-Gen. v. BBC* [1981] A.C. 303, *per* Viscount Dilhorne at 336; "Hypothetical and Premature Questions", 1968 S.L.T. (News) 81; Walker, *Civil Remedies*, pp. 109, 111.

[55] *Humphries v. S*, 1986 S.L.T. 683.

[56] *Mackinnon's Trs v. MacNeill* (1897) 24 R. 981.

[57] *Blyth Dry Docks & Shipbuilding Co. Ltd v. Commrs for Port of Calcutta*, O.H., Lord Emslie, Feb. 12, 1971, not reported on this point, 1972 S.L.T. (Notes) 7; and see Maxwell, p. 194, n. 8. Lord Emslie's dictum was cited with approval by T.G. Coutts, Q.C. in *Lord Advocate v. Black*, 1995 S.L.T 540 at 542 in which he made it clear that the question of whether there is a proper pursuer before the court is *pars judicis* even if the point was not pleaded at first instance.

[58] *Clark v. Campbell* (1873) 1 R. 281, *per* L.P. Inglis at 283.

[59] *Buchan v. Lumsden* (1837) 9 Sc.Jur. 449; *Blyth Dry Docks, supra*, n. 57; *Macgregor v. Macfarlane* (1914) 31 Sh.Ct.Rep. 104; *McCallum v. Cohen* (1915) 32 Sh.Ct.Rep. 39; *Livingstone v. Gillies*, 1930 S.L.T. (Sh. Ct.) 25. *Cf. Connell v. Ferguson* (1857) 19 D. 482, *per* Lord Deas at 486–487.

[60] *Connell, supra*, n. 59.

[61] See para. 6.04.

[62] OCR, r. 7.2(3), (4); SCR rr. 18(8), 18A. See paras 3.56 to 3.59.

[63] *Wardrope v. Duke of Hamilton* (1876) 3 R. 876 at 878; *Clydesdale Bank Ltd v. Paton* (1896) 23 R.(H.L.) 22, *per* Lord Watson at 26; *C v. W*, 1950 S.L.T. (Notes) 8. See para. 10.60.

[64] *Cadbury Bros Ltd v. T. Mabon Ltd*, 1962 S.L.T. (Sh. Ct.) 28.

even if some destructive averment, undermining the basic relevancy of the case, is plain to see[65]: nor will the court apply and enforce statutory provisions as to limitation of action[66]; for these are both matters which parties may waive or plead without prejudice to the public interest or the interests of third parties. The sheriff may dismiss a summary cause if it appears to him either that it is clearly incompetent or that there is a patent defect of jurisdiction.[67] It has been said that in the most exceptional circumstances he may dismiss an undefended ordinary cause on similar grounds,[68] the incompetency warranting dismissal being an incompetency of remedy, expressed in a crave which the court has no power to grant: oppression is said not to be a ground for intervention unless it appears in the form of the crave, perhaps where an unconscionable remedy is sought *ad factum praestandum*.[69] A decree in an undefended action cannot, however, be regarded as embodying a judgment in favour of its competency.[70] If an action is brought in the name of a child or by a child to whom there is no person entitled to act as his legal representative (within the meaning of Part I of the Children (Scotland) Act 1995), or where there is such a person and he or she is unable or refuses to bring or defend such proceedings or to take such a step, it is *pars judicis* to appoint a curator *ad litem*.[71] It is *pars judicis* to propone a declinature on the ground of relationship, which cannot be waived.[72]

2.16 In the course of a proof, where a witness is asked a question the reply to which may be incriminating it is the duty of the sheriff to tell the witness that he need not answer the question.[73] It may be *pars judicis* to question the admissibility as a witness of a person who ought not to have been present in court.[74] There may be cases in which the sheriff should raise the question whether public interest immunity attaches to any documentary or oral evidence which it is proposed to adduce.[75] Objections under the Stamp Act 1891 are taken by the court and cannot be waived by the parties.[76] Upon the production of an instrument chargeable with any duty as evidence in the sheriff's civil court, the sheriff must take notice "of any omission or insufficiency of the stamp thereon",[77] but he is "only bound to intervene to protect the Revenue where there is an undoubted case of insufficient stamping or an attempted evasion of the Stamp Act."[78] If not duly stamped, the instrument may be received in evidence only if it may be

---

[65] *United Dominions Trust Ltd v. McDowell*, 1984 S.L.T. (Sh. Ct.) 10, at 14–15.

[66] *Burns v. Glasgow Corporation*, 1917 1 S.L.T. 301.

[67] SCR, r. 18(4).

[68] *Terry v. Murray*, 1947 S.C. 10, *per* Lord Mackay at 15. (The decision in this case is overruled by the Family Law (Scotland) Act 1985, s. 3(1)(d).).

[69] *United Dominions Trust*, *supra*, n. 65.

[70] *Hopkinson Ltd v. McGrory* (Glasgow Sh. Ct, April 1952, unreported), *cit. George Hopkinson Ltd v. Carr*, 1955 S.L.T. (Sh. Ct.) 80.

[71] Age of Legal Capacity (Scotland) Act 1991, s. 1(3)(f), as amended by the Children (Scotland) Act 1995, s. 105(4) and Sched. 4, para. 53(2). See paras 4.23 *et seq.*

[72] *Blair v. Sampson*, Jan. 26, 1814, F.C. (1814–15, High Ct of Justiciary, App. 501), *per* Lord Gillies at 504; *Gordon v. Gordon's Trs* (1866) 4 M. 501, at 509; *Duke of Athole v. Robertson* (1869) 8 M. 299, *per* Lord Neaves at 303. See para. 2.125.

[73] *Dickson*, para. 1789.

[74] *Macdonald v. Mackenzie*, 1947 J.C. 169, *per* Lord Mackay at 175, Lord Jamieson at 176–177.

[75] *Rogers v. Home Secretary* [1973] A.C. 388, *per* Lord Reid at 400.

[76] *Cowan v. Stewart* (1872) 10 M. 735 at 737.

[77] Stamp Act 1891, s. 14(1). See Walkers, Chap. 20.

[78] *Francesco v. De Meo*, 1908 S.C. 7, *per* Lord Ardwall at 11; *O'Brien v. O'Brien* (1910) 26 Sh.Ct.Rep. 268.

legally stamped after execution, and on payment to the sheriff clerk of the duty, the penalty and one pound.[79]

(3) Defenders. As to the persons convened as defenders, at common law the court has in general no interest to notice whether or not the defender in a personal action is subject to the jurisdiction.[80] As explained above, however, in terms of the Civil Jurisdiction and Judgments Act 1982 the court is bound to notice not only whether the action is concerned with a matter over which another court has exclusive jurisdiction but also, where the defender does not enter an appearance, whether the court has any jurisdiction which is compatible with the 1982 Act[81] and whether the defender has been duly served with the proceedings.[82] Further, the State Immunity Act 1978 obliges the court to give effect to the immunity conferred on foreign States by section 1 of the Act, even though the State concerned does not appear in the proceedings in question.[83] **2.17**

Contempt of court

Contempt of court is: **2.18**

> "the name given to conduct which challenges or affronts the authority of the court or the supremacy of the law itself whether it takes place in or in connection with civil or criminal proceedings. The offence of contempt of court is an offence *sui generis* and, where it occurs, it is peculiarly within the province of the court itself, civil or criminal as the case may be, to punish it under its power which arises from the inherent and necessary jurisdiction to take effective action to vindicate its authority and preserve the due and impartial administration of justice."[84]

Many forms of conduct may constitute contempt of court.[85] In civil proceedings in the sheriff court such conduct may include failure to obtemper an order of the court, abuse of process, breach of an undertaking, tampering with documents in the custody of the court, conduct by a witness in defiance or disregard of the court's authority, and in certain circumstances the publication of material relevant to the proceedings. Any failure to obtemper an order of the court which is wilful or intentional,[86] or inexcusably careless,[87] or which involves misconduct or a flagrant disregard of the due course and administration of justice,[88] **2.19**

---

[79] See *supra*, n. 77.
[80] *Wall's Trs v. Drynan* (1888) 15 R. 359, *per* L.P. Inglis at 363.
[81] para. 2.11.
[82] para. 2.14.
[83] State Immunity Act 1978, s. 1(2); *Property Managers and Factors (Edinburgh) Ltd v. Federal Republic of Nigeria* (Edinburgh Sh. Ct, Aug. 22, 1983, unreported). See also Anton with Beaumont, p. 113.
[84] *H.M. Advocate v. Airs*, 1975 J.C. 64 at 69.
[85] *Encyclopaedia*, iv, paras 963–975; Gordon, *Criminal Law* (2nd ed.), Chap. 51; Maxwell, pp. 96–98; Nicholson (2nd ed.), pp. 100–105; A. Allidge and D. Eady, *The Law of Contempt* (1982), Chap. 8; N. Lowe, *Borrie and Lowe's Law of Contempt* (3rd ed., 1995); McKain, Bonnington & Watt, *Scots Law for Journalists* (6th ed., 1995), Chap. 9.
[86] *Muir v. Milligan* (1868) 6 M. 1125; *Leys v. Leys* (1886) 13 R. 1223; and *Johnston v. Johnston*, 1996 S.L.T. 499.
[87] *Hall v. Associated Newspapers Ltd*, 1979 J.C. 1; *Muirhead v. Douglas*, 1979 S.L.T. (Notes) 17.
[88] *Simpson, Boath & Co., Petrs*, 1981 S.C. 153.

may be dealt with under the inherent jurisdiction as a contempt of court warranting punishment. Abuse of process is misuse of the procedure of the court in a way which, although not inconsistent with the literal application of its procedural rules, would nevertheless be manifestly unfair to a party to litigation before it, or would otherwise bring the administration of justice into disrepute among right-thinking people.[89] The circumstances in which abuse of process can arise are very varied. It is an abuse of process for a pursuer unreasonably to initiate or continue an action when it has no or substantially no chance of success,[90–91] as where it is manifestly incompetent and irrelevant[92] or is brought in order to bring under review a final decision against the pursuer by another court of competent jurisdiction in previous proceedings in which he had a full opportunity of contesting that decision[93]; or for a defender with no defence in fact or in law to use the procedure of the court to delay the enforcement of a right which is undeniable.[94] The court has a duty to prevent any abuse of its process,[95] and may punish it as contempt. Where an undertaking is given to the court by a party, a breach of the undertaking may be treated as contempt[96] especially, it is thought, where on the faith of the undertaking the court has made or refrained from making an order or has sanctioned a course of action or inaction.[97] Any wrongful removal of a process or part thereof,[98] any failure to return a lawfully-borrowed process when required by the court,[99] and any refusal by a person to return a document to which he has been referred in court[1] may be dealt with as contempt of court. A witness may be held to be in contempt by wilfully refusing to appear,[2] or coming into court intoxicated,[3] or refusing to take the oath or affirm,[4] or to answer any competent and relevant question,[5] or by prevaricating.[6] But conduct which takes place in or in connection with proceedings which are wholly irregular or without warrant cannot be contempt of court.[7]

---

[89] *Hunter v. Chief Constable of West Midlands Police* [1982] A.C. 529, *per* Lord Diplock at 536. On abuse of civil process as an actionable wrong, see *Encyclopaedia*, i, paras 51–77; Walker, *Delict*, Chap. 24; Walker, *Civil Remedies*, pp. 998 *et seq.*

[90–91] *Stewart v. Stewart*, 1984 S.L.T. (Sh. Ct.) 58; *Edwards v. Edwards* [1958] P. 235, *per* Sachs J. at 248.

[92] *Manson v. Chief Constable of Strathclyde* (*The Scotsman*, Dec. 16, 1983); *cf. Moore v. Sec. of St. for Scotland*, 1985 S.L.T. 38.

[93] *Manson, Moore, supra*, n. 92; *Hunter, supra*, n. 89.

[94] *Stewart, supra*, n. 91.

[95] *Hunter, supra*, n. 89; *Castanho v. Brown & Root (U.K.) Ltd* [1981] A.C. 557, *per* Lord Scarman at 571.

[96] *Graham v. Robert Younger Ltd*, 1955 J.C. 28. (The procedure in this case by way of appeal to the High Court of Justiciary should not now be followed in civil proceedings: see *Cordiner, Petr*, 1973 J.C. 16 at 18–19; *McIver v. McIver*, 1996 S.C.L.R. 225; para. 2–25.) The Inner House has questioned the wisdom of recording an undertaking by a party to obey the orders of a sheriff court given that parties are bound to obey the orders of the court in so far as they affect them: *Johnston v. Johnston*, 1996 S.L.T 499 at 501.

[97] Halsbury, ix, para. 75.

[98] *Watt v. Thomson* (1868) 6 M. 1112; (1870) 8 M.(H.L.) 77; (1873) 11 M. 960; (1874) 1 R.(H.L.) 21.

[99] *Levison v. Jewish Chronicle Ltd*, 1924 S.L.T. 755.

[1] *Gregson v. Grant*, 1910 2 S.L.T. 16.

[2] *Petrie v. Angus* (1889) 2 White 358.

[3] *Allan* (1826) Shaw 172.

[4] *Wylie v. H.M.Advocate*, 1966 S.L.T. 149.

[5] *Kerr* (1822) Shaw 68; *H.M.Advocate v. Airs*, 1975 J.C. 64.

[6] *MacLeod v. Speirs* (1884) 5 Coup. 387.

[7] *Paxton v. H.M.Advocate*, 1984 S.L.T. 367.

The publication of averments appearing in pleadings before the record is closed may be dealt with as contempt of court.[8] Under the Contempt of Court Act 1981 it is a contempt of court to use a tape-recorder in court or to bring it into court for use, without leave, or to publish such a recording to any section of the public.[9] Under the same Act a publication which creates a substantial risk that the course of justice will be seriously impeded or prejudiced may be treated as a contempt of court as tending to interfere with the course of justice regardless of intent to do so ("the strict liability rule") if at the time of the publication the proceedings in question are active, in respect that the record has been closed, or a motion or application has been enrolled or made, or the date for a hearing has been fixed or a hearing has been allowed, or appellate proceedings have been commenced.[10] The Act provides a defence of innocent publication or distribution,[11] and further provides that contemporary reports of legal proceedings[12] and discussions of public affairs[13] do not constitute contempt under "the strict liability rule" in specified circumstances. The court has a discretion to order the postponement of a report of proceedings where it appears to be necessary to avoid a substantial risk of prejudice to those or other proceedings, pending or imminent.[14] A detailed discussion of these provisions is beyond the scope of this book.[15] **2.20**

In dealing with contempt the court should exercise the greatest restraint and discretion, and when determining whether any conduct constitutes contempt must be seen to exclude from its consideration all matters which might prejudice or be thought to prejudice its decision.[16] If the conduct under consideration may also constitute a criminal offence, the sheriff should normally ascertain whether the Crown intends to bring criminal proceedings before deciding to deal with the matter himself as a contempt; and if the Crown institutes a prosecution, the sheriff will not so deal with it.[17] If the sheriff deals with the matter, and if the conduct in question was not personally witnessed by the sheriff and is denied by the alleged contemnor, it would appear to be necessary to hold a proof in which, since the proceedings might result in the imposition of punishment, the case must be proved beyond reasonable doubt[18] and the alleged contemnor cannot in general be compelled to give evidence.[19] The evidence of only one witness is sufficient if the contempt arises in civil proceedings.[20] **2.21**

---

[8] *Macleod v. Justices of the Peace of Lewis* (1892) 20 R. 218; *Graham v. Farquhar* (1893) 1 S.L.T. 63; *Young v. Armour*, 1921 1 S.L.T. 211.

[9] Contempt of Court Act 1981, s. 9.

[10] *ibid.* s. 1; s. 2 (as amended by the Cable and Broadcasting Act 1984, Sched. 5, para. 39(1) and the Broadcasting Act 1990, Sched. 20, para. 31(1)); Sched. 1, paras 12, 14, 15; *Att.-Gen. v. English* [1983] 1 A.C. 116.

[11] *ibid.* s. 3.

[12] *ibid.* s. 4.

[13] *ibid.* s. 5; *Att.-Gen. v. English*, *supra*, n. 10.

[14] *ibid.* s. 4(2).

[15] See A. Arlidge and D. Eady, *The Law of Contempt* (1982); N. Lowe, *Borrie and Lowe's Law of Contempt* (3rd ed., 1995); McKain, Bonnington & Watt, *Scots Law for Journalists* (6th ed., 1995), Chap. 9.

[16] *Milburn*, 1946 S.C. 301, *per* L.P. Normand at 315.

[17] *H.M. Advocate v. Airs*, 1975 J.C. 64 at 69. *Cf. Szczepanski v. Szczepanski* (1985) 15 Fam.L. 120; *Caprice v. Boswell* (1986) 16 Fam.L. 52.

[18] The fact that the standard of proof is beyond reasonable doubt and that a sheriff must hold a proof before finding contempt of court, unless satisfied beyond reasonable doubt that the defender's admissions proved contempt of court, was established by the Inner House in *Johnston v. Johnston*, 1996 S.L.T. 499. See also *Gribben v. Gribben*, 1976 S.L.T. 266.

[19] *Comet Products U.K. Ltd v. Hawkex Plastics Ltd* [1971] 2 Q.B. 67.

[20] *Byrne v. Ross*, 1992 S.C.L.R. 898.

2.22 If the conduct in question is admitted or, where necessary, proved and the sheriff decides to make a finding of contempt, the subsequent procedure should be based on the guidance issued by the Lord Justice-General in 1975.[21] The nature of the contempt should be distinctly stated in court and recorded in the interlocutor sheets. The sheriff should ordain the defender to appear at the bar at a specified date and time and either inform him of the wisdom of obtaining professional advice[22] and of his right to apply for legal aid[23] or, where appropriate, make arrangements through the clerk of court for him to be represented at the hearing. The objects of so deferring further consideration of the matter are not only to afford the offender the opportunity of obtaining legal advice (and, if necessary, legal aid)[24] and considering his position, but also to secure that his conduct is seen to be dealt with objectively. Where the offender is aged not less than 16 but under 21 and the sheriff considers that it may be necessary to impose a sentence of imprisonment or detention, he should seek to obtain a social enquiry report from the local authority.[25] The offender may be either released on such conditions, if any, as the court may impose or, in the rarest cases, detained in custody.

2.23 If the offender has been released and fails to appear at the bar at the appointed time, the sheriff may either sentence him in his absence[26] or grant a warrant for his apprehension. The offender or his legal representative should be given a full opportunity of explaining and apologising for his conduct and of making a statement in mitigation.[27] If his contempt has consisted in prevarication or refusing to depone, the offender may where practicable be permitted to give further evidence.

2.24 The court's power to punish contempt should be exercised with the greatest of care and the wisest discretion.[28] Offenders are normally punished by admonition, fine and imprisonment or detention, or any of these.[29] The maximum sentence which may be imposed by the sheriff in the course of or in connection with proceedings other than criminal proceedings on indictment is three months' imprisonment or a fine at Level 4 of the Standard Scale or both.[30] If a custodial sentence is imposed it must be for a fixed term[31] and may be made to run consecutively to any sentence the offender is currently serving, but it has been observed that in that event it cannot be aggregated with the latter sentence for parole

---

[21] Printed in Nicholson, *Sentencing* (2nd ed.), pp. 104–105.

[22] It is thought that he should be given an opportunity to obtain legal representation notwithstanding that s. 204(1) of the Criminal Procedure (Scotland) Act 1995, which restricts the passing of custodial sentences on unrepresented persons, is not applicable to a sentence for contempt; Criminal Procedure (Scotland) Act 1995, s. 307(1).

[23] Legal Aid (Scotland) Act 1986, s. 30, as amended by the Criminal Procedure (Consequential Proceedings) (Scotland) Act 1995, Sched. 4, para. 63(9) and by the Law Reform (Miscellaneous Provisions) (Scotland) Act 1990, Sched. 8, para. 36(12).

[24] *ibid.*

[25] Contempt of Court Act 1981, s. 15(3), applying s. 207 of the Criminal Procedure (Scotland) Act 1995.

[26] *Stark's Trs v. Duncan* (1906) 8 F. 429.

[27] *Royle v. Gray*, 1973 S.L.T. 31.

[28] *ibid.*

[29] *Kelso School Board v. Hunter* (1874) 2 R. 228, *per* Lord Deas at 232.

[30] Contempt of Court Act 1981, s. 15(2)(a).

[31] *ibid.* s. 15(1).

purposes.[32] The court may order the discharge of the offender before the expiry of the fixed term imposed.[33] Section 207 of the Criminal Procedure (Scotland) Act 1995 applies in relation to the detention of young offenders and sections 58, 59 and 61 of that Act are applicable to persons suffering from mental disorder.[34]

The sheriff's exercise of his jurisdiction to deal with cases of contempt in civil proceedings is subject to appeal to the Inner House of the Court of Session and it appears not to the sheriff principal.[35] **2.25**

II. The Subject-matter of the Cause

The jurisdiction of the sheriff court in point of subject-matter extends over all causes except those reserved to the Court of Session or to other courts or tribunals. In certain cases it has privative jurisdiction; in others its jurisdiction is excluded; and in others it has concurrent jurisdiction with the Court of Session. Those three aspects of the jurisdiction of the sheriff court in point of subject-matter are discussed in the following paragraphs of this part of this chapter. **2.26**

Privative jurisdiction

The value rule

Subject to one exception, the sheriff court has privative jurisdiction in all causes not exceeding £1,500 in value exclusive of interest and expenses which are competent in the sheriff court. Such a cause must be brought and followed forth in the sheriff court only, and is not subject to review by the Court of Session[36] unless it has been brought as a summary cause (with the exception of a small claim) and has been appealed to the sheriff principal who has, after final judgment, certified the cause as suitable for appeal to the Court of Session.[37] If the cause is not competent in the sheriff court, as where the defender is not subject to its jurisdiction, the limit of value does not apply and the cause may be brought in the Court of Session if the defender is subject to the jurisdiction of that court.[38] A Lord Ordinary of the Court of Session may hear by summary trial any dispute or question not affecting the status of any person which might competently be the subject of any cause in the Outer House, or which might competently have been the subject of any such cause but for the provisions of section 7 of the 1907 Act.[39] **2.27**

---

32 *Manson, Petr*, High Court of Justiciary, May 27, 1977, unreported.

33 See n. 31.

34 Contempt of Court Act 1981, s. 15(3) as substituted by the Criminal Procedure (Consequential Provisions) (Scotland) Act 1995, Sched. 4, para. 36.

35 *McIver v. McIver*, 1996 S.C.L.R. 225, disapproving dicta in *Forbes v. Forbes*, 1994 S.L.T. 16 at 18.

36 1907 Act, s. 7, as amended by 1971 Act, Sched. 2, S.I. 1976 No. 900, Law Reform (Miscellaneous Provisions) (Scotland) Act 1980, Sched. 3, and S.I. 1988 No. 1993; *Allan v. Alexander's Trs* (1908) 16 S.L.T. 491; *Dickson & Walker v. John Mitchell & Co.*, 1910 S.C. 139.

37 1971 Act, s. 38, as amended by the Law Reform (Miscellaneous Provisions) (Scotland) Act 1985, s. 18(4).

38 *Strachan v. Pharmaceutical Society of Great Britain* (1901) 8 S.L.T. 373; *Pagan & Osborne v. Haig*, 1910 S.C. 341. This rule is now of limited application, in view of the jurisdictional rules in the Civil Jurisdiction and Judgments Act 1982: see Chap. 3.

39 Court of Session Act 1988, s. 26(4).

2.28 The value of the cause may have to be considered if there is a question whether the action should be raised in the sheriff court or the Court of Session, or whether a decision in the sheriff court may be appealed to the Court of Session. The statutory rule is that the sheriff court has privative jurisdiction, subject to the exception noted above, in causes competent in that court which do not exceed £1,500 in value "exclusive of interest and expenses".[40] The interest thus excluded is not only interest from the date of citation, but all interest which is merely an accessory of the principal sum sued for.[41] A cause "not exceeding £1,500 in value" is one the subject-matter of which does not exceed the value of £1,500.[42] Questions as to how the value of the cause is to be determined may arise in actions for payment, in actions *ad factum praestandum*, and in appeals to the Court of Session where a counter-claim has been stated or where there has been a change of circumstances subsequent to the raising of the action. These questions are considered in the following paragraphs.

2.29 **(1) Action for payment.** In an action for payment of money the crave gives only a *prima facie* means of ascertaining the value, since the value is that of the true subject of the cause as determined by the court,[43] and it may be gathered from the whole of the record.[44] Thus the sum sued for is not conclusive should the nature of the action be such that something of greater value, taking the case outside the limit, is at stake and is dependent on the result of the case.[45] A common example is where the sum sued for is rent[46] or other periodic payment[47] and the decision will rule a question of continuing liability which takes the case beyond the limit of value.[48] Where no such question arises, the value of such a cause is the amount sued for.[49] Apart from questions of continuing liability, a case containing a small pecuniary crave may involve a question of greater value which

---

[40] 1907 Act, s. 7, as amended: see n. 36.

[41] *Bowie v. Donaldson*, 1922 S.C. 9. It is not clear whether interest which is treated as part of and included in the principal sum sued for should be excluded.

[42] *Hopkirk v. Wilson* (1855) 18 D. 299 at 300; *Buie v. Stiven* (1863) 2 M. 208, *per* L.J.-C. Inglis at 218. (Note that prior to 1988 the equivalent sum was £500 and before that it was £50.)

[43] *Dickson & Walker v. John Mitchell & Co.*, 1910 S.C. 139, *per* L.P. Dunedin at 145–146. In A.S. (Alteration of Sheriff Court Fees) 1971, Sched. 2, para. 18(f) (now revoked) "value" was held to mean the value as determined by the court, and not the sum sued for (*Bennett v. Livingston Development Corporation*, Sh. Pr. O'Brien, Linlithgow Sh. Ct, Oct. 29, 1979, unreported); but see Vol. 2 of this work.

[44] *Purves v. Brock* (1867) 5 M. 1003, *per* L.P. Inglis at 1004; *General Guarantee Corporation v. Alexander*, 1918 S.C. 662. The court will not, however, consider the question by reference to what may come out at the proof: *Soutar v. Mulhern*, 1907 S.C. 723.

[45] *Scottish Special Housing Association v. Maxwell*, 1960 S.C. 391, approving Dobie, p. 49.

[46] *Drummond v. Hunter* (1869) 7 M. 347; *Cunningham v. Black* (1883) 10 R. 441; *Duke of Argyll v. Muir*, 1910 S.C. 96; *Scottish Special Housing Association v. Maxwell*, 1960 S.C. 391. *Cf. Welsh v. Duncan* (1893) 20 R. 1014.

[47] *Stevenson v. Sharp*, 1910 S.C. 580 (payment under letter of obligation); *Abrahams Ltd v. Campbell*, 1911 S.C. 353 (rent due under contract); *Hamilton v. Hamilton* (1877) 4 R. 688 (aliment); *Paisley Parish Council v. Glasgow and Row Parish Councils*, 1907 S.C. 674 (relief of payment of aliment).

[48] *Scottish Special Housing, supra.*

[49] *Macfarlane v. Friendly Society of Stornoway* (1870) 8 M. 438 (single claim for aliment); *Heddle v. Gow* (1880) 18 S.L.R. 96 (single assessment); *North British Ry v. McArthur* (1889) 17 R. 30 (rent); *Standard Shipowners' Mutual Association v. Taylor* (1896) 23 R. 870 (not shown that continuing liability over limit); *Stirling Parish Council v. Perth Parish Council* (1898) 25 R. 964 and *Melrose Parish Council v. Hawick Parish Council*, 1912 S.C. 1029 (no continuing liability to aliment).

takes it beyond the limit[50]; but it must appear on the face of the proceedings that there is such a live, practical question to be determined[51] which is part of the subject-matter of the action and not an extrinsic consequence of it.[52]

The following appear to be further general rules for determining value which are applicable in particular circumstances. Where a crave for payment of a sum under the limit is combined with a crave which may raise a very large question from a pecuniary point of view, the value of the cause is taken to be above the limit.[53] Where in one action two or more pursuers having community of interest[54] sue for separate sums,[55] or several defenders having community of interest are sued for separate sums,[56] or where actions have been conjoined,[57] the whole sums claimed are aggregated to determine the value of the cause. In a process of competition the value of the cause is in general determined by the amount of the claim.[58] Where the pursuer sues for payment of the balance of an account, the value of the cause will be determined by the amount craved[59]; but if he gives credit to the defender for a sum due by him on a separate transaction, the value is the sum craved plus the credited amount.[60] Where the defender is entitled in terms of the contract sued on to make deductions from the sum craved, the value will be taken to be the balance.[61] **2.30**

(2) Action *ad factum praestandum*. The determination of the value of an action *ad factum praestandum* depends on the nature of the crave. If there is a crave for payment of a definite sum of money as an alternative to the crave for decree *ad factum praestandum* the sum specified will be taken to be the value of the cause,[62] but if the sum alternatively craved is indefinite the value will be deemed to exceed the limit.[63] The value was formerly deemed to exceed the limit if there was no alternative pecuniary crave,[64] **2.31**

---

50 *Raimes, Clark & Co. v. Swan's Tr.* (1902) 10 S.L.T. 316 (condition adjected to payment of dividend); *Airchisan v. McDonald*, 1911 S.C. 174 (liability of official not called as defender to pay on charge for club debt); *McDonald v. Ross*, 1929 S.C. 240 (paternity); *Brady v. Napier & Son*, 1944 S.C. 18 (irregular execution of diligence); *Scottish Special Housing Association v. Maxwell*, 1960 S.C. 391 (test case).

51 *Standard Shipowners' Murual Association v. Taylor* (1896) 23 R. 870 (no question apparent from process); *Stirling Parish Council v. Perth Parish Council* (1898) 25 R. 964 (insufficient that question of statutory construction involved).

52 *Brown & Critchley v. Decorative Art Journals Co.*, 1922 S.C. 192.

53 *Thomson v. Barclay* (1883) 10 R. 694, commented on in *North British Ry v. McArthur* (1889) 17 R. 30.

54 The rule does not apply where there is no community of interest: *Bruce v. Henderson* (1889) 17 R. 276; *Brotherston v. Livingston* (1892) 20 R. 1.

55 *Nelson, Donkin, & Co. v. Browne* (1876) 3 R. 810, *per* Lord Deas at 812; *Birrell v. Taylor* (1884) 12 R. 151; *Campbell v. Train*, 1910 S.C. 147, *per* L.P. Dunedin at 149; *Sneddon v. Addie & Sons' Collieries*, 1927 S.N. 164.

56 *Dykes v. Merry and Cuninghame* (1869) 7 M. 603; *Nelson, Donkin, & Co. v. Browne* (1876) 3 R. 810.

57 *Campbell v. Train*, 1910 S.C. 147.

58 *Henderson v. Grant* (1896) 23 R. 659; *cf. Dobbie v. Thomson* (1880) 7 R. 983.

59 *Stevens, Son & Co. v. Grant* (1887) 5 R. 19.

60 *Inglis v. Smith* (1859) 21 D. 822.

61 *Campbell's Trs v. Kinloch*, 1925 S.L.T. 189.

62 *Singer Manufacturing Co. v. Jessiman* (1881) 8 R. 695; *Dickson v. Bryan* (1889) 16 R. 673; *Lamonby v. Foulds Ltd*, 1928 S.C. 89.

63 *Shotts Iron Co. v. Kerr* (1871) 10 M. 195; *Aberdeen v. Wilson* (1872) 10 M. 971.

64 *Purves v. Brock* (1867) 5 M. 1003; *Galloway v. McGhie* (1869) 41 Sc.Jur. 400; *Henry v. Morrison* (1881) 8 R. 692; *Broatch v. Pattison* (1898) 1 F. 303.

unless it was clear from the pleadings that it was below the limit.[65] Now, however, an action *ad factum praestandum* other than one in which there is claimed in addition, or as an alternative, to a decree *ad factum praestandum* a decree for payment of money exceeding £1,500 in amount (exclusive of interest and expenses) should be brought as a summary cause.[66] In a summary cause action *ad factum praestandum* the value of the cause determines whether there is to be a percentage reduction of the fees chargeable under Chapter IV of the Table of Fees.[67] It is thought that it is for the party claiming that there should be a reduction to raise the matter when the sheriff hears parties on the question of liability for expenses, and to satisfy the court that the value of the cause is within the limit to which the reduction claimed applies.

2.32 **(3) Other actions.** In actions of accounting, where the crave is for payment of a specified sum or such other sum as may be found due, the sum specified does not determine the value, which may be held to exceed the limit.[68] It has been suggested that on the analogy of the cases where a pecuniary alternative to a crave for delivery is left indefinite, the value of an accounting should be regarded as over the limit unless it clearly appears from the record that it is in fact under the limit.[69] The value of an action of declarator may be deemed to exceed the limit, notwithstanding that a sum below the limit has been specified in an ancillary crave.[70]

2.33 **(4) Counterclaim.** The question whether the value of the cause is affected by the statement of a counterclaim may arise on appeal to the Court of Session. In *Bowie v. Donaldson*[71] it was observed *obiter* that no counterclaim, however large, could make appealable a cause which was otherwise unappealable for want of value: it was said that a pursuer who sues for a sum under the limit could not be subjected to appeal by the existence of a counterclaim over the limit, and that the defender could obtain a decision in the Court of Session by raising a substantive action. It has been submitted, however, that the value of the cause should be the total of the claim and the counterclaim.[72] It is thought that the latter view is correct, subject to the observations that the true value of a claim may not be the sum specified[73] and that where one claim is admitted the value of the cause may be only the difference between the claims.[74] A counterclaim may be dealt with as if it had been stated in a substantive cause,[75] the

---

[65] *General Guarantee Corporation v. Alexander*, 1918 S.C. 662.

[66] 1971 Act, s. 35(1)(c). Note that S.I. 1988 No. 1993 increased the amount from £1,000 to £1,500. See also *Rutherford v. Virtue*, 1993 S.C.L.R. 886 showing the incompetence of bringing an action *ad factum praestandum* as an ordinary cause and attempting to cure it by adding an amendment craving damages.

[67] A.S. (Fees of Solicitors in the Sheriff Court) (Amendment and Further Provisions) 1993, Sched. 1, General Regulations, reg. 14(f).

[68] *Stott v. Gray* (1834) 12 S. 828.

[69] Dobie, p. 51.

[70] *Edinburgh Tramways Co. v. Torbain* (1876) 3 R. 655, (1877) 4 R. (H.L.) 87; commented on, *Aitchison v. McDonald*, 1911 S.C. 174, *per* L.P. Dunedin at 176.

[71] 1922 S.C. 9, *per* Lord Salvesen at 13.

[72] Lewis, p. 21; Dobie, p. 50; *Murphy v. Muir*, 1927 S.L.T. (Sh. Ct.) 55. For the purpose of the percentage reduction of solicitors' fees in certain summary causes the value of any action in which a counterclaim has been lodged is the total of the sums craved in the writ and the sum claimed in the counterclaim (A.S. (Fees of Solicitors in the Sheriff Court) (Amendment and Further Provisions) 1993, Sched. 1, General Regulations, reg. 14(f)).

[73] See para. 2.29.

[74] *Kinnaird & Sons v. Millar* (1931) 47 Sh.Ct.Rep. 320.

[75] OCR, r. 19.4(a).

principles to be applied as regards the expenses of trying it are the same as if it had been tried in a separate action,[76] and it continues as a separate cause if the pursuer abandons the cause.[77] The right to state a counterclaim would therefore appear not to be a limited privilege controlled by the value and continued existence of the pursuer's claim. If the defender raised instead a substantive action, the pursuer could be subjected to appeal by the conjoining of the actions.[78]

(5) Change of circumstances. On appeal to the Court of Session the question may arise whether the value of the cause is affected by a change of circumstances subsequent to the raising of the action which results in an alteration reducing the demand with which the pursuer came into court. The effect of such an alteration appears to vary according to the circumstances causing it. It would appear that the value of the cause used to be regarded as its value at the date either of litiscontestation (*i.e.* of lodging defences), or of the closing of the record. Thus an admission before the closing of the record that the defender was liable for only part of the sum sued for, so that the outstanding difference was below the statutory limit, was held not to affect the value of the cause[79]; and restriction of the sum sued for below the limit was held to reduce the value where it was made before the closing of the record,[80] but not to do so where it was made thereafter.[81] In some later cases, however, the criterion of value was taken to be the value of the matter in dispute at the date of the appeal.[82] But these cases have been criticised,[83] so that the matter is left in some uncertainty. 2.34

Other matters

There are many matters in respect of which jurisdiction is conferred upon the sheriff court either exclusively or subject to a right of appeal to the Court of Session. These matters are noted elsewhere in this book. It has been observed that there is a class of cases which are only competent in the sheriff court, and in which an action brought in the Court of Session would be dismissed as incompetent. 2.35

> "The general character of such cases is that they relate to questions as to property within the sheriffdom in which there is a necessity for immediate decision, such, for example, as warrants for the sale of a pledge or the sale of perishable articles when the right of possession is disputed. There can be no doubt that cases between landlord and tenant of property situated within the sheriff's territory have always been regarded as specially suited for decision in the sheriff court."[84]

Under his common-law powers as a judge ordinary of the bounds the sheriff may undertake miscellaneous duties which cannot be appropriately

---

[76] *Macfarlane v. Macdougall*, 1932 S.L.T. (Sh. Ct.) 36.
[77] OCR, r. 19.3.
[78] *Gottlieb v. Fons Patent Inkwell Ltd*, 1917 1 S.L.T. 331.
[79] *Wilson v. Wallace* (1858) 20 D. 764; *Armour v. Munro* (1899) 7 S.L.T. 21.
[80] *Cairns v. Murral* (1884) 12 R. 167.
[81] *Buie v. Stiven* (1863) 2 M. 208; *Tait v. Lees* (1903) 5 F. 304.
[82] *David Allen & Sons Billposting Ltd v. Dundee and District Billposting Co. Ltd*, 1912 S.C. 970; *cf. Muirhead v. Gilmour*, 1909 1 S.L.T. 235 and see comments on *Tait v. Lees*, *supra*, in *Melrose Parish Council v. Hawick Parish Council*, 1912 S.C. 1029.
[83] *Lamonby v. Foulds Ltd*, 1928 S.C. 89.
[84] *Duncan v. Lodijenski* (1904) 6 F. 408, *per* Lord McLaren at 410.

performed by any other authority. Such duties are considered elsewhere in this book.[85] Numerous other duties are performed by the sheriff under statutory powers which are also considered elsewhere.[86]

Exclusion of jurisdiction

2.36 The jurisdiction of the sheriff court in point of subject-matter extends over all causes except those reserved to the Court of Session or to other courts or tribunals. Among such courts and tribunals[87] are the Court of the Lord Lyon,[88] the Scottish Land Court,[89] the Lands Tribunal for Scotland,[90] the Restrictive Practices Court,[91] industrial tribunals[92] and rent assessment committees.[93] Church causes[94] and peerage claims[95] are excluded from the jurisdiction of the sheriff court. Its jurisdiction is further excluded by the rules of private international law that the Scottish courts will not adjudicate upon the transactions of foreign sovereign states,[96] will not enforce the penal or revenue laws of another state[97] and will not entertain proceedings which have as their object rights *in rem* in, or tenancies of, immoveable property outwith Scotland.[98] There is an obligation on the court to declare of its own motion that it has no jurisdiction if rule 4 of Schedule 8 to the Civil Jurisdiction and Judgments Act 1982 gives exclusive jurisdiction to another court.[99] If the parties have agreed that a court is to have jurisdiction to settle any disputes which have arisen or which may arise in connection with a particular legal relationship, that court shall have exclusive jurisdiction.[1] If the sheriff court has no jurisdiction which is compatible with the Civil Jurisdiction and Judgments Act 1982 and the defender does not enter an appearance, the court must declare of its own motion that it has no jurisdiction.[2] This part of the present chapter is concerned with matters which are privative to the Court of Session, by reason either of their subject-matter or of the form of remedy sought.

---

[85] paras 25.03 to 25.05.

[86] Chap. 26.

[87] For an account of the principal special courts and tribunals see Walker, *Scottish Legal System* (7th ed.), Chap. 8.

[88] Innes of Learney, Chap. 2.

[89] G. R. Lamb, "The Scottish Land Court", 1958 S.L.T. (News) 129; Maxwell, p. 89; Gill, Chap. 36; *Carvie's Trs v. Still*, 1972 S.L.T. 29.

[90] Lands Tribunal Act 1949, ss. 1–4; Land Compensation (Scotland) Act 1963, ss. 1, 8; Conveyancing and Feudal Reform (Scotland) Act 1970, ss. 1–7, 50; *Smith v. Taylor*, 1972 S.L.T. (Lands Tr.) 34.

[91] Restrictive Practices Court Act 1976.

[92] W. Leslie, *Employment Tribunal Practice in Scotland* (looseleaf).

[93] Rent (Scotland) Act 1984, s. 44 and Sched. 4, replacing Rent (Scotland) Act 1971, s. 38, Sched. 5; *Wilson v. Cumming*, 1970 S.L.T. (Sh. Ct.) 44.

[94] Other than matters of a civil nature: see Maxwell, pp. 93–95.

[95] Maxwell, p. 98. It appears that where a question of peerage arises incidentally in litigation regarding other matters, the appropriate court has power to determine the question for its own purpose: Mitchell, *Constitutional Law* (2nd ed., 1968), p. 111.

[96] *Buttes Gas and Oil Co. v. Hammer* [1982] A.C. 888.

[97] Anton with Beaumont, pp. 101–105, 229–231.

[98] *ibid.* pp. 193–194; Civil Jurisdiction and Judgments Act 1982, Sched. 8, r. 4(1)(a) as amended by S.I. 1993 No. 603. See also the other instances of exclusive jurisdiction mentioned in Sched. 8, r. 4 to the 1982 Act. See Anton & Beaumont, *C.J.*, pp. 144–153 and 273–278. See paras 3.23 to 3.28 and 3.11.

[99] Civil Jurisdiction and Judgments Act 1982, Sched. 8, r. 7. See para. 3.113.

[1] Sched. 8, r. 5. On prorogation, see Anton & Beaumont, pp. 153–165 and 278–280. See paras 3.51 to 3.53.

[2] Civil Jurisdiction and Judgments Act 1982, Sched. 8, r. 8. See para. 3.113.

The matters excepted from the sheriff's jurisdiction and reserved to the Court of Session are certain actions relating to personal status, actions of adjudication, inhibitions, actions of reduction, actions of proving the tenor of a lost document, the majority of applications relative to trusts, petitions for the winding-up of a company with a paid-up capital exceeding £120,000, patent actions, and appeals against administrative acts and omissions. These matters are considered in the following paragraphs. Other matters reserved to the Court of Session are Exchequer causes,[3] appeals and other functions relative to administrative courts and tribunals,[4] stated cases in arbitrations,[5] certain proceedings which are directed by statute to be brought in the Court of Session,[6] and matters appropriate to the *nobile officium* of the court.[7] An action against a defender who is not subject to the jurisdiction of the sheriff court may be brought in the Court of Session if he is subject to that court's jurisdiction, irrespective of the value of the cause.[8] **2.37**

As to the construction of statutory provisions relative to jurisdiction, it is a general rule that there is not to be presumed, without express words, an authority to deprive the Court of Session of a jurisdiction which it had previously exercised, or to extend what was once the privative jurisdiction of the Court of Session to the sheriff court.[9] **2.38**

Status

The Court of Session has exclusive jurisdiction in all proceedings for declarator of marriage or nullity of marriage,[10] for declarator of freedom and putting to silence,[11] for reduction of a decree of divorce,[12] and in actions under the Hague Convention on the Civil Aspects of International Child Abduction for the return of a child wrongfully removed or retained.[13] Only the Court of Session may entertain an action brought by a person domiciled in Scotland or claiming any heritable or moveable **2.39**

---

[3] Maxwell, pp. 636, 641.

[4] *ibid.* pp. 642–648, 655–656.

[5] *ibid.* p. 541.

[6] *e.g.* Merchant Shipping (Liner Conferences) Act 1982, s. 7(1).

[7] Maxwell, pp. 126–129 and index.

[8] *Strachan v. Pharmaceutical Society of Great Britain* (1901) 8 S.L.T. 373; *Pagan & Osborne v. Haig*, 1910 S.C. 341. See para. 2.27, n. 37.

[9] *Dunbar & Co. v. Scottish County Investment Co.*, 1920 S.C. 210, *per* Lord Salvesen at 217; *Brown v. Hamilton D.C.*, 1983 S.C. (H.L.) 1, *per* Lord Fraser of Tullybelton at 45. See also Ersk., I, ii, 7; *Dewar v. John Dewar & Sons Ltd* (1899) 2 F. 249, *per* L.P. Balfour at 253; *Pagan & Osborne v. Haig*, 1910 S.C. 341, *per* Lord Mackenzie at 346. Clear or necessary implication from the terms of the statute has been said to suffice: *L.M. & S. Ry v. Turnbull*, 1926 S.L.T. 264 at 268; *Duke of Fife's Trs v. George Wimpey & Co.*, 1943 S.C. 377, *per* Lord Patrick at 382; *cf. Brodie v. Ker*, 1952 S.C. 216 at 224. See also *Jacobs v. Prett* (1875) 20 L.R. Eq. 1, *per* Sir G. Jessel M.R. at 6–7.

[10] Court of Session Act 1830, s. 33; 1907 Act, s. 5(1) as amended by the Law Reform (Parent and Child) (Scotland) Act 1986, Sched. 2; Domicile and Matrimonial Proceedings Act 1973, s. 7.

[11] Court of Session Act 1850, s. 16, s. 19; Domicile and Matrimonial Proceedings Act 1973, s. 7.

[12] *Acutt v. Acutt*, 1935 S.C. 525.

[13] Child Abduction and Custody Act 1985, ss. 4, 8 and 27. The Act also gives force of law to the European Convention on Recognition and Enforcement of Decisions concerning Custody of Children and on the Restoration of Custody of Children as set out in Sched. 2 (see s.12) and defines the appropriate court in Scotland for registering foreign custody decisions, varying, revoking or enforcing them, and to give interim directions to secure the welfare of the child, as being the Court of Session (see ss. 16–19 and 27(2)).

property situate in Scotland, for declarator that he is a British subject.[14] The Court of Session and the sheriff court have concurrent jurisdiction in actions of divorce,[15] actions for declarator of parentage, non-parentage, legitimacy, legitimation or illegitimacy,[16] and actions of declarator under section 1 of the Presumption of Death (Scotland) Act 1977. The court may make in any proceedings an incidental finding as to parentage, non-parentage, legitimacy, legitimation or illegitimacy for the purposes of those proceedings.[17]

Adjudication

2.40 Section 5(4) of the 1907 Act confers on the sheriff court jurisdiction in "actions relating to questions of heritable right or title (except actions of adjudication save in so far as now competent and actions of reduction)". Actions of adjudication are of two types: an action of adjudication in implement, which has the object of effectually vesting heritable property in a party who cannot otherwise obtain a valid title: and an action of adjudication for debt, in which a debtor's heritable property is attached for debt, the adjudged land being vested in the creditor subject to a right of redemption by the debtor. Both forms of action are competent only in the Court of Session.[18] The exception referred to in section 5(4) relates to adjudications *contra haereditatem jacentem*, which are competent in the sheriff court[19] but are now unknown in practice. The Grant Committee recommended that both actions of adjudication in implement and actions of adjudication for debt should be competent in the sheriff court,[20] but the recommendation has not been implemented. A statutory sheriff court process of adjudication on non-payment of a ground annual is noted elsewhere.[21]

Inhibition

2.41 Inhibition is a preventive diligence whereby a debtor is prohibited from burdening, alienating or otherwise affecting his heritable property to the prejudice of the creditor inhibiting. It may be used both on the dependence of an action in the sheriff court[22] and in execution of the decree, but it proceeds on a warrant contained in a writ under the signet of the Court of Session, and in order to transfer the property to the pursuer must be followed by an action of adjudication in the Court of Session. Both the McKechnie Committee[23] and the Grant Committee[24] recommended that the sheriff should be given the same powers as the Court of Session to grant a warrant for inhibition, but these recommendations have not been implemented.

---

[14] Legitimacy Declaration Act 1858, s. 9, as amended by the British Nationality Act 1948, s. 31, Sched. 4 and by the British Nationality Act 1981, Sched. 7.

[15] Court of Session Act 1830, s. 33; 1907 Act, s. 5(2B), added by the Divorce Jurisdiction, Court Fees and Legal Aid (Scotland) Act 1983, s. 1; Domicile and Matrimonial Proceedings Act 1973, s. 8.

[16] Law Reform (Parent and Child) (Scotland) Act 1986, s. 7.

[17] *ibid.* s. 7(5).

[18] Adjudication in implement originated in the *nobile officium* of the court: Stair, IV, li, 9. As to adjudication for debt, see Diligence Act 1661 and Adjudications Act 1672.

[19] *Ker v. Primrose* (1709) Mor. 46; Ersk., II, xii, 53; Bell, *Comm.*, i, 751, 752.

[20] Grant, paras 121–123, rec. 21.

[21] Chap. 26.

[22] See paras. 11.36 to 11.42.

[23] McKechnie, paras 190–191, rec. 63.

[24] Grant, para. 125, rec. 23.

Reduction

While only actions of reduction relating to questions of heritable right or title are expressly excepted by statute from the sheriff's jurisdiction,[25] all actions of reduction remain exclusively within the jurisdiction of the Court of Session,[26] which is competent to entertain actions for reduction of any documents or proceedings unless reduction is excluded by the nature of the documents or proceedings themselves, or by statutory enactment.[27] In the sheriff court an action of reduction, and any action which is in substance, although not in form, a reduction will not be allowed to proceed.[28] The sheriff is, however, empowered to set aside deeds or writings to which objection is taken by way of exception in ordinary[29] and summary[30] causes, and, where objection is similarly taken, a debtor's gratuitous alienations or unfair preferences.[31] He may also set aside or vary transactions intended to defeat claims for aliment or financial provision.[32] **2.42**

Proving the tenor[33]

An action of proving the tenor is an action by which the terms of a writing which is lost or destroyed are sought to be established.[34] It is privative to the Court of Session.[35] If, however, a document is not in a party's possession and could not have been recovered by him, its terms may, in certain circumstances, be proved incidentally in the course of a depending action in the sheriff court.[36] **2.43**

Trusts

The Court of Session has jurisdiction over the whole subject-matter of all Scottish trusts.[37] The statutory jurisdiction in respect of trusts belongs almost exclusively to the Court of Session, which may also on occasion exercise its *nobile officium*.[38] The sheriff court has, however, concurrent jurisdiction with the Court of Session in appointing new trustees,[39] in removing trustees who are insane or incapable of acting by reason of physical or mental disability or being absent from the United Kingdom continuously for a period of at least six months,[40] in authorising **2.44**

---

[25] 1907 Act, s. 5(4).

[26] *Young v. O'Rourk* (1826) 4 S. 617 (N.S. 625); *Porteous v. Cordiners of Glasgow* (1830) 8 S. 908; *Young v. Roberton* (1830) 9 S. 59; *Dickson v. Murray* (1866) 4 M. 797; *Donald v. Donald*, 1913 S.C. 274, *per* L.J.-C. Macdonald at 278.

[27] *Kerr v. Hood*, 1907 S.C. 895, *per* Lord Ardwall at 902.

[28] *Cornhill Insurance Co. Ltd v. Fraser, Owen & Co. Ltd* (1936) 53 Sh. Ct.Rep. 168; *Wolfsan v. Edelman*, 1952 S.L.T. (Sh. Ct.) 87.

[29] OCR, 21.3: see paras 12.66 to 12.72.

[30] SCR, r. 41.

[31] Bankruptcy (Scotland) Act 1985, ss. 34(4), 36(5), 73(1); *Report on Bankruptcy and Related Aspects of Insolvency and Liquidation* (Scot. Law Com. No. 68), para. 12.27.

[32] Family Law (Scotland) Act 1985, s. 18. See, *e.g. Tahir v Tahir (No. 2)* 1995 S.L.T. 451.

[33] Walkers, Chap. 19; Walker, *Civil Remedies*, pp. 1245–1247.

[34] Ersk., IV, i, 54.

[35] Ersk., IV, i, 58; *Dunbar & Co. v. Scottish County Investment Co.*, 1920 S.C. 210.

[36] *Elliott v. Calpern*, 1927 S.C. 29; *Hutcheon's Exr v. Hutcheon* (1941) 58 Sh.Ct.Rep. 158; *Crichton v. Wood*, 1981 S.L.T. (Notes) 66; Walkers, paras 229–230.

[37] Maxwell, p. 91; Wilson and Duncan (2nd ed.), pp. 377–379; Anton with Beaumont, pp. 157–158; Anton & Beaumont, paras 5.10, 5.50, 9.27 and 10.34–10.35.

[38] Walker, *Civil Remedies*, pp. 1196 *et seq.*

[39] Trusts (Scotland) Act 1921, ss. 22, 24A, as amended and inserted by the Law Reform (Miscellaneous Provisions) (Scotland) Act 1980, s. 13.

[40] *ibid.* ss. 23, 24A.

completion of title by the beneficiary of a lapsed trust,[41] and in actions against a person in his capacity as settlor, trustee or beneficiary of a trust domiciled in Scotland created by the operation of a statute, or by a written instrument, or created orally and evidenced in writing.[42] Such proceedings may be brought in the "appropriate" sheriff court. In the case of a trust other than a marriage contract, the "appropriate" sheriff court is a court of the sheriffdom where the truster, or any of the trusters, was domiciled at the date of the coming into operation of the trust; and in the case of a marriage contract it is a court of the sheriffdom where either spouse is, or was when he died, domiciled. If in either case that provision cannot apply, or if the applicant does not possess sufficient information to enable him to determine which is an appropriate sheriff court, the application should be presented to the sheriff court at Edinburgh.[43] A trust instrument may confer jurisdiction, which is treated as exclusive, on a sheriff court in any proceedings brought against a settlor, trustee or beneficiary if relations between these persons or their rights or obligations under the trust are involved.[44] If the trust instrument confers jurisdiction on the courts of the United Kingdom or of Scotland then such proceedings may be brought in any court in Scotland.[45] Section 9 of the Law Reform (Miscellaneous Provisions) (Scotland) Act 1990 provides that the trustees of a public trust may apply to the court for approval of a scheme for the variation or reorganisation of the trust purposes in certain circumstances. The court to which application should be made must at present be the Court of Session.[46] However, provision is made for application to be made to the sheriff court in the case of a public trust having an annual income not exceeding such amount as may be prescribed by the Secretary of State.[47] This provision is not yet in force and will come into force from such day as the Lord Advocate may appoint.[48] The appropriate sheriff court will be that for the place with which the trust has its closest and most real connection, which failing for the place where any of the trustees resides, which failing the court of Lothian and Borders at Edinburgh.[49]

Companies

2.45 Where a company is registered in Scotland under the Companies Acts, the Court of Session has jurisdiction to deal with matters of company administration which require an application to a court. Where, however, the amount of the share capital of a company paid up or credited as paid up does not exceed £120,000, the sheriff court of the sheriffdom in which the registered office of the company is situated has concurrent jurisdiction with the Court of Session to wind up the

---

[41] Trusts (Scotland) Act 1921, ss. 24, 24A.

[42] Civil Jurisdiction and Judgments Act 1982, Sched. 1, Art. 5(6); Sched. 3C, Art. 5(6); Sched. 4, Art. 5(6); Sched. 8, r. 2(7). See Anton & Beaumont, *C.J.*, paras 5.52–5.58 and 10.34–10.35.

[43] Trusts (Scotland) Act 1921, 5.24A.

[44] Civil Jurisdiction and Judgments Act 1982, Sched. 1, Art. 17; Sched. 3C, Art. 17(2); Sched. 4, Art. 17; Sched. 8, r. 5(3). See Anton & Beaumont, *C.J.*, paras 7.27 and 10.77.

[45] Civil Jurisdiction and Judgments Act 1982, Sched. 8, r. 5(4). Anton & Beaumont, *C.J.*, para. 10.78. The reference to "any court in Scotland" indicates that the legislature did not intend to restrict this exclusive jurisdiction to the Court of Session.

[46] Law Reform (Miscellaneous Provsions) (Scotland) Act, 1990, s. 9(4).

[47] *ibid.* s. 9(5).

[48] *ibid.*

[49] *ibid.*

company and to entertain other applications under the Companies Acts and other legislation.[50]

Patents, trade marks, etc.

2.46 In Scotland proceedings relating primarily to patents are competent in the Court of Session only and the jurisdiction of the sheriff court relating to patents extends only to questions which are incidental to the issue in proceedings which are otherwise competent there.[51] The Court of Session has a statutory jurisdiction in respect of the rectification and correction of the trade marks register[52] and in appeals from the registrar of trade marks.[53] Proceedings for orders for delivery up of infringing goods, materials or articles[54] or an order as to disposal of infringing goods[55] may be brought in the sheriff court.[56] The Court of Session has a statutory jurisdiction in respect of registered designs.[57] The Court of Session also has jurisdiction to hear appeals on points of law from the Copyright Tribunal in Scotland.[58] References and appeals on design right matters can be made to the Court of Session.[59] As a matter of practice, copyright infringement actions are normally dealt with in the Court of Session but there is no reason why they cannot be dealt with in a sheriff court.[60] The sheriff court has jurisdiction under the Copyright, Designs and Patents Act 1988 in certain secondary matters pertaining to copyright,[61] rights in performances[62] and to the unregistered design right[63]. It is also provided by the Civil Jurisdiction and Judgments Act 1982 that the Court of Session (but not the sheriff court) has jurisdiction in proceedings principally concerned with the registration in the United Kingdom or the validity in the United Kingdom of patents, trade marks, designs or other similar rights required to be deposited or registered.[64]

Arbitration

2.47 The Civil Jurisdiction and Judgments Act 1982 provides that in proceedings concerning an arbitration which is conducted in Scotland or in which the procedure is governed by Scots law, a person may be sued in the Court of Session, not in the sheriff court,[65] but the person may also be sued in the sheriff courts of the place where he or she is domiciled.[66]

---

[50] See paras 2.71, 2.72.

[51] Patents Act 1977, s. 98(1).

[52] Trade Marks Act 1994, ss. 64 and 75.

[53] *ibid.* ss. 75 and 76.

[54] *ibid.* s. 16.

[55] *ibid.* s. 19.

[56] *ibid.* s. 20.

[57] Registered Designs Act 1949, s. 27, as substituted by Copyright, Designs and Patents Act 1988, Sched. 4.

[58] Copyright, Designs and Patents Act 1988, s. 152.

[59] *ibid.* s. 251.

[60] For an example of a copyright infringement action in the sheriff court see *Robert Allan & Partners v. Scottish Ideal Homes*, 1972 S.L.T. (Sh. Ct.) 32. That such jurisdiction exists is confirmed by reg. 4 of the Copyright, Designs and Patent Rules 1990 (S.I. 1990 No. 380).

[61] *i.e.* proceedings under ss. 99, 102(5) and 114; s. 115.

[62] *i.e.* proceedings under ss. 195 and 204; s. 205.

[63] *i.e.* proceedings under ss. 230, 231 and 235(5); s. 232.

[64] Civil Jurisdiction and Judgments Act 1982, Sched. 8, r. 2(14); Patents, Designs and Marks Act 1986, Sched. 2, Pt I, para. 1(2)(j). See para. 3.108.

[65] Civil Jurisdiction and Judgments Act 1982, Sched. 8, r. 2(13): see para. 3–107.

[66] *ibid.* Sched. 8, r. 1. See also Anton & Beaumont, *C.J.*, paras 10.48–10.50.

Supervisory jurisdiction

2.48 The Court of Session alone has power, in the exercise of its supervisory jurisdiction, to review decisions of inferior courts and tribunals and administrative bodies. The sheriff court has no such general supervisory jurisdiction.[67] Certain statutes expressly confer jurisdiction upon the sheriff to determine specific questions arising from the manner of the exercise of particular powers by statutory bodies,[68] but there is no process whereby the sheriff may review and quash any decisions of other courts or bodies without express statutory power to do so.

Concurrent jurisdiction with the Court of Session

2.49 Previous sections of this chapter have considered the privative jurisdiction of the sheriff court and matters in which its jurisdiction is excluded. This section attempts to define the jurisdiction of the sheriff court in point of subject-matter in all cases which are not within the privative jurisdiction of the Court of Session or the sheriff court or any other court or tribunal. In such cases the sheriff court has concurrent jurisdiction with the Court of Session. An action in which there is concurrent jurisdiction may be remitted from the sheriff court to the Court of Session or *vice versa* in accordance with rules considered elsewhere.[69]

2.50 It sometimes happens that an action before the sheriff is in some way related to an action which is in dependence before the Court of Session. If that is thought to cause difficulty, various courses may be available. If both actions are between the same parties or parties representing the same interest, and raise the same question, one of them may be dismissed on a plea of *lis alibi pendens*.[70] Alternatively, if the appropriate conditions as regards remit or removal are fulfilled,[71] the sheriff court action may be sent to the Court of Session. If none of these courses is appropriate, considerations of courtesy and good sense may often point in favour of sisting the sheriff court action or deferring any decision therein which might affect the proceedings in the Court of Session. In some circumstances, however, it may be appropriate for the sheriff court action to proceed.[72]

Obligations

2.51 A sheriff court is competent, in terms of subject matter, to hear any actions concerning contract, delict, quasi-delict or unjustified enrichment. Whether it has personal jurisdiction in such matters is determined by the Civil Jurisdiction and Judgments Act 1982.[73]

Moveable rights

2.52 In all actions relating to moveable property other than those not exceeding £1,500 in value exclusive of interest and expenses[74] and those

---

[67] *Brown v. Hamilton D.C.*, 1983 S.C. (H.L.) 1; *Edinburgh D.C. v. Round and Robinson*, 1987 S.L.T. (Sh. Ct.) 117.

[68] See Chap. 26.

[69] paras 13.57 to 13.67.

[70] paras 2.94 to 2.98.

[71] See n. 69.

[72] *Borders R.C. v. M*, 1986 S.L.T. 222.

[73] See Chap. 3, esp. the provisions on prorogation (Art. 17), general ground of jurisdiction (Art. 2) and the special jurisdiction in contract (Art. 5(1)) and delict (Art. 5(3)) discussed in paras 3.51 to 3.53, 3.06 to 3.22 and 3.92 to 3.93.

[74] See paras 2.27 to 2.34.

concerning incorporeal moveable property which have already been noted,[75] the jurisdiction of both the sheriff court and the Court of Session is without limit as regards the value of the subject involved.[76] It is accordingly competent to sue in the sheriff court for any sum by way of debt or damages.

Heritable rights

The jurisdiction of the sheriff in matters relating to heritage is, subject to exceptions as regards adjudication and reduction, as extensive as in the case of moveables. The 1907 Act confers jurisdiction in "actions relating to questions of heritable right or title (except actions of adjudication save in so far as now competent and actions of reduction) including all actions of declarator of irritancy and removing, whether at the instance of a superior against a vassal or of a landlord against a tenant."[77] The exceptions of actions of adjudication[78] and reduction[79] have already been considered. The sheriff's jurisdiction accordingly includes actions relating to nuisance,[80] interdict[81] or damages[82] arising from the undue exercise of the right of property; to the constitution and exercise of servitudes[83]; and to questions between landlord and tenant.[84] It has always included questions relating to the possession of heritable subjects,[85] and questions of personal liability in contract[86] or delict[87] in which heritage is incidentally involved.[88] By statute the sheriff has a power, similar to that possessed by the Court of Session in the exercise of the *nobile officium*, to order the clerk of court to execute deeds relating to heritage. Where the grantor of any deed relating to the heritable property cannot be found or refuses or is unable or otherwise fails to execute the deed, the sheriff may make an order dispensing with the execution of the deed by the grantor and directing the sheriff clerk to execute the deed.[89] **2.53**

Among the questions between landlord and tenant which are within his jurisdiction, the sheriff may determine whether a valid lease exists[90]; may adjudicate on claims for rent and counterclaims for damages thereunder[91]; and may enforce the stipulations of the lease,[92] as by ordering the tenant **2.54**

---

[75] See para. 2.46.
[76] Ersk., I, iv, 3.
[77] 1907 Act, s. 5(4).
[78] See para. 2.40.
[79] See para. 2.42.
[80] Competent before the 1907 Act by the Sheriff Courts (Scotland) Act 1838, s. 15.
[81] Civil Jurisdiction and Judgments Act 1982, Sched. 8, r. 2(10); see para. 3.104.
[82] See n. 80.
[83] *ibid.*
[84] Certain questions are excluded from the sheriff's jurisdiction by statute: see para. 2.36, n. 92. Sequestration for rent is competent in the sheriff court only: *Duncan v. Lodijensky* (1904) 6 F. 408.
[85] *Sutherland v. Thomson* (1876) 3 R. 485.
[86] *Anderson v. McGown*, 1911 S.C. 441; *Duff v. West Craig Ltd* (1935) 51 Sh.Ct.Rep. 315.
[87] *Cf. Brady v. Miller's Properties Ltd* (1935) 51 Sh.Ct.Rep. 315.
[88] See n. 86.
[89] 1907 Act, s. 5A, inserted by Law Reform (Miscellaneous Provisions) (Scotland) Act 1985, s. 17. See Chap. 26.
[90] *Horn v. McLean* (1830) 8 S. 329; *Robertson v. Cockburn* (1875) 3 R. 21; *Fingland & Mitchell v. Howie*, 1926 S.C. 319.
[91] *McDougall v. Buchanan* (1867) 6 M. 120; *Macdonald v. Mackessack* (1888) 16 R. 168 (to stock farm); *Whitelaw v. Fultan* (1871) 10 M. 27 (to furnish shop); *Wright v. Wightman* (1875) 3 R. 69 (to furnish a house).
[92] See n. 90.

to plenish the subjects.[93] He may also order the inspection and repair of the subjects[94] where necessary,[95] as where there is some present danger of the existing state of matters being changed by the necessary use of the subjects,[96] although it has been said that he may not delegate to a reporter his duty of decision, apart from consent or acquiescence.[97] The sheriff may also make orders relative to heritable property which are urgently required, such as orders as to the management of a farm neglected[98] or deserted[99] by the tenant.

2.55 The 1907 Act also confers on the sheriff jurisdiction in actions of division of commonty and of division or division and sale of common property, and provides that the Division of Commonties Act 1695 is to be read and construed as if it conferred jurisdiction upon the sheriff court in the same manner as upon the Court of Session.[1] The March Dykes Acts 1661 and 1669 confer on the sheriff a practically exclusive jurisdiction in actions for the repair and rebuilding of march dykes[2] and for straightening marches[3]; and while an action for the erection of a march dyke may be brought in the Court of Session,[4] it would normally be more convenient to bring it in the sheriff court. Under the Runrig Lands Act 1695 actions for the division of runrig lands, which are practically obsolete, are competent in the sheriff court. The sheriff possesses jurisdiction in other actions relating to heritable rights, such as actions of maills and duties, where his jurisdiction is concurrent with that of the Court of Session if the creditor's right has been constituted by an instrument other than a standard security and is otherwise exclusive; in actions of poinding of the ground[5]; and in certain statutory applications.[6]

Family proceedings

2.56 The sheriff court has jurisdiction over a wide range of proceedings relative to family relationships,[7] including many actions between husband and wife, actions concerning parental responsibilities and parental rights under section 11 of the Children (Scotland) Act 1995 (hereinafter referred to as Section 11 orders), actions of affiliation and aliment, declarators of

---

[93] See n. 91.

[94] *Dickson v. Graham* (1887) 4 R. 717 (authority to landlord to execute repairs at sight of man of skill); *Lees v. Marr Typefounding Co.* (1887) 4 R. 1088 (inspection and repair).

[95] *Jenkins v. Gascoigne*, 1907 S.C. 1189.

[96] *Mags of Kilmarnock v. Reid* (1897) 24 R. 388, *per* L.P. Robertson at 392; *Sutherland v. Squair* (1898) 25 R. 656, *per* Lords Trayner and Moncreiff at 660.

[97] *Maclagan v. Marchbank* (1911) 27 Sh.Ct.Rep. 282; *McFarlane v. Crawford* (1919) 35 Sh.Ct.Rep. 78 at 83–84.

[98] *Brock v. Buchanan* (1851) 13 D. 1069.

[99] *Gibson v. Clark* (1895) 23 R. 294.

[1] 1907 Act, s. 5(3). See paras 23.37 to 23.41.

[2] *Strang v. Steuart* (1864) 2 M. 1015; 4 M. (H.L.) 5; *Paterson v. MacDonald* (1880) 7 R. 958; *Secker v. Cameron*, 1914 S.C. 354. See paras. 23.44 to 23.46.

[3] *Earl of Kintore v. Earl of Kintore's Trs* (1886) 13 R. 997.

[4] *Pollock v. Ewing* (1869) 7 M. 815.

[5] As to maills and duties, see para. 23.28; as to poinding of the ground, paras. 23.26, 23.27.

[6] On the Heritable Securities (Scotland) Act 1894, see paras 23.29 to 23.26. For other statutory applications, see Chap. 26.

[7] The traditional term "consistorial actions" is not used in this book, since some of the actions within that class which are mentioned in the Court of Session Acts 1830, s. 33 and 1850, s. 16, are incompetent in the sheriff court, and the sheriff has jurisdiction in causes relative to family relationships which are outside that class.

parentage and the like, applications for adoption,[8] applications relative to children under Part II of the 1995 Act (which largely re-enacts the Social Work (Scotland) Act 1968),[9] and applications regarding the registration of marriage and births.

The sheriff court has concurrent jurisdiction with the Court of Session in actions for divorce,[10] actions for separation,[11] actions for aliment[12] where jurisdiction is not restricted by the provisions of the Child Support Act 1991,[13] applications for variation of Court of Session awards of aliment, periodical allowance or Section 11 orders,[14] applications under the Maintenance Orders Act 1950[15] and the Matrimonial Homes (Family Protection) (Scotland) Act 1981, the majority of actions pertaining to parental responsibilities and parental rights, applications for adoption and actions for declarator of parentage and the like. The sheriff court has exclusive jurisdiction in applications for the recovery of maintenance under sections 4(1) and 31(1) of the Maintenance Orders (Reciprocal Enforcement) Act 1972; in applications to sanction the re-registration of the birth of a child legitimated by subsequent marriage of the parents[16]; and in appeals against the refusal of the Registrar General to authorise the correction of an alleged error in a register of marriages or births.[17] The jurisdiction of the sheriff court as regards the principal matters which are within the scope of this book is considered below under the headings of divorce and separation; children; maintenance; and declarators of parentage, etc. **2.57**

(1) Divorce; separation.[18] A sheriff court has jurisdiction to entertain an action for divorce or separation if (and only if) (a) either party to the marriage in question (i) is domiciled in Scotland at the date when the action is begun, or (ii) was habitually resident there throughout the period of one year ending with that date; and (b) either party to the marriage (i) was resident in the sheriffdom for a period of 40 days ending with that date, or (ii) had been resident in the sheriffdom for a period of not less than 40 days ending not more than 40 days before that date, and has no known residence in Scotland at that date.[19] Here, "domiciled" is used in its traditional sense, not in the special sense defined in the Civil Jurisdiction and Judgments Act 1982. The expression "habitually resident" is an increasingly important jurisdictional connecting factor and in other **2.58**

---

[8] See Chap. 28.

[9] See Chap. 26. See also Norrie, *Children's Hearings in Scotland* (1997).

[10] 1907 Act, s. 5(2B), inserted by Divorce Jurisdiction, Court Fees and Legal Aid (Scotland) Act 1983, s. 1. See paras 22.02 to 22.32.

[11] 1907 Act, s. 5(2), as substituted by Family Law (Scotland) Act 1985, Sched. 1, para. 1 as amended by the Law Reform (Parent and Child) (Scotland) Act 1986, Sched. 2.

[12] *ibid.*

[13] See s. 8 of the Child Support Act 1991 in particular; Wilkinson and Norrie, *The Law Relating to Parent and Child in Scotland* (1993), pp. 298–300. The restriction of jurisdiction effected by the 1991 Act should be borne in mind wherever aliment is referred to in this chapter.

[14] Law Reform (Miscellaneous Provisions) (Scotland) Act 1966, s. 8 as amended; OCR, Chap. 33: see paras 22.92 to 22.95.

[15] On maintenance orders generally, see Clive (4th ed.), pp. 176–210.

[16] Registration of Births, Deaths and Marriages (Scotland) Act 1965, s. 20.

[17] *ibid.* s. 42(5).

[18] See Clive, Chap. 28.

[19] Domicile and Matrimonial Proceedings Act 1973, s. 8(2), as amended by Divorce Jurisdiction, Court Fees and Legal Aid (Scotland) Act 1983, Sched. 1, para. 18.

contexts is spawning a large and growing case law.[20] Even if the court does not have jurisdiction on these grounds, it may entertain a cross-action or further action for divorce or separation which is begun at a time when an original action is pending in respect of the marriage.[21] The period during which an action is pending includes any period while the taking of an appeal is competent and the period while any proceedings on appeal are pending.[22] These provisions are without prejudice to any jurisdiction of a sheriff court to entertain an action of divorce or separation remitted to it in pursuance of any enactment or rule of court.[23]

2.59 If the court has jurisdiction in an action for divorce or separation, it has jurisdiction to entertain applications for the making, or for the variation or recall of, various ancillary orders by virtue of section 10(1) of the Domicile and Matrimonial Proceedings Act 1973.[24] Such orders include those relating to children, aliment and financial provision on divorce.[25] Further, if the Court of Session has jurisdiction under section 10 of the 1973 Act to entertain an application for the variation and recall of an order made by it, and the order is one which may be varied or recalled in a sheriff court, then the sheriff has jurisdiction to vary or recall the order.[26] The sheriff court may entertain an application for financial provision following a foreign divorce provided that the applicant was domiciled or habitually resident in Scotland on the date when the application was made and the other party to the marriage fulfilled the same condition, or was domiciled or habitually resident in Scotland when the parties last lived together as husband and wife, or on the date when the application was made, was an owner or tenant of, or had a beneficial interest in, property in Scotland which had at some time been a matrimonial home of the parties, provided that either (i) one of the parties was, on the date when the application was made, habitually resident in the sheriffdom, or (ii) on the date when the application was made, the other party was an owner or tenant of, or had a beneficial interest in property situated wholly or partially within the sheriffdom, which had at some time been a matrimonial home of the parties.[27]

---

[20] See Clive, pp. 573–574. See also Clive, "The Concept of Habitual Residence" (1997) J.R. 137 in which the author expresses the view that habitual residence should be left undefined at the Hague Conference on Private International Law and by the legislatures and courts of Member States. While there is merit in this view, there is a risk of divergence from state to state as to what constitutes habitual residence. Problems tend to arise when a person has been resident for less than a year in the jurisdiction concerned. This is not relevant in the immediate context but is in the context of jurisdiction over children and has led to many reported cases with outcomes which are difficult to reconcile: see, *e.g.* on international child abduction *Singh v. Singh*, 1997 G.W.D. 20–930; *Cameron v. Cameron*, 1996 S.C. 17; *Findlay v. Findlay (No. 2)*, 1995 S.L.T. 492; *Re B (Child Abduction: Habitual Residence)* [1994] 2 F.L.R. 915; *Re R (Wardship: Child Abduction)* [1993] 1 Fam. 249; *Re N (Child Abduction: Habitual Residence)* [1993] 2 F.L.R. 124; *Re B (Minors) (Abduction) (No. 2)* [1993] 1 F.L.R. 993; *A v. A (Child Abduction)* [1993] 2 F.L.R. 225; *Re F (A Minor) (Child Abduction)* [1992] 1 F.L.R. 548; *V v. B (A Minor) (Abduction)* [1991] 1 F.L.R. 266; and on intra-U.K. custody cases under the Family Law Act 1986, see *e.g. Scullion v. Scullion*, 1990 S.C.L.R. 577; *Morris v. Morris*, 1993 S.C.L.R. 144; and *Rellis v. Hart*, 1993 S.L.T 738.

[21] Domicile and Matrimonial Proceedings Act 1973, s. 8(3).

[22] *ibid.* s. 12(4).

[23] *ibid.* s. 8(4).

[24] As amended by Children (Scotland) Act 1995, Sched. 4, para. 20(2)(a).

[25] Domicile and Matrimonial Proceedings Act 1973, s. 10(1A).

[26] *ibid.* s. 10(2).

[27] Matrimonial and Family Proceedings Act 1984, s. 28(2)(c). See Anton with Beaumont, pp. 593–595.

In order to avoid conflicts of jurisdiction, provision is made for the sisting of actions when proceedings in respect of the marriage are continuing in another jurisdiction.[28] The parties to an action of divorce or separation must inform the court of any concurrent proceedings in respect of the marriage which are capable of affecting its validity or subsistence, and in certain circumstances the court may, or must, sist the proceedings. The relevant rules are considered in detail in Chapter 22. 2.60

(2) Children. The sheriff has jurisdiction under section 11 of the Children (Scotland) Act 1995 to make orders in relation to: (a) parental responsibilities; (b) parental rights; (c) guardianship; or (d) subject to section 14(1) and (2) of the 1995 Act, the administration of a child's property. In the case of any action in the sheriff court, being an action for divorce or an action in relation to parental responsibilities or parental rights (within the meaning of sections 1(3) and 2(4) respectively of the 1995 Act) in relation to a child or the guardianship or adoption of a child the sheriff may, of his own accord, at any stage remit the action to the Court of Session.[29] The sheriff court has concurrent jurisdiction with the Court of Session in actions of aliment[30] where jurisdiction is not restricted by the Child Support Act 1991.[31] 2.61

The sheriff court may make a Section 11 order irrespective of whether or not the proceedings are independent of any other action.[32] Where the proceedings are not ancillary to another action, jurisdiction is chiefly governed by the Family Law Act 1986 (which applies also to orders made under Part I of that Act). Under the Act the court may only entertain such an application if, on the date of the application, the child concerned is habitually resident[33] in the sheriffdom[34]; or if on that date the child is not habitually resident in any part of the United Kingdom but is present in Scotland and either the pursuer or the defender in the application is habitually resident in the sheriffdom[35]; or if on that date the child is present in the sheriffdom and the sheriff considers that, for the protection of the child, it is necessary to make such an order immediately[36]. The qualifications of these general rules and the other provisions of the Act relative to sheriff court practice are noted in Chapter 22. The Act also provides that an application for an order relating to the guardianship of a child may be entertained by the sheriff if, on the date of the application, the child is habitually resident in the sheriffdom. That rule does not, however, apply to an application for the appointment or removal of a judicial factor or of a curator *bonis* or any application made by such factor or curator.[37] Section 14(2) of the Children (Scotland) Act 1995 grants the 2.62

---

[28] Domicile and Matrimonial Proceedings Act 1973, Sched. 3, as amended. Clive, pp. 577–579. See paras 22.27 to 22.31.

[29] 1971 Act, s. 37(2A) (added by Law Reform (Miscellaneous Provisions) (Scotland) Act 1980, s. 16(b), and amended by Divorce Jurisdiction, Court Fees and Legal Aid (Scotland) Act 1983, Sched. 1, para. 12, Law Reform (Parent and Child) (Scotland) Act 1986, Sched. 1, para. 11, Age of Legal Capacity (Scotland) Act 1991, Sched. 1, para. 35 and Children (Scotland) Act 1995, Sched. 4, para. 18(3)).

[30] Family Law (Scotland) Act 1985, s. 2.

[31] para. 2.57.

[32] Children (Scotland) Act 1995, s. 11(1).

[33] On "habitually resident", see n. 20.

[34] Family Law Act 1986, s. 9.

[35] *ibid.* s. 10.

[36] *ibid.* s. 11.

[37] *ibid.* s. 16(1), (2), as amended by Age of Legal Capacity (Scotland) Act 1991.

sheriff jurisdiction to entertain an application for an order relating to the administration of a child's property provided the child is habitually resident in, or the property is situated in, the sheriffdom.

2.63 **(3) Maintenance.** The proceedings relating to maintenance in which the sheriff court has jurisdiction are noted above.[38] A sheriff court's jurisdiction over parties in matters relating to maintenance is derived from the terms of Schedules 1, 3C, 4 and 8 to the Civil Jurisdiction and Judgments Act 1982. The court has jurisdiction in such matters if the defender is "domiciled" within its jurisdiction in the sense of the 1982 Act, which is explained below[39]; or if the maintenance creditor is "domiciled" or habitually resident[40] there; or if the matter is ancillary to proceedings concerning the status of a person. An action of affiliation and aliment is treated as a matter relating to maintenance which is not ancillary to proceedings concerning the status of a person.[41]

2.64 **(4) Declarator of parentage, etc.** An action for declarator of parentage, non-parentage, legitimacy, legitimation or illegitimacy may be brought in the Court of Session or the sheriff court.[42] Such an action may be brought in the sheriff court if and only if either of two conditions is fulfilled. The first is that the child was born in the sheriffdom.[43] In order to understand the second condition, which refers to the jurisdiction of the Court of Session, it is necessary to notice that such an action may be brought in the Court of Session if and only if the child was born in Scotland; or the alleged or presumed parent of the child[44] is domiciled[45] in Scotland on the date when the action is brought, or was habitually resident[46] in Scotland for not less than one year immediately preceding that date, or died before that date and either (i) was at the date of death domiciled in Scotland, or (ii) had been habitually resident in Scotland for not less than one year immediately preceding the date of death.[47] The terms of the second condition applicable to the sheriff court are that such an action may be brought in the sheriff court if and only if an action could have been brought in the Court of Session under the foregoing rules and the alleged or presumed parent or the child was habitually resident in the sheriffdom on the date when the action is brought or on the date of his death.[48]

Declarator of death

2.65 The sheriff court has concurrent jurisdiction with the Court of Session in actions for declarator of death of missing persons brought under the Presumption of Death (Scotland) Act 1977.[49] Decree in such an action is

---

[38] paras 2.56, 2.57.
[39] paras 3.06 to 3.12.
[40] On "habitually resident", see para. 2.58.
[41] See 1982 Act, Sched. 8, r. 2(5).
[42] Law Reform (Parent and Child) (Scotland) Act 1986 ("1986 Act"), s. 7(1). See Anton with Beaumont, pp. 484–486.
[43] 1986 Act, s. 7(3).
[44] "The alleged or presumed parent" includes a person who claims or is alleged to be or not to be the parent: 1986 Act, s. 7(6).
[45] "Domiciled" is here used in its traditional sense and not in the special sense defined in the 1982 Act.
[46] On "habitually resident", see n. 20.
[47] 1986 Act, s. 7(2).
[48] *ibid.* s. 7(3)(h).
[49] Presumption of Death (Scotland) Act 1977, s. 1(1).

effective against any person and for all purposes including the dissolution of a marriage to which the missing person is a party and the acquisition of rights to or in property belonging to any other person.[50] Such an action may be brought in the sheriff court on either of two jurisdictional grounds. The first is that the missing person was domiciled[51] in Scotland on the date on which he was last known to be alive, or had been habitually resident[52] there throughout the period of one year ending with that date and his last known place of residence in Scotland was in the sheriffdom. The alternative ground is established where the pursuer in the action is the spouse of the missing person; is domiciled in Scotland at the date of raising of the action, or was habitually resident there throughout the period of one year ending with that date; and was resident in the sheriffdom for a period of not less than 40 days ending with the date of raising of the action.[53] The procedure in such actions is described in Chapter 20.

Succession; trusts

The Sheriff of Chancery[54] has jurisdiction to entertain a petition for completion of title to heritage in terms of section 10 of the Conveyancing (Scotland) Act 1874 at the instance of a person seeking to have himself served heir to a person who died before September 10, 1964.[55] All sheriff courts exercise jurisdiction in the appointment and confirmation of executors. Where the deceased has died intestate and there is no executor nominate, the executor is appointed by decerniture of the sheriff on an application made to the court of the sheriffdom in which the deceased was domiciled, or, if he died domiciled furth of Scotland or without any fixed or known domicile, in the sheriff court of Edinburgh.[56] All executors, whether appointed by the deceased or by the court, are authorised to ingather and distribute the heritable and moveable estate of the deceased by confirmation by the court.[57] **2.66**

The jurisdiction of the sheriff court as to trusts has already been noted.[58] **2.67**

Judicial factors[59]

The Judicial Factors (Scotland) Act 1880, as amended, provides that the sheriff's jurisdiction in appointing judicial factors is concurrent with that **2.68**

---

[50] Presumption of Death (Scotland) Act 1977, s. 3(1).

[51] In this statute also, "domiciled" is used in its traditional sense.

[52] On "habitually resident", see n. 20.

[53] Presumption of Death (Scotland) Act 1977, s. 1(4).

[54] The jurisdiction of every other sheriff in relation to the service of heirs was transferred to the Sheriff of Chancery by the Sheriff of Chancery (Transfer of Jurisdiction) Order 1971 (S.I. 1971 No. 743).

[55] *Duthie's Trs, Petrs*, 1966 S.L.T. (Sh. Ct.) 24; *Findlay, Petr*, 1975 S.L.T. (Sh. Ct.) 46; *Robertson, Petr*, 1978 S.L.T. (Sh. Ct.) 30. See Meston, *The Succession (Scotland) Act 1964* (3rd ed., 1982), p. 84.

[56] Confirmation of Executors (Scotland) Act 1858, s. 3, as amended by A.S. (Confirmation of Executors) 1964, para. 6(2)(h).

[57] See Currie, *Confirmation of Executors* (8th ed., 1995).

[58] para. 2.44.

[59] The law and practice relating to judicial factors is outside the scope of this book: see Walker, *Judicial Factors*; D. Addison, *Judicial Factors* (1995). As to jurisdiction in relation to children, see Anton with Beaumont, pp. 564–565. In relation to adults, see Anton with Beaumont, pp. 567–568; Scottish Law Commission Discussion Paper No. 94, Sept. 1991, pp. 302–304 and 329–333 and the subsequent *Report on Incapable Adults* (SLC No. 151), pp. 15–16, 45 and 134–136.

of the Court of Session.[60] In the Act the expression "judicial factor" includes a curator *bonis*, a factor *loco tutoris*, a factor *loco absentis*, a factor on trust or other estates, and a guardian where caution is required, but does not include a judicial factor appointed under section 11A of the Judicial Factors (Scotland) Act 1889.[61] Under the latter section a creditor of a party deceased may apply for the appointment of a judicial factor on the party's estate: the application is made by summary petition to the Court of Session or to the sheriff of the sheriffdom within which the deceased resided or carried on business during the year immediately preceding the date of the petition.[62] At common law the Court of Session and the sheriff court may appoint a judicial factor in order to provide for the administration of property in dispute, or, if parties agree, for its sale and administration of the price, until parties' rights have been settled by agreement or litigation.[63]

2.69 Proceedings for the appointment of judicial factors in the sheriff court must be brought "in an appropriate sheriff court". In the case of a petition for the appointment of a judicial factor on a trust estate, that expression has the same meaning as in sections 22 to 24 of the Trusts (Scotland) Act 1921. That meaning is defined in section 24A of the 1921 Act, which has already been noted above.[64] In any other case it means (i) where the petition is for the appointment of a judicial factor (other than a factor *loco absentis*) to an individual, a sheriff court of the sheriffdom in which the individual is resident; (ii) where the petition is for the appointment of a factor *loco absentis* to an individual, a sheriff court of the sheriffdom in which the individual was last known to the petitioner to be resident; or (iii) where the petition is not as mentioned in (i) or (ii), the sheriff court at Edinburgh.[65]

Bankruptcy

2.70 The Court of Session and the sheriff court have, in general, concurrent jurisdiction in bankruptcy.[66] The Court of Session has exclusive jurisdiction to recall an award of sequestration.[67] In practice sequestration proceedings are carried on almost exclusively in the sheriff court. Separate jurisdictional rules apply to the sequestration of individuals and to the sequestration of other entities. In respect of the sequestration of the estate of a living debtor or of a deceased debtor,[68] the sheriff has jurisdiction if the debtor had an established place of business[69] in the sheriffdom, or was

---

[60] Judicial Factors (Scotland) Act 1880, s. 4, as amended by Law Reform (Miscellaneous Provisions) (Scotland) Act 1980, s. 14(1).

[61] *ibid.* s. 3, as amended.

[62] Judicial Factors (Scotland) Act 1889, s. 11A, inserted by Bankruptcy (Scotland) Act 1985, Sched. 7, para. 4.

[63] Walker, *Judicial Factors*, Chap. 9.

[64] para. 2.44.

[65] Judicial Factors (Scotland) Act 1880, s. 4(1) and (1A), as substituted and inserted by Law Reform (Miscellaneous Provisions) (Scotland) Act 1980, s. 14(1)(b).

[66] Bankruptcy (Scotland) Act 1985, s. 9.

[67] *ibid.* s. 16.

[68] "Debtor" includes the executor of a deceased debtor or a person entitled to be appointed as his executor: *ibid.* s. 73(1).

[69] "Business" means the carrying on of any activity, whether for profit or not: Bankruptcy (Scotland) Act 1985, s. 73(1). The qualification "established" is intended to emphasise the requirement of the settled nature of the place of business: *Report on Bankruptcy and Related Aspects of Insolvency and Liquidation* (Scot. Law Com. No. 680), para. 6.19. The expression "established place of business" is used in s. 409(1) of the Companies Act 1985: *Re Oriel Ltd* [1986] 1 W.L.R. 180.

habitually resident[70] there, at "the relevant time", which is any time in the year immediately preceding the date of presentation of the petition or the date of death, as the case may be.[71] In respect of the sequestration of a trust, partnership, body corporate (but not a company incorporated under the Companies Acts), unincorporated body or limited partnership, the sheriff has jurisdiction if the entity had an established place of business in the sheriffdom at the relevant time, or was constituted or formed under Scots law and at any time carried on business in the sheriffdom.[72] If the sheriff has jurisdiction to sequestrate the estate of a partnership, he also has jurisdiction to sequestrate the estate of any of the individual partners: if a petition is presented in the sheriffdom for the sequestration of the estate of the firm of which he is, or was at the relevant time before his decease, a partner and the process of that sequestration is still current, the sheriff has jurisdiction to sequestrate his estate.[73] Sequestration proceedings are outside the scope of this book.

Companies

Where the amount of a company's share capital paid up or credited as paid up does not exceed £120,000,[74] the sheriff court of the sheriffdom in which the company's registered office[75] is situated has concurrent jurisdiction with the Court of Session to wind up the company,[76] and to entertain other applications under the Companies Acts and other legislation. That rule is subject to the following qualifications. The Court of Session may, if it thinks expedient having regard to the amount of the company's assets to do so, (i) remit to a sheriff court any petition presented to the Court of Session for winding up such a company; or (ii) require such a petition presented to a sheriff court to be remitted to the Court of Session. The Court of Session may also require a petition presented to one sheriff court to be remitted to another sheriff court.[77] In a winding up in the sheriff court the sheriff may submit a stated case for the opinion of the Court of Session on any question of law arising in that winding up.[78] In the case of such a company the sheriff court also has concurrent jurisdiction with the Court of Session to make an administration order[79] or a disqualification order.[80] Applications for the appointment of a receiver do not appear to be competent in the sheriff court.[81] **2.71**

Among the many applications under the Companies Acts which may be made to the sheriff court where it has jurisdiction to wind up the company are: applications in respect of the alteration of a company's objects[82]; **2.72**

---

70 On "habitually resident", see n. 20.

71 Bankruptcy (Scotland) Act 1985, s. 9(1), (4) and (5).

72 *ibid.* s. 9(2) and (4).

73 *ibid.* s. 9(3) and (4); and see s. 6(5).

74 This sum may be altered by statutory instrument: Insolvency Act 1986, s. 120(5).

75 "Registered office" means the place which has longest been the company's registered office during the six months immediately preceding the presentation of the petition for winding up: Insolvency Act 1986, s. 120(4).

76 Insolvency Act 1986, s. 120(3).

77 *ibid.*

78 *ibid.*

79 Insolvency Act 1986, ss. 8(1), 9(1) and 251; Companies Act 1985, s. 744.

80 Company Directors Disqualification Act 1986, ss. 2(2), 3(4), 4(2), 6(3) and 10(1).

81 Insolvency Act 1986, s. 51(2); J. H. Greene and I. M. Fletcher, *The Law and Practice of Receivership in Scotland* (1987), para. 1.

82 Companies Act 1985, ss. 4 (as inserted by the Companies Act 1989, s.110(2)), 5 and 6.

confirmation of the reduction of its share capital[83]; variation of shareholders' rights[84]; rectification of the register of members[85]; arrangements and reconstructions[86]; takeover offers[87]; various incidental applications following on a voluntary liquidation[88]; the realisation of heritable estates affected by preferable securities[89]; the declaration of personal liability in respect of both fraudulent and wrongful trading[90]; the assessment of damages against delinquent directors and others[91]; restoring to the register a company struck off as defunct[92]; and the granting of relief against the company where members are unfairly prejudiced.[93] Proceedings under the Companies Acts are beyond the scope of this book.[94]

Partnerships

2.73 Both the Court of Session[95] and the sheriff court[96] may, on an application by a partner, decree a dissolution of the partnership in terms of section 35 of the Partnership Act 1890 on the ground that (a) a partner is insane or (b) is in any other way permanently incapable of performing his part of the partnership contract, or (c) is guilty of conduct prejudicially affecting the carrying on of the business, or (d) wilfully or persistently commits a breach of the partnership agreement or otherwise so conducts himself that it is not reasonably practicable for the other partner or partners to carry on the business in partnership with him, or (e) the business can only be carried on at a loss, or (f) circumstances have arisen which render it just and equitable that the partnership be dissolved.[97] The appropriate form of process is an action of declarator coupled with a crave for dissolution of the partnership.[98] The sheriff court may also appoint a judicial factor on the estate of a partnership.[99] Actions of declarator of dissolution of a partnership on the ground of breach of the partnership agreement, as by a partner's insolvency,[1] actions of declarator of partnership[2] and actions of accounting against co-partners[3] are among other actions relating to partnership which may be brought in the sheriff court.[4]

---

[83] Companies Act 1985, ss. 135–140 (s. 140(2), as amended by the Insolvency Act 1986, Sched. 13, Pt 1).

[84] *ibid.* s. 127.

[85] *ibid.* s. 359.

[86] *ibid.* ss. 425–427A, as amended.

[87] *ibid.* ss. 428–430F, as substituted by the Financial Services Act 1986, s. 172 and Sched. 12.

[88] Insolvency Act 1986, ss. 6(1),(4),(5),(6), 100(3), 101(3), 108, 110, 112, 165(1)(b), 201(3), 204(5).

[89] *ibid.* s. 185(1)(b).

[90] *ibid.* ss. 213–215. *Dyer v. Hyslop*, 1995 S.C.L.R. 161.

[91] *ibid.* s. 212.

[92] Companies Act 1985, s. 653(2); ss. 653(2A) and 653(2B), as inserted by the Deregulation and Contracting Out Act 1994, Sched. 5, para. 3.

[93] Companies Act 1985, ss. 459–461, as amended (particularly by the Companies Act 1989, Sched. 19, para. 11).

[94] Palmer's *Company Law* (Looseleaf edition), esp. Pt 15, pp.15241 *et seq.*

[95] *Semple v. Macnair and Crawford* (1907) 15 S.L.T. 448; *Hackston v. Hackston*, 1956 S.L.T. (Notes) 38; *Roxburgh v. Dinardo*, 1981 S.L.T. 291.

[96] *Duthie v. Milne*, 1946 S.L.T. (Sh. Ct.) 14.

[97] On the Partnership Act 1890, s. 35, see Miller, *Partnership* (2nd ed., Brough, 1994), pp. 473–498. On s. 35(f) see National Health Service (Amendment) Act 1949, s. 7(4).

[98] Miller, *Partnership* (2nd ed.), p. 474.

[99] Such appointments are made at common law and in terms of s. 35 and/or s. 39 of the Partnership Act 1890. See D. Addison, *Judicial Factors*, paras 34.1–34.3.

[1] See Dobie, *Styles*, p. 261.

[2] *ibid.* p. 353.

[3] *ibid.* p. 6.

[4] For further examples, see Walker, *Civil Remedies*, Chap. 35.

Admiralty

Provided a legal ground of jurisdiction against the defender can be established, the sheriff court is a competent tribunal in which to try any civil maritime cause.[5] When the High Court of Admiralty was abolished in 1830 its jurisdiction was conferred on the Court of Session[6] and the sheriff courts.[7] Section 4 of the 1907 Act, as amended, now provides that the powers and jurisdictions formerly competent to the High Court of Admiralty in all civil maritime causes and proceedings shall be competent to the sheriffs. Civil maritime causes and proceedings include causes relative to charterparties, freights, salvages, wrecks, collisions of ships, bottomries, policies of marine insurance, contracts concerning the loading and unloading of ships, actions for the delivery of goods shipped or for their value,[8] and causes falling within the definition of Admiralty causes in rule 46.1 of the Rules of the Court of Session. Thus, in all such causes and proceedings the sheriff court has jurisdiction which is privative in causes below £1,500 in value[9] and otherwise concurrent with that of the Court of Session. **2.74**

Prize jurisdiction is vested in the Admiralty Court which is part of the Queen's Bench Division of the High Court of England.[10] The sheriff court has concurrent jurisdiction in cases of apportionment of salvage in accordance with the provisions of section 229 of the Merchant Shipping Act 1995. **2.75**

The territorial jurisdiction of the sheriff in maritime causes is regulated principally by section 4 of the 1907 Act.[11] As to his jurisdiction over defenders, Schedule 9 to the Civil Jurisdiction and Judgments Act 1982 excludes from Schedule 8 Admiralty causes in so far as the jurisdiction is based on arrestment *in rem* or *ad fundandam jurisdictionem* of a ship, cargo or freight.[12] In so far as the sheriff's jurisdiction relates to the arrest of a ship or vessel, it is thought to be preserved.[13] The Administration of Justice Act 1956 provides special grounds of jurisdiction in actions arising out of ship collisions,[14] and restricts the extent to which arrestment of a ship may be used on the dependence or *in rem*.[15] In dealing with maritime causes the court applies not Scottish municipal law, but maritime law which is the same in both Scotland and England.[16] In procedure, however, it follows its own rules and practice.[17] **2.76**

---

5 1907 Act, s. 4, as amended by the Criminal Procedure (Scotland) Act 1975, Sched. 10, Pt I, *Sheaf Steamship Co. v. Compania Transmediterranea*, 1930 S.C. 660, *per* L.J.-C. Alness at 665.

6 Court of Session Act 1830, s. 21.

7 *ibid.* s. 22; Sheriff Courts (Scotland) Acts 1838, s. 21, 1877, s. 8(4).

8 Ersk., I, iii, 33; Bell, *Comm.*, i, 546.

9 See paras 2.27 to 2.34.

10 Court of Session Act 1825, s. 57; Administration of Justice Act 1970, s. 2; Supreme Court Act 1981, s. 6.

11 See para. 2.02.

12 Civil Jurisdiction and Judgments Act 1982, Sched. 9, para. 6.

13 *ibid.* Sched. 1, Art. 57; Anton & Beaumont, *C.J.*, para. 5.09.

14 Administration of Justice Act 1956, s. 45.

15 *ibid.* s. 47.

16 *Currie v. McKnight* (1896) 24 R.(H.L.); *Constant v. Christensen*, 1912 S.C. 1371; *Quinn v. Peacock & Co.* (1916) 33 Sh.Ct.Rep. 205; *Clydesdale Bank v. Walker & Bain*, 1926 S.C. 72, *per* L.J.-C. Alness at 82, Lord Anderson at 89.

17 *Sheaf Steamship Co. v. Compania Transmediterranea*, 1930 S.C. 660.

Air

2.77 The jurisdiction of the sheriff court relative to the air space over the sheriffdom has already been noted.[18] Jurisdiction in actions of damages in respect of carriage by air is conferred by the Carriage by Air Act 1961[19] in a self-contained code within the limits of which a pursuer must found his jurisdiction.[20] It gives him at his option courts at four different places in the territories of the High Contracting Parties to the Warsaw Convention, as amended, where he may sue an action for damages: first, where the carrier is ordinarily resident; secondly, where the carrier has his principal place of business; third, where the carrier has an establishment by which the contract has been made; and fourth, at the place of destination. In respect of damage resulting from the death, injury or delay of a passenger or the destruction, loss, damage or delay of baggage, the action may be brought before any of these courts or the court within the jurisdiction of which the carrier has an establishment if the passenger has his ordinary or permanent residence in the same territory. Questions of procedure are governed by the law of the court seised of the case.

Diligence[21]

2.78 As to diligence against heritage, it has already been noted that a warrant for inhibition may be granted,[22] and an action of adjudication for debt may be brought,[23] only in the Court of Session. As to diligence against moveables, arrestment on the dependence and in execution may proceed from the Court of Session or the sheriff court, and any action of furthcoming necessary to effect the transfer of the assets arrested may be brought in either court according to the value of the cause.[24] Personal poindings proceed subject to the authority of the sheriff,[25] but the debtor's remedies of suspension and interdict may be sought in either the Court of Session or the sheriff court, depending in general on the basis of the charge[26] and the value of the suspension.[27]

Crime; illegality

2.79 In exercising his civil jurisdiction the sheriff may adjudicate upon allegations of criminal or illegal conduct which are relevantly made in the proceedings before him, as where reparation is sought on the ground of assault,[28] theft,[29] reset,[30] embezzlement,[31] or breach of

---

[18] para. 2.02. Provision may be made by Order in Council as to the courts in which proceedings may be taken for enforcing any claim in respect of aircraft: Civil Aviation Act 1982, s. 91.

[19] Carriage by Air Act 1961, Sched. 1, substituted by Carriage by Air and Road Act 1979, Sched. 1, art. 28; *Rothman's of Pall Mall (Overseas) Ltd v. Saudi Arabian Airlines Corporation* [1981] Q.B. 368.

[20] *Rothman's, supra, per* Roskill L.J. at 385.

[21] See, generally, Chap. 29.

[22] para. 2.41.

[23] para. 2.40.

[24] Maxwell, p. 84.

[25] Debtors (Scotland) Act 1987, ss. 18(2), 21(1), 22(3),(5), 23, 24, 27, 28(4)–(6), 29(2)–(3).

[26] 1907 Act, s. 5(5), as amended by Law Reform (Miscellaneous Provisions) (Scotland) Act 1980, s. 15(a) and Sched. 3; A.S. (Summary Suspension) 1993 (S.I. 1993 No. 3128), para. 2. See paras 24.11 to 24.15.

[27] See paras 2.27 to 2.34.

[28] *Marco v. Merrens*, 1964 S.L.T. (Sh. Ct.) 74.

[29] *Dalhanna Knitwear Co. Ltd v. Mohammed Ali*, 1967 S.L.T. (Sh. Ct.) 74.

[30] *ibid.*

[31] *Buick v. Jaglar*, 1973 S.L.T. (Sh.Ct.) 6.

[32] *e.g.* offences under road traffic or health and safety statutes or regulations.

statutory duty.[32] The same matter may properly be adjudicated upon both in the criminal and in the civil court without justifying a plea of *res judicata* in either, apart from rare cases where the parties, ground of action and remedy sought are the same.[33] In civil proceedings the fact that a person has been convicted is admissible evidence that he committed the offence, and a person proved to have been convicted is taken to have committed the offence unless the contrary is proved,[34] except where the civil action is for defamation and the question is whether or not he committed the offence: in the latter case, the conviction is conclusive evidence that he did so.[35] It is thought that where any criminal conduct is in issue in a civil case, the standard of proof is on a balance of probabilities.[36] When in the course of civil proceedings it appears to the sheriff that a criminal offence may have been committed, he may send the relevant papers to the procurator fiscal in order that the latter may make further inquiries.[37]

The sheriff may impose penalties in proceedings for breach of interdict[38] and in other cases of contempt of court,[39] and may forfeit caution in actions for contravention of lawburrows.[40] **2.80**

III. REMEDIES

This section of the chapter attempts to classify in broad terms the remedies which may competently be sought and the applications which may competently be made in the sheriff court. A distinction is drawn between the subject-matter of remedies and applications on the one hand, and the procedure whereby they are sought or made on the other[41]; while they cannot be entirely separated, this book deals, as far as possible, only with procedure. In Scots law there is no exact correlation between particular remedies and particular procedures or forms of action: while some remedies have procedural peculiarities not shared by others, Scots law has never had a strict system of forms of action, in which claims for particular remedies have each their own form of procedure.[42] The classification which is attempted here is accordingly designed only to provide a survey of the remedies and applications which are competent, and is not the basis of the plan of the book. **2.81**

The remedies and applications competent in the sheriff court may be classified into proceedings properly remedial; proceedings administrative, executorial or accessory; and miscellaneous common law and statutory proceedings.[43] These classes of proceedings are briefly noticed in the following paragraphs. Any procedural specialties are considered elsewhere, as indicated in the footnotes. **2.82**

---

[33] Walkers, p. 47; Maxwell, p. 95.
[34] Law Reform (Miscellaneous Provisions) (Scotland) Act 1968, s. 10.
[35] *ibid.* s. 12, as amended by the Defamation Act 1996, s. 12(2).
[36] Macphail, *Evidence*, paras 22.32–22.35.
[37] *Donnelly v. Donnelly*, 1986 S.L.T. 305 at 306.
[38] See para. 21.99.
[39] See paras 2.18 to 2.25.
[40] See para. 24.05.
[41] Walker, *Civil Remedies*, Chap. 1.
[42] *ibid.* p. 10.
[43] *ibid.* p. 18.

Proceedings properly remedial

2.83 These include actions declaratory, rescissory, petitory, possessory, preventive and competitive, and claims peculiar to family proceedings[44] or Admiralty jurisdiction. Declaratory actions are considered elsewhere.[45] Actions of reduction fall within the exclusive jurisdiction of the Court of Session, but the sheriff has power to set aside certain deeds or writings to which objection is taken by way of exception in ordinary and summary causes.[46]

2.84 "Petitory actions are so called, not because something is sought to be awarded by the judge (for in that sense all actions must be petitory), but because some demand is made upon the defender, in consequence either of a right of property or credit in the pursuer."[47] They include actions for payment of money, including actions for payment of debt or damages, and actions of count, reckoning and payment[48]; actions *ad factum praestandum*[49]; actions of interdict[50]; claims for restitution; actions of constitution; applications for sequestration or liquidation; applications by secured creditors[51]; and actions of sequestration for rent,[52] poinding of the ground,[53] and maills and duties.[54]

2.85 Possessory actions are those "wherein an absolute right is not insisted for, but possession is claimed to be attained, retained, or recovered."[55] Such actions in relation to heritage include summary cause actions for recovery of heritable property.[56] Actions of interdict, of maills and duties, of poinding of the ground and for delivery of moveable property may also be classed as possessory actions, if based on a simple right of possession and not on an absolute right in the pursuer. Questions of possession now normally arise as incidental to actions in which the question of absolute right is raised, and the distinction between petitory and possessory actions is now of little practical importance.[57] The preventive actions of suspension of diligence, and of interdict, and the competitive action of multiplepoinding,[58] are traditionally classified as possessory actions but may also be classified as petitory actions.

---

[44] See Chap. 22.
[45] See Chap. 20.
[46] See paras 2.42, 12.66 to 12.72 (ordinary cases).
[47] Ersk., IV, i, 47.
[48] See Chap. 21.
[49] *ibid.*
[50] *ibid.*
[51] See paras. 23.14 to 23.24.
[52] *ibid.*
[53] *ibid.*
[54] *ibid.*
[55] Stair, IV, iii, 47.
[56] See 1st ed., Chap. 25, and Vol. 2 of this work.
[57] It may have a bearing on the question whether a decree can found a plea of *res judicata*: *McCallum v. Forth Iron Co.* (1861) 23 D. 729, *per* Lord Kinloch at 731; *Duke of Sutherland v. Reed* (1890) 18 R. 252, *per* Lord Adam at 259; *Davidson v. Shipmasters' Society of Aberdeen* (1897) 5 S.L.T. 34.
[58] See paras 24.11 to 24.15 (suspension of diligence), 21.83 to 21.99 (interdict), 21.52 to 21.71 (multiplepoinding).

Administrative, executorial or accessory proceedings

Administrative proceedings are those in which are invoked the court's jurisdiction relative to trusts,[59] succession,[60] judicial factors,[61] guardians,[62] adoption,[63] companies,[64] partnerships,[65] division or division and sale of heritage, division of commonty and regulation of march fences.[66] Executorial proceedings are those concerned with the execution of decrees and the doing of diligence: poindings, and actions of furthcoming.[67] Accessory proceedings are those "which do not subsist by themselves, but merely prepare the way for or are subservient to other actions."[68] Those competent in the sheriff court are actions of exhibition, the object of which is to obtain exhibition of writs in which the pursuer has an interest, and actions of transumpt, in which the object is the exhibition of the writs so that transumpts or copies may be judicially made out and delivered to the pursuer. Both appear to be virtually unknown in modern practice.[69] **2.86**

Miscellaneous

A wide variety of other civil proceedings may be brought in the sheriff court, both at common law and under statute. While many of these may be classified as administrative, others do not readily fall under any of the previous headings. The statutory proceedings include: actions of lawburrows[70]; appeals against administrative decisions of local or other authorities; the ordering or prohibiting of works; the exercise of powers in relation to feus, tenancies and burdened estates; and the assessment of compensation, apportionment of costs, arbitrations and settlement of disputes. An attempt is made in a later chapter to provide a list of miscellaneous statutory proceedings.[71] **2.87**

IV. Exclusion of Exercise of Jurisdiction Otherwise Competent

> "When a party with a title and an interest to do so brings an action before a court with jurisdiction to decide the questions raised in it the court is normally bound to entertain the action. If the defender maintains that the court should not do so, he must satisfy the court that special circumstances exist which make it inappropriate that the court should exercise its jurisdiction."[72] **2.88**

---

59 para. 2.44.
60 para. 2.66.
61 para. 2.68.
62 paras 2.61, 2.62.
63 See Chap. 28.
64 paras 2.45, 2.71, 2.72.
65 para. 2.73.
66 See Chap. 23.
67 On actions of furthcoming, see paras 21.45 to 21.51.
68 Ersk., IV, i, 52.
69 See para. 24.01.
70 See paras 24.02 to 24.05.
71 Chap. 26.
72 *Argyllshire Weavers Ltd v. A. Macaulay (Tweeds) Ltd*, 1962 S.C. 388, *per* Lord Guthrie at 403. See also *Clements v. Macaulay* (1866) 4 M. 583, *per* L.J.-C. Inglis at 593; *Forbes v. Underwood* (1886) 13 R. 465, *per* L.P. Inglis at 467–468.

Examples of such circumstances are considered in this section of this chapter.

Forum non conveniens

2.89 Subject to what is said below as to the effect of the Civil Jurisdiction and Judgments Act 1982,[73] the defender may plead that the action should be dismissed or sisted on the ground of *forum non conveniens.* The principle of *forum non conveniens*, for long recognised in Scots law, has recently been recognised in England, and Scots and English law may now be regarded as indistinguishable on the point.[74] The basic principle is that the plea can never be sustained unless the court is satisfied that there is some other tribunal outside Scotland,[75] having competent jurisdiction, which is the appropriate forum for the action, that is, in which the case may be tried more suitably for the interests of all the parties and the ends of justice.[76] The question at issue is not one of mere practical convenience. The court

> "has to consider how best the ends of justice in the case in question and on the facts before it, so far as they can be measured in advance, can be respectively ascertained and served. . . . This object, under the words '*forum non conveniens*' is to find that *forum* which is the more suitable for the ends of justice, and is preferable because pursuit of the litigation in that forum is more likely to secure those ends."[77]

2.90 In general, the burden of satisfying the court that the case should not be allowed to proceed lies upon the defender who tables the plea.

> "It is, however, of importance to remember that each party will seek to establish the existence of certain matters which will assist him in persuading the court to exercise its discretion in his favour, and that in respect of any such matter the evidential burden will rest on the party who asserts its existence. Furthermore, if the court is satisfied that there is another available forum which is prima facie the appropriate forum for the trial of the action, the burden will then shift to the [pursuer] to show that there are special circumstances by

---

[73] para. 2.93.

[74] *The Abidin Daver* [1984] A.C. 398, *per* Lord Diplock at 411; *Spiliada Maritime Corporation v. Cansulex Ltd* [1987] A.C. 460 at 475, 477, *per* Lord Goff of Chieveley whose speech reviews the authorities and contains the most comprehensive modern analysis of the principle.

[75] Where a prior action between the same parties, raising the same point, is before the same or another Scottish court, the appropriate plea is *lis alibi pendens*: see paras 2.94 to 2.98.

[76] *Sim v. Robinow* (1892) 19 R. 665, *per* Lord Kinnear at 668. See also *Longworth v. Hope* (1865) 3 M. 1049, *per* L.P. McNeill at 1053; *Clements v. Macaulay* (1866) 4 M. 583, *per* L.J.-C. Inglis at 593; *Forbes v. Underwood* (1886) 13 R. 465, *per* L.P. Inglis at 467–468; *Société du Gaz de Paris v. Armateurs Francais*, 1925 S.C. 332, *per* L.J.-C. Alness at 334–348, approved *per* Lord Dunedin, 1926 S.C. (H.L.) 13 at 18; *Argyllshire Weavers Ltd v. A. Macaulay (Tweeds) Ltd*, 1962 S.C. 388, *per* Lord Guthrie at 403; *Credit Chimique v. James Scott Engineering Ltd*, 1979 S.C. 406 at 410; *Spiliada, supra*; *Sokha v. Secretary of State for the Home Department*, 1992 S.L.T. 1049 at 1052–1054; *Morrison v. Panic Link Ltd*, 1993 S.L.T. 602; *PTKF Kontinent v. VMPTO Progress*, 1994 S.L.T. 235; in *Connelly (A.P.) v. RTZ Corporation plc* [1997] 4 All E.R. 335, Lord Goff once again repeats his restatement of the *Sim v. Robinow* dicta which he originally gave in *Spiliada, supra.*

[77] *Société du Gaz de Paris, supra*, 1926 S.C. (H.L.) 13, *per* Lord Sumner at 22, putting the rule in "its authoritative form" (*The Atlantic Star* [1974] A.C. 436 *per* Lord Kilbrandon at 475).

reason of which justice requires that the trial should nevertheless take place in this country."[78]

Since the Scottish court has jurisdiction to entertain the action, the burden on the defender is not only to show that that court is not the natural or appropriate court for the litigation, but to establish that there is another available forum which is clearly or distinctly more appropriate than the Scottish court. The court will look first to see what factors there are which point in the direction of another forum as being the "natural" forum "with which the action [has] the most real and substantial connection".[79] Connecting factors in this sense include not only factors affecting convenience or expense, such as availability of witnesses, but also other factors such as the law governing the relevant transaction[80] and the places where the parties respectively reside or carry on business.[81] If the court concludes that there is no other available forum which is clearly more appropriate for the litigation of the action, it will repel the defender's plea; but if it concludes that there is some other available forum which prima facie is clearly more appropriate, it will ordinarily sustain the plea unless there are circumstances by reason of which "justice" requires that it should not do so. In this inquiry, the court will consider all the circumstances of the case, including circumstances which go beyond those taken into account when considering connecting factors with other jurisdictions.[82] Since the cases in which the plea has been sustained have, almost without exception, special features, it is difficult to formulate any further principles as to the factors relevant to the plea and the actions in which it is appropriate. The matter is extensively discussed elsewhere.[83] **2.91**

The plea of *forum non conveniens* is a preliminary plea, to be disposed of after it has been conceded or determined that the court has jurisdiction[84] but before the merits of the cause are considered.[85] The plea may be stated in the form: "This court being *forum non conveniens*, the action should be dismissed [or sisted]" and should be founded on relevant averments in the answers to the condescendence.[86] Where the plea is sustained, the court **2.92**

---

78 *Spiliada, supra*, at 476.

79 *The Abidin Daver* [1984] A.C. 398, *per* Lord Keith of Kinkel at 415.

80 *Jubert v. Church Commissioners for England*, 1952 S.C. 160; *Crédit Chimique v. James Scott Engineering Ltd*, 1979 S.C. 406.

81 *Spiliada, supra*, at 478. In *Connelly (A.P.) v. RTZ Corporation, supra*, the House of Lords (Lord Hoffmann dissenting) decided to invoke the "justice" exception and not uphold the plea of *forum non conveniens*. In this case Namibia was clearly the natural forum—it was a "clearly more appropriate" forum than England. However, the plaintiff would neither have been able to get legal aid in Namibia, nor been able to pursue the litigation on a contingency fee basis there. One or other of these opportunities was available in England. Owing to the nature and complexity of the case, it was not possible for the plaintiff to pursue his remedy in Namibia without financial assistance. Substantial justice would therefore be denied if the plea of *forum non conveniens* were upheld.

82 *Spiliada, supra*, at 478.

83 *Spiliada, supra*, at 478–484; Anton with Beaumont, pp. 212–218; Lord Wark, "Forum Non Conveniens", in *Encyclopaedia*, vii, pp. 180–186. Beaumont, "Great Britain" in Fawcett (ed.), *Declining Jurisdiction in Private International Law* (Clarendon, Oxford, 1995), pp. 207–220; U.K. Note to Hague Conference on Private International Law, Annex D to Preliminary Document No. 3, April 1996.

84 *Montgomery v. Zarifi*, 1917 S.C. 627 at 640, 644 (*affd*, 1918 S.C. (H.L.) 128).

85 *Boe v. Anderson* (1857) 20 D. 11, *per* L.P. McNeill at 24; *Montgomery, supra.*

86 *Crédit Chimique v. James Scott Engineering Ltd*, 1979 S.C. 406.

may dismiss the action; but the procedure to be followed is to a certain extent in the discretion of the court.[87] The court may sist the action where that course may facilitate a solution by the foreign tribunal of the controversy between the parties[88] or the enforcement of the foreign decree.[89]

2.93 By virtue of the provisions of the Civil Jurisdiction and Judgments Act 1982 the Scottish rules of *forum non conveniens* do not now apply where an action is brought in a Scottish court and proceedings involving the same cause of action and between the same parties are brought in the courts of another State Party to the Brussels or Lugano Convention. In that situation, any court other than the court first seised must of its own motion decline jurisdiction in favour of that court; but if the jurisdiction of the court first seised is contested, another court may stay the action before it to await the result of that contest, instead of declining jurisdiction and dismissing the action.[90] The Act also provides for a situation in which "related actions" are brought in the courts of different Member States. "Related actions" are those which are so closely connected that it is expedient to hear and determine them together to avoid the risk of irreconcilable judgments resulting from separate proceedings. Any court other than the court first seised may, while the actions are pending at first instance, stay its proceedings, or may on the application of one of the parties decline jurisdiction if the law of the court first seised permits the consolidation of related actions and the court first seised has jurisdiction over both actions.[91] Where actions come within the exclusive jurisdiction of several courts, any court other than the court first seised must decline jurisdiction in favour of that court.[92] It is submitted that a Scottish court is "seised" of an action for the purpose of these provisions at the date of citation of the defender[93]; the citation of the defender is the commencement of the action, and thereafter it is in dependence.[94] The 1982 Act does, however, preserve the power of the court to decline jurisdiction on the ground of *forum non conveniens* where to do so is not inconsistent with the Brussels Convention or, as the case may be, with the Lugano Convention.[95]

Lis alibi pendens (within Scotland)

2.94 There is always an equitable power and duty of control in each tribunal to see that there is not on the whole an improper and oppressive accumulation of litigation or diligence.[96] If, accordingly,

---

[87] *Atkinson & Wood v. Mackintosh* (1905) 7 F. 598, *per* Lord Pearson at 601.

[88] *Orr-Ewing's Trs v. Orr-Ewing* (1885) 13 R. (H.L.) 1, *per* Lord Watson at 27; *Foster v. Foster's Trs*, 1923 S.C. 212, *per* L.P. Clyde at 219.

[89] *Jubert v. Church Commissioners for England*, 1952 S.C. 160; *Crédit Chimique*, *supra*.

[90] Civil Jurisdiction and Judgments Act 1982, Sched. 1, Art. 21. See para. 3.60.

[91] *ibid.* Art. 22. See para. 3.61.

[92] *ibid.* Art. 23. See para. 3.62.

[93] Maxwell Report, para. 5.226. Under English law the date when the courts are definitively seised for the purposes of Art. 21 is the date of service of process, see *Dresser U.K. Ltd v. Falcongate Ltd* [1992] 1 Q.B. 523; *Neste Chemicals SA v. D.K. Line SA*; *The Sargasso* [1994] 3 All E.R. 180.

[94] See para. 6.06.

[95] Civil Jurisdiction and Judgments Act 1982, s. 49 as amended by the Civil Jurisdiction and Judgments Act 1991, Sched. 2, para. 24; see also s. 22(1) and para. 3.63. *Forum non conveniens* can be pleaded where the alternative forum is in another part of the United Kingdom, see Drake J. in *Cumming v. Scottish Daily Record and Sunday Mail Ltd*, *The Times*, June 8, 1995.

[96] *Cochrane v. Paul* (1857) 20 D. 178, *per* Lord Neaves at 179. See also para. 2.113, n. 15.

the court in any action is satisfied that the question raised in the action is already at issue in a prior suit between the same parties or parties representing the same interests which is depending before the same court or another court of competent jurisdiction in Scotland, the second action may be dismissed on the preliminary plea of *lis alibi pendens*.[97] The plea is stated in the form "*Lis alibi pendens*", and must be supported by relevant averments.[98] The plea may be waived by implication, as by a minute prorogating the jurisdiction.[99] The circumstances in which the plea may be successfully proponed are noted in the following paragraphs.

(1) The two actions must raise for determination precisely the same question.[1] Where, however, there are counter-declarators each raising exactly the same question, the plea may be repelled on the ground that the defender in the prior declarator is not bound to wait for the pursuer's pleasure in proceeding with it.[2] **2.95**

(2) The prior action must be between the same parties or parties representing the same interest.[3] **2.96**

(3) The prior action must be in dependence at the date when the plea comes before the court for consideration. If by that time the double dependence has been brought to an end the plea should not, or at least need not, be sustained.[4] An action begins to depend as soon as the defender is cited: the citation of the defender is the commencement of the action,[5] and thereafter the prior *lis* is in dependence until the final decree for taxed expenses is pronounced,[6] except where it has been dismissed on a plea of no jurisdiction.[7] The plea is elided by abandonment[8] or disclaimer[9] of the prior action before the plea falls to be considered. Abandonment and disclamation may be effected by minute in the prior action,[10] and abandonment may alternatively be effected by intimation in the later action by minute[11] or perhaps, if the prior action has not been called or tabled, by averment in the condescendence.[12] An **2.97**

---

[97] *Rothfield v. Cohen*, 1919 1 S.L.T. 138.

[98] *Flannigan v. British Dyewood Co.*, 1971 S.C. 110 at 111, 114.

[99] *Longmuir v. Longmuir* (1850) 12 D. 926.

[1] *Mags of Kilrenny v. Johnston* (1828) 6 S. 624; *Wilson v. Junor* (1907) 15 S.L.T. 182; *Stewart v. Stewart* (1906) 8 F. 769; *Alston v. Alston's Trs*, 1919 2 S.L.T. 22; *Wilson v. Dunlop, Bremner & Co. Ltd*, 1921 1 S.L.T. 35.

[2] *Howden v. Viscountess Hawarden* (1864) 2 M. 637; *Wishart v. Howatson* (1897) 5 S.L.T. 84; *Harland Engineering Co. v. Stark's Trs*, 1913 2 S.L.T. 448.

[3] *Alston, supra*; Lord Wark, "*Lis Alibi Pendens*" in *Encyclopaedia*, ix, p. 299.

[4] *McAulay v. Cowe* (1873) 1 R. 307; *Nelson v. Gordon* (1874) 1 R. 1093 at 1097; *Alston, supra*; *Flannigan v. British Dyewood Co.*, 1971 S.C. 110; *Dickson v. United Dominions Trust Ltd (No. 2)*, 1983 S.L.T. 189; *Saudi Distribution Services Ltd v. Kane*, 1985 S.L.T. (Sh. Ct.) 9.

[5] Ersk., III, vi, 3; *Aitken v. Dick* (1863) 1 M. 1038; *Kennedy v. Macdonald* (1876) 3 R. 813 (more fully reported, 13 S.L.R. 525); *Alston v. Macdougall* (1887) 15 R. 78; *Gibson v. Clark* (1895) 23 R. 294; *Smith v. Stewart*, 1960 S.C. 329, *per* L.P. Clyde at 334. See para. 6.06.

[6] *Aitken, Kennedy, Flannigan, supra.*

[7] *Watt v. Coughlan* (1902) 10 S.L.T. 89.

[8] *Earl of Hopetoun v. Scots Mining Co.* (1859) 21 D. 218 at 221; *McAulay, supra*; *Nelson, supra*.

[9] *Alston v. Alston's Trs*, 1919 2 S.L.T. 22.

[10] *ibid.*

[11] *Nelson v. Gordon* (1874) 1 R. 1093.

[12] *Laidlaw v. Smith* (1834) 12 S. 538; *McAulay v. Cowe* (1873) 1 R. 307.

extrajudicial communication by a solicitor is insufficient to put an end to a regular action in a question of *lis alibi pendens.*[13]

2.98 (4) The prior action must be in dependence either in the same court[14] or in another court of competent jurisdiction in Scotland. The plea does not apply to proceedings before foreign courts.[15]

Arbitration; Agreement

2.99 The court will not exercise jurisdiction as to the merits of a dispute which falls to be referred to arbitration, either by virtue of a valid contract between the parties to submit the matter in dispute to arbitration, or in terms of a statutory provision that certain questions or differences be determined by arbitration. The law of Scotland "has, from the earliest times, permitted private parties to exclude the merits of any dispute between them from the consideration of the court by simply naming their arbiter."[16] In that situation the court, if satisfied as to the effect of the contractual provision as to reference to arbitration,[17] has no discretion to permit an action to proceed because it considers that course to be more appropriate than arbitration.[18] The jurisdiction of the court is not, however, wholly ousted by such a contract: it only introduces a new plea into the cause on which the court must decide by virtue of its inherent jurisdiction.[19] If a valid contract of arbitration is found to exist, it

> "deprives the court of jurisdiction to inquire into and decide the merits of the case, while it leaves the court free to entertain the suit and to pronounce a decree in conformity with the award of the arbiter. Should the arbitration from any cause prove abortive, the full jurisdiction of the court will revive, to the effect of enabling it to hear and determine the action upon its merits. When a binding reference is pleaded *in limine*, the proper course to take is either to refer the question in dispute to the arbiter named or to stay procedure until it has been settled by arbitration."[20]

A party may raise an action with a view to effecting diligence and then move for it to be sisted pending arbitration. In practice many arbitrations take place within the framework of a civil litigation.[21] If the arbitration agreement is of an international commercial character and comes within the scope of the UNCITRAL Model Law on International Commercial Arbitration of June 21, 1985, as adapted for application in Scotland, then

---

[13] *Nelson, supra*, n. 2.

[14] In such a case the appropriate form of plea is "*Lis pendens*": *Levy v. Gardiner*, 1965 S.L.T. (Notes) 86.

[15] *Cochrane v. Paul* (1857) 20 D. 178, *per* Lord Neaves at 179; *Martin v. Stopford-Blair's Exrs* (1879) 7 R. 329, *per* L.P. Inglis at 331; *Atkinson & Wood v. Mackintosh* (1905) 7 F. 598, *per* Lord Kinnear at 601; *Rothheld v. Cohen*, 1919 1 S.L.T. 138; *Argyllshire Weavers Ltd v. A. Macaulay (Tweeds) Ltd*, 1962 S.C. 388 at 391, 400; *The Atlantic Star* [1974] A.C. 436, *per* Lord Kilbrandon at 475.

[16] *Hamlyn & Co. v. Talisker Distillery* (1894) 21 R. (H.L.) 21, *per* Lord Watson at 27.

[17] See para. 2.101.

[18] *Sanderson & Son v. Armour & Co.*, 1922 S.C. (H.L.) 117, *per* Lord Dunedin at 126; *Roxburgh v. Dinardo*, 1981 S.L.T. 291 at 292.

[19] *Wilson v. Glasgow Tramways Co.* (1877) 5 R. 981, *per* Lord Gifford at 992.

[20] *Hamlyn, supra, per* Lord Watson at 25; and see *Sanderson & Son, supra, per* Lord Dunedin at 125, 126; A. E. Anton, "Arbitration: International Aspects", 1986 S.L.T. (News) 45, 53, at 47.

[21] *Graeme Borthwick Ltd v. Walco Developments (Edinburgh) Ltd*, 1980 S.L.T. (Sh. Ct.) 93; *Motordrift A/S v. Trachem Co. Ltd*, 1982 S.L.T. 127.

the Scottish courts are obliged to sist the proceedings in favour of arbitration if one of the parties so requests.[22] If the arbitration agreement does not come within the scope of the UNCITRAL Model Law or the New York Convention then the Scottish courts have a discretion whether to sist the proceedings in favour of arbitration but are likely to do so.[23] It may be that the courts will sist their proceedings in favour of a form of dispute resolution falling short of a classical arbitration agreement.[24]

A party who wishes to found on an arbitration clause in order to have an action sisted so that its subject-matter may be decided by arbitration should specifically aver the terms of the clause and the dispute or difference which he maintains falls within its ambit and should be submitted to arbitration[25] and state a plea-in-law appropriate to the circumstances averred, as "*Ante omnia* the cause should be sisted to allow the matter to proceed to arbitration"[26] or, "In respect that the dispute between the parties falls to be resolved by arbitration in terms of [the specified clause of the contract], the present action should be sisted."[27] Pleas of no jurisdiction,[28] or seeking dismissal of the action,[29] are incorrect. It is unusual, but not incompetent, for a pursuer to raise an action and then plead that it be sisted for arbitration.[30] The plea-in-law is a preliminary plea.[31] It is not necessarily waived by agreement to a preliminary proof before answer on a restricted issue.[32] Lord Watson's observation in *Hamlyn & Co.*[33] that the reference is pleaded *in limine* has been understood to mean that it should be pleaded before the closing of the record,[34] upon the view that parties may make alterations to their pleadings up to that point[35] and that amendment thereafter is permitted only in so far as it is necessary to determine the real question in controversy between the parties[36] and not in order to effect the transfer **2.100**

---

[22] See Law Reform (Miscellaneous Provisions) (Scotland) Act 1990, s. 66 and Sched. 7, discussed in Davidson, *International Commercial Arbitration: Scotland and the UNCITRAL Model Law* (W. Green, Edinburgh, 1991) and Beaumont, "Great Britain" in Fawcett (ed.), *Declining Jurisdiction in Private International Law* (Clarendon, Oxford, 1995), pp. 207–233 and 228–229.

[23] See Beaumont, "Great Britain", *supra*.

[24] See Beaumont, "Great Britain", *supra*, at p. 228; *Channel Tunnel v. Balfour Beatty Group* [1993] A.C. 334 at 355–357.

[25] *Mackay & Son v. Leven Police Commissioners* (1893) 20 R. 1093, *per* Lord Adam at 1102, Lord Kinnear at 1103; *Steuart v. Young's Paraffin Light and Mineral Oil Co.* (1898) 6 S.L.T. 69; *Allied Airways (Gandar Dower) Ltd v. Sec. of St. for Air*, 1950 S.C. 249.

[26] *Redpath Dorman Long Ltd v. Tarmac Construction Ltd*, 1982 S.C. 14 at 15.

[27] *Wilson & McFarlane v. Stewart & Co.* (1898) 25 R. 655.

[28] *Hamlyn & Co. v. Talisker Distillery* (1894) 21 R. (H.L.) 21, *per* Lord Watson at 25 (*cit.* para. 2.99); and see *Brodie v. Ker*, 1952 S.C. 216 at 223.

[29] Dismissal appears to be contrary to modern practice except in unusual circumstances, as in *N.B. Ry v. Newburgh and North Fife Ry*, 1911 S.C. 710; *Taylor v. Brick*, 1982 S.L.T. 25.

[30] *D. & J. McDougall Ltd v. Argyll & Bute D.C.*, 1987 S.L.T. 7.

[31] *Laidlaw v. Dunlop* (1831) 9 S. 579.

[32] *D. & J. McDougall Ltd*, *supra*, n. 21.

[33] See *supra*, n. 19.

[34] *Wm Louden & Sons Ltd v. Frank Doonin Ltd*, Sh. Pr. Reid, Glasgow Sh. Ct, May 9, 1979, unreported; *Halliburton Manufacturing and Service Ltd v. Bingham Blades & Partners*, 1984 S.L.T. 388; *Stanley Howard (Construction) v. Davis*, 1988 S.L.T. (Sh. Ct.) 30; *Raphael v. Wilcon Homes Northern*, 1994 S.C.L.R. 940 (O.H.); and *ERDC Construction Ltd v. H.M. Love & Co.*, 1995 S.L.T. 254 (but the Second Division made the point that an arbiter is not necessarily bound by the rules of practice and procedure which apply to litigation in the courts: see 259, 266 and 270).

[35] *Coyle v. National Coal Board*, 1959 S.L.T. 114 at 116.

[36] O.C.R., r. 18.2(2)(a) and (c); see paras 10.04, 10.05.

of the questions in controversy from the court to another forum. It is only after the record is closed that the plea is considered,[37] and that an application for a sist is normally disposed of.[38]

2.101 Before the court gives effect to the plea, it must be established that a valid contract exists[39] and that there is a specific dispute or difference[40] to which the reference clause applies.[41] If the contract has been effectively rescinded, the reference clause falls with the rest of the contract[42]; but it is not elided by disputed *ex parte* averments that the contract is at an end by virtue of repudiation[43] or frustration.[44] To substitute procedure by way of arbitration for procedure in court requires clear and distinct language.[45] Where the clause is held to apply to the dispute which is the subject-matter of the action, the court will sist the action in order to enable the assistance of the court to be invoked in the event of the arbitration breaking down or of other questions arising, or in order to implement the award.[46] Where the subject-matter of the action consists of several disputes and the clause applies only to some of them, the procedure to be adopted will depend on the court's assessment of convenience and the various other considerations of each case.[47] The court may sist the cause until the questions raised for the arbiter's decision have been decided[48]; or, where there is no dispute as to liability *quoad* the subject-matter of the questions to which the clause does not apply, it may grant decree *de plano* thereanent and sist the action to allow the others to proceed to arbitration.[49] Where the clause is not applicable to the subject-matter of the action, the court will repel the plea and dispose of the whole cause.[50]

---

[37] *Robertson & Co. v. Robertson*, Sh. Pr. Caplan, Paisley Sh. Ct, Dec. 4, 1986, unreported; *cf. Walker v. Crawford* (1902) 10 S.L.T. 362.

[38] *Clydesdale Bank Ltd v. D. & H. Cohen*, 1943 S.C. 244; *Halliburton Manufacturing and Service Ltd, supra.*

[39] *Ransohoff & Wissler v. Burrell* (1897) 25 R. 284; *Hoth v. Cowan*, 1926 S.C. 58.

[40] *Mackay & Son v. Leven Police Commrs* (1893) 20 R. 1093, *per* Lord Adam at 1102, Lord Kinnear at 1103; *Stewart v. Young's Paraffin Light and Mineral Oil Co.* (1898) 6 S.L.T. 69; *Woods v. Co-operative Insurance Society*, 1924 S.C. 692; *Allied Airways (Gander Dower) Ltd v. Sec. of St. for Air*, 1950 S.C. 249.

[41] *Crawford Bros v. Commrs of Northern Lighthouses*, 1925 S.C. (H.L.) 22.

[42] *Hegarty & Kelly v. Cosmopolitan Insurance Corporation Ltd*, 1913 S.C. 377; *Sanderson & Son v. Armour & Co.*, 1922 S.C. (H.L.) 117.

[43] *Sanderson & Son, supra; Paterson v. United Scottish Herring Drifter Insurance Co.*, 1927 S.N. 75 141; *Dryburgh v. Caledonian Insurance Co.*, 1933 S.N. 85; *Cant v. Eagle Star Insurance Co.*, 1937 S.L.T. 444; *Heyman v. Darwin Ltd* [1942] A.C. 356.

[44] *Scott & Sons v. Del Sel*, 1923 S C. (H.L.) 37; *Charles Mauritzen Ltd v. Baltic Shipping Co.*, 1948 S.C. 646; *Heyman, supra.*

[45] *Calder v. Mackay* (1860) 22 D. 741, *per* L.J.-C. Inglis at 744; *McConnell & Reid v. Smith*, 1911 S.C. 635, *per* Lord Dundas at 638; *Brodie v. Ker*, 1952 S.C. 216 at 224.

[46] *Hamlyn & Co. v. Talisker Distillery* (1894) 21 R. (H.L.) 21, *per* Lord Watson at 27; *Muir v. Muir* (1906) 8 F. 365; *Robertson v. Brandes, Schonwaid & Co.* (1906) 8 F. 815; *W. & A. Robertson v. Gerrard* (1908) 16 S.L.T. 100; *James Howden & Co. Ltd v. Powell Duffryn Steam Coal Co. Ltd*, 1912 S.C. 920, *per* L.P. Dunedin at 931; *Caledonian Railway Co. v. Clyde Shipping Co.*, 1917 S.C. 107, *per* L.P. Strathclyde at 114; *Palmer v. S.-E. Lancashire Insurance Co. Ltd*, 1932 S.L.T 68; *Roxburgh v. Dinardo*, 1981 S.L.T. 291; *Motordrift A/S v. Trachem Co. Ltd*, 1982 S.L.T. 127.

[47] *Barr v. Commrs of Queensferry* (1899) 1 F. 630.

[48] *ibid.*

[49] *Redpath Dorman Long Ltd v. Tarmac Construction Ltd*, 1982 S.L.T. 442.

[50] *Miller & Son v. Oliver & Boyd* (1906) 8 F. 390.

A party who contends that the issues in the action fall to be determined by arbitration in terms of a statutory provision should state an appropriate preliminary plea-in-law to the effect that the action should be sisted,[51] and support it by relevant and specific averments.[52] The court will construe the provision founded on in accordance with the rule that the right of the subject to invoke the common law courts of the country for the decision of any question properly falling within their jurisdiction can only be excluded by express provision or clear implication, either in a contract or in a statute.[53] If the court finds that the provision is not imperative but only enabling, it will repel the plea.[54] A plea to arbitration founded on an imperative provision, unlike a plea founded on a contractual submission, cannot be waived, and the court is bound to take notice of the provision at whatever stage the question of arbitration is raised.[55] If the court determines that the provision is in imperative terms and that it is applicable to the dispute between the parties, it will sist the cause.[56] **2.102**

> "Whenever a court is satisfied that the parties are at issue on a question the decision of which is confided by Parliament to some other tribunal, the powers of the court to investigate and determine that question cannot (at any rate in the meantime) be put into operation; the action will normally be sisted to await the expiscation of the matter by that other tribunal, and, this having been done, the court will then resume its interrupted task—usually by pronouncing an order to effectuate the decision of the other tribunal."[57]

Jurisdiction clauses

The jurisdiction of the court may be excluded by a contractual provision to the effect that the courts of a foreign legal system have exclusive jurisdiction.[58] **2.103**

Res judicata

The exercise of jurisdiction is excluded where the court sustains a plea of *res judicata*. The rule may be stated thus: when a matter has been the subject of judicial determination pronounced *in foro contentioso* by a competent tribunal, that determination excludes any subsequent action in regard to the same matter between the same parties or their authors, **2.104**

---

[51] *e.g. Fairholme's Trs v. Graham*, 1943 S.L.T. 158 at 159; *Houison-Craufurd's Trs v. Davies*, 1951 S.C. 1 at 8; *Lanarkshire C.C. v. East Kilbride T.C.*, 1967 S.C. 235 at 238.

[52] *Brodie v. Ker*, 1952 S.C. 216 at 227.

[53] *Brodie, supra*, at 224; *Fairholme's Trs, supra*, at 160.

[54] *Lanarkshire C.C., supra*; *Irving v. Aberdeen and District Milk Marketing Board* (1941) 59 Sh.Ct.Rep. 1.

[55] *Houison-Craufurd's Trs., supra*, at 8, 10, 15; *Brodie, supra*, at 227; *Taylor v. Brick*, 1982 S.L.T. 25.

[56] *Houison-Craufurd's Trs, supra*; *Brodie, supra*; *Maclean v. Galloway*, 1979 S.L.T. (Sh. Ct.) 32.

[57] *Brodie, supra, per* the consulted judges at 223. In *Taylor v. Brick, supra*, the Lord Ordinary took notice of an imperative provision which had not been pleaded and dismissed the action.

[58] See paras 3.51 to 3.53 and Beaumont, "Great Britain", *supra*, at pp. 223–227. These references also consider the discretion given to the Scottish courts to decline to exercise jurisdiction where the parties have entered into a non-exclusive jurisdiction clause. For a recent case, see *Morrison v. Panic Link Ltd*, 1993 S.L.T. 602, affd by an Extra Division, 1994 S.L.T. 232.

and on the same grounds.[59] "The plea is common to most legal systems, and is based upon considerations of public policy, equity and common sense, which will not tolerate that the same issue should be litigated repeatedly between the same parties on substantially the same basis."[60] It is the interest of the State that there should be an end to litigation, and it is a hardship that a man should be vexed twice for the same cause.[61] The plea is usually stated in the short form "*Res judicata*", although in some circumstances a more detailed plea may be appropriate,[62] and it must be founded on relevant averments in the answers to the condescendence. The plea is not a preliminary plea but a plea on the merits, since it professes to show that the pursuer is not entitled, at any time or in any form or in any court, to the object of his suit.[63] If the plea is established *quoad* the whole cause,[64] the defender is accordingly entitled to decree of absolvitor.[65] For the plea to succeed, the five conditions referred to in the following paragraphs must be satisfied. If these conditions are satisfied, the plea may be elided only by a successful plea of *res noviter veniens ad notitiam*.[66] In certain statutory applications the plea of *res judicata* may be inapplicable by virtue of particular statutory rules of procedure.[67]

2.105 (1) The prior determination must have been made by a competent tribunal, which may be a foreign[68] or an inferior court, or a statutory tribunal or an arbiter. The plea is not open if the tribunal in pronouncing the determination exceeded its jurisdiction.[69] A decree competently pronounced in the sheriff court may found a plea of *res judicata* in subsequent proceedings in a superior court.[70] It is thought that a competent decree

---

[59] Dickson, para. 385; *Earl of Perth v. Lady Willoughby de Eresby's Trs* (1875) 2 R. 538, *per* Lord Gifford at 555–556; *Esso Petroleum Co. v. Law*, 1956 S.C. 33, *per* Lord Carmont at 38. On the whole matter, see Maclaren, pp. 396 *et seq.*; *Encyclopaedia*, xii, pp. 550 *et seq.*; P. R. Beaumont, "*Res Judicata* and Estoppel in Civil Proceedings", 1985 S.L.T. (News) 133, 141. Only a selective citation from the many authorities is attempted in the following footnotes.

[60] *Graham v. Sec. of St. for Scotland*, 1951 S.C. 368, *per* L.P. Cooper at 387.

[61] *Lockyer v. Ferryman* (1877) 4 R. (H.L.) 32, *per* Lord Blackburn at 42; *Vervaeke v. Smith* [1983] 1 A.C. 145, *per* Lord Simon of Glaisdale at 161.

[62] *McFeetridge v. Stewarts & Lloyds Ltd*, 1913 S.C. 773 at 775–776; *Wilson v. Murphy*, 1936 S.L.T. 564; *Ryan v. McBurnie*, 1940 S.C. 173 at 175; *Anderson v. Wilson*, 1972 S.C. 147 at 148. Pleas seeking dismissal were stated in *Matuszcsyk v. National Coal Board*, 1955 S.C. 418 at 419, and *Young v. Young's Trs*, 1957 S.C. 318; see n. 65.

[63] *Geils v. Geils* (1851) 1 Macq. 36, *per* Lord Truro L.C. at 39–40.

[64] It has been stated that there is a rule that a successful plea of *res judicata* will exclude all consideration of the merits of the action: *Davies v. Davies*, Sh. Pr. O'Brien, Edinburgh Sh. Ct, July 1, 1982, unreported. The plea may, however, be directed against a particular issue: see *Hutchison v. Mags of Innerleithen*, 1933 S.L.T. 52; *Anderson v. Wilson*, 1972 S.C. 147 at 148.

[65] The plea was sustained and decree of absolvitor pronounced in *Rutherfurd v. Nisbett's Trs* (1832) 11 S. 123: *Marquis of Huntly v. Nicol* (1858) 20 D. 374; *Cray v. McHardy* (1862) 24 D. 1043; *Forrest v. Dunlop* (1875) 3 R. 15; and *McPhee v. Heatherwick*, 1977 S.L.T. (Sh. Ct.) 46. Decree of dismissal was pronounced in *Matuszczyk v. National Coal Board*, 1955 S.C. 418, and *Young v. Young's Trs*, 1957 S.C. 318 (the rubric in *Young* is inaccurate), apparently upon the view that the question there was one of competency.

[66] See paras 2.110, 2.111.

[67] *McGregor v. D*, 1981 S.L.T. (Notes) 97; *Kennedy v. S*, 1986 S.L.T. 679.

[68] *Hamilton v. Dutch East India Co.* (1732) 1 Pat. App. 69. The plea rests upon the authority of statute in the case of judgments to which are applicable the Foreign Judgments (Reciprocal Enforcement) Act 1933 or the Civil Jurisdiction and Judgments Act 1982: see Anton with Beaumont, pp. 234–237.

[69] *Pollock v. Thomson* (1858) 21 D. 173.

[70] *Brand v. Police Commrs of Arbroath* (1890) 17 R. 790; *Murray v. Seath*, 1939 S.L.T. 348; *Hynds v. Hynds*, 1966 S.C. 201; *Anderson v. Wilson*, 1972 S.C. 147 at 149.

pronounced in a summary cause may sustain the plea in a subsequent action.[71] A judgment in a criminal court may be *res judicata* in a civil action only in the exceptional circumstances that the parties are the same, the ground of action the same, and the remedy sought the same.[72] An arbiter's complete and final decision, however expressed, on the questions submitted to him may found the plea.[73]

(2) The prior determination must have been pronounced *in foro contentioso*, without fraud or collusion.[74] It is not, however, necessary that the action should have been fully litigated to make the decree pronounced a decree *in foro*. In the sheriff court it is sufficient that defences should have been lodged in an ordinary cause[75] or, it is thought, that a defence should have been noted in a summary cause.[76] A decree of absolvitor[77] and a decree by default will support the plea.[78] It is not material that the prior determination should have proceeded upon a compromise, consent or joint minute.[79] The plea cannot be based on a decree in absence[80] or a decree of dismissal.[81] A decree in an undefended consistorial action is 2.106

[71] *McPhee v. Heatherwick*, 1977 S.L.T. (Sh. Ct.) 46. This case was not followed by Sheriff Lockhart in *McSheehy v. MacMillan*, 1993 S.L.T. (Sh. Ct.) 10 but he does not disapprove the point made in the text. Sheriff Lockhart decided that the subsequent summary cause was not barred by a plea of *res judicata*, even though the facts of the case were on all fours with those in *McPhee v. Heatherwick* because the parties and the subject-matter were not the same. The former case related to the individual's uninsured pecuniary loss whereas the latter claim, although brought in the name of the same individual, was to enable the individual's insurance company to recover the insured pecuniary losses.

[72] *Young v. Mitchells* (1874) 1 R. 1011; *Kennedy v. Wise* (1890) 17 R. 1036; *Wilson v. Murphy*, 1936 S.L.T. 564. In other circumstances a civil action may follow a verdict (*Wood v. N.B. Ry* (1899) 1 F. 562; *Wilson v. Bennet* (1904) 6 F. 269; *Procurators of Glasgow v. Colquhoun* (1900) 2 F. 1192; *Wilson v. Murphy*, 1936 S.L.T. 564). A party who is proved to have been convicted is taken to have committed the offence unless the contrary is proved except in an action of defamation, where the conviction is conclusive evidence of the commission of the offence (Law Reform (Miscellaneous Provisions) (Scotland) Act 1968, s. 10(2)(a); also s. 12, as amended by the Defamation Act 1996, s. 12(2)). As to the inadmissibility of acquittals in civil actions, see Macphail, *Evidence*, paras 11.18–S11.19A.

[73] *Fraser v. Lord Lovat* (1850) 7 Bell's App. 171, *per* Lord Brougham at 182; *Miller & Son v. Oliver & Boyd* (1906) 8 F. 390, *per* Lord Kinnear at 404–405; *Farrans v. Roxburgh C.C.*, 1969 S.L.T. 35; *Crudens Ltd. v. Tayside Health Board*, 1979 S.C. 142.

[74] *Lockyer v. Ferryman* (1876) 3 R. 882, *per* Lord Gifford at 911–912.

[75] *Esso Petroleum Co. v. Law*, 1956 S.C. 33.

[76] SCR, r. 20.

[77] *Stewart v. Greenock Harbour Trs* (1868) 6 M. 954, *per* Lord Deas at 958; *Glasgow and S.-W. Ry Co. v. Boyd & Forrest*, 1918 S.C. (H.L.) 14.

[78] *Forrest v. Dunlop* (1875) 3 R. 15.

[79] *Glasgow and S.-W. Ry, supra, per* Lord Dunedin at 26; *Young v. Young's Trs*, 1957 S.C. 318 at 320–321; *Hynds v. Hynds*, 1966 S.C. 201 at 202; *McPhee v. Heatherwick*, 1977 S.L.T. (Sh. Ct.) 46; *Luxmoore v. Red Deer Commission*, 1979 S.L.T. (Notes) 53. In the case of a declarator of public right of way a decree of absolvitor obtained as a result of a compromise will not support the plea to the effect of precluding any other member of the public from raising a new action about the same road or way: *White v. Lord Morton's Trs* (1866) 4 M. (H.L.) 53; *Jenkins v. Robertson* (1867) 5 M. (H.L.) 27; *Young, supra.*

[80] Ersk., IV, iii, 6; *Mackintosh v. Smith and Lowe* (1865) 3 M. (H.L.) 6, *per* Lord Westbury L.C. at 10; *Fulton v. Earl of Eglinton and Winton* (1895) 22 R. 823, *per* L.P. Robertson at 824; *Paterson v. Paterson*, 1958 S.C. 141 at 145; *Gibson & Simpson v. Pearson*, 1992 S.L.T. 894 at 897.

[81] *Russel v. Gillespie* (1859) 3 Macq. 757, (1859) 21 D. (H.L.) 13; *Stewart v. Greenock Harbour Trs* (1868) 6 M. 954, *per* Lord Deas at 958; *Duke of Sutherland v. Reed* (1890) 18 R. 252; *Menzies v. Menzies* (1893) 20 R. (H.L.) 108, *per* Lord Watson at 111; *Cunningham v. Skinner* (1902) 4 F. 1124; *Govan Old Victualling Society Ltd v. Wagstaff* (1907) 14 S.L.T. 716; *Paterson v. Paterson*, 1958 S.C. 141. *Cf. Wallace v. Braid* (1900) 2 F. 754, *per* Lord Young at 761; *Malcolm Muir Ltd v. Jamieson*, 1947 S.C. 314, *per* Lord Mackay at 321. In *Farrans v. Roxburgh C.C.*, 1969 S.L.T. 35, the arbiter's decree of dismissal was held to be a final pronouncement exhausting the reference.

a decree in absence,[82] as is a decree pronounced in an ordinary action in the sheriff court after a notice of intention to defend has been lodged but before the lodging of defences.[83] A decree in absence does, however, eventually become entitled to all the privileges of a decree *in foro* after a given period of time[84] and thus becomes *res judicata* against the defender.

2.107 (3) The subject-matter of the two actions must be the same.[85]

2.108 (4) The *media concludendi*, or points in controversy between the parties, in the two actions must be the same. The *media concludendi* are not the same unless the specific point raised in the second action has been directly raised and decided in the first. An unsuccessful pursuer has a right to raise a further action against the same defenders relating to the same subject-matter, provided that the second action is based on different grounds.[86] Whether the *media concludendi* are the same will appear from a study of the pleadings and decision in the previous action: the court looks at the essence and reality of the matter rather than the technical form and considers the question, what was litigated and what was decided.[87] A new *medium concludendi* will elide the plea of *res judicata* unless it is irrelevant[88] or is obnoxious to the plea of "competent and omitted".[89] In an action of reparation based on the alleged fault or negligence of the defenders, common law negligence and breach of statutory duty are not different *media concludendi* for the purposes of *res judicata*.[90]

2.109 (5) Except where the earlier decree is a decree *in rem*, the parties to the second action must be identical with, or representative of,[91] the parties to the first action, or have the same interest.[92] When considering who are the parties to the second action, the court has regard to the reality and the

---

[82] *Paterson v. Paterson*, 1958 S.C. 141.

[83] *Esso Petroleum Co. v. Lan*, 1956 S.C. 33.

[84] Court of Session Act 1868, s. 24; OCR, r. 7.5. See para. 7.18.

[85] *Leith Dock Commrs v. Miles* (1866) 4 M.(H.L.) 14, *per* Lord Chelmsford at 19; *Murray v. Murray*, 1957 S.L.T. 41; *Richardson v. Richardson*, 1957 S.L.T. (Notes) 45; *Hynds v. Hynds*, 1966 S.C. 201 at 203–204; *Mitchell's Trs v. Aspin*, 1971 S.L.T. 29 at 33, 36 (affd, 1971 S.L.T. 166); *Anderson v. Wilson*, 1972 S.C. 147; *Bacon v. Blair*, 1972 S.L.T. (Sh. Ct.) 11.

[86] *Phosphate Sewage Co. v. Lawson & Son's Tr.* (1878) 5 R. 1125, *per* L.P. Inglis at 1139; *Scott v. Macdonald* (1885) 12 R. 1123; *N.B. Ry v. Lanarkshire and Dumbartonshire Ry* (1897) 24 R. 564, *per* Lord Kinnear at 572; *Edinburgh and District Water Trs v. Clippens Oil Co.* (1899) 1 F. 899, *per* L.P. Robertson at 907, Lord Kinnear at 909; *Burton v. Chapel Coal Co.*, 1909 S.C. 430; *Matuszczyk v. National Coal Board*, 1955 S.C. 418 at 421–422.

[87] *Edinburgh and District Water Trs, supra*; *Glasgow and S.-W. Ry v. Boyd & Forrest*, 1918 S.C. (H.L.) 14, *per* Lord Shaw of Dunfermline at 31–32 (this case shows that if the first action is a simple petitioning one then there is no need for an identity of grounds of claim in the second action for *res judicata* to operate); *Grahame v. Sec. of St. for Scotland*, 1951 S.C. 368, *per* L.P. Cooper at 387; *Weissenbruch v. Weissenbruch*, 1965 S.L.T. 139; *Crudens v. Tayside Health Board*, 1979 S.C. 142; *Gibson & Simpson v. Pearson*, 1992 S.L.T. 894 at 896; *Margrie Holdings Ltd v. City of Edinburgh District Council*, 1994 S.L.T. 971, *per* L.P. Hope at 974. The relevance of a material change of circumstances is considered by Lord Johnston in *Short's Tr. v. Chung (No.2)*, *The Times*, May 18, 1998.

[88] *Earl of Perth v. Lady Willoughby de Eresby's Trs* (1877) 5 R. (H.L.) 26.

[89] See paras 2.112, 2.113.

[90] *Matuszczyk, supra*.

[91] *Earl of Leven and Melville v. Cartwright* (1861) 23 D. 1038; *McCaig v. Maitland* (1887) 14 R. 295; *Elder's Trs v. Elder* (1895) 22 R. 505; *Coutts v. Wear*, 1914 2 S.L.T. 86; *Ryan v. McBurnie*, 1940 S.C. 173.

[92] *Gray v. McHardy* (1862) 24 D. 1043; *Duke of Atholl v. Glover Incorporation of Perth* (1899) 1 F. 658; *Allen v. McCombie's Trs*, 1909 S.C. 710.

substance of that action.[93] Where the first judgment is a judgment *in rem*, which includes for this purpose a judgment affecting status, a plea of *res judicata* will be upheld not only against the original parties but against any other person who desires to litigate with regard to the same matter.[94]

Res noviter veniens ad notitiam

If the five conditions considered in the foregoing paragraphs are satisfied, the plea of *res judicata* may be elided only by a successful plea of *res noviter veniens ad notitiam.*[95] A party is not debarred by the plea of *res judicata* from again presenting a case before the courts founded upon new and material matters of fact (relevant to support the crave of the initial writ) or new and material evidence (relevant to establish facts on which proof has already been led) which have come to his knowledge and of which he is able to prove that, through no fault of his, he was previously ignorant.[96] "Anything proponed to the court by a party after the proper time has gone by, which the court is asked to entertain on the ground that the party did not and could not know of it at the time, is *res noviter veniens ad notitiam*."[97] "Nothing can be *res noviter* that was within the power of the party to discover with ordinary care."[98] Accordingly, when a party relies on *res noviter* **2.110**

> "he must not merely aver that something material has newly come to his knowledge, but he must aver it with such circumstantiality as will show that he could not by the exercise of reasonable diligence have known of it in time to have made use of it in the original action. He must give particulars of its discovery and of the circumstances which bear upon the possibility of his having acquired earlier knowledge of it."[99]

Thus, a general allegation of perjury, unsupported by facts and circumstances, is not a relevant averment for a plea of *res noviter.*[1]

> "The allowance of *res noviter* is always more or less in the nature of an indulgence. Accordingly, it may present to the court a delicate problem of discretion. But it is an indispensable condition of the allowance that the *res noviter* should be material to the justice of the cause; and it is inconceivable that it should be refused if it is seen to be such that to exclude it from the materials of judgment would prevent justice being done. The grounds which justify, or fall short **2.111**

---

93 *Ryan, supra*, at 177 and *McSheehy v. MacMillan*, 1993 S.L.T. (Sh. Ct.) 46.

94 *Administrator of Austrian Property v. Von Lorang*, 1926 S.C. 598, *per* Lord Sands at 620, 622, 627, approved, 1927 S.C. (H.L.) 80, *per* Viscount Haldane at 88, Viscount Dunedin at 91; Walkers, pp. 46–47.

95 In the Court of Session *res noviter* is a ground for reduction of a decree (Maxwell, p. 583) and a ground on which a new jury trial may be granted (Jury Trials (Scotland) Act 1815, s. 6; Maxwell, pp. 559–560).

96 *Glasgow and S.-W. Ry v. Boyd & Forrest*, 1918 S.C. (H.L.) 14, *per* Lord Shaw of Dunfermline at 31; *Miller v. Mac Fisheries*, 1922 S.C. 157, *per* L.P. Clyde at 162; *Ross v. Ross*, 1928 S.C. 600, *per* L.P. Clyde at 602.

97 *Miller, supra, per* L.P. Clyde at 160.

98 *Campbell v. Campbell* (1865) 3 M. 501, *per* L.P. McNeill at 504.

99 *McCarroll v. McKinstery*, 1926 S.C.(H.L.) 1, *per* Lord Sumner at 7; see also *Phosphate Sewage Co. v. Molleson* (1879) 6 R.(H.L.) 113, *per* Lord Cairns L.C. at 117.

1 *Turnbull v. Campbell* (1859) 21 D. 1021; *Mackintosh's Tr. v. Stewart's Tr.* (1906) 8 F. 467; *Maltman v. Tarmac Civil Engineering Ltd*, 1967 S.C. 177.

of justifying, the allowance of *res noviter* vary somewhat according to the circumstances in which the *res noviter* is proponed."[2]

While new evidence may be *res noviter*, it appears that the discovery of additional evidence in support of a fact originally averred, and supported by testimony, in the party's case may not be *res noviter*.[3] It has been suggested that a second action may be justified where the result in the prior action has been reached by a total failure of all parties to realise that the rights adjudicated on had been settled in a contrary sense by an Act of Parliament of which no stock had been taken.[4]

Competent and omitted

2.112 The plea of "competent and omitted" is based on considerations similar to those underlying the plea of *res judicata*.[5] Where a defender has put forward a defence that is unsuccessful, he cannot in a subsequent process challenge the prior judgment on grounds which it was competent to plead in the prior process, but which he omitted to do.[6] Where he is the pursuer in the subsequent process and the omitted grounds are the only grounds of the action, the court will sustain the plea of "competent and omitted" stated by the defender and dismiss the cause.[7] The plea may also be directed against particular pleas or grounds of action,[8] and may be stated by a pursuer.[9] The plea should specify the grounds on which it is contended that the other party is barred from insisting in the process or pleading any particular plea, and should be supported by relevant averments.[10] The plea will be sustained only if the party against whom it is stated is seeking to challenge a prior judgment given against him[11] or his representative[12] and if the omitted ground would have been a good defence in the prior process.[13]

2.113 The plea cannot be maintained against a party who was the pursuer in a prior process, because the judgment in favour of the defender is not an

---

[2] *Miller v. Mac Fisheries*, 1922 S.C. 157, *per* L.P. Clyde at 160–161; see also *Ross v. Ross*, 1928 S.C. 600, *per* L.P. Clyde at 603; *Maltman v. Tarmac Civil Engineering Ltd*, 1967 S.C. 177, *per* Lord Cameron at 190.

[3] *Miller, supra.*

[4] *Glasgow and S.-W. Ry v. Boyd & Forrest*, 1918 S.C. (H.L.) 14, *per* Lord Shaw of Dunfermline at 31. It may be that in such a case the plea of *res judicata* would be elided if statutory provisions provided a new *medium concludendi*. In *Stewart v. Celot* (1871) 9 M. 1057, a rule of foreign law ascertainable by the party at the time of the prior action but not then pleaded by him was held not to be *res noviter*.

[5] Stair, IV, i, 50; *Rorie v. Rorie*, 1967 S.L.T. 75 at 78.

[6] *Macdonald v. Macdonald* (1842) 1 Bell's App. 819, *per* Lord Campbell at 829; *Dickson v. United Dominions Trust Ltd*, 1988 S.L.T. 19, *per* Lord McCluskey at 24. See *Encyclopaedia*, xii, pp. 567–568; P. R. Beaumont, "Competent and Omitted", 1985 S.L.T. (News) 345. The plea cannot be taken against the Crown: see para. 4.76.

[7] Maclaren, pp. 395–396, and Maxwell, p. 197, classify "Competent and Omitted" as a defence on the merits, but in modern practice it appears to be regarded as a dilatory plea: see the pleas stated in *Murray v. Seath*, 1939 S.L.T. 348 at 349, *Rorie v. Rorie*, 1967 S.L.T. 75, and *Cantors Properties (Scotland) Ltd v. Swears & Wells Ltd*, 1978 S.C. 310 at 314.

[8] *Rennie v. James*, 1908 S.C. 681.

[9] *Carmichael v. Anstruther* (1866) 4 M. 841 at 844.

[10] For examples, see *Murray, supra*, at 349; *Rorie, supra*, at 75; *Cantors Properties, supra*, at 314.

[11] *Cantors Properties (Scotland) Ltd v. Swears & Wells Ltd*, 1977 S.L.T. (Notes) 30 (affd, 1978 S.C. 310); *Dickson v. United Dominions Trust Ltd*, 1988 S.L.T. 19 at 24.

[12] *Glasgow Shipowners Association v. Clyde Navigation Trs* (1885) 12 R. 695.

[13] *N.B. Ry v. Lanarkshire and Dumbartonshire Ry* (1897) 24 R. 564; *Cantors Properties, supra*, 1978 S.C. 310.

absolute affirmation of his rights but is merely negative of the grounds put forward by the pursuer, and cannot extend beyond those grounds. A pursuer who raises an action upon one ground and is defeated may therefore raise further actions upon different grounds, whether or not he knew of them at the former time, provided that they are separate *media concludendi.*[14] It has been suggested that the pursuer's entitlement to do so is subject to the power of the court by award of expenses or otherwise to restrain an undue and excessive accumulation of actions.[15] The raising of a multiplicity of actions is also inhibited by the principle that a defender should not be vexed more than once for the same breach of contract or delict, which underlies the established rule of practice that a single act amounting either to a delict or a breach of contract cannot be made the ground of two or more actions for the purpose of recovering damages arising within different periods but caused by the same act:

> "Though the delict or breach of contract be of such a nature that it will necessarily be followed by injurious consequences in the future, and though it may for this reason be impossible to ascertain with precise accuracy at the date of the action or of the verdict the amount of loss which will result, yet the whole damage must be recovered in one action, because there is but one cause of action."[16]

Prescription; limitation of actions

Introduction

The court may sustain a plea by the defender that the exercise of its jurisdiction is excluded by virtue of the fact that the pursuer's claim has been extinguished by prescription, or has been rendered unenforceable by the running of time. The rules of prescription, whereby after a stated period of time certain rights are wholly extinguished, are rules of substantive law which are beyond the scope of this book.[17] On the other hand the rules as to limitation of actions, whereby after a stated period of time certain rights are unenforceable, are rules of procedural law. While it is *pars judicis* to take a plea of prescription,[18] it is for the defender to take a plea of limitation. A defender does not invariably wish to rely on a defence of limitation, and may prefer to contest the issue on the merits.[19] The modern law as to limitation of actions of damages for personal injuries, death or defamation is contained in Part II of the Prescription and Limitation (Scotland) Act 1973, as amended. While a substantive obligation to make reparation in respect of any of these prescribes after the lapse **2.114**

---

[14] *Macdonald v. Macdonald* (1842) 1 Bell's App. 819, *per* Lord Campbell at 829; *Earl of Perth v. Lady Willoughby de Eresby's Trs* (1875) 2 R. 538, *per* Lord Neaves at 545, Lord Gifford at 556 (affd (1877) 5 R.(H.L.) 26); *Phosphate Sewage Co. v. Molleson* (1879) 6 R. (H.L.) 113, *per* Lord Blackburn at 121; *Edinburgh and District Water Trs v. Clippens Oil Co. Ltd* (1899) 1 F. 899.

[15] Maclaren, p. 401, Maxwell, p. 198, citing *Bruce v. Duncan* (1793) Hume 596; see also Stair, IV, xl, 16; *Cochrane v. Paul* (1857) 20 D. 178, *per* Lord Neaves at 179; and the Vexatious Actions (Scotland) Act 1898, discussed in paras 4.122, 4.123.

[16] *Stevenson v. Pontifex & Wood* (1887) 15 R. 125, *per* L.P. Inglis at 129; and see *Dunlop v. McGowans*, 1980 S.C.(H.L.) 73, *per* Lord Keith of Kinkel at 81. It may be that the rule is too sweeping and over-harsh on pursuers in certain cases: *Aberdeen Development Co. v. Mackie, Ramsey & Taylor*, 1977 S.L.T. 177. As to provisional damages in personal injuries actions, see paras 21.29 to 21.34.

[17] See Walker, *Prescription and Limitation of Actions.*

[18] *ibid.* p. 4.

[19] *Ketteman v. Hansel Properties Ltd* [1987] 2 W.L.R. 312, *per* Lord Griffiths at 339.

of five years,[20] the limitation period for bringing an action in respect of time is three years, subject to a number of important qualifications which are noted in the following paragraphs. The provisions of Part II are closely analysed in the undernoted work,[21] which also notes a number of other statutory limitations on the time for bringing certain actions which are seldom encountered in sheriff court practice.[22]

Personal injuries actions

2.115 The following rules apply to an action of damages where the damages claimed consist of or include damages in respect of personal injuries,[23] and the action is brought by the injured person or any other person.[24] Subject to certain qualifications,[25] no such action may be brought unless it is commenced[26] within a period of three years after one or other of certain specified dates.[27] The first of these dates is the date on which the injuries were sustained. Alternatively, where the act or omission to which the injuries were attributable was a continuing one, the date is that on which the injuries were sustained or the date on which the act or omission ceased, whichever is the later.[28] Finally, provision is made for circumstances in which certain facts were not apparent to the pursuer on the dates already mentioned. This date is that on which the pursuer[29] became aware of certain facts, or on which, in the opinion of the court, it would have been reasonably practicable for him in all the circumstances to become aware of them. These facts are all of the following[30]:

(1) that the injuries in question were sufficiently serious to justify his bringing an action of damages on the assumption that the person against whom the action was brought did not dispute liability and was able to satisfy a decree;
(2) that the injuries were attributable in whole or in part to an act or omission[31]; and
(3) that the defender was a person to whose act or omission the injuries were attributable in whole or in part or the employer or principal of such a person.

2.116 The qualifications of the general three-year rule are twofold. First, in the computation of the three-year period (often called "the triennium")

---

[20] Prescription and Limitation (Scotland) Act 1973 (hereafter "the 1973 Act"), Sched. 1, paras 1(d), 2(g), (gg) (inserted by Law Reform (Miscellaneous Provisions) (Scotland) Act 1985, s. 12(5)).

[21] See Walker, *Prescription and Limitation of Actions*.

[22] *ibid.* Chap. 6.

[23] "Personal injuries" includes any disease and any impairment of a person's physical or mental condition (1973 Act, s. 22(1), substituted by Prescription and Limitation (Scotland) Act 1984 (hereafter "the 1984 Act"), s. 3), and has been held to extend to injury to feelings (*Barclay v. Chief Constable Northern Constabulary*, 1986 S.L.T. 562).

[24] 1973 Act, s. 17(1). S. 17 was substituted by the 1984 Act, s. 2.

[25] See para. 2.116.

[26] An action is "commenced" on the date of citation of the defender: see para. 6.06.

[27] 1973 Act, s. 17(2).

[28] *ibid.* s. 17(2)(a).

[29] Where the pursuer is an assignee, the reference to the pursuer here is to be construed as a reference to the assignor of the right of action: 1973 Act, s. 22(2), substituted by the 1984 Act, s. 3, and amended by the Law Reform (Miscellaneous Provisions) (Scotland) Act 1985, s. 12(4).

[30] 1973 Act, s. 17(2)(b).

[31] Knowledge that any act or omission was or was not, as a matter of law, actionable is irrelevant: 1973 Act, s. 22(3), substituted by the 1984 Act, s. 3.

there must be disregarded any time during which the person who sustained the injuries was under legal disability by reason of nonage[32] or unsoundness of mind.[33] The second qualification relates to the discretionary power of the court to override time-limits, which is considered below.[34]

Death actions

The following rules apply to any action in which, following the death of any person from personal injuries, damages are claimed in respect of the injuries or the death.[35] Subject to certain qualifications,[36] no such action may be brought unless it is commenced[37] within a period of three years after (a) the date of death of the deceased; or (b) the date (if later than the date of death) on which the pursuer[38] in the action became, or on which, in the opinion of the court, it would have been reasonably practicable for him in all the circumstances to become, aware of both of the following facts—(i) that the injuries of the deceased were attributable in whole or in part to an act or omission[39]; and (ii) that the defender was a person to whose act or omission the injuries were attributable in whole or in part or the employer or principal of such a person.[40] **2.117**

There are three qualifications to the rule.[41] The first is that where the pursuer is a relative[42] of the deceased, there must be disregarded in the computation of the triennium any time during which the relative was under legal disability by reason of nonage[43] or unsoundness of mind.[44] Secondly, subject to the discretionary power of the court to override time-limits, where an action of damages has not been brought by or on behalf of a person who has sustained personal injuries within the triennium and that person subsequently dies in consequence of those injuries, no such action may be brought in respect of the injuries or death.[45] The third qualification relates to the court's discretionary power to override time-limits.[46] **2.118**

Defamation actions

Subject to certain qualifications, no action of defamation[47] may be brought unless it is commenced[48] within a period of three years after **2.119**

---

[32] Under the Age of Legal Capacity (Scotland) Act 1991, full capacity is attained at the age of 16. Prior to this, "nonage" comprehended both pupillarity and minority (*Fyfe v. Croudace Ltd,* 1986 S.L.T. 528). Transitional provisions were made under s. 8 of the 1991 Act.

[33] 1973 Act, s. 17(3).

[34] para. 2.121.

[35] 1973 Act, s. 18(1). S. 18 was substituted by the 1984 Act, s. 2.

[36] See para. 2.118.

[37] See n. 26.

[38] See n. 29.

[39] See n. 31.

[40] 1973 Act, s. 18(2).

[41] *ibid.* s. 18(2).

[42] "Relative" has the same meaning as in Sched. 1 to the Damages (Scotland) Act 1976, as amended by the Law Reform (Parent and Child) (Scotland) Act 1986, Sched. 1: 1973 Act, s. 18(5).

[43] See n. 32.

[44] 1973 Act, s. 18(3).

[45] *ibid.* s. 18(4).

[46] See para. 2.121.

[47] "Defamation" includes *convicium* and malicious falsehood: 1973 Act, s. 18A(4)(a), inserted by the Law Reform (Miscellaneous Provisions) (Scotland) Act 1985, s. 12(2).

[48] See n. 26.

the date when the publication or communication in respect of which the action is to be brought first came to the notice of the pursuer.[49] The rule is qualified by the discretionary power of the court to override time limits,[50] and the following provisions. In the computation of the triennium there must be disregarded any time during which the person alleged to have been defamed was under legal disability by reason of nonage[51] or unsoundness of mind.[52] The three-year rule does not affect any right of action which accrued before December 30, 1985.[53]

Harassment actions

2.120 Section 18B of the 1973 Act[54] provides, subject to certain qualifications, that no action of harassment (within the meaning of section 8 of the Protection from Harassment Act 1997) which includes a claim for damages may be brought unless it is commenced within a period of three years after the date on which the alleged harassment ceased or the date (if later) on which the pursuer became or on which, in the opinion of the court, it would have been reasonably practicable for him in all the circumstances to have become, aware, that the defender was a person responsible for the alleged harassment or the employer or principal of such a person.[55] Again, in the computation of the triennium, there must be disregarded any time during which the person who is alleged to have suffered the harassment was under legal disability by reason of nonage or unsoundness of mind.[56]

Power of the court to override time-limits

2.121 Section 19A of the 1973 Act provides that where a person would be entitled, but for any of the provisions discussed above, to bring an action, the court may, if it seems to it equitable to do so, allow him to bring the action notwithstanding that provision.[57] The discretion conferred on the court is unfettered, although in every case the relaxation of the statutory bar can and must depend solely upon equitable considerations relevant to the exercise of a discretionary jurisdiction in the particular case, having regard to the fact that it is for the party seeking relief to satisfy the court that it is, in the view of the court and in the circumstances of the case and of the legitimate rights and interests of the parties, equitable to do so.[58] In some cases it may be necessary for the question of the applicability of section 19A to be decided on the result of a preliminary proof on the relevant averments and pleas of parties.[59] If the court decides not to exercise its discretion in favour of the pursuer,

---

[49] 1973 Act, s. 18A(1) and (4)(b). As to "pursuer", see n. 29.

[50] See para. 2.121.

[51] See n. 32.

[52] 1973 Act, s. 18A(2).

[53] *ibid.* s. 18A(3). Before that date the relevant period was five years: *ibid.* s. 6(1), Sched. 1, para. 1(d).

[54] Inserted by the Protection from Harassment Act 1997, s.10(1).

[55] 1973 Act, s. 18B(1) and (2).

[56] *ibid.* s. 18B(3).

[57] *ibid.* s. 19A(1), inserted by Law Reform (Miscellaneous Provisions) (Scotland) Act 1980, s. 23(a), and amended by 1984 Act, Sched. 1, para. 8(a) and Law Reform (Miscellaneous Provisions) (Scotland) Act 1985, s. 12(3). S. 19A(1) has retrospective effect: s. 19A(2) and (3).

[58] *Donald v. Rutherford*, 1984 S.L.T. 70, *per* Lord Cameron at 75; *Forsyth v. A.F. Stoddart & Co. Ltd*, 1985 S.L.T. 51; *Anderson v. Glasgow D.C.*, 1987 S.L.T. 279. Earlier cases include *Whyte v. Walker*, 1983 S.L.T. 441 and the cases cited in para. 10.41.

[59] *Donald, supra, per* Lord Cameron at 78, Lord Dunpark at 79; *Anderson, supra.*

the defender is assoilzied.[60] Section 19A has often been considered in questions as to the amendment of pleadings after the expiry of the triennium.[61]

Pleading

If the defender states a limitation plea, the pursuer should aver the circumstances on which he relies as indicating that the action is not time-barred or that the court should exercise its discretion to override the time-limit. Thus, where he has become aware of the specified facts after the date of injury or death or the date of cessation of the act or omission, he must aver both the date on which he became aware of the specified facts and the date on which it would have been reasonably practicable for him in all the circumstances to become aware of them.[62] **2.122**

Mora, taciturnity and acquiescence

Delay in prosecuting a claim for a period shorter than a relevant statutory period of prescription or limitation[63] is not in itself a defence to the action, but the pursuer may be barred from insisting in it if the delay has been prejudicial to the defender[64] or if it gives rise to an inference of acquiescence on the part of the pursuer.[65] In such circumstances the following plea is competent to the defender: "The pursuer being barred by *mora*, taciturnity and acquiescence from insisting in the present action, the defender should be assoilzied."[66] The plea must be supported by appropriate averments inferring prejudice or acquiescence.[67] The plea is a plea to the merits.[68] If the relevance of the averments supporting it is not challenged, or if they are attacked as irrelevant and the plea attacking them is repelled, the plea can be disposed of only on an admission by the pursuer of facts leading to the irresistible inference of prejudice or acquiescence, or after inquiry into the facts.[69] If the plea is sustained, decree of absolvitor is pronounced.[70] The plea is very seldom stated, however, and there appears to be no modern reported instance of the plea being sustained.[71] It more frequently occurs that where delay has taken place to the prejudice of the defender, and where in consequence the weighing of the value of evidence and the drawing of inferences from it are rendered more anxious and difficult, the court scrutinises the evidence **2.123**

---

60 *Donald, supra, per* Lord Cameron at 77 (the report at 71 appears to be inaccurate); *Forsyth, supra,* at 52, 55; *Anderson, supra,* at 287.

61 See para. 10.41.

62 *Hamill v. Newalls Insulation Co.*, 1987 S.L.T. 478.

63 See paras 2.114 to 2.122.

64 *Assets Co. Ltd v. Bain's Trs* (1904) 6 F. 692, *per* L.P. Kinross at 705 (revd on the facts (1905) 7 F. (H.L.) 104).

65 *Moncrieff v. Waugh* (1859) 21 D. 216.

66 *Bethune v. A. Stevenson & Co. Ltd*, 1969 S.L.T. (Notes) 12. See Walker, *Prescription and Limitation of Actions*, Chap. 8.

67 *Assets Co. Ltd, supra; Halley v. Wall,* 1956 S.C. 370, *per* L.P. Clyde at 374.

68 *Halley, supra.*

69 *Bethune, supra; Halley, supra.*

70 *Robson v. Bywater* (1870) 8 M. 757 at 759, 766; *Spence v. Paterson's Trs* (1873) 1 R. 46 at 48, 50, 60.

71 In *Lees' Trs v. Dun*, 1912 S.C. 50, 1913 S.C. (H.L.) 12, the Lord Ordinary's interlocutor sustaining the plea of *mora* was recalled by the Inner House, whose interlocutor was affirmed by the House of Lords. In *Bethune, supra,* Lord Hunter, after proof before answer, found it unnecessary to dispose of the plea (Jan. 16, 1972, unreported).

with particular care.[72] If an action has been timeously raised the court has no power to dismiss it because the pursuer delays in prosecuting it.[73]

Declinature

2.124 The exercise of the jurisdiction of the court may be excluded by objection taken to its exercise by a particular sheriff. The taking of such an objection is called proponing a declinature; and the two grounds on which it may be done are (1) that of relationship to one of the parties, and (2) that of interest in the matter at issue.

Relationship

2.125 Declinature on the ground of relationship is based on the Declinature Acts 1594 and 1681, the effect of which is that a sheriff may not sit in causes where the pursuer or defender is his father, brother, son, father-in-law, brother-in-law, son-in-law, uncle or nephew. Nor may he sit where he is so related to the party's mandatary.[74] The rule does not extend to other relationships.[75] Where it applies, however, it cannot be waived by the parties[76] and the sheriff must decline to sit.[77] The declinature may be proponed at any stage of the case, and the effect of the rule is that all prior proceedings before the sheriff are a nullity and his interlocutors are recalled.[78]

Interest

2.126 The rules regarding declinature on the ground of interest are based on the common law, with one statutory modification. The common law rules have been stated thus:

> "The general and salutary rule is that no man can be a judge in his own cause, and that rule within certain limits is rigorously applied. The reason of it is obvious, viz., to ensure not merely that the administration of justice shall be free of bias but that it shall be beyond suspicion. It is subject, however, to qualifications and exceptions. The result of the authorities which were cited to us may be stated as follows:
>
> 1. As a general rule a pecuniary interest, if direct and individual, will disqualify, however small it may be.
> 2. An interest although not pecuniary may also disqualify, but the interest in that case must be substantial.

---

72 *C.B. v. A.B.* (1885) 12 R. (H.L.) 36, *per* Earl Selborne L.C. at 40; *Bain v. Assets Co.* (1905) 7 F. (H.L.) 104, *per* Earl of Halsbury L.C. at 108–109; *Bosville v. Lord Macdonald*, 1910 S.C. 597, *per* L.P. Dunedin at 608–609; *McKenzie's Exrx v. Morrison's Trs*, 1930 S.C. 830, *per* L.J.-C. Alness at 835; *Woods v. A.C.S. Motors Ltd*, 1930 S.C. 1035 *per* Lord Hunter at 1037; *Rutherford v. Harvey & McMillan*, 1954 S.L.T. (Notes) 28; *Clark v. Pryde*, 1959 S.L.T. (Notes) 16. In the Court of Session an action otherwise appropriate for jury trial may be sent for proof before a judge on the ground that he is more likely than a jury to give fair weight to the consequences of the delay when determining the reliability of the evidence: *Rutherford, Clark, supra*; *Hunter v. John Brown & Co.*, 1961 S.C. 231.

73 *Esso Petroleum Co. Ltd v. Hall Russell & Co. Ltd*, 1995 S.C.L.R. 36.

74 *Ommanney v. Smith* (1851) 13 D. 678; *Commrs of Highland Roads v. Machray, Croall & Co.* (1858) 20 D. 1165; *Campbell v. Campbell* (1866) 4 M. 867 at 923.

75 *Gordon v. Gordon's Tr.* (1866) 4 M. 501 at 509. Parties may nevertheless acquiesce in a judge's wish not to sit: *Sinclair v. Brown* (1841) 3 D. 871 at 874.

76 Ersk., I, ii, 31; *Shaw Stewart v. Corbet*, May 30, 1820, F.C. (note p. 146); *Ommanney, Commrs of Highland Roads, supra*; *Duke of Athole v. Robertson* (1869) 8 M. 299, *per* Lord Neaves at 303.

77 *Duke of Athole, supra.*

78 *Ommanney, supra.*

3. Where the interest which is said to disqualify is not pecuniary, and is neither substantial nor calculated to cause bias in the mind of the judge, it will be disregarded, especially if to disqualify the judge would be productive of grave public inconvenience."[79]

Declinature may also be stated on grounds of enmity or malice, or bribery and corruption.[80] If the disqualifying interest is not waived by the parties, or is only discovered after decree, the decree may be recalled or reduced.[81]

(1) Pecuniary interest.[82] The general rule that a pecuniary interest, if direct and individual, will disqualify, however small it may be, is subject to a statutory exception where the judge is a partner in a life or fire insurance company, or the holder merely as a trustee of shares in any incorporated company, which is a party to the litigation.[83] The general rule accordingly applies to the holding of shares in any company other than a life or fire insurance company,[84] and in any unincorporated company[85] even as trustee. The tender of declinature by judges who are shareholders in incorporated companies "is a matter of constant experience",[86] but the parties may waive any objection by joint minute.[87] **2.127**

(2) Interest other than pecuniary. When the interest is not pecuniary it must, in order to disqualify, be substantial or calculated to cause bias in the mind of the judge.[88] Few of the older reported cases on non-pecuniary interest[89] appear to discuss the way in which that test should be applied, but it is now clear that if a judge has a bias which renders him otherwise than an impartial judge he is disqualified from performing his duty. Further, if there are circumstances so affecting him as to be calculated to create in the mind of a reasonable man a suspicion of his impartiality, those circumstances are themselves sufficient to disqualify although in fact no bias exists.[90] The basic principle is that it is of supreme importance that the administration of the law should be pure and unsuspect,[91] and the guiding consideration is that the administration of justice should reason- **2.128**

---

[79] *Wildridge v. Anderson* (1897) 2 Adam 399, *per* Lord Moncreiff at 410–411; approved, *Gorman v. Wright*, 1916 S.C.(J.) 44, *per* L.J.-C. Scott Dickson at 47.

[80] *Duke of Athole v. Robertson* (1869) 8 M. 299.

[81] *Sellar v. Highland Ry*, 1919 S.C. (H.L.) 19.

[82] I.S. Dickinson, "Disqualification of Judges on Account of Interest" (1984) 29 J.L.S. 446.

[83] Court of Session Act 1868, s. 103 (passed after *Borthwick v. Scottish Widows' Fund* (1864) 2 M. 595: see 613). The A.S., Feb. 1, 1820, which provides a further exception where the judge is a shareholder in a chartered bank in Scotland, does not apply to the sheriff courts.

[84] *Sellar v. Highland Ry*, 1918 S.C. 838, at 846; 1919 S.C. (H.L.) 19.

[85] *Smith v. Liverpool and London and Globe Insurance Co.* (1887) 14 R. 931.

[86] *Sellar, supra*, 1918 S.C. 838, *per* Lord Sands at 843.

[87] *Smith, supra, per* L.P. Inglis at 938; *Sellar, supra*, 1919 S.C.(H.L.) 19, *per* Lord Buckmaster at 21.

[88] *Wildridge, Gorman, supra*; *Laughland v. Galloway*, 1968 J.C. 26; *R. McDermid Ltd v. Muir Crawford (Builders) Ltd*, 1978 S.L.T (Sh. Ct.) 18.

[89] *Encyclopaedia*, v, pp. 456–457.

[90] *Law v. Chartered Institute of Patent Agents* [1919] 2 Ch. 276, approved *Bradford v. McLeod*, 1986 S.L.T. 244. See also *Gorman v. Wright*, 1916 S.C.(J.) 44, *per* Lord Guthrie at 48; *Tennant v. Houston*, 1987 S.L.T. 317. The conditions for declinature of jurisdiction were reiterated in *Black v Scott Lithgow Ltd*, 1990 S.L.T. 612, *per* L.P. Hope at 616 and followed by Sh. Pr. Cox in *Dumfries and Galloway Regional Council v. O*, 1994 S.C.L.R. 661.

[91] *Smith, supra, per* Lord Adam at 939.

ably appear to be disinterested as well as be so in fact.[92] In general, however, the fact that a judge has determined the issues in the action and in so doing has expressed views on the conduct of the parties and of the witnesses, neither constitutes bias nor the appearance of bias in relation to subsequent applications in the action.[93] Interest in a similar cause which may be brought has been held not to be a ground of declinature[94]; and as to whether acting as advocate in the same cause before appointment to the Bench is a ground of declinature, practice has varied.[95] It is submitted that the consideration that the administration of justice should reasonably appear to be disinterested would nowadays lead to the conclusion that in such cases the sheriff should not sit, unless of consent of parties to adjudicate on matters entirely incidental to the merits of the cause.[96] A sheriff is not entitled to decline jurisdiction because a case may give rise to questions of the credibility, reliability or integrity of a solicitor who regularly appears before him.[97] However, in such a case it would generally be desirable to arrange that the case should be heard by a visiting sheriff.

2.129 **(3) Procedure.** A declinature may be proponed either by the judge himself[98] or by either or both of the parties.[99] A declinature on the ground of interest may be waived by joint minute[1] but one proponed on the ground of relationship may not.[2] A declinature on the ground of relationship may be stated at any time,[3] but a declinature on other grounds must in general be stated at once.[4] Since a judge may not rule on a declinature proponed by or against himself,[5] it may be that the grounds of declinature should be recorded in an interlocutor pronounced by the sheriff and reviewed by the sheriff principal, who may either sustain the declinature and remit the cause to another sheriff, or repel it and remit to the sheriff to proceed.[6] In practice the formal proponing of a declinature appears to be a rare occurrence, no doubt because any objection on the ground of interest is ordinarily waived by the parties or because the existence of a possible ground of declinature is in general apparent before the sitting of the court and the cause in question is allocated to another sheriff.[7] Where

---

92 *Public Utilities Commission of D.C. v. Pollak* (1952) 343 U.S. 451, *per* Frankfurter J. at 467, *cit. R. v. Liverpool J.J., ex p. Topping* [1983] 1 W.L.R. 119 at 125.

93 *Bahai v. Rashidian* [1985] 1 W.L.R. 1337, *per* Sir J. Donaldson M.R. at 1342; discussed by Lord President Hope in *Black v Scott Lithgow Ltd*, 1990 S.L.T. 612 at 616 and by Sh. Pr. Cox in *Dumfries and Galloway Regional Council v. O*, 1994 S.C.L.R. 661 at 663.

94 *Belfrage v. Davidson's Trs* (1862) 24 D. 1132; *Henderson's Trs v. Dunfermline District Committee of Fife C.C.* (1896) 12 Sh.Ct.Rep. 58.

95 *Innes's Reps v. Duke of Gordon* (1827) 6 S. 279 at 294–295 (sustained); *King v. King* (1841) 4 D. 124 at 127 (repelled); *Hall v. Hall* (1891) 18 R. 690 at 690n (apparently not proponed); *Free Church of Scotland v. McRae* (1905) 7 F. 686 (sustained); *McCardle v. McCardle's J.F.* (1906) 8 F. 419 (L.O. disinclined to act: cause transferred by L.P.).

96 As in *Burgh of Ayr v. British Transport Commission*, 1956 S.L.T. (Sh. Ct.) 3 at 7–8. *Cf.* Stair, IV, xxxix, 14; IV, xxxvii, 15.

97 *McDonald v. Kelly*, 1995 S.C.L.R. 187.

98 *Gordon v. Gordon's Trs* (1866) 4 M. 501 at 509.

99 *Porterfield v. Stewart* (1821) 1 S. 9 at 10 (N.E. 6 at 7); *Moubray's Trs v. Moubray* (1883) 10 R. 460.

1 para. 2.127.

2 para. 2.125.

3 *Ommanney v. Smith* (1851) 13 D. 678.

4 *Duke of Athole v. Robertson* (1869) 8 M. 299.

5 *Blau v. Sampson*, Jan. 26, 1814, F.C. (1814–15, High Ct of Justiciary, App. 501).

6 *Henderson's Trs v. Dunfermline District Committee of Fife C.C.* (1896) 12 Sh.Ct.Rep. 58.

7 *Bradford v. McLeod*, 1986 S.L.T. 244, *per* Lord Dunpark at 249.

an objection to the exercise of jurisdiction by a sheriff principal is not, or cannot be, waived, the Secretary of State may either authorise another sheriff principal to dispose of the cause or appoint a temporary sheriff principal to do so.[8]

Miscellaneous

Exclusion or restriction by statute

In certain cases, for reasons of public policy, statutes provide that an action is excluded, either on certain grounds or unless certain conditions are satisfied. Thus, a public prosecutor may be sued for damages only in very limited circumstances[9]; and a person who has habitually and persistently instituted legal proceedings without any reasonable grounds for doing so may be restrained by the Court of Session from instituting proceedings unless he obtains the leave of a Lord Ordinary, whose decision on the matter is final.[10] **2.130**

Failure to exhaust statutory remedy

The exercise of the court's jurisdiction may be excluded by the application of the principle that unless exceptional circumstances are present it is incompetent for a pursuer to resort to the courts where he has not had recourse to a statutory procedure designed for the redress of his complaint.[11] The principle is more frequently invoked in the Court of Session than in the sheriff court.[12] **2.131**

Recompense

It would at least require special and strong circumstances to justify an action of recompense where there was, or had been, an alternative remedy open to the pursuer.[13] **2.132**

Concurrent criminal proceedings

Where criminal proceedings have been or are clearly about to be instituted which have as their subject-matter issues which are closely related to those in a civil action, the civil court should not improperly intrude into the domain of the criminal court by making any order or decision which would prejudice the criminal proceedings.[14] If the Crown institute a prosecution in respect of conduct which may have constituted a contempt of a court, that court will not deal with the matter as a contempt.[15] **2.133**

---

[8] 1971 Act, ss. 10(1A), 11(1A), substituted by Law Reform (Miscellaneous Provisions) (Scotland) Act 1980, s. 10(a) and (b).

[9] Criminal Procedure (Scotland) Act 1995, s. 170. But see also *Bell v. McGlennan*, 1992 S.L.T. 237. See also *Mowbray v. Valentine*, 1998 S.C.L.R. 305.

[10] Vexatious Actions (Scotland) Act 1898, as amended by the Law Reform (Miscellaneous Provisions) (Scotland) Act 1980, s. 19; see paras 4.122, 4.123.

[11] *British Railways Board v. Glasgow Corporation*, 1976 S.C. 224 at 237; *Edinburgh D.C. v. Round and Robinson*, 1987 S.L.T. (Sh. Ct.) 117.

[12] The authorities are collected and analysed by C.T. Reid, "Failure to Exhaust Statutory Remedies", 1984 J.R. 185.

[13] *Varney (Scotland) Ltd v. Lanark T.C.*, 1974 S.C. 245, *per* Lord Fraser at 259–260; see also L.J.-C. Wheatley at 252–253 and Lord Kissen at 257.

[14] *Imperial Tobacco Ltd v. Att.-Gen.* [1981] A.C. 718.

[15] para. 2.21.

Registration of custody decision

2.134 In the case of proceedings for, or for the variation or discharge of, a parental responsibilities order made under section 86 of the Children (Scotland) Act 1995, the powers of the court are restricted where an application has been made to the court for the registration of a custody decision under section 16 of the Child Abduction and Custody Act 1985, or where such a decision has been registered, having been made in proceedings commenced before the proceedings before the court were instituted.[16]

Transfer, remit or removal of cause

2.135 An action raised in a sheriff court may in certain circumstances be transferred to another sheriff court or remitted or removed to the Court of Session.[17]

---

[16] Child Abduction and Custody Act 1985, s. 20, as amended.
[17] See paras 13.51 to 13.66.

CHAPTER 3

JURISDICTION OVER PERSONS AND ESTATE

INTRODUCTION

This chapter is concerned with the rules which regulate the civil jurisdiction of the sheriff court over the persons whom a pursuer seeks to convene as defenders or over the conduct or property in respect of which a pursuer seeks a remedy or makes an application. The subject is dominated by the Civil Jurisdiction and Judgments Act 1982, which came into force on January 1, 1987[1] and effected many complex and wide-ranging changes in the law. This chapter attempts only a guide to the principal provisions of the Act. For a thorough exposition of the statutory provisions and detailed comment on the many problems of interpretation which they present, the reader is referred to Anton & Beaumont's *Civil Jurisdiction in Scotland: Brussels and Lugano Conventions.*[2] The background to the Act can be understood in the context of the official report, known as the Maxwell Report, which preceded it.[3] The policy adopted in this chapter is to try to note any important developments which have taken place since the first edition of this work and since the writing of the second edition of *Civil Jurisdiction.* **3.01**

The 1982 Act gives the force of law in the United Kingdom to several Conventions and Protocols: the Convention on jurisdiction and the enforcement of judgments in civil and commercial matters (the 1968 Convention), including the Protocol annexed to that Convention, signed at Brussels on September 27, 1968 (the Annexed Protocol) and the Protocol on the interpretation of that Convention by the European Court, signed at Luxembourg on June 3, 1971 (the 1971 Protocol). These Conventions and Protocols were agreed by the original six Member States of the then European Economic Community—Belgium, France, Germany, Italy, Luxembourg and the Netherlands—under power given by Article 220 of the EEC Treaty. Various Accession Conventions have amended the 1968 Convention, the Annexed Protocol, and the 1971 Protocol, and have enabled new Member States of the European Union to become parties to these instruments, namely Denmark, Ireland and the United Kingdom (1978), Greece (1982), Portugal and Spain (1989), and Austria, Finland and Sweden (1996).[4] These instruments are referred to in **3.02**

---

[1] Civil Jurisdiction and Judgments Act 1982 (Commencement No. 3) Order 1986 (S.I. No. 2044). The Act is hereafter referred to as "the 1982 Act".

[2] Hereafter *Civil Jurisdiction* (2nd ed., W. Green, 1995).

[3] *The Report of the Scottish Committee on Jurisdiction and Enforcement* (HMSO, 1980).

[4] The 1996 Accession Convention was signed in Brussels on Nov. 29, 1996 ([1997] O.J. C15/02), but has only been ratified by the Netherlands as at July 1997. It has not yet been implemented into U.K. law by amending the 1982 Act. Austria, Finland and Sweden are, however, parties to the Lugano Convention. The 1996 Accession Convention makes no substantive changes to the 1968 Convention but does add some new provisions to the Annexed Protocol.

the Act as "the Brussels Conventions" and the English texts are set out in Schedules 1, 2, 3, 3A, and 3B. In this chapter the "Brussels Convention" means the original 1968 Convention as amended by all the accession conventions up to and including the 1996 Accession Convention. Part I of the Act makes provision for the implementation of the Brussels Conventions, sections 2 and 3, and the parallel Lugano Convention, sections 3A and 3B and Schedule 3C. The latter operates in relation to the Member States of the European Union and the European Free Trade Association States (Iceland, Norway and Switzerland), and perhaps in the future other States which are permitted to ratify the Convention, but not for matters internal to the European Union which are still governed by the Brussels Convention. Part II enacts provisions, set out in Schedule 4, as to the allocation of jurisdiction among the courts of the different parts of the United Kingdom (England and Wales, Scotland and Northern Ireland) in proceedings where the subject-matter is within the scope of the Brussels Convention and the parties are "domiciled"[5] in different parts of the United Kingdom. Of primary importance to the Scottish practitioner is Part III of the Act, which provides rules as to jurisdiction in Scotland. These rules, which are contained in Schedule 8, apply to a wide range of proceedings: they are not restricted to proceedings whose subject-matter is within the scope of the Brussels Convention but cover, with a few important exceptions listed in Schedule 9, the whole law of civil jurisdiction in Scotland. They have effect, however, subject to Parts I and II of the Act[6]: that is, they apply only when and to the extent that the question of jurisdiction is not governed by the rules of the Brussels or Lugano Conventions or of Schedule 4.

3.03 Broadly speaking, the Brussels Convention provides jurisdictional rules which must be followed by United Kingdom courts in proceedings to which the Convention applies whenever the defender (or a defender, if there is more than one) is domiciled in another European Union State which has ratified the Convention (a "Contracting State"),[7] or, arguably, when the defender is domiciled in the United Kingdom and the pursuer is not domiciled there (at least where the pursuer is domiciled in a Contracting State),[8] or when certain rules as to "exclusive" jurisdiction apply.[9] The Lugano Convention applies when the defender is domiciled in one of the Contracting States to that Convention which are not Contracting States to the Brussels Convention, or where the defender is domiciled in

---

5 "Domicile" has a special meaning: see paras 3.06 *et seq.*

6 1982 Act, s. 20(1).

7 The Contracting States are: Belgium, Denmark, France, Germany, Greece, Ireland, Italy, Luxembourg, the Netherlands, Portugal, Spain, and the United Kingdom: 1982 Act, s. 1(3).

8 The argument turns on the interpretation of Art. 2 of the Brussels Convention. The English Court of Appeal took the view that if the alternative forum to England was a non-Convention country and the parties were not connected with a Convention country other than the U.K., then it was free to decline jurisdiction based on the principle of *forum non conveniens*: see *Re Harrods (Buenos Aires) Ltd* [1992] Ch. 72 and *The Po* [1991] 2 Lloyd's Rep. 206. The approach of the Court of Appeal has been heavily criticised by a number of commentators who argue that Art. 2 of the Convention is general in its terms and that Arts 21–23 preclude any place for *forum non conveniens* when the Convention's jurisdiction rules are applicable: see Briggs (1991) 107 L.Q.R. 180; Kaye (1992) J.B.L. 47; Gaudemet-Tallon (1991) 80 Rev. crit. de droit int. privé 491. For a creative and very well researched examination of this issue, see Kennett (1995) 54 C.L.J. 552.

9 The exclusive jurisdiction rules in Art. 16 and the prorogation provisions in Art. 17 when parties have selected the courts of one of the Contracting States.

the United Kingdom and the pursuer is domiciled in a State party to the Lugano Convention which is not party to the Brussels Convention, or where the "exclusive" jurisdiction rules in the Lugano Convention[10] (prorogation, under Article 17, as well as the exclusive jurisdiction rules in Article 16) select a jurisdiction which is within a Contracting State to the Lugano Convention which is not a Contracting State to the Brussels Convention. The rules in Schedule 4 must be applied by the Scottish courts when the subject-matter of proceedings is within the scope of the Brussels Convention and, either the parties are domiciled in the United Kingdom provided at least one of them is domiciled in a part other than Scotland, or the proceedings fall within Article 16 of Schedule 4. Schedule 8 applies to a wide range of proceedings where the defender is domiciled in Scotland or in another jurisdiction which is neither another Contracting State to the Brussels or Lugano Conventions nor another part of the United Kingdom, or where the Scottish courts have exclusive jurisdiction irrespective of the defender's domicile. The rules in Schedules 4 and 8 are borrowed, with varying modifications and qualifications, from the Brussels Convention. In the majority of cases in the sheriff court Schedule 8 will in fact be the place to find the applicable jurisdictional law. Moreover, in so far as the rules in Schedule 8 correspond with the Brussels Convention rules, it will often be unnecessary for the Scottish court and the Scottish practitioner to decide the by no means easy problem of whether the case is or is not governed by the rules of the Brussels or Lugano Conventions or of Schedule 4, for the test of jurisdiction in these instances will be the same.[11] Since, however, the rules in Schedule 8 have effect subject to Parts I and II of the Act, it is necessary to consider first the jurisdictional provisions of the Brussels and Lugano Conventions and the scheme in Schedule 4 for the allocation of jurisdiction within the United Kingdom, before examining the provisions in Part III as to jurisdiction in Scotland. A review of the operation of the Brussels and Lugano Conventions was commenced by the Contracting States in 1997 with a view to amending the Conventions.[12]

The Brussels Convention

Interpretation of the Convention[13]

Judicial notice is taken of the Convention.[14] Any question as to the meaning or effect of any provision of the Convention may, and in some cases must, be referred by a court other than a court of first instance to the European Court for a preliminary ruling in accordance with the 1971 Protocol. A sheriff can only refer a case under the Brussels Convention to the European Court when hearing an appeal against enforcement of a maintenance order granted in a Brussels Convention Contracting State.[15] **3.04**

---

[10] Arts 16 and 17.

[11] Lord Maxwell, reviewing the first edition of *Civil Jurisdiction in Scotland* (W. Green, 1984) by Anton, in 1984 S.L.T. (News) 338.

[12] See the Consultation Paper prepared by Beaumont and McEleavy and published by Scottish Courts Administration and the Lord Chancellor's Department in April 1997 entitled, *The Operation of the Brussels and Lugano Conventions*.

[13] See *Civil Jurisdiction*, Chap. 2.

[14] 1982 Act, s. 2(1).

[15] See Art. 37 of the Convention, Chap. 38 of Ordinary Cause Rules, and the Sheriff Court Enforcement Act of Sederunt (S.I. 1986 No. 1947), para. 6(10) and (11).

A sheriff principal, exercising the appellate jurisidiction in civil matters, has the power to refer a question of interpretation of the Brussels Convention to the European Court for a preliminary ruling but is not obliged to do so. If the question is not referred to the European Court, it must be determined in accordance with the principles laid down by any relevant decision of the European Court.[16] Judicial notice must be taken of any decision of, or expression of opinion by, the European Court on any such question.[17] This chapter will refer to relevant cases of the European Court which have been decided since *Civil Jurisdiction*. The reports by Mr P. Jenard on the Brussels Convention and the 1971 Protocol, and the report by Professor Peter Schlosser on the 1978 Accession Convention and the reports on the subsequent accession conventions, which are published in the *Official Journal of the European Communities*,[18] may be considered in ascertaining the meaning or effect of any provision of the Convention, and must be given "such weight as is appropriate in the circumstances".[19]

Scope of the Convention

3.05 Article 1 of the Convention provides that it applies "in civil and commercial matters whatever the nature of the court or tribunal". The Convention does not define "civil and commercial matters" but Article 1 specifically excludes certain matters by stating that the Convention "shall not extend, in particular, to revenue, customs or administrative matters", and does not apply to: "(1) the status or legal capacity of natural persons, rights in property arising out of a matrimonial relationship, wills and succession; (2) bankruptcy, proceedings relating to the winding-up of insolvent companies or other legal persons, judicial arrangements, compositions and analogous proceedings; (3) social security; (4) arbitration".[20] The question of the scope of the Convention is, however, difficult, and reference should be made to the undernoted work.[21]

---

16 1982 Act, s. 3(1).

17 *ibid.* s.3(2). The official reports of the European Court of Justice's cases are the European Court Reports (E.C.R.) and these are available in all European Documentation Centres (Aberdeen, Dundee, Edinburgh and Glasgow Universities). These reports are also available in the library of the Faculty of Advocates, and in the court libraries at Edinburgh and Glasgow sheriff courts. Unreported cases since June 1997 are available on the official web site of the European Court of Justice: see http://europa.eu.int/cj/en/index.htm. Summaries of cases ordered according to subject-matter can be found in *Civil Jurisdiction*, pp. 429–592 and in chronological order in the *Scots Law Times*, Appendix to the News.

18 This is available in any European Documentation Centre, and in the libraries referred to in n. 17, *supra*, and is referred to by the abbreviation O.J. followed by the year and then "C" or "L" depending on which series it is published in. See [1979] O.J. C59/1–70, C59/71–151, [1986] O.J. C298/1 and [1990] O.J. C189/35.

19 1982 Act, s. 3(3).

20 *ibid.* Sched. 1, Art. 1.

21 See *Civil Jurisdiction*, Chap. 3. In relation to revenue matters it is important to note that though they fall outside the scope of the Brussels and Lugano Conventions they do fall within the scope of Sched. 8 to the 1982 Act: see *Lord Advocate v. Tursi*, 1997 S.C.L.R. 264. The European Court has considered the scope of "civil matters" in the context of the boundary with public law and criminal law in Case C-172/91, *Sonntag v. Waidmann* [1993] E.C.R. I-1963, paras 20–28. The dividing line between "rights in property arising out of a matrimonial relationship", outwith the scope of the Convention, and of "maintenance", within its scope, was examined by the European Court in Case C-220/95, *Van den Boogaard* [1997] 3 W.L.R. 284.

Domicile[22]

In the matters to which the Convention applies, the general principle is that "persons domiciled in a Contracting State shall, whatever their nationality, be sued in the courts of that State".[23] In the context of the Act, "domicile" is a concept with a special meaning different from that attached to it by the common law rules of private international law in Scotland. Under the Act, the rules for ascertaining a person's domicile differ according to whether the person is an individual or a corporation, partnership or unincorporated body of persons. Provision is also made as to the domicile of trusts, and of the Crown. The domicile principle is qualified by rules creating exclusive jurisdiction; rules conferring concurrent jurisdictions; rules as to jurisdiction in matters relating to insurance and consumer contracts; rules relating to prorogation of and submission to jurisdiction; and provisions as to declinature of jurisdiction. **3.06**

Individuals

An individual is domiciled in the United Kingdom if and only if (a) he is resident in the United Kingdom, and (b) the nature and circumstances of his residence indicate that he has a substantial connection with the United Kingdom.[24] "Substantial connection" is not defined, but if he is resident in the United Kingdom and has been so resident for the last three months or more, condition (b) is presumed to be fulfilled unless the contrary is proved.[25] **3.07**

A similar test is employed in order to allocate jurisdiction among the courts of the "parts" of the United Kingdom (England and Wales, Scotland and Northern Ireland).[26] An individual is domiciled in a particular part of the United Kingdom if and only if (a) he is resident in that part, and (b) the nature and circumstances of his residence indicate that he has a substantial connection with that part.[27] If an individual is domiciled in the United Kingdom but condition (b) is not satisfied in relation to any particular part of the United Kingdom, he is treated as domiciled in the part of the United Kingdom in which he is resident.[28] If an individual is resident in a particular part of the United Kingdom and has been so resident for the last three months or more, condition (b) is presumed to be fulfilled unless the contrary is proved.[29] **3.08**

---

22 See *Civil Jurisdiction*, Chap. 4.

23 1982 Act, Sched. 1, Art. 2.

24 *ibid.* s. 41(2). An individual for this purpose includes a sole trader trading under a business name: see *Northamber plc v. Ian Benson (t/a Kyle Micros)*, 1990 S.C.L.R. 140, 141 (Sh. Murphy).

25 1982 Act, s. 41(6).

26 *ibid.* s. 50.

27 *ibid.* s. 41(3). In *Bank of Dubai Ltd v. Abbas* [1997] I.L.Pr. 308 the English Court of Appeal interpreted s. 41(3) as meaning that a person is resident in a particular part of the United Kingdom if that part is for him or her "a settled or usual place of abode" (at 311). This connotes "some degree of permanence or continuity". Lord Justice Saville, as he then was, stressed that cases turn on their own circumstances. In this case residence in England was not established but he did envisage circumstances where it could be established "immediately" (at 312), *e.g.* where a person comes to England to retire, buys a house, moves into it, sells all his foreign possessions and cuts his foreign ties. Of course the situation Lord Saville is describing in his example would be enough for the person to acquire an English common law domicile immediately.

28 1982 Act, s. 41(5).

29 *ibid.* s. 41(6).

3.09 In order to ascertain which sheriff court has jurisdiction over an individual, it is necessary to determine the place in which the individual is domiciled. An individual is domiciled in a particular place in the United Kingdom if and only if he (a) is domiciled in the part of the United Kingdom in which that place is situated, and (b) is resident in that place.[30] Thus, a person may be sued in a particular sheriff court if he is resident in that court's district or sheriffdom[31] and either the nature and circumstances of his residence indicate that he has a substantial connection with Scotland or, subject to his rebutting the statutory presumption, he has been resident in Scotland for the last three months or more.

3.10 In order to determine whether a party is domiciled in another Contracting State, the court must apply the law of that State.[32]

3.11 A person who is domiciled in a Contracting State may be sued in the courts of another Contracting State only by virtue of the rules set out in sections 2 to 6 of Title II of the Convention, which are noted in subsequent paragraphs. In particular, he cannot be sued in Scotland by virtue of rules[33] enabling jurisdiction to be founded on the presence of property belonging to him or on the arrestment of moveable property. It is thought, however, that in so far as the sheriff's jurisdiction founded on arrestment in terms of section 6(c) of the 1907 Act relates to the arrest of a ship or vessel, it is preserved by Article 57 of the Brussels and Lugano Conventions.[34]

3.12 An individual is domiciled in a state other than a Contracting State if and only if (a) he is resident in that state, and (b) the nature and circumstances of his residence indicate that he has a substantial connection with that state.[35] If he is so domiciled, the jurisdiction of the courts of each Contracting State are determined by the law of that state, subject only to the provisions as to "exclusive" jurisdictions.[36] In most cases the law of Scotland is now to be found in Schedule 8.

Corporations and associations

3.13 Rules are provided for determining the domicile of a "corporation" or "association". A "corporation" is a body corporate, and includes a partnership subsisting under the law of Scotland; and an "association" is an unincorporated body of persons.[37] The "seat" of a corporation or association is treated as its domicile.[38] There are both general and special rules.

---

[30] 1982 Act, s. 41(4). It may be possible for a person to be domiciled in more than one part of the United Kingdom at the same time: see *Daniel v. Foster*, 1989 S.C.L.R. 378 (Sh. Palmer).
[31] See para. 2.03.
[32] 1982 Act, Sched. 1, Art. 52.
[33] *ibid.* Sched.1, Art. 3.
[34] See *Civil Jurisdiction*, paras 3.31–3.35, 5.09, 10.36–10.38 and 11.04. Case C-406/92, *The Tatry* [1994] E.C.R. I-5439 shows that this jurisdiction is subject to Brussels and Lugano Convention rules on *lis pendens* and related actions in Arts 21 and 22 if the matter falls within the scope of those Conventions. The case is noted by Briggs (1996) L.M.C.L.Q. 161 and (1994) Y.Eur.L. 579; and Hartley (1995) Eur.L.R. 409.
[35] 1982 Act, s. 41(7).
[36] *ibid.* Sched. 1, Art. 4.
[37] *ibid.* s. 50.
[38] *ibid.* s. 42(1).

The general rules make provision for determining the seat of a corporation or association (i) in the United Kingdom; (ii) in a part of the United Kingdom; (iii) in a place in a part of the United Kingdom; and (iv) in a state other than the United Kingdom. **3.14**

A corporation or association has its seat in the United Kingdom if and only if (1) it was incorporated or formed under the law of a part of the United Kingdom and has its registered office or some other official address in the United Kingdom; or (2) its central management and control is exercised in the United Kingdom.[39] **3.15**

A corporation or association has its seat in a particular part of the United Kingdom if and only if it has its seat in the United Kingdom and (1) it has its registered office or some other official address[40] in that part; or (2) its central management and control is exercised in that part; or (3) it has a place of business[41] in that part.[42] **3.16**

In order to decide whether a particular sheriff court has jurisdiction, it is necessary to ascertain whether the corporation or association has a seat in a place within the sheriffdom. It has its seat in a particular place in the United Kingdom if and only if it has its seat in the part of the United Kingdom in which that place is situated and (1) it has its registered office[43] or some other official address in that place; or (2) its central management and control is exercised in that place; or (3) it has a place of business in that place.[44] **3.17**

A corporation or association has its seat in a state other than the United Kingdom if and only if (1) it was incorporated or formed under the law of that state and has its registered office or some other official address there; or (2) its central management and control is exercised in that state. It is not, however, to be regarded as having its seat in a Contracting State other than the United Kingdom if it is shown that the courts of that state would not regard it as having its seat there.[45] Accordingly, a corporation or association may have a number of seats. For example, a company which has its seat in the United Kingdom and places of business in different sheriffdoms in Scotland will have a seat in each of those sheriffdoms. It is also possible for a company to have seats in more than one state. **3.18**

Special rules are provided to determine where a corporation or association has its seat for the purposes of Article 16(2) of the Conventions and the corresponding Articles 5A and 16(2) of Schedule 4 and rules 2(12) and 4(1)(b) of Schedule 8, whereby exclusive jurisdiction is conferred over proceedings relating to the formation or dissolution of such bodies, or to **3.19**

---

39 1982 Act, s. 42(3).

40 "Official address" means an address which it is required by law to register, notify or maintain for the purpose of receiving notices or other communications: 1982 Act, s. 42(8).

41 "Business" includes any activity carried on by a corporation or association, and "place of business" is construed accordingly: 1982 Act, s. 42(8).

42 1982 Act, s. 42(4).

43 The jurisdiction of the court is not elided by a change in the situation of the registered office to a place beyond the sheriffdom which has not been intimated to the registrar of companies in terms of the Companies Act 1985, s. 287(2): *Ross v. Invergordon Distillers Ltd*, 1961 S.C. 286; 1961 S.L.T. 358.

44 1982 Act, s. 42(5).

45 *ibid.* s. 42(6), (7).

the decisions of their organs. For these purposes a corporation or association has its seat in the United Kingdom if and only if (1) it was incorporated or formed under the law of a part of the United Kingdom; or (2) its central management and control is exercised in the United Kingdom.[46] To have its seat in a particular part of the United Kingdom, it must have its seat in the United Kingdom and one of two conditions must be fulfilled: (1) it was incorporated or formed under the law of that part, provided that if it was formed under a law applying in more than one part, it has its seat in the part in which its registered office is situated; or (2) if it was incorporated or formed under the law of a state other than the United Kingdom, its central management and control is exercised in that part.[47] Thus, a corporation or association has its seat in Scotland for the purposes of Article 16(2) and the related provisions only if it was incorporated or formed under the law of Scotland; or, where that was done under a law applying in more than one part of the United Kingdom, if its registered office is situated in Scotland; or, where that was done under the law of a state other than the United Kingdom, its central management or control is exercised in Scotland. The jurisdiction of the sheriff court is determined by the further rule that a corporation or association has its seat in a particular place in Scotland if and only if it has its seat in Scotland and (1) it has its registered office or some other official address in that place; or (2) it has no registered office or other official address in Scotland, but its central management and control is exercised in that place.[48]

3.20 In addition to these rules for the purposes of Article 16(2) and the related provisions, there are special rules to determine domicile in relation to certain insurance and consumer contracts within the Brussels Convention, which are noticed below.

Trusts[49]

3.21 A person domiciled in a Contracting State may be sued in his capacity as settlor, trustee or beneficiary of a trust in the courts of the Contracting State in which the trust is domiciled.[50] Any proceedings brought in the United Kingdom by virtue of that rule must be brought in the courts of the part of the United Kingdom in which the trust is domiciled.[51] A trust is domiciled in a part of the United Kingdom if and only if the system of law of that part is the system of law with which the trust has its closest and most real connection.[52]

The Crown

3.22 The seat of the Crown in right of Her Majesty's government in the United Kingdom is treated as its domicile; and, subject to any special provisions made by Order in Council, it has its seat in every part of, and every place in, the United Kingdom.[53] Thus, where an action against the Crown in the sheriff court is competent, it may be sued in any sheriff court in Scotland.

---

[46] 1982 Act, s. 43(2).
[47] *ibid.* s. 43(3), (5).
[48] *ibid.* s. 43(4).
[49] See *Civil Jurisdiction*, paras 5.52–5.58 and 10.34–10.35.
[50] 1982 Act, Sched. 1, Art. 5(6).
[51] *ibid.* s. 10(2); Sched. 4, Art. 5(6).
[52] *ibid.* s. 45(3).
[53] *ibid.* s. 46(1), (3).

Qualifications of the domicile principle

Exclusive jurisdiction

Article 16 of the Convention provides that in certain categories of proceedings the courts of a specified Contracting State shall have exclusive jurisdiction, regardless of domicile. In such cases the prorogation of the jurisdiction of another court is incompetent.[54] Most of the principles embodied in Article 16 are reflected in Schedule 4, Article 16, and in Schedule 8, rule 4. It will therefore be convenient to notice the relevant terms of these Schedules in the following paragraphs. **3.23**

Article 16(1)(a) of the Convention provides that in proceedings which have as their object rights *in rem* in, or tenancies of, immoveable property,[55] the courts of the Contracting State in which the property is situated have exclusive jurisdiction. The 1989 Accession Convention introduced an exception to the exclusive jurisdiction for proceedings which have as their object tenancies of immoveable property concluded for temporary private use for a maximum period of six months. If the landlord and tenant are both natural persons and are domiciled in the same state then the courts of that state have jurisdiction. The pursuer can choose those courts or the courts of the place of the immoveable property. Schedule 4, Article 16, and Schedule 8, rule 4(1)(a), are in identical terms except that the reference to the courts of the Contracting State is replaced in the former by a reference to the courts of the part of the United Kingdom in which the property is situated, and in the latter by a reference to the courts of the place where the property is situated. In Scotland, accordingly, such proceedings may be brought in the Court of Session or in the sheriff court of the place where the property is situated. **3.24**

Article 16(2) of the Convention provides that the courts of a Contracting State in which a company, legal person or association[56] has its seat[57] have exclusive jurisdiction "in proceedings which have as their object the validity of the constitution, the nullity or the dissolution of companies or other legal persons or associations of natural or legal persons, or the decisions of their organs." Schedule 4, Article 16, and Schedule 8, rule 4(1)(b) make substitutions similar to those already noted for the reference to the courts of the Contracting State, and omit the reference to **3.25**

---

[54] 1982 Act, Sched. 1, Art. 17.

[55] See *Civil Jurisdiction*, paras 7.07–7.11, 10.64–10.66 which includes the salient points from *Barratt International Resorts Ltd v. Martin*, 1994 S.L.T. 434. In Case C-294/92, *Webb v. Webb* [1994] ECR I-1717, 1996 S.L.T. (News) A1–A2, the European Court held that: "An action for a declaration that a person holds immoveable property as trustee and for an order requiring that person to execute such documents as should be required to vest the legal ownership in the plaintiff does not constitute an action *in rem* within the meaning of Article 16(1) of the Convention." The case has been noted by Beaumont (1995) 44 I.C.L.Q. 219; Briggs (1994) L.Q.R. 526 and (1995) Y.Eur.L. 563; and Rogerson (1994) 53 C.L.J. 462. The scope of rights *in rem* was further clarified by the European Court in Case C-292/93, *Lieber v. Gobel* [1994] ECR I-2535: "A claim for compensation for use of a dwelling after the annulment of a transfer of ownership is not included in the matters governed by Article 16(1) of the Convention." Noted by Briggs (1994) Y.Eur.L. 572. In *Jarrett v. Barclays Bank* [1997] I.L.Pr. 531, the English Court of Appeal decided that a timeshare should be treated as a tenancy for the purposes of Art. 16(1) rather than a right *in rem*.

[56] See *Civil Jurisdiction*, paras 7.12–7.17, 10.46, 10.47, 10.67–10.69.

[57] The rules for determining the seat of the entity for the purposes of art. 16(2) and the related provisions have already been noted: see para. 3.19.

"the decisions of their organs". Thus, in Scotland the Court of Session and the sheriff court of the place where the entity has its seat have exclusive jurisdiction in the proceedings to which rule 4(1)(b) applies. Proceedings which have the decisions of the organs of an entity as their object may be brought in the courts of the part of the United Kingdom in which the entity has its seat[58] or, in Scotland, in the court for the place where it has its seat[59]; but none of these courts has exclusive jurisdiction in such proceedings. The reference in the Convention and Schedule 4 to proceedings which have as their object the dissolution of companies or other legal persons or associations does not include proceedings relating to the winding up of insolvent bodies, which are excluded from the Convention by Article 1(2), and thus from Schedule 4.[60] Schedule 5 excludes from Schedule 4 proceedings for the winding up of a company under the Companies Act 1985 [61]; and Schedule 9 excludes from Schedule 8 proceedings in respect of the winding up of a company or other legal person, and proceedings relating to a company where, by any enactment, jurisdiction in respect of those proceedings is conferred on the court having jurisdiction to wind it up.[62]

3.26 Article 16(3) of the Convention provides that in proceedings which have as their object the validity of entries in public registers,[63] the courts of the Contracting State in which the register is kept have exclusive jurisdiction. Article 16 of Schedule 4 provides that in such proceedings the courts of the part of the United Kingdom in which the register is kept are to have exclusive jurisdiction. In Schedule 8, rule 4(1)(c) provides that the courts for the place where the register is kept are to have exclusive jurisdiction. Thus, the Court of Session and the sheriff court of that place will have concurrent jurisdiction. The jurisdiction of the Court of Session in proceedings concerning the validity of entries in registers of patents, trade marks, designs or other similar rights is preserved.[64]

3.27 Article 16(4) of the Convention provides that in proceedings concerned with the registration or validity of patents, trade marks, designs, or other similar rights[65] required to be deposited or registered, exclusive jurisdiction is conferred on the courts of the Contracting State in which the deposit or registration has been applied for, has taken place or is under the terms of an international convention deemed to have taken place. There is no equivalent provision in Schedule 4. In Schedule 8 it is provided that the Court of Session, but not the sheriff court, has a non-exclusive jurisdiction in proceedings principally concerned with the registration in the United Kingdom or the validity in the United Kingdom of patents, trade marks, designs or other similar rights required to be deposited or registered.[66]

---

[58] 1982 Act, Sched. 4, Art. 5A.
[59] *ibid.* Sched. 8, r. 2(12).
[60] *ibid.* s. 16(1)(a).
[61] *ibid.* Sched. 5, para. 1, as amended by the Companies Act 1985, Sched. 2.
[62] *ibid.* Sched. 9, para. 4. See *infra*, para. 3.81.
[63] 1982 Act, Sched. 8, r. 4(2).
[64] See *Civil Jurisdiction*, paras 7.19–7.21, 9.26, 10.51. See *Chiron Corp. v. Evans Medical Ltd* [1996] F.S.R. 863 and *Coin Controls Ltd v. Suzo International (U.K.) Ltd*, judgment of Laddie J. on Mar. 26, 1997.
[65] 1982 Act, Sched. 8, r. 2(14).
[66] *Civil Jurisdiction*, para. 12.11.

Article 16(5) of the Convention provides that in proceedings concerned with the enforcement of judgments,[67] the courts of the Contracting State in which the judgment has been or is to be enforced have exclusive jurisdiction. Article 16 of Schedule 4 substitutes for the reference to the courts of the Contracting State a reference to the courts of the part of the United Kingdom in which the judgment has been or is to be enforced, and rule 4(1)(d) of Schedule 8 substitutes a reference to the courts for the place where the judgment has been or is to be enforced. **3.28**

Concurrent jurisdictions

The general principle that the courts of the domicile of the defender have jurisdiction is supplemented by provisions whereby in certain categories of proceedings concurrent jurisdiction is conferred on courts other than those of the defender's domicile. **3.29**

Article 5(1) of the Convention provides that a person domiciled in a Contracting State may, in another Contracting State, be sued in matters relating to a contract,[68] in the courts for the place of performance of the obligation in question.[69] The 1989 Accession Convention added a particular provision concerning individual contracts of employment.[70] It also created a new contract jurisdiction in Article 6(4) of the Convention whereby a contract action may be combined with an action against the same defendant in matters relating to rights *in rem* in immoveable property, in the court of the Contracting State in which the property is situated.[71] **3.30**

Article 5(2) of the Convention provides that a person domiciled in a Contracting State may, in another Contracting State, be sued in matters relating to maintenance,[72] in the courts for the place where the maintenance creditor is domiciled or habitually resident or, if the matter is ancillary to proceedings concerning the status of a person, in the court which, according to its own law, has jurisdiction to entertain those proceedings, unless that jurisdiction is based on the nationality of one of the parties.[73] **3.31**

The European Court has decided that the term "maintenance creditor" covers any person applying for maintenance, including a person bringing a maintenance action for the first time.[74] The vexed dividing line between a maintenance order (within the scope of the Convention) and a decision relating to rights in property arising out of a matrimonial relationship **3.32**

---

[67] *Civil Jurisdiction*. paras 7.22, 10.72.

[68] *ibid.*, paras 5.17–5.28, 10.21–10.23.

[69] Discussed *infra*, para. 3.92.

[70] See para. 5.22 of *Civil Jurisdiction* and *infra*, para. 3.92.

[71] See para. 5.73 of *Civil Jurisdiction*.

[72] See *Civil Jurisdiction*, paras 5.29–5.37, 10.29–10.31.

[73] The meaning of "habitual residence" has not been adjudicated upon by the European Court. Some Contracting States are advocating that domicile in Art. 2 may be replaced by "habitual residence" in the revision of the Brussels and Lugano Conventions which commenced in 1997. Habitual residence is a key concept in the Hague Child Abduction Convention which has now been analysed in numerous cases. Reference is made here to only two of the most recent and authoritative cases and an up-to-date and authoritative systematic article: *Cameron, Petr*, 1996 S.C.L.R. 25; *Re S (A Minor) (Custody: Habitual Residence)* [1997] 3 W.L.R. 597 (H.L.); and Clive, "The Concept of Habitual Residence", 1997 J.R. 137.

[74] See Case C-295/95, *Farrell v. Long* [1997] 3 W.L.R. 613.

(outwith the scope of the Convention) was discussed by the European Court in the recent *van den Boogaard* case.[75] In a divorce case if "the provision awarded is designed to enable one spouse to provide for himself or herself or if the needs and resources of each of the spouses are taken into consideration in the determination of its amount, the decision will be concerned with maintenance. On the other hand, where the provision awarded is solely concerned with dividing property between the spouses, the decision will be concerned with rights in property arising out of a matrimonial relationship".[76] This distinction is not likely to be of great importance at the jurisdiction stage but can be very significant if a spouse wishes to rely on the Brussels or Lugano Conventions to get the financial orders arising from a Scottish divorce enforced in another Contracting State. The test is rather subjective as it refers to the "aim" of the award. In *van den Boogaard* the European Court accepted that the English court's ordering of a lump sum and transfer of ownership of certain items of property in divorce proceedings was a matter of maintenance within the scope of the Convention. In Scotland it seems likely that orders under section 9(1)(c),(d) and (e) of the Family Law (Scotland) Act 1985 would be regarded as maintenance. It is less clearcut how the other principles in section 9, which seem to be a division of matrimonial property, would be viewed bearing in mind that the courts have a discretion under section 8(2) to modify the amount arrived at, using the section 9 principles, by what is reasonable having regard to the resources of the parties.[77]

3.33 Article 5(3) of the Convention provides that a person domiciled in a Contracting State may, in another Contracting State, be sued "in matters relating to tort, delict or quasi-delict,[78] in the courts for the place where the harmful event occurred."[79]

3.34 Article 5(4) of the Convention provides that a person domiciled in a Contracting State may, in another Contracting State, be sued as regards a civil claim for damages or restitution which is based on an act giving rise to criminal proceedings,[80] in the court seised of those proceedings, to the extent that that court has jurisdiction under its own law to entertain civil proceedings. It seems that this provision has very limited jurisdictional implications for the Scottish courts. Compensation orders made under sections 249 to 253 of the Criminal Procedure (Scotland) Act 1995 do not appear to be made by criminal courts in the exercise of a civil jurisdiction.[81] At a trial for an offence under section 7 of the Sea Fisheries (Scotland) Amendment Act 1885 the sheriff may be called upon to consider and dispose of the question of compensation to the injured party and, having considered the evidence led at the trial and any additional evidence, may give decree as in an ordinary action[82]; but this procedure is thought to be seldom invoked.

---

[75] Case C-220/95, *Van den Boogaard v Laumen* [1997] 3 W.L.R. 284.
[76] *ibid.* at para. 22.
[77] See Thomson, *Family Law in Scotland* (3rd ed., Butterworths, 1996), pp.120–149 for the details on financial provision on divorce.
[78] See *Civil Jurisdiction*, paras 5.38–5.42, 9.18, 10.24 and 10.25.
[79] Discussed at para. 3.93.
[80] See *Civil Jurisdiction*, paras 5.43–5.45, 10.26–10.28.
[81] Previously ss. 58 to 67 of the Criminal Justice (Scotland) Act 1980.
[82] Sea Fisheries (Scotland) Amendment Act 1885, s. 8, as amended.

Article 5(5) of the Convention provides that a person domiciled in a Contracting State may, in another Contracting State, be sued as regards a dispute arising out of the operations of a branch, agency or other establishment,[83] in the courts for the place in which the branch, agency or other establishment is situated. The undertakings entered into by the branch do not need to be performed in the State in which the branch is established.[84] **3.35**

The provisions of the Convention and of Schedule 4 as to trusts, and the provisions of the Act as to the domicile of a trust, have already been noted.[85] **3.36**

Articles 5(7) of the Convention and of Schedule 4 apply to disputes concerning the payment of remuneration claimed in respect of the salvage of a cargo or freight (not of a vessel) in which it is claimed that the defender has an interest in the cargo or freight or had such an interest at the time of salvage.[86] Under the Convention a person domiciled in a Contracting State may, in another Contracting State, be sued as regards such a dispute in the court under the authority of which the cargo or freight in question (a) has been arrested to secure such payment, or (b) could have been arrested but bail or other security has been given. Article 6A of the Convention provides that where by virtue of the Convention a court of a Contracting State has jurisdiction in actions relating to liability arising from the use or operation of a ship, that court, or any other court substituted for this purpose by the internal law of that state, also has jurisdiction over claims for limitation of such liability. **3.37**

Procedural provisions

(1) Plurality of defenders.[87] The object of this and the two following sets of provisions is to secure that all relevant issues may be determined at the same time by the same court. Article 6(1) of the Convention provides that a person domiciled in a Contracting State may also be sued, where he is one of a number of defenders, in the courts for the place where any one of them is domiciled.[88] Article 6(1) of Schedule 4 similarly applies where a person domiciled in one part of the United Kingdom is sued in the courts of another part. Rule 2(15)(a) of Schedule 8 is also derived from Article 6(1) of the Convention: a person may be sued, where he is one of a number of defenders, in the courts for the place where any one of them is domiciled. This provision effects an alteration of the sheriff court rule that jurisdiction may be exercised over a co-defender over whom the sheriff court does not have jurisdiction, only where he is subject to the jurisdiction of another sheriff court.[89] Under rule 2(15)(a), where in an action competent in the sheriff court the sheriff has jurisdiction over one of a plurality of defenders on the ground of domicile, he has jurisdiction over all the others. **3.38**

---

[83] See *Civil Jurisdiction*, paras 5.46–5.51, 10.32 and 10.33.

[84] See Case C-439/93, *Lloyd's Register of Shipping* [1995] E.C.R. I-961, noted by Briggs (1995) Y.Eur.L. 496 and Hartley (1996) Eur.L.R. 162.

[85] para. 3.21.

[86] See *Civil Jurisdiction*, paras 5.59–5.60, 5.74, 9.21.

[87] *ibid.* paras. 5.62–5.66, 9.20 and 10.53.

[88] On the operation of Art. 6(1), where there has been a prorogation agreement, see *Civil Jurisdiction*, para. 5.65.

[89] 1907 Act, s. 6(a).

3.39 **(2) Third-party proceedings.**[90] Article 6(2) of the Convention provides that a person domiciled in a Contracting State may also be sued as a third party in an action on a warranty or guarantee or in any other third party proceedings, in the court seised of the original proceedings, unless these were instituted solely with the object of removing him from the jurisdiction of the court which would be competent in his case. Article 6(2) of Schedule 4 and rule 2(15)(b) of Schedule 8 are similarly worded. The jurisdiction of the Scottish courts is thus very considerably extended. Except in collusive actions raised with the object of bringing in a third party over whom the court would not otherwise have jurisdiction, the sheriff court has jurisdiction over the third party if it has jurisdiction on any ground over the defender: no reference is made to the domicile of any party to the action. The procedural rules relative to third parties are considered elsewhere.[91]

3.40 **(3) Counterclaims.**[92] Article 6(3) of the Convention provides that a person domiciled in a Contracting State may also be sued "on a counter claim arising from the same contract or facts on which the original claim was based, in the court in which the original claim is pending". The European Court has decided that this provision applies only to claims by defenders which seek the pronouncement of a separate judgment or decree, not to situations where the defender raises, as a pure defence, a claim which he or she allegedly has against the pursuer.[93]

Insurance[94]

3.41 The general ground of jurisdiction set out in Article 2, domicile of the defender, and the various concurrent grounds of special jurisdiction in Articles 5, 6 and 6A, with the exception of the branch, agency or establishment jurisdiction in Article 5(5), are not applicable to jurisdiction in matters relating to insurance. Instead a closed body of jurisdiction rules for matters relating to insurance is provided in Section 3 of the Convention (Articles 7 to 12A). The rationale of these rules is that the policy-holder or consumer lacks bargaining power and should be assisted by limits being set to the places where he may be sued and extensions to the places where he may sue.[95] Section 3 of the Convention, which contains the rules relative to insurance, has been described as "a complex body of rules with several unsatisfactory features".[96] Its provisions have not been incorporated into Schedule 4 or Schedule 8. Thus, jurisdiction in insurance cases is allocated among the courts of the parts of the United Kingdom in accordance with the general provisions of Schedule 4; and in Scotland jurisdiction in such cases is regulated by the normal grounds of jurisdiction of the Scottish courts, as set out in Schedule 8.

3.42 Many of the provisions of the Convention concerning jurisdiction against insurers apply to an insurer who is domiciled or deemed to be domiciled in a Contracting State. An insurer who is not domiciled in a

---

90 See *Civil Jurisdiction*, paras 5.67–5.71, 9.20 and 10.54.

91 paras 12.42 to 12.65.

92 See *Civil Jurisdiction*, paras 5.72, 9.20, 10.55, 10.56; Maxwell Report, para. 5.90.

93 See Case C-341/93, *Danvaern Production v. Schufabriken Otterbeck* [1995] E.C.R. I-2053, noted by Briggs (1995) Y.Eur.L. 498 and Hartley (1996) Eur.L.R. 166.

94 See *Civil Jurisdiction*, paras 6.01–6.24; Maxwell Report, paras 5.92–5.125.

95 See *Civil Jurisdiction*, para. 6.01.

96 *ibid.* para. 6.02.

Contracting State but has a branch, agency or other establishment in one of the Contracting States is deemed to be domiciled in that State in disputes arising out of the operation of the branch, agency or establishment. The provisions may be summarised as follows.

(1) An insurer domiciled or deemed to be domiciled in a Contracting State may be sued in the courts of the State where he is domiciled.[97] Thus, an insurer actually, or deemed to be, domiciled in the United Kingdom may be sued in Scotland in any court having jurisdiction under the general rules of Scots law.

(2) An insurer domiciled or deemed to be domiciled in a Contracting State may be sued in another Contracting State, in the courts for the place where the policyholder is domiciled.[98] Thus, a policyholder domiciled in Scotland may sue, in the courts for the place where he is domiciled, an insurer actually, or deemed to be, domiciled in another Contracting State.

(3) An insurer domiciled or deemed to be domiciled in Scotland may be sued, if he is a co-insurer, in the courts of a Contracting State in which proceedings are brought against the leading insurer.[99] Thus, where the leading insurer is being sued in Scotland, the co-insurer may be sued in the court where the leading insurer is being sued.

(4) In respect of insurance of immoveable property, an insurer who is actually or deemed to be domiciled in a Contracting State may in addition be sued in the courts for the place where the harmful event occurred. The same applies if moveable and immoveable property are covered by the same insurance policy and both are adversely affected by the same contingency.[1] Thus, an insurer actually or deemed to be domiciled in another Contracting State may be sued in Scotland, where the harmful event occurred in Scotland, in the courts for the place where it occurred.

(5) In respect of liability insurance, similarly, an insurer actually or deemed to be domiciled in a Contracting State may be sued in the courts for the place where the harmful event occurred.[2] He may also, if the law of the court permits it, be joined in proceedings which the injured party has brought against the insured.[3] Thus, an insurer actually or deemed to be domiciled in another Contracting State may in respect of liability insurance be sued in Scotland, where the harmful event occurred in Scotland, in the courts for the place where it occurred; or, where the injured party has brought proceedings against the insured in Scotland, in the court dealing with these proceedings.

(6) An insurer who is actually domiciled in another Contracting State but who has a branch, agency or other establishment in Scotland may be sued, as regards a dispute arising out of its operations, in the courts of the place in which it is situated.[4]

---

[97] 1982 Act, Sched. 1, Art. 8.
[98] *ibid.*
[99] *ibid.*
[1] *ibid.* Art. 9.
[2] *ibid.*
[3] *ibid.* Art. 10.
[4] *ibid.* Arts 5(5), 7.

3.43 An insurer may bring proceedings only in the courts of the Contracting State in which the defender is domiciled, irrespective of whether he is the policyholder, the insured or a beneficiary. Where, however, an insurer is being sued, he may bring a counterclaim in the court in which the action against him is proceeding.[5]

3.44 The rules mentioned in the two preceding paragraphs may be departed from by a reference to arbitration,[6] or by an agreement on jurisdiction under Article 12. Such an agreement (1) must be entered into after the dispute has arisen; or (2) must allow the policyholder, the insured or the beneficiary to bring proceedings in courts other than those indicated in Articles 8 to 11; or (3) must be concluded between a policyholder and an insurer both of whom are at the time of conclusion of the contract domiciled or habitually resident in the same Contracting State, and must have the effect of conferring jurisdiction on the courts of that state even if the harmful event were to occur abroad, provided that such an agreement is not contrary to the law of that State; or (4) must be concluded with a policyholder who is not domiciled in a Contracting State, except in so far as the insurance is compulsory or relates to immoveable property in a Contracting State; or (5) must relate to a contract of insurance in so far as it covers one or more of the risks set out in Article 12A.[7] Article 12A sets out certain risks in contracts of marine or aviation insurance, including loss or damage (other than bodily injury to passengers) caused by, or caused to, sea-going ships, offshore installations or aircraft, or loss of or damage to goods (other than passengers' baggage) in transit on such ships or aircraft.

3.45 The rules mentioned above do not apply where an insurer is not actually domiciled, or deemed to be domiciled, in the United Kingdom or another Contracting State, or where a defender in an action brought by an insurer is not domiciled in the United Kingdom or another Contracting State. In such cases the Convention has no application, and jurisdiction is determined by the law of the state in which the action is brought.[8]

Consumer contracts

3.46 As with matters relating to insurance, consumer contracts are given their own uniquely applicable set of rules. These are set out in Section 4 of the Convention, Articles 13–15, and they preserve the application of the branch, agency and establishment jurisdiction in Article 5(5). In the Convention,[9] a consumer contract is defined as a contract concluded by a person (called "the consumer") "for a purpose which can be regarded as being outside his trade or profession" which is (1) a contract for the sale of goods on instalment credit terms; or (2) a contract for a loan repayable by instalments, or for any other form of credit, made to finance the sale of goods; or (3) any other contract for the supply of goods or a contract for the supply of services and (a) in the state of the consumer's domicile the conclusion of the contract was preceded by a specific invitation addressed to him or by advertising, and (b) the consumer took in that state the steps

---

[5] 1982 Act, Sched. 1, Art. 11.
[6] *ibid.* Art. 1.
[7] *ibid.* Art. 12.
[8] *ibid.* Arts. 4, 7.
[9] See *Civil Jurisdiction*, paras 6.25–6.33.

necessary for the conclusion of the contract.[10] The rule does not apply to contracts of transport[11] or insurance.[12] It is intended that the consumer shall be the purchaser in case (1), the borrower in case (2), and the person supplied in case (3), but there is no specific statement to that effect.[13]

The consumer is assisted by being enabled to sue in several places, while the places where he may be sued are restricted. He may bring proceedings against the other party to the contract if he is domiciled in a Contracting State in the courts of that state, or in the courts of the Contracting State in which the consumer is domiciled (Article 14), or in a dispute arising out of the operations of a branch, agency or establishment in the courts for the place where the establishment is situated (Article 5(5) as preserved by Article 13). If the other party is not domiciled in a Contracting State, but has a branch, agency or other establishment in one of the Contracting States, and the dispute arises out of the operations of the establishment, that person is deemed to be domiciled in that state and the consumer is then free to bring the proceedings there or in the courts of his or her own domicile.[14] However, if the defender is not domiciled in a Contracting State and does not have a branch, agency or establishment in a Contracting State then Article 4 is applicable and the law of the Contracting State in which proceedings are brought governs: in Scotland the rules set out in Schedules 4 or 8 to the 1982 Act, as appropriate.[15] Proceedings may be brought against the consumer only in the courts of the Contracting State in which the consumer is domiciled. The other party may, however, bring a counterclaim against the consumer in the court in which the original claim is pending.[16] **3.47**

The foregoing provisions may be departed from only by an agreement (1) which is entered into after the dispute has arisen; or (2) which allows the consumer to bring proceedings in courts other than those indicated above; or (3) which is entered into by the consumer and the other party to the contract, both of whom are at the time of the conclusion of the contract domiciled or habitually resident in the same Contracting State, and which confers jurisdiction on the courts of that state, provided that such an agreement is not contrary to the law of that state.[17] **3.48**

In Schedule 4,[18] Article 13 omits from the definition of consumer contract provision 3(a) above and explicitly excludes contracts of insurance as well as contracts of transport. It also omits the provision as to the other party's deemed domicile. Articles 14 and 15 substitute references to the courts of a part of the United Kingdom for references to the courts of a Contracting State. Section 10(3) of the Act further provides that any **3.49**

---

[10] 1982 Act, Sched. 1, Art. 13. In Case C-269/95, *Benincasa v. Dentalkit Srl* [1997] I.L.Pr. 343, judgment of July 3, 1997, the European Court held that a pursuer "who has concluded a contract with a view to pursuing a trade or profession, not at the present time but in the future, may not be regarded as a consumer."

[11] 1982 Act, Sched. 1, Art. 14.

[12] See *Civil Jurisdiction*, para. 6.25.

[13] Maxwell Report, para. 5.128.

[14] 1982 Act, Sched. 1, Art. 14 read in conjunction with the second para. of Art. 13.

[15] *ibid.* Art. 5(5). See Case C-318/93, *Brenner and Noller v. Dean Witter Reynolds* [1994] E.C.R. I-4275, noted by Briggs (1994) Y.Eur.L. 578.

[16] 1982 Act, Sched. 1, Art. 14.

[17] *ibid.* Art. 15.

[18] See *Civil Jurisdiction*, paras 9.23–9.25.

proceedings with respect to consumer contracts which are brought in the United Kingdom by a consumer on the ground that he is himself domiciled there must be brought in the courts of the part of the United Kingdom in which he is domiciled.

3.50 In Schedule 8, rule 3[19] states the rules as to jurisdiction in Scotland in proceedings concerning a consumer contract. Its terms are broadly similar to those of Articles 13, 14 and 15 of Schedule 4. Where it departs from the rules in Articles 13, 14 and 15 of the Convention, the latter rules must be applied in relation to a person domiciled in another Contracting State.[20] In the definition of "consumer contract" there are substituted for sub-paragraphs (a) and (b) of provision 3 the condition that (i) the consumer took in Scotland the steps necessary for the conclusion of the contract; or (ii) proceedings are brought in Scotland by virtue of section 10(3) of the Act, that is, on the ground that the consumer is domiciled in Scotland. The consumer may bring proceedings against the other party only in (i) the courts for the place in which that party is domiciled; or (ii) the courts for the place in which he is himself domiciled; or (iii) any court having jurisdiction by virtue of rule 2(6) or (9) of Schedule 8. Rule 2(6) confers jurisdiction as regards a dispute arising out of the operations of a branch, agency or other establishment, on the courts of the place in which the establishment is situated. Rule 2(9) confers jurisdiction in certain proceedings in respect of moveable property on the courts for the place where the property is situated.[21] Proceedings may be brought against the consumer by the other party only in the courts for the place where the consumer is domiciled or any court having jurisdiction under rule 2(9). The references to rule 2(9) are thought to be inapplicable in relation to a defender domiciled in a Contracting State other than the United Kingdom.[22] The other party may bring a counterclaim in the court in which the original claim is pending. Rule 3(6) states that the provisions of rule 3 may be departed from only by an agreement (i) which is entered into after the dispute has arisen, or (ii) which allows the consumer to bring proceedings in a court other than a court indicated in rule 3.

Prorogation and submission

3.51 General rules[23] regarding prorogation of, and submission to, jurisdiction are contained in Articles 17 and 18 of the Convention. Article 17[24] provides that if the parties, one or more of whom is domiciled in a Contracting State, have agreed that a court or the courts of a Contracting State are to have jurisdiction to settle any disputes which have arisen or which may arise in connection with a particular legal relationship, that court or those courts have exclusive jurisdiction. Such an agreement

---

[19] See *Civil Jurisdiction*, paras 10.58–10.61.

[20] *ibid.*, para. 10.59.

[21] See para. 3.103.

[22] See *Civil Jurisdiction*, para. 10.59.

[23] Specific provision is made for prorogation agreements in insurance and consumer contracts: see paras 3.44, 3.45, and 3.48 to 3.50.

[24] For detailed comment on this complex provision, see *Civil Jurisdiction*, paras 7.23–7.27. In Case C-269/95 *Benincasa v Dentalkit Srl* [1997] I.L.Pr. 343, judgment of July 3, 1997, the European Court has held that: "The courts of a Contracting State which have been designated in a jurisdiction clause validly concluded under the first paragraph of Article 17 . . . also have exclusive jurisdiction where the action seeks in particular a declaration that the contract containing the clause is void." Article 17 was discussed by Lord Sutherland in *Barratt International Resorts Ltd v. Martin*, 1994 S.L.T. 434.

conferring jurisdiction must be either in writing or evidenced in writing or, in a form which accords with practices which the parties have established between themselves, or in international trade or commerce, in a form which accords with a usage of which the parties are or ought to have been aware and which in such trade or commerce is widely known to, and regularly observed by, parties to contracts of the type involved in the particular trade or commerce concerned.[25] Where such an agreement is concluded by parties, none of whom is domiciled in a Contracting State, the courts of the other Contracting States have no jurisdiction over their disputes unless the court or courts chosen have declined jurisdiction. The court or courts of a Contracting State on which a trust instrument has conferred jurisdiction have exclusive jurisdiction in any proceedings brought against a settlor, trustee or beneficiary, if relations between these persons or their rights or obligations under the trust are involved. Agreements or provisions of a trust instrument conferring jurisdiction have no legal force if they are contrary to the provisions of Articles 12 or 15 (which relate to prorogation in insurance and consumer contracts), or if the courts whose jurisdiction they purport to exclude have exclusive jurisdiction by virtue of Article 16.[26] The penultimate paragraph of Article 17 is an obscure provision which is not repeated in Schedules 4 and 8, to the effect that if an agreement conferring jurisdiction was concluded for the benefit of only one of the parties, that party retains the right to bring proceedings in any other court which has jurisdiction by virtue of the Convention.[27] The 1989 Accession Convention added a new paragraph at the end of Article 17 whereby in individual contracts of employment prorogation agreements are valid only if agreed after the dispute has arisen or if the employee can use it to seise a court other than that of the employer's domicile.

In Schedule 4, Article 17[28] not only refers to a part of the United Kingdom instead of to a Contracting State, but differs from Article 17 of the Convention in other respects. It does not provide that the prorogation agreement confers an exclusive jurisdiction, it makes no reference to the form of the agreement, and the reference to Article 12 is deleted. **3.52**

In Schedule 8, rule 5[29] closely follows Article 17 of the Brussels Convention. Rule 5(1) states that if the parties have agreed that a court **3.53**

---

[25] The wording of Art. 17 was amended by the 1978 and 1989 Accession Conventions. The wording in the text refers to the latter version which is now in force in all the Contracting States to the Brussels Convention. In any case the European Court has construed the wording of the 1978 Accession Convention in a way broadly consistent with the wording of the 1989 Acccssion Convention: see Case C-106/95, *Mainschiffahrts-Genossenschaft v. Les Gravieres Rhenanes* [1997] I.L.Pr. 411. For a recent decision on what constitutes agreement in writing, see *Crédit Suisse Financial Products v. Société Générale d'Entreprises* [1997] I.L.Pr. 165 (CA).

[26] On Art. 16, see paras 3.23 to 3.28.

[27] The U.K. Government is seeking its removal in the negotiations for the revision of the Brussels and Lugano Conventions which commenced in 1997.

[28] See *Civil Jurisdiction*, para. 9.27. Notwithstanding the lack of reference to "exclusive" jurisdiction in Sched. 4, Art. 17, it seems correct to take the view that if the prorogation clause purports to give jurisdiction to the courts of only one part of the United Kingdom, to the exclusion of any other courts, then the courts of that part have exclusive jurisdiction: see *Jenic Properties Ltd v. Andy Thornton Architectural Antiques*, 1992 S.L.T. (Sh. Ct.) 5 and *McCarthy v. Abowall (Trading) Ltd*, 1992 S.L.T. (Sh. Ct.) 65. If parties wish to create an exclusive jurisdiction then they should be careful to use unambiguous language because otherwise there is a significant risk that the courts will construe it as a non-exclusive jurisdiction clause: see *Morrison v. Panic Link*, 1994 S.L.T. 232.

[29] *Civil Jurisdiction*, paras 10.73–10.79.

is to have jurisdiction to settle any disputes which have arisen or which may arise in connection with a particular legal relationship, that court is to have exclusive jurisdiction. Rule 5(2) makes provision as to the form of such an agreement: it must be either in writing or evidenced in writing or, in trade or commerce, in a form which accords with practices in that trade or commerce of which the parties are or ought to have been aware.[30] Rule 5(3) confers an exclusive jurisdiction on a court upon which a trust instrument has conferred jurisdiction in any proceedings brought against a settlor, trustee or beneficiary, if relations between these persons or their rights or obligations under the trust are involved. In terms of rule 5(5) an agreement or provision of a trust instrument conferring jurisdiction which purports to exclude an exclusive jurisdiction is invalid. Rule 5(4), which has no counterpart in Article 17 of the Brussels Convention, further provides that where an agreement or trust instrument confers jurisdiction on the courts of the United Kingdom or of Scotland, proceedings may be brought in any court in Scotland. The court may, however, decline jurisdiction on the ground of *forum non conveniens*.[31] Rule 5(6) follows the text of the last paragraph of Article 17 as inserted by the 1989 Accession Convention in matters relating to individual contracts of employment.

3.54 Article 18 of the Brussels Convention[32] provides that a court of a Contracting State before whom a defender enters appearance shall have jurisdiction; but that rule does not apply where appearance was entered solely to contest the jurisdiction, or where another court has exclusive jurisdiction by virtue of Article 16. Similarly, Article 18 of Schedule 4 provides that, subject to the same qualifications, a court of a part of the United Kingdom before which a defender enters an appearance shall have jurisdiction. Rule 6 of Schedule 8 likewise follows Article 18 of the Convention: it provides that apart from jurisdiction derived from other provisions of Schedule 8, a court before whom a defender enters appearance shall have jurisdiction; but that this rule does not apply where appearance was entered solely to contest jurisdiction, or where another court has exclusive jurisdiction by virtue of rule 4 of Schedule 8, or where rule 4(3) applies.[33] The lodging of a notice of intention to defend does not imply acceptance of the jurisdiction of the court.[34]

Declinature of jurisdiction

3.55 Article 19 of the Convention provides that where a court of a Contracting State is seised of a claim which is principally concerned with a

---

[30] Although this wording is derived from the 1978 Accession Convention version of the Brussels Convention, it is clear from Case C-106/95, *supra*, n. 25, that the European Court construes the trade or commerce exception to the need for writing in a way that is broadly consistent with the version of Art. 17 as amended by the 1989 Accession Convention noted in para. 3.51.

[31] 1982 Act, s. 22(1).

[32] See *Civil Jurisdiction*, paras 7.28, 9.28, and 10.80. Despite the use of the word "solely" in the English version of Art. 18 it is clear that a defender can contest the merits as well as the jurisdiction without submitting to the jurisdiction of the court, provided the defences on jurisdiction are lodged before or at the same time as the defences on the merits: see Case 150/80, *Elefanten Schuh v. Jacqmain* [1981] E.C.R. 1671. The U.K. Government is seeking to have the word "solely" omitted from Art. 18 in the revision conference for the Brussels and Lugano Conventions which commenced in 1997.

[33] On Sched. 8, r. 4, see paras 3.24 to 3.26, 3.28 and 3.111.

[34] OCR, r. 9.1(2); see also SCR, r. 51. *Cf. Thorburn v. Dempster* (1900) 2 F. 583. See paras 9.108, 9.119.

matter over which the courts of another Contracting State have exclusive jurisdiction by virtue of Article 16, it must declare of its own motion that it has no jurisdiction.[35] In Schedule 4, Article 19 places a similar duty on a court of a part of the United Kingdom in relation to a matter over which the courts of another part have exclusive jurisdiction, and in Schedule 8, rule 7 is in similar terms. A further series of rules is based on Article 20 of the Convention, which provides that where a defender domiciled in one Contracting State is sued in a court of another Contracting State and does not enter an appearance, the court must declare of its own motion that it has no jurisdiction unless its jurisdiction is derived from the provisions of the Convention. Article 20 of Schedule 4 requires a court of a part of the United Kingdom to make a similar declaration where a defender domiciled in another part of the United Kingdom is sued before it and does not enter an appearance. In Schedule 8, rule 8 enacts a novel principle in Scots law by providing that where in any case a court has no jurisdiction which is compatible with the 1982 Act, and the defender does not enter an appearance, the court must declare of its own motion that it has no jurisdiction.

There are two sets of rules relative to the verification by the court of origin, in cases where a defender domiciled in another Contracting State has not entered appearance, of the fact that he was duly served with the proceedings.[36] The question of which set of rules applies depends on whether the defender is domiciled in a Contracting State which is a party to the Hague Convention of November 15, 1965 on the Service Abroad of Judicial and Extrajudicial Documents in Civil or Commercial Matters.[37] Most of the Contracting States are parties to the Hague Convention.[38] If the defender is domiciled in one of these states, Article 15 of the Hague Convention applies. It provides that where a writ of summons or equivalent document had to be transmitted abroad for service and the defender has not appeared, judgment may not be given until it is established that (a) the document was served by a method prescribed by the internal law of the state addressed for the service of documents in domestic actions upon persons who are within its territory, or (b) the document was actually delivered to the defender or to his residence by another method provided for by the Hague Convention. That Convention further provides that each Contracting State is free to declare, and the United Kingdom has in fact declared, that the judge, notwithstanding the foregoing provisions, may give judgment even if no certificate of service or delivery has been received, if all the following conditions are fulfilled: (a) the document was transmitted by one of the methods provided for in the Hague Convention, (b) a period of time of not less than six months, considered adequate by the judge in the particular case, has elapsed since the date of the transmission of the document, and (c) no certificate of any kind has been received, even though every reasonable effort has been made to obtain it **3.56**

---

[35] See *Civil Jurisdiction*, paras 7.29, 7.30, 9.29, and 10.81–10.82.

[36] *ibid.* paras 7.31–7.36, 9.30 and 10.83.

[37] The text of the Hague Convention is printed in *Civil Jurisdiction*, pp. 663–670. See Hague Conference on Private International Law, *Practical Handbook on the Operation of the Hague Convention of 15 November 1965 on the Service Abroad of Judicial and Extrajudicial Documents in Civil or Commercial Matters* (Apeldoorn, Antwerp, 1983, with supplements).

[38] The parties to the Hague Convention include Belgium, Denmark, Finland, France, Germany, Greece, Ireland, Italy, Luxembourg, The Netherlands, Norway, Portugal, Spain, Sweden, Switzerland, and the United Kingdom. Austria and Iceland among Lugano Convention Contracting States are not parties to the Hague Convention.

through the competent authorities of the state addressed. Notwithstanding these provisions, the judge may order, in case of urgency, any provisional or protective measures.

3.57 The methods of service provided for by the Hague Convention are as follows:

(1) Service by or through a central authority in the state addressed on the request of an authority in the state of origin.[39] In the United Kingdom the latter authority is the Foreign and Commonwealth Office.
(2) Service through the diplomatic or consular agents of the state of origin.[40]
(3) Postal service, provided that the state of destination does not object.[41]
(4) Service by judicial officers, officials or other competent persons of the state of destination (*e.g. huissiers*) at the request of such officers in the state of origin or of any person interested in the judicial proceedings.

3.58 Where the defender is domiciled in a Contracting State which is not a party to the Hague Convention, or where the defender's address is unknown,[42] the rule laid down by Article 20 of the Brussels Convention applies. It provides that the court must stay the proceedings so long as it is not shown either (1) that the defender has been able to receive the document instituting the proceedings or an equivalent document in sufficient time to enable him to arrange for his defence; or (2) that all necessary steps have been taken to this end. The methods of service which are competent for the purposes of this rule are specified in Article IV of the Annexed Protocol to the Brussels Convention, which makes provision for the service of documents drawn up in one Contracting State which have to be served on persons in another Contracting State. They are to be transmitted in accordance with the procedures laid down in the conventions and agreements concluded between the Contracting States. They may also be sent by the appropriate public officers of the state in which the document has been drawn up directly to the appropriate public officers of the state in which the addressee is to be found. In the sheriff court, the Ordinary and Summary Cause Rules now contain appropriate provisions relative to the citation of, and service of documents on, persons outwith Scotland,[43] and the granting of decree in undefended causes.[44] In 1997 the Convention on the Service in the Member States of the European Union of judicial and extrajudicial documents in civil or commercial matters was opened for signature.[45]

---

[39] Arts 3–7.
[40] Art. 8.
[41] Art. 10.
[42] Art. 1 of the Hague Convention provides that the Convention does not apply where the address of the person to be served with the document is not known.
[43] See paras 6.29 to 6.32, and Vol. 2 of this work; *Civil Jurisdiction*, para. 10.83.
[44] See para. 7.12, and Vol. 2 of this work.
[45] See the Consultation Paper on *The Draft EU Convention on the Service in the Member States of the European Union of Judicial and Extra-Judicial Documents in Civil or Commercial Matters*, Scottish Courts Administration, March 1997.

In Schedule 4, Article 20 contains a rule similar to the rule in Article 20 **3.59** of the Convention as to a defender domiciled in a state which is not a party to the Hague Convention. Thus, in proceedings before a Scottish court in which a defender domiciled in another part of the United Kingdom or in another Contracting State has not entered an appearance, the court must sist the proceedings until it is satisfied that the defender had adequate notice of them or that all necessary steps to that end have been taken.

Articles 21 to 23 of the Convention deal with three situations in which **3.60** proceedings are concurrently in dependence in the courts of different Contracting States[46]. In these situations a court has no general discretion to decline jurisdiction on the ground of *forum non conveniens*, but has only limited powers to decline jurisdiction in the circumstances prescribed by these articles. The first situation arises where proceedings involving the same cause of action and between the same parties are brought in the courts of different Contracting States. Here, any court other than the court first seised must of its own motion decline jurisdiction in favour of that court. If, however, the jurisdiction of the court first seised is contested, the other court may stay its proceedings instead of declining jurisdiction.[47] The European Court has given an extensive application to Article 21 by saying "same cause of action" extends to the situation where one party is bringing a positive action in one court and the other party is bringing a negative declaration in another court, by not regarding the distinction between *in personam* and *in rem* actions as a factor worthy of disapplying Article 21, and by applying the Article to disputes governed by specific Conventions which lack any provision on *lis pendens*, for example the Arrest Convention.[48] The European Court permits the laws of the Contracting States to determine at what time their courts are definitively seised for the purpose of Article 21.[49] This can lead to variations from place to place, encourages a race to the court house and can involve expensive litigation determining what the law of the relevant Contracting State is on the point.[50] It is hoped that the negotiations on the revision of the Brussels and Lugano Conventions which commenced in 1997 will at least lead to an agreement on uniform criteria for determining on which date courts are seised of proceedings. The relationship between Articles 17 and 21 has not yet been clarified by the European Court but there is authority in England and Scotland for the view that the court second seised should not decline to exercise jurisdiction if it is the court given exclusive jurisdiction by the parties in a prorogation agreement which is valid in terms of Article 17.[51]

---

[46] See *Civil Jurisdiction*, paras 7.37–7.42, and 9.31.

[47] 1982 Act, Sched. 1, Art. 21.

[48] See Case C-406/92, *The Tatry* [1994] E.C.R. I-5439. For the application of the European Court's case law in Scotland and England, see *Bank of Scotland v. SA Banque Nationale de Paris*, 1996 S.L.T. 103; *William Grant & Sons International Ltd v. Marie Brizard & Roger International SA*, 1996 S.C.L.R. 987; *Group Torras v. Al-Sabah* [1996] 1 Lloyd's Rep. 7; *Sarrio SA v. Kuwait Investment Authority* [1997] I.L.Pr. 441; *Mecklermedia Corporation v. D.C. Congress GmbH*, judgment of Mar. 7, 1997, *The Times*, 27 March 1997. Further light will be shed on Art. 21 by the European Court in Case C-351/96, *Drouot Assurances SA v. Consolidated Metallurgical Industries (CMI Industrial Sites), GIE Reunion Europeenne and Protea Assurance*.

[49] See Case 129/83, *Zelger v. Salinitri* [1984] E.C.R. 239.

[50] See *Groupo Torras v. Al-Sabah* [1996] 1 Lloyd's Rep. 7.

[51] See *Continental Bank v. Aeakos Compania* [1994] 1 W.L.R. 588 (CA) and *Bank of Scotland v. Banque Nationale de Paris*, 1996 S.L.T. 103.

3.61 In the second situation, governed by Article 22 of the Convention, "related actions" are brought in the courts of different Contracting States. Actions are deemed to be "related" where they are so closely connected that it is expedient to hear and determine them together to avoid the risk of irreconcilable judgments resulting from separate proceedings.[52] In this situation a court other than the court first seised may, while the actions are pending at first instance, stay its proceedings. It may also, on the application of one of the parties, decline jurisdiction if the law of the court first seised permits the consolidation of related actions and that court has jurisdiction over both actions.

3.62 In the third situation, governed by Article 23 of the Convention, actions are raised which come within the exclusive jurisdiction of several courts. Here, any court other than the court first seised must decline jurisdiction in favour of that court.

3.63 In Schedules 4 and 8 there are no rules corresponding to Articles 21 to 23 of the Convention. Thus, where an action has been brought in the sheriff court and proceedings are brought in another Scottish court, or in England or Northern Ireland, or in a state other than a Contracting State, the Scottish principle of *forum non conveniens* will continue to apply in order to determine the course which that sheriff court should follow relative to the action before it.[53]

3.64 The various provisions of Articles 19 to 23 of the Convention relative to the duty of the court to declare that it has no jurisdiction or to decline jurisdiction underlie a number of rules as to pleading and the granting of undefended decrees which have been introduced into the Ordinary and Summary Cause Rules.[54] In ordinary causes, the initial writ must include in the condescendence an article stating the ground of jurisdiction of the court and the facts upon which the ground of jurisdiction is based.[55] The initial writ must also contain averments about any agreement which the pursuer has reason to believe may exist prorogating jurisdiction over the subject-matter of the cause to another court[56]; and about any proceedings which the pursuer has reason to believe may be pending before another court involving the same cause of action and between the same parties as those named in the initial writ.[57] There are analogous provisions in the Summary Cause rules.[58] The Ordinary and Summary Cause Rules further provide, however, that the sheriff must not grant decree in an undefended action unless it

---

[52] In Case C-406/92, *The Tatry* [1994] E.C.R. I-5439, the European Court commented on the application of Art. 22 that it is not necessary that there is a risk that the two proceedings will produce mutually exclusive legal consequences: it is sufficient if there is a risk of conflicting decisions. See also the English Court of Appeal in *Fox v. Taher* [1997] I.L.Pr. 441. For Scottish authority on Art. 22, see *Bank of Scotland v. Banque Nationale de Paris*, 1996 S.L.T. 103 and *William Grant & Sons International Ltd v. Marie Brizard & Roger International SA*, 1996 S.C.L.R. 987.

[53] See *infra*, n. 88. On *forum non conveniens* generally, see Anton with Beaumont, *Private International Law* (2nd ed., 1990), pp. 212–218 and Beaumont, in *Declining Jurisdiction in Private International Law* (Fawcett (ed.)) (Oxford University Press, 1995), pp. 207–220.

[54] See *Civil Jurisdiction*, para. 10.82 and Appendix 3.

[55] OCR, r. 3.1(5).

[56] *ibid.* r. 3.1(3).

[57] *ibid.* r. 3.1(4).

[58] SCR, rr. 2(2),(3),(4); 55(5): see Vol. 2 of this work.

appears *ex facie* of the initial writ that a ground of jurisdiction exists under the 1982 Act.[59]

Provisional and protective measures[60]

The jurisdictional rules of the Convention do not apply to applications for provisional measures. Article 24 provides that application may be made to the courts of a Contracting State for such provisional, including protective, measures as may be available under the law of that state, even if, under the Convention, the courts of another Contracting State have jurisdiction as to the substance of the matter. In Schedule 4, Article 24 makes similar provision with regard to applications relative to the courts of the different parts of the United Kingdom. Sections 27 and 28 of the Act provide a rule for Scotland where proceedings have been commenced, or, where appropriate, are to be commenced, in England and Wales or Northern Ireland or another Contracting State, and their subject-matter is within the scope of the Convention. In the case of such proceedings an application in Scotland for a warrant for arrestment or inhibition on the dependence, or for interim interdict or for an order under section 1 of the Administration of Justice (Scotland) Act 1972 as amended, must be made to the Court of Session, and not to the sheriff court. **3.65**

The Act also provides, however, that any power of a court in Scotland to grant protective measures pending the decision of any hearing shall apply to a case where (a) the subject of the proceedings includes a question as to the jurisdiction of the court to entertain them, or (b) the proceedings involve the reference of a matter to the European Court under the 1971 Protocol.[61] That provision is applicable to the sheriff court, and whether or not the subject-matter of the proceedings is within the scope of the 1968 Convention. **3.66**

Lugano Convention[62]

The Lugano Convention was opened for signature on September 16, 1988. It has been ratified by all the Member States of the European Union including the United Kingdom and by Iceland, Norway and Switzerland. It has a fairly limited sphere of operation. Its jurisdictional provisions are only of relevance in Scotland when one of the defenders is domiciled in Iceland, Norway or Switzerland and the question arises whether one of the special grounds of jurisdiction in Articles 5, 6 and 6A confers jurisdiction on the Scottish courts; or one of the parties is domiciled in Iceland, Norway or Switzerland and the special rules on matters relating to insurance or to consumer contracts are applicable; or the courts of one of those countries have been submitted to (Article 18), or prorogated (Article 17), or have exclusive jurisdiction under Article 16; or where **3.67**

---

[59] OCR, r. 7.2(2)(a); SCR, r. 55(5); and r. 29 of the Sheriff Court Summary Application Rules 1993.

[60] See *Civil Jurisdiction*, paras 7.43–7.48, 9.32. 11.03, 11.04 and 11.05. See also Case C-391/95, *Van Uden Maritime BV v. Kommanditgesellschaft in Firma DECO-LINE, Peter Determann KG*, Opinion of Att.-Gen. Leger on June 10, 1977.

[61] 1982 Act, s. 24(2). For an examination of provisional and protective measures available in Scotland, see *Civil Jurisdiction*, paras 11.02–11.05 and, on s. 28, *Union Carbide Corporation v. B.P. Chemicals Ltd*, 1995 S.C.L.R. 524.

[62] See *Civil Jurisdiction*, Chap. 12.

identical or related proceedings are pending in one of those states (Articles 21 to 23).[63] The sphere of application could widen if more states are invited to accede to the Lugano Convention in accordance with the procedure laid down in Article 62. Unanimous agreement of all the signatory states is required for this to happen but it may not be long before Poland and perhaps some other Central European states, initially Hungary and the Czech Republic, become parties to the Convention.

3.68 The content of the Lugano Convention's rules of jurisdiction is almost identical to that of the Brussels Convention. There are three relatively minor differences: the wording of the special provision on individual employment contracts in Article 5(1),[64] on the exception to exclusive jurisdiction for short term tenancies of immoveable property in Article 16(1)(b),[65] and on prorogation agreements in relation to individual contracts of employment in the last paragraph of Article 17.[66] It is hoped that these discrepancies will be removed by the outcome of the review of the Brussels and Lugano Conventions which commenced in 1997. The text of the Brussels Convention is preferable on Article 5(1) and the last paragraph of Article 17 and the text of the Lugano Convention is preferable on Article 16(1)(b). Questions on the interpretation of the Lugano Convention cannot be referred to the European Court for a preliminary ruling. United Kingdom courts are, however, required to take account of any principles laid down in any relevant decision delivered by a court of any other Lugano Contracting State concerning provisions of the Convention and may consider the official report on the Convention, the Jenard and Moller Report.[67]

JURISDICTION WITHIN THE UNITED KINGDOM[68]

Introduction

3.69 Section 16 of the 1982 Act provides that the provisions set out in Schedule 4 are to have effect for determining, for each part of the United Kingdom, whether the courts of law for that part, or any particular court of law for that part, have or has jurisdiction where (a) the subject-matter of the proceedings is within the scope of the Brussels Convention, and (b) the defender is domiciled in the United Kingdom or the proceedings are of a kind mentioned in Article 16, which is concerned with exclusive jurisdiction regardless of domicile.[69] Schedule 4 contains a modified version of Title II of the Brussels Convention, which comprises Articles 2–24. In Schedule 4 the modifications by way of omission are indicated by dots, and those by way of addition or substitution are printed in heavy type.[70]

---

[63] The exceptions are Belgium and Greece.

[64] See Art. 54B of the Lugano Convention. Until the 1996 Accession Convention to the Brussels Convention has been ratified by the U.K. and the new Member States of the European Union, however, the Lugano Convention will have a wider sphere of operation and Austria, Finland and Sweden must be bracketed with Iceland, Norway and Switzerland in the text of this paragraph.

[65] See *Civil Jurisdiction*, para. 5.22.

[66] *ibid.* para. 7.11.

[67] See s. 3B of the 1982 Act as amended by the Civil Jurisdiction and Judgments Act 1991 and Protocol 2 to the Lugano Convention set out in Sched. 3C to the 1982 Act.

[68] See *Civil Jurisdiction*, paras 9.01–9.32.

[69] 1982 Act, s. 16(1).

[70] *ibid.* s. 16(2).

In determining any question as to the meaning or effect of any provision contained in Schedule 4 a court must have regard to any relevant principles laid down by the European Court in connection with Title II of the Brussels Convention and to any relevant decision of that court as to the meaning or effect of any provision of that Title. Courts in the United Kingdom cannot refer a question on the interpretation of Schedule 4 to the European Court even if the provision is identical to its counterpart in the Brussels Convention.[71] The Jenard and Schlosser Reports[72] may be considered and must, so far as relevant, be given such weight as is appropriate in the circumstances.[73] The provisions of section 16 and Schedule 4 have effect subject to the Brussels Convention and section 17, which makes provision for the exclusion of certain proceedings from the application of section 16 and Schedule 4.[74] **3.70**

Excluded proceedings

Section 17 of the 1982 Act provides that Schedule 4 shall not apply to proceedings of any description listed in Schedule 5, or to proceedings in Scotland under any enactment which confers jurisdiction on a Scottish court in respect of a specific subject-matter on specific grounds.[75] The following proceedings are listed in Schedule 5: **3.71**

(1) Proceedings for the winding up of a company under the Insolvency Act 1986 or the Companies Act (Northern Ireland) 1960, or proceedings relating to a company as respects which jurisdiction is conferred on the court having winding up jurisdiction under either of those Acts.[76]
(2) Proceedings concerned with the registration of validity of patents, trade marks, service marks,[77] designs or other similar rights required to be deposited or registered.
(3) Proceedings under section 6 of the Protection of Trading Interests Act 1980.
(4) Proceedings on appeal from, or for review of, decisions of tribunals.

---

[71] See Case C-346/93, *Kleinwort Benson* [1995] E.C.R. I-615, noted by Beaumont (1995) 63 S.L.G. 111, and Briggs (1995) Y.Eur.L. 492. The case was within the scope of Sched. 4 and questions on the interpretation of Art. 5(1) and (3) of the Brussels Convention were referred by the English Court of Appeal under the 1971 Protocol. The European Court decided it did not have jurisdiction as its decision would not be binding on the English courts. It was also influenced by the fact that Sched. 4 does not reproduce the Convention's terms exactly. It is worth remembering that the European Court is not bound by its own decisions. In the context of Art. 177 of the EC Treaty the European Court (13 judges) has recently accepted a reference from a national court of a question of Community law when the case was outwith the scope of Community law and the national law applied Community law to a matter purely internal to the Member State referring the question: see Case C-28/95, *Leur-Bloem v. Inspecteur der Belastingdienst/Ondernemingen Amsterdam 2* [1998] 1 C.M.L.R. 157, judgment of July 17, 1997. Indeed in *Leur-Bloem* the Netherlands Government had pointed out that the decision of the European Court on the interpretation of Community law would not be binding on the Dutch court in that case because the meaning of the Community directive was "only a factor" in the interpretation of the Dutch law (see para. 21). It is very difficult to reconcile the Court's decision in *Leur-Bloem* with its decision in *Kleinwort Benson*.

[72] See para. 3.04.

[73] 1982 Act, s. 16(3).

[74] *ibid.* s. 16(4).

[75] *ibid.* s. 17(1). See *Civil Jurisdiction*, paras 9.11–9.12.

[76] *ibid.* Sched. 5, as amended by the Companies Act 1985, Sched. 2.

[77] Patents, Designs and Marks Act 1986, Sched. 2, Pt 1, para. 1(2)(j).

(5) Proceedings for, or otherwise relating to, an order under any of a number of statutory provisions relative to maintenance and similar payments to local and other public authorities.
(6) Proceedings under conventions on jurisdiction relative to specific matters which override the general rules in the Brussels Convention.
(7) Proceedings in Scotland in an Admiralty cause where the jurisdiction of the Court of Session or, as the case may be, of the sheriff is based on arrestment *in rem* or *ad fundandam jurisdictionem* of a ship, cargo or freight.
(8) Proceedings for the rectification of the register of aircraft mortgages kept by the Civil Aviation Authority.
(9) Proceedings brought in any court in pursuance of an order under section 23 of the Oil and Gas (Enterprise) Act 1982.
(10) Proceedings such as are mentioned in the Financial Services Act 1986.

Schedule 4

3.72 The leading article of Schedule 4 states that subject to the provisions of the Schedule, persons domiciled in a part of the United Kingdom are to be sued in the courts of that part.[78] Persons domiciled in one part of the United Kingdom may be sued in the courts of another part only by virtue of the rules in the Schedule as to concurrent jurisdictions, jurisdiction over consumer contracts, exclusive jurisdiction and prorogation of jurisdiction.[79] The principal modifications of the Convention in these groups of rules in the Schedule are noted below. There are no rules in Schedule 4 as to jurisdiction in matters relating to insurance.

3.73 In the rules as to concurrent jurisdictions, Article 5(3) of Schedule 4 additionally confers jurisdiction based on the place where a threatened wrong is likely to be committed.[80] Article 5(8) confers concurrent jurisdiction in certain proceedings relating to property on the courts of the part of the United Kingdom in which the property is situated. The proceedings referred to are those concerning a debt secured on immoveable property, or which are brought to assert, declare or determine proprietary or possessory rights, or rights of security, in or over moveable property, or to obtain authority to dispose of moveable property. Article 5A provides that proceedings which have as their object a decision of an organ of a company or other legal person or of an association of natural or legal persons may, without prejudice to the other provisions of the Schedule, be brought in the courts of the part of the United Kingdom in which that company, legal person or association has its seat.

3.74 The modified rules in Schedule 4 relative to jurisdiction over consumer contracts have already been noted.[81]

3.75 Article 16 of Schedule 4, which deals with exclusive jurisdiction, omits the paragraph in Article 16 of the Brussels Convention dealing with patents.[82]

---

[78] 1982 Act, Sched. 4, Art. 2.
[79] *ibid.* Art. 3.
[80] See paras 3.33, 3.93.
[81] para. 3.49.
[82] para. 3.27.

The modifications in Article 17 of Schedule 4, which deals with prorogation, have also been noted above,[83] as have the provisions of Schedule 4 as to submission to jurisdiction,[84] verification of jurisdiction[85] and due service,[86] and provisional and protective measures.[87] The provisions of the Brussels Convention as to *lis pendens* and related actions are omitted from Schedule 4.[88] 3.76

Jurisdiction in Scotland[89]

Introduction

Part III of the 1982 Act provides rules of jurisdiction for the Scottish courts, many of which are derived from the Brussels Convention, often with important additions and modifications. These rules are not, however, restricted to proceedings whose subject-matter is within the scope of the Brussels Convention but cover, with a few important exceptions, the whole law of civil jurisdiction in Scotland. The rules are contained in Schedule 8, and the exceptions in Schedule 9. It is to be noted that the rules in Schedule 8 have effect subject to Parts I and II of the Act.[90] Thus, Schedule 8 will have effect, unqualified by the Brussels and Lugano Conventions or Schedule 4 in proceedings to which it applies which are outwith the scope of the Brussels Convention. But in matters within the scope of the Convention where the defender is domiciled in another Contracting State or in another part of the United Kingdom, the rules in Schedule 8 will not apply only. In the majority of cases, most of which will involve two parties domiciled in Scotland, Schedule 8 will be the place to find the appropriate jurisdictional rules; and in so far as the rules in Schedule 8 correspond with the Brussels Convention rules, it will often be unnecessary to decide whether the case is or is not governed by the rules of the Brussels or Lugano Conventions or of Schedule 4, for the test of jurisdiction in these instances will be the same.[91] 3.77

Section 6 of the 1907 Act ceases to have effect to the extent that it determines jurisdiction in relation to any matters to which Schedule 8 applies.[92] Schedule 8 does not, however, affect the competence as respects 3.78

---

[83] para. 3.52.
[84] para. 3.54.
[85] para. 3.55.
[86] para. 3.59.
[87] para. 3.65.
[88] para. 3.63. Drake J. reversed his own mistake and decided that *forum non conveniens* does apply in the context of Sched. 4 in *Cumming v. Scottish Daily Record, The Times*, June 8, 1995, noted by Collins (1995) 111 L.Q.R. 541 and Beaumont (1995) 63 S.L.G. 111. The time for testing whether a defender is domiciled in a particular Contracting State under Articles 2 and 6 has not been established by the European Court. In England the majority of the Court of Appeal has decided that the place where a defendant is domiciled is to be determined at the date of the issue of the writ. Pill L.J., dissenting, favoured the date of service on the defendant: see *Canada Trust Co. v. Stolzenberg (No. 2)* [1998] 1 W.L.R. 547.
[89] See *Civil Jurisdiction*, Chap. 10.
[90] 1982 Act, s. 20(1). The fact that the scope of Sched. 8 is not restricted to the scope of the Brussels Convention is illustrated by *Lord Advocate v. Tursi*, 1997 S.C.L.R. 264 and *Lord Advocate v. West End Construction*, 1990 S.C.L.R. 777.
[91] para. 3.03.
[92] 1982 Act, s. 20(3).

subject-matter or value of the Court of Session or of the sheriff court.[93] Nor does it affect the operation of any enactment which confers jurisdiction on a Scottish court in respect of a specific subject-matter on specific grounds, or the jurisdiction of any court in respect of any matter mentioned in Schedule 9.[94] Nothing in Schedule 8 prevents a court from declining jurisdiction on the ground of *forum non conveniens*,[95] but the court may not do so if that would be inconsistent with the Brussels or Lugano Conventions.[96] Thus, declinature on that ground is incompetent in matters within the scope of the Convention where the defender is domiciled in another Contracting State, or where the court has exclusive jurisdiction by virtue of Article 16 of the Convention. Nothing in Schedule 8 affects the operation of any enactment or rule of law under which a court may decline to exercise jurisdiction because of the prorogation by parties of the jurisdiction of another court.[97] Where a court has jurisdiction in any proceedings by virtue of Schedule 8, it also has jurisdiction to determine any matter which is ancillary or incidental to the proceedings, or requires to be determined for the purposes of a decision in the proceedings.[98] Nothing in Schedule 8 affects the power of the court to vary or recall a maintenance order which it has granted, or to vary or discharge a maintenance order registered in the sheriff court under Part II of the Maintenance Orders Act 1950, or to vary or revoke a registered order within the meaning of Part I of the Maintenance Orders (Reciprocal Enforcement) Act 1972.[99] In Schedule 8, words resulting from modifications of Title II of the Brussels Convention by way of addition or substitution, and provisions not derived from that Title, are printed in heavy type; and the marginal notes show, where appropriate, of which provision of Title II a provision of Schedule 8 is a modified version.[1] No indication is given, however, when a provision of Title II is omitted from Schedule 8. Section 20(5) of the Act, as to the interpretation of Schedule 8, is in the same terms as section 16(3) which deals with the interpretation of Schedule 4.[2] Thus the courts in Scotland must have regard to decisions of the European Court interpreting the jurisdictional provisions of the Brussels Convention which have been utilised in Schedule 8 but they cannot refer a case to the European Court for a preliminary ruling.

Proceedings excluded from Schedule 8

3.79 The proceedings excluded from Schedule 8 are listed in Schedule 9. The list may be varied by Order in Council.[3] The listed proceedings are as follows.

Status and capacity of natural persons

3.80 Paragraph I of Schedule 9 excludes "proceedings concerning the status or legal capacity of natural persons (including proceedings for separation) other than proceedings which consist solely of proceedings of affiliation

---

[93] 1982 Act, s. 20(2).
[94] *ibid.* s. 21(1).
[95] *ibid.* s. 22 (1). See *supra*, n.88.
[96] *ibid.* s. 49.
[97] *ibid.* s. 22(2).
[98] *ibid.* s. 22(4).
[99] *ibid.* s. 23.
[1] *ibid.* s. 20(4).
[2] See para. 3.70.
[3] 1982 Act, s. 21(2),(3).

and aliment."[4] We have already considered the jurisdiction of the sheriff court in actions for divorce or separation and ancillary applications,[5] actions for declarator of parentage, non-parentage, legitimacy or illegitimacy,[6] and actions for declarator of death.[7]

Residence of children

Proceedings for regulating the residence of children are excluded from Schedule 8.[8] The jurisdiction of the sheriff court in such proceedings is to a large extent regulated by the Family Law Act 1986, whose provisions are considered above.[9] **3.81**

Guardianship

Proceedings relating to guardianship of children, and all proceedings relating to the management of the affairs of persons who are incapable of managing their own affairs, are excluded from Schedule 8.[10] The jurisdictional grounds on which the sheriff court could entertain proceedings relating to guardianship (tutory and curatory as it then was) at common law were obscure,[11] and for most practical purposes do not need to be relied on, even though preserved by the Family Law Act 1986, because of the explicit jurisdictional provisions in that Act, which are considered above.[12] The sheriff court may also make orders relating to guardianship in actions for divorce or separation.[13] The sheriff's jurisdiction in appointing guardians to the property of an incapax is explained above.[14] **3.82**

Insolvency proceedings

The following are also excluded from Schedule 8: proceedings in respect of sequestration in bankruptcy; or the winding up of a company or other legal person; or proceedings in respect of a judicial arrangement or judicial composition with creditors.[15] We have considered above the sheriff's jurisdiction in bankruptcy,[16] the winding up of companies[17] and the dissolution of partnerships.[18] Judicial composition with creditors is regulated by Schedule 4 to the Bankruptcy (Scotland) Act 1985.[19] **3.83**

Certain proceedings relating to companies

"Proceedings relating to a company where, by any enactment, jurisdiction in respect of those proceedings is conferred on the court having **3.84**

---

[4] 1982 Act, Sched. 9, para. 1, as amended by Family Law (Scotland) Act 1985, Sched. 2.
[5] paras 2.58 to 2.60.
[6] para. 2.64.
[7] para. 2.65.
[8] 1982 Act, Sched. 9, para. 2. (Sched. 9 still refers to "custody" and not to "residence".)
[9] para. 2.62; see also para. 22.03.
[10] 1982 Act, Sched. 9, para. 3.
[11] *Family Law—Report on Custody of Children, Jurisdiction and Enforcement within the United Kingdom* (Law Com. No. 138, Scot. Law Com. No. 91).
[12] para. 2.62. See also Anton with Beaumont, *Private International Law* (2nd ed., W. Green, 1990), pp. 564–565.
[13] para. 2.61.
[14] paras 2.68, 2.69. See also Anton with Beaumont, *Private International Law* (2nd ed., 1990), pp. 567–568.
[15] 1982 Act, Sched. 9, para. 4.
[16] para. 2.70.
[17] paras 2.71, 2.72.
[18] para. 2.73.
[19] Bankruptcy (Scotland) Act 1985, s. 56.

jurisdiction to wind it up" are also excluded from Schedule 8.[20] Such proceedings include applications for an administrative order; or for the appointment of a receiver (apparently not competent in the sheriff court); or for a disqualification order.[21]

Certain admiralty causes

3.85 Also excluded are admiralty causes in so far as the jurisdiction is based on arrestment *in rem* or *ad fundandam jurisdictionem* of a ship, cargo or freight.[22] Otherwise, the rules in Schedule 8 are applicable in an admiralty cause, unless it is brought in terms of rules implementing a convention on a particular matter.[23] Other aspects of jurisdiction in Admiralty causes are noted above.[24]

Commissary proceedings

3.86 Since commissary proceedings are excluded from Schedule 8, by paragraph 7 of Schedule 9, the sheriff court to which a petition for appointment as executor must be presented continues to be, where the deceased was domiciled (in the traditional sense) in Scotland at the date of his death, the court of the sheriffdom in which he was domiciled; and, where he was domiciled furth of Scotland or without any fixed or known domicile having property in Scotland, the sheriff court at Edinburgh.[25]

Miscellaneous proceedings

3.87 Schedule 9 also excludes the following from Schedule 8: proceedings for the rectification of the register of aircraft mortgages kept by the Civil Aviation Authority[26]; proceedings under section 7(3) of the Civil Aviation (Eurocontrol) Act 1962; proceedings brought in pursuance of an order under section 23 of the Oil and Gas (Enterprise) Act 1982 [27]; proceedings under section 6 of the Protection of Trading Interests Act 1980; appeals from, or review of, decisions of tribunals; proceedings under conventions on jurisdiction relative to specific matters which override the general rules in the Brussels Convention; and proceedings which are not in substance proceedings in which a decree against any person is sought.[28] The latter exclusion is directed towards "proceedings where there is not necessarily a contradictor and where it would be inappropriate, if not impracticable, to apply the ordinary rules of jurisdiction in patrimonial matters."[29] Many proceedings of an administrative nature in the sheriff court fall into this category.[30]

---

20 1982 Act, Sched. 9, para. 5.
21 See para. 2.71.
22 1982 Act, Sched. 9, para. 6.
23 *ibid.* para. 14.
24 paras 2.74 to 2.76.
25 Confirmation of Executors (Scotland) Act 1858, s. 3, as amended by the A.S. (Confirmation of Executors) 1964 (S.I. 1964 No. 1143), para. 6(2)(b) and as read with the Sheriff Courts (Scotland) Act 1876, s. 35, and the 1971 Act, Sched. 1, para. 1.
26 Civil Aviation Act 1982, s. 86.
27 See para. 3.71.
28 1982 Act, Sched. 9, paras 8–14.
29 See *Civil Jurisdiction*, para. 10.08 (on p. 248).
30 See Chaps 25, 26.

Schedule 8

The scope and interpretation of Schedule 8 have already been explained.[31] Schedule 8 begins by stating a general rule based on the domicile principle, and adds rules as to special or alternative grounds of jurisdiction; jurisdiction over consumer contracts; exclusive jurisdiction; prorogation; and declinature of jurisdiction. There are no rules as to jurisdiction over matters relating to insurance. In the following paragraphs, where a rule in Schedule 8 is derived from an Article of the Brussels Convention and has already been noted in the discussion of that Article in this chapter, a footnote refers the reader to the relevant earlier paragraph. **3.88**

General rule

The general rule is in these terms: "Subject to the following Rules, persons shall be sued in the courts for the place where they are domiciled."[32] Thus, the sheriff court will have jurisdiction over a person who is domiciled in the sheriffdom. The meaning of "domicile" in the context of the 1982 Act has already been explained.[33] Where a defender is domiciled in a sheriffdom with more than one sheriff court district the pursuer may seek to sue him in any court of that sheriffdom; but a sheriff clerk may decline to cite a defender domiciled in another court district, and the sheriff at a particular court is entitled to exercise a discretion whether to issue a warrant of citation if the defender is more suitably amenable to another court of the sheriffdom.[34] The qualification that the general rule is "subject to the following Rules" means that it is subject to the rules as to jurisdiction over consumer contracts, exclusive jurisdiction, prorogation and declinature. It is not subject to rule 2, as to special or alternative grounds of jurisdiction, because those are grounds on which "a person may also be sued". **3.89**

Special jurisdiction

Rule 2 provides that subject to rules 3 (jurisdiction over consumer contracts), 4 (exclusive jurisdiction) and 5 (prorogation) "a person may also be sued" in 15 specified types of proceedings or sets of circumstances: accordingly, in each of these 15 cases the pursuer may sue the defender by virtue of these provisions instead of suing him in the courts for the place where he is domiciled. Several of the 15 cases are derived from Articles 5 and 6 of the Brussels Convention but others are not. Accordingly the latter cannot be invoked where the subject-matter of the proceedings falls within the scope of the Brussels Convention and the defender is domiciled in another Contracting State to the Brussels or Lugano Convention or, unless there is an identical provision in Schedule 4, in another part of the United Kingdom. **3.90**

Itinerants. Rule 2(1) provides that a person who has no fixed residence may be sued in a court within whose jurisdiction he is personally cited.[35] **3.91**

---

[31] paras 3.77, 3.78.
[32] 1982 Act, Sched. 8, r. 1.
[33] paras 3.06 to 3.09.
[34] *Tait v. Johnston* (1891) 18 R. 606; *Davidson v. Davidson* (1891) 18 R. 884; *McCormick v. Campbell* (1924) 42 Sh.Ct.Rep. 124; *South Side Sawmills Ltd v. Buchanan*, 1963 S.L.T. (Sh. Ct.) 19; para. 6.02. On remitting of cases from the Court of Session to the sheriff court, see *Civil Jurisdiction*, para. 10.18, n. 41.
[35] 1982 Act, Sched. 8, r. 2(1).

This rule has no counterpart in the Brussels or Lugano Conventions or in Schedule 4. It enacts, and extends to the sheriff court, the common law rule as to the jurisdiction of the Court of Session over itinerants.[36] It is the only rule in Schedule 8 which requires personal citation of the defender within the territory as a condition of jurisdiction. The rule does not apply to an individual who is domiciled in the United Kingdom but has no substantial connection with any part of it: such an individual is treated as domiciled in the part of the United Kingdom in which he is resident.[37]

3.92 **Contract.** Rule 2(2) provides that in matters relating to a contract a person may be sued in the courts for the place of performance of the obligation in question.[38] This rule is derived from Article 5 of the Brussels Convention and corresponds to Article 5(1) of Schedule 4.[39] Under rule 2(2) the sheriff has jurisdiction over the defender if, applying the place of performance of the particular contractual obligation which gives rise to the pursuer's claim, or if the claim concerns more than one obligation the place of performance of the principal obligation in question,[40] is situated within the sheriffdom. It is a matter of contention whether rule 2(2) is applicable where there is more than one place of performance of the obligation in question.[41] If the sheriff court is trying to determine where is the "place of performance" it must apply the law applicable to the contract under Scots private international law.[42] The parties are free to specify the place of performance of the obligation in question[43] but not if the place of performance has no real connection with the reality of the contract and where the obligations arising under the contract could not be performed in accordance with its terms. In such a scenario the parties are really prorogating a court and should comply with the terms of Article 17 of the Brussels Convention.[44] In matters relating to individual contracts of employment the place of performance of the obligation in question is defined by Rule 2(2), in a phrase derived from Article 5(1) of the Brussels Convention, as the place where the "employee habitually carries out his work". This in turn has been defined by the European Court as meaning the place where the employee has established the "effective centre of his working activities".[45]This can be localised in one place even though the employee works in several places[46] but if that proves impossible then the employee can sue in the courts for the place where the business which engaged him was or is now situated.

---

[36] For the Scottish authorities, see Anton with Beaumont, *Private International Law* (2nd ed., 1990), p. 182.

[37] 1982 Act, s. 41(5).

[38] *ibid.* Sched. 8, r. 2(2). He may also be sued in the courts for the place where he is domiciled: *ibid.*, r. 1.

[39] para. 3.30.

[40] See *Civil Jurisdiction*, para. 5.21, and *Source Ltd v. Tuv Rheinland Holding AG* [1997] I.L.Pr. 514 (CA).

[41] *ibid.* para. 5.25. The Inner House has stated that it is not, *Bank of Scotland v. Seitz*, 1990 S.L.T. 584 but the opposite view is taken in England, *Boss Group Ltd v. Boss France SA* [1996] 4 All.E.R. 970 (CA), noted by Forsyth (1995) 54 C.L.J. 515 and Turkki (1996) Eur.L.R. 419.

[42] See Case C-288/92, *Custom Made Commercial* [1994] E.C.R. I-2913, noted by Briggs (1994) Y.Eur.L. 573. For the Scottish rules on choice of law in contract, see the Rome Convention as implemented into U.K. law by the Contracts (Applicable Law) Act 1990, discussed in Anton with Beaumont, *Private International Law* (2nd ed., 1990), Chap. 11.

[43] See Case 56/79, *Zelger v. Salinitri* [1980] E.C.R. 89.

[44] See Case C-106/95, *Mainschiffahrts-Genossenschaft v. Les Gravieres Rhenanes* [1997] I.L.Pr. 411.

[45] See Case C-78/95, *Rutten v. Cross Medical Ltd* [1997] I.L.Pr. 199.

[46] *ibid.*

Delict or quasi-delict. By virtue of rule 2(3), in matters relating to delict or quasi-delict a person may be sued in the courts for the place where the harmful event occurred.[47] This rule is derived from Article 5(3) of the Brussels Convention.[48] It differs from Article 5(3) of Schedule 4 in making no provision for jurisdiction where a threatened wrong is likely to occur, but proceedings for interdict are dealt with separately in rule 2(10).[49] Under rule 2(3) a sheriff court now has jurisdiction over the defender if the place where the damage occurred (the place of harm) or the place of the event giving rise to the damage (the place of acting) is situated within the sheriffdom.[50] The place of harm has been further defined to exclude the place of damage of indirect victims[51] and the place where financial damage is suffered by a direct victim if it is consequential upon initial damage arising and suffered by the victim in another place.[52] In the context of defamation, the courts of the place where the publisher of the allegedly defamatory publication is established have jurisdiction to consider the whole claim. The pursuer can alternatively sue in each legal system where the publication was distributed and his or her reputation was allegedly damaged but the courts of each place can adjudicate only on the injury caused in that place to the victim's reputation.[53] The European Court has stated that Article 5(3) applies to all actions "which seek to establish the liability of a defendant and which are not related to a 'contract' within the meaning of Article 5(1)."[54] The dividing line between the special jurisdictions in contract and delict has been further discussed in two recent English Court of Appeal decisions[55] and by Lord Gill.[56] 3.93

Civil claims in criminal proceedings. Rule 2(4) provides that a person may be sued as regards a civil claim for damages or restitution which is based on an act giving rise to criminal proceedings, in the court seised of those proceedings to the extent that that court has jurisdiction to entertain civil proceedings.[57] This provision is likewise derived from Article 5 of the Brussels Convention, and conforms to Article 5(4) of Schedule 4, but it is thought to have very limited jurisdictional implications for the Scottish courts.[58] 3.94

---

[47] 1982 Act, Sched. 8, r. 2. He may also be sued in the courts for the place where he is domiciled: Sched. 8, r. 1.

[48] para. 3.33.

[49] para. 3.104.

[50] See *Civil Jurisdiction*, paras 5.39–5.40.

[51] See Case C-220/88, *Dumez France* [1990] E.C.R. I-49, discussed in *Civil Jurisdiction*, para. 5.41.

[52] See Case C-364/93, *Marinari* [1995] E.C.R. I-2719, noted by Briggs (1995) Y.Eur.L. 511; and Hartley (1996) Eur.L.R. 164.

[53] See Case C-68/93, *Shevill v. Press Alliance* [1995] E.C.R. I-415, noted by Briggs (1995) Y.Eur.L. 487.

[54] Case 189/87, *Kalfelis v. Bankhaus Schroder* [1988] E.C.R. 5565, para. 17. Applied in Scotland by the Inner House to a Sched. 4 case: *Davenport v. Corinthian Motor Policies at Lloyds*, 1991 S.L.T. 774; see *Civil Jurisdiction*, para. 9.18.

[55] *Kleinwort Benson Ltd v. Glasgow City Council* [1996] Q.B. 678 and *Source Ltd v. Tuv Rheinland Holding AG* [1997] I.L.Pr. 514. It would seem from these cases that in England if a plaintiff has a choice of cause of action in contract or tort then for jurisdictional purposes it is not possible to rely on the special jurisdiction in tort because the case concerns a "matter relating to a contract" in terms of the Brussels Convention.

[56] *William Grant & Sons International Ltd v. Marie Brizard & Roger International SA*, 1996 S.C.L.R. 987. The European Court may cast further light on the issue in Case C-51/97, *La Reunion Européennee v. Spliethoff's Bevrachtingskantoor*.

[57] 1982 Act, Sched. 8, r. 2(4). He may also be sued in the courts for the place where he is domiciled: Sched. 8, r. 1.

[58] para. 3.34.

3.95 **Maintenance.** Rule 2(5), as to matters relating to maintenance,[59] is derived in part from Article 5(2) of the Brussels Convention which has already been discussed.[60]

3.96 **Branch, agency or establishment.** Rule 2(6) provides that a person may be sued as regards a dispute arising out of the operations of a branch, agency or other establishment in the courts for the place in which the branch, agency or other establishment is situated.[61] This rule is derived from Article 5(5) of the Brussels Convention and is similar to Article 5(5) of Schedule 4,[62] with the modification that it applies generally, and not merely as against persons domiciled in another Contracting State or in another part of the United Kingdom. It has been observed that the rule may be useful where it is difficult to discover whether the defender, notably a defending company, is "domiciled" in Scotland or in a particular sheriffdom of Scotland in the sense of the 1982 Act.[63] In terms of rule 2(6) the sheriff court of the sheriffdom in which the establishment is situated will have jurisdiction over the defender in a dispute arising out of its operations.

3.97 **Trusts.** In terms of rule 2(7), a person may be sued in his capacity as settlor, trustee or beneficiary of a trust domiciled in Scotland created by the operation of a statute, or by a written instrument, or created orally and evidenced in writing, in the Court of Session or the appropriate sheriff court within the meaning of section 24A of the Trusts (Scotland) Act 1921.[64] This provision has already been discussed.[65]

3.98 **Arrestment of moveables; *situs* of immoveables.** In terms of rule 2(8), a person who is not domiciled in the United Kingdom may be sued in the courts for any place where (i) any moveable property belonging to him has been arrested; or (ii) any immoveable property in which he has any beneficial interest is situated. This rule has no counterpart in the Brussels and Lugano Conventions, which provide that rules enabling jurisdiction to be founded on such grounds are not applicable as against persons domiciled in another Contracting State.[66] Rule 2(8) is accordingly applicable only in relation to defenders domiciled neither in the United Kingdom nor in any Contracting State. A sheriff court will have jurisdiction over such a defender if the moveable property is arrested, or the immoveable property is situated, within the sheriffdom.

3.99 Rule 2(8) is thought to refer to the existing common law rules as to arrestment to found jurisdiction, which are fully considered in the undernoted works.[67] They may be briefly summarised as follows. By the process of arrestment to found jurisdiction, also called arrestment

---

[59] 1982 Act, Sched. 8, r. 2(5).

[60] paras 3.31, 3.32.

[61] 1982 Act, Sched. 8, r. 2(6). He may also be sued in the courts for the place where he is domiciled: Sched. 8, r. 1.

[62] para. 3.35.

[63] See *Civil Jurisdiction*, para. 10.33.

[64] 1982 Act, Sched. 8, r. 2(7).

[65] para. 3.36.

[66] 1982 Act, Sched. 1, Art. 3.

[67] Graham Stewart, Chap. 12; Anton with Beaumont, *Private International Law* (2nd ed., 1990), pp. 188–193. See also the discussion of arrestment on the dependence in paras 11.10 to 11.42.

jurisdictionis fundandae causa or arrestment *ad fundandam jurisdictionem*, a person may be subjected to the jurisdiction of the Scottish courts by the arrestment of moveable property belonging to him, or of a debt owed to him, provided that the following conditions are satisfied. The action must be one in which the decree is of a class that can be expressed in terms of money. The subjects arrested must be of some, albeit small, commercial value[68]; must belong to or be owed to the defender (the "common debtor") in the capacity in which he is being sued[69]; and must be in the hands of a third party (the "arrestee", who is neither the pursuer[70] nor the defender[71]) who is liable to account for them to the defender[72] and is himself subject to the jurisdiction. The subjects arrested need not have any connection with the action.[73] A debt due to the defender by a third party may, in general, be arrested,[74] as may a ship within port.[75]

The effect of arrestment to found jurisdiction is only to subject the defender to the jurisdiction of the court in the particular action in which it is used: it does not subject him to the jurisdiction in any other action.[76] Nor does it create a nexus over the subjects arrested. Accordingly the arrestee is not precluded by the arrestment from parting with the property, or paying the debt, which has been arrested.[77] If the pursuer desires to retain the subjects to be available for satisfaction of any decree which he may obtain against the defender, he must obtain and use a warrant for arrestment on the dependence of the action, in order to prevent the arrestee from parting with them until the action is at an end[78]; and, if and when he gets a decree, it may be necessary for him to obtain a decree of furthcoming against the arrestee. If the subject arrested to found jurisdiction is a ship, and the pursuer desires to retain it in port, he should apply for a warrant to arrest on the dependence and to dismantle, which should be signed by the sheriff.[79] An arrestment to found jurisdiction which was not authorised may be retrospectively validated by a subsequent ratification of the action.[80] **3.100**

Arrestment to found jurisdiction in an ordinary action proceeds on a warrant which may be applied for in the crave of the initial writ. Averments to justify the granting of the warrant must be included in **3.101**

---

68 *Shaw v. Dow & Dobie* (1869) 7 M. 449, *per* L.P. Inglis at 455; (1869) 6 S.L.R. 297.

69 *Parnell v. Walter* (1889) 16 R. 917.

70 *Heron v. Winfields Ltd* (1894) 22 R. 182; 2 S.L.T. 349.

71 *Hutchison v. Hutchison*, 1912 1 S.L.T. 219.

72 *Kerr v. R. & W. Ferguson*, 1931 S.C. 736; 1931 S.L.T. 475, 540.

73 *Sheaf Steamship Co. v. Compania Transmediterranea*, 1930 S.C. 660; 1930 S.L.T. 445.

74 *Ross v. Ross* (1887) 5 R. 1013; *American Mortgage Co. of Scotland v. Sidway*, 1908 S.C. 500; (1908) 15 S.L.T. 850.

75 Anton, *Private International Law* (1st ed., 1967), pp. 115–117; *West Cumberland Farmers Ltd v. Ellon Hinengo Ltd*, 1988 S.L.T. 294; and *PTKF Kontinent v. VMPTO Progress*, 1994 S.L.T. 235.

76 *Anderson v. Harboe* (1871) 10 M. 217.

77 *Craig v. Brunsgaard, Kjosterud & Co.* (1896) 23 R. 500; 3 S.L.T. 265; *Ward & Co. v. Samyang Navigation Co.*, 1975 S.C. (H.L.) 26; 1975 S.L.T. 126.

78 See paras 11.10 to 11.42. Care must be taken to execute both warrants: *Sutherlands of Peterhead (Road Hauliers) Ltd v. Allard Hewson & Co. Ltd*, 1972 S.L.T. (Notes) 83.

79 *Lucovich* (1885) 12 R. 1090; *McConnachie*, 1914 S.C. 853; 1914 2 S.L.T. 71; Dobie, *Styles*, p. 46. To justify arrestment of a ship the court must be satisfied at the very least that the averments in the summons disclose some intelligible and discernible cause of action: see *West Cumberland Farmers Ltd v. Ellon Hinengo Ltd*, 1988 S.L.T. 294 and *PTKF Kontinent v. VMPTO Progress*, 1994 S.L.T. 235, 237.

80 *Ward & Co., supra.*

the condescendence.[81] If, after the action is raised, the pursuer calls an additional defender whom he desires to subject to the jurisdiction by arrestment, he should lodge a minute setting forth the facts and craving a warrant for arrestment to found jurisdiction.[82] In a summary cause, where the necessary averments are included in the summons, the summons signed by the sheriff clerk is warrant for arrestment to found jurisdiction.[83] The warrant is executed before or at the same time as the service of the initial writ or summons,[84] and in the same way as a warrant for arrestment on the dependence.[85] Care should be taken to follow the correct procedure where it is desired to serve an arrestment on the Lord Advocate.[86]

3.102 The rule that a person not domiciled in the United Kingdom or in another Contracting State may be sued in the courts for any place where any immoveable property in which he has any beneficial interest is situated, is derived from the common law rule that the Court of Session has jurisdiction over a person if he has at the date of citation a beneficial right or interest in heritable property situated in Scotland,[87] in the character in which he is sued.[88] The court has jurisdiction not only in actions relating to the heritable property but in all actions of a patrimonial character brought against the defender. The rule is fully examined in the undernoted work.[89]

3.103 **Actions relating to moveables.** Rule 2(9) provides that in proceedings which are brought to assert, declare or determine proprietary or possessory rights, or rights of security, in or over moveable property, or to obtain authority to dispose of moveable property, a person may be sued in the courts of the place where the property is situated.[90] A sheriff court therefore has jurisdiction over the defender in such proceedings when the moveable property is situated within the sheriffdom. Like rule 2(8), rule 2(9) has no counterpart in the Brussels or Lugano Conventions, which provide that rules enabling jurisdiction to be founded on such grounds are not applicable as against persons domiciled in another Contracting State.[91] Rule 2(9) does, however, correspond to the terms of Article 5(8)(b) of Schedule 4,[92] so this basis of jurisdiction is applicable in relation to a defender domiciled in any part of the United Kingdom or in a state other than a Contracting State, but not in relation to a defender domiciled in another Contracting State.

3.104 **Interdict.** Rule 2(10) provides that in proceedings for interdict, a person may be sued in the courts for the place where it is alleged that the wrong is

---

[81] OCR, r. 3.4. See also OCR, Chap. 6 on arrestment.

[82] *MacKenzie v. R. McKenzie & Co.* [1956] C.L.Y. 12121 (OH).

[83] SCR, r. 3(2); see Vol. 2 of this work.

[84] *Walls' Trs v. Drynan* (1888) 15 R. 359; *North v. Stewart* (1890) 17 R. (H.L.) 60.

[85] paras 11.18 to 11.20.

[86] para. 4.71; 1980 S.L.T. (News) 146.

[87] *Bowman v. Wright* (1877) 4 R. 322; *Caledonian Fish Selling Marine Stores Co. Ltd v. Allard Hewson & Co. Ltd*, 1970 S.C. 168; 1970 S.L.T. 195; *Llewellyn v. Hebbert*, 1983 S.L.T. 370; *Forth Tugs Ltd v. Wilmington Trust Co.*, 1987 S.L.T. 153; *Permanent Houses (Holdings) Ltd v. Caledonian Properties Ltd*, 1987 S.L.T. 553.

[88] *Mackenzie v. Drummond's Exrs* (1868) 6 M. 932.

[89] Anton, *Private International Law* (1st ed., 1967), pp. 102–105.

[90] 1982 Act, Sched. 8, r. 2(9). He may also be sued in the courts for the place where he is domiciled: Sched. 8, r. 1.

[91] 1982 Act, Sched. 1, Art. 3.

[92] para. 3.73.

likely to be committed.[93] A sheriff court therefore has jurisdiction where that place is within the sheriffdom. By virtue of rule 1, the defender may also be sued in the courts for the place where he is domiciled. Rule 2(10) corresponds with part of Article 5(3) of Schedule 4.[94] It is not clear whether proceedings relating to a threatened wrong fall within Article 5 of the Brussels and Lugano Conventions.[95]

Debt secured over immoveables. Rule 2(11) provides that in proceedings concerning a debt secured over immoveable property, a person may be sued in the courts for the place where the property is situated.[96] There is a corresponding provision in Article 5(8)(b) of Schedule 4,[97] but not in the Brussels or Lugano Conventions. This basis of jurisdiction is accordingly applicable in relation to a defender domiciled in any part of the United Kingdom or in a state other than a Contracting State, but not in relation to a defender domiciled in a Contracting State. 3.105

Decisions of organs of companies, etc. Under rule 2(12), in proceedings which have as their object a decision of an organ of a company or other legal person or of an association of natural or legal persons, a person may be sued in the court for the place where that company, legal person or association has its seat. The meaning of "seat" for the purposes of this rule is explained above.[98] Rule 2(12) is derived from Article 16(2) of the Brussels Convention,[99] but unlike that article it does not confer an exclusive jurisdiction. In conferring a non-exclusive jurisdiction in these matters it corresponds to Article 5A of Schedule 4.[1] The non-exclusive jurisdiction accordingly applies in relation to a defender domiciled in the United Kingdom or in a state other than a Contracting State, but it does not apply to a defender domiciled in another Contracting State. An exclusive jurisdiction is conferred by rule 4(1)(b) of Schedule 8 relative to proceedings concerning the constitution of companies and other entities,[2] while proceedings in respect of winding-up and certain other proceedings relating to a company are excluded from Schedule 8 by Schedule 9.[3] 3.106

Arbitration. In terms of rule 2(13) the Court of Session, but not the sheriff court, has jurisdiction in proceedings concerning an arbitration which is conducted in Scotland or in which the procedure is governed by Scots law. The Brussels Convention does not apply to "arbitration",[4] and there is no corresponding provision in Schedule 4.[5] 3.107

Patents, trade marks, etc. By virtue of rule 2(14) the Court of Session, but not the sheriff court, has a non-exclusive jurisdiction in proceedings 3.108

---

[93] 1982 Act, Sched. 8, r. 2(10).
[94] para. 3.33.
[95] See *Civil Jurisdiction*, para. 5.38, n. 92.
[96] 1982 Act, Sched. 8, r. 2(11). He may also be sued in the courts for the place where he is domiciled: Sched. 8, r. 1.
[97] para. 3.73.
[98] para. 3.19.
[99] para. 3.25.
[1] para. 3.73.
[2] para. 3.25.
[3] paras 3.83, 3.84.
[4] 1982 Act, Sched. 1, Art. 1.
[5] See Maxwell Report, pp. 199 and 259; *Civil Jurisdiction*, paras 10.48–10.50. For a consideration of the international aspects of arbitration see Anton, 1986 S.L.T. (News) 45, 53 and Anton with Beaumont, *Private International Law* (2nd ed., 1990), Chap. 12.

principally concerned with the registration in the United Kingdom or the validity in the United Kingdom of patents, trade marks, service marks, designs or other similar rights required to be deposited or registered.[6]

3.109 **Procedural provisions.** Rule 2(15)[7] sets out provisions as to plurality of defenders, third party proceedings and "counterclaims" which are derived from the Brussels Convention and are designed to secure that all relevant issues may be determined at the same time by the same court. These provisions, which are applicable irrespective of the domicile of the defender, have already been noticed.[8]

Jurisdiction over consumer contracts

3.110 Rule 3 of Schedule 8,[9] which states the rules as to jurisdiction in Scotland in proceedings concerning a consumer contract, has already been noticed.[10]

Exclusive jurisdiction

3.111 The provisions of rule 4(1) of Schedule 8 as to exclusive jurisdiction in certain proceedings concerned with immoveable property,[11] companies and other entities,[12] public registers[13] and the enforcement of judgments[14] have already been noted. To ensure that the court does not assume jurisdiction on any ground other than those specified in rule 4(1), rule 4(3) forbids the court to exercise jurisdiction in a case where immoveable property,[15] the seat of an entity, a public register or the place where a judgment has been or is to be enforced is situated outside Scotland and where rule 4(1) would apply if the property, seat, register or place of enforcement were situated in Scotland.

Prorogation and submission

3.112 Rule 5 of Schedule 8, which deals with prorogation of jurisdiction generally,[16] rule 3(6), which imposes additional restrictions on prorogation agreements relative to consumer contracts,[17] and rule 6, which is concerned with submission,[18] have been noticed above.

Declinature of jurisdiction

3.113 Rule 7 of Schedule 8, which is derived from Article 19 of the Brussels Convention, provides that where a court is seised of a claim which is principally concerned with a matter over which another court has exclusive jurisdiction by virtue of rule 4, or where it is precluded from

---

6 1982 Act, Sched. 8, r. 2(14); Patents, Designs and Marks Act 1986, Sched. 2, Pt 1, para. 1(2)(j). See para. 3.27.
7 1982 Act, Sched. 8, r. 2(15).
8 paras 3.38 to 3.40.
9 1982 Act, Sched. 8, r. 3.
10 para. 3.50.
11 para. 3.24.
12 para. 3.25.
13 para. 3.26.
14 para. 3.28.
15 See *Civil Jurisdiction*, paras 10.63–10.64.
16 para. 3.53.
17 para. 3.50.
18 para. 3.54.

exercising jurisdiction by rule 4(3), it must declare of its own motion that it has no jurisdiction. Rule 8 provides that where in any case a court has no jurisdiction which is compatible with the 1982 Act, and the defender does not enter an appearance, the court must declare of its own motion that it has no jurisdiction. The relevant rules of pleading and the rules of court providing that the sheriff must not grant decree in an undefended action unless it appears *ex facie* of the writ that a ground of jurisdiction exists under the 1982 Act, have already been noted.[19]

[19] para. 3.64.

PART II

PARTIES

CHAPTER 4

PARTIES

INTRODUCTION

Before any proceeding is brought into court, the practitioner must consider whether his client is the proper person to raise it, and against what person or persons it should be brought. In order for a person to maintain or defend an action, three attributes are necessary: capacity, which is full possession of the qualifications which the law requires for participation in legal process; title, which is a formal legal relationship to the subject-matter of the action; and interest, which is some benefit from asserting the right with which the action is concerned or from preventing its infringement.[1] Further, in view of diverse legal rights and duties attaching to different persons and bodies, special rules of procedure are provided to regulate legal proceedings brought by or against particular parties. There are additional rules governing the subject of parties after an action has been raised. This chapter deals with capacity, title and interest to sue and be sued, and with the procedural rules regarding some of the more important categories of particular parties. The procedural rules governing the position of parties generally after the raising of an action are considered in Chapter 12. **4.01**

CAPACITY

The general rule of law is that any person, natural or artificial, fully possesses the qualifications to sue and defend and thus may sue in the sheriff court, or be sued there if subject to its jurisdiction. Some persons, however, lack this capacity, totally or partially, and thus are prevented, either absolutely or conditionally, from suing or being sued. **4.02**

Persons who cannot sue

Enemy aliens

No one is disabled from suing an action in the Scottish courts because he is of foreign domicile or nationality.[2] A party who is resident outside the United Kingdom may be required to sist a mandatary responsible for the conduct of the case and the payment of any expenses in which the party may be found liable, but the requirement is based on his residence outwith the United Kingdom and not on his domicile or nationality.[3] Special rules apply, however, when a state of war exists between the United Kingdom and the country of residence of the pursuer or **4.03**

---

[1] Mackay, *Practice*, i, 279; Thomson and Middleton, pp. 50–52. See paras 4.30, (title), 4.33, (interest).

[2] Anton, *Private International Law* (1st ed.), p. 138.

[3] See para. 11.68.

prospective pursuer.[4] Upon the principle "that the enemy is not to be benefited even to the smallest extent",[5] a person who is voluntarily resident or who is carrying on business in hostile territory, whether he is a subject of the United Kingdom or of a neutral or a hostile state, may not raise an action during the continuance of the state of war[6]; and any action which he has raised before the existence of the state of war cannot be continued but will be sisted *in hoc statu* for the duration of the war.[7] Such a person may, however, be sued in the Scottish courts, and is entitled to defend the action against him.[8]

Persons who cannot be sued

Foreign states[9]

4.04 The law as to the immunity of foreign states from the jurisdiction of the courts of the United Kingdom is codified by the State Immunity Act 1978. Part I of the Act provides a catalogue of cases in which there is no entitlement to immunity, most of the cases being subject to conditions and exceptions,[10] and states a general rule that in other cases a foreign or Commonwealth state is immune from the jurisdiction of the courts of the United Kingdom.[11] The court must give effect to that immunity even though the state does not appear in the proceedings in question.[12] The Act also specifies the circumstances in which a state is deemed to have submitted to the jurisdiction,[13] provides procedural rules where a state is defender as to the service of process and giving judgment in default of appearance[14] and grants to states a variety of procedural advantages primarily relating to the enforcement of judgments.[15] Reference should be made to the undernoted works.[16]

Foreign heads of state and diplomats[17]

4.05 The State Immunity Act 1978 broadly assimilates the position of foreign heads of state, their families and private servants to that of the head of a diplomatic mission, his family and servants under the Diplomatic Privileges Act 1964.[18] That Act divides persons entitled to diplomatic immunity into

---

[4] Maxwell, pp. 134–135. For a discussion of the rules see Anton, *supra*, pp. 138–141.

[5] Bell, *Comm.*, i, 326.

[6] *Arnauld v. Boick* (1704) Mor. 10159; *Porter v. Freudenherg* [1915] 1 K.B. 857, *per* Lord Reading C.J. at 869; *Sovfracht (V/O) v. Van Udens Scheepvart en Agentuur Maatschappij* [1943] A.C. 203, *per* Lord Thankerton at 214–217.

[7] *Carron v. Covan & Co.*, Nov. 28, 1809, F.C.; *Craig Line Steamship Co. Ltd v. N.B. Storage and Transit Co.*, 1915 S.C. 113; *Van Uden v. Burrell*, 1916 S.C. 391.

[8] *Cooper & Co. v. Deutsche Bank, Berlin* (1914) 31 Sh.Ct.Rep. 67.

[9] On the recognition of foreign states, see *Gur Corporation v. Trust Bank of Africa Ltd* [1986] 3 All E.R. 449.

[10] ss. 2 to 11; *Forth Tugs Ltd v. Wilmington Trust Co.*, 1987 S.L.T. 153.

[11] State Immunity Act 1978, ss. 1(1), 14(1). The Act is a comprehensive code and s. 1 is not subject to any overriding provisions even in the case of alleged breach of fundamental human rights under international law (*Al-Adsani v. Kuwait, The Times*, Mar. 29, [1996] C.L.Y. 3663).

[12] *ibid.* s. 1(2); *Property Managers & Factors (Edinburgh) Ltd v. Federal Republic of Nigeria*, Edinburgh Sh. Ct, Aug. 22, 1983, unreported.

[13] *ibid.* s. 2.

[14] *ibid.* s. 12.

[15] *ibid.* s. 13; *Alcom Ltd v. Republic of Colombia* [1984] A.C. 580: *Forth Tugs Ltd v. Wilmington Trust Co.*, 1987 S.L.T. 153.

[16] Dicey and Morris, pp. 156–171. Anton with Beaumont, pp. 111–117.

[17] Dicey and Morris, pp. 171–178. Anton with Beaumont, pp. 117–120.

[18] State Immunity Act 1978, s. 20.

three categories: diplomatic agents, who enjoy immunity from criminal jurisdiction and also from civil and administrative jurisdiction, except in respect of certain actions relating to immoveables and succession and to professional or commercial activities outside their official functions[19]; members of the administrative and technical staff of the mission, who enjoy the like immunity except that their immunity from civil and administrative jurisdiction does not extend to acts performed outside the course of their duties[20]; and members of the service staff of the mission, who enjoy immunity only in respect of acts performed in the course of their duties.[21] If in any proceedings any question arises whether or not any person is entitled to any privilege or immunity under the Act, a certificate issued by or under the authority of the Secretary of State stating any fact relating to that question is conclusive evidence of that fact.[22] Consular officers and consular employees, and persons performing similar duties in the service of a Commonwealth government or the Government of the Republic of Ireland are immune from jurisdiction except in civil actions (a) arising out of contracts concluded by them in which they did not contract expressly or impliedly as agents of the sending state, or (b) by a third party for damage arising from an accident in the United Kingdom caused by a vehicle, vessel or aircraft.[23] Their immunity from jurisdiction may be expressly waived; and their initiation of proceedings in a matter where immunity might be enjoyed precludes the invocation of immunity in respect of any counterclaim directly connected with the principal claim.[24]

International organisations, etc.

The International Organisations Acts 1968 and 1981 empower the Crown by Order in Council to confer complete immunity from suit and legal process upon any international organisation of which the United Kingdom is a member; to confer the like immunity from suit and legal process as is accorded to the head of a diplomatic mission or its representatives, high officers and others; and to confer on specified subordinate officers and servants a limited immunity from suit and legal process extending only to things done or omitted to be done in the course of the performance of official duties.[25] Orders in Council made under the International Organisations (Immunities and Privileges) Act 1950 continue in force notwithstanding the repeal of that Act.[26] Many Orders in Council have been made under these Acts conferring immunity from suit on many international organisations and (in most cases) on their representatives, officers and staffs.[27] It has been held that no immunity from suit attaches to the European Community.[28] **4.06**

---

[19] Diplomatic Privileges Act 1964, Sched. 1, art. 31. See *Empson v. Smith* [1966] 1 Q.B. 426; *R. v. Guildhall Mags' Ct, ex p. Jarret-Thorpe* [1977] C.L.Y. 1663; *Shaw v. Shaw* [1979] Fam. 62.

[20] *ibid.* Sched. 1, art. 37(2).

[21] *ibid.* Sched. 1, art 37(3).

[22] *ibid.* s. 4.

[23] Consular Relations Act 1968, Sched. 1, art. 43; s. 12, substituted by the Diplomatic and Other Privileges Act 1971, Sched.

[24] *ibid.* art. 45.

[25] International Organisations Act 1968, Sched. 1, as amended.

[26] *ibid.* s. 12(5).

[27] For a list see Halsbury, Vol. 18, para. 1598.

[28] *J.H. Rayner Ltd v. Dept of Trade* [1989] Ch. 72 at 196–203; *cf. Maclaine Watson & Co. v. International Tin Council* [1989] Ch. 253 at 283. But see comments of Lord Oliver of Aylmerton in *J.H. Rayner Ltd v. Dept of Trade* [1990] 2 A.C. 418 at 516.

Persons under disability in respect of suing or being sued

Insane persons

4.07 An insane person has no *persona standi in judicio*[29] or character entitling him to appear in a law suit whether as pursuer or defender.[30] An action cannot be raised in his name, except, perhaps, in an emergency,[31] and the proper course is to apply to the court for the appointment of a curator *bonis*, at whose instance the action may proceed.[32] Where a proposed defender is insane and has a curator *bonis*, the action should be brought against the curator *bonis*.[33] If he has no curator *bonis*, he alone should be called as defender and the court, on his incapacity being brought to its notice, will in general sist the cause until a curator *bonis* is appointed[34]; but the court may, it is thought, in special circumstances and in actions affecting status,[35] appoint a curator *ad litem*. The same courses appear to be open to the court when a party becomes insane during the dependence of the action.[36] Where in an action of divorce or separation it appears to the sheriff that the defender is suffering from mental disorder, he must appoint a curator *ad litem*.[37] The duties of a curator *ad litem* are considered below.[38] Rules of court regulate the citation of persons in actions of divorce or separation where the defender is suffering from mental disorder.[39]

4.08 Where a question has arisen as to the mental capacity of a party not under curatory to sue or defend a particular action, it may be treated as a question of fact to be resolved by the leading of evidence.[40] All human beings are presumed to be sane,[41] and in certain circumstances the onus on a party alleging incapacity may be a very heavy one.[42] The competency of inquiring into the general medical condition of a party to an action has not been decided,[43] and a motion that a party allegedly *incapax* should be ordained to be medically examined before giving evidence has been refused.[44]

4.09 The disposal of moncy payable as damages to persons under legal disability is regulated by rules 36.14 to 36.17 of the Ordinary Cause Rules,

---

[29] *Moodie v. Dempster*, 1931 S.C. 553, *per* L.P. Clyde at 554.

[30] Trayner, p. 456. *Reid v. Reid* (1839) 1 D. 400; *Thomson v. Thomson* [1887] 14 R. 634; *Moodie, supra*; *McGaughey v. Livingstone*, 1991 S.C.L.R. 412.

[31] *McGaughey, supra*, at 413F.

[32] *Moodie, supra, per* L.P. Clyde at 555. A curator *bonis* may also be appointed to a person who is prevented from managing his affairs by physical incapacity: see Walker, *Judicial Factors*, p. 24.

[33] *Anderson's Trs v. Skinner* (1871) 8 S.L.R. 325; *Latta*, 1977 S.L.T. 127 at 130. *Cf. Govan v. Thomson*, Dec. 20, 1814, F.C.

[34] *Anderson's Trs., supra*; *Moodie v. Dempster*, 1931 S.C. 553.

[35] *Moodie, supra, per* Lord Sands at 555; *Drummond's Trs v. Peel's Trs*, 1929 S.C. 484; *Finlay v. Finlay*, 1962 S.L.T. (Sh. Ct.) 43.

[36] *Moodie, supra*. If a minor pursuer becomes insane after instructing the raising of an action with the consent and concurrence of his curator, a curator *ad litem* is unnecessary: *Hutchison v. Dougall's Trs*, 1912 2 S.L.T. 516.

[37] OCR, r. 33.16; Divorce (Scotland) Act 1976, s. 11. See para. 22.24.

[38] paras 4.24 to 4.28.

[39] OCR, r. 33.13. See para. 22.21.

[40] *AB v. CB*, 1937 S.C. 408 (preliminary proof); *Gibson v. Gibson*, 1970 S.L.T. (Notes) 60 (undefended proof continued and medical evidence adduced).

[41] Bell, *Prin.*, s. 2103; Dickson, para. 114(1).

[42] *AB, supra, per* L.J.-C. Aitchison at 418.

[43] *AB, supra*.

[44] *McIntyre v. McIntyre*, 1920 1 S.L.T. 207.

which are considered below.[45] Where in an action of damages arising from personal injury or death a sum of money becomes payable to an insane person, it is in general ordered to be paid to his curator *bonis*.

Children

Prior to the commencement of the Age of Legal Capacity (Scotland) Act 1991 the law distinguished between pupil and minor children. A child was in pupillage from birth until the age of 14, if a male, and until 12, if a female. Minority, in this narrow sense as distinct from the wider sense applicable to all persons under age, began when pupillarity ended, and continued until majority,[46] *i.e.* the age of 18 in both males and females.[47] It was commonly said that a pupil had no *persona standi in judicio*,[48] and could not appear by himself as pursuer or defender.[49] A pupil was subject to the guardianship of tutors. His tutor, who was the guardian of his person as well as his property, acted for him in all legal transactions. Thus, where the pupil was litigant, his tutor was *dominus litis* in that he was in complete control of the case, with power to compromise or continue the proceedings. If the pupil was legitimate, both parents were his tutors and either might act without the other. If he was illegitimate, his mother was his tutrix but his father had no rights as tutor unless he subsequently married the mother.[50] On the death of a parent a child might have a nominated tutor, or where both parents were dead a tutor-at-law or a factor *loco tutoris* appointed by the court.[51] In certain circumstances parental rights and powers might be vested in a local authority or voluntary organisation.[52] **4.10**

Under the Age of Legal Capacity (Scotland) Act 1991 as amended by the Children (Scotland) Act 1995 any reference in any rule of law, enactment or document to the tutor of a pupil child is now to be construed as referring to a person entitled to act as the legal representative of a child and no further appointments are to be made to the office of factor *loco tutoris*.[53] For this purpose a child is a person under the age of 16 years.[54] A parent of a child has the responsibility and right to act as the child's legal representative.[55] By parent is meant, subject to exceptions for adoptive parents and persons deemed to be parents under the Human Fertilisation and Embryology Act 1990, the child's genetic father or mother; but a father has parental responsibilities and rights, including those of legal representation, only if married to the mother at the time of the child's conception or subsequently.[56] Parental responsibilities may, however, be imposed and rights conferred on any person by order of the Court,[57] a natural father may acquire such responsibilities and rights by **4.11**

---

[45] paras 21.37 to 21.42.

[46] Ersk., I, vii, 1.

[47] Age of Majority (Scotland) Act 1969, s. 1(1).

[48] *Keith v. Archer* (1836) 15 S. 116, *per* Lord Corehouse at 117. But this was true only in a qualified sense as Lord Corehouse makes clear. See *Peel v. Drummond's Trs*, 1929 S.C. 484, *per* Lord President Clyde at 493.

[49] *Earl of Craven v. Lord Elibank's Trs* (1854) 16 D. 811, *per* L.J.-C. Hope at pp. 820–821.

[50] Law Reform (Parent and Child) (Scotland) Act 1986, ss. 2(1), (4), 8.

[51] Walker, *Judicial Factors*, Chap. 2.

[52] Social Work (Scotland) Act 1968, ss. 16–18.

[53] Age of Legal Capacity (Scotland) Act 1991, s. 5 (1) and (4).

[54] *ibid.* s. 5(1) and Children (Scotland) Act 1995, ss. 1(2)(a) and 2(7).

[55] Children (Scotland) Act 1995, ss. 1(1) and 2(2).

[56] *ibid.* ss. 15(1) and 3(1).

[57] *ibid.* s. 11.

agreement,[58] or exercise them by arrangement,[59] and a parent may appoint a guardian to act in the event of death to whom such responsibilities and rights will accrue.[60]

4.12 A child who has general understanding of what it means to instruct a solicitor in connection with any civil matter has legal capacity to sue or defend in any civil proceedings and a child of 12 or more is presumed to have that understanding.[61] It appears that in a child under 12 sufficiency of understanding will require to be proved and that in a child of or over that age the presumption of understanding is open to rebuttal. A child who lacks such understanding, actual or presumed, has no legal capacity to bring or defend, or take any steps in, civil proceedings.[62] The capacity to sue and defend conferred on children of sufficient understanding is irreconcilable with the right of legal representation conferred on parents. That right is therefore to be regarded as extinguished when the child attains understanding as is the parental responsibility of legal representation although the person who would have had that responsibility may act with the child's consent.[63] The raising of an action by or, it would seem, in the name of a child who does not have the requisite understanding or his defending an action or taking any step in proceedings is void[64] except where under any rule of law or practice existing before the Age of Legal Capacity (Scotland) Act 1991 that might have been done in the name of a child who had no legal representative or whose legal representative was unable (by reason of conflict of interest or otherwise) or refused to act.[65] In such a case the court may appoint a curator *ad litem*.[66] The general rule of the law prior to 1991 that there was no fundamental nullity in an instance in the name of pupil child but merely a defect curable by the appointment of a curator *ad litem* and his entering the process[67] is therefore, in effect, preserved.

4.13 The result of the new statutory regime is that the position of a child who has legal capacity is assimilated to that of an adult except that the person who, had he lacked capacity, would have been his legal representative may with his consent act as such. On a strict, if anomalous, interpretation of the 1991 Act it also appears that, in contrast with the position of a capax adult, a curator *ad litem* may be appointed to such a child.[68] Subject to the changes which have been noticed in the preceding paragraphs, the position of children who lack capacity and their legal representative is, on the other hand, assimilated to that of pupil children and their tutors under the previous law. The previous law on pupils and tutors can therefore be taken, subject to those changes, as representing the present law in relation to children under incapacity and their legal representatives. It is on that basis that the law is discussed in the following paragraphs.

---

[58] Children (Scotland) Act 1995, s. 4.
[59] *ibid.* s. 3(5).
[60] *ibid.* s. 7.
[61] Age of Legal Capacity (Scotland) Act 1991, ss. 2(4) and 4(a).
[62] *ibid.* s. 1(i).
[63] Children (Scotland) Act 1995, s. 15(6).
[64] Age of Legal Capacity (Scotland) Act 1991, ss. 2(5) and 9(c).
[65] *ibid.* s. 1(3)(f)(i).
[66] *ibid.* s. 1(3)(f)(ii).
[67] *Drummond v. Peel's Trs*, 1928 S.C. 484, *per* L.P. Clyde at 493.
[68] See *supra*, n. 66, and *infra*, para. 4.20.

4.14 Where the child has a legal representative, an action should be brought in the name of his representative suing in that capacity.[69] A legal representative who raises an action in the interest of the child he represents and who is unsuccessful is liable personally for judicial expenses to which the defender is found entitled.[70] Where a child on whose behalf an action has been raised by his legal representative attains the age of 16, or attains the requisite understanding for capacity during the dependence of the action, he may be sisted as pursuer, in place of his representative; and in the event of a final decree in favour of the defender, expenses may be awarded against the representative up to the date of sisting the child as pursuer, and against the child subsequent to that date.[71] If, under the former law, an action was brought in name of a pupil child, the court might appoint a curator *ad litem* after the case was brought into court, and the action would proceed if the curator *ad litem* concurred.[72] If the defender objected that the action had not been raised by the tutor, and the court refused to appoint a curator *ad litem*, the action could not proceed.[73] But if the defender did not object to the instance, he was thereafter personally barred from challenging the decree on that ground.[74] It remains the law that the action cannot proceed unless a curator *ad litem* is appointed and enters the process and it is thought that the saving provisions of the Age of Legal Capacity (Scotland) Act 1991[75] have the effect that the defender's failure to object continues to constitute personal bar, with the result that decree cannot be challenged. The object of appointing a curator *ad litem* to a child pursuer is to overcome his legal incapacity where the circumstances make the appointment necessary in his interests.[76] Examples of such circumstances, which are not exhaustive,[77] are: where the child has no representative[78]; where the whereabouts of the child's legal representative are unknown[79]; where the representative himself is *incapax*[80]; where the representative has an adverse interest[81]; and where the representative refuses to sue except, perhaps, where there are no circumstances indicating that he is not acting with regard to the child's interests.[82] The duties of a

---

[69] Statements that proceedings ought to be in the pupil's name as well as in that of the tutor (Bell, *Prin.*, s. 2082; *Whitehall v. Whitehall*, 1958 S.C. 252, *per* Lord Mackintosh at 259) do not appear to be in accordance with modern practice *quoad* pursuers (*Encyclopaedia of Styles*, i, 85; Dobie, *Styles*, p. 218; *Davis's Tutor v. Glasgow Victoria Hospitals*, 1950 S.C. 382; *McGlone v. British Railways Board*, 1966 S.C.(H.L.) 1 at 2; *McKinnell v. White*, 1971 S.L.T. (Notes) 61).

[70] *White v. Steel* (1894) 21 R. 649; *Wilkinson v. Kinneil Cannel and Coking Coal Co. Ltd* (1897) 24 R. 1001.

[71] *Wilkinson, supra*, at 1009.

[72] *Keith v. Archer* (1836) 15 S. 116, *per* Lord Corehouse at 118. The term "tutor *ad litem*" is sometimes found where the ward is a pupil (*Aitken's Trs v. Miles*, 1921 S.C. 454), but "curator *ad litem*" appears to be now in general use: see Ersk., I, vii, 13; Maclaren, p. 187.

[73] *Carrigan v. Cleland* (1907) 15 S.L.T. 543.

[74] *Sinclair v. Stark* (1828) 6 S. 336 at 338; *Ward v. Walker*, 1920 S.C. 80; *Drummond's Trs v. Peel's Trs*, 1929 S.C. 484, *per* L.P. Clyde at 493.

[75] s. 1(3)(f)(i). See *supra*, para. 4.12.

[76] *Kirk v. Scottish Gas Board*, 1968 S.C. 328, *per* Lord Guthrie at 330–331.

[77] *ibid.*

[78] *Ward v. Walker*, 1920 S.C. 80; *Hughes v. Lord Advocate*, 1963 S.C.(H.L.) 31 at 32.

[79] *Steen v. Macnicol*, Feb. 28, 1967, unreported, *cit. Kirk, supra*, at 331.

[80] *Rankine* (1821) 1 S. 118 (N.E. 117).

[81] *McConochie v. Binnie* (1847) 9 D. 791; *Kirk, supra.*

[82] *Keith v. Archer* (1836) 15 S. 16, *per* Lord Balgray at 118; *Bogie v. Bogie* (1840) 3 D. 309; *Park v. Park* (1876) 3 R. 850; *Ross v. Tennant's Trs* (1877) 5 R. 182. *Cf. Munro's Trs v. Munro*, 1971 S.C. 280. A factor's rejection of counsel's advice to accept an offer in settlement of a claim for damages was held not to demonstrate a conflict of interest which would justify the appointment of a curator *ad litem*. *Kay v. Ayrshire and Arran Health Board, The Scotsman*, Jan. 15, 1982 (not otherwise reported on this point).

curator *ad litem*,[83] and the procedure to be followed where damages are awarded to a child,[84] are considered below.

4.15 Where a child is called as defender, his representative must also be called. The reason for the rule formulated in terms of the previous law still, with necessary changes, applies, and is:

> "that as by the law of Scotland there is scarcely any pupil who may not have either a tutor-nominate or a relation entitled to the office of tutor-at-law, the citation of such parties is insisted on, so that they may be made aware that the interests of the pupil are called into question in a court of law, and that they may, if they think it their duty, attend to such interests."[85]

Different rules apply according as the child has, or has not, a legal representative.

4.16 Where the child has a known legal representative, both should be called as defenders, and where the child is known to have a representative but the representative's identity is not known, the action should be brought against the child and his legal representatives generally[86]: otherwise the decree will be null,[87] even where a curator *ad litem* has been appointed.[88] If the legal representative is called as defender, is cited and appears in the process, a decree against the defenders is binding on the child[89]; and if, having been called and cited, the legal representative fails to appear and the court appoints a curator *ad litem*, a decree against the child will be valid.[90]

4.17 Where a child is known to have no legal representative,[91] or where it is not known whether he has a legal representative,[92] the action must be brought against the child "and his legal representatives, if he any has".[93] In the Court of Session the latter are cited edictally,[94] but there is no edictal citation in the sheriff court.[95] If no legal representative appears and no curator *ad litem* is appointed, any decree obtained is a valid decree in absence.[96]

4.18 Even although there is no appearance for the defenders in an action raised against a child, it is competent to appoint a curator *ad litem* to the

---

[83] paras 4.23 to 4.26.

[84] para. 21.43.

[85] *Thomson's Trs v. Livingston* (1863) 2 M. 114, *per* Lord Jerviswoode at 115. Lord Jerviswoode was speaking, in relation to the law as it then was, of a pupil child whose father was dead, but the same reasoning applied to the citation of the father as administrator-at-law.

[86] Maclaren, pp. 169–170.

[87] *Earl of Craven v. Lord Elibank's Trs* (1854) 16 D. 811.

[88] *Thomson's Trs v. Livingston* (1863) 2 M. 114.

[89] *Earl of Craven, supra*, at 820–821.

[90] *Agnew v. Earl of Stair* (1822) 1 Shaw's App. 333.

[91] *Crighton v. Lord Rossie* (1573) Mor. 2178.

[92] Maxwell, p. 137.

[93] *Thomson's Trs v. Livingston* (1863) 2 M. 114. "Curators as well as tutors are called presumably to meet the not unusual situation where the actual age of the defender is unknown to the pursuer" (Maxwell, p. 138, n. 1).

[94] Maclaren, p. 171.

[95] Provision was made for edictal citation in the 1907 Act, Sched. I, r. 15; but there is no corresponding provision in the current OCR.

[96] *Sinclair v. Stark* (1828) 6 S. 336; *Dick v. McIlwham* (1828) 6 S. 798; *Sinclair or MacDonald v. Brown* (1835) 13 S. 594, 2 Sh. & McL. 103, (1837) 15 S. 770, (1841) 3 D. 871; *Grieve or Dingwall v. Burns* (1871) 9 M. 582; *Drummond's Trs v. Peel's Trs*, 1929 S.C. 484, *per* Lord Hunter at 507.

child, whether or not he has any legal representatives. There may, however, be cases where the court considers it unnecessary or inexpedient to make such an appointment; and a curator *ad litem*, if appointed, is not obliged to lodge defences but must consider whether a defence should be put in or not and may decide to allow decree to pass against the child,[97] the decree having effect as a decree in absence.[98]

If an action raised against a child is defended on his behalf, any decree against him is a decree *in foro*. Reduction on the grounds of minority and lesion is no longer available.[99] **4.19**

As already noticed[1] the position of children not under incapacity is the same as that of adults with two exceptions—(1) a person who would have had the responsibility of legal representation may act if the child consents and (2) a curator *ad litem* may be appointed. The latter exception requires further consideration. Under the Age of Legal Capacity (Scotland) Act 1991 nothing in that Act affects any existing rule of law or practice whereby the court may appoint a curator *ad litem* to a person under the age of 16 years.[2] The preservation of the existing law is not qualified by any reference to the capacity of the person to whom the appointment is made and it appears to override the abolition of curatory by reason of age alone. A curator *ad litem* may therefore be appointed to a child although that child is under no incapacity. It is, however, submitted that the functions of such a curator *ad litem* can be no greater than the giving of advice and assistance. Anything else would be inconsistent with the capacity possessed by the child. Where an action is raised against a child who is presumed or can be shown to have the requisite understanding it is unnecessary to call his legal representatives as defenders. It may nonetheless be prudent to do so lest dispute should arise. They may be called "for any interest they may have". **4.20**

Young persons

The Age of Legal Capacity (Scotland) Act 1991 has replaced for persons between 16 and 18 the previous law applicable to minors in the sense of persons between pupillarity and majority. At common law a minor was subject to no legal incapacity, but his appearance as a litigant was governed by particular procedural rules. The minor was *dominus litis*, and it was the function of his curator, who was not the guardian of his person and did not act for him in legal transactions, to give or withhold consent to the proceedings. If the minor was legitimate, both parents were his curators, and either might act without the other. If he was illegitimate, his mother was his curatrix, but his father had no rights as curator unless he subsequently married the mother. If the minor was a married woman, her husband, if of full age and subject to no legal incapacity, was her curator: if her husband was also in minority her father or other curator was entitled to continue to act as such until she attained majority or her husband's curatory commenced. **4.21**

---

[97] *Drummond's Trs v. Peel's Trs*, 1929 S.C. 484, esp. *per* Lord Hunter at 505. On the duties of a curator *ad litem* see paras 4.23 to 4.26.

[98] *Sinclair v. Stark* (1828) 6 S. 336; *Drummond's Trs, supra.*

[99] Age of Legal Capacity (Scotland) Act 1991, s. 1(5).

[1] para. 4.13.

[2] s. 1(3)(f)(ii).

4.22 Curatory of minors is abolished by the age of Legal Capacity (Scotland) Act 1991. Under that Act no one may be the subject of curatory by reason of age alone[3] and a person of or over the age of 16 has legal capacity to bring or defend or take any steps in civil proceedings.[4] The provisions of the Act on ratification of proposed transactions and setting aside of prejudicial transactions do not apply to such proceedings.[5] The parental responsibility of guidance applies but there is no corresponding parental right.[6] It is undecided whether the abolition of the curatory of minors renders it incompetent to appoint a curator *ad litem* to exercise that responsibility in place of or in the absence of a parent or guardian. The court may, in any event, impose the responsibility of guidance on a person other than the parent or guardian.[7] With that exception, the position of a person of 16 years or over but under 18 in relation to civil proceedings is no different in its essentials from that of an adult.

Curator ad litem

4.23 The circumstances in which the court may appoint a curator *ad litem* have already been considered.[8] The court may make the appointment *ex proprio motu* or on the application of any interested party.[9] Apart from the appointment of a curator *ad litem* to a defender in an action of divorce or separation who is suffering from mental disorder, which is mandatory,[10] it is for the court, in its discretion, to determine whether in the circumstances of the particular case justice demands that an appointment be made.[11] In so determining, the court may take account of the interests not only of the child or *incapax* but also of others concerned in the issue, whether as parties to the action or otherwise.[12] Since the appointment is of a curator *ad litem pendentem*, applications for appointment presented in anticipation of litigation are not granted.[13] The appointment is normally made at the outset of proceedings,[14] but may be made at any time thereafter.[15] The person appointed is normally a solicitor, but any competent person may be appointed. He takes and signs the declaration *de fideli administratione officii*[16] and is allowed to see the process. He does not find caution since he has no power to intermeddle with the ward's estate[17] and cannot be made personally liable for any part of the expenses of process.[18]

---

3 s. 5(3).
4 s. 1(1)(b).
5 s. 3(2)(d).
6 Children (Scotland) Act 1995, s. 1(1)(b)(ii) and 2(b).
7 *ibid.* s. 11(1).
8 paras 4.07 (insane person), 4.14 to 4.18, 4.20 (child), 4.21 (young person).
9 *Drummond's Trs v. Peel's Trs*, 1929 S.C. 484, *per* Lord Moncrieff at 519; Dobie, *Styles*, p. 320.
10 OCR, r. 33.16.
11 *Drummonds Trs, supra, per* L.P. Clyde at 497–499, L.J.-C. Alness at 505, Lord Sands at 512–513, Lord Morison at 516, Lord Murray at 518; *Kirk v. Scottish Gas Board*, 1968 S.C. 328, *per* Lord Guthrie at 331; *Cunningham v. Smith* (1880) 7 R. 424, *per* Lord Shand at 426.
12 *Drummond's Trs, supra, per* Lord Sands at 513, Lord Murray at 518, Lord Mackay at 523.
13 *Baird* (1741) Mor. 16346; *Youngs, Petrs* (1828) 7 S. 220 *per* L.J.-C. Boyle; *Wallace* (1830) 9 S. 40; *Ward v. Walker*, 1920 S.C. 80; *Drummond's Trs, supra, per* L.P. Clyde at 493.
14 *Youngs, Petrs* (1828) 7 S. 220, *per* L.J.-C. Boyle; *Drummond's Trs, supra, per* L.P. Clyde at 493.
15 *Hamilton* (1861) 24 D. 31; *Finlay v. Finlay*, 1962 S.L.T. (Sh. Ct.) 43.
16 *Christie* (1873) 1 R. 237; Sellar's *Forms*, Vol. i, p. 267.
17 Ersk., I, vii, 13.
18 See para. 4.27.

Since the curator *ad litem* is an officer of the court, appointed in order that the court may be satisfied that the case is properly conducted,[19] it is his duty to exercise his judgment independently and protect or safeguard the interests of his ward so far as they are affected by the particular action.[20] He has no control over the person of the ward, and thus cannot consent to the sampling and testing of the ward's blood.[21] The duties of a curator *ad litem* to a defender in an action of divorce or separation who is suffering from mental disorder are considered elsewhere.[22] **4.24**

The curator's powers are confined to the process for which he was appointed, and are limited in the same way as those of a regular guardian of the ward would be, in any event as regards the continuance or compromise of the action. Thus, the curator *ad litem* to a child under incapacity or, it is thought, to an insane person is *dominus litis*. It is his first duty to consider whether the action ought in the interests of the ward to be proceeded with.[23] Accordingly, he has power to settle the action[24]; and where his ward is a defender, he must consider whether a defence should be put in or not.[25] If defences have already been lodged on behalf of such a ward, the curator must satisfy himself that the defence has so far been properly conducted and that it should be continued, or that the defence ought no longer to be insisted in, and, in either event, to report to the court accordingly; and, if the defence is to be insisted in, to satisfy himself that it continues to be properly conducted in the interests of the ward, and to make such reports to the court from time to time as he considers necessary or as the court may require.[26] **4.25**

In any process the curator *ad litem* may retrospectively validate the prior actings of the ward in the process.[27] Whether in any process in which solicitors are not already acting on behalf of the ward the curator should himself conduct the ward's case or should be represented by solicitors and, if necessary, counsel is a question of circumstances. The disposal of money payable to persons under legal disability is regulated by O.C.R., rules 36.14 to 36.17, which are considered below.[28] Where in an action of damages arising from personal injury or death a sum of money becomes payable to an insane person, it is in general ordered to be paid to his curator *bonis*. **4.26**

Since the curator *ad litem* is appointed by the court from considerations of public policy, he is in a peculiar position in regard to expenses.[29] If he is not assured of sufficient funds to enable him to safeguard the interests of his ward, he may apply to the court for an order on an **4.27**

---

19 Maclaren, p. 184.
20 *Drummond's Trs, supra, per* L.P. Clyde at 496, Lord Hunter at 504.
21 *Docherty v. McGlynn*, 1983 S.L.T. 645 at 647.
22 See paras 22.24, 22.25; *Drumore, Petrs* (1741) Mor. 16349; Ersk., I, vii, 13.
23 *Ward v. Walker*, 1920 S.C. 80, *per* Lord Skerrington at 86.
24 *Dewar v. Dewar's Trs* (1906) 14 S.L.T. 238.
25 *Drummond's Trs, supra, per* Lord Moncrieff at 486, L.J.-C. Alness at 501, Lord Hunter at 505, Lord Sands at 512, 514, Lord Murray at 518; *Munro's Trs v. Munro*, 1971 S.C. 280 at 284.
26 *Drummond's Trs, supra, per* L.P. Clyde at 496; *Finlay v. Finlay*, 1962 S.L.T. (Sh. Ct.) 43.
27 *Youngs* (1828) 7 S. 220; *Keith v. Archer* (1836) 15 S. 116; *Drummond's Trs, supra, per* L.P. Clyde at 494, 495; *Munro's Trs, supra*, at 284.
28 paras. 21.37 to 21.42.
29 *Dunlop v. Brown* (1903) 11 S.L.T. 522.

appropriate party to supply him with funds.[30] Where no funds are available in the process, it may be his duty to apply for legal aid on behalf of his ward.[31] He is entitled to remuneration for his professional services[32]; and such remuneration may be recovered from the party requiring his appointment or from a defender on acceptance of a tender "with the expenses of process".[33] He cannot be made personally liable for any part of the expenses of process.[34] Where he is successful, he may be awarded expenses on the general principle that expenses follow the event. Where he is unsuccessful, there is no absolute rule. He is not in every case entitled to an award of expenses even though he is unsuccessful, but he appears to be in a more favourable position in regard to expenses than the ordinary unsuccessful litigant.[35] In some cases he may recover his expenses from the party who required his appointment,[36] or whose actings brought about his appointment.[37] It has been said that the court will always try to secure his expenses out of any available fund if at all possible.[38]

4.28 If the curator *ad litem* seeks discharge of his appointment *pendente lite*, he should lodge a minute setting forth the circumstances.[39] If a minor becomes insane *pendente lite* the appointment of his curator *ad litem* falls.[40] When the action is terminated, the appointment ceases.[41]

TITLE AND INTEREST

4.29 A party to an action must not only have the capacity to maintain or defend it: he must also have both a title and an interest to do so.[42] "Title" and "interest", "although they are different, often very much run into each other".[43] In broad terms, "title" connotes a formal legal relationship to the subject-matter of the action, and "interest" some benefit from asserting the right with which the action is concerned or from preventing its infringement.[44] The title and interest of pursuers to sue and of defenders to defend any particular action are thus matters to be regulated by the substantive law affecting the merits of that action, and are beyond the scope of this book. The law of procedure is concerned only with the general concepts of title and interest to sue and defend, and with the general rules of procedure provided to regulate legal proceedings brought by or against particular parties. This section of the chapter considers separately title and interest to sue, and title and interest to

---

30 *Studd v. Cook* (1883) 10 R. (H.L.) 53; *Smith v. Smith's Tr.* (1900) 8 S.L.T. 226; *Cathcart v. Cathcart's Trs* (1906) 13 S.L.T. 909; *Percy v. Percy*, 1923 S.L.T. 295.

31 Maxwell, p. 229; *Walls v. Walls*, 1953 S.L.T. 269.

32 *Rennie* (1849) 11 D. 1021; *Pirie v. Collie* (1851) 13 D. 841.

33 *Campbell v. Alexander & Sons Ltd*, 1934 S.L.T. 52.

34 *Fraser v. Pattie* (1847) 9 D. 903.

35 *Dunlop, supra.*

36 *Johnstone* (1885) 12 R. 468; *Walker v. Walker* (1903) 5 F. 320; Campbell, *supra.*

37 *Rooney v. Cormack* (1895) 23 R. 11.

38 Maclaren, p. 186; Maxwell, p. 229.

39 *Walls v. Walls*, 1953 S.L.T. 269.

40 *Moodie v. Dempster*, 1931 S.C. 553.

41 Ersk., I, vii, 13; *Drummond's Trs v. Peel's Trs*, 1929 S.C. 484, *per* Lord Hunter at 505.

42 *D. & J. Nicol v. Dundee Harbour Trs*, 1915 S.C.(H.L.) 7, *per* Lord Dunedin at 12.

43 *Summerlee Iron Co. Ltd v. Lindsay*, 1907 S.C. 1161, *per* L.P. Dunedin at 1165.

44 Mackay, *Practice*, i, 279; Thomson and Middleton, pp. 50–52. See paras 4.30 (title), 4.33 (interest).

defend; and the final part of the chapter deals with the procedural rules concerning proceedings brought by or against particular parties.

Title to sue

"Title to sue" is difficult to define, but for a person to have a title to sue he must be a party (in the widest sense) to some legal relation which gives him some right which the person against whom he raises the action either infringes or denies.[45] **4.30**

The pursuer must correctly set out his title in the condescendence and, if he fails to do so when his title is challenged, his action will be dismissed.[46] If his title is founded on a document it should be specified in the condescendence and lodged in process at the time of returning the initial writ under rule 9.3.[47] A preliminary proof on the question of title may be necessary.[48] **4.31**

The pursuer must have a title to sue at the date of the raising of the action (which is the date of the service of the initial writ on the defender)[49] and a continuing title to pursue the action to final judgment.[50] At the date of the raising of the action the pursuer must have a title to sue or at least a substantial right which requires merely a subsequent formality to complete it.[51] If he has not, the lack cannot be cured by a subsequent assignation[52] or retrocession[53] or by the consent and concurrence of the person to whom the right of action truly belongs.[54] If basically the title is in the pursuer, although it is not complete or is subject to some qualification, he may complete the steps required to clear his title of defects or qualifications during the action.[55] In an appropriate case the action may be sisted to enable him to establish his title.[56] If the pursuer's title becomes defective only after the action has been raised, the court may allow the instance to be amended by the addition of a pursuer to whose title no objection can be taken.[57] Where a pursuer averred that after the action had been raised the defenders had deprived him of title in order to stifle the action, the court allowed a proof before answer.[58] **4.32**

---

[45] *D. & J. Nicol v. Dundee Harbour Trs*, 1915 S.C.(H.L.) 7, *per* Lord Dunedin at 12–13; *Air 2000 Ltd v. Secretary of State for Transport (No. 2)*, 1991 S.L.T. 335, *per* Lord Clyde at 337L–338C.

[46] *Mackintosh v. Mackintosh* (1835) 13 S. 884; *Hutchison v. Ferrier* (1846) 8 D. 1228; *Kilmarnock Mags v. Mather* (1869) 7 M. 548; *Bentley v. Macfarlane*, 1964 S.C. 76, *per* Lord Guthrie at 83; *Microwave Systems (Scotland) Ltd v. Electro-Physiological Instruments Ltd*, 1971 S.C. 140. On the plea of "No title to sue", see para. 9.116.

[47] OCR, r. 21.1(1); *Horne & Ross v. Ram* (1848) 11 D. 141; *Shaw v. Shaw's Trs* (1876) 3 R. 813.

[48] *Leith-Buchanan v. Hogg*, 1930 S.N. 130.

[49] *Alston v. Macdougall* (1887) 15 R. 78; *Jack v. MacKay*, 1990 S.C.L.R. 816 (pursuer deceased when action raised). See para. 6.06.

[50] *Donaghy v. Rollo*, 1964 S.C. 278.

[51] *Symington v. Campbell* (1894) 21 R. 434; *David Boswell Ltd v. William Cook Engineering Ltd*, 1989 S.L.T. (Sh. Ct.) 61.

[52] *Symington, supra.*

[53] *Bentley v. Maclarlane*, 1964 S.C. 76.

[54] *Hislop v. MacRitchie's Trs* (1881) 8 R. (H.L.) 95; *Eagle Lodge Ltd v. Keir and Cawder Estates Ltd*, 1964 S.C. 30.

[55] *Symington, supra, per* Lord Adam at 437; *Doughty Shipping Co. Ltd v. N.B. Ry.*, 1909 1 S.L.T. 267; *Bentley, supra*, L.P. Clyde at 79; *Craham v. Craham*, 1968 S.L.T. (Notes) 42; *Lanarkshire Health Board v. Banafaa*, 1987 S.L.T. 229; *David Boswell Ltd, supra.*

[56] *Shaw v. Shaw's Trs* (1876) 3 R. 813; *McLean v. Glasgow Corporation*, 1933 S.L.T. 396.

[57] *Donaghy, supra*; OCR, r. 18.2(2)(b).

[58] *McDowall v. McGhee*, 1913 2 S.L.T. 238.

Interest to sue

4.33 Besides a title to sue, the pursuer must have an interest to pursue the action, which has been defined above as some benefit from asserting the right with which the action is concerned or from preventing its infringement.[59] The grounds of the rule that interest is necessary as well as title are that it is the function of the courts to decide practical questions, and that no person is entitled to subject another to the trouble and expense of a litigation unless he has some real interest to enforce or protect.[60] The interest need not be pecuniary or patrimonial, but it may be the interest in any right recognised by law.[61] It may be small[62] or contingent[63] but it must not be remote.[64] It is for the court to decide whether a sufficient interest has been shown.[65] A plea of no title to sue always leaves it open to the party proponing it to contend that the title fails through lack of sufficient interest to maintain the action; and it is generally, though by no means invariably, on the ground of lack of interest that a plea of no title to sue succeeds.[66] It is rare for a pursuer to have a title but no interest.[67] In general, an interest to sue implies a title,[68] but it does not necessarily confer a title to sue a particular person or action.[69]

Title and interest to defend

4.34 Every person who is called as a defender has a title to state and to be heard on his defences to the action.[70] The pursuer's denial of his right to do so would be a denial of the pursuer's own interest to bring an action against him.[71] The defender, however, may have insufficient interest to maintain his defences.[72]

4.35 A person who has not been called as a defender may have a title and interest to defend, and may apply to be sisted as a party if decree in the action would in any way affect his rights.[73] He must, however, have both a title and an interest to defend.[74]

---

[59] para. 4.29.

[60] *Swanson v. Manson*, 1907 S.C. 426, *per* Lord Ardwall at 429.

[61] Mackay, *Manual*, p. 125: *e.g. Edinburgh Mags v. Macfarlane* (1857) 20 D. 156; *Gunstone v. Scottish Women's Amateur Athletic Association*, 1987 S.L.T. 611.

[62] *Strang v. Steuart* (1864) 2 M. 1015, *per* L.J.-C. Inglis at 1029; *Browne v. Orr* (1872) 10 M. 397.

[63] *Strathallan v. Glenlyon's Trs* (1837) 15 S. 971; *Raes v. Meek* (1889) 16 R.(H.L.) 31 at 33; *Hannah v. Hannah's Trs*, 1958 S.L.T. (Notes) 9; *Hayes v. Robinson*, 1984 S.L.T. 300.

[64] *Agnew v. Laughlan*, 1948 S.C. 656.

[65] *Earl of Zetland v. Hislop* (1882) 9 R.(H.L.) 40.

[66] *Agnew, supra*, at 661.

[67] For examples, see *Gould v. McCorquodale* (1869) 8 M. 165, L.P. Inglis at 170; *Maguire v. Burges*, 1909 S.C. 1283.

[68] *Doherty v. Norwich Union Fire Insurance Society Ltd*, 1974 S.C. 213 at 220.

[69] *Bellenden v. Earl of Winchelsea* (1825) 3 S. 367; *D. & J. Nicol v. Dundee Harbour Trs*, 1915 S.C.(H.L.) 7, *per* Lord Dunedin at 12.

[70] *Low v. Scottish Amicable Building Society*, 1940 S.L.T. 295 at 296; *McLauchlan v. McLauchlan's Trs*, 1941 S.L.T. 43 at 44.

[71] *Murray's Trs v. Trs for St Margaret's Convent* (1906) 8 F. 1109, *per* Lord Kinnear at 1116–1117.

[72] *Schaw v. Black* (1889) 16 R. 336: *McLaughlan, supra.*

[73] *Glasgow Shipowners' Association v. Clyde Navigation Trs* (1885) 12 R. 695; *Gas Power and By Products Co. Ltd v. Power Gas Corpn Ltd*, 1911 S.C. 27; *Zurich General Accident and Liability Insurance Co. v. Livingston*, 1938 S.C. 582.

[74] *Muir v. Glasgow Corporation*, 1917 2 S.L.T. 106.

If all those parties whose appearance or failure to appear is necessary to have the question at issue disposed of have not been called, the defender may plead that all parties have not been called. It is also *pars judicis* to notice that all such parties have not been called.[75] Additional defenders may be added by amendment.[76] **4.36**

SPECIAL CLASSES OF PARTIES

This section of the chapter considers the special rules of procedure which regulate legal proceedings brought by or against particular parties. **4.37**

(1) Several pursuers

An action in which two or more pursuers join is competent provided that two conditions are satisfied: (1) the ground of action by each pursuer must be identical; and (2) there must be no material prejudice to the defender by the pursuers' combining in one action.[77] The rule is justifiable on the ground that if an action is brought by a single pursuer a defender may more easily come to a settlement while, if there are several persons suing on different claims, any one of them by holding out may not only subject the defender to needless expense but prevent any settlement being reached.[78] Thus, separate pursuers cannot sue the same defender in one action for payment of debts arising out of separate and independent grounds of action.[79] Nor may they sue for payment to one pursuer or alternatively to another, and thus advance competing claims to the same debt.[80] Two or more pursuers injured by the same wrong of the same defender and claiming on the same grounds of action may join in one action, each claiming for himself respectively in a separate crave a separate sum of damages.[81] **4.38**

If an action is raised by pursuers whose grounds of action are not identical, the court may allow the instance to be amended by the removal of some of the pursuers, or of all but one pursuer,[82] or it may dismiss the action as incompetent.[83] **4.39**

Surviving relatives who wish to sue for damages arising from a death must sue together in one action, in order to enable the court to consider **4.40**

---

[75] On the plea of "All parties not called", see para. 9.117.

[76] OCR, r. 18.2(2)(d). See paras 10.11, 10.12.

[77] *Buchan v. Thomson*, 1976 S.L.T. 42 at 44. See also *Feuars in Orkney v. Stewart* (1741) Mor. 11986; *Brims & Mackay v. Pattullo*, 1907 S.C. 1106; *Smith-Shand's Trs v. Forbes*, 1921 S.C. 820; and cases cited *infra*.

[78] *Paxton v. Brown*, 1908 S.C. 406, *per* Lord McLaren at 414–415.

[79] *Paxton, supra, per* L.P. Dunedin at 412; *Feld British Agencies Ltd v. James Pringle Ltd*, 1961 S.L.T. 123; *Fishof v. Cheapside Bonding Co. Ltd*, 1972 S.L.T. (Notes) 7.

[80] *Interplan (Joiners and Shopfitters) Ltd v. Brown*, Sh.Pr. Caplan, Paisley Sh. Ct, June 26, 1984, unreported.

[81] *Harkes v. Mowat* (1862) 24 D. 701; *Cowan & Sons v. Duke of Buccleuch* (1876) 4 R.(H.L.) 14; *Mitchell v. Grierson* (1894) 21 R. 367; *Gray v. Caledonian Ry*, 1912 S.C. 339; *Browne v. Thomson & Co.*, 1912 S.C. 359. *Cf. Killin v. Weir* (1905) 7 F. 526; see also *Boulting v. Elias*, 1990 S.L.T. 596 (not competent where grounds of debt separate and independent).

[82] *Paxton, Smith-Shand's Trs, supra.*

[83] *Killin, Feld, Fishof, supra.*

their claims as interrelated family claims.[84] Provision is made by rules 36.1 to 36.7 of the Ordinary Cause Rules for the intimation of such actions to any other persons having title to sue and for the sisting of such persons as additional pursuers.[85]

(2) Several defenders

4.41 It is contrary to practice to sue in one action two or more defenders on separate and unconnected grounds inferring separate individual liability. Such an action may be dismissed as incompetent.[86] An action may, however, be laid against two or more defenders if their liability to the pursuer is alternative, or joint and several, or joint. The nature of their liability to the pursuer should be described in the crave. The matters discussed in paragraphs 4.42 to 4.44 are applicable both to joint obligants and to joint delinquents. The special procedural considerations relative to each of these classes are dealt with in subsequent paragraphs.[87]

4.42 The meaning of a decree for payment against two or more defenders jointly and severally is that, as regards the pursuer, each is made liable *in solidum* (*i.e.* for the whole debt), but that *inter se* they are liable *pro rata* (*i.e.* each for his own share): therefore a decree against each for full payment to the pursuer will still leave open to each a claim for contribution against the others. When an action is brought against several persons without the addition of words descriptive of the nature of their liability, then, if one of the defenders is assoilzied or if the pursuer passes from his action against him, the pursuer may continue to insist in the action against the remaining defenders. Each of these defenders would, however, only be liable jointly (*i.e.* for a share) unless the crave contained words denoting several liability (*i.e.* for the whole). The pursuer would therefore lose part of his claim unless he used the words "jointly and severally" in the crave to describe the nature of the defenders' liability. The word "severally" implies that against whatever number of defenders the pursuer proceeds, each is liable for the whole sum sued for, and the word "jointly" secures to those against whom the decree is made operative the right of rateable relief against the persons who have not paid.[88] From a procedural point of view there is no difference between a crave for payment against the defenders "jointly and severally" or a crave for payment against the defenders "jointly and severally or severally".[89] The pursuer has the option of recovering from any defender either the whole sum decerned for or a part of it; and, if the pursuer takes the

---

[84] *Darling v. Gray* (1892) 19 R.(H.L.) 31, *per* Lord Watson at 32; *Pollok v. Workman* (1900) 2 F. 354; *Allen v. McCombie's Trs*, 1909 S.C. 710; *Slorach v. Kerr*, 1921 S.C. 285; *Kinnaird v. McLean*, 1942 S.C. 448; *McNeil v. National Coal Board*, 1966 S.C. 72.

[85] See paras 21.14 to 21.18.

[86] *Liquidators of Western Bank v. Douglas* (1860) 22 D. 447, *per* L.J.-C. Inglis at 497; *Exchange Loan Co. v. Levenson* (1904) 21 Sh.Ct.Rep. 33. *Cf. Miller, Peel, Hughes, Rutherford & Co. v. Forrester* (1897) 5 S.L.T. 71, doubted, *Feld British Agencies Ltd v. James Pringle Ltd*, 1961 S.L.T. 123, *per* Lord Guthrie at 128.

[87] Two defenders may be jointly and severally liable where one is in breach of contract and the other has committed a delict, both thereby contributing to produce one wrong: *Belmont Laundry Co. Ltd v. Aberdeen Steam Laundry Co. Ltd* (1898) 1 F. 45; *Rose Street Foundry and Engineering Co. v. Lewis & Sons*, 1917 S.C. 341; both commented on in *Grunwald v. Hughes*, 1965 S.L.T. 209.

[88] *Fleming v. Gemmill*, 1908 S.C. 340, *per* Lord McLaren at 345; *Mackenzie v. Macallister*, 1909 S.C. 367, *per* L.P. Dunedin at 371.

[89] *Fleming, supra*; *Royal Bank of Scotland v. McKerracher*, 1968 S.L.T. (Sh. Ct.) 77.

former course, that defender has a right of relief against those defenders who have not paid, which he may make good if he can. A pursuer cannot, however, competently crave a joint and several decree against two or more defenders sued for separate causes of action.[90]

If an action competently brought against defenders jointly and severally fails against one defender, as by his being assoilzied[91] or by the case against him being held to be irrelevant,[92] or if one defender effects a settlement with the pursuer,[93] the action may proceed against the remaining defenders. If the action fails against one defender and the case is to be remitted to the Court of Session,[94] the remit should be delayed until any expenses found due to that defender are taxed and he has obtained an extract.[95] If the pursuer obtains a decree against one defender which turns out to be worthless, such as a decree in absence or a decree following on acceptance of a tender which is not satisfied, he is entitled to continue the action against the remaining defenders, adding appropriate averments explaining that his claim has not been satisfied. The test is not whether the pursuer has obtained a decree for the amount of his debt but whether he has in fact received satisfaction[96]: the action will fail only if the remaining defenders can aver and prove that the decree already granted has been extracted and satisfied by payment.[97] Any defender may be found liable for the whole sum. Some defenders may be assoilzied and the others decerned against jointly and severally.[98] A joint decree only may be pronounced.[99] The existence of a decree against one of several parties liable jointly and severally is no bar to an action against the others, except in so far as the party decerned against has actually satisfied the debt.[1] **4.43**

When an action is raised against a defender who considers that he is entitled to relief by another who has not been sued in that action, the defender should intimate the action to that other at once,[2] and should consider whether to plead that all parties are not called[3] or to invoke third party procedure.[4] **4.44**

---

[90] *Barr v. Neilson* (1868) 6 M. 651; *Ellerman Lines Ltd v. Clyde Navigation Trs*, 1909 S.C. 690, *per* L.P. Dunedin at 691–692.

[91] *Gibson v. Irvine* (1900) 7 S.L.T. 391; *Baird's Trs v. Leechman* (1903) 10 S.L.T. 515; *Gavin v. Henderson & Co.*, 1910 S.C. 357.

[92] *Robinson v. Reid's Trs* (1900) 2 F. 928, *per* Lord Moncreiff at 931; *Reilly v. Smith* (1904) 6 F. 662; *Rae v. Swanson* (1905) 21 Sh.Ct.Rep. 291; *Mackenzie, supra*. There may be cases in which the action will fail unless there is a relevant case against all the defenders: *Mackersy v. Davis & Sons* (1895) 22 R. 368.

[93] *Douglas v. Hogarth* (1901) 4 F. 148; *McNair v. Dunfermline Corporation*, 1953 S.C. 183; *Arrow Chemicals Ltd v. Guild*, 1978 S.L.T. 206; Walker, *Delict*, pp. 116–118; Walker, *Civil Remedies*, pp. 1103–1105.

[94] On remits see paras 13.57 to 13.66.

[95] *Gavin, supra*.

[96] *Royal Bank of Scotland v. McKerracher*, 1968 S.L.T. (Sh. Ct.) 77; *Arrow Chemicals Ltd v. Guild*, 1978 S.L.T. 206; see para. 4.48.

[97] *Hamilton Leasing Ltd v. Clark*, 1974 S.L.T. (Sh. Ct.) 95.

[98] *Fleming, supra*.

[99] *Gillespie v. Paisley Road Trust* (1900) 7 S.L.T. 350.

[1] *Steven v. Broady Norman & Co.*, 1928 S.C. 351.

[2] *Duncan's Trs v. Steven* (1897) 24 R. 880; *Dorman, Long & Co. v. Harrower* (1899) 1 F. 1109, *per* Lord Kinnear at 1115; *Alexander v. Perth C.C.* (1939) 56 Sh.Ct.Rep. 20 at 26–28. As to actions of relief, see paras 24.09, 24.10.

[3] See para. 9.117.

[4] See paras 12.42 to 12.65.

4.45 In actions for the enforcement of contractual obligations, different rules apply according to whether the obligants are liable only *pro rata* or jointly and severally.[5]

4.46 If the obligants are liable only *pro rata*, it would appear that all the obligants who are subject to the jurisdiction of the Scottish courts must be called. If some only are called they may insist, under the plea "All parties not called", that the others should be made defenders before the action proceeds.[6]

4.47 If, however, the obligation is joint and several and expressed in writing, any one obligant may be sued for the whole debt.[7] But if the debt has to be constituted, all the obligants must be called unless any are not subject to the jurisdiction of the Scottish courts. The fact that they are not all subject to the jurisdiction of the sheriff court in which the action is brought is not a sufficient ground for not calling all the obligants.[8] Having convened them all, however, the pursuer may pass from the action *quoad* any of them.[9]

4.48 Where two or more persons[10] have contributed to the commission of a delict, they are liable jointly and severally.[11] The pursuer may sue any one of them,[12] or some or all of them, for the whole damage arising from their combined wrongdoing or from the common harmful result.[13] If he elects not to sue all of them, the plea of "All parties not called" cannot be maintained.[14] If he elects to sue only one of them, he must crave the whole loss which he expects to suffer and hopes to recover, and if he recovers the damages awarded the obligations of reparation owed to him by the other wrongdoers are thereby extinguished.[15] But if the single party sued and decerned against does not satisfy the decree, the pursuer may go on to sue the others.[16] If the pursuer elects to sue several parties who are liable jointly and severally, he may transact with some of these in appropriate terms and may consent to their being assoilzied, without impairing his

---

[5] As to joint, and joint and several, obligations see Gloag, *Contract*, Chap. 12; Walker, *Contracts*, Chap. 27; W. W. McBryde, *The Law of Contract in Scotland* (1987), Chap. 16. A joint and several crave has been held competent in an action of delivery: *Sinclair v. Fleming* (1909) 25 Sh.Ct.Rep. 268.

[6] *Johnstone v. Arnotts* (1830) 8 S. 383; Mackay, *Practice*, i, 351, approved, *Neilson v. Wilson* (1890) 17 R. 608, *per* Lords Shand and Young (*diss.*) at 616; Gloag, *Contract*, pp. 204–205.

[7] Ersk., III, iii, 74; Bell, *Prin.*, s. 56; *Richmond v. Grahame* (1847) 9 D. 633.

[8] *Neilson v. Wilson* (1890) 17 R. 608. Where the sheriff has jurisdiction over one of a number of defenders on the ground of domicile, he has jurisdiction over all the others: Civil Jurisdiction and Judgments Act 1982, Sched. 8, para. 2(15)(a); see *supra*, para. 3.38.

[9] *Fleming v. Gemmill*, 1908 S.C. 340; *Mackenzie v. Macallister*, 1909 S.C. 367; *James Allan & Sons (Contractors) Ltd v. Gourlay*, 1956 S.L.T. (Sh.Ct.) 77.

[10] See Walker, *Delict*, pp. 111–123.

[11] Ersk., III, i, 15; Bell, *Prin.*, s. 550. Where the liability of one of two co-delinquents is limited by statute, the other should be sued for the whole damages and both sued jointly and severally for the limited amount: *Duthie v. Caledonian Ry* (1898) 25 R. 934.

[12] *National Coal Board v. Thomson*, 1959 S.C. 353, *per* L.J.-C. Thomson at 361–362.

[13] *Fleming v. Gemmill*, 1908 S.C. 340; *Ellerman Lines Ltd v. Clyde Navigation Trs*, 1909 S.C. 690.

[14] *Liquidators of Western Bank v. Douglas* (1860) 22 D. 447; *Croskery v. Gilmour's Trs* (1890) 17 R. 697. The party sued may convene the others by third party procedure: see paras 12.42 to 12.65.

[15] *Balfour v. Baird*, 1959 S.C. 64.

[16] *Steven v. Broady Norman & Co.*, 1928 S.C. 351.

right to pursue his action against the rest for the balance of his claim.[17] But no transaction between an injured person and one co-delinquent can deprive another co-delinquent of any right of relief he has against the first.[18]

Where in any action of damages in respect of loss or damage arising from any wrongful acts or negligent acts or omissions two or more persons are, in pursuance of the judgment of the court, found jointly and severally liable in damages or expenses, they are liable *inter se* to contribute to such damages or expenses in such proportions as the court may deem just.[19] Each defender who is sued jointly and severally should state a plea-in-law seeking apportionment in terms of the statute. Where any person has paid any damages or expenses in which he has been found liable in such an action, he is entitled to recover from any other person who, if sued to judgment relevantly, competently and timeously, might also have been held liable in respect of the loss or damage on which the action was founded, such contribution, if any, as the court may deem just.[20] The person seeking contribution may base his claim on a decree of a Scottish court as a result of which the debt in question is enforceable against him: it is not necessary that the proceeding should have resulted from a judicial decision upon a contested issue of liability.[21] **4.49**

Where more than one specific wrong is founded on, committed by different parties, and the wrongs are disconnected, with different parties liable in respect of their own wrongful acts only, these parties cannot be sued jointly and severally since they are severally liable only.[22] It has been suggested that they may be called in one writ, in which a separate decree is asked against each of them in respect of the wrong done by each,[23] but that would appear to be at least doubtful.[24] It may be appropriate to sue defenders severally where it is clear that only one of them caused the wrong complained of, but it is not clear which.[25] In practice, if the circumstances are such as to raise liability which may be maintained against two or more parties, but may also be maintained against one of them separately, or if there is any doubt whether only one, or more than one, defender is liable, the defenders are sued jointly and severally, on the view that the court is thus permitted to grant decree either against all the **4.50**

---

17 *Douglas v. Hogarth* (1901) 4 F. 148; Walker, *Delict*, pp. 116–118; Walker, *Civil Remedies*, pp. 1103–1105. See para. 4.43.

18 *Corvi v. Ellis*, 1969 S.C. 312, *per* Lord Guthrie at 321; *Magee & Co. (Belfast) Ltd v. Bracewell Harrison & Coton*, 1981 S.L.T. 107. *Cf. Hardy v. British Airways Board*, 1983 S.L.T. 45.

19 Law Reform (Miscellaneous Provisions) (Scotland) Act 1940, s. 3(1). See Walker, *Delict*, pp. 119–123; Walker, *Civil Remedies*, pp. 1243–1244.

20 *ibid.* s. 3(2); *Singer v. Gray Tool Co. (Europe) Ltd*, 1984 S.L.T. 149. See Walker, *op. cit.* The obligation to make a contribution by virtue of s. 3(2) prescribes after two years: Prescription and Limitation (Scotland) Act 1973, s. 8A, inserted by Prescription and Limitation (Scotland) Act 1984, s. 1.

21 *Comex Houlder Diving Ltd v. Colne Fishing Co. Ltd*, 1987 S.L.T. 443.

22 *Barr v. Neilson* (1868) 6 M. 651; *Sinclair v. Caithness Flagstone Co.* (1898) 25 R. 703; *Hook v. McCallum* (1905) 7 F. 528; *Fleming v. McGillivray*, 1946 S.C. 1; *Turnbull v. Frame*, 1966 S.L.T. 24. *Cf. Belmont Laundry Co. v. Aberdeen Steam Laundry Co.* (1898) 1 F. 45; *Rose Street Foundry and Engineering Co. v. Lewis & Sons*, 1917 S.C. 341.

23 Lewis, p. 85; Dobie, p. 109. *Cf.* Walker, *Delict*, pp. 98, 123.

24 See para. 4.41.

25 The case against each would have to be relevantly averred: *cf. Stout v. U.K. Atomic Energy Authority*, 1979 S.L.T. 54.

defenders jointly and severally, or against any one or more of them while absolving others. It is still common in practice to sue such defenders "jointly and severally or severally" because formerly, if a pursuer sued defenders "jointly and severally" only, his action failed if he did not establish a case of joint fault.[26] But it is now competent to sue defenders "jointly and severally" and obtain decree against only one of them.[27]

4.51 Where the pursuer's case against one defender is dismissed, another defender has no title to insist that the dismissed defender should remain a party to the cause.[28]

(3) The Crown

4.52 The position of the Crown as a litigant is regulated by the Crown Proceedings Act 1947 (hereafter "the 1947 Act") which in many respects equates the position of the Crown with that of ordinary litigants. The Crown has, however, a number of privileges both in regard to the substantive law enforceable by or against the Crown and in regard to procedure. This book is concerned only with the latter.[29]

4.53 "The Crown" in this context means Her Majesty's Government in the United Kingdom,[30] and includes the Lord Advocate, any government department and any servant of Her Majesty including a Minister of the Crown.[31] The Act does not apply to proceedings by or against Her Majesty in her private capacity.[32] A certificate of a Secretary of State to the effect that any alleged liability of the Crown arises otherwise than in respect of Her Majesty's Government in the United Kingdom, or to the effect that any proceedings by the Crown are proceedings otherwise than in right of Her Majesty's Government in the United Kingdom, is for the purposes of the Act conclusive as to the matters so certified.[33]

Jurisdiction

4.54 The general rule is that civil proceedings against the Crown may be instituted in the sheriff court in like manner as if the proceedings were against a subject, but the rule is qualified by the provisions of the Act and by "any enactment limiting the jurisdiction of the sheriff court (whether by reference to the subject-matter of the proceedings or otherwise)."[34] For

---

26 *Douglas v. Hogarth* (1901) 4 F. 148, *per* Lord Trayner at 150.

27 *Fleming v. Gemmill*, 1908 S.C. 340, *per* Lords McLaren and Pearson at 345; *Mackenzie v. Macallister*, 1909 S.C. 367, *per* L.P. Dunedin at 371; Lees, *Pleading*, p. 25, para. 59. *Cf. Arrow Chemicals Ltd v. Guild*, 1978 S.L.T. 206 at 208. In *Brodie v. Coplan* (1906) 14 S.L.T. 35, a joint and several decree was granted although not concluded for.

28 *McDermott v. Western SMT Co.*, 1937 S.C. 239. See para. 4.42.

29 The best introduction to the 1947 Act from a Scottish standpoint is still W. I. R. Fraser (later Lord Fraser of Tullybelton), *An Outline of Constitutional Law* (2nd ed., 1948), Chap. 11. As to the substantive law, see Glanville Williams, *Crown Proceedings (1948); H. Street, Governmental Liability* (1953); P. W. Hogg, *Liability of the Crown* (1971); Walker, *Delict* (2nd ed.), pp. 73–78; Walker, *Principles* (4th ed.), Chap. 3.12. As to proceedings by and against the Crown in the English courts see Halsbury (4th ed.), Supp., Vol. 11, *s.v.* "Crown Proceedings and Crown Practice".

30 1947 Act, s. 40(2)(c).

31 *ibid.* ss. 38(4), 51(2); 38(2): see *Smith v. Lord Advocate*, 1980 S.C. 227 at 230.

32 *ibid.* s. 40(1), 38(3).

33 *ibid.* s. 40(3); *Trawnik v. Lennox* [1985] 1 W.L.R. 532; *R. v. Sec. of St. for Foreign and Commonwealth Affairs, ex p. Trawnik, The Times*, Feb. 21, 1996; [1986] C.L.Y. 950.

34 1947 Act, s. 44.

the purposes of the Civil Jurisdiction and Judgments Act 1982 the Crown is domiciled in every part of, and every place in, the United Kingdom, subject to any special provisions made by Order in Council.[35] Thus, where an action against the Crown in the sheriff court is competent, it may be sued in any sheriff court in Scotland. It would appear that if an action were to be raised against the Crown in a sheriff court far from the local origin of the cause of action,[36] it might be remitted to the Court of Session in terms of section 44 of the 1947 Act,[37] or to another sheriff court.[38]

The jurisdiction of the sheriff court is qualified by the proviso in section 44 of the 1947 Act that any proceedings against the Crown in the sheriff court must be remitted to the Court of Session if a certificate by the Lord Advocate is produced to the effect that the proceedings may involve an important question of law, or may be decisive of other cases, or are for other reasons more fit for trial in the Court of Session. Where any proceedings have been so remitted, and it appears to the Court of Session that the remit has occasioned additional expense to the pursuer, the court is directed to take account of the additional expense so occasioned in deciding any question of expenses.[39] **4.55**

Form of proceedings

In general, the ordinary forms of action in the sheriff court, such as actions for payment or for declarator, are available to and against the Crown, in the same way as they are available to and against any other party; and the 1947 Act provides a general rule that in any civil proceedings by or against the Crown the court has power to make all such orders as it has power to make in proceedings between subjects, and otherwise to give such appropriate relief as the case may require.[40] "Order" includes a judgment, decree, rule, award or declaration.[41] These general rules are, however, qualified as follows. **4.56**

(1) In proceedings against the Crown the court cannot grant an interdict or make an order for specific performance, but it may in lieu thereof make an order declaratory of the rights of the parties.[42] The Crown may be expected, as a general rule, to obey a declaratory order of the court, even where it is adverse to the Crown's interest, so that in practice such an order may be almost as effective as an interdict.[43] Whether the court has jurisdiction to make an interim declaratory order, which might similarly be almost as effective as an interim interdict, has not been decided in Scotland. The English courts do not make such orders, upon the view that an order declaratory of the rights of the parties must in its nature be a final **4.57**

---

[35] Civil Jurisdiction and Judgments Act 1982, s. 46(1), (3)(a); see para. 3.22.

[36] Events giving rise to an action may have occurred outside Scotland: *Cameron v. Lord Advocate*, 1952 S.C. 165; *Burmah Oil Co. (Burmah Trading) Ltd v. Lord Advocate*, 1964 S.C.(H.L.) 117.

[37] See para. 4.55.

[38] OCR, r. 26.1: see paras 13.51 to 13.56.

[39] 1947 Act, s. 44.

[40] *ibid.* s. 21(1).

[41] *ibid.* s. 38(2).

[42] *ibid.* s. 21(1), as applied to Scotland by ss. 42 and 43. *McDonald v. Secretary of State for Scotland*, 1994 S.C. 234.

[43] Fraser, *op. cit.*, p. 165.

order.[44] It has been tentatively suggested that the English decisions may not be applicable in Scotland.[45] In any event the Scottish courts will not make an interim declaratory order if it would prejudge the merits of the case or would be hypothetical, made upon the assumption that the pursuer's averments are correct.[46] In certain circumstances the status quo may be for the time being preserved, or the commission of an alleged threatened wrong for the time being prevented, by the Crown's tendering an undertaking in terms which are acceptable to the court.[47] A pursuer seeking a declaratory order should formulate it with precision.[48] A writ seeking a bare declarator, without any additional remedy, is not for that reason incompetent.[49]

4.58 (2) In proceedings against the Crown for the recovery of land or other property the court cannot make an order for the recovery of the land or the delivery of the property, but may in lieu thereof make an order declaring that the pursuer is entitled as against the Crown to the land or property or to the possession thereof.[50]

4.59 (3) The court cannot in any civil proceedings grant any interdict or make any order against an officer of the Crown if the effect of granting the interdict or making the order would be to give any relief against the Crown which could not have been obtained in proceedings against the Crown.[51] Thus the Act cannot be circumvented by raising an action against an officer of the Crown as an individual, and not against the Crown itself.[52]

4.60 (4) A person is not entitled to avail himself of any set-off[53] or counterclaim in any proceedings by the Crown for the recovery of taxes, duties or penalties, or to avail himself in proceedings of any other nature by the Crown of any set-off or counterclaim arising out of a right or claim to repayment in respect of any taxes, duties or penalties.[54]

4.61 (5) A person is not entitled without the leave of the court to avail himself of any set-off or counterclaim in any proceedings by the Crown if the

---

44 *Underhill v. Ministry of Food* [1950] 1 All E.R. 591; *International General Electrical Co. of New York Ltd v. Commr's of Customs and Excise* [1962] Ch. 784. In *Clarke v. Chadburn* [1985] 1 W.L.R. 78 a declaration was made in interlocutory proceedings.

45 *Ayr T.C. v. Secretary of State for Scotland*, 1965 S.C. 394 at 399; and see Fraser, *op. cit.*, p. 166.

46 *Ayr T.C., supra*; *Robertson v. Lord Advocate* (Mar. 25, 1950), 1965 S.C. 400. In applications for judicial review in the Court of Session "in certain cases, the notorious difficulty of the interim declarator can be circumvented by a combination of the speed of the review process and the opportunity for the court to pronounce on the issue raised at the first hearing" (Lord Davidson, 1986 S.L.T. (News) 283 at 284).

47 *Ayr Mags v. Lord Advocate*, 1950 S.C. 102 at 105; *Robertson, supra.*

48 *MacCormick v. Lord Advocate*, 1953 S.C. 396, *per* L.P. Cooper at 409; and see para. 20.05.

49 *Gibson v. Lord Advocate*, 1975 S.C. 136 at 145; and see para. 20.04. *Cf. Griffin v. Lord Advocate*, 1950 S.C. 448 at 452.

50 1947 Act, s. 21(1), as applied to Scotland by ss. 42 and 43.

51 *ibid.* s. 21(2), as applied to Scotland by ss. 42 and 43. A health board is neither "the Crown" nor "an officer of the Crown": *British Medical Association v. Greater Glasgow Health Board*, 1988 S.L.T. 538, 1989 S.L.T. 493, 1989 S.C.(H.L.) 65. See I. S. Dickinson, "Interim Relief against the Crown", 1986 S.L.T. (News) 280.

52 *R. v. Sec. of St. for Home Dept., ex p. Kirkwood* [1984] 1 W.L.R. 913.

53 On "set-off" see *Laing v. Lord Advocate*, 1973 S.L T. (Notes) 81.

54 1947 Act, s. 35(2)(b), subs. by s. 50.

subject-matter of the set-off or counterclaim does not relate to the government department on whose behalf the proceedings are brought.[55]

(6) The Crown, in any proceedings against a government department, or against the Lord Advocate on behalf of a government department, is not, without the leave of the court, entitled to avail itself of any set-off or counterclaim if the subject-matter thereof does not relate to that department.[56] The Crown may, accordingly, set off a claim which relates to a government department where the action relates to that department. The Crown may also put forward claims by other departments of government, but the leave of the court must be obtained to make such counterclaims permissible or effective. For this purpose government departments are not separate entities in law from the Crown.[57] The court in deciding whether to grant leave will balance the common law right against the statutory provision[58] and may take account of the degree of similarity between the nature of the claims on either side.[59] The provision is applicable both where the pursuer is solvent and where he is a trustee in bankruptcy or a liquidator. In the latter cases, a decision on the request for leave may be approached by asking first, "Why should leave not be granted?" and then considering the other circumstances arising from the case.[60] **4.62**

Representation

Actions by or against the Crown are normally instituted by or against the Lord Advocate. His title to represent the Crown, including all government departments, appears from the Crown Suits (Scotland) Act 1857, which is declaratory of the common law[61] and provides that every action, suit or proceeding instituted in Scotland on behalf of or against Her Majesty, or in the interest of the Crown, or on behalf of or against any public department, may be lawfully raised in the name and at the instance of or directed against the Lord Advocate for the time being.[62] The purpose of the Act is procedural only: it does not enlarge the right to sue the Crown.[63] No action which has been raised by or against the Lord Advocate for the time being is affected by any change in the person holding the office of Lord Advocate.[64] The Solicitor General for Scotland may discharge the functions of the Lord Advocate if the office of Lord Advocate is vacant or if the Lord Advocate is unable to act owing to absence or illness.[65] **4.63**

Before instituting or defending any action, the Lord Advocate must have the authority of Her Majesty or of the public department on whose behalf he acts; but it is not competent to any private party to challenge his **4.64**

---

55 1947 Act, s. 35(2)(c).

56 *ibid.* s. 35(2)(d); *Atlantic Engine Co. (1920) Ltd*, 1955 S.L.T. 17.

57 *Smith v. Lord Advocate*, 1980 S.C. 227; *cf.* J. D. B. Mitchell, *Constitutional Law* (2nd ed., 1968), pp. 204–205, 307–308.

58 *Smith v. Lord Advocate*, 1980 S.C. 227.

59 *Laing v. Lord Advocate*, 1973 S.L.T. (Notes) 81.

60 *Smith*, *supra*. See also *Atlantic Engine Co. (1920) Ltd v. Lord Advocate*, *supra*; *Laing v. Lord Advocate*, *supra*.

61 *Smith v. Lord Advocate*, 1980 S.C. 227 at 231–232.

62 Crown Suits (Scotland) Act 1857 (hereafter "the 1857 Act"), s. 1.

63 *Macgregor v. Lord Advocate*, 1921 S.C. 847, *per* Lord Anderson at 848; *Smith v. Lord Advocate*, 1932 S.L.T at 378.

64 1857 Act, s. 5.

65 Law Officers Act 1944, s. 2.

title to do so on the ground that such authority has not been granted or that evidence of such authority is not produced.[66] It would appear to be competent to challenge on the ground that the body for whom he acts is not a public department within the meaning of the 1857 Act.[67]

4.65 The public departments for which the Lord Advocate may act in terms of the 1857 Act are broadly defined by section 4 as including the Treasury, other named government departments "and all the like public departments, bodies, or boards, and all and every officer and officers, person and persons acting on the behalf or in the interest of or entitled at the date of the passing of this Act to sue on the behalf of or in the interest of any such public department."[68] For the purposes of English proceedings the Treasury publishes a list of departments authorised to sue and be sued under the 1947 Act.[69] The public departments defined by section 4 do not include such bodies as public corporations, local authorities or independent boards such as hospital boards or the Supplementary Benefits Commission.[70]

4.66 The style normally followed in the instance is: "The Right Honourable A.B. [*or* the Lord C. of D. *as the case may be*], Her Majesty's Advocate, as representing the Secretary of State for the Environment [*or as the case may be*], Crown Office, 25 Chambers Street, Edinburgh EH1 1LA."[71] Official communications, specifications and other documents which require to be served on or sent to the Lord Advocate should likewise be forwarded to the Crown Office.[72]

4.67 The Lord Advocate may sue or defend, on behalf of the public, actions regarding encroachments by private or public bodies on the shores of the realm.[73] An action of declarator under the Presumption of Death (Scotland) Act 1977[74] should be intimated to the Lord Advocate, or he may be called as a defender in such an action.[75] When it appears that the Crown has a prima facie interest in the subject-matter of an action, the court should appoint intimation of the action to the Lord Advocate or, where appropriate, to the procurator fiscal, and continue or, if necessary, sist the action pending his decision whether to appear or take any other measures.[76] The concurrence of the Lord Advocate, represented in the sheriff court by the procurator fiscal, is necessary in proceedings for breach of interdict, for contravention of lawburrows, and for breach of sequestration for rent where penal consequences are sought.

---

[66] 1857 Act, ss. 2, 3.

[67] J. D. B. Mitchell, *Constitutional Law* (2nd ed., 1968), p. 311; Walker, *Delict*, p. 77.

[68] *Cameron v. Lord Advocate*, 1952 S.C. 165 at 169; *Glasgow Corporation v. Central Land Board*, 1956 S.C. (H.L) 1.

[69] 1947 Act, s. 17(1). It was referred to in *Lord Advocate v. Argyllshire C.C.*, 1950 S.C. 304.

[70] *Smith v. Lord Advocate*, 1932 S.L.T. 374; *Ronson Nominees Ltd v. Mitchell*, 1982 S.L.T. (Sh. Ct.) 18; *British Medical Association v. Greater Glasgow Health Board*, 1988 S.L.T. 538, 1989 S.L.T. 493, 1989 S.C.(H.L.) 65.

[71] *Hannah v. Lord Advocate*, 1970 S.L.T. (Sh. Ct.) 46.

[72] [1953] C.L.Y. 4528.

[73] *Cameron and Gunn v. Ainslie* (1848) 10 D. 446; *Young v. N.B. Ry* (1887) 14 R. (H.L.) 53.

[74] See paras 4.63 to 4.68.

[75] *Horak v. Lord Advocate*, 1984 S.L.T. 201.

[76] *Ogston v. Stewart* (1896) 23 R.(H.L.) 16, *per* Lord Watson at 18; *Smith v. Foster*, 1949 S.C. 269 at 273–274; *Peden v. Peden*, 1957 S.C. 409 at 411.

There is no statutory prohibition against ministers suing or being sued in their own names instead of through the Lord Advocate but, with one exception, that is contrary to established practice.[77] The exception is the Secretary of State for Scotland, who may be a party to legal proceedings in which is involved any department for which he is responsible. His title to sue or be sued appears to depend on the common law.[78] It is sufficient to describe him as "The Secretary of State for Scotland" without naming him.[79] Statutory appeals from administrative tribunals to the Court of Session proceed in the name of the relevant minister.[80] **4.68**

Government departments which are not represented by their own permanent solicitors or by the Solicitor to the Secretary of State for Scotland are represented by solicitors in private practice nominated by the Lord Advocate. Departments may also be represented by their standing junior counsel, appointed by the Lord Advocate, and by a Law Officer or senior counsel instructed for the particular case. **4.69**

Arrestment

Section 46 of the 1947 Act provides that arrestment in the hands of the Crown or of a government department or of any officer of the Crown as such is competent in any case where arrestment in the hands of a subject would have been competent, subject to two provisos. The first is that it is not competent to arrest in execution the earnings of any serving member of the armed forces. There is, however, statutory provision for certain deductions from service pay where aliment or other sums are payable under decree of court.[81] The second proviso is that nothing in section 46 warrants the arrestment of any money which is subject to the provisions of any enactment prohibiting or restricting assignation or charging or taking in execution.[82] **4.70**

Where it is desired to serve an arrestment on the Lord Advocate as acting under the Crown Suits (Scotland) Act 1857 on behalf of the Crown or, as the case may be, on behalf of any minister or public department,[83] the correct designation is as follows. In the arrestment the arrestee should be designated as "The Lord Advocate, Crown Office, 25 Chambers Street, Edinburgh EH1 1LA" and the designation should also state on whose behalf the Lord Advocate is designated as arrestee, whether the Crown or a particular secretary of state, minister or department. If the Lord Advocate is designated as the arrestee without any further description or qualification, he will regard the arrestment as attaching only to debts owed to the debtor in question by him or by one of his own departments.[84] **4.71**

---

77 See *Sandeman's Trs*, 1947 S.C. 304.

78 Fraser, *op. cit.*, p. 162.

79 Reorganisation of Offices (Scotland) Act 1939, s. 1(8).

80 *e.g. Minister of Social Security v. Connolly*, 1967 S.L.T. 121.

81 Army Act 1955, ss. 150–152; Air Force Act 1955, ss. 150–152, all as amended, esp. by Armed Forces Act 1971, s. 59 and Armed Forces Act 1991, s. 14; Naval Forces (Enforcement of Maintenance Liabilities) Act 1947, s. 1, as amended, esp. by Armed Forces Act 1991, s. 15; Naval Discipline Act 1957, s. 128E, inserted by Armed Forces Act 1971, s. 61(1).

82 1947 Act, s. 46, as amended by Law Reform (Miscellaneous Provisions) (Scotland) Acts 1966, s. 2(1), and 1985, s. 49.

83 See paras 4.63 to 4.68.

84 1980 S.L.T. (News) 146.

Recovery of documents

4.72 With regard to the recovery of documents in the hands of the Crown, section 47 of the 1947 Act provides that subject to and in accordance with Acts of Sederunt applying to the Court of Session and the sheriff court, commission and diligence for the recovery of documents in the possession of the Crown may be granted in any action whether or not the Crown is a party thereto, in like manner and in all respects as if the documents were in the possession of a subject. That general rule, however, is subject to two provisos. (1) The general rule is "without prejudice to any rule of law which authorises or requires the withholding of any document on the ground that its disclosure would be injurious to the public interest." (2) The existence of a document must not be disclosed if, in the opinion of a minister of the Crown, it would be injurious to the public interest to disclose its existence. These provisions are not restricted to proceedings to which the Crown is a party: they apply equally to civil proceedings between private individuals. They do not apply, however, to documents which do not emanate from or come into the possession of a servant or agent of the Crown in the ordinary course of his official duties.[85]

4.73 The first proviso preserves the existing rule of law which appeared to have been authoritatively settled in *Duncan v. Cammell Laird & Co.*[86] In *Glasgow Corporation v. Central Land Board*,[87] however, it was made clear that the law as stated in *Duncan* was not the law of Scotland, and the further House of Lords decision in *Conway v. Rimmer*[88] brought the law of England broadly into line with the law of Scotland. The modern law in both jurisdictions appears to be that where there is a ministerial objection to a call for the production of a document in the possession of the Crown, the test to be applied is whether the public interest in the administration of justice not being frustrated outweighs the ministerial objection. The objection may be that it is against the public interest to disclose the contents of particular documents, or that the documents belong to a class which should be withheld irrespective of their contents. Where the objection is taken in respect of a class of documents, the court, in considering whether to override the objection, can take into account not only the interests of the particular applicant for recovery, but the interests of the public as a whole in so far as other members of the public might find themselves in the same position as the applicant.[89] The court may inspect the document before it is made available to the parties in order to verify whether it should be produced and, if so, whether steps could be taken to limit exposure only to its relevant parts.[90] If the court decides to order production, the minister should be given an opportunity to appeal before the document is produced.

4.74 The power to overrule ministerial objections has been considered in a number of subsequent cases, and courts in both jurisdictions have been

---

85 *Whitehall v. Whitehall*, 1957 S.C. 30.
86 [1942] A.C. 624.
87 1956 S.C.(H.L.) 1.
88 [1968] A.C. 910.
89 *Friel v. Chief Constable of Strathclyde*, 1981 S.C. 1.
90 *Science Research Council v. Nassé* [1980] A.C. 1028; *Air Canada v. Sec. of St. for Trade (No. 2)* [1983] 2 A.C. 394.

slow to exercise it.[91] A great variety of expressions has been used in the reported cases to explain the considerations that ought to influence judges in deciding whether to order inspection. It has been observed that it is not possible to state a test which could be applied in all cases, because circumstances vary greatly; and that the most that can usefully be said is that, in order to persuade the court even to inspect the documents the party seeking disclosure ought at least to satisfy the court that they are very likely to contain material which would give substantial support to his contention on an issue which arises in the case, and that without them he might be deprived of the means of proper presentation of his case.[92]

The court's refusal to permit the recovery of evidence as a result of objection by the Crown used to be said to be based on the doctrine of Crown privilege, but it is now clear that there is no question of any privilege in the ordinary legal sense of the word. The real question is whether the public interest requires that the document shall not be produced and whether that public interest is so strong as to override the ordinary right and interest of a litigant that he shall be able to lay before a court of justice all relevant evidence. It is open to any person interested to raise the question, and there may be cases where the judge should himself raise the question if no one else has done so.[93] A full discussion of this important subject is beyond the scope of this book.[94] **4.75**

Special pleas

The Crown cannot be prejudiced by the negligence of its officers in the conduct of litigation to which it is a party. It may state any exception, reply or defence previously omitted, and that by way of exception or reply without raising an action of reduction.[95] Accordingly a plea of bar founded on such negligence cannot be maintained against the Crown[96]; an action of warrandice will not lie against the Crown[97] and its officers cannot prejudice the Crown by prorogating the jurisdiction of an incompetent court.[98] The Crown may not, however, plead its officers' negligence as a ground for reducing a right founded on prescription[99]; **4.76**

---

[91] *Rogers v. Home Secretary* [1973] A.C. 388; *Alfred Crompton Amusement Machines Ltd v. Commissioners of Customs and Excise* [1974] A.C. 405; *Norwich Pharmacal Co. v. Commissioners of Customs and Excise* [1974] A.C. 133; *Burmah Oil Co. v. Bank of England* [1980] A.C. 1090; *Air Canada v. Sec. of St. for Trade (No. 2)* [1983] 2 A.C. 394; *Friel v. Chief Constable of Strathclyde, supra*; *Anderson v. Palombo*, 1984 S.L.T. 332, 1986 S.L.T. 46 at 48; *P. Cannon (Garages) Ltd v. Lord Advocate*, 1983 S.L.T. (Sh. Ct.) 50; *Balfour v. Foreign and Commonwealth Office* [1994] 1 W.L.R. 681.

[92] *Air Canada, supra, per* Lord Fraser of Tullybelton at 435.

[93] *Rogers, supra, per* Lord Reid at 400; *Air Canada, supra, per* Lord Fraser of Tullybelton at 436.

[94] See Lord Mackay of Clashfern, "The Development of the Law on Public Interest Immunity" (1983) 2 C.J.Q. 337.

[95] Crown Proceedings Act 1600; Stair, IV, xxxv, 2; Ersk., I, ii, 27; *Crawford v. Kennedy* (1694) Mor. 7866.

[96] *Lord Advocate v. Meiklam* (1860) 22 D. 1427; *Lord Advocate v. Miller's Trs* (1884) 11 R. 1046, *per* Lord Fraser at 1053; *Lord Advocate v. Duke of Hamilton* (1891) 29 S.L.R. 213; *Alston's Trs v. Lord Advocate* (1896) 3 S.L.T. 150; *Lord Advocate v. Mirrielees' Trs*, 1943 S.C. 587, *per* Lord Keith at 594; 1945 S.C.(H.L.) 1.

[97] Ersk., II, iii, 27.

[98] *Eyres v. Hunter* (1711) Mor. 7596.

[99] Stair, II, xii, 25; Ersk., III, vii, 31; *Earl of Leven v. Balfour* (1711) Mor. 10930.

and both the positive[1] and the negative[2] prescriptions run against the Crown.

Course of proceedings

4.77 Subject to the special rules noted in this section of this chapter, all civil proceedings by or against the Crown in the sheriff court are instituted and proceeded with in accordance with the normal rules and practice of the court.[3] When the Crown is called as a defender in any action, it may not lodge a minute instead of defences.[4] The Crown may take advantage of the provisions of an Act of Parliament although not named therein; and in any civil proceedings against the Crown the provisions of any Act of Parliament which could, if the proceedings were between subjects, be relied upon by the defender as a defence to the proceedings, whether in whole or in part, or otherwise, may, subject to any express provision to the contrary, be so relied upon by the Crown.[5]

Expenses

4.78 There is no distinction between the Crown and a subject in the matter of expenses. When decree is given for the Crown, the Crown may move for and recover expenses of process in the like manner as and under the like rules, regulations and provisions as are in force touching expenses of process in proceedings between subject and subject; and similarly, when decree is given against the Crown, the subject obtaining the decree may move for and, if awarded, recover expenses. It is also competent to recover expenses of diligence to which the Crown is a party in the like manner and to the like extent as such expenses may be recovered in cases between subject and subject.[6] With regard to the taxation of a judicial account of expenses, the Crown is subject to the same rules as a private litigant.[7] The Crown is exempted from payment of the fees regulated by the Sheriff Court Fees Order 1997 only in the enforcement of the criminal law or in the exercise of powers or the performance of duties arising out of or relating to that enforcement.[8] Accordingly, those fees are generally payable by the Crown in civil cases.

Enforcement of orders of court

4.79 Any order made in favour of the Crown against any person in any civil proceedings to which the Crown is a party may be enforced in the same

---

[1] Bell, *Prin.*, s. 2025; *H.M. Advocate v. Graham* (1844) 7 D. 183; *Lord Advocate v. Hunt* (1867) 5 M.(H.L.) 1; *Buchanan v. Lord Advocate* (1882) 9 R. 1218, *per* Lord Deas at 1233.

[2] *Earl of Fife's Trs v. Commissioners of Woods and Forests* (1849) 11 D. 889; *Deans of Chapel Royal v. Johnstone* (1869) 7 M.(H.L.) 19.

[3] *Cf.* 1947 Act, ss. 13, 42–43.

[4] *Ramsay v. McLaren*, 1936 S.L.T. 35.

[5] 1947 Act, ss. 31, 43(a). As to the extent to which the Crown is bound by statute, see *Edinburgh Mags v. Lord Advocate*, 1912 S.C. 1085; *Lord Advocate v. Strathclyde R.C.*; *Lord Advocate v. Dumbarton D.C.*, O.H., Sept. 4, 1986, unreported; 1947 Act, s. 40(2)(f); *Encyclopaedia*, v, paras 791–792; Fraser, *op. cit.*, pp. 175–176; J. D. B. Mitchell, *Constitutional Law* (2nd ed., 1968), p. 183; H. Street, *Government Liability* (1953), Chap. 6(1); P. W. Hogg, *Liability of the Crown* (1971), Chap. 7; P. P. Craig, *Administrative Law* (1983), Chap. 18(2).

[6] Court of Exchequer (Scotland) Act 1856, s. 24; *Macleod's Judicial Factor v. Busfield*, 1914 2 S.L.T. 268. See Maclaren, *Expenses*, pp. 137–139.

[7] *Officers of Ordnance v. Edinburgh Mags* (1860) 22 D. 446; *Lord Advocate v. Stewart* (1899) 36 S.L.R. 945; Maclaren, *Expenses*, pp. 429–430.

[8] Sheriff Court Fees Order 1997 (S.I. 1997 No. 687), para. 6.

manner as an order made in an action between subjects, and not otherwise.[9]

Where the court makes an order, including an award of expenses, in favour of any person against the Crown or against a government department or against an officer of the Crown as such, he is not entitled to enforce it by any diligence or execution.[10] Instead, the following procedure is prescribed. The person in whose favour the order is made applies to the sheriff clerk for a certified copy of the order. He may so apply at any time after the expiration of 21 days from the date of the order or, in a case where there is an award of expenses and the expenses require to be taxed, at any time after taxation, whichever is the later. The sheriff clerk issues the certified copy of the order and the person in whose favour it is made then serves a copy of the order on the person for the time being named in the record as the solicitor, or the person acting as solicitor, for the Crown or government department or officer concerned. If the order decerns for the payment of any money by way of damages or otherwise or of any expenses, the appropriate government department pays to the person entitled or to his solicitor the amount appearing from the order to be due to him together with the interest, if any, lawfully due thereon, unless the court by which the order is made, or any court to which an appeal against the order lies, directs that payment of the whole or any part of the amount payable is to be suspended.[11] **4.80**

Where decree in absence has been granted against the Crown, the decree is not operative without the leave of the court obtained on an application of which notice has been given to the Crown.[12] **4.81**

(4) Office Holders

Except where statute otherwise provides, actions by or against the holder of an office should be in the name of the office-holder designed as an individual. Accordingly, it has been held that an action against the holder of an office by description of the office without naming the holder as an individual is incompetent.[13] **4.82**

(5) Corporate bodies[14]

A corporation sues and is sued in its own name. The mode of its incorporation, whether by charter,[15] statute,[16] registration under the Companies Acts[17] or otherwise should normally be specified in the instance. The charter or statute of incorporation should be consulted and any relevant provisions followed. **4.83**

---

[9] 1947 Act, s. 26(1).
[10] *ibid.* s. 45(4).
[11] *ibid.* s. 45(1)–(3).
[12] *ibid.* s. 35(2)(a), substituted by s. 50.
[13] *McLaren v. Procurator Fiscal for the Lothians and Borders*, 1991 S.C.L.R. 872.
[14] See Walker, *Principles*, Chaps 3.11, 3.13.
[15] *e.g.* "Carron Company, a company incorporated by royal charter."
[16] *e.g.* "The Governor and Company of the Bank of Scotland, incorporated by Act of Parliament": see Bell, *Comm.*, i, 102.
[17] *e.g.* "The A.B. Company plc, incorporated under the Companies Acts."

Name

4.84 Care should be taken to state the name of the corporation correctly.[18] The name of a public limited company ends with the words "public limited company" or "plc"[19]; and the name of a company limited by shares or by guarantee (not being a public company) must have "Limited" or "Ltd" as its last word[20] unless exempt from that requirement.[21]

4.85 A change of name by a company does not render defective any legal proceedings by or against it; and any legal proceedings that might have been continued or commenced against it by its former name may be continued or commenced against it by its new name.[22] Thus, a change of name does not invalidate proceedings which have already commenced or taken place before the change of name occurred. But proceedings which do not take place or commence until after the change of name should be brought in the new name: if brought in the former name, leave to amend the instance should be sought in terms of rule 18.2(2)(b) of the Ordinary Cause Rules.[23] Where the whole estate of a company is given over to and taken possession of by another company, the business being continued on the same footing, there is a general presumption that the liabilities go along with the assets, so that the second company may be sued for the debts of the first.[24]

4.86 Where a company carries on a business under a trading or descriptive name it may sue or be sued in such name alone[25]; and special rules are provided as to diligence[26] and as to the service of documents.[27]

4.87 Where a company carries on business under a name other than its corporate name, and fails to disclose on business letters and other specified documents its corporate name and an address at which service of any document relating in any way to the business will be effective, the following rule applies. If the company brings legal proceedings to enforce a right arising out of a contract made in the course of the business, and the defender shows that as a result of the non-disclosure he has a claim against the pursuer arising out of the contract which he has been unable to pursue or he has suffered some financial loss in connection with the contract, the proceedings must be dismissed unless the court is satisfied that it is just and equitable to permit them to continue.[28] That rule does not, however, appear to affect the company's ability to counterclaim when it is being sued by the other party to the contract.[29]

---

18 See para. 9.78.
19 Companies Act 1985, ss. 25(1), 27.
20 *ibid.* ss. 25(2), 27. Welsh equivalents are specified for companies with their registered offices in Wales.
21 *ibid.* s. 30: *e.g.* The Scottish Special Housing Association (see 1986 S.L.T. (News) 107).
22 Companies Act 1985, s. 28(7).
23 *Richards & Wallington (Earthmoving) Ltd v. Whatlings Ltd,* 1982 S.L.T. 66.
24 *Britton v. Maple & Co. Ltd,* 1986 S.L.T. 70.
25 OCR, r. 5.7(1).
26 *ibid.*
27 OCR, r. 5.7(2): see para. 6.43.
28 Business Names Act 1985, s. 5(1).
29 *ibid.* s. 5(2), which seems obscurely worded: *cf.* Registration of Business Names Act 1916, s. 8(1)(c). The principal Scottish decisions on the 1916 Act are cited in *Thomas Montgomery & Sons v. W. B. Anderson & Sons Ltd,* 1979 S.L.T. 101.

Receivership

Where a receiver is appointed, he has, in relation to such part of the property of the company as is attached by the floating charge by virtue of which he was appointed, any powers given to him by the instrument creating the charge and the powers specified in Schedule 2 to the Insolvency Act 1986 provided these are not inconsistent with any provision in the instrument. The statutory powers include the power to take such proceedings as may seem to him expedient for the purpose of taking possession of, collecting and getting in the property from the company or a liquidator thereof or any other person.[30] The receiver also has power under the Schedule to bring or defend any action or other legal proceedings in the name and on behalf of the company.[31] The receiver cannot sue in his own name for payment of a debt due to the company: such an action must be raised in the name of the company.[32] The instance customarily runs in the name of the company with the addition of the words "(In Receivership)" and the name and designation of the receiver as such,[33] but in such an action that style is confusing.[34] **4.88**

The view has been expressed that during receivership the directors' powers are in abeyance[35]; but it is thought that the directors may institute proceedings where so doing does not threaten or imperil the property attached by the charge.[36] **4.89**

Winding-up

A liquidator in a winding-up by the court has power with the sanction either of the court or of the liquidation committee to bring or defend any action or other legal proceeding in the name and on behalf of the company.[37] The exercise of his power to do so is subject to the control of the court, and any creditor or contributory may apply to the court with respect to any exercise or proposed exercise of the power.[38] Where there is no liquidation committee, the court may provide by order that the liquidator may exercise the power without the sanction or intervention of the court.[39] The liquidator in a voluntary winding-up may exercise the power without sanction.[40] The instance should run in the name of the company and the liquidator.[41] As pursuer in an action for payment, **4.90**

---

[30] Insolvency Act 1986, s. 55, Sched. 2, para. 1. See *Taylor v. Scottish and Universal Newspapers Ltd*, 1981 S.C. 408; *Forth & Clyde Construction Co. Ltd v. Trinity Timber & Plywood Co. Ltd*, 1984 S.L.T. 94. *Cf. McPhail v. Lothian R.C.*, 1981 S.C. 119; W.A.W., "The Receiver and Book Debts", 1982 S.L.T. (News) 129; J. H. Greene and I. M. Fletcher, *The Law and Practice of Receivership in Scotland* (1987), paras 2.09–2.11, 3.03.

[31] Insolvency Act 1986, s. 55, Sched. 2, para. 5. Such proceedings have included an application for the recall of an arrestment: *Forth & Clyde Construction Co. Ltd, supra.*

[32] *Taylor, supra; Myles J. Callaghan Ltd v. Glasgow D.C.*, 1988 S.L.T. 227.

[33] *e.g. Emerald Stainless Steel Ltd v. South Side Distribution Ltd*, 1982 S.C. 61.

[34] *Myles J. Callaghan Ltd, supra.*

[35] *Imperial Hotel (Aberdeen) Ltd v. Vaux Breweries Ltd*, 1978 S.C. 86.

[36] *Newhart Developments Ltd v. Co-operative Commercial Bank Ltd* [1978] 1 Q.B. 814, referred to with approval in *Taylor, supra; Hastings Black Construction Ltd v. A.I.R. (Air Conditioning and Refrigeration) Ltd*, Glasgow Sh. Ct, Oct. 4, 1984, unreported; *cit.*, Greene and Fletcher, *op. cit.*, paras 2.22, 2.23.

[37] Insolvency Act 1986, s. 167(1), Sched. 4, Pt II, para. 4.

[38] *ibid.* s. 167(3).

[39] *ibid.* s. 169(1).

[40] *ibid.* s. 165(3), Sched. 4., Pt II, para. 4. See s. 116 as to a creditors' voluntary winding-up.

[41] *e.g.* "The C.D. Company plc, having its registered office at [*address*] and E.F. [*designed*] the official liquidator thereof."

the liquidator must afford as much specification of his claim as would be required of a normal debtor.[42]

4.91 Restrictions are placed on litigation against the company. If, at any time after the presentation of a winding-up petition and before a winding-up order has been made, any action or proceeding is pending against the company, the company or any creditor or contributory may apply to the court having jurisdiction to wind up the company to restrain further proceedings in the action or proceeding, and the court may sist or restrain the proceedings accordingly on such terms as it thinks fit.[43] On the application of the liquidator in a voluntary winding-up, the court may direct that no action or proceeding shall be proceeded with or commenced against the company except by leave of the court and subject to such terms as the court may impose.[44] In a winding up by the court, when a winding-up order has been made or a provisional liquidator has been appointed, no action or proceeding may be proceeded with or commenced against the company or its property except by leave of the court and subject to such terms as the court may impose.[45] Leave is not required for a counterclaim restricted to a set-off against the sum due by the defender to the company.[46]

4.92 Where proceedings are started in name of a company as pursuer without proper authority the company can as a general rule ratify the act of the person who started the proceedings and adopt the proceedings. Such ratification may be done by the liquidator of the company.[47]

Companies Act 1985, Pt XIV

4.93 Where under Part XIV of the Companies Act 1985 a report has been made by inspectors appointed to investigate a company's affairs, or information or documents have been obtained, and it appears therefrom to the Secretary of State that civil proceedings ought to be brought in the name of the company, he may himself bring such proceedings in the company's name and on its behalf, but he must indemnify the company against any costs or expenses incurred by it in or in connection with the proceedings.[48]

(6) Partnerships

4.94 A partnership may sue or be sued in the firm name, whether that name is social or descriptive. A social name consists of personal names, which need not be those of the partners. A partnership with such a name is a "proper" firm, and may sue or be sued in that name without the addition of the names of any of the individual partners.[49] While it is unnecessary to add the names of the individual partners, it is competent

---

[42] *M. Publications Ltd v. Melland*, 1981 S.L.T. (Notes) 72.

[43] Insolvency Act 1986, s. 126(1). As to companies registered under s. 680 of the Companies Act 1985, see s. 126(2) and Palmer, para. 87–58.

[44] Insolvency Act 1986, s. 113.

[45] *ibid.* s. 130(2). See also s. 130(3) as to companies registered under s. 680 of the 1985 Act. Palmer, para. 87–62 should be consulted.

[46] *G. & A. (Hotels) Ltd v. THB Marketing Services Ltd*, 1983 S.L.T. 497.

[47] *Alexander Ward & Co. v. Samyang Navigation Co. Ltd*, 1975 S.C.(H.L.) 26.

[48] Companies Act 1985, s. 438. See *Selangor United Rubber Estates Ltd v. Cradock* [1968] 1 W.L.R 1555; [1969] 1 W.L.R. 1773.

[49] *Forsyth v. Hare & Co.* (1834) 13 S. 42.

to do so and in certain circumstances it may be thought advisable, for example in order to identify those who were the partners at a material time, or in order to ensure that a decree against the firm will be a warrant for diligence against the individual partners. If it is decided to add them to the instance, their names and designations should be followed by the words "the partners of said firm as such partners and as individuals."

If the firm name is not social but descriptive, the firm is a "descriptive" firm and may be sued in that name alone.[50] It is competent, though unusual, to add the names of the partners of the firm; or for all the partners to sue or be sued with the addition to their names and designations of the words "carrying on business under the style of [*the descriptive name*]".[51] **4.95**

Where a partnership carries on business under a name which does not consist of the surnames or corporate names of all the partners, failure to disclose on business letters and other specified documents each partner's name and an address at which service may be effected will attract the application of section 5 of the Business Names Act 1985.[52] **4.96**

Where a minority of the partners of a firm sue or defend without the consent of the majority, which may be admitted or apparent from a minute of disclamation, the action may be dismissed or the defences repelled.[53] **4.97**

Where the surviving partners of a firm which has been dissolved involuntarily by death or, it is thought,[54] otherwise sue to recover debts due to the firm, it is usual in practice to make reference in the instance to the fact that the firm is now dissolved, but it is not obligatory to use the firm name.[55] The usual style is: "A.B. [*designed*] and C.D. [*designed*], the whole [surviving] partners of the now dissolved firm of [*firm name*] which carried on business [as *nature of business, if not apparent*] at [*address*] as such partners and as individuals."[56] Where a firm is voluntarily dissolved, the right to sue for the firm's debts is normally assigned to a named person who sues as such assignee and avers the details of the assignation in the condescendence: otherwise, the partners of the dissolved firm, and no others, may sue in the style given above.[57] In an action for the recovery of a debt owed by a firm now dissolved, all the former partners **4.98**

---

50 OCR, r. 5.7(1). See *Borland v. Lochwinnoch Golf Club*, 1986 S.L.T. (Sh. Ct.) 13. Although, in contrast with OCR (1985), r. 14(1), the current rule refers to "a person" rather than "any person or persons"; it comprehends firms and associations as well as individual traders because the singular includes the plural. See also Sheriff Court (Scotland) Act 1907, s. 3(e). In the Court of Session the names of at least three partners must be added: *Antermony Coal Co. v. Wingate* (1866) 4 M.1017. R. 5.7 also makes provision as to diligence and the service of writs, etc.

51 *Plotzker v. Lucas*, 1907 S.C. 315.

52 See para. 4.87.

53 *Marquis of Breadalbane v. Toberonochy Slate Quarry Co.* (1916) 33 Sh.Ct.Rep. 154; *Hutcheon and Partners v. Hutcheon*, 1979 S.L.T. (Sh. Ct.) 61. *Cf. British Anchor Pottery Co. Ltd v. Cowan & Co.* (1950) 66 Sh.Ct.Rep. 279.

54 Thomson and Middleton, p. 62.

55 *Nicoll v. Reid* (1877) 5 R. 137.

56 *J. & F. Anderson v. Balnagown Estates Co.*, 1939 S.C. 168.

57 *Wilson v. Cook*, 1954 S.L.T. (Sh. Ct.) 17; *D. Forbes Smith & Johnston v. Kate*, 1975 S.L.T. (Sh. Ct.) 33.

who can be traced and competently sued should be called. The object of the rule is to protect their rights *inter se*.[58]

(7) Individual traders

4.99 A single individual who carries on a business under the name of a proper firm may sue or be sued either in his own name alone, or in his own name with the firm name added, thus: "A.B. [*designed*], carrying on business under the name of A.B. & Co. at [*address*]." If he carries on business under a trading or descriptive name, he may sue or be sued in that name alone.[59] If he carries on business under a name other than his own and fails to disclose on business letters and other specified documents his name and an address at which service may be effected, section 5 of the Business Names Act 1985 will apply to any action he brings to enforce a right arising out of a contract made in the course of the business.[60]

(8) Trade unions and employers' associations

4.100 A trade union[61] is not and must not be treated as if it were a body corporate, but it may sue and be sued, just as an unincorporated employers' association[62] may sue and be sued, in its own name, whether in proceedings relating to property or founded on contract or delict or any other cause of action.[63] An employers' association may be either a body corporate[64] or an unincorporated association.[65] Other unincorporated associations are considered in the next paragraph.

(9) Unincorporated associations

4.101 A voluntary association other than those considered above can sue and be sued in its own name in the sheriff court. First, it may so sue and be sued if it is carrying on a business under a trading or descriptive name.[66] The object of this rule is to provide a convenient way for actions involving such associations, among others, to proceed in the sheriff court, and "business" is construed in the widest sense as an occupation or duty which requires attention.[67] The rule also makes provision for the execution of diligence and for the service of writs and other documents. Secondly, if the association is not carrying on a business under a trading or descriptive name it may nevertheless sue or be sued in its own name alone, since it falls within the statutory definition of a person who may be a pursuer or defender.[68] If the rules of the association prescribe the manner in which it may sue or be sued, the instance may be expressed accordingly.[69] In all cases where an association is sued, however, the pursuer should consider how a decree in his favour could be enforced. Since a decree against the

---

[58] *McNaught v. Milligan* (1885) 13 R. 366; *Neilson v. Wilson* (1890) 17 R. 608; *Jones Sewing Machine Co. Ltd v. Smart*, 1987 G.W.D. 5–162 (apparently not reported elsewhere).

[59] OCR, r. 5.7(1). As to "business" see *Borland v. Lochwinnoch Golf Club*, 1986 S.L.T. (Sh.Ct.) 13. R. 5.7 also makes provision as to diligence and the service of writs, etc.

[60] See para. 4.87.

[61] Defined in the Trade Union and Labour Relations (Consolidation) Act 1992, s. 1.

[62] *ibid.* s. 127.

[63] *ibid.* ss. 10 (trade unions), 127 (unincorporated employers' association).

[64] See paras 4.83 *et seq.*

[65] Trade Union and Labour Relations (Consolidation) Act 1992, s. 127.

[66] OCR, r. 5.7(1). There is no equivalent rule in the Court of Session.

[67] *Borland v. Lochwinnoch Golf Club, supra.*

[68] 1907 Act, s. 3(e), (n), (o); *Greengairs Rovers F.C. v. Blades* (1910) 26 Sh.Ct.Rep. 280.

[69] *Whitecraigs Golf Club v. Ker*, 1923 S.L.T. (Sh. Ct.) 23.

association alone is not a warrant for diligence against an official or member not called in the action,[70] it is advisable to include as defenders any known office-bearers.[71] If the members of the association are all known and are few in number, all may be named in the instance.[72]

The method of raising proceedings by or against a friendly society is regulated by statute.[73] **4.102**

(10) Trustees

Where an action is brought by or against trustees, they must be individually named and designed in the instance, with the appropriate qualification,[74] *e.g.* "A.B. [*designed*], C.D. [*designed*] and E.F. [*designed*] as trustees acting under the trust disposition and settlement by the deceased G.H. [*designed*] dated [*state date*] and registered in the Books of Council and Session [*state date*]." If persons who are not trustees are erroneously named in the instance, the title to sue of those who have been correctly named is not thereby affected,[75] but the names wrongly stated should be removed by amendment. **4.103**

Where an action is brought by a majority of the trustees, the non-concurring trustees should be called as defenders or for their interest. Where an action is brought against the trustees, and a minority desire to escape liability for expenses, they should disclaim the defences put in by lodging a minute of disclaimer.[76] **4.104**

(11) Executors

The powers possessed by executors-dative and executors-nominate are the same as those possessed by trustees.[77] Thus a majority as well as all of them may sue an action. They should be individually named and designed and their qualification added, as by trust disposition and settlement and confirmation, or by decree-dative and testament-dative following thereon. An executor has a title to sue although he has not completed confirmation before the action is raised[78]: it is only necessary for him to do so before extract.[79] Where an executor refuses to sue, the beneficiaries may compel him to give the use of his name and prosecute the action themselves, giving him an indemnity for expenses.[80] **4.105**

---

[70] *Aitchison v. McDonald*, 1911 S.C. 174. The subsequent alterations of the rule, explained in *Borland, supra*, do not appear to have affected this decision.

[71] As in *Bryson & Co. Ltd v. Glasgow Civil Service and Mercantile Guild* (1915) 32 Sh.Ct.Rep. 23.

[72] As in *Alyth Light Symphony Band v. Ross*, 1930 S.L.T. (Sh. Ct.) 34.

[73] Friendly Societies Act 1974, s. 103.

[74] *Bell v. Trotter's Trs* (1841) 3 D. 380.

[75] *McDonald v. Burns* (1938) 54 Sh.Ct.Rep. 229, *sub nom. Trustees for the Religious Community of Poor Clares Colletines, Edinburgh v. Burns*, 1939 S.L.T. (Sh. Ct.) 2.

[76] *Cf. Bennett v. MacLellan* (1891) 18 R. 955 at 957; *Campbell v. Campbell's Trs*, 1957 S.L.T. (Sh. Ct.) 53.

[77] Trusts (Scotland) Act 1921, s. 2; Succession (Scotland) Act 1964, s. 20; *Graham v. Graham*, 1968 S.L.T. (Notes) 42.

[78] *Symington v. Campbell* (1894) 21 R. 434, *per* Lord Adam at 437; *Bentley v. Macfarlane*, 1964 S.C. 76, *per* L.P. Clyde at 79.

[79] *Chalmers' Trs v. Watson* (1860) 22 D. 1060 at 1064; *Bone v. Morrison* (1866) 5 M. 240; *Mackay v. Mackay*, 1914 S.C. 200; McLaren, *Wills and Succession*, ii, para. 1616.

[80] *Blair v. Stirling*, 1894 1 S.L.T. 599; *Morrison v. Morrison's Exrx*, 1912 S.C. 892.

(12) Representatives

4.106 Where a person wishes to pursue a claim against the estate of a deceased person and no one has been confirmed as executor, he should raise an action for decree *cognitionis causa tantum* calling as defenders all the known next-of-kin of the deceased.[81] In the instance they should be individually named and designed, and the capacity in which they are sued stated.[82] If a defender dies while an action is in dependence, the pursuer may have the action transferred against his representatives *cognitionis causa tantum*.[83]

(13) Judicial factors[84]

4.107 A judicial factor sues and is sued as such, the particulars of his appointment being specified in the instance. He has a title to sue before obtaining extract of his appointment.[85]

(14) Assignees

4.108 An assignee may sue in his own name with the addition in the instance of "assignee of X.Y. [*designed*]" and the date and other details of the assignation being given in the condescendence. He may also sue with the consent and concurrence of his cedent,[86] or sist himself as pursuer in an action commenced by his cedent.[87] An application by way of plea or motion by the defender in an action raised by the cedent, that the assignee should be sisted as a party or ordained to find caution for the defender's expenses will be refused where the true interest in the cause remains with the cedent[88] or where the assignee undertakes to meet any award of expenses against the cedent or where the only reason for the application is that the question of contribution between the defender and the assignee as joint wrongdoers may be decided in the same process.[89]

4.109 A pursuer who has no title to sue at the date of the raising of the action cannot acquire one by a subsequent assignation or retrocession.[90]

(15) Bankruptcy

4.110 The permanent trustee may bring, defend or continue any legal proceedings relating to the estate of the debtor if he considers that to do so would be beneficial for the administration of the estate; but if there are commissioners he may do so only with the consent of the commissioners, the creditors or the court.[91] He may sue or be sued in his own name, his qualification as trustee being stated in the instance.[92] When an action has

---

[81] *Smith v. Tasker*, 1955 S.L.T. 347; *Stevens v. Thomson*, 1971 S.L.T. 136.
[82] *Kay v. Morrison's Reps*, 1984 S.L.T. 175.
[83] *Davidson, Pirie & Co. v. Dihle's Reps* (1900) 2 F. 640.
[84] See Walker, *Judicial Factors*, pp. 90–91.
[85] *Calver v. Howard, Baker & Co.* (1894) 22 R. 1.
[86] See para. 4.114.
[87] *Mavor v. Governors of Aberdeen Educational Trust* (1902) 10 S.L.T. 156; *Cole-Hamilton v. Boyd*, 1962 S.C. 247 at 248, 260 (1963 S.C.(H.L.) 1); *Bentley v. Macfarlane*, 1964 S.C. 76, *per* L.P. Clyde at 79.
[88] *McCuaig v. McCuaig*, 1909 S.C. 355.
[89] *Cairney v. Mags of Callander*, 1958 S.L.T. (Notes) 40. The latter reason may in any event now lack force in view of the availability of third-party procedure.
[90] *Symington v. Campbell* (1894) 21 R. 434; *Bentley, supra*; *Cobham v. Minter*, 1986 S.L.T. 336 (defender convening third party). See para. 4.32.
[91] Bankruptcy (Scotland) Act 1985, s. 39(2)(b).
[92] *Howden v. Rocheid* (1868) 6 M. 300.

already been raised, it may be intimated to the trustee on the motion of the opposite party or by the court *ex proprio motu.*[93] The trustee may sist himself as pursuer or defender and maintain the action or defence.[94] A creditor may compel the trustee to give his name as pursuer of an action against a debtor of the bankrupt on giving security for expenses, or to grant an assignation of the claim.[95]

The bankrupt has no title to sue, without the concurrence of his trustee, any action in which there is or may be competition with his creditors or the trustee representing them for any part of the assets sequestrated.[96] In those actions where he has a title to sue or defend, he may be named in the instance in normal terms. He may be required to find caution for expenses.[97] **4.111**

(16) *Dominus litis*

A *dominus litis* is a person standing behind a nominal party to the action, who has an interest in the subject-matter of the action which is so direct and dominant that he is in control of that party's conduct of the proceedings in the action.[98] It is said that where the nominal pursuer is not the true *dominus litis*, it is in the discretion of the court to order caution to be found, or to order the true *dominus litis* to sist himself, under the penalty that, if he does not, the action will be dismissed.[99] In modern practice it would appear to be uncommon to require the *dominus litis* to sist himself. In *Hepburn v. Tait*,[1] Lord Justice-Clerk Moncreiff observed that he did not know of any case in which the *dominus litis* had been sisted as a party; and reported examples of that procedure appear to be rare.[2] The procedure has, however, been considered in cases of two classes[3]: where the pursuer has alienated or been divested of the subject of the action in favour of a transferee[4]; and where the pursuer of an *actio popularis* has been a man of straw.[5] **4.112**

It appears that in practice the plea of *dominus litis* is given effect to either by requiring the nominal pursuer to find caution for expenses before proceeding with the action[6] or, more usually, by making the *dominus litis* liable for the expenses after the conclusion of the action.[7] A preliminary **4.113**

---

[93] *Hallowell v. Niven* (1843) 5 D. 675.

[94] *Thom v. Bridges and Macqueen* (1857) 19 D. 721; *Grindall v. John Mitchell (Grangemouth) Ltd*, 1987 S.L.T. 137 (bankrupt suing for *solatium* for personal injuries, trustee suing for patrimonial loss); *Watson v. Thompson*, 1990 S.L.T. 374, 1991 S.L.T. 683 (trustee sisted with respect to claim for *solatium*).

[95] *Henderson v. Robb* (1889) 16 R. 341.

[96] *Dickson v. United Dominion Trust*, 1988 S.L.T. 19, *per* Lord McCluskey at 22F–G; *Thomson v. Yorkshire Building Society*, 1994 S.C.L.R. 1014 at 1017B.

[97] See paras 11.54, 11.55.

[98] *Cairns v. McGregor*, 1931 S.C. 84.

[99] Mackay, *Practice*, i, p. 505; Maxwell, p. 154; Dobie, p. 112.

[1] (1874) 1 R. 875 at 877.

[2] *Fraser v. Dunbar* (1839) 1 D. 882.

[3] *Drysdale v. Reid* (1920) 36 Sh.Ct.Rep. 124.

[4] *Fraser, supra*; *Waddell v. Hope* (1843) 6 D. 160; *McCuaig v. McCuaig*, 1909 S.C. 355, *Rutherford v. Licences and General Insurance Co.*, 1939 S.L.T. 47; *Cairney v. Mags of Callander*, 1958 S.L.T. (Notes) 40: see para. 4.108.

[5] *Jenkins v. Robertson* (1869) 7 M. 739; and see *Robertson v. Duke of Atholl* (1905) 8 F. 150, where the alleged *domini litis* were sisted as pursuers on their own application.

[6] para. 11.56.

[7] *Hepburn, supra.* The plea has not been sustained where the *domini* undertook to meet any expenses awarded against the pursuer: *Cairney, supra.*

proof of the averments supporting the plea of *dominus litis* may be allowed.[8] Where the *dominus litis* has not been sisted, he may nevertheless be found liable in the expenses incurred by his intervention in the action[9] if his participation as *dominus litis* is evident or admitted.[10] It is more usual, however, to raise a separate action for payment.[11]

(17) Consent and concurrence

4.114 A pursuer may sue with the consent and concurrence of another in the following circumstances. He may sue with the consent and concurrence of another with a view to excluding some anticipated or reasonably possible objection to his title by the party concurring, whereby the defender might be subsequently prejudiced, as where an assignee to a debt or demand sues the debtor therein with the concurrence of the cedent. The object in such a case is to guarantee the pursuer's title to receive payment and discharge of the debt against any objection by the person concurring, who is, by the fact of his concurrence, barred from stating it. Also, where the pursuer has a right and interest of his own, which is qualified by or dependent upon some *jus tertii* or some limitation or condition which may be an obstacle or impediment to his suing, such a defect may be cured by the consent and concurrence of the appropriate person.[12] The concurring pursuer enters into an agreement with all parties that, so far as he is concerned, the principal pursuer shall control any interest he may have in the matter in dispute, and that he will be bound by the issue as that is determined in the action between the principal pursuer and the defender.[13] But a person who has no right or title to sue an action cannot do so by obtaining the consent and concurrence of the person to whom alone such right or title belongs.[14]

4.115 A party who merely grants his consent and concurrence has no title to appeal against any interlocutor pronounced in the cause[15]; nor does he incur any liability for expenses.[16] If, however, he takes a prominent part in the litigation, expenses may be awarded against him[17] or he may be found jointly and severally liable in expenses with the pursuer.[18]

(18) Defender called for his interest

4.116 It is sometimes desirable to call, along with the defender, some person who has an *ex facie* legal, or a probable personal, interest in the subject-matter of the action. Such a person should be called as a defender with the addition in the instance of the words "for his interest" or "for any interest

---

[8] *Jenkins, Robertson, Rutherford, supra.*

[9] *Nairn v. S.-E. Lancashire Insurance Co.*, 1930 S.C. 600.

[10] *Walker v. Walker* (1903) 5 F. 320; *McMillan v. Mackinlay*, 1926 S.C. 673; *Main v. Rankin & Sons*, 1929 S.C. 40; *Davidson v. Whatmough*, 1930 S.L.T. 536.

[11] *Swirles v. Isles*, 1930 S.C. 696; *Cairns, Rutherford, supra.*

[12] *Hislop v. MacRitchie's Trs* (1879) 7 R. 384, *per* Lord Young at 393, 394; (1881) 8 R. (H.L.) 95, *per* Lord Selborne L.C. at 98, Lord Watson at 105.

[13] *Martin v. Lindsay* (1894) 21 R. 759.

[14] *Hislop v. MacRitchie's Trs, supra.*

[15] *Martin, supra.*

[16] *Whitehead v. Blaik* (1893) 20 R. 1045; *Armstrong v. Thompson* (1895) 2 S.L.T. 537; *Currie v. Cowan & Co.*, 1911 2 S.L.T. 467; *Gordon v. Henderson* (1922) 38 Sh.Ct.Rep. 293.

[17] *Fraser v. Cameron* (1892) 19 R. 564; *cf. Docherty v. Glasgow Tramways and Omnibus Co.* (1895) 2 S.L.T. 406.

[18] *Wilkinson v. Kinneil Cannel and Coking Coal Co.* (1897) 24 R. 1001 (pupil attaining minority *pendente processu*); *Rodger v. Weir*, 1917 S.C. 300; *McMillan v. Mackinlay*, 1926 S.C. 673.

he may have". The object of so doing is twofold. It provides against the statement by the defender of the plea of "All parties not called". It also provides against the person's claiming in future disputes that he had no notice of what was pending: he receives due notice of the action and is given an opportunity of stating a defence if he has an interest to do so.[19] He is not, however, bound to appear, and if he does not, no operative decree can be pronounced against him.[20]

(19) Legally-aided parties

Where a party is in receipt of civil legal aid in the cause in question, the words "Assisted Person", normally placed in brackets, must follow his name on every step of process.[21] Where the assisted person is a pursuer, he must lodge his legal aid certificate along with the initial writ. Where he is not the pursuer, he must lodge his certificate when he receives it and intimate the lodging to all the other parties to the cause. In the case of an appeal to the Court of Session or from the sheriff to the sheriff principal, the certificate must be lodged and likewise intimated before the appeal is heard.[22] If a party becomes an assisted person during the dependence of a cause, he must forthwith lodge his certificate in process and intimate to the other parties that he has done so.[23] If the party ceases to be an assisted person, or the conditions upon which he has been granted civil legal aid have been varied, he must forthwith serve notice of the fact by registered or recorded delivery letter on all the other parties.[24] **4.117**

(20) Party litigants

In general, any person may conduct his own cause in the sheriff court, in accordance with the fundamental principle that everyone has the constitutional right of access to the courts.[25] The exceptions to the general rule are children,[26] insane persons,[27] persons voluntarily resident or carrying on business in hostile territory,[28] and firms, companies and other artificial entities.[29] A party who conducts his own cause, other than a practising solicitor,[30] is known as a party litigant. **4.118**

A party litigant is inevitably at a great disadvantage in coping with the rules of practice and procedure, which he must observe in the same way as a solicitor. Unlike a solicitor, however, he may borrow a process only by leave of the sheriff and subject to such conditions as the sheriff may impose; but he may inspect the process and obtain copies, where practicable, from the sheriff clerk.[31] While the sheriff clerk may assist a party litigant on matters of procedure, he is not required to act as his agent or to **4.119**

---

[19] *Scottish Heritages Co. Ltd v. N.B. Property Investment Co. Ltd* (1885) 12 R. 550; *Smith v. Lord Advocate*, 1932 S.L.T. 374.

[20] *Campbell v. McAllister* (1893) 1 S.L.T. 14; *Smith, supra.*

[21] A.S. (Civil Legal Aid Rules) 1987 (No. 492), rr. 3(1), 1(2).

[22] *ibid.* r. 3(2), (3).

[23] *ibid.* r. 3(4).

[24] *ibid.* r. 3(5).

[25] *Lord Advocate v. Rizza*, 1962 S.L.T. (Notes) 8. The effect of an order under the Vexatious Actions (Scotland) Act 1898 is considered *infra*, paras 4.122 and 4.123.

[26] See paras 4.10 *et seq.*

[27] See paras 4.07 to 4.09.

[28] See para. 4.03.

[29] See para. 1.32.

[30] *Macbeth, Currie & Co. v. Matthew*, 1985 S.L.T. (Sh. Ct.) 44.

[31] OCR, r. 11.3(3).

keep him advised on the progress of the case[32]: the party litigant must appear personally when necessary and must himself perform the various duties which would otherwise be carried out by a solicitor.

4.120 In view of his disadvantages the sheriff allows the party litigant considerable latitude or indulgence in the presentation of his case, so long as that does not result in prejudice to his opponent.[33] While it is proper for the sheriff to assist the party litigant to present his case in evidence, he may not decide in his favour on a ground not explored at the proof, of which the opposing party has had no notice.[34] The sheriff gives the reasons for his rulings in particularly clear and simple terms, and when giving his judgment deals with special care with the party litigant's case.[35]

4.121 There are special rules as to the expenses allowable to party litigants.[36]

(21) Vexatious litigants

4.122 The general right of access to the courts is qualified where the Court of Session has made an order in terms of section 1 of the Vexatious Litigants (Scotland) Act 1898 in order to control the oppressive raising of actions.[37] If the Lord Advocate satisfies either Division of the Court of Session that a person has habitually and persistently instituted vexatious legal proceedings without any reasonable ground for instituting such proceedings, whether in the Court of Session or in any inferior court, and whether against the same person or against different persons, the court may order that no legal proceedings shall be instituted by that person in the Court of Session or any other court, unless he obtains the leave of a judge sitting in the Outer House.[38] The court may be so satisfied upon a consideration not only of the number of actions raised, but of the way in which the person has conducted himself within the legal process.[39] The court gives the person an opportunity of being heard.[40] If the court makes an order, a copy is published in the *Edinburgh Gazette*,[41] and it is also notified to sheriff clerks in the Scottish Court Service Circular.

4.123 Once an order is made, the person may not institute legal proceedings in the sheriff court or any other court without the leave of the Outer House judge, which may be given only if he satisfies the judge that the legal proceeding is not vexatious and that there is a prima facie ground for it.[42] A decision of the judge to refuse leave is final.[43] The order appears to remain in force indefinitely, but not to apply to proceedings which are in dependence when it is made.

---

32 *Miller v. Chapelside Chemical Co.* (1887) 3 Sh.Ct.Rep. 83 at 88.

33 *Moore v. Secretary of State for Scotland*, 1985 S.L.T. 38 at 39–40.

34 *Kay's Tutor v. Ayrshire and Arran Health Board*, 1985 S.L.T. 435 at 440; 1987 S.L.T. 577.

35 *Cf. Bowman v. McKeown, The Times*, Nov. 23, 1978; [1978] C.L.Y. 2399.

36 Litigants in Person (Costs and Expenses) Act 1975; A.S. (Expenses of Party Litigants) 1976 (S.I. 1976 No. 1606), amended by A.S. (Expenses of Party Litigants) 1983 (S.I. 1983 No. 1438).

37 *Lord Advocate v. Rizza*, 1962 S.L.T. (Notes) 8; *Lord Advocate v. Henderson*, 1983 S.L.T. 518.

38 Vexatious Actions (Scotland) Act 1898, s. 1, read with the Administration of Justice (Scotland) Act 1933, s. 3(1).

39 *Lord Advocate v. Cooney*, 1984 S.L.T. 434.

40 *Lord Advocate v. Arnold*, 1951 S.C. 256, *sub nom. Lord Advocate v. Gracie*, 1951 S.L.T. 116.

41 1898 Act, s. 1. The court directs such publication in its interlocutor.

42 *ibid.*

43 1898 Act, s. 1A, inserted by the Law Reform (Miscellaneous Provisions) (Scotland) Act 1980, s. 19.

MANDATES

Where a mandatary is joined with the pursuer in raising the action, the writ proceeds at the instance of both, thus: "A.B. [*designed*] and C.D. [*designed*], his mandatary." The circumstances in which the court may ordain a party to sist a mandatary are considered below.[44] **4.124**

Where a question arises as to the authority of a solicitor to appear for a party, it may be resolved by the party's appearance in court with the solicitor.[45] The court may ordain the party or the solicitor to produce a written mandate, and allow him a reasonable time for that purpose.[46] Where the party is the pursuer, the order may be made under certification that, if the mandate is not produced, the action will be dismissed.[47] It will be dismissed without expenses against the pursuer, since the pursuer is not liable for expenses caused by an action which it may be assumed he did not authorise,[48] but expenses may be awarded against the solicitor who raised the action on the basis that it is to be presumed that he did so without a mandate. Where the party is the defender, the solicitor's possession of the service copy of the initial writ implies a mandate[49]; but if an order to produce a mandate is not obtempered, the sanction would appear to be decree by default.[50] The mandate produced must be construed according to its own terms.[51] A solicitor who initiates[52] or defends[53] an action without a sufficient mandate, or who fails to produce such a mandate when called upon to do so,[54] may be found liable in expenses. **4.125**

Similarly, where a question arises as to the authority of a party to sue or defend an action on behalf of another, as where he does so as factor or trustee, or on behalf of himself and others, an order should be made for the production of a mandate and a reasonable time allowed.[55] **4.126**

Counsel has a presumed mandate to appear for a party whom he has been instructed by a qualified solicitor to represent.[56] He cannot be required to produce a mandate, his gown being a sufficient mandate.[57] It has been said that the presumption that he is duly authorised to appear and represent his client can only be rebutted by a disclaimer[58]; and, on the other hand, that the presumption cannot shut the door against positive and circumstantial averments as to matters altogether behind the province of counsel.[59] **4.127**

---

[44] See paras 11.67 to 11.80.

[45] *Hepburn v. Tait* (1874) 1 R. 875.

[46] *Fischer & Co. v. Anderson* (1896) 23 R. 395; *Ferguson, Davidson & Co. v. Paterson and Dobbie* (1898) 1 F. 227.

[47] *Hepburn, supra.*

[48] *Ferguson, Davidson & Co., supra*; Lees, *Pleading*, p. 151, para. 380.

[49] *Muir v. Stevenson* (1850) 12 D. 512.

[50] *Fischer & Co., supra.*

[51] *Goodall v. Bilsland*, 1909 S.C. 1152. For examples of insufficient mandates, see *Goodall*; *Bonny v. Gillies* (1829) 8 S. 13.

[52] *Cowan v. Farnie* (1836) 14 S. 634; *Robertson v. Ross* (1873) 11 M. 910.

[53] *McCall v. Sharpe and Bayne* (1862) 24 D. 393.

[54] *Philip v. Gordon* (1848) 11 D. 175.

[55] *Shinas v. Fordyce* (1777) 5 Brown's Supp. 572; *Fischer & Co., supra.*

[56] Mackay, *Manual*, p. 286.

[57] Bankton, IV, iii, 26; Ersk., III, iii, 33.

[58] *Oyston v. Turnbull* (1875) 13 S.L.R. 69.

[59] *Ferguson, Davidson & Co., supra.*

CHAPTER 5

THE ORDINARY COURT

Introduction

The ordinary court is the tribunal in which the sheriff exercises his civil jurisdiction. In strict theory every civil proceeding proceeds in the ordinary court, although certain stages of its procedure, and in some cases all the stages, may not take place in the public courtroom. The proceedings competent in the ordinary court take a variety of forms of which the principal are ordinary actions or causes,[1] summary causes, small claims, summary applications, adoptions, bankruptcy and liquidation proceedings, commissary proceedings and miscellaneous statutory appeals and applications. In modern practice, however, the term "ordinary court" is usually reserved for those causes which are governed by the Ordinary Cause Rules 1993 and, in some instances, the matters mentioned above other than summary causes and small claims. Summary causes and small claims usually tend nowadays to be regarded as falling outwith the concept of the ordinary court. 5.01

The term "ordinary court" is commonly applied to the regular sittings of the court at which the sheriff regulates the procedural progress of the ordinary causes and summary applications currently in dependence before the court and hears applications relative thereto, and the days of these sittings are often referred to as "ordinary court days". Similarly, "summary cause court" is used to describe the sittings at which summary causes are called and incidental applications heard, which need not necessarily take place on "ordinary court days". Such usages are convenient and generally understood, and will be used in this book; but they are not strictly correct, because properly speaking all the sittings of the court at which civil business is considered, whether by way of proof, debate, motion or otherwise, whether in court or in chambers and whatever the form of process, are sittings of the ordinary court. Thus the original First Schedule to the 1907 Act was headed "Rules for regulating procedure in the ordinary court", and contained rules for summary causes (in the form then prescribed) as well as for ordinary causes; and the various actions or causes referred to in the 1907 and 1971 Acts include "every civil proceeding competent in the ordinary sheriff court".[2] 5.02

The unitary and flexible character of the sheriff court system of civil procedure may also be seen in the fact that an action which is brought as an ordinary cause, summary cause or small claim need not necessarily remain within that category. If it has been brought under the wrong form 5.03

---

[1] The terms "cause" and "action" originally had distinct meanings, but are now used interchangeably: McGlashan, p. 141; 1907 Act, s. 3(d).

[2] 1907 Act, s. 3(3); 1971 Act, s. 45(3).

of process by a simple formal error which has caused the defender no prejudice, the sheriff has an inherent power to transfer it to the roll appropriate to the correct form of process, and it is thereafter treated as an action brought under that form.[3] Further, the 1971 Act provides that in certain circumstances an ordinary cause may be treated as a summary cause[4]; a summary cause may be treated as an ordinary cause[5]; a small claim as a summary or ordinary cause[6]; and a summary or ordinary cause as a small claim.[7] An ordinary cause may also in certain circumstances be remitted to the Court of Session.[8] For that to happen a sheriff must first decide whether the importance or difficulty of the case makes it appropriate for such a remit, and then must decide, in the exercise of his discretion, whether the whole circumstances are such as to persuade him to order a remit.[9]

The business of the court

5.04 It follows that the business of the ordinary court is of a very extensive and varied character. It may be divided into the following classes.

Ordinary causes

5.05 "Ordinary cause" was not originally a statutory term, and "ordinary actions" were defined as "those which proceed in the regular and solemn order of law, without omitting any of its accustomed formalities".[10] They were distinguished from "summary actions" which were "those wherein extraordinary dispatch is required, and where the interests of the party might suffer by abiding the ordinary *induciae*, and therefore proceed without reference to the ordinary court days, or time of vacation".[11] The distinction between "ordinary" and "summary" forms of process with reference to the procedure in them is now statutory, but they may still be differentiated as respectively formal and expeditious in character.

5.06 "Ordinary causes" are now those whose procedure is regulated by the First Schedule to the 1907 Act, as substituted in 1993, which applies to any action or proceedings commenced on or after January 1, 1994.[12] They include those actions in which are followed the forms and procedure applicable to petitory actions craving payment of a sum of money exceeding the limit specified in relation to summary causes.[13] Part III of this book is concerned with the normal procedure followed in such actions, and with those incidental and interim procedures which particular circumstances frequently require. "Ordinary causes" also include other forms of action which to a greater or lesser extent require some departure

---

[3] *Borthwick v. Bank of Scotland*, 1985 S.L.T. (Sh. Ct.) 49. See para. 13.50.
[4] 1971 Act, s. 37(1)(a): see para. 13.46.
[5] *ibid.* s. 37(2): see para. 13.47, and Vol. 2 of this work.
[6] *ibid.* s. 37(2B), inserted by the Law Reform (Miscellaneous Provisions) (Scotland) Act 1985, s. 18(3)(a); see para. 13.48.
[7] 1971 Act, s. 37(2C), inserted as above; see para. 13.49.
[8] *ibid.* s. 37(1)(b): see paras 13.57 to 13.66.
[9] *Mullan v. Anderson*, 1993 S.C.L.R. 506 (Bench of Five Judges), overruling *Data Controls (Middlesborough) Ltd v. British Railways Board*, 1991 S.C.L.R. 359.
[10] McGlashan, p. 142.
[11] *ibid.*
[12] A.S. (Ordinary Cause Rules, Sheriff Court) 1993 (S.I. 1993 No. 1956), as amended.
[13] At the time of writing, £1,500: 1971 Act, s. 35(1), as amended by S.I. 1988 No. 1993.

from the course of procedure prescribed for the petitory actions considered in Part III. These other forms of action, which are considered in Part IV, include petitory actions other than those dealt with in Part III, declaratory actions, family proceedings, actions connected with heritable subjects and miscellaneous other actions.

Summary causes

The modern summary cause was introduced by section 35 of the 1971 Act.[14] Summary causes, which are not to be confused with summary applications, are fully considered in Volume 2 of this work. **5.07**

Small claims

The small claim is a form of summary cause which was introduced with effect from November 30, 1988.[15] It is used for the purpose of such descriptions of summary cause proceedings as are prescribed by the Lord Advocate by order.[16] Small claims are also fully considered in Volume 2 of this work. **5.08**

Summary applications[17]

A great variety of matters are brought before the sheriff by way of summary application. "Summary application" means and includes all applications of a summary nature brought under the common law jurisdiction of the sheriff, and all applications, whether by appeal or otherwise, brought under any Act of Parliament which provides, or which, according to any practice in the sheriff court, allows that it shall be disposed of in a summary manner, but which does not more particularly define in what form it shall be heard, tried and determined.[18] The procedure in summary applications generally is described in Chapter 25. Statutory applications are among the matters considered in Chapter 26. **5.09**

Other matters

Miscellaneous statutory appeals also form a large category of civil business, and are likewise considered in Chapter 26. Commissary proceedings, sequestrations and liquidations are so fully examined in other works familiar to the practitioner that it is thought to be unnecessary to include them in this book.[19] **5.10**

Sittings of the court

Court days

The sheriff principal may by order prescribe the number of courts to be held at each of the places in the sheriffdom at which a court is required to be held,[20] and the days on which and the times at which those courts are to be held.[21] When the court is held in a building belonging to a local or **5.11**

---

[14] The financial limit has been amended as noted in n. 13.

[15] S.I. 1988 No. 1976.

[16] 1971 Act, s. 35(2), substituted by the Law Reform (Miscellaneous Provisions) (Scotland) Act 1985, s. 18(1).

[17] Not to be confused with summary causes: see para. 5.07.

[18] 1907 Act, s. 3(p).

[19] See Currie (commissary and confirmation), McBryde (bankruptcy), Flint (liquidation).

[20] *i.e.* in terms of s. 3 of the 1971 Act.

[21] 1971 Act, s. 17(1).

other public authority, the sittings of the court must be so arranged as not to interfere with the normal use of the building.[22]

Court holidays

5.12 The court is not required to sit on a Saturday or Sunday or on a court holiday.[23] The court holidays are prescribed by the sheriff principal who may, and in practice does, prescribe as court holidays in respect of criminal business 10 days (other than Saturdays and Sundays) in a calendar year and any special day proclaimed to be a bank holiday either throughout the United Kingdom or in a place or locality within the sheriffdom.[24] In practice the sheriff principal annually fixes as court holidays the statutory bank holidays in Scotland[25] plus Easter Monday, December 26, 27 or 28,[26] and certain local holidays[27]; and the court does not sit at all on those days.

Civil sessions

5.13 In terms of the Sheriff Courts (Scotland) Act 1971 there should be three sessions in each year for the disposal of civil business: a winter session, a spring session and a summer session. There should not be a vacation of longer than two weeks at Christmas time, four weeks in the spring and eight weeks in the summer. According to the Act the dates of the sessions are to be prescribed by the sheriff principal.[28] In practice the foregoing provisions of the 1971 Act are now seriously outdated and, while a certain amount of lip-service may still be paid to them, the fact of the matter is that most sheriff courts now sit continuously throughout the year with sheriffs and court staff taking leave, in accordance with their personal entitlement, at such times of the year as are convenient.

Vacations

5.14 The same is largely true in respect of the statutory provisions relating to vacations. Except in some of the smaller courts the provisions in the 1971 Act now reflect a leisured time when the volume of business was much less than is the case now; and the consequence is that in the larger courts so-called vacation courts are a thing of the past, and civil business of all kinds is conducted more or less continuously throughout the year. However, it remains appropriate to note the current statutory requirements in relation to vacations, and vacation courts. They are as follows. The sheriff principal should fix the dates of vacation courts: at least one day during the vacation immediately following the spring session, and at least two days during the vacation immediately following the summer session, for the disposal of civil business.[29] At a vacation court the business of an

---

[22] 1971 Act, s. 25(2).

[23] Criminal Procedure (Scotland) Act 1995, s. 8(1).

[24] *ibid.* s. 8(2). A special day may be so proclaimed under the Banking and Financial Dealings Act 1971, s. 1(3).

[25] These are: New Year's Day, if it be not a Sunday or, if it be a Sunday, Jan. 3; Jan. 2, if it be not a Sunday or, if it be a Sunday, Jan. 3; Good Friday; the first Monday in May; the first Monday in August; and Christmas Day, if it be not a Sunday or, if it be a Sunday, Dec. 26: Banking and Financial Dealings Act 1971, s. 1 and Sched. 1.

[26] If Christmas Day is a Friday, Dec. 28 is a holiday; if it is a Saturday, Dec. 27 and 28 are holidays; if it is a Sunday, Dec. 26 and 27 are holidays.

[27] *e.g.* Lanimer Day in Lanark; the Riding of the Marches in Linlithgow.

[28] 1971 Act, s. 17(2).

[29] *ibid.* s. 17(3).

ordinary court will be conducted.[30] Civil proceedings of all kinds may proceed during vacation as during session, and interlocutors may be pronounced during vacation in any such proceedings.[31] The foregoing provision appears strange to anyone accustomed to the year-round business of most sheriff courts today, but is a relic from a time when, without express statutory provision, courts could not competently conduct civil business during designated vacation periods.

Civil days

The sheriff principal also prescribes the descriptions of business to be disposed of at the courts of his sheriffdom.[32] In practice the days in each session when the sheriff or sheriffs in each court preside in the ordinary court and sit to take proofs, debates and other hearings in civil proceedings are set out in a scheme of civil and criminal business for that session which is drafted by the sheriff clerk at that court in consultation with the sheriff or sheriffs there, and adjusted and approved by the sheriff principal. The sheriff may, however, deal with civil business at any time which does not prejudice other business which has been set down in terms of the approved scheme. He may deal with such matters as motions continued from the ordinary court, or urgent applications, at any time on any court day; and often a period of time before the hour when he takes his seat on the bench in the morning is set aside for such matters. **5.15**

Ordinary court

The ordinary court, at which cases in dependence other than summary causes are called before the sheriff and motions heard and orders made relative to the procedure therein, normally sits on the same day or days each week during session,[33] but separate days may be prescribed for dealing respectively with different classes of business, such as family and non-family causes. In some larger courts, however, the volume of business is now such that provision is made in the court programme for incidental civil business to be dealt with on a daily basis. The summary cause court, at which summary causes and small claims are called for the same purpose, may sit on the same day as the ordinary court or on a different day. **5.16**

Time of sitting

The sheriff normally takes his seat on the bench at or as soon as possible after a specified time between 10 and 10.30 a.m., and sits if necessary until about 4 p.m. with a luncheon adjournment at or about the hour when the sheriff clerk's office closes for lunch.[34] The times of sitting are, however, flexible: the sheriff may sit earlier or continue to sit later, and frequently does so in order to finish a case or to accommodate witnesses or others who have come from a distance. Moreover, on occasions the volume of business in some courts necessitates that certain classes of business are set down to start earlier than 10 a.m. The effect of late sitting on court **5.17**

---

[30] See para. 5.16.

[31] 1971 Act, s. 17(3).

[32] *ibid.* s. 17(1)(a).

[33] In some of the less busy courts it sits on alternate weeks, and in others every fourth week.

[34] Each office's hours are fixed by the sheriff clerk.

shorthand-writers and staff must nevertheless be considered. The strain of continuous note-taking should not be underestimated, and the staff are generally entitled to expect to be able to leave the building, having completed all their duties for the day, at the end of the normal office hours.

Necessity

5.18 Although the court is normally held in the sheriff court house during conventional court hours, in cases of necessity or urgency the court may sit anywhere in the sheriffdom, and at any time. For example, there is no reason in principle why the court should not be convened at the home of an infirm witness, or sit on a Saturday, or why the sheriff should not grant an interim interdict or other order at his home in the evening or during the weekend. The introduction of child protection orders under section 57 of the Children (Scotland) Act 1995 has led to an increase in the number of occasions when a sheriff is required to conduct a hearing at his home in the evening or at weekends.

Publicity of proceedings

Principle

5.19 In principle, the court must administer justice in public.[35] The doors of the courtroom are kept unlocked, and members of the public are entitled to be admitted and to come and go as freely as possible, having regard to the facilities available, the possibility of disorder, the need for security and the danger and fire risk involved if too many people are permitted inside the courtroom.[36] The principle is subject to statutory exceptions, and to exceptions recognised by the common law and the practice of the courts which are justifiable on the ground that justice could not be done if the court were to sit in public, or that the nature of the business being conducted is administrative or procedural in character.

Statutory exceptions

5.20 Among the more important statutory exceptions to the principle are the following. Adoption proceedings must take place in private unless the court otherwise directs.[37] Proceedings under Part II of the Children (Scotland) Act 1995 are to be heard in chambers,[38] as is a parent's appeal against a decision of an education authority's appeal committee.[39] Decrees in undefended actions of divorce or separation where acceptable evidence in the form of affidavits is lodged,[40] and in simplified divorce applications,[41] are granted in chambers.

---

[35] The principle is reflected in the Court of Session Act 1693 whereby Court of Session advisings must take place "with open doors" except "in some special cases". *Cf. Scott v. Scott* [1913] A.C. 417.

[36] *cf. R. v. Denbigh Justices, ex p. Williams* [1974] Q.B. 759, *per* Lord Widgery C.J. at 764–765.

[37] Adoption Act 1978, s. 57.

[38] 1995 Act, s. 93(5). Section 44 of that Act contains certain prohibitions on the reporting and publication of matters arising in proceedings under Part II of the Act: see para. 5.29.

[39] Education (Scotland) Act 1980, s. 28F(3)(c), inserted by the Education (Scotland) Act 1981, s. 1(1).

[40] OCR, r. 33.28.

[41] *ibid.* rr. 33.79 and 33.80.

Applications in chambers at common law

Certain applications of a preliminary kind may be heard in chambers. These include applications to shorten or extend the period of notice,[42] and applications for interim interdict[43] or for interim orders under the Matrimonial Homes (Family Protection) (Scotland) Act 1981.[44] In practice, however, since some preliminary applications such as, for example, for interim interdict, may properly raise matters of public interest, they will often be dealt with in open court. Applications of a purely administrative character, such as applications regarding money payable to a person under disability,[45] are usually dealt with in chambers. **5.21**

Evidence behind closed doors at common law

The court may sit behind closed doors during certain actions of divorce or separation, not so much in the interests of public decency as in the interests of justice, in that publicity would be likely to interfere with the ascertainment of the truth by inhibiting witnesses from speaking frankly.[46] It is thought that the court may also sit behind closed doors in the interests of national security; or in the event of a disturbance; or when evidence concerning secret processes is to be given; or where publicity would prejudice other proceedings, as where evidence in a civil case is heard behind closed doors because criminal investigations are proceeding in relation to the same subject-matter.[47] **5.22**

Examinations under section 198 of the Insolvency Act 1986 are in practice heard behind closed doors, as are proceedings relative to the making of a parental responsibilities order.[48] **5.23**

Any person creating a disturbance may be excluded, and it is thought that children of tender years may also be excluded if the sheriff considers that in all the circumstances it is in the interests of justice, or in their own best interests, that they should not be present.[49] **5.24**

Press reporters

Where the court sits behind closed doors, or is ordered to be cleared in the course of a hearing, it is normally understood that press and other reporters may remain on the understanding that they will respect the sheriff's intention in excluding the public, as by refraining from disclosing the identity of the witness.[50] It is thought that in rare cases, as where **5.25**

---

42 OCR, r. 5.1.

43 See paras 21.85 to 21.93.

44 See paras 22.77 *et seq.*

45 OCR, rr. 36.14 to 36.17. See para. 21.37.

46 *cf. Scott v. Scott* [1913] A.C. 417.

47 *McGeachy v. Standard Life Assurance Co.*, 1972 S.C. 145; and see the Contempt of Court Act 1981, s. 4(2): see para. 5.30.

48 Children (Scotland) Act 1995, s. 86. Section 93(5) refers to such matters being heard "in chambers" but in practice a closed courtroom is normally used because it provides facilities for taking evidence from witnesses which would not be available in a sheriff's chambers. See also *Sloan v. B*, 1991 S.L.T. 530 at 551C–G.

49 In criminal proceedings the presence in court of children under 14 years of age is restricted by the Criminal Procedure (Scotland) Act 1995, s. 50(1),(2); but there is no equivalent statutory provision for civil proceedings.

50 It is thought that the general principle exemplified in the practice of the High Court in trials for rape (see Macphail, *Evidence*, para. 7.07; *H v. Sweeney*, 1982 J.C. 70, *per* Lord Avonside at 92–93) is equally applicable in civil proceedings.

national security is involved, the sheriff may exclude reporters and clear the court completely.

Real evidence

5.26 It is unnecessary for items of real evidence such as a book, newspaper or film to be exhibited to the public in open court. They must be produced and identified there, but where it is necessary for the sheriff to consider them he may do so out of court.[51] In some circumstances it may be desirable to allow representatives of the press to be present when a film is being shown to the sheriff out of court.[52]

Recording of proceedings

5.27 It is a contempt of court to use a tape recorder in court or to bring it into court for use, without leave, or to publish such a recording to any section of the public.[53]

Reporting of proceedings

5.28 The reporting of civil proceedings in the sheriff court by the press and broadcasting media is restricted by four statutes, namely the Judicial Proceedings (Regulation of Reports) Act 1926, the Children and Young Persons (Scotland) Act 1937, the Children (Scotland) Act 1995 and the Contempt of Court Act 1981. The Judicial Proceedings (Regulation of Reports) Act prohibits the publication of indecent matter in relation to any judicial proceedings and, in relation to actions of divorce and of separation and aliment, forbids the publication of any particulars other than: (i) the names, addresses and occupations of the parties and witnesses; (ii) a concise statement of "the charges, defences and counter-charges" in respect of which evidence has been given; (iii) submissions on any point of law arising in the course of the proceedings, and the decision of the court thereon; and (iv) the "summing-up" of the judge, the judgment of the court and observations made by the judge in giving judgment.

5.29 The Children and Young Persons (Scotland) Act 1937 makes provision by section 46, as amended, for the protection by the court of the identity of young persons.[54] In any proceedings, the court may direct that except in so far as (if at all) the court may by direction permit, no report may reveal the name, address, or school, or include any particulars calculated to lead to the identification, of any person under the age of 17 years concerned in the proceedings, either as being the person by or against or in respect of whom the proceedings are taken, or as being a witness therein; and no

---

[51] *cf. Carmichael v. Ashrif*, 1985 S.C.C.R. 461.

[52] *cf. R. v. Waterfield* [1975] 1 W.L.R. 711.

[53] Contempt of Court Act 1981, s. 9.

[54] Section 46 was amended by the Children and Young Persons Act 1963, s. 57(1), and the Social Work (Scotland) Act 1968, Sched. 2, Pt II, para. 7. It applies not only to newspapers but also, with the necessary modifications, to sound and television broadcasts (1963 Act, s. 57(4)) and to cable programmes (Cable and Broadcasting Act 1984, Sched. 5, para. 5(3)). It does not apply to criminal proceedings, having been repealed in that regard by the Criminal Procedure (Scotland) Act 1975, s. 461 and Sched. 10, Pt I. However, it has not been affected by more recent legislation save to the extent that the maximum penalty for a contravention of the section has been increased from a fine of £50 to a fine at level 4 on the standard scale: Criminal Procedure (Consequential Provisions) (Scotland) Act 1995, Sched. 5.

picture may be published as being or including a picture of any such person.[55] The Children (Scotland) Act 1995 makes provision by section 44 for the protection of the identity of children involved in a children's hearing and in various proceedings under Part II of the Act. Publication is prohibited of any matter which is intended to, or is likely to, identify any child concerned, or any address or school as being of that child. However, the foregoing requirements may, in the interests of justice, be dispensed with by the sheriff in any proceedings before him, by the Court of Session in any appeal under section 51(11) of the Act, or by the Secretary of State in relation to any proceedings at a children's hearing, all to such extent as may be considered appropriate.[56]

The Contempt of Court Act 1981 confers on the court a discretion to order the postponement of a report of the proceedings, or a part of them, for such period as the court thinks necessary, where that course appears to be necessary for avoiding a substantial risk of prejudice to the administration of justice in those proceedings, or in any other proceedings, pending or imminent.[57] The Act also provides that where a court "(having power to do so)" allows a name or other matter to be withheld from the public in proceedings before the court, the court may give such directions prohibiting the publication of that name or matter in connection with the proceedings as appear to the court to be necessary for the purpose for which it was so withheld.[58] While the question whether the sheriff "has power to do so" has not been authoritatively decided, it is not uncommon in criminal practice for the address of a witness who has been or is likely to be offered violence to be withheld from the public but disclosed to the court in writing. Further provisions of the Act have already been noted.[59] 5.30

The books of court

The records of the various civil proceedings brought in the sheriff court are kept by the sheriff clerk. Some records are ordered to be kept by statute, but many are kept in accordance with long practice, and may change in form or content as the sheriff clerk finds convenient. Increasingly, many such records are now being kept in computerised form. It is thought that the following records are kept in most sheriff courts. 5.31

Register of ordinary causes

Every initial writ in an ordinary cause is noted by the sheriff clerk in the register of ordinary causes and has allotted to it a serial number to which the letter "A" is prefixed and the year suffixed, thus: "A 123/1998". The register is accordingly often referred to as "the A register". The first entry records the serial number, the date of the first warrant, the names of the parties, the nature of the action and, where there is a pecuniary crave, the sum sued for. Thereafter, there are recorded in due course the date of lodging of any notice of intention to defend, the date of an options hearing, and the date of decree. The register may be divided into two parts, one for family actions and the other for all other ordinary causes. In some courts that distinction is marked by giving family actions a "D" prefix. 5.32

---

55 *C v. S*, 1989 S.L.T. 168.
56 1995 Act, s. 44(5).
57 Contempt of Court Act 1981, s. 4(2).
58 *ibid.* s. 11.
59 See para. 2.20.

Register of summary applications

5.33 Appeals to the sheriff, special summary applications under statutes and other miscellaneous applications are similarly entered in a register known as "the B register", the serial numbers being prefixed by the letter B. The register may be subdivided for different classes of business, the serial numbers of the cases in each class being given an appropriate prefix, as "2B", "3B" and so on.

Family proceedings

5.34 A number of registers are kept for different categories of family proceedings: a simplified divorce register; various maintenance orders registers,[60] including a Maintenance Orders (Reciprocal Enforcement) Act 1972 Register[61]; and an Adoption Register.[62]

Roll book of court

5.35 The proceedings in ordinary actions, summary applications and other causes, other than summary causes and others assigned to special registers, are recorded in the roll book of court. At the discretion of the sheriff clerk it may be in bound or looseleaf form, and may have separate divisions for different classes of business, as for cases calling in the ordinary court, appeals to the sheriff principal, and hearings on applications for interim interdict.

Act book of court

5.36 In the past, there was kept in every sheriff court an act book of court in which all interlocutors were entered, either in full or in summary form. The principal purpose of the act book was to enable any interested party, such as a solicitor in a case which had been taken to avizandum, to come to the court house and find out what interlocutors had been pronounced. The date of any interlocutor was the date of its being entered in "the books of court",[63] which meant the act book of court. Since it was the entry in the act book which advised parties that an interlocutor had been issued, the time-limit for appealing ran from that date. When it became the duty of the sheriff clerk to send parties copies of interlocutors which had notes appended thereto,[64] the function of the act book as a source of information became unimportant. In any event, the date of an interlocutor is now either the date when it is pronounced in court or, where a case has been taken to avizandum, the date when the interlocutor is received by the sheriff clerk.[65] In some courts the act book no longer exists, while in others it is now used only to a limited extent. In some instances, for example, the

---

[60] Under various Acts of Sederunt and statutory instruments; see *e.g.*, A.S. (Maintenance Orders Act 1950, Courts of Summary Jurisdiction Rules) 1951 (S.I. 1951 No. 552), r. 2(3); A.S. (Enforcement of Judgments under the Civil Jurisdiction and Judgments Act 1982) 1986 (S.I. 1986 No. 1947), para. 6(5); and others set out in *Parliament House Book*, Div. K.

[61] Required by A.S. (Maintenance Orders (Reciprocal Enforcement) Act 1972 Rules) 1974 (S.I. 1974 No. 929), para. 13(1).

[62] Required by A.S. (Child Care and Maintenance Rules) 1997 (S.I. 1997 No. 291), para. 2.13.

[63] Sheriff Courts (Scotland) Act 1876, s. 50; 1907 Act, original First Sched., r. 83; OCR (1983 Rules), r. 89(3).

[64] Now OCR, r. 12.2(5)(b)(ii).

[65] *ibid.* r. 12.2(5)(a).

act book of court records acts of court and practice notes by the sheriff principal, the commissions of sheriffs and honorary sheriffs, and all interlocutors of importance, including those to which the sheriff principal or sheriff has appended a note.

Book of summary causes

The sheriff clerk is required to keep a Book of Summary Causes in which must be entered a note of all summary causes and minutes under rules 19(1) and 92(1) of the Summary Cause Rules, setting forth a list of specified particulars.[66] **5.37**

Other registers

Other registers kept by the sheriff clerk include registers of clubs,[67] and a register of applications under the Mental Health (Scotland) Act 1984. The sheriff clerk also keeps a register of writs, deeds and other documents registered for preservation or execution,[68] a register of protests of bills,[69] fee books and books relative to commissary business and criminal matters. At most courts the sheriff clerk keeps a register of sheriff officers having a commission to practise at that court. **5.38**

The rolls of court

Under the procedures which were in place prior to the coming into force of the Ordinary Cause Rules 1993 the rolls of court were an important element of procedure for ordinary causes. Essentially, all cases calling in the ordinary court were grouped in rolls, or lists, which brought together those cases which were at a certain stage of procedure. Thus, the ordinary court prior to January 1, 1994, would commonly be made up of cases on the tabling roll, the adjustment roll, the continued adjustment roll, the procedure roll, a miscellaneous roll, and a family proceedings or consistorial roll. Some courts also had other rolls such as a diet roll in which were grouped cases awaiting the assignation of a diet for hearing a proof or debate. **5.39**

Some of the foregoing rolls were provided for, or at least were recognised, by the pre-1993 Ordinary Cause Rules. Thus, for example, rules 119 and 120 of the 1983 Rules provided, in relation to multiple-poindings, that in certain circumstances the sheriff should continue a cause to the procedure roll. In general, however, most of the rolls which were in use prior to the coming into force of the 1993 Rules were the creatures of usage and convenience, and had no statutory or other authority. **5.40**

By contrast, the Ordinary Cause Rules 1993 totally removed some of the old procedures such as tabling and virtually unlimited adjustment, and so took away the need for rolls to accommodate such procedures. Moreover, the general thrust of the 1993 Rules is to make provision for fixed **5.41**

---

66 SCR, r. 16(1). See Vol. 2 of this work.

67 Required by the Licensing (Scotland) Act 1976, s. 102(1), and the Gaming Act 1968, Sched. 10, para. 2.

68 Public Records (Scotland) Act 1809: see J.M. Halliday, *Conveyancing Law and Practice in Scotland* (2nd ed.), Vol. 1, para. 4–62.

69 Referred to in the Writs Execution (Scotland) Act 1877, s. 2.

diets when certain steps of procedure must take place. Thus, in place of tabling and adjustment rolls there is now provision[70] for the sheriff clerk to fix a date and time for an options hearing by which time all adjustment of pleadings ought to have been completed. Likewise, in relation to multiplepoindings (referred to by way of example in the previous paragraph) the sheriff clerk is now required to fix a precise date and time for a first hearing.[71] It is understood that, notwithstanding the changes brought about by the 1993 Rules, some courts still have a procedure roll which acts as a convenient repository for cases in respect of which nobody is instantly prepared to decide what should happen next. There is now no authority for such a practice but, given its uncertain historical origins, it is probably not incompetent and may in some circumstances serve a useful purpose.

5.42 Notwithstanding what has just been said, some courts find it convenient and appropriate to programme certain classes of cases for different days, or different times of day, in the course of a week. Thus, for example, different dates, or times of day, may be allocated for ordinary options hearings and for options hearings in family actions. Such a course can be justified by reason of the fact that, in the latter type of case, the parties are required to attend personally.[72] In that situation it is unlikely to be reasonable to expect parties to take part in an options hearing when the court is likely to be full of solicitors and others waiting their turn to deal with actions for payment and all other kinds of non-family actions. However, programming of the kind just described does not involve any return to the old rolls of court.

The process

5.43 In every action the pleadings and productions lodged are kept together and form the process.[73] The rules as to the contents of the process, the custody and borrowing of the process, and the substitution of lost documents of process, are considered in the context of the normal procedure in a defended action.[74] The two following sections of this chapter consider the steps of process known as motions and minutes. During the dependence of an action applications are made to the court by motion or minute; and minutes may also be used by parties to define their positions or to direct matters to the attention of the court.

Motions

5.44 In general, before the court makes an order relative to the procedure in a depending action, a party or parties must apply to the court to make such an order, though in some instances the court may make an order *ex proprio motu*. An application of the foregoing kind is usually made by motion, though in some instances applications must be made by way of minute.[75] In the interval between the commencement of proceedings and their final determination, motions are made in a wide variety of circumstances, many of which are considered in Chapters 11 to 15.

---

[70] OCR, r. 9.2.
[71] *ibid.* r. 35.9.
[72] *ibid.* r. 33.36.
[73] *ibid.* r. 9.5.
[74] See paras 8.09 to 8.17.
[75] See paras 5.56 to 5.71.

The rules governing motions are set out in Chapter 15 of the Ordinary Cause Rules 1993, as amended in 1996. A motion may be made (a) orally, with leave of the court, during any hearing of a cause, or (b) by lodging a written motion in Form G6.[76] **5.45**

A written motion must be lodged with the sheriff clerk within five days after the date of intimation required by the rules,[77] and it must be accompanied by a certificate of intimation in Form G8 and, so far as practicable, any document referred to in the written motion and not already lodged in process.[78] If the period for lodging opposition to the motion has been varied[79] to a period of five days or less, the written motion and the certificate of intimation must be lodged no later than the day on which the period for lodging opposition expires.[80] **5.46**

Intimation of motions

Except in the case of a joint written motion by all parties,[81] a party who intends to lodge a written motion must intimate it in Form G7, together with a copy of any document referred to in the motion, to every other party.[82] Intimation of a motion may be given by any of the methods of service provided for in Chapter 5 of the Rules.[83] Alternatively, where intimation is being made to a party represented by a solicitor, it may be given to that solicitor by (i) personal delivery, (ii) facsimile transmission, (iii) first class ordinary post, or (iv) delivery to a document exchange.[84] In the case of intimation by the first or second of the methods just described, intimation will be deemed to have been given on the day of transmission or delivery where it is given before 5 p.m. on any day, and on the day after such transmission or delivery where it is given after 5 p.m. on any day.[85] In the case of intimation by the third or fourth methods described above, intimation will be deemed to have been given on the day after posting or delivery.[86] **5.47**

Generally, a party who wishes to oppose a motion must lodge a notice of opposition within seven days of the date of intimation of the motion.[87] However, the sheriff may, on the application of a party intending to lodge a written motion, vary that period of seven days, or may dispense with intimation altogether.[88] Any such application must be made in the written motion, and must give reasons supporting variation or dispensation.[89] Where the sheriff varies the period within which notice of opposition is to be lodged, the form of intimation (Form G7) must state the date by which such notice requires to be lodged.[90] **5.48**

---

76 OCR, r. 15.1(1).
77 See para. 5.47.
78 OCR, r. 15.1(2).
79 See para. 5.48.
80 OCR, r. 15.1(3).
81 *ibid.* r. 15.2(7).
82 *ibid.* r. 15.2(1).
83 *ibid.* r. 15.2(2)(a); see paras 6.17 *et seq.*
84 *ibid.* r. 15.2(2)(b).
85 *ibid.* r. 15.2(3)(a).
86 *ibid.* r. 15.2(3)(b).
87 See para. 5.49.
88 OCR, r. 15.2(4).
89 *ibid.* r. 15.2(5).
90 *ibid.* r. 15.2(6).

Opposition to motions

5.49 Where a party seeks to oppose a written motion he must (a) complete a notice of opposition in Form G9; (b) intimate a copy of that notice to every other party; and (c) lodge the notice with the sheriff clerk within seven days after the date of intimation of the motion or within such other period as the sheriff may have determined after an application to vary the standard period.[91] Intimation of opposition to a motion is governed by the same rules as to the method and time of intimation as apply in relation to the intimation of a motion.[92]

Consent to motions

5.50 Where a party consents to a written motion, he must either endorse the motion to that effect or give notice of his consent in writing to the sheriff clerk.[93]

Hearing of motions

5.51 Where no notice of opposition is lodged with the sheriff clerk within the period specified in rule 15.3(1)(c), or ordered by virtue of rule 15.2(4), the motion will be determined by the sheriff in chambers without the appearance of parties, unless the sheriff otherwise directs.[94] However, it is open to a sheriff principal to direct that a sheriff clerk may determine any motion other than a motion which seeks a final interlocutor.[95] In practice all of the sheriffs principal have prescribed an identical, but limited, number of motions which may be determined by a sheriff clerk. These are all motions of an uncontentious kind, such as to authorise re-service of an initial writ in terms of rule 5.9. However, the sheriffs principal have also provided that, if the granting of such a motion is likely to involve any order relating to expenses, it must be referred to the sheriff.[96] Moreover, if the sheriff clerk himself considers that a motion which may be dealt with by him should not be granted, he must refer it to the sheriff who will then determine it in the manner described above.[97] If a sheriff requires to hear a party on a motion which is not opposed, the sheriff clerk must: (a) fix a date, time and place; and (b) inform the party of that date, time and place, and of the reasons for the sheriff wishing to hear him.[98]

5.52 Where a notice of opposition has been lodged within the appropriate period of time, and has been intimated to every other party, the sheriff clerk must assign a date, time and place for the motion to be heard. The date and time must be on the first suitable court day after the lodging of the notice of opposition.[99] The sheriff clerk must also intimate that date, time and place to the parties.[1]

---

[91] OCR, r. 15.3(1); and see para. 5.48.
[92] *ibid.* r. 15.3(2): see para. 5.47.
[93] *ibid.* r. 15.4.
[94] *ibid.* r. 15.5(1).
[95] *ibid.* r. 15.5(2).
[96] The relevant provisions made by the sheriffs principal are to be found in the Acts of Court and Practice Notes which are set out in *Parliament House Book*, D601 *et seq.*
[97] OCR, r. 15.5(3).
[98] *ibid.* r. 15.5(4).
[99] *ibid.* r. 15.5(5)(a).
[1] OCR, r. 15.5(5)(b).

Where a motion in respect of which no notice of opposition has been lodged has been determined by the sheriff in chambers, or where a motion of a kind specified by the sheriff principal has been determined by the sheriff clerk, the sheriff clerk must forthwith intimate the interlocutor determining the motion to all parties.[2] Where a sheriff dispenses altogether with intimation of a motion,[3] he must make such order as he thinks fit for intimation of his determination of the motion to every party in respect of whom intimation has been dispensed with.[4] **5.53**

Unless the sheriff requires to hear a party in respect of an unopposed motion, where all parties expressly consent to a written motion the sheriff may determine that motion in chambers without the appearance of parties.[5] Subject to the same qualification, where a joint motion of all parties in Form G6 has been lodged with the sheriff clerk the sheriff may also determine that motion in chambers without the appearance of parties.[6] **5.54**

Expenses

The majority of interlocutors pronounced in respect of motions are silent as to the expenses of the motion, mainly because the question is seldom raised at that stage. However, a motion for expenses may be made, and may be granted if it is appropriate to do so. Normally, questions of expenses are likely to arise when a motion itself relates to steps of procedure which have occasioned significant expense, such as, for example, a motion to allow a record to be opened up and amended in terms of a minute of amendment and answers. In such a case any award of expenses will usually relate to the whole of the amendment procedure. **5.55**

Minutes

Minutes fall to be distinguished from motions in that, with some exceptions, they constitute a form of application to the court in which a particular juridical determination is sought, and where that determination may require a specific crave, averments as to fact, and appropriate pleas-in-law. Many examples of applications which require to be brought by way of minute are to be found in relation to family proceedings, and they are considered in detail in Chapter 22. Procedural rules for minutes which take the form of an application to the court of the kind just described are now to be found in Chapter 14 of the Ordinary Cause Rules 1993, and they are considered below. **5.56**

There are, however, some forms of minute which do not themselves seek a particular juridical determination, but instead state the intention, or define the position, of a party or parties. In some instances they will require an ancillary motion in order to enable a party, or parties, to invite the court to give effect to what is contained in the minute. An example of that kind of minute is a minute of amendment. There are also minutes of a kind (for example, a minute of tender) which simply express a party's position on a certain matter, and which will usually lie *in retentis*, and in **5.57**

---

2 OCR, r. 15.5(6).
3 As provided for in r. 15.2(4); see para. 5.48.
4 OCR, r. 15.5(7).
5 *ibid.* r. 15.5(8).
6 *ibid.* r. 15.5(9).

the case of a minute of tender unopened, until the merits of the cause have been determined by the court. Finally, there are joint minutes in which parties jointly state their intentions, or define their positions. In some instances such minutes will express agreed terms on which a case is to be disposed of, and in such a case parties will usually make a joint motion to the court to interpone authority to the joint minute, and to grant decree in accordance with those agreed terms. In other cases, however, a joint minute may not of itself require further action such as a motion. A joint minute of admissions is an example of this since a minute of this kind merely details certain matters on which parties have reached agreement, and in respect of which proof will as a result be unnecessary. Joint minutes of admissions are commonly used in, for example, family proceedings, and express provision is made for such joint minutes in rule 33.26 of the Ordinary Cause Rules. Joint minutes of admissions may also be used in actions for damages for personal injury as a way of detailing agreement on matters such as wage loss, the content of medical records, and so on. Minutes of amendment, minutes of abandonment, and joint minutes are all expressly excluded from the provisions of Chapter 14 of the Rules.[7] Curiously, other forms of minute which do not directly involve an application to the court, such as minutes of tender, are not so excluded. However, the structure and content of the rules in Chapter 14 are appropriate only to minutes which embody particular applications, and it may therefore be assumed that those rules do not apply to minutes which are entirely different in character and function.

Form of minute

5.58 Where an application may be made by minute, the form of the minute and the procedure to be adopted must, unless otherwise provided in the Rules, be in accordance with Chapter 14.[8] Such a minute must contain a crave; where appropriate, a condescendence in the form of a statement of facts supporting the crave; and, where appropriate, pleas-in-law.[9]

Lodging of minutes

5.59 Before intimating any minute, the minuter must lodge it in process.[10] On the lodging of the minute along with any document founded on or adopted in it,[11] the sheriff may do any one of three things. He may make an order for answers to be lodged; he may order intimation of the minute without making an order for answers; or, where he considers it appropriate for the expeditious disposal of the minute or for any other specified reason, he may fix a hearing.[12] Where any answers are ordered to be lodged they must, unless the sheriff orders otherwise, be lodged within 14 days after the date of intimation of the minute.[13] Where the sheriff fixes a hearing the interlocutor fixing that hearing must specify whether: (a) answers are to be lodged; (b) the sheriff will hear evidence at that hearing; and (c) the sheriff will allow evidence by affidavit.[14] Any answers

---

[7] OCR, r. 14.1(2).
[8] *ibid.* r. 14.1(1).
[9] *ibid.* r. 14.2.
[10] *ibid.* r. 14.3(1).
[11] *ibid.* r. 21.1(1)(b).
[12] *ibid.* r. 14.3(2).
[13] *ibid.* r. 14.3(3).
[14] *ibid.* r. 14.3(4).

or affidavit evidence which are so ordered must be lodged within such time as is specified in the sheriff's interlocutor.[15] When the sheriff pronounces an interlocutor following on the lodging of a minute in process, the sheriff clerk must forthwith return the minute to the minuter along with the interlocutor in question.[16]

Certain of the provisions in Chapter 14 do not apply where, as described above, the sheriff fixes a hearing because he considers that that is appropriate for the expeditious disposal of the minute or for any other specified reason.[17] The provisions in question are those in rule 14.7 (relating to the opposition of a minute where no order for answers has been made),[18] those in rule 14.8 (relating to the hearing of minutes where no notice of opposition is lodged or where no answers are lodged),[19] and those in rule 14.10 (relating to the situation where a notice of opposition has, or answers have, been lodged).[20] **5.60**

Intimation of minutes

The party lodging a minute must, on receiving it back from the sheriff clerk, make intimation to every other party. In addition, if the minute includes a crave seeking leave for a person to be sisted as a party to the action or to appear in the proceedings, or for the cause to be transferred against the representatives of a party who has died or is under a legal capacity, intimation must be made to any such person or persons.[21] Intimation itself must consist of a notice in whichever is appropriate of Forms G7A (where answers lodged), G7B (where no order for answers or no hearing fixed) or G7C (where hearing fixed), together with a copy of the minute, any interlocutor, and any document referred to in the minute.[22] Rule 14.4 is curiously worded because it appears to suggest, in paragraph (1)(a), that the notice may be intimated by any of the methods provided for in rule 14.5,[23] but it does not make any provision for the method of intimation of the minute and other documents which must accompany the notice. It is also to be noted that rule 14.5 itself refers to intimation of "a minute" and not to intimation of "a notice" although the latter, and not the former, would be consistent with what is contained in rule 14.4(1)(a). In practice it is inconceivable that anyone would consider intimating the minute, the interlocutor, and documents referred to in the minute separately from, and in a different manner from, the form of notice required by the rules. It must therefore be assumed that the inconsistencies within rule 14.4, and between it and rule 14.5, were not intentional, and are simply examples of careless drafting. **5.61**

Methods of intimation

Subject to what has just been said, intimation of a minute may be given by any of the methods of service provided for in Chapter 5 of the Rules[24] **5.62**

---

[15] OCR, r. 14.3(5).
[16] *ibid.* r. 14.3(7).
[17] *ibid.* r. 14.3(6).
[18] See para. 5.64.
[19] See para. 5.65.
[20] See para. 5.67.
[21] OCR, rr. 14.4(1) and 14.13(1).
[22] *ibid.* r. 14.4(1).
[23] See para 5.62.
[24] OCR, r. 14.5(1)(a); see paras 6.17 *et seq.*

or, where intimation is to a party represented by a solicitor, to that solicitor by any of the following means, namely personal delivery, facsimile transmission, first class ordinary post, or delivery to a document exchange.[25] Where intimation is given to a solicitor by either the first or the second of the foregoing means, it will be deemed to have been given on the day of transmission or delivery where it is given before 5 p.m. on any day, and to have been given on the day after transmission or delivery where it is given after 5 p.m. on any day.[26] Where intimation is given by either the third or fourth means described above, it will be deemed to have been given on the day after the date of posting or delivery.[27]

Return of minute with evidence of intimation

5.63 Where intimation of any minute has been given, the minute and a certificate of intimation in Form G8 must be returned to the sheriff clerk within five days after the date of intimation.[28]

Opposition where no order for answers made

5.64 Where a party seeks to oppose a minute in respect of which no order for answers has been made, he must, within 14 days of the intimation of the minute to him, do three things. He must: (a) complete a notice of opposition in Form G9; (b) lodge that notice with the sheriff clerk; and (c) intimate a copy of that notice to every other party.[29] The rules relative to methods of intimation of a minute, and return of a minute with evidence of intimation, apply to intimation of opposition to a minute.[30] The sheriff may, however, on cause shown reduce, or dispense with, the period for lodging a notice of opposition with the sheriff clerk.[31]

Hearing of minutes where no opposition or no answers lodged

5.65 Where no notice of opposition has been lodged or where no answers have been lodged within the time allowed, the minute will be determined by the sheriff in chambers without the attendance of parties unless the sheriff otherwise directs.[32] Where the sheriff requires to hear a party on a minute, the sheriff clerk must fix a date, time and place for the party to be heard, and inform that party of the date, time and place, and of the reasons for the sheriff wishing to hear him.[33]

Intimation of interlocutor

5.66 Where a minute has been determined in the manner described in the previous paragraph the sheriff clerk must forthwith intimate the interlocutor containing that determination to the parties.[34]

---

[25] OCR, r. 14.5(1)(b).
[26] *ibid.* r. 14.5(2)(a).
[27] *ibid.* r. 14.5(2)(b).
[28] *ibid.* r. 14.6.
[29] *ibid.* r. 14.7(1).
[30] *ibid.* r. 14.7(2): see paras 5.62 to 5.63.
[31] *ibid.* r. 14.7(3).
[32] *ibid.* r. 14.8(1).
[33] *ibid.* r. 14.8(2).
[34] *ibid.* r. 14.9.

Notice of opposition or answers lodged

Where a notice of opposition has, or answers have, been lodged to the minute, the sheriff clerk must assign a date, time and place for a hearing on the first suitable court day after the date of the lodging of the notice of opposition or answers, and must intimate that date, time and place to the parties.[35] The interlocutor fixing the foresaid hearing must specify whether the sheriff will hear evidence at the hearing or receive evidence by affidavit.[36] **5.67**

Procedure for hearing

A certified copy of the interlocutor assigning any hearing under Chapter 14 of the Rules, and requiring evidence to be led, is sufficient warrant to a sheriff officer to cite a witness on behalf of a party.[37] At the hearing the sheriff will hear parties on the minute and any answers lodged, and may determine the minute, or may appoint such further procedure as he considers necessary.[38] It is not unusual for answers to be ordered, a period for adjustment of the minute and answers to be allowed, and a "proof" thereon to be fixed. **5.68**

Consent to minute

Subject to a sheriff's entitlement to hear a party on a minute in respect of which no notice of opposition has, and no answers have, been lodged,[39] where all parties to the action indicate to the sheriff, by endorsement of the minute or otherwise in writing, their intention to consent to the minute, the sheriff may forthwith determine the minute in chambers without the appearance of parties.[40] **5.69**

Procedure following grant of minute

Where the minute includes a crave seeking leave for a person to be sisted as a party to the action or to appear in the proceedings, or for the cause to be transferred against the representatives of a party who has died or is under a legal incapacity, the sheriff, on granting the minute, may order an options hearing to be fixed or may appoint such further procedure as he thinks fit.[41] Where an options hearing is ordered the sheriff clerk must fix a date and time for such a hearing, which date, unless the sheriff otherwise directs, must be on the first suitable court day occurring not sooner than 10 weeks after the date of the interlocutor of the sheriff ordering that hearing.[42] The sheriff clerk is then required to intimate forthwith to the parties in Form G5: (i) where appropriate, the last date for lodging defences; (ii) where appropriate, the last date for adjustment; and (iii) the date of the options hearing. He must also prepare and sign an interlocutor recording those dates.[43] For the purpose of fixing the date for the options hearing the date of granting the minute is deemed to be the date of expiry of the period of notice.[44] **5.70**

---

35 OCR, r. 14.10(1).
36 *ibid.* r. 14.10(2).
37 *ibid.* r. 14.11(1).
38 *ibid.* r. 14.11(2).
39 See para. 5.65.
40 OCR, r. 14.12.
41 *ibid.* r. 14.13(1).
42 *ibid.* r. 14.13(2)(a).
43 *ibid.* r. 14.13(2)(b) and (c).
44 *ibid.* r. 14.13(3).

Minutes in old cases

5.71 Most sheriff courts still have extant a small number of actions which were commenced prior to the coming into force of the Ordinary Cause Rules 1993 on January 1, 1994. In so far as further procedures have to take place in such cases, those procedures will continue to be governed by the Ordinary Cause Rules 1983. However, a problem has come to light in circumstances where, subsequent to the coming into force of the Children (Scotland) Act 1995, a party seeks to proceed by way of minute in order to vary an award of custody or access which was originally granted in an action which proceeded under the pre-1993 Rules. Section 15(2) of the 1995 Act effectively says that any such minute for variation is to proceed as if the original order had been made under section 11 of the 1995 Act, but the Ordinary Cause Rules 1993 are silent as to whether the procedure in such a minute is to be governed under those Rules or under the 1983 Rules. That raises questions as to the applicability of certain rules in Chapter 33 (dealing with family actions) and the rules in Chapter 14 which have just been described. It has been held by a sheriff at first instance[45] that the 1993 Rules apply in such a case, but it is submitted that the position is far from clear, and probably requires to be put beyond doubt by an amendment to the Rules.[46]

Interlocutors

Definition

5.72 An interlocutor is an order or determination pronounced by the sheriff, whether in the course of an action or at its conclusion, and embodied in writing. The term "interlocutor" formerly referred only to an order pronounced between the commencement of the action and its determination, while the term "decerniture", "decreet" or "decree" was applied to the order which finally determined the whole, or part, of the cause.[47] In modern practice, however, "interlocutor" is applied indiscriminately to the judgments or orders of the sheriff, whether they exhaust the question at issue or not.[48] An order which finally determines the whole, or part, of the cause may also be described as a "decree", or "final judgment".[49]

5.73 This section of this chapter is concerned with the general rules as to the nature, form and correction of interlocutors, and their effect. The special rules relative to interim decrees,[50] summary decrees,[51] decrees in absence,[52] decrees by default[53] and decrees *in foro*,[54] interlocutors pronounced after debate,[55] final interlocutors[56] and appealable interlocutors[57] are considered elsewhere.

---

45 *Gallacher v. Gallacher*, 1996 S.C.L.R. 174.
46 See the commentary to the foregoing case.
47 Stair, IV, xlvi, 2; Mackay, *Practice*, i, pp. 581–582; Maclaren, p. 1089; *Doherty v. Norwich Union Fire Insurance Society Ltd*, 1974 S.C. 213 at 219.
48 Bell, *Dictionary*, p. 577. See also Lees, *Interlocutors*.
49 "Decree": OCR *passim*; "final judgment": 1907 Act, ss. 3(h), 27 and 28.
50 paras 11.81.
51 paras 14.71 to 14.74.
52 paras 7.02 *et seq.*
53 paras 14.02 to 14.14.
54 para. 2.106.
55 paras 13.23 to 13.24.
56 paras 17.02, 17.30, 18.33 to 18.37 and 18.94.
57 paras 18.10 to 18.49; 18.95, 18.96.

Form of interlocutors

On what written. In undefended actions the interlocutor is normally written by the clerk of court on the initial writ, to which a printed form for the purpose is attached, or it may be written on a separate paper which is then attached to the writ. In defended actions, the interlocutors and any notes appended thereto[58] are entered by the clerk of court on the interlocutor sheets and duplicate interlocutor sheets, which are steps of process kept by the sheriff clerk in the process folder.[59] The interlocutor sheets cannot be borrowed, but remain in the custody of the sheriff clerk.[60] **5.74**

Place and date of issue. The interlocutor is headed with the place of sitting of the court and the date. The sheriff may in fact produce or sign the interlocutor when he is not at the seat of the court, or even when he is furth of the sheriffdom,[61] but the interlocutor bears to be issued at the seat of the court. The date of the interlocutor is the date when it is pronounced in court or, where a case has been taken to avizandum, the date when the interlocutor is received by the sheriff clerk.[62] Accordingly, in the latter case the sheriff does not date the interlocutor when he signs it: the date is inserted by the sheriff clerk when he receives it. There is old authority[63] to the effect that, if the sheriff indicates the terms of his order or judgment orally from the bench, but they are not embodied in a written interlocutor until a subsequent day, the latter date is the date which the interlocutor must bear. However, it is thought that current practice is always to prepare a written interlocutor on the date when an order is pronounced with the result that the interlocutor will bear that date. **5.75**

Parties. The parties who were present or represented at the hearing leading to the interlocutor are also recorded in the heading of the interlocutor, against the abbreviations "Act." for the actor or pursuer,[64] and "Alt." for the other party or parties. Normally, only the surnames of counsel and solicitors are noted,[65] with an initial or initials if necessary to avoid confusion. However, it is now common to distinguish female practitioners by the addition of "Miss", "Mrs" or "Ms" as appropriate. A party litigant is noted as "Party". Where counsel has appeared, it is appropriate to add "Advocate" or "Queen's Counsel", as appropriate, after that person's name. It is incorrect to add the word "Counsel". **5.76**

The order. Under the heading, the record of the order pronounced is expressed in whatever language and form suits the particular case.[66] In general, however, it is framed in the present tense, usually in one sentence, which must be carefully punctuated. It begins with the words "The Sheriff", or "The Sheriff Principal", and states the order pronounced. In some instances the old practice of using initial capitals for the words **5.77**

---

[58] As to notes, see paras 5.85 to 5.86.
[59] OCR, Chap. 11. See para. 8.09.
[60] *ibid.* r. 11.2(2).
[61] *ibid.* r. 12.2(1).
[62] *ibid.* r. 12.2(5)(a).
[63] *Cleland v. Clason and Clark* (1849) 11 D. 601 and 614 (affd (1850) 7 Bell's App. 153).
[64] *Buxton v. Buxton* (1845) 7 D. 1063, *per* Lord Jeffrey at 1065.
[65] The Dean of the Faculty of Advocates is correctly noted as "*Decanus*", but in modern practice he is simply noted as "Dean of Faculty".
[66] Maclaren, p. 1095.

(usually verbs) at the beginning of each division of the interlocutor is still followed.[67] However, many sheriffs now prefer a more contemporary style which uses initial capitals only when strictly necessary. In either event, what is important is that the interlocutor should set out the order or decision with clarity and without ambiguity. Each division of an interlocutor may also be numbered, where that would assist clarity.

5.78 The interlocutor must record an order accurately when it has been orally pronounced by the sheriff from the bench: otherwise parties would leave the court under an erroneous impression as to the terms of the interlocutor which was to be signed.[68] It is submitted that if it appears to the sheriff, before he signs the interlocutor, that the order which he pronounced in court was incorrect, he may pronounce an interlocutor in different terms only in exceptional circumstances; where none of the parties, in proper reliance on the order, has acted to his detriment; and after giving parties an opportunity to address him further.[69] Where the order has been pronounced in the ordinary court, it is framed on the basis of the notes made by the clerk of court.

5.79 The interlocutor should state on whose initiative the order was made. If made by the sheriff *ex proprio motu*, or by all parties on joint motion, that should be stated. If made on the motion of one party, that should likewise be recorded, since it may in due course have a bearing on a question of expenses. The terms of the interlocutor may also bar that party from later challenging it, whether by appeal or otherwise,[70] unless it erroneously fails to give effect to the motion.[71]

5.80 Where the interlocutor is pronounced on the motion of one party, it should also bear whether the other parties opposed, consented to, or did not object to, the motion. If the motion was opposed, the interlocutor may use such formulae as: "The Sheriff, on the pursuer's motion and having heard the defender in reply . . ." or, where the motion is a written motion, "having heard parties' procurators on the pursuer's motion no. x of process . . .". (While it is still common for clerks of court to use the word "procurator", many sheriffs and others regard the word as old-fashioned, and unlikely to be intelligible to the lay public. Consequently, it is now probably preferable to use the word "solicitor".)

5.81 If the motion was consented to, the interlocutor may say: "on the pursuer's motion [no. x of process, if a written motion], and of consent . . .". An interlocutor pronounced of consent must so state, and that practice should be followed even where the motion has been endorsed or there has been written intimation of consent to the sheriff clerk.[72] An interlocutor which bears to have been pronounced of consent is not liable to reduction if it is not *ex facie* defective or if no averment of

---

[67] *Fleming v. Eadie & Son* (1897) 25 R. 3, *per* L.J.-C. Macdonald at 5.

[68] *Tolland v. William Reid (Sports) Ltd*, 1970 S.L.T. (Notes) 19. See also *Manders v. Lacon Floors Ltd*, 1993 S.C.L.R. 311; *Eurocopy (Scotland) plc v. British Geological Survey*, 1997 S.C.L.R. 392.

[69] *cf. Re Barrell Enterprises* [1973] 1 W.L.R. 19 at 23–24; *Pittalis v. Sherefettin* [1986] Q.B. 868.

[70] *Watson v. Russell* (1894) 21 R. 433.

[71] *Ruthven v. Ruthven* (1905) 42 S.L.R. 562.

[72] See OCR, r. 15.4.

fraud against a party in the obtaining of it is made.[73] If it is not timeously objected to,[74] it will be read as a contract between the parties as to the procedure to be followed,[75] and will exclude appeal by either party[76] unless, on an appeal by a party who bears to have consented, it is maintained that the interlocutor is incorrect and no consent, was given.[77] The same is thought to be true of an interlocutor pronounced on joint motion. Where the other party merely does not object to the motion, the interlocutor states: "on the pursuer's motion, the defender not objecting".

If the interlocutor proceeds on the basis of an undertaking given by or on behalf of a party, it is advisable that it should record the terms of the undertaking in order to remove all scope for subsequent argument as to its precise terms. The sheriff may appoint the other party to intimate the interlocutor to the giver of the undertaking. The interlocutor may include a suitable form of words explaining the consequences of any breach of the undertaking. **5.82**

Signature. Most interlocutors are signed by the sheriff who pronounced them.[78] However, provision now exists whereby, in accordance with any directions given by the sheriff principal, any interlocutor other than a final interlocutor may be written and signed by the sheriff clerk.[79] Any such interlocutor is to be treated for all purposes as if it had been written and signed by the sheriff,[80] and any extract of such an interlocutor will not be invalid by reason only of its being written and signed by a sheriff clerk.[81] If an interlocutor extends to more than one page, the sheriff signs it at the end and initials the foot of each of the previous pages. He also initials any corrections, additions or interlineations[82]; but if an unauthenticated alteration truly expresses his order, the lack of authentication will not invalidate the interlocutor.[83] The interlocutor cannot be extracted until it is signed.[84] **5.83**

In a case where all proceedings following on an unsigned interlocutor allowing proof were held to be null and void, two of the four judges **5.84**

---

[73] *Lauder v. National Bank of Scotland Ltd*, 1918 1 S.L.T. 43. Where a solicitor has consented to decree without his client's authority, reduction will be allowed if a miscarriage of justice would result: *Zannetos v. Glenford Investment Holdings Ltd*, 1982 S.L.T. 453.

[74] *McLaren v. Ferrier* (1865) 3 M. 833. It is, however, doubtful whether an error of substance in an interlocutor may be corrected by the sheriff who pronounced it, other than of consent: see *Lauder, supra*; paras 5.87 to 5.90.

[75] *Paterson v. Kidd's Trs* (1896) 23 R. 737.

[76] *McLaren, Watson, Paterson, Lauder, supra*; *Fleming v. Eadie & Son* (1897) 25 R. 3; *Barton v. Caledon Shipbuilding and Engineering Co. Ltd*, 1947 S.L.T. (Notes) 12.

[77] *Whyte, Lauder, supra.*

[78] Interlocutors Act 1686. An interlocutor was signed by a judge who had not heard the case in *Petrie v. Forsyth* (1874) 2 R. 214 (of consent), and in *Maclean of Ardgour v. Maclean*, 1941 S.C. 613 at 710. As to procedure on the death, etc., of a sheriff, see para. 16.39.

[79] OCR, r. 12.1. The sheriffs principal have all made provision for the writing and signing by sheriff clerks of interlocutors giving effect to determinations by sheriff clerks as authorised under OCR, r. 15.5(2). The relevant Acts of Court and Practice Notes are to be found in the *Parliament House Book*, D601 *et seq.* No provision has as yet been made for the writing and signing by sheriff clerks of interlocutors determined by the sheriff. However, there is some specific provision in the Rules for the writing and signing of formal interlocutors by sheriff clerks: see, for example, r. 9.2(2)(b).

[80] OCR, r. 12.1(a).

[81] *ibid.* r. 12.1(b).

[82] As to corrections, see paras 5.87 to 5.90.

[83] *Clark & Macdonald v. Bain* (1895) 23 R. 102.

[84] Interlocutors Act 1686.

constituting the court observed that the rule requiring signature was limited to "essential" interlocutors.[85] In a later case the House of Lords indicated that while the rule that extracts of unsigned interlocutors may not be given out was imperative, the rule that interlocutors must be signed was directory only, and that they could be signed subsequent to being pronounced.[86] It may be, accordingly, that an interlocutor may be signed at any time before extract of that or a subsequent interlocutor, or before the transmission of the process when an appeal is taken[87]; but it seems at least prudent that interlocutors should be signed "while they are fresh in remembrance".[88]

Note

5.85 Formerly, the sheriff was required to append to all interlocutors, except those of a formal nature, a note setting out the grounds upon which he had proceeded.[89] In practice this rule was often not followed if only because it was quite impracticable to do so in circumstances where, in a busy court, a sheriff might be making decisions in respect of more than a hundred cases in the course of a day. Occasionally, however, the practicalities of the situation in which sheriffs often found themselves were ignored when a case came before the Inner House on appeal, and adverse criticism was sometimes directed at sheriffs who had failed to give effect to the requirements of rule 89(1).[90] However, the reality of the situation was recognised when the 1993 Rules were being prepared and, except in respect of cases which have gone to proof, a sheriff is now required to append a note to an interlocutor, giving reasons for his decision, only where he himself decides to do so or when he is requested to do so by a party.[91] He authenticates the note by initialling it at the foot of each page and at the end.[92] Where an appeal is marked against an interlocutor to which the sheriff has not appended a note, the person marking the appeal must, in his note of appeal, add a request that the sheriff write a note setting out the reasons for his decision.[93] The sheriff thereafter provides a note in appropriate terms. Where an interlocutor with a note appended thereto is pronounced by the sheriff otherwise than in the presence of the parties, as is almost invariably the case, the sheriff clerk must forthwith provide the parties with a copy of the interlocutor and note free of charge.[94]

5.86 The note is not part of the interlocutor.[95] While it may explain the interlocutor, it cannot control or limit its effect,[96] except in very special circumstances.[97] Thus, if an interlocutor is clearly competent, it cannot be

---

[85] *Smith v. McAulay* (1846) 9 D. 190: see Lords Fullerton and Mackenzie at 191–192.

[86] *Fergusson v. Skirving* (1852) 1 Macq. 232, and the version of the speech of Lord St Leonards, L.C. in 1 Stuart M. & P. 824 at 828–829.

[87] *cf.* OCR, r. 12.2(2).

[88] Stair, IV, ii, 18.

[89] OCR (1983 Rules), r. 89(1).

[90] See, *e.g. Kinnaird v. Donaldson*, 1992 S.C.L.R. 694.

[91] OCR, r. 12.2(4). The rule as to notes to final interlocutors is considered in paras 17.02 to 17.30, 18.33 to 18.37 and 18.94.

[92] Lees, *Interlocutors*, pp. 3–4.

[93] OCR, r. 31.4(2)(d).

[94] *ibid.* r. 12.2(5)(b)(ii).

[95] *McCaffer v. Allan* (1896) 33 S.L.R. 601, *per* Lord Young.

[96] *Marquis of Huntly v. Nicol* (1896) 23 R. 610, *per* Lord McLaren at 616; *Moubray's Trs v. Moubray* (1896) 23 R. 809.

[97] *Maclean of Ardgour v. Maclean*, 1941 S.C. 613 at 710; *Pollok School v. Glasgow Town Clerk*, 1947 S.C. 605. See T.B. Smith, *Judicial Precedent in Scots Law* (1952), pp. 88–92.

made incompetent by any opinions expressed in the note[98]; and where an interlocutor has allowed proof before answer the sheriff who hears the proof before answer is not bound by any opinions expressed in the note to that interlocutor by the sheriff who issued it.[99]

Correction of interlocutors

Clerical or incidental errors. At any time before extract the sheriff may correct any clerical or incidental error in his interlocutor or note.[1] A clerical error is an error made in copying or writing.[2] An incidental error is thought to be one the correction of which would not alter the interlocutor in substance such as an error in expression,[3] or an inadvertent failure to record part of the sheriff's decision.[4] It is submitted that the power to correct incidental errors does not enable the sheriff to correct errors of judgment whether of fact or law or to have second thoughts, but does enable him to give true effect to his first thoughts or intentions.[5] Parties' solicitors should examine interlocutors as soon as they are issued and apply immediately for the correction of any clerical or incidental errors which they may perceive. Any correction should be authenticated by the sheriff but lack of authentication will not invalidate the interlocutor.[6] The correction should also be intimated to the parties if made by the sheriff *ex proprio motu* after the interlocutor has been issued. 5.87

Other errors. It seems clear that the sheriff cannot *ex proprio motu*, and without prior intimation to the parties, correct any error other than a "clerical or incidental" error in an interlocutor which has been issued and seen by the parties.[7] Nor may he purportedly do so by making conflicting provision in a subsequent interlocutor.[8] The common law power of the Court of Session to alter an interlocutor which contains an error other than one which is merely clerical or incidental appears to be derived from the *nobile officium*,[9] and reported examples of the recall or amendment by the Inner House of its own interlocutors[10] are thought not to be in all circumstances reliable guides to proper practice in the sheriff court. In the sheriff court, unlike the Court of Session,[11] there is no settled and 5.88

---

98 *Sydie v. A.A. Stuart & Sons (Contractors) Ltd*, 1968 S.L.T. (Sh. Ct.) 93.

99 *Forbes v. Forbes's Trs*, 1957 S.C. 325 at 337–338; *Coutts v. J.M. Piggins Ltd*, 1983 S.L.T. 320. But see D.I.C.A.-C., "The meaning of proof before answer", 1958 S.L.T. (News) 109.

1 OCR, r. 12.2(2). Court of Session decisions on RCS, rr. 4.15(6) and 4.16(7), which confer a more extensive power of correction than OCR, r. 12.2(2), exercisable only on cause shown, may be misleading.

2 *Assessor for Strathclyde Region v. Dass Nicholson*, 1981 S.L.T. (Notes) 116.

3 *Cuthill v. Burns* (1862) 24 D. 849 at 859. "Incidental" was construed as "accidental" in *Project Contract Services Ltd v. Fraoli*, 1980 S.C. 261, *per* Sh. Pr. Reid at 262. The Sheriff Courts (Scotland) Act 1876, s. 34, used the expression "any merely clerical or accidental error".

4 *Eurocopy (Scotland) plc v. British Geological Survey*, 1997 S.C.L.R. 392.

5 *cf. Mutual Shipping Corporation v. Bayshore Shipping Co. Ltd* [1985] 1 W.L.R. 625, *per* Sir John Donaldson M.R. at 632–633.

6 *Clark & Macdonald v. Bain* (1895) 23 R. 102.

7 *White v. McEwen's Trs* (1873) 11 M. 602.

8 *Manders v. Lacon Floors Ltd*, 1993 S.C.L.R. 311.

9 *White, supra, per* Lord Mure. Court of Session interlocutors may also be corrected or altered before extract by virtue of RCS, rr. 4.15(6) and 4.16(7).

10 Authorities cited in Maclaren, p. 1096; Maxwell, pp. 620–621; see also *Haberstich v. McCormick & Nicholson*, 1974 S.C. 241.

11 *e.g. Harvey v. Lindsay* (1875) 2 R. 980, *per* Lord Deas at 982; *Bruce v. Bruce*, 1945 S.C. 353, *per* Lord Moncrieff at 357.

formulated practice regarding the alteration in substance of interlocutors which have been issued.[12] In the Court of Session alteration is excluded at common law unless application is made *de recenti* or unless both parties consent.[13]

5.89 It has been observed, however, that an error in an interlocutor of an inferior court may be corrected *de recenti* and in presence of the parties.[14] It is submitted that such a correction, if competent, could only be made before extract[15] or before transmission of a process in which an appeal has been taken. It has also been maintained, under reference to decisions on Court of Session practice, that the sheriff may, of consent, recall or correct an interlocutor which has been pronounced in error.[16] While as a general rule no court may recall its own interlocutor,[17] it is thought that it might be difficult to ground a practical objection to the sheriff's making a correction of which he approves, *de recenti* and of consent of the parties, in circumstances analogous to those of a reported Court of Session decision.[18]

5.90 On the other hand it is clear that the sheriff may not issue an interlocutor explaining a supposed ambiguity in a prior interlocutor.[19]

Effect of interlocutors

5.91 It is the obligation of every person against or in respect of whom an interlocutor is pronounced by a court of competent jurisdiction to obtemper[20] it unless and until it is recalled, varied, suspended or reduced, or unless extract of it is suspended. Any failure to obtemper an interlocutor which is wilful or intentional[21] or inexcusably careless[22] or which involves misconduct or a flagrant disregard of the due course and administration of justice[23] may be dealt with under the inherent jurisdiction of the court as a contempt of court warranting punishment. If the person affected by the interlocutor believes it to be irregular or void he should not assume that he may disregard it with impunity, but should seek a remedy at once by way of appeal, suspension or reduction.[24] It has been submitted above that an interlocutor

---

[12] A statement by Bankton (IV, xxxvi, 1) that interlocutory judgments before inferior courts are rectified by these courts themselves upon application, appears to have been seldom cited in modern times: *Campbell & Henry v. Hunter* (1910) 27 Sh.Ct.Rep. 26.

[13] *Kennedy v. Clyde Shipping Co.*, 1908 S.C. 895; *Bruce, supra*; *McChesney v. Harper*, 1993 S.C.L.R. 170.

[14] *White, supra, per* L.J.-C. Moncreiff at 603.

[15] *Hutchison*, 1965 S.C. 240 at 242.

[16] Lees, *Interlocutors*, p. 35, citing *Gillon's Trs v. Gillon* (1903) 40 S.L.R. 461 (but *cf.* Lees, *Pleading*, p. 138); Dobie, p. 248, citing *Gillon's Trs* and *Rottenburg v. Duncan* (1896) 24 R. 35.

[17] *Collie & Co. v. Mitchell*, 1935 S.L.T. 16. An interlocutor pronounced *ad interim* may be recalled. After amendment of pleadings the sheriff may permit procedure which is inconsistent with an earlier interlocutor: see para. 10.06. The Court of Session on appeal may direct the sheriff to recall an incompetent interlocutor: *Mackay v. Mackenzie* (1894) 21 R. 894; *James Y. Keanie Ltd v. Maycrete Sales Ltd*, 1949 S.L.T. (Notes) 28.

[18] In addition to the cases cited *supra*, see *Scott v. Mills's Trs*, 1923 S.C. 726; *Cumming v. Stewart*, 1928 S.C. 709 (judgments pronounced in ignorance of party's death).

[19] *Edington v. Astley* (1829) 8 S. 192; *Davidson & Syme, W.S. v. Booth*, 1971 S.L.T. (Notes) 11; *Manders v. Lacon Floors Ltd*, 1993 S.C.L.R. 311.

[20] *i.e.* obey. The word is now used only in Scots law.

[21] *Muir v. Milligan* (1868) 6 M. 1125; *Leys v. Leys* (1886) 13 R. 1223.

[22] *Hall v. Associated Newspapers Ltd*, 1979 J.C. 1; *Muirhead v. Douglas*, 1979 S.L.T. (Notes) 17.

[23] *Simpson, Boath & Co., Petrs*, 1981 S.C. 153.

[24] *cf. Hadkinson v. Hadkinson* [1952] P. 285, *per* Romer L.J. at 288; *Isaacs v. Robertson* [1985] 1 A.C. 97.

pronounced in error may in certain circumstances be corrected *de recenti* and of consent.[25] That possibility apart, however, it is doubtful whether the sheriff may recall an irregular interlocutor of his own (other than one made *ad interim*), *ex debito justitiae* in the exercise of the inherent jurisdiction of the court, and thus avoid the necessity for the party aggrieved to have recourse to such remedies.[26] Failure to obtemper an interlocutor pronounced during the dependence of an action may also result in decree by default against the party responsible.[27]

A party who has acquiesced in the operation of an interlocutor ordering some procedural step of process may not be permitted subsequently to challenge it.[28] **5.92**

Non-compliance with rules of court: dispensing power

Chapter 2 of the Ordinary Cause Rules 1993 confers on the sheriff a general discretionary power to relieve a party from the consequences of failure to comply with a provision in the Rules. The general rule is in these terms: "The sheriff may relieve a party from the consequences of failure to comply with a provision in these Rules which is shown to be due to mistake, oversight or other excusable cause, on such conditions as he thinks fit."[29] There are provisions in identical terms, *mutatis mutandis*, relative to the Rules of the Court of Session,[30] and in approximately the same terms in the Summary Cause Rules,[31] though the Summary Cause Rules reflect the provisions of rule 1 in the 1983 Rules, and accordingly include the words "not being wilful non-observance", words which are now omitted from the provision in the 1993 Rules. Rule 2.1 applies only to non-compliance with the Ordinary Cause Rules in force at the time of the failure,[32] and not to non-compliance with a statute or Act of Sederunt.[33] Failure to comply with a requirement prescribed by any such enactment or to comply with an order of the sheriff may result in decree by default.[34] Applications are often made to the court to exercise its discretionary dispensing power under rule 2.1 in such cases, but the power conferred by that rule does not extend to such cases since it is restricted to a failure to comply with a provision in the Rules. A limited amount of relief is allowed by rule 16.3 which, in relation to decrees by default, allows the sheriff, on cause shown, to prorogate the time for lodging any production or part of process, or for giving intimation, or for implementing any order, but it is not clear that that rule allows such a wide discretion as that provided for in rule 2.1.[35] **5.93**

---

[25] para. 5.89.

[26] As to the correction of interlocutors, see paras 5.87 to 5.90. *Cf. Isaacs, supra*.

[27] OCR, r. 16.2(1)(b): see paras 14.02 to 14.14. However, a failure to comply with an order of the court during the dependence of an action may not necessarily lead to decree by default: see para. 5.93.

[28] *Ferguson's Tr. v. Reid*, 1931 S.C. 714; *Macaskill v. Nicol*, 1943 S.C. 17; *Burgh of Ayr v. British Transport Commission*, 1956 S.L.T. (Sh. Ct.) 3 at 7: but see *McCue v. Scottish Daily Record and Sunday Mail Ltd*, 1998 S.C.L.R. 742 (Bench of Five Judges).

[29] OCR, r. 2.1(1).

[30] RCS, r. 2.1.

[31] A.S. (Summary Cause Rules, Sheriff Court) 1976 (S.I. 1976 No. 476), para. 5. See Vol. 2 of this work.

[32] *Barnes (Flexible Packaging) Ltd v. Okhai (Flexible Packaging) Ltd*, 1978 S.L.T. (Notes) 72.

[33] *Speirs v. Peat*, 1987 S.C.L.R. 369.

[34] OCR, r. 16.2(1); see paras 14.02 to 14.14.

[35] See *Group 4 Total Security Ltd v. Jaymarke Developments Ltd*, 1995 S.C.L.R. 303.

5.94 At one time there was authority[36] for the proposition that the dispensing power conferred by what is now rule 2.1 should only very rarely be employed in highly special circumstances. However, that view was expressly disapproved by a Court of Five Judges in *Grier v. Wimpey Plant and Transport Ltd*,[37] where it was said[38] that the dispensing power was too narrowly construed in *Grieve v. Batchelor and Buckling*.

5.95 What will, or will not, be deemed to amount to a "mistake, oversight or other excusable cause" such as to persuade a court to exercise its discretion in favour of a party who, either personally or through his solicitor, has failed to comply with a provision in the Rules will depend very much on the whole circumstances of the case and, possibly, on the nature and importance of the rule concerned. Following on the introduction of the 1993 Rules there were several reported instances where decree by default was granted at first instance in circumstances where a solicitor had failed to lodge a certified copy of the record in process not later than two days prior to the date of an options hearing.[39] On appeal some sheriffs principal expressed the view that the timeous lodging of a record is essential if the options hearing system, as introduced by the 1993 Rules, is to operate effectively, and accordingly refused appeals against decrees by default.[40] That approach was supported by the Inner House in *DTZ Debenham Thorpe v. Henderson Transport Services*.[41] However, it does not necessarily follow that decree by default must always be granted where there has been a failure to lodge a record at the correct time. If the failure has been slight, if the defender has not even been present so as to move the court to grant such a decree, and if the consequence of dismissing an action is that it may thereafter be time-barred, it may be reasonable to grant the relief which is provided for by rule 2.1.[42] Furthermore, it is not necessarily a bar to the exercise of the dispensing power that a failure to comply with the rules has been deliberate, but in fact mistaken.[43]

5.96 Where a sheriff at first instance has declined to exercise the dispensing power provided for by rule 2.1, it should not be assumed by the party in default that matters can be put right on appeal, possibly by advancing arguments which were not before the sheriff, and possibly by accepting liability for the expenses of the appeal. The grounds on which an appellate court may be entitled to review such a decision are the same as apply in any case where what is in issue is the exercise of a discretion:

> "As the matter was at the sheriff's discretion in terms of rule 16.2(2), the question for this court is whether it has been shown that she misdirected herself in law, failed to take into account a relevant and material factor, left some relevant and material factor out of account, or reached a result which was wholly unreasonable."[44]

---

[36] *Grieve v. Batchelor and Buckling*, 1961 S.C. 12.

[37] 1994 S.L.T. 714: see also *Eurocopy (Scotland) plc v. British Geological Survey*, 1997 S.C.L.R. 392.

[38] *Grier* at 719H–I, *per* L.J.-C. Ross.

[39] OCR, r. 9.11(2).

[40] See, *e.g. Mahoney v. Officer*, 1994 S.C.L.R. 1059; *Morran v. Glasgow Council of Tenants Associations*, 1994 S.C.L.R. 1065.

[41] 1995 S.C.L.R. 345.

[42] *Price v. Fernando*, 1995 S.C.L.R. 23; see also *Burtonport Fishermen's Co-operative v. Sans Unkles*, 1994 S.C.L.R. 844.

[43] *Eurocopy (Scotland) plc v. British Geological Survey*, 1997 S.C.L.R. 392.

[44] *DTZ Debenham Thorpe v. Henderson Transport Services*, 1995 S.C.L.R. 345 at 348D. See also *Royal Life Insurance v. Douglas*, 1998 S.C.L.R. 405.

The dispensing power may be exercised by the sheriff principal as well as by the sheriff.[45] Where the sheriff, or sheriff principal, has relieved a party from the consequences of failure to comply with a provision in the Rules by virtue of the power conferred by rule 2.1(1), he may make such order as he thinks fit to enable the cause to proceed as if the failure to comply with the provision had not occurred.[46] The nature of any such order will, of course, depend on the circumstances and on the stage of the proceedings at the relevant time. **5.97**

Control of conduct of proceedings

The sheriff is the master of the procedure before him, with a general command over the process and the regulation of the business of the court, power to keep the litigation within bounds,[47] control over the incidental procedure in the course of the action[48] and a controlling and censorial power over those practising in the court.[49] He cannot, however, take active control of the litigation once it has been brought into court, or disregard or innovate upon the rules of practice and procedure.[50] On the other hand, one of the objectives which the Ordinary Cause Rules 1993 seek to achieve is a greater measure of judicial control than was formerly the case during the early stages of a litigation prior to a debate or a proof. Consequently, sheriffs are likely to be fairly interventionist at, for example, the stage of an options hearing; but that is simply in accordance with the current Rules. In exceptional circumstances the sheriff may grant relief where there has been a failure to comply with the rules of court,[51] and he may depart from the accepted and traditional practice of the court when the interests of justice so require[52]; but in general his function is rather to see to it that the rules are observed and that the progress of the proceedings is orderly and expeditious, and to discourage any delay which might be to the detriment of the interests of justice. **5.98**

It is the will of Parliament[53] that the disposal of business in the sheriff court should be speedy and efficient; and the sheriff is therefore bound to be cautious before acceding to requests for continuations, amendments, postponements and all the other expedients which increase expense, delay the court's decision in the particular case and the dispatch of business in general, dislocate the judicial arrangements of the court and are inimical to the proper administration of justice. In particular, where at the proof the case will turn upon the recollection of witnesses to past events, the sheriff should exercise such powers as he possesses to encourage the progress of the action with all proper diligence.[54] **5.99**

---

[45] *Hardy v. Robinson*, 1985 S.L.T. (Sh. Ct.) 40. See also, for example, *Crendon Timber Engineering Ltd v. Miller Construction Ltd*, 1996 S.L.T. (Sh. Ct.) 102.

[46] OCR, r. 2.1(2).

[47] *Stewart v. Stewart* (1906) 8 F. 769, *per* L.P. Dunedin at 775; *Park v. Wilsons and Clyde Coal Co.*, 1929 S.C. (H.L.) 38, *per* Lord Buckmaster at 50.

[48] *Mackenzie v. Mackenzie*, 1951 S.C. 163, *per* L.P. Cooper at 166.

[49] *Hamilton v. Anderson* (1858) 3 Macq. 363, *per* Lord Chelmsford L.C. at 373; *Matthews v. Munster* (1888) 20 Q.B.D. 141, *per* Lord Esher M.R. at 143.

[50] See *Brennan v. Central SMT Co.*, 1947 S.L.T. (Notes) 4; *Stewart v. Lothians Construction (Edinburgh) Ltd*, 1972 S.L.T. (Notes) 75; *Mitchell Construction Co. (Scotland) Ltd v. Brands Transport and Demolition Ltd*, 1975 S.L.T. (Notes) 58.

[51] See paras 5.93 to 5.97.

[52] *Park, supra.*

[53] Expressed in ss. 15(1) and 16(1) of the 1971 Act.

[54] *cf. Birkett v. James* [1978] A.C. 297, *per* Lord Diplock at 321.

5.100 The sheriff should, however, be cautious before selecting and imposing any sanction on a party who has been responsible for delay or has disregarded a rule or order of court. A party whose conduct has brought about delay or dislocation in the proceedings, or has entailed unnecessary and improper charges on the other party, as by the amendment of pleadings[55] or the discharge or adjournment of a diet of debate[56] or proof,[57] may be penalised by a suitable interim award of expenses.[58] Consideration may be given to the question whether the conduct to be penalised is that of the party or of his solicitor. An adverse award of expenses will affect the party unless his solicitor is found personally liable in expenses. An award of expenses against a legally aided party may be ineffective.[59] Where the conduct under consideration is that of the party's solicitor, the sheriff may direct that these expenses should not be charged against the parties,[60] and may find the solicitor personally liable for these expenses.[61] A solicitor who is conscious of default may undertake to pay personally any expenses awarded against his client.[62] This may certainly result in a less censorious view being taken by the court than might otherwise be the case. A solicitor or party litigant who fails to return a borrowed part of process may be fined up to £50.[63] An order may be made for payment of an interim award of expenses against a pursuer, as a condition precedent of his being allowed to proceed, or against a defender, under certification that if he fails to do so, decree as craved will be pronounced; but such orders are appropriate only in very special circumstances.[64]

5.101 Sanctions other than an award of expenses should be used with great caution. A decree by default[65] may be quite inappropriate if, as is frequently the case, there has been no fault on the part of the litigant himself; and it also seems to be generally wrong in principle that the court should dispose of a depending action on procedural grounds, without determining the issues between the parties on the merits. It is only rarely appropriate to treat failure to obtemper an order of the court as a contempt.[66]

5.102 Fortunately, however, the standards of the profession and the fact that the objective of the orderly administration of justice is shared by Bench and Bar alike normally result in the conduct of litigation in a spirit of co-operation and not in acute consciousness that penalties will be instantly imposed for failures to comply with rules or orders of court. Business is in general conducted on the basis that "courts do not exist for the sake of discipline, but for the sake of deciding matters in controversy."[67]

---

[55] See paras 10.29, 10.30.

[56] *Edinburgh Modern Quarry Co. Ltd v. Eagle Star Insurance Co. Ltd*, 1965 S.L.T. (Notes) 91.

[57] See para. 16.35.

[58] *Mackenzie v. Mackenzie*, 1951 S.C. 163, *per* L.P. Cooper at 166.

[59] See the power to modify a party's liability under the Legal Aid (Scotland) Act 1986, s. 18(2).

[60] *Kelly v. Fyfe Douglas Co. Ltd*, 1965 S.L.T. (Notes) 87.

[61] *Stewart v. Stewart*, 1984 S.L.T. (Sh. Ct.) 58 at 59: see para. 19.23

[62] *McLean v. Thomas O'Connor Autos*, 1967 S.L.T. (Sh. Ct.) 41.

[63] OCR, r. 11.4(1): see para. 8.16.

[64] See paras 11.86 to 11.89.

[65] See paras 14.02 to 14.14.

[66] See paras 2.18 to 2.25.

[67] *Cropper v. Smith* (1884) 26 Ch. D. 700, *per* Bowen L.J. at 710.

PART III

THE ORDINARY COURT AND THE ORDINARY CAUSE

CHAPTER 6

COMMENCEMENT OF THE ACTION

INTRODUCTION

The essential requirements for the commencement of an ordinary action in the sheriff court are: (1) an initial writ, which is an authenticated initiating document containing a statement of the nature and extent of the pursuer's claim or demand; and (2) service of the initial writ, which is to give the defender notice of the writ and an opportunity to intimate an intention to defend. Accordingly, once it has been decided, after due investigation[1] and selection of the appropriate form of remedy,[2] that an ordinary action should be brought in the sheriff court, it is necessary in the first instance to select the sheriff court in which the action is to be brought, draft the initial writ and arrange for service on the defender, The form, content and authentication of the initial writ are examined in Chapter 9. The rules as to service of the writ are considered in this chapter. The procedure where the defender does not lodge a notice of intention to defend and the action proceeds as undefended, is explained in Chapter 7. The procedure where he does lodge such a notice and the cause proceeds as a defended action is the subject of the remaining chapters in this Part of the book. **6.01**

CHOICE OF SHERIFF COURT

The choice of the sheriffdom in which it is proposed to bring the action will be determined by the relevant rules as to jurisdiction.[3] An action may be competently raised in any sheriff court of that sheriffdom, since the resident sheriff at any court has jurisdiction throughout the sheriffdom.[4] Service on the defender, however, proceeds on a warrant of citation issued from the court in question, and the sheriff and sheriff clerk at that court are entitled to exercise a discretion not to issue a warrant if the defender or the property or conduct with which the action is concerned is more suitably amenable to another court of the sheriffdom.[5] Where an initial **6.02**

---

[1] On the duty of a solicitor to investigate before raising an action, see *Writers to the Signet v. Mackersy*, 1924 S.C. 776.

[2] On the choice of the appropriate remedy, see Walker, *Civil Remedies*, p. 16.

[3] On jurisdiction, see Chaps 2 and 3.

[4] *Simpson v. Bruce*, 1984 S.L.T. (Sh. Ct.) 38.

[5] *Tait v. Johnston* (1891) 18 R. 606; *Davidson v. Davidson* (1891) 18 R. 884; *McCormick v. Campbell* (1924) 42 Sh.Ct.Rep. 124; *South Side Sawmills Ltd v. Buchanan*, 1963 S.L.T. (Sh. Ct.) 19. An Act of Court, No. 1 of 1977, of the Sheriffdom of Lothian and Borders provided that where a cause was presented for a warrant to cite in a court in the sheriffdom where it would not normally fall to be dealt with and the sheriff clerk was unwilling to grant a warrant, the sheriff clerk had, if requested, to bring the writ before the sheriff for special reason to be shown for a warrant to cite to be granted by that court. This Act of Court was revoked (*per incuriam?*) by the Act of Court (Consolidation etc.) No. 1 of 1990, and not re-enacted. No other sheriffdom deals with this matter by Act of Court.

writ in an action for interdict is presented at an apparently unsuitable court, the sheriff may wish to ascertain whether a caveat has been lodged at the more suitable court.

6.03 Once the action has been brought it may, in certain circumstances, be transferred to another sheriff court or remitted or removed to the Court of Session.[6]

SIGNIFICANCE OF DUE SERVICE

Convening of defender: defective service

6.04 Due service of the initial writ (often referred to as the execution of the writ, or the citation of the defender) has a twofold significance: it apprises the defender of the nature of the proceedings against him and gives him an opportunity to lodge a notice of intention to defend, if he so wishes[7]; and, as a general rule, it marks the commencement of the action. As to the former consideration, it is *pars judicis* to notice that the citation of the defender has been irregular.[8] If it appears to the sheriff that there has been any failure or irregularity in service on a defender, the sheriff may authorise the pursuer to re-serve the initial writ on such conditions as he thinks fit.[9] But the sheriff may only make such an order before the case has reached the stage of final decree.[10] On the other hand, a party who appears may not state any objection to the regularity of the service upon himself, and his appearance remedies any defect in the service.[11] The rationale of the latter rule is that the purpose of citation is to convene a defender before the court, and once he has in fact been convened and is before the court, it matters not how his appearance was secured.[12] The rule accordingly applies even where the citation is seriously defective.[13] It is also applicable whether the defender appears before the sheriff or at an appeal before the sheriff principal.[14] It should be noted that "appearance" by a defender means that a notice of intention to defend has been lodged.[15] It has been suggested that the proper course for a defender who is irregularly cited and does not choose to waive the point by appearing is either to ignore the citation or to return it to the sender and, if the pursuer proceeds to take decree in absence, to raise a suspension or reduction.[16] The execution of citation may have to be reduced.[17] A party who is sisted in place of a defender who has been irregularly cited may state an objection to the regularity of the service on that defender.[18]

---

[6] See paras 13.52 to 13.66.

[7] *Corstorphine v. Kasten* (1898) 1 F. 287, *per* Lord Adam at 296; *McGraddie v. Clark*, 1966 S.L.T. (Sh. Ct.) 36.

[8] *Hamilton v. Murray & Co.* (1830) 9 S. 143.

[9] OCR, r. 5.9. He is unlikely to authorise re-service unless the pursuer so moves. See para. 6.47.

[10] *Black v. Black*, 1990 S.C.L.R. 433.

[11] OCR, r. 5.10(1). He is not precluded from pleading that the court has no jurisdiction: r. 5.10(2).

[12] *Struthers v. Kirkintilloch Mags*, 1951 S.L.T. (Notes) 77.

[13] *National Cash Register Co. Ltd v. Hunter* (1915) 32 Sh.Ct.Rep. 121; *Struthers, supra*; *Thomson v. Wiggins Teape Ltd*, 1981 S.L.T. (Sh. Ct.) 85.

[14] *Johnston v. Johnston*, 1965 S.L.T. (Sh. Ct.) 29.

[15] *Cairney v. Bulloch*, 1994 S.L.T. (Sh. Ct.) 37, 1993 S.C.L.R. 901.

[16] *Thomson, supra*; Mackay, *Manual*, p. 221.

[17] para. 6.46.

[18] *Morrison v. Vallance's Exrs*, 1907 S.C. 999.

Acceptance of service

Formal service of the writ may not be necessary. Once a warrant for service has been granted, the defender or his solicitor may accept service. At the same time he may, and usually does, dispense with the period of notice. He does so by endorsing a holograph docquet to that effect on the initial writ.[19] A defender who is sent an initial writ for that purpose must return it to the pursuer on demand.[20] **6.05**

Commencement of action

The second function of due service of the initial writ is that, as a general rule, it marks the commencement of the action. The principal qualifications of that general rule are that the court has power to grant an interim interdict before service,[21] and that arrestments on the dependence or to found jurisdiction may be used before service.[22] Such qualifications apart, an action does not commence until the defender is cited,[23] or until that is deemed to have been achieved.[24] Only then is the action in dependence.[25] It is, therefore, vital to ensure that the initial writ is served before the expiry of any relevant period of prescription or limitation. Citation is "a *sine qua non* before effective action is allowed".[26] Until it has been accomplished, or is deemed to have been accomplished, no step can be taken in the action, except that a further warrant to cite may be granted on the pursuer's motion: no other motion may be entertained, and decree in absence will not be pronounced.[27] If no steps are taken in the action for a year and a day after the last day on which a notice of intention to defend may be lodged, the instance falls: that is, the initial writ is at an end and has no existence whatever.[28] **6.06**

WARRANT OF CITATION

Form of warrant

In order to effect service of the initial writ, whether formally or by acceptance of service, it is necessary to obtain a warrant of citation. The warrant is usually a printed form which is attached to the initial writ. In an ordinary cause, with three exceptions, the warrant of citation must be framed in accordance with Form O1 in Appendix 1 to the Ordinary Cause Rules.[29] **6.07**

---

[19] For styles, see Greens *Litigation Styles*, E04–16. See also Lewis, p. 98; Dobie, *Styles*, p. 72. The docquet may be combined with one for dispensing with the period of notice: see *Litigation Styles*, E04–18.

[20] *Campbell v. Macpherson* (1905) 22 Sh.Ct.Rep. 88.

[21] See paras 21.85 to 21.90. An interim interdict prohibiting the removal of a child under s. 35(3)(a) of the Family Law Act 1986 may be granted at any time after the warrant of citation is signed.

[22] para. 11.23.

[23] Ersk., III, vi, 3; *Alston v. Macdougall* (1887) 15 R. 78; *Walls' Trs v. Drynan* (1888) 15 R. 359, *per* L.P. Inglis at 362–363; *North v. Stewart* (1870) 17 R. (H.L.) 60, *per* Lord Watson at 63; *McTernan v. Bennell* (1898) 1 F. 333, *per* Lord Low at 336–337; *Miller v. National Coal Board*, 1960 S.C. 376, *per* L.P. Clyde at 383; *Smith v. Stewart & Co.*, 1960 S.C. 329, *per* L.P. Clyde at 334; *McGraddie v. Clark*, 1966 S.L.T. (Sh. Ct.) 36.

[24] See paras 6.20 to 6.22, 6.25.

[25] *Aitken v. Dick* (1863) 1 M. 1038, *per* Lord Deas and Lord Ardmillan at 1041.

[26] *Johnson v. Taylor Bros & Co. Ltd* [1920] A.C. 144, *per* Lord Dunedin at 154.

[27] *McGraddie, supra.*

[28] *McKidd v. Manson* (1882) 9 R. 790.

[29] OCR, r. 3.3(1).

The exceptions are a family action,[30] an action of multiplepoinding[31] and an action in which a time to pay direction[32] under the Debtors (Scotland) Act 1987 may be applied for by the defender.[33] There may be added to the warrant any other appropriate grant or order, such as a grant of a warrant to arrest on the dependence or to found jurisdiction, or an interim interdict.[34]

Signature of warrant

6.08 A warrant for citation or for arrestment on the dependence may be signed by the sheriff for the sheriff clerk.[35] In practice it is usually signed by the sheriff clerk. Before granting a warrant, the sheriff clerk should check whether the initial writ discloses adequate grounds of jurisdiction, and should draw any apparent defect to the attention of the pursuers solicitor.[36] If for any reason the sheriff clerk refuses to sign a warrant—for example because he considers that the action would be more appropriately raised in the court of another district[37]—the writ may be presented to the sheriff for his consideration and signature if appropriate.[38] A warrant for citation on a person whose address is not known,[39] warrants containing an order shortening or extending the period of notice,[40] warrants for arrestment on the dependence in actions for aliment or on a claim for financial provision,[41] warrant for intimation in a family action where an improper association is averred,[42] or any other order such as an interim interdict or a warrant for arrestment to found jurisdiction or a warrant to dismantle a ship, may only be signed by the sheriff.[43] If the sheriff refuses to grant a warrant he pronounces an interlocutor to that effect, an appeal against which is competent only with leave.[44]

Error in warrant

6.09 If the wrong form of warrant is used[45] or the period of notice is misstated[46] but the defender nevertheless appears, the error will be regarded as immaterial.

---

[30] A "family action" is defined in OCR, r. 33(1). See para. 22.02

[31] On actions of multiplepoinding, see paras 21.52 *et seq.*

[32] A "time to pay direction" is an order permitting the defender to pay a sum of money under a decree in the cause either by instalments or by deferred lump sum: Debtors (Scotland) Act 1987, s. 1(1). See, further, paras 7.03 *et seq.*

[33] The form of warrant in a family action is in Form F14 (OCR, r. 33.10), in an action of multiplepoinding is in Form M1 (OCR, r. 35.5), and in an action in which a time to pay direction may be applied for is in Form O2 (OCR, r. 3.3(2)).

[34] See OCR, App. 1, Form O1.

[35] OCR, r. 5.1(1).

[36] Maxwell Report, para. 5.201.

[37] See para. 6.02.

[38] OCR, r. 5.1(3).

[39] OCR, r. 5.6(1): see paras 6.33 to 6.35.

[40] OCR, r. 5.1(2)(a): see para. 6.12.

[41] OCR, r. 5.1(2)(b). These warrants relate to claims to which section 19 of the Family Law (Scotland) Act 1985 applies.

[42] OCR, r. 5.1(2)(c).

[43] OCR, r. 5.1(2).

[44] *Davidson v. Davidson* (1891) 18 R. 884.

[45] *Muir & Weir v. Petrie* (1910) 22 Sh.Ct.Rep. 151; *MacGregor v. McKinnon* (1915) 32 Sh.Ct.Rep. 3 at 8; OCR, r. 5.10(1); paras 6.04, 13.50, 26.19.

[46] *Stevenson v. Wilson* (1941) 58 Sh.Ct.Rep. 74; OCR, r. 5.10(1); para. 6.04.

Period of effectiveness of warrant

The warrant remains effective for a year and a day.[47] 6.10

PERIOD OF NOTICE

General rules

The period of notice which must be inserted in the warrant and form of citation is the period after service within which the defender, if he intends to defend, must lodge a notice of intention to defend. The general rules as to the length of the period of notice are set out in rule 3.6, while rule 5.6 makes provision for the citation of persons whose addresses are not known.[48] Rule 3.6(1) provides that, subject to rule 5.6(1) and the power of the sheriff to shorten or extend the period of notice,[49] causes shall proceed after the following periods of notice have been given to the defender: (a) 21 days where the defender is resident or has a place of business within Europe, or (b) 42 days where the defender is resident or has a place of business outside Europe. 6.11

Shortening or extension of period

The sheriff may, on cause shown, shorten or extend the period of notice on such conditions as to the form or manner of service as he thinks fit,[50] but in any case, where the period of notice is reduced, at least two days' notice must be given.[51] The rule appears to require two days' clear notice, the date of service and the date by which a notice must be lodged both being excluded from the computation of the period.[52] 6.12

Calculation of period

Where citation is effected upon any of the general rules, the defender is obliged to lodge a notice of intention to defend within 21 or 42 days after the date of citation.[53] The latter date is accordingly excluded from the computation of the period, and the notice must be lodged on or before the last day of the period.[54] Where a period of notice expires on a Saturday, Sunday, public or court holiday, the period of notice is deemed to expire on the first following day on which the sheriff clerk's office is open for civil court business.[55] In all cases of postal service the period of notice starts to run from the beginning of the day after the date of posting.[56] Where, for example, the day of posting is Wednesday, May 3, the first day of the period of notice will be Thursday, May 4. It may be inadvisable, however, to assume that the period of service will not expire until the end of the last 6.13

---

47 *Hodgson v. Hodgson's Trs*, 1984 S.L.T. 97 at 98.

48 See paras 6.33 to 6.35.

49 para. 6.12.

50 OCR, r. 3.6(2).

51 OCR, r. 3.6(3).

52 *Watson Gow & Co. v. Glasgow Assessor*, 1910 S.C. 807; *McMillan v. H.M. Advocate*, 1983 S.L.T. 24.

53 OCR, r. 3.6(1); App. 1, Form O4.

54 *Pugh v. Duke of Leeds* (1777) 2 Cowp. 714; *Stair Memorial Encyclopaedia of the Laws of Scotland*, Vol. 36, paras 823 and 826(9).

55 OCR, r. 3.6(4).

56 *ibid.* r. 5.3(2). This contrasts with the rule in the Court of Session that the period of notice runs from the end of the day after the date of posting: RCS 1994, rr. 13.4 and 16.4(6); and see Greens' *Annotated Rules of the Court of Session*, nn. 13.4.4 and 16.4.8.

day of the period, and that it will suffice to push the notice through the letterbox of the sheriff clerk's office after it has closed for civil court business but before midnight at the end of that day. It seems arguable that it is not possible to "lodge" a notice "with" the sheriff clerk unless it is accepted by the sheriff clerk when the office is open. The rule that the period is extended where it expires on a day when the office is closed[57] may support that view.

Execution of Citation

Documents to be served

6.14 Citation is effected by the delivery, or deemed delivery,[58] to the defender of a copy of the initial writ, known as a service copy, to which are attached a copy of the warrant of citation and a form of citation signed by the sheriff officer or solicitor who serves the copy writ and warrant, and a form of notice of intention to defend.[59] In an action in which the defender may apply for a time to pay direction under the Debtors (Scotland) Act 1987, a notice (which includes a form of application for such a direction) must also be served.[60] No other document should be served on or sent to the defender along with the service copy of the initial writ. The practice of attaching a variety of unauthorised notices to the service copy or of sending them with the service copy in the citation envelope is objectionable, and is expressly prohibited in North Strathclyde.[61]

Service copy

6.15 Any amendments made to the initial writ before the granting of the warrant—for example where the court has granted an interim interdict in terms of an amended crave—must be shown on the service copy. It is thought that any clerical error in the body of the service copy would not normally invalidate the proceedings and that any prejudice thereby suffered by the defender might be dealt with by an appropriate award of expenses.[62] The name and address of the pursuer's solicitor, if any, must be stated on the back of the service copy[63] for the information of the defender or his solicitor.[64] It has been held sufficient for the name and town of the solicitor's firm to appear on the back of the service copy.[65] A typed or written version of the signature of the pursuer's solicitor need not appear at the end of the pleas-in-law on the service copy.[66] In any event a defender who appears is thereby barred from taking any objection to the regularity of the service upon himself,[67] including an objection to the

---

57 OCR, r. 3.6(4).
58 See paras 6.20 to 6.22, 6.25.
59 OCR, r. 5.2; App. 1, Forms O1, O4 and O7. Where the action is a family action or an action of multiplepoinding the forms of warrant and citation and the notice will be different: see rr. 5.2(1)(a) and (b), and 33.10, 33.11, 35.5 and 35.6. Where the action is one in which the defender may apply for a time to pay direction under the Debtors (Scotland) Act 1987, the form of citation will be different: r. 5.2(1)(c) and (2).
60 OCR, r. 3.3(3).
61 North Strathclyde Act of Court (Consolidation, etc.) 1992, para. 1.04.
62 *Lochrie v. McGregor*, 1911 S.C. 21 at 24.
63 OCR, r. 3.1(7).
64 *Muir's Sequestration* (1911) 27 Sh.Ct.Rep. 327.
65 *Muir v. National Bank Ltd* (1943) 59 Sh.Ct.Rep. 51.
66 *Muir, supra.*
67 OCR, r. 5.10(1). See para. 6.04.

accuracy of the service copy[68] or to the absence of any signature on the service copy or of any name and address on its back.[69]

Form of citation

The form of citation is prefixed to the service copy. Special forms are provided for a family action,[70] an action of multiplepoinding[71] and an action in which the defender may apply for a time to pay direction under the Debtors (Scotland) Act 1987.[72] In other ordinary actions the form must be in accordance with Form O4 in Appendix 1 to the Rules. The form is signed by the person serving the documents, who must be either a sheriff officer or a solicitor. The latter adds his designation and business address.[73] **6.16**

Methods of citation

Different methods of citation are prescribed according to whether the defender (a) has an address in Scotland[74] or (b) has an address furth of Scotland[75] or (c) is a person whose address is not known.[76] Special provision is made for the citation of the Crown and certain other entities.[77] **6.17**

Citation of defender with address in Scotland

A defender who has an address in Scotland may be cited either (i) by post or (ii) by an officer of court. In practice, postal citation is the more common method. Citation by officer of court is the safer method since it normally avoids any dispute as to whether the documents were tendered to the defender. It is, however, more expensive than postal citation, and the additional expense will not be allowed on taxation unless the sheriff deciding the case is of opinion that it was not expedient in the interests of justice that postal citation should be made.[78] **6.18**

Postal citation. Postal service may be made at the known address or place of business of the person[79] upon whom the documents are to be served, or at his last known address if it continues to be his legal domicile or proper place of citation.[80] It may be effected by sending the documents by registered letter[81] or by recorded delivery first class service.[82] In practice the latter is almost invariably used. On the face of the envelope there must be written or printed the following notice or a notice to the like effect[83]: **6.19**

---

68 *Thompson v. Wiggins Teape Ltd*, 1981 S.L.T. (Sh. Ct.) 85.
69 *National Cash Register Co. Ltd v. Hunter* (1915) 32 Sh.Ct.Rep. 121.
70 OCR, rr. 5.2(1)(a) and 33.11.
71 OCR, rr. 5.2(1)(b) and 35.6.
72 OCR, rr. 5.2(1)(c) and (2).
73 OCR, App. 1, Form O4.
74 paras 6.18 to 6.28.
75 paras 6.29 to 6.32.
76 paras 6.32 to 6.36.
77 paras 6.37 to 6.44.
78 Citation Amendment (Scotland) Act 1882 (hereinafter the "1882 Act"), s. 6; *Macleod v. Davidson* (1887) 14 R. 298.
79 "Person" includes corporation, company, firm or other body requiring to be cited: 1882 Act, s. 7.
80 1882 Act, s. 3.
81 *ibid.*
82 Recorded Delivery Service Act 1962, ss. 1, 2 and Sched.; OCR, r. 5.3(1).
83 OCR, r. 5.3(3).

"This letter contains a citation or intimation to [*specify the court*]. If delivery of the letter cannot be made at the address shown it is to be returned immediately to: The Sheriff Clerk [*insert address of sheriff clerk's office*]."

The certificate of citation must have attached to it any relevant postal receipts.[84] Postal citation may be effected by an officer of court or by a solicitor.[85]

6.20 Where the letter is posted and not returned, the posting constitutes a legal and valid citation, unless the defender proves that the letter was not left or tendered at his known residence or place of business, or at his last known address if it continues to be his legal domicile or proper place of citation.[86] Since the defender is barred by appearing from stating objections to service,[87] he may so prove only in proceedings following the taking of a decree in absence. Those proceedings would be suspension or reduction.[88] Proof that the letter was not left or tendered at any of the places mentioned will not invalidate the citation if the defender has in fact received it or if it has been delivered to a person authorised by him to receive it.[89] Since it is the posting of the letter which constitutes legal and valid citation, the date of posting is the date of citation.[90] The rule that in all cases of postal service the period of notice starts to run on the day after the date of posting, has already been considered.[91]

6.21 If delivery of the letter is not made for any reason, for example because the house or place of business at the address is shut up, or the addressee is not known there or has gone away, or the letter is refused, the letter must be immediately returned through the post office to the sheriff clerk, with the reason for the failure to deliver marked on it. The sheriff clerk must intimate its return to the pursuer, and the sheriff may order service of new.[92] In practice the pursuer's solicitor usually instructs re-service by a sheriff officer without any formal court order. It is possible for a letter not to be returned until after the expiry of the period of notice. In that event the action will have commenced on the assumption that a valid citation has been effected, and the pursuer may have taken decree in absence. It is then for the defender, when he becomes aware of the existence of the action, to establish if he can, by reduction or otherwise, that the citation was not in fact valid and effective.[93] If the letter is

---

[84] OCR, r. 5.3(4).

[85] 1882 Act, s. 3; Execution of Diligence (Scotland) Act 1926, s. 4; Solicitors (Scotland) Act 1980, s. 65(2). The solicitor may be a party to the cause: *Addison v. Brown* (1906) 8 F. 443.

[86] 1882 Act, s. 3. A pursuer who accepts delivery of a letter addressed to a defender and does not see that he gets it cannot plead that the citation is good: *Morrison v. Vallance's Exrs*, 1907 S.C. 999; *Johnston v. Johnston*, 1965 S.L.T. (Sh. Ct.) 29.

[87] OCR, r. 5.10(1).

[88] *Thomson v. Wiggins Teape Ltd*, 1981 S.L.T. (Sh. Ct.) 85; Mackay, *Manual*, p. 221. See further para. 6.04.

[89] *Steuart v. Ree* (1885) 12 R. 563.

[90] *Alston v. Macdougall* (1887) 15 R. 78; s. 7 of the Interpretation Act 1978 is inapplicable. This contrasts with the position in the Court of Session where the date of execution of service (citation) by post is the day after the date of posting: RCS 1994, r. 16.4(6). This is consistent with s. 7 of the Interpretation Act 1978; see Greens *Annotated Rules of the Court of Session*, n. 16.4.8.

[91] OCR, r. 15.3(2); see para. 6.13.

[92] 1882 Act, s. 4.

[93] *McGraddie v. Clark*, 1966 S.L.T. (Sh. Ct.) 36.

returned after the expiry of the period of notice but before decree in absence has been signed, the pursuer may refrain from making, or may withdraw, an application for decree in absence, and instruct re-service by a sheriff officer.

If the sheriff is satisfied that the letter has been tendered at the defender's proper address and refused, he may hold the tender equal to a good citation.[94] Before so holding, he must be satisfied that the letter has been tendered to and deliberately[95] refused by the defender himself or by someone who was authorised by him to do so[96] or who may reasonably be taken to have been acting on his behalf.[97] A letter which is accepted and thereafter returned to the sheriff clerk is not "refused".[98] The sheriff may consider not only the reason for failure to deliver which is marked on the letter, but other documents tendered and any information given orally at the bar.[99] He is entitled, if in his discretion he thinks fit, to regard the letter as having been tendered and deliberately refused and to allow the action to proceed on the assumption that a valid service has been executed.[1] He should dispose of the question by pronouncing an interlocutor.[2] Decree in absence may be granted.[3] It is then for the defender to establish, by reduction[4] or otherwise, that the citation was not valid and effective. **6.22**

Citation by officer of court. An initial writ may be served by an officer of court.[5] "An officer of court" means in practice a sheriff officer[6] of the court which granted the warrant of citation or of the sheriff court district within which it is to be executed.[7] He must not have any personal interest in the action.[8] He executes the citation in the presence of a witness[9] who signs the certificate of citation along with him.[10] A person under the age of 16 years is not a competent witness.[11] **6.23**

---

[94] 1882 Act, s. 4.

[95] *McGraddie v. Clark, supra,* at 38.

[96] *Bruce v. British Motor Trading Corporation,* 1924 S.C. 908 at 923; and see *Steuart v. Ree* (1885) 12 R. 563.

[97] *Smith v. Conner & Co. Ltd,* 1979 S.L.T. (Sh. Ct.) 25 at 28; *cf. Roberts v. Crawford* (1884) 22 S.L.R. 135.

[98] *Foote v. Foote,* 1963 S.L.T. (Sh. Ct.) 51.

[99] *Spaulding & Co. v. Marjoribanks* (1903) 11 S.L.T. 71; *Busby v. Clark* (1904) 7 F. 162; *Matheson v. Fraser,* 1911 2 S.L.T. 493.

[1] *McGraddie, supra.*

[2] *Bruce, supra,* at 923, 927.

[3] *Hannah v. Lord Advocate,* 1970 S.L.T. (Sh. Ct.) 46.

[4] *e.g. Bruce, supra.*

[5] 1882 Act, s. 3.

[6] See para. 1.28; Dobie, p. 117. A decree, charge, warrant or other order or writ following upon an initial writ or decree may also be served by a sheriff officer: OCR, r. 5.4(1). The qualifications, training, examination, discipline and, to some extent, functions of a sheriff officer are governed by the Debtors (Scotland) Act 1987 and the Act of Sederunt (Messengers-at-Arms and Sheriff Officers) Rules 1991 (S.I. 1991 No. 1397).

[7] OCR, r. 5.8.

[8] *Dalgleish v. Scott* (1822) 1 S. 506 (N.E. 469).

[9] OCR, r. 5.2(4).

[10] OCR, App. 1, Form O6.

[11] The rule of law used to be that a pupil (a boy under 14 and a girl under 12) was not a competent witness: Dobie, p. 126; *Davidson v. Charteris* (1738) Mor. 16899. Section 1 of the Age of Legal Capacity (Scotland) Act 1991 abolished the distinction between pupils and minors in respect of transactions by persons under 16. A transaction is defined in s. 9 of the Act as including "the taking of any step in civil proceedings". It must be concluded that witnessing a citation, though not done in the capacity of a party, is taking such a step.

6.24 The sheriff officer may serve the writ on the defender either personally[12] or at his dwelling-place or place of business.[13] It is doubtful whether service by any of these modes may be competently executed on a Sunday.[14]

6.25 Personal service applies only to service on a natural person, *i.e.* an individual; it does not apply to a non-natural person such as a company.[15] Personal service is effected when the sheriff officer tenders to the defender the service copy writ with the copy of the warrant of citation and the form of citation attached to it. He may do so wherever he happens to find the defender. The service is complete when the tender is made: it cannot be defeated by the defender refusing to receive the documents[16] or deliberately obstructing or avoiding service.[17] The fact of refusal or prevention of service should be mentioned in the certificate of citation.[18]

6.26 The alternative to service on the defender personally is to leave the documents in the hands of a resident at the defender's dwelling-place or an employee at his place of business.[19] His dwelling-place is his usual place of residence.[20] If he has more than one, service at any one of them may be sufficient.[21] The fact of the person receiving the documents at the dwelling-place or place of business may exclude inquiry into the question whether he was a resident or employee; since by receiving them he may be deemed to have acted in that capacity.[22] Leaving the documents *at* the dwelling-place or place of business is not enough; they must be placed in the hands of the relevant person.

6.27 Where a sheriff officer has been unsuccessful in executing either personal service or service at the dwelling-place or place of business by leaving the documents with the appropriate person he may, after making diligent enquiries, serve the documents either (a) by depositing them in the dwelling-place or place of business or (b) by affixing them to the door of the dwelling-place or place of business.[23] Rule 5.4(4) provides that if he effects service by either of those methods he must as soon as possible after such service send by ordinary first class post to the address at which he thinks it most likely that the defender may be found a letter containing copies of the documents. "Depositing" in the dwelling-place or place of business means putting the documents through the letterbox or in the place by other lawful means such as by pushing them under and inside the door.[24] "Affixing" to the door of the premises is still permitted in the

---

12 OCR, r. 5.4(1)(a); and see para. 6.25.
13 OCR, r. 5.4(1)(b); and see paras 6.26, 6.27.
14 *Oliphant v. Douglas* (1633) Mor. 15002; Stair, III, i, 37; III, iii, 11; IV, xlvii, 27; Bell, *Comm.*, ii. 460; *McNiven v. Glasgow Corporation*, 1920 S.C. 584.
15 *Rae v. Calor Gas Ltd*, 1995 S.L.T. 244; 1995 S.C.L.R. 261 (IH).
16 Stair, IV, xxxviii, 15.
17 *Busby v. Clark* (1904) 7 F. 162.
18 Dove Wilson, p. 111.
19 OCR, r. 5.4(1).
20 *Corstorphine v. Kasten* (1898) 1 F. 287.
21 *Douglas and Heron v. Armstrong* (1779) Mor. 3700; *Macdonald v. Sinclair* (1843) 5 D. 1253.
22 *A v. B* (1834) 12 S. 347.
23 OCR, r. 5.4(3).
24 *Docherty v. Docherty*, 1981 S.L.T. (Notes) 24.

sheriff court,[25] although it is no longer an authorised means of service in the Court of Session.[26]

Where the initial writ has been served by a sheriff officer, the certificate of citation[27] must be signed by the officer and the witness and must specify whether the citation was personal or, if otherwise, the mode of citation and the name of any person to whom the citation was delivered.[28] Where citation is effected by depositing or affixing to the door, the certificate must also contain a statement of the mode of service previously attempted, the circumstances which prevented such service being effected and a statement that copies of the documents were sent by letter in accordance with rule 5.4(4).[29] **6.28**

Citation of defender furth of Scotland

The citation of defenders outwith Scotland is regulated by the provisions of rule 5.5. The sheriff court provisions are quite unsatisfactory compared with those in the Court of Session. Rule 5.5(1)(a) is concerned with service at a known residence or place of business in England, Wales, Northern Ireland, the Isle of Man, the Channel Islands or any country with which the United Kingdom does not have a convention providing for the service of writs in that country. Service may be executed in either of two ways. It may be executed in accordance with the rules for personal service under the domestic law of the place in which service is to be executed.[30] If it is so executed in a place other than another part of the United Kingdom, the Channel Islands or the Isle of Man, the pursuer must lodge a certificate by a person who is conversant with the law of the country concerned and who practises or has practised as an advocate or solicitor in that country or is a duly accredited representative of the government of that country. The certificate must state that the form of service employed is in accordance with the law of the place where the service was executed.[31] Alternatively, service may be executed by posting in Scotland copies of the documents in a registered letter, addressed to the defender at his residence or place of business.[32] The pursuer must observe the general rules as to posting, forms and translations which are noted below.[33] **6.29**

Rule 5.5(1)(b) is concerned with service in a country which is a party to the Hague Convention on the Service Abroad of Judicial and **6.30**

---

[25] OCR, r. 5.4(3)(b).

[26] See RCS 1994, r. 16.1(1). The sheriff court provisions should be brought into line with those of the Court of Session. Affixing was abolished in the latter court because of obvious problems with this form of service, such as removal of the documents by unauthorised persons.

[27] See para. 6.45.

[28] OCR, r. 5.2(5).

[29] OCR, r. 5.2(6).

[30] OCR, r. 5.5(1)(a)(i).

[31] OCR, r. 5.5(6).

[32] OCR, r. 5.5(1)(a)(ii). The recorded delivery service, as an alternative to registered post under the Recorded Delivery Service Act 1962 is available only in the United Kingdom, the Channel Islands and the Isle of Man (but not the Republic of Ireland). The Royal Mail provides an international recorded delivery service, but this is not authorised by the 1882 Act, the Recorded Delivery Service Act 1962 or any rules of court. It might be considered by the Rules Councils whether the international recorded delivery service might be included as an alternative to registered post for service by post abroad.

[33] para. 6.32.

Extrajudicial Documents in Civil and Commercial Matters dated November 15, 1965[34] or the Convention in Schedule 1 or 3C to the Civil Jurisdiction and Judgments Act 1982. The Hague Convention sets out methods of service (and these are the methods set out in heads (ii) to (v) of rule 5.5(1)(b)). It will always be necessary to confirm, however, that the method used is permitted in the country in which service is to be executed. The expression "civil or commercial matter" is not defined in the Hague Convention. A special commission in 1989 indicated that it should be interpreted in an autonomous manner without reference exclusively to the law of the requesting or requested state. The theory underlying the Hague Convention is that a defender resident in the state where service is to be executed cannot complain if he is duly served in accordance with the law of that state.[35] The Hague Convention applies only where the address of the person to be served is known.[36] Reference should be made to the undernoted guide to the operation of the Hague Convention.[37] The Conventions in Schedules 1 and 3C of the 1982 Act provide for service (a) in accordance with any Conventions (which would include the Hague Convention) or agreements between the Contracting States or (b) where permitted, by a public officer (*e.g.* an *huissier*) to whom it has been sent by a public officer here (sheriff officer or sheriff clerk).[38] The implication in rule 5.5(1)(b) that any of the methods listed there may be used in any country which is party to one of these three Conventions is, therefore, inaccurate; and rule 5.5(1)(c) is inconsistent with paragraph 1 of Article IV of the Protocols to the Brussels and Lugano Conventions.[39] The draftsman of the Ordinary Cause Rules 1993[40] did not interfere with the substance of rule 12(1)(b) in the 1983 Rules in drafting rule 5.5 of the 1993 Rules because of lack of time. But it seems clear that rule 5.5(1)(b) and its predecessor represent a misunderstanding of the Conventions. Rule 5.5 should probably be brought into line with rule 16.2 of the Rules of the Court of Session 1994. Rule 5.5(1)(b) prescribes the following five methods of executing service.

(1) A method prescribed by the internal law of the country where service is to be executed for the service of documents in domestic actions upon persons who are within its territory.[41] Here, the pursuer must lodge a certificate as to the form of service such as is described in paragraph 6.29.[42] The provision in rule 5.5(1)(b)(i) for service by a method prescribed by the

---

[34] Cmnd 3986 (1969), printed in Anton, *C.J.*, pp. 286–298. The following countries, *inter alia*, are parties to the Convention: Antigua and Barbuda, Barbados, Belgium, Botswana, Canada, China, Cyprus, the Czech Republic, Denmark, Egypt, Finland, France, Federal Republic of Germany, Greece, Israel, Italy, Japan, Luxembourg, Malawi, The Netherlands, Norway, Pakistan, Portugal, Seychelles, the Slovak Republic, Sweden, Turkey, the United Kingdom (including the Channel Islands, the Isle of Man and most of the dependent territories) and the United States of America (including Guam, Puerto Rico and the Virgin Islands). See further, Green's *Annotated Rules of the Court of Session*, n. 16.2.3.

[35] Anton and Beaumont, *C.J.*, para. 7.36.

[36] Hague Convention, Art. I.

[37] Hague Academy of Private International Law, *Practical Handbook on the Operation of the Hague Convention of 15 November 1985 on the Service Abroad of Judicial and Extrajudicial Documents in Civil or Commercial Matters* (Antwerp, Apeldoorn, 1983, with supplements). See also Green's *Annotated Rules of the Court of Session*, n. 16.2.3.

[38] See 1982 Act, Sched. 1, Annexed Protocol, Art. IV and Sched. 3C, Protocol No. 1, Art. IV.

[39] *ibid.*

[40] N. M. P. Morrison, Q.C. in the Lord President's Private Office.

[41] OCR, r. 5.5(1)(b)(i).

[42] OCR, r. 5.5(5).

internal law of the country concerned is erroneous because it is not an alternative to the other methods listed in rule 5.5(1)(b), although it is expressed as such. The three Conventions provide for the methods of service (and this provision is not one of them), but the method used must be one which the country concerned permits in its jurisdiction.

(2) By or through a central authority in the country where service is to be executed at the request of the Foreign Office.[43] Here, the pursuer must send a copy of the writ and warrant for service with form of citation attached, with a request for service[44] to be effected by the method indicated in the request, to the Secretary of State for Foreign and Commonwealth Affairs.[45] He must also lodge in process a certificate of execution of service signed by the authority which has effected service.[46] That certificate appears to be intended to take the place of the certificate of citation required by rule 5.2(3). The method which will be used will be one permitted by the internal law of the country concerned or a particular requested method so long as it is not incompatible with the internal law.

(3) By or through a British Consular authority at the request of the Foreign Office.[47] This method should be used only as one of last resort. Here again, the pursuer must send the documents with a request to the Foreign and Commonwealth Office, and must in due course lodge a certificate of execution of service, as described in the immediately preceding sub-paragraph.[48]

(4) Where the law of the country in which the defender resides permits, by posting in Scotland copies of the documents in a registered or recorded delivery letter or the nearest equivalent which the available postal services permit, addressed to the defender at his residence.[49] This method is available only where the defender is a natural person with a known residence. Here, the pursuer must observe the general rules as to posting, forms and translations which are noted below.[50]

(5) Where the law of the country in which service is to be executed permits, service by an *huissier*, other judicial officer, or competent official of the country where service is to be made.[51] This method is surer than postal service and quicker and more reliable than transmission through the central authorities. Here, the pursuer's solicitor or the officer must send to the official in the country in which service is to be effected a copy of the writ and warrant for service with form of citation attached, with a request for service to be executed by delivery to the defender or his residence. He must also lodge in process a certificate of execution of service by the official who has effected service,[52] which appears to be intended to take the place of the certificate of citation prescribed by rule 5.2.

---

[43] OCR, r. 5.5(1)(b)(ii).

[44] The model form of request in the Hague Convention should be used for service in a Hague Convention country. For the form, see Green's *Annotated Rules of the Court of Session*, n. 16.2.3.

[45] OCR, r. 5.5(3)(a). The request should be sent to the Treaty and Nationality Department of the Foreign and Commonwealth Office.

[46] OCR, r. 5.5(3)(b). For service in a Hague Convention country, the model form of certificate should be used. For the form, see Green's *Annotated Rules of the Court of Session*, n. 16.2.3.

[47] OCR, r. 5.5(1)(b)(iii).

[48] OCR, r. 5.5(3)(b).

[49] OCR, r. 5.5(1)(b)(iv).

[50] para. 6.32.

[51] OCR, r. 5.5(1)(b)(v).

[52] OCR, r. 5.4(4).

6.31 Rule 5.5(1)(c) is concerned with service in a country with which the United Kingdom has a Convention on the service of writs in that country other than the Conventions mentioned in paragraph 6.30. In such a case, service may be executed by one of the methods approved in the relevant Convention.[53] A list of countries with which the United Kingdom has such Conventions is given in the undernoted guide.[54] It is understood that the approved methods of service may be ascertained from the Foreign and Commonwealth Office, Treaty and Nationality Department.

6.32 Any document which requires to be posted in Scotland for the purposes of rule 5.5 must be posted by a solicitor or an officer of court, and the forms for citation and certificate of citation in rule 5.2 apply to a postal citation under rule 5.5(1)(b)(iv) as they apply to a citation under rule 5.2. On the face of the envelope used for postal service under rule 5.5 there must be written or printed a notice in the same or similar terms as that required in the case of ordinary service under rule 5.3(3).[55] Every writ or document and every citation and notice on the face of the envelope must be accompanied by a translation in an official language[56] of the country in which service is to be executed unless English is an official language of that country.[57] The translation must be certified as a correct translation by the person making it and the certificate must contain the full name, address and qualifications of the translator and be lodged along with the execution of citation or certificate of execution.[58]

Citation of defender whose address is not known

6.33 **Granting of warrant.** Rule 5.6 makes provision for the citation of a defender whose address is not known to the pursuer. In an action of divorce or separation intimation to certain other persons is required by rule 33.7.[59] Rule 5.6 prescribes two alternative modes of citation: by newspaper advertisement, or by displaying documents on the walls of court. The initial writ should contain a crave for warrant for citation by the mode selected, and where newspaper advertisement is chosen should specify the newspaper. The instance should state that the defender's whereabouts are not known.[60] In the condescendence the pursuer should state the domicile of the defender and the ground of jurisdiction of the court.[61] He should also state that the defender's present address is not known to him and specify his last known address, which determines the choice of newspaper and which in each case is inserted in the prescribed notice. The pursuer must aver what steps have been taken to ascertain the defender's whereabouts.[62] It is the sheriff, and not the sheriff clerk, who grants the warrant for citation in each case.[63] In the ordinary case citation by newspaper advertisement should be preferred to the less obviously useful method of display on the walls of

---

[53] OCR, r. 5.5(1)(c).
[54] See *supra*, n. 37; and see Green's *Annotated Rules of the Court of Session*, n. 16.2.5.
[55] OCR, r. 5.5(2): see para. 6.19.
[56] See Vol. 2 of this work.
[57] OCR, r. 5.5(6).
[58] OCR, r. 5.5(7).
[59] See paras 22.15, 22.16.
[60] OCR, r. 3.1(6).
[61] OCR, r. 3.1(5).
[62] OCR, r. 3.1(6).
[63] OCR, r. 5.6(1).

court. In any event the sheriff should not grant a warrant unless he is satisfied that his court has jurisdiction and that reasonable efforts have been made to trace the defender. He may require to hear the pursuer's solicitor on these matters before disposing of the application for the warrant.[64]

Newspaper advertisement. Citation is effected by the publication of an advertisement in a newspaper circulating in the area of the defender's last known address[65] and possibly in an area in which he might be thought to be. It is recommended that where there may be any doubt as to whether the newspaper proposed in the crave for the warrant actually circulates in that area, the sheriff clerk should ascertain the position before the sheriff considers the application for the warrant. The advertisement must be in Form G3 as set out in Appendix 1 to the Rules.[66] Form G3 is in the following terms: 6.34

> NOTICE TO [C.D.] Court ref. no.
>
> An action has been raised in Sheriff Court by [A.B.], Pursuer, calling as a Defender [C.D.] whose last known address was (*insert last known address of defender*). If [C.D.] wishes to defend the action [*where notice is given in a family action add:* or make any claim or seek any order] he [*or* she] should immediately contact the sheriff clerk at [*insert address*] from whom the service copy initial writ may be obtained. If he [*or* she] fails to do so decree may be granted against him [*or* her].
>
> Signed
>
> [X.Y.], (*add designation and business address*)
> Solicitor for the pursuer
> *or*
> [P.Q.], (*add business address*)
> Sheriff officer

The period of notice is fixed by the sheriff and runs from the date of publication of the advertisement.[67] The pursuer lodges with the sheriff clerk: (a) a service copy of the initial writ and a copy of the warrant of citation, which the defender may uplift from the sheriff clerk[68]; and (b) a copy of the newspaper containing the advertisement.[69]

Display on the walls of court. The alternative to citation by newspaper advertisement is citation by displaying on the walls of court a copy of the instance and crave of the initial writ, warrant of citation and notice in Form G4 in Appendix 1 to the Rules.[70] Form G4 is in these terms: 6.35

---

[64] See note by the Judicial Procedure Committee of the Council of the Law Society of Scotland (1982) 27 J.L.S. 523–524, and subsequent letter (1983) 28 J.L.S. 60.
[65] OCR, r. 5.6(1)(a).
[66] *ibid.*
[67] OCR, r. 5.6(1).
[68] OCR, r. 5.6(2).
[69] OCR, r. 5.6(4).
[70] OCR, r. 5.6(1)(b).

NOTICE TO [C.D.] Court ref. no.

An action has been raised in Sheriff Court by [A.B.], Pursuer, calling as a Defender [C.D.] whose last known address was (*insert last known address of defender*). If [C.D.] wishes to defend the action [*where notice is to be given in a family action add:* or make any claim or seek any order] he [*or* she] should immediately contact the sheriff clerk at (*insert address*) from whom the service copy initial writ may be obtained. If he [*or* she] fails to do so decree may be granted against him [*or* her].

Date (*insert date*) Signed

Sheriff clerk (depute)

Telephone no. (*insert telephone number of sheriff clerk's office*)

The period of notice is fixed by the sheriff and runs from the date of display on the walls of court.[71] The pursuer supplies to the sheriff clerk for the purpose of display a certified copy of the instance and crave of the initial writ and the warrant of citation.[72] He also lodges with the sheriff clerk a service copy of the initial writ and a copy of the warrant of citation, which the defender may uplift from the sheriff clerk.[73]

6.36 **Address known after citation.** If a defender has been cited by newspaper advertisement or by display on the walls of court and after the cause has commenced his address becomes known, the sheriff may allow the initial writ to be amended subject to such conditions as to re-service, intimation, expenses, or transfer of the cause as the sheriff thinks fit.[74]

Citation of particular parties

6.37 The following are rules as to the citation of certain parties. Other rules as to special classes of parties are contained in Chapter 4.

6.38 **Lord Advocate.** The Lord Advocate is cited at the Lord Advocate's Chambers, Crown Office, 25 Chambers Street, Edinburgh EH1 1LA.[75]

6.39 **Local authorities.** Any legal proceedings against a council or islands council are deemed to have been duly served on the council if served on the officer of the council appointed by it for that purpose.[76]

6.40 **Companies registered under the Companies Acts.** A document may be served on a company registered under the Companies Acts by leaving it at, or sending it by post to, the company's registered office.[77] Service may also be effected at a place of business of the company in certain situations.[78]

---

[71] OCR, r. 5.6(1).
[72] OCR, r. 5.6(5).
[73] OCR, r. 5.6(2).
[74] OCR, r. 5.6(3).
[75] See paras 4.66, 4.71.
[76] Local Government (Scotland) Act 1973, ss. 190 and 235(1), (3).
[77] Companies Act 1985, ss. 725(1) and 735(1)(a).
[78] OCR, r. 5.4(1)(b) (sheriff officer); and r. 5.7(1) (person carrying on business under trading or descriptive name), on which, see para. 6.43.

Oversea companies. An oversea company[79] which establishes a place of business in Great Britain[80] must within a month deliver to the Registrar of Companies for registration certain particulars, including the names and addresses of some one or more persons resident in Great Britain authorised to accept on behalf of the company service of process and any notices required to be served on it.[81] Any process or notice required to be served on the company is sufficiently served if addressed to any such person and left at or sent by post to that person's address as so delivered to the registrar.[82] If, however, the company has failed to deliver the name and address of any such person, or if all those whose names and addresses have been so delivered are dead or have ceased to reside in Great Britain or refuse to accept service on the company's behalf or for any reason cannot be served, a document may be served on the company by leaving it at, or sending it by post to, any place of business established by the company in Great Britain.[83] **6.41**

Other corporations. Special provisions as to the mode of citation of other corporations may be made in the statutes under which they were created. **6.42**

Persons carrying on a business under a trading or descriptive name. Any person[84] or persons carrying on a business under a trading or descriptive name may be sued in such trading or descriptive name alone.[85] The initial writ may be served at any place of business or office at which such business is carried on within the sheriffdom of the sheriff court in which the cause is brought. In the event of there being no place of business within that sheriffdom, service may be effected at any place where such business is carried on, including the place of business or office of the clerk or secretary of any company, corporation or association or firm.[86] **6.43**

Friendly societies. The service of proceedings brought against a friendly society is regulated by statute.[87] **6.44**

Certificate of citation

When citation is executed, a certificate of citation is annexed to the initial writ.[88] It may be, and usually is, a form partly printed and partly written or typewritten.[89] It must be in Form O6 in Appendix 1 to the Rules, except in family actions or actions of multiplepoinding.[90] Form O6 is in these terms: **6.45**

---

[79] Defined by s. 744 of the Companies Act 1985.

[80] *South India Shipping Corporation v. Export-Import Bank of Korea* [1985] 1 W.L.R. 585.

[81] Companies Act 1985, s. 691(1)(b)(ii).

[82] *ibid.* s. 695(1).

[83] *ibid.* s. 695(2).

[84] "Person" includes company, corporation, or association and firm of any description nominate or descriptive, or any Board corporate or unincorporate: 1907 Act, s. 3(e).

[85] OCR, r. 5.7(1).

[86] OCR, r. 5.7(2).

[87] Friendly Societies Act 1974, s. 103.

[88] OCR, r. 5.2(3).

[89] *Hunter* (1908) 15 S.L.T. 716.

[90] OCR, r. 5.2(3). In a family action the certificate is in Form F16; and in an action of multiplepoinding, it is in Form F3.

[*Insert place and date*] I, hereby certify that upon the day of I duly cited [C.D.], Defender, to answer to the foregoing writ. This I did by (*state method of service; if by officer and not by post, add:* in presence of [L.M.] [*insert designation*], witness hereto with me subscribing; *and where service executed by post, state whether by registered post or first class recorded delivery service*).

Signed
[P.Q.], Sheriff officer,
[L.M.], Witness;
or
[X.Y.] (*add designation and business address*),
Solicitor for the pursuer

In the case of postal service, the certificate has attached to it any relevant postal receipts.[91] The certificate should not be signed by a trainee solicitor[92]; and one solicitor should not sign a certificate on behalf of another.[93] The requirements of rule 5.2 as to the contents of the certificate when citation, other than postal citation, is by sheriff officer have already been noted.[94]

Objections to execution of citation

6.46 A party who appears may not state any objection to the regularity of the service upon himself, and his appearance remedies any defect in the service.[95] It should be noted that "appearance" means lodging a notice of intention to defend.[96] Where a defender who has not appeared wishes to challenge a decree which has been taken in absence, it may be necessary for him to set aside the certificate of citation, because as a general rule a certificate which is *ex facie* regular is normally accepted as correct and conclusive until it is successfully challenged by reduction or by exception where that method is available.[97] It appears[98] that such a challenge may be unnecessary not only where the objection is patent on the face of the certificate[99] but also where it is instantly verifiable[1] or, perhaps, where it is agreed that citation was not validly effected.[2]

RE-SERVICE

6.47 If it appears to the sheriff that there has been any failure or irregularity in service upon a defender, he may authorise the pursuer to re-serve the initial writ upon such conditions as the sheriff thinks fit.[3] The authorisation of re-service is usually preferable to the dismissal of the action.[4] Re-service may only be ordered by the sheriff before the case has reached the stage of final decree.[5]

---

[91] OCR, r. 5.3(4).
[92] *Wilson* (1885) 13 R. 342.
[93] *Tait v. Johnston* (1891) 18 R. 606.
[94] para. 6.28.
[95] OCR, r. 5.10(1): see paras 6.04, 6.09.
[96] *Cairney v. Bulloch*, 1994 S.L.T. (Sh. Ct.) 37; 1993 S.C.L.R. 901.
[97] *Stewart v. Macdonald* (1860) 22 D. 1514, *per* L.J.-C. Inglis at 1522; *Tait v. Johnston* (1891) 18 R. 606; *Gibson v. Clark* (1895) 23 R. 294; *Reid v. Clark*, 1914 2 S.L.T. 68 at 70; *John G. Kincaid & Co. v. Taggart*, 1974 S.C. 15; *Boslem v. Paterson*, 1982 S.L.T. 216.
[98] *Reid, supra.*
[99] *Kirkonnel v. Barnbarroch* (1628) Mor. 3682.
[1] *Boslem, supra* (defender dead at date of citation).
[2] *cf. McAllister v. H.M. Advocate*, 1985 S.L.T. 399; *Welsh v. H.M. Advocate*, 1986 S.L.T. 664.
[3] OCR, r. 5.9.
[4] *Johnston v. Johnston*, 1965 S.L.T. (Sh. Ct.) 29.
[5] *Black v. Black*, 1990 S.C.L.R. 433.

Chapter 7

PROCEDURE WHERE ACTION UNDEFENDED

This chapter considers the procedure in undefended ordinary actions other than those in which the sheriff may not grant decree without evidence.[1] The pursuer in such an action, like any other pursuer, cannot force the defender to appear in the process; and if he does not, the pursuer's only remedy is to take a decree in absence[2] for whatever it may be worth.[3] The defender may apply to be reponed against such a decree. The following paragraphs deal with the procedure in applying for and granting a decree in absence, and with its effect; the procedure in relation to an application for a time to pay direction under the Debtors (Scotland) Act 1987; amendment in undefended actions; and the procedure with regard to reponing. **7.01**

Decree where liability undisputed

Response to service: time to pay

If a defender in an ordinary action chooses not to respond timeously in any way to service of the initial writ upon him, then he will have no further opportunity (before decree in absence is sought) to state his position in regard to the matters raised unless he later seeks to be allowed to lodge a late notice of intention to defend.[4] After decree has passed, the defender may appeal, or seek to be reponed, or to suspend (by process in the Court of Session) the operation of any diligence on a decree, pending its reduction.[5] But a defender need not lodge a notice of intention to defend if the action is one to which the provisions of the Debtors (Scotland) Act 1987 apply and all that he seeks is an order for time to pay.[6] In the latter case he may apply for a time to pay direction and, where appropriate, to have any arrestment used on the dependence of the action recalled or restricted.[7] **7.02**

Applications for time to pay directions

A defender in a cause which is otherwise undefended may, in a case covered by the provisions of the 1987 Act, apply for time to pay (or to recall or restrict an arrestment) by completing and lodging with the sheriff clerk the appropriate part of Form O3 before the expiry of the period of **7.03**

---

[1] The numerically largest class of undefended actions necessitating the consideration of evidence by the court are undefended family actions: see Chap. 22. It has been doubted whether it is competent to grant decree in absence in an action of rectification proceeding under the provisions of s. 8 of the Law Reform (Miscellaneous Provisions) (Scotland) Act 1985: see *Belhaven Brewery Co. Ltd v. Swift*, 1996 S.L.T. (Sh. Ct.) 127.

[2] The term "decree in absence" means absence from the process: *Miller v. Chapelside Chemical Co.* (1887) 3 Sh.Ct.Rep. 83.

[3] *Drummond's Trs v. Peel's Trs*, 1929 S.C. 484, *per* Lord Morison at 516.

[4] See para. 7.14.

[5] On the finality and effect of decree, see paras 7.18 to 7.19.

[6] OCR, r. 7.3(1),(2).

[7] *ibid.*

notice.[8] As previously noted,[9] in cases where such an application is competent, citation of the defender will have been in Form O5; and along with the citation, initial writ, and notice of intention to defend, there will have been served on the defender a notice in Form O3 telling the defender how to apply for time to pay. Part of Form O3 contains the form of application. Where the pursuer does not object to the application, he minutes for decree in accordance with the normal rule,[10] and the sheriff may grant decree or other order in terms of the application and minute.[11] But where the pursuer does object to the application, he likewise minutes for decree making his opposition clear: thereafter the sheriff clerk must fix a hearing on the application and intimate the hearing to both parties.[12] At the hearing the sheriff may determine the application whether or not any of the parties appear.[13]

Normal rule

7.04 If the defender (i) does not lodge a notice of intention to defend, (ii) does not (in an appropriate case) lodge an application for a time to pay direction under the 1987 Act, (iii) has lodged such an application for a time to pay direction and the pursuer does not object to the application or to any recall or restriction of an arrestment sought in the application, the sheriff may, on the pursuer endorsing a minute for decree on the initial writ, at any time after the expiry of the period for lodging that notice or application, grant decree in absence or other order in terms of the minute so endorsed (and any application) without requiring the attendance of the pursuer in court.[14] On granting decree in absence or thereafter the sheriff may grant decree for expenses.[15] In the sheriff court, accordingly, the pursuer may apply for decree in absence only if the defender has not lodged a notice of intention to defend: if he lodges such a notice but thereafter fails to lodge defences, the pursuer may apply for decree by default.[16] In the Court of Session, on the other hand, the pursuer may apply for decree in absence if the defender fails to enter appearance or if, having duly entered appearance, he fails to lodge defences[17]; and a decree by default may be pronounced only after the lodging of defences.[18]

Minute for decree

Procedure

7.05 Upon the expiry of the period for lodging the notice of intention to defend or (where appropriate) an application for a time to pay direction, the sheriff clerk completes and signs a certificate, on a printed form

---

[8] OCR, r. 7.3(2).
[9] See Chap. 6.
[10] See para. 7.04.
[11] OCR, r. 7.3(3).
[12] *ibid.* r. 7.3(4).
[13] *ibid.* r. 7.3(5).
[14] *ibid.* r. 7.2(1). The rule does not apply to causes in which decree may not be granted without evidence, or to an undefended family action for an order under s. 11 of the Children (Scotland) Act 1995 to which r. 33.31 applies: r. 7.2(2)(b). Nor can it be invoked in a case in which service has been effected in a country to which the Hague Convention on the Service Abroad of Judicial and Extrajudicial documents in Civil and Commercial Matters applies: OCR, r. 7.2(2)(b)(ii) and (4).
[15] OCR, r. 7.4.
[16] See paras 14.02 to 14.14 on decree by default.
[17] RCS, r. 19.1; Maxwell, pp. 248–250.
[18] Maxwell, p. 250. The difference in practice between the two courts seems difficult to justify.

attached to the initial writ, that no such notice or application has been lodged. On the same form the pursuer or his solicitor thereafter endorses a minute craving decree or such other order as is required.

Time

Although the defender is obliged to send to the pursuer a copy of his notice of intention to defend at the same time as he lodges the principal notice with the sheriff clerk,[19] it is prudent for the pursuer's solicitor to ascertain from the sheriff clerk's office, immediately on the expiry of the period for lodging a notice, whether one has in fact been lodged; and if none has been lodged, to complete the minute for decree with the least possible delay. Since the case does not require to be called in court,[20] the pursuer need not await a sitting of the court but may endorse the minute "at any time" after the expiry of the period of notice.[21] Any delay gives the defender an opportunity to lodge a notice late, in the hope that his motion for it to be received will be unopposed.[22] If an arrestment on the dependence has been used prior to service it will fall unless the action is served within 20 days from the date of arrestment, and decree in absence is pronounced within 20 days after the expiry of the period of notice.[23] In any event, the minute must be endorsed within a year and a day of the last day of the period of notice, otherwise the action will fall.[24] **7.06**

Restriction of crave

If the pursuer wishes to restrict the crave of the writ, he may do so either in the minute craving decree in absence, or in a separate minute. It is not usually necessary for a restriction of the crave to be intimated to the defender, or for the writ to be re-served. A restriction which has the effect of making the action appropriate for summary cause procedure may have a bearing on the expenses to be awarded unless it is made because the defender has made a payment after service of the action. Where the defender has paid the principal sum after service, the pursuer may restrict the crave to one for expenses only. Where the defender has made a payment to account after service, and interest is craved from a date earlier than the date of decree, it is thought that the pursuer should specify in his minute the interest which he seeks. The widely followed style which seeks "decree as craved less £x paid to account" is not specific as to interest. It is recommended that the pursuer should make clear what is required, *e.g.* by minuting for decree "under deduction of £x and the relative interest from this date" (*i.e.* the date of the minute). It is thus evident that the pursuer seeks decree for payment of the sum sued for less £x, with interest at the rate sued for on the sum sued for from the date specified in the crave until the day before the date of the minute, and on the sum sued for less £x from the date of the minute until payment. **7.07**

---

[19] See paras 8.04 to 8.06.

[20] OCR, r. 7.2(1). If it is called in court, it is not thereby deprived of the characteristics of an "undefended cause" within the meaning of the Rules: *Terry v. Murray*, 1947 S.C. 10, *per* L.J.-C. Cooper at 12.

[21] *Belfrage v. Blyth* (1910) 24 Sh.Ct.Rep. 295.

[22] See para. 7.14.

[23] OCR, r. 6.2(1).

[24] *McKidd v. Manson* (1882) 9 R. 790; *Belfrage, supra*; *Hillhead Garage Ltd v. Bunten & Miller* (1924) 40 Sh.Ct.Rep. 208; *Hughes v. Scott* (1940) 56 Sh.Ct.Rep. 176; *McCulloch v. McCulloch*, 1990 S.L.T. (Sh.Ct.) 63, 1990 S.C.L.R. 155; *Royal Bank of Scotland v. Mason*, 1994 S.C.L.R. 558; *Cringean v. McNeil*, 1996 S.L.T. (Sh. Ct.) 137.

Alternative craves[25]

7.08 Where the writ states alternative craves, the minute must specify the crave on which decree is desired. In the normal case the pursuer should minute for an order in terms of the primary crave and, if that is not implemented, should thereafter minute for decree in terms of the alternative crave. Thus, in an action craving (1) delivery and (2) failing delivery, payment, the sheriff may order the defender to deliver as craved within a specified period, under certification that on his failure to do so decree will be pronounced in terms of the alternative crave. That interlocutor is intimated to the defender and, if he does not duly implement its terms, the pursuer may minute for decree in terms of the alternative crave, narrating in his minute that the defender has failed to obtemper the order, and the sheriff may grant decree in terms of the alternative crave.[26] Upon the grant of decree in terms of the alternative crave the pursuer is personally barred from enforcing the decree in terms of the primary crave.[27]

Several defenders

7.09 Where two or more defenders are sued jointly and severally, and only some of them lodge notices of intention to defend, the pursuer may minute for decree in absence against the non-compearing defender or defenders and continue the action against the compearing defenders unless he receives satisfaction from the non-compearing defender or defenders.[28] The sheriff should not hold the non-compearing defender as confessed without granting decree in absence: the expression "holds as confessed" is best avoided in this context.[29] The sheriff may, however, after hearing parties refuse to grant decree in absence *in hoc statu* if to do so might prove inequitable and result in prejudice to any of the other defenders.[30]

Expenses

7.10 The pursuer usually seeks decree for expenses in the minute by which he seeks decree in absence.[31] He may seek expenses as taxed by the auditor of court[32]; but usually he elects to crave the appropriate inclusive fee and outlays, and taxation is then unnecessary.[33]

Granting of decree

Procedure

7.11 The decree is already partly printed on the same form as that which contains the sheriff clerk's certificate and the minute for decree.[34] When the minute for decree is endorsed, the sheriff clerk drafts the terms of the decree

---

[25] See para. 9.86.

[26] See, *e.g. Wilkinson v. Wilkinson* (1963) Sh.Ct.Rep. 47; Dobie, *Styles*, pp. 321–322.

[27] *Bosco Design Services Ltd v. Plastic Sealant Services Ltd*, 1979 S.C. 189.

[28] *Royal Bank of Scotland v. McKerracher*, 1968 S.L.T. (Sh. Ct.) 77; *Hamilton Leasing Ltd v. Clark*, 1974 S.L.T. (Sh. Ct.) 95.

[29] *Squire Light and Sound Ltd v. Vidicom Systems Ltd*, 1987 S.C.L.R. 538. The decree used to proceed on the confession of the justice of the pursuer's claim which was inferred from the defender's failure to appear: see Trayner, pp. 481–482.

[30] *Morrison v. Somerville* (1860) 22 D. 1082; *Symington, Son & Co. Ltd v. Larne Shipbuilding Co. Ltd*, 1911 2 S.L.T. 32.

[31] OCR, r. 7.4.

[32] If so, no formal remit to the auditor is required, although in practice this is often done.

[33] A.S. (Fees of Solicitors in the Sheriff Court) 1993, Sched., Table of Fees, Chap. 1, Pt 1, para. 1.

[34] See para. 7.04.

(including, if appropriate, the terms of any time to pay direction) and places the writ before the sheriff. Where, however, a solicitor sues for payment of a professional account and the action is undefended, the sheriff should remit the account to the auditor of court for taxation, and the solicitor should thereafter seek decree for the amount of the taxed account.[35]

Powers of sheriff

As indicated, the foregoing procedure applies only in cases where decree may be granted without evidence; and it does not apply to an undefended family action for an order under s. 11 of the Children (Scotland) Act 1995.[36] Several other constraints on the power of the sheriff to grant decree in absence are imposed by rules enacted in consequence of the Civil Jurisdiction and Judgments Act 1982. **7.12**

(i) The sheriff must not grant decree unless it appears *ex facie* of the initial writ that a ground of jurisdiction exists under the Civil Jurisdiction and Judgments Act 1982.[37] If, after hearing the pursuer's solicitor and considering any motion for amendment and re-service, the sheriff is not satisfied that the writ discloses such a ground of jurisdiction, he should dismiss the action.

(ii) In the case of a defender domiciled in another part of the United Kingdom[38] or in another Contracting State,[39] the sheriff must not grant decree in absence until it has been shown that the defender has been able to receive the initial writ in sufficient time to arrange for his defence or that all necessary steps have been taken to that end.[40] It is thought that where the sheriff is not satisfied as to those matters he may continue consideration of the minute for decree in order to enable the pursuer's solicitor to obtain further information.

(iii) Where an initial writ has been served in a country to which the Hague Convention on the Service Abroad of Judicial and Extra-Judicial Documents in Civil or Commercial Matters dated November 15, 1965, applies, decree cannot be granted until it is established to the satisfaction of the sheriff that the requirements of Article 15 of that Convention have been complied with.[41] The terms of Article 15 of the Hague Convention have already been noted.[42] The effect of the rule is that the sheriff may grant decree in absence where he is satisfied either that service was effected under rule 5.5(1)(b)(i) of the Ordinary Cause Rules; or that service was effected under rule 5.5(1)(b)(ii), (iii), (iv) or (v) and the writ was actually delivered to the defender or to his residence; or that the conditions referred to in a declaration made in terms of Article 15 have been fulfilled. Here again, it may be appropriate to continue consideration of the minute in order to give the pursuer's solicitor an opportunity to provide further information.

Before signing the decree the sheriff may take notice of other matters which are *pars judicis*, including whether the subject-matter of the action **7.13**

---

[35] See discussion of this matter in paras 21.72 to 21.74.

[36] OCR, r. 7.2(2)(b)(iii).

[37] *ibid.* r. 7.2(2)(a).

[38] The question whether a person is domiciled in another part of the United Kingdom is determined in accordance with ss. 41 and 42 of the 1982 Act: OCR, r. 7.2(3)(a); see paras 3.07 to 3.09.

[39] The question whether a person is domiciled in another Contracting State is determined in accordance with the 1982 Act, Sched. 1 or 3C, Art. 52: OCR, r. 7.2(3)(b); see para. 3.10. "Contracting State" has the meaning assigned to it by the 1982 Act, s. 1: OCR, r. 7.2(3)(c); see para. 3.03.

[40] OCR, r. 7.2(3): see para. 3.58.

[41] *ibid.* r. 7.2(4).

[42] See para. 3.56.

and the remedy sought are within the jurisdiction of the court, whether the defender has been validly cited, and other matters of competency.[43] If he pronounces decree, however, he does not imply a judgment in favour of the competency of the action.[44] He is not entitled to dismiss the action on the ground of irrelevancy.[45] Nor may he *ex proprio motu* grant decree for any sum less than that minuted for by the pursuer.[46] If he is minded to refuse decree in the terms minuted for, he should give the pursuer's solicitor an opportunity to be heard.

Late notice of intention to defend[47]

7.14 It sometimes happens that the defender lodges a notice of intention to defend out of time, between the expiry of the period of notice and the time when the writ is to be placed before the sheriff for signature of the decree. If the pursuer's solicitor has already docqueted the notice to the effect that he has no objection to its being lodged late, or if the defender has also lodged a motion craving the court to allow the notice to be received late, to which motion the pursuer's solicitor has consented or has not lodged a notice of opposition,[48] the sheriff clerk should ascertain from the sheriff whether he nonetheless wishes to hear parties. If he does not, the clerk should prepare an interlocutor allowing the notice to be received late and place this before the sheriff in chambers for signature.[49] If neither of these procedures has been followed, the sheriff clerk should ascertain from the pursuer's solicitor whether he has any objection to the notice being lodged late and, if he has, should arrange an early diet for a hearing before the sheriff on a motion by the defender to allow the notice to be received late.[50]

Form of decree

7.15 It is recommended that the common style, "Grants decree as craved together with £x of expenses" should be avoided in anything other than the simplest action for payment. In other cases it may cause doubt, confusion and further expensive procedure.[51] It is at least desirable that the order of the court should be clearly expressed in the interlocutor; and in actions of interdict the precise terms of the interdict granted must appear *ad longum* in the interlocutor.[52]

Extract of decree

7.16 The date of the decree in absence would now appear to be the date of the interlocutor containing that decree.[53] The sheriff clerk may issue an extract of the decree on the expiry of 14 days following the granting of

---

[43] See paras 2.09 to 2.17.

[44] *Hopkinson Ltd v. McGrory*, Acting Sh. Pr. (later Lord) Walker, Glasgow Sh. Ct, Apr. 1952, unreported, *cit. George Hopkinson Ltd v. Carr*, 1955 S.L.T. (Sh. Ct.) 80.

[45] *Cadbury Bros Ltd v. T. Mabon Ltd*, 1962 S.L.T. (Sh. Ct.) 28; *United Dominions Trust v. McDowell*, 1984 S.L.T. (Sh. Ct.) 10 at 14–15.

[46] *Terry v. Murray*, 1947 S.C.10, overruled as to actions for aliment by Family Law (Scotland) Act 1985, s. 3(1)(d).

[47] See paras 8.01 *et seq.*

[48] See para. 8.05.

[49] *ibid.*

[50] *ibid.*

[51] *Project Contract Services Ltd v. Fraoli*, 1980 S.C. 261; *Nelson v. Dowden*, Sh. Pr. Dick, Glasgow Sh. Ct, Oct. 20, 1981, unreported (decree for custody and interdict).

[52] *Pirie & Sons v. Earl of Kintore* (1906) 8 F. (H.L.) 16, *per* Earl of Halsbury L.C. at 18; *Nelson, supra.*

[53] See discussion regarding the dates of interlocutors in para. 5.75.

the decree,[54] but the sheriff may on cause shown order the extract to be issued at an earlier date.[55] The words "in absence" should be inserted in the extract.[56] The lodging of a reponing note[57] does not appear to prevent the issue of extract, but a reponing note when duly lodged and served on the pursuer has effect to sist diligence.[58]

Where decree in absence has been granted against the Crown, the decree is not operative without the leave of the court, obtained on an application of which notice has been given to the Crown.[59] 7.17

Finality and effect of decree

A decree in absence which has not been recalled, or brought under review by suspension or by reduction, becomes final, and is entitled to all the privileges of a decree *in foro*: (a) on the expiry of six months from its date or from the date of a charge under it, where the service of the initial writ or of the charge has been personal; (b) in any event, on the expiry of 20 years from its date.[60] 7.18

A decree in absence differs from a decree *in foro* in that the defender may be reponed against a decree in absence[61]; and a decree in absence cannot support a plea of *res judicata*.[62] A decree in absence does not imply an admission by the defender of the pursuer's claim,[63] and the extract is in the general case only competent evidence of the facts that the defender was absent from the process and that that decree was pronounced.[64] Nor can the decree be regarded as embodying a judgment in favour of the competency of the action.[65] Both a decree in absence and a decree *in foro* may in various circumstances be brought under review by appeal, suspension or reduction,[66] but not by judicial review.[67] 7.19

Amendment

The sheriff has the same power to allow amendment in undefended actions as he has in defended actions. In an undefended action he may 7.20

---

[54] OCR, r. 30.4(1)(a). But where the sheriff has, in pronouncing decree, reserved any question of expenses, extract of that decree may be issued only after the expiry of 14 days from the date of the interlocutor disposing of the question of expenses unless the sheriff otherwise directs: r. 30.4(c).

[55] *ibid.* r. 30.4(2).

[56] Sheriff Courts (Scotland) Extracts Act 1892, Sched., para. 1.

[57] See paras 7.23 *et seq.*

[58] OCR, r. 8.1(4).

[59] Crown Proceedings Act 1947, s. 35(2)(a). On proceedings by and against the Crown, see paras 4.52 to 4.81.

[60] OCR, r. 7.5. The rule does not apply to a decree in an action of removing brought by a lessor against a lessee under s. 9 of the Land Tenure Reform (Scotland) Act 1974: see s. 9(7).

[61] On reponing generally, see paras 7.23 *et seq.*

[62] See para. 2.106; *Gibson & Simpson v. Pearson*, 1992 S.L.T. 894; 1992 S.C.L.R. 771.

[63] *Mackintosh v. Smith and Lowe* (1864) 2 M. 1261, *per* L.P. McNeill at 1264 (affd 3 M. (H.L.) 6); *William Bain & Co. (Joinery) Ltd v. Gilbert Ash (Scotland) Ltd*, Sh. Pr. Dick, Glasgow Sh. Ct, Jan. 28, 1982, unreported.

[64] *William Bain & Co. (Joinery) Ltd, supra*; W.J. Lewis, *Manual of the Law of Evidence in Scotland* (1925), p. 72.

[65] *Hopkinson Ltd v. McGrory*, Acting Sh. Pr. (later Lord) Walker, Glasgow Sh. Ct, Apr. 1952, unreported, *cit. George Hopkinson Ltd v. Carr*, 1955 S.L.T. (Sh. Ct.) 80.

[66] Walker, *Civil Remedies*, pp. 207–209. See also *Johnstone & Clark (Engineers) Ltd v. Lockhart*, 1995 S.L.T. 440.

[67] *Bell v. Fiddes*, 1996 S.L.T. 51.

allow the pursuer to amend the initial writ in any way permitted by rule 18(2) of the Ordinary Cause Rules,[68] which regulates his powers in relation to the amendment of pleadings in defended actions.[69] The relative motion does not require to be intimated. The sheriff may order the amended initial writ to be re-served on the defender on such period of notice as he thinks fit.[70] But he may dispense with re-service where the amendment clearly causes no prejudice to the defender: as where its purpose is to amend an immaterial clerical error; or to reduce the sum sued for and amend the condescendence accordingly; or to alter the defender's address in the instance to that at which the writ has been validly served by sheriff officer. In any other case, however, re-service is appropriate; and it is to be noted that an apparently small amendment, for example in a party's name,[71] may have serious consequences. The defender is not liable for the expense occasioned by the amendment of the initial writ unless the sheriff so orders.[72]

7.21 Amendment of the initial writ in an undefended action does not have the effect of validating diligence used on the dependence of the action so as to prejudice creditors of the party against whom the diligence has been executed who are interested in defeating such diligence.[73] Thus, no amendment has the effect of making a diligence used on the dependence good, so as to give the pursuer a preference over other creditors.[74] Amendment does, however, preclude any objection to diligence used on the dependence when stated by a party or by any person by virtue of a title acquired or in right of a debt contracted by him subsequent to the execution of such diligence.[75] Objections by a person representing the defender by a title are thought to be obviated only if his title is subsequent in date to the execution of the diligence.[76]

7.22 Rule 27(3) of the Ordinary Cause Rules 1983, which provided that any diligence which was competent on the original initial writ would be competent on an amended writ has been repealed and not re-enacted in the Ordinary Cause Rules 1993, no doubt because its meaning was unclear. Arrestments on an incompetent writ are invalid: if it is amended so as to become competent, new arrestments should be used after amendment.[77]

Reponing: general

Initial procedure

7.23 Where decree in absence[78] has been pronounced, the defender may apply to be reponed.[79] He does so by lodging with the sheriff clerk a note setting out

---

[68] OCR, r. 7.6(1)(a).
[69] See Chap. 10.
[70] OCR, r. 7.6(1)(b).
[71] See para. 9.78.
[72] OCR, r. 7.6(2).
[73] *ibid.* r. 7.6(3)(a).
[74] *Fischer & Co. v. Andersen* (1896) 23 R. 395, *per* Lord Young at 397.
[75] OCR, r. 7.6(3)(b).
[76] Dobie, p. 239.
[77] *Fischer & Co., supra, per* Lord Young at 398.
[78] Where a notice of intention to defend has been lodged, reponing is incompetent: *Stewart v. Lothians Construction (Edinburgh) Ltd*, 1972 S.L.T. (Notes) 75.
[79] *i.e.* to be placed in the position he would have occupied if he had acted timeously and the decree had not been granted.

his proposed defence and explaining his failure to appear (a "reponing note")[80]; and by serving a copy of the note on the pursuer.[81] He no longer requires to consign any funds in the hands of the sheriff clerk. When the reponing note is lodged, the sheriff pronounces an interlocutor ordering service of the note on the pursuer and appointing a diet for hearing parties.[82]

Applicant

Although the rules refer only to an application by the defender, a party other than the defender, who is entitled to be sisted as a party to the action, may apply to be reponed.[83] Thus, a defender's executrix,[84] a trustee for a defender's creditors,[85] and a former partner of the defenders' firm[86] have been reponed. In the following paragraphs the applicant is referred to as "the defender". **7.24**

When competent

Reponing is competent in any undefended cause other than those mentioned in rule 33.1(1)(a) to (h)[87] of the Ordinary Cause Rules 1993, or a cause to which Chapter 37[88] thereof applies.[89] Where it is competent, the defender may apply to be reponed at any time before implement in full of the decree in absence.[90] The decree must not have become final,[91] because the sheriff cannot repone the defender against a decree *in foro*.[92] A long delay between the date of the decree and the lodging of the reponing note is not in itself fatal to the application,[93] but, if the defender has been aware of the decree for a considerable time before he lodges the note, the sheriff may scrutinise with particular care his explanation of his failure to appear.[94] **7.25**

The defender cannot be reponed if the decree has been implemented "in full". It is thought that the decree is implemented in full where the pursuer has obtained all that he was awarded under the decree, whether by the voluntary act of the defender or by the use of diligence by the pursuer,[95] or where the pursuer has secured it by a poinding. If by such means the pursuer has recovered or secured part of what has been decerned for, the defender **7.26**

---

[80] OCR, r. 8.1(1). For a style of a reponing note, see Bennett, *Style Writs in the Sheriff Court* (1988), p. 110. That style was drafted before abolition of the rule that a defender seeking to be reponed is required to lodge caution.

[81] OCR, r. 8.1(2).

[82] It seems anomalous that the procedure for recall of a decree in absence is much more strict in the sheriff court than in the Court of Session where, in general, the decree is recalled automatically if within 7 days the defender merely enrols for recall and for defences to be received and pays the pursuer £25; see RCS, r. 19.2.

[83] *Pearson & Jackson v. Alison* (1871) 9 M. 473; *cf. Ross v. Ross* (1901) 2 S.L.T. 117.

[84] *Pearson & Jackson, supra.*

[85] *Barrie v. Hosie* (1933) 49 Sh.Ct.Rep. 114; *LNE Ry v. Reid Bros* (1944) 61 Sh.Ct.Rep. 22. *Cf. Primrose Thomson & Co. v. Crawford* (1911) 29 Sh.Ct.Rep. 243.

[86] *British Anchor Pottery Co. Ltd v. Cowan & Co.* (1950) 66 Sh.Ct.Rep. 279.

[87] Certain family actions.

[88] Causes under the Presumption of Death (Scotland) Act 1977.

[89] OCR, r. 8.1(1).

[90] *ibid.*

[91] As to when a decree in absence becomes final, see paras 7.18 to 7.19.

[92] *West v. Hair* (1926) 43 Sh.Ct.Rep. 118.

[93] In *Davidson v. Anderson*, 1921 S.C. 369, a decree in absence pronounced in 1908 was recalled in 1920.

[94] *Smart v. Miller*, 1966 S.L.T. (Sh. Ct.) 80.

[95] Dobie, p. 137.

can be reponed against the decree only *quoad* that which has not been recovered or secured, and the sheriff in such a case may recall the decree "so far as not implemented".[96] Thus, where a poinding has been executed, although it has not been reported or followed by a sale, the decree is implemented, so that a reponing note is incompetent to the extent to which the poinded goods satisfy the decree.[97] An arrestment which has not been followed by a decree of furthcoming does not, however, bar reponing.[98]

Effect on diligence

7.27 A reponing note, when duly lodged and served on the pursuer, has effect to sist diligence,[99] but does not recall it. Thus, an arrestment on the dependence stands[1]; and where a poinding has been executed, it is effective *quoad* the goods poinded, and the lodging of the reponing note cannot prevent the sheriff from granting a warrant of sale.[2]

Disposal of reponing note

Hearing

7.28 The sheriff hears parties on the reponing note at the diet fixed in the interlocutor pronounced on the lodging of the note.[3] If the pursuer opposes the application, or if the sheriff is in doubt as to any matter stated in the note, the defender may amplify or explain its terms.[4] It has also been held that a reponing note may be amended[5] and that if an error is discovered in a reponing note, a fresh or substitute note may be lodged.[6] But amendment or substitution of a note is not to be encouraged; on the contrary, since a defender seeking to be reponed comes to the court as a supplicant and since reponing is entirely within the discretion of the sheriff,[7] the defender's case must be carefully prepared. Documents in support of it,[8] and the proposed defences themselves,[9] may be lodged and considered by the sheriff. Even if the defender does not appear, however, the sheriff must consider the terms of the reponing note and exercise his discretion before granting or refusing it.[10] In highly exceptional circum-

---

[96] OCR, r. 8.1(3).

[97] *Stephenson & Co. v. Dobbins and Bibby* (1852) 14 D. 510; *Anderson v. Anderson* (1855) 17 D. 804; *Rowan v. Mercer* (1863) 4 Irv. 377; *McNiven v. Orr* (1905) 22 Sh.Ct.Rep. 9; *M.H. Credit Corp. Ltd v. Gill*, Sh. Pr. O'Brien, Linlithgow Sh. Ct, Dec. 1983, unreported.

[98] *Paul v. Macrae* (1887) 3 Sh.Ct.Rep. 338.

[99] OCR, r. 8.1(4). An application for sequestration following upon a decree in absence is not a form of diligence: *G & A Barnie v. Stevenson*, 1993 S.C.L.R. 318. It is thought that if a reponing note is refused, the marking of an appeal against that refusal has no effect whatever on any diligence: see *Chris Hart (Business Sales) Ltd v. Campbell*, 1993 S.C.L.R. 383.

[1] Dobie, pp. 136–137.

[2] *M.H. Credit Corp., supra.*

[3] See paras 7.23 *et seq.*

[4] *Dixon Street Motors v. Associated Rentals Ltd*, 1980 S.L.T. (Sh. Ct.) 46; *Guardian Royal Exchange Group v. Moffat*, 1986 S.L.T. 262, *per* Sh. Pr. Dick at 264.

[5] This should be done by minute of amendment, but it appears that any amendment of substance may be allowed at first instance only if the sheriff is persuaded to use the general dispensing power (OCR, r. 2.1) on the assumption that the explanation for the default falls within its scope: *Risi v. Lennox Properties Ltd*, 1993 S.C.L.R. 227. See also *Ratty v. Hughes*, 1996 S.C.L.R. 160 where it was held that an amended reponing note will not be acceptable at appeal where it contains material that was not before the sheriff at first instance.

[6] *Johnston v. Dewart*, 1992 S.L.T. 286; 1991 S.C.L.R. 447.

[7] *Hoggan v. McKeachie*, 1960 S.C. 461 at 462; *Orr Pollock (Printers) Ltd v. Mulholland*, 1983 S.L.T. 558; *Guardian Royal Exchange Group, supra*, at 266.

[8] *Orr Pollock, supra.*

[9] *Biggart v. Wilson*, 1948 S.L.T. (Sh. Ct.) 26.

[10] *Orr Pollock, supra.*

stances, where the defender's explanation of his failure to appear involved disputed allegations of misrepresentation, a proof has been allowed[11] or contemplated.[12] Generally, however, the matter of reponing is decided on the terms of the note and any statements made or documents lodged at the hearing. "A proper and practical approach is to set out in the reponing note a full and clear explanation covering all factors in the defenders' conduct likely to influence the sheriff's decision on the note."[13]

Relevant issues

As to the matters on which the sheriff must be satisfied before granting the reponing note, the rule is entirely silent. The sheriff has a wide discretion: he "may, on considering the reponing note, recall the decree".[14] Accordingly, some of the earlier case law on reponing, which developed at a time when the rule was expressed in different terms, is of limited relevance today. In particular, it should be noted that it is no longer the law that only where a defender has demonstrated a reasonable excuse for failure to enter the process timeously is it necessary for the sheriff to consider whether he has a statable defence.[15] But since a reponing note must set out both the proposed defence and an explanation for the failure to appear, it is clear that the sheriff must consider both of these matters when considering the note as a whole.[16] **7.29**

Proposed defence. Rule 8(1) in its original form was introduced by the 1907 Act,[17] and it appears to have been assumed from an early date that the sheriff should consider the proposed defence[18] because it was set forth in the reponing note together with the explanation which the sheriff was required to consider.[19] But differing views have been expressed in the Inner House as to the extent to which the sheriff must scrutinise the proposed defence. In *Guardian Royal Exchange v. Moffat*[20] it was said that the grounds of defence stated in the reponing note must be examined against the background of the evidence proposed to be led in support of these grounds in a proof, and that that warranted the application of the tests of relevancy, proper specification and fair notice. But in *Consultants and Technologists North Sea Ltd v. Scott*,[21] where it was conceded that the defender must demonstrate the existence of a statable defence, and *Guardian Royal Exchange Group* was not cited, the court stated that it was wrong to look in a reponing note for the specification required in a debate on relevancy on a closed record, and approved dicta which had not **7.30**

---

[11] *Biggart, supra*; *Johnston v. Dewart, supra*.

[12] *Smart v. Miller*, 1966 S.L.T. (Sh. Ct.) 80.

[13] *Schroder Leasing Ltd v. Fraser*, Sh. Pr. Caplan, Paisley Sh. Ct, Apr. 25, 1986, unreported.

[14] OCR, r. 8.1(3); *Cozy Legs of Scotland v. Razno & Co. Ltd*, 1991 S.L.T. (Sh. Ct.) 52; *Banks v. Cruden Building*, 1992 S.C.L.R. 779; *Scottish Enterprise v. Southbank Glass Co. Ltd*, 1992 S.C.L.R. 785; *Forbes v. Johnstone*, 1995 S.C. 220; 1995 S.L.T. 158; 1995 S.C.L.R. 154.

[15] The previous rule was set out in *Rayment v. Jack*, 1988 S.L.T. 647, but was superseded in 1990 when the OCR 1983 were amended. See also *Forbes v. Johnstone, supra*, in which dicta in *McDonough v. Focus DIY Ltd*, 1994 S.L.T. 596 following *Rayment v. Jack* were disapproved and the case of *Mullen v. Harmac Ltd*, 1994 S.L.T. 926 was overruled.

[16] *Forbes v. Johnstone, supra*.

[17] 1907 Act, Sched. 1, rr. 29 and 30.

[18] Wallace, p. 135; *Fraser v. Savings Investment Trust Ltd* (1912) 28 Sh.Ct.Rep. 224.

[19] *Nisbet v. Macleod* (1923) 39 Sh.Ct.Rep. 248.

[20] 1986 S.L.T. 262.

[21] 1986 S.L.T. 685.

been cited in *Guardian Royal Exchange Group*. These dicta were to the effect that the court would be most reluctant, in any case in which prima facie there appeared to be a proper defence put forward, to allow decree to pass against the defender without investigation of the defence[22]; and that as a reponing note does not generally contain more than an outline of the defence, it should not be scrutinised too critically on the matter of relevancy.[23] It has been held that while the sheriff must consider the note before deciding whether or not to recall the decree, it is unlikely that a sheriff would exercise his discretion to recall it unless he was satisfied that the defence was a statable one.[24]

7.31 It is thought that the rules as to reponing could with advantage be restated, either in order to bring sheriff court practice back into line with that of the Court of Session, where the defender is entitled as of right to recall of the decree on timeous application and payment of a small sum to the pursuer,[25] or in order to give the sheriff express directions as to the consideration which ought to be given to the proposed defence. Under the present rule, however, the sheriff must give some consideration to the proposed defence, and it would appear to be inappropriate to grant a reponing note where the proposed defence, which the rule requires to be stated, is merely dilatory,[26] or clearly absurd,[27] or incontestably bad. As to the test to be applied to the proposed defence, it is respectfully submitted that *Consultants and Technologists North Sea Ltd* should be followed, since it is based on a consideration of authority and full argument on both sides.[28]

7.32 The question of the defence must be decided on the particular facts of each case. It has been held, however, that where the pursuer's claim is a liquid claim which the defender admits, and the proposed defence consists of a counterclaim which is illiquid, the reponing note should be refused, since if the action had proceeded as defended the pursuer could have moved for and obtained decree for the sum sued for.[29]

7.33 **Explanation of failure to appear.** The expression "failure to appear" refers to failure by the defender to lodge a notice of intention to defend which led to the decree in absence.[30] Sheriffs used to adopt a fairly strict approach to a defender's explanation of his failure to appear.[31] In modern practice, however, a failure caused by the defender's solicitor or some other person for whom he is responsible is unlikely to be held against him,[32] and even his own carelessness will not necessarily prevent him from being reponed.[33] The courts adopt a benevolent attitude to explanations, recognising that few of

---

[22] *McKelvie v. Scottish Steel Scaffolding Co.*, 1938 S.C. 278, *per* Lord Moncrieff at 281.

[23] *Nisbet, supra, per* Sh. Pr. Mackenzie at 250.

[24] *Forbes v. Johnstone, supra*, a decision of the Inner House.

[25] See *supra*, para. 7.23, n. 82. Sheriff court practice used to be similar (Sheriff Courts (Scotland) Acts 1853, s. 2; 1876, s. 14(1); see Dove Wilson, pp. 132–136); but the Grant Committee did not favour "automatic reponing" (Report, para. 738).

[26] *Wailes Dove Bitumatic Ltd v. Plastic Sealant Services Ltd*, 1979 S.L.T. (Sh. Ct.) 41.

[27] *Nisbet, supra, per* Sh. Pr. Mackenzie at 250.

[28] In *Guardian Royal Exchange Group, supra*, the citation of authority was incomplete and the defender was a party litigant.

[29] *Reiach v. Sinclair*, 1954 S.L.T. (Sh. Ct.) 71.

[30] *Schroder Leasing Ltd, supra.*

[31] *McColl v. McDonald*, 1933 S.L.T. (Sh. Ct.) 4 used to be frequently cited.

[32] *Graham v. Wylie & Lochhead Ltd*, Second Div., Feb. 17, 1949, unreported, *cit. Burke v. C. Alexander & Partners (Transport) Ltd* (1957) 73 Sh.Ct.Rep. 153 at 156–157.

[33] *McKelvie, supra.*

them justify the failure,[34] and are prepared to be satisfied with something less than a good or sound explanation.[35] While each case falls to be regarded on its own merits,[36] the defender must tender some explanation[37]; and the courts will not accept an explanation which demonstrates that the failure was due to a reckless indifference to,[38] or a deliberate disregard of,[39] the rules of procedure. And if the nature of the explanation and the nature of the defence, considered together, suggest that the defender's purpose is merely to delay the pronouncement of a decree against him, the reponing note will be refused.[40] It is not a requirement of the rules that the sheriff must be satisfied that the explanation provides a reasonable explanation for the non-appearance, and it might result in an injustice if a defender who had a perfectly sound defence were to be denied the opportunity of entering the process simply because the explanation for his non-appearance was not a reasonable one.[41]

Decision

Interlocutor. If the sheriff, following consideration of the note and having taken account of all the circumstances and balanced one consideration against another, decides to exercise his discretion in favour of the defender, he may recall the decree so far as not implemented subject to such order as to expenses as he thinks fit; and if he does so the case thereafter proceeds in all respects as if the defender had lodged a notice of intention to defend and the period of notice had expired on the date on which the decree in absence was recalled.[42] He normally pronounces an interlocutor in which he grants the reponing note, recalls the decree in absence so far as not implemented, appoints defences to be lodged within a specified time (or allows the defences tendered to be received), allows a period for adjustment, appoints an options hearing and makes orders as to expenses.[43] If the sheriff intends to attach a condition to a reponing, he should continue the application until after the period allowed for compliance with the condition, and only then grant or refuse the reponing.[44] If the sheriff is not satisfied that the defender should be reponed, he pronounces an interlocutor refusing the reponing note. 7.34

Expenses. On the disposal of the reponing note the sheriff may make such order as to expenses as he thinks fit.[45] If the decree in absence is 7.35

---

[34] *Neilson & Marshall, supra.*

[35] *Wailes Dove Bitumatic Ltd, supra.*

[36] *Graham, supra, per* L.J.-C. Thomson.

[37] *Wailes Dove, supra,* not following *Olsen v. Keddie,* 1976 S.L.T. (Sh. Ct.) 64. *Wailes Dove* was followed, and *Olsen* not followed, in *Ram v. Yadh,* Sh. Pr. Dick, Glasgow Sh. Ct, Mar. 5, 1982, unreported.

[38] *Purves v. Strathclyde Industrial Services,* Sh. Pr. Caplan, Dumbarton Sh. Ct, Oct. 21, 1983, unreported.

[39] *S. D. Ellison & Co. (Scotland) v. Asgher,* Sh. Pr. Caplan, Paisley Sh. Ct, Feb. 14, 1985, unreported.

[40] *Neilson & Marshall, supra; Purves, supra.*

[41] *Forbes v. Johnstone,* 1995 S.C. 220; 1995 S.L.T. 158; 1995 S.C.L.R. 154.

[42] OCR, r. 8.1(3).

[43] See para. 7.35.

[44] *Appleyard (Aberdeen) Ltd v. Morrison,* 1979 S.L.T. (Sh. Ct.) 65. The Ordinary Cause Rules do not themselves make any provision for attaching conditions to the allowance of a reponing note, and the competency of such a course may therefore be in some doubt.

[45] OCR, r. 8.1(3), which appears to be restricted to the situation where reponing is allowed. But where it is refused, the sheriff clearly has power at common law to award expenses against the reponer.

recalled, the decerniture for expenses which was pronounced in absence is recalled also. In some cases the question of expenses is not considered because the pursuer's solicitor omits to move for expenses. Where a motion is made, the sheriff sometimes finds the defender liable to the pursuer in the expenses of the action since the date of service. An order making payment of expenses by the defender a condition precedent to reponing should be pronounced only after careful consideration,[46] and consideration should be given to continuing the application to be reponed until after a period allowed for lodging of the account of expenses, taxation and report.[47]

Appeal

7.36 Any interlocutor or order recalling, or incidental to the recall of, a decree in absence, is final and not subject to review.[48] The sheriff cannot competently grant leave to appeal against such an interlocutor,[49] unless, perhaps, it contains an order which is open to appeal with leave.[50] It is possible that an appeal may be entertained against an incompetent interlocutor,[51] or one to which a condition has been adjected and not complied with, so that the interlocutor has become effective as a refusal to repone.[52]

7.37 An interlocutor refusing a reponing note may be appealed without leave to the sheriff principal[53] or to the Court of Session.[54] If the sheriff principal recalls the decree, his decision is final[55]: if he refuses to recall, there is an appeal to the Court of Session.[56] A reponing note has been amended for the purposes of an appeal,[57] but it has also been held (on a full examination of authority) that it is not appropriate to have regard on appeal to material which was not before the sheriff and that an amended reponing note would not be received on appeal.[58] Since the decision to refuse a reponing note is discretionary, an appellate court is entitled to override it only where the court below has erred in law, or taken into account an irrelevant factor, or left out of account a relevant factor, or if its decision was unreasonable or unjudicial.[59] A defender who succeeds in having a decree recalled on appeal, having failed to present his case fully to the sheriff, may be found liable in the expenses of the appeal.[60]

---

[46] See para. 11.89. Such orders were made in *Burke v. C. Alexander & Partners (Transport) Ltd* (1957) 73 Sh.Ct.Rep. 153, and *Olsen v. Keddie*, 1976 S.L.T. (Sh. Ct.) 64.

[47] *Appleyard (Aberdeen) Ltd, supra.* But see comment in n. 44.

[48] OCR, r. 8.1(5). See also *Manders v. Lacon Floors Ltd*, 1993 S.C.L.R. 311, in which it was held that that part of an interlocutor recalling a decree in absence which dealt with expenses was "incidental" to that recall and was thus final.

[49] *Mess v. Mutch* (1928) 45 Sh.Ct.Rep. 54.

[50] *Appleyard (Aberdeen) Ltd, supra.*

[51] See 18.12.

[52] *Appleyard (Aberdeen) Ltd, supra.*

[53] 1907 Act, s. 27(e). For a history of this provision, see *W. Jack Baillie Associates v. Kennedy*, 1985 S.L.T. (Sh. Ct.) 53 at 54–55.

[54] 1907 Act, s. 28(1)(c).

[55] OCR, r. 8.1(5).

[56] 1907 Act, s. 28(1)(c).

[57] *Purves v. Strathclyde Industrial Services*, Dumbarton Sh. Ct, Oct. 21, 1983, unreported, where the amendment was not challenged as incompetent; *McGarry v. O'Connor*, 1991 S.L.T. (Sh. Ct.) 43.

[58] *Ratty v. Hughes*, 1996 S.C.L.R. 160. See also *Dryburgh v. Currys Group* PLC, 1988 S.C.L.R. 316.

[59] *Guardian Royal Exchange Group v. Moffat*, 1986 S.L.T. 262 at 266.

[60] *Schroder Leasing Ltd v. Fraser*, Sh. Pr. Caplan, Paisley Sh. Ct, Apr. 25, 1986, unreported; but see *Ratty, supra.*

No second reponing note

Only one reponing note may be lodged. Where a reponing note has been refused and the time for appeal has expired without any appeal having been taken, it is incompetent to present a further reponing note, and the interlocutor refusing the first reponing note cannot be submitted to review in an appeal against a subsequent interlocutor.[61] **7.38**

[61] *Ram v. Yadh*, Sh. Pr. Dick, Glasgow Sh. Ct, Mar. 5, 1982, unreported.

CHAPTER 8

BASIC PROCEDURE UNTIL OPTIONS HEARING OR PROCEDURAL HEARING

INTENTION TO DEFEND

Notice of intention to defend in actions other than family actions and multiplepoindings

8.01 Rule 9.1 of the Ordinary Cause Rules provides that, in actions other than family actions or multiplepoindings, if a defender intends to challenge the jurisdiction of the court, to state a defence or to make a counterclaim, he must before the expiry of the appropriate period of notice lodge with the sheriff clerk a notice of intention to defend in Form O7 of Appendix 1.[1] At the same time the defender must send to the pursuer a copy of the notice of intention to defend.[2]

Notice of intention to defend in family actions[3]

8.02 There are separate provisions in the Ordinary Cause Rules for a notice of intention to defend in family actions. The relevant rule is rule 33.34 which applies in four separate situations. The first is where a defender seeks to oppose any crave in the initial writ.[4] The second is where a defender seeks to make a claim for (i) aliment, (ii) an order for a financial provision within the meaning of section 8(3) of the Family Law (Scotland) Act 1985 (*e.g.* a claim for payment of a capital sum or a periodical allowance); or (iii) an order under section 11 of the Children (Scotland) Act 1995 (*e.g.* a residence order or a contact order).[5] The third situation is where a defender seeks (i) an order under section 16(1)(b) or (3) of the Family Law (Scotland) Act 1985 (setting aside or varying an agreement as to financial provision), (ii) an order under section 18 of the 1985 Act (relating to avoidance transactions), or (iii) an order under the Matrimonial Homes (Family Protection) (Scotland) Act 1981 (*e.g.* an exclusion order).[6] The fourth situation is where a defender seeks to challenge the jurisdiction of the court.[7] The defender must, in any of these situations, before the expiry of the period of notice, lodge a notice of intention to defend in Form F26 of Appendix 1 to the Ordinary Cause Rules.[8] This form differs from the equivalent form in non-family actions in respect that it requires the defender to state within the body of the form which of the four situations applies to his case.[9] If the defender wishes either to oppose

---

1 OCR, r. 9.1(1).
2 *ibid.*
3 For family actions generally, see Chap. 22.
4 OCR, r. 33.34(1)(a).
5 OCR, r. 33.34(1)(b).
6 OCR, r. 33.34(1)(c).
7 OCR, r, 33,34(1)(d).
8 OCR, r. 33.34(2)(a).
9 OCR, App. 1, Form F26, Pt B.

an order sought by the pursuer under section 11 of the Children (Scotland) Act 1995 or to seek such an order himself, the form requires him to state therein the order(s) which he is opposing or seeking together with his reasons therefor.[10] If he is either opposing or seeking a section 11 order he must also crave warrant to intimate to the child or children concerned or to dispense with such intimation.[11]

Notice of appearance in multiplepoindings

8.03 Because of the peculiar nature of an action of multiplepoinding,[12] any person interested in the action is required by the rules to lodge a notice of appearance rather than a notice of intention to defend.[13] The rule provides that any party who intends to lodge either (a) defences to challenge the jurisdiction of the court or the competency of the action, (b) objections to the condescendence of the fund *in medio*, or (c) a claim on the fund must, before the expiry of the period of notice, lodge a notice of appearance in Form M4 of Appendix 1 to the Ordinary Cause Rules.[14]

8.04 When lodging either a notice of intention to defend or a notice of appearance the defender should pay the appropriate fee to the sheriff clerk.[15] If the fee is not paid, the sheriff clerk may return the notice to the defender.[16] In some courts the sheriff clerk may be prepared to receive the notice, mark it as "tendered" (not "lodged") and draw the non-payment of the fee to the attention of the sheriff. It is thought that the latter course is liable to lead to confusion. If it is followed and the fee is thereafter paid before the expiry of the period of notice, the notice must be marked as "lodged" on the date when the fee is paid. If the fee is not paid until after the expiry of the period of notice, the defender would require to apply by motion to the sheriff to exercise his dispensing power under rule 2.1.[17] A clear general rule that a notice will not be accepted without fee seems preferable.

8.05 If the appropriate period of notice expires on a *dies non*, rule 9.1 may be complied with on the first day thereafter on which the sheriff clerk's office is open for ordinary civil business.[18] While the time for compliance with the rule cannot be prorogated by the sheriff under rule 16.3, which applies only to defended causes,[19] in practice a late notice may be accepted on the defender's so moving. To achieve this the defender lodges a motion craving the court to allow the notice to be received late. If the pursuer

---

[10] OCR, App. 1, Form F26, Pt C.

[11] *ibid.*

[12] See paras 21.52 *et seq.*

[13] OCR, r. 35.8.

[14] *ibid.*

[15] Sheriff Court Fees Order 1997 (S.I. 1997 No. 687), para. 2(1) provides that a notice of intention to defend and a notice of appearance in a multiplepoinding fall within the definition of "writ" for the purposes of the Order. At the time of writing the fee payable in terms of the Order for a defenders "first writ" in cases other than divorces is £45. In divorces it is £72.

[16] That course was not disapproved in *Orr Pollock & Co. (Printers) Ltd v. Mulholland*, 1983 S.L.T. 558.

[17] See paras 5.93 to 5.97.

[18] *Mackenzie v. Munro* (1894) 22 R. 45; *McMurray v. Wallis* (1950) 66 Sh.Ct.Rep. 234; *Lanark C.C. v. Docherty*, 1959 S.L.T. (Sh. Ct.) 12; *Craig-Na-Brro Sales v. Munro Furniture Ltd*, 1974 S.L.T. (Sh. Ct.) 107.

[19] Lewis, p. 110; Dobie, p. 139; *Watson v. Foley*, 1955 S.L.T. (Sh. Ct.) 28; *Craig-Na-Brro Sales, supra. Cf. Reilly Glen & Co. v. Beaton*, 1964 S.L.T. (Sh. Ct.) 73.

consents to the motion[20] or does not intimate opposition to it, the sheriff may grant it in chambers without requiring the defender to appear.[21] However, because allowing the notice to be received late is a matter for the sheriff's discretion involving the exercise of the dispensing power under rule 2.1, the sheriff may require that the case calls in court in order that the defender may explain why the notice was not lodged timeously, even though the motion is unopposed or even consented to.[22] If the motion is refused and the pursuer thereafter minutes for decree,[23] which is granted, the defender's only remedy is to seek to be reponed.[24]

The effect of lodging a notice of intention to defend is that the cause becomes at once a defended cause[25]; and if the defender does not go on to defend, the pursuer is entitled to decree by default[26] rather than decree in absence.[27] It is thought that, accordingly, a notice cannot be withdrawn.[28] A defender who lodges a notice cannot state any objection to the regularity of the service upon himself, and the lodging of the notice remedies any defect in the service.[29] The lodging of the notice does not imply acceptance of the jurisdiction of the court,[30] and the defender is not thereby precluded from pleading that the court has no jurisdiction.[31] A defender who lodges defences cannot plead that he did not authorise the lodging of the preceding notice in his name.[32] **8.06**

Fixing date for options hearing, etc.

When a notice of intention to defend is lodged the sheriff clerk must fix a date for the options hearing in the case.[33] This date must be not sooner than 10 weeks after the expiry of the period of notice.[34] At the same time the sheriff clerk intimates to the parties in Form G5 of Appendix 1 to the Ordinary Cause Rules (i) the last date for lodging defences,[35] (ii) the last date for adjustment,[36] and (iii) the date of the options hearing,[37] and prepares and signs an interlocutor recording these dates.[38] **8.07**

---

[20] In terms of OCR, r. 15.4.

[21] In terms of OCR, r. 15.5(1).

[22] *ibid.*

[23] In terms of OCR, r. 7.2(1).

[24] In terms of OCR, r. 8.1. See *Watson, supra.*

[25] Fyfe, para. 376, p. 155; Dobie, p. 139; *Reilly Glen & Co., supra.*

[26] In terms of OCR, rr. 16.2 (non-family actions, see paras 14.02 *et seq*) and 33.37 (family actions, see para. 14.14). *Miller v. Chapelside Chemical Co.* (1887) 3 Sh.Ct.Rep. 83. Sheriff court procedure differs in this respect from Court of Session procedure, where a pursuer cannot obtain a decree by default until after defences have been lodged: see RCS, rr. 19.1(2)(b), 20.1, and Maxwell, p. 248.

[27] In terms of OCR, Chap. 7.

[28] In any event the practice of withdrawing the notice before the lodging of defences appears to be obsolete: *cf.* Dove Wilson, pp. 127–128; *Gray v. Low* (1856) 18 D. 628; *Cuthbert v. Stuart-Gray* (1904) 21 Sh.Ct.Rep. 31.

[29] OCR, r. 5.10(1). This rule uses the term "appears" which harks back to the days when the document lodged by a defender was a notice of appearance, but there can be no doubt that it should be read as referring to the lodging of a notice of intention to defend.

[30] OCR, r. 9.1(2).

[31] OCR, r. 5.10(2).

[32] *AB v. CD* (1905) 21 Sh.Ct.Rep. 303.

[33] OCR, r. 9.2(1). For options hearing, see paras 8.36 to 8.43.

[34] *ibid.*

[35] This date should be 14 days after the expiry of the period of notice: OCR, r. 9.6(1).

[36] This date should be 14 days before the date of the options hearing: OCR, r. 9.8(1).

[37] OCR, r. 9.2(2)(a).

[38] OCR, r. 9.2(2)(b).

Fixing date for child welfare hearing[39]

8.08 When a notice of intention to defend is lodged in certain family actions the sheriff clerk is required to fix a child welfare hearing not sooner than 21 days after the lodging of the notice, or earlier if the sheriff so directs.[40] A child welfare hearing must be fixed (a) if a defender wishes to oppose any order in terms of section 11 of the Children (Scotland) Act 1995 ("section 11 order") craved by the pursuer or to seek the same order,[41] (b) if a defender seeks a section 11 order which is not craved by the pursuer,[42] or (c) in any other circumstances where the sheriff considers that such a hearing should be fixed.[43] The sheriff clerk intimates the date of the hearing to all parties in Form F41 of Appendix 1 to the Ordinary Cause Rules,[44] which may in some courts be incorporated in the notice of the options hearing, Form G5. The fact that a child welfare hearing is fixed has no effect on the fixing of an options hearing as this must be done in every action in which a notice of intention to defend is lodged.[45] However, it is possible that at the child welfare hearing or a continuation thereof the action may be disposed of,[46] in which case the options hearing previously fixed would never take place. The interlocutor following the child welfare hearing should make it clear whether the case is being continued to the options hearing or whether the options hearing is being discharged.[47]

The Process

8.09 The various documents which have to be lodged with the sheriff clerk, such as the initial writ, the notice of intention to defend, the defences and productions are collectively known as "the process". The individual items are generally referred to as "parts of" or "steps in" the process. Each part or step is given a number and is usually referred to by that number.

Process folder

8.10 When the sheriff clerk receives a notice of intention to defend in an action he must prepare a process folder.[48] This folder is made of heavy cardboard and is expandable so that it is capable of containing the documents which form a normal process. Exceptionally bulky documentary productions may be kept separately from the process folder. The folder contains a number of plastic holders into which documents may be inserted. Each holder has a numbered tag attached to it. The folder also contains a borrowing sheet on which any person borrowing a part of process must specify the part borrowed and sign a receipt for it. On the outside of the folder is an inventory of process consisting of a numbered list, the numbers corresponding to the numbers on the plastic holders. The sheriff clerk must place any production or part of process lodged into the folder[49] and enter each item

---

[39] For child welfare hearing, see paras 22.37, 22.38.
[40] OCR, r. 33.22A(1).
[41] OCR, r. 33.22A(1)(a).
[42] OCR, r. 33.22A(1)(b).
[43] OCR, r. 33.22A(1)(c).
[44] OCR, r. 33.22A(2).
[45] *Henderson v. Adamson*, 1998 S.C.L.R. 365.
[46] *Hartnett v. Hartnett*, 1997 S.C.L.R. 525.
[47] *Henderson, supra, per* Sh. Pr. Risk at 369B–C.
[48] OCR, r. 9.5(1).
[49] OCR, rr. 9.5(2), 11.2(1).

into the inventory of process appending thereto the date of lodging. The process folder *must* include (a) interlocutor sheets, (b) duplicate interlocutor sheets, (c) a production file (in practice there is one production file for each party), (d) a motion file, and (e) as already mentioned, an inventory of process.[50] When the process folder is first opened it will contain the notice of intention to defend and an interlocutor and duplicate interlocutor stating the date of the options hearing, the last date for lodging defences and the last date for adjustment.[51] The next item to be put in the file will almost certainly be the initial writ which must be returned, unbacked and unfolded, by the pursuer to the sheriff clerk within seven days after the expiry of the period of notice.[52] If any document is founded on or adopted as incorporated in the initial writ it must, so far as it is in the pursuer's possession or within his control, be lodged at the same time as the initial writ is returned.[53]

All parts of process must be written, typed or printed on A4 size paper of durable quality and must be lodged with the sheriff clerk unbacked and unfolded.[54] **8.11**

The words "Assisted Person" must follow the name of any party in receipt of civil legal aid on every step of process,[55] and it is the responsibility of his solicitor to see that this is done.[56] The party's legal aid certificate must be lodged in process.[57] **8.12**

After a notice of intention to defend has been lodged, any party lodging a part of process must, at the same time, intimate such lodging to every other party who has entered the process by delivering to them a copy of the part of process concerned, including, where practicable, copies of any documentary production.[58] Delivery may be by any of the methods of service provided in Chapter 5 of the Ordinary Cause Rules,[59] or, if the party to whom intimation is to be made is represented by a solicitor, it may be by (i) personal delivery, (ii) facsimile transmission, (iii) first class ordinary post, or (iv) delivery to a document exchange, to that solicitor.[60] In the case of personal delivery or facsimile transmission intimation is deemed to have been given on the day of delivery or transmission where it was given before 5 p.m. on that day but, if later, is deemed to have been given on the following day.[61] If intimation is by post or document exchange, it is deemed to have been given on the day after posting or delivery.[62] In all cases, if the deemed date of intimation falls on a Saturday, Sunday or public or court holiday, it is deemed to have been given on the next day on which the sheriff clerk's office is open for civil business.[63] **8.13**

---

50 OCR, r. 9.5(1).
51 In conformity with OCR, r. 9.2(2)(b).
52 OCR, r. 9.3.
53 OCR, r. 21.1(1)(a).
54 OCR, r. 11.1
55 A.S. (Civil Legal Aid Rules) 1987 (S.I. 1987 No. 492), r. 3(1).
56 *James Sim Ltd v. Haynes*, 1968 S.L.T. (Sh. Ct.) 76.
57 A.S. (Civil Legal Aid Rules) 1987, r. 3(2)–(4). See para. 4.117.
58 OCR, r. 11.6(1).
59 OCR, r. 11.6(2)(a).
60 OCR, r. 11.6(2)(b).
61 OCR, r. 11.6(3)(a).
62 OCR, r. 11.6(3)(b).
63 OCR, r. 11.6(4).

Custody and borrowing of process

8.14 The initial writ, interlocutor sheets, borrowing receipts and the process folder remain in the custody of the sheriff clerk.[64] The pursuer, his solicitor or the solicitor's authorised clerk may, on cause shown, be authorised by the sheriff clerk to borrow the initial writ.[65] All other items of process may be borrowed by a solicitor or by his authorised clerk.[66] A party litigant is entitled to borrow a process only with leave of the sheriff and subject to such conditions as the sheriff may impose,[67] but he may inspect a process and obtain copies, where practicable, from the sheriff clerk.[68] When borrowing any part of process, the borrower writes on the borrowing sheet[69] the number of the item which he has borrowed, the date and a legible signature. An authorised clerk should add the name of his principal and firm. Both the sheriff clerk and the solicitor should ensure that the signature is cancelled when the borrowed item is returned. All parts of process which have been borrowed must be returned to the sheriff clerk not later than 12.30 p.m. on the day preceding a proof.[70] The sheriff may also, on the motion of any party, ordain any other party who has borrowed a part of process to return it within such time as the sheriff thinks fit.[71]

8.15 In the sheriffdom of Lothian and Borders every process or part thereof which has been borrowed must be returned to the sheriff clerk not later than 4 p.m. on the second working day before the date on which it is required in court.[72] No process or part thereof may be borrowed or be available for inspection during the period from that time until the day after the date on which it is required in court.[73] These directions do not apply where a process or a part thereof is due to be returned prior to a diet of proof, as then rule 29.13 applies.[74] In Glasgow and Strathkelvin all processes must be returned to the sheriff clerk not later than noon on the day preceding any diet or the date on which they appear on the rolls of the court; and where there is an appeal to the sheriff principal any parts of process in the case must be returned to the sheriff principal's clerk not later than 10 a.m. on the day before the diet of hearing.[75] In South Strathclyde, Dumfries and Galloway all processes must be returned to the sheriff clerk not later than noon on the second day preceding any diet or the date on which they appear on the rolls of the court.[76] In North Strathclyde all processes must be returned to the sheriff clerk not later than noon of the second day preceding any diet or

---

[64] OCR, r. 11.2(2).
[65] OCR, r. 11.2(3).
[66] OCR, r. 11.3(1).
[67] OCR, r. 11.3(3)(a).
[68] OCR, r. 11.3(3)(b).
[69] See para. 8.10.
[70] OCR, r. 29.13.
[71] OCR, r. 11.3(4).
[72] Lothian and Borders Act of Court (Consolidation, etc.) 1990, No. 1, para. 3(1). See *Parliament House Book*, D1002.
[73] Lothian and Borders Act of Court (Consolidation, etc.) 1990, No. 1, para. 3(2).
[74] *ibid.* para. 3(3). For OCR, r. 29.13, see para. 8.14.
[75] Glasgow and Strathkelvin, "Practice by Solicitors which would Assist the Running of the Sheriff Court at Glasgow", paras 4, 11. See *Parliament House Book*, D606, 607.
[76] South Strathclyde, Dumfries and Galloway Practice Note, June 25, 1982, Sched., para. 1. See *Parliament House Book*, D803.

the date on which they appear on the rolls of court.[77] No process or any part thereof may be borrowed within the period from noon on the second working day preceding any diet at which it is required until after that diet.[78] Where an ordinary cause or summary application process is required for an ordinary court diet, that process is not available for inspection during the period from noon on the second working day preceding that ordinary court diet until after that diet.[79] At the time of writing there are no acts of court or practice notes relating to the process in the sheriffdoms of Tayside, Central and Fife or Grampian, Highland and Islands.

Rule 11.4(1) provides that when a solicitor or party litigant has borrowed a process or any part of a process and fails to return it for any diet at which it is required, the sheriff may impose on him a fine not exceeding £50, which is payable to the sheriff clerk.[80] In the case of a solicitor, such a fine is a penalty personal to him. The order imposing the fine is not subject to appeal,[81] but it may, on cause shown, be recalled by the sheriff who granted it.[82] Any wrongful removal of a process or part thereof,[83] and any failure to return a lawfully borrowed process when required by the court,[84] may be dealt with as contempt of court. Failure to implement an order for return of the process may also result in the granting of decree against the party in default, in terms of rule 16.2 or rule 33.7.[85] A refusal by a party or a witness to return a document to which he has been referred in court may be dealt with as contempt of court even if the document is not in process.[86] All remedies competent to enforce the return of a borrowed process may proceed on the warrant of the court from whose custody the process was obtained.[87] It would therefore appear that a process caption, which is a summary warrant of incarceration, may be issued for the purpose of compelling the return of a process.[88] In general, however, it is competent and expedient to deal with irregularities either in terms of rule 11.4(1) or, in a more serious case, by way of contempt of court.[89] **8.16**

Lost documents

When any part of process is lost or destroyed, a copy thereof, authenticated in such manner as the sheriff thinks fit, may be substituted, and for the purposes of the action to which the process relates the copy is treated as having the same force and effect as the original.[90] **8.17**

---

77 North Strathclyde Act of Court (Consolidation, etc.) 1992, para. 1.02. See *Parliament House Book*, D702.
78 North Strathclyde Act of Court (Consolidation, etc.) 1992, para. 1.01.
79 *ibid.* para. 1.03.
80 OCR, r. 11.4(1).
81 OCR, r. 11.4(2).
82 OCR, r. 11.4(1).
83 *Watt v. Thomson* (1868) 6 M. 1112; (1870) 8 M. (H.L.) 77; (1873) 11 M. 960; (1874) 1 R. (H.L.) 21.
84 *Levison v. Jewish Chronicle Ltd*, 1924 S.L.T. 755.
85 *Levison, supra.*
86 *Gregson v. Grant*, 1910 2 S.L.T. 16.
87 OCR, r. 11.3(2).
88 *Broatch v. Pattison* (1898) 1 F. 303 at 305; Maclaren, pp. 416–418.
89 See paras 2.18 to 2.25.
90 OCR, r. 11.5. As to the mode of authentication, see Vol. 2 of this work.

The Defences

Lodging of defences

Time

8.18 Defences must be lodged within 14 days after the expiry of the period of notice.[91] If defences are not timeously lodged the defender may lodge a motion to have the time for lodging them prorogated in terms of rule 16.3.[92] If no motion for prorogation has been made, the pursuer may move for decree by default under rule 16.2 (in the case of actions other than family actions) or rule 33.7 (in the case of a family action). A decree by default pronounced in such circumstances is not, however, a basis for a plea of *res judicata*.[93]

Litiscontestation

8.19 The effect of lodging defences is that litiscontestation takes place, and any decree pronounced thereafter is a decree *in foro contentioso*.[94] "Both parties become subject to the procedure of the court and neither can escape from its toils until the action is judicially disposed of."[95]

Documents

8.20 On lodging defences, the defender must send a copy of the defences to the pursuer.[96] He must lodge along with his defences any documents founded upon or incorporated in the defences, so far as they are in his possession or within his control.[97] If the defender is an assisted person he must lodge his legal aid certificate when he receives it.[98]

Plurality of defenders[99]

8.21 Where there is more than one defender or set of defenders, each with a separate ground of defence, each should lodge separate defences; but defenders having a common interest should combine as far as possible in conducting their defence, since otherwise questions may arise as to their entitlement to full expenses in the event of success. Such defenders should therefore lodge joint defences where it is practicable to do so.

Sisting of defenders

8.22 A party who has not been called as a defender may enter the process by minute[1] and thereafter be sisted as a defender and allowed to lodge defences

---

[91] OCR, r. 9.6(1).

[92] As to the considerations which may be relevant when such a motion is made, see para. 14.08.

[93] *Esso Petroleum Co. Ltd v. Law*, 1956 S.C. 33. See para. 2.106.

[94] *Gow v. Henry* (1899) 5 F. 48, *per* Lord Young at 52; *Woodbury v. Sutherland's Trs*, 1938 S.C. 689, *per* Lord Robertson at 692; *Esso Petroleum Co. Ltd, supra, per* Lord Carmont at 36–38; *Argyllshire Weavers Ltd v. A. Macaulay (Tweeds) Ltd*, 1962 S.C. 388, *per* Lord Hunter at 394. Dicta in *Clydesdale Bank v. D. & H. Cohen*, 1943 S.C. 244, *per* L.J.-C Cooper at 246 and Lord Mackay at 247, appear to indicate that litiscontestation takes place at the closing of the record. See Mackay, *Practice*, i, p. 442; Maclaren, p. 403; Trayner, s.v. "*Litis contestatia*"; *Encyclopaedia*, ix, s.v. "Litiscontestation"; *Stair Encyclopaedia*, Vol. 17, paras 1034, 1387.

[95] *Argyllshire Weavers Ltd, supra, per* Lord Hunter at 394–395.

[96] OCR, r. 11.6(1) which applies generally to all parts of process.

[97] OCR, r. 21.1(1)(b).

[98] A.S. (Civil Legal Aid Rules) 1987, r. 3(2)(b).

[99] See paras 4.41 to 4.51.

[1] Minute procedure is governed by OCR, Chap. 14. See paras 5.57 *et seq.*

if he can show a title and interest to defend.[2] Otherwise a defender will not normally be allowed to appear in the process by minute without applying for the special authority of the court.[3] Where he considers that he has no interest to litigate but desires to explain his position to the court without making statements prejudicial to the other parties, he may in exceptional circumstances be permitted to do so by minute.

Withdrawal of defences

Defences which have been lodged may be withdrawn by minute, in which case decree in the pursuer's favour will be granted.[4] Alternatively, the defender may, at any calling of the case, intimate that he is not insisting on his defence and that he is consenting to decree being granted as craved. Where it is stated that defences have been lodged without authority, time should be allowed for the production of a mandate.[5] **8.23**

Form of defences

The technique of drafting defences is considered in Chapter 9. Third-party procedure and counterclaim procedure are considered in Chapter 12. Here, only the formal requirements of the Ordinary Cause Rules concerning the form of defences are noted. Defences, which do not include a counterclaim, must be in the form of answers in numbered paragraphs corresponding to the articles of the condescendence, and must have appended a note of the defender's pleas-in-law.[6] Every statement of fact made by one party must be answered by the other party, and if a statement made by one party of a fact within the knowledge of the other party is not denied by that other party, the latter is held as admitting the fact so stated.[7] This does not, of course, mean that every statement has to be specifically denied. A general denial is quite sufficient. If the defender in an action other than a family action wishes to counterclaim against the pursuer, the counterclaim should be stated in the defences. Such defences commence with a crave and include, as well as answers to the condescendence, a separate statement of facts in numbered paragraphs and appropriate pleas-in-law.[8–9] **8.24**

ADJUSTMENT OF PLEADINGS

Object

After defences have been lodged, the parties may proceed forthwith to adjust their pleadings. The primary object of adjustment is to make such alterations to the parties' averments and pleas-in-law as are necessary to **8.25**

---

[2] *Macfie v. Scottish Rights of Way Society* (1884) 11 R. 1094; *Glasgow Shipowners' Association v. Clyde Navigation Trs* (1885) 12 R. 695; *Bruce v. Calder* (1903) 20 Sh.Ct.Rep. 288; *Macpherson v. Macdonald Fraser & Co. Ltd* (1905) 12 S.L.T. 824. See para. 12.15.

[3] *Campbell v. Ayr C.C.* (1905) 13 S.L.T. 193; *Ramsay v. McLaren*, 1936 S.L.T. 35.

[4] *Ower v. Crichton* (1902) 10 S.L.T. 279.

[5] *Fischer & Co. v. Andersen* (1896) 23 R. 395. On mandates, see paras 4.122 to 4.127.

[6] OCR, r. 9.6(2).

[7] OCR, r. 9.7.

[8–9] OCR, r. 19.1(3). Strictly speaking a counterclaim is not competent in a family action, but OCR, r. 33.34(2)(b) provides that a defender in such an action should crave in his defences any order sought by him in much the same way as a counterclaim is pleaded in a non-family action.

ensure that when the record is closed the issues between the parties and the stand which each party is taking on these issues may be readily understood from a reading of the pleadings.[10] The technique of adjustment is considered in Chapter 9. The following paragraphs are concerned with the rules relating to adjustment.

Extent of alteration permitted by adjustment

8.26 Each party may by adjustment alter his averments and pleas-in-law. In addition, the pursuer in a cause in which all parties have lodged defences or answers may, prior to the closing of the record and without leave of the sheriff, alter any sum sued for by amending the crave of the initial writ and any record.[11] The pursuer must immediately intimate any such amendment in writing to all other parties.[12]

8.27 Adjustment, unlike the amendment of pleadings,[13] does not require the leave of the court. With the possible exception of scandalous averments which may be deleted by order of the court before the record is closed,[14] the court cannot exercise any control over the averments which may be added by adjustment. Accordingly, if a pursuer has raised his action within a statutory time-limit, he may add by adjustment after the expiry of the time-limit averments which radically alter his case.[15]

Making of adjustments

8.28 All adjustments of the pleadings are exchanged between the parties and are not lodged in process.[16] Parties are responsible for maintaining a record of adjustments made during the period of adjustment.[17] If any hearing is fixed before the options hearing each party must lodge in process a copy of his pleadings as adjusted not later than two days before the date of the hearing.[18]

Open record

8.29 An open record is a document in which the original pleadings are consolidated, showing the heading, instance and crave of the initial writ, each article of the condescendence followed by the corresponding answer for the defender, or answers for each of several defenders, and the pleas-in-law for all parties. To facilitate the reading of the open record the answers for the defender or defenders may be inset from the margin used for the pleadings of the pursuer. If the defences include a counterclaim, the pleadings must be set out in the order: (a) the crave of the initial writ; (b) the condescendence and answers relating to the initial writ; (c) the pleas-in-law of the parties relating to the crave of the initial writ; (d) the crave of the counterclaim; (e) the statement of facts and answers relating to the counterclaim; and (f) the pleas-in-law of the parties relating to the counterclaim.[19] Rule 9.10 is headed "Open Record" and provides

---

10 Sir Allan G. Walker, "Written Pleadings" (1963) 79 Sc.L.Rev. 161, at 162–163.
11 OCR, r. 18.1(1). As "any record", see para. 8.29.
12 OCR, r. 18.1(2).
13 Chap. 10.
14 *C v. W*, 1950 S.L.T. (Notes) 8; see para. 10.60.
15 *Sellars v. IMI Yorkshire Imperial Ltd*, 1986 S.L.T. 629.
16 OCR, r. 9.8(2).
17 OCR, r. 9.8(3).
18 OCR, r. 9.4.
19 OCR, r. 19.2A.

that the sheriff may at any time before the closing of the record, on the application of a party to the action or *ex proprio motu*, order any party to lodge in process a record of the pleadings as adjusted and amended to the date of the order. In practice this procedure is seldom invoked.

Adjustment period

Parties may adjust their pleadings until 14 days before the date of the options hearing.[20] No adjustment is permitted after that period except with leave of the sheriff.[21] In practice such leave is sometimes sought *ex post facto* at the options hearing. If an action is sisted during the period for adjustment, any period for adjustment prior to the sist counts as part of the adjustment period.[22] When the sist is recalled the sheriff clerk fixes a new date for the options hearing[23] and parties are free to adjust until 14 days before that date. The new date for the options hearing should take account of the period for adjustment which has elapsed before the action was sisted. **8.30**

The fact that an options hearing has been fixed and a case is in the course of adjustment does not prevent any party making an incidental application to the court such as, for example, a motion for some interim order.[24] As has already been noted, parties must lodge in process a copy of their pleadings as adjusted not later than two days before the hearing of any such application.[25] **8.31**

Rules as to pleading and publication

The contents of the pleadings before the closing of the record are the subject of rules as to pleading and publication. A party's averments as to the contents of his opponent's pleadings before the closing of the record will be excluded from probation if the opponent states a plea to that effect, and there will thus be no enquiry into the circumstances in which the averment was made. The party may, however, cross-examine his opponent and his witnesses on any such averment, since it was a statement made by or on behalf of the opponent and may therefore have a bearing on their credibility.[26] The publication of averments appearing in pleadings before the record is closed may be contempt of court,[27] and if they contain any defamatory statements the publisher is also liable to an action of damages.[28] **8.32**

Record for Options Hearing

At the end of the period of adjustment the pursuer must "make a copy of the pleadings and any adjustments and amendments in the form of a **8.33**

---

[20] OCR, r. 9.8(1).
[21] OCR, r. 9.8(4).
[22] OCR, r. 9.9(1).
[23] OCR, r. 9.9(2)(a).
[24] OCR, r. 9.2(3).
[25] OCR, r. 9.4. See para. 8.28.
[26] *Lennox v. National Coal Board*, 1955 S.C. 438; *cf. Kirkham v. Cementation Co. Ltd*, 1964 S.L.T. (Notes) 33.
[27] *Graham v. Farquhar* (1893) 1 S.L.T. 63; *Young v. Armour*, 1921 1 S.L.T. 211.
[28] *Richardson v. Wilson* (1879) 7 R. 237; *Macleod v. Justices of the Peace of Lewis* (1892) 20 R. 218.

record".[29] The form of the record is not prescribed by the rules except in a case where the defender has included a counterclaim in his defences. In practice it consists essentially of the heading, instance and crave of the initial writ; each article of the condescendence as adjusted, followed by the corresponding answer or answers, as adjusted; the pleas-in-law for the pursuer, which follow the last answer; the pleas-in-law for the defender or defenders and any third party. In a case where there is a counterclaim the Ordinary Cause Rules provide that the record, after the heading and instance, should consist of (a) the crave of the initial writ, (b) the condescendence and answers relating to the initial writ, (c) the pleas-in-law of the parties relating to the crave of the initial writ, (d) the crave of the counterclaim, (e) the statement of facts and answers relating to the counterclaim, and (f) the pleas-in-law of the parties relating to the counterclaim.[30] It is recommended that, for ease of reading, the answers for the defender and any third party (and for the pursuer in the counterclaim) should be inset from the margin used for the pleadings of the pursuer (or defender).

8.34 The pursuer must lodge a certified copy of the record not later than two days before the options hearing.[31] This means that there must be at least two clear days between the lodging and the options hearing.[32] A fee is payable on the lodging of the certified copy record.[33] A failure timeously to lodge a record is a default which entitles the sheriff to grant decree of dismissal in favour of the defender, the question whether to do so or to exercise the dispensing power under rule 2.1(1) being one for the discretion of the sheriff.[34] If a pursuer seeks to persuade a sheriff that the dispensing power should be exercised to allow a certified copy record to be lodged late, it is essential that he addresses the sheriff fully, giving him all relevant information to enable him to exercise his discretion.[35] If an action has been settled prior to the options hearing, even though no minute of acceptance of tender or joint minute has actually been lodged, the sheriff should not dismiss the action because the pursuer has failed timeously to lodge a record.[36] If decree by default is granted in the defender's favour it should be dismissal and not absolvitor.[37]

Note of Basis of Preliminary Plea

8.35 If a party's pleadings include a preliminary plea[38] and the party intends to insist on that plea, he must, not later than three days before the options

---

[29] OCR, r. 9.11(1).
[30] OCR, r. 19.2A.
[31] OCR, r. 9.11(2).
[32] *Ritchie v. Maersk Co. Ltd*, 1994 S.C.L.R. 1038; *DTZ Debenham Thorpe v. I. Henderson Transport Services*, 1995 S.L.T. 553, *per* L.P. Hope giving the opinion of the court at 555A.
[33] Sheriff Court Fees Order 1997 (S.I. 1997 No. 687), Sched. 1, para. 22. At the time of writing the fee is £57.
[34] *Andrew Welsh Ltd v. Thornholme Services*, 1994 S.C.L.R. 1021; *Mahoney v. Officer*, 1994 S.C.L.R. 1059; *Morran v. Glasgow Council of Tenants' Associations*, 1994 S.C.L.R. 1065; *Group 4 Total Security Ltd v. Jaymarke Developments Ltd*, 1995 S.C.L.R. 303; *DTZ Debenham Thorpe, supra*; *D.A. Baird & Son v. Nisbet*, 1995 S.C.L.R. 1127. *Cf. Burtonport Fishermens's Co-operative v. Sans Unkles*, 1994 S.C.L.R. 844; *Gordon v. Mayfair Homes Ltd*, 1994 S.C.L.R. 862; *Price v. Fernando*, 1995 S.C.L.R. 23.
[35] *Royal Life Insurance Ltd v. Douglas*, 1998 S.C.L.R. 405.
[36] *David Witner & Sons Ltd v. George Craig & Sons Ltd*, 1995 S.L.T. 1331.
[37] *Group 4 Total Security Ltd, supra.*
[38] A preliminary plea includes a plea that an action should be sisted pending arbitration: *Dinardo Partnership Ltd v. Thomas Tait & Sons Ltd*, 1995 S.C.L.R. 941.

hearing, lodge in process a note of the basis for the plea and intimate a copy of that note to every other party.[39] Such a note is usually referred to as a "rule 22 note". If no rule 22 note is lodged, the party is deemed to be no longer insisting on his preliminary plea and the sheriff must repel the plea at the options hearing.[40] The requirement to lodge a rule 22 note for the options hearing applies even though the parties are agreed that the case should go to the additional procedure with the result (if the sheriff agrees to that course) that a further period for adjustment will be allowed.[41] A failure to lodge a rule 22 note is not a default within the meaning of rule 16.2(1).[42]

Options Hearing

The options hearing, which is an innovation introduced by the Ordinary Cause Rules 1993, is a very important step in the progress of a defended action. In many cases it will be the first occasion when the action actually calls in court. "At the options hearing the sheriff shall seek to secure the expeditious progress of the case by ascertaining from parties the matters in dispute" and certain other information.[43] The other information includes material to enable the sheriff to decide what the extent of the proof should be and whether a joint minute should be lodged.[44] It is the duty of the parties to provide the sheriff with sufficient information to enable him to conduct the hearing in the manner provided for in the rule.[45] It is also the duty of the parties to endeavour to reach agreement on uncontroversial evidence.[46] An options hearing is a diet for the purposes of a decree by default,[47] and a failure of a party to be present or represented at an options hearing may result in decree being pronounced against him.[48] **8.36**

In the case of a family action the Ordinary Cause Rules provide that the parties must, except on cause shown, personally attend the options hearing.[49] However, a failure by a party to attend in person, where that party is represented at the hearing, has been held not to amount to default within the meaning of rule 33.37 on the basis that the rule applies only where a party fails "to appear *or be represented*" at a diet.[50] **8.37**

There is limited scope for the sheriff to continue an options hearing. He may either on the motion of a party or *ex proprio motu*, on cause shown, continue the hearing on one occasion only for a period not exceeding 28 days or to the first suitable court day thereafter.[51] There must be some good reason for granting a continuation; the agreement of the parties is **8.38**

---

[39] OCR, r. 22.1(1).
[40] OCR, r. 22.1(3). See *Bell v. John Davidson (Pipes) Ltd*, 1995 S.C.L.R. 192.
[41] *Colvin v. Montgomery Preservations Ltd*, 1995 S.C.L.R. 40. For additional procedure, see paras 8.44 to 8.52.
[42] *Group 4 Total Security Ltd v. Jaymark Developments Ltd*, 1995 S.C.L.R. 303, *per* Sh. Pr. Risk at 307D.
[43] OCR, r. 9.12(1).
[44] *ibid*, referring to OCR, r. 9.12(3).
[45] OCR, r. 9.12(2).
[46] *Weatherall v. Jack*, 1995 S.C.L.R. 189.
[47] OCR, r. 9.12(7).
[48] As in *Colonial Mutual Group (U.K. Holdings) Ltd v. Johnston*, 1995 S.C.L.R. 1165.
[49] OCR, r. 33.36.
[50] *Grimes v. Grimes*, 1995 S.C.L.R. 268.
[51] OCR, r. 9.12(5).

not sufficient.[52] If a continuation is granted parties may adjust further up until 14 days prior to the continued hearing.[53] If further adjustment or amendment is made to the pleadings during the period of continuation, a certified copy of the pleadings as adjusted or amended must be lodged in process not later than two days before the continued options hearing.[54] No fee is payable in respect of this certified copy, provided, as will almost invariably be the case, a fee has been paid when the certified copy record was lodged for the original options hearing.[55] If a party has lodged a rule 22 note for the original options hearing, there is no need to lodge a further note for the continued hearing unless the basis for the preliminary plea has changed following further adjustment.[56] The opinion has been expressed that if a preliminary plea has been repelled at the original options hearing because of a lack of a rule 22 note, it may be reinstated prior to the continued hearing provided that a rule 22 note is lodged for that hearing.[57]

8.39 At the options hearing or a continuation thereof if one has been allowed,[58] unless the sheriff sends the case to the additional procedure[59] he must close the record.[60] If no adjustments have been made since the certified copy record was lodged under rule 9.11(2)[61] that record becomes the closed record.[62] Where adjustments have been made since the lodging of the certified copy, the sheriff may order that a closed record including such adjustments be lodged within seven days after the date of the interlocutor closing the record.[63] The form of closed record under the standard procedure is not prescribed.[64] However, it is a reasonable inference from the terms of rule 9.11(1), which governs the form of the record to be lodged for the options hearing, that, like the record under the additional procedure,[65] the closed record under the standard procedure should contain only the pleadings of the parties and should not contain any interlocutors.

Closed record

8.40 "On the theory of our procedure, the closing of the record is still a crucial step as it marks the borderline between pleading and proof."[66] The pleadings as they appear in the closed record place before the court a statement of the case binding on the parties respectively as a true and complete disclosure of their contentions, and thus restrict both the scope of any inquiry by means of evidence and the issues for discussion by oral argument. After the record is closed, accordingly, the pleadings may not be altered except by amendment, which requires the leave of the court.[67]

---

52 *Andrew Welsh Ltd v. Thornholme Services*, 1994 S.C.L.R. 1021.

53 OCR, r. 9.8(1). It is not competent for a sheriff to allow a longer period for adjustment: *Ferguson and Menzies Ltd v. J.W. Soils Supplies Ltd*, 1998 G.W.D. 30–1529.

54 OCR, r. 9.11(3).

55 Sheriff Court Fees Order 1997 (S.I. 1997 No. 687), para. 2(3).

56 OCR, r. 22.1(5).

57 *Ferguson and Menzies Ltd, supra, per* Sh. Pr. Cox.

58 See para. 8.38.

59 See paras 8.44 to 8.52.

60 OCR, r. 9.12(3).

61 See para. 8.34.

62 OCR, r. 9.12(6)(a).

63 OCR, r. 9.12(6)(b).

64 *cf.* OCR, r. 10.5(3) which prescribes that the closed record under the additional procedure should contain only the pleadings of the parties.

65 OCR, r. 10.5(3). See para. 8.47.

66 *Thomson v. Glasgow Corporation*, 1962 S.C. (H.L.) 36, *per* L.J.-C Thomson at 52.

67 See Chap. 10.

The closed record plays a critical and predominant part in the subsequent stages of the action. Each party is limited to the case he has pleaded on record,[68] and the court is limited to granting the remedy craved, and to deciding the case on the basis of the pleadings.[69] The closed record is also the basis for the court's decision as to further procedure: the question whether to order debate or a form of inquiry will be determined on a consideration of the parties' submissions with reference to the pleadings and any rule 22 note.[70] If debate is allowed, the court's decision is based on and limited by the pleadings.[71] If inquiry is allowed, the ambit of any commission and diligence for the recovery of oral, documentary or real evidence is dependent on the pleadings,[72] and the determination of the questions of where the burden of proof lies, which party is to lead evidence first,[73] and questions of admissibility of evidence at the inquiry. After judgment, the closed record together with the decree will show whether the court's determination will ground a successful plea of *res judicata* in subsequent proceedings.[74] **8.41**

Further procedure

According to the strict letter of the Ordinary Cause Rules, after the record has been closed at the options hearing or continued options hearing, there are only three things which the sheriff may do. First, he may "appoint the cause to a proof and make such orders as to the extent of the proof, the lodging of a joint minute of admissions or agreement, or such other matter as he thinks fit".[75] Secondly, he may, after having heard parties and considered any rule 22 note[76] appoint the cause to a proof before answer[77] and make orders thereanent in the same way as in the case of a proof.[78] Finally, he may, after having heard parties and considered any rule 22 note, appoint the cause to debate "if satisfied that there is a preliminary matter of law which justifies a debate".[79] The question whether a case should be sent to debate is one of law and not a matter for the sheriff's discretion.[80] The phrase "which justifies a debate" means that there is a substantial argument which, if successful, would lead to decree in favour of one of the parties or would limit the extent of proof to a considerable degree.[81] It is not sufficient to justify sending a case to debate that a responsible solicitor says that there is a point to be debated or that parties agree on a debate; the sheriff must decide the question on the basis of consideration of the rule 22 note and of the oral submissions made to him at the options hearing.[82] Even though the sheriff takes the **8.42**

---

[68] *McBain v. Wallace & Co.* (1881) 8 R. (H.L.) 106, *per* Lord Watson at 117.
[69] See para. 17.03.
[70] See para. 8.42.
[71] See paras 13.01 to 13.25.
[72] See paras 15.24, 15.51.
[73] See para. 8.64.
[74] *Edinburgh and District Water Trs v. Clippens Oil Co. Ltd* (1899) 1 F. 899, *per* Lord Kinnear at 909; *Glasgow and S.W. Ry v. Boyd & Forrest*, 1918 S.C. (H.L.) 14, *per* Lord Shaw of Dunfermline at 32; *Graham v. Sec. of St. for Scotland*, 1951 S.C. 368, *per* L.P. Cooper at 387.
[75] OCR, r. 9.12(3)(a).
[76] See para. 8.35.
[77] For proof before answer, see paras 8.57 to 8.59.
[78] OCR, r. 9.12(3)(b).
[79] OCR, r. 9.12(3)(c).
[80] *Gracey v. Sykes*, 1994 S.C.L.R. 909.
[81] *Gracey, supra; The Blair Bryden Partnership v. Adair*, 1995 S.C.L.R. 358.
[82] *Gracey, supra*; *The Blair Bryden Partnership, supra.*

view that the preliminary plea is clearly well-founded, he is not entitled to sustain it at the options hearing; he must send the case to debate.[83]

8.43 Although rule 9.12 provides for only the three options narrated above, in practice it is not uncommon for the rule to be "liberally" interpreted. Thus, if settlement is imminent, the case may be continued to a hearing on the "procedure roll" to enable settlement to be achieved. The case may be sisted for negotiations. More dubiously, if for some reason it seems pointless to have an options hearing (for example, a party may just have changed his agent) the options hearing may be discharged and a new one fixed. There can be no doubt that this latter proceeding is contrary to the letter of the rule, but it has certain practical attractions. While it is not to be encouraged, there may be occasions when it is in the broad interests of justice to adopt it.

Additional Procedure

8.44 The procedure which has been described so far in this chapter is what is called the "standard procedure".[84] The sheriff may, having heard parties at the options hearing, on the motion of any party or *ex proprio motu*, send a case to the procedure under Chapter 10 of the Ordinary Case Rules if he is satisfied "that the difficulty or complexity of the cause makes it unsuitable for [the standard procedure]".[85] Chapter 10 procedure is known as "additional procedure".[86] It is submitted that, by analogy with the allowance of a continuation of the options hearing, a case should be sent to the additional procedure only if it is difficult or complex; the agreement of the parties is not sufficient.[87]

8.45 If the sheriff orders that a case should proceed under the additional procedure he continues the adjustment period for an additional eight weeks.[88] At any time before the expiry of this period the sheriff may close the record if parties, jointly or of consent, lodge a motion to that effect.[89] The eight-week period may be extended by the sheriff if he is satisfied that there is sufficient reason for doing so.[90] Before such an extension can be granted a party must lodge a motion seeking it and lodge a copy of the record adjusted to the date of the lodging of the motion.[91] The motion must set out the reasons for seeking an extension and specify the period sought.[92] The rules relating to the exchange and record of adjustments apply to any period of adjustment under the additional procedure in the same way as they do to the original period prior to the options hearing.[93] As in the case of adjustment prior to the options hearing, if a case is sisted while being adjusted under the additional procedure, any period of adjustment before the sist is reckoned as part of the period of adjustment.[94]

---

[83] *Ritchie v. Cleary*, 1995 S.C.L.R. 561.
[84] This is the procedure covered by OCR, Chap. 9.
[85] OCR, r. 9.12(4).
[86] See the heading to OCR, Chap. 10.
[87] *cf. Andrew Welsh Ltd v. Thornholme Services*, 1994 S.C.L.R. 1021.
[88] OCR, r. 10.1(1).
[89] OCR, r. 10.3(1).
[90] OCR, r. 10.3(2).
[91] *ibid.*
[92] OCR, r. 10.3(3).
[93] OCR, r. 10.1(2).
[94] OCR, r. 10.2.

Under the additional procedure, as under the standard procedure, the sheriff may, at any time before the closing of the record, either on the motion of a party or *ex proprio motu*, order any party to lodge an open record of the pleadings containing any adjustments or amendments made as at the date of the order.[95] **8.46**

At the end of the period of adjustment (whether it be eight weeks or an extended period) the record automatically closes without the attendance of parties.[96] The sheriff clerk prepares and signs an interlocutor closing the record and fixing a date for the procedural hearing under rule 10.6, which date should be on the first suitable court day occurring not sooner than 21 days after the closing of the record.[97] He also intimates the date of the hearing to all parties.[98] Within 14 days after the date of the interlocutor closing the record the pursuer must lodge in process a certified copy of the closed record[99] along with the appropriate fee.[1] It is specifically provided that the closed record should contain only the pleadings of the parties.[2] This is in contradistinction to the form of closed record customarily lodged under former procedure where there were usually appended to the pleadings all the interlocutors pronounced in the cause to the date of the closing of the record.[3] **8.47**

Note of Basis of Preliminary Plea

If a party's pleadings in a case under the additional procedure contain a preliminary plea and he wishes to insist on that plea, he must, not later than three days before the procedural hearing lodge a note of the basis for the plea and intimate a copy thereof to every other party.[4] A failure to do so means that the party is deemed to be no longer insisting on his plea and the sheriff must repel it at the procedural hearing.[5] There is a certain ambiguity in rule 22.1 and it is arguable that, if a rule 22 note has been lodged for the options hearing in a case which is then sent to the additional procedure, no further note requires to be lodged for the procedural hearing.[6] However, it is suggested that sound practice dictates that in all cases where a preliminary plea appears in the pleadings for a procedural hearing a rule 22 note should be lodged if the party intends to insist on the plea.[7] **8.48**

Procedural Hearing

The procedural hearing performs exactly the same function for a case under the additional procedure as does the options hearing for a case **8.49**

---

[95] OCR, r. 10.4.
[96] OCR, r. 10.5(1).
[97] OCR, r. 10.5(1)(a). For procedural hearing, see para. 8.49.
[98] OCR, r. 10.5(1)(b).
[99] OCR, r. 10.5(2).
[1] Sheriff Court Fees Order 1997 (S.I. 1997 No. 687), Sched. 1, para. 23. At the time of writing the fee is £57.
[2] OCR, r. 10.5(3).
[3] See Glasgow and Strathkelvin, "Practice by Solicitors which would Assist the Running of the Sheriff Court at Glasgow", para. 7, which no longer applies even though it is still printed in the *Parliament House Book* at D607.
[4] OCR, r. 22.1(1).
[5] OCR, r. 22.1(3).
[6] This was held to be so in *Hart v. Thorntons W.S.*, 1995 S.C.L.R. 642.
[7] *cf.* OCR, r. 22.1(5) which provides that a new rule 22 note is required for a continued options hearing only if the basis of the plea has changed.

under the standard procedure. The provisions of rule 10.6(1) to (3) are *mutatis mutandis* in terms identical with those of rule 9.12(1) to (3). Thus the sheriff must "seek to secure the expeditious progress of the cause by ascertaining from parties the matters in dispute" and certain other information.[8] The other information includes material to enable the sheriff to decide what the extent of the proof should be and whether a joint minute should be lodged.[9] It is the duty of the parties to provide the sheriff with sufficient information to enable him to conduct the hearing in the manner provided for in the rule.[10] A procedural hearing is a diet for the purposes of a decree by default in a family action,[11] and a failure of a party to be present or represented at a procedural hearing in such an action may result in decree being pronounced against him or the action proceeding as undefended, depending on the nature of the action.[12] For a reason which is obscure the Ordinary Cause Rules do not provide that a procedural hearing is a diet for the purposes of a decree by default in any action other than a family action.[13] However, this should not be taken as a licence for a party not to be present or represented at such a hearing. Despite the absence of a specific rule it is difficult to see why a sheriff should not be prepared to grant decree by default against such a party.

8.50 There is no requirement in the Ordinary Cause Rules that parties in a family action must attend a procedural hearing in person.[14]

8.51 As is the case with an options hearing, according to the strict letter of the Ordinary Cause Rules, there are only three things which the sheriff may do at the conclusion of a procedural hearing. He may "appoint the cause to a proof and make such orders as to the extent of the proof, the lodging of a joint minute of admissions or agreement, or such other matter as he thinks fit".[15] He may, after having heard parties and considered any rule 22 note,[16] appoint the cause to a proof before answer and make orders thereanent in the same way as in the case of a proof.[17] Finally, he may, after having heard parties and considered any rule 22 note, appoint the cause to debate "if satisfied that there is a preliminary matter of law which justifies a debate".[18] However, it is suggested that, as in the case of an options hearing, other disposals may in practice be made, even though these may be strictly outwith the letter of the rules.[19]

8.52 It should be noted that there is no provision in rule 10.6 for any continuation of the procedural hearing.[20] This suggests that it was not within the contemplation of the compilers of the rules that a continuation should be granted. No doubt it was considered that, given the flexible

---

[8] OCR, r. 10.6(1).
[9] *ibid.*, referring to OCR, r. 10.6(3).
[10] OCR, r. 10.6(2).
[11] OCR, r. 10.6(4).
[12] OCR, r. 33.37(2). For decree by default in family actions, see para. 14.14.
[13] *cf.* OCR, r. 9.12(7) which provides that an options hearing is a diet for the purposes of a decree by default in both family and non-family actions.
[14] *cf.* OCR, r. 33.36 which imposes such a requirement on parties in the case of an options hearing.
[15] OCR, r. 10.6(3)(a).
[16] See para. 8.48.
[17] OCR, r. 10.6(3)(b).
[18] OCR, r. 10.6(3)(c).
[19] See para. 8.43.
[20] *cf.* OCR, r. 9.12(5) which specifically permits a continuation of an options hearing.

provisions for extending the period of adjustment,[21] there should never be a need for any continuation. However that may be, in practice it is not unknown for the sheriff, at the request of all parties, to grant a continuation with a further period of adjustment. This is almost certainly incompetent but there is as yet no decision on the matter, and, if all parties agree to the continuation, there is unlikely to be any appeal so that an authoritative decision can be given.

ALLOWANCE OF DEBATE

Interlocutor allowing debate

Although there is no specific provision in the Ordinary Cause Rules to **8.53** that effect, it is suggested that an interlocutor allowing debate should always indicate in clear terms which pleas-in-law are to be debated. If a party has offered a proof before answer instead of a debate the interlocutor should state this fact as it may have an important bearing on expenses in the event of a proof before answer being ordered after the debate.

ALLOWANCE OF PROOF

Interlocutor allowing proof

Where proof is necessary, the sheriff pronounces an interlocutor **8.54** allowing a proof and fixing a date for the taking of the proof.[22] The interlocutor also specifies the place for taking the proof. This is usually the ordinary court house, but there seems nothing to prevent the proof being taken, in an emergency, at any place within the sheriff court district, so long as the public are not excluded.[23]

If certain averments are to be excluded from probation, or if the proof is **8.55** to be before answer or a preliminary proof limited to certain averments, that should also be specified in the interlocutor allowing proof. If the proof is to be before answer the interlocutor should specify which pleas-in-law are to be reserved until after the proof. Where the defender has confined himself to a denial of the pursuer's averments, the proper interlocutor is: "Allows the pursuer a proof of his averments, and to the defender a conjunct probation."[24] Where the defender admits the pursuer's claim but makes counter-averments, the proper interlocutor is: "Allows the defender a proof of his averments and to the pursuer a conjunct probation", and the defender accordingly leads in the proof.[25] A conjunct probation is allowed to a party for the purpose of contradicting the other party's case, and is to be distinguished from a proof-in-chief, which is allowed for the purpose of supporting the party's own case on record. Where both parties make averments and are allowed a proof, the interlocutor in modern practice is: "Allows both parties a proof of their respective averments", which enables each party to lead evidence in

---

[21] OCR, r. 10.3(2). See para. 8.45.
[22] OCR, r. 29.5. The interlocutor is appealable: see para. 18.42.
[23] Dove Wilson, p. 163. If the court sits in private premises, a press reporter may be invited to represent the public.
[24] *Mags of Edinburgh v. Warrender* (1862) 1 M. 13.
[25] *Malcolm v. Campbell* (1889) 17 R. 255; *Penman v. White*, 1957 S.C. 338.

support of his own case and at the same time his evidence in anticipation of or reply to his opponent's case.[26]

8.56 Rule 29.5 requires the sheriff to fix a date for taking the proof.[27] He may do this at an options hearing or procedural hearing. He may, however, at such a hearing pronounce an interlocutor allowing a proof and appointing the cause to the procedure roll of an ordinary court to be held on a specified future date, in order that a date for the proof may then be fixed. This is a common occurrence if the proof is likely to be lengthy or counsel are to be instructed. In such cases it is essential that parties' solicitors liaise with the sheriff clerk as well as with each other and counsel's clerks when seeking to establish suitable dates. The fixing of the date must, however, be done by the sheriff and not as an administrative matter by the sheriff clerk.

Proof before answer

8.57 A proof before answer is a proof in which questions of law and of the relevancy of the averments are reserved until after evidence has been led.[28] The consequence of allowing proof before answer is that, although the facts averred are proved, they may be held insufficient in law to support the crave of the writ or the pleas in defence, and the final decision may be against the party proving them.[29] The allowance of proof before answer does not authorise the admission of incompetent evidence, which ought to be objected to when it is tendered.[30]

8.58 The sheriff may order proof before answer at the options hearing or procedural hearing. If the case goes to debate the sheriff will order proof before answer after debate[31] where he is satisfied either (a) that the law is clear, but it is desirable to ascertain the facts before applying it, because it cannot be said in advance of the leading of the evidence whether the facts averred are sufficient to support the pleas to which they are related[32]; or (b) that the law applicable to the case cannot be stated with precision until the facts are ascertained and seen in their proper setting.[33] Where the position in law may depend on an appreciation of the precise facts which are ultimately found, it is normally not considered possible or, if possible, appropriate to express a general opinion on the law which might be of no effect on a certain view of the facts or which would have to be alternative with regard to a variety of views of the facts. If the sheriff is satisfied that particular averments are irrelevant, he should exclude them from probation.[34] If he is in doubt as to their relevancy he should allow a proof before

---

[26] Maclaren, pp. 537–538.

[27] OCR, r. 29.5 also provides that the sheriff "may limit the mode of proof". It is submitted that this is no longer appropriate as proof by writ or oath was abolished by the Requirements of Writing (Scotland) Act 1995, s. 11.

[28] *Robertson v. Murphy* (1867) 6 M. 114; *Belmont Laundry Co. Ltd v. Aberdeen Steam Laundry Co. Ltd* (1898) 1 F. 45 at 48; Mackay, *Practice*, ii, 15–23; Maclaren, p. 553.

[29] *McRostie v. Halley* (1850) 12 D. 816.

[30] *Robertson, supra; Haldane v. Speirs* (1872) 10 M. 537; *Duke of Argyll v. Duchess of Argyll*, 1962 S.C. (H.L.) 88, *per* Lord Guest at 98.

[31] On procedure at debate, see paras 13.01 to 13.25.

[32] *e.g.* where it is alleged that there has been an abuse of a position of trust: *Honeyman's Exrs v. Sharp*, 1978 S.C. 223 at 230.

[33] *Davie v. Stark* (1876) 3 R. 1114, *per* L.J.-C. Moncrieff at 1116; *Moore v. Stephen & Sons*, 1954 S.C. 331, *per* L.J.-C. Thomson at 335, Lord Patrick at 336; D.I.C.A.-C., "The Meaning of Proof before Answer", 1958 S.L.T. (News) 109.

[34] *Inglis v. National Bank of Scotland Ltd*, 1909 S.C. 1038.

answer.[35] The sheriff who hears the proof before answer which is allowed is not bound by any opinions expressed by the sheriff who allowed it.[36]

"Proof before answer" in its original sense means proof before answer as to the relevancy.[37] Whether proof before answer may be allowed as to other preliminary pleas appears to depend on the circumstances of the particular case. A proof before answer reserving a plea to competency may be allowed where, as in certain actions of damages founded on the contraction of progressive disease which are claimed to be time-barred, the evidence relating to the merits will also be relevant to the questions raised by the plea[38]; but only in very exceptional circumstances is it appropriate to allow proof reserving a plea to jurisdiction.[39] The more usual course is to allow a preliminary proof before answer on the question of competency[40] or jurisdiction[41] where the parties are in dispute as to the facts on which the plea is founded. It appears that, exceptionally, where a plea of no title to sue is stated, a preliminary proof on title,[42] or a proof before answer reserving the plea to title,[43] may be allowed. **8.59**

Preliminary proof

The court may order a separate preliminary proof of averments supporting a preliminary plea which, if sustained, would exclude proof of the merits of the action. Such proof should be allowed of disputed averments supporting a plea of no jurisdiction, except where the jurisdiction and the merits are bound up together.[44] It may also be allowed where it is pleaded that the pursuer's claim has been discharged[45] or is barred by virtue of a statutory limitation[46] or other provision,[47] or that another **8.60**

---

[35] *Hackett v. Allan*, Sh. Pr. Caplan, Dunoon Sh. Ct, May 15, 1984, unreported.

[36] *Forbes v. Forbes' Trs*, 1957 S.C. 325, *per* Lord Guthrie at 337–338; *cf.* D.I.C.A.-C., *op. cit.*, and 1965 S.L.T. (News) 45.

[37] *Robertson v. Murphy* (1867) 6 M. 114; *Fleming v. Eadie & Son* (1897) 25 R.3, *per* Lord Young at 5–6; Mackay, *Practice*, ii, 20: *cf. Macvean v. Maclean* (1873) 11 M. 506, *per* Lord Neaves and L.J.-C. Moncrieff at 509.

[38] *Clark v. R. B. Tennent Ltd*, 1962 S.C. 578; *Shaw v. Renton & Fisher Ltd*, 1977 S.L.T. (Notes) 60. Proof proceeded under reservation of competency in *Blyth Dry Docks and Shipbuilding Co. Ltd v. Commissioners for Port of Calcutta*, 1972 S.L.T. (Notes) 7, and in the very exceptional circumstances of *Hope Bros v. Morrison*, 1960 S.C. 1.

[39] *McLeod v. Tancred Arrol & Co.* (1890) 17 R. 514; *Donald v. Baird* (1907) 15 S.L.T. 427; *Dallas & Co. v. McArdle*, 1949 S.C. 481; *Methven Simpson Ltd v. Gray & Goskirk* (1905) 22 Sh.Ct.Rep. 342 at 348–349.

[40] *Bernard's Exrx v. National Union of Mineworkers*, 1971 S.C. 32; *McIntyre v. Armitage Shanks Ltd*, 1979 S.C. 248; *Black v. British Railways Board*, 1983 S.L.T. 146; *Donald v. Rutherford*, 1984 S.L.T. 70, *per* Lord Cameron at 78, Lord Dunpark at 79.

[41] *Carter v. Allison*, 1966 S.C. 257 at 259.

[42] *Eagle Lodge Ltd v. Keir and Cawder Estates Ltd*, 1964 S.C. 31, *per* Lord Carmont at 39–40.

[43] *Asher v. Macleod*, 1948 S.L.T. 227 (plea to title not printed in 1948 S.C. 55).

[44] *McLeod v. Tancred Arrol & Co.* (1890) 17 R. 514, *per* Lord Lee at 516; *Donald v. Baird* (1907) 15 S.L.T. 427; *Dallas & Co. v. McArdle*, 1949 S.C. 481; *Methven Simpson Ltd v. Gray & Goskirk* (1905) 22 Sh.Ct.Rep. 342 at 348–349.

[45] *Gow v. Henry* (1899) 2 F. 48; *Docherty v. McAlpine & Sons* (1899) 2 F. 128; *Hunter v. Darngavil Coal Co.* (1900) 3 F. 10; *McLean v. Hassard* (1903) 10 S.L.T. 593; *Sinclair v. Lochgelly Iron and Coal Co. Ltd* (1905) 13 S.L.T. 103; *Buchanan v. Alexander Cross & Sons Ltd*, 1911 2 S.L.T. 33; *Gray v. Rivet Bolt and Nut Co. Ltd*, 1912 2 S.L.T. 341; *Davies v. Hunter*, 1933 S.L.T. 158.

[46] *Gardner v. Hastie*, 1928 S.L.T. 497, *per* Lord Fleming at 499; *D. & J. McDougall Ltd v. Argyll and Bute D.C.*, 1986 S.L.T. 564; *Bernard's Exrx v. National Union of Mineworkers*, 1971 S.C. 32; *McIntyre v. Armitage Shanks Ltd*, 1979 S.C. 248; *Black v. British Railways Board*, 1983 S.L.T. 146; *Donald v. Rutherford*, 1984 S.L.T. 70, *per* Lord Cameron at 78, Lord Dunpark at 79.

[47] *Gilillan v. Lanark C.C.* (1902) 9 S.L.T. 432; *Duncan v. Fife Coal Co.* (1905) 7 F. 958.

party is the true *dominus litis*,[48] or that the pursuer is incapable of giving instructions for the raising and prosecution of the action.[49] A preliminary proof may be allowed of averments relating to an issue which, if proved, would determine the primary question in controversy between the parties and render other averments irrelevant, with considerable saving of judicial time and expense.[50] In general, however, with the exception of the situation noted in the next paragraph, the court does not favour preliminary proofs on the merits of a case but confines itself to allowing preliminary proofs where an issue is raised in the pleadings which could bar the action from proceeding.[51] A preliminary proof will not be allowed on an issue which is so involved in the merits of the case that it cannot easily be separated therefrom,[52] unless on the parties' joint motion.[53] The interlocutor should specify which party is to lead in the preliminary proof.[54]

Preliminary proof on liability or quantum

8.61 In any case with a pecuniary crave the sheriff may, on the motion of any party or *ex proprio motu*, order that proof on liability or any specified issue be heard separately from proof on the question of the amount for which decree may be pronounced, and he may determine the order in which the proofs should be heard.[55] Whether to allow separate proofs is a matter for the discretion of the sheriff.[56] At the conclusion of the first proof in any such action the sheriff may pronounce such interlocutor as he thinks fit.[57]

Renunciation of probation

8.62 If proof is allowed following an options hearing, a procedural hearing or a debate, the parties may be in substantial agreement on the material facts and may be willing to waive the taking of oral evidence and to submit the cause for decision on their averments and any agreed documents, with the result that what is technically a proof becomes in fact a debate. This they may do by lodging a joint minute stating that they renounce probation and, where appropriate, setting forth a statement of admitted facts and productions.[58] The sheriff may then order the case to be debated.[59] This course may be adopted at any time on or after the closing of the record.[60] Since the joint minute is a contract to renounce probation, one party will not thereafter be allowed, without the other's consent, to

---

[48] *Jenkins v. Robertson* (1869) 7 M. 739; *Robertson v. Duke of Atholl* (1905) 8 F. 150; *Rutherford v. Licences and General Insurance Co. Ltd*, 1934 S.L.T. 47.

[49] *AB v. CB*, 1937 S.C. 408, 696.

[50] *Battu v. Battu*, 1979 S.L.T. (Notes) 7.

[51] *Burroughs Machines Ltd v. Davie Crawford & Partners*, 1976 S.L.T. (Notes) 35.

[52] *McCafferty v. McCabe* (1898) 25 R. 872; *McKinnan v. Keith*, 1912 2 S.L.T. 501; *Oates v. Redpath Brown & Co.*, 1926 S.L.T. 211; *Gardner v. Hastie*, 1928 S.L.T. 497; *Burroughs Machines Ltd v. Davie Crawford & Partners*, 1976 S.L.T. (Notes) 35; *Shaw v. Renton & Fisher Ltd*, 1977 S.L.T. (Notes) 60; *Bonner v. Colvilles Ltd*, 1968 S.L.T. (Sh. Ct.) 5.

[53] *Wallace v. Morrison & Co. Ltd*, 1927 S.N. 170.

[54] *Donald v. Baird* (1907) 15 S.L.T. 427; *Rutherford v. Licences and General Insurance Co. Ltd*, 1934 S.L.T. 47; *AB v. CB*, 1937 S.C. 408; *Battu v. Battu*, 1979 S.L.T. (Notes) 7; *D. & J. McDougall Ltd v. Argyll and Bute D.C.*, 1986 S.L.T. 564 at 566.

[55] OCR, r. 29.6(1). *Cf.* RCS, r. 36.1 which is in similar terms but, unlike its predecessor under the RCS 1965, is not restricted to cases with a pecuniary crave.

[56] *Dyer v. Balfour Beatty Construction (Northern) Ltd*, 1997 S.C.L.R. 783.

[57] OCR, r. 29.6(2).

[58] OCR, r. 29.4(1).

[59] OCR, r. 29.4(2).

[60] OCR, r. 29.4(1).

lead evidence[61] or to amend with a view to leading evidence,[62] except where it is in the interests of justice that a proof should be allowed.

Form of proof

Until the coming into force of section 11 of the Requirements of Writing (Scotland) Act 1995 proof of a case or part of a case might be restricted to a party's writ or oath. Section 11 abolished that form of proof with the result that all proofs are now proofs *prout de jure*. In such a proof evidence may be led in support or disproof of an averment which might have been excluded from probation on the ground of irrelevance or lack of specification if a plea to that effect had been timeously stated and sustained,[63] for objection cannot be taken to the proving of an averment which has been remitted to probation.[64] In Mackay's *Practice* it is said, in relation to Court of Session practice, that the question of relevancy is foreclosed; and although questions of law may be argued after the proof, the party against whom the facts are proved can no longer maintain that no proof should have been allowed, and the facts proved disregarded.[65] On the other hand, it has been judicially observed that an interlocutor allowing to both parties a proof of their averments leaves all questions of relevancy open to further consideration.[66] It has also been observed that the learned author was not considering the sheriff court rules of procedure which provide specifically for findings in law,[67] and that it is difficult to see why a finding in law if erroneous should not be attacked on appeal once it is made notwithstanding that there is no related plea to relevancy.[68] **8.63**

Decision as to which party must lead[69]

If nothing to the contrary is said in an interlocutor issued before the commencement of the proof, the pursuer must lead. He does so in the normal case, where the initial burden of proof rests upon him. Where the pursuer's averments, if relevant and sufficient to support the crave, are admitted by the defender, so that the initial burden of proving his averments rests upon the defender, the defender may be ordained to lead. Where each party, as disclosed by his own averments, must rebut a presumption in order to succeed, the question of who is to lead may depend upon a comparison of the strengths of the two presumptions.[70] Usually, however, the question is decided by the court in the exercise of its discretion, having regard to considerations of prejudice and convenience as well as to presumptive issues of onus.[71] The undernoted cases[72] may **8.64**

---

61 *Picken v. Arundale & Co.* (1872) 10 M. 987, *per* L.P. Inglis at 990–991.

62 *Carswell & Son v. Finlay* (1887) 24 S.L.R. 643, *per* L.P. Inglis at 645.

63 *Barr v. Bain* (1896) 23 R. 1090.

64 *Scott v. Cormack Heating Engineers Ltd*, 1942 S.C. 159, *per* L.P. Normand at 162.

65 Mackay, *Practice*, ii, 18.

66 *Duke of Hamilton's Trs v. Woodside Coal Co.* (1897) 24 R. 294, *per* Lord McLaren at 296.

67 OCR, r. 12.2(3)(a).

68 *Newcastle Building Society v. White*, Sh. Pr. Caplan, Kilmarnock Sh. Ct, May 16, 1985, unreported.

69 Maclaren, p. 554; Walkers, pp. 65–66; Maxwell, pp. 264–265.

70 *Millar v. Mitchell* (1860) 22 D. 833, *per* Lord Neaves at 846, 847; *Penman v. White*, 1957 S.C. 338; Walkers, p. 66, nn. 2, 3.

71 *Docherty v. Royal Bank of Scotland*, 1962 S.L.T. (Notes) 102; *Johnstone's Exrs v. Harris*, 1977 S.L.T. (Notes) 10.

72 *Millar, Penman, Docherty, Johnstone's Exrs, supra*; *Gibson v. Adams* (1875) 3 R. 144; *Krupp v. Menzies*, 1907 S.C. 903; *Donald v. Baird* (1907) 15 S.L.T. 427; *Rutherford v. Licences and General Insurance Co. Ltd*, 1934 S.L.T. 47; *AB v. CB*, 1937 S.C. 408; *Morrison v. Lipp's Exrs*, 1947 S.L.T. (Notes) 59; *Hunter v. McLean*, 1948 S.L.T. (Notes) 83; *Wills' Trs v. Cairngorm Canoeing and Sailing School Ltd*, 1973 S.L.T. (Notes) 63; *Battu v. Battu*, 1979 S.L.T. (Notes) 7.

therefore be of only limited assistance in deciding the question. The question may arise in relation to a preliminary proof.[73]

> "A direction that a specified party shall lead in a proof never imports an anticipatory decision by the court as to where the ultimate onus of proof lies. It may, and often does, import the view of the court, formed upon a consideration of the averments, as to where the initial onus lies; but sometimes it imports no more than this, that considerations of convenience point to the desirability of the specified party leading his evidence first."[74]

8.65 A motion that the defender should lead may be made at any time before the diet of proof.[75] It may, however, be refused if the defender would be prejudiced by being ordained to lead "at the eleventh hour",[76] and a motion made after the proof is called will be refused.[77] The defender may agree to lead.[78] If there is no agreement, or if nothing to the contrary is said in an interlocutor issued before the proof, the pursuer must lead.

Other courses

8.66 Apart from proceeding to proof, proof before answer or debate an action may, in exceptional circumstances, follow a different course. In certain cases the cause may be remitted to the Court of Session.[79] In other cases proof may be obviated or abbreviated by a judicial remit,[80] or a judicial reference.[81] The parties may at any stage require the cause to be treated as a summary cause, and in that event it is so treated for all purposes and proceeds accordingly.[82] Where there are several actions arising out of the same cause of action, it is competent for the court at or after the closing of the record to appoint one of them to be the leading action and to sist the other actions pending the determination of the leading action.[83] To take a case along any of these courses a party would lodge the appropriate motion. The stage at which the motion should be lodged depends on the circumstances of the individual case. It might be as early as when defences are lodged[84] or as late as after proof has been allowed.[85]

---

[73] *Donald, Rutherford, AB, Battu, supra; D. & J. McDougall Ltd v. Argyll and Bute D.C.*, 1986 S.L.T. 564, *per* Lord Mackay of Clashfern at 566.

[74] *Macfarlane v. Macfarlane*, 1947 S.L.T. (Notes) 34, *per* L.P. Cooper.

[75] *Wills' Trs, supra.* It is thought that the reasoning in *Marquis of Breadalbane v. McNab* (1902) 20 Sh.Ct.Rep. 51 at 52–53, which is inconsistent with *Wills' Trs*, would not now be followed.

[76] *Wills' Trs, supra.*

[77] *Hope Bros v. Morrison*, 1960 S.C. 1, *per* Lord Sorn at 3.

[78] As, *e.g.* in *Mackay v. Campbell*, 1966 S.L.T. 329 although that case did not actually proceed to proof.

[79] Under the Sheriff Courts (Scotland) Act 1971, s. 37(1)(b). See paras 13.57 to 13.66.

[80] OCR, r. 29.2. See paras 13.26 to 13.34.

[81] See paras 13.35 to 13.40.

[82] Under the Sheriff Courts (Scotland) Act 1971, s. 37(1)(a). See para. 13.46.

[83] RCS, r. 22.3(6) makes specific provision for this procedure in the Court of Session. Although there is no similar rule in the OCR it is submitted that there is no reason in principle why this course should not be followed in appropriate circumstances.

[84] The defences might admit so much of the sum craved as to leave in dispute only an amount appropriate for a summary cause. Or they might include a counterclaim making the case suitable for remit to the Court of Session.

[85] Even at this stage a party may lodge a minute of amendment which affects the future progress of the case.

Chapter 9

WRITTEN PLEADINGS

The Nature and Functions of Pleadings

Definition

"The pleadings" means the written statements by the parties of their grounds of action and defence, which, when finally adjusted, form the closed record.[1] They may be referred to as "written pleadings" to distinguish them from "oral pleading", which consists of the arguments used in debate, at hearings on evidence and on appeal, and the conduct of the examination of witnesses. The first written pleading is the initial writ, which embodies the pursuer's claim, and the next is the defences, which contain the defender's answer to the pursuer's claim. There may be more than one set of defences where there is more than one defender; and in further separate pleadings a defender may make a counterclaim against the pursuer and the pursuer may answer it, and a third party may lodge answers to a case stated against him in the defences. The initial writ, the defences and any other pleadings are adjusted and when finally adjusted are printed in the closed record. They may not thereafter be altered except by amendment, which requires the leave of the court. 9.01

The formal requirements of the Ordinary Cause Rules concerning the initial writ, the defences and the adjustment of the pleadings are considered in Chapter 8, and the law and practice regarding counterclaims, third party procedure and amendment of pleadings are dealt with in later chapters. The purpose of this chapter is to consider, first, matters which are common to all written pleadings—the nature and functions of pleadings, the principal rules of pleading and the form and language of pleadings; and secondly, the techniques of pleading required in every ordinary action—the drafting of the initial writ and the defences, and the adjustment of the pleadings. 9.02

---

[1] J. M. Lees, *A Handbook of Written and Oral Pleading in the Sheriff Court* (2nd ed., 1920, reprinted by Caledonian Books 1988), p. 1, para. 1. Lees is the only book on the subject of written pleading in the Scottish courts. Essays on the subject include the "Introduction to Murray's Jury Court Reports", Vol. V (1831); C. (later L.J.-C.) Scott Dickson, "Pleading" (1897) 9 J.R. 26; D. (later Lord) Dundas, "Observations on the Art of Advocacy" (1903) 15 J.R. 329 at pp. 329–333; J. A. (later L.P.) Clyde, "Practice and Procedure in the Court of Session" (1906) 18 J.R. 319 at pp. 325, 329; R. W. Millar, "Civil Pleading in Scotland" (1932) 30 Mich. L.R. 545, 709 (with notes by L.P. Clyde); Lord Blades, "The Art of Pleading" (1948) 64 Sc.L.R. 25, 53; A. G. (later Sh. Pr. Sir Allan G.) Walker, "Written Pleadings" (1963) 79 Sc.L.R. 161; Professor R. Black, *An Introduction to Written Pleading* (Law Society of Scotland, 1982). The writer is also indebted to an unpublished lecture on Written Pleadings by Mr J. A. D. Hope, Q.C. (now Lord Hope of Craighead), and to Sir Jack I. H. Jacob's writings on English civil pleadings, especially his essay "The System of Pleadings" in Bullen and Leake and Jacob's *Precedents of Pleadings in the Queen's Bench Division of the High Court of Justice* (12th ed., 1975).

Functions of pleadings

Definition of the issues

9.03 "The objects sought to be attained by our system of pleading are, (1) the full disclosure of the facts; and (2) the full statement of the grounds of action and defence in law, as connected with those facts."[2] Each party states in his pleadings the material facts and the propositions of law on which he relies in support of his claim or defence, and thus there are elicited any matters on which the parties are agreed and the matters on which they differ. "The points on which the parties differ are the issue [or issues], and the matters which are said to be 'put in issue' are the material points which must be determined in order that the case may be decided."[3] The function of our system of written pleading is, accordingly, to ascertain and demonstrate with precision the matters on which the parties differ and those on which they agree; and thus to arrive at certain clear issues on which both parties require a judicial decision.

9.04 The presentation of each party's case in the written pleadings has the important effect of giving notice of his case to the court and to his opponent, and of providing for the party himself a summary of the matters which he must prove and the arguments which he must present in order to succeed in his claim or defence. The pleadings also provide the basis for the court's decisions on questions of procedure; and, since they place on record the precise questions raised in the action, they are considered when a plea of *res judicata* is raised with reference to the action in any future litigation.

Notice to the court

9.05 The importance of giving notice of each party's case to the court arises from the consideration that the court is limited to granting the remedy craved and to deciding the case on the basis of the pleadings.[4] Except in regard to the limited category of matters which are *pars judicis*,[5] the court does not play an active role in relation to the raising of the issues for its consideration and determination. The court, by examining the pleadings, ascertains from the parties themselves what are the matters in dispute between them.

> "It is no part of the duty or function of the court to enter upon any inquiry into the case before it other than to adjudicate upon the specific matters in dispute which the parties have raised by their pleadings. . . . The court does not provide its own terms of reference or conduct its own inquiry into the merits of the case, but accepts and acts upon the terms of reference which the parties have chosen and specified in their pleadings."[6]

9.06 It follows that the pleadings provide each party with his first opportunity to present his case to the sheriff; and that the sheriff's first

---

[2] McGlashan, p. 217.
[3] Lees, *Pleading*, p. 1, para. 2.
[4] See para. 17.03.
[5] See paras 2.09 to 2.17.
[6] Sir Jack I. H. Jacob, "The Present Importance of Pleadings" (1960) 13 *Current Legal Problems* 171 at p. 174, reprinted in Jacob, *The Reform of Civil Procedural Law* (1982), p. 243 at 246.

impression of the party's case will normally be derived from his reading of the party's pleadings before he goes into court and hears any evidence or oral argument. He will be entitled to assume that each party has put forward in his pleadings the best case he has in the best way he can. It is therefore of considerable practical importance that the pleadings should be cast in the manner most likely to impress the sheriff favourably by displaying an understanding on the part of the draftsman of the functions, rules, forms and language of pleading.

Notice to the opponent

"The function of pleadings is to give fair notice of the case which has to be met so that the opposing party may direct his evidence to the issue disclosed by them."[7] **9.07**

> "It is a fundamental rule of our pleading that a party is not entitled to establish a case against his opponent of which the other has not received fair notice upon record. It follows that a defender cannot be held liable upon a ground which is not included in the averments made against him by the pursuer. These are not mere technical rules since their disregard would tend to create injustice, by imposing liability upon a defender for reasons which he had no opportunity to refute."[8]

Each party, accordingly, frames and prepares his own case for proof and conducts his examination and cross-examination of the witnesses upon the basis that he has been given fair and proper notice of the issues which the other intends to raise and that the other will not take him by surprise by introducing different issues. "Averments give notice of the facts which the pursuer will attempt to prove, and he is not entitled to prove other facts not averred by him."[9] The degree of specification which is sufficient for fair notice is considered below.[10]

Notice to the party

A party's own pleadings, if properly drafted, provide for his solicitor a convenient method of compiling the essential elements of his own case and constitute a useful summary of the facts he must prove and the arguments he must adduce when presenting the case in court. If the pleadings have been soundly framed, the draftsman will have defined the facts which form the ground of action or defence and will have considered whether his client has a valid claim or defence, and no vital matter will have been overlooked. Further, once the pleadings have been finally adjusted, the pleader should be able to see at once the matters which remain in dispute and precisely what facts he must prove in order to support his own case and rebut the case he has to meet. His pleadings should accordingly form a reliable basis for his preparation of the evidence he will require for the proof and of the submissions he will make to the sheriff at any debate and at the hearing on evidence. **9.08**

---

[7] *Esso Petroleum Co. v. Southport Corporation* [1956] A.C. 218, *per* Lord Normand at 238. See also *Lord Advocate v. Johnston*, 1985 S.L.T. 533, *per* L. J.-C. Wheatley giving the opinion of the court at 534–535.

[8] *Morrison's Associated Cos Ltd v. James Rome & Sons Ltd*, 1964 S.C. 160, *per* Lord Guthrie at 190.

[9] *Ward v. Coltness Iron Co.*, 1944 S.C. 318, *per* L.P. Normand at 322.

[10] See paras 9.27 to 9.30.

Basis of procedural decisions

9.09 The pleadings not only define the issues for the benefit of the court and the parties: they also provide the basis for the court's decisions on many important procedural questions both before and at the stage of proof. The question whether to order debate or a form of inquiry or a remit to the Court of Session or to a man of skill will be determined on a consideration of the parties' submissions with reference to the pleadings. If debate is allowed, the court's decision is based on and limited by the pleadings.[11] If inquiry is allowed, the mode of inquiry is dependent on the pleadings,[12] as are the ambit of any commission and diligence for the recovery of oral, documentary or real evidence,[13] and the determination of the questions of where the burden of proof lies, which party is to lead evidence first,[14] and questions of the admissibility of evidence at the inquiry.

Res judicata

9.10 Where a plea of *res judicata* is stated, its validity as regards identity of *media concludendi* normally depends upon a consideration of the pleadings and decision in the previous action: the question always is, what was litigated and what was decided. The court must read the whole of the pleadings in each case and grasp the substance of each, and then compare the two.[15] The pleadings accordingly constitute a permanent record of the issues litigated in the action, and together with the decree will show whether the court's decision will ground a successful plea of *res judicata* in subsequent proceedings.

Importance of written pleadings

9.11 Since written pleadings have to fulfil the various functions described in the foregoing paragraphs, their importance in civil litigation cannot be over-emphasised.

> "A party is not well served if his pleading is drafted in a hurried, shoddy, slipshod, unthinking manner, on the basis that whatever is stated in the pleading will do and may be developed by [adjustment or recovery of documents or evidence at the proof] or may be amended in due course; and conversely a party is well served whose pleading states his case with clarity and precision, with [proper specification], with understanding of the law, an insight into the substantive rights of the parties, and intelligent anticipation of how the case of the party will need to be prepared and presented to the court. The one kind of pleading lays bare the weakness of the party's case; the other kind clothes it with strength and substance. The drafting of a pleading is the equivalent of laying the foundation on which to build the claim or defence of a party, and as the foundation is laid, whether badly or well and truly, so will the claim or defence be weak and fall or be well sustained and upheld. Pleadings should therefore be

---

[11] See paras 13.01 to 13.25.
[12] See paras 8.54 to 8.66.
[13] See paras 15.24, 15.51.
[14] See para. 8.64.
[15] *Edinburgh and District Water Trs v. Clippens Oil Co.* (1899) 1 F. 899, *per* L.P. Robertson at 907, Lord Kinnear at 909. See para. 2.108.

drafted with all due care and circumspection, and they require the exercise of much skill and not a little art, to fulfil their whole function."[16]

Responsibility of the pleader

It follows that the drafting of pleadings is a responsibility which must be carefully discharged. Before putting pen to paper (or perhaps, more commonly nowadays, voice to dictating machine), the pleader must be satisfied that he understands both the facts and the legal basis of his case. He must identify the facts which he requires to prove, and the legal arguments which he will have to present, in order to succeed, and then decide on the most precise, clear and effective method of presenting his case in accordance with the rules, forms and language of pleading. It is of cardinal importance that he should draft the pleadings in good faith. He should state matters as facts only if he has before him evidence to support his averments, and he should never make averments for which he has no evidence "in the hope that something may turn up in the course of the case to justify them".[17] In particular, allegations of fraud, bad faith or immoral conduct should not be pleaded unless expressly instructed and unless there is in the papers before the pleader clear and sufficient evidence to support them.[18] A solicitor undertaking the conduct of a cause in the sheriff court, like an advocate in the Court of Session, "takes on himself an office in the performance of which he owes a duty, not to his client only, but also to the court, to the members of his own profession, and to the public."[19] The pleader's signature of his pleadings will be understood by the court as a voucher that the case which he has pleaded is not a mere fiction.[20] **9.12**

THE PRINCIPAL RULES OF PLEADING

The principal rules of pleading are these. (1) Pleadings must state facts only, and not evidence or, in general, law. (2) Every statement of fact made by one party must be answered by the other party. An understanding of this rule requires a consideration of the law and practice as to implied admissions and the making of admissions. (3) The pleadings must be specific. (4) The pleadings must be relevant. **9.13**

Facts

General rule

The condescendence of the initial writ and the answers in the defences should state only the facts upon which the party relies. The condescendence must state the ground of jurisdiction[21] and the facts upon which the ground of jurisdiction is based.[22] It should also state the facts which form **9.14**

---

[16] Bullen and Leake and Jacob, p. 17, adapted.

[17] *Boustead v. Gardner* (1879) 7 R. 139, *per* L.J.-C. Moncreiff at 145.

[18] *Milne & Co. v. Aberdeen District Committee* (1899) 2 F. 220, *per* Lord Kinnear at 231; Black, p. 18. *Cf. Associated Leisure Ltd v. Associated Newspapers Ltd* [1970] 2 Q.B. 450, *per* Lord Denning M.R. at 456.

[19] *Batchelor v. Pattison and Mackersy* (1876) 3 R. 914, *per* L.P. Inglis at 918.

[20] *cf. Great Australian Gold Mining Co. v. Martin* (1877) 5 Ch.D. 1, *per* James L.J. at 10. See para. 9.49.

[21] OCR, r. 3.1(5)(a).

[22] OCR, r. 3.1(5)(b).

the ground of action,[23] and the defences must contain answers to the condescendence[24] which, similarly, must be factual in content. Each party must, accordingly, plead all the facts which he must prove in order to establish his ground of action or defence. "Our Scottish procedure pays observance, not lip service, to pleadings. A pursuer or petitioner must set out in his final pleadings averments which, if established on the basis of the law on which he founds, warrant the remedy which he seeks."[25] There should be no argumentative[26] or scandalous[27] matter. Such matter may be ordered to be withdrawn, and its author penalised in expenses or otherwise.[28]

No evidence

9.15 The requirement that the parties should aver only the facts which form the grounds of action or defence means that they must aver only the facts which they offer to prove, and not the evidence by which they propose to prove them.[29] "The beauty of the Scotch system is, that, without disclosing what is properly called evidence, you must at least state the line of defence, and the main facts and points in the enquiry on which you rest, so that the other party shall be fully able previously to investigate the case, and be prepared for it."[30] Since the function of evidence is to prove or disprove the facts in issue and not to identify what these issues are, averments of evidence have no place in pleadings.

No law

9.16 A further corollary of the rule that the parties must plead only facts in their pleadings is that matters of law should not be pleaded there.[31] The legal propositions on which a party relies should be stated in his pleas-in-law.

Exceptions to the rule

9.17 There are both real and apparent exceptions to this rule. The major real exception is that in actions of damages for negligence the established modern practice is to aver specifically the legal duties owed to the pursuer by the defender at common law or by virtue of statutory provisions. The practice has been criticised,[32] but it remains the usual and approved style of pleading such actions.[33] The minor real exception is that a Private Act of Parliament passed before 1850 must be averred and proved unless it contains a provision to the effect that it is to be judicially noticed as a Public Act.[34]

---

[23] OCR, r. 3.1(1) and App. 1, Form G1.

[24] OCR, r. 9.6(2).

[25] *Mackenzie v. West Lothian D.C.*, 1979 S.C. 433, *per* L.J.-C. Wheatley at 437–438.

[26] *Sproat v. Mure* (1826) 5 S. 66 (N.E. 61); *Connell v. Ferguson* (1861) 23 D. 683, *per* Lord Neaves at 686.

[27] *Herdman v. Young* (1744) Mor. 13987; *Wardrope v. Duke of Hamilton* (1876) 3 R. 876, *per* L.P. Inglis at 878; *Clydesdale Bank Ltd v. Paton* (1896) 23 R.(H.L.) 22, *per* Lord Watson at 26; *MacGregor v. MacGregor*, 1946 S.L.T. (Notes) 13; *C v. W*, 1950 S.L.T. (Notes) 8.

[28] *Herdman, Wardrope, supra.* See para. 10.60.

[29] *Roy v. Wright* (1826) 5 S. 107 (N.E. 98); *Tullach v. Davidson* (1858) 20 D. 1045, *per* Lord Cowan at 1056.

[30] *Neilson v. Househill Coal and Iron Co.* (1842) 4 D. 1187, *per* L.J.-C. Hope at 1193.

[31] *Roy v. Wright* (1826) 5 S. 107 (N.E. 98).

[32] D. M. Walker, "Pleadings in Negligence" (1956) 72 Sc.L.R. 241; Walker, *Delict*, p. 187, n. 88.

[33] Lord Kissen, "Delict", 1966 S.L.T. (News) 45.

[34] Interpretation Act 1978, s. 3; Walkers, *Evidence*, p. 219.

Foreign law

The apparent exception to the rule occurs where foreign law is pleaded. Apart from the limited category of cases in which the Scottish courts are required to take judicial notice of foreign law,[35] foreign law is a matter of fact for the Scottish courts and is presumed to be the same as Scots law except in so far as may be relevantly averred and proved to the contrary. A party founding upon foreign law must therefore relevantly aver the substance of the foreign rule upon which he founds, why it is in point, and its effect in relation to the facts before the court.[36] **9.18**

Admissions

General rule

It is a general rule of pleading that every statement of fact made by one party must be answered by the other party.[37] A party is accordingly obliged to respond to each averment made by his opponent in one of three ways: by admitting it, denying it, or stating that the matter is not known and not admitted. The following paragraphs deal with the circumstances in which an admission may be implied, and the considerations relevant to the making of explicit admissions. **9.19**

Implied admissions

A party will be deemed to have admitted a fact averred by his opponent in the following situations. **9.20**

(a) If a party leaves unanswered a statement of fact made by his opponent, he is deemed to have admitted it.[38] **9.21**

(b) If a statement made by one party of a fact within the knowledge of the other party is not denied by that other party, the latter is held as admitting the fact so stated.[39] It has been held that this rule extends to facts within the knowledge of the other party's solicitors, and that knowledge acquired by them as his agents is knowledge of the other party.[40] On the other hand it appears that a fact is held to be within a party's knowledge only if the fact is his state of knowledge,[41] or the **9.22**

---

35 Macphail, *Evidence*, paras 2.04 to 2.07.

36 *Valery v. Scott* (1876) 3 R. 965, *per* Lord Deas at 967; *Owners of the "Immanuel" v. Denholm & Co.* (1887) 15 R. 152, *per* L.J.-C. Moncreiff at 156; *Roe v. Roe* (1915) 32 Sh.Ct.Rep. 30; *Stuart v. Potter, Choate & Prentice*, 1911 1 S.L.T. 377, *per* Lord Salvesen at 382; *McElroy v. McAllister*, 1949 S.C. 110, *per* L.J.-C. Thomson at 117–118, Lord Mackay at 123, L.P. Cooper at 137; *Prawdzu-Lazarska v. Prawdzic-Lazarski*, 1954 S.C. 98, *per* L.P. Cooper at 101–102; *Rodden v. Whatlings Ltd*, 1961 S.C. 132; *Scottish National Orchestra Society Ltd v. Thomson's Exr*, 1969 S.L.T. 325 at 331; *Pryde v. Proctor and Gamble Ltd*, 1971 S.L.T. (Notes) 18; *Bonnor v. Balfour Kilpatrick Ltd*, 1974 S.C. 223; *Emerald Stainless Steel Ltd v. South Side Distribution Ltd*, 1982 S.C. 61. But see *Bain v. Whitehaven Ry* (1850) 7 Bell's App. 79; Walkers, *Evidence*, p. 447.

37 OCR, r. 9.7.

38 *Scottish N.-E. Ry v. Napier* (1859) 21 D. 700, *per* L.J.-C. Inglis at 703; A. G. Walker, "Written Pleadings" (1963) 79 Sc.L.R. 161 at 169.

39 OCR, r. 9.7. *Ellis v. Fraser* (1840) 3 D. 264 at 271; *Pegler v. Northern Agricultural Implement Co.* (1877) 4 R. 435; *Central Motor Engineering Co. v. Galbraith*, 1918 S.C. 755; *Gilmour v. Scottish Clan Motorways Ltd*, 1928 S.N. 19.

40 *Mohammed v. Mohammed*, 1954 S.L.T. (Sh. Ct.) 93.

41 *Central Motor Engineering Co., supra, per* L.P. Strathclyde at 765, Lord Mackenzie at 770.

existence of a simple legal relationship with another,[42] or any other matter about which he does not have to make inquiries in order to ascertain the truth.[43] The expression "Not admitted" or "No admission is made" is not the equivalent of a denial of a fact within the other party's knowledge, and is construed as an admission.[44]

9.23 (c) Where one party answers the other's averment with the words "Believed to be true that . . ." he will be deemed to have admitted the fact averred by the other.[45]

9.24 (d) In general, averments which are not explicit admissions should not be construed as such,[46] but an averment that the defender performed all statutory duties incumbent upon him will be construed as an admission of the applicability of the statute founded on by the pursuer,[47] and a narrative of matters which are not seriously in dispute may be construed as implicitly admitting the other party's account of them.[48] Admissions may be held sufficient to support a reasonable inference adverse to the defender, as that a driver was an employee of the defender acting in the course of his employment.[49]

Making of admissions

9.25 Care is required in the making of admissions, because admissions in the closed record exclude evidence and are conclusive against the party making them in the cause in which they are made,[50] except in certain family actions,[51] and may be proved against him in a subsequent civil cause in which he is also a party[52]; and admissions deleted from the pleadings before the record is closed, although not binding on the party making them, may be the subject of cross-examination by his opponent.[53] Admissions must, however, be read along with any qualifications and explanations which accompany them, unless these are disproved[54] or found to be irrelevant.[55]

9.26 While admissions must be framed with care, the rules of proper conduct of civil litigation demand that pleaders should be as candid as possible, since the function of pleadings is to focus the issues on which the parties are truly in dispute. One party is not entitled simply to deny all the other's

---

42 *Ellis, supra.*

43 *O'Connor v. W. G. Auld & Co. (Engineering) Ltd*, 1970 S.L.T. (Notes) 16.

44 *Ellis, supra*; *Callaghan v. J. & A. Weir Ltd* (1955) 71 Sh.Ct.Rep. 312; *Clark v. Clark*, 1967 S.C. 296 at 305.

45 *Scottish N.-E. Ry v. Napier* (1859) 21 D. 700.

46 *Cruickshank Fraser & Co. v. Caledonian Ry* (1876) 3 R. 484.

47 *McNaught v. British Railways Board*, 1979 S.L.T. (Notes) 99.

48 *Paterson v. Scottish Solicitors Discipline Tribunal*, 1984 S.L.T. 3 at 4.

49 *Hayhoe v. Hydro Plant*, 1976 S.L.T. (Sh. Ct.) 78.

50 Stair, IV, xlv, 5–6; Erskine, IV, ii, 33; *Scottish Marine Insurance Co. v. Turner* (1853) 1 Macq. 334, *per* Lord Truro at 340.

51 *Macfarlane v. Macfarlane*, 1956 S.C. 472.

52 Walkers, *Evidence*, p. 31; Maxwell, p. 188.

53 *Lennox v. National Coal Board*, 1955 S.C. 438; *Carter v. Allison*, 1966 S.C. 257, *per* Lord Fraser at 265. *Cf. Healey v. A. Massey & Son*, 1961 S.C. 198 (statements in legal aid memorandum).

54 *Picken v. Arundale & Co.* (1872) 10 M. 987; *Armour & Melvin v. Mitchell*, 1934 S.C. 94, *per* L.J.-C. Aitchison at 96; Walkers, *Evidence*, pp. 42–43, Maxwell, p. 188 and cases there cited.

55 *Robertson & Co. v. Bird & Co.* (1897) 24 R. 1076; *Rothwell v. Stuart's Trs* (1898) 1 F. 81.

averments and put him to proof of his case. It has been said that a plain denial of the pursuer's cardinal averment always entitles the defender to put the pursuer to the proof of it[56]; but such a denial must not be dishonestly stated. Not only must a party admit any averment which he knows to be true: he should also admit any other averments which are not truly in issue or in doubt.[57] The withholding of admissions may be reflected in the court's ultimate awards of interest and expenses,[58] and may have other serious consequences: a solicitor who withholds an admission of a fact within his knowledge is liable to incur severe criticism[59]; and if the party admits in court a matter which has been denied in his pleadings, the force of the defence will be weakened and his credibility prejudiced.[60]

Specification

A party's averments in his condescendence or answers must specify sufficient facts to allow the party to lead all the evidence he desires to lead at the inquiry, and to give his opponent fair notice of what the party hopes to establish in fact; and they must present, together with the pleas-in-law, a relevant claim or defence. If a party's pleadings are attacked in debate and found by the court to be deficient in specification or relevancy, then his action may be dismissed or his defences may be repelled and decree granted against him *de plano*, without inquiry into the merits of his claim or defence.[61] A plea to specification is very frequently combined with a plea to relevancy as a ground for dismissal or decree *de plano*. Pleas to relevancy and specification are in practice more frequently stated by defenders than by pursuers, and for that reason the discussions of specification and relevancy in the following paragraphs are concerned with the specification and relevancy of the pursuer's averments in his condescendence. The same requirements of specification and relevancy are, however, equally applicable to the pleadings of defenders. **9.27**

The Ordinary Cause Rules direct that the condescendence must state the ground of jurisdiction[62] and the facts upon which the ground of jurisdiction is based.[63] It should also state the facts which form the ground of action.[64] A condescendence which is seriously lacking in such specification may not render the action fundamentally null,[65] but it will not pass the tests of specification and relevancy. While the condescendence should not refer to the evidence which the pursuer proposes to lead, it must specify the material facts which the pursuer offers to prove.[66] It is a fundamental rule of pleading that a party is not entitled to establish a case **9.28**

---

[56] *Mohammed v. Mohammed*, 1954 S.L.T. (Sh. Ct.) 93.

[57] *Ellon Castle Estates Co. Ltd v. Macdonald*, 1975 S.L.T. (Notes) 55; *Foxley v. Dunn*, 1978 S.L.T. (Notes) 35; *Lossie Hydraulic Co. v. Ecosse Transport Ltd*, 1980 S.L.T. (Sh. Ct.) 94. See para. 9.114.

[58] *Ganley v. Scottish Boatowners Mutual Insurance Association*, 1967 S.L.T. (Notes) 45; *J. C. Forbes Ltd v. Duignan*, 1974 S.L.T. (Sh. Ct.) 74.

[59] *Mohammed, supra.*

[60] *McDonald v. Glass* (1883) 21 S.L.R. 45.

[61] See para. 13.48.

[62] OCR, r. 3.1(5)(a).

[63] OCR, r. 3.1(5)(b).

[64] OCR, r. 3.1(5)(9) and (a) and App. 1, Form G.1.

[65] *Bank of Scotland v. W. & G. Fergusson* (1898) 1 F. 96; *British Railways Board v. Strathclyde R.C.*, 1981 S.C. 90.

[66] See para. 9.14.

against his opponent of which the other has not received fair notice upon record.[67] It follows that a defender cannot be held liable upon a ground which is not included in the averments made against him by the pursuer,[68] unless he has failed to object timeously to the introduction of evidence in support of such a ground.[69] That situation apart, the pursuer may later be entitled to put forward as a ground for judgment a case which is a variation, modification or development of what is averred, but not one which is new, separate and distinct,[70] or wholly inconsistent with his own averments.[71] When a duty in general terms is averred, followed by a particularisation of the way or ways in which it is alleged that that duty has been breached, the inquiry on the facts is restricted to the specific breach or breaches of which notice has been given, and evidence directed to some other unspecified way in which the general duty may have been breached is excluded.[72]

9.29 The defender may seek dismissal of the action upon a plea of lack of specification.[73] That plea finds its proper application in a case where the defender does not know the case against him and objects to being taken by surprise at the proof.[74] It is possible for a condescendence to be relevant, in respect that it states facts sufficient to render the action relevant in law, but to be lacking in specification in respect that it does not give fair notice of all the facts which the pursuer intends to establish. The degree of specification which will be deemed sufficient for fair notice depends on the particular circumstances of each case. Enough specification must be given to enable the other party to identify what is being alleged against him and to prepare his case. Any material dates, times and places which ought reasonably to be known to the pursuer should be specified[75]; but in certain circumstances averments may be sufficiently specific if facts peculiarly within the defender's knowledge cannot be averred because of practical difficulties.[76] When deciding whether the defender has been given fair notice of the pursuer's case the court will consider the matter broadly,[77] and will regard a complaint of lack of fair notice as justifiable only if it is likely to result in material prejudice to the defender.[78]

---

[67] See para. 9.07.

[68] *Morrison's Associated Cos Ltd v. James Rome & Sons Ltd*, 1946 S.C. 160, *per* Lord Guthrie at 190.

[69] *McGlone v. British Railways Board*, 1966 S.C.(H.L.) 1; *Brown's Exrx v. N.B. Steel Foundry*, 1968 S.L.T. 121.

[70] *Burns v. Dixon's Iron Works*, 1961 S.C. 102, *per* L.J.-C. Thomson at 108–109; *O'Hanlon v. John G. Stein & Co.*, 1965 S.C.(H.L.) 23, *per* Lord Guest at 42; *McIntosh v. Walker Steam Trawl Fishing Co. Ltd*, 1971 S.L.T. (Notes) 75; *McCusker v. Saveheat Cavity Wall Insulation Ltd*, 1987 S.L.T. 24.

[71] *Johnstone v. Clyde Navigation Trs* (1949) 82 Ll.L.Rep. 187, *per* Lord Reid at 195; *Gunn v. McAdam & Son*, 1949 S.C. 31; *Lawrence v. Sir William Arrol & Co.*, 1958 S.C. 348; *Hamilton v. John Brown & Co. (Clydebank) Ltd*, 1969 S.L.T. (Notes) 18; *Carroll v. Scots Shipbuilding & Engineering Co. Ltd*, 1969 S.L.T. (Notes) 46. See also Walkers, *Evidence*, pp. 80–82.

[72] *Morrison's Associated Cos Ltd v. James Rome & Sons Ltd*, 1946 S.C. 160, *per* L.P. Clyde at 182.

[73] See para. 9.123.

[74] *Macdonald v. Glasgow Western Hospitals*, 1954 S.C. 453, *per* L.P. Cooper at 465.

[75] A. G. Walker, "Written Pleadings" (1963) 79 Sc.L.R. 161 at 169.

[76] *Gunn v. McAdam & Sons*, 1949 S.C. 31; *Johnson v. Gill*, 1978 S.C. 74.

[77] *McMenemy v. James Dougal & Sons Ltd*, 1960 S.L.T. (Notes) 84.

[78] *Avery v. Hew Park School for Boys*, 1949 S.L.T. (Notes) 6.

In many cases the defender is entitled to have the grounds of action specified in some detail. Where a charge of fraud is made, the facts and circumstances from which fraud may be inferred must be distinctly stated.[79] So too, clear averments are required when contempt of court is being alleged.[80] In an action for declarator of paternity, a defender who denies intercourse at a time which could account for the birth of the child is entitled to know when and where the alleged acts of intercourse took place[81]; and in an action of separation founded on adultery the averments should be "as precise and pointed as they can be made".[82] In an action founded on warranty, the exact words of the warranty must be given,[83] and the special quality warranted.[84] If it is averred that goods were sold for a particular purpose, that purpose must be specified.[85] Where it is averred that a contract was subject to conditions by implication from a previous course of dealings, clear specification of the previous course of dealings must be given.[86] In actions of defamation the words used[87] and the places where, occasions when[88] and persons before whom[89] they were uttered, and any innuendo,[90] must be specified. In an action founded on fault, a specific fault or breach of duty must be averred[91]; and an averment of foreseeability must be supported by averments of the facts and circumstances from which foreseeability is to be inferred,[92] such as specific previous complaints[93] or similar incidents.[94] In an action founded on breach of statutory duty the pursuer should specify the particular statutory provision of which he claims the defender to be in breach, and in what respect he is in breach.[95] A distinction, however, is to be drawn between cases in which it is necessary for a pursuer to bring himself within a statutory provision by specific reference to the statute in averment (*e.g.* a Factories Act case) and those in which it is sufficient for the pursuer to **9.30**

---

[79] *Shedden v. Patrick* (1852) 14 D. 721 at 727 (affd (1854) 17 D.(H.L.) 18); *Wright v. Guild & Wyllie* (1893) 30 S.L.R. 785, *per* L.J.-C Macdonald at 787; *Thomson & Co. v. Pattison Elder & Co.* (1895) 22 R. 432; *Milne & Co. v. Aberdeen District Committee* (1899) 2 F. 220; and see *Stair Encyclopaedia*, Vol. 11, para. 704.

[80] *Byrne v. Ross*, 1993 S.L.T. 307.

[81] *Barr v. Bain* (1896) 23 R. 1090; *Tolan v. Stewart* (1913) 30 Sh.Ct.Rep. 280.

[82] *Tulloh v. Tulloh* (1861) 23 D. 639, *per* L.J.-C. Inglis at 644; and see Clive, para. 27.030.

[83] *Robeson v. Waugh* (1874) 2 R. 63; *Mackie v. Riddell* (1874) 2 R. 115.

[84] *Rose v. Johnston* (1878) 5 R. 600.

[85] *Hamilton v. Robertson* (1878) 5 R. 839; *Dunlop v. Crawford* (1886) 13 R. 973.

[86] *McCrone v. Boots Farm Sales Ltd*, 1981 S.C. 68; *GEA Airexchangers Ltd v. James Howden & Co. Ltd*, 1984 S.L.T. 264.

[87] *Martin v. McLean* (1844) 6 D. 981.

[88] *Walker v. Cumming* (1868) 6 M. 318.

[89] *Broomfield v. Greig* (1868) 6 M. 992; *Bisset v. Ecclesfield* (1864) 2 M. 1096.

[90] *Reid v. Moore* (1893) 20 R. 712; *Murdison v. Scottish Football Union* (1896) 23 R. 449, *per* Lord Kinnear at 463. These were cases in which the pursuer sought jury trial. It has been observed that in the sheriff court, where civil jury trial is incompetent, "all that is required of the pleader is to give reasonable notice of the derogatory imputation that the material complained of is said to bear. The precise articulation of the innuendo becomes less important" (*Hackett v. Allan*, Sh. Pr. Caplan, Dunoon Sh. Ct, May 15, 1984, unreported).

[91] *Harper v. James Dunlop & Co. Ltd* (1902) 5 F. 208, *per* Lord Kinnear at 213 and many later cases, *e.g. Gilfillan v. National Coal Board*, 1972 S.L.T. (Sh. Ct.) 39; *Davie v. Edinburgh Corporation*, 1977 S.L.T. (Notes) 5.

[92] *Robb v. Dundee D.C.*, 1980 S.L.T. (Notes) 91.

[93] *Bryce v. Allied Ironfounders Ltd*, 1969 S.L.T. (Notes) 29.

[94] *W. Alexander & Sons v. Dundee Corporation*, 1950 S.C. 123; *Murray v. Nicholls*, 1983 S.L.T. 194.

[95] For a discussion of the requirements of relevancy in an action based on breach of statutorily implied terms of a contract, see *Britain Steamship Co. Ltd v. Lithgows Ltd*, 1975 S.L.T. (Notes) 20.

aver facts and circumstances bringing himself within the ambit of the statute.[96] In an action of damages the pursuer must specify the details of the losses which in the aggregate form the sum claimed in the crave of the initial writ.[97]

9.31 The degree of specification which is to be afforded in any case is a matter which requires careful judgment by the pleader. If his pleadings are successfully criticised on the ground of lack of specification, he may have to seek leave to amend, or the action may be dismissed. If his pleadings are sufficient to take the case to proof, they may yet be insufficient for him to lead all the evidence he needs in order to succeed. He is not entitled to make averments which are not supportable by information before him, "in the hope that something may turn up in the course of the case to justify them".[98] He must beware of making averments which require him to undertake a more extensive onus of proof than a strict application of the requirements of the law demands,[99] although failure to discharge a superfluous onus does not involve failure to succeed if other averments sufficient to warrant the remedy sought are established in proof.[1] He may make averments which are not essential with a view to the disclosure of information under a commission and diligence. If he avers more than is necessary for success, or claims more than can be clearly proved to be due to the pursuer, he may provoke opposition when he had a chance of obtaining a decree in absence. If it is necessary to make averments which are guarded in their language, they must nevertheless give the defender fair notice of the line of action.

Relevancy

9.32 "The object of a condescendence is not merely to give fair notice to the other side of what the framer hopes to establish in fact, but—coupled with the note of pleas-in-law—to present a relevant case, that is, to disclose a position in fact and law which requires or justifies the remedy asked. It is as if the pursuer came into court and said: 'This is a summary of my case.' The summary must be sufficiently full to enable the court to determine whether, assuming the facts to be verified either (a) *instanter* by admission or by probative documents, or (b) by evidence to be subsequently led, the pursuer has a good case in law. If the pursuer fails in this, his case is dismissed without enquiry into the matters of fact alleged on either side."[2]

---

[96] *Devos NV Gebroeder v. Sunderland Sportswear Ltd*, 1987 S.L.T. 331; *Mac Electrical and Heating Engineers Ltd v. Calscot Electrical (Distributors) Ltd*, 1989 S.C.L.R. 498; and see para. 9.68.

[97] In an action of damages for personal injuries no overall figures are usually stated in practice for the elements of wage loss and *solatium*, but some basis for the assessment of wage loss is given in the form of a statement of pre-accident wages and time off work, and for the assessment of *solatium* in the form of a statement of the nature and consequences of the injuries (*Jamieson v. Allan McNeil & Son*, 1974 S.L.T. (Notes) 9).

[98] *Boustead v. Gardner* (1879) 7 R. 139, *per* L.J.-C. Moncrieff at 145.

[99] See *Sinclair v. National Coal Board*, 1963 S.C. 586; *Nimmo v. Alexander Cowan & Sons*, 1967 S.C.(H.L.) 79.

[1] *Keenan v. Rolls-Royce Ltd*, 1969 S.C. 322, *per* Lord Cameron at 341.

[2] R. W. Millar, "Civil Pleading in Scotland" (1932) 30 Mich.L.R. 545 at 561–562, n. 74, *per* L.P. Clyde.

In stating a plea to relevancy the pleader in effect

> "says: 'What the opposite party says may be true, or it may not, but even if it be assumed that it is all true, nevertheless he cannot prevail against me, either because an essential fact is unrepresented in his averments, or because the facts he avers would not, even if proved, justify the application of the legal principle to which he appeals.' The plea to the relevancy, in short, avoids, or at least postpones, any joinder of issue on the merits of the case."[3]
>
> "The effect of the relevancy plea is neatly shown in the American lawyer's classification of defences into three types. There is 'No, I didn't'—a denial of the facts; then there is 'Yes, but'—the facts are admitted but the action cannot succeed because of some other facts—the condonation of adultery, for example; thirdly there is 'So what?'—even if the facts are true they do not afford the remedy sought—that is exactly the idea of relevancy."[4]

An action will not be dismissed as irrelevant unless it must necessarily fail even if all the pursuer's averments are proved.[5] Actions of damages for negligence will be dismissed on that ground only in a very clear case,[6] such as one in which the facts bearing on liability are within the knowledge of the pursuer, and it is clear that his averments are irrelevant.[7] Pleadings in simple traffic accident cases are not scrutinised with strictness.[8] In all cases, the court in reaching a decision on relevancy will consider those averments by the defender which the pursuer admits,[9] but not those which he denies.[10] A bare general denial of the defender's averments as to a matter essential to the relevancy of the pursuer's case about which the pursuer himself has made no averments may, however, be considered.[11] In certain circumstances his failure to make his meaning perfectly distinct, in the face of an averment in answer by the defender, may be taken into account.[12] The court will prefer the most reasonable and ordinary construction of the words employed in the averments under consideration, and will "avoid such an analysis as, pushed to an extreme, would evacuate simple and plain statements and tear their plain meaning to pieces."[13] It is undesirable, even if proper, that the interpretation of pleadings should in a matter of relevancy depend upon concessions given or glosses offered at the bar in order to modify or alter what would appear **9.33**

---

3 Millar, *op. cit.*, at 568, n. 96, *per* L.P. Clyde.

4 W. A. Wilson, *Introductory Essays on Scots Law* (2nd ed., 1984), p. 66.

5 *Jamieson v. Jamieson*, 1952 S.C.(H.L.) 44, *per* Lord Normand at 50, Lord Reid at 63.

6 *Miller v. SSEB*, 1958 S.C.(H.L.) 20, *per* Viscount Simonds at 32, Lord Keith of Avonholm at 33; *McArthur v. Raynesway Plant Ltd*, 1980 S.L.T. 74; *Murray v. Edinburgh D.C.*, 1981 S.L.T. 253, *per* Lord Maxwell at 256; *McGeouch v. Strathclyde R.C.*, 1985 S.L.T. 321; *Meechan v. British Railways Board*, 1989 S.C.L.R. 772. But see *Gibson v. Strathclyde R.C.*, 1992 S.C.L.R. 902.

7 *Blaikie v. British Transport Commission*, 1961 S.C. 44. For examples of the dismissal of such actions, see *Davie v. Edinburgh Corporation*, 1977 S.L.T. (Notes) 5; *Robb v. Dundee D.C.*, 1980 S.L.T. (Notes) 91.

8 *Adamson v. Roberts*, 1951 S.C. 681; *Prentice v. Chalmers*, 1985 S.L.T. 168, *per* Lord Hunter at 170; *Barrow v. Bryce*, 1986 S.L.T. 691.

9 *Pringle v. Bremner and Stirling* (1867) 5 M.(H.L.) 55, *per* Lord Chelmsford L.C. at 58, Lord Colonsay at 61.

10 *Hamilton v. Santi* (1916) 32 Sh.Ct.Rep. 73.

11 *Murray v. Edinburgh D.C.*, 1981 S.L.T. 253, *per* Lord Maxwell at 256.

12 *Potter & Co. v. Braco de Prata Printing Co. Ltd* (1891) 18 R. 511, *per* L.P. Inglis at 517.

13 *Baikie v. Glasgow Corporation*, 1919 S.C.(H.L.) 13, *per* Lord Shaw at 17.

to be the plain construction of the pleadings,[14] or in order to explain or restate a case obscured by muddled, confused and contradictory pleadings.[15]

9.34 The nature of the averments which will be sufficiently relevant to entitle the pursuer to an inquiry will depend on the nature and circumstances of each case. In an action of damages for negligence it is necessary, first, that the essential facts relied on should be set out with reasonable clarity; secondly, that the duties alleged to have been breached should be plainly stated and should be duties which the court can be satisfied at least might have been incumbent upon the defender in law in the circumstances averred; thirdly, that it should be reasonably apparent how any alleged loss is claimed to be attributable to any one or more alleged breaches of duty; and, fourthly, that in so far as the nature of any head of patrimonial loss permits, at least some notice should be given of the amount claimed under that head and, in any event, of the basis of quantification proposed to be relied upon.[16]

9.35 There are many cases in which substantial justice requires that a case may be stated alternatively on inconsistent averments of fact; but in other cases it would be incompatible with substantial justice to the opposite party that a case should be allowed to proceed on such inconsistent averments without the party making them being forced to choose between the alternative cases he seeks to make. There are two factors which are of importance when considering whether it is legitimate to permit a party to state his case alternatively on inconsistent averments of fact: the first is whether the party making the averments can justifiably assert that he is excusably in ignorance of the precise facts in question,[17] and the second is whether he is the pursuer or the defender, more latitude in normal circumstances being allowed to a defender.[18]

9.36 In cases where there is an alternative averment of fact, relevancy must depend on the alternative which is weaker in law, that being the only one which the pursuer absolutely offers to prove.[19] So where there are two alternative and inconsistent factual grounds of action, one of which is not supported by relevant averments, the whole action is dismissed.[20] "If legal liability arises only on proof that the fact is A and if all that a pursuer offers to prove is that it is either A or B his pleadings are irrelevant. The relevancy of the case is tested on the weaker alternative."[21] Where, however, legal liability could be established on either of two legal grounds (such as, for example, two separate contractual provisions) if the facts respectively material to

---

[14] *Brown v. Caterpillar Tractor Co. Ltd*, O.H., Lord Cameron, Nov. 30, 1971, unreported.

[15] *Fryers v. Joseph Simmers & Sons*, 1986 G.W.D. 5–105.

[16] *Jamieson v. Allan McNeil & Son*, 1974 S.L.T. (Notes) 9; and see *Stevenson v. Glasgow Corporation*, 1908 S.C. 1034, *per* Lord Kinnear at 1041.

[17] *Finnie v. Logie* (1859) 21 D. 825, *per* L.P. McNeill at 839; *Clarke v. Edinburgh and District Tramways Co. Ltd*, 1914 S.C. 775; *Valley v. Wiggins Teape Ltd*, 1979 S.L.T. (Notes) 50.

[18] *Smart v. Bargh*, 1949 S.C. 57, *per* L.P. Cooper at 61–62; *M v. M*, 1967 S.L.T. 157.

[19] *Hope v. Hope's Trs* (1898) 1 F. (H.L.) 1, *per* Lord Watson at 3, Lord Shand at 5.

[20] *Finnie, supra*; *Murray v. Wyllie*, 1916 S.C. 356; *Percival v. Bairds & Scottish Steel Ltd*, 1952 S.L.T. (Sh. Ct.) 80.

[21] *Haigh & Ringrose Ltd v. Barrhead Builders Ltd*, 1981 S.L.T. 157, *per* Lord Stott at 157.

either were averred and proved, and no facts material to one ground are averred, the pursuer may nevertheless prove the facts averred which are material to the other ground.[22] Where a pursuer pleaded a case against four defenders in the alternative, not specifying which of them was responsible for the act complained of, the action so far as directed against two of them was dismissed.[23]

An alternative averment of fact should be clearly stated as such. If it is made on the basis of an assumption as to certain other facts it should begin: "Alternatively, *esto* [the assumed facts], . . ." A pursuer may aver facts stated in the defences which he denies, thus: "Alternatively, *esto*, as averred by the defender, [the assumed facts] (which is denied) . . .", and may thereby avail himself of facts averred by the defender which, if proved, would entitle the pursuer to decree on a ground alternative to the substantive ground on which the action was raised.[24] If the defender's statement of the facts is thereafter established in evidence, the pursuer will succeed even if the defender leads no evidence.[25] Averments which are not alternative must not be self-contradictory.[26] **9.37**

If a pursuer founds on alternative legal grounds, he must distinguish them by clear and precise language in separate articles of the condescendence and separate pleas-in-law.[27] **9.38**

A pursuer who founds on more than one legal ground cumulatively must similarly distinguish the grounds in the condescendence and pleas-in-law. Each of the articles which state the second and subsequent grounds should begin: "Further, . . ." and not: "Further and in any event . . .", because the words "and in any event" are only appropriate to a case which can survive as an alternative to a primary case which has failed.[28] **9.39**

The Form of Pleadings

General form

The forms of pleadings are prescribed by the Ordinary Cause Rules and by practice. Each pleading contains a heading, a description of the pleading, the names of the parties, a statement of facts and pleas-in-law, and is signed by the party or his solicitor and presented to the court on acceptable paper. An initial writ must contain an instance. An initial writ and defences including a counterclaim must contain a crave or craves. These constituent parts of a pleading are discussed in the following paragraphs. They may be seen in the following specimen initial writ: **9.40**

---

[22] *Haigh, supra; Stewarts' Exrs v. Stewart*, 1994 S.L.T. 466.
[23] *Stout v. U.K. Atomic Energy Authority*, 1979 S.L.T. 54. The other two defenders had agreed to a proof before answer.
[24] *M v. M*, 1967 S.L.T. 157.
[25] *McGlynn v. National Coal Board*, O.H., Lord Stott, July 9, 1971, unreported.
[26] *McSourley v. Paisley Mags* (1902) 10 S.L.T. 86; *Stanley Ltd v. Hanway*, 1911 2 S.L.T. 2.
[27] *Keenan v. Glasgow Corporation*, 1923 S.C. 611.
[28] *O'Sullivan v. Kerr*, O.H., Lord Emslie, June 10, 1970, unreported.

SHERIFFDOM OF LOTHIAN AND BORDERS AT EDINBURGH
INITIAL WRIT
in causa
JOHN BROWN, residing at 1 White Street, Blackburgh, BHI 2AD—*Pursuer*
against
JAMES GREEN, residing at 2 Auburn Road, Edinburgh, EH4 3QZ—*Defender*

The pursuer craves the Court:
1.
2. [The specific decree, warrant or order asked.]

CONDESCENDENCE

1.
2.
3. [The facts which form the grounds of action.]
4.
5.

PLEAS-IN-LAW

1.
2.
3.

IN RESPECT WHEREOF

[*Signed*] A. GOOD LAWMAN
A. Good Lawman, S.S.C.,
3 Stair Square, Edinburgh EH3 9PQ.
Solicitor for Pursuer.

Defects in form

9.41 Any defect in the *contents* of a pleading may be cured by amendment by leave of the court.[29] However, it is not clear whether a defect in the *form* of a pleading may be similarly cured or renders the pleading fundamentally null. It is thought that the consequence of a defect in form depends on whether the defect lies in a failure to comply with a provision of the Rules or with the practice of the court and, if the former, whether the provision is directory or mandatory; and that only a breach of a mandatory provision of the Rules as to form would be held to render a pleading fundamentally null. As to the initial writ, rule 3(1) of the 1983 Ordinary Court Rules provided that ordinary causes should be commenced by initial writ "as nearly as may be" in accordance with Form A as set out in the Appendix to the Rules. In relation to that rule it was suggested that the terms of the rule "do not suggest that the form is so rigid that a variant should be regarded as radically incompetent."[30] It will be noted that the

---

[29] OCR, r. 18.2. See para. 10.04.

[30] *Simpson v. Royal Burgh of Inverurie*, Sh. Pr. Gimson, Aberdeen Sh. Ct, Feb. 7, 1974, unreported: the absence of a crave in an appeal against a closing order under the Housing (Scotland) Act 1966 where the writ made clear the purpose of the application and the nature of the order sought, was held not to render the writ a nullity, and the pursuer was allowed to add a crave by amendment. The fact that this was a summary application rather than an ordinary action does not affect the principle. See also *Wilson v. Lothian Regional Council*, 1995 S.L.T. 991.

existing rule 31(1) does not contain the words "as nearly as may be". It is submitted, however, that where an initial writ entirely lacked an instance or condescendence or pleas-in-law it would be held that the defect could not be cured by amendment in terms of rule 18.2,[31] that the requirements of the Rules in these respects were mandatory, and thus that the writ was a nullity.[32] In the Outer House of the Court of Session it has recently been held that a summons without a conclusion is not a nullity and that a conclusion may be inserted by amendment.[33] By analogy an initial writ without a crave would also be curable by amendment. It may be that certain breaches of the Rules would be held to be a breach of a directory requirement only, which was curable by the exercise of the sheriff's dispensing power.[34] Similarly, it may be that such matters as a failure to head or sign defences, or to insert pleas-in-law in a third party's answers and sign them, which would be breaches of rules of practice only, would be regarded as irregularities which might be waived or cured in the exercise of the court's inherent jurisdiction to regulate questions of procedure.[35] It is thought that the court would not readily treat a defect in the form of a pleading as fundamental, rendering the pleading a nullity, but would be anxious to exercise its dispensing power or inherent jurisdiction in favour of curing the defect, except where the defect has so prejudiced the other party that the issue must be decided in his favour *ex debito justitiae*.[36] But in view of the apparent scarcity of decisions on such matters, the requirements of the Rules and of the practice of the court should be observed with great care, so that the form of the pleading does not prejudice or embarrass the party's case.

The parts of a pleading

Heading

Every pleading is headed with the name of the sheriffdom and the place of sitting of the court in which the action is raised, *e.g.* "SHERIFFDOM OF LOTHIAN AND BORDERS AT EDINBURGH". In the case of the initial writ the heading (and indeed the whole layout of the writ) is prescribed by the Ordinary Cause Rules,[37] and in the case of other pleadings by the practice of the court. **9.42**

Description of pleading

Beneath the heading[38] the pleading bears its own description, for example "INITIAL WRIT", "DEFENCES" or "ANSWERS". Only the description of the **9.43**

---

[31] OCR, r. 18.2(2), literally construed, appears to indicate that amendment is competent only where the initial writ already contains an instance, condescendence or plea-in-law.

[32] *cf. Bank of Scotland v. W. & G. Fergusson* (1898) 1 F. 96, *per* L.P. Robertson at 101–102; *British Railways Board v. Strathclyde R.C.*, 1981 S.C. 90. *Carnbroe Chemical Co. Ltd v. Lanark Middle Ward* (1927) 43 Sh.Ct.Rep. 163 where a party was allowed to cure by amendment the absence of a condescendence and pleas-in-law, was disapproved in *Simpson, supra*.

[33] *Wilson v. Lothian R.C.*, 1995 S.L.T. 991.

[34] OCR, r. 2.1(1). See paras 5.93 to 5.97.

[35] See paras 2.07, 2.08.

[36] *cf. Re Pritchard, dec'd* [1963] Ch. 502, *per* Hodson L.J. at 523 *cit. Brady v. Barrow Steel Works Ltd* [1965] 2 Q.B. 182.

[37] OCR, r. 3.1(1), App. 1, Form G1.

[38] In Form G1 (as in Form A of the 1983 OCR) the description is shown as coming above the heading. However, almost invariable practice over many years suggests that the heading should come above the description.

answers for a third party are prescribed by the Rules.[39] Where necessary, the description of the pleading should indicate, in addition to the nature of the pleading, the party for whom it is lodged. Where one of several defenders is separately represented, the description of his defences should run:

DEFENCES
for
E.F., [*designed*]—*Second-named Defender*
in the action at the instance of
A.B., [*designed*]—*Pursuer*
against
C.D., [*designed*]—*First-named Defender*
and
the said E.F.

Indeed it is preferable that defences should always be in this form even if there is only one defender, and not simply:

DEFENCES
in causa
A.B., [*designed*]—*Pursuer*
against
C.D., [*designed*]—*Defender*.

A third party's answers should be described[40]:

ANSWERS
for
E.F., [*designed*]—*Third Party*
in the action at the instance of
A.B., [*designed*]—*Pursuer*
against
C.D., [*designed*]—*Defender*

Instance

9.44 Below the description of the pleading are the words "*in causa*" or "in the action at the instance of", followed by the name and designation of the party by whom the action is brought, then the word "against" and the name and designation of the person called in the action. The contents of the instance are fully considered in the context of the drafting of the initial writ.[41]

---

39 OCR, r. 20.5(2).
40 *ibid.*
41 paras 9.77 to 9.81.

Crave

Both an initial writ[42] and defences including a counterclaim[43] should contain a crave, which sets forth the specific decree, warrant or order asked. The contents of the crave are considered below.[44] 9.45

Statement of facts

Every pleading must contain a statement of the facts on which the party's claim or defence is founded, set out in consecutively numbered paragraphs. In an initial writ, these paragraphs form the condescendence[45]; in all defences[46] and in a third party's pleading,[47] the answers; and in defences including a counterclaim, as well as answers, a statement of facts.[48] In each case they should be headed as such. The draftsman of a condescendence or statement of facts in effect dictates the number of paragraphs in which his opponent may answer the draftsman's claim and state his own case, because the paragraphs of the opponent's answers must correspond to the paragraphs of the condescendence or statement of facts. The draftsman should therefore compose his condescendence or statement of facts in short paragraphs, in order to enable the cases of both parties to be stated with clarity and precision. An all too common fault in sheriff court pleadings is that the draftsman confines himself to only three paragraphs, with formal matters in the first and third and all the facts forming his ground of claim in the second. The other party in reply is forced to state his whole defence in his own second paragraph. Both parties then extensively adjust. The result is long, discursive and confused narratives on either side which do nothing to clarify, and much to obscure, the issues between the parties. The drafting of a condescendence is considered below.[49] 9.46

Pleas-in-law

Each party is required to include in his pleadings after his statement of facts a note of his pleas-in-law stated in consecutively numbered sentences.[50] Certain pleas-in-law are in practice stated in an abbreviated form,[51] but as a general rule a plea-in-law should be a distinct legal proposition specifically applicable to the facts of the case.[52] An abstract proposition is not a plea-in-law, nor is a statement that in the circumstances narrated in the statement of facts the party is entitled to the decree which he seeks.[53] When read together with the facts averred in the statement of facts, the plea-in-law should substantiate the party's right to the remedy he seeks or his entitlement to decree of dismissal or 9.47

---

42 OCR, r. 3.1(1) and App., Form G1.
43 OCR, r. 19.1(3).
44 paras 9.92 to 9.98.
45 OCR, r. 3.1(1) and App., Form G1.
46 OCR, r. 9.6(2).
47 OCR, r. 20.5(2)(a).
48 OCR, r. 19.1(3)(b).
49 paras 9.99 to 9.103.
50 OCR, r. 3.1(1) and App. 1, Form G1 (initial writ), r. 9.6(2) (defences without a counterclaim), r. 19.1(3)(c) (defences including a counterclaim). In practice, pleas-in-law are also stated in a third party's answers and in a pursuer's answers to a counterclaim.
51 See paras 9.115 *et seq.*
52 *Young & Co. v. Graham* (1860) 23 D. 36, *per* L.J.-C. Inglis; *Mitchell v. Aberdeen Insurance Corporation*, 1918 S.C. 415, *per* L.J.-C. Scott Dickson at 430, Lord Dundas at 435.
53 *Young & Co., supra.*

absolvitor. The pleas-in-law focus the legal issues in the action, and the decree of the court is expressed in its interlocutor by sustaining or repelling them. Apart from such matters as questions of competency which it is *pars judicis* to notice even in the absence of a plea,[54] the court will not sustain a plea which is not stated on record, and a party seeking to put forward an argument unsupported by an appropriate plea must seek leave to amend his pleadings by adding the plea.[55] The pleas stated should therefore be those which have a direct bearing on the case or upon the mode of proof by which it is contended that the court should arrive at its decision.

9.48 The following are thought to be useful general rules[56]:

(1) Each legal proposition upon which a party founds in asking for a decree, including a decree of dismissal or absolvitor, or in asking for an interim order such as interim interdict or for a restriction of proof, ought to be represented by a plea-in-law.
(2) Each plea-in-law must be supported by averments of all the facts which the law says are necessary to make the plea-in-law successful. If the averments which the law requires in order that the plea-in-law should be sustained are not there, the plea-in-law may be repelled after debate.
(3) Any averment which is not relevant to a plea-in-law is irrelevant and ought not to be in the pleadings.[57]

The drafting of pleas-in-law is considered below.[58]

Signature of pleading

9.49 The Rules require only that the initial writ should be signed by the pursuer or his solicitor, that the solicitor should add his designation and business address and that the solicitor's name and address should be stated on the back of every service copy of the writ.[59] In practice, however, every pleading is signed at the end of the pleading by the solicitor for the party, or by the party himself if he is a party litigant. Counsel do not sign sheriff court pleadings, although they may draft them. A rubber stamp is not acceptable. It is customary to add above the signature the words "IN RESPECT WHEREOF", which have been said to signify that in respect of the foregoing pleading the party or his solicitor appends his signature.[60] But whether these words are included or not, the signature indicates the responsibility of the signatory for the contents of the pleading.[61] If a solicitor signs, he adds his designation and business address. A document exchange box number is not acceptable as an address. Although it is not strictly necessary for a typed or written version of the signature to appear on the service copy of the initial writ,[62] in practice the signature, designation and address should be printed, typed or written on all copies of every pleading.

---

[54] See para. 2.14.
[55] *Robb v. Logiealmond School Board* (1875) 2 R. 417, *per* L.P. Inglis at 422; *Kelly v. Edmund Nuttall Sons & Co. (London) Ltd*, 1965 S.C. 427 at 434.
[56] *cf.* A. G. Walker, "Written Pleadings" (1963) 79 Sc.L.R. 161 at 166.
[57] On relevancy, see paras 9.32 to 9.34.
[58] See paras 9.104, 9.115 to 9.128.
[59] OCR, r. 3.1(7) and App. 1, Form G1.
[60] Lees, *Pleading*, pp. 57–58, para. 141.
[61] See para. 9.12.
[62] *Muir v. National Bank Ltd* (1943) 59 Sh.Ct.Rep. 51.

Paper used for pleadings

The rules provide that the initial writ shall be written, typed or printed on A4 size paper of durable quality and not be backed.[63] It must be returned to the sheriff clerk unfolded.[64] Although there is no specific provision in the rules about the form of paper to be used for any other pleading, in practice the defences and every other part of process should be on A4 size paper, unfolded and unbacked. This is so that it can be inserted into the process folder which the sheriff clerk is obliged to prepare as soon as a notice of intention to defend is lodged.[65] 9.50

The Language of Pleadings

General rule

In any statement of facts, the material facts should be set out in a logical order in language which is as clear and precise as possible. Apart from a few very rare exceptions, the past tense should be used throughout. Sentences should be short. If the draftsman finds himself writing a sentence containing participial phrases (such as "The pursuer, being . . ." or "having . . ."), or colons, semicolons or brackets, that is usually an indication that the sentence is too long. Each material fact should be stated positively in a separate sentence. Admissions may be more readily elicited from an opponent by a series of short sentences than by a few lengthy sentences. The pleader's language should be succinct in expression and moderate in tone: verbose, extravagant and needlessly offensive language is disapproved by the court, and it is more effective for a pleader at proof to present in evidence a strong case from a drily but fairly stated record than a weak case from a highly-coloured record. 9.51

The following advice is commended[66]: 9.52

> "The names of persons and places, if material, must be accurately given. Avoid pronouns, it often is not clear whom you mean by 'he.' Repeat ['the pursuer'] or 'the said Johnson,' whenever 'he' would be ambiguous. . . . Call things by their right names, so far as you can, but in any event always allude to the same thing by the same name. Keep to the same phraseology throughout the pleading; a change of phrase suggests a change of meaning. . . .
>
> Facts should be alleged as facts. Use terse, short, curt, blunt sentences, all in the indicative mood. Be positive. Do not beat about the bush. Go straight to the point. If you mean to allege a particular fact, state it boldly, plainly and concisely. Avoid all 'ifs,' all introductory averments and all circumlocution. A pleading is not the place for fine writing, but simply for hard, downright, business-like assertion . . .
>
> Avoid, too, the passive voice, always use the most direct and straightforward construction, and that, as a rule, will be the active voice. . . .
>
> If a fact is material, it should be stated as a positive fact, and in a separate sentence.

---

[63] OCR, r. 3.1(2).
[64] OCR, r. 9.3.
[65] OCR, r. 9.5.
[66] Odgers, *Principles of Pleading and Practice* (20th ed., 1971), pp. 105–107.

Then, again, it always conduces to clearness to observe the strict order of time. In any case not of the simplest, dates are of the greatest importance. The only way to tell a long or complicated story clearly and intelligently is to keep to strict chronological order."

Useful expressions

9.53 The following paragraphs note briefly a number of expressions in common use in Scottish written pleadings. When correctly employed they are helpful, since their meanings are well understood and they save space. Those which may be used both when stating and when answering a claim include the following.

9.54 "**Believed and averred.**" If a material fact, which the party must establish in order to succeed in his claim or defence, is not known to him, he may aver that he believes it to be true if that is a reasonable inference from other facts known to or ascertained by him which he avers as matter of categorical assertion.[67] That may be appropriate where the material fact is within his opponent's knowledge[68]; but it is inappropriate where it is wholly within the party's own knowledge.[69] An averment of belief which is not supported by other averments from which it may reasonably be inferred is irrelevant.[70] It has been said to be appropriate to introduce with the words "Believed and averred" an averment which is not vital to the party's case but which is designed to test his opponent's case in cross-examination.[71] However, it is open to question whether such an averment is consistent with the general principle that only averments relevant to a party's case should appear in the pleadings.

9.55 "***Brevitatis causa***" ("For the sake of brevity") is used where a document is referred to and held as repeated in the pleading, but not quoted.[72]

9.56 "***Esto***" ("Be it that"; "Let it be assumed that") is employed when introducing an alternative case, either in the statement of facts[73] or in the pleas-in-law.[74]

9.57 "***Separatim***" ("Separately"). Where two paragraphs of a statement of facts or two pleas-in-law conflict with each other, the second is usually prefaced by the word "*Separatim*". Where the second plea-in-law not only conflicts with the first but is based on a version of the facts alternative to that primarily averred in the party's pleadings, the second is usually prefaced by "*Separatim. Esto . . .*".[75]

---

67 *Brown v. Redpath Brown & Co. Ltd*, 1963 S.L.T. 219; *Magee & Co. (Belfast) Ltd v. Bracewell Harrison & Coton*, 1980 S.L.T. (Notes) 102.

68 *Brown, supra*; *Shaw v. Rentan & Fisher Ltd*, 1977 S.L.T. (Notes) 60.

69 *McCrone v. Macbeth, Currie & Co.*, 1968 S.L.T. (Notes) 24.

70 *Leslie v. Leslie*, 1983 S.L.T. 186, *per* Lord Dunpark at 188; *Strathmore Group Ltd v. Credit Lyonnais*, 1994 S.L.T. 1029, *per* Lord Osborne at 1032.

71 *McCrindle v. Sandilands*, 1980 S.L.T. (Notes) 12.

72 See para. 9.67.

73 See para. 9.46.

74 See paras 9.57, 9.104, 9.128.

75 *e.g.* a defender's plea of contributory negligence in an action of damages for personal injuries: "*Separatim. Esto* the said accident was partly caused by the fault of the defender (which is denied), it having been also partly caused by the fault of the pursuer, any damages awarded should be reduced in terms of the Law Reform (Contributory Negligence) Act 1945."

The following phrases are useful when an opponent's averments are being answered. They are further considered in the paragraphs below on the drafting of defences. 9.58

"Admitted." When admitting an averment by the other party, it is sufficient to say "Admitted that", followed by a repetition of the averment. 9.59

"Believed to be true." This expression may be used in answer to an averment outwith the party's knowledge which he accepts to be true in order to narrow the issues in dispute; but it will be construed as an admission, and thus dispenses with the necessity of the other party's proving the averment in question.[76] 9.60

"Not known and not admitted." Where a fact averred by his opponent is not within the party's knowledge, the reply may be "Not known and not admitted that", followed by a repetition of the averment. 9.61

"Denied." Similarly, where a fact averred by the other party is denied, the reply may be "Denied that", followed by a repetition of the averment. 9.62

"***Quoad ultra***" ("As regards the rest"). Where it is intended to convey that the remainder of the averments in the paragraph being answered are denied, or admitted, or believed to be true, or not known and not admitted, the pleader may say "*Quoad ultra* denied" or "*Quoad ultra* not known and not admitted" or whatever the reply to the remainder may be, as more fully explained below.[77] 9.63

"Explained and averred." Any explanation which is considered to be necessary in the course of an answer to the other party's averments may be introduced by the words "Explained and averred that . . .". Where the explanation falls into two parts, which must be stated in the same paragraph, the second part may begin, "Explained further and averred that . . .". The latter formula may also be useful at adjustment, when replying to an adjustment adding new matter. 9.64

Expressions to be avoided

"Averred that . . ." is unnecessary and bad pleading, because any statement made in the statement of facts is an averment. "Denied as stated" ought not to be used, as explained below.[78] "The said" is sometimes necessary to avoid ambiguity,[79] but it is superfluous where the noun can refer to only one object or person.[80] 9.65

Abbreviations

The use of intelligible and fully-explained abbreviations may save space. A lengthy company name may be abbreviated and subsequently used in the 9.66

---

[76] *Scottish N.E. Ry v. Napier* (1859) 21 D. 700, *per* L.J.-C. Inglis at 703; Lees, *Pleading*, p. 49, para. 119; *Binnie v. Rederij Theodoro BV*, 1993 S.C. 71.

[77] See paras 9.109, 9.110.

[78] See para. 9.111.

[79] See para. 9.52.

[80] *e.g.* in an action concerned with only one elephant who is called Dorabella it is unnecessary constantly to refer to the beast as "the said elephant" or "the said Dorabella".

pleading, thus: "The Lewis and Dobie Printing and Publishing Company Limited (hereinafter referred to as 'L. & D.') . . .". The company may thereafter be referred to as "L. & D." (not "the said L. & D.").

Documents

9.67 Where a party's case is founded on a document, or part of a document, the document must be produced and specifically described. Its critical provisions must be accurately and clearly specified, and either quoted in the averments or, if overlong, expressly incorporated and held as repeated in them by reference *brevitatis causa*.[81] A document which is not incorporated by reference or otherwise in the averments cannot be looked at by the court when considering the relevancy of the averments, unless a joint minute is lodged dispensing with probation of the document.[82] The whole document[83] should be produced. The rules provide that when a document is founded upon by a party or adopted as incorporated in his pleadings, it must, so far as in the possession or within the control of the party founding upon it or adopting it be lodged in process as a production by him[84] at the time of returning the initial writ under rule 9.3.[85] When the document is founded upon or adopted in a minute, defences, counterclaim or answers it is to be lodged in process at the same time as the lodging of the minute, etc.[86] If the document is founded on or adopted in the course of adjustment of any pleadings, it is to be lodged in process at the time when such adjustment is intimated to any other party.[87] The foregoing requirements are without prejudice to any power of the sheriff to order the production of any document or grant a commission and diligence for recovery of it.[88] Should a party fail to lodge a document at the time required by the rules he may be found liable in the expenses of any order for production or recovery of it obtained by any other party.[89] If the document is not produced, it cannot be considered.[90] A party is not entitled to incorporate in his averments by reference a document containing statements of fact and opinion which his opponent cannot properly answer.[91] A reference to a document "for its terms" is not an averment of fact upon which a plea-in-law can be based.[92] Where one party makes

---

[81] *Gordon v. Davidson* (1864) 2 M. 758, *per* L.J.-C. Inglis at 769; *Green v. Maxwell Property Development Co.*, 1976 S.L.T. (Sh. Ct.) 65; *Redpath Dorman Long Ltd v. Tarmac Construction Ltd*, 1982 S.C. 14, *per* Lord Ross at 18; *Grampian Hydraulics (Buckie) Ltd v. Dauntless Marine Engineering & Supply Co. Ltd*, 1992 S.L.T. (Sh. Ct.) 45; *Halliday v. Rolland Decorators Ltd*, 1994 S.C.L.R. 305.

[82] *Ribble Paper Mills Ltd v. Clyde Paper Mills Ltd*, 1972 S.L.T. (Notes) 25; *Stone v. Macdonald*, 1979 S.C. 363, *per* Lord Ross at 365; *Trade Development Bank v. David W. Haig (Bellshill) Ltd*, 1983 S.L.T. 107, *per* Lord Stewart at 109; *Eadie Cairns v. Programmed Maintenance Painting*, 1987 S.L.T. 777; *Grampian Hydraulics (Buckie) Ltd v. Dauntless Marine Engineering & Supply Co. Ltd*, 1992 S.L.T. (Sh. Ct.) 45; *McIlwraith v. Lochmaddy Hotel Ltd*, 1995 S.C.L.R. 595, *per* Lord Prosser at 497.

[83] *Murray's Trs v. Wilson's Exrs*, 1945 S.C. 51; *Unigate Foods Ltd v. Scottish Milk Marketing Board*, 1975 S.C.(H.L.) 75, *per* Lord Fraser of Tullybelton at 106.

[84] OCR, r. 21.1(1).

[85] *ibid.* para. (a).

[86] *ibid.* para. (b).

[87] *ibid.* para. (c).

[88] OCR, r. 21.1(2).

[89] OCR, r. 21.2.

[90] *Hayes v. Robinson*, 1984 S.L.T. 300, *per* Lord Ross at 301.

[91] *Connell v. Ferguson* (1861) 23 D. 683, *per* Lord Neaves at 685; *Westwood v. Keay* (1950) 66 Sh.Ct.Rep. 147; *Barton v. William Low & Co.*, 1968 S.L.T. (Notes) 27.

[92] A. G. Walker, "Written Pleadings" (1963) 79 Sc.L.R. 161 at 174.

averments relating to a document his opponent may reply that the document "is referred to for its terms" and may be understood to indicate that he admits the existence of the document but does not admit its terms.[93] On the other hand, it has been said that reference to a document for its terms, particularly if coupled with a general denial, does not imply an admission that the document exists or ever existed.[94] The reply, "The alleged document is referred to for its terms", has been said to indicate that the existence of the document is not admitted and must be proved.[95] In the present state of the authorities[96] it may be preferable to set forth the party's attitude to the document in specific terms rather than to employ either of these expressions.

Statutes and statutory instruments

Where the party's case is founded on his opponent's breach of a provision of a statute or statutory instrument, the party's averments relating thereto should specify the provision founded on, briefly quoting therefrom where necessary for intelligibility, and make clear the grounds on which he seeks to establish that his opponent is guilty of a breach of the provision. Where a pursuer alleges a breach of more than one provision, the cases relating to the different breaches should be separately and distinctly averred in different articles of the condescendence. Where the pursuer founds on common law as well as statute, his common law grounds should similarly be separately averred.[97] **9.68**

Calls

One party may require another to lodge before the closing of the record a document on which the latter founds in his pleadings, by calling on him to produce it. This is done by means of an averment in such terms as, "The defender is called on to produce [the document founded on]." Such a call is legitimate where the document founded on is within the other party's possession or control, having regard to the provisions of rule 21.1(1) and (2). **9.69**

A party who has stated a plea to the relevancy of another party's averments may in a similar way call on the latter to make averments about certain specified matters, "as a warning to call the opponent's attention to the state of his averments, that he might have no reason afterwards to complain that he was taken by surprise, or that he understood that no **9.70**

---

[93] *Pringle v. Bremner and Stirling* (1867) 5 M.(H.L.) 55; *H. Widdop & Co. Ltd v. J. & J. Hay Ltd*, 1961 S.L.T. (Notes) 35; *cf. Healey v. A. Massey & Son*, 1961 S.C. 198; *Mitchell Construction Co. (Scotland) Ltd v. Brands Transport and Demolition Ltd*, 1975 S.L.T. (Notes) 58.

[94] *McConnel v. Pringle* (1960) 76 Sh.Ct.Rep. 67 at 69.

[95] Lees, *Pleading*, at p. 49, para. 119.

[96] *Pringle v. Bremner and Stirling* (1867) 5 M.(H.L.) 55; *H. Widdop & Co. Ltd v. J. & J. Hay Ltd*, 1961 S.L.T. (Notes) 35; *cf. Healey v. A. Massey & Son*, 1961 S.C. 198; *Mitchell Construction Co. (Scotland) Ltd v. Brands Transport and Demolition Ltd*, 1975 S.L.T. (Notes) 58.

[97] *Carruthers v. Caledonian Ry* (1854) 16 D. 425, *per* L.P. McNeill at 428; *McGrath v. Glasgow Coal Co. Ltd*, 1909 S.C. 1250; *Keenan v. Glasgow Corporation*, 1923 S.C. 611, *per* L.J.-C. Alness at 619, Lord Ormidale at 621; *Gaitens v. Blythswood Shipping Co.*, 1948 S.L.T. (Notes) 49; *Lindsay v. Anchor Line Ltd* [1948] C.L.Y. 4715; *Culbert v. Ramsay*, 1951 S.L.T. (Notes) 16. *Hughes' Tutrix v. Glasgow D.C.*, 1982 S.L.T. (Sh. Ct.) 70, appears to be inconsistent with these authorities.

greater specification was wanted."[98] A call on another party to make an averment which he does not need to make in order to be relevant is valueless and has no effect.[99] So also is a call which is unrelated to any plea-in-law. A party is not bound to answer a call in the form of a question.[1] A call is not an averment of fact, and does not amount either to a denial of any of the other party's averments or to the making of any averments different from these.[2]

The Technique of Drafting Pleadings

9.71 The earlier sections of this chapter have considered the nature and functions of pleadings, the principal rules of pleading and the form and language of pleadings. This final section deals with the detailed technique of drafting pleadings, in relation to the features common to all ordinary actions: the initial writ, the defences, and the adjustment of the pleadings.

9.72 In drafting pleadings the Scottish practitioner has two modern books of styles which he may follow or adapt as necessary. These are *Greens Litigation Styles*[3] and Bennett's *Style Writs for the Sheriff Court.*[4] The *Encyclopaedia of Scottish Legal Styles*, the forms in Appendix 2 of Lewis's *Sheriff Court Practice* and Sheriff Dobie's *Sheriff Court Styles* remain valuable to a limited extent, but these works are out of print and are considerably out of date. Some forms of crave may be adapted from the forms of conclusion in Form 13.2–B of the Appendix to the Rules of the Court of Session,[5] and guidance may sometimes be found in the reports of Court of Session cases in *Session Cases*, the *Scots Law Times* and *Scottish Civil Law Reports* where extracts from the pleadings are often printed. It is recommended that the practitioner should compile and put into his word processing database his own collection of styles by noting such reports and acquiring copies of pleadings which have been approved, or at least not disapproved, by the court in earlier cases. As he builds up his collection he will gradually save himself valuable time, labour and research. It must, of course, be remembered that the use of a style is no substitute for careful original thought as to the material facts and legal basis of the particular case before the pleader, and that a style should not simply be followed but should be adapted to suit the circumstances of the case.

9.73 Even an experienced draftsman will usually be able to improve on his first draft of a pleading. It is therefore recommended that the draftsman should take time to revise his first draft, ideally after an interval of time, before approving the final version. It is usually unhelpful, except perhaps in the case of the very simplest pleading, merely to dictate the pleading into a dictating machine without previously drafting and revising it by

---

[98] *Gordon v. Donaldson* (1864) 2 M. 758, *per* L.J.-C. Inglis at 768; *Bryce v. Allied Ironfounders Ltd*, 1969 S.L.T. (Notes) 29; *M. Publications (Scotland) Ltd v. Meiland*, 1981 S.L.T. (Notes) 72.

[99] *Bonnor v. Balfour Kilpatrick Ltd*, 1974 S.C. 223, *per* Lord Kincraig at 227, L.P. Emslie at 228.

[1] *Gordon, supra.*

[2] *Bonnor, supra.*

[3] W. Green: looseleaf and disk, regularly updated.

[4] 2nd ed., Butterworth, 1994.

[5] Printed in *Parliament House Book*, Div. C.

hand: the result tends to be diffuse pleading and loose syntax, often reflections of loose thinking. It is of course also possible to draft and revise pleadings on a word-processor, and this is the usual practice in many offices. However, this should be done only after the careful study of the papers, research into the law, and attention to precision and clarity in drafting which are essential to successful pleading.

The initial writ

The initial writ must be in accordance with Form G1 of Appendix 1 to the Ordinary Cause Rules.[6] It consists of: (1) the heading, which identifies the court[7]; (2) the description, which identifies the pleading; (3) the instance, which identifies the parties; (4) the crave, which specifies the claim; (5) the condescendence, which sets out the factual basis of the claim; and (6) the pleas-in-law, which are the legal propositions which justify the claim being granted.[8] The logical structure of the initial writ is that the pleas-in-law connect the facts averred in the condescendence to the remedy sought in the crave.[9] **9.74**

The heading

The heading states the name of the sheriffdom and the place of sitting of the court, for example "SHERIFFDOM OF LOTHIAN AND BORDERS AT EDINBURGH". **9.75**

The description

In an ordinary action the initial writ bears the description "INITIAL WRIT". In other applications to the court it may bear a description appropriate to the nature of the application, such as "NOTE OF APPEAL", "APPLICATION" or "PETITION".[10] Below the description are usually written the words "*in causa*". **9.76**

The instance

The instance identifies the person by whom the action is brought, and any person who requires to be called in the action. The former is "the pursuer", a term which means and includes any person making a claim or demand, or seeking any warrant or order competent in the sheriff court.[11] The latter is "the defender", which means and includes any person who is required to be called in any action.[12] "Person" includes company, corporation, or association and firm of any description nominate or descriptive, or any Board corporate or unincorporate.[13] **9.77**

Wherever possible, the full name and correct designation of each party should be stated in the instance. Immaterial errors in the instance may be disregarded by the court,[14] but "while the court will not be swayed by **9.78**

---

[6] OCR, r. 3 (1).

[7] In Form G1 (as in Form A of the previous OCR) the description is shown as coming above the heading. However, almost invariable practice over many years suggests that the heading should come above the description.

[8] See specimen initial writ, para. 9.40.

[9] W. A. Wilson, *Introductory Essays on Scots Law* (2nd ed., 1984), p. 64.

[10] See para. 9.43.

[11] 1907 Act, s. 3(n).

[12] *ibid.* s. 3(o).

[13] *ibid.* s. 3(e).

[14] *Anderson v. Stoddart*, 1923 S.C. 755.

technical or immaterial mistakes, it must be kept in view that accuracy is the foundation of procedure, and practitioners must realise that laxity which springs from carelessness will not necessarily be condoned."[15] A serious error in the name of a pursuer may render invalid any arrestment on the dependence,[16] and in an undefended case a serious error in the name of a defender may render any decree against him inoperable.[17] The court may allow certain errors in the instance to be amended.[18] As a general rule a person can sue or be sued under the name which he himself uses and by which on account of that usage he is generally known.[19] Parties' full forenames and surnames should be stated, where these are known, and not their initials.[20] A married woman's name should be stated as her maiden name with her husband's surname (or husbands' surnames, if she has been married more than once) added as an alternative (or as successive alternatives), thus: Mrs A.B. or C.; or Mrs A.B. or C. or D.[21] The words "Assisted Person", normally placed in brackets, must follow the name of a party in receipt of legal aid, in the instance and in every subsequent step of process.[22]

9.79 The proper designation of a person is, as a general rule, a statement of his present occupation, if any, and his address.[23] If the address given is the party's residence the address should be preceded by the words "residing at". If the address is not the party's residence its nature should be stated, for example "having a place of business at". The court may require a party to state his true address.[24] In general, accommodation addresses such as a party's solicitor's office or a Post Office or document exchange box number should not be used in the instance, and a pursuer who wishes to use one should fully explain his reasons in the condescendence.[25] Where a party is in prison, the court may dispense with the necessity for designing him as "at present a prisoner in" a named prison subject, in the case of a defender, to suitable arrangements being made to secure that service is duly effected.[26] If the defender's whereabouts are not known to the pursuer, that should be stated in the instance.

9.80 Where a party sues or is sued in any special character, for example as trustee, such character must be set forth in the instance, as well as the

---

15 *Overseas League v. Taylor*, 1951 S.C. 105, *per* L.J.-C. Thomson at 107; *Kinloch v. Lourie* (1853) 16 D. 197, *per* Lord Cowan at 200.

16 *Richards & Wallington (Earthmoving) Ltd v. Whatlings Ltd*, 1982 S.L.T. 66.

17 *Spalding v. Valentine* (1883) 10 R. 1092; *Brown v. Rodger* (1884) 12 R. 340; *Cruickshank v. Gow & Sons* (1888) 15 R. 326; *Anderson, supra.* A decree taken in error against a party not liable is, however, no bar to subsequent proceedings against the true debtor (*Links & Co. Ltd v. Jesner* (1953) 69 Sh.Ct.Rep. 261; *cf. MacLellan & Co. Ltd v. Jesner*, 1952 S.L.T. (Sh. Ct.) 39.

18 OCR, rr. 7.6 (undefended action: see paras 7.20 to 7.22), 18.2 (defended action: see paras 10.07 to 10.10).

19 *Overseas League v. Taylor*, 1951 S.C. 105, *per* L.J.-C. Thomson at 107; *Kinloch v. Lourie* (1853) 16 D. 197, *per* Lord Cowan at 200. See also *Atlas Appointments Ltd v. Tinsley*, 1994 S.C.L.R. 729; 1997 S.C.L.R. 482.

20 Maclaren, p. 293; *Forsyth v. Scott's Trs*, 1947 S.L.T. (Sh. Ct.) 46.

21 Clive, para. 11.021.

22 A.S. (Civil Legal Aid Rules) 1987, r. 3(1).

23 *Joel v. Gill* (1859) 22 D. 6, *per* L.J.-C. Inglis at 12. The practice of stating the party's occupation appears to have died out (Black, *Introduction to Written Pleading*, p. 5).

24 *Murdoch v. Young*, 1909 2 S.L.T. 450; *Baird v. Baird*, 1914 2 S.L.T. 260; *Stein v. Stein*, 1936 S.C. 268; *McColl v. McColl*, 1949 S.L.T. (Notes) 11; *Rowlett v. Rowlett* [1955] C.L.Y. 3510; *Doughton v. Doughton*, 1958 S.L.T. (Notes) 34.

25 *Doughton, supra.*

26 *cf.* Court of Session Practice Note, July 23, 1952 (printed in *Parliament House Book*, Div. C; (1952) 68 S.L.R. 229; 1952 S.L.T. (News) 158).

name and designation of the individual.[27] The steps by which he acquired that character may be averred in the condescendence.[28] If his name and designation are not set forth in the instance, the instance will not be in proper form and the action may be held to be incompetent.[29]

If there is more than one defender, each should be named and designed separately, and should be described as "First-named Defender", "Second-named Defender" and so on. If the pursuer wishes to have defenders found liable jointly and severally this should be stated in the crave[30] and *not*, as has recently, for some reason, become fashionable, in the instance. The procedural rules concerning the manner in which different kinds of parties may sue and be sued have been considered in Chapter 4. **9.81**

The crave

The crave of the initial writ sets forth "the specific decree, warrant, or order asked".[31] It should therefore claim something which it is competent for the court to grant, and which may be enforced; for the court will not grant a decree which is incompetent or unenforceable.[32] It should also be so framed that an interlocutor expressed in terms of the crave gives the required order, and an extract may be prepared from it without difficulty. It must therefore be precise: this is especially important in an action *ad factum praestandum*[33] or for interdict,[34] where the defender is entitled to understand clearly what he is required to do or refrain from doing. It is incorrect to crave a decree in favour of the defender.[35] **9.82**

The crave should ask neither too little nor too much. While "a litigant is entitled to sue, and to keep on suing, until he has obtained satisfaction for his wrong",[36] it is advisable where possible to crave all the requisite remedies in a single action. Any number of craves may be combined in one initial writ: they should, however, be distinctly stated and consecutively numbered. A decree for less than has been craved is competent even in actions concerning property.[37] In actions of count, reckoning and payment it is competent to obtain decree for a sum greater than is craved.[38] Damages for all the losses arising from one ground of action must be recovered in the one claim: it is not competent to bring a further action on such grounds as that the damages were inadequate, or that it has later been ascertained that the injuries and loss are more serious than were **9.83**

---

27 OCR, App. 1, Form G1; *Kay v. Morrison's Reps*, 1984 S.L.T. 175.

28 *Hunter v. LMS Ry*, 1938 S.L.T. 598, *per* Lord Jamieson at 599; 1939 S.L.T. 297.

29 *Kay, supra.*

30 See para. 9.90.

31 OCR, App. 1, Form G1.

32 *Gall v. Loyal Glenbogie Friendly Society* (1900) 2 F. 1187; *Henderson v. Patrick Thomson Ltd*, 1911 S.C. 246, *per* L.P. Dunedin at 249.

33 *Robertson v. Cockburn* (1875) 3 R. 21, *per* L.J.-C. Moncrieff at 23; *Middleton v. Leslie* (1829) 19 R. 801, *per* L.P. Robertson at 802; and see para. 21.77.

34 *Kelso School Board v. Hunter* (1874) 2 R. 228, *per* Lord Deas at 232, Lord Ardmillan at 235; and see para. 21.84.

35 *T v. T*, 1987 S.L.T. (Sh. Ct.) 74.

36 *Steven v. Broady Norman & Co.*, 1928 S.C. 351, *per* Lord Anderson at 365. Further actions must of course be for different remedies or on different grounds or against different defenders, otherwise the plea of *res judicata* would apply (see paras 2.104 to 2.109); and damages for all the losses arising from one ground of action must be recovered in the one claim (see n. 39).

37 *McTaggart v. McDouall* (1867) 5 M. 534.

38 *Spottiswoode v. Hopkirk* (1853) 16 D. 59; and see para. 21.04.

suspected at the time of the original claim and award.[39] It is also desirable in a pecuniary crave to ask for the most that may be exigible. Since personal injuries may prove to be more serious than they at first appear, and solatium is incapable of exact ascertainment,[40] the pursuer's claim should cover the highest award which may reasonably be expected. On the other hand a crave which asks too much may induce the defender to defend when otherwise he would not have done so, and may be reflected in the court's ultimate award of expenses. The court may allow the crave to be amended.[41]

9.84 Further general rules relative to the crave are considered in the following paragraphs. Rules applicable to particular types of action are considered elsewhere.[42] Many of the forms of conclusion in Form 13.2–B of the Appendix to the Rules of the Court of Session[43] may be adapted for use in initial writs.

9.85 The pursuer's solicitor, in framing the crave of the initial writ so as to secure the decree his client requires for the enforcement or protection of his rights, may combine any number of craves[44] or state alternative or eventual craves, provided that they may all be disposed of in the same course of procedure[45] and the different grounds of action are distinguished by clear and precise language in the condescendence and pleas-in-law.[46] The craves should be clearly distinguished and consecutively numbered.

9.86 **Alternative craves.** Alternative craves, for alternative decrees incompatible with each other, are competent: for example for damages failing specific implement,[47] or for damages failing delivery.[48] If decree in terms of the primary crave is pronounced but not obtempered by the defender, the pursuer may move for decree in terms of the alternative crave. Upon the grant of decree in terms thereof the pursuer is personally barred from enforcing the decree in terms of the primary crave.[49] Alternative craves which are irreconcilable, proceeding on alternative averments inconsistent with each other, are competent.[50]

9.87 **Eventual craves.** A pursuer may also state eventual craves: for example for interdict and damages following declarator.[51]

---

[39] *Stevenson v. Pontifex and Wood* (1887) 15 R. 125; *Aberdeen Development Co. v. Mackie, Ramsay & Taylor*, 1977 S.L.T. 177. The rule is inapplicable to breaches of instalment contracts or to continuing wrongs: see Walker, *Civil Remedies*, pp. 393, 878. As to provisional damages in personal injuries actions, see paras 21.29 to 21.32.

[40] *Traynor's Exrs v. Baird's & Scottish Steel Ltd*, 1957 S.C. 311, *per* Lord Guthrie at 314.

[41] OCR, rr. 7.6(1) (undefended action: see paras 7.20 to 7.22), 18.2(2)(a) (defended action: see paras 9.89, 10.13).

[42] See Chaps 20–24.

[43] Printed in *Parliament House Book*, Div. C.

[44] *Glasgow Corporation v. Railwaymen's Club* (1915) 31 Sh.Ct.Rep. 220; *McGregor v. Mackechnie* (1918) 34 Sh.Ct.Rep. 174; Maclaren, p. 295.

[45] *Murphy v. Richards & Co.*, 1922 S.L.T. (Sh. Ct.) 135; *Macdonald v. Baird & Co. Ltd* (1927) 43 Sh.Ct.Rep. 73.

[46] *Keenan v. Glasgow Corporation*, 1923 S.C. 611, *per* L.J.-C. Alness at 619, Lord Ormidale at 621.

[47] See para. 21.77.

[48] *ibid.*

[49] *Bosco Design Services Ltd v. Plastic Sealant Services Ltd*, 1979 S.C. 189.

[50] *Green or Borthwick v. Borthwick* (1896) 24 R. 211; *Spence v. Spence*, 1914 S.C. 887.

[51] See *Jameson v. Sharp* (1887) 14 R. 643, *per* L.P. Inglis at 648, as to eventual conclusions in actions of furthcoming.

Ancillary craves. A crave which is dependent upon, or an incidental step of procedure towards, the pursuer's obtaining an effective decree sought by another crave, and which thus falls if the claim expressed by the main crave is abandoned or dismissed, may be termed an ancillary crave.[52] 9.88

Crave for money

Specific amount. A crave for payment of money must specify a definite sum,[53] which should be stated in words and figures. In a defended action the pursuer may alter the sum sued for by amendment without leave of the sheriff before the record is closed.[54] 9.89

Lump sum. In an action against a single defender it is competent to crave payment of a lump sum which is averred to be the aggregate of specific amounts respectively due in respect of separate acts.[55] It is also competent to crave a lump sum against several defenders where there is truly one wrong contributed to by several defenders: in such a case the crave runs "jointly and severally".[56] But it is incompetent to have a crave for a lump sum in favour of separate pursuers, or against several defenders in respect of different grounds of action.[57] 9.90

Payment in foreign currency. The sum craved is as a general rule expressed in sterling. The Scottish courts nevertheless recognise the principle that a foreign creditor who is entitled to payment of a debt due in the currency of his own country or of a particular foreign country should not be bound to accept payment of the debt in the currency of his debtor's country if any prejudice is thereby caused to the creditor.[58] It is therefore competent for such a creditor suing in Scotland to conclude, *primo loco*, for payment in the currency of account in his contract with the debtor. For the purposes of enforcement in Scotland it is necessary to provide in the decree, and accordingly it is at least desirable to provide in the crave, for the conversion of the foreign currency into sterling. The pursuer may therefore crave payment of the debt in the currency of account or the sterling equivalent thereof at the date of payment or at the date of extract, whichever is the earlier, thus: 9.91

> "To grant decree for payment by the defender to the pursuer of the sum of [amount in foreign currency] with interest thereon at the rate of [state rate] from [state date] until payment or the sterling equivalent of the said sum and interest at the date of payment or at the date of extract whichever is the earlier."[59]

---

52 *Skerret v. Oliver* (1896) 23 R. 468; *Harvey v. Smith* (1904) 6 F. 511, *per* Lord Kinnear at 523.

53 But see para. 21.04 as to the crave in an action of count, reckoning and payment.

54 OCR, r. 18.1(1); see para. 8.26.

55 *Western SMT Co. Ltd v. Greenock Mags*, 1957 S.L.T. (Notes) 22; *Lord Advocate v. Duncan Lagan (Contractors) Ltd*, 1964 S.L.T. (Notes) 35.

56 See para. 4.42.

57 See paras 4.38, 4.41.

58 *Commerzbank Aktiengesellschaft v. Large*, 1977 S.C. 375. It would appear to be wrong in principle that a creditor under a contract providing for payment in sterling should be permitted to sue in the Scottish courts for payment in a foreign currency merely because a fluctuation in the value of sterling had made it to his advantage to do so: *L/F Føroya Fiskasola v. Charles Mauritzen Ltd*, 1978 S.L.T. (Sh. Ct.) 27.

59 *Commerzbank AG, supra*, at 381.

Upon decree being pronounced in these terms it is in the option of the defender whether to satisfy the judgment in the currency of account or in the sterling equivalent.

9.92 The procedure is regulated by rule 30.3. A party requesting extract of the decree does so by minute endorsed on or annexed to the initial writ stating the rate of exchange prevailing, either on the date of the decree sought to be extracted, or on the date on which the extract is ordered, or within three days before the date on which the extract is ordered, together with the sterling equivalent at that rate for the principal sum and interest decerned for.[60] With the minute requesting extract must be lodged a certificate in Form G18 of Appendix 1 to the Ordinary Cause Rules, from the Bank of England or a bank authorised under the Banking Act 1987 certifying the rate of exchange and the sterling equivalent.[61] The extract decree issued by the sheriff clerk must mention such a certificate.[62]

Crave for interest

9.93 Where interest is included in a decree or extract, it is deemed to be at a rate specified by Act of Sederunt.[63] The rate currently specified is 8 per cent per annum.[64] Thus, where interest is craved but not specified, 8 per cent per annum is at present deemed to be the rate. Although interest runs *ex lege* from the date of the decree or of its affirmation on appeal,[65] it is advisable that it should be expressly craved at a specified rate.[66] A pactional rate different from the deemed rate may be craved,[67] but if it is, it is appropriate that there should be averments to justify the different rate.[68] In the event of an action being undefended, interest not craved cannot be included in the decree: if claimed by amendment, the court will, it is thought, require service of the amended writ on the defender.[69] In cases where interest runs from an earlier date than that of decree, it must be craved from that date in order that it may be recovered, except in actions of damages for personal injuries.[70]

Crave for expenses

9.94 Expenses should be expressly craved *ob majorem cautelam* in all cases in which they are desired, for while in a defended action it is competent to award expenses without these being craved,[71] the power to award

---

[60] OCR, r. 30.3(1).

[61] OCR, r. 30.3(2).

[62] OCR, r. 30.3(3).

[63] Administration of Justice (Scotland) Act 1972, s. 4, which permits amendment by Act of Sederunt of the Sheriff Courts (Scotland) Act 1892, s. 9.

[64] A.S. (Interest in Sheriff Court Decrees and Extracts) 1993 (S.I. 1993 No. 769).

[65] *Roger v. J. & P. Cochrane & Co.*, 1910 S.C. 1.

[66] Maclaren, p. 298.

[67] *Bank of Scotland v. Davis*, 1982 S.L T. 20. A crave for interest based on a bank base rate at the date of extract or payment was approved in *Royal Bank of Scotland plc v. Geddes*, 1983 S.L.T. (Sh. Ct.) 32; but see S. A. Bennett, 1983 S.L.T. (News) 85.

[68] *Petroleum Industry Training Board v. Jenkins*, 1982 S.L.T. (Sh. Ct.) 43; but see *Royal Bank of Scotland plc v. Briggs*, 1982 S.L.T. (Sh. Ct.) 46.

[69] OCR, r. 7.6(1).

[70] *Orr v. Metcalfe*, 1973 S.C. 57. See para. 21.13.

[71] *Torrance v. Craufuird* (1822) 1 S. 301 (N.E. 280); *Heggie & Co. v. Stark and Selkrig* (1826) 4 S. 510 (N.E. 518); *Scott v. Wilson* (1829) 7 S. 566; *Western Bank v. Buchanan* (1865) 4 M. 97, *per* Lord Deas at 99.

expenses being inherent in the court,[72] it is doubtful whether they may be awarded in an undefended action which has no crave for expenses.[73] In some circumstances, however, expenses are craved only in the event of some party appearing and opposing or appearing and causing expense as, for example, in certain actions of declarator and in actions of constitution.[74]

Expenses are normally craved by adding at the end of the crave the words "and with expenses" or "and to find the defender [or defenders] liable in expenses". Where the craves are alternative, the latter form is preferable, since the former may be thought to imply that decree for expenses will not be sought if the defender complies with the primary crave. Where the crave is for decree for payment by defenders jointly and severally, the former style should be used, since it is doubtful whether, if the latter is used, any defender will be liable for more than his own share of the pursuer's expenses. **9.95**

Crave for warrants

For arrestment on the dependence. The rules relating to arrestment on the dependence of an action are discussed in Chapter 11. Where such arrestment is competent it may be obtained by including in the crave a crave for warrant to arrest on the dependence.[75] A warrant to arrest is in practice sought in most actions with pecuniary craves, upòn the view that it may be put in force or not, as may be found expedient. A warrant granted without a crave therefor in the initial writ has been held to be valid.[76] **9.96**

For arrestment to found jurisdiction. The rules concerning arrestment to found jurisdiction are discussed in Chapter 3. Application for a warrant for arrestment to found jurisdiction may be made in the crave of the initial writ, and averments to justify the granting of the warrant must be included in the condescendence.[77] **9.97**

For intimation. Where it is necessary for intimation to be made to any person, such as an alleged paramour or other person in terms of rule 33.7, or any other person having a title to sue an action under the Damages (Scotland) Act 1976 in terms of rule 36.3, a crave for warrant for intimation should be added at the end of the crave. **9.98**

The condescendence

Form A of the Appendix to the Ordinary Cause Rules gives the following direction as to the condescendence: "State in numbered paragraphs the facts which form the ground of action." The condescendence is accordingly a statement of the material facts on which the pursuer founds **9.99**

---

[72] *Heggie & Co., supra*; *Ledgerwood v. McKenna* (1868) 7 M. 261; *Mitchell v. Baird* (1902) 4 F. 809, *per* Lord Kinnear at 811; *McQuarter v. Fergusson*, 1911 S.C. 640, *per* L.P. Dunedin and Lord Kinnear at 646.

[73] *Heggie & Co., supra, per* Lord Glenlee at 519.

[74] *Smith v. Kippen* (1860) 22 D. 1495; *Earl of Rosslyn v. Lawson* (1872) 9 S.L.R. 291; *Harper v. Connor's Trs* (1927) 43 Sh.Ct.Rep. 138; *Ferrier v. Crockart*, 1937 S.L.T. 206.

[75] See para. 11.16.

[76] *Muir & Son v. Robert Muir & Co. Ltd*, 1910 1 S.L.T 414.

[77] OCR, r. 3.4. See paras 3.98 to 3.102.

the claim which he has formulated in the crave. The pursuer should therefore set forth in the condescendence his title,[78] and the circumstances in which he is compelled to assert it, or the grounds of the defender's liability and the necessity for raising an action against him.[79] The legal propositions which the pursuer claims to be applicable to the facts averred in the condescendence are enunciated in the pleas-in-law. The condescendence and pleas-in-law may be subsequently altered by adjustment[80] or amendment,[81] but it is advisable to frame them only after a careful appreciation of the relevant facts and law, so that they will require the minimum of subsequent alteration.

9.100 The condescendence is divided into paragraphs (customarily called "articles") numbered consecutively. A number of essential matters are usually averred in the opening articles. Article 1 usually states the designations of the parties and any special capacities in which they are suing and being sued. Any special capacity is set forth in the instance, and the details of how the party came to possess that special capacity are given in the condescendence, in order that they may be proved, or admitted, or denied.[82]

9.101 It is essential to state, preferably in article 1 or 2, the ground of jurisdiction of the court and the facts upon which that ground is based.[83] If the pursuer has reason to believe that an agreement exists prorogating jurisdiction over the subject-matter of the cause to another court he must aver details of that agreement.[84] If he has reason to believe that proceedings are pending before another court involving the same cause of action and between the same parties as those named in the initial writ, he must aver details of those proceedings.[85] Such averments may conveniently appear in an early article of condescendence. If there is no reason to believe either of these matters, there is no need to aver the negative. There should also be averred, in one of the opening articles, the facts necessary to establish the pursuer's title to sue[86] and the defender's capacity to be sued, where these are likely to be challenged or are not immediately apparent from the facts subsequently averred.

9.102 The following articles set out the material facts in a logical order. What is an appropriate statement of these facts must depend on the nature and particular circumstances of each case[87]; but the primary consideration in drafting is that it is the function of written pleadings to enable the parties and the court to ascertain with precision those matters on which the parties are at issue and those on which they are agreed, and thus to arrive at the question which the parties wish

---

[78] *Mackintosh v. Mackintosh* (1835) 13 S. 884; *Hutchison v. Ferrier* (1846) 8 D. 1228; *Kilmarnock Mags v. Mather* (1869) 7 M. 548; *Bentley v. Macfarlane*, 1964 S.C. 76, *per* Lord Guthrie at 83; *Microwave Systems (Scotland) Ltd v. Electro-Physiological Instruments Ltd*, 1971 S.C. 140; *Fraser v. Church of Scotland General Trs*, 1986 S.L.T. 692, *per* Lord Dunpark at 697.

[79] Maclaren, p. 311.

[80] See paras 8.26, 8.27.

[81] See Chap. 10.

[82] *Hunter v. LMS Ry*, 1938 S.L.T. 598, *per* Lord Jamieson at 599; 1939 S.L.T. 297.

[83] OCR, r. 3.1(5). See R. Black, "Styles for Averring Jurisdiction under the Civil Jurisdiction and Judgments Act 1982", 1987 S.L.T. (News) 1.

[84] OCR, r. 3.1(3).

[85] OCR, r. 3.1(4).

[86] See the cases cited *supra*, n. 78.

[87] See Black, *Introduction to Written Pleading*, pp. 12–19.

decided. Thus, in an action of damages for breach of contract or negligence, the condescendence will set out the relationship between the parties and a chronological narrative of the facts. A series of short articles is preferable to one long article: the defender may make admissions in reply to short articles more readily than to long articles. Such admissions both help to focus the issues and assist the party obtaining them, for "every admission a litigant can obtain for his averments saves proof and avoids risk".[88] Next, a link is formed between the narrative and the pleas-in-law by a separate article or articles stating the facts from which the pleas-in-law directly emerge: in the case of a breach of contract, there are averred the terms or conditions which the pursuer claims to have been breached and the respects in which he maintains that they were breached[89]; and in the case of negligence, the duty incumbent on the defender and the way in which he failed to discharge it.[90] Each ground of liability, whether at common law or under statute, should be the subject of a separate article, and the relevant part of any statute or statutory instrument founded on should be quoted.[91] A further separate article explains the way in which the sum sued for is made up, and specifies the various heads under which damages are claimed. The final article briefly explains that the action is necessary because the defender has failed to meet the pursuer's demands, although given a reasonable opportunity to do so.

It has already been pointed out that the condescendence should state only facts and not evidence, or law except in those cases in which averments of legal duty are customarily made, or argumentative or scandalous matter[92]; and that it should be framed in short sentences, in dry and succinct language and, generally, in the past tense.[93] **9.103**

The pleas-in-law

The nature and function of pleas-in-law have already been considered.[94] The pursuer's pleas-in-law are stated after the condescendence, and are numbered consecutively. The facts necessary to sustain each plea-in-law should have been distinctly stated in the condescendence.[95] The pleas-in-law are not necessarily stated in any particular order, but the customary order[96] is as follows. The pursuer states, first, the pleas which he claims justify a decision in his favour[97]; then the pleas which refute the defender's **9.104**

---

[88] Lees, *Pleading*, p. 31, para. 77.

[89] *Britain Steamship Co. Ltd v. Lithgows Ltd*, 1975 S.L.T. (Notes) 20, *per* Lord Maxwell at 22.

[90] This manner of pleading in negligence actions has been criticised, but it remains the usual and approved practice. See para. 9.17.

[91] See para. 9.68.

[92] See paras 9.14 to 9.18.

[93] See para. 9.51.

[94] See paras 9.47, 9.48.

[95] *McGrath v. Glasgow Coal Co. Ltd*, 1909 S.C. 1250.

[96] Lees, *Pleading*, pp. 56–57, para. 138; A. G. Walker, "Written Pleadings" (1963) 79 Sc.L.R. 161 at pp. 166–167.

[97] Where the pursuer in an action of damages for personal injuries founds on breaches of duty at common law and under statute, and clearly distinguishes these grounds in separate articles of the condescendence, it is sufficient to plead fault as the ground of action: *Durnin v. William Coutts & Son*, 1955 S.L.T. (Notes) 9; *Cobban v. British Transport Commission* [1955] C.L.Y. 3535. The usual style is, however: "The pursuer having sustained loss, injury and damage through fault *et separatim* breach of statutory duty on the part of the defenders, is entitled to reparation from them therefor."

substantive case; then pleas dealing with the relevancy of the defences. No pleas are necessary concerning any warrants craved, or expenses. There is no need, and indeed it is bad pleading, to add the words "with expenses" to a plea-in-law. Where two pleas conflict with each other, the second is usually prefaced by "*Separatim*" or "*Separatim. Esto . . .*".[98]

Authentication

9.105 Rule 3.1(7) provides that the initial writ shall be signed by the pursuer or his solicitor, and Form G1 requires such signature at the end of the pleas-in-law. It is usual to add before the signature the words "IN RESPECT WHEREOF".[99] If the solicitor signs, Form G1 requires the addition, after his signature, of his designation and business address and the words "Solicitor for Pursuer". Another solicitor holding a practising certificate may sign the writ on behalf of the pursuer's solicitor,[1] but the latter's name, designation and address must appear after the signature. It must also be stated on the back of every service copy of the writ[2] for the information of the defender or his solicitor.[3] A typed or written version of the signature need not appear on the service copy.[4] It has been held sufficient for the name and town of the solicitor's firm to appear on the back of the service copy.[5] A defender who appears is thereby barred from objecting to the absence of any signature on the service copy and the absence of any name and address on its back.[6]

The defences

9.106 The defences must be in the form of answers in paragraphs corresponding to the articles of the condescendence, and must have appended a note of the defender's pleas-in-law.[7] In practice they are also headed and signed.

The heading

9.107 The defences begin by stating the name of the sheriffdom and the place of sitting of the court.[8] Then comes the word "DEFENCES" followed by a distinct identification of the defender for whom they are lodged,[9] then the words "in the action at the instance of" and the names and designations of the parties as in the instance, thus:

---

[98] See para. 9.57.
[99] See para. 9.49.
[1] *Muir's Sequestration* (1911) 27 Sh.Ct.Rep. 327; *cf. Stonehaven Town Council v. E. Williams Promotions*, 1954 S.L.T. (Sh. Ct.) 105.
[2] OCR, r. 3.1(7).
[3] *Muir's Sequestration, supra.*
[4] *Muir v. National Bank Ltd* (1943) 59 Sh.Ct.Rep. 51, but see para. 9.49.
[5] *Muir, supra.*
[6] *National Cash Register Co. Ltd v. Hunter* (1915) 32 Sh.Ct.Rep. 121.
[7] OCR, r. 9.6(2). See para. 9.108.
[8] See para. 9.75.
[9] *Fernie v. Bell* (1894) 2 S.L.T. 311. See para. 9.43.

DEFENCES

for

JAMES BLACK, 2 Burgh Place,
Edinburgh, EH3 4DC—*First-named Defender*

in the action at the instance of

JOHN WHITE, 1 Academy Street,
Whiteness, WS1 2AB—*Pursuer*

against

the said JAMES BLACK—*First-named Defender*

and

JOSEPH GREEN, 3 Canada Road,
Edinburgh, EH5 6EF—*Second-named Defender*

If the defender is legally aided the words "Assisted Person" must follow his name in brackets in the heading and in every step of process.[10]

The answers

It is possible that a defender who intends to challenge the jurisdiction of the court may be entitled to lodge defences relating only to the question of jurisdiction in the first instance. The lodging of a notice of intention to defend does not imply acceptance of the jurisdiction of the court.[11] The Maxwell Report envisaged that the rules would be amended to entitle the defender to lodge defences relating only to jurisdiction, and to proceed to defend on the merits if these defences were unsuccessful.[12] The rules have not, however, been amended to that extent. They continue to provide that defences must be in the form of answers in paragraphs corresponding to the articles of the condescendence,[13] and that every statement of fact made by one party must be answered by the other party.[14] Defences framed without regard to these rules may attract criticism.[15] It may be that a defender who intends only to contest jurisdiction without stating a defence on the merits, as he seems entitled to do by rule 9.1(2), should lodge defences which are in conformity with these rules to the extent that they state fully his challenge to jurisdiction but are only skeletal on the merits. In any event a defender who intends to contest jurisdiction must state a specific plea-in-law in the defences lodged.[16] **9.108**

The answers are headed "ANSWERS TO CONDESCENDENCE". Subject to the possible qualification relative to defences designed only to contest jurisdiction, discussed immediately above, the general rules are as follows. The answers must be framed in paragraphs corresponding to the articles of the condescendence.[17] In each paragraph the defender must answer every statement of fact made by the pursuer in the corresponding **9.109**

---

[10] A.S. (Civil Legal Aid Rules) 1987, r. 3(1).
[11] OCR, r. 9.1(2).
[12] Maxwell Report, para. 5.195.
[13] OCR, r. 9.6(2).
[14] OCR, r. 9.7.
[15] *Thorburn v. Dempster* (1900) 2 F. 583.
[16] See para. 9.119.
[17] OCR, r. 9.6(2).

paragraph of the condescendence,[18] and must add any averments which the defender intends to prove. The defender cannot withhold his defence on the merits on the ground that he has stated a preliminary plea which would dispose of the action if sustained.[19] He is obliged to respond to each averment by the pursuer in one of three ways: by admitting it, or denying it, or stating that the matter is not known and not admitted. It is good practice to begin each paragraph of the answers with any admissions which should properly be made by the defender.[20] Every averment, or part of an averment, in the corresponding paragraph which is to be admitted should be specifically repeated, preceded by the words "Admitted that". A brief explanation or qualification which is related to the averment admitted may be added to the admission, thus: "Admitted that [*here repeat the averment or part thereof to be admitted*] under explanation that [*here state the explanation or qualification*]." Any averments made by the pursuer of facts outwith the defender's knowledge should thereafter be answered with the words "Not known and not admitted that", followed by a repetition of the averments concerned. The words "Believed to be true that" may be similarly employed in answer to an averment of a fact outwith the defender's knowledge which he concedes to be true in order to narrow the issues in dispute.[21] The pursuer's remaining averments are denied by stating: "*Quoad ultra* denied."

9.110 The foregoing order may, however, be varied according to circumstances: a paragraph consisting mainly of facts outwith the defender's knowledge may be answered by stating which of the averments within his knowledge are admitted or denied, and ending, "*Quoad ultra* not known and not admitted." It is, however, in general undesirable to use the phrase, "*Quoad ultra* admitted", because additions to the paragraph made by adjustment may thus be held to be admitted, or may require the redrafting of the answer. The omission of a denial of the pursuer's narrative, where it is inconsistent with the narrative pleaded by the defender, may at least cause difficulties later.[22] In that situation a useful form of denial is, "*Quoad ultra* denied except in so far as coinciding herewith."[23]

9.111 It is rarely appropriate to use the phrase "It is specifically denied that . . .". If the pleader has stated a general denial, or has used the phrase "*Quoad ultra* denied", a further specific denial is unnecessary; but it may serve to draw attention to the fact that the averment in question has been denied. The phrase "Denied as stated" should be avoided altogether. It is liable to be construed as a meaningless superfluity,[24] or as meaning that the facts as averred by the pursuer are distorted[25] or that the ambit of the

---

[18] OCR, r. 9.7.

[19] *Thorburn, supra,* was concerned with a plea to jurisdiction, and its effect may be modified by the option to contest jurisdiction only which is apparently intended to be conferred by the rules (see para. 9.108). It seems to remain authority for the general proposition that the rules require preliminary defences and defences on the merits to be stated at the same time.

[20] On the making of admissions, see paras 9.19 to 9.26.

[21] See para. 9.60.

[22] *Music Hire Service (Manchester) Ltd v. Roccio,* 1961 S.L.T. (Notes) 13.

[23] *Campbell v. Campbell* (1863) 1 M. 217; A. G. Walker, "Written Pleadings" (1963) 79 Sc.L.R. 161 at 170.

[24] C. Scott Dickson, "Pleading" (1897) 9 J.R. 4 at p. 26; *Morrison v. McArdle,* 1967 S.L.T. (Sh. Ct.) 58.

[25] Lees, *Pleading,* p. 48, para. 119.

denial is circumscribed by the averments which follow[26]; and it is no longer employed by good pleaders.[27]

9.112 In a case where the defender wishes to put forward a substantive case or line of defence in answer to the pursuer's averments, the defender's answer, having dealt with the pursuer's averments, goes on to state, normally by averments by way of explanation beginning "Explained and averred that . . .", the facts which the defender intends to prove. In each answer the defender states that part of his case which is appropriate to the chapter of the pleadings of which the corresponding article of condescendence forms part: thus, any averments to support a plea of no jurisdiction or no title to sue are normally made in answer 1. In drafting the defender's case, the same principles apply as in the case of the condescendence: "without disclosing what is properly called evidence, you must at least state the line of defence, and the main facts and points in the enquiry on which you rest, so that the other party shall be fully able previously to investigate the case, and be prepared for it."[28] As a general rule, the defender cannot withhold his defence on the merits on the ground that he has stated a preliminary plea which would dispose of the action if sustained[29]; and a ground of defence which is not stated on record cannot, in general, be sustained by the court.[30] Like a pursuer, a defender may urge pleas which are inconsistent with each other, so long as they are taken alternatively, and so long as the facts upon which the pleas are founded are stated alternatively.[31] Although averments in answer may not be treated as equivalent to admissions,[32] an averment that the defender performed all statutory duties incumbent upon him may be construed as an admission of the applicability of the statute founded on by the pursuer: if the defender disputes its applicability, he must aver or at least clearly imply that it does not apply.[33] He must also give notice of any statutory defence on which he wishes to rely,[34] and of any other issue, such as contributory negligence,[35] where the onus of proof lies on the defender. He cannot lead evidence in rebuttal of evidence led in support of the pursuer's averments unless he himself has made averments on the matter in his answers.[36] He may, however, be entitled to found on evidence inconsistent with his pleadings if it has been led without timeous objection.[37]

---

[26] *Jack Davis Publicity Ltd v. Kennedy*, Sh. Pr. Caplan, Paisley Sh. Ct, Dec. 18, 1984, unreported.

[27] See Black, *Introduction to Written Pleading*, p. 22.

[28] *Neilson v. Househill Coal and Iron Co.* (1842) 4 D. 1187, *per* L.J.-C. Hope at 1193.

[29] *Thorburn v. Dempster* (1900) 2 F. 583. See paras 9.108, 9.109.

[30] *Robb v. Logiealmond School Board* (1875) 2 R. 417, *per* L.P. Inglis at 422; *Quinn v. Caraeron & Robertson*, 1956 S.C. 244, *per* Lord Russell at 240. As to matters which are *pars judicis*, see paras 2.09 to 2.17.

[31] Maclaren, p. 375, approved, *Smart v. Bargh*, 1949 S.C. 57; *Middleton v. Middleton*, 1972 S.C. 188.

[32] *Wilson v. Clyde Rigging and Boiler Scaling Co.*, 1959 S.C. 328. It is doubted whether *Lord Advocate v. Gillespie*, 1969 S.L.T. (Sh. Ct.) 10 was correctly decided.

[33] *McNaught v. British Railways Board*, 1979 S.L.T. (Notes) 99.

[34] *Moffat v. Marconi Space and Defence Systems Ltd*, 1975 S.L.T. (Notes) 60.

[35] *Taylor v. Simon Carves Ltd*, 1958 S.L.T. (Sh. Ct.) 23 (applied, *Fookes v. Slaytor* [1978] 1 W.L.R. 1293).

[36] *O'Connor v. W. G. Auld & Co. (Engineering) Ltd*, 1970 S.L.T. (Notes) 16.

[37] *Brown's Exrx v. N.B. Steel Foundry Ltd*, 1968 S.L.T. 121.

9.113 The defender's averments, like the pursuer's, must be relevant and specific.[38] If a general plea to the relevancy and specification of the defender's averments is stated by the pursuer and sustained by the court, the defences will be repelled and decree granted in favour of the pursuer, except in cases where decree cannot be granted without proof.[39] If particular averments are held to be irrelevant or lacking in specification, they will be excluded from probation.[40] The question whether defences are relevant and specific depends on the particular case they are designed to meet.

9.114 **Skeleton defences.** There is no principle or rule of practice which requires a defender in every case, as a matter of relevancy, to state more than a general denial of the pursuer's averments: there are cases in which such a "skeleton" defence may be a perfectly fair and relevant defence to a pursuer's claim,[41] although it would not permit the defender at a proof to make out any substantive case in answer to the pursuer's averments either by positive evidence or by cross-examination.[42] It may also be perfectly proper, if there is initially doubt about the facts or the law, to put in skeleton defences to preserve the position while investigations are made. But as soon as the facts and the law are elucidated, either the defences should be expanded if in their skeleton form they are not a fair and relevant defence to the pursuer's claim, or they should be withdrawn if it appears that there is no defence to the action. If a defender who has no defence either in fact or in law uses the procedures of the court not to establish his right but to delay the enforcement of a right which is undeniable, he is guilty of an abuse of process and his solicitor may be required to pay what his conduct has cost the other party to the litigation.[43] If a defender chooses to rely on a skeleton defence which is clearly evasive or incomplete, the court, if called on to determine its relevancy, will construe it very strictly against him.[44] If the defences

> "are clearly seen to be skeletal in form then the court can readily conclude that at best they do not represent a full and candid statement of the defence. This calls into question whether there is a defence at all. The court will be reluctant to expose a pursuer to the expense and delay consequent upon allowing a proof if it is not at all clear that there is an actual issue to go to proof."[45]

---

[38] See paras 9.27 to 9.39.

[39] *Brown v. George Wilson (Stonehouse) Ltd*, 1982 S.L.T. (Sh. Ct.) 96; *RHM Bakeries (Scotland) Ltd v. Strathclyde R.C.*, 1985 S.L.T. 3.

[40] See paras 8.58, 13.21.

[41] *Redpath v. McCall*, 1963 S.L.T. (Sh. Ct.) 47; *Ganley v. Scottish Boatowners Mutual Insurance Association*, 1967 S.L.T. (Notes) 45; J. C. *Forbes Ltd v. Duignan*, 1974 S.L.T. (Sh. Ct.) 74; *Jarvie v. Laird*, 1974 S.L.T. (Sh. Ct.) 75; *Lossie Hydraulic Co. v. Ecosse Transport Ltd*, 1980 S.L.T. (Sh. Ct.) 94 at 96–97; *McManus v. Spiers Dick and Smith Ltd*, 1989 S.L.T. 806; *Gray v. Boyd*, 1996 S.L.T 60. It is doubted whether *Turner's Ltd v. Hay*, 1963 S.L.T. (Sh. Ct.) 45, was correctly decided.

[42] *Ganley, supra.*

[43] *Stewart v. Stewart*, 1984 S.L.T. (Sh. Ct.) 58.

[44] *Ellon Castle Estates Co. Ltd v. Macdonald*, 1975 S.L.T. (Notes) 66; *Foxley v. Dunn*, 1978 S.L.T. (Notes) 35; *Lossie Hydraulic Co., supra*; *Edward Gibbon (Aberdeen) Ltd v. Edwards*, 1992 (Sh. Ct.) 86 and contrast *Grampian Hydraulics (Buckie) Ltd v. Dauntless Marine Engineering & Supply Co. Ltd*, 1992 (Sh. Ct.) 45.

[45] *George Wallace (Builders) Ltd v. Clydebank Parish Church Congregational Board*, Sh. Pr. Caplan, Paisley Sh. Ct., May 24, 1984, unreported.

> "Any system of pleading has some imperfections, but it is an instrument, not a master, and it is for the court to see that any imperfections are not taken advantage of so as to lead to injustice."[46]

An exiguous or uncandid defence consisting mainly of a general denial may be held to be irrelevant if it contains an admission of facts which require explanation[47] or an admission,[48] implied admission,[49] averment[50] or plea-in-law[51] inconsistent with the denial. When determining the relevancy of such a defence the court will consider any material probative documents which are produced[52] and any explanations or concessions made at the bar.[53]

Pleas-in-law

The pleas-in-law for the defender fall into two classes: (i) preliminary pleas and (ii) pleas on the merits, which are respectively applicable to dilatory defences and peremptory defences.[54] A preliminary plea is one which, unless met, leads to the disposal of the action without inquiry into the merits of the dispute which the action is intended to raise, unless the preliminary defence is so bound up with the merits that inquiry is necessary in order to ascertain the facts. Where the facts of the preliminary defence itself are alone in dispute, an inquiry into these facts is allowed without going into the merits, as where a plea that the defender is not subject to the jurisdiction of the court is inquired into by way of a preliminary proof which does not investigate the merits of the case.[55] If a preliminary plea is sustained, the action is dismissed or (if the preliminary plea is to the effect that some other form of resolution of the dispute, such as arbitration, has been agreed between the parties) sisted. If the action is dismissed, the pursuer may bring a new action on the same ground without being open to the plea of *res judicata*.[56] A plea on the merits cannot be either sustained or repelled without inquiry into the facts, unless these are agreed; and if sustained, decree of absolvitor is granted to the defender. Both types of plea must be supported by relevant averments in the pleadings, except those preliminary pleas to competency and relevancy which are based, not upon specific averments, but upon the nature of the case as laid or the pleadings as a whole. **9.115**

Preliminary pleas

Those usually met with may be divided into three categories: objections to the instance; objections to the jurisdiction of the court to entertain the action; and pleas against the action itself. **9.116**

---

46 *MacShannon v. Rockware Glass Ltd* [1978] A.C. 795, *per* Lord Keith of Kinkel at 830.
47 *Roberts v. Logan*, 1966 S.L.T. 77.
48 *Lloyd's Bank Ltd v. Bauld*, 1976 S.L.T. (Notes) 53; *D. Roy (Roots and Floors) Ltd v. McCorquodale*, 1979 S.L.T. (Sh. Ct.) 33.
49 *Ulferts Fabriker A.B. v. Form and Colour Ltd*, 1977 S.L.T. (Sh. Ct.) 19; *Brown v. George Wilson (Stonehouse) Ltd*, 1982 S.L.T. (Sh. Ct.) 96.
50 *Foxley, supra*; *Grampian Hydraulics (Buckie) Ltd, supra.*
51 *Lossie Hydraulic Co., supra.*
52 *Lloyd's Bank Ltd, supra.*
53 *Ellon Castle Estates Co. Ltd, supra.*
54 *Geils v. Geils* (1851) 1 Macq. 36, *per* Lord Truro L.C. at 39–40.
55 See paras 8.59, 8.60.
56 *Menzies v. Menzies* (1893) 20 R.(H.L.) 108, *per* Lord Watson at 110–111, *Govan Old Victualling Society Ltd v. Wagstaff* (1907) 44 S.L.R. 295.

Objections to the Instance

9.117 *No title to sue.*[57] The objection that the pursuer has no title to sue the action means that, even on the assumption that the defender is liable to have a decree pronounced against him in the circumstances condescended on, the pursuer is not the person who has a title to call upon the court to pronounce such a decree.[58] The plea is not appropriate where the pursuer's title is the *de quo* of the action, and not merely a precondition of some other remedy.[59] The usual form of the plea is: "The pursuer having no title to sue, the action should be dismissed."[60] The grounds of objection must be specifically averred[61]; and if the pursuer fails to set forth his title on record when thus challenged, his action will be dismissed.[62]

9.118 *All parties not called.* This defence means that all parties whose appearance or failure to appear is necessary to have the question at issue effectively disposed of have not been called.[63] It is *pars judicis* to notice that all such parties have not been called.[64]

Objections to Jurisdiction

9.119 *No jurisdiction.* A plea in the short form "No jurisdiction" has been criticised,[65] but it continues to be the usual way in which the defender contests the jurisdiction of the court. Where his objection is that he is not subject to the jurisdiction of the court, the appropriate form is: "The defender not being subject to the jurisdiction of the court, the action should be dismissed."[66] An objection that the action itself is not of a kind within the jurisdiction of the sheriff court may be stated in the form: "The sheriff court having no jurisdiction in the case, the action should be dismissed", or in the form of a plea to competency.[67] In any event, a defender contesting the jurisdiction of the court must do so timeously by stating a specific plea-in-law in the defences lodged.[68]

---

57 On title and interest to sue, see paras 4.29 to 4.33. The plea is fully discussed by Maxwell, pp. 192–193.

58 Maclaren, p. 380.

59 *Luss Estates Co. v. B.P. Oil Grangemouth Refinery Ltd*, 1981 S.L.T. 97.

60 *Bentley v. MacFarlane*, 1964 S.C. 76. *Cf. Alexander Ward & Co. Ltd v. Samyang Navigation Co. Ltd*, 1975 S.C.(H.L.) 26 at 27.

61 *North British Ry v. Brown, Gordon & Co.* (1857) 19 D. 840.

62 *Bentley, supra, per* Lord Guthrie at 83; *Microwave Systems (Scotland) Ltd v. Electro-Physiological Instruments Ltd*, 1971 S.C. 140.

63 *Wilson v. IBA*, 1979 S.C. 351, *per* Lord Ross at 356; *Firth v. Anderson*, 1954 S.L.T. (Sh. Ct.) 27; and see Maxwell, pp. 193–194 and cases there cited. Parties who are not called, but who have an interest to defend the action, have a right to sist themselves as defenders: see para. 12.18.

64 *Connell v. Ferguson* (1857) 19 D. 482, *per* Lord Deas at 486–487.

65 *Love v. Love*, 1907 S.C. 728, *per* Lord Dundas at 729; *Ponton's Exrs v. Ponton*, 1913 S.C. 598, *per* Lord Dundas at 600; *Mitchell v. Aberdeen Insurance Committee*, 1918 S.C. 415, *per* Lord Dundas at 433.

66 *cf. Carter v. Allison*, 1966 S.C. 257 at 259.

67 Dobie, *Styles*, p. 365.

68 Ersk., I, ii, 27; *Wall's Trs v. Drynan* (1888) 15 R. 359, *per* L.P. Inglis at 363; *Assets Co. Ltd v. Falla's Tr.* (1894) 22 R. 178; *Young v. Evans*, 1968 S.L.T. (Notes) 57; *Alexander Ward & Co. v. Samyang Navigation Co.*, 1975 S.C.(H.L.) 26, *per* Lord Hailsham at 49, Lord Kilbrandon at 52–53. *Obiter dicta* in *Fraser-Johnston Engineering Co. v. Jeffs*, 1920 S.C. 222, *per* L.P. Clyde and Lord Mackenzie at 229 to the effect that the plea may be added at adjustment, appear to be inconsistent with these authorities: see Black, p. 27. See also *A v. B* (1873) 10 S.L.R. 290; *Cheek v. Santa Fe (U.K.) Ltd*, 1978 S.L.T. (Sh. Ct.) 60. *Cf.*, however, the rule concerning the pleading of an arbitration clause (para. 2.100).

Other objections. Other objections to the jurisdiction of the court may be stated by the pleas of *forum non conveniens*[69] and *lis alibi pendens*,[70] both normally stated in short form,[71] and by a plea that the action is excluded by an arbitration clause or other agreement.[72] The latter plea may be stated in the form: "In respect that the dispute between the parties falls to be resolved upon a reference under [the arbitration clause referred to in the answers], and such reference having been made, the action should be sisted."[73] **9.120**

PLEAS AGAINST THE ACTION ITSELF

Incompetency. This is an objection to the form of the initial writ either in general or in a particular set of circumstances, as distinguished from irrelevancy, which is an objection to the averments in the condescendence.[74] An action may be incompetent because, for example, it seeks a remedy not known to the law[75]; or because some other process is alone appropriate to the circumstances[76]; or because of the manner in which it is laid.[77] A plea to the competency should specify the ground on which the objection is taken.[78] A party by acting inconsistently with his plea to competency may be held to have waived it[79]; and a party cannot challenge the competency of a process which he himself has initiated.[80] Since it is *pars judicis* to notice questions of competency, even in the absence of a plea,[81] the court may dismiss an action as incompetent although no plea to competency has been stated.[82] Where one of several craves is held to be incompetent, the incompetent crave and the relative averments should be deleted.[83] **9.121**

Irrelevancy. The requirement of relevancy in pleading has already been discussed.[84] The question whether an action is irrelevant is determined by an application to the pursuer's averments of the legal principles relative to its subject-matter. A plea may be directed against the action as a whole, thus: "The pursuer's averments being irrelevant and insufficient in law to support the crave of the initial writ, the action should be dismissed." Or it may be directed against the relevancy of particular averments: "The pursuer's averments in article 4 of the condescendence relating to **9.122**

---

[69] See paras 2.89 to 2.93.
[70] See paras 2.94 to 2.98.
[71] But *cf. Crédit Chimique v. James Scott Engineering Group Ltd*, 1979 S.C. 406 at 407.
[72] See para. 2.100.
[73] *cf. Lanarkshire C.C. v. East Kilbride C.C.*, 1967 S.C. 235 at 238; *Wilson & McFarlane v. Stewart & Co.* (1898) 25 R. 655.
[74] Maclaren, pp. 387–388.
[75] *Jack v. Jack*, 1962 S.C. 24.
[76] *e.g.* an ordinary action for payment of a sum within the pecuniary limit for summary causes is incompetent.
[77] *e.g.* an action against more than one defender with separate conclusions against each based on separate and independent grounds of debt (*Liquidators of Western Bank v. Douglas* (1860) 22 D. 447, *per* L.J.-C. Inglis at 496–497).
[78] *Coxall v. Stewart*, 1976 S.L.T. 275.
[79] *N.B. Ry v. Carter* (1870) 8 M. 998.
[80] *Davie v. Edinburgh Mags*, 1951 S.C. 720.
[81] See para. 2.14.
[82] *Hamilton v. Murray* (1830) 9 S. 143; *Buchanan v. Lumsden* (1837) 9 Sc.Jur. 449; *Macgregor v. Macfarlane* (1914) 31 Sh.Ct.Rep. 104; *McCallum v. Cohen* (1915) 32 Sh.Ct.Rep. 39.
[83] *Heriot-Hill v. Heriot-Hill* (1906) 14 S.L.T. 182; *Chalmers v. Chalmers*, 1982 S.L.T. 79.
[84] See paras 9.32 to 9.39.

[*here specifying their matter*] being irrelevant, should not be remitted to probation."[85] On the basis of a general plea to the relevancy of the action as a whole, attacks on specific averments may be made at debate and these averments may be, and if plainly irrelevant ought to be, excluded from probation.[86] A limited plea to the relevancy of specific averments is, however, particularly appropriate where the attack on relevancy is to be confined to these averments: the statement of a more general plea could affect the disposal of the question of the expenses of the debate.[87] The court will not *ex proprio motu* dismiss an action on the ground of irrelevancy.[88]

9.123 *Lack of specification.* The requirement of specification has also been discussed.[89] A plea to specification is very frequently combined with a plea to relevancy, thus: "The pursuer's averments being irrelevant *et separatim* lacking in specification, the action should be dismissed", or, "The pursuer's averments relating to [*specifying the matter*] being irrelevant *et separatim* lacking in specification, should not be remitted to probation." The various modes of disposing of pleas to relevancy and specification are considered elsewhere.[90]

9.124 *Competent and omitted.*[91] This plea should specify the grounds on which it is contended that the pursuer is barred from insisting in the process or pleading any particular plea.[92]

Pleas on the merits

9.125 These depend on the circumstances of each case, and thus are as numerous and various as the grounds of action and defence. Those which are based on practice and procedure include the following.

9.126 *Res judicata.*[93] It is normally stated in this short form, but in certain circumstances it is desirable to adopt a more detailed form.[94]

Compensation. In the event of a counterclaim being stated for which decree is craved by the defender, pleas-in-law necessary to support the counterclaim must be included in the counterclaim.[95]

Prescription.[96] If a defender wishes to found upon a prescription he must state a plea to that effect, which the court will normally either sustain or repel before proof is allowed.[97]

Mora, taciturnity and acquiescence. The plea, "The pursuer being barred

---

[85] *cf. Bark v. Scott*, 1954 S.C. 72 at 73; *Edgar v. Lord Advocate*, 1965 S.C. 67 at 68; *Bryce v. Allied Ironfounders Ltd*, 1969 S.L.T. (Notes) 29.

[86] *Inglis v. National Bank of Scotland*, 1909 S.C. 1038. If the sheriff is in doubt as to their relevancy he should allow a proof before answer: *Hackett v. Allan*, Sh. Pr. Caplan, Dunoon Sh. Ct, May 15, 1984, unreported.

[87] *Hackett, supra.*

[88] *Cadbury Bros Ltd v. T. Mabon Ltd*, 1962 S.L.T. (Sh. Ct.) 28.

[89] See paras 9.27 to 9.31.

[90] See paras 13.15 to 13.21.

[91] See paras 2.104 to 2.108.

[92] *Murray v. Seath*, 1939 S.L.T. 348; *Rorie v. Rorie*, 1967 S.L.T. 75; *Cantors Properties (Scotland) Ltd v. Swears & Wells Ltd*, 1980 S.L.T. 165; *cf. Fowler v. Brown*, 1916 S.C. 597.

[93] See paras 2.102 to 2.109.

[94] *McFeetridge v. Stewarts & Lloyds Ltd*, 1913 S.C. 773 at 775, 776; *Anderson v. Wilson*, 1972 S.C. 147 at 148.

[95] OCR, r. 19.1(3)(c).

[96] See para. 2.114.

[97] Walkers, *Evidence*, pp. 135–136.

by *mora* taciturnity and acquiescence from insisting in the present action, the defender should be assoilzied", is competent where it is supported by averments of facts and circumstances from which prejudice or acquiescence may be inferred.[98]

The defender normally negatives formally the pursuer's principal plea on the merits (*e.g.* "The pursuer not having suffered loss, injury or damage through fault on the part of the defenders, the defenders are entitled to absolvitor"), but otherwise the defender ought not merely to state the same pleas as the pursuer turned into the negative form: he should so frame his pleas as to show distinctly which of the pursuer's pleas he controverts, and what separate propositions he sets up on his own behalf. Whenever the question is one of fact, and the facts are disputed, he should state the plea, "The pursuer's averments, so far as material, being unfounded in fact, the defender should be assoilzied." When he invokes third-party procedure, he should state pleas-in-law relative to his averments that the third party is liable to him by way of contribution, relief or indemnity.[99] **9.127**

Order

The customary order in which the defender's pleas-in-law are stated is as follows: objections to jurisdiction; competency; objections to the instance; relevancy; any plea of prescription; then substantive pleas on the merits, including those relative to the pursuer's case, to substantive defences and to any third party notice; and finally pleas to *quantum* and interest.[1] Where two pleas are conflicting, the expression "*Separatim*" or "*Separatim. Esto . . .*" is usually prefixed to the second.[2] **9.128**

Signature

Although there is no statutory direction that the defences should be signed, it is customary for the defender or his solicitor to add his signature after the last plea-in-law, under the words "IN RESPECT WHEREOF", and for the solicitor to add his address.[3] **9.129**

Adjustment of pleadings

After defences have been lodged, the parties may proceed forthwith to adjust their pleadings. The Rules and practice relative to adjustment have already been noted.[4] The primary object of adjustment is to make such alterations to the parties' averments and pleas-in-law as are necessary to ensure that when the record is closed the issues between the parties and the stand which each party is taking on these issues may be readily understood from a reading of the pleadings.[5] **9.130**

---

[98] See para. 2.114.

[99] See para. 12.54.

[1] Lees, *Pleading*, p. 57, para. 138; A. G. Walker, "Written Pleadings" (1963) 79 Sc.L.R. 161 at 167. *Cf.* Black, p. 30.

[2] *e.g.* a plea of contributory negligence in an action of damages for personal injuries: "*Separatim. Esto* the said accident was partly caused by the fault of the defender (which is denied), it having been also partly caused by the fault of the pursuer, any damages awarded should be reduced in terms of the Law Reform (Contributory Negligence) Act 1945." See para. 9.57.

[3] See para. 9.49.

[4] See paras 8.25 to 8.32.

[5] A. G. Walker, "Written Pleadings" (1963) 79 Sc.L.R. 161 at 162–163.

9.131 The procedure is normally initiated by the pursuer. He must answer every statement of fact made by the defender by admitting or denying it or stating that it is not known and not admitted, and adding further explanations, on the same principles as the defender's answers to the pursuer's condescendence.[6] These answers are normally added at the end of each article of the condescendence, beginning, "With reference to the defender's averments in answer, admitted that . . .", and ending, "*Quoad ultra* the defender's averments in answer are denied except in so far as coinciding herewith."[7] The denial is of importance because the rules as to implied admissions[8] apply to the pursuer's averments in answer to the defender as they do to the defender's answers to the condescendence.[9] The pursuer may not found on averments by the defender which he denies, either at debate[10] or after proof.[11] In addition to answering the defender's averments the pursuer may amplify, delete, correct, recast or otherwise alter the averments in the condescendence, add further averments, and add or delete pleas-in-law. Any plea to the relevancy of the defences or of specific averments in the defences should be added at the end of the pursuer's original list of pleas.

9.132 The defender may thereafter adjust by altering his answers and pleas-in-law where necessary to meet any new matter introduced by the pursuer's adjustments. He may, if he has not already done so, add a counterclaim, or averments and pleas-in-law directed against a third party with a view to seeking an order for service of a third party notice. The pursuer, having considered any such adjustments by the defender, may further adjust the condescendence and pleas-in-law, and each party may continue to adjust until the closing of the record, in order to perfect the statement of his own case or to meet the case presented by his opponent. Where there are more than two parties, one may adopt all or part of another's case against a third, as where a pursuer adopts part of a first defender's case against a second defender; but care should always be taken that expansion of the pleadings does not impair the intelligibility of the record, so that "the wood is largely lost among the trees".[12] It is important to bear in mind at all stages of adjustment that it is necessary to re-read the whole pleadings. Failure to do so may easily result in averments in answer to an opponent's point remaining in the pleadings when the averment of that point itself has been deleted.

---

[6] See paras 9.109 to 9.112.

[7] Walker, *supra*, at pp. 172–173.

[8] See paras 9.20 to 9.24.

[9] *Central Motor Engineering Co. v. Galbraith*, 1918 S.C. 755; *Gilmour v. Scottish Clan Airways*, 1928 S.N. 19; *Park Motors v. Blackmore*, 1964 S.L.T. (Sh. Ct.) 30.

[10] *Hamilton v. Santi* (1915) 32 Sh.Ct.Rep. 73.

[11] *Lee v. National Coal Board*, 1955 S.C. 151; but see para. 9.37.

[12] *Gunn v. McAdam & Son*, 1949 S.C. 31, *per* L.P. Cooper at 38.

CHAPTER 10

AMENDMENT OF PLEADINGS

I. INTRODUCTION

Amendment[1] is the means by which a pursuer may at any stage before final judgment alter the instance or crave of the initial writ, and by which any party may alter his pleadings after the record has been closed and before final judgment. Adjustment, on the other hand, is the means by which each party may alter his averments and pleas-in-law before the record is closed. While adjustment does not require the leave of the court, leave is required for all amendments other than an amendment of the crave of the initial writ in order to alter any sum sued for prior to the closing of the record.[2] Any reference to amendment in this chapter excludes amendments of the latter kind. In theory, the pleadings as they appear in the closed record place before the court each party's revised and perfected statement of his case and finally fix the limits of the dispute.[3] In practice, however, motions for leave to amend after the closing of the record are now so frequent that "amendment seems to have become the rule rather than the exception among present-day pleaders".[4] The modern provisions as to amendment of pleadings are contained in rule 18.2 of the Ordinary Cause Rules. These are significantly different from those contained in rules 78 and 80 of the original rules enacted in Schedule 1 to the 1907 Act, and are very similar to those of Chapter 24 of the Rules of the Court of Session. Any decisions under the old rules 79 and 80 are therefore no longer of value, and it is likely that rule 18.2 should be applied in the same way and to the same extent as the analogous provisions of Chapter 24. Decisions relating to rule 64 of the 1983 Ordinary Cause Rules, which was the immediate predecessor of the present rules, are of relevance since there are broad similarities between the provisions of the former rule 64 and the present rule 18.2. **10.01**

Before any amendment may be made, two conditions must be satisfied: it must be a competent amendment, and the sheriff must be satisfied that it is in the interests of justice that he should exercise his discretion in favour of allowing the amendment.[5] The sheriff may attach conditions to the allowance of an amendment, including a finding of liability for the expenses thereby occasioned. This chapter considers the extent to which amendment is competent, and the factors which the sheriff may consider in the exercise of his discretion as to the allowance of the amendment and the attachment of conditions. Proposed amendments raising an issue as to **10.02**

---

[1] As to amendment in undefended actions see paras 7.20 to 7.22.
[2] OCR, r. 18.1: see para. 8.23.
[3] See paras 8.30, 8.31.
[4] 1981 J.R. 84, *per* Lord Ross at 86.
[5] *Thomson v. Glasgow Corporation*, 1962 S.C. (H.L.) 36, *per* L.J.-C. Thomson at 51.

time-bar, which may involve questions of both competency and discretion, are then separately discussed. Finally, the chapter deals with the effect of amendment, and the procedure to be followed.

II. Competency

General provisions

10.03 The sheriff and, on appeal, the sheriff principal[6] and the Court of Session,[7] may allow amendment at any time before final judgment.[8] In practice, however, motions for leave to amend at the later stages of an action are often contested, and may be refused.[9] Rule 18.2 states that the sheriff may, at any time before final judgment, allow amendment of the initial writ which may be necessary for the purpose of determining the real question in controversy between the parties, notwithstanding that in consequence of such amendment the sum sued for is increased or restricted after the closing of the record[10] or a different remedy from that originally craved is sought.[11] The sheriff may also allow any amendment of the condescendence, defences, answers or pleas-in-law which may be necessary for determining in the existing cause the real question in controversy between the parties.[12]

10.04 Under these provisions, the test of the competency of a proposed amendment is whether it is necessary for the purpose of determining in the existing cause the real question in controversy between the parties. Under the old rules it was always accepted in the sheriff court that amendments of actions which were radically incompetent should not be allowed.[13] There was, however, room for considerable debate over what constituted a radical incompetence in an action.[14] Under the present rule it is clear that many defects in the instance, held under the earlier rules to be incurable by amendment,[15] are now so curable.[16] The question of the extent to which other defects are curable by amendment under the present rule has not yet been the subject of authoritative decision. In *Rutherford v. Virtue*,[17] Sheriff Principal Nicholson held that the changes brought about by the Ordinary Cause Rules since 1979 did not allow amendment of actions which were fundamentally incompetent. One view may be that a broad interpretation should be applied to all the provisions of the rule,

---

[6] Interpretation Act 1978, ss. 5, 23, Sched. 1, s.v. "Sheriff".

[7] *Paterson v. Wallace*, 1909 S.C. 20 at 24, 25; *Henderson v. Campbell Bros*, 1937 S.C. 91. The powers of the sheriff principal and the Court of Session to allow additional proof after amendment are considered in paras 10.25, 18.81, 18.98.

[8] OCR, r. 18.2(1).

[9] See paras 10.18 to 10.28.

[10] OCR, r. 18.2(2)(a)(i). Prior to the closing of the record the sum sued for may be altered without leave of the sheriff: OCR, r. 18.1; para. 8.23.

[11] OCR, r. 18.2(2)(a)(ii).

[12] OCR, r. 18.2(2)(c).

[13] *Tennent Caledonian Breweries Ltd v. Gearty*, 1980 S.L.T. (Sh. Ct.) 71. *Cf.* Maclaren, p. 455: "If a summons or other proceeding is *ab initio* null, it is impossible to amend it", citing *Campbell v. Fotheringham* (1826) 4 S. 766 (N.E. 774); *Ferguson, Davidson & Co. v. Paterson and Dobbie* (1898) 1 F. 227; *Gordon v. Purves* (1902) 10 S.L.T. 446, (1903) 11 S.L.T. 38.

[14] *Bank of Scotland v. W. & G. Fergusson* (1898) 1 F. 96.

[15] *e.g. Clugston v. Scottish Women's Friendly Society* (1914) 30 Sh.Ct.Rep. 150.

[16] See paras 10.07 to 10.12.

[17] 1993 S.C.L.R. 886.

and not only to those whose analogous predecessors have been authoritatively so read,[18] with the result that any defect may be cured by amendment; but that view might lead to such absurd results as the amendment of writs which were devoid of form, content or meaning. A more tenable view, it is submitted, is that the rule requires that there must be an "existing cause" before amendment may competently be allowed, and that in certain circumstances, at least, there cannot be said to be an "existing cause". It may be that there cannot be an "existing cause" where the pursuer has no title at all to initiate the action[19]; or where the citation of the defender has been invalid[20]; or where the subject-matter of the cause is not within the jurisdiction of the court[21]; or where the remedy sought is one which the court has no power to grant; or where there has been a breach of a mandatory provision of the Rules as to the form of the initial writ.[22] It may be that other matters which are *pars judicis*, such as *turpis causa*, prescription, or immunity conferred by the State Immunity Act 1978, and which would entitle the sheriff to dismiss the action as incompetent *ex proprio motu*,[23] would also have the effect of rendering the action a nullity which is incapable of amendment.

If there is an "existing cause", the principal criterion of the competency of an amendment proposed in terms of rule 18.2(2)(a) or (c) is whether it is necessary for the purpose of determining in that cause the real question in controversy between the parties. In view of the wide powers of amendment of the instance and crave conferred by rule 18.2(2)(b),[24] it would appear that neither the cause nor the question in controversy need be the cause or question between the original parties to the action.[25] Since a different remedy from that craved may be sought, an amendment is not incompetent because it raises a different question from that upon which the pursuer came into court.[26] An amendment is not, however, "necessary" in terms of the rule where there is no longer any question in controversy between the parties: thus, if it is admitted that there is no relevant defence on the merits, the defender will not be allowed to add by amendment a technical preliminary plea which would only cause further litigation and expense without a different ultimate result.[27] Nor is an amendment "necessary" which is clearly irrelevant,[28] or which renders the action incompetent,[29] or which would not remedy the defect it is intended to remove,[30] or which affects the onus of proof where that is a matter of **10.05**

---

[18] *Donaghy v. Rollo*, 1964 S.C. 278.

[19] *Bentley v. Macfarlane*, 1964 S.C. 76, *per* L.P. Clyde at 79; but this seems at least very doubtful: see *Donaghy, supra*; paras 10.09, 10.10. It seems clear that there cannot be an "existing cause" if there is literally no pursuer in the instance at all.

[20] *e.g.* where it appears that at the time of the purported citation the defender was already dead: *Boslem v. Paterson*, 1982 S.L.T. 216.

[21] *Morley v. Jackson* (1888) 16 R. 78. *Cf. Graham v. Galli*, 1980 S.L.T. (Sh. Ct.) 2.

[22] See para. 9.41. But see *Wilson v. Lothian R.C.*, 1995 S.L.T. 991.

[23] See paras 2.09 to 2.14.

[24] See paras 10.07 to 10.13.

[25] *cf. Ford v. Ford* (1912) 28 Sh.Ct.Rep. 226; *Flynn v. Faulds* (1948) 64 Sh.Ct.Rep. 265.

[26] *cf. Gibson's Trs v. Fraser* (1877) 4 R. 1001, *per* L.P. Inglis at 1004; *McKenzie v. Jones* (1926) 42 Sh.Ct.Rep. 289; *Kirkwood v. Campbell* (1926) 43 Sh.Ct.Rep. 7.

[27] *Paterson v. Wallace*, 1909 S.C. 20.

[28] *Dick & Stevenson v. Woodside Steel and Iron Co.* (1888) 16 R. 242.

[29] *Interplan (Joiners and Shopfitters) Ltd v. Brown*, Sh. Pr. Caplan, Paisley Sh. Ct, June 6, 1984, unreported. As to the appropriate procedure where the competency or relevancy of a proposed amendment is challenged, see para. 10.52.

[30] *Bank of Scotland v. W. & G. Fergusson* (1898) 1 F. 96, *per* Lord Kinnear at 103.

indirect and secondary importance.[31] And an amendment which is designed only to allow the party to adduce, at an additional proof allowed by an appeal court, further evidence on the question considered by the court below which was available to the party before he closed his proof, is not necessary for determining that question and will be refused.[32]

10.06 In some cases the question has arisen whether it is competent to allow an amendment which is inconsistent with an interlocutor already pronounced. It seems clear that an appellate court cannot competently allow an amendment which is inconsistent with an interlocutor already pronounced which has not been brought under review.[33] When parties contracted to renounce probation, amendment on appeal with the view of leading additional proof was refused[34]; and where a case was made the subject of a judicial reference, an amendment with a view to the introduction of a new question which was outside the contract of reference was refused.[35] It has been held in one case, however, that where a proof has been allowed the sheriff cannot competently allow an amendment which adds a preliminary plea.[36] It is respectfully submitted that that is not correct. An interlocutor allowing proof or proof before answer allows only proof of the averments in the pleadings as they stand at the date of that interlocutor. Rule 18.2 empowers the sheriff to allow at any time before final judgment any amendment which may be necessary for the purpose of determining in the existing cause the real question in controversy between the parties. Such amendment may render all that has gone before entirely nugatory and permit procedure on the amended pleadings which may be different from that which was allowed on the unamended pleadings.[37] In the Court of Session and the sheriff court such amendment has been held[38] or assumed[39] to be competent in many cases,[40] and an amendment adding a preliminary plea has been allowed where issues had been approved[41] or a proof before answer allowed.[42] It is immaterial that the proof before answer was allowed of consent.[43] "In practice, it is not uncommon that, after a proof before answer has been allowed, amendments are made to the record which necessitate the case being restored to the [debate] roll."[44] The consideration that such an amendment would result in debate on the amended closed record and

---

[31] *Muldoon v. Carntyne Steel Castings Co. Ltd*, 1965 S.L.T. (Notes) 63.

[32] *Brown v. Hastie & Co. Ltd* (1904) 6 F. 1001.

[33] *Arthur v. Lindsay* (1895) 22 R. 417; *McGown v. Cramb* (1897) 24 R. 481; *Terrell v. Ker* (1900) 2 F. 1055.

[34] *Carswell & Son v. Finlay* (1887) 24 S.L.R. 643. *Cf. Thomson v. Hughson & Co.* (1861) 23 D. 679.

[35] *Brown's Trs v. Horne*, 1907 S.C. 1027.

[36] *Alexander Low and Sans v. Mckenzie*, 1972 S.L.T. (Sh. Ct.) 10. A similar view was expressed in *Kinnersly v. Husband*, Sh. Pr. O'Brien, Edinburgh Sh. Ct, Mar. 24, 1987, unreported.

[37] *McKenna v. British Transport Commission*, 1960 S.L.T. (Notes) 30; *Napier Co. (Arbroath) Ltd v. S.M. Frangos*, 1995 S.C.L.R. 804.

[38] *McKenna, supra*; *Spalding v. Inveresk Paper Co. Ltd*, 1971 S.L.T. (Notes) 47.

[39] *McFarquhar v. British Railways Board*, 1967 S.L.T. (Notes) 102; *Rae v. Rae*, Sh. Pr. Dick, Glasgow Sh. Ct, Jan. 26, 1984, unreported; *East Hook Purchasing Corp. Ltd v. Ben Nevis Distillery (Fort William) Ltd*, 1985 S.L.T. 442.

[40] In *Muldoon v. Carntyne Steel Castings Co. Ltd*, 1965 S.L.T. (Notes) 63, Lord Fraser reserved his opinion as to the competency of such amendment.

[41] *McKenna, supra*; *Nicol v. McIntosh*, 1987 S.L.T. 104.

[42] *East Hook Purchasing Corp. Ltd, supra.*

[43] *Duke of Argyll v. Duchess of Argyll*, 1962 S.C. (H.L.) 88, *per* Lord Guest at 97–98.

[44] *ibid.*

possible appeals, which could substantially delay the progress of the action, might cause the court to exercise its discretion by refusing to allow the amendment,[45] but it seems clear that such amendment is competent. It may be, however, that a sheriff is not entitled to allow an amendment which would have the effect of altering a course of procedure determined by an appellate court.[46]

Amendment of instance

General

Where persons are sisted as pursuers or defenders, or the cause is transferred against the representative of a deceased party,[47] amendment of the instance is unnecessary. Similarly, where one of several pursuers desires to retire from the case, he should ordinarily lodge a minute of abandonment, since the defender may be entitled to decree of absolvitor *quoad* that pursuer[48]: his name is not deleted from the instance by amendment. The rules make provision for necessary amendments of the instance as follows. **10.07**

The sheriff may allow any amendment which may be necessary: (1) to correct or supplement the designation of any party to the cause[49]; or (2) to enable any party who has sued or has been sued in his own right to sue or be sued in a representative capacity; or (3) to enable any party who has sued or has been sued in a representative capacity to sue or be sued in his own right or in a different representative capacity.[50] **10.08**

New pursuer

The sheriff may also allow any amendment which may be necessary: (1) to add the name of an additional pursuer; or (2) to add the name of a person whose concurrence is necessary; or (3) where the cause has been commenced or presented in the name of the wrong person as pursuer or where it is doubtful whether it has been commenced or presented in the name of the right person,[51] to allow any other person to be sisted as pursuer in substitution for, or in addition to, the original pursuer.[52] Although the expression "to be sisted" is used in the rule, a minute of sist is unnecessary and the new pursuer may be introduced by amendment on the application of the original pursuer, provided that the original pursuer is still alive and his solicitor is authorised by the new pursuer to introduce him into the action.[53] The provisions of the rule set out in (3) above are intended, in the interests of the parties and in the interests of the court, to do away with unnecessary procedure, and its terms should be given a wide reading.[54] Thus, a new pursuer may be added where the title of the original pursuer was defective at the raising of the action or became defective thereafter.[55] **10.09**

---

45 As in *McFarquhar*, *supra*. See also *Spalding*, *supra*.
46 *Kerr v. John Brown & Co. Ltd*, 1965 S.C. 144.
47 paras 12.10, 12.14, 12.15.
48 Fyfe, p. 249.
49 An immaterial clerical error in a party's name may be corrected by amendment: *Riach v. Wallace* (1899) 1 F. 718; *Watt v. Smith's Trs* (1901) 9 S.L.T. 215.
50 OCR, r. 18.2(2)(a)(i)–(iii).
51 *Anderson v. Balnagown Estates Co.*, 1939 S.C. 168.
52 OCR, r. 18.2(2)(b)(iv)–(v).
53 *Interplan (Joiners and Shopfitters) Ltd v. Brown*, Sh. Pr. Caplan, Paisley Sh. Ct, June 26, 1984, unreported.
54 *Rackstraw v. Douglas*, 1919 S.C. 354, *per* L.J.-C. Scott Dickson at 357.
55 *Donaghy v. Rollo*, 1964 S.C. 278; *cf. Bentley v. Macfarlane*, 1964 S.C. 76, *per* L.P. Clyde at 79. See *A. C. Stewart and Partners v. Coleman*, 1989 S.L.T. 430.

10.10 Where a person is to be sisted by amendment in substitution for an original pursuer, the court when allowing the amendment may dismiss the action so far as laid at the instance of the original pursuer[56] and may deal with any question of expenses as between the defender and the original pursuer. Where an action is incompetent in respect that it has been raised by pursuers whose grounds of action are not identical, some of them, or all but one of them, may be removed by amendment.[57] Amendment has been said to be incompetent where it becomes clear that the pursuer did not authorise the action,[58] or where at the commencement of the action the pursuer had no title to institute it[59]; but these propositions appear to be inconsistent with the liberal interpretation of the rule in *Donaghy v. Rollo*.[60] If, however, no pursuer is named in the instance at all, the action is probably a nullity which is incapable of amendment.[61]

New defender/third party

10.11 Rule 18.2 also makes provision for calling a new defender in any case in which it appears that all parties having an interest have not been called,[62] or that the cause has been directed against the wrong person.[63] The new defender must be subject to the jurisdiction of the court.[64] The following rules apply.

(1) The sheriff may allow an amendment which (a) inserts in the initial writ an additional or substitute party and (b) directs existing or additional craves, averments and pleas-in-law against that party.[65]

(2) The sheriff may also allow an amendment which may be necessary to direct a crave against a third party brought into the action under Chapter 20 (third party procedure).[66]

(3) Rule 18.5 provides that where an amendment has been allowed to bring in an additional or substitute defender, or to direct a crave against a third party, or where it has been made when all parties have not been called or the wrong person has been called, the sheriff should order, normally in the same interlocutor, that a copy of the amended initial writ or record, as the case may be, be served by the party who made the amendment on the additional or substitute party. Together with the amended writ or record, there requires to be served in a cause in which a time to pay direction under the Debtors (Scotland) Act 1987 may be applied for, a notice in Form O8 specifying the date by which a notice of intention to defend must be lodged in process, a notice in Form O3 and a notice of intention to defend in Form O7.[67] In any other cause, there requires to be served a notice in Form O9 specifying the date by which a notice of intention to defend must be lodged in process and a notice of intention to defend in Form O7.[68] The party who made the amendment is required to lodge in process (i) a copy of

---

56 *Donaghy, supra.*
57 *Paxton v. Brown*, 1908 S.C. 406; *Smith-Shand's Trs v. Forbes*, 1921 S.C. 820.
58 *Ferguson, Davidson & Co. v. Paterson and Dobbie* (1898) 1 F. 227; *Gordon v. Purves* (1902) 10 S.L.T. 446, (1903) 11 S.L.T. 38.
59 *Bentley v. Macfarlane*, 1964 S.C. 76, *per* L.P. Clyde at 79.
60 1964 S.C. 278.
61 para. 10.04.
62 See para. 9.117.
63 OCR, r. 18.2(2)(d).
64 Fyfe, p. 253; Dobie, p. 236.
65 OCR, r. 18.2(2)(d).
66 OCR, r. 18.2(2)(vi).
67 OCR, r. 18.5(1)(a)(i).
68 OCR, r. 18.5(1)(a)(ii).

the initial writ or record as amended, (ii) a copy of the notice sent in Form O8 or Form O9, and (iii) a certificate of service.[69] Once the foregoing requirements of service and lodging are complied with, the cause as amended bringing in the new or additional party shall proceed in every respect as if that party had originally been made a party to the cause.[70] When a notice of intention to defend is lodged by virtue of rule 18.5(1)(a), the sheriff clerk fixes a diet for a hearing under rule 9.12 (options hearing).[71]

(4) Where a minute of amendment is lodged by a pursuer under rule 18.2(2)(d) (all parties not called or case directed against the wrong person), he may apply by motion for warrant to use any form of diligence which could have been used on the defender in a separate action.[72] A copy certified by the sheriff clerk of the interlocutor granting warrant for diligence on the dependence in respect of such an application is sufficient authority for the execution of that diligence.[73]

(5) Where the cause has been directed against the wrong defender, it is competent to allow the deletion of that defender's name by amendment, to dismiss the action so far as laid against him and to dispose of any questions of expenses between him and the pursuer. In some circumstances, however, it may be that the pursuer should abandon the action against that defender in terms of rule 23.[74]

Similarly, where the pursuer of an action against more than one defender no longer wishes to insist in the action against one of them, it may be a question of circumstances whether he should formally abandon the action so far as laid against that defender, or should be permitted to delete that defender's name from the instance by amendment with the consequences of dismissal and the disposal of questions of expenses as described above. **10.12**

Amendment of crave

The sheriff may allow the crave to be amended so as to seek a different remedy from that originally craved.[75] Thus, a crave for damages may be added as an alternative to a crave for specific performance.[76] After the closing of the record,[77] he may allow the crave to be amended so as to increase or restrict the sum sued for.[78] The lodging by the defender of a minute consenting to decree does not prevent the pursuer from thereafter amending to increase the sum sued for.[79] **10.13**

III. Discretion

An amendment which is competent may be refused if the sheriff in the exercise of his discretion considers that it is in the interests of justice to **10.14**

---

[69] OCR, r. 18.5(1)(b).
[70] OCR, r. 18.5(2).
[71] OCR, r. 18.5(3).
[72] OCR, r. 18.4(1).
[73] OCR, r. 18.4(2).
[74] See para. 14.29.
[75] OCR, r. 18.2(2)(a)(ii).
[76] *Summerlee Iron Co. Ltd v. Caledanian Ry*, 1911 S.C. 458.
[77] Before the closing of the record the sum sued for may be amended without lodging a minute of amendment: OCR, r. 18.1. See para. 8.23.
[78] OCR, r. 18.2(2)(a)(i).
[79] *Cowie v. Carron Co.*, 1945 S.C. 280.

do so. It is thought that the general rule may be stated thus. Amendment should be allowed if it is necessary for the purpose of determining in the existing cause the real question in controversy between the parties, and if allowance would not result in injustice to the other party not capable of being compensated by an award of expenses and the attachment of any other conditions which seem just.[80] The critical issue is usually whether the opponent of the party seeking leave to amend would be unfairly prejudiced by allowance of the amendment. Among the factors which the sheriff may take into account when determining how to exercise his discretion are the stage which the action has reached[81] and the nature of the amendment, which together will often indicate the nature of the prejudice which the amendment would cause to the other party; and the conditions which he might in his discretion attach in allowing the amendment. These factors are in practice interrelated, but for convenience the subject of the court's discretion as to allowing amendment is considered first in the context of the various stages of procedure at which leave to amend may be sought. The various conditions which may be attached in allowing amendment are separately dealt with thereafter.

Stage at which leave to amend sought

10.15 The sheriff has to consider, in the light of the structure of the procedural system and the whole history of the case to date, whether allowance of the amendment will operate to give the amender an unfair advantage over his opponent. Procedure by amendment after the closing of the record presumably and generally operates to the prejudice of the other party, but the prejudice is not regarded as unfair where the other party may be regarded as compensated by an award of expenses.[82] In some cases, however, and in particular once the proof has begun, the sheriff may consider that no attached conditions and no award of expenses would remove the prejudice which the other party would suffer.[83]

Before inquiry imminent

10.16 Amendment after the closing of the record and before the proof becomes imminent usually presents no difficulty, and is normally allowed upon the view that the other party suffers no prejudice by the allowance of the amendment which cannot be compensated by the party making it being found liable in the expenses thereby occasioned. Such an amendment "is, in theory, a belated adjustment for which the laggard has to pay . . . A party can on terms restate his case, aver further and even different facts, add new and different grounds of action and so forth. This is all regarded as further adjustment on terms."[84] Where an interlocutor allowing proof or proof before answer has been pronounced, the sheriff

---

[80] *Thomson v. Glasgow Corporation*, 1962 S.C. (H.L.) 36, *per* L.J.-C. Thomson at 52, Lord Patrick at 55; *Ketteman v. Hansel Properties Ltd* [1987] 2 W.L.R. 312, *per* Lord Keith of Kinkel at 323 (an English appeal).

[81] *Gibson's Trs v. Fraser* (1877) 4 R. 1001, *per* L.P. Inglis at 1004; *Stodard v. British Transport Commission*, 1956 S.L.T. 71.

[82] *Thomson v. Glasgow Corporation*, 1962 S.C. (H.L.) 36, *per* L.J.-C. Thomson at 52.

[83] *Thomson, supra, per* Lord Patrick at 55.

[84] *Thomson, supra, per* L.J.-C. Thomson at 52–53. See also *Spalding v. Inveresk Paper Co. Ltd*, 1971 S.L.T. (Notes) 47.

may allow an amendment which adds a preliminary plea although it would result in the withdrawal of the allowance of proof or proof before answer and the ordering of further debate.[85] Where an interlocutor appointing parties to debate has been pronounced prior to amendment, the addition of further preliminary pleas by amendment before the diet of debate may be allowed.[86]

Debate

If a party decides before a diet of debate that his pleadings require amendment, he should either lodge a minute of amendment and a motion for leave to amend for calling in the ordinary court before the diet, or if it is too late to do so, he should intimate to his opponent before the diet that when the case calls for debate he proposes to move for leave to amend. At the diet he should so move and either lodge a minute of amendment or state in what respect or to what extent he desires to amend.[87] In the course of debate amendment is frequently allowed, often in consequence of arguments presented by the opponent of the party seeking to amend.[88] The amendment allowed may be minor, involving only a formal alteration of the record, or substantial, involving the addition or deletion of material averments and pleas-in-law.[89] In general it is not right or just to dismiss an action, or to award expenses against a party, by reason of a formal defect in his pleadings which is capable of being put right by a simple amendment without any prejudice being suffered by the other party.[90] It is for the party who is considering amendment to make up his mind before the debate is concluded whether he wishes to amend or not[91]; if he does, he should make a formal motion for leave to do so and, if the proposed amendment is other than of a minor nature for which the court does not require a minute, either tender a minute of amendment then or ask for a continuation in order to draft and lodge a minute.[92] It is not for the court to amend his record for him,[93] or *ex proprio motu* to give him an opportunity to amend.[94] Moreover, the sheriff is entitled only to allow amendment if asked for and to the extent asked for by a party.[95] When averments have been excluded from probation after debate it is incorrect to seek to amend by expanding and elaborating upon these averments: the appropriate course is to appeal and proffer the amendment in the appeal court.[96] **10.17**

---

85 para. 10.06.

86 *Spalding, supra.*

87 *Colbron v. United Glass Ltd,* 1965 S.L.T. 366.

88 *Thomson, Spalding, supra.*

89 *Spalding, supra.*

90 *Music Hire Service (Manchester) Ltd v. Roccio,* 1961 S.L.T. (Notes) 13; *GUS Property Management Ltd v. Littlewoods Mail Order Stores Ltd,* 1982 S.C. (H.L.) 157, *per* Lord Keith of Kinkel at 178.

91 *Gibson v. Strathclyde R.C.,* 1992 S.C.L.R. 902, *per* L.J.-C. Ross at 907B.

92 *Macdonald v. Greenock Dockyard Co. Ltd,* 1959 S.L.T. (Sh. Ct.) 6, approved, *Lord Advocate v. Johnston,* 1983 S.L.T. 290. *Cf. Wilson v. Mersey Insulation Co. Ltd,* 1987 S.L.T. 238 and *Kennedy v. Norwich Union Fire Insurance Society Ltd,* 1994 S.L.T. 617.

93 *Conway v. Dalziel* (1901) 3 F. 918, *per* Lord McLaren at 922; *Barton v. Wm Low & Co. Ltd,* 1968 S.L.T. (Notes) 27.

94 *Lord Advocate v. Johnston, supra.* The courses adopted in *Armia Ltd v. Daejan Developments Ltd,* 1978 S.C. 152 at 172, 1979 S.C. (H.L.) 56, 1979 S.L.T. 147, and *Lanarkshire Health Board v. Banafaa,* 1987 S.L.T. 229, appear to have been exceptional.

95 *Creed v. Christie and Ferguson,* 1991 S.L.T. (Sh. Ct.) 44.

96 *Urquhart v. British Railways Board,* 1982 S.L.T. 308.

When inquiry imminent

10.18 "In deciding whether or not a record should be amended the court seeks to do justice both to the pursuer and to the defender. When a minute of amendment is lodged very late in the course of a litigation, the time may have come when it would be unjust to the other party to allow the minute to be received, with consequent postponement of the diet of proof or trial, consequent delay in the final determination of the case and additional expense occasioned by further precognition of the witnesses. Moreover, the investigation of circumstances newly averred long after the date of the occurrence giving rise to the action may result in serious prejudice to the other party, which should not be allowed."[97]

Last-minute amendments on the eve of proof which would involve the discharge of the diet and investigation by the opponent of a new case against him are therefore refused except in highly special circumstances.[98] But a late minute of amendment containing new matter which the party could not earlier have ascertained with the exercise of reasonable diligence and which may be answered before the proof, may be allowed.[99] A late minute of amendment may be allowed, and the diet of proof discharged, where the amendment adds a new case which is made on a state of facts which is the same in material respects as the existing case.[1] The consequence of the postponement of the final decision of the case may not be alone sufficient to justify refusal of an amendment relating to an important matter in an action involving status.[2]

At inquiry

10.19 The subject of amendment at inquiry is considered here on the assumption that a motion for leave to amend is made by the pursuer, since it is usually the pursuer who makes any such motion. Similar considerations to those about to be discussed would, however, apply to a motion made by the defender. Since a party is not entitled to establish a case against his opponent of which the latter has not received fair notice upon record, a defender cannot be held liable upon a ground which is not included in the averments made against him by the pursuer.[3] The pursuer may succeed on a ground which is a variation, modification or development of what is averred, but not on a ground which is new, separate and distinct.[4] If in the course of the proof such a ground emerges on which he wishes to rely, the proper and only course is to ask for leave to amend so as fairly to raise it,[5] and the proper time to do so is the time when the

---

[97] *Dryburgh v. National Coal Board*, 1962 S.C. 485, *per* Lord Guthrie at 492. See also *Muldoon v. Carntyne Steel Castings Co. Ltd*, 1965 S.L.T. (Notes) 63.

[98] *Dryburgh*, *supra*, *per* L.P. Clyde at 491. See also *Strachan v. Caledonian Fish-Selling and Marine Stores Co.*, 1963 S.C. 157; *McGhie v. British Transport Commission*, 1964 S.L.T. (Notes) 56; *Fairley v. National Coal Board*, 1965 S.L.T. (Notes) 17; *Greenhorn v. J. Smart (Contractors) Ltd*, 1979 S.C. 427 at 432; *Urquhart v. British Railways Board*, 1982 S.L.T. 308; *Ashcroft's Curator Bonis v. Stewart*, 1988 S.L.T. 163; *Wood v. Philips*, 1994 S.L.T. 142.

[99] *Daig v. Randsgrove Ltd*, 1980 S.L.T. (Notes) 16.

[1] *Jones v. McDermott (Scotland)*, 1986 S.L.T. 551.

[2] *Duke of Argyll v. Duchess of Argyll*, 1962 S.C. (H.L.) 88, *per* Lord Reid at 95.

[3] *Morrison's Associated Cos Ltd v. James Rome & Sons Ltd*, 1964 S.C. 160.

[4] *Burns v. Dixon's Iron Works*, 1961 S.C. 102; *O'Hanlon v. John G. Stein & Co. Ltd*, 1965 S.C. (H.L.) 23 at 42; *Hamilton v. John Brown & Co. (Clydebank) Ltd*, 1969 S.L.T. (Notes) 18; *McIntosh v. Walker Steam Trawl Fishing Co. Ltd*, 1971 S.L.T. (Notes) 75.

[5] *Lawrence v. Sir William Arrol & Co.*, 1958 S.C. 348 at 352–353. See also *Black v. John Williams & Co. (Wishaw)*, 1924 S.C. (H.L.) 22; *"Vitruvia" S.S. Co. v. Ropner Shipping Co.*, 1924 S.C. (H.L.) 31; *Gunn v. McAdam & Son*, 1949 S.C. 31 at 39–40.

difficulty arises.[6] An unexplained delay in putting forward a proposed amendment may be a circumstance adverse to allowing it; and if it is allowed, the party amending may be found liable in expenses from the date when he ought to have made a motion for leave to amend.[7]

After a proof has begun, allowance of an amendment becomes increasingly difficult in proportion to the significance and extent of disclosure of the facts of the other side's case: the other side may be so grossly prejudiced by amendment that they could not be properly compensated by attached conditions or an award of expenses. As a general rule it is wrong to allow a party to amend so as to take advantage of what his opponent has, in reliance on the closed record, legitimately put forward in support of his own case.[8] Examples of other circumstances adverse to the allowance of an amendment are that the matters which it is proposed to aver were, or should have been, known to the pursuer before he raised his action[9]; and that the other side has been deprived, by lack of notice, of the opportunity of investigating and testing these matters.[10] On the other hand, the absence of timeous objection to the evidence on which the amendment is founded may be a consideration in favour of allowing the amendment.[11] **10.20**

Allowance of an amendment in the course of a proof might have unusual procedural consequences. Witnesses might have to be recalled, or a party might have to be allowed to reopen his case and lead further evidence.[12] The other side might legitimately seek to lodge answers to the minute of amendment: that would entail the discharge or continuation of the diet of proof[13] and, if the relevancy of the averments in the minute or answers were to be challenged, argument on relevancy before a decision is reached as to whether the amendment should be allowed.[14] **10.21**

While case at avizandum

Since he may allow amendment at any time before final judgment[15] it is technically possible for the sheriff to do so after he has taken the case to avizandum, but unless in highly exceptional circumstances that would be so prejudicial to the other side as to be an inappropriate exercise of his discretion.[16] **10.22**

---

[6] *Rafferty v. Weir Housing Corporation Ltd*, 1966 S.L.T. (Notes) 23.

[7] *Campbell v. Cordale Investment Ltd*, 1985 S.L.T. 305.

[8] *Thomson v. Glasgow Corporation*, 1962 S.C. (H.L.) 36; *McLinden v. British Steel Corporation*, 1972 S.L.T. (Sh. Ct.) 25; *Chapman v. James Dickie & Co. (Drop Forgings) Ltd*, 1985 S.L.T. 380; *Hodge v. British Coal Corporation*, 1992 S.L.T. 484.

[9] *Thomson, Chapman, supra*; *Moran v. King*, 1975 S.L.T. (Notes) 77; *Hodge v. British Coal Corporation, supra*.

[10] *McLean v. Victoria Spinning Co. Ltd*, 1971 S.L.T. (Notes) 10; *Moran, supra*.

[11] *Boyle v. West of Scotland Ship-Breaking Co. Ltd*, 1963 S.L.T. (Sh. Ct.) 54.

[12] *Campbell, supra*. *Cf. Roy v. Carron Co.*, 1967 S.L.T. (Notes) 84.

[13] *Titchener v. British Railways Board*, 1981 S.L.T. 208 at 210.

[14] It appears that such argument should be heard on the motion for leave to amend, since the proof cannot be interrupted by a diet of debate on a preliminary plea added by amendment: see para. 16.56.

[15] OCR, r. 18.2.

[16] *Oswald v. Fairs*, 1911 S.C. 257 at 264. *Cf. Gray v. SSPCA* (1980) 17 R. 789; *Govan Rope and Sail Co. Ltd v. Weir & Co.* (1897) 24 R. 368.

While appeal pending

10.23 After an appeal has been taken and before the hearing of the appeal the appeal court may allow amendment of the record.[17] If, however, the amendments are of material importance the appeal court may decide not to hear argument on the pleadings as amended, but may recall the sheriff's interlocutor and remit the case to the sheriff to hear argument on the amended pleadings.[18] In order that that possible course of action may be explored before the appeal is put out for hearing, any party lodging a motion for a record to be amended in terms of a minute of amendment and any answers thereto pending the hearing of an appeal should at the same time lodge an application for an order for further procedure.[19]

During hearing of appeal

10.24 The appeal court may allow amendment at the commencement of the hearing of the appeal[20] or during its course. An amendment which entails only the addition of a plea-in-law after debate in the court below, in order to focus an argument more precisely,[21] or only a technical alteration of the pleadings which does not affect the substance of a proof led in the court below,[22] is likely to be allowed; but the addition after proof of a plea unsupported by relevant averments of fact which would involve unjustifiable disregard of the rules of fair notice will be refused,[23] as will a belated and unjustifiable attempt to make a radical amendment, as by adding a plea to competency after proof.[24] A party who has amended more than once before the sheriff may not be allowed to do so again on appeal if his opponent would be prejudiced by further delay in the determination of the case.[25] Amendment has also been refused where defenders sought to rectify a mistaken view of the law and the amendment if allowed might have led to the dismissal of the action after the expiry of a period of limitation, when the pursuer could no longer pursue other remedies.[26] The appeal court may be reluctant to allow an amendment which raises a new case or contention on which the court below has had no opportunity of expressing an opinion.[27]

10.25 An amendment which requires the allowance of additional proof may be allowed. In the Court of Session the additional evidence is heard by a

---

[17] The sheriff principal and the Court of Session have the same powers to allow amendment as has the sheriff: see para. 10.03. Their powers to allow additional proof are noted in paras 10.25, 18.81, 18.98.

[18] *Wallace v. Scottish Special Housing Association*, 1981 S.L.T. (Notes) 60.

[19] RCS, rr. 24.2(5), 38.21 which may with advantage be applied *mutatis mutandis* in the sheriff court: *Redpath Dorman Long Ltd v. Cummins Engine Co. Ltd*, 1981 S.C. 370 at 375.

[20] *e.g. Kelly v. Edmund Nuttall Sons & Co. (London) Ltd*, 1965 S.C. 427 at 434.

[21] *Kelly, supra.*

[22] *McFadyen v. Wilson*, Sh. Pr. Caplan, Kilmarnock Sh. Ct., Jan. 20, 1984, unreported. *Cf. Rose v. Johnston* (1878) 5 R. 600, where an amendment was proposed by the court.

[23] *Winnik v. Dick*, 1984 S.L.T. 185 at 188, 189.

[24] *Paxton v. McKain*, 1983 S.L.T. (Sh. Ct.) 88. In *Thomson v. Hughson & Co.* (1861) 23 D. 679 the court approved the amendment of a plea which had been allowed in the court below but on the footing that the pursuer would be allowed to abandon the action and would be entitled to expenses from the date of lodging defences.

[25] *Jack Davis Publicity Ltd v. Kennedy*, Sh. Pr. Caplan, Paisley Sh. Ct, Dec. 18, 1984, unreported.

[26] *Bonnor v. Balfour Kilpatrick Ltd*, 1974 S.C. 223.

[27] *Duke of Portland v. Wood's Trs*, 1927 S.C. (H.L.) 1; *Bentley v. Macfarlane*, 1964 S.C. 76 at 83–84; *Martin v. Bell-Ingram*, 1986 S.L.T. 575 at 585; *McGuffie v. Forth Valley Health Board*, 1991 S.L.T. 231.

judge of the Division.[28] In the sheriff court the sheriff principal may allow further proof.[29] In practice an appellate court is unlikely to allow amendment after proof to introduce a new case which would gravely prejudice the opponent of the amending party and require the hearing of further proof,[30] or to introduce new evidence on a matter which has already been the subject of judicial investigation.[31] They may, however, open up a concluded proof on a minute disclosing additional and material evidence, written or parole, which has emerged since the proof was closed and could not by reasonable diligence have been obtained before.[32] In an action of damages for personal injuries the court may do so in very exceptional circumstances, where the new matter sought to be introduced is not only relevant but of marked materiality.[33]

A party who seeks leave to amend at the hearing of an appeal should ordinarily either tender a minute of amendment or indicate to the court the nature of the averments which he would wish to make if an opportunity for amendment were allowed: failure to do either may result in the court's refusing to allow a minute to be received.[34] **10.26**

It is competent for the sheriff principal, when the case is before him on appeal on any point, to open the record *ex proprio motu* if the record appears to him not to have been properly made up.[35] It is, however, difficult to imagine in what circumstances he would do so, instead of leaving it to the parties to move to amend.[36] **10.27**

After appeal hearing but before judgment

Since an amendment may be allowed at any time before final judgment,[37] it is theoretically possible for amendment to be allowed between the conclusion of the hearing of the appeal and the signature of the appeal court's interlocutor disposing of the subject-matter of the cause[38]; but there appear to be few cases in which an appeal court has exercised its discretion in favour of allowing amendment at that stage.[39] **10.28**

---

28 Court of Session Act 1868, ss. 62, 72; *Gairdner v. Macarthur*, 1915 S.C. 589; *Pirie v. Leask*, 1964 S.C. 103. The court may also receive a minute of *res noviter* and allow additional evidence to be heard in very exceptional circumstances: *Coul v. Ayr C.C.*, 1909 S.C. 422; *Mitchell v. Sellar*, 1915 S.C. 360 at 361; *Pirie, supra.*

29 1907 Act, s. 27. See paras 18.81, 18.82.

30 *Thomson v. Glasgow Corporation*, 1962 S.C. (H.L.) 36. In *Guinness, Mahon & Co. v. Coats Iron and Steel Co.* (1891) 18 R. 441, cit. Lewis, p. 174, Dobie, p. 240, the court appear to have considered that under s. 29 of the Court of Session Act 1868 they had no discretion to refuse to allow the amendment.

31 *Cook v. Robertson's Exr*, 1960 S.L.T. (Sh. Ct.) 4.

32 *Miller v. MacFisheries*, 1922 S.C. 157 at 161; *Castlehill Ltd v. Scott*, Sh. Pr. Reid, Glasgow Sh. Ct., Oct. 2, 1979, unreported, where defenders in an action for payment tendered in support of their defence of part-payment a minute of amendment and a writ accidentally discovered after the proof which could be construed as an admission by the pursuers of a payment to account.

33 *Rieley v. Kingslaw Riding School*, 1975 S.C. 28 at 40–42. Further proof was elided by agreement (at 55).

34 *Menzies v. Menzies* (1890) 17 R. 881; *Lamont v. Hall*, 1964 S.L.T. (Sh. Ct.) 25 at 27; *Grant v. Peter C. Cauld & Co.*, 1985 S.L.T. 545 at 548–549.

35 1907 Act, s. 27.

36 *Hutchison v. Davidson*, 1945 S.C. 395.

37 OCR, r. 18.2.

38 1907 Act, s. 3(h) (definition of "final judgment").

39 *Mackenzie v. Munro* (1869) 7 M. 676 at 687; *Duke of Argyll v. Duchess of Argyll*, 1962 S.C. 140 at 148, revsd 1962 S.C. (H.L.) 88. *Cf. Moyes v. Burntisland Shipping Co.*, 1952 S.C. 429, and cases cited in para. 10.22.

Attachment of conditions

Expenses

10.29 In allowing an amendment under rule 18.2 the sheriff may attach such conditions as seem just. He must, however, find the party making the amendment liable in the expenses thereby occasioned unless it is just and equitable that these expenses should be otherwise dealt with.[40] It would appear to be for the party lodging the minute to show that it is just and equitable that the expenses should be otherwise dealt with. The expenses occasioned to the other party by the amendment include, where it is necessary to answer it, the expense of preparing answers.[41] In appropriate circumstances the sheriff may find the party making the amendment liable not only in the expenses occasioned by the amendment but also in other expenses, on the basis that it is for the court to control the incidental procedure in the course of the action and to penalise by a suitable award of expenses conduct on the part of one party which entails unnecessary and improper charges upon the other.[42] Where the amendment is tendered at a diet of debate or at a hearing of an appeal, and renders the diet or hearing abortive, the party amending may also be found liable in the expenses of the debate or appeal.[43] Where the averments in the amendment could have been added by the party at the stage of adjustment, or where the amendment cures a radical defect in the party's pleadings or supersedes the procedure which has occurred since the closing of the record, he may be found liable in the expenses incurred since the closing of the record,[44] or in the expenses of any procedure which has been rendered abortive.[45] Where the amendment renders abortive the whole procedure to date, or cures a defect in the form of a writ, or involves a complete change of front, the party may be required to pay the whole expenses of process to date[46]; but such an award must be compensatory, not penal, in effect.[47] Payment of any expenses awarded is not a condition of the amendment being allowed unless expressly stated to be so in the interlocutor. Elsewhere in this book the subject of interim awards of expenses is examined, and it is there suggested that a condition of payment should be added only where there has been a failure or delay on the part of a litigant or his solicitor of such a nature that, although decree by default is inappropriate and it is in the interests of justice that the action should proceed, it is just and equitable that all or part of the expenses incurred by his opponent should be paid before the action proceeds further.[48]

---

[40] OCR, r. 18.6. See paras 10.15, 10.16.

[41] *Campbell v. Henderson*, 1949 S.C. 172 at 183–184.

[42] *Mackenzie v. Mackenzie*, 1951 S.C. 163 at 165–166.

[43] *Murdison v. Scottish Football Union* (1896) 23 R. 449; *Mackenzie, supra*; *Calbron v. United Glass Ltd*, 1965 S.L.T. 366.

[44] *Keith v. Outram & Co.* (1877) 4 R. 958; *Cray v. SSPCA* (1890) 17 R. 789; *Morgan, Gellibrand & Co. v. Dundee Gem Line S.S. Co. Ltd* (1890) 18 R. 205; *Murdison, supra*; *Stevens v. Motherwell Entertainments Ltd*, 1914 S.C. 957; *Campbell, supra.* The condition of payment of the expenses imposed in the five earlier cases would seldom be attached in modern practice: see end of this paragraph.

[45] *Moyes v. Burntisland Shipbuilding Co.*, 1952 S.C. 429 at 435, 440.

[46] *Black v. John Williams & Co. (Wishaw)*, 1924 S.C. (H.L.) 22 at 27; *Campbell, supra*; *Kerr v. Alexander*, Sh. Pr. O'Brien, Edinburgh Sh. Ct, July 14, 1978, unreported (amendment on appeal of defective writ combining craves for interdict and lawburrows: pursuer found liable in expenses to date). *Cf. Haughton v. N.B. Ry* (1892) 20 R. 113.

[47] *Clippens Oil Co. Ltd v. Edinburgh and District Water Trs* (1905) 7 F. 914, *per* L.P. Dunedin at 916; *Woodbury v. Sutherland's Trs*, 1939 S.L.T. 93 at 95.

[48] para. 11.89.

On the other hand it is possible that an amendment may be made which is a proper and even a necessary one, but which involves little or no further expense. In such cases no award,[49] or only a nominal[50] or modified[51] award of expenses may be appropriate. Where in special circumstances it is impossible to ascertain until a later stage of procedure what expenses, if any, have been incurred by the opposite party for which he should be compensated by an award of expenses, the equitable course is to reserve all questions of expenses in connection with the amendment.[52] Ordinarily, however, questions of expenses should be dealt with as soon as the amendment is completed[53]: otherwise, the usual result is that the expenses of the amendment are lost sight of and become part of the expenses in the cause.[54] A finding that the expenses occasioned by the amendment should be part of the expenses in the cause may be appropriate where amendment is needed because of an unforeseen turn of events and is not due to fault on the part of any party. **10.30**

Other conditions

The sheriff may not only make a finding as to liability for expenses, but attach such other conditions as seem just.[55] It has been suggested that finding caution,[56] making consignation, disclosure of an address, or production of a mandate or other document might be made conditions.[57] The conditions must be pertinent to the subject of the action.[58] Where a party who is allowed to amend on conditions does so, he cannot thereafter appeal against the conditions imposed. If he objects to them, he should seek leave to appeal. If leave to appeal is refused, he should raise the matter on appeal after the final decision of the case.[59] **10.31**

IV. Time-bar

When considering the extent to which amendment may be permitted after the expiry of a time-limit imposed by the law of prescription or of limitation of actions it will be convenient to examine first the general principles which are applicable to all actions, and then the special statutory rules which apply to actions of damages in respect of personal injuries or death. In practice it is in actions of the latter class that the vast majority of questions arise as to the effect of a time-bar on an amendment. **10.32**

---

49 *Murdison v. Scottish Football Union* (1896) 23 R. 449, *per* Lord McLaren at 460–461; *Gillespie v. Duncan* (1933) 50 Sh. Ct.Rep. 60.

50 *Macdonald v. Forsyth* (1898) 25 R. 870.

51 *Woodbury v. Sutherland's Trs*, 1939 S.L.T. 93.

52 *Clippens Oil Co. Ltd v. Edinburgh and District Water Trs* (1905) 7 F. 914; *William Beardmore & Co. Ltd v. Park's Exrx*, 1932 S.L.T. 218.

53 *Williamson v. John Williams (Wishaw) Ltd*, 1971 S.L.T. (Sh. Ct.) 2; see para. 19.16.

54 Thomson and Middleton, p. 368.

55 OCR, r. 18.6.

56 Caution for expenses was required in *Paton v. McKnight* (1897) 24 R. 554.

57 Dove Wilson, p. 245; Lewis, p. 175.

58 *Duthie Bros & Co. v. Duthie* (1892) 19 R. 905, where special conditions were imposed; *Castlehill Ltd v. Scott*, Sh. Pr. Reid, Glasgow Sh. Ct, Oct. 2, 1979, unreported (see para. 10.25): interim decree pronounced and payment of sum and interest decerned for made condition precedent of amendment requiring additional proof.

59 *Duthie Bros & Co., supra.*

General principles

Date of amendment

10.33 It is sometimes necessary to determine whether an amendment is timeous in relation to the expiry of a time-limit. The correctness of the present rule for determining that question has been seriously doubted. The rule, which appears from *Boyle v. Glasgow Corporation*,[60] seems to be that the amendment is not time-barred if before the expiry of the time-limit the minute of amendment is lodged in process and intimation is made to the other side of the motion for the minute to be received and answered. It has been pointed out, however, that the lodging of a minute of amendment *per se* achieves nothing. Before a minute of amendment can become part of the pleadings in a case, the court must be asked (1) to allow the minute of amendment to be received and, if necessary, answered; and (2) to allow the record to be opened up and amended in terms of the minute of amendment and any answers which have been lodged. Unless and until motions to such an effect are granted, the minute of amendment which has been lodged in process has no effect on the pleadings. Even though it is allowed to be received, it is possible that neither party may move to have the record amended in terms of the minute of amendment, and unless and until such a motion is made and granted, the minute does not become part of the case of the party lodging it.[61] It is respectfully submitted that these considerations have great force; but the rule in *Boyle*'s case must, of course, be followed unless and until it is altered.[62]

The general principles in Pompa's Trustees

10.34 General principles as to the making of amendments by a pursuer after the expiry of a time-limit were stated by Lord Justice-Clerk Cooper in a dictum in *Pompa's Trustees v. Edinburgh Magistrates*[63] which has been very frequently cited. It may be paraphrased thus: after the expiry of a time-limit which would have prevented him from raising proceedings afresh, a pursuer will not in general be allowed by amendment (i) to substitute the right defender for the wrong defender; or (ii) to cure a radical incompetence in his action; or (iii) to change the basis of his case. These three restrictions will be examined in the following paragraphs. The view has been cogently expressed that the statement on restrictions (ii) and (iii) has not in practice proved to be a satisfactory statement of the law.[64] It appears from more recent authority, however, that the dictum is not to be understood as a test of the competency of amendment, but as a statement of general principles to which the court will have regard when deciding whether to exercise its wide discretionary power to allow amendment or not. In the absence of a statutory provision making it incompetent to amend in an action which has itself been brought within the time-limit, the allowance of an amendment is a pure question for the discretion of the court in all the circumstances of the particular case, provided that the amendment is one which is necessary for determining in the existing action

---

60 1975 S.C. 238.
61 *Morrison v. Scotstoun Marine Ltd*, 1979 S.L.T. (Notes) 76.
62 *Morrison, supra*; *Robertson v. Crane Hire (Paisley) Ltd*, 1982 S.L.T. 505.
63 1942 S.C. 119 at 125.
64 *Prescription and the Limitation of Actions* (Scot. Law Com. No. 74), para. 5.2.

the real question in controversy between the parties.[65] The three restrictions in *Pompa's Trustees* are now examined in turn.

Substitution of right defender for wrong defender. The first restriction, that a pursuer will not in general after the expiry of a time-limit be permitted by amendment to substitute the right defender for the wrong defender, is a restatement of one of the main general principles of the law of prescription and limitation.[66] It would be an improper, and to that extent an incompetent, exercise of the court's discretion to allow a pursuer by amendment to defeat the protection afforded to a defender by the statute prescribing the time-bar.[67] But while a pursuer may not substitute the right defender for the wrong defender, he may substitute one representative of the right defender for another representative of the right defender.[68] He may also by amendment correct some trivial spelling mistake,[69] or some misdescription which is not misleading,[70] in the name or designation of the defender. In an action for decree *cognitionis causa tantum* in which all the known next-of-kin of the deceased should be called, he may by amendment add to the instance persons to complete the class of next-of-kin who are the proper representatives of the deceased's estate.[71] 10.35

Curing of radical incompetence. The restriction as to the curing of a radical incompetence in the pursuer's action leaves considerable scope for argument as to what constitutes a "radical incompetence" in an action.[72] It is clear that an amendment which removes what is essentially a technical irregularity in the form of a crave is not one which cures a radical incompetence in the action.[73] Decisions collected above which may have a bearing on the question whether there is an "existing cause" may afford examples of actions in which a radical incompetence may exist.[74] 10.36

Change of basis of case. There is also room for debate over whether a proposed amendment "changes the basis of" the pursuer's case. In *McPhail v. Lanarkshire County Council* it was said that a permissible amendment is one which changes "not the basis of the action so much as the method of formulating the ground of action" so that "the pursuer may well claim, not to have offered a new front, but only to have presented the old front from a new angle, not to have changed the foundation of his action, but only to have made certain alterations in the superstructure."[75] It was also said that since in that particular case the substance of the action remained unchanged, the amendment was permissible.[76] An amendment which did not alter "the essence" of the pursuer's case was allowed in 10.37

---

[65] *Hynd v. West Fife Co-operative Ltd*, 1980 S.L.T. 41 (decided in 1975); *Greenhorn v. J. Smart & Co. (Contractors) Ltd*, 1979 S.C. 427; *Sellars v. IMI Yorkshire Imperial Ltd*, 1986 S.L.T. 629.

[66] See, *e.g. Miller v. National Coal Board*, 1960 S.C. 376.

[67] *Hynd, supra.*

[68] *Pompa's Trs, supra.*

[69] *McCullough v. Norwest Socea Ltd*, 1981 S.L.T. 201 at 203.

[70] *Watson v. Frame* (1983) 28 J.L.S. 421 (O.H.: change from "Security Guard Dog Services Ltd" to "GDS Security Ltd (formerly Guard Dog Services (Scotland) Ltd)").

[71] *Stevens v. Thomson*, 1971 S.L.T. 136.

[72] *Prescription and the Limitation of Actions* (Scot. Law Com. No. 74), para. 5.2.

[73] *Stevens, supra.*

[74] para. 10.04.

[75] 1951 S.C. 301, *per* L.P. Cooper at 309.

[76] *ibid., per* Lord Keith at 310.

O'Hare v. Western Heritable Investment Co.[77] There is, however, no clear-cut dividing line of really practical application for determining whether amendment should be allowed, and the question in a particular case is inevitably one of degree.[78] Amendments have been allowed which required fairly substantial changes in a pursuer's averments of fact,[79] and, in another case, in a pursuer's legal formulation of the duty owed to him and the person upon whom it rested[80]; but the addition of an entirely new ground of liability may be disallowed,[81] and where it was sought by amendment to make substantial changes both in the averments of fact and in the averments of liability, which "would have altered the averments both of fact and of fault almost out of recognition",[82] amendment was refused.[83] Even if a case is irrelevant, however, amendment may be allowed after the expiry of a time-limit, if the basis or substance of the case remains the same.[84] The matter is one for the discretion of the court, and it has been observed that the court might exercise its discretion so as to allow an amendment which radically altered a pursuer's case after the expiry of a time-limit. Such a course might be followed where, for example, the defenders had deliberately concealed material facts from the pursuer until after the expiry of the time-limit, so that he had been in ignorance of the proper case to make.[85]

10.38 The court, in considering whether to exercise its discretion to allow amendment, has regard to the object of the relevant statutory provision as to time-bar. In *Greenhorn*[86] it was observed that if the pursuer's case as amended were allowed to proceed the defenders would be deprived of the protection which they were intended to enjoy under the relevant provision,[87] the clear policy of which was to protect defenders against stale claims which after the passage of time would be difficult to investigate and resist. On the other hand, an action in relation to a claim to which section 6(1) of the Prescription and Limitation (Scotland) Act 1973 applies may be extensively amended after the expiry of the five-year period: so long as the obligation remains the same, its expression or the grounds for it may be altered.[88]

10.39 The sum sued for may be increased, and any necessary averments to support the new figure added, by amendment after the expiry of a

---

[77] 1965 S.C. 97, *per* L.J.-C. Grant at 104. See also *Corman v. National Coal Board*, 1975 S.L.T. (Notes) 8; *Meek v. Milne*, 1985 S.L.T. 318.

[78] *Anderson v. British Railways Board*, 1973 S.L.T. (Notes) 20; *Hynd, Greenhorn, supra*; *Jones v. McDermott (Scotland)*, 1986 S.L.T. 551.

[79] *Emslie v. Tognarellli's Exrs*, 1969 S.L.T. 20.

[80] *Mackenzie v. Fairfields Shipbuilding and Engineering Co.*, 1964 S.C. 90.

[81] On *Kelly v. Holloway Bros (London) Ltd*, 1960 S.L.T. (Notes) 69, see *Anderson, supra*, and *Davies v. BICC Ltd*, 1980 S.L.T. (Sh. Ct.) 17. *Cf. McCluskie v. National Coal Board*, 1961 S.C. 87; *Hynd, supra*; *McCrattan v. Renfrew D.C.*, 1983 S.L.T. 678.

[82] *Mackenzie, supra, per* Lord Hunter at 95.

[83] *Dryburgh v. National Coal Board*, 1962 S.C. 485, where, however, the court seems to have been principally concerned to penalise the pursuer for excessive delay and to prevent the last-minute postponement of the proof; *Rollo v. British Railways Board*, 1980 S.L.T. (Notes) 103.

[84] *Mowatt v. Shore Porters Society*, 1965 S.L.T. (Notes) 10.

[85] *Sellars v. IMI Yorkshire Imperial Ltd*, 1986 S.L.T. 629, *per* L.J.-C. Ross at 635.

[86] 1979 S.C. 427 at 432. See also *Grimason v. National Coal Board*, 1986 S.L.T. 286 at 289.

[87] Prescription and Limitation (Scotland) Act 1973, s. 17(1) before amendment by the Prescription and Limitation (Scotland) Act 1984, s. 2.

[88] *British Railways Board v. Strathclyde R.C.*, 1981 S.C. 90; *Macleod v. Sinclair*, 1981 S.L.T. (Notes) 38; *Lawrence v. J. D. McIntosh & Hamilton*, 1981 S.L.T. (Sh. Ct.) 73.

time-limit. If the amendment is one which is necessary for determining in the existing action the real question in controversy between the parties, the question whether it should be allowed is a matter for the discretion of the court in all the circumstances of the particular case.[89] If objection is to be taken to an amendment on the ground of time-bar and a plea is set out to this effect in the answers, the appropriate way of dealing with the matter is for the judge to decide, as a matter of discretion, whether or not to allow the amendment, including the allegedly time-barred averments, at the time when he is dealing with the motion to amend the record.[90]

Actions in respect of personal injuries or death

Prescription and Limitation (Scotland) Act 1973, s. 19A

The limitation period of three years is applicable to actions of damages in respect of personal injuries and to actions of damages where death has resulted from personal injuries. In personal injuries actions, the period runs from the date of injury or, if later, from the date on which the pursuer became aware, or on which in the opinion of the court it would have been reasonably practicable for him in all the circumstances to become aware, of specified relevant facts.[91] In death actions, similarly, time runs against an executor or relative from the date of death or, if later, from the date on which he became aware, or on which in the opinion of the court it would have been reasonably practicable for him in all the circumstances to become aware, of specified relevant facts.[92] The court has, however, a general power to override these time-limits: section 19A of the 1973 Act[93] provides that where a person would be entitled, but for any of these provisions, to bring an action, the court may, if it seems equitable to do so, allow him to bring that action notwithstanding that provision. The discretion conferred on the court is unfettered, although in every case the relaxation of the statutory bar can and must depend solely upon equitable considerations relevant to the exercise of a discretionary jurisdiction in the particular case, having regard to the fact that it is for the party seeking relief to satisfy the court that it is, in the view of the court and in the circumstances of the case and of the legitimate rights and interests of the parties, equitable to do so.[94] **10.40**

The court has the same measure of discretion in allowing an amendment to be made to bring in a new defender after the expiry of a time-limit prescribed by section 17, 18 or 18A of the 1973 Act, as amended.[95] The **10.41**

---

89 *Mackie v. Glasgow Corporation*, 1924 S.L.T. 510; *Hynd, supra.*

90 *Gibson v. Droopy and Brown Ltd*, 1989 S.L.T. 173; *Jones v. Lanarkshire Health Board*, 1990 S.L.T. 19, upheld in Inner House—see 1991 S.L.T. 714.

91 Prescription and Limitation (Scotland) Act 1973 (hereafter "the 1973 Act"), s. 17, substituted by the Prescription and Limitation (Scotland) Act 1984 (hereafter "the 1984 Act"), s. 2. In the computation of any period, any time during which the person who sustained the injury was under legal disability by reason of nonage or unsoundness of mind is to be disregarded: 1973 Act, s. 17(3) as substituted by the 1984 Act, s. 2. See paras 2.115, 2.116.

92 1973 Act, s. 18, substituted by the 1984 Act, s. 2. See paras 2.117, 2.118.

93 Inserted by the Law Reform (Miscellaneous Provisions) (Scotland) Act 1980, s. 23, and amended by the 1984 Act, Sched. 1, para. 8. S. 19A also applies to defamation actions, to which a limitation period of three years is applied by s. 18A of the 1973 Act, inserted by s. 12(2) of the Law Reform (Miscellaneous Provisions) (Scotland) Act 1985. See paras 2.119, 2.121.

94 *Donald v. Rutherford*, 1984 S.L.T. 70, *per* Lord Cameron at 75; *Forsyth v. A. F. Stoddart & Co. Ltd*, 1985 S.L.T. 51; *Anderson v. Glasgow D.C.*, 1987 S.L.T. 79.

95 *McCullough v. Norwest Socea Ltd*, 1981 S.L.T. 201 at 204; *Carson v. Howard Doris Ltd*, 1981 S.C. 278; *Harris v. Roberts*, 1983 S.L.T. 452; *Donald, supra.*

minute of amendment should contain material which would justify the exercise of the discretion.[96] In an exceptional case the court may hear evidence before reaching its decision.[97] In personal injuries actions courts have often considered: (1) the conduct of the pursuer since the accident and up to the time of his seeking the court's authority to bring the action against the new defender out of time, including any explanation for his not having done so timeously; (2) any likely prejudice to the pursuer if authority to bring the action out of time were not granted; and (3) any likely prejudice to the new defender from granting authority to bring the action out of time.[98] Such factors will often be relevant, but it has been authoritatively declared that the discretion is unfettered,[99] and the considerations which the court will take into account will therefore depend on the circumstances of each particular case. If the action against the original defender is fundamentally null, the pursuer should not seek to amend it but should abandon it and raise a new action against the proposed new defender, including in his condescendence averments of any matters which he submits would justify the court in exercising the discretionary power conferred by section 19A.[1]

New pursuer

10.42 Where it is sought to introduce, by minute of amendment or by minute of sist, a new pursuer into an action timeously brought, the introduction of the new pursuer will be treated as the bringing or commencement of an action for the purposes of the running of the time-bar in terms of section 17 or 18 of the 1973 Act, as amended.[2] If, therefore, the attempted introduction takes place outside the statutory time-limit, the action so far as at the instance of the new pursuer will be time-barred.[3] In a death action, a "connected person" will be sisted, but the crave will not be amended to allow the addition of a crave for his claim,[4] unless the time-bar can be overridden by the court's exercising its discretion in terms of section 19A.

V. Effect of Amendment

Diligence

10.43 No amendment allowed under rule 18.2 has the effect of validating diligence used on the dependence of a cause so as to prejudice the rights of creditors of the party against whom the diligence has been executed who are interested in defeating such diligence.[5] The amendment does not

---

96 *Carson, supra.*

97 *Hobbs v. Fawcett*, 1983 S.L.T. (Sh. Ct.) 15; *Dormer v. Melville Dundas & Whitson Ltd*, 1987 S.C.L.R. 655.

98 *Carson, supra*; *Henderson v. Singer (U.K.) Ltd*, 1983 S.L.T. 198; *Munro v. Anderson-Grice Engineering Co. Ltd*, 1983 S.L.T. 295; *Williams v. Forth Valley Health Board*, 1983 S.L.T. 376; *Whyte v. Walker*, 1983 S.L.T. 441; *Harris, supra*—all decided before *Donald v. Rutherford*, 1984 S.L.T. 70.

99 *Donald, Forsyth, supra*; see also *Carson, supra.*

1 *Boslem v. Paterson*, 1982 S.L.T. 216.

2 *McLean v. British Railways Board*, 1966 S.L.T. 39; *McArthur v. Raynesway Plant Ltd*, 1980 S.L.T. 74; *Marshall v. Black*, 1981 S.L.T. 228.

3 *McLean, McArthur, supra.*

4 *Marshall, supra.*

5 OCR, r. 18.7(a).

preclude any objection to such diligence by a party or any person by virtue of a title acquired or in right of a debt contracted by him subsequent to the execution of such diligence.[6]

Abandonment by pursuer on amendment by defender

Where a defender amended a plea at debate, the Inner House held that he might do so on the footing that the pursuer was allowed to abandon the action and was entitled to expenses since the date of lodging defences.[7] **10.44**

Pleading contents of minute

A party's averments as to any averment made by his opponent in a minute of amendment will be excluded from probation if the opponent states a plea to that effect. There will thus be no inquiry into the circumstances in which the averment in the minute was made. The party may, however, cross-examine the opponent on any such averment.[8] **10.45**

VI. Procedure

Minor amendments

Minor amendments may be made without notice by motion made orally at the bar in the course of an ordinary court, debate, proof, hearing on evidence or appeal, and may be answered at the bar.[9] If, however, the amendment is of importance or is contentious, the sheriff may appoint the party seeking to amend to lodge a minute of amendment, and may allow the other party time to consider the amendment and lodge answers if necessary before the question of leave to amend is decided. **10.46**

Usual procedure

Minute and motion

Until the coming into force of the present rules, there was no prescribed procedure to be followed in the making of amendments except, in part, where an action was by amendment directed against a new defender.[10] The procedure is now governed by rule 18.3. The rule provides that a party seeking to amend must lodge a minute of amendment specifying the party for whom it is lodged and setting forth exactly the sentences and words which he wishes to delete, alter or add, referring in each case to the number of the paragraph of his condescendence or answers, and the line of the paragraph where the proposed alteration occurs. At the same time he must lodge a motion to allow the minute to be received[11] and to allow the amendment in terms of the minute and, where appropriate, to grant an order under rule 18.5(1)(a) (for service of the amendment on an additional or substitute party).[12] The motion should also allow, where the minute of **10.47**

---

6 OCR, r. 18.7(b).

7 *Thomson v. Hughson & Co.* (1861) 23 D. 679. See also *Railton v. Jacques* (1834) 13 S. 26.

8 *Kirkham v. Cementation Co. Ltd*, 1964 S.L.T. (Notes) 33. *Cf. Lennox v. National Coal Board*, 1955 S.C. 438.

9 *Whyte v. Walker*, 1983 S.L.T. 441 at 442; *Boyle v. Gray*, 1993 S.C.L.R. 272.

10 By the former OCR 64(1)(a).

11 OCR, r. 18.3(1)(a).

12 OCR, r. 18.3(1)(b)(i).

amendment may require to be answered, that any other person may lodge answers thereto within a specified period.[13]

Hearing of motion

10.48 The normal procedure for motions in terms of Chapter 15 of the Ordinary Cause Rules is followed.[14] If opposition to the motion is not intimated the sheriff may deal with it in chambers without requiring to hear parties.[15] He will pronounce an interlocutor allowing the record to be opened up, amended in terms of the minute and closed of new. If a notice of opposition is lodged, the motion must call in court.[16] If the motion is to allow the minute of amendment to be received and the record amended in terms thereof without any mention of answers, the other party may wish to intimate opposition to the motion simply in order to be given an opportunity to answer. Apart from this, opposition to a motion to allow a minute to be received is usually premature, and should ordinarily be reserved until a motion is made for amendment of the record, except in the following cases. (1) It should not be reserved where the normal procedure would necessitate the discharge of a diet of proof to which the opposing party would object.[17] (2) Where a party intends to oppose an amendment after the expiry of a time-limit on the ground that it seeks to state a new case, it is preferable that the opposition should be stated at the hearing of the motion to allow the minute to be received, because answers to a minute which should not be allowed may result in useless expense as they do not affect the substance of the issue whether the proposed amendment is tantamount to a new case or merely a reformulation of the original.[18]

10.49 Once the sheriff has pronounced an interlocutor allowing a minute of amendment to be received and answered, he may allow a period of adjustment of the minute of amendment and answers and, in so doing, he must fix a date for the parties to be heard on the minute and answers as adjusted.[19] Where a party seeks to add a preliminary plea by amendment or answers to an amendment or by adjustment thereto, a note of the basis for the plea requires to be lodged at the same time as the minute, answers or adjustment, as the case may be.[20] Any person who fails to comply with this requirement is deemed to be no longer insisting in the preliminary plea and the plea must be repelled by the sheriff.[21] Any adjustments should be added to the process copies of the minute and answers, initialled and dated by the solicitor for the party making them or, if substantial, be stated in a separate note of adjustments.

Answers

10.50 Answers should specify the party for whom they are lodged, thus: "Answers / for the Defender [or as the case may be] / to / Minute of Amendment for the Pursuer [or as the case may be] *in causa* [etc.]." Like

---

[13] OCR, r. 18.3(1)(b)(ii).
[14] See paras 5.44 to 5.55.
[15] OCR, r. 15.5(1).
[16] OCR, r. 15.5(5).
[17] See para. 10.56.
[18] *Sellars v. IMI Yorkshire Imperial Ltd*, 1986 S.L.T. 629, *per* Lord Dunpark at 637–638.
[19] OCR, r. 18.3(2).
[20] OCR, r. 18.8(1).
[21] OCR, r. 18.8(2) and see *Sutherland v. Duncan*, 1996 S.L.T. 428.

the minute of amendment, answers should specify exactly the words which the party wishes to add, delete or alter. A party answering a minute of amendment may not only make consequential amendments to his own pleadings, including a plea directed against the case as proposed to be amended, or against the averments in the minute, but take advantage of the answers to introduce new matter into his own case. The extent to which he does so may have a bearing on the question of liability for the expenses of the amendment. The party lodging the minute may by adjustment state any appropriate plea directed against the averments in the answers.

Motion for leave to amend

At the hearing which the sheriff fixes in terms of rule 18.3(2), the party who has lodged the minute normally makes an oral motion to allow the record to be opened up and amended in terms of the minute (if no answers have been lodged) or in terms of the minute and answers (if no adjustment has taken place) or in terms of the minute and answers as adjusted, and of new closed. A written motion would be perfectly competent but would in most cases be unnecessarily cumbersome, as the procedure for intimation and notice of opposition under Chapter 15 of the Ordinary Cause Rules would require to be complied with. If it is clear that the party lodging the minute should be found liable in the expenses thereby occasioned,[22] the motion may concede that these expenses should be allowed to the other party or parties.[23] Alternatively, the motion may ask the court to hear parties on the question of the expenses occasioned by the amendment, or to reserve that question. **10.51**

Hearing and disposal of motion for leave to amend

It is at the stage of the motion for leave to amend the record that any opposition to amendment should normally be stated.[24] An opposing party may have stated in his answers a preliminary plea directed against the averments in the minute, but whether he opposes amendment on the ground stated in his plea or on any other ground, his grounds of opposition to amendment should in general be fully argued and disposed of at the hearing of the motion.[25] It is wrong to allow the record to be amended and to appoint parties to debate on the closed record as amended where the real question is whether the amendment should be allowed at all.[26] If it would be inconvenient to hear parties on the motion during an ordinary court, the sheriff may continue consideration of the motion to another diet, which would be a continued motion roll hearing. Where, however, the ground of opposition is that the averments proposed to be added by amendment would render the whole action or defence irrelevant, it is inappropriate that the question of relevancy should be debated on the motion roll. If the sheriff is on other grounds disposed **10.52**

---

[22] OCR, r. 18.6.

[23] *Spalding v. Inveresk Paper Co. Ltd*, 1971 S.L.T. (Notes) 47.

[24] *e.g. Spalding, supra; McGrattan v. Renfrew D.C.*, 1983 S.L.T. 678.

[25] *Stevens v. Thomson*, 1971 S.L.T. 136 at 137; *Greenhorn v. J. Smart & Co. (Contractors) Ltd*, 1979 S.C. 427 at 429; *Marshall v. Black*, 1981 S.L.T. 228 at 229; *Grimason v. National Coal Board*, 1986 S.L.T. 286 at 287. *Cf. McCluskie v. National Coal Board*, 1961 S.C. 87 at 88; *Anderson v. British Railways Board*, 1973 S.L.T. (Notes) 20; *Mazs v. Dairy Supply Co. Ltd*, 1978 S.L.T. 208; *McArthur v. Raynesway Plant, Ltd*, 1980 S.L.T. 74.

[26] *Greenhorn, supra.*

to allow the amendment, he should do so and appoint parties to debate on the amended closed record. To reach a decision on such a question of relevancy on the motion roll is incorrect not merely because of shortage of time but also because the parties' rights of appeal are different as regards, on the one hand, a decision on a motion for leave to amend, where leave to appeal is required, and on the other, the disposal of a preliminary plea after debate by dismissing the action or by repelling the defences and granting decree as craved, which may be appealed without leave.[27]

10.53 At the hearing of the motion for leave to amend the sheriff hears parties on the motion, on questions of expenses and any other conditions to be attached in the event of allowance of the amendment, and on further procedure. If the motion for leave to amend is not opposed, it is still in the discretion of the sheriff to disallow amendment, or to allow it on conditions as to expenses and otherwise in terms of rule 18.6,[28] but it is thought that it is only in highly exceptional circumstances that he would take a course which was not urged by a party or parties. The question of expenses must be considered if amendment is allowed,[29] and should be considered if amendment is refused: if it is not dealt with, it may be later lost sight of, and the expenses occasioned by the amendment will then become part of the expenses in the cause. If the sheriff allows amendment, he may order a fresh copy of the record as amended to be typed or printed (or, as it is usually put, "reprinted") and certified and lodged, or he may dispense with reprinting of the record. It is appropriate to order reprinting when the amendments are so numerous or of such a nature or length that to make or attach written or typed amendments on the record would make it difficult or inconvenient to read. If the sheriff dispenses with reprinting, the amendments should be added to the process copy of the record. In either case the closed record should be headed "Closed Record (As Amended)".

10.54 Since the sheriff when allowing the amendment allows the record to be opened up and amended, then closes the record of new, there is a question as to the application of rule 10.5(2), which provides that not later than 14 days after the closing of the record the pursuer must lodge in process a certified copy of the closed record. There are *obiter dicta* expressing reservations as to whether the predecessor of the rule applied other than to the first closing of the record, and expressing the opinion that the date for lodging an amended closed record may depend on the order of the sheriff.[30] It is recommended that the sheriff should in his interlocutor allowing amendment specify a period within which the pursuer must either amend the process copy of the record or, where the sheriff orders reprinting, lodge an amended and certified copy of the record as amended.

10.55 In his interlocutor allowing amendment the sheriff will make any necessary order for further procedure, and where preliminary pleas have been added in the amendment process he will require to consider any note lodged under rule 18.8(1) and: (1) appoint the cause to a debate if satisfied

---

27 paras 10.59, 18.34.

28 Thomson and Middleton, p. 367; *Wm Beardmore & Co. Ltd v. Park's Exrx*, 1932 S.L.T. 218.

29 OCR, r. 18.6.

30 *Eriks Allied Polymer Ltd v. Hydracrat Ltd*, Sh. Pr. Gillies, Hamilton Sh. Ct, Dec. 8, 1982, unreported, on rule 52 of original Sched. 1 to the 1907 Act, as substituted by A.S. (Sheriff Court Rules Amendment) 1950.

that there is a preliminary matter of law which justifies a debate; or (2) consider whether the preliminary pleas are to be reserved and a proof before answer allowed; or (3) where a proof before answer has already been allowed before amendment, consider whether the pleas are to be reserved and the diet provisionally delayed is to stand; or (4) if proof has been allowed, consider whether the allowance of proof should be recalled and an allowance of proof before answer substituted; or (5) where proof or proof before answer has been allowed, consider whether he is satisfied that there is a preliminary matter of law which requires a debate with the consequence that the allowance of proof or proof before answer will be recalled.

Abbreviated procedure

It is sometimes possible to shorten the procedure described in the foregoing paragraphs. By arrangement with the other party or parties it may be ascertained whether they are to lodge answers, or the minute and answers may be lodged simultaneously, or adjustment may be dispensed with, or all parties may agree to amendment and reservation of all questions of expenses.[31] Where a motion to allow a minute of amendment to be received and answered is lodged at a very late stage before a diet of proof and amendment is opposed, and it appears that the diet of proof will have to be discharged if the minute is to be received and answered, the sheriff may hear parties on the grounds of opposition to amendment at the stage of the hearing of the motion to allow the minute to be received.[32] If he decides that the minute should be received, he should not consider questions of relevancy arising from the minute until answers are lodged and the minute and answers adjusted.[33] In an appropriate case he may also, of consent, dispose of a motion to allow a minute of amendment to be received as if it were a motion for leave to amend in terms of the minute tendered, in order to avoid the expense and delay which would be occasioned if, in normal course, he simply allowed the minute to be received.[34] **10.56**

An abbreviated procedure should never, however, be imposed by the sheriff without the consent of all interested parties where this might result in prejudice to any of the parties. So, for example, where on the morning of a proof a party moves to have the record opened up and amended in terms of a minute of amendment, there are three options open to the sheriff: (1) he may refuse the amendment and allow the proof to proceed; or (2) he may allow the minute to be received and give the other party time to answer, thereby discharging the proof; or (3) he may allow the amendment and refuse the other party time to answer. If the minute of amendment raises a new question of law or fact which requires to be answered for the other party to press his claim or resist the claim against him, as the case may be, then if the sheriff is minded to allow the amendment he should discharge the proof to allow the other party time to consider whether to lodge answers.[35] **10.57**

---

31 Thomson and Middleton, p. 367.

32 *e.g. Dryburgh v. National Coal Board*, 1962 S.C. 485; *Mackenzie v. Fairfields Shipbuilding and Engineering Co. Ltd*, 1964 S.C. 90; *Hynd v. West Fife Co-operative Ltd*, 1980 S.L.T. 41.

33 *Mackenzie, supra.*

34 *Bannor v. Balfour Kilpatrick Ltd*, 1974 S.C. 223 at 229.

35 *Ogilvie v. Perth Kitchen Centres Ltd*, 1993 S.L.T. (Sh. Ct.) 60.

Further minutes of amendment

10.58 After one minute of amendment has been disposed of, a party may move for a further minute or minutes of amendment to be received. The new minute may alter or delete averments made in the original minute.[36] It should be headed "Second [or as the case may be] Minute of Amendment", and the same procedure may be followed as for the first minute, the closed record being ultimately headed "Closed Record (As Amended and Further Amended)". Sometimes, however, a further minute of amendment is an indication of inadequate preparation or investigation by the party tendering it, and the sheriff may be disposed to scrutinise any grounds of opposition with care and to refuse it if the opponent would be prejudiced by further delay in the determination of the case.[37]

Appeal

10.59 An appeal against a decision on a motion to allow a minute of amendment to be received, or on a motion for leave to amend, requires the leave of the sheriff. In so far as the decision has been an exercise of discretion, the appeal court will not interfere unless it is shown that the sheriff has taken account of an irrelevant factor, or has ignored an important factor, or has reached a decision which is either unreasonable or injudicial.[38]

VII. Deletion of Scandalous and Irrelevant Averments

10.60 It is *pars judicis* to notice and order the deletion of any averment the making of which is an abuse of the process of the court in respect that it is scandalous and irrelevant.[39] The order should preferably be made before the closing of the record.[40] Section 4 of the Sheriff Courts (Scotland) Act 1853, which required the sheriff before closing the record to strike out of the record any matter which he might deem to be either irrelevant or unnecessary, was repealed by the Statute Law Revision Act 1892, but its repeal has no bearing on the sheriff's inherent jurisdiction to prevent abuse of process.[41] Averments which have been deleted in the Court of Session on the ground of their scandalous and irrelevant character have included offensive and plainly improper allegations of immorality,[42] professional misconduct[43] or neglect of duty[44] on the part of third parties, or relative to collateral matters, which did not bear directly on the issues between the parties before the court. In modern practice the irrelevance of averments such as these will normally attract a plea by the opponent of the party making them that on the ground of their irrelevance they should be

---

36 *Lynch v. Stewart* (1871) 9 M. 860; *Duke of Argyll v. Duchess of Argyll*, 1962 S.C. (H.L.) 88.

37 *Jack Davis Publicity Ltd v. Kennedy*, Sh. Pr. Caplan, Paisley Sh. Ct, Dec. 18, 1984, unreported.

38 *Hynd v. West Fife Co-operative Ltd, supra.*

39 *Hamilton v. Anderson* (1858) 20 D. (H.L.) 16; *Wardrope v. Duke of Hamilton* (1876) 3 R. 876 at 878; *Clydesdale Bank Ltd v. Paton* (1896) 23 R. (H.L.) 22 at 26; *McIsaac v. Leonard* (1915) 31 Sh. Ct.Rep. 303; *Sellars v. IMI Yorkshire Imperial Ltd*, 1986 S.L.T. 629.

40 *Clydesdale Bank Ltd, supra.*

41 See paras 2.11, 2.16.

42 *M v. S*, 1909 1 S.L.T. 192; *C v. M*, 1923 S.C. 1; *MacGregor v. MacGregor*, 1946 S.L.T. (Notes) 13.

43 *C v. W*, 1950 S.L.T. (Notes) 8.

44 *Wardrope, supra* (averments in a sheriff court record).

excluded from probation; and in general they may be satisfactorily dealt with by sustaining such a plea after debate.[45] A tender made on an open record has, however, been deleted by order of the court on a motion to that effect.[46] There appears to be no modern reported example of the pronouncing of an order for the deletion of scandalous and irrelevant averments in the sheriff court.

---

[45] *A v. C*, 1922 S.L.T. 34.

[46] *Key v. Scottish Chemist Supply Co.*, 1956 S.L.T. (Notes) 43; *cf. Rodgers v. Clydesdale*, 1995 S.C.L.R. 1163.

CHAPTER 11

INTERIM PROTECTIVE AND REMEDIAL PROCEDURES

This chapter is concerned with protective and remedial procedures of a provisional nature which may be employed pending the disposal of the action and may play an important part in its progress by regulating the rights of the parties or the procedure in the cause before its final determination. **11.01**

Objectives

The protective procedures described below include orders for interim interdict, for the preservation of documents and other property, and for the appointment of a factor, and interim orders pending appeal. These are designed to achieve various objectives in the interests of justice, such as to preserve or restore the *status quo ante* the commencement of the action, to prevent the commission or continuation of wrongs, and to secure the preservation or proper management of property pending the final outcome of the proceedings. The court's power to grant protective measures pending the decision of any hearing extends to a case where the subject of the proceedings includes a question as to the jurisdiction of the court to entertain them, or where the proceedings involve the reference of a matter to the European Court under the 1971 Protocol on the interpretation of the Convention on jurisdiction and the enforcement of judgments in civil and commercial matters.[1] **11.02**

Interim remedial procedures include orders to provide security for the sum sued for, or for expenses, and interim decrees and interim awards of expenses. The objective of the provision of security for the sum sued for is to satisfy, at least in part, before judgment a party's legitimate concern that his opponent will be able to meet any decree which may be pronounced against him. In an action claiming payment of money other than expenses the pursuer may be able to obtain payment in the event of success in consequence either of having used arrestment or inhibition on the dependence or of having obtained consignation of, or caution for, the sum sued for. In any defended action, since both parties may be concerned to obtain security for their expenses, either may in certain circumstances be required to find caution for expenses or to sist a mandatary. The objective of an interim decree may be to confer on a party an immediate legitimate advantage by disposing of part of the merits of the cause in his favour, as where it appears that a sum of money is admittedly or plainly due and presently exigible; or to regulate the rights of the parties pending the disposal of the action, as in family proceedings by interim orders for the residence of or contact with children or for the interim aliment of a spouse and children. The objective of an interim award of expenses is to **11.03**

---

[1] Civil Jurisdiction and Judgments Act 1982, s. 24(2). The Act does not define "protective measures". The classification of the procedures discussed in this chapter is that of the writer.

dispose of a question of expenses upon a matter which is entirely distinct from, and cannot be affected by, the ultimate decision on the merits,[2] and to enable the party in whose favour it is made to enforce it without awaiting the conclusion of the litigation.

I. Protective Procedures

Interim interdict

11.04 Interim interdict may be granted at any stage of the action, with the object of preserving the existing state of matters or prohibiting any wrong which is either being done or apprehended. The court appears to have power to grant interim interdict in the course of any action, but the power is seldom applied for or exercised other than in actions in which perpetual interdict is sought. The subject is therefore considered in Chapter 21.

Preservation of documents and other property

11.05 The sheriff appears to have power at common law to make orders for the interim preservation of property, since section 29 of the 1907 Act refers to warrants to place effects in custody *ad interim* and to warrants for interim preservation of property as being among those the immediate execution of which is not prevented by an appeal. In any event, however, wide powers are conferred by statute. By virtue of section 1 of the Administration of Justice (Scotland) Act 1972 the court has power to order the inspection, photographing, preservation, custody and detention of documents and other property (including, where appropriate, land) which appear to the court to be property as to which any question may relevantly arise in any existing proceedings or in proceedings which are likely to be brought, and to order the production and recovery of any such property, the taking of samples thereof and the carrying out of any experiment thereon or therewith. The power is conferred without prejudice to the common law powers of the court, but is qualified by various specified rules as to privilege from disclosure. This matter is considered in the treatment of the law as to the recovery of evidence in Chapter 15.[3]

Appointment of factor

(1) Common law jurisdiction

11.06 The sheriff appears to have power at common law to appoint, or make a remit to, a person to take temporary charge of property during the course of a litigation in which it is involved, where such an arrangement is necessary for its management and preservation.[4] It has been suggested that such powers may be exercised only of consent.[5]

---

[2] *Waddel v. Hope* (1843) 6 D. 160 at 169.

[3] See paras 15.84 to 15.92.

[4] *Drysdale v. Lawson* (1842) 4 D. 1061; *Affleck v. Affleck* (1862) 24 D. 291; Dove Wilson, p. 422; Walker, *Judicial Factors*, p. 140.

[5] *Pollock v. Campbell*, 1962 S.L.T. (Sh. Ct.) 89. But see *Brock v. Buchanan* (1851) 13 D. 1069; *Gibson v. Clark* (1895) 23 R. 294.

(2) Statutory jurisdiction

The sheriff has no power at common law to appoint a judicial factor.[6] The Judicial Factors (Scotland) Act 1880, as amended, provides that the sheriff's jurisdiction in appointing judicial factors is concurrent with that of the Court of Session.[7] The sheriff court therefore has power, like the Court of Session, to appoint a judicial factor in order to provide for the administration of property in dispute, or, if parties agree, for its sale and administration of the price, until parties' rights have been settled by agreement or litigation. The procedure of appointment of a judicial factor as an incident in a pending cause may be found in the Act of Sederunt (Judicial Factors Rules) 1992.[8] The application is made by summary application.[9] The practice of the Court of Session is described in the undernoted work.[10] **11.07**

Interim orders pending appeal

Notwithstanding an appeal, the sheriff or sheriff principal from whose decision appeal has been taken has power to regulate all matters relating to interim possession, to make any order for the preservation of any property to which the action relates or for its sale if perishable, or provision for the preservation of evidence, or to make in his discretion any interim order which a due regard to the interests of the parties may require.[11] Such orders are not subject to review except by the appellate court at the hearing of the appeal.[12] **11.08**

Family proceedings

Interim protective procedures in family proceedings are considered in Chapter 22. **11.09**

II. Remedial Procedures

Security for the sum sued for

(1) Arrestment on the dependence

Nature.[13] Arrestment on the dependence is a procedure whereby the pursuer[14] in an action with a pecuniary crave, other than one for expenses, may prevent a third party holding moveable property for the defender or owing money to the defender from parting with the property or money **11.10**

---

6 *Rowe v. Rowe* (1872) 9 S.L.R. 492; *Pollock, supra.* In *Muir v. More Nisbett* (1881) 19 S.L.R. 59, it was apparently not argued that the sheriff-substitute had no power to appoint a judicial factor.

7 See paras 2.68, 2.69.

8 S.I. 1992 No. 272, as amended by S.I. 1994 No. 2354 and S.I. 1996 No. 2167.

9 1992 A.S., para. 4.

10 Walker, *Judicial Factors*, Chap. 9.

11 OCR, r. 31.10(1).

12 OCR, r. 31.10(2). See para. 18.69.

13 Only an exposition of the procedural aspects of arrestment on the dependence is attempted in the following pages. For a full discussion of arrestment, which forms a substantial part of the law of diligence, see Graham Stewart, Chaps 1–12; Maher & Cusine, *Diligence*, Chap. 4; *Stair Encyclopaedia*, Vol. 18, paras 247–314.

14 A warrant for arrestment on the dependence may also be sought by a defender when making a counterclaim (OCR, r. 19.2(1)) or applying for an order for the service of a third-party notice (OCR, r. 20.3). In the former case it is specifically provided that the warrant has the like effect as it would have in an initial writ (r. 19.2(4): see para. 12.34). In this chapter it is assumed that the warrant is applied for by a pursuer.

pending the disposal of the action, with the object that the pursuer in the event of his succeeding in the action may obtain therefrom payment of his debt either in whole or in part. The effect of arrestment is not only to prohibit the defender (the common debtor) from alienating, and the third party (the arrestee) from parting with the subject. It also affects the subject with an inchoate diligence which may or may not be completed, for in order to transfer the subject arrested to the pursuer or to enable goods to be sold for his benefit it is necessary that arrestment be followed by a process of furthcoming. Arrestment on the dependence is one of two kinds of arrestment[15] which form part of the diligence of arrestment and furthcoming, which is "an adjudication preceded by an attachment",[16] and whose purpose and effect is "to enable the arresting creditor to enforce for his own benefit obligations which are prestable to the common debtor by the arrestee".[17] The pursuer, by the attachment of the subject, prevents its being disposed of before decree; and in the event of decree being pronounced in his favour, he may follow up the arrestment and work out the diligence by means of a decree in an action of furthcoming whereby the subject is adjudged, or effectually transferred, to him. In practice a process of furthcoming is seldom necessary since the defender, to avoid the expense of such an action, usually grants a mandate authorising the arrestee to release the subject to the pursuer.[18] The expense of arrestment on the dependence cannot be recovered as part of the expenses of process, on the principle that the using of diligence on the dependence, however necessary it may be to make a pursuer's decree effectual when obtained, has nothing to do with obtaining that decree, which is the sole object of the action.[19]

11.11 **Actions in which competent.** Arrestment on the dependence, although commonplace in practice, is an extraordinary remedy which is not to be extended further than has been sanctioned by law and usage.[20] It is competent only where the writ contains a crave for payment of a sum of money other than expenses,[21] since only such a crave can be secured by the diligence.[22] An alternative pecuniary crave is sufficient.[23] In the ordinary case of an action with a pecuniary crave, averments justifying arrestment are unnecessary. Nor are they necessary in an action of count, reckoning and payment, although the crave is for payment of such sum as the accounting demonstrates to be due.[24] At common law, arrestment on the dependence of

---

[15] The other is arrestment in execution. Arrestment to found jurisdiction is not now a diligence "in the proper sense of the word": *Fraser-Johnston Engineering Co. v. Jeffs*, 1920 S.C. 222, *per* L.P. Clyde at 228; see also *Alexander Ward & Co. v. Samyang Navigatian Co. Ltd*, 1975 S.C.(H.L.) 26, *per* Lord Kilbrandon at 54.

[16] *Lucas's Trs v. Campbell and Scott* (1894) 21 R. 1096, *per* Lord Kinnear at 1103; *Lord Advocate v. Royal Bank of Scotland*, 1977 S.C. 155, *per* L.P. Emslie at 169, Lord Cameron at 175; *cf. Iona Hotels Ltd (In Receivership) v. Craig*, 1990 S.C. 330.

[17] *Shankland & Co. v. McGildowny*, 1912 S.C. 857, *per* Lord Kinnear at 868.

[18] Payment under such a mandate is not challengeable as an unfair preference where there has been a decree for payment or a warrant for summary diligence: Bankruptcy (Scotland) Act 1985, s. 36(2)(d). As to arrestments executed within 60 days before the date of sequestration, see s. 37(4).

[19] *Symington v. Symington* (1874) 1 R. 1006; *Black v. Jehangeer Framjee & Co.* (1887) 14 R. 678; *Roy v. Turner* (1891) 18 R. 717. See para. 11.25.

[20] *Stafford v. McLaurin* (1875) 3 R. 148, *per* Lord Deas and Lord Ardmillan at 150.

[21] *Stafford, supra.*

[22] *Weir v. Otto* (1870) 8 M. 1070.

[23] *Gordon v. Duncan* (1827) 5 S. 544 (N.E. 511).

[24] *Telford's Exr v. Blackwood* (1866) 4 M. 369; *Stafford v. McLaurin* (1875) 3 R. 148, *per* L.P. Inglis at 149; *Fisher v. Weir*, 1964 S.L.T. (Notes) 99.

an action for the enforcement of a future or contingent debt, although not incompetent, is not warranted unless there is something special in the circumstances of the case to justify it, such as that the defender is *vergens ad inopiam*[25] or *in meditatione fugae*[26] or intending to remove his effects beyond the power of his creditors[27]; and the special circumstances must be specifically averred.[28] By statute, however, in an action for aliment, or an action where a claim has been made for an order for financial provision in a divorce, the court has power, on cause shown, to grant warrant for arrestment on the dependence of the action and, if it thinks fit, may limit the arrestment to any particular property or to funds not exceeding a specified value.[29]

Subjects arrestable. In general, all moveable property belonging to the defender in the hands of third parties who are subject to the jurisdiction of the Scottish courts[30] may be arrested, provided that at the time of the arrestment the third party is under an obligation to account to the defender therefor.[31] "It is the obligation to account which is the proper subject of attachment."[32] **11.12**

(i) Corporeal moveables. With regard to goods, however, the property arrested must not be in the possession of the defender's employee or any other person who cannot retain it without his consent.[33] But if the third party possesses the goods in such a capacity as to give him a right of retention,[34] or if he has been empowered to dispose of them,[35] they may in general be arrested in his hands. If, however, the third party's possession of the goods is of a short or temporary character, it may be a question of fact whether the defender has lost possession to such an extent as will render arrestment competent.[36] A pursuer cannot, subject to one exception, arrest goods belonging to the defender in his (the pursuer's) own hands; nor may he place them with a depositary and arrest them there, since the depositary is under no obligation to deliver them to the defender.[37] The only case in which a pursuer may arrest goods in his own possession is that of a seller of goods the property in which has passed to the defender.[38] A warrant for arrestment on the dependence does not **11.13**

---

[25] "Approaching to want or insolvency" (Trayner). See *Pow v. Pow*, 1987 S.L.T. 127.
[26] "Meditating flight; intending to leave the country" (Trayner).
[27] *Symington v. Symington* (1875) 3 R. 205; *Burns v. Burns* (1879) 7 R. 355; *Gillanders v. Gillanders*, 1966 S.C. 54; *Brash v. Brash*, 1966 S.C. 56; *Tweedie v. Tweedie*, 1966 S.L.T. (Notes) 89; *Wilson v. Wilson*, 1981 S.L.T. 101.
[28] A statement in *Speirs v. Speirs* (1938) 54 Sh.Ct.Rep. 208, that averment is unnecessary is inconsistent with current practice: *Brash, Wilson, supra*. See also *Millar v. Millar* (1907) 15 S.L.T. 205; *Noble v. Noble*, 1921 1 S.L.T. 57. Those decisions are otherwise superseded by s. 19 of the Family Law (Scotland) Act 1985.
[29] Family Law (Scotland) Act 1985, s. 19.
[30] Ersk., III, vi, 3; *Douglas, Heron & Co. v. Palmer* (1777) 5 Br. Supp. 449; *Brash v. Brash*, 1966 S.C. 56.
[31] *Young v. Aktiebolaget Ofverums Bruk* (1890) 18 R. 163.
[32] Bell, *Comm.*, ii, 71; *Riley v. Ellis*, 1910 S.C. 934, *per* L.P. Dunedin at 941–942; *Shankland & Co. v. McGildowny*, 1912 S.C. 857, *per* L.P. Dunedin at 862, Lord Kinnear at 866–867; *Caldwell v. Hamilton*, 1919 S.C.(H.L.) 100, *per* Lord Dunedin at 109.
[33] Bell, *Comm.*, ii, 70; *Cuningham v. Home* (1760) Mor. 747 (employee); *Davidson v. Murray* (1784) Mor. 761 (tenant of furnished property).
[34] Sale of Goods Act 1979, s. 39 (unpaid seller); *N.B. Ry v. White* (1881) 9 R. 97 (carrier).
[35] *Brown v. Blaikie* (1850) 13 D. 149 (agent instructed to sell house contents).
[36] *Neilson v. Smith* (1821) Hume 31 (horse in smithy); *Hume v. Baillie* (1852) 14 D. 821, *Hutchison v. Hutchison*, 1912 1 S.L.T. 219 (personal luggage of resident in hotel).
[37] *Heron v. Winfields Ltd* (1894) 22 R. 182.
[38] Sale of Goods Act 1979, s. 40.

have effect as authority for the detention of a ship unless the action is for the enforcement of a claim to which section 47 of the Administration of Justice Act 1956 applies[39] and either the ship is the ship with which the action is concerned or all the shares in the ship are owned by the defender.[40]

11.14 *(ii) Incorporeal moveables.* Debts due to the defender[41] by a third party[42] may in general be arrested, unless they are heritably secured. Thus, the unpaid price of goods sold by the defender may be arrested in the hands of the purchaser,[43] and funds held by a bank in name of the defender may be arrested in the hands of the bank.[44] An arrestment of sums at credit of a debtor's account made at a branch of a bank in Scotland is probably not effective against sums held to his credit by a branch of the same bank in England.[45] A defender's shares in a limited company are arrestable in the hands of the company,[46] and his interest in a partnership is arrestable in the hands of the partnership.[47] Sums held by agents or on special deposit are arrestable by lodging an arrestment in the hands of a principal.[48] A defender's interest as beneficiary in a trust estate is arrestable in the hands of the trustees[49]; and in an insurance policy, in the hands of the insurers.[50] Since it is the obligation to account which is the subject of attachment, an obligation to account at the time of arrestment is attachable, and "it is not necessary that there should be a debt presently due. A claim, whether actual or contingent, whether liquid or illiquid, may be arrested."[51] The obligation must be, however, to account in Scotland.[52]

11.15 **Subjects not arrestable.** Since arrestment is only possible where there is a present liability to account, a pure future debt,[53] or a future and

---

[39] As defined in s. 47(2) of the Administration of Justice Act 1956 as amended by the Merchant Shipping Act 1995, Sched. 13.

[40] Administration of Justice Act 1956, s. 47(1); *The "Aifanourios"*, 1980 S.C. 346; *Catoil International Inc. v. Arkwright-Boston Manufacturers Mutual Insurance Co.*, 1985 S.L.T. 68; *Interatlantic (Namibia) (Pty) Ltd v. Okeanski Ribolov Ltd*, 1996 S.L.T. 819.

[41] Funds due to a company incorporated after the debt sued for was incurred cannot be arrested: *F J. Neale (Glasgow) Ltd v. Vickery*, 1973 S.L.T. (Sh. Ct.) 88.

[42] An assignee cannot arrest a debt owing by his assignor: *O'Hare v. Reaich*, 1956 S.L.T. (Sh. Ct.) 78.

[43] *Benjedward's Creditors* (1753) Mor. 743.

[44] Wallace and McNeil, *Banking Law* (10th ed., 1991), pp. 207–212; Crerar, *Banking* (1997), pp. 166–171.

[45] *Stewart v. Royal Bank*, 1994 S.L.T. (Sh. Ct.) 27. See also *Bank of Scotland v. Seitz*, 1990 S.L.T. 584.

[46] *Sinclair v. Staples* (1860) 22 D. 600; *American Mortgage Co. of Scotland Ltd v. Sidway*, 1908 S.C. 500. A subsidiary company may arrest shares in its holding company: *Stenhouse London Ltd v. Allwright*, 1972 S.C. 209. The stock of the Royal Bank of Scotland is attachable only by adjudication: *Royal Bank of Scotland v. Fairholm* (1770) Mor.App. "Adjudication", No. 3.

[47] Bell, *Comm.*, ii, 508; *Parnell v. Walter* (1889) 16 R. 917, *per* Lord Kinnear at 925; *American Mortgage Co. of Scotland Ltd, supra*; Miller, *Partnership* (2nd ed.), pp. 408 *et seq.*

[48] *Lord Advocate v. Bank of India*, 1991 S.C.L.R. 320, see further 1993 S.C.L.R. 178.

[49] *Learmonts v. Shearer* (1866) 4 M. 540; *Gracie v. Gracie*, 1910 S.C. 899.

[50] *Bankhardt's Trs v. Scottish Amicable Life Assurance Society* (1871) 9 M. 443.

[51] *Boland v. White Cross Insurance Association*, 1926 S.C. 1066, *per* L.J.-C. Alness at 1071. See also *Park, Dobson & Co. v. William Taylor & Son*, 1929 S.C. 571; *Agnew v. Norwest Construction Co.*, 1935 S.C. 771; *Commercial Bank of Scotland Ltd v. Eagle Star Insurance Co. Ltd*, 1950 S.L.T. (Notes) 30.

[52] *McNairn v. McNairn*, 1959 S.L.T. (Notes) 35; *J. Verrico & Co. Ltd v. Australian Mutual Provident Society*, 1972 S.L.T. (Sh. Ct.) 57.

[53] *Riley v. Ellis*, 1910 S.C. 934, *per* L.P. Dunedin at 942.

contingent debt,[54] is not arrestable. A claim of damages for wrongful dismissal was held to be validly arrested although at the time of the arrestment the common debtor had neither brought an action nor intimated a claim[55]; but this has been doubted,[56] and it may be that at least certain other claims of damages are not arrestable until asserted.[57] By statute it is not competent to arrest on the dependence "any earnings or any pension": "earnings" means any sums payable by way of wages or salary, and "pension" includes any annuity in respect of past services and any pension or allowance payable in respect of disablement or disability.[58] Benefits payable under social security legislation are not arrestable.[59] At common law, alimentary funds are not arrestable[60] to the extent of a reasonable provision considering the recipient's station in life; but they are arrestable in so far as the aliment is in excess of a reasonable sum.[61] They are also arrestable when the debt in respect of which the arrestment is used is an alimentary debt, albeit one incurred prior to the current term of the aliment which is arrested[62]: it may be that a sum of ready money may be retained to meet the recipient's current expenses.[63] Arrears of an alimentary fund are arrestable, except so far as they may be required to meet alimentary debts.[64] Bills, promissory notes[65] and property of no mercantile value[66] cannot be arrested; and property which is held jointly cannot be arrested for a debt of one of the joint owners.[67] Arrestment in the hands of the Crown is considered elsewhere.[68]

Procedure. *(i) Warrant for arrestment.* The pursuer usually obtains a warrant for arrestment on the dependence by inserting an application therefor in the crave of the initial writ. Unless the action is one for the enforcement of a future or contingent debt he is not required to make any averments in justification of his application.[69] If the action is one in which arrestment is prima facie competent the court grants the warrant automatically without inquiry, together with the warrant for citation.[70] It is incompetent for a defender to lodge a caveat against a warrant for arrestment on the dependence.[71] The warrant may be signed by the sheriff or the sheriff clerk. If for any reason the sheriff clerk refuses to **11.16**

---

[54] *Kerr v. R. & W. Ferguson*, 1931 S.C. 736, *per* Lord Sands at 743.

[55] *Riley v. Ellis*, 1910 S.C. 934.

[56] Gloag and Henderson, para. 53.9.

[57] *Riley, supra, per* L.P. Dunedin at 942; *Shankland & Co. v. McGildowny*, 1912 S.C. 857, *per* Lord Kinnear at 866–867; *Caldwell v. Hamilton*, 1919 S.C.(H.L.) 100, *per* Lord Dunedin at 109.

[58] Law Reform (Miscellaneous Provisions) (Scotland) Act 1966, s. 1.

[59] Social Security Administration Act 1992, s. 187, as amended by Jobseekers Act 1995, Sched. 2.

[60] Bell, *Prin.*, s. 2276.

[61] *Livingstone v. Livingstone* (1886) 14 R. 43; *Cuthbert v. Cuthbert's Trs*, 1908 S.C. 967, *per* Lord McLaren at 971.

[62] *Earl of Buchan v. His Creditors* (1835) 13 S. 1112; *Lord Ruthven v. Pulford & Sons*, 1909 S.C. 951.

[63] *Lord Ruthven, supra, per* Lord McLaren at 954.

[64] *Muirhead v. Miller* (1877) 4 R. 1139.

[65] Bell, *Comm.*, ii, 68.

[66] *Trowsdale's Tr. v. Forcett Ry* (1870) 9 M. 88; *Millar & Lang v. Polak* (1907) 14 S.L.T. 788; *Millar & Lang v. Poole* (1907) 15 S.L.T. 76.

[67] *Lord Ruthven, supra.*

[68] paras 4.70, 4.71.

[69] See para. 11.11.

[70] See OCR, App. 1, Form O1.

[71] *Wards v. Kelvin Tank Services Ltd*, 1984 S.L.T. (Sh. Ct.) 39.

sign, the writ may be presented to the sheriff for his consideration and signature if appropriate.[72] The certified copy initial writ with the warrant thereon is sufficient warrant to arrest on the dependence if it is otherwise competent to do so.[73] If the action is not one in which arrestment is prima facie competent, as where it is for the enforcement of a future or contingent debt or where there is no pecuniary crave, it is submitted that the court should grant warrant for citation alone, and should grant warrant for arrestment only after service of the initial writ and upon consideration of a motion which has been duly intimated to the defender.[74]

11.17 *(ii) Precept of arrestment.* If a warrant for arrestment on the dependence has not been obtained along with the warrant for citation, a precept of arrestment may be issued by the sheriff clerk. It may be issued on production to the sheriff clerk of either (a) an initial writ, containing a crave for payment of money, on which a warrant of citation has been issued but without a warrant to arrest having been included, or (b) a document of liquid debt.[75] The precept may be prepared by the pursuer's solicitor,[76] or by the sheriff clerk on the basis of a printed form, and is signed by the sheriff clerk.

11.18 *(iii) Schedule and execution of arrestment.* The authority to arrest on the dependence is the warrant granted with the warrant for citation, or the precept of arrestment issued by the sheriff clerk, or the certified copy initial writ with warrant thereon lodged by the pursuer in a defended action.[77] Arrestment on the dependence is competent at any time: it may be used before service of the action[78] and at any time thereafter up to the issue of the extract of the final decree. Until the pursuer is in the position of being able to arrest in execution he may arrest on the dependence.[79] The warrant or precept of arrestment is executed by a sheriff officer.[80] It may be executed anywhere in Scotland without endorsation by a sheriff clerk, and may be executed either by an officer of the court which granted it or by an officer of the sheriff court district within which it is to be executed.[81] The sheriff officer must be in possession of his warrant at the time of execution.[82] He serves on the arrestee a schedule or short copy of the warrant, and returns an execution, either endorsed on the warrant or separately, narrating that the arrestment was duly executed.[83]

---

72 OCR, r. 5.1(1), (3).
73 OCR, r. 3.5(1).
74 *cf. Wilson v. Wilson*, 1981 S.L.T. 101.
75 OCR, r. 3.5(2).
76 See Lewis, p. 539: Dobie, *Styles*, p. 46.
77 OCR, r. 3.5(1).
78 See para. 11.23.
79 Graham Stewart, pp. 21–22: Maher & Cusine, *Diligence*, para. 4.02.
80 OCR, r. 5.4. S. 8 of the Sheriff Courts (Scotland) Extracts Act 1892, which authorises arrestment in execution by a messenger-at-arms, does not apply to arrestment on the dependence. If the sheriff within whose jurisdiction the warrant requires to be executed is satisfied that no sheriff officer is reasonably available, he may grant authority to any person whom he may deem suitable (not including the law agent of the party presenting the warrant) to execute it: Execution of Diligence (Scotland) Act 1926, s. 3.
81 OCR, r. 5.8.
82 *MacKillop v. Mactaggart*, 1939 S.L.T. 65.
83 Bell, *Prin.*, s. 2277.

Diligence, and in particular arrestment on the dependence, demands a high degree of precision and accuracy if it is to be effective.[84] By statute, the schedule must be signed by the officer and bear the date of the execution and the name and designation of the witness.[85] Only one witness is required.[86] At common law, while there is no rule that every clerical blunder will vitiate a diligence,[87] the omission of anything essential in the execution will be fatal.[88] An erroneous or defective execution may, however, be replaced by a correct one before being produced in judgment.[89] The schedule and the execution both narrate the warrant for the arrestment (giving its date and designing the parties), the arrestee, the sum or subjects arrested and the date of execution.[90] They must be in conformity with the warrant and craves of the initial writ.[91] A misnomer, which is more than a trivial spelling mistake, of the pursuer[92] or of the arrestee[93] is fatal, as is a misdescription of the capacity in which the funds or subjects are due to the common debtor,[94] or any ambiguity in the description of the funds intended to be attached.[95] A misnomer of the common debtor,[96] however, or a misdescription of the capacity in which the arrestee holds any sum arrested,[97] is not fatal where there is no risk of misunderstanding. **11.19**

As to the description of the subjects arrested, there are specified as arrested a certain sum of money "more or less" and a general description of other effects lying in the arrestee's hands which must be stated to belong to the common debtor.[98] The effect of the qualification "more or less" is to attach all funds due to the common debtor in the hands of the arrestee, notwithstanding that they are considerably in excess of the sum sued for.[99] If it is desired to attach any specific fund or subject which is known to be in the arrestee's hands, there may be added to the general description "and particularly" with a specification of the specific fund or **11.20**

---

[84] *Richards & Wallington (Earthmoving) Ltd v. Whallings Ltd*, 1982 S.L.T. 66; *Allied Irish Banks v. CPT Sales & Services*, 1993 S.C.L.R. 778.

[85] Citation Acts 1592, c. 59, 1693, c. 21. There is no declaration of nullity if any of these is omitted.

[86] Debtors (Scotland) Act 1838, s. 32; Citations (Scotland) Act 1846, s. 1.

[87] *Hannan v. Kendal*, O.H., Lord Kincairney, Mar. 30, 1897, printed in Graham Stewart, pp. 849–850.

[88] Bell, *Prin.*, s. 2277.

[89] *Henderson v. Richardson* (1848) 10 D. 1035; *Hamilton v. Monkland Iron and Steel Co.* (1863) 1 M. 672.

[90] Graham Stewart, p. 34. The McKechnie Committee received evidence that in a large number of cases the arrestee does not appreciate the import of an arrestment served on him, and they recommended that there should be a standard form of arrestment containing an explanatory note with information to the arrestee as to its effect and his duties and obligations under it (Report, para. 153, rec. 37).

[91] *Mactaggart v. MacKillop*, 1938 S.L.T. 100. Where warrant has been granted both for arrestment on the dependence and for arrestment to found jurisdiction, care should be taken to execute both: *Sutherlands of Peterhead v. Allard Hewson & Co.*, 1972 S.L.T. (Notes) 83.

[92] *Richards & Wallington (Earthmoving) Ltd v. Whatlings Ltd*, 1982 S.L.T. 66; *Allied Irish Banks, supra.*

[93] *Henderson's Trs* (1831) 9 S. 618.

[94] *Wilson v. Mackie* (1875) 3 R. 18; *Gibb v. Lee* (1908) 16 S.L.T. 260.

[95] *Lattimore v. Singleton, Dunn & Co.*, 1911 2 S.L.T. 360.

[96] *Hannan, supra; Pollock, Whyte & Waddell v. Old Park Forge Ltd* (1907) 15 S.L.T. 3.

[97] *Huber v. Banks*, 1986 S.L.T. 58.

[98] See Graham Stewart, App., p. 846; *Marshall & Sons v. Robertson* (1904) 21 Sh.Ct.Rep. 243.

[99] *Ritchie v. McLachlan* (1870) 8 M. 815. See also *Bremner v. TSB (Scotland) plc*, 1993 S.L.T. (Sh. Ct.) 3; 1992 S.C.L.R. 662.

subject: the absence of such specification will not render the arrestment invalid, but it may impair its efficiency by failing to direct the vigilance of the arrestee.[1]

11.21 *(iv) Arrestee.* The arrestee must be subject to the jurisdiction of the Scottish courts.[2] The rules as to service on the arrestee are as follows.

(1) Where the arrestee is an individual, the schedule may be served personally or at his dwelling-place.[3]

(2) Where the arrestee is a limited company, it may be served by leaving it at or sending it by post to the registered office of the company.[4]

(3) In the case of a bank, service of the arrestment should be made at its registered office or the schedule should be delivered to an official at its head office. In all cases, notice by way of another schedule should be served on the branch where the account of the common debtor is kept.[5] Where the arrestee is Girobank plc the schedule should be served on Girobank plc, 93 George Street, Edinburgh EH2 3JL.

(4) Where the arrestee is a corporation to which no special statutory provision regarding service is applicable, the schedule should be served at its place of business[6] by leaving it with a responsible official.[7]

(5) Where the arrestee is a firm with a social name, it should be served at the place of business by leaving it with any partner or employee; if a firm with a descriptive name, it may be served at any place of business and personally on or at the dwelling-places of three partners, if there are as many.[8]

(6) Where the arrestees are trustees, the schedule should be served on such trustees as are entitled to act,[9] and should state that the arrestment is served on each as trustee, not as an individual.[10]

(7) Where it is desired to serve an arrestment on the Lord Advocate as acting under the Crown Suits (Scotland) Act 1857 on behalf of the Crown or, as the case may be, on behalf of any minister or public department, the arrestee should be designed as "The Lord Advocate, Crown Office, 25 Chambers Street, Edinburgh EH1 1LA, as acting under the Crown Suits (Scotland) Act 1857." The designation should also state on whose behalf the Lord Advocate is designated as arrestee, whether the Crown or a particular secretary of state, minister, or department. If the Lord Advocate is designated as arrestee without any further description or qualification, he will regard the arrestment as attaching only to debts owed to the debtor in question by him or by one of his own departments.[11]

11.22 *(v) Sending copy schedule by post.* Rule 6.1 provides that if a schedule of arrestment has not been personally served upon an arrestee, the arrestment only has effect if a copy of the schedule is also sent in a registered or recorded delivery letter to the last known place of residence of the arrestee, or, if such place of residence is unknown, or if the arrestee is a firm or

---

[1] *Macintyre v. Caledonian Ry* (1909) 25 Sh.Ct.Rep. 329 at 333.
[2] See para. 11.12.
[3] *Campbell v. Watson's Tr.* (1898) 25 R. 690, *per* Lord Trayner at 695.
[4] Companies Act 1985, s. 725(1).
[5] Wallace and McNeil, *Banking Law* (10th ed., 1991), p. 207; Crerar, *Banking* (1997), p. 165.
[6] *Campbell, supra*; *Abbey National Building Society v. Strang*, 1981 S.L.T. (Sh. Ct.) 4.
[7] Graham Stewart, pp. 32–33; Maher & Cusine, para. 4.23.
[8] Graham Stewart, p. 32.
[9] Bell, *Prin.*, s. 2276; *Gracie v. Cracie*, 1910 S.C. 899.
[10] *Burns v. Gillies* (1906) 8 F. 460.
[11] 1980 S.L T. (News) 146.

corporation, to the arrestee's principal place of business if known, or, if not known, to any known place of business of the arrestee. The officer must in his execution certify that that has been done and specify the address to which the copy of the schedule was sent.[12] That rule does not provide a method of curing the invalidity of an attempt at personal service. The sending of the copy is not in itself an arrestment, but is merely a supplementary step prescribed in the use of an arrestment validly served otherwise than personally.[13] It appears that while a delay in posting the copy will not render the arrestment invalid, the execution of the arrestment will not be completed until the rule has been complied with.[14] It is thought that the rule is inapplicable in the case of a limited company where there has been compliance with section 725(1) of the Companies Act 1985.[15]

(vi) Arrestment prior to service. Arrestment on the dependence may be **11.23** used not only at any time after service of the initial writ while the action is pending, but also before service. Arrestment prior to service is, however, regulated by the provisions of rule 6.2. The arrestment ceases to have effect unless the initial writ is served within 20 days from the date of arrestment and in the case of undefended causes, decree in absence has been pronounced within 20 days after the expiry of the period of notice.[16] When an arrestment on the dependence prior to service has been executed, the party who executed it must forthwith report the execution to the sheriff clerk.[17] The reason for the latter requirement appears to be that the execution must be in the sheriff clerk's hands as the debtor may at any moment apply to have the arrestment recalled or loosed,[18] or to have rectified anything which he may have to complain of in regard to its use.[19] Such failure renders the arrestment null. It is not competent to use the dispensing power to cure such a nullity.[20]

Effect.[21] The effects of a valid arrestment on the dependence are to **11.24** prohibit the common debtor from alienating and the arrestee from parting with the subject, and to affect the subject with an inchoate diligence, which may or may not be completed by a process of furthcoming, decree in which is the completion of the pursuer's right to the subject: it adjudges to the pursuer so much of the fund attached as may pay his debt, or if the subject is corporeal it authorises a sale and payment out of the proceeds.[22] An arrestment confers no real right: if the arrestee parts with the subject he is liable to the pursuer for its value, but a bona fide purchaser from the arrestee takes a good title.[23] If the pursuer obtains decree in the action, he has a preferable right over the subject arrested. There may accordingly

---

[12] OCR, r. 6.1.
[13] *Corson v. Macmillan*, 1927 S.L.T. (Sh. Ct.) 13.
[14] *Hart v. Grant & Wylie* (1907) 23 Sh.Ct.Rep. 186.
[15] See para. 11.21.
[16] OCR, r. 6.2(1).
[17] OCR, r. 6.2(2); *Henley's Tyre and Rubber Co. Ltd v. Swan*, 1929 S.L.T. (Sh. Ct.) 47.
[18] *Johnson v. Johnson* (1910) 26 Sh.Ct.Rep. 134 at 138.
[19] Dove Wilson, p. 212.
[20] *Cluny Investment Services v. Macandrew & Jenkins*, 1992 S.C.L.R. 478.
[21] A detailed consideration of the effect of arrestment is beyond the scope of this book. See Graham Stewart, Chap. 6; *Stair Encyclopaedia*, Vol. 8, paras 284–291; Gloag and Henderson, paras 53.3–53.10; Maher & Cusine, *Diligence*, paras 5.36–5.38.
[22] Bell, *Prin.*, s. 2283; Graham Stewart, pp. 125, 126.
[23] Graham Stewart, pp. 126–127.

be more than one arrestment of the same subject: if the first arrester completes his diligence he will have priority, but when his claim is satisfied the second will have a preference for any balance.[24] The pursuer takes the subject under those burdens which affect the debtor's real right.[25]

11.25 The arrestment operates as a valid security for the sum sued for, the interest craved thereon and the expenses of the action,[26] but not the expenses of the arrestment itself[27] or of the furthcoming.[28] Where funds have been arrested, the arrestee remains the proprietor of the funds until he pays them over: he is not obliged to earmark, separate or identify these funds in his general funds or to invest them, so long as he can always make them available.[29] While the arrestment attaches only the obligation to account to the defender at the time the arrestment is laid on, the effect of the arrestment continues until the action is finally disposed of: it accordingly continues after decree of absolvitor if the pursuer appeals.[30] If the action is finally disposed of in favour of the defender, the arrestment falls when the final decree is extracted. It is thought[31] that where a plea of no jurisdiction is sustained and the cause is transferred to another sheriff court in terms of rule 26.1(3), the arrestment remains effective since there is no final decree and the transferred cause proceeds in the other court in all respects as if it had been originally brought there.[32] If the action is finally disposed of in favour of the pursuer, the arrestment prescribes in three years from the date of the decree excluding the time during which a time to pay direction or order or interim order is in effect[33]; and arrestments used on a future or contingent debt prescribe in three years from the time when the debt becomes due and the contingency is purified.[34] The course of prescription may be interrupted if the arrestment is "pursued or insisted on" within the three years, as by raising an action of furthcoming or multiplepoinding.[35] Where the pursuer obtains decree, he may raise an action of furthcoming on the arrestment on the dependence: it is unnecessary to use an arrestment in

---

[24] *W.H. Hill & Sons Ltd v. Manning's Tr.*, 1951 S.L.T. (Sh. Ct.) 29.

[25] *Mansfield v. Walker's Trs* (1833) 11 S. 813 at 822.

[26] *McDonald v. Wingate* (1825) 3 S. 494 (N.E. 344); *May v. Malcolm* (1825) 4 S. 76 (N.E. 79) (decree in name of agent-disburser).

[27] *Symington v. Symington* (1874) 1 R. 1006; *Black v. Jehangeer Framjee & Co.* (1887) 14 R. 678; *Roy v. Turner* (1891) 18 R. 717. See para. 11.10. The McKechnie Committee recommended that it should be within the discretion of the court to award the pursuer the expenses of arrestment on the dependence if he obtains a decree (even if only for expenses) or can show good cause why the arrestment was used: *Report of the Committee on Diligence*, Cmnd 456 (1958), para. 181, rec. 58.

[28] *May, supra.* The expenses of the furthcoming were formerly made good out of the arrested fund or subject in terms of the original r. 129 enacted in the 1907 Act, First Sched., but there is no similar provision in the current Ordinary Cause Rules. *Cf.* SCR, r. 64. See paras 21.47, 21.50.

[29] *Glen Music Co. Ltd v. Glasgow D.C.*, 1983 S.L.T. (Sh. Ct) 26.

[30] *Countess of Hadinton v. Richardson* (1822) 1 S. 387.

[31] See Lewis, p. 102; Dobie, p. 265.

[32] OCR, r. 26.1(7).

[33] Debtors (Scotland) Act 1838, s. 22 as amended by Debtors (Scotland) Act 1987, Sched. 6, para. 3; *Paterson v. Cowan* (1826) 4 S. 477 (N.E. 482); Graham Stewart, pp. 223–224.

[34] Debtors (Scotland) Act 1987, s. 221. The latter phrase of this subsection appears to apply only to contingent debts: in *Jameson v. Sharp* (1887) 14 R. 643, where the arrestment of a vested interest in a trust was held to be prescribed, it seems not to have been argued that this provision (being former Act of 1838, s. 22) was applicable. "Perhaps the 'or' is exegetical and 'future' is used to mean 'contingent'; that would explain the 'and' between 'due' and 'the contingency' " (Wilson, *Debt* (2nd ed.), para. 17.7).

[35] *Jameson, supra.*

execution.[36] Where there is a competition of arrestments, the appropriate action is a multiplepoinding.[37]

Arrestment attaches all funds due to the common debtor in the hands of the arrestee at the time of the arrestment, notwithstanding that they are considerably in excess of the sum sued for.[38] It has frequently been criticised on that ground. **11.26**

> "The use of inhibition and arrestment may be productive of the most serious injury to the mercantile credit and interests of the party against whom they are used: and it might frequently happen that reparation for such injury could not be obtained."[39]
>
> "The evil done by the diligence is the same, whether the arrestment has been successful or not. That evil is the creation in the minds of arrestees of doubt as to the stability of the common debtor. The average man who receives an arrestment schedule does not stop to discriminate whether that imports an arrestment in execution, or merely an arrestment on the dependence. Most probably he does not know the difference between the two. Even if he does, the impression conveyed to his mind is that the defender is wrongously refusing to pay a claim made against him, and is being sued in court to compel payment; and to the mind of the commercial man in the street I fear an action in court infers resistance to a just claim. If the process of arrestment is repeated, it is not difficult to see how easily the reputation of a commercial firm might be injured in the eye of the commercial community".[40]
>
> "There is no greater hardship connected with litigation than the arbitrary and uncalled-for use of this powerful means of persecution."[41]

Thus, notwithstanding that a pursuer may obtain warrant for arrestment without inquiry,[42] and that arrestments are subject to recall or restriction by the court[43] and damages may be recovered for the wrongful use of arrestment,[44] it has been strongly recommended that agents should dissuade litigants from heaping on arrestments to a needless extent or from vindictive motives.[45] The McKechnie Committee, who considered representations as to "the excessive and sometimes oppressive use of this form of diligence where it is used without limitation of effect",[46] recommended that an arrestment on the dependence should arrest only a specified sum reached by reference to the amount of the creditor's claim with the addition of a reasonable sum in

---

[36] *Gordon v. Hill* (1841) 3 D. 517, *per* Lord Mackenzie at 522; *Liquidators of Benhar Coal Co. v. Turnbull* (1883) 10 R. 558, *per* L.P. Inglis at 562; *Abercrombie v. Edgar & Crerar Ltd*, 1923 S.L.T. 271; *Mactaggart v. MacKillop*, 1938 S.L.T. 100; Graham Stewart, p. 231. *Cf. North v. Stewart* (1890) 17 R. (H.L.) 60, *per* Lord Watson at 63; *Kerr v. R. & W. Ferguson*, 1931 S.C. 736, *per* Lord Morison at 745.

[37] Bell, *Prin.*, s. 2283.

[38] *Ritchie v. McLachlan* (1870) 8 M. 815 (followed in *Bremner v. TSB (Scotland)*, 1993 S.L.T. (Sh. Ct.) 3); 1992 S.C.L.R. 662.

[39] *Beattie & Son v. Pratt* (1880) 7 R. 1171, *per* Lord Ormidale at 1173.

[40] *Dick & Parker v. Langloan Iron and Chemical Co. Ltd* (1904) 21 Sh.Ct.Rep. 139 at 140.

[41] Lees, *Pleading*, p. 30.

[42] para. 11.16.

[43] paras 11.27, 11.28.

[44] para. 11.35.

[45] Lees, *Pleading*, p. 30.

[46] Report, para. 43.

respect of expenses.[47] That recommendation, however, has not been implemented.

11.27 **Procedure for preventing the use or effect of arrestment.** *(i) Where arrestment is threatened.* It is incompetent for a defender to lodge a caveat against a warrant for arrestment on the dependence.[48] He may, however, obtain interdict against the threatened use of arrestment on the dependence in two situations: (1) where it can be instantly verified that the arrestment would be wrongful in the sense discussed below,[49] that is, executed without warrant, or irregularly, or maliciously and without probable cause[50]; or (2) where he has consigned the principal sum sued for.[51] While it may be that a sheriff could competently interdict the use of arrestment on the dependence of an action in his own court, the safer course is to apply to the Court of Session. Where the application is for interdict of arrestment on the dependence of any action in any court including the Court of Session, or for interdict of both arrestment and inhibition on the dependence, the Court of Session alone has jurisdiction.[52]

11.28 *(ii) Where arrestment has been used.* Section 21 of the Debtors (Scotland) Act 1838 provides that it shall be competent for the sheriff to recall or to restrict arrestments on caution or without caution, as to the sheriff shall appear just.[53] In practice arrestments may also be loosed on caution or consignation. While a recall removes the arrestment altogether, the loosing of an arrestment entitles the arrestee to make over the subject to the defender, but if it remains in the arrestee's hands when the pursuer obtains decree it is still subject to furthcoming.[54] In practice an application for the recall, restriction or loosing of an arrestment is seldom made, because normally the pursuer is ready to withdraw an arrestment when it is shown to him that sufficient to cover his claim is caught by another of his arrestments.[55]

11.29 Arrestments will normally be recalled on caution being found by the defender that on decree being pronounced against him there will be made forthcoming to the pursuer the arrested fund or subject or its value or, more commonly, the whole debt sued for (including principal, interest and expenses) to the extent of the arrested fund. Caution for the whole debt is more commonly used as it has the effect of relieving all the arrestments, however numerous they may be. But if anything less than full caution is offered and a motion is made for recall or restriction of an arrestment, the amount of the caution which will be required by the sheriff on recalling or restricting the arrestment will depend on the circumstances of each case.[56] If the arrestment is recalled, the caution required may be for the value of the property arrested; or, if that exceeds the debt, to the extent of the debt;

---

47 Report, para. 44, rec. 1.

48 *Wards v. Kelvin Tank Services Ltd*, 1984 S.L.T. (Sh. Ct.) 39.

49 See para. 11.35.

50 *Beattie & Son v. Pratt* (1880) 7 R. 1171.

51 *Duff v. Wood* (1858) 20 D. 1231.

52 *Beattie & Son, supra.*

53 It appears that application may also be made to the Inner House of the Court of Session (*Drummond & Dobie v. Boyd* (1834) 12 S. 454); but this seems to be unknown in modern practice.

54 Bell, *Comm.*, ii, 67; Bell, *Prin.*, ss. 2279, 2281; Graham Stewart, pp. 195–197.

55 McKechnie Report, para. 45.

56 *Henderson v. George Outram and Co. Ltd*, 1993 S.C.L.R. 162.

or, if a random sum is sued for, to the extent of a sum modified by the sheriff, taking into consideration the nature of the action, the amount arrested and the circumstances of the common debtor.[57] Caution may be ordered not only for the sum sued for, but also for expenses.[58] It is thought that the sheriff may order consignation of an appropriate sum in place of caution.[59] When considering the extent to which an arrestment should be restricted the court will not lend its authority to the freezing of a party's assets beyond the limit of what in the circumstances seems reasonable,[60] and will endeavour to recognise the interests of both parties.[61] When an arrestment is recalled or restricted by the court the sheriff clerk issues a certificate which sets out the consequences of the order.[62]

An arrestment may be recalled or restricted with or without caution where it is nimious (*i.e.* where it is a superfluous and vexatious precaution) or oppressive, or has been effected or made possible by the fraud or wrong of the pursuer,[63] or where the subjects are not arrestable. In considering what is nimious the court will be influenced by the nature of the action and will in general recall or restrict the arrestment where the craves are extravagant or the sum sought to be attached is disproportionate to the pursuer's interest.[64] The court may recall the arrestment as oppressive where there are ample funds to meet the pursuer's claim, and no prospect of its being defeated by other creditors[65]; or where it appears that the primary purpose of the arrestment is not to protect the legitimate interests of the pursuer but to embarrass the defender[66]; or, perhaps, where the pursuer has delayed excessively in prosecuting the action.[67] Where the arrestment is held to be nimious or oppressive, it will be recalled, in some cases *simpliciter*, but much more generally on caution.[68] If the pursuer has arrested in bad faith, the arrestment may be recalled without caution.[69] If the subjects are clearly not arrestable,[70] or if the arrestment can attach nothing on any view of the facts,[71] the arrestment will be recalled; but as a general rule a question as to the validity of the arrestment must be tried in thc furthcoming, not in an application for recall of the arrestment.[72] **11.30**

---

[57] Graham Stewart, pp. 202–204; *Fisher v. Weir*, 1964 S.L.T. (Notes) 99 (action of count, reckoning and payment).

[58] *Miller v. McLean* (1831) 9 S. 923; *Stewart v. Macbeth & Gray* (1882) 10 R. 382; *McPhedron and Currie v. McCallum* (1888) 16 R. 45.

[59] *James v. James* (1886) 13 R. 1153; *McPhedron and Currie, supra*; *Ellis v. Menzies & Co.* (1901) 9 S.L.T. 243; *Fisher, supra*; Dove Wilson, p. 213.

[60] *Tweedie v. Tweedie*, 1966 S.L.T. (Notes) 89.

[61] *Noble v. Noble*, 1921 1 S.L.T. 57 at 59–60.

[62] Maher & Cusine, para. 4.25.

[63] Bell, *Prin.*, s. 2280.

[64] Graham Stewart, p. 198; *Cullen v. Buchanan* (1862) 24 D. 1280; *Levy v. Gardiner*, 1964 S.L.T. (Notes) 68; *Henderson, supra.*

[65] Graham Stewart, p. 199; *Magistrates of Dundee v. Taylor and Grant* (1863) 1 M. 701.

[66] *Levy, supra.*

[67] *Telford's Exr v. Blackwood* (1866) 4 M. 369 at 371; *Mowat v. Kerr*, 1977 S.L.T. (Sh. Ct.) 62.

[68] *Barclay, Curle & Co. v. Sir James Laig & Sons Ltd*, 1908 S.C. 82, *per* L.P. Dunedin at 86.

[69] *Rintoul & Co. v. Bannatyne* (1862) 1 M. 137; *Alexander v. Graham* (1842) 5 D. 218. In *Henley's Tyre and Rubber Co. Ltd v. Swan*, 1929 S.L.T. (Sh. Ct.) 48, an arrestment used in breach of an arrangement between the parties was held to be invalid and inept. See also *Lapsley v. Lapsley* (1915) 31 Sh.Ct.Rep. 330. *Cf. Svenska Petroleum AB v. HOR Ltd*, 1986 S.L.T. 513.

[70] *Lord Ruthven v. Drummond*, 1908 S.C. 1154.

[71] *Shivas' Tr. v. Shivas' Trs* (1883) 27 J. of J. 556.

[72] *Vincent v. Chalmers & Co.'s Tr.* (1887) 5 R. 43.

11.31 As to title to apply for recall, an application for recall of arrestments is competent only at the instance of any party in the cause against whom they have been used,[73] and incompetent at the instance of a third party who alleges that the arrested fund or subject belongs to him.[74] Nor may the defender as a rule raise in his application the question of the right to the fund arrested.[75] These are issues which may be tried in the furthcoming or in a multiplepoinding.[76] The arrestee and any other party who has an interest in having the arrestment taken off may apply only to the Court of Session.[77]

11.32 Modern practice no longer adheres to the procedure for recall or restriction of arrestments laid down in section 21 of the Debtors (Scotland) Act 1838. That section makes it competent for any sheriff from whose books a warrant of arrestment has been issued to recall or restrict arrestments on the petition of the defender duly intimated to the pursuer: the sheriff is directed to allow answers to be given in to the petition, and to proceed with the further disposal of the cause in the same manner as in summary causes (*i.e.* summary applications).[78] In modern practice an initial writ appears to be required only where there is no pending process in which a motion can be made.[79] Where the action has been commenced, the procedure is by motion, intimated to the pursuer and, if thought fit, to the arrestee.[80] In either case, written answers are said to be necessary only if the pursuer moves for them.[81] It is respectfully submitted, however, that where the procedure is by motion written answers are not appropriate, and that the practice of the sheriff court need be no more elaborate than that of the Court of Session, where questions relating to the recall of arrestments are disposed of without proof and upon a prima facie presentation of the facts.[82] The sheriff may consider oral explanations as to the circumstances, made at the bar, and any other facts and circumstances which, in his judicial capacity, have come to his knowledge, such as the nature of other processes depending before his court in which the parties are interested.[83] It appears to be competent to restrict arrestments on a motion for recall.[84]

11.33 Although section 21 of the 1838 Act refers only to review of the sheriff's judgment in the Court of Session, it has been held that an appeal without

---

[73] *Stewart* v. *Macbeth & Gray* (1882) 10 R. 382 at 382.

[74] *Brand* v. *Kent* (1892) 20 R. 29; *"Nordsoen"* v. *Mackie, Koth & Co.*, 1911 S.C. 172; *Tait* v. *Main*, 1989 S.L.T. (Sh. Ct.) 81; 1989 S.C.C.R. 106.

[75] *McMorran* v. *Glover* (1937) 53 Sh.Ct.Rep 87. See para. 11.30.

[76] *Vincent* v. *Chalmers & Co.'s Tr.* (1887) 5 R. 43; *"Nordsoen"*, *supra.*

[77] Graham Stewart, pp. 209–210.

[78] *Johnson* v. *Johnson* (1910) 26 Sh.Ct.Rep. 134 at 136.

[79] Dobie, *Styles*, p.48, note; Grant Report, para. 646. See *Gatoil International Inc.* v. *Arkwright-Boston Manufacturers Mutual Insurance Co.*, 1985 S.L.T. 68.

[80] *Mowat* v. *Kerr*, 1977 S.L.T. (Sh. Ct.) 62; Dobie, *Styles*, p. 335. It appears that intimation of an initial writ or motion may be dispensed with in exceptional circumstances: *Mellis* (1872) S.L.R. 630.

[81] *Gordon* v. *Bruce & Co.* (1897) 24 R. 844; *Mowat*, *supra.*

[82] *Vincent* v. *Chalmers & Co.'s Tr.* (1877) 5 R. 43, *per* L.P. Inglis at 44; *Noble* v. *Noble*, 1921 1 S.L.T. 57 at 59; *Azcarate* v. *Iturrizaga*, 1938 S.C. 573, *per* L.P. Normand at 581; RCS, rr. 13.10 and 13.11.

[83] *Uden* v. *Burrell* (1914) 30 Sh.Ct.Rep. 224.

[84] *Conzemius Ltd* v. *Findlay* (1924) 41 Sh.Ct.Rep. 337. Restriction on a motion for recall seems to be familiar in modern practice, although it may not be illustrated in the reports.

leave to the sheriff principal is competent.[85] However, in the most recent case to consider the matter, Sheriff Principal Ireland held that, at least in the case of an application by incidental motion, leave to appeal *is* required.[86] The expenses of an application for recall fall upon the party applying for recall if the arrestment was properly used and is recalled on caution or consignation,[87] or if the application is refused[88]; but if the arrestment is nimious or oppressive,[89] or if there are circumstances in which the arrester ought to have withdrawn it extrajudicially without conditions, the arrester will be liable in the expenses of an application for recall,[90] even although he is successful on the merits.[91] In practice, however, any question as to expenses is frequently reserved until the merits of the action are disposed of.[92]

Breach of arrestment. If, notwithstanding an arrestment, the arrestee voluntarily pays the debt or delivers the goods arrested to the defender or other party, he commits a breach of the arrestment and is liable to the extent of the sum attached thereby,[93] unless he was ignorant of the arrestment.[94] If he pays or delivers to a party other than the pursuer, he is liable to pay to the pursuer the value of the subject attached, or the sum secured by the arrestment if that is less than the value of the subject attached,[95] or—if the value of the subject cannot be ascertained—the whole debt due to the pursuer.[96] If he pays or delivers to the pursuer, who receives the subject in the knowledge that the payment or delivery is made without the authority of the defender and in breach of the arrestee's duty to retain the subject and in the knowledge that the amount of the defender's indebtedness to the pursuer is disputed, the court may ordain the pursuer to return the subject to the arrestee upon the view that prejudice has been caused to certain rights of the defender, such as to seek recall of the arrestment after finding caution or otherwise.[97] It may be that the only person who may not be required to repay arrested funds received from an arrestee is a party who has received them in ignorance of the arrestment.[98] It is possible that an arrestee who pays or delivers in breach of the arrestment may be criminally liable to punishment for breach of arrestment as for a contempt of court but only, it is thought, in an extreme case where there is clearly no misunderstanding or inadvertency on his part.[99] 11.34

---

85 *Irvine v. Gow* (1910) 26 Sh.Ct.Rep. 174; *Kennedy v. Kennedy* (1910) 27 Sh.Ct.Rep. 71; *Swan v. Kirk*, 1932 S.L.T. (Sh. Ct.) 9; *Mowat v. Kerr*, 1977 S.L.T. (Sh. Ct.) 62. *Cf. McGarva v. McBrierly*, 1917 1 S.L.T. 324.

86 *Tait v. Main*, 1989 S.L.T. (Sh. Ct.) 81; 1988 S.C.C.R. 106.

87 Graham Stewart, p. 212.

88 *Crawford v. Ritchie* (1837) 16 S. 107; *Mowat, supra.*

89 *Hamilton v. Bruce's Trs* (1857) 19 D. 745; *Cullen v. Buchanan* (1862) 24 D. 1280; *Magistrates of Dundee v. Taylor and Grant* (1863) 1 M. 701; *Mackintosh v. Miller* (1864) 2 M. 452; *Radford & Bright Ltd v. D. M. Stevenson & Co.* (1904) 6 F. 429.

90 Maclaren, *Expenses*, p. 117.

91 *Clark v. Loos* (1855) 17 D. 306, *per* L.J.-C. Hope at 307.

92 Maher & Cusine, para. 4.55.

93 Bell, *Prin.*, s. 2278; *McEwen v. Blair and Morrison* (1822) 1 S. 313 (N.E. 289).

94 *Laidlaw v. Smith* (1838) 16 S. 367 (affd (1841) 2 Rob. 490).

95 Breach of Arrestment Act 1581, c. 23. (This Act has not fallen into desuetude: *McSkimming v. Royal Bank of Scotland*, 1996 S.C.L.R. 547.) *Grant v. Hill* (1792) Mor. 786; Graham Stewart, p. 222.

96 *Macarthur v. Bruce* (1760) Mor. 803.

97 *High-Flex (Scotland) Ltd v. Kentallen Mechanical Services Co.*, 1977 S.L.T. (Sh. Ct.) 91.

98 *ibid.* at 94.

99 *Inglis and Bow v. Smith and Aikman* (1867) 5 M. 320; Hume, *Lectures*, vi, pp. 112–113.

11.35 **Wrongful arrestment.**[1] The extent to which arrestment on the dependence is used requires to be carefully considered by the pursuer's solicitor. If arrestments are used nimiously or oppressively they are liable to be recalled or restricted.[2] Further, it must be kept in mind that all diligence is *periculo petentis.*[3] While the pursuer, since he has an absolute right to the warrant, will incur no liability in damages merely because his action fails, an arrestment which is without warrant or irregularly executed is a quasi-delict which may render the pursuer liable to an action of damages.[4] A pursuer is so liable if he arrests without legal warrant,[5] as where there is no warrant at all[6] or the warrant is defective[7] or irregularly executed.[8] In such circumstances the warrant may also be reduced by the Court of Session.[9] Where the arrestment has been legally and regularly executed, it is actionable only if executed maliciously and without probable cause.[10]

(2) Inhibition on the dependence

11.36 **Nature.**[11] By inhibition on the dependence the pursuer may prevent the defender from dealing with his heritable property to the pursuer's prejudice pending the disposal of the action.[12] "Inhibition is a preventive diligence whereby a debtor is prohibited from burdening, alienating directly or indirectly, or otherwise affecting, his lands or other heritable property to the prejudice of the creditor inhibiting."[13] Like arrestment, inhibition may be used both on the dependence of an action and in execution of the decree, and, in order to transfer the property to the pursuer, must be followed by a further process: in the case of inhibition, by an action of adjudication in the Court of Session.[14] At common law, inhibition on the dependence is competent in the actions in which arrestment on the dependence is competent[15]—where the writ contains a pecuniary crave other than one for expenses[16] and, if the action is for the enforcement of a future or contingent debt, where its use is justified by special circumstances.[17] It may also be used where the crave of the initial writ is one which can be secured by inhibition, for example implement of an obligation in respect of heritage.[18] By statute, in an

---

[1] See Graham Stewart, pp. 773–776; *Stair Encyclopaedia*, Vol. 1, para. 124; Walker, *Delict*, pp. 863–864.

[2] See para. 11.30.

[3] Bell, *Prin.*, s. 553(4).

[4] *Azcarate v. Iturrizaga*, 1938 S.C. 573 at 579.

[5] *Wilson v. Mackie* (1875) 3 R. 18, *per* L.P. Inglis at 19.

[6] *ibid.*

[7] *Wilson, supra*; *Kennedy v. Fort William Police Commissioners* (1877) 5 R. 302, *per* Lord Ormidale at 305.

[8] *Borjesson v. Carlberg* (1878) 5 R. (H.L.) 215.

[9] *MacKillop v. Mactaggart*, 1939 S.L.T. 65.

[10] *Wolthekker v. Northern Agricultural Co.* (1862) 1 M. 211.

[11] See Graham Stewart, Chaps 26, 27; G. L. Gretton, *The Law of Inhibition and Adjudication* (2nd ed., 1996).

[12] Inhibition on the dependence may also be available to a defender who has stated a counterclaim or has duly served a third-party notice: *c.f.* OCR, rr. 19.2(1), 20.3(1); RCS, rr. 25.2(1), 26.3(1).

[13] Graham Stewart, p. 526.

[14] The McKechnie Report recommended a simplified procedure whereby a separate action of adjudication would be unnecessary (paras 182–185, rec. 59 and App. 6). The recommendation has not been implemented.

[15] *Wilson v. Wilson*, 1981 S.L.T. 101. See para. 11.11.

[16] *Weir v. Otto* (1870) 8 M. 1070; *Burns v. Burns* (1879) 7 R. 355.

[17] *Symington v. Symington* (1875) 3 R. 205; *Burns, supra*; and see para. 11.11.

[18] *Bristow v. Menzies* (1840) 2 D. 611; *Seaforth's Trs v. Macauley* (1844) 7 D. 180.

action for aliment, or in an action where a claim has been made for an order for financial provision, the Court of Session has power, on cause shown, to grant warrant for inhibition on the dependence of the action and, if it thinks fit, to limit the inhibition to any particular property.[19] It has been observed that in family actions with ancillary financial craves inhibition is a more effective and more suitable method of preserving the pursuer's prospects of securing substantial financial provisions than an interdict against the disposal of property, since an inhibition both prevents the disposal of the property and does not involve questions of contempt of court.[20]

Procedure.[21] Inhibition on the dependence of a sheriff court action proceeds upon a warrant of the Court of Session contained in letters of inhibition issued under the Signet.[22] These are obtained by the presentation in the Petition Department of the Court of Session of an application in the appropriate form[23] accompanied by the initial writ with the warrant of citation and execution of citation appended. The application is signed by the pursuer's solicitor. If everything is in order the warrant to inhibit is granted and signed and dated by the Deputy Principal Clerk of Session[24] or a clerk of session authorised by him[25] and is signeted.[26] If the Deputy Principal Clerk of Session refuses to sign and date the warrant the applicant may request that the application be placed before a Lord Ordinary, whose decision thereon is final.[27] If the application is for letters of inhibition on the dependence of an action to which a claim under section 19 of the Family Law (Scotland) Act 1985 applies, the application must be placed before a Lord Ordinary whose decision thereon is final.[28–29] **11.37**

The letters must then be served on the defender by a messenger-at-arms personally or at his dwelling-place if within Scotland,[30] or edictally if he is furth of Scotland. A notice of inhibition must be registered in the Register of Inhibitions and Adjudications setting forth the names and designations of the persons by and against whom the inhibition is raised and the date of signeting. If the letters and execution of service are also registered not later than 21 days from the date of registration of the notice, the inhibition takes effect from the date of registration of the notice: otherwise it takes effect only from the date of registration of the letters and execution of service. Without the latter registration, the **11.38**

---

19 Family Law (Scotland) Act 1985, s. 19.

20 *Wilson, supra, per* Lord Maxwell at 102–103; *Pow v. Pow*, 1987 S.L.T. 127.

21 See W. W. McBryde and N. J. Dowie, *Petition Procedure in the Court of Session* (2nd ed.), Chap. 12.

22 The McKechnie and Grant Reports recommended that the sheriff should be given the same powers as the Court of Session to grant a warrant for inhibition, such warrant to have the same effect as a Court of Session warrant or letters of inhibition (McKechnie, paras 190–191, rec. 63; Grant, para. 125, rec. 23). The recommendations have not been implemented.

23 RCS, r. 59.1(d); Form 59.1-D.

24 RCS, r. 59.1(3)(a).

25 RCS, r. 1.3(4).

26 RCS, r. 59.1(3)(b).

27 RCS, r. 59.1(4).

28–29 RCS, r. 59.1(5).

30 *Morton v. Dean Smith* (1902) 9 S.L.T. 396.

inhibition has no effect.[31] The expenses of inhibition on the dependence, like the expenses of arrestment on the dependence, cannot be recovered as part of the expenses of process, since "the using of diligence on the dependence, however necessary it may be to make a pursuer's decree effectual when obtained, has nothing to do with obtaining that decree, which is the sole object of the action."[32]

11.39 **Effect.**[33] Inhibition of itself gives the inhibitor no title to, and effects no transfer of, the subjects: its effect is to preserve the heritable property as part of the defender's estate, and therefore attachable by the pursuer in the event of his succeeding in the action. Any voluntary deed posterior to the effective date of the inhibition and affecting the defender's heritable property is voidable at the instance of the pursuer to the extent that his interests are prejudiced. The pursuer is also given the practical advantage that a purchaser of the subjects covered by the inhibition is entitled before paying the price to have the inhibition discharged by payment of the pursuer's debt.[34] The inhibition does not, however, affect deeds which the defender was under an antecedent obligation to grant,[35] or the ordinary administration of the property[36] or property acquired after the date of registration of the inhibition (unless in the case of an heir under entail or other indefeasible title).[37]

11.40 **Extinction.** If the action is abandoned[38] or settled[39] the pursuer must bear the cost of discharging the inhibition. If the defender is assoilzied, the inhibition is recalled by petition to the Outer House of the Court of Session,[40] which will grant warrant to the Keeper of the Register to have the inhibition marked as recalled. If the inhibition has not been registered, the court on granting recall may prohibit registration.[41]

11.41 **Recall.** While the action remains in dependence, the inhibition may be recalled or restricted on cause shown by the defender.[42] The procedure is

---

[31] Titles to Land Consolidation (Scotland) Act 1868, s. 155; Conveyancing (Scotland) Act 1924, s. 44 as amended; McBryde and Dowie, p. 48. On registration of an interest in land any subsisting entry in the Register of Inhibitions and Adjudications adverse to the interest is entered in the title sheet (Land Registration (Scotland) Act 1979, s. 6(1)(c)).

[32] *Symington v. Symington* (1874) 1 R. 1006, *per* L.P. Inglis at 1007–1008. The McKechnie Report recommended that it should be within the discretion of the court to award the pursuer the expenses of inhibition if he obtains a decree (even if only for expenses) or can show good reason why the inhibition was used (para. 181, rec. 58). The recommendation has not been implemented.

[33] The effect of inhibition is a subject beyond the scope of this book: see G. L. Gretton, *The Law of Inhihition and Adjudication* (2nd ed., 1996); Graham Stewart, Chap. 27; *Stair Encyclopaedia*, Vol. 8, paras 159–171; Gloag and Henderson, para. 53.24; Wilson, *Debt*, p. 237; G. L. Gretton (1982) 27 J.L.S. 13, 1983 S.L.T. 145, 228; J. A. D. Hope, 1983 S.L.T. (News) 177.

[34] *Dryburgh v. Gordon* (1896) 24 R. 1.

[35] *Livingstone v. McFarlane* (1842) 5 D. 1.

[36] Bell, *Comm.*, ii, 142.

[37] Titles to Land Consolidation (Scotland) Act 1868, s. 157.

[38] *Robertson* (1896) 4 S.L.T. 114.

[39] *Robertson v. Park, Dobson & Co.* (1896) 24 R. 30; *Milne v. Birrell* (1902) 4 F. 879.

[40] RCS, r. 14.2(g).

[41] *Russell v. Johnston* (1827) 6 S. 255; *Dove v. Henderson* (1865) 3 M. 339.

[42] It may be that in special circumstances capable of instant verification the Court of Session would be prepared to interdict the threatened use of inhibition on the dependence, so making it unnecessary for the defender to wait until it is used and then apply for recall: *Beattie & Son v. Pratt* (1880) 7 R. 1171.

by petition to the Outer House.[43] Among good grounds of recall are: that the procedure has been defective or irregular[44]; that the pursuer's averments in justification of the use of inhibition are lacking in specification[45]; that, in the case of a future or contingent debt, there are no special circumstances to justify the inhibition[46]; that the inhibition is nimious or oppressive[47]; and that the creditor already has sufficient security for his debt.[48] The court may grant recall either unconditionally or on condition that the defender makes consignation or finds caution, or may restrict the inhibition to particular subjects.[49] The interlocutor grants authority for a certified copy of it to be recorded in the Register of Inhibitions and Adjudications. In practice the defender frequently makes consignation of, or offers sufficient caution for, the debt, and the inhibition is recalled. The expenses of recall are in the discretion of the court. If the inhibition has been recalled as nimious or oppressive the petitioner for recall will be entitled to his expenses[50]; but if the inhibition was warranted and is only recalled on caution, the expenses will fall on the petitioner.[51]

Prescription. An inhibition prescribes on the lapse of five years from the date on which it takes effect.[52] 11.42

(3) Consignation; caution

In certain circumstances the pursuer may obtain the security of an order of the court requiring the defender to find caution for the sum sued for, or to consign in the hands of the sheriff clerk[53] the whole or part of the sum sued for[54] to await the result of the action. Such orders may be made in circumstances which do not warrant the granting of an interim decree.[55] Exceptionally a form of security other than caution or consignation may be ordered by the sheriff.[56] 11.43

When competent to order. Consignation is a matter within the discretion of the court, but it will not be ordered unless it is clear that a sum will be ultimately due by the defender[57]: as where the debt sued for is admitted or clearly shown to be due, but the defender claims deductions which are disputed[58] or disputes the pursuer's title to sue.[59] It must also be clear that there is no legal obstacle to the defender's complying with the order.[60] 11.44

---

43 RCS, r. 14.2(g).

44 Graham Stewart, pp. 541–546.

45 *Beton v. Beton*, 1961 S.L.T. (Notes) 19.

46 *Dove v. Henderson* (1865) 3 M. 339; *Stevens v. Campbell* (1873) 11 M. 772.

47 *Mackintosh v. Miller* (1864) 2 M. 452.

48 *Hamilton v. Bruce's Tr.* (1857) 19 D. 745.

49 *McInally v. Kildonan Homes Ltd*, 1979 S.L.T. (Notes) 89.

50 *Hamilton, Mackintosh, supra.*

51 Maclaren, *Expenses*, p. 117; Graham Stewart, p. 573.

52 Conveyancing (Scotland) Act 1924, s. 44(3)(a) as amended. As to the effective date, see para. 11.38.

53 OCR, r. 27.4(1)(b).

54 It is also competent to order consignation of a corporeal moveable, such as a picture or a statue (*Mackenzie v. Balerno Paper Mill Co.* (1883) 10 R. 1147 at p. 1153), which is usually placed in a public store.

55 As to interim decrees, see paras 11.81 to 11.85.

56 OCR, r. 27.4(2).

57 *Donaldson v. Findlay, Bannatyne & Co.* (1846) 5 Bell's App. 105; *George Cohen, Sons & Co. v. Jamieson & Paterson*, 1963 S.C. 289.

58 *Cumming v. Williamson* (1842) 4 D. 1304.

59 *Rolfe v. Drummond* (1862) 1 M. 39.

60 *Cowan v. Liquidators of Western Bank* (1860) 22 D. 1260.

11.45 Consignation or caution may be ordered by virtue of the following provisions. Where an objection to a deed or writing founded on by any party in a cause is stated and maintained by way of exception, and an action of reduction would be competent, the sheriff may order the objector to find caution, or to make consignation as he shall direct.[61] Where a buyer of goods has availed himself of his alternative remedy under section 11(5) of the Sale of Goods Act 1979 by electing to retain goods which he might have rejected and to claim damages only, he may, in an action by the seller for the price, be required in the discretion of the court to consign the price or part thereof, or to give other reasonable security for its due payment.[62] The Bills of Exchange Act 1882 preserves the law and practice whereby, when a party proceeds by summary diligence, the debtor may be required, as a condition of obtaining a sist of diligence, or suspension of a charge, or threatened charge, to make such consignation, or to find such caution, as the court may require.[63] Consignation may be required in various actions necessitating special procedure,[64] as explained elsewhere in this book. The requirement of caution in the recall of arrestments[65] and in various special actions is also discussed elsewhere.

11.46 **Interlocutor.** The defender may be required to make consignation by an interlocutor pronounced by the sheriff after considering a motion by the pursuer.[66] An interlocutor ordaining consignation is a decree *ad factum praestandum*. As such it is enforceable by imprisonment,[67] and appealable to the sheriff principal without leave.[68] It should state the time within which consignation is to be made.[69] It may appoint consignation *simpliciter*, with no alternative to failure to obtemper it, in which case it will be enforceable by imprisonment[70]; or it may certify particular consequences of failure, as that the defender will be held as confessed to the extent of the sum specified,[71] or that decree will be pronounced in terms of the crave of the initial writ.[72]

11.47 **Voluntary consignation.** The defender may make consignation voluntarily if he considers it to be in his interests to do so, as where he states an objection *ope exceptionis* in terms of OCR, r. 21.3,[73] or where in answer to a claim for payment he pleads overcharge and attests his willingness to pay

---

[61] OCR, r. 21.3(2), on which see para. 12.72; *Winter v. Kerr* (1895) 12 Sh.Ct.Rep. 77.

[62] Sale of Goods Act 1979, s. 58; *Lee & Brown v. Menzies* (1896) 12 Sh.Ct.Rep. 273; *Motor Plants Ltd v. D. Stewart & Co.*, 1909 1 S.L.T. 478; *Gorrie & Son v. Northern Laundry Co. Edinburgh Ltd* (1910) 27 Sh.Ct.Rep. 66; *Gunn, Collie & Topping v. Purdie*, 1946 S.L.T. (Sh. Ct.) 11; *Porter Spiers (Leicester) Ltd v. Cameron* [1950] C.L.Y. 5329; *George Cohen, Sons & Co. v. Jamieson & Paterson*, 1963 S.C. 289; *Frimokar (U.K.) Ltd v. Mobile Technical Plant (International) Ltd*, 1990 S.L.T. 180.

[63] Bills of Exchange Act 1882, s. 100.

[64] In actions of accounting (para. 21.09), multiplepoinding (paras 21.66, 21.67) and sequestration for rent (para. 23.20).

[65] See paras 11.28 to 11.33.

[66] Example: "The pursuer moves the Court to ordain the defender within such time as the Court may appoint to consign in the hands of the Clerk of Court the sum of £xxx admittedly due by him." (See Dobie, *Styles*, p. 331.) Modern practice would probably prefer the words "sheriff clerk" rather than "clerk of court".

[67] *Mackenzie v. Balerno Paper Mill Co.* (1883) 10 R. 1147.

[68] 1907 Act, s. 27(b); *Menzies v. Templeton* (1895) 12 Sh.Ct.Rep. 323 at 324; *Dallas v. J. & F. Anderson*, 1977 S.L.T. (Sh. Ct.) 88 at 89.

[69] *McLintock v. Prinzen & Van Glabbeek* (1902) 4 F. 948.

[70] *Mackenzie, supra*, at 1148.

[71] *Cf. Strachan v. Steuart* (1870) 9 M. 116.

[72] *Gorrie & Son v. Northern Laundry Co. Edinburgh Ltd* (1910) 27 Sh.Ct.Rep. 66.

[73] *Brodie & Hall Ltd v. Di Placido* (1938) 55 Sh.Ct.Rep. 82.

the sum he thinks reasonable by consignation of it. If eventually the question of expenses is raised, the defender's position may be strengthened by consignation.[74] It is, however, incompetent to make consignation before an action is raised.[75]

Effect of consignation. The interlocutor is not an order "for payment of a sum of money on account of a debt, but it is an order to lodge the money in court until it is seen if any debt is due."[76] **11.48**

> "The sheriff clerk becomes custodier or trustee for the party in whose favour the process may ultimately be decided. If the defender succeeds, he will get it back, if he fails, the other party will be entitled to it. It is in fact conditional payment—the condition being that the creditor who has brought the action will succeed in making the claim good, to meet which the consignation has been made . . . [T]here is no difference between consignation judicially ordered and consignation arranged by the parties, for in either case the money, through the medium of the clerk of court, is placed *in manibus curiae*."[77]

The consigned money is thus specifically appropriated to the purposes of the action, and is subject to the orders of the court as to its disposal. The interest of a party in the consigned money may, however, be arrested by his creditors in the hands of the sheriff clerk,[78] unless in special circumstances the creditor is personally barred from using arrestment.[79]

Custody of consigned money. The sheriff clerk is responsible for the safe custody of all consignations made with him.[80] He must enter their full particulars in a consignation register which may be inspected by interested parties, and he must within 10 days after consignation lodge on deposit receipt all consignations amounting to not less than £5.[81] These and further detailed provisions as to consignations are made by the Sheriff Courts Consignations (Scotland) Act 1893, as amended. **11.49**

Judgment. If the pursuer is successful in the action, the decree should in general decern against the defender in the usual form, and grant warrant to the clerk of court to pay the consigned money to the pursuer in *pro tanto* extinction of the sums found due by the defender. But if, of consent of parties or under order of court, the sum consigned falls to be held as the sum in dispute, or as a surrogatum for the sum or subject in dispute, there need then be no decerniture on the merits against the defender, but only a warrant granted to the clerk of court to pay over the consigned money to the pursuer.[82] **11.50**

No decree, warrant or order for payment to any person may be granted in a case in which money has been consigned into court until there has been lodged with the sheriff clerk a certificate by an authorised officer of **11.51**

---

[74] Lees, *Pleading*, p. 144.
[75] *Alexander v. Campbell's Trs* (1903) 5 F. 634; *AB & Co. v. CD* (1908) 25 Sh.Ct.Rep. 106.
[76] *Mackenzie v. Balerno Paper Mill Co.* (1883) 10 R. 1147, *per* L.P. Inglis at 1151; see also L.J.-C. Moncrieff at 1153.
[77] *Littlejohn v. Reynolds* (1890) 6 Sh.Ct.Rep. 321 at 326.
[78] *Pollock v. Scott* (1844) 6 D. 1297.
[79] See Graham Stewart, pp. 89–91.
[80] Sheriff Courts Consignations (Scotland) Act 1893, s. 5.
[81] *ibid.* s. 4.
[82] Lees, *Interlocutors*, pp. 23, 61–62.

the Inland Revenue stating that all taxes or duties payable to the Commissioners of Inland Revenue have been paid or satisfied.[83]

Caution for expenses

(1) General[84]

11.52 Whether a party to an action should or should not find caution or security for the expenses that may be awarded against him is a matter entirely within the discretion of the court.[85] The court will not make such an order unless the interests of justice appear to require it.[86] The court may in its discretion ordain either the pursuer or the defender to find caution,[87] but in practice an order is made only in cases where the party against whom it is asked is an undischarged bankrupt or is a nominal pursuer, or where special circumstances exist. In addition, the court has statutory power to order a pursuer limited company to find caution. These cases are considered in the following paragraphs.

11.53 Poverty alone is not a sufficient ground for ordering caution for expenses, since such an order "would be nothing short of shutting the doors of the court upon" the poor litigant.[88] "It would clearly be wrong that a litigant with a statable case should in effect be excluded from the court by an order for caution with which he could not comply, unless in exceptional circumstances."[89] Provisional insolvency,[90] and absolute insolvency in the the sense of an excess of liabilities over assets, appear never to have been held sufficient to justify an order for caution[91]; and a discharged bankrupt may sue without finding caution.[92] Apart from the case of an undischarged bankrupt, the court will order caution only in exceptional circumstances.[93] On the other hand, if the litigant does not have a statable case and is unable to meet an award of expenses, it would be unfair to oblige his opponent to continue the litigation without any prospect of recovering expenses in the event of success.[94] There is no fixed rule that a party in receipt of legal aid should not be called on to find caution except in special circumstances.[95] A defender is not

---

83 OCR, r. 30.2(1). See para. 17.31.

84 Maclaren, *Expenses*, Chap. 5.

85 *Stevenson v. Midlothian D.C.*, 1983 S.C.(H.L.) 50.

86 *Thom v. Andrew* (1888) 15 R. 780, *per* Lord Young at 782; *Cooney v. Kirkpatrick*, 1989 S.L.T. 457.

87 *ibid.*

88 *Walker v. Kelty's Tr.* (1839) 1 D. 1066, *per* L.P. Hope at 1070; *Jenkins v. Robertson* (1869) 7 M. 739, *per* Lord Kinloch at 747; *Weir v. Buchanan* (1876) 4 R. 8; *Ritchie v. McIntosh* (1881) 8 R. 747, *per* Lord Young at 748; *Macdonald v. Simpsons* (1882) 9 R. 696, *per* Lord Young at 697, Lord Craighill at 698; *Cooper v. Frame & Co.* (1893) 20 R. 920, *per* Lord McLaren at 922, Lord Adam at 923; *Will v. Sneddon, Campbell & Munro*, 1931 S.C. 164, *per* L.J.-C. Alness at 168.

89 *Stevenson v. Midlothian D.C.*, 1983 S.C.(H.L.) 50, *per* Lord Fraser of Tullybelton at 58.

90 *Weir v. Buchanan* (1876) 4 R. 8.

91 *Hegard v. Hegard*, 1981 S.L.T. (Notes) 45.

92 *Cooper, supra*; *Cunningham v. Skinner* (1902) 4 F. 1124.

93 *Arch Joinery Contracts v. Arcade Building Services*, 1992 S.L.T. 755.

94 *Rush v. Fife R.C.*, 1985 S.L.T. 451.

95 *Stevenson, supra*, where a legally-aided pursuer was ordained to find caution. Orders for security for costs have been made against assisted persons by the English courts, *e.g. Friedmann v. Austay (London) Ltd* [1954] 1 W.L.R. 466; *Wyld v. Silver* [1962] 1 W.L.R. 863; *Caldwell v. Sumpters* [1972] Ch. 478. The Court of Session has not exercised the power conferred on it by the Legal Aid (Scotland) Act 1986, s. 38(1)(a) (formerly the Legal Aid (Scotland) Act 1967, s. 16(1)(b)(ii)) to make provision by Act of Sederunt as to the cases in which and the extent to which a person receiving legal aid may be required to find caution and the manner in which caution in such cases may be found.

ordinarily required to find caution,[96] since he is exercising his right to defend himself.

(2) *Bankruptcy*[97]

Pursuer. As a general rule, if the pursuer is bankrupt or becomes bankrupt in the course of the action, whether under sequestration or by a trust deed, the court will ordain him to find caution for the defender's expenses in the event of the action being unsuccessful.[98] The ratio of the rule is that a bankrupt who is legally divested of his estate is usually seeking to recover for himself something which properly belongs to his estate which has been sequestrated.[99] Numerous cases have been treated as exceptions to the general rule, and the citation of such cases which do not lay down general principles is unlikely to be helpful except in a case where the circumstances are identical.[1] Caution is usually required in actions of defamation,[2] but not in certain actions where the pursuer has, notwithstanding the bankruptcy, a substantial interest in the result,[3] or where he is only nominally the pursuer and in substance the defender.[4] In cases where the pursuer was made bankrupt by the defender, directly or indirectly, practice has varied according to circumstances.[5] As a general rule, a bankrupt applying to the court for his discharge will not be ordained to find caution for the expenses of the application.[6] A discharged **11.54**

---

96 *Johnston v. Wallace* (1954) 71 Sh.Ct.Rep. 80; *cf. Robertson v. McCaw*, 1911 S.C. 650.

97 See Goudy, *Bankruptcy*, pp. 20, 365–367.

98 *Ritchie v. McIntosh* (1881) 8 R. 747; *Clarke v. Muller* (1884) 11 R. 418; *Munro v. Mudie* (1901) 9 S.L.T. 53; *Neil v. South-East Lancashire Insurance Co.*, 1930 S.C. 629.

99 *Ritchie, supra. Cf. Cooper v. Frame & Co.* (1893) 20 R. 920, *per* Lord McLaren at 922; *Stevenson v. Midlothian D.C.*, 1983 S.C.(H.L.) 50, *per* Lord Fraser of Tullybelton at 58.

1 *Neil, supra, per* L.J.-C. Alness at 632.

2 Required: *Clarke, supra*; *Collier v. Ritchie & Co.* (1884) 12 R. 47; *Scott v. Roy* (1886) 13 R. 1173; *Watson v. Williamson* (1895) 3 S.L.T. 21; *Brown v. Oliver & Co.* (1895) 3 S.L.T. 43; *Powell v. Long* (1896) 23 R. 955; *Munro v. Mudie* (1901) 9 S.L.T. 53; *Cook v. Kinghorn* (1904) 12 S.L.T. 186; *Miller v. J. M. Smith Ltd* (1908) 16 S.L.T. 268; *Johnston v. Laird & Son*, 1915 2 S.L.T. 24; *Hill v. Sneddon, Campbell & Munro*, 1931 S.C. 164. Not required: *Scott v. Johnston* (1885) 12 R. 1022; *Briggs v. Amalgamated Press Ltd*, 1910 2 S.L.T. 298; *Paterson v. Wright* (1937) 53 Sh.Ct.Rep. 108 (no trustee appointed).

3 Required: *Buchanan v. Peyton* (1897) 4 S.L.T. 324 (claim for share of profits of invention); *Gilmour v. Donnelly* (1899) 7 S.L.T. 267 (reduction of decree of cessio); *Dunsmore's Tr. v. Stewart* (1891) 19 R. 4 (appeal against rejection of claim in sequestration of another bankrupt); *Douglas v. McKinlay* (1902) 5 F. 260 (bankrupt suing as consenting curator); *Birnie v. McBain*, 1914 1 S.L.T. 359 (bankrupt suing as executor with no executry funds); *Stevenson v. Midlothian D.C.*, 1983 S.C. (H.L.) 50 (bankrupt not suing for benefit of estate, but no arguable case and evidence of impecuniosity and unreasonable behaviour). Not required: *McAlister v. Swinburne* (1873) 1 R. 166 (declarator that discharge granted before sequestration); *Burnett v. Murray* (1877) 14 S.L.R. 616 (claim in respect of business carried on after sequestration: see also *Kennedy v. Crawford* (1899) 7 S.L.T. 26; *McCall v. Gattens* (1905) 13 S.L.T. 149; *Dingley v. Black* (1934) 51 Sh.Ct.Rep. 171); *Ritchie v. McIntosh* (1881) 8 R. 747 (accounting against trustee); *Rogerson v. Rogerson's Tr.* (1885) 22 S.L.R. 673 (reduction of voluntary assignation to trustee); *Thom v. Andrew* (1888) 15 R. 780 (damages for breaking into premises and removing contents: see also *McQuator v. Wellwood* (1908) 16 S.L.T. 110); *Derrick v. Derrick* (1900) 8 S.L.T. 321 (damages for adultery); *Paton v. Paton's Trs* (1901) 8 S.L.T. 455 (claim against father's estate after trustee divested of interest); *Thom v. Caledonian Ry* (1902) 9 S.L.T. 440 (claim for damages admitted except *quoad* amount); *McCall v. Gattens* (1905) 13 S.L.T. 149 (claim for wages under agreement made after sequestration); *Cooney v. Kirkpatrick*, 1989 S.L.T. 457 (action of lawburrows by undischarged bankrupt).

4 *Stephen v. Skinner* (1860) 22 D. 1122 (suspension of charge on decree).

5 *Fraser v. McMurrich*, 1924 S.C. 93; *Rennie v. Campbell Bros*, 1929 S.L.T. 27; *Gallagher v. Edinburgh Corporation*, 1929 S.L.T. 356; *Neil v. South-East Lancashire Insurance Co.*, 1930 S.C. 629.

6 *Melrose-Drover Ltd v. Heddle* (1905) 7 F. 852; *Scott v. Scott's Tr.*, 1914 S.C. 704.

bankrupt can sue, without finding caution, for sums which his trustee failed to recover.[7]

11.55 **Defender.** As a general rule a bankrupt defender, being bound to defend himself having been brought into court by the pursuer, is not ordered to find caution[8]; and he may proceed with an appeal, as appellant or respondent, without caution.[9] Caution may, however, be required where he is virtually the pursuer in the action[10]; or where he has apparently no material interest to defend[11]; or where he has voluntarily divested himself of his estate after the raising of the action[12]; or pèrhaps where the defence appears to be of doubtful merit.[13]

(3) Nominal pursuer

11.56 Where the pursuer is not *dominus litis*, the plea of *dominus litis* may be given effect to either by requiring the pretended pursuer to find caution for expenses before proceeding with the action or, more usually, by making the *dominus litis* liable for the expenses after the conclusion of the action.[14] Caution may be required if there is reason to believe that the nominal pursuer will be unable to satisfy a decree for expenses and is "manifestly a mere catspaw"[15] put forward by a wealthier *dominus litis* in order that the latter may avoid liability for expenses[16]; or, probably, if for the same purpose the nominal pursuer has assigned his whole right in the subject of the action to a third party who is the true *dominus litis*.[17] But a pursuer who is the genuine representative of an association or committee will not be required to find caution.[18]

(4) Limited company[19]

11.57 While a pursuer who is a natural person will not be required to find caution solely on the ground of poverty, there is no such general rule in the case of a pursuer which is a limited company, in view of the ability of individuals to carry on operations for their benefit behind the shield of limited liability.[20] Section 726 of the Companies Act 1985 subjects limited

---

[7] *Cooper v. Frame & Co.* (1893) 20 R. 920.

[8] *Taylor v. Fairlie's Trs* (1833) 6 W. & S. 301; *Stephen v. Skinner* (1860) 22 D. 1122; *Lawrie v. Pearson* (1888) 16 R. 62; *Crichton Bros v. Crichton* (1902) 5 F. 178; *Drew v. Robertson* (1903) 11 S.L.T.

[9] *Ferguson v. Leslie* (1873) 11 S.L.R. 16; *Buchanan v. Stevenson* (1880) 8 R. 220; *Johnstone v. Henderson* (1906) 8 F. 689; *Mackay v. Boswall-Preston*, 1916 S.C. 96.

[10] *Ferguson Lamont & Co.'s Tr. v. Lamont* (1889) 17 R. 282; *Robb v. Dickson* (1901) 9 S.L.T. 224; *Professional and Civil Service Supply Association Ltd v. Lawson*, 1913 2 S.L.T. 55; *Govers & Co. v. Findlay & Wallace*, 1923 S.L.T.(Sh. Ct.) 127.

[11] *Smith's Trs v. McCheyne* (1879) 16 S.L.R. 592; *Finklestone v. Smellie* (1916) 32 Sh.Ct.Rep. 244; *Macrae's Tr. v. Macrae* (1945) 62 Sh.Ct.Rep. 48.

[12] *Stevenson v. Lee* (1886) 13 R. 913; *Macnaughtan v. Thurman* (1907) 24 Sh.Ct.Rep. 80; *Swan & Sons Ltd v. Speirs* (1925) 41 Sh.Ct.Rep. 218.

[13] *Finklestone, Macrae's Tr., supra.*

[14] *Hepburn v. Tait* (1874) 1 R. 875, *per* L.J.-C. Moncreiff at 877.

[15] *Porteous v. Pearl Life Assurance Co.* (1901) 8 S.L.T. 430.

[16] *Jenkins v. Robertson* (1869) 7 M. 739; *Robertson v. Duke of Atholl* (1905) 8 F. 150.

[17] *Walker v. Kelty's Tr.* (1839) 1 D. 1066, affd (1843) 2 Bell's App. 57, suggests that this may be so. *Cf. McCuaig v. McCuaig*, 1909 S.C. 355.

[18] *Potter v. Hamilton* (1870) 8 M. 1064.

[19] Halsbury, Vol. 7, para. 779, Vol. 37, para. 301; *Stair Encyclopaedia*, Vol. 4, para. 1002.

[20] *Hegard v. Hegard*, 1981 S.L.T. (Notes) 45.

companies who are pursuers or plaintiffs[21] to the liability to find security, and thus affords "some protection for the community against litigious abuses by artificial persons manipulated by natural persons".[22] Section 726(2) provides that where in Scotland a limited company is pursuer in an action or other legal proceeding, the court having jurisdiction in the matter may, if it appears by credible testimony that there is reason to believe that the company will be unable to pay the defender's expenses if successful in his defence, order the company to find caution and sist the proceedings until caution is found.

A company required to find caution must be truly, as well as nominally, *in petitorio*.[23] A company which appeals as unsuccessful defender[24] or opposes an appeal as successful pursuer[25] is not a pursuer in the sense of the section. The "credible testimony" which is required in support of a motion for caution may include copies of the company's balance sheets[26] and other documents relating to the company lodged with the Registrar of Companies.[27] That no accounts or annual returns appear to have been lodged, or that the company appears to have no assets or to have ceased to trade or never to have traded, are matters which the court may consider in the absence of a satisfactory explanation by the company's advocate.[28] Credible testimony may also be found in facts alleged on record or at the bar by one party and not disputed or satisfactorily explained by the other[29]; but a bare assertion by an advocate is probably not "testimony".[30] Where the company is in liquidation the liquidator is a party to the proceedings and may be found liable in expenses, but is entitled to relief out of the company's assets, if there are any.[31] Where no suggestion is made against the solvency of the liquidator, the court will not order the company to find caution.[32] **11.58**

Even where the court is satisfied upon credible testimony that there is reason to believe that the company will be unable to pay the defender's expenses, the court still has a discretion whether or not to order caution.[33] **11.59**

---

[21] s. 726 of the Companies Act 1985 does not apply in relation to companies registered or incorporated in Northern Ireland or outside Great Britain: s. 745(1). It would appear that such companies may be ordered to find caution at common law: see para. 11.52; *cf. DSQ Property Co. Ltd v. Lotus Cars Ltd* [1987] 1 W.L.R. 127.

[22] *Pearson v. Naydler* [1977] 1 W.L.R. 899, *per* Megarry V.-C. at 904, 905; *R. v. Westminster City Council, ex p. Residents' Association of Mayfair* [1991] C.O.D. 182. The amount ordered must be sufficient in the circumstances of the case to be just as between the parties: *Roburn Construction v. William Irvine (South) & Co.* [1991] B.C.C. 726.

[23] *English's Coasting and Shipping Co. Ltd v. British Finance Co. Ltd* (1886) 13 R. 430 (company pursuing action of reduction of certain steps of diligence held truly defenders).

[24] *Sinclair v. Glasgow and London Contract Corporation Ltd* (1904) 6 F. 818.

[25] *Star Fire and Burglary Insurance Co. Ltd v. Davidson & Sons Ltd* (1902) 4 F. 997.

[26] *Edinburgh Entertainments Ltd v. Stevenson*, 1925 S.C. 848.

[27] *Dean Warwick Ltd*, 1981 S.L.T. (Notes) 18.

[28] *ibid.*

[29] *New Mining and Exploring Syndicate Ltd v. Chalmers & Hunter*, 1909 S.C. 1390; *Dean Warwick Ltd, supra.*

[30] *Edinburgh Modern Quarry Co. Ltd v. Eagle Star Insurance Co. Ltd*, 1965 S.L.T. (Notes) 91.

[31] *Kilmarnock Theatre Co. v. Buchanan*, 1911 S.C. 607.

[32] *Motor Plants Ltd v. D. Stewart & Co. Ltd*, 1909 1 S.L.T. 478; *Stewart v. Steen*, 1987 S.L.T. (Sh. Ct.) 60; *Arch Joinery Contracts v. Arcade Building Services*, 1992 S.L.T. 755.

[33] *Brownrigg Coal Co. Ltd v. Sneddon*, 1911 S.C. 1064, *per* Lord Salvesen at 1068, Lord Mackenzie at 1069; *Sir Lindsay Parkinson & Co. Ltd v. Triplan Ltd* [1973] Q.B. 609; *Roburn Construction v. William Irvine (South) & Co.* [1991] B.C.C. 726.

Different views have been expressed as to whether the discretion may be exercised having regard to all the circumstances of the case,[34] or must be exercised unless there are special circumstances which justify refusing an order.[35] Matters which, upon the former view at least, the court may take into account include: whether the company's claim is made in good faith[36]; whether it has reasonable prospects of success; whether there is an admission by the defender in the pleadings or otherwise that money is due; whether the company's want of means has been brought about by any conduct by the defender, such as delay in payment or in doing his part of the work; whether the motion is being used oppressively, for example so as to stifle a genuine claim; and whether the motion is made at a late stage of the proceedings.[37]

11.60 As to the amount of the caution, in England it is recommended that the security for costs ordered should be for the probable amount of costs taking into account the chance of the case collapsing, but the amount is in the discretion of the court.[38] It must be just as between the parties.[39] A company may be ordered to find additional caution in the course of an action.[40]

11.61 An interlocutor ordering caution would appear to be appealable only with leave of the sheriff.[41] However, if leave to appeal is refused by the sheriff and the party then fails to find caution with the result that decree is then pronounced against him, an appeal against that decree (which, as the decree is a final judgment, may be taken without leave[42]) may bring under review the interlocutor ordaining the party to find caution in respect of which leave to appeal was refused.[43] The appellate court will not reverse the sheriff's judgment unless satisfied that he has plainly erred.[44]

11.62 While section 726(2) empowers the court to "sist the proeeedings until caution is found", there appears to be no reason why the court, in addition to sisting process while an order for caution is running, should not dismiss the action or grant absolvitor upon failure of the company to comply with the order.[45] It is within the court's discretion whether to sist the action. It is open to the court to impose a time-limit for the finding of

---

[34] *Sir Lindsay Parkinson & Co. Ltd, supra, per* Lord Denning M.R. at 626, Lawton L.J. at 628–629; *Roburn Construction, supra.*

[35] *Kruger Stores (Pty) Ltd v. Kopman* (1957) 1 S.A.L.R. 645 at 648; *Peppard & Co. Ltd v. Bogoff* [1962] I.R. 180, *per* Kingsmill Moore J. at 188; *Sir Lindsay Parkinson & Co. Ltd, supra, per* Cairns L.J. at 626.

[36] *Brownrigg Coal Co. Ltd v. Sneddon, supra; Sir Lindsay Parkinson & Co. Ltd, supra, per* Lord Denning M.R. at 626.

[37] *Sir Lindsay Parkinson & Co. Ltd, supra, per* Lord Denning M.R. at 626.

[38] Halsbury, Vol. 37, para. 307; *Pearson v. Naydler* [1977] 1 W.L.R. 899, *per* Megarry V.-C. at 907; *Bacal Contracting Ltd v. Modern Engineering (Bristol) Ltd* [1980] 2 All E.R. 655.

[39] *Roburn Construction, supra.*

[40] *Merrick Homes Ltd v. Duff,* 1996 S.L.T. 932.

[41] See *Jack v. Carmichael* (1894) 10 Sh.Ct.Rep. 242; *Govers & Co. v. Findlay & Wallace,* 1923 S.L.T. (Sh. Ct.) 127; *Dallas v. J. & F. Anderson,* 1977 S.L.T. (Sh. Ct.) 88.

[42] 1907 Act, ss. 27, 28.

[43] *McCue v. Scottish Daily Record and Sunday Mail Ltd,* 1998 S.C.L.R. 742.

[44] *New Mining and Exploring Syndicate Ltd v. Chalmers & Hunter,* 1909 S.C. 1390, *per* L.P. Dunedin at 1392; *Brawnrigg Coal Co. Ltd v. Sneddon,* 1911 S.C. 1064, *per* Lord Dundas at 1067.

[45] Wilton, *Company Law and Practice*, pp. 419, 420; OCR, r. 16.2(1); and see para. 11.65.

caution. If no time-limit is imposed caution must be found within a reasonable time.[46]

(5) Special circumstances

Since the court has a discretion whether or not to order caution for expenses to be given, there may be circumstances in which the court may not require caution although the case falls within one of the foregoing categories, and other circumstances in which the court may require caution although the case does not fall within any of these categories.[47] The court may require caution upon a consideration of the cumulative effect of a number of factors none of which of itself might be sufficient to justify an order.[48] It is, however, settled that poverty alone is not a sufficient ground for ordering caution[49]; and a defender is not ordinarily required to find caution.[50] The power to order caution for expenses is excluded by several international conventions.[51] **11.63**

(6) Procedure

The procedure for having a party ordained to find caution is set out in the Ordinary Cause Rules.[52] The party seeking to have his opponent ordained to find caution should lodge a motion.[53] The motion should set out the grounds on which the application is made.[54] If the grounds are special, it may be desirable to aver them on record[55] or by minute[56]; but that is unnecessary where the other party is not prejudiced by inadequate notice of the grounds.[57] Intimation of the motion to the other parties, intimation of opposition and a hearing of the motion will follow the standard rules for motion procedure.[58] If the grounds are disputed the sheriff may, without awaiting the closing of the record, allow parties a preliminary proof thereon[59] in which it is for the party seeking caution to establish the grounds.[60] While the motion may be made at any stage of the action,[61] and may be renewed,[62] it should not be delayed since it may be refused if there is a risk that the order would cause hardship to the party in **11.64**

---

[46] *Metric Modules International Ltd v. Laughton Construction Co. Ltd*, 1995 S.C.L.R. 676. See also OCR, r. 27.3 and para. 11.65.

[47] *e.g. Fraser v. Mackenzie* (1874) 12 S.L.R. 74 (sole partner of firm sequestrated and assuming new partner); *Hardie v. Brown, Barker & Bell* (1907) 15 S.L.T. 539 (suspension of *ex facie* regular decree); *Murdoch v. Young*, 1909 2 S.L.T. 450 (pursuer failing to disclose address); *Kennedy v. Hamilton Bros Oil and Gas Ltd*, 1986 S.L.T. 110 (caution ordered after proof partly heard); other cases cited in Maclaren, *Expenses*, Chap. 5.

[48] *Will v. Sneddon, Campbell & Munro*, 1931 S.C. 164.

[49] See para. 11.53.

[50] *ibid.*

[51] See *e.g.* Carriage of Goods by Road Act 1965, s. 10, Sched., art. 31(5); *Central Trading Corporation v. James Mills (Montrose) Ltd*, 1982 S.L.T. (Sh. Ct.) 30.

[52] OCR, Chap. 27.

[53] OCR, r. 27.2(1).

[54] OCR, r. 27.2(2).

[55] *Macrae v. Sutherland* (1889) 16 R. 476; *Gallagher v. Edinburgh Corporation*, 1929 S.L.T. 356.

[56] *Horn & Co. v. Tangyes Ltd* (1906) 8 F. 475; *Nakeski-Cumming v. Gordon's Judicial Factor*, 1923 S.C. 770.

[57] *Hegard v. Hegard*, 1981 S.L.T. (Notes) 45.

[58] OCR, Chap. 15. See paras 5.44 to 5.55.

[59] *Jenkins v. Robertson* (1869) 7 M. 739; *Robertson v. Duke of Atholl* (1905) 8 F. 150; *Horn & Co., supra; Dallas, supra.*

[60] *Dallas, supra.*

[61] In *Kennedy, supra*, caution was ordered after proof had been partly heard.

[62] *Thom v. Andrew* (1888) 15 R. 780, *per* Lord Young at 783.

the conduct of his case[63] or would in effect preclude him from going on with it.[64]

11.65 An interlocutor which orders a party "to find caution for expenses" is an order for caution for future expenses only.[65] The interlocutor may order caution for expenses already incurred also,[66] but only where a motion for such caution has been expressly made.[67] As to the amount of caution fixed, a litigant with a statable case should not be in effect excluded from the court by an order for caution with which he cannot comply, unless in exceptional circumstances.[68] The interlocutor should specify the period within which caution is to be found.[69] If a party fails to find caution within the specified period any other party in the case may apply by motion for what is in effect decree by default.[70] If it is the pursuer who is in default decree of absolvitor may be applied for and granted.[71] If the defaulting party is a defender or third party the other party may move for decree by default "or such other finding or order as the sheriff thinks fit".[72] A party ordered to find caution normally does so by obtaining a bond of caution.[73] The bond must be obtained from an insurance company authorised under either section 3 or section 4 of the Insurance Companies Act 1982 to carry on insurance business of a certain class,[74] and this must be stated in the bond.[75] The bond obliges the cautioner to make payment of the sums for which it is cautioner as validly and in the same manner as the party for whom it is cautioner.[76] The bond of caution must be lodged in process[77] and may not be borrowed.[78] The sheriff clerk must satisfy himself that the bond of caution is in proper form.[79] A party who is dissatisfied with the sufficiency or form of caution may apply by motion to have the party who has been ordered to find caution held in default.[80] Exceptionally the sheriff may order a form of caution other than a bond of caution.[81] An order to find caution may be renewed,[82] modified or superseded on a change of circumstances[83]; and a party may, excep-

---

[63] *Simpson v. Allan* (1894) 1 S.L.T. 590; *McCrae v. Bryson*, 1922 S.L.T. 664.

[64] *Maltman v. Tarmac Civil Engineering Ltd*, 1967 S.L.T. (Notes) 102.

[65] *Douglas v. McKinlay* (1902) 5 F. 260.

[66] *Govers & Co. v. Findlay & Wallace*, 1923 S.L.T. (Sh. Ct.) 127; *Swan & Sons Ltd v. Speirs* (1925) 41 Sh.Ct.Rep. 218.

[67] *Douglas, supra, per* Lord McLaren at 262.

[68] *Stevenson v. Midlothian D.C.*, 1983 S.C.(H.L.) 50.

[69] OCR, r. 27.3. A time-limit may be specified even where the action is sisted in terms of the Companies Act 1985, s. 726(2): *Metric Modules International Ltd v. Laughton Construction Co. Ltd*, 1995 S.C.L.R. 676. The time for finding caution may be prorogated on cause shown: OCR, r. 16.3.

[70] OCR, r. 27.9.

[71] OCR, r. 27.9(a). *Gray v. Ireland* (1884) 11 R. 1104; *Tenlon v. Seaton* (1885) 12 R. 1179; *Macdougall v. Cunningham* (1901) 9 S.L.T. 100. In *British Artificial Silk Machines Ltd v. Liquidators of Scottish Amalgamated Silks Ltd*, 1935, unreported, *cit.* Thomson and Middleton, p. 369, the action was dismissed; but see *Cunningham v. Skinner* (1902) 4 F. 1124.

[72] OCR, r. 27.9(b).

[73] OCR, r. 27.4(1)(a)

[74] OCR, r. 27.5.

[75] OCR, r. 27.6(2).

[76] OCR, r. 27.6(1)

[77] OCR, r. 27.4(3).

[78] OCR, r. 27.4(5).

[79] OCR, r. 27.7(1).

[80] OCR, r. 27.7(2).

[81] OCR, r. 27.4(2).

[82] *Gray v. Ireland* (1884) 11 R. 1104.

[83] *MacBean v. West End Clothiers Co. Ltd*, 1918 S.C. 221; *Whyte v. City of Perth Co-operative Society*, 1932 S.C. 482; *Merrick Homes v. Duff*, 1996 S.L.T. 932.

tionally, be allowed to consign a specific sum instead of finding caution where to require caution might amount to a denial of justice.[84] An interlocutor ordering caution is appealable only with leave of the sheriff,[85] and will not be recalled unless it can be shown that it is so unreasonable that no reasonable sheriff, properly directed, could or should have pronounced it.[86] If leave to appeal is refused by the sheriff and the party then fails to find caution with the result that decree is then pronounced against him, an appeal against that decree (which, as the decree is a final judgment, may be taken without leave[87]) may bring under review the interlocutor ordaining the party to find caution in respect of which leave to appeal was refused.[88]

The cautioner is liable for expenses incurred while he holds office. A new cautioner must be sisted in his place if he becomes bankrupt[89] or if he withdraws, unless his withdrawal was induced by the other party.[90] **11.66**

Sist of mandatary

(1) General rule

Where a party to any proceedings is resident outside the United Kingdom, the court may order him to sist a mandatary.[91] The object of having a mandatary sisted is twofold. The absent party's opponent in the action has an interest to obtain some assurance that any expenses in which the absentee may be found liable will be paid; and the court has an interest in having within its jurisdiction a person responsible to it for the proper conduct of the case. The court may, accordingly, order the absent party to sist a mandatary and thus to bring into the process a representative who will act in his stead as a party to the cause, and will be personally liable not only for any expenses awarded against the absent party but also for the implement of any order the court may pronounce in regulating the procedure in the action.[92] Such a judicial mandatary differs from an agent to whom a mandate is given merely to sue or defend, who is not a party to the action.[93] Nor is a judicial mandatary a cautioner for the subject-matter[94] or the expenses[95] of the suit, although in many cases the **11.67**

---

84 *Harvey v. Farquhar* (1870) 8 M. 971; *Morrison v. Morrison's Exrx*, 1912 S.C. 892. It is incorrect to order consignation whenever caution is asked for and granted: *Dallas v. J. & F. Anderson*, 1977 S.L.T. (Sh. Ct.) 88.

85 *Jack v. Carmichael* (1894) 10 Sh.Ct.Rep. 242; *Govers & Co., supra*; *Derber v. J. Smith Stewart & Co. Ltd*, 1957 S.L.T. (Sh. Ct.) 53; *Dallas, supra.*

86 *Will v. Sneddon, Campbell & Munro*, 1931 S.C. 164; *Stevenson v. Midlothian D.C.*, 1983 S.C. (H.L.) 50; *Rush v. Fife R.C.*, 1985 S.L.T. 451.

87 1907 Act, ss. 27, 28.

88 *McCue v. Scottish Daily Record and Sunday Mail*, 1998 S.C.L.R. 742.

89 *AB v. CD* (1836) 15 S. 158.

90 *Oliver v. Robertson* (1869) 8 M. 82.

91 For the origins of this practice see Ersk., III, iii, 33, n. 140 (Ivory's ed.).

92 *Renfrew and Brown v. Mags of Glasgow* (1861) 13 D. 1003, *per* L.J.-C. Inglis at 1005; *Lawson's Trs v. British Linen Co.* (1874) 1 R. 1065. Responsibility for expenses has been said to be "the main and determining consideration" (*Dessau v. Daish* (1897) 24 R. 976, *per* Lord McLaren at 980; *Bell v. Strathern & Blair*, 1953 S.L.T. (Notes) 23). The mandatary's liability for the proper conduct of the litigation "is one of no great importance, because, when a party is abroad, he is necessarily represented by a law-agent whose liability in this respect is of a more serious kind" (Dove Wilson, p. 229).

93 See paras 4.125, 4.126.

94 *Gordon v. Gordon* (1823) 2 S. 572 (N.E. 493); *Renfrew and Brown, supra.*

95 *Overbury v. Peek* (1863) 1 M. 1058, *per* Lord Deas at 1060. A party suing with a mandatary may be ordained to find caution for expenses: *Cullen v. Brown* (1860) 22 D. 1090.

substance of a motion to ordain a party to sist a mandatary may be that he should find caution for expenses.[96]

11.68 The operation of the rule depends, first, on the existence of a proper judicial proceeding to which the absentee is a party[97]; and secondly, on the party's residence outwith the United Kingdom.[98] It does not depend on his domicile or nationality[99] or on an absence which is temporary,[1] or occasional in the course of business[2] or involuntary in the course of the public service.[3] If the party returns and undertakes to remain until the conclusion of the action, the need for a mandatary may be elided.[4] The operation of the rule does not depend on the party's impecuniosity[5]; but a bankrupt who is resident outwith the United Kingdom may not be exempted from its operation on the ground of his insolvency.[6]

(2) Discretion of court

11.69 Whether a mandatary should be sisted is a question for the discretion of the court.[7] A party from whom expenses may readily be recovered may not be required to sist a mandatary. Thus a mandatary is not required where the party owns heritable property in Scotland[8] which is reasonably sufficient to meet the expenses of process and against which diligence can be effectively executed,[9] unless it is the subject of the action.[10] The ownership of moveable estate appears not to be a bar to the sisting of a

---

[96] *Simla Bank v. Home* (1870) 8 M. 781, *per* L.P. Inglis at 783.

[97] A party abroad may use diligence without a mandatary, but may be required to sist a mandatary if litigation follows: *Ewing v. Hare and Glasgow* (1823) 2 S. 534 (N.E. 467); *Lockhart v. Ferrier* (1832) 11 S. 236; *Ross v. Shaw* (1849) 11 D. 984.

[98] It has been held that pursuers resident in the Republic of Ireland need not sist mandataries (*Doohan v. NCB*, 1959 S.C. 310; *Harley v. Kinnear Moodie & Co. Ltd*, 1964 S.L.T. 64); but in view of the repeal in the Republic of the Judgments Extension Act 1868 and the Inferior Courts Judgments Extension Act 1882 by the Courts of Justice Act 1936, which was not cited in *Doohan* or *Harley*, that does not appear to be correct: see Anton with Beaumont, *Private International Law*, pp.752–753, and *Bell, supra*.

[99] *Railton v. Mathews Leonard* (1844) 6 D. 1348; *Faulks v. Whitehead* (1854) 16 D. 718; *Bruce v. Smith* (1865) 1 S.L.R. 53; *Dessau v. Daish* (1897) 24 R. 976; *Withers v. Lattimore* (1920) 37 Sh.Ct.Rep. 147.

[1] *McDonald's Trs v. Steuart* (1891) 18 R. 491.

[2] *Steel v. Steel and Buchanan* (1826) 4 S. 527 (N.E. 535).

[3] *Simla Bank v. Home* (1870) 8 M. 781; *Graham v. Graham's Trs* (1901) 4 F. 1; *Elliot v. Erikson*, 1960 S.L.T. (Sh. Ct.) 28.

[4] *Faulks, supra*; *Bracken v. Blasque* (1891) 18 R. 819; *cf. Nero v. Gunn & Cameron* (1886) 2 Sh.Ct.Rep. 342; *Dickey v. British Mexican Ry* (1893) 1 S.L.T. 273.

[5] *Dessau, supra*; *Boss v. Lyle Shipping Co.*, 1980 S.L.T. (Sh. Ct.) 65. A legally-assisted party may be ordained in appropriate circumstances to sist a mandatary: *Harley v. Kinnear Moodie & Co. Ltd*, 1964 S.L.T. 64 at 66.

[6] *Overbury v. Peek* (1863) 1 M. 1058.

[7] *Dessau, supra*; *Gordon's Trs v. Forbes* (1904) 6 F. 455; *NV Ondix International Ltd v. Landay Ltd*, 1963 S.C. 270; *Vidlocker v. McWilliam*, 1964 S.L.T. (Notes) 6. It has been observed that the court would appear to have a discretionary power of its own motion to require a mandatary to be sisted (Mackay, *Practice*, i, p. 460). In practice, however, an action raised without a mandatary proceeds without one until the opposite party objects; and it is thought that if the opposite party waives the objection the absentee party cannot ask to have the case delayed until he sists a mandatary (Dove Wilson, p. 226; Wallace, p. 219).

[8] *Smith v. Norval* (1828) 6 S. 852; *Renfrew and Brown v. Mags of Glasgow* (1861) 23 D. 1003, *per* L.J.-C. Inglis at 1005.

[9] *Fairley v. Elliot* (1839) 1 D. 399; *Caledonian and Dunbartonshire Ry v. Turner* (1849) 12 D. 406; *Vidlocker v. McWilliam*, 1964 S.L.T. (Notes) 6.

[10] *Sandilands v. Sandilands* (1848) 10 D. 1091; *Lawson's Trs v. British Linen Co.* (1874) 1 R. 1065; *Morton v. Smith* (1902) 9 S.L.T. 396.

mandatary, notwithstanding that it is accessible to diligence.[11] Again, a mandatary may not be required where the party lives in a country where any award of expenses may be readily enforced. It is submitted that just as a mandatary was not generally required in a case falling within the Judgments Extension Act 1868[12] or the Inferior Courts Judgments Extension Act 1882,[13] so also a mandatary is not essential where the litigant resides in a country to which is extended Part II of the Administration of Justice Act 1920, Part I of the Foreign Judgments (Reciprocal Enforcement) Act 1933 or Part I or Part II of the Civil Jurisdiction and Judgments Act 1982.[14]

The court is more reluctant to require a mandatary in the case of a defender than in the case of a pursuer,[15] since a defender is brought into court at the pursuer's instance, and does not have the same responsibility as a pursuer as to the conduct of the litigation.[16] A pursuer who is in the position of a defender,[17] or who sues as a consenter[18] or as a co-pursuer jointly and severally liable for expenses with solvent co-pursuers resident in the United Kingdom,[19] may not be required to sist a mandatary. A defender has not normally been ordained to sist a mandatary until after the disposal of any pleas to competency[20] or jurisdiction,[21] but the discretion of the court to require him to do so is affirmed by statute in cases where the subject of the proceedings includes a question as to the jurisdiction of the court to entertain them.[22] He may be required to sist a mandatary if he has gone abroad in the course of the action, especially where it seems possible that he may have done so to escape the consequences of the litigation.[23] A motion for the sist of a mandatary may be refused if the party appears to have a good prima facie case,[24] or where the party has a fund *in manibus curiae* sufficient to meet any claims for expenses that would be made against him,[25] or where it appears that the real object of the motion is to delay or stop the proceedings.[26] It has been said that as a general rule a claimant in a multiplepoinding who is resident **11.70**

---

[11] *Vidlocker, supra.*

[12] *Lawson's Trs, supra; Dessau, supra.*

[13] *Lawson v. Young* (1891) 7 Sh.Ct.Rep. 319; *McGildowney v. Hart* (1910) 27 Sh.Ct.Rep. 37; *Boss v. Lyle Shipping Co. Ltd*, 1980 S.L.T. (Sh. Ct) 65.

[14] Anton with Beaumont, *Private International Law*, p. 753.

[15] *Simla Bank v. Home* (1870) 8 M. 781; *D'Ernesti v. D'Ernesti* (1882) 9 R. 655; *NV Ondix International v. Landay Ltd*, 1963 S.C. 270; *Vidlocker v. McWilliam*, 1964 S.L.T. (Notes) 6.

[16] *Taylor v. Taylor*, 1919 1 S.L.T. 169.

[17] *Aitkenhead v. Bunten & Co.* (1892) 19 R. 803 (respondent in appeal); *Seaman v. Butters*, 1911 2 S.L.T. 198 (complainer in suspension); *NV Ondix International, supra.*

[18] *Gale v. Bennett* (1857) 19 D. 665.

[19] *Antermony Coal Co. v. Wingate & Co.* (1866) 4 M. 544; *Rob's Trs v. Hutton* (1866) 4 M. 546; *Armour v. Glasgow Royal Infirmary* (1908) 16 S.L.T. 435.

[20] *Clark v. Campbell* (1873) 1 R. 281.

[21] *D'Ernesti, supra; cf. Ranken v. Nolan* (1842) 4 D. 832.

[22] Civil Jurisdiction and Judgments Act 1982, s. 24(2)(a).

[23] Required: *Young v. Carter* (1907) 14 S.L.T. 411, 829; *Dampskibsselskabet Neprune v. Blasquez* (1908) 15 S.L.T. 1046; *Bank of Scotland v. Rorie* (1908) 16 S.L.T. 130; *Irvine v. Reid* (1921) 37 Sh.Ct.Rep. 108; *Holmes v. McMurrich*, 1920 S.C. 632. Not required: *Morton v. Smith* (1902) 9 S.L.T. 396; *Florence v. Smith*, 1913 S.C. 393.

[24] *Smith v. Norval* (1828) 6 S. 852; *McLean v. McGarvey* (1908) 16 S.L.T. 174; *NV Ondix Internatianal, supra; Vidlocker, supra; Harrison v. Butters*, 1968 S.L.T. (Notes) 90. The fact that a party has been granted a legal aid certificate has been held to be evidence that he has a prima facie case: *Boss v. Lyle Shipping Co.*, 1980 S.L.T. (Sh. Ct.) 65.

[25] *Buik v. Pattullo* (1855) 17 D. 568.

[26] *ibid.*

abroad will not be ordained to sist a mandatary,[27] but it is submitted that the better view is that while the court is often ready to treat such a claimant with indulgence,[28] a claimant in a liquidation,[29] sequestration,[30] multiplepoinding,[31] or other process of distribution[32] whose claim has been rejected or opposed may be in the position of a pursuer or defender according to circumstances.[33]

11.71 In an action of divorce the liability of an absent party, whether pursuer or defender, to sist a mandatary depends generally on the same grounds as in other processes.[34] The courts have not, however, made an order where there has been a serious risk that it might make it impossible for the party to pursue or defend,[35] especially where the party has been domiciled in Scotland. And the consideration of the interest of the absent party's opponent in obtaining some security for expenses, which is said to be the main and determining consideration,[36] may perhaps be met by an award of interim expenses.[37]

(3) Who may be mandatary

11.72 The mandatary must be solvent and must occupy at least the same position in life as the party for whom he is sisted: it is not a valid objection that he is unable to pay the expenses of process.[38] He must reside in the United Kingdom or, it is thought, in a country in which a decree of the court will be enforceable against him as effectually as if he resided in Scotland.[39] He must not be a party to the cause.[40] Whether any person is duly appointed to act as mandatary by the party depends on the extent of the authority given him by the party,[41] and in every case, if a mandate is required, an express mandate under the hand of the party must be produced.[42]

(4) Liability of mandatary

11.73 The mandatary is responsible to the court for the proper and decorous conduct of the cause, and is personally liable in the expenses of the cause.[43]

---

[27] *Stow's Trs v. Silvester* (1900) 8 S L.T. 253.

[28] *Gordon's Trs v. Forbes* (1904) 6 F. 455; *Elmslie v. Pauline* (1905) 7 F. 541.

[29] *Stern v. Bruce Peebles & Co. Ltd*, 1909 2 S.L.T. 297.

[30] *Ford* (1844) 6 D. 1163.

[31] *Buik, supra*; *North British Ry v. White* (1881) 9 R. 97; *Town and County Bank v. Lilienlield* (1900) 8 S.L.T. 227.

[32] *Lowson v. Lowson* (1902) 4 F. 692 (objector to accounts of judicial factor).

[33] *Stern, supra.*

[34] *D'Ernesti v. D'Ernesti* (1882) 9 R. 655, *per* L.P. Inglis at 657; *Tingman v. Tingman* (1854) 17 D. 122 (order on defender leaving country during dependence of action).

[35] *D'Ernesti, supra*; *Scott v. Scott*, 1924 S.C. 843.

[36] *Dessau v. Daish* (1893) 24 R. 976, *per* Lord McLaren at 980; *Bell v. Strathern & Blair*, 1953 S.L.T. (Notes) 23.

[37] *Low v. Low* (1905) 12 S.L.T. 817. If the interim decree is not obtempered, a mandatary may be required: *Taylor v. Taylor*, 1919 1 S.L.T. 169.

[38] *Duncan v. Duncan* (1830) 8 S. 641; *Stephenson v. Dunlop* (1841) 4 D. 248; *Railton v. Mathews* (1844) 7 D. 105; *McKinlay v. McKinlay* (1849) 11 D. 1022; *Overbury v. Peek* (1863) 1 M. 108; *Grant v. Macdonald* (1867) 4 S.L.R. 189.

[39] *Goodhall v. Mackill* (1891) 8 S.L.R. 40; *Blow v. Ecuadorian Association Ltd* (1903) 5 F. 444.

[40] *Barstow v. Smith* (1851) 13 D. 854.

[41] *Dempster v. Potts* (1836) 14 S. 521; *Knight v. Freeto* (1863) 2 M. 386.

[42] *Gunn & Co. v. Couper* (1871) 10 M. 116.

[43] *ibid.*

> "As regards the merits, he is a mere representative, but he is personally answerable for all the other conditions of the contract of litiscontestation. He is liable to implement any order the Court may pronounce in regulating the conduct of the process; he is personally liable for fines and for expenses which may be found due in the course of the process, and he is personally liable for the whole expenses of the process."[44]

He is liable conjunctly and severally with the party for whom he is sisted in the expenses found due to the opposite party, including expenses incurred prior to his being sisted if decerned for subsequent to his being sisted, and expenses incurred while he held office although decerned for subsequent to his withdrawal[45]; and he may recover from the mandant any expenses he may have disbursed on his account.[46] He is not entitled to stipulate any conditions as to the effect of his sisting himself, even where he is sisted upon the failure of a previous mandatary, but must do so simply, leaving the consequences to follow according to law,[47] unless, perhaps, his principal is an assisted person.[48] Whether a new mandatary's so sisting himself liberates the original mandatary has not been decided.[49] A mandatary may at any time put an end to his obligation by lodging a minute of withdrawal in process,[50] and thus will not be liable in expenses subsequently incurred[51]; but if he withdraws at a stage when the other party has necessarily incurred expenses in anticipation of the action proceeding, as on the morning of a proof, he may be liable for all necessary expenses incurred by the other party in consequence of his not withdrawing sooner.[52] On the death of the mandatary *pendente processu* his estate is liable for expenses up to the date of the death.[53] On the death of his principal, an order for intimation of the process to the principal's representatives should be made, and if they decline to sist themselves, the mandatary may be held liable in expenses to the date of the principal's death.[54] The fact that a party was an assisted person with a contribution to the legal aid fund assessed at nil has been held to be a ground for not requiring a mandatary[55]; but it may be that the mandatary of an assisted person should be liable only for the proper conduct of the litigation and for any expenses in which the assisted person is found liable.[56]

---

[44] *Renfrew and Brown v. Mags of Glasgow* (1861) 23 D. 1003, *per* L.J.-C. Inglis at 1005.

[45] *Lindsay v. Lindsay* (1827) 5 S. 288; *Renfrew and Brown, supra*; *Erskine v. Walker's Trs* (1883) 10 R. 717; *Barr v. British Transport Commission*, 1963 S.L.T. (Notes) 39.

[46] Mackay, *Practice*, i, p. 466.

[47] *Pease, Wrays and Trigg v. Smith and Jameson* (1822) 1 S. 452 (N.E. 420); *Robertson & Co. v. Exley, Dimsdale & Co.* (1833) 11 S. 320.

[48] *Herzberg v. Herzberg*, 1952 S.L.T. (Sh. Ct.) 65; *Harley v. Kinnear Moodie & Co. Ltd*, 1964 S.L.T. 64.

[49] Ersk. III, iii, 33, n. 140 (Ivory's ed.). In *Anderson v. Bank of Scotland* (1836) 14 S. 316, on the pursuer's sisting a new mandatary and finding caution for all past expenses the court declared the original mandatary free from all responsibility to the defenders.

[50] See para. 11.80.

[51] *Cairns v. Anstruther* (1838) 1 D. 24, affd (1841) 2 Rob. App. 29; *Marshall v. Cannon* (1848) 21 Sc.Jur. 63; *Erskine v. Walker's Trs* (1883) 10 R. 717.

[52] *Chapman v. Balfour* (1875) 2 R. 291.

[53] *Barclay and Ewart's Reps v. Barclay* (1850) 12 D. 1253.

[54] *Cairns, Marshall, Erskine, supra.*

[55] *Harley v. Kinnear Moodie & Co. Ltd*, 1964 S.L.T. 64.

[56] See *Herzberg v. Herzberg*, 1952 S.L.T (Sh. Ct.) 65, which was apparently not cited in *Harley, supra.*

11.74 So far as the merits of the case are concerned, the mandatary is a mere representative, and all the security he affords as to the merits is that the judgment on the merits shall be binding on his principal.[57] His liability to implement the orders of the court does not extend to liability for an interim award of aliment for a wife in a divorce action.[58] He cannot settle the case without special authority.[59]

(5) Procedure

11.75 If a mandatary has been appointed before the raising of the action, the action may be raised in the name of the party and his mandatary. If that is not done, it is competent for the opposing party to move that a mandatary should be sisted. He may state a plea-in-law in such terms as, "*Ante omnia* the pursuer should be ordained to sist a mandatary", and allow the pursuer an opportunity to sist a mandatary; or he may lodge a motion with or without stating such a plea. The motion may be made at any stage of the case, including the stage of appeal.[60] It may be for an order ordaining the opposite party to sist a mandatary, or for an order ordaining him to do so by a specified date. The latter form of motion is to be preferred, because an interlocutor simply ordaining a party to sist a mandatary is a preliminary order which may be recalled and is unenforceable without supplementary procedure.[61]

11.76 An order to sist a mandatary has been obviated by the party's undertaking to remain in Scotland either permanently or until the action was disposed of[62]; by his consigning of a sum sufficient to cover the opposite party's expenses[63]; and in special circumstances by the party's appearing personally in court[64] or finding caution to attend all diets of court[65]; but not by his undertaking to attend all diets of court and to obey all orders of court at his solicitor's office[66]; or by consigning the sum sued for.[67] If the motion is refused, the refusal is *in hoc statu* and the motion may be renewed on a change of circumstances.[68]

11.77 If the motion is granted, a reasonable time should be,[69] and additional time may be,[70] allowed and the process may or may not be sisted, according to circumstances, until the order is obeyed.[71] Within the time allowed the mandatary must lodge a minute of sist in his own name craving leave to

---

57 *Renfrew and Brown v. Mags of Glasgow* (1861) 23 D. 1003, *per* L.J.-C. Inglis at 1005.
58 *Webster v. Webster* (1896) 33 S.L.R. 369.
59 *Thoms v. Bain* (1888) 15 R. 613.
60 *Aitkenhead v. Bunten & Co.* (1892) 19 R. 803.
61 *NV Ondix International v. Landay Ltd*, 1963 S.C. 270.
62 *Faulks v. Whitehead* (1854) 16 D. 718; *Hall v. Newland's Trs* (1859) 22 D. 333; *Bracken v. Blasque* (1891) 18 R. 819. *Cf. Dickey v. British Mexican Ry* (1893) 1 S.L.T. 273.
63 *Bell v. Strathern & Blair*, 1953 S.L.T. (Notes) 23.
64 *Clarke v. Newmarch* (1836) 14 S. 488 at 498, 499, explained in *Railton v. Mathews* (1844) 6 D. 1348.
65 *Earl of Hopetoun v. Horner* (1842) 4 D. 877, explained in *Railton, supra.*
66 *Nero v. Gunn & Cameron* (1886) 2 Sh.Ct.Rep. 342.
67 *Brown v. Lindley* (1833) 12 S. 18.
68 *Aitkenhead v. Bunten & Co.* (1892) 19 R. 803; *Scott v. Scott*, 1924 S.C. 843; *Bell, supra*; *N.V. Ondix International v. Landay Ltd*, 1963 S.C. 270.
69 *Black v. Malcolm* (1830) 8 S. 599.
70 *Murray v. Murray* (1845) 7 D. 1000.
71 Dove Wilson, p. 230.

be sisted.[72] The minute must be unconditional,[73] except perhaps where the mandant is an assisted person.[74] Production of a mandate at the bar, without a minute of sist, is insufficient.[75] An express mandate under the hand of the party need not be produced unless demanded by the opposite party.[76] If the proposed mandatary is not objected to as insufficient, or if any such objection is repelled,[77] the court pronounces an interlocutor sisting him as a party to the cause. In all papers subsequent to the sist, the name of the mandatary should be included along with that of the mandant.[78] While the foregoing appear to be the settled procedural rules as to the effecting of a sist of a mandatary, there is no authority for holding that any particular form of words, or paper, or interlocutor is necessary to constitute against an individual the liabilities of a mandatary: an individual may incur these liabilities without any minute or interlocutor sisting him as a mandatary if he acts as such and calls himself by that name and carries on the process in that character.[79]

If a mandatary is not timeously sisted in terms of the court's interlocutor, it is usual to grant a further reasonable opportunity for so doing on cause shown.[80] But if the time allowed expires without the order of the court having been obtempered, the court usually pronounces decree of absolvitor[81] or in terms of the crave of the writ,[82] with expenses, according to whether the failure is on the part of the pursuer or the defender. **11.78**

An interlocutor ordering the sist of a mandatary is not appealable without leave of the sheriff.[83] If leave to appeal is refused by a further interlocutor, the first and the proper stage at which an appeal may be taken is when final decree is granted in consequence of failure to obtemper the order.[84] If the appeal court considers that a mandatary should not have been, or is no longer, required, these interlocutors and the final decree will be recalled.[85] If it considers that a mandatary is required, and a minute of sist of a mandatary satisfactory to the court is tendered, the final decree may be recalled, the mandatary sisted and the case remitted to the sheriff.[86] **11.79**

---

[72] Subsequent procedure is governed by OCR, Chap. 14 which applies generally to minutes. See paras 5.56 to 5.71.

[73] *Pease, Wrays, and Trigg v. Smith & Jameson* (1822) 1 S. 452 (N.E. 420); *Robertson & Co. v. Exley, Dimsdale & Co.* (1833) 11 S. 320.

[74] See para. 11.73.

[75] *Thomson v. Woodthorpe* (1863) 1 M. 635.

[76] *Gunn & Co. v. Couper* (1871) 10 M. 116.

[77] If the grounds of objection are not admitted or instantly verifiable, the sheriff may remit to a reporter and act upon his report (Dove Wilson, p. 228; Fyfe, para. 269, p. 110).

[78] Maclaren, p. 433.

[79] *Cullen v. Brown* (1860) 22 D. 1090.

[80] *Murray v. Murray* (1845) 7 D. 1000; *Masinimport v. Scottish Mechanical Light Industries Ltd*, 1972 S.L.T. (Notes) 76.

[81] OCR, r. 16.2(2); *Train v. Little*, 1911 S.C. 736; *Masinimport, supra.*

[82] OCR, r. 16.2(2); *Robb v. Independent West Middlesex Assurance Co.* (1853) 5 D. 1025; *Morton v. Dean Smith* (1902) 9 S.L.T. 396 at 397.

[83] *Lawson v. Young* (1891) 7 Sh.Ct.Rep. 319; *Neill v. Smith* (1953) 70 Sh.Ct.Rep. 105.

[84] *Boss v. Lyle Shipping Co.*, 1980 S.L.T. (Sh. Ct.) 65; *cf. McCue v. Scottish Daily Record and Sunday Mail Ltd*, 1998 S.C.L.R. 742.

[85] *Boss, supra; Hall v. Newland's Trs* (1859) 22 D. 333.

[86] *Thomson v. Woodthorpe* (1863) 1 M. 635; *Masinimport v. Scottish Mechanical Light Industries Ltd*, 1st Div., May 15, June 7 and Sept. 25, 1973, unreported: see para. 11.89.

(6) Termination of mandate

11.80 The mandatary may resign his office at any time by lodging a minute stating his intention to resign, upon which the court will grant him leave to withdraw from the process: he cannot resign merely by giving notice to the other side.[87] He continues to be liable for expenses to the date of his withdrawal.[88] His office is also brought to an end by his death[89] or insolvency.[90] Upon his resignation,[91] death[92] or insolvency[93] the opponent is entitled to move that a new mandatary be sisted; and failure to sist a new mandatary has the same consequence as failure to obtemper an order to sist a mandatary.[94] The mandatary's office also falls on the death of his principal,[95] but not on his principal's insolvency, notwithstanding that decree is pronounced against the principal in respect of his failure to find caution for expenses.[96] After his mandate has terminated he is not entitled to reappear after the withdrawal or death of the mandant and contend that no expenses should be awarded against him.[97] The right of continuing a process for the purposes of determining the question of expenses appears to be confined to the case of an agent-disburser.[98]

Interim decree

11.81 The court may pronounce an interim decree either for the purpose of making some interim provision until the merits of the case are decided, or for the purpose of determining a part of the case before finally disposing of it. Interim decrees of the former class include interim interdicts,[99] orders for interim preservation of property,[1] interim appointments of factors,[2] interim orders pending appeal[3] and orders relative to consignation[4]; and in the field of family proceedings, interim protective measures and interim orders for the residence of or contact with children and for the interim aliment of the spouse and children.[5] Interim decrees of this former class are considered elsewhere.

11.82 Interim decrees of the latter class, pronounced for the purpose of determining a part of the case before finally disposing of it, may be made in any action in which the court considers it expedient to do so.[6] Special provision is made by rules of court for the interim payment of damages to

---

[87] *Neilson v. Wilson* (1822) 1 S. 314 (N.E 290); *Martin v. Underwood* (1827) 5 S. 783 (N.E. 730).

[88] *Erskine v. Walker's Trs* (1883) 10 R. 717. See para. 11.73.

[89] *Barclay and Ewart's Reps v. Barclay* (1850) 12 D. 1253. See para. 11.73.

[90] *Harker v. Dickson* (1856) 18 D. 793; *Tradden v. Sweetman* (1862) 24 D. 1360.

[91] *Gordon v. Gordon* (1822) 2 S. 93 (N.E. 86); *Robb v. Independent West Middlesex Assurance Co.* (1843) 5 D. 1025.

[92] *Pease, Wrays and Trigg v. Smith and Jameson* (1822) 1 S. 452 (N.E. 420).

[93] *Harker, Tradden, supra.*

[94] See para. 11.78; *Gordon* (pursuer), *Robb* (defender), *supra.*

[95] See para. 11.73.

[96] *Cullen v. Brown* (1860) 22 D. 1090.

[97] *Gordon v. Gordon* (1823) 2 S. 572 (N.E. 493).

[98] Mackay, *Practice*, i, p. 466. On the privileges of an agent-disburser, see paras 19.26 to 19.28.

[99] See paras 21.85 to 21.93.

[1] See para. 11.05.

[2] See paras 11.06, 11.07.

[3] See para. 11.08.

[4] See paras 11.43 to 11.51.

[5] See Chap. 22.

[6] Mackay, *Practice*, i, p. 583.

pursuers in actions of damages for personal injuries, which are separately considered elsewhere.[7] Such actions apart, the most common form of interim decree is for payment of money in an ordinary petitory action, where it appears from the pleadings that a sum of money is admittedly[8] or plainly[9] due and presently exigible[10]: the pursuer may move for, and the court may grant, an interim decree for payment of that sum, which goes out on the footing that the sum decerned for ought to have been paid, leaving the disputed balance to be the subject of future litigation.[11] Again, if one portion of a case can be decided in favour of the pursuer after debate, while the rest of the case can be disposed of only after proof or other further procedure, the sheriff, having decided that portion of the case in favour of the pursuer after debate, may pronounce an interim decree in his favour and allow a proof or order the appropriate procedure quoad the rest of the case.[12] An interim decree *ad factum praestandum* is in general competent,[13] but it has been held that in an action in which interim interdict is sought such a decree is incompetent if sought for the purpose of restoring the status quo and making the interim interdict ineffective.[14]

An interim decree may be pronounced both before[15] and after[16] the record is closed, and on appeal[17]; but the pronouncing of interim decree is a matter of discretion,[18] and there may be cases in which very nice considerations may arise as to whether interim decree, even for an admitted balance, ought to be given.[19] Interim decrees pronounced before the record is closed generally proceed upon an unqualified admission of partial liability. Interim decree should not be granted if there is a reasonably foreseeable prospect that it may cause unfair prejudice to the defender, or if it would foreclose the court's determination of an aspect of the case which remains seriously in issue.[20] It is said to be a relevant consideration that the defender has a contingent claim on the pursuer for the expenses of the action, if the defence succeeds in respect of the matters still in dispute.[21] It is thought that where the sheriff pronounces an interim decree which in part disposes of the merits of the cause he should append a note to his interlocutor[22] except, perhaps, where he has pronounced it of consent. **11.83**

---

[7] OCR, rr. 36.8–36.10.

[8] *Sinclair v. Sinclair* (1833) 12 S. 61; *Crawfurd v. Ballantine's Trs* (1833) 12 S. 113; *McKinlay v. McKinlay* (1849) 11 D. 1022; *Conacher v. Conacher* (1857) 20 D. 252.

[9] *Cameron v. McNeill* (1822) 1 S. 389 (N.E. 364); *Jack Davis Publicity Ltd v. Kennedy*, Sh. Pr. Caplan, Paisley Sh. Ct, Dec. 18, 1984, unreported: action for payment of costs of services—services admittedly performed and pursuers' averments of costs thereof not specificially challenged—defender alleging failure to credit payments to account—interim decree granted for sum sued for less alleged payments to account.

[10] *Banks v. Lang* (1845) 17 Sc.Jur. 536.

[11] *McAllister v. Duthie* (1867) 5 M. 912, *per* L.P. Inglis at 913.

[12] Maclaren, p. 1091; *Niven v. Clyde Fasteners Ltd*, 1986 S.L.T. 344.

[13] 1907 Act, s. 27; *Scottish Flavour Ltd v. Watson*, 1982 S.L.T. 78.

[14] *Lindsay v. Stivens*, 1967 S.L.T. (Sh. Ct.) 84.

[15] *McKinlay v. McKinlay* (1849) 11 D. 1022; *Conacher v. Conacher* (1857) 20 D. 252; *George Hotel (Glasgow) Ltd v. Prestwick Hotels Ltd*, 1961 S.L.T. (Sh. Ct.) 61. S. 4 of the Court of Session Act 1825, referred to in *Conacher*, does not apply to the sheriff court.

[16] *Elliott v. Aiken* (1869) 7 M. 894.

[17] *Jack Davis Publicity Ltd, supra.*

[18] *Dalziel v. Scott* (1831) 3 Sc.Jur. 591; *Banks v. Lang* (1845) 17 Sc.Jur. 536.

[19] *McAllister v. Duthie* (1867) 5 M. 912, *per* L.P. Inglis at 913.

[20] *Murray v. Kilmaurs Snooker Club*, Sh. Pr. Caplan, Kilmarnock Sh. Ct, Sept. 18, 1986, unreported.

[21] Dobie, p. 163.

[22] OCR, r. 12.2(4).

11.84 An interim decree is appealable to the sheriff principal[23] if it is an interlocutor (a) granting or refusing interdict, (b) granting interim decree for payment of money other than decree for expenses,[24] (c) making an order *ad factum praestandum*,[25] or (d) against which the sheriff grants leave to appeal. An interim decree is appealable to the Court of Session[26] if it is an interlocutor (a) granting interim decree for payment of money other than a decree for expenses,[27] or (b) against which the sheriff principal or sheriff grants leave to appeal. An appeal against an interim decree for payment of money brings up for review any previous interlocutor disposing of part of the merits, of which it is the logical sequence.[28]

11.85 An appealable interim decree in which no question of expenses is reserved may be appealed within 14 days of its date[29] and is thereafter extractable[30]; but the sheriff may, and frequently does, grant a motion to allow earlier extract on cause shown,[31] if the motion is made in the presence of the parties or if he is satisfied that proper intimation of its terms has been made in writing to all other parties.[32] The sheriff may also supersede extract.[33]

Interim award of expenses

(1) General

11.86 It is always competent to pronounce interim decree for the expenses of any part of or procedure in a cause.[34] Expenses are in the discretion of the sheriff,[35] who accordingly has full power to determine at what stage, against whom and to what extent expenses are to be awarded. Expenses are often awarded in respect of matters which are distinct and separate from the merits of the cause.[36] Thus, when allowing an amendment of pleadings in terms of rule 18.2, the sheriff is directed to find the party making the amendment liable in the expenses thereby occasioned unless it is just and equitable that the expenses occasioned by the amendment should be otherwise dealt with.[37] The sheriff may also make an interim award of expenses against an unsuccessful party in incidental applications and discussions, as when he disposes of an opposed motion which has reference to a point that is quite separable from the merits,[38] or when after

---

23 1907 Act, s. 27. See paras 18.38 to 18.49.

24 Including an interlocutor granting warrant to an officer of court to pay out to a party money in his hands (*Baird v. Glendinning* (1874) 2 R. 25) or granting warrant to a party to uplift consigned money (*Sinclair v. Baikie* (1884) 11 R. 413), but excluding an interlocutor ordaining consignation (*Maxton v. Bone* (1866) 13 R. 912) or granting warrant to uplift money in the hands of a third party (*Hughes's Trs v. Hughes*, 1925 S.C. 25).

25 *e.g.* an interlocutor ordaining consignation: *Mackenzie v. Balerno Paper Mill Co.* (1883) 10 R. 1147; *Menzies v. Templeton* (1896) 12 Sh.Ct.Rep. 323.

26 1907 Act, s. 28(1)(a) and (d). See paras 18.95, 18.96.

27 See n. 24.

28 *Cross & Sons v. Borders* (1879) 6 R. 934. See also *McCue v. Scottish Daily Record and Sunday Mail Ltd*, 1998 S.C.L.R. 742.

29 OCR, r. 31.1.

30 OCR, r. 30.4(1)(b)(iii).

31 OCR, r. 30.4(2).

32 OCR, r. 30.4(3).

33 OCR, r. 30.4(4).

34 *Waddel v. Hope* (1843) 6 D. 160 at 169; *Vaughan v. Davidson* (1854) 16 D. 922.

35 Maclaren, *Expenses*, p. 4; and see para. 19.03.

36 *Waddel, Vaughan, supra.*

37 OCR, r. 18.6. See paras 10.29, 10.30.

38 Maclaren, *Expenses*, p. 44; *Stair Encyclopaedia*, Vol. 17, para. 1069.

debate he disposes of or reserves preliminary pleas and orders further procedure.[39] He may also make an interim award of expenses against a party whose conduct has brought about the discharge or adjournment of a diet of debate[40] or proof.[41] Where expenses are incurred through the failure of a party's solicitor, the sheriff may direct that these expenses shall not be charged against the parties,[42] and may find the solicitor personally liable for these expenses.[43]

(2) Particular actions

In an action of multiplepoinding, after consignation or deposit of the fund *in medio* the holder may apply for his exoneration and discharge,[44] and on his exoneration and discharge the sheriff may allow him his expenses out of the fund as a first charge thereon[45] and grant decree therefor although the action continues to proceed. **11.87**

(3) Modification

When making an interim award of expenses the sheriff may modify, or fix, the amount of expenses awarded so as to avoid the further expense of remitting the successful party's account to taxation. He may do so of consent, at a figure agreed by the parties; but otherwise his power to do so should be sparingly used and only where there has been little expenditure and he really knows what expenditure there has been and is in a position to judge as to what part of it should be allowed.[46] Where the interim award is modified, no further expenses in respect of the part modified can be obtained by the party receiving the interim modified award should he ultimately be successful in the cause.[47] **11.88**

(4) Enforcement: payment as condition precedent

Interim decree may be granted for the taxed, agreed or modified amount of any expenses awarded during the dependence of the action. The interim decree may be extracted and enforced before the action is concluded,[48] and interest runs on it when extracted and charged upon.[49] But payment of an interim award of expenses is not a condition precedent of a pursuer's being allowed to proceed, unless the court specifically so orders.[50] The earlier practice of the Court of Session in regard to making payment of expenses a condition precedent of further proceedings when allowing amendment of pleadings is no longer **11.89**

---

39 Thomson and Middleton, pp. 85–86; *Stair Encyclopaedia*, Vol. 17, para. 1069; and see para. 13.24.

40 A.S. (Fees of Solicitors in the Sheriff Court) (Amendment and Further Provisions) 1993, Sched. 1, General Regulations, reg. 5(c); *Edinburgh Modern Quarry Co. Ltd v. Eagle Star Insurance Co. Ltd*, 1965 S.L.T. (Notes) 91; and see para. 13.03.

41 A.S. 1993, *supra*, Sched. 1, reg. 5(c); and see paras 16.35 to 16.37.

42 *Kelly v. Fyfe Douglas Co. Ltd*, 1965 S.L.T. (Notes) 87.

43 *Stewart v. Stewart*, 1984 S.L.T. (Sh. Ct.) 58 at 59; and see para. 19.23.

44 OCR, r. 35.15(2).

45 OCR, r. 35.15(3).

46 *Clarke v. McNab* (1888) 15 R. 670.

47 *Viscountess Strangford v. Hurlet & Campsie Alum. Co.* (1861) 23 D. 534; *Cameron & Waterston v. Muir & Son* (1861) 23 D. 535.

48 Fyfe, para. 786, p. 331; Dobie, p. 311.

49 *Dalmahoy and Wood v. Mags of Brechin* (1859) 21 D. 210; *Wallace v. Henderson* (1876) 4 R. 264.

50 Maclaren, p. 43.

followed[51] except in very special circumstances,[52] since the effect of such a course is often to deny to a party the very indulgence which the court is professing to dispense.[53] It is thought that other early decisions in which such orders were made in other circumstances[54] are not necessarily reliable guides to the modern practice of the courts. In modern practice it appears that such an order is made only where there has been a failure or delay on the part of a litigant or his solicitor of such a nature that, although decree by default is inappropriate and it is in the interests of justice that the action should proceed, it is just and equitable that all or part of the expenses incurred by his opponent should be paid before the action proceeds further.[55] It appears to be an important consideration that the litigant should be financially capable of complying with the order: it is thought that it is incorrect to make such an order if its practical consequence would be the termination of the action due to the impecuniosity of the litigant.[56] An order may be made against a defender for the payment of all or part of the pursuer's expenses under certification that if he fails to do so decree as craved will be pronounced.[57]

---

[51] *Fleming v. Paterson*, 1948 S.C. 564; *Smellie v. Smellie*, 1953 S.L.T. (Notes) 53; *Edinburgh Modern Quarry Co. Ltd v. Eagle Star Insurance Co. Ltd*, 1965 S.L.T. (Notes) 91.

[52] *Fleming v. McGillivray*, 1946 S.C. 1 at 12; *Colbron v. United Glass Ltd*, 1965 S.L.T. 366.

[53] *Moyes v. Burntisland Shipping Co.*, 1952 S.C. 429, *per* L.J.-C. Thomson at 435.

[54] Cases cited in Maclaren, *Expenses*, p. 7, nn. 5–11.

[55] *McGregor v. Rooney*, O.H., Lord Hunter, Feb. 5, 1971, unreported (decree by default in sheriff court due to negligence of defender's solicitor, defender pursuing action for reduction of decree—condition precedent to further procedure in action of reduction that defender-pursuer pay the whole of the taxed or agreed amount of pursuer-defender's expenses in both actions: *cf. Campbell v. McCance*, 1928 S.N. 145); *Masinimport v. Scottish Mechanical Light Industries Ltd*, 1st Div., May 15, 1973, unreported (decree of absolvitor in O.H. upon failure of pursuers to sist mandatary (1972 S.L.T. (Notes) 76)—decree recalled—pursuers appointed to sist mandatary within 28 days under certification that otherwise decree of absolvitor would be pronounced of new; pursuers found liable to defender in expenses from date of O.H. interlocutor appointing pursuers to sist mandatary taxed on solicitor and client, client paying, scale-payment of taxed or agreed amount of expenses condition precedent of pursuers proceeding with action—sequel, 1976 S.C. 102); *Olsen v. Keddie*, 1976 S.L.T. (Sh. Ct.) 64 (sheriff principal reponing defender against decree in absence).

[56] *Moyes, supra.*

[57] *Stevens v. Motherwell Entertainments Ltd*, 1914 S.C. 957; *McLean v. Thomas O'Connor Autos*, 1967 S.L.T. (Sh. Ct.) 41; *Olsen, supra.*

CHAPTER 12

INCIDENTAL PROCEDURE—I

In addition to the interim protective and remedial procedures considered in the last chapter, there are a number of incidental proceedings which may take place at various stages of a defended ordinary action. These are considered in this and the following chapter. **12.01**

I. PROCEDURE BEFORE COMMENCEMENT OF ACTION

Disclosure of identity of defender

Powers of the court

Section 1 of the Administration of Justice (Scotland) Act 1972, as amended, confers on the Court of Session and the sheriff court power to make various orders prior to the commencement of proceedings. The court may order the inspection, photographing, preservation, custody and detention of documents and other property (including, where appropriate, land) which appear to the court to be property as to which any question may relevantly arise not only in any existing civil proceedings before that court but in civil proceedings which are likely to be brought, and to order the production and recovery of any such property, the taking of samples thereof and the carrying out of any experiment thereon or therewith. The court may also order the disclosure of information as to the identity of persons who might be witnesses or defenders. We consider here only the procedure for obtaining an order to disclose the identity of a defender. The other provisions of section 1 are examined in Chapter 15 in the context of the recovery of evidence.[1] **12.02**

The court has power to order any person to disclose such information as he has as to the identity of any persons who appear to the court to be persons who might be defenders in any civil proceedings which appear to the court to be likely to be brought.[2] The power is conferred without prejudice to the existing powers of the court,[3] but subject to section 1 (4) of the Act which preserves the law and practice relative to the privilege of witnesses and havers, confidentiality of communications and withholding or non-disclosure of information on the grounds of public interest, and section 47 of the Crown Proceedings Act 1947 which makes provision as to the recovery of documents in the hands of the Crown.[4] The court may exercise the power on the application at any **12.03**

---

[1] paras 15.02, 15.03 (identity of witnesses); 15.84 to 15.92 (inspection, etc., of property).

[2] Administration of Justice (Scotland) Act 1972, s. 1(1A)(b), inserted by Law Reform (Miscellaneous Provisions) (Scotland) Act 1985, s. 19.

[3] The identification of potential defenders was ordered in *De Duca v. Sillitoe* (1936) 52 Sh.Ct.Rep. 18. See also Macphail, *Evidence*, paras 25.08–S25.11.

[4] On s. 47 of the Crown Proceedings Act 1947, see paras 4.72 to 4.75.

time of any person who appears to the court to be likely to be a party to or minuter in proceedings which are likely to be brought; and may exercise the power unless there is special reason why the application should not be granted.[5]

Procedure

12.04 An application under section 1(1A)(b) of the 1972 Act is made by summary application.[6] Before the coming into force of the Summary Application Rules 1993[7] detailed rules for applications for orders under section 1(1A)(b) of the 1972 Act were contained in the Ordinary Cause Rules.[8] Power to make such rules is clearly provided by the 1972 Act itself.[9] However, such detailed rules are not now contained in either the 1993 Ordinary Cause Rules or the Summary Application Rules. It may be considered that the general provisions of the Summary Application Rules together with the wide powers which a sheriff has to regulate procedure in a summary application[10] enable him to take any of the steps provided by the old rules. Thus he may make an order for intimation to any person who appears to him to have an interest in the summary application.[11] It is suggested that he may grant the order sought in whole or in part, as amended, or subject to such conditions, including caution, as he thinks fit.[12] It is further suggested that the order should specify the party or parties who are to obtemper it and the time within which they are required to do so, and where the sheriff has granted an order, the applicant should serve upon the person to whom it is directed and intimate to any other person to whom intimation of the application has been made, a certified copy of the interlocutor granting the order.[13]

Appointment of factor pending litigation

12.05 The sheriff appears to have power to appoint a judicial factor in order to provide for the administration of property in dispute, or, if parties agree, for its sale and administration of the price, until parties' rights have been settled by agreement or litigation.[14] The procedure would appear to be by way of petition presented to the sheriff court at Edinburgh, which should be as nearly as may be in the form in use in ordinary actions.[15] It would no doubt be appropriate to follow the practice of the Court of Session as far as possible.[16] In view of the sheriff's statutory power to

---

[5] Administration of Justice (Scotland) Act 1972, s. 1(2). See para. 15.90.

[6] A.S. (Sheriff Court Summary Application Rules) 1993, r. 30(2). It should be noted that the provisions of OCR, r. 28.2 (which on the face of it apply to all applications under s. 1 of the 1972 Act) do not apply to applications under s. 1(1A)(b). The whole of Chap. 28 of the OCR applies to "the recovery of evidence in a cause depending before the sheriff" (OCR, r. 28.1(1)) and an application under s. 1 (1A)(b) is by definition not in a pending case but in respect of "proceedings which appear to the court to be likely to be brought".

[7] On January 1, 1994.

[8] 1983 OCR, r. 84A (inserted by S.I. 1986 No. 1966).

[9] 1972 Act, s. 1(3).

[10] SAR, r. 32.

[11] SAR, r. 5.

[12] These powers were specifically provided in 1983 OCR, r. 84A(7).

[13] These powers were specifically provided in 1983 OCR, r. 84A(8) and (10).

[14] See para. 11.07.

[15] Judicial Factors (Scotland) Act 1880, s. 4(1) and (1A)(b)(ii), as substituted and inserted by Law Reform (Miscellaneous Provisions) (Scotland) Act, 1980. s. 14(1)(b).

[16] RCS, Chap. 61.

order the preservation of property in terms of section 1 of the Administration of Justice (Scotland) Act 1972,[17] it is thought that such petitions will rarely be necessary.

Road Traffic Act 1988, section 151

In terms of section 151(5) of the Road Traffic Act 1988 the insurer under a motor insurance policy is bound to pay to the person entitled to the benefit of a judgment against the insured any sum payable thereunder in respect of the liability covered by the policy. The insurer's liability to do so is not, however, enforceable in various circumstances set out in section 152. He is not liable to pay any sum in respect of any judgment unless, before or within seven days after the commencement of the proceedings in which the judgment was given, he had notice of the bringing of the proceedings.[18] **12.06**

II. Parties

Calling and sisting new parties

During the course of the action persons other than the parties named in the instance of the initial writ may enter the process. New pursuers or defenders may be added by amendment[19]; third parties may be called by means of third party procedure[20]; representatives of an original party may be called; and persons maintaining an interest to enter the process may be sisted. The following paragraphs deal with the two latter situations. **12.07**

Representative of party

The question of adding or substituting a representative of a party may arise when the party dies,[21] or is sequestrated,[22] or becomes insane,[23] or parts with or is divested of his interest in the subject-matter of the action.[24] **12.08**

Death of party. On the death of a party during the dependence of the action, all procedure in the cause, including any procedure on appeal, is suspended and any steps that may be taken or interlocutors pronounced in the cause in ignorance of the death are null and void. That is so even where there remain other parties on the same side of the litigation as was the deceased party. Any further proceedings are inept unless the representatives of the deceased party sist themselves, or the action is transferred against them.[25] But unless the subject-matter of the cause is such as transmits to representatives, they are not entitled to sist themselves[26]; and unless the court has jurisdiction over them they are not bound to appear.[27] **12.09**

---

[17] See paras 15.84 to 15.92.
[18] Road Traffic Act 1988, s. 152(1)(a).
[19] See paras 10.09 to 10.12.
[20] See paras 12.42 to 12.65.
[21] paras 12.09 to 12.11.
[22] para. 12.12.
[23] para. 12.13.
[24] paras 12.14 to 12.17.
[25] *Davidson v. Robertson* (1827) 5 S. 751 (N.E. 702); *Marshall v. Hynd* (1828) 6 S. 384 at 389n.; *Ferrier v. Berry* (1828) 6 S. 982; *Mercer v. Maxwell* (1850) 12 D. 756; *Thompson v. Crawfurd*, 1979 S.L.T. (Notes) 91.
[26] *Gibson v. Barbour's Reps* (1846) 8 D. 427; *Green or Borthwick v. Borthwick* (1896) 24 R. 211. They may, however, be sisted under reservation of all questions as to their right to continue the action: *Martin's Exrx v. McGhee*, 1914 S.C. 628.
[27] *Mackenzie v. Drummond's Exrs* (1868) 6 M. 932.

12.10 *Sist of representatives.* If the representatives desire to sist themselves, the procedure is by minute narrating the death and the representatives' title, and craving to be sisted in room of the deceased party.[28] The procedure is the same as with any other minute.[29] The representatives may be sisted at any stage,[30] even after judgment has been pronounced.[31] But the rules as to the intimation to and sisting of persons in actions of damages arising from a death are procedural only and do not affect or override the rules regarding time-bar.[32] If the representatives do not move to be sisted, the opposite party may move the court to appoint intimation of the dependence of the action to be made to them, in order that they may, if so advised, sist themselves as parties to the action within a specified period.[33] Since they cannot be compelled to sist themselves, intimation should not be made under certification.[34]

12.11 *Transfer of cause.* Where any depending cause cannot proceed owing to the death of any party and the party's representatives do not sist themselves in his place, any other party may apply by minute to have the cause transferred in favour of or against, as the case may be, any person who represents that party's estate.[35] The cause is depending, and the procedure is accordingly competent, at any time after service of the initial writ[36] and before final judgment disposing of the merits and amount of expenses.[37] The procedure is the same as with any other minute.[38] It appears that the only objection which may be relevantly stated to the minute is that the objectors are not the proper representatives of the deceased: any defences they may have should be proponed later.[39] It appears that if the representatives do not carry on the action, the opposite party is entitled to take decree of constitution against the deceased's estate, where the deceased was the defender[40]; or, where the deceased was the pursuer, decree of absolvitor.[41]

12.12 **Bankruptcy: liquidation.** In the event of a party to the cause being sequestrated during the dependence of the action, the permanent trustee may continue the action if he considers that to do so would be beneficial for the administration of the estate; but if there are commissioners he may do so only with the consent of the commissioners, the creditors or the court.[42] He may sist himself as pursuer or defender and maintain the action or defence.[43] By doing so he adopts the contract of litiscontestation, and renders himself liable to the opposite party in all expenses incurred prior as well as subsequent to his being sisted.[44] If the trustee

---

28 OCR, r. 25.1.
29 OCR, Chap. 14. See paras 5.56 to 5.71.
30 *X v. Y*, 1945 S.L.T. (Sh. Ct.) 2 (pursuer dying in witness-box).
31 *Gibson's Trs v. Gibson* (1869) 7 M. 1061; *Scott v. Mills's Trs*, 1923 S.C. 726; *Cumming v. Stewart*, 1928 S.C. 709; *Thompson v. Crawfurd*, 1979 S.L.T. (Notes) 91.
32 *Marshall v. Black*, 1981 S.L.T. 228; see paras 21.14 to 21.18.
33 *Finklestone v. Smellie* (1916) 32 Sh.Ct.Rep. 244.
34 W.J.D., "Death of a defender" (1950) 66 Sc.L.Rev.33 at p. 34.
35 OCR, r. 25.2.
36 *Watson v. Watson* (1898) 6 S.L.T 201; see para. 6.06.
37 *Aitken v. Dick* (1863) 1 M. 1038; *Forbes v. Clinton* (1872) 10 M. 449.
38 OCR, Chap. 14. See paras 5.56 to 5.71.
39 *Wilson v. Agnew* (1828) 6 S. 927; *Parks v. Earl of Stair* (1854) 16 D. 1165.
40 *Davidson, Pirie & Co. v. Dihle's Reps* (1900) 2 F. 640; see para. 4.106, *supra.*
41 Thomson and Middleton, p. 409.
42 Bankruptcy (Scotland) Act 1985, s. 39(2)(b).
43 *Thom v. Bridges and Macqueen* (1857) 19 D. 721.
44 *Ellis v. Ellis* (1870) 8 M. 805.

does not sist himself, the sheriff may, either *ex proprio motu* or on the motion of the opposite party, order intimation of the dependence of the action to him, and appoint him, if so advised, to crave to be sisted.[45] If the trustee does not crave to be sisted, the bankrupt may, where he continues to have a title to sue or defend, continue the action. As a general rule, he will be ordained to find caution where he is the pursuer, but not where he is the defender.[46] In a winding-up by the court the liquidator has (subject to general rules) the same powers as a trustee on a bankrupt estate,[47] and may be similarly sisted.[48]

Insanity. Where a party becomes insane during the dependence of the action, no further steps can be taken in his name, and any subsequent interlocutors pronounced in ignorance of his incapacity are null and void. On his incapacity coming to the notice of the court, the sheriff should normally sist the cause until a curator *bonis* is appointed.[49] The curator when appointed is entitled to apply by minute to be sisted if he so wishes.[50] If the curator *bonis* does not seek to be sisted, any other party may apply by minute to have the cause transferred in favour of or against, as the case may be, the curator *bonis*, as in the case of the representative of a deceased party.[51] Otherwise the action will be ordered to be intimated to the curator *bonis*, and if he does not appear in the process within the time specified, the opposite party may take decree against the insane party, which will have similar effect to a decree granted in absence of a party.[52] Where in an action of divorce or separation it appears to the sheriff that the defender is suffering from mental disorder, he must appoint a curator *ad litem* to the defender.[53] In special circumstances also, it is thought, the court may appoint a curator *ad litem* instead of sisting the cause for the appointment of a curator *bonis*.[54] 12.13

Person maintaining interest

Transmission of interest. Where any party to the cause has alienated or been divested of his interest in the subject-matter of the action in favour of a transferee, the transferee is as a rule entitled to take his place.[55] The opposite party is entitled to apply to have the transferee added to the instance in addition to the original party. If the parties' interests in the subject-matter of the action are unaffected by the transaction, the sisting of the third party is inappropriate.[56] Where the party who has alienated or been divested of his interest is the pursuer, and the transferee does not have himself sisted, the defender may move for an order on him to sist himself. The facts on which the motion is founded may be stated in 12.14

---

45 *Hallowell v. Niven* (1843) 5 D. 655.

46 See paras 11.54, 11.55.

47 Insolvency Act 1986, s. 169(2).

48 See paras 4.90 to 4.92.

49 *Moodie v. Dempster*, 1931 S.C. 553; and see para. 4.07.

50 OCR, r. 25.1 applies to a party who comes under a legal disability as it does to a party who dies.

51 OCR, r. 25.2. See para. 12.11.

52 Thomson and Middleton, p. 410.

53 OCR, r. 33.16; Divorce (Scotland) Act 1976, s. 11; see paras 22.24 to 22.26.

54 *Moodie, supra, per* Lord Sands at 555; and see para. 4.07.

55 *Parker v. Welsh* (1894) 2 S.L.T. 122; *Fearn v. Cowpar* (1899) 7 S.L.T. 68 (assignees); *Mavor v. Governors of Aberdeen Educational Trust* (1902) 10 S.L.T. 156 (disponee).

56 *Waddel v. Hope* (1843) 6 D. 160.

the motion.[57] If the transferee fails to sist himself within the time specified in the interlocutor, the action may be dismissed,[58] or the defender may by motion[59] obtain an order on the pursuer to find caution for expenses as a condition of proceeding with the action.[60] Where the party who has alienated or been divested of his interest is the defender, the pursuer may move for intimation to be made to the transferee in order that he may sist himself if so advised. If he does not do so, the action proceeds against the original defender, and the pursuer may by amendment call the transferee as an additional defender.[61]

12.15 **Other interested parties.** A person other than a representative or transferee of a party may be sisted on his own application if he shows that he has a title[62] and an interest to be made a party to the cause.[63] Thus a person who has not been called as a defender may enter the process by minute[64] and thereafter be sisted as a defender and allowed to lodge defences.[65] The minute should specify the applicant's title and interest to enter the process and the grounds of the defence which he proposes to state.[66] If the sheriff is satisfied that title and interest have been shown he may grant the applicant leave to enter the process as a party minuter and to lodge defences.[67] He may also make such order as to expenses as he thinks fit.[68] If the application to enter the process is made after the closing of the record it may be granted only if the sheriff is satisfied as to the reason why earlier application was not made.[69] When the party minuter has lodged defences an options hearing is fixed as if the period of notice had expired on the date for lodging defences.[70] At the options hearing or at any time thereafter the sheriff may grant decree or any other order he thinks fit.[71] A decree or other order against a party minuter has the same effect as against a defender.[72] In some circumstances it may be inappropriate to grant an application to be sisted.[73]

12.16 It is *pars judicis* to give an opportunity of appearing to any party that the court sees in the course of the process to be interested in the result.[74]

---

[57] OCR, r. 15.1(1)(b), Form G6 provides for the reason for seeking an order to be stated in the written motion.
[58] *Fraser v. Dunbar* (1839) 1 D. 882.
[59] See para. 11.64.
[60] Thomson and Middleton, p. 410.
[61] *ibid.* pp. 410–411; Maxwell, p. 233.
[62] *Muir v. Glasgow Corporation,* 1917 2 S.L.T. 106.
[63] *e.g. Addison v. Brown,* 1910 1 S.L.T. 185 (attestor of cautioner).
[64] OCR, r. 13.1(1).
[65] *Lord Blantyre v. Lord Advocate* (1876) 13 S.L.R. 213; *Macfie v. Scottish Rights of Way Society* (1884) 11 R. 1094; *Glasgow Shipowners' Association v. Clyde Navigation Trustees* (1885) 12 R. 695; *Bruce v. Calder* (1903) 20 Sh.Ct.Rep. 288; *Macpherson v. Macdonald Fraser & Co. Ltd* (1905) 12 S.L.T. 824; *Ross v. Ross,* 1909 2 S.L.T. 117; *Gas Power and By-Products Co. Ltd v. Power Gas Corporation Ltd,* 1911 S.C. 27; *Alexander v. Picken,* 1946 S.L.T. 91; *Glasgow Corporation v. Regent Oil Co. Ltd,* 1971 S.L.T. (Sh. Ct.) 61.
[66] OCR, r. 13.1(2).
[67] OCR, r. 13.1(3)(a).
[68] OCR, r. 13.1(3)(b).
[69] OCR, r. 13.1(4).
[70] OCR, r. 13.2(1).
[71] OCR, r. 13.2(2).
[72] OCR, r. 13.2(3).
[73] *Laing's Sewing Machine Co. v. Norrie & Sons* (1877) 5 R. 29 (undefended action of interdict: *cf. Gas Power and By-Products Co. Ltd, supra*); *Aberdeen Grit Co. Ltd v. Aberdeen Corporation,* 1948 S.L.T. (Notes) 44 (other competent and appropriate procedure available).
[74] *Lord Blantyre, supra, per* Lord Deas at 214.

Where such a person has not applied to be sisted, the court may order intimation to him, to enable him if so advised to sist himself as a party.[75]

The special considerations relative to the sisting of persons as additional pursuers in actions of damages under the Damages (Scotland) Act 1976,[76] and the sisting of parties in family proceedings,[77] are examined elsewhere. **12.17**

Expenses

A party who sists himself or is sisted as a party is not allowed to make any conditions as to his liability for expenses.[78] A party who sists himself as a defender and is discovered to have no title to defend is liable in expenses from the date of his minute.[79] A party who sists himself in room of another may be liable for the full expenses of the opposite party before, as well as after, he has sisted himself.[80] Once he has been allowed to appear in the case, it is of no significance as regards his liability for expenses whether he has been formally sisted or not.[81] **12.18**

Disclamation

Any person whose name has been used as a party to a cause without his authority may disclaim the proceedings by lodging in process a minute of disclaimer.[82] The usual procedure for minutes is followed.[83] The minute does not take effect until it is sustained[84]; and it may be refused.[85] If the minute is sustained disclaimer takes place.[86] A person who promptly disclaims is usually not liable for expenses incurred before disclaimer,[87] and is not liable for any incurred thereafter. He may be awarded expenses against those who used his name without authority,[88] or he may exercise a right of relief against them.[89] They may also be liable in expenses to the opposite party.[90] **12.19**

If the court sustains a sole pursuer's minute of disclaimer which dates back to the raising of the action, another person cannot be sisted as pursuer since there has never been any competent action in court.[91] The **12.20**

---

75 *Orr-Ewing's Trs* (1884) 12 R. 343; (1885) 13 R.(H.L.) 1; *cf. Shaw* v. *Caledonian Ry* (1888) 15 R. 504.
76 See paras 21.14 to 21.18.
77 See paras 22.15 to 22.17.
78 *Buchanan* v. *Corbett, Borthwick & Co.* (1827) 5 S. 805 (N.E. 745); *Wallace* v. *Earl of Eglinton* (1836) 14 S. 599; *Ellis* v. *Ellis* (1870) 8 M. 805.
79 *Hope* v. *Landward Committee of Parish Council of Inveresk* (1906) 8 F. 896.
80 *Torbet* v. *Borthwick* (1849) 11 D. 694; *Ellis, supra*; *Skinner's Tr.* v. *Keith* (1887) 14 R. 563.
81 *Gill* v. *Anderson* (1859) 21 D. 723. *Cf. Cullen* v. *Brown* (1860) 22 D. 1090.
82 Dobie, *Styles*, p. 322.
83 OCR, Chap. 14. See paras 5.56 to 5.71.
84 *e.g. Cambuslang West Church Committee* v. *Bryce* (1897) 25 R. 322.
85 *e.g. Eadie* v. *Glasgow Corporation*, 1908 S.C. 207.
86 For a style of interlocutor, see *Cambuslang West Church Committee, supra.*
87 *Menzies* v. *Caldwell* (1834) 12 S. 772.
88 *Cambuslang West Church Committee, supra; Muir & Rutherford* (1933) 49 Sh.Ct.Rep. 214; *Faulie* v. *Fairlie's Trs* (1903) 11 S.L.T. 51; *Edington* v. *Dunbar Steam Laundry Co.* (1903) 11 S.L.T. 117.
89 *Cowan* v. *Farnie* (1836) 14 S. 634.
90 *Noble* v. *Magistrates of Inverness* (1825) 3 S. 516 (N.E. 358); *Philip* v. *Gordon* (1848) 11 D. 175.
91 *Ferguson, Davidson & Co.* v. *Paterson and Dobbie* (1898) 1 F. 227; *Gordon* v. *Purves* (1902) 10 S.L.T. 446, (1903) 11 S.L.T. 38. See also *Noble, supra.*

minority of the members of a corporation cannot dissociate themselves by disclaimer from an action by or against the corporation,[92] but partners,[93] trustees[94] and members of an association[95] may disclaim. A defender who lodges defences cannot disclaim a notice of intention to defend which has been lodged in his name.[96] A party may disclaim a minute of disclaimer.[97]

III. Advocates

Instruction of counsel

General rule

12.21 Counsel are entitled to practise in the sheriff court on the instructions of a solicitor, and they regularly advise, draw pleadings and appear in sheriff court proceedings. There are, however, restrictions on the fees which are allowed in the taxation of accounts as between party and party where counsel is employed. Counsel's fees and the solicitor's fees for the instruction of counsel are allowed only where the sheriff has sanctioned the employment of counsel. The solicitor's fees cover the instruction of counsel to revise the record and to conduct a debate or proof or an appeal before the sheriff principal. Except on cause shown, fees to counsel and the solicitor for only two consultations in the course of the case are allowed.[98]

Timeous instruction

12.22 Close co-operation between counsel and his instructing solicitor is essential for the effective conduct of the litigation. It is therefore recommended that the restrictions placed on the recovery of counsel's fees on taxation should not discourage solicitors from instructing counsel at any stage when to do so is likely to avoid delay or expense, or to enhance the prospects of success. Ideally, counsel should be instructed to draft the original pleading; and he should certainly be instructed to adjust the pleadings before the record is closed. If he is instructed only after the record is closed, he may well advise that some amendment of the pleadings is essential, and delay and expense may be thereby incurred which might have been avoided if he had been instructed earlier. Immediately after any interlocutor allowing proof, counsel should be instructed to write a note on the line of evidence, which is "the most important step in preparing for a proof".[99] The note should be instructed as early as possible, because counsel may advise that additional evidence is required or that documents should be recovered by commission and diligence. About six weeks before the proof there should be a consultation with counsel, at which all the information sought in the note on the line of evidence should be available, and decisions should be taken as to the witnesses to be cited and the productions to be lodged.

---

92 *Eadie v. Glasgow Corporation, supra.*
93 See para. 4.97.
94 *Fairlie, supra.*
95 *Cambuslang West Church Committee, supra.*
96 *AB v. CD* (1905) 21 Sh.Ct.Rep. 303.
97 *Tulloch v. Baud* (1859) 21 D. 807.
98 A.S. (Fees of Solicitors in the Sheriff Court) (Amendment and Further Provisions) 1993, Sched. 1, General regulations, reg. 12(b).
99 Lord Blades, "The Art of Pleading" (1948) 64 S.L.R. 25, 53 at 53–54.

Mode of instruction[1]

12.23 Instructions to counsel sent through the post or by DX should be addressed to "The Clerk to Mr [*or* Mrs *or* Miss] X", or, if counsel has not been selected, to "[*Name of advocate's clerk*], Parliament House, Edinburgh EH1 1RF [*or* DX ED 302, Edinburgh]". The names of the advocates' clerks appear in *The Faculty of Advocates Directory*, *The Scottish Law Directory* (the "White Book") and the "Blue Book" (the directory of the Law Society of Scotland). In very urgent cases instructions will be treated in the same way as the normal direct deliveries by hand to counsel's box or chambers, without acknowledgment of receipt. Counsel may be instructed to act in sheriff court proceedings by a local solicitor without the intervention of an Edinburgh solicitor. On taxation, fees paid to an Edinburgh solicitor are likely to be disallowed as unreasonable.[2] It appears that there used to be a rule of professional etiquette that a solicitor who instructed counsel should give reasonable notice of the fact that he had done so to the opposite party, so that the latter might instruct counsel also, if he chose.[3] In modern practice, however, there seems to be no legal or professional obligation on a solicitor to inform his opponent when he intends to instruct counsel. Some solicitors give notice as a matter of courtesy, but it is not regarded as discourteous to refrain from doing so. It is thought that the quality of preparation by a solicitor who has decided to conduct a case himself should not be affected by the professional status of the advocate on the other side. Whether notice has been given does not appear to be a relevant factor in the sheriff's consideration of a motion to sanction the employment of counsel.[4]

Motion to sanction employment of counsel

12.24 A motion to sanction the employment of counsel should usually be made orally at the conclusion of the proof or debate in which counsel has appeared. The sheriff then deals with it in his subsequent interlocutor. If an oral motion has not been made, a written motion should be lodged whenever that interlocutor is issued.[5] Regulation 12(a) of the General Regulations contained in Schedule 1 to the Act of Sederunt (Fees of Solicitors in the Sheriff Court) (Amendment and Further Provisions) 1993 appears to permit sanction at any time up to the date of taxation.[6] Sanction has sometimes been obtained after some delay subsequent to the date of the interlocutor but before taxation,[7]

---

[1] 1984 S.L.T. (News) 175; (1984) J.L.S. 303.

[2] *cf.* A.S. (Fees of Solicitors in the Sheriff Court) (Amendment and Further Provisions) 1993, Sched. 1, General Regulations, reg. 8; *Sinclair v. Bayley-Lunnon*, 1969 S.L.T. (Sh. Ct.) 18 (a case decided when the criterion was "necessary" rather than, as it is now, "reasonable").

[3] *Leny v. Milne* (1899) 15 Sh.Ct.Rep. 76, *per* Sh. Pr. A. J. G. Mackay at 77; *Encyclopaedia*, xiii, para. 1445.

[4] *Leny*, *supra*; para. 12.25.

[5] *Turner v. Wilson*, 1954 S.C. 296 at 305–306.

[6] *Calder Chemicals Ltd v. Brunton*, Sh. Pr. O'Brien, Edinburgh Sh. Ct, Aug. 8, 1984, unreported (sequel to 1984 S.L.T. (Sh. Ct.) 96), where no objection was taken to the competency of the motion.

[7] *Purvis v. Douwie* (1869) 7 M. 764, *McKerchar v. McQuarrie* (1887) 14 R. 1038 (both briefly reported, and the competency of the sheriff-substitutes' certificates seems at least doubtful: see *Baird v. SMT Co. Ltd*, 1948 S.C. 526); *Swanson v. Gardner & Co. Ltd* (1916) 33 Sh.Ct.Rep. 117 (after decree extracted); *Eagle Star Insurance Co. Ltd v. Edward*, 1982 S.L.C.R. 145 (sanction by Scottish Land Court after account lodged for taxation); *Calder Chemicals Ltd*, *supra*.

and in a few exceptional cases it has been obtained after taxation.[8] Application for sanction should be made to the sheriff who conducted the case. An appellate court will sanction the employment of counsel before the sheriff only where the applicant shows not only that the employment was right but also that there are very good reasons why the motion was not made before.[9] The party moving for sanction should make clear to the court precisely the extent to which sanction is desired: whether for senior and junior counsel, or for senior only, or for junior only; and whether for the employment of counsel throughout the case, or for a particular step of procedure only.[10]

Decision

12.25 Whether to sanction the employment of counsel is a matter within the discretion of the sheriff. An appeal court is unlikely to interfere with his decision unless there has been an obvious miscarriage of justice or the expenses have become a great deal more valuable than the merits.[11] The criterion for giving sanction is not that of necessity, because in the sheriff court, unlike the Court of Session, it is not necessary for a party who desires legal representation to be represented by counsel or a solicitor-advocate. The test appears to be whether the employment of counsel is appropriate by reason of circumstances of difficulty or complexity, or the importance or value of the claim.[12] A claim of small value may involve imputations on the personal or professional character of a party of such seriousness that representation by counsel is appropriate.[13] It has been said that where the case is one of serious difficulty, or one of very large value, or one which relates to personal character, the employment of counsel may generally be sanctioned, and the onus is thrown on the other side to show why it should not be.[14] Sanction may, however, be refused where the case is not intrinsically difficult or complex and counsel has had to display a degree of forensic skill and ingenuity only because of the basic weakness of his client's position,[15] or because his client has failed to follow prescribed procedure.[16] Sanction is usually granted where counsel have appeared on both sides,[17] but it may also be granted where counsel has appeared on one side only.[18]

---

[8] *McKerchar, supra*; *Reid v. North Isles District Committee of Orkney C.C.*, 1912 S.C. 627; *Harris v. Lamont*, 1925 S.L.T. (Sh. Ct.) 141 (a decision which is "not justifiable": Dobie, p. 335); *Baird, supra*.

[9] *Taylor v. Drummond* (1848) 11 D. 223; *Hunt v. Rutherford* (1855) 17 D. 305; *Mackenzie v. Blakeney* (1879) 7 R. 51; *Wood's Trs v. Wood* (1900) 2 F. 870; *Reid, Baird, Turner, supra*.

[10] See para. 12.26.

[11] *Caldwell v. Dykes* (1906) 8 F. 839; *Elliott v. N.B. Ry* (1921) 38 Sh.Ct.Rep. 17 at 27; *Mason v. Foster Wheeler Power Products Ltd*, 1984 S.L.T. (Sh. Ct.) 5.

[12] *Leny v. Milne* (1899) 15 Sh.Ct.Rep. 76, *per* Sh. Pr. A. J. G. Mackay at 77; *Cochran v. Paton & Co.* (1919) 36 Sh.Ct.Rep. 3; *Elliott, supra* (case in nature of a test case); *Clarkson v. Hastie*, 1962 S.L.T. (Notes) 8; *Calder Chemicals Ltd, supra* (point of law on which no authoritative decision directly in point: see 1984 S.L.T. (Sh. Ct.) 96).

[13] *Gunn, Collie & Topping v. Purdie*, 1946 S.L.T. (Sh. Ct.) 11.

[14] *Leny, supra*.

[15] *Scottish Milk Agency Ltd v. Leiper* (1931) 47 Sh.Ct.Rep. 106; *Jack Davis Publicity Ltd v. Kennedy*, Sh. Pr. Caplan, Paisley Sh. Ct., Dec. 18, 1984, unreported.

[16] *W. Jack Baillie Associates Ltd v. Kennedy*, 1985 S.L.T. (Sh. Ct.) 53.

[17] *Turner, supra*; *Encyclopaedia*, xiii, para. 1445.

[18] *Cochran, supra*; Elliott, *supra*.

Interlocutor

While no special method of sanctioning the employment of counsel is prescribed, the sanction must be expressed by the sheriff in writing,[19] and cannot be conferred by implication from the instruction of counsel by both parties.[20] A note, certificate or other properly authenticated writing may suffice,[21] but the proper practice is to grant or refuse the motion expressly in an interlocutor. Where an appeal has been taken, it is incompetent to grant a certificate after the transmission of the process.[22] Where necessary, the interlocutor should specify whether the sanction is for senior and junior counsel, or for senior only, or for junior only.[23] It should also make clear whether the sanction is for the employment of counsel throughout while the case is at first instance, in which case the appropriate formula may be "Certifies the cause as suitable for the employment of counsel", or only for the employment of counsel at a particular stage of procedure, when the formula may be, for example, "Sanctions the employment of counsel at the debate." Where the sheriff's interlocutor is recalled on appeal *quoad* the merits, the fees to counsel sanctioned by the interlocutor may nevertheless be allowed on taxation.[24] Since sanction is primarily a matter for the judge who presided over the proceedings,[25] it is thought that the sheriff may not sanction the employment of counsel in a previous appeal to the sheriff principal, in the absence of a remit from the sheriff principal in appropriate terms.[26] Similarly, it is thought that the formula "Certifies the cause as suitable for the employment of counsel", when used by the sheriff, cannot sanction counsel's employment in a subsequent appeal to the sheriff principal, since the nature of the arguments on appeal cannot be predicted by the sheriff. It is submitted that the correct practice is for a motion to sanction the employment of counsel in an appeal to be made to, and dealt with by, the sheriff principal.[27] 12.26

Withdrawal of solicitor

A solicitor may cease to act for a party in a variety of circumstances. The party may decide to change his solicitor, or to dispense with the services of a solicitor and act in person as a party litigant; or the solicitor may decide that he will no longer act for the party. The solicitor may so decide for a number of reasons, perhaps the commonest being that he is unable to obtain instructions. Where a party has decided to change his solicitor, or to act in person, or where a solicitor decides that he will no longer act for a party, the retiring solicitor must intimate that fact at once by letter to the sheriff clerk and to all the other parties to the action.[28] The letter is lodged in process by the sheriff clerk.[29] Where his former client's 12.27

---

19 *Wood's Trs v. Wood* (1900) 2 F. 870.

20 *Hunt v. Rutherford* (1855) 17 D. 305; *aliter Harris v. Lamont*, 1925 S.L.T. (Sh. Ct.) 141.

21 *Daniel Logan & Son v. Rodger*, 1952 S.L.T. (Sh. Ct.) 99.

22 *Baird v. SMT Co. Ltd*, 1948 S.C. 526.

23 *Mason v. Foster Wheeler Power Products Ltd*, 1984 S.L.T. (Sh. Ct.) 5. *Cf. Alpine v. Heritors of Dumbarton* (1908) 16 S.L.T. 388; *Garden, Haig-Scott & Wallace v. Prudential Approved Society for Women*, 1927 S.L.T. 393 at 397–398.

24 *Taylor v. Steel-Maitland*, 1913 S.C. 978.

25 *Reid v. North Isles District Committee of Orkney C.C.*, 1912 S.C. 627.

26 See *Harris, supra.*

27 *e.g. Westwood v. Keay* (1949) 66 Sh.Ct.Rep. 147 at 153.

28 OCR, r. 24.1(1).

29 OCR, r. 24.1(2).

address is different from that stated in the instance and is known to him the withdrawing solicitor must disclose it to the other party or parties in order that intimation may be made as described in paragraph 12.28 below.[30] A solicitor who has decided not to continue to act sometimes lodges and intimates a formal motion for leave to withdraw. It is submitted that such motions are unnecessary. It is thought that a solicitor may resign at any time on giving reasonable notice to his client where that is possible, and the leave of the court is not required.[31] If such motions are entertained, it would seem that they should logically be heard in chambers in the absence of the other parties, because the reasons for withdrawal might reveal matters which are confidential between solicitor and client, and because, the purpose of the motion apparently being for the sheriff to decide what is the best thing to be done as between solicitor and client, there is no room for third parties to be brought in. There does not appear to be any reported case in which a sheriff hearing such a motion has considered whether the solicitor's reasons for withdrawal were adequate and has refused leave to withdraw in order to protect the interests of the client.

12.28 When a solicitor has intimated his withdrawal by letter as described in the preceding paragraph, the sheriff, either of his own volition or on the motion of a party, pronounces an interlocutor ordaining the solicitor's ex-client to appear or be represented at a specified date to state whether or not he intends to proceed with the action, under certification that if he fails to appear or be represented the sheriff may grant decree or make such order as he thinks fit.[32] The diet fixed must be not less than 14 days after the date of the interlocutor unless the sheriff orders otherwise.[33] Intimation of this "peremptory diet" is made "forthwith" by the party moving for it or by any other party appointed by the sheriff.[34] A certificate of intimation must be lodged in process.[35] If the party whose solicitor has withdrawn fails to attend the peremptory diet the sheriff may grant decree or make such other order or finding as he thinks fit.[36]

IV. Counterclaim

Competency of counterclaim

12.29 If the defender wishes to prosecute a claim against the pursuer, he may either bring a separate or cross-action against the pursuer or, where it is competent to do so, make a counterclaim against him.[37] Rule 19.1 of the Ordinary Cause Rules provides that in an action other than a family

---

30 *Sime, Sullivan & Dickson's Tr. v. Adam*, 1908 S.C. 32.

31 *Scott v. Christie* (1856) 19 D. 178; *Urquhart v. Grigor* (1857) 19 D. 853.

32 OCR, r. 24.2(1).

33 OCR, r. 24.2(2).

34 OCR, r. 24.2(3).

35 *ibid.*

36 OCR, r. 24.3.

37 In some circumstances a counterclaim may be unnecessary. Where a defender is sued for the contract price, having withheld payment on the ground that he has suffered damage through the pursuer's breach of contract, a counterclaim is unnecessary if he estimates his damage at less than the contract price: *British Motor Body Co. Ltd v. Thomas Shaw (Dundee) Ltd*, 1914 S.C. 922; *James Allan & Sons (Contractors) Ltd v. Gourlay*, 1956 S.L.T. (Sh. Ct.) 77. The jurisdiction of the court to entertain "counterclaims" under the Civil Jurisdiction and Judgments Act 1982 is noted in para. 3.40.

action or an action of multiplepoinding, a defender may counterclaim against a pursuer (a) where the counterclaim might have been made in a separate action in which it would not have been necessary to call as defender any person other than the pursuer, and (b) in respect of any matter (i) forming part of or arising out of the grounds of the action by the pursuer, or (ii) the decision of which is necessary for the determination of the question in controversy between the parties, or (iii) which, if the pursuer had been a person not otherwise subject to the jurisdiction of the court, might have been the subject-matter of an action against that pursuer in which jurisdiction would have arisen by reconvention.

Counterclaims by or against the Crown

The Crown Proceedings Act 1947 makes special provision as to counterclaims in actions brought by or against the Crown. These have already been considered.[38] **12.30**

Counterclaim in family actions

Strictly speaking there is no such thing as a counterclaim in a family action but rule 33.34 of the Ordinary Cause Rules which deals with defences in a family action provides that the defender may set out certain claims in his defences. This rule is considered elsewhere.[39] **12.31**

Procedure

Lodging

The defender makes his counterclaim against the pursuer in the defences, when they are lodged or during adjustment, or by amendment at any other stage, with leave of the sheriff and subject to such conditions, if any, as to expenses or otherwise as the sheriff thinks fit.[40] The sheriff may deal with the counterclaim as if it had been stated in a separate action.[41] He may regulate procedure in relation to the counterclaim as he thinks fit,[42] grant decree for the counterclaim in whole or in part or for the difference between it and the sum sued for by the pursuer,[43] or he may dismiss it.[44] He also has a discretion to allow or refuse any amendment of the defender's answers or pleas-in-law which is consequential on the lodging of the counterclaim.[45] **12.32**

Form

The defences which include a counterclaim must commence with a crave setting out the counterclaim in such form as, if it had been made in a separate action, would have been appropriate in the initial writ in that separate action, and must include answers to the condescendence of the initial writ, a statement of facts in numbered paragraphs setting out the facts on which the counterclaim is founded, incorporating by reference, if necessary, any matter contained in the defences, and appropriate **12.33**

---

[38] See paras 4.60 to 4.62.
[39] See para. 22.52.
[40] OCR, r. 19.1(2).
[41] OCR, r. 19.4(a).
[42] OCR, r. 19.4(b).
[43] OCR, r. 19.4(c).
[44] para. 12.37.
[45] OCR, r. 18.2(c).

pleas-in-law.[46] Where a record requires to be lodged in an action in which a counterclaim is included in the defences, the pleadings must be set out in the order of the crave of the initial writ, the condescendence and answers relating thereto, the pleas-in-law of the parties relating to the craves of the initial writ, the crave of the counterclaim, the statement of facts and answers relating thereto, and the pleas-in-law relating to the counterclaim.[47]

Warrants

12.34 The defender who makes a counterclaim may apply for a warrant for arrestment on the dependence which would have been permitted had the warrant been sought in an initial writ in a separate action.[48] The application, if made at the time of making the counterclaim, is made by inserting after the crave of the counterclaim the words "Warrant for arrestment on the dependence applied for".[49] If it is made at a later stage it is by precept of arrestment.[50] The application is granted by the sheriff clerk writing on the defences, the defences as adjusted or the minute of amendment the words "Grants warrant as craved", and adhibiting below those words his signature together with the date.[51] The warrant has the like effect as it would have in an initial writ.[52]

Subsequent procedure

12.35 The sheriff may (a) deal with the counterclaim as if it had been stated in a separate action[53]; (b) regulate procedure as he thinks fit[54]; and (c) grant decree for the counterclaim in whole or in part or for the difference between it and the claim sued for.[55] It is thought that the sheriff's power to regulate procedure includes power to hear and try the counterclaim along with, or before, or after, the claim in the pursuer's initial writ, as he may consider just and expedient in the circumstances[56]; and, if he directs evidence to be led with regard to either claim separately from the other, to hold that such evidence shall, so far as competent and relevant, be evidence with regard to the other claim.[57]

12.36 The sheriff may dispose of the pursuer's action—as by dismissing it,[58] or by granting decree for a sum admittedly due[59] or in respect of which no relevant defence has been stated[60]—and allow the counterclaim to proceed as if it were a substantive action.[61] Where a sum is admittedly due to the pursuer, or no relevant defence has been stated, it is normally correct to grant decree in the pursuer's favour in the principal action without delay,

---

[46] OCR, r. 19.1(3).
[47] OCR, r.19.2A.
[48] OCR, r. 19.2(1).
[49] OCR, r. 19.2(2)(a).
[50] OCR, r. 19.2(2)(b). For precept of arrestment, see para. 11.17.
[51] OCR, r. 19.2(3).
[52] OCR, r. 19.2(4).
[53] OCR, r. 19.4(a).
[54] OCR, r. 19.4(b). See *Heritage House Ltd v. Brown*, 1995 S.L.T. (Sh. Ct.) 101.
[55] OCR, r. 19.4(c).
[56] *cf.* RCS, r. 25.5(1).
[57] *cf.* RCS, r. 25.5(2).
[58] *McKay v. McIntosh*, 1952 S.L.T. (Sh. Ct.) 88; *Feld British Agencies Ltd v. James Pringle Ltd*, 1961 S.L.T. 123.
[59] *Armour & Melvin v. Mitchell*, 1934 S.C. 94; *Grant v. McAlister* (1948) 64 Sh.Ct.Rep. 261.
[60] *Fulton Clyde Ltd v. J. F. McCallum & Co.*, 1960 S.C. 78.
[61] OCR, r. 19.4(a).

..d not to postpone doing so or to supersede extract until the determination of a counterclaim which is not an answer to the pursuer's claim. The latter courses may be justifiable in exceptional circumstances, as where the court is satisfied that the pursuer may seek to avoid the enforcement of any decree pronounced against him in the counterclaim or may be unable to satisfy such a decree [62] Similarly, where decree is pronounced in the pursuer's favour in the principal action, there is normally no reason to reserve the question of the expenses of the principal action and await the result of the counterclaim before awarding the pursuer the expenses to which he is entitled in the principal action.[63]

Another course which may be open to the sheriff is to dismiss the counterclaim and either allow the pursuer's action to proceed, or grant decree as craved if there is no relevant defence.[64] It has been held, in unusual circumstances, that where a counterclaim has been dismissed the defender cannot raise a separate action stating the same claim until the principal action has been finally disposed of.[65] It is thought, however, that the defender may raise such an action if he states therein that he abandons his right to proceed with the counterclaim.[66] **12.37**

An interlocutor disposing of the whole merits, but not of the whole expenses, of the principal action or counterclaim cannot be appealed without the leave of the sheriff.[67] The principles to be applied as regards the expenses of trying a counterclaim are the same as if it had been tried in a separate action.[68] **12.38**

The lodging of a counterclaim may have other procedural consequences. It may affect the running of prescription.[69] It may have a bearing on the determination of the value of the cause.[70] It may bring about the recall of an order upon the pursuer to sist a mandatary.[71] And if admitted or proved to the extent that the pursuer's claim is reduced below the pecuniary limit for summary causes, the pursuer may be awarded expenses on the lower scale.[72] In certain circumstances, however, that might be an unfair result, especially where the net award is below the pecuniary limit for small claims. **12.39**

Abandonment

The pursuer cannot be prevented from abandoning his action by reason only of a counterclaim by the defender.[73] Abandonment by the pursuer does not affect the counterclaim, which continues as a separate **12.40**

---

[62] *cf. Montecchi v. Shimco (U.K.) Ltd* [1979] 1 W.L.R. 1180; *Continental Illinois National Bank and Trust Co. of Chicago v. Papanicolaou* [1986] 2 Lloyd's Rep. 441.

[63] *Grant v. McAllister, supra.*

[64] *Christie v. Birrells*, 1910 S.C. 986; *Smart v. Wilkinson*, 1928 S.C. 383; *Commissioner for Arran and Easton Trs v. Carmichael* (1949) 66 Sh.Ct.Rep. 64; *Alexander Allan & Sons v. McGee*, 1990 S.L.T. (Sh. Ct.) 2.

[65] *Stevenson v. Fraser & Carmichael* (1914) 30 Sh.Ct.Rep. 277.

[66] Dobie, pp. 153–154.

[67] *Palombo v. James Jack (Hyndford) Ltd*, 1977 S.L.T. (Sh. Ct.) 95.

[68] *MacFarlane v. MacDougall*, 1932 S.L.T. (Sh. Ct.) 36.

[69] *Beveridge & Kellas v. Abercromby*, 1996 S.C.L.R. 558. For a claim to be made timeously it is necessary that it should be made in appropriate proceedings and brought to the attention of the other party. *Cf.* the terms of OCR, r. 19.1.

[70] See para. 2.30.

[71] *NV Ondix International v. James Landay Ltd*, 1963 S.C. 270.

[72] *Phoenix Fireplace Builders v. McCubbin*, 1953 S.L.T. (Sh. Ct.) 75.

[73] OCR, r. 19.3(1). On abandonment see paras 14.15 to 14.30.

cause.[74] Any expenses payable by the pursuer as a condition of, or in consequence of, abandonment do not include the expenses of the counterclaim.[75]

12.41 The defender may abandon his counterclaim. The procedure is *mutatis mutandis* the same as for abandonment of an action by a pursuer.[76]

V. Third-Party Procedure

Object

12.42 Third-party procedure is available in both the Court of Session and the sheriff court in order that in appropriate cases certain questions arising out of one matter, including questions of liability between the defender and a third party, and claims by the defender against a third party for contribution, relief or indemnity, may be disposed of by the court in one action, thereby saving time and expense.[77] The procedure also enables the third party to be heard on any matter in which he has a relevant interest in relation to the case between the pursuer and the defender.[78] In each court the provisions of the rules are concerned with procedure only, not with matters of substantive right.[79] They apply not only to a claim by a defender, but also to a claim by a third party and to a claim by a pursuer in respect of a counterclaim by a defender.[80]

12.43 In the Court of Session third-party procedure was introduced by rule 20 of the Rules of Court enacted on July 19, 1934, abolished by the Act of Sederunt of May 25, 1937,[81] and reintroduced by the Act of Sederunt (Rules of Court Amendment) 1963, the terms of which were re-enacted in rule 85 of the Rules of Court 1965, and subsequently amended.[82] The provisions currently applicable are contained in Chapter 26 of the Rules of the Court of Session 1994. In the sheriff court, provision is made for third-party procedure in certain summary causes brought under the Consumer Credit Act 1974 by Part II of the Act of Sederunt (Consumer Credit Act 1974) 1985, and in all ordinary causes by rule 20.1 of the Ordinary Cause Rules. The provisions of rule 20.1 are virtually identical to the provisions of rule 26.1 of the Rules of the Court of Session, and decisions on the Court of Session rule must apply in sheriff court practice.

---

[74] OCR, r. 19.3(2).

[75] OCR, r. 19.3(1).

[76] OCR, r. 23.2 applying the provisions of r. 23.1 to counterclaims. For abandonment under r. 23.1, see para. 14.21.

[77] *Findlay v. National Coal Board*, 1965 S.L.T. 328; *Winchester v. Ramsals*, 1966 S.C. 41; *Beedie v. Norrie*, 1966 S.C. 207, *per* L.P. Clyde at 210; *Buchan v. Thomson*, 1976 S.L.T. 42, *per* Lord Fraser at 44; *Nimmo's Exrs v. White's Exrs*, 1976 S.L.T. 70; *Anderson v. Anderson*, 1981 S.L.T. 271. As to jurisdiction over third parties by virtue of the Civil Jurisdiction and Judgments Act 1982, see para. 3.39.

[78] *Barton v. William Love & Co. Ltd*, 1968 S.L.T. (Notes) 27.

[79] *Findlay, supra*, at 330; *Aitken v. Norrie*, 1966 S.C. 168, *per* L.P. Clyde at 174; *Beedie, supra*; *R. & W. Watson Ltd v. David Traill & Sons Ltd*, 1972 S.L.T. (Notes) 38.

[80] OCR, r. 20.1(2). *Cf.* RCS, r. 26.1(2). For an example of a third party convening a second third party, see *Nicol Homeworld Contracts Ltd v. Charles Gray Builders Ltd*, 1986 S.L.T. 317.

[81] "Third Party Notice", 1937 S.L.T. (News) 98.

[82] 1965 R.C. 85 is discussed by Maxwell, pp. 233–236, and B. Gill, "Aspects of Relevancy in Third Party Procedure", 1968 S.L.T. (News) 65.

Competency

Rule 20.1 provides: **12.44**

"(1) Where, in an action, a defender claims that—

(a) he has in respect of the subject-matter of the action a right of contribution, relief or indemnity against any person who is not a party to the action, or

(b) a person whom the pursuer is not bound to call as a defender should be made a party to the action along with the defender in respect that such person is—

(i) solely liable, or jointly or jointly and severally liable with the defender, to the pursuer in respect of the subject-matter of the action, or

(ii) liable to the defender in respect of a claim arising from or in connection with the liability, if any, of the defender to the pursuer,

he may apply by motion for an order for service of a third party notice upon that other person in Form O10 for the purpose of convening that other person as a third party to the action.

(2) Where—

(a) a pursuer against whom a counterclaim has been made, or

(b) a third party convened in the action, seeks in relation to the claim against him, to make against a person who is not a party, a claim mentioned in paragraph (1) as a claim which could be made by a defender against a third party, he shall apply by motion for an order for service of a third party notice in Form O10 in the same manner as a defender under that paragraph; and rules 20.2 to 20.6 shall, with the necessary modifications, apply to such a claim as they apply in relation to such a claim by a defender."

First branch of Ordinary Cause Rule 20.1(1)

The rule has three branches or limbs, which apply to different sets of circumstances. The first applies in a case where "a defender claims that he has in respect of the subject-matter of an action a right of contribution, relief, or indemnity against any person who is not a party to the action." Here, the defender claims that he himself has a right against the third party, but does not claim that the pursuer has any such right: the third party is not a defender in the main action, but only in what is truly a separate action of relief by the defender against him, which is incorporated in the main process. Thus a third party may be competently convened by a defender in an action of damages for personal injuries after the expiry of three years from the date of the act or neglect giving rise to the action[83]; and where there are two or more pursuers, a pursuer may be convened as a third party.[84] **12.45**

The defender may invoke the first branch of the rule if he has a title and interest to do so when the proceedings against the third party are commenced by the service of the third-party notice.[85] He has a title if **12.46**

---

[83] *Findlay v. National Coal Board*, 1965 S.L.T. 328; *Travers v. Neilson*, 1967 S.C. 155.

[84] *Buchan v. Thomson*, 1976 S.L.T. 42.

[85] *Cobham v. Minter*, 1986 S.L.T. 336.

his claim is based upon a right which he then has,[86] and he may have an interest although he has no enforceable right to recover from the third party until after he has paid the pursuer.[87] He may claim a right of contribution only where he and the third party are co-obligants to the same principal.[88] As to when he may claim a right of relief, different views have been expressed. One view is that the third party must have undertaken to bear or share the obligation to the pursuer, so that the pursuer could, if he wished, have sued the third party direct, and that the third party's liability to the defender must be commensurate or co-extensive with the defender's liability to the pursuer.[89] The other view is that the expression "right of relief" is not to be construed as a term of art,[90] and that third-party procedure may be invoked by a defender seeking recourse in respect only of certain components of the pursuer's claim.[91] The latter view appears to be consistent with the objective of the avoidance of multiplicity of actions in appropriate cases which is the rationale of third-party procedure.

12.47 An employer who is sued by an employee in respect of personal injuries suffered in consequence of a defect in equipment provided by the employer may convene a third party to whose fault the defect is wholly or partly attributable, and claim up to 100 per cent relief from that party.[92]

12.48 A defender sued in contract cannot claim any right of relief in terms of section 3(2) of the Law Reform (Miscellaneous Provisions) (Scotland) Act 1940, since section 3 is concerned with contribution among joint wrongdoers.[93] Similarly a defender sued on the ground of negligence cannot claim such a right on the ground that the third party was in breach of duty to the defender, because the basis of a third party's liability to make a contribution under section 3(2) is a relationship in negligence with the pursuer alone.[94] A defender sued on the ground of negligence may not claim such a right in terms of section 3(2) against a person who has been sued and has been held not liable on the merits or upon a preliminary plea (including a plea of time-bar): he may, however, do so against a person who has been sued by the pursuer but released from the process as the result of the pursuer's abandonment of the action as laid against him.[95]

Second branch of Ordinary Cause Rule 20.1(1)

12.49 The second branch of the rule applies where a defender claims "that a person whom the pursuer is not bound to call as a defender should be made a party to the action along with the defender in respect that such a person is solely liable, or jointly and severally liable with the defender, to the pursuer in respect of the subject-matter of the action." In this case the

---

86 *Cobham, supra.*

87 *Findlay, Beedie, R. & W. Watson, Cobham, supra.*

88 *Lanarkshire Speedway and Sports Stadium Ltd v. Gray*, 1970 S.L.T. (Notes) 54.

89 *ibid.*

90 *Nimmo's Exrs v. White's Exr*, 1976 S.L.T. 70; *Anderson v. Anderson*, 1981 S.L.T. 271; *Nicol Homeworld Contracts Ltd v. Charles Gray Builders Ltd*, 1986 S.L.T. 317.

91 *Anderson, supra.*

92 Employers' Liability (Defective Equipment) Act 1969, s. 1; *Yuille v. Daks Simpson Ltd*, 1984 S.L.T. 115.

93 *National Coal Board v. Knight Bros*, 1972 S.L.T. (Notes) 24.

94 *R. & W. Watson Ltd v. David Traill & Sons Ltd*, 1972 S.L.T. (Notes) 38.

95 *Singer v. Gray Tool Co. (Europe) Ltd*, 1984 S.L.T. 149.

defender is not himself claiming any right against the third party, but claims that the third party is liable to the pursuer in respect of the pursuer's claim and should accordingly be made a party to the action.[96] The pursuer cannot, however, recover damages directly from the third party unless he amends his pleadings to include a crave for decree against the third party, supported by appropriate averments and pleas-in-law.[97] The third party, although he thereby becomes in effect an additional defender, remains designated a third party.[98] Sometimes the latter rule is overlooked, and the pursuer amends to design the third party as an additional defender.[99] That course is undesirable because it obscures the means by which the third party entered the process; it causes the other parties to amend their references to the third party in their own pleadings; and where the pursuer directs his action against only one of a number of third parties, it is confusing that that third party should be designed as a defender while the others are not.

If the defender claims only that the third party is solely liable to the pursuer, and the pursuer does not amend to crave decree against the third party, with appropriate averments and pleas-in-law, the action so far as directed against the third party will be dismissed.[1] If the defender claims that the third party is jointly and severally liable with him to the pursuer, and the pursuer does not so amend, the possible consequences include the following. (1) The court holds the third party wholly liable, and assoilzies the defender. (2) The court holds the third party jointly and severally liable with the defender: the court then decerns against the defender for payment to the pursuer of the damages awarded, finds the defender entitled to a right of relief against the third party to the extent of the appropriate proportion of the award of damages, and decerns against the third party for payment to the defender of the specific sum representing that proportion of the award. In each of these two cases the pursuer may raise separate proceedings against the third party: in the latter case he may do so if the defender does not satisfy the decree. In either case, however, his right against the third party will generally at that stage be time-barred. **12.50**

In general, the pursuer may not amend to include a crave for decree against the third party, with appropriate averments and pleas-in-law, after the expiry of a statutory period of limitation[2]; but in an action in respect of personal injuries or death the period may run from a date later than the date on which the injuries were sustained or the death occurred, or the court may exercise its statutory discretion to dispense with the limitation rules.[3] It is sufficient if the crave is amended before the expiry of the limitation period, and the appropriate averments and pleas are added **12.51**

---

[96] *Buchan v. Thomson*, 1976 S.L.T. 42, *per* Lord Fraser at 45.

[97] *Findlay v. National Coal Board*, 1965 S.L.T. 328; *Beedie v. Norrie*, 1966 S.C. 207; *Thomson v. Greig*, 1967 S.L.T. (Notes) 113.

[98] *Jack v. Glasgow Corporation*, 1965 S.L.T. 227; *Aitken v. Norrie*, 1966 S.C. 168, *per* Lord Kissen at 171. *Cf. Thomson, supra.*

[99] *e.g. Carson v. Howard Doris Ltd*, 1981 S.L.T. 273; *Robertson v. Crane Hire (Paisley) Ltd*, 1982 S.L.T. 505; *Harris v. Roberts*, 1983 S.L.T. 452.

[1] *Aitken v. Norrie, supra; Connor v. Andrew Main & Sons*, 1967 S.L.T. (Notes) 71.

[2] *Aitken v. Norrie, supra.*

[3] Prescription and Limitation (Scotland) Act 1973, ss. 17, 18 (both substituted by Prescription and Limitation (Scotland) Act 1984, s. 2) and 19A (inserted by Law Reform (Miscellaneous Provisions) (Scotland) Act 1980, s. 23, and amended by 1984 Act); *Harris v. Roberts*, 1983 S.L.T. 452. See para. 10.40.

subsequently.[4] It appears from the decision of the Second Division in *Boyle v. Glasgow Corporation*,[5] which is applicable and binding in the sheriff court, that the case against the third party will not be time-barred if the pursuer, before the expiry of the limitation period, lodges a minute of amendment and intimates to the third party his motion asking for the minute to be received and answered within a specified period.

Third branch of Ordinary Cause Rule 20.1(1)

12.52 The third branch of the rule applies when a defender claims "that a person whom the pursuer is not bound to call as a defender should be made a party to the action along with the defender in respect that such a person is liable to the defender in respect of a claim arising from or in connection with the liability, if any, of the defender to the pursuer". This branch is really wide enough to include the other two branches and removes any doubt about the meaning of the phrase "right of contribution, relief or indemnity" in the first branch.[6]

Advantage to defender

12.53 It is thought that the only cases where it is to a defender's advantage to convene a third party are those where the defender has a right of contribution, relief, indemnity or other claim (under the first or third branch of the rule), or where there are reasonable prospects of liability being apportioned between the defender and the third party (under the second branch). In such cases it is in the defender's interests to convene the third party rather than to be obliged to intimate to the third party his claim against him and every step of the pursuer's action, and subsequently to raise an action of relief,[7] to which an extinctive prescriptive period of two years applies.[8] But where it appears that liability must be attributed either solely to the defender or solely to the third party (as in certain accident cases where the accident must have been caused by the sole fault of either one or the other), there is no advantage to the defender in convening a third party. It is preferable for the defender to blame the third party without convening him to the process and thereby giving him an opportunity to exonerate himself. If the court thereafter holds that liability rests solely with the unconvened third party, the defender will be assoilzied. If the third party were to be convened and exculpated, the defender being held wholly liable, the defender would be found liable to the third party in expenses. The defender by blaming the third party without convening him may encourage the pursuer to amend by convening him as an additional defender, if he is not barred from doing so by statutory rules of limitation; and if the pursuer were to so amend he might incur at least some liability for the third party's expenses if he were assoilzied.

---

[4] *Cross v. Noble*, 1975 S.L.T. (Notes) 33.

[5] 1975 S.C. 238; followed in *Stewart v. Highlands & Islands Development Board*, 1991 S.L.T. 787 and *Kinnaird v. Donaldson*, 1992 S.C.L.R. 694.

[6] See *Green's Annotated Rules of the Court of Session*, para. 26.1.6.

[7] *Dorman Long & Co. v. Harrower* (1899) 1 F. 1109, *per* Lord Kinnear at 1115; *Alexander v. Perth C.C.* (1939) 56 Sh.Ct.Rep. 20 at 26, 28; *Central SMT Co. Ltd v. Cloudsley*, 1974 S.L.T. (Sh. Ct.) 70 at 72. See para. 24.07.

[8] Prescription and Limitation (Scotland) Act 1973, s. 8A, inserted by Prescription and Limitation (Scotland) Act 1984, s. 1.

Procedure

Averments

Where a defender intends to apply by motion for an order for service of a third-party notice before closing of the record, he must, before lodging the motion, set out in his defences, either by adjustment of them or in a separate statement of facts annexed thereto, averments setting out the grounds on which he maintains that the proposed third party is liable to him by contribution, relief or indemnity, or should be made a party to the action, and appropriate pleas-in-law.[9] Where the application is made after the closing of the record, he must, on lodging the notice, lodge a minute of amendment containing that material unless these grounds and pleas have been set out in his defences in the closed record.[10] A motion for an order for service of a third-party notice must be lodged before the commencement of the hearing on the merits of the cause.[11] **12.54**

Order for service

A defender may seek to have more than one third party convened.[12] A third-party notice must be served on the third party within 14 days after the date of the interlocutor allowing service.[13] If service is not made within that period, the order for service ceases to have effect. No service of the notice may then be made, unless a further order for service has been applied for and granted.[14] **12.55**

Warrant for arrestment

A defender applying for an order for service of a third-party notice may also apply for a warrant for arrestment to found jurisdiction or arrestment on the dependence, which would have been permitted had the warrant been sought in an initial writ in a separate action.[15] Averments supporting the application for such a warrant must be included in the defences or in a separate statement of facts.[16] The application may be made at the time of applying for the third-party notice or at any stage in the cause thereafter.[17] A certified copy of the interlocutor granting warrant for the diligence so applied for is sufficient authority for execution.[18] **12.56**

Service of notice

The third-party notice must be as nearly as may be in terms of Form O10 as set out in Appendix 1 to the Rules.[19] Somewhat strangely, the Ordinary Cause Rules 1993, unlike the former Rules, make no express provision for the mode of service of a third-party notice. It is submitted, however, that service will, as formerly, be competent if effected by any of the methods which are competent for service of an initial writ. That will **12.57**

---

[9] OCR, r. 20.2(1).
[10] OCR, r. 20.2(2).
[11] OCR, r. 20.2(3).
[12] *Findlay v. National Coal Board*, 1965 S.L.T. 328.
[13] OCR, r. 20.4(1).
[14] OCR, r. 20.4(2).
[15] OCR, r. 20.3(1).
[16] OCR, r. 20.3(2).
[17] OCR, r. 20.3(3).
[18] OCR, r. 20.3(4).
[19] OCR, r. 20.1(1).

involve postal service or service by sheriff officer.[20] A copy of the pleadings (including any adjustments and amendments) must be served with the third-party notice.[21] It is thought that the copy pleadings accompanying the notice must accurately show the state of the pleadings at the date of the order, and in particular the defender's averments and pleas directed against the third party: otherwise the nature of the action, and of the defender's claim against the third party, will not "more fully appear" from the copy pleadings in terms of the notice,[22] and the service will be inept and of no effect.[23] Where the pleadings are not readily intelligible because the defender's averments and pleas directed against the third party have been added at adjustment or by amendment, the sheriff may consider it appropriate to order the defender to make up an open record of the pleadings as adjusted or amended to the date of the order, and to serve it along with the third-party notice.

12.58 A copy of the third-party notice with a certificate of service attached must be lodged in process by the defender.[24]

Terms of notice

12.59 The third-party notice informs the third party that if he wishes to resist either the claim of the pursuer against the defender,[25] or the claim of the defender against the third party,[26] he must lodge answers in the action within 28 days and must pay a court fee.[27] The period of 28 days may be varied by the sheriff on cause shown.[28]

Answers for third party

12.60 The third party's answers are headed "Answers for E.F. (designed), Third Party / in the action at the instance of A.B. (designed), Pursuer / against / C.D. (designed), Defender", and must include answers to the averments of the defender against him in the form of numbered paragraphs corresponding to the numbered articles annexed to the summons and incorporating, if the third party so wishes, answers to the averments of the pursuer, or where a separate statement of facts has been lodged by the defender, in the form of numbered paragraphs corresponding thereto, and appropriate pleas-in-law.[29] The third party's answers are drafted on the same principles as a defender's answers.[30]

12.61 Since one of the objects of third-party procedure is to enable the third party to be heard on any matter in which he has a relevant interest in relation to the case between the pursuer and the defender,[31] the third party may resist the claim of the pursuer against the defender.[32] He may, if he so

---

20 For detailed provisions regarding modes of service, see OCR, rr. 5.3–5.6.
21 OCR, r. 20.4(3).
22 See OCR App. 1, Form O10, first para.
23 *cf. Miller v. National Coal Board*, 1960 S.C. 376.
24 OCR, r. 20.4(4).
25 See para. 12.61.
26 See para. 12.62.
27 OCR, App. 1, Form O10.
28 OCR, r. 20.5(1).
29 OCR, r. 20.5(2).
30 See paras 9.108 to 9.113.
31 *Barton v. William Low & Co. Ltd*, 1968 S.L.T. (Notes) 27.
32 OCR, App. 1, Form O10.

desires, answer the averments of the pursuer in the same way as if the third party had been called as a defender, and may adopt the averments of one party against another. Thus, for example, the third party may state a preliminary plea-in-law directed against the pursuer's case,[33] or defences challenging its merits.[34] In a personal injuries action the third party may adopt the pursuer's averments of fault against the defender and also blame the pursuer.[35]

In his answers the third party may himself make, as against any person who is not already a party to the action, a further "third party" claim of the nature specified in rule 20.1(2)[36]; and in that event the provisions of rules 20.2 to 20.6 apply *mutatis mutandis* to the claim between the third party and such other person.[37] There is no provision in the Ordinary Cause Rules equivalent to that in rule 26.7 (5) of the Rules of the Court of Session which provides that the same procedure shall be followed, as between the defender and the third party, or as between the pursuer and the third party, as would have been followed in an ordinary action between those parties as pursuer and defender therein respectively. The third-party notice, however, states that the third party may resist the claim of the defender against him, and it is thought that a third party convened under the first or third branch of rule 20.1(1) may state a counterclaim against the defender, since the third party is in effect the defender in a separate action brought against him which has been procedurally linked with the action brought against the defender by the pursuer.[38] **12.62**

Further procedure

Where a third party lodges answers the sheriff clerk fixes a date and time under rule 9.2 for an options hearing, as if the third party had lodged a notice of intention to defend and the period of notice had expired on the date of lodging answers.[39] At the options hearing or at any time thereafter the sheriff may grant such decree or other order as he thinks fit.[40] A decree or other order against the third party has effect and is extractable in the same way as a decree or other order would be against a defender.[41] Parties are not confined by the terms of the third-party notice and the state of the pleadings when it was served, to the contentions then made: by adjustment subsequent to a third-party notice alleging sole fault, the defender and the third party may make averments of joint fault *inter se* in pursuance of the provisions of section 3 of the Law Reform (Miscellaneous Provisions) (Scotland) Act 1940.[42] The averments of one party against another may be adopted by any other party to the action, provided that such other party adds any necessary pleas-in-law, and that where the pursuer adopts the defender's averments against the third party in a case under the second branch of rule 20.1(1), the crave is appropriately amended.[43] **12.63**

---

[33] *Barton, supra.*
[34] *Winchester v. Ramsay*, 1966 S.C. 41.
[35] *Algeo v. Melville Dundas & Whitson Ltd*, 1973 S.L.T. (Notes) 90.
[36] *e.g. Nicol Homeworld Contracts Ltd v. Charles Gray Builders Ltd*, 1986 S.L.T. 317.
[37] OCR, r. 20.1(2).
[38] *Buchan v. Thomson*, 1976 S.L.T. 42; *cf. Mair v. Simpson's Motors Ltd*, 1966 S.C. 198.
[39] OCR, r. 20.6(1).
[40] OCR, r. 20.6(2).
[41] OCR, r. 20.6(3).
[42] *Beedie v. Norrie*, 1966 S.C. 207.
[43] *Findlay v. National Coal Board*, 1965 S.L.T. 328 at 329.

Where the third party has stated a plea to the competency of his being convened or to the relevancy of any averments of a right of contribution, relief or indemnity, or connecting him with the subject-matter of the action, the sheriff may, after closing the record and hearing parties in debate on the plea, dismiss the action so far as directed against the third party.

Proof

12.64 In cases where inquiry is necessary, it is thought that the sheriff may allow the case so far as directed against the third party to proceed to proof or proof before answer either along with or separately from the action between the pursuer and the defender, or may deal with the matter otherwise as in his discretion he thinks fit.[44] In certain cases it may be appropriate to allow a proof or proof before answer directed to the question of the third party's liability to the defender, and *quoad ultra* to allow the pursuer and the defender a proof of their averments on record but sist the action in so far as it relates to the defender's liability to the pursuer until the determination of the question of the third party's liability to the defender.[45] There is no provision in Chapter 20 of the Ordinary Cause Rules corresponding to the provision in rule 26.7(4) of the Rules of the Court of Session that in any case where the merits of the pursuer's case are challenged by the third party the latter is entitled to appear and take part in the cause as if he were a defender. It is thought, however, that where the third party challenges the merits of the pursuer's case[46] the Court of Session rule should be followed and the sheriff should permit him to appear at the proof of the pursuer's case and take part in the cause and lead evidence therein, and should order that such evidence, so far as competent and relevant, shall be evidence for or against the pursuer, or for or against the defender, and shall be available to all parties in the cause.[47]

Judgment

12.65 The court necessarily has full power to pronounce a judgment or judgments in favour of or against any of the various parties to a cause in which a third-party notice has been served, and, since the power to award expenses is inherent in the court,[48] to deal with expenses as between them. Thus, where the pursuer has craved decree against the third party, the sheriff may after proof pronounce a decree in favour of the pursuer against the third party, or may assoilzie the third party from any liability to the pursuer in respect of the subject-matter of the action, as if he had been a party to the original action, but without prejudice to any liability of the third party to the defender.[49] Any decree, interlocutor or order against the third party takes effect and is extractable in the same way as a decree, interlocutor or other order against the defender.[50]

---

[44] *cf.* RCS, r. 26.7(3).
[45] *Cookney v. Laverty*, 1967 S.L.T. (Notes) 89 (opinion not reported in 1968 S.C. 207 at 210).
[46] See para. 12.61.
[47] *Winchester v. Ramsay*, 1966 S.C. 41.
[48] See para. 9.94.
[49] *Aitken v. Norrie*, 1966 S.C. 168 at 176–177.
[50] OCR, r. 20.6 (3).

VI. Objection to Documents by Way of Exception

Rule

Actions of reduction are incompetent in the sheriff court, and fall exclusively within the jurisdiction of the Court of Session.[51] A writing which has a defect which renders it void or *ipso jure* null may, however, be set aside in the sheriff court at common law: an objection in respect of such a nullity may be stated in any pleading whenever it is founded on in any court, and the judge is bound to give immediate effect to the objection, the absolute nullity rendering reduction unnecessary, although sometimes convenient. Examples of writings which are void or *ipso jure* null are those which are executed without the necessary statutory solemnities, or are unstamped or understamped; or are contrary to public morals, or to statutes declaring that no action can be maintained on them.[52] **12.66**

Before the enactment of section 11 of the Sheriff Courts (Scotland) Act 1877, when a question arose in a sheriff court action as to the validity of a deed by reason of a defect other than one which rendered it void or *ipso jure* null, the sheriff was obliged to sist the cause until an action of reduction was brought in the Court of Session to settle the question.[53] Since the coming into effect of section 11 of the 1877 Act, however, certain documents may be set aside in the sheriff court "*ope exceptionis*" or "by way of exception", which means that they may be set aside at the instance of any party otherwise than by the raising of an action of reduction.[54] Section 11 was modified and replaced by rules 50 and 51 of the original Schedule annexed to the 1907 Act. The modern rule, which is in broadly similar terms, is that when a deed or writing is founded on by a party, any objections to it by any other party may be stated and maintained by exception, without reducing it.[55] The purpose of the rule is that, in cases to which it applies, an objection to a deed or writing founded on may be made good in the same process, thus avoiding the delay, trouble, expense and multiplication of procedure involved in raising and litigating in the Court of Session, while the sheriff court process is sisted, an action of reduction the expense of which might be wholly disproportionate to the amount at stake.[56] **12.67**

Competency

Nature of document

The characteristics which a document must possess to make it a subject of objection under rule 21.3 are these. **12.68**

(1) It must be "a deed or writing". It may be a probative deed.[57] But

---

[51] See para. 2.47.

[52] Mackay, *Practice*, ii, pp. 21–128; Dove Wilson, p. 216.

[53] Dove Wilson, pp. 60–61.

[54] *Dickson v. Murray* (1866) 4 M. 797, *per* L.J.-C. Inglis at 799; *Mackenzie v. Calder* (1868) 6 M. 833 at 834.

[55] OCR, r. 21.3(1). R.C. 53.8, which is similarly worded, in addition confers on the court a discretionary power to refuse to allow an objection to be stated if the court considers that the matter would be more conveniently tried in a separate action of reduction.

[56] *Donald v. Donald*, 1913 S.C. 274, *per* L.J.-C. Macdonald at 278, Lord Salvesen at 280; *Hopkinson Ltd v. Sanders*, 1941 S.L.T. (Sh. Ct.) 36 at 39. *Cf. Oswald v. Fairs*, 1911 S.C. 257, *per* L.P. Dunedin at 264; *Doherty v. Norwich Union Fire Insurance Society*, 1974 S.C. 213 at 219–220.

[57] *Hopkinson Ltd v. Sanders*, 1941 S.L.T. (Sh. Ct.) 36. *Cf. Inland Revenue v. Gibb*, 1963 S.L.T. (Notes) 66.

since the sheriff court does not have any inherent power to reduce its own decrees,[58] and the Court of Session has exclusive inherent power to reduce its own decrees as well as those of inferior courts,[59] an *ex facie* regular decree of court cannot be set aside by way of exception, whether it be a decree *in foro*,[60] a decree in absence[61] or a decree of registration of a protested bill of exchange.[62]

(2) It must be "founded on" by a party.

(3) It must be so founded on "in a cause", *i.e.* in any civil proceeding competent in the sheriff court.[63]

(4) It must not touch the interests of persons who are not parties to the cause, and cannot be compelled to make themselves parties to it. Only where no parties and no question, other than the parties and the question before the court, can be involved, may an objection be stated under the rule.[64] Thus, for example, the rule cannot be founded on in order to set aside a will[65]; or a bond where a co-obligant is absent from the process[66]; or an *ex facie* valid certificate by auditors of the value of a company's shares in the absence of the auditors[67]; or in order to rectify the register of a limited company in the absence of the company or other interested parties.[68]

12.69 The rule is thought to be unqualified in two respects. First, while certain *obiter dicta* in *Donald v. Donald*[69] have sometimes been understood to mean that objections may not be stated by way of exception to a document forming the basis of the action or defence,[70] it is submitted that there is no reason to read the rule as being impliedly qualified in that way.[71] Objections have been stated to such documents in many cases.[72] Secondly, although actions of reduction relating to questions of heritable right or title are expressly excluded from the sheriff's jurisdiction,[73] that does not affect the sheriff's right to entertain an objection stated by way of exception to a deed or writing in such a question when it would otherwise be appropriate to do so.[74]

---

[58] *Doherty v. Norwich Union Fire Insurance Society Ltd*, 1974 S.C. 213 at 218.

[59] *Innes v. Dunbar* (1534) Mor. 7320; *Jarvie's Trs v. Bannatyne*, 1927 S.C. 34, *per* L.P. Clyde at 38; *Doherty, supra.*

[60] *Leggat Bros v. Gray*, 1912 S.C. 230.

[61] *Neil v. McNair* (1901) 3 F.(J.) 85 at 89, *Jarvie's Trs, supra.*

[62] *Smith v. Hutchison*, 1926 S.L.T. (Sh. Ct.) 50.

[63] 1907 Act, s. 3(d).

[64] *Donald v. Donald* 1913 S.C. 274, explained in *Kilmaurs Dairy Association Ltd v. Brisbane and Beattie's Dairies* (1927) 43 Sh.Ct.Rep. 210; *Brodie & Hall Ltd v. Di Placido* (1938) 55 Sh.Ct.Rep. 82; *Hopkinson Ltd v. Sanders*, 1941 S.L.T. (Sh. Ct.) 36 (approved in *Bank of Ireland v. Dewar*, Sh. Pr. Caplan, Paisley Sh. Ct., May 8, 1986, unreported); and *Cavendish Pharmacies Ltd v. Stephenson Ltd*, 1998 S.L.T. (Sh.Ct.) 66.

[65] *Donald, supra*; *Bradford Equitable Building Society v. Thomson*, 1965 S.L.T. (Sh. Ct.) 54. *Cf. Roberts v. Fettes* (1901) 10 S.L.T. 319.

[66] *Lucarelli v. Buchanan*, 1954 S.L.T. (Sh. Ct.) 46.

[67] *Kelly v. Kelly*, 1986 S.L.T. 101. See also *Cavendish Pharmacies Ltd, supra.*

[68] *National Bank of Scotland Glasgow Nominees Ltd v. Adamson*, 1932 S.L.T. 492. See also *Scottish Amalgamated Silks Ltd v. Macalister*, 1930 S.L.T. 593.

[69] 1913 S.C. 274.

[70] *e.g. Scottish Amalgamated Silks Ltd v. Macalister*, 1930 S.L.T. 593 at 595; *National Bank of Scotland Glasgow Nominees Ltd v. Adamson*, 1932 S.L.T. 492 at 496; *Brown v. Hamilton D.C.*, 1983 S.C. (H.L.) 1, *per* Lord Dunpark at 23.

[71] *Black v. Campbell & Cameron Ltd* (1938) 54 Sh.Ct.Rep. 169 at 171–172; *Hopkinson Ltd v. Sanders*, 1941 S.L.T. (Sh. Ct.) 36; *Doherty v. Norwich Union Fire Insurance Society Ltd*, 1974 S.C. 213 at 219.

[72] *Hopkinson Ltd v. Sanders, supra.*

[73] 1907 Act, s. 5(4).

[74] Dobie, p. 27.

Under the predecessors of rule 21.3 it has been held competent to state and maintain by way of exception objections to the following documents which displayed the characteristics discussed in paragraph 12.68: a receipt[75]; a discharge of a claim of damages[76]; an arbiter's award[77]; a sheriff officer's execution[78]; and contracts of sale,[79] of hire,[80] and of hire-purchase.[81] Other documents with the necessary characteristics which may apparently be set aside by way of exception include a resolution of a trade incorporation,[82] minutes of a meeting of a friendly society at which an election took place,[83] and an *ex facie* valid assignation.[84] The issue of the validity of an alienation by a debtor which is alleged to be voidable under the common law or under statutory bankruptcy rules may be litigated by way of exception in the sheriff court.[85] It is possible that in an appropriate case[86] a decision of a statutory tribunal might be set aside by way of exception.[87] As already explained, a writing which has a defect which renders it void or *ipso jure* null may in any event be set aside at common law.[88] **12.70**

Title and interest to object

The party stating the objection may be either the pursuer or the defender.[89] There are several reported examples of a pursuer in a personal injuries action seeking to set aside a discharge of his claim which is founded on by the defenders.[90] The objector must, however, have a title and interest to state and maintain his objection. Thus, where a tenant took exception to a lease founded on against him and averred that he was truly the proprietor, but was unable to show a title to the property, it was held that his defence could not be tried by way of exception and the process was sisted to enable him to bring an action of declarator and reduction.[91] **12.71**

---

75 *Neil v. McNair* (1901) 3 F.(J.) 85 at 89; *Donald v. Donald,* 1913 S.C. 274, *per* L.J.-C. Macdonald at 278.

76 *Winter v. Kerr* (1895) 12 Sh.Ct.Rep. 77; *Mackie v. Strachan, Kinmond, & Co.* (1896) 23 R. 1030; *Mathieson v. Hawthorns & Co. Ltd* (1899) 1 F. 468; *Neil, supra*; *Donald, supra, per* Lord Salvesen at 280; *Hopkinson Ltd, supra,* at 39.

77 *Nivison v. Howat* (1883) 11 R. 182; *McLaughlan, Brown & Co. v. Morrison* (1902) 18 Sh.Ct.Rep. 206 at 211–212; *Sundt & Co. v. Watson* (1914) 31 Sh.Ct.Rep. 156; *Kilmaurs Dairy Association Ltd v. Brisbane and Beattie's Dairies* (1927) 43 Sh.Ct.Rep. 210; *Blythe Building Co. Ltd v. Mason's Exrx* (1936) 53 Sh.Ct.Rep. 180. See also *Wilson v. Glasgow Tramways Co.* (1878) 5 R. 981; *Brown & Sons v. Associated Fireclay Cos,* 1937 S.C.(H.L.) 42.

78 *Scott v. Cook* (1886) 24 S.L.R. 34. *Cf. Inland Revenue v. Gibb,* 1963 S.L.T. (Notes) 66.

79 *Black v. Campbell & Cameron Ltd* (1938) 54 Sh.Ct.Rep. 169.

80 *Bell Bros (H.P.) Ltd v. Aitken,* 1939 S.C. 577.

81 *Hopkinson Ltd, supra.*

82 *Sadler v. Webster* (1893) 21 R. 107.

83 *McGowan v. City of Glasgow Friendly Society,* 1913 S.C. 991.

84 *Macfarlane v. Macfarlane,* 1947 S.L.T. (Notes) 34.

85 *Report on Bankruptcy and Related Aspects of Insolvency and Liquidation* (Scot. Law Com. No. 68), paras 12–27, 12–28.

86 *Caledonian Ry v. Glasgow Corporation* (1905) 7 F. 1020; *Adair v. Colville & Sons,* 1926 S.C.(H.L.) 51, *per* Viscount Dunedin at 55–56; *Bellway Ltd v. Strathchlyde R.C.,* 1979 S.C. 92; *Watt v. Lord Advocate,* 1979 S.C. 120, *per* L.P. Emslie at 130.

87 *Construction Industry Training Board v. James Duncan (Plumbers) Ltd,* Glasgow Sh. Ct., March 13, 1985, unreported.

88 para. 12.66.

89 *Dickson v. Murray* (1866) 4 M. 797, *per* L.J.-C. Inglis at 799.

90 See para. 12.70.

91 *Duke of Argyll v. Muir,* 1910 S.C. 96.

Procedure

12.72 The party stating the objection must give fair notice of the objection and the ground on which it is based,[92] by stating an appropriate plea-in-law[93] and supporting it with relevant averments.[94] The sheriff may, where an action of reduction would be competent, order the objector to find caution or to give such other security as the sheriff directs.[95] It appears that an action of reduction, and thus such an order, is unnecessary where the defect in the document objected to renders it void or *ipso jure* null.[96] The sheriff has power to direct the finding of caution or other security in order to prevent objections being taken for the mere purpose of creating delay.[97] It has been suggested that if a party is seeking to avoid liability by a challenge made by way of exception in the sheriff court, the sheriff should order him to find caution or to make consignation if the party would be required to do so in the Court of Session on challenging the validity of the document by direct action there.[98] If the sheriff considers that the objection cannot competently be maintained in the process before him, he may sist[99] the cause to enable the objector to bring an action of reduction or other appropriate proceeding. He may do so *ex proprio motu.*[1]

---

[92] *Oswald v. Fairs*, 1911 S.C. 257, *per* L.P. Dunedin at 264.

[93] *e.g. Bell Bros (H.P.) Ltd v. Aitken*, 1939 S.C. 577 at 582.

[94] *Mathieson v. Hawthorns & Co. Ltd* (1899) 1 F. 468; *Black v. Campbell & Cameron Ltd* (1938) 54 Sh.Ct.Rep. 169.

[95] OCR, r. 21.3(2); *Brodie & Hall Ltd v. Di Placido* (1938) 55 Sh.Ct.Rep. 82. As to caution and consignation, see paras 13.41 to 13.48.

[96] See para. 12.66.

[97] Dove Wilson, p. 61.

[98] *Winter v. Kerr* (1896) 12 Sh.Ct.Rep. 77 at 80.

[99] *Duke of Argyll v. Muir*, 1910 S.C. 96; *Donald v. Donald*, 1913 S.C. 274; *Bradford Equitable Building Society v. Thomson*, 1965 S.L.T. (Sh. Ct.) 54.

[1] *Bradford Equitable Building Society, supra.*

Chapter 13

INCIDENTAL PROCEDURE—II

I. Debate

Circumstances in which debate ordered

Not later than three days before the options hearing under rule 9.12 or the procedural hearing under rule 10.6 a party intending to insist on a preliminary plea must lodge a note of the basis of the plea in process, and intimate a copy of it to every other party.[1] This should be done in the case of an options hearing even when it is thought likely that the case may proceed under the additional procedure.[2] Where a procedural hearing is held under Chapter 10 it has been held by a sheriff at first instance that a further note is not required.[3] However, it is submitted that it is generally desirable that a new note should be lodged before a procedural hearing.[4] A preliminary plea includes one seeking a sist for arbitration.[5] Where an options hearing is continued under rule 9.12(5) and a preliminary plea is then added by adjustment similar provisions apply in relation to the steps to be taken before the continued options hearing.[6] Where a note of the basis of a preliminary plea has been lodged under rule 22.1(1) and the options hearing is continued under rule 9.12(5), unless the basis of the plea is changed following further adjustment, a party insisting on it is not required to lodge a further note for the continued options hearing.[7] At the options hearing or at the continued options hearing (except where Chapter 10 procedure is ordered) the sheriff closes the record, and having heard the parties and considered any note lodged under rule 22.1, may appoint the cause to debate, if satisfied there is a preliminary matter of law which justifies that.[8] A debate is justified where the sheriff is persuaded that there is a substantial argument which, if successful, would lead to decree in favour of the pursuer or defender, or would limit the method or extent of the proof to a considerable degree.[9] It is for the party seeking to maintain his plea to satisfy the sheriff by reference to the note and by oral argument that there is a preliminary point of law which justifies a debate.[10] However it is not open to the sheriff at the options hearing to sustain what he considers to be a well-founded argument and to dismiss the action.[11] **13.01**

---

1 OCR, r. 22.1(1): see para. 8.48.
2 *Colvin v. Montgomery Preservations*, 1995 S.L.T. (Sh. Ct.) 15.
3 *Hart v. Thorntons WS*, 1995 S.C.L.R. 642.
4 See the commentary at 1995 S.C.L.R. 646.
5 *Dinardo Partnership v. Thomas Tait & Sons*, 1995 S.C.L.R. 941.
6 OCR, r. 22.1(2).
7 OCR, r. 22.1(5).
8 OCR, r. 9.12(3)(c).
9 *Gracey v. Sykes*, 1994 S.C.L.R. 909.
10 *The Blair Bryden Partnership v. Adair*, 1995 S.L.T. (Sh. Ct.) 98.
11 *Ritchie v. Cleary*, 1995 S.C.L.R. 561.

13.02 If a party fails to lodge a rule 22 note, he is deemed to be no longer insisting on the preliminary plea, and it should be repelled by the sheriff at the options hearing or procedural hearing.[12] If a plea unsupported by a note is not repelled then it may be belatedly repelled at debate.[13] A failure to comply with rule 22.1 may be relieved by the operation of rule 2.1(1),[14] and ignorance of the rule may be so excused.[15] While at any debate the parties may raise matters in addition to those set out in the note,[16] that does not permit the introduction of a wholly new plea or the resurrection of a plea which has fallen.[17] A similar rule to that provided by rule 22 applies when a preliminary plea is added in the course of amendment.[18] The note should be lodged at the same time as the minute of amendment, answers thereto or adjustment of either which adds the preliminary plea.[19] A failure to lodge a note results in the preliminary plea being repelled.[20] The sheriff may also order parties to debate where at any time on or after the closing of the record they lodge a joint minute renouncing probation.[21]

Steps before debate

Discharge of diet

13.03 If, after a diet of debate has been fixed, the parties come to be agreed that the debate should not proceed for any reason, for example where the action has been settled or will almost certainly be settled, or where they are agreed that the action should be disposed of by a proof (any preliminary plea having been repelled of consent) or by a proof before answer,[22] they should immediately intimate the position by telephone to the sheriff clerk and confirm the intimation in writing.[23] They should also lodge a joint motion asking the court to discharge the diet of debate and pronounce such further order as may be appropriate, which may be specified in the motion. The reasons for the motion should be stated in the motion.[24] If the parties reach agreement too late for that procedure to be followed, they should informally intimate to the sheriff clerk that they do not wish the debate to proceed, and thus enable the court to arrange for the disposal of other business on the date fixed for the debate, if the court considers that to be appropriate. It remains a matter for the discretion of the court whether the diet is to be discharged. When a motion is made to discharge a diet of debate and fix a new diet, the sheriff is bound to have regard to his duty to prevent unnecessary delay in the progress of the particular litigation and to avoid, in the interests of other litigants, the waste of judicial time. Such a motion will therefore be granted only where the sheriff considers that to do so is a proper exercise of his discretion on

---

[12] OCR, r. 22.1(3).
[13] *Bell v. John Davidson (Pipes)*, 1995 S.L.T. (Sh. Ct.) 18.
[14] *Colvin v. Montgomery Preservations*, 1995 S.L.T. (Sh. Ct.) 15
[15] *Sutherland v. Duncan*, 1996 S.L.T. 428. This case related to a failure to lodge a note in terms of OCR, r. 18.8, rather than OCR, r. 22.1 but the principle is the same.
[16] OCR, r. 22.1(4).
[17] *Bell v. John Davidson (Pipes)*, *supra*.
[18] OCR, r. 18.8.
[19] OCR, r. 18.8(1).
[20] OCR, r. 18.8(2).
[21] OCR, r. 29.4.
[22] On whether to agree a proof before answer before debate, see Kearney, pp. 83–84.
[23] Glasgow and Strathkelvin Practice Notes (1982) (*Parliament House Book*, D-606): a statement of good practice which should be generally followed.
[24] OCR, r. 15.1(1)(b), Form G6.

the statement of facts advanced in justification of the motion.[25] A solicitor who is no longer prepared to act for his client at the debate should follow the normal procedure for a solicitor who withdraws from acting for a client.[26] If a party or his solicitor abandons, fails to attend, or is not prepared to proceed with a diet of debate the sheriff has power to decern against that party for payment of such expenses as is considered reasonable.[27]

Preparation for debate

The following advice is commended, particularly to the recently-qualified practitioner: **13.04**

> "I have always thought it a good rule, when preparing for a debate—first to prepare one's own case, then to prepare one's opponent's case, and finally to revise one's own argument in the light of the argument which one's opponent will probably put forward. If one does that there should be no difficulty in dealing promptly and effectively with any difficulties which the sheriff may suggest in the course of one's address."[28]

> "It was our habit when preparing for a debate in the Court of Session—and no doubt it is still the habit there—to assume that neither we nor the judges knew anything at all about the branch of law which was under discussion, even when the subject was one which cropped up daily in the courts. We did not consider that we were equipped for a legal debate unless we were able, should it be necessary to do so, to trace the development of the law in question from its origin to the present day by reference to the statutes and leading cases which referred to it. This might involve a search of the statute indices, of the digests of cases in the Court of Session and in other courts, of the institutional writers and of the text-books. Without this careful search it is very easy to overlook some statutory provision or judicial dictum which may upset one's whole argument if one should hear of it for the first time in court. Having got the legal background of the problem at our finger-tips, we then tried to apply the general legal principles to the particular circumstances of the case—to analyse in detail those decided cases upon which we particularly relied, and to show, if we could, that they should be interpreted in such a way as to support our argument. And above all, we were taught never to mention a case in court unless we were prepared to describe what it was about in our own words and to say exactly how it applied to the point under discussion."[29]

Joint minute

Where it is proposed to ask the sheriff at debate to make a decision on **13.05**
the basis not only of the pleadings but also of the provisions of a document or documents, that can only be achieved in one of the following ways. (1)

---

[25] *Merson v. Coia*, 1959 S.L.T. (Sh. Ct.) 33. *Cf. Sinclair v. Samuels*, 1948 S.L.T. (Notes) 44.

[26] OCR, Chap. 24. See paras 12.27, 12.28.

[27] A.S. (Fees of Solicitors in the Sheriff Court) (Amendment and Further Provisions) 1993, Sched. 1, General Regulations, reg. 5(c).

[28] Sh. Pr. Sir Allan G. Walker, Q.C., "Pleaders and Pleading in the Sheriff Court" (1951) 67 Sh.Ct.Rep. 33 at 36. The whole article repays study. See also Kearney, pp. 81–84 and R. G. McEwan, *Pleading in Court* (2nd ed.).

[29] Sh. Pr. A. G. Walker, *supra*, at 37, 38. On the last point see also *Clark v. Watson*, 1982 S.L.T. 450 at 451.

Where the critical provisions have been quoted *verbatim* in the pleadings. (2) Where the critical provisions have been accurately specified in the pleadings and have been expressly incorporated and held as repeated therein *brevitatis causa*, the document or documents having been lodged in process.[30] (3) Where neither of these courses has been followed in the drafting of the pleadings, a joint minute must be lodged dispensing with probation of the document or documents and, if necessary, agreeing copies as principals.[31] The sheriff cannot consider a document at debate unless one of these courses has been adopted.

List of authorities

13.06 It is good practice for the solicitor for each party to lodge with the sheriff clerk a note of all the authorities to which reference is to be made in the course of the argument for the party whom he represents. That should be done by 10 a.m. on the day of the debate or earlier.[32] The object is that the books should be on the bench in time for the hearing and the sheriff should be able to look at each authority while the advocate is referring to it.

Diet of debate

Attendance of parties

13.07 As at a diet of proof, the case is called; the advocates, and the parties if they are present, take their places[33]; and the sheriff may grant decree by default if one party fails to appear or be represented[34] or if none of the parties appears. If none appears, the decree by default is a decree of dismissal.[35] A party is not represented by an advocate who has no instructions.[36] A party is, however, represented by an instructed advocate who is not in a position to proceed; but any motion he makes for a postponement of the debate may be refused.[37] Where a party or his solicitor on one side attends a diet of debate and the other is absent or not prepared to proceed, the sheriff has power to decern against the latter party for payment of such expenses as the sheriff may consider reasonable.[38] As at a diet of proof, it is often prudent not to grant decree by default or decern for expenses at once, in ignorance of the reason for a party's failure to appear or to be represented.[39]

---

30 *Gordon v. Davidson* (1864) 2 M. 758, *per* L.J.-C. Inglis at 769; *Green v. Maxwell Property Development Co.*, 1976 S.L.T. (Sh. Ct.) 65.

31 *Ribble Paper Mills Ltd v. Clyde Paper Mills Ltd*, 1972 S.L.T. (Notes) 25; *Stone v. Macdonald*, 1979 S.C. 363 at 365; *Trade Development Bank v. David W. Haig (Bellshill) Ltd*, 1983 S.L.T. 107 at 109.

32 This is requested in the Sheriffdom of Glasgow and Strathkelvin (*Parliament House Book*, D-606) and required in the Sheriffdoms of South Strathclyde (not later than two clear working days prior to the diet), Dumfries and Galloway, North Strathclyde, and Lothian & Borders (at least 24 hours to the diet) (*Parliament House Book*, D-803, D-703 and D-1007, respectively).

33 See paras 16.45, 16.46.

34 OCR, r. 16.2(1)(c),(2). See paras 16.47, 16.48.

35 OCR, r. 16.2(3).

36 *cf. W. B. Anderson & Sons Ltd. v. Aytoun*, 1960 S.L.T. (Notes) 60.

37 *Merson v. Coia*, 1959 S.L.T (Sh. Ct.) 33; *cf. Sinclair v. Samuels*, 1948 S.L.T. (Notes) 44.

38 A.S. (Fees of Solicitors in the Sheriff Court) (Amendment and Further Provisions) 1993, Sched. 1, General Regulations, reg. 5(c).

39 *cf. Saleem v. Hamilton District Licensing Board*, 1993 S.L.T. 1092; *McGowan v. Cartner*, 1995 S.C.L.R. 312. See para. 16.48.

Order of speeches

Where only one party has stated a preliminary plea or pleas, that party's advocate opens the debate. Where both parties have stated preliminary pleas, the defender opens, since if his plea is sustained it is not necessary to consider the soundness of his defence.[40] If, however, the pursuer has stated a general plea to the relevancy of the defences while the defender has stated only a plea of limited scope such as a plea to the relevancy of particular averments by the pursuer which he specifies and claims should not be remitted to probation, it may be appropriate for the pursuer's advocate to speak first. Any departure from the usual order of speeches should be considered by the parties' advocates before the debate and proposed to the sheriff at the beginning of the hearing. **13.08**

After the opening speech, the other party makes a speech in reply, and if he is the pursuer and has stated a preliminary plea, may present argument in support of that plea. The sheriff then invites the first speaker to reply, in a third speech, and if the first speaker does so, the second speaker may make a final speech. If there is no third speech, the second speaker cannot make a final speech; and if there is a third speech, but it does not introduce new matter, a fourth speech may be unnecessary. In the event of two counsel appearing for one party on the basis that both are to speak (a most unusual occurrence in the sheriff court), the junior counsel makes the first speech for that party, and the senior the second. It is for senior counsel to make the ultimate decision on the conduct of the case and the arguments to be presented.[41] If the sheriff is so unmoved by junior counsel's speech as to doubt whether any reply is required from the other side, he should hear senior counsel before deciding not to call on the other side.[42] If junior counsel makes the second speech in the debate, the other side may intimate that they do not wish to exercise their right of reply, and thus eliminate a final speech by senior counsel. **13.09**

Content of speeches

The opening speaker states who appears for the parties, gives the sheriff a brief description of the nature of the case and explains how it comes to be on the debate roll, indicating the pleas which are to be debated. He should then read the relevant parts of the record unless, as is often the case, the sheriff intimates that he has previously read it. If the record is to be read, it is read as follows: the crave, if necessary; then each material paragraph[43] of the condescendence as far as the beginning of the reply to the averments in answer, which usually begins "With reference to the averments in answer"; then the corresponding paragraph of the answers; then the remainder of the condescendence starting from the beginning of the reply to the averments in answer; and finally the plea or pleas-in-law which are to be debated. Where the only plea to be debated is a general plea to the relevancy of the pursuer's pleadings, it is often unnecessary to read the defender's averments in answer and the pursuer's averments in reply. **13.10**

---

[40] Lees, *Pleading*, p. 61.

[41] *Wolf and Wolf v. Forfar Potato Co.*, 1984 S.L.T. 100.

[42] *Greenhorn v. J. Smart & Co. (Contractors) Ltd*, 1979 S.C. 427 at 431.

[43] *e.g.* in a personal injuries action, where there are no preliminary pleas directed against the averments relating to damages, these should be omitted.

13.11 After any reading of the pleadings, the opening speaker should explain what his argument is going to be. It may be useful to introduce the argument in the form of numbered propositions, stating whether they are main or subsidiary propositions, and whether any of them are alternatives. Since the advocate's object is to make his argument intelligible and persuasive, and to avoid any misunderstanding, his critical propositions, at whatever state of the argument they are introduced, should be stated at dictation speed.[44] In a case of any complexity, where to take down in longhand propositions read out at dictation speed would be irksome and time-consuming, it may be desirable to tender to the sheriff and the other side a typed statement of propositions.[45] The advocate should also state to the sheriff exactly what interlocutor he wants the sheriff to pronounce and, in particular, which pleas he wishes the sheriff to sustain or repel. The speech in reply is presented in the same way, omitting the introductory matter and the reading of the record; and it may be difficult to formulate in advance a series of propositions in rebuttal of those stated in the first speech.

13.12 The party challenging the sufficiency of his opponent's case must, for the purposes of the argument, accept as true his opponent's averments of fact, and argue that even if the facts averred by his opponent can be proved, his opponent is not entitled in law to succeed. The foundation of the argument should have been stated in his preliminary plea or pleas, supported by the terms of the rule 22 note.[46] Courts are not in general strict in refusing to entertain an argument on the ground that no plea-in-law supports it as a matter of form, but a plea of "No jurisdiction" must have been timeously stated.[47] It is frequently appropriate for the other side to take objection to the absence of a plea-in-law supporting an argument against them.[48] Rather than refuse to entertain the argument, the court will normally require the appropriate plea to be added by amendment,[49] and impose any appropriate conditions as to expenses or otherwise, including adjournment of the diet of debate.

13.13 It is important that the case should be adequately argued from both sides of the bar. If it is not, the sheriff cannot properly fulfil his judicial function.

> "He is entitled to assume that the argument on each side has been fully presented: that every point has been made and nothing omitted. His function, and it is sometimes not an easy one to discharge, is to consider each argument impartially, and to decide between the two. If he has to concern himself with the omissions and mistakes of the pleaders, it is impossible for him to approach the decision as impartially and as judicially as he should."[50]

---

[44] Sheriff Principal Sir Allan G. Walker, Q.C., "Appeals in the Sheriff Court" (1973) 18 J.L.S. 222 at 225. Like the same author's "Pleaders and Pleading in the Sheriff Court" (1951) 67 Sc.L.Rev. 33, this article in its entirety is warmly commended to the recently-qualified practitioner. See also Kearney, pp. 85–90.

[45] *cf. R. v. Goldstein* [1983] 1 W.L.R. 151 at 157.

[46] The pleader is not restricted to the points made in the Rule 22 note (OCR, r. 22.1(4)) but see *Bell v. John Davidson (Pipes) Ltd*, 1995 S.L.T. (Sh. Ct.) 18.

[47] *Alexander Ward & Co. Ltd v. Samyang Navigation Co. Ltd*, 1975 S.C.(H.L.) 26, *per* Lord Kilbrandon at 52–53. See para. 9.118.

[48] *McLaughlin v. Scott's Shipbuilding and Engineering Co. Ltd*, 1960 S.L.T. (Notes) 58.

[49] *Robb v. Logiealmond School Board* (1875) 2 R. 417, *per* L.P. Inglis at 422. The addition of a preliminary plea must be supported by a Rule 18 note: OCR, r. 18.8. See para. 13.02.

[50] Walker (1951) 67 Sc.L.Rev. 33 at 38–39.

Precise references should be given to the pages in any authorities which are relied on, and their relevance to the argument should be carefully explained. The advocate should also cite any authorities which appear to be against him, face up to the difficulties which they create, and deal with them as best he can.[51]

The topic of amendment at debate has already been considered.[52] If a party in the course of debate indicates that he is restricting his claim or defence to particular matters, he should seek leave to amend his pleadings accordingly; and if he does not do so, it is appropriate for the sheriff to insist on amendment.[53] 13.14

Decision

Disposal of preliminary pleas

It is the sheriff's duty to adjudicate on the pleas argued, and it is improper for him to suggest leave to amend be sought,[54] or the scope of amendment.[55] The disposal of preliminary pleas has already been considered,[56] and particular consideration given to pleas to title,[57] the plea of "All parties not called",[58] and pleas to jurisdiction[59] and competency.[60] The subjects of relevancy[61] and specification,[62] general and limited pleas to relevancy[63] and lack of specification,[64] the circumstances in which an action will be dismissed as irrelevant,[65] and the nature of the averments which will be sufficient to entitle the pursuer to an inquiry[66] have also been discussed, as have the nature of proof before answer,[67] and the circumstances in which the sheriff will order proof before answer after debate.[68] Other questions which have already been noticed, as to whether the mode of proof should be restricted in any other way,[69] or whether there should be a preliminary proof,[70] or as to which party is to lead at any inquiry,[71] are often resolved after debate. Reference is also made elsewhere to the courses open to the sheriff when, after making avizandum, he finds authorities which were not cited to him but appear to have a bearing on the arguments.[72] It may be convenient to recapitulate some of these 13.15

---

51 Walker (1973) 18 J.L.S. 222 at p. 224. On reference to authorities, see *Clark v. Watson*, 1982 S.L.T. 450 at 451; and on the citation of adverse authorities, see para. 16.42.

52 para. 10.17.

53 *Jack Davis Publicity Ltd v. Kennedy*, Sh. Pr. Caplan, Paisley Sh. Ct., Dec. 18, 1984, unreported.

54 *Alexander Allan & Son v. McGee*, 1990 S.L.T. (Sh. Ct.) 2.

55 *Creed v. Christie & Ferguson*, 1991 S.L.T. (Sh. Ct.) 44.

56 para. 9.115.

57 para. 9.117.

58 para. 9.118.

59 paras 9.119, 9.120.

60 para. 9.121.

61 paras 9.32 to 9.39 (initial writ); 9.113, 9.114 (defences).

62 paras 9.27 to 9.31.

63 para. 9.122.

64 para. 9.123.

65 para. 9.33.

66 para. 9.34.

67 para. 8.57.

68 para. 8.58.

69 paras 8.54 to 8.56.

70 para. 8.60.

71 paras 8.64, 8.65.

72 para. 17.29.

matters in the following paragraphs. Unless the contrary is stated, it is assumed that the preliminary plea under consideration has been stated by the defender.

13.16 Where the sheriff sustains a preliminary plea which is stated by a defender and directed against the whole action, the action is dismissed. A decree of dismissal, accordingly, is a decree dismissing the action as laid, but not dealing with the merits of the case so as to prevent them from being retried between the same parties. The pursuer may therefore bring a new action against the defender on the same ground without being met by a plea of *res judicata*; but in practice he hardly ever does so. Decrees of dismissal are to be contrasted with decrees of absolvitor which are decrees on the merits pronounced in favour of a defender and are *res judicata*. Where the sheriff sustains a similar general preliminary plea stated by a pursuer, he repels the defences and grants a decree of condemnator in the pursuer's favour. But debate on a defender's preliminary plea does not necessarily lead at once to the disposal of the action. The sheriff has the following options, depending on the nature of the dispute and of any averments challenged.

13.17 (*i*) If the parties are agreed as to the facts and are at issue only on the question or questions of law raised by the defender's plea, the sheriff may either sustain the plea and dismiss the action, or repel the plea and grant decree.

13.18 (*ii*) If the parties are at issue on both law and fact, the sheriff may dispose of the preliminary plea by ruling on the legal issues. He may either sustain the plea and dismiss the action upon the view that the pursuer's case, even if soundly based in fact, is unsound in law; or he may repel the plea upon the view that the defender's objection to the legal basis of the pursuer's case is unsound, and order a proof in order to enable the parties to attempt to prove their averments of fact.

13.19 (*iii*) It is, however, frequently necessary to inquire into the facts before disposing of a preliminary plea. Where the facts on which the preliminary plea is based are in dispute and are capable of being inquired into separately from an inquiry into the merits, a proof may be allowed of these facts alone without going into the merits. For example, a plea that the defender is not subject to the jurisdiction of the court may be inquired into by way of a preliminary proof which does not investigate the merits of the case.[73]

13.20 (*iv*) A situation more commonly encountered in practice is that the sheriff is unable to rule on the question raised by the preliminary plea without knowing more about the facts relative to the merits than the averments challenged disclose. He may be satisfied either (a) that the law is clear, but it is desirable to ascertain the facts before applying it, because it cannot be said in advance of the leading of evidence whether the facts averred are sufficient to support the pleas to which they are related; or (b) that the law applicable to the case cannot be stated with precision until the facts are ascertained and seen in their proper setting. In that situation he will reserve his opinion on the legal question argued and allow a proof

---

[73] See para. 8.60.

before answer, at which the parties may lead their evidence and thereafter argue not only as to what facts have been established but also how the legal question should be answered.[74]

The preliminary plea most often encountered in practice is the "general plea to the relevancy"[75] which, when stated by a defender, grounds the argument that even if all the pursuer's averments were proved, the pursuer would clearly not be entitled to the remedy which he seeks, and thus the action would necessarily fail and therefore should be dismissed.[76] Similarly, the pursuer may state a plea to the relevancy of the defences, to the effect that the defence, even if proved, would not be adequate in law, and that the defences should therefore be repelled and decree granted in the pursuer's favour. If, after debate, the sheriff repels the plea to relevancy and allows a proof, as distinct from a proof before answer, it may be that the question of relevancy cannot thereafter be reopened and the party against whom the facts are proved can no longer maintain that no proof should have been allowed, and that the facts proved should be disregarded.[77] If, on the other hand, the sheriff reserves the question and allows a proof before answer as to the relevancy, the consequence is that, although the facts averred are proved, they may be held insufficient in law to support the claim (or the pleas in defence), and the final decision may be against the party proving them. It is rare for decree of dismissal to be pronounced after proof before answer, but not incompetent.[78] If a plea directed against the relevancy of particular averments is sustained after debate, the averments are not remitted to probation, so that no evidence based upon them may be led at the proof.[79] If the sheriff considers the relevancy of the averments to be doubtful, a proof before answer is appropriate.[80] To reserve such a plea may seem illogical, on the ground that a decision whether or not to exclude averments from probation can only be made before proof; but the practice appears to be fairly general and to be justifiable on grounds of expediency, particularly where the averments are concerned with a branch of the case which may be of material significance. **13.21**

Comment

It may be said in favour of the system of preliminary pleas that it is well understood by the legal profession and that a procedure whereby an action may be dismissed or defences repelled after debate has the great merit of obviating a fruitless inquiry into the facts which would waste the time of the court and cause the parties further "vexation, delay and expense".[81] Criticisms were formerly made of the system of preliminary pleas. These criticisms were twofold: first that preliminary pleas were frequently used in order to delay the progress of a case; and secondly that **13.22**

---

[74] See paras 8.57 to 8.59.
[75] See para. 9.122.
[76] See paras 9.32 *et seq.*
[77] See para. 8.63.
[78] See para. 17.12.
[79] See para. 9.122.
[80] ***P. & W. MacLellan Ltd v. Peattie's Trs*** (1903) 6 F. 1031; ***Hackett v. Allan***, Sh. Pr. Caplan, Dunoon Sh. Ct., May 15, 1984, unreported.
[81] "The burthens inseparably attendant on judicial procedure" (Bentham, *Works* (Bowring ed.), Vol. ii, p. 19.

a general plea did not give sufficient notice of the point to be made at debate.[82] These criticisms have—or should have—been obviated by the introduction of the options hearing and rule 22 note.

Form of interlocutor

13.23 In his interlocutor pronounced after debate the sheriff, if sustaining or repelling a preliminary plea, specifies the plea and the result. Among the more common expressions used are the following: "Sustains the defender's first plea-in-law and Dismisses the action"; or, if he has decided to allow a proof before answer, "before answer, Allows both parties a proof of their respective averments"[83]; or, if he has decided to exclude certain averments from probation on the ground that they are irrelevant or lacking in specification, but to allow a proof before answer on the remainder of the case, "Excludes from probation the pursuer's averments in article 3 [or as the case may be] of the condescendence [relative to a particular matter, or, repeating the averments *verbatim*] and to that extent Sustains the defender's first plea-in-law; *quoad ultra* before further answer Allows both parties a proof of their respective averments"; or, if allowing a preliminary proof before answer, "Allows a preliminary proof before answer of the parties' averments relating to the defender's first plea-in-law". Where the sheriff holds a crave to be incompetent, the appropriate course is to delete the incompetent crave and the relative averments.[84] In an interlocutor pronounced after debate on relevancy it is inappropriate to make findings in fact[85]; or to express a view on the irrelevancy of a party's pleadings and *ex proprio motu* allow him an opportunity to amend, where no motion for leave to amend has been made in the course of the debate, since the question of relevancy must be decided on the averments as they stand[86]; or to allow amendment where a party has made a motion for leave to amend in the event of the sheriff's decision on relevancy being against him.[87] Where the interlocutor allows proof before answer, the sheriff who hears the proof before answer is not bound by any opinions expressed in the note to the interlocutor.[88]

Expenses

13.24 It is usually desirable to reserve the question of expenses in an interlocutor pronounced after debate, and to appoint parties to be heard thereon after the interlocutor has been issued.[89] The question should then be disposed of, and should not simply be reserved until the conclusion of the case.[90] A general award of expenses in favour of a defender carries the expenses of a debate in which he has been unsuccessful, if those expenses

---

[82] See Macphail, *Sheriff Court Practice* (1st ed.), paras 13–21, 13–22.

[83] For variants, see para. 8.55.

[84] *Heriot-Hill v. Heriot-Hill* (1906) 14 S.L.T. 182; *Chalmers v. Chalmers*, 1983 S.L.T. 535.

[85] *Scottish Special Housing Association v. Maxwell*, 1960 S.C. 391.

[86] *Lord Advocate v. Johnston*, 1983 S.L.T. 290; *Gibson v. Strathclyde Regional Council*, 1992 S.C.L.R. 902 at 907B, *per* L.J.-C. Ross. But *cf. Kennedy v. Norwich Union Fire Insurance Society*, 1993 S.C.L.R. 735 at 742B, *per* Lord McCluskey. See para. 10.17.

[87] *Lord Advocate v. Johnston, supra, per* Lord Hunter at 294. *Cf. Gibson, supra*; *Kennedy, supra*.

[88] See para. 5.86.

[89] See paras 16.103, 17.23.

[90] See para. 19.16.

have not been awarded to the pursuer.[91] If a proof before answer has been offered and refused, that having been recorded in a previous interlocutor,[92] and the interlocutor allows a proof before answer, the refusal of the offer may have a bearing on the question of expenses.

Appeal

The interlocutor is appealable without leave if it grants decree or dismisses the action and finds expenses due,[93] or if it allows or refuses or limits the mode of proof.[94] If the loser considers that a different result might have been obtained if he had timeously amended his pleadings, and he has material which would support different averments, he should appeal and lodge a minute of amendment and a motion to allow it to be received and answered, which will be considered by the appeal court. If the appeal court allows the amendment it may remit the case to the sheriff for further hearing on the amended pleadings.[95] **13.25**

II. Procedures Which Shorten or Obviate Proof

This section of the chapter considers certain procedures which in appropriate cases may or must be substituted for the conventional model of proof by witnesses before the sheriff. **13.26**

Judicial remit

Types of remit

It is incompetent for a judge to delegate to another his duty of reaching a decision on a question of law, but in certain cases he may competently remit to make inquiries into any matter of fact. Remits in substitution for the leading of evidence, with which this section of this chapter is concerned, may be distinguished from executive remits and informative remits. An executive remit may be made to the auditor of court,[96] or to the Accountant of Court[97] or to any other officer of the court for the purpose of carrying out the functions of the court. In such cases the approval of the court is necessary to give effect to what is done under the remit. An informative remit may be made by the court in order to advise itself of the state of facts where proof is not in the first instance allowed,[98] or where it is necessary to see whether an order of court has been complied with.[99] Examples of executive or informative remits are noted elsewhere in this book. **13.27**

---

[91] *Earl of Lauderdale v. Wedderburn*, 1911 S.C. 4; see para. 19.55.

[92] See paras 8.41, 8.42.

[93] 1907 Act, s. 27. A decree of dismissal is a final interlocutor within the definition in s. 3(h). If expenses are found due in an interlocutor subsequent to that which disposes of the plea, appeal against the later interlocutor opens both to review: see para. 18.36.

[94] 1907 Act, s. 27(d).

[95] see para. 10.23.

[96] *e.g.* the remit of an account of expenses to tax and to report; see para. 19.35.

[97] *e.g.* in applications for the discharge of a judicial factor.

[98] *e.g.* a remit to a reporter in an application for an interim order relating to the residence of or contact with a child (see para. 22.35), or to an accountant in an action of count, reckoning and payment (see para. 21.11).

[99] *e.g.* in actions *ad factum praestandum* (see paras 21.75 to 21.82) or in actions of interdict (see para. 21.95).

Remit in place of proof by witnesses

13.28 A judicial remit in place of proof by witnesses takes place where the sheriff remits to a person of skill or other person to report on any matter of fact. The object of such a judicial remit is to provide a basis of fact for the sheriff's judgment in law[1] in circumstances where the hearing of evidence in court would be an expensive and inappropriate procedure, as where it would not be possible for the court itself to examine adequately the subject in question, or a state of matters could be described in court only by calling much oral evidence, or it would be necessary for the parties to adduce persons of skill as witnesses.[2] The procedure seems to have been more widely used in the nineteenth than in the twentieth century.[3]

Competency

13.29 A remit is incompetent where the ascertainment of the facts involves the consideration of questions of law.[4] A remit may be moved for by any party or on joint motion,[5] and it follows that the sheriff cannot remit *ex proprio motu*. The remit need not exhaust all the issues of fact in dispute between the parties, and on issues beyond the terms of the remit proof may be allowed.

Appointment of reporter

13.30 The name of the proposed person of skill or other person (hereinafter referred to as "the reporter") is included in a joint motion or a motion consented to by all parties, the parties having agreed on him and having ascertained that he is willing to act if appointed. If the motion is by one party only and is not consented to by the other parties a nomination may be made by the court. The reporter is normally a person with the special skill, knowledge or experience appropriate to an inquiry into the matters of fact which are to be the subject of the remit. Any subsequent dispute as to the amount of the reporter's remuneration[6] may be avoided by agreeing a fee or rate of payment prior to his appointment.

Time for remitting

13.31 The appropriate time for remitting is normally after the record has been closed and any preliminary pleas requiring to be debated have been disposed of, and before proof. Provision for the inspection of a perishable subject or transient condition before the closing of the record would probably now normally be made by an order under section 1 of the Administration of Justice (Scotland) Act 1972, and not by a judicial remit.[7] After proof has begun, a remit should not be made except of consent, as it is otherwise incompetent to interrupt the course of the proof by other procedure.[8]

---

[1] Dobie, p. 173.

[2] *Quin v. Gardner & Sons Ltd* (1888) 15 R. 776, *per* Lord Shand at 780; *Macdonald v. Cameron* (1882) 10 R. 172; *Broxburn Oil Co. v. Morrison* (1903) 5 F. 694, (1903) 10 S.L.T. 728.

[3] *Evidence* (Scot. Law Com. Memo. No. 46, 1980), para. R. 14.

[4] *Quin, supra.*

[5] OCR, r. 29.2(1).

[6] See para. 13.34.

[7] *cf. Magistrates of Kilmarnock v. Reid* (1897) 24 R. 388.

[8] See para. 16.56.

Procedure after remit

The sheriff having pronounced an interlocutor making the remit, it is for the parties, not the court, to instruct the reporter. The reporter should receive a copy of the interlocutor and a copy of the pleadings, and he is entitled, as a general rule, to see any step of process. In carrying out his remit the reporter is left to act very much on his own discretion, so long as he acts with fairness to both parties. Before he examines the subject of the remit it may be appropriate for him to give notice to both sides to attend if they wish. He does not formally take evidence, but each party may give him such information as he may require.[9] If the reporter dies before completing his report, a remit may be made to a new reporter in his place.[10] **13.32**

Conclusiveness of report

The report is conclusive with respect to the matter of the remit if the remit was made by joint motion or of consent of all parties.[11] It is thought that, in accordance with earlier practice where a report was obtained of consent and was therefore conclusive as to the facts reported on, the parties are entitled to be heard upon the report before it is adopted by the sheriff, and the sheriff is entitled to direct the reporter to revise his report where he has not exhausted the original remit or where further information on the matters remitted to him is desired.[12] **13.33**

Expenses

The expense of the execution of the remit is in the first instance paid by the party on whose motion it was made,[13] or, if on joint motion or of consent of all parties, equally unless the sheriff otherwise directs.[14] After the reporter has prepared his report and his account of his fee and expenses, the sheriff pronounces an interlocutor with an appropriate finding as to expenses of the execution of the remit and appointing the pursuer to uplift and lodge the report.[15] The parties alone are responsible to the reporter for his remuneration: their solicitors are not personally liable therefor without special agreement.[16] If all the parties have been ordered to contribute equally to the expenses and one party pays the whole fee and uplifts the report from the reporter, his opponent cannot compel him to lodge the report until the opponent pays the first party the half of the fee due from the opponent.[17] The reporter may withhold his report until his account for his fee and expenses is paid. If he does not receive payment he may enter the process and obtain decree for payment against the parties jointly and severally,[18] or against a party who has not paid his proportion of the fee.[19] If it is maintained that his charges are **13.34**

---

9 *Pearce Bros v. Irons* (1869) 7 M. 571.
10 *Lord Blantyre v. Glasgow Paisley and Greenock Ry* (1851) 13 D. 570.
11 OCR, r. 29.2(2); *Gibson v. Ewan* (1852) 15 D. 211; *Pearce Bros, supra.*
12 Fyfe, p. 193; Dobie, p. 175.
13 OCR, r. 29.2(3)(a).
14 OCR, r. 29.2(3)(b).
15 *Ballantine v. Reddie* (1884) 22 S.L.R. 136; *Davidson v. Watson*, 1925 S.C. 883.
16 A.S. (Fees of Solicitors in the Sheriff Court) (Amendment and Further Provisions)1993 Sched. 1, General Regulations, reg. 10.
17 *Sutherland v. Goalen* (1855) 17 D. 509.
18 *Ballantine, supra.*
19 *Sutherland, supra.*

excessive, the sheriff may remit his account to the auditor for taxation and thereafter fix the amount and allow the pursuer to uplift and lodge the report. Alternatively the reporter may allow his report to be uplifted without having received payment of his account, and after the sheriff has pronounced decree in the action and remitted the successful party's account of expenses to the auditor for taxation, representations against the amount of the fee may be made to the auditor or in a note of objections to the auditor's report. The sheriff may allow the reporter to lodge a minute answering the note of objections.[20]

Judicial reference

Nature of reference

13.35 A judicial reference is a rare occurrence in modern practice. It takes place when the parties agree to refer to an arbiter or referee selected by them some matter or issue in the action. The matter remitted must be in issue in the cause[21]: it may be the whole cause or any part of it, and, unlike a remit to a man of skill, it may include not only matters of fact but also questions of law.

Procedure

13.36 Since a judicial reference requires the consent of all parties and the authority of the court, a joint minute is prepared showing the terms of the remit, to which the authority of the court requires to be interponed. A solicitor should obtain a special mandate before agreeing to such procedure[22] or signing such a minute.[23] It is in the discretion of the court to interpone authority or not.[24] When the court has interponed authority, the reference becomes irrevocable[25] unless recalled of consent,[26] and the court will not allow an amendment of the record which enlarges the scope of the reference.[27] A judicial reference is competent at any stage so long as the cause is in dependence, but if it is made later than the closing of the record only such questions raised on record as the court has not already disposed of may be remitted to the referee.[28]

13.37 If authority is interponed, the sheriff remits the process to the referee. The referee's jurisdiction is determined by the terms of the minute.[29] The proceedings before him are conducted in the same manner as in an arbitration, and are largely within his discretion. But the original cause remains: the reference is not a substitute for the action, but a step in the action itself.[30] Accordingly, diligence used on the dependence of the action remains in force, and warrants for diligence on the dependence remain effectual[31]; witnesses and havers can be cited only on warrant granted by

---

20 *Morrison v. Ramsay* (1948) 64 Sh.Ct.Rep. 160.
21 *Mackenzie v. Girvan* (1840) 3 D. 318 at 329.
22 *Black v. Laidlaw* (1844) 5 D. 1254.
23 *Livingston v. Johnson* (1830) 8 S. 594.
24 *Brakinrig v. Menzies* (1841) 4 D. 274 at 280.
25 *Reid v. Henderson* (1841) 3 D. 1102.
26 *Walker & Co. v. Shaw-Stewart* (1855) 2 Macq. 424.
27 *Brown's Trs v. Horne*, 1907 S.C. 1027, *per* Lord Kinnear at 1033.
28 *Brown's Trs, supra.*
29 *Mackenzie v. Girvan* (1840) 3 D. 318.
30 *Shiels v. Shiels' Trs* (1874) 1 R. 502.
31 *Stewart v. Earl of Galloway* (1770) Mor. 7004.

the court on a motion to that effect[32]; and the referee's decision takes the form of a report to the court which suggests the terms of an interlocutor. A motion is lodged for decree in terms of the report, and if no valid objection is taken, his decision is made effective by the pronouncing of an interlocutor in the terms suggested.[33] The reference falls if the process falls.[34] If the referee dies before making an award the process reverts to its position as at the date of the remit[35]; but if a party dies the reference does not fall.[36]

The referee's decision must either be adopted or be rejected by the court; **13.38**
and, if adopted, the court's judgment is not subject to review on the merits of the award.[37] Objections to the report may be lodged and the parties heard thereon. The court may remit the report back to the referee to make necessary alterations in point of form or to correct manifest ambiguity or inaccuracy in statement. The court may reject the award in virtue of its jurisdiction over the action out of which the reference has arisen,[38] but may do so only on the recognised grounds of objection ordinarily applicable to arbiter's awards.[39]

Expenses

The referee is entitled to decide the question of liability for the expenses of **13.39**
the reference and, if power is included in the reference to him, the expenses of the process.[40] The referee and his clerk are entitled to remuneration.[41] If the account has not been agreed, the court may fix it after taxation by the auditor, and grant decree therefor against both parties, jointly and severally. If one party has paid the fee of the referee or clerk, the court may decern the other party to reimburse his share.[42]

Appeal

The sheriff's interlocutor interponing authority to the referee's report is **13.40**
not subject to review on the merits of the award.[43] It is possible for the parties to exclude rights of appeal if they do so expressly in their minute of reference,[44] or if, in place of making a reference, they expressly agree by joint minute to submit specified matters in dispute to the final decision of the sheriff as arbiter.[45]

Reference under Social Security Administration Act 1992

A compulsory reference by statute may occur in any proceedings **13.41**
involving any question as to the payment of certain contributions under the Social Security Administration Act 1992, or for the recovery of any sums due to the Secretary of State or the National Insurance Fund. Where

---

32 *Mackenzie, supra, per* Lord Moncreiff at 329.
33 *Mackenzie, Brakinrig, supra*; *Gillon v. Simpson* (1859) 21 D. 243.
34 *Gillon, supra.*
35 *Mackenzie, supra, per* Lord Moncreiff at 329.
36 *Watmore v. Burns* (1839) 1 D. 743.
37 *Mackenzie v. Girvan* (1840) 3 D. 318.
38 *Hilton v. Walkers* (1867) 5 M. 969.
39 *Mackenzie, Brakinrig, Hilton, supra.*
40 *Paul v. Henderson* (1867) 5 M. 613; *Hilton, supra*; *Fairley v. McGown* (1836) 14 S. 470.
41 *Henderson v. Paul* (1867) 5 M. 628; *Macintyre Bros v. Smith,* 1913 S.C. 129.
42 *Edinburgh Oil Gas-Light Co. v. Clyne's Trs* (1835) 13 S. 413; *Drummond v. Leslie* (1835) 13 S. 648.
43 *Mackenzie, supra.*
44 *Shiels v. Shiels' Trs* (1874) 1 R. 502.
45 *Lindsay v. Walker's Trs* (1877) 4 R. 870; *Gordon v. Bruce & Co.* (1897) 24 R. 844; *Steel v. Steel* (1898) 25 R. 715 at 720. *Cf. Dykes v. Merry & Cunninghame* (1869) 7 M. 603.

a decision of any of a number of specified questions is necessary for the determination of such proceedings, that question must be referred to the Secretary of State for determination.[46] The action should be sisted until his decision is received. It is necessary to refer the question to the Secretary of State although he may be the pursuer in the action.[47]

III. Conjunction of Processes

13.42 Where two or more actions are raised in relation to the same subject-matter, the parties' solicitors should consider whether it is possible to avoid multiplication of procedure and expense. It is often agreed that one action should be litigated as the leading action, and the others sisted[48] pending its determination.[49] An alternative arrangement is that the parties move the court to assign the same date as a diet of proof in each action; the parties agree to select one action as the leading action; and proof is led on all the branches of that case, parties further agreeing either that the proof in that action shall be held to be the proof in the others, or, where some supplementary evidence in each of the others is necessary, that the evidence to be led in the leading action shall so far as competent and relevant be held to be the evidence in the others. Such agreement is expressed by joint minutes lodged in each of the other processes.[50] It is usually possible for parties' solicitors to make some such arrangement with the approval of the sheriff. If that is not possible, the court may be moved to conjoin the actions. The effect of conjunction is that the cases conjoined become one process. It can only be done if the cases are in dependence before the same sheriff court. If any are not, the party seeking conjunction must first secure their removal to the court where he wishes conjunction to take place.[51]

13.43 Whether the motion for conjunction should be granted is a matter entirely within the discretion of the sheriff. Conjunction may be appropriate if the actions raise the same issue,[52] and conjunction will achieve convenience and economy in the conduct of the actions.[53] It is not appropriate, however, if there is the least risk that conjunction may produce confusion, perplexity, embarrassment or prejudice because of the complexity of the actions, or because of the shades of distinction between the questions which they raise.[54] In modern practice conjunction is usually resorted to only where different pursuers have raised separate actions of damages arising out of the same circumstances.[55]

---

[46] Social Security Administration Act 1992, s. 117.

[47] *Secretary of State for Social Services v. Caro Accessories Ltd*, Sh. Pr. Gillies, Airdrie Sh. Ct, Sept. 19, 1983, unreported.

[48] On sist of process, see paras 13.71 to 13.83.

[49] *cf.* RCS, r. 22.3(6).

[50] See para. 16.30.

[51] See paras 13.51 to 13.56.

[52] *McDowall v. Campbell* (1838) 16 S. 629; *Duke of Buccleuch v. Cowan* (1866) 4 M. 475, *per* L.J.-C. Inglis at 480 (affd (1876) 4 R.(H.L.) 14).

[53] *Gatt v. Angus Shipping Co. Ltd* (1907) 14 S.L.T. 749; *Wilson v. Rapp*, 1911 S.C. 1360.

[54] *Duke of Buccleuch, Gatt, supra*; Thomson and Middleton, p. 387.

[55] *e.g. Simpson v. Imperial Chemical Industries Ltd*, 1983 S.L.T. 601. See also *Gatt, Wilson, supra*; *Neil v. Edinburgh & Leith Tramways Co.* (1903) 10 S.L.T. 524; *Boyle v. Olsen*, 1923 S.C. 1235.

Before the hearing of the motion, all the cases are placed before the same sheriff. If the sheriff grants the motion, he pronounces an interlocutor in each process conjoining it with the other or others. The actions thereby become one process.[56] The interlocutors are thereafter written on the interlocutor sheet of the principal action, or on a new interlocutor sheet, and all steps taken are applicable to all the processes.[57] The steps of process in the other action or actions are marked as numbers of the leading process.[58] Where it later appears in the course of procedure that it is inexpedient that the processes should continue conjoined, the court may disjoin them.[59] **13.44**

IV. TRANSFER OF CAUSES

Transfer to another roll

Statutory provisions

It sometimes appears in the course of procedure that an action which has been properly raised under one form of process, whether as an ordinary cause, summary cause or small claim, would proceed more conveniently if it were treated as falling under another form. In certain circumstances the sheriff or sheriff principal[60] may, or must, make an appropriate direction. **13.45**

Ordinary cause to summary cause.[61] An ordinary cause is treated as a summary cause only if all parties so move. If at any stage on joint motion they move the sheriff to direct that the cause be treated as a summary cause, he must so direct. The cause is then treated for all purposes (including appeal) as a summary cause, and proceeds accordingly. The cause is remitted to a summary cause roll occurring not more than seven days after the date of the direction or, if no appropriate summary cause roll occurs within that period, to the roll first occurring. The initial writ is deemed to be a summary cause summons.[62] **13.46**

Summary cause to ordinary cause. At any stage of a summary cause the sheriff must direct that it be treated as an ordinary cause if so moved on the joint motion of the parties[63]; and he may so direct on the motion of any of the parties if he is of opinion that the importance or difficulty of the cause makes it appropriate to do so.[64] He may so direct of his own accord only where the summary cause is an action for the recovery of possession of heritable or moveable property.[65] When the direction is made, the case is treated for all purposes (including appeal) as an ordinary cause and proceeds accordingly. The sheriff's decision to make, or not to make, such a direction is not subject to review.[66] The cause is remitted to the ordinary cause roll first **13.47**

---

[56] *Campbell and Cowan & Co. v. Train*, 1910 S.C. 147, *per* Lord Kinnear at 149–150.

[57] Dove Wilson, pp. 258–259.

[58] Maclaren, pp. 499, 501.

[59] *Turner v. Tunnock's Trs* (1864) 2 M. 509; *Yellowlees v. Alexander* (1882) 9 R. 765; *McDonald v. McDonald* (1912) 29 Sh.Ct.Rep. 157.

[60] 1971 Act, s. 37(4).

[61] 1971 Act, s. 37(1)(a).

[62] SCR, r. 23(1).

[63] 1971 Act, s. 37(2)(a).

[64] 1971 Act, s. 37(2)(b).

[65] Proviso to 1971 Act, s. 37(2).

[66] 1971 Act, s. 37(3)(b), as substituted by Law Reform (Miscellaneous Provisions) (Scotland) Act 1980, s. 16.

occurring not sooner than seven days after the date of the direction.[67] There is no provision in the rules deeming any part of the summary cause process to be an initial writ or defences. In practice it is desirable to order the pursuer to lodge an initial writ in accordance with Form G1 of the Ordinary Cause Rules. The crave should be based on, but not materially different from, the claim in the summary cause summons.[68] The condescendence may be based on, and if desirable may expand, the averments in the statement of claim. Thereafter defences are ordered, a period for adjustment is allowed and an options hearing fixed. The case is treated as an ordinary cause for the purpose of dealing with expenses. If the sheriff decerns for a sum below the summary cause limit, he may nevertheless direct that the pursuer's expenses be taxed on the scale appropriate to an ordinary cause.[69] The matter is, however, within the discretion of the sheriff. It is possible, for example, that a pursuer may not receive expenses on the ordinary cause scale if, a remit having been made on joint motion to enable him to sue for more than the summary cause limit, he obtains decree for a sum under the limit; or if he has moved for a remit because of the complexity of the issues but has failed to focus the issues properly in his pleadings.[70]

13.48 **Small claim to summary or ordinary cause.** At any stage the sheriff must direct that a small claim be treated as a summary cause or ordinary cause if so moved on the joint motion of the parties[71]; and he may do so, if he is of opinion that a difficult question of law or a question of fact of exceptional complexity is involved, of his own accord or on the motion of any party.[72] When he so directs, the small claim is treated for all purposes (including appeal) as a summary cause or ordinary cause.[73] His decision is not subject to review.[74]

13.49 **Summary or ordinary cause to small claim.**[75] Where a cause is not a small claim by reason only of the monetary limit applicable to a small claim, the sheriff must direct that it be treated as a small claim if so moved at any stage on the joint motion of the parties. In that event the cause is treated for all purposes (including appeal) as a small claim and proceeds accordingly. The sheriff may not so direct of his own accord or on the motion of one or only some of the parties.

Sheriff's inherent power

13.50 The statutory provisions discussed above prescribe the circumstances in which a case which has been properly raised and correctly assigned to the appropriate roll of civil causes may or must be transferred to another roll.

---

[67] SCR, r. 23(2). Extra court fees are payable: Sheriff Court Fees Order 1997, para. 5(1).

[68] It is incorrect to convert by this means a summary cause action for recovery of possession of heritable property into an ordinary action for summary ejection: *Monklands D.C. v. Baird*, 1987 S.C.L.R. 88.

[69] A.S. (Fees of Solicitors in the Sheriff Court) (Amendment and Further Provisions) 1993, Sched. 1, General Regulations, reg. 2.

[70] *Forsyth v. John Dickinson Group Ltd*, 1984 S.L.T. (Sh. Ct.) 51.

[71] 1971 Act, s. 37(2B)(b), added by Law Reform (Miscellaneous Provisions) (Scotland) Act 1985, s. 18(3).

[72] 1971 Act, s. 37(2B)(a).

[73] 1971 Act, s. 37 (2B).

[74] 1971 Act, s. 37(3)(a), as substituted by Law Reform (Miscellaneous Provisions) (Scotland) Act 1980, s. 16 and amended by Law Reform (Miscellaneous Provisions) (Scotland) Act 1985, s. 18(3)(b).

[75] 1971 Act, s. 37(2C), added by Law Reform (Miscellaneous Provisions) (Scotland) Act 1985, s. 18(3).

They do not deal with a situation in which an action which can only be properly raised under one form of process has been raised in error under the wrong form of process. There appear to be two views of such a situation. One view is that the action is a total nullity upon which no further procedure can follow.[76] The other, less drastic, view is that the sheriff has an inherent power to transfer the action to the correct roll, which he may exercise where the defender has suffered no prejudice by the error, as where the action has been raised within any statutory time-limit, the nature of the claim and the remedy sought have been made clear to the defender, and the error has been formal rather than substantial or the procedural rule contravened has been directory rather than mandatory.[77] The latter view appears to be supported by the observations in *Bliersbach v. MacEwan* that in the circumstances of that case any error in the initiation of the proceedings as a summary application instead of as an ordinary cause could easily have been remedied before the sheriff-substitute, who could have transferred the cause to the ordinary roll.[78] In any event it is submitted that the latter view is to be preferred, since it is in accordance with the tendency of modern practice to relieve a party of the consequences of merely technical irregularity.[79]

Transfer to another sheriff court

Rule 26.1 of the Ordinary Cause Rules confers on the sheriff certain powers to transfer a cause to another sheriff court. The theory of the rule is that the whole sheriff courts of Scotland are to be regarded practically as one system, and that a sheriff court cause, in whatever district it is initiated, may be tried in that sheriff court which affords the maximum of convenience, at the minimum of expense, to all concerned.[80] **13.51**

Grounds for transfer

Convenience of parties and witnesses. Rule 26.1 empowers the sheriff to transfer a cause to another sheriff court, whether in the same sheriffdom or another, in three situations. First, where a cause in which there are two or more defenders has been brought in the sheriff court of the residence or place of business of one of them, the sheriff may transfer the cause to any other sheriff court which has jurisdiction over any of the defenders.[81] He may do so, however, only on the motion of one or more of the parties, and only where he considers it expedient to do so having regard to the convenience of the parties and their witnesses.[82] **13.52**

Secondly, where a plea of no jurisdiction is sustained, the sheriff may transfer the cause to the sheriff court before which it appears to him it ought to have been brought.[83] Here again, however, he may do so only on the motion of one or more of the parties, and only where he considers it expedient having regard to the convenience of the parties and their **13.53**

---

[76] *Tennent Caledonian Breweries Ltd v. Gearty*, 1980 S.L.T. (Sh. Ct.) 71; *Rutherford v. Virtue*, 1993 S.C.L.R. 886.
[77] *Borthwick v. Bank of Scotland*, 1985 S.L.T. (Sh. Ct.) 49.
[78] 1959 S.C. 43, *per* L.P. Clyde at p. 48; 1959 S.L.T. 81, *per* Sheriff McKechnie at 82.
[79] *Paxton v. Brown*, 1908 S.C. 406, *per* L.P. Dunedin at 414.
[80] Fyfe, p. 66; approved, *Wilson v. Hay*, 1977 S.L.T. (Sh. Ct.) 52.
[81] OCR, r. 26.1(2). *Graham v. Young*, 1927 S.L.T. (Sh. Ct.) 25.
[82] OCR, r. 26.1(4).
[83] OCR, r. 26.1(3).

witnesses.[84] This branch of the rule forms a very reasonable exception to the ordinary rule that an action falls to be dismissed when a plea of no jurisdiction is sustained: in a country with many local courts and a mobile population it not infrequently happens that a pursuer raises his action in the wrong court, and the operation of this branch of the rule may save some time and expense.[85] The transfer of the cause does not, however, foreclose the question of the jurisdiction of the court to which the cause is transferred, and it is conceivable that in some circumstances the defender might be entitled to renew his plea to jurisdiction there.

13.54 **On cause shown.** Thirdly, the sheriff may "on cause shown" remit any cause to another sheriff court.[86] Whether or not cause is shown is a matter for the discretion of the sheriff. It is suggested that questions of convenience and expediency should be taken into account. The terms of this branch of the rule are sufficiently wide to enable causes to be transferred between courts of concurrent jurisdiction; or from a court having no jurisdiction to a court possessing jurisdiction; or vice versa.[87] It is essential, however, that either the transferring court or the court to which the cause is transferred should have jurisdiction over the defender. Otherwise, the matter is one for the sheriff's discretion,[88] and an appeal court will be slow to interfere.[89]

Procedure

13.55 On making an order transferring a cause to another sheriff court under any branch of rule 26.1, the sheriff must state his reasons for so doing in the interlocutor, not in the note.[90] He may make the order subject to such conditions as to expenses or otherwise as he thinks fit.[91] His interlocutor transferring the cause is, with his leave, subject to review by the sheriff principal, but is not further subject to review.[92] It is thought that an interlocutor from which reasons are omitted is not merely uninformative but incompetent, in respect that it fails to comply with rule 26.1(5)(a).

13.56 Rule 26.1(6) provides that the sheriff court to which the cause is transferred must accept it. It is thought, however, that if no reasons for the transfer are stated in the interlocutor purporting to transfer the cause, the sheriff court to which it is purportedly transferred may refuse to accept it: the sheriff may direct the sheriff clerk not to enrol it but to return it to the original court, where the sheriff may pronounce an interlocutor of new, including his reasons for transfer. Where reasons have been stated as required by rule 26.1(5)(a) the receiving court accepts the cause and it proceeds in that court in all respects as if it had been originally brought there.[93] It is thought that an arrestment on the dependence remains effective.[94]

---

[84] OCR, r. 26.1(4).

[85] *Wilson v. Ferguson*, 1957 S.L.T. (Sh. Ct.) 52.

[86] OCR, r. 26.1(1).

[87] *Walden v. Campbell*, 1940 S.L.T. (Sh. Ct.) 39, although it should be noted that this case was decided under a rule whose wording was not the same as that of OCR, r. 26.1(1).

[88] *Wilson v. Hay*, *supra*.

[89] *Chiesa v. Greenshields*, 1958 S.L.T. (Sh. Ct.) 58. As in *Walden*, *supra*, the wording of the rule under which this case was decided was different from that of OCR, r. 26.1(1).

[90] OCR, r. 26.1(5)(a); *Walden*, *supra*; *Wilson v. Hay*, *supra*.

[91] OCR, r. 26.1(5)(b).

[92] OCR, r. 26.1(8).

[93] OCR, r. 26.1(7).

[94] See para. 11.25.

Remit to the Court of Session

13.57 The remit of causes from the sheriff court to the Court of Session is regulated by a number of statutory provisions. In addition to a general provision empowering the sheriff to remit, there are particular provisions regulating certain family proceedings, proceedings against the Crown, actions of declarator of death, and remits by order of the Court of Session. There are procedural provisions applicable to all remits.

General provision

13.58 Section 37(1)(b) of the 1971 Act empowers the sheriff or the sheriff principal[95] to remit to the Court of Session any ordinary cause brought in the sheriff court, subject to three qualifications: (1) that the value of the cause exceeds the limit of privative jurisdiction of the sheriff court (currently £1,500)[96]; (2) that he is moved to do so by any of the parties to the cause; and (3) that he is of opinion that the importance or difficulty of the cause makes it appropriate to do so.[97]

13.59 The question of remit from the sheriff court to the Court of Session was considered at length in the recent Full Bench case of *Mullan v. Anderson*.[98] Unfortunately, there was a certain division of judicial opinion about the way in which a sheriff should approach the question whether to remit to the Court of Session. There was no dispute about the fact that "importance" is to be given a wide meaning and includes importance to the parties.[99] However, one view was expressed to the effect that the importance or difficulty of a case are not the only relevant factors to be considered by a sheriff when considering whether to remit. According to that view, the proper approach for a sheriff to take is to decide in the first place whether the importance or difficulty of the case makes it appropriate to remit and, if that question is answered in the affirmative, to consider whether to exercise his discretion to remit having regard to all relevant factors.[1] The contrary view expressed was that the sheriff is entitled to take into account only the importance or difficulty of the case but that when considering the appropriateness of a remit, he should relate his detailed picture of importance or difficulty to the characteristics of the two courts and in so doing is entitled to have regard to broader circumstances such as extra delay or expense.[2] It is perhaps open to question whether there is any substantial practical difference between the two views at the end of the day. The Lord Justice-Clerk was also of the view that the availability of a jury trial in the Court of Session was a factor favouring remit to the Court of Session.[3] In reaching a decision in a particular case as to "the importance or difficulty of the cause" it is necessary to take account only of the terms of the pleadings and the parties' submissions thereon, and it is irrelevant to speculate as to any undisclosed reason which the parties may have for making or opposing the motion, or as to possible developments in the subsequent procedural

---

[95] 1971 Act, s. 37(4).

[96] See paras 2.27, 2.28.

[97] 1971 Act, s. 37(1)(b), as amended by Law Reform (Miscellaneous Provisions) (Scotland) Act 1980, s. 16.

[98] 1993 S.L.T. 835, overruling *Data Controls (Middlesborough) v. BRB*, 1991 S.L.T. 426. See also *Butler v. Thom*, 1982 S.L.T. (Sh. Ct.) 57.

[99] *Mullan supra*, at 839L, 842G, 846H, 850C.

[1] *ibid.* at 838J, 841B.

[2] *ibid.* at 845D, 848J.

[3] *ibid.* at 840G.

progress of the action.[4] An action should not be remitted on a ground which would justify a remit in every case of its kind.[5] An action of damages for very severe personal injuries, brought on behalf of a pupil, was remitted in view of the paucity of contemporary Scottish reported decisions discussing the principles applicable to the assessment of damages and the appropriate level of award in such a case.[6] An action raised by the relatives of a deceased against the man acquitted of his murder was remitted because of the importance of the case to the defender and the fact that a civil court was being asked to consider a question already considered by the High Court of Justiciary. These factors outweighed the pursuers' right to choose the sheriff court as the forum in which the action was to be brought.[7] An action in which a plea of no jurisdiction has been sustained cannot be remitted.[8]

13.60 From a decision to remit, or not to remit, under section 37(1)(b) an appeal lies to the Court of Session.[9]

Family proceedings

13.61 The sheriff or the sheriff principal[10] may, of his own accord, at any stage remit to the Court of Session any action in the sheriff court which is an action for divorce or an action in relation to parental responsibilities or parental rights in relation to a child or the guardianship or adoption of a child.[11] A decision to remit, or not to remit, such an action is not subject to review.[12] If remitting, the sheriff must give his reasons for doing so in detail.[13] When family proceedings raising the same issue are in dependence in both courts, it may be desirable to sist the sheriff court process until the Court of Session process is determined. But where the issues in each process overlap one another, and an issue in the sheriff court process will not necessarily be determined in the Court of Session process, it may be appropriate to remit the sheriff court process so that a single proof may take place in regard to both.[14] A petition for the adoption of a child, which was opposed by the child's natural mother, was remitted because the child was also the subject of an action between the same parties in the Court of Session relative to the custody of the child.[15]

---

[4] *Butler, supra.*

[5] *Dunbar v. Dunbar*, 1912 S.C. 19, *per* Lord Kinnear at 21.

[6] *Butler, supra.*

[7] *Mullan, supra.*

[8] *Lindsay v. Lindsay* (1939) 56 Sh.Ct.Rep. 88 at 95.

[9] 1971 Act, s. 37(3), as substituted by Law Reform (Miscellaneous Provisions) (Scotland) Act 1980, s. 16, and amended by Law Reform (Miscellaneous Provisions) (Scotland) Act 1985, s. 18.

[10] 1971 Act, s. 37(4).

[11] 1971 Act, s. 37(2A), added by Law Reform (Miscellaneous Provisions) (Scotland) Act 1980, s. 1 and amended by Divorce Jurisdiction, Court Fees and Legal Aid (Scotland) Act 1983, Sched. 1, paras 11, 12, Law Reform (Parent and Child) (Scotland) Act 1986, Sched. 1 and Children (Scotland) Act 1995, Sched. 4, para. 18(3).

[12] 1971 Act, s. 37(3), as substituted by Law Reform (Miscellaneous Provisions) (Scotland) Act 1980, s. 16, and amended by Law Reform (Miscellaneous Provisions) (Scotland) Act 1985, s. 18.

[13] *Brown v. Brown*, 1948 S.C. 5.

[14] *Campbell v. Campbell*, 1960 S.L.T. (Notes) 20.

[15] *A v. B*, Linlithgow Sh. Ct, Oct. 9, 1985, unreported. It is thought to be unnecessary to remit a straightforward application by a grandparent for contact: *cf. Cook v. McGinnes*, 1982 S.L.T. (Sh. Ct.) 101, where the sheriff subsequently remitted on the pursuer's motion and of consent, not *ex proprio motu*.

Action of declarator of death

An action of declarator under section 1 of the Presumption of Death (Scotland) Act 1977 may be remitted to the Court of Session at any stage of the proceedings. The sheriff may remit, either of his own accord or on the application of any party to the action, where he considers a remit desirable because of the importance or complexity of the matters at issue. He must remit if so directed by the Court of Session, who may give such a direction on the application of any party to the action, where the court for the same reasons considers a remit desirable.[16] An application for variation or recall of a decree in an action of declarator may be likewise remitted.[17] **13.62**

Proceedings against the Crown

Any proceedings against the Crown in the sheriff court must be remitted to the Court of Session if a certificate by the Lord Advocate is produced to the effect that the proceedings may involve an important question of law, or may be decisive of other cases, or are for other reasons more fit for trial in the Court of Session. Where any proceedings have been so remitted, and it appears to the Court of Session that the remit has occasioned additional expense to the pursuer, the court is directed to take account of the additional expense so occasioned in deciding any question of expenses.[18] **13.63**

Transmission by order of the Court of Session

Contingency. The Court of Session may order the transmission to that court of a sheriff court process on the ground of contingency.[19] When there is contingency between a process depending in the Court of Session and a process depending in the sheriff court, the latter may be transmitted to the Court of Session by order of that court. There is no contingency unless a decision in one of the actions would decide the other in whole or in part.[20] An application for transmission may be made in the Court of Session by motion at the instance of a party to the cause depending before the Court of Session, or by minute at the instance of any other person having an interest, including a party to the cause depending before the sheriff.[21] A copy of the sheriff court pleadings and interlocutors is lodged with the motion or minute.[22] Although there is no specific provision in the Rules of Court it is suggested that if the court decides that there is contingency between the processes, it should grant warrant to the sheriff clerk for transmission of the sheriff court process. The process is transmitted by the sheriff clerk and receipt of it is intimated to all parties by the Deputy Principal Clerk.[23] The party on whose motion the case was transmitted must make up a Court of Session process and lodge it within 14 days after the date of receipt.[24] He must then apply for such further procedure as he desires, the action thereafter proceeding as if it were a **13.64**

---

[16] Presumption of Death (Scotland) Act 1977, s. 1(6). On declarators of death, see paras 20.06 to 20.18.

[17] *ibid.* s. 4(4).

[18] Crown Proceedings Act 1947, s. 44.

[19] Court of Session Act 1988, s. 33.

[20] *Duke of Athole v. Robertson* (1869) 8 M. 299; *Wilson v. Junor* (1907) 15 S.L.T. 182; *James Sutherland & Sons v. Pottinger*, 1989 S.L.T. 679. For examples of cases where contingency has been held to be present, see Maxwell, p. 240.

[21] RCS, r. 32.2(1).

[22] RCS, r. 32.2(2).

[23] RCS, r. 32.3.

[24] RCS, r. 32.4(1).

Court of Session action.[25] A decision made on an application for transmission is not appealable, but an application that has been refused may, in the event of a change of circumstances, be renewed.[26]

13.65 **Necessity.** The Rules of the Court of Session make provision for the transmission to the Court of Session of any process depending, or that may have depended, in any inferior court.[27] This would arise when the lower court process is required as evidence in the Court of Session. When any of the parties to a cause in the Court of Session deems it necessary that any such process should be lodged in the Court of Session process, the party applies by motion to the court for a warrant to authorise and direct the clerk of the inferior court, on production of a certified copy of the interlocutor, to deliver up the process to the Deputy Principal Clerk.[28] The motion must be duly intimated to the opposite party in the Court of Session process or to his solicitor as required by rule 23.3 of the Rules of the Court of Session, and intimated to the custodier of the inferior court process at least two days before it is enrolled.[29] The Deputy Principal Clerk must grant a receipt for any process transmitted to him and lodge it in the Court of Session process.[30] No process transmitted under this provision may be borrowed.[31] After the process ceases to be required the Deputy Principal Clerk must return it to the sheriff clerk.[32]

Procedure

13.66 When the process is transmitted by order of the Court of Session, the sheriff makes no order. In the other cases described above, the sheriff pronounces an interlocutor remitting the cause to the Court of Session. In cases other than a mandatory remit in terms of section 44 of the Crown Proceedings Act 1947 he should append to his interlocutor a note fully explaining his reasons for remitting.[33] Within four days after the interlocutor is pronounced, the sheriff clerk transmits the process to the Deputy Clerk of Session.[34] Within the same period the sheriff clerk sends written notice of the remit to each party and certifies on the interlocutor sheet that he has done so[35]; but failure to do so does not affect the validity of the remit.[36] The procedure in the Court of Session immediately after transmission is regulated by rules 32.3 and 32.4 of the Rules of the Court of Session. Once the case has been transmitted, it cannot be transferred back to the sheriff without the authority of the Court of Session, with a view to obtaining incidental orders from the sheriff, such as an interlocutor sanctioning the employment of counsel.[37] If the Court of Session considers that the sheriff should not have remitted the cause, it may remit it back to him.[38]

---

[25] RCS, r. 32.4(2).
[26] RCS, r. 32.2(3).
[27] RCS, r. 35.10(1).
[28] *ibid.*
[29] RCS, r. 35.10(2).
[30] RCS, r. 35.10(3).
[31] RCS, r. 35.10(4).
[32] RCS, r. 35.10(5).
[33] *Brown v. Brown*, 1948 S.C. 5 at 11.
[34] OCR, r. 26.2(1).
[35] OCR, r. 26.2(2).
[36] OCR, r. 26.2(3).
[37] *Baird v. SMT Co.*, 1948 S.C. 526.
[38] *Dunbar v. Dunbar*, 1912 S.C. 19; *Lamont v. Lamont*, 1939 S.C. 484; *Campbell v. Campbell*, 1956 S.C. 285.

Remit from the Court of Session

Where an action is before the Court of Session which could competently have been brought before a sheriff, the court may remit the action to the sheriff within whose jurisdiction it could have been brought. The court may take that course at its own instance or on the application of any of the parties to the action, but will do so only where, in the opinion of the court, the nature of the action makes it appropriate to do so.[39] "The nature of the action" refers, it is thought, to the circumstances of the particular case, and not to the class of causes to which it belongs. A remit may be appropriate where, for example, other related proceedings are in dependence in the sheriff court, and for reasons of efficiency and convenience it is desirable that all the proceedings should be dealt with in the sheriff court,[40] but the existence of such proceedings is not determinative.[41] The power may be exercised in large and difficult cases as well as in small and simple ones and the fact that a claim is small and simple is not *per se* enough to justify a remit.[42] The power may possibly be exercised even where novel and complicated issues of fact and law arise.[43] Where there is concurrent jurisdiction the pursuer will not be deprived of his choice of forum on grounds applicable in every case of the kind, and the practical and procedural advantages to be found in adopting one forum rather than another, such as the availability of optional procedure and the right to civil jury trial, should be considered by the court.[44] A straightforward claim should not be remitted in the absence of any factor showing that its nature was such that the sheriff court was more appropriate, and actions whose nature made them inappropriate for the sheriff court should not be remitted.[45] A remit may be appropriate where the expense of defending an action in the Court of Session would cause difficulties for the defender.[46] On receipt of the process the sheriff clerk records the date of receipt on the interlocutor sheet; fixes a hearing to determine further procedure on the first court day occurring not earlier than 14 days after the date of receipt; and forthwith sends written notice of the date of the hearing to the parties.[47] **13.67**

V. Reference to the European Court

The Court of Justice of the European Communities has jurisdiction to give preliminary rulings concerning (1) the interpretation of the Community Treaties; (2) the validity and interpretation of acts of the institutions of the Community; (3) the interpretation of the statutes of bodies established by an act of the Council of Ministers of the Community where those statutes so provide; and the interpretation of the Conventions defined in section 1(1) of the Civil Jurisdiction and Judgments Act 1982. Where a question as to any of these matters is raised before any court or **13.68**

---

[39] Law Reform (Miscellaneous Provisions) (Scotland) Act 1985, s. 14.

[40] H.L. Deb., Vol. 467, col. 194, *per* Lord Mackay of Clashfern, Lord Advocate.

[41] *Rae v. Rae*, 1991 S.L.T. 44.

[42] *McIntosh v. BRB (No.1)*, 1990 S.C. 338.

[43] *Watson v. Babcock Power*, 1987 S.C.L.R. 624.

[44] *McIntosh, supra*, disapproving *Hamilton v. British Coal Corporation*, 1990 S.L.T. 287 and *Wescott v. James Dickie & Co.*, 1991 S.L.T. 200.

[45] *McIntosh, supra*.

[46] *Gribb v. Gribb*, 1993 S.L.T. 178.

[47] OCR, r. 26.3.

tribunal of a Member State, and that court or tribunal considers that a decision on the question is necessary to enable it to give judgment, it *may* request the European Court to give a ruling on the question. Where any such question is raised before any court or tribunal of a Member State against whose decisions there is no judicial remedy under national law (*i.e.* no right of appeal), that court or tribunal *must* bring the matter before the European Court.[48]

13.69 The grounds on which the discretion to refer should be exercised were considered in the leading English case on the matter.[49] It was observed that the discretion should be exercised only where the court has ascertained the relevant facts or the best formulation of the question and is satisfied that a decision of the question will be necessary to enable it to give judgment. There is no jurisdiction to refer the question if it does not fall within the terms of the Treaties; and it is unnecessary to refer it if the case may be decided on grounds other than those raised by the question, or if the answer to the question is reasonably clear and free from doubt. It was also suggested that in exercising its discretion whether to decide a question itself or to refer it to the European Court the national court should take into account the delay and expense involved, the difficulty and importance of the point, the importance of not overloading the European Court, the need to formulate the question clearly, and the wishes of the parties. In Scotland a reference will not normally be appropriate until the pleadings have been adjusted and the real question in dispute focused in the pleadings, and preliminary issues of title, competency or relevancy have been resolved.[50] In some circumstances it may be necessary and desirable to make a reference before proof.[51]

13.70 In the sheriff court a reference may be made by the sheriff *ex proprio motu* or on the motion of any party to the proceedings.[52] The reference must be made in the form of a request for a preliminary ruling of the European Court, framed as nearly as may be in terms of a prescribed form.[53] When the sheriff decides that a reference be made, he must continue the cause *simpliciter* for the purpose and draft a reference within four weeks thereafter.[54] On the reference being drafted, the sheriff clerk must forthwith send a copy to each of the parties[55]; and within four weeks from the date when the copies have been sent, each party may lodge with the sheriff clerk and send to each of the other parties a note of any adjustments he desires to have made in the draft reference.[56] Within 14 days after the latest date on which any such note may be lodged the sheriff, after considering any adjustments, makes up and signs the reference,[57] and the sheriff clerk forthwith intimates the making of the reference to the parties.[58] It seems unfortunate that there

---

[48] European Economic Community Treaty, Art. 177(1); European Coal and Steel Community Treaty, Art. 41; European Atomic Energy Community Treaty, Art. 150(1); Civil Jurisdiction and Judgments Act 1982, Sched. 2, Art. 3.

[49] *H. P. Bulmer Ltd v. J. Bollinger SA* [1974] Ch. 401, followed in *Wither v. Cowie*, 1990 S.C.C.R. 741 and applied in *BCP Group v. Customs and Excise Commissioners*; *Swallowfield v. Customs and Excise Commissioners* [1994] S.T.C. 41.

[50] *Prince v. Secretary of State for Scotland*, 1985 S.C. 8.

[51] *Kaur v. Lord Advocate*, 1980 S.C. 319 at 336.

[52] OCR, r. 38.2(1).

[53] OCR, r. 38.2(2), Form E1.

[54] OCR, r. 38.3(1).

[55] OCR, r. 38.3(2).

[56] OCR, r. 38.3(3).

[57] OCR, r. 38.3(4).

[58] OCR, r. 38.3(5).

may thus be a delay of up to 10 weeks from the date of the decision to make the reference. Unless the sheriff otherwise orders, the proceedings are sisted until the European Court has given a preliminary ruling on the question or questions referred to it.[59] The sheriff may recall the sist, however, for the purpose of making an interim order which a due regard to the interests of the parties may require.[60] The sheriff clerk transmits a certified copy of the reference to the Registrar of the European Court,[61] but he must not do so, unless the sheriff otherwise directs, where an appeal against the making of the reference is pending.[62] An appeal is to be treated as pending until the time for making an appeal has expired or, if an appeal is brought within that time, until the appeal is disposed of.[63] In the European Court the parties, the parties' Member States, the European Commission and, where appropriate, the Council of Ministers are entitled to submit statements of case or written observations to the Court. When the Court has given its judgment a certified copy is transmitted to the court which made the reference.[64]

VI. Sist of Process

General rules

It is a general principle of civil procedure that an action should be litigated without interruption to a conclusion in conformity with the settled rules of practice and procedure, and each party is entitled to insist upon the cause proceeding to judgment.[65] In certain circumstances, however, it is in the interests of justice that a stop should be put on the further conduct of the proceedings, so that the parties are precluded from taking any further steps therein until the arrival of a certain date or the occurrence of a particular event or, most usually, for an indefinite period "until the further orders of court". Such a stoppage of procedure is called a sist of process,[66] and it is made under an order of the court pronounced in the exercise of its discretionary jurisdiction.[67] A sist of process does not affect arrestment on the dependence.[68] **13.71**

Procedure

The court may sist the cause on the motion[69] or plea[70] of either party, or on joint motion, or *ex proprio motu*.[71] A motion by one party should be made promptly, as soon as practicable after the grounds for making it **13.72**

---

59 OCR, r. 38.4(1).
60 OCR, r. 38.4(2).
61 OCR, r. 38.5(1).
62 OCR, r. 38.5(2).
63 OCR, r. 38.5(3).
64 D. Anderson, *References to the European Court* (Sweet & Maxwell, 1995).
65 *Purves v. N.B. Ry* (1848) 10 D. 853; *Connell v. Grierson* (1865) 3 M. 1166, *per* Lord Deas at 1167; *Auld & Macdonald v. George Wimpey & Co. Ltd*, 1977 S.L.T. (Notes) 23; *Keel v. Keel*, 1985 S.L.T. (Sh.Ct.) 52.
66 *Thornton v. North Star Fishing Co. Ltd*, 1983 S.L.T. 530.
67 *Connell, supra; Phosphate Sewage Co. v. Molleson* (1876) 3 R.(H.L.) 77; *Keel, supra*. Exceptionally, a sist may be mandatory in certain family proceedings (see para. 22.28), and is mandatory where a party has become an enemy alien (see para. 4.03).
68 *Robert Taylor & Partners (Edinburgh) v. William Gerrard*, 1996 S.L.T. (Sh. Ct.) 105.
69 Dobie, *Styles*, p. 337.
70 *ibid.* p. 368.
71 *Clark's Exr v. Clark*, 1953 S.L.T. (Notes) 58.

have arisen or come to the party's knowledge, otherwise it may be refused if a sist would occasion undue prejudice to the other party.[72] Where a plea is stated, a motion may be made when the defences containing the plea are lodged,[73] or the plea may be disposed of after debate.[74]

Exercise of discretion

13.73 A sist of process is a serious interference with the orderly progress of procedure, and the onus is on the party moving for it to satisfy the court that it is in the interests of justice that the proceedings should not be allowed to continue.[75] A sist may be granted in a wide variety of circumstances.[76] Some of those most frequently encountered in practice are discussed in the following paragraphs. The question whether or not an action should be sisted must, however, always be a matter for the discretion of the sheriff. He must balance the reasons urged on either side, and must not, by simply following a practice of adopting a fixed rule of policy, disable himself from exercising his discretion in the light of the particular circumstances of each case.[77] An interlocutor sisting a case should state the reason for the sist.[78]

Application for legal aid

13.74 Unless there are special circumstances, an action will ordinarily be sisted to enable a party to apply for legal aid. Special circumstances in a particular case may include: the nature of the litigation; the amount or availability of resources at the applicant's command; and any undue delay by the applicant in applying for legal aid.[79] When a case has been sisted to enable a party to apply for legal aid, there may be a delay before the application is disposed of by the legal aid authorities, and the applicant's opponent may lodge a motion for the sist to be recalled. On the hearing of such a motion the applicant's solicitor must give the court the fullest possible information about the reasons for the delay, and must be prepared to satisfy the court that the delay has not been occasioned by any shortcoming on the part of the applicant, such as failure to co-operate with the legal aid authorities by furnishing them with all necessary information.[80] A party who has made, or who intends in good faith to make, a proper and timeous application for legal aid is likely to be seriously prejudiced if the court refuses or recalls a sist while his application is being processed.

Settlement

13.75 Actions are very often sisted on joint motion where parties have reached, or are about to reach, an agreement for settlement. In particular, personal injuries actions are frequently raised shortly before the expiry of the limitation period only in order to preserve the pursuer's position, the parties already being engaged in negotiation for the settlement of his

---

[72] *McCrae v. Bryson*, 1922 S.L.T. 664.
[73] *Motordrift A/S v. Trachem Co. Ltd*, 1982 S.L.T. 127.
[74] *Greenock Port and Harbour Trs v. British Oil and Cake Mills Ltd*, 1944 S.C. 70.
[75] *Connell, supra*; *Keel, supra*.
[76] Many examples are given in Maclaren, pp. 481–487.
[77] *Graham v. National Coal Board*, 1964 S.L.T. (Sh. Ct.) 53; *Keel, supra*.
[78] *Jones v. Jones*, 1993 S.C.L.R. 151.
[79] *Keel, supra*.
[80] *McCulloch v. Neilson*, Sh. Pr. Gillies, Hamilton Sh. Ct, Nov. 11, 1983, unreported.

claim, and are sisted on a joint or unopposed motion as soon as they are commenced. Exceptional cases may occur from time to time when, in spite of the fact that both parties concur in asking for a sist, the court is satisfied that it is in the interests of justice that the motion should be refused. In general, however, when both parties are agreed that the action will probably be settled, and concur in asking for a sist, a sist is granted, usually at a considerable saving of expense and judicial time.[81]

Aribtration

An action may be sisted in order that its subject-matter, or part of it, may be decided by arbitration. The circumstances in which that course may be adopted have already been discussed.[82] **13.76**

Family proceedings

Provision for mandatory or discretionary sists in consistorial actions is made by the Domicile and Matrimonial Proceedings Act 1973, which is considered below.[83] **13.77**

Other proceedings

It is appropriate in certain circumstances to sist a cause to await the outcome of other proceedings. An action may be sisted to enable a pursuer to establish his title to sue, as by raising an action of proving the tenor[84] or of declarator,[85] or by obtaining confirmation as executor.[86] Similarly, an action may be sisted to enable a defender to establish his title to defend.[87] Again, a sist may be granted to enable a party to take appropriate proceedings, the decision in which may vindicate the position he has taken up in the action,[88] or will be a necessary preliminary to the decision of the action.[89] **13.78**

Whether it is otherwise appropriate to sist a cause to await the decision in another action is a question of circumstances. It is in any event improper to sist until the pleadings in both actions are fully adjusted.[90] Where there are two actions in dependence raising the same issue, that which is the less appropriate for trying the issue may be sisted.[91] Where an issue in one action between the parties depends on the outcome of another action in which one or both parties are also parties, the former action may be sisted.[92] It may be appropriate to sist an action in the sheriff court, the **13.79**

---

[81] *Mair v. National Coal Board*, 1962 S.L.T. (Sh. Ct.) 53; *Graham v. National Coal Board*, 1964 S.L.T. (Sh. Ct.) 53.

[82] paras 2.99 to 2.102.

[83] paras 22.27 to 22.31.

[84] *Officers of Ordnance v. McDonald* (1825) 3 S. 629 (N.E. 442); *Shaw v. Shaw's Trs* (1876) 3 R. 813.

[85] *McLean v. Glasgow Corporation*, 1933 S.L.T. 396.

[86] *Bridges v. Ewing* (1833) 11 S. 335.

[87] *Earl of Lauderdale v. Wedderburn* (1903) 11 S.L.T. 194.

[88] *Blake's Trs v. Jolly*, 1920 1 S.L.T. 304.

[89] *Loudon v. Young* (1856) 18 D. 856; *Smellie v. Thomson* (1868) 6 M. 1024; *Duke of Argyll v. Muir*, 1910 S.C. 96; *Clark's Exr v. Clark*, 1953 S.L.T. (Notes) 58.

[90] *Clydesdale Bank v. D. & H. Cohen*, 1943 S.C. 244; *N. G. Napier Ltd v. Corbett* (1959) 79 Sh.Ct.Rep. 23.

[91] *Davidson v. Davidson's Trs*, 1952 S.L.T. (Notes) 3 (same parties in both actions); *Girvan, Petr*, 1985 S.L.T. 92 (one party claiming custody of child in both actions).

[92] *AB v. CB*, 1911 2 S.L.T. 99; *Greenock Port and Harbour Trs v. British Oil and Cake Mills Ltd*, 1944 S.C. 70; *Central SMT Co. Ltd v. Lanarkshire C.C.*, 1949 S.C. 450.

record having been closed, if the legal issue in the case is about to be settled authoritatively in a superior court. But while parties may agree to a sist to await the result of another action, it would be improper, against the wishes of one of them, to sist merely to await the result of another action between different parties where the decision in that action would not be binding upon the court,[93] or where it is not clear that the decision in that action would affect the result of the case.[94] Thus, where two pursuers sue the same defender in separate actions, even for loss arising from the same fault, one action cannot be sisted to await the outcome of the other if that course is opposed by the pursuer of the action which it is proposed to sist.[95] It may be proper to sist an action in order to prevent prejudice to a party who has raised other proceedings[96]; it may, on the other hand, be incorrect to sist where to do so would enable a party to gain an unfair advantage by taking other proceedings, as where a defender seeks an opportunity to make an illiquid counterclaim liquid.[97] Where a plea of *forum non conveniens* is sustained, the court may sist the action where that course may facilitate a solution by the foreign tribunal of the controversy between the parties or the enforcement of the foreign decree.[98]

Other considerations

13.80 A sist is appropriate where circumstances have arisen since the action was raised which may render the action unnecessary or may lead to its early disposal, as where an action for divorce and residence is raised after the raising of an action for residence,[99] or where a party has become bankrupt and his trustee requires time to investigate the circumstances before deciding whether to sist himself as a party.[1] An action may be sisted in so far as it relates to a severable branch of the case.[2] The court will not grant a sist where it is better and more convenient that the action should be dismissed and a new and separate action brought.[3] It may be necessary to sist an action in order to enable a document to be after stamped.[4]

Appeal

13.81 An interlocutor sisting an action may be appealed, without leave, from the sheriff to the sheriff principal or the Court of Session,[5] or from the sheriff principal to the Court of Session.[6] An appeal against the refusal of a sist is competent only with leave.[7]

---

93 *N. G. Napier Ltd, supra.*
94 *Maitland v. Maitland* (1885) 12 R. 899.
95 *Higgins v. Glasgow Corporation*, 1954 S.L.T. (Sh. Ct.) 73.
96 *James Finlay Corporation Ltd v. McCormack*, 1986 S.L.T. 106.
97 *Thomson v. Paxton* (1849) 11 D. 1113; *Pegler v. Northern Agricultural Implement Co.* (1877) 4 R. 435; *Mackie v. Mackie* (1897) 5 S.L.T. 42. But see *Munro v. Macdonald's Exrs* (1866) 4 M. 687; *Ross v. Ross* (1895) 22 R. 461.
98 para. 2.92.
99 *Paterson v. Paterson* (1899) 2 F. 81.
1 Dobie, p. 177.
2 *Cookney v. Laverty*, 1967 S.L.T. (Notes) 89.
3 *N.B. Ry v. N.B. Grain Storage and Transit Co.* (1897) 11 R. 687.
4 Stamp Act 1891, s. 14; *Elliot v. Erikson* (1960) 76 Sh.Ct.Rep. 104 at 107 (not fully reported on this point, 1960 S.L.T. (Sh. Ct.) 28); Walkers, *Evidence*, Chap. 20.
5 1907 Act, s. 27(c).
6 1907 Act, s. 28(1)(b).
7 1907 Act, ss. 27(f), 28(1)(d).

Recall of sist

Once the action has been sisted, no step of procedure, however formal, may be taken, and no interlocutor pronounced, until the sist is recalled. If some incidental step of procedure is desired before the purpose for which the action was sisted has been achieved, it is necessary to move the court to recall the sist, pronounce the order desired, and of new sist the cause. It is always competent for any party at any time to lodge a motion for recall of the sist and re-enrolment of the cause for further procedure.[8] It is desirable that the motion should specify what the further procedure is to be. If it does not do so the motion may have to call in court even though it is unopposed. A litigant who has consented to a sist is entitled to withdraw his consent at any time and move for recall of the sist, unless he has agreed not to do so, as by an extrajudicial agreement or by having consented to a sist until the occurrence of some event.[9] **13.82**

Recall is in the discretion of the court. It is often granted where the court is satisfied that the purpose of the sist has been served; or that there has been a material change of circumstances; or that it is in the interests of justice that the sist should be recalled in respect that its continuance is likely to cause or produce prejudice. An appeal against the recall of a sist is competent only with leave.[10] **13.83**

---

[8] Dobie, *Styles*, p. 337.

[9] *Orr v. Glasgow, Airdrie and Monklands Junction Ry* (1857) 20 D. 327 at 338; *Higgins v. Glasgow Corporation*, 1954 S.L.T. (Sh. Ct.) 73.

[10] 1907 Act, ss. 27(f), 28(1)(d).

CHAPTER 14

DISPOSAL OF ACTION WITHOUT PROOF

The majority of the actions raised in the sheriff court are disposed of without proof. Many are undefended actions in which no proof is required.[1] Of the defended actions, some are disposed of after debate[2]; and in a few others, a judicial remit or reference, or a reference to oath, takes the place of a conventional proof by witnesses before the sheriff.[3] This chapter is concerned with the disposal of defended actions without proof by means of decree by default, abandonment, settlement, or summary decree. **14.01**

I. DECREE BY DEFAULT

General rule

It is a general principle of civil procedure that an action, once commenced, should be litigated to a conclusion in conformity with the settled rules of practice and procedure, and within the shortest possible time consistent with the interests of justice and the preservation of the equitable rights of the parties. A party cannot be allowed so to retard or impede the progress of the action as to infringe these interests and prevent the due administration of justice. There must therefore be an effective and appropriate sanction to compel the parties' due compliance with the rules and orders of court and their due appearance or representation at those callings of the case at which their attendance is required. In sheriff court practice, in a defended cause other than an action of multiplepoinding and a cause under the Presumption of Death (Scotland) Act 1977,[4] failure so to comply or attend may be treated as a "default". The sanction for such default is that decree, with expenses, may be pronounced against the defaulter: in the case of a pursuer, decree of absolvitor or dismissal; and in the case of a defender, decree as craved.[5] If none of the parties appears at a diet and the sheriff considers it appropriate to dispose of the action at that stage, the only decree which he may pronounce is a decree of dismissal.[6] In all these cases, the action is disposed of without proof, irrespective of the merits of the cause. The sheriff is, however, endowed with a discretion to prorogate, on cause shown, the time for lodging any production or part of process, for giving intimation or for implementing any order.[7] The following paragraphs **14.02**

---

[1] See Chap. 7. Special rules apply to certain family actions (see Chap. 22).

[2] para. 13.16.

[3] paras 13.26 to 13.41.

[4] OCR, r. 16.1(b),(c). Decree by default in family actions is covered by a separate rule (OCR, r. 16.1(a) referring to OCR, r. 33.37). This is considered at para. 14.14.

[5] OCR, r. 16.2(2).

[6] OCR, r. 16.2 (3); see para. 14.07.

[7] OCR, r. 16.3.

consider the nature of a decree by default; the circumstances in which it may be pronounced; the exercise of the sheriff's discretionary powers; and appeals.

Nature of decree by default

14.03 A decree by default with a finding of expenses is a final judgment.[8] It may be pronounced in any defended action other than, as already noted,[9] an action of multiplepoinding (to which Chapter 35 of the Ordinary Cause Rules applies) or a cause under the Presumption of Death (Scotland) Act 1977 (to which Chapter 37 of the Rules applies).[10] Separate rules apply to family actions and these are considered below.[11] A defended cause is one in which a notice of intention to defend has been lodged.[12] In the sheriff court, if the defender does not lodge defences by the specified date in terms of Ordinary Cause Rule 9.6(1), the pursuer may move for decree by default.[13] A decree by default pronounced in those circumstances is not, however, habile to found a plea of *res judicata* since it is not a decree pronounced *in foro contentioso*.[14] It is only when defences are lodged that litiscontestation takes place, and only a decree by default which is pronounced thereafter is a decree *in foro* which, as long as it subsists, may found a plea of *res judicata*.[15] By contrast, a decree in absence (or a decree by default granted before defences are lodged) becomes entitled to the privileges of a decree *in foro* only after a substantial interval.[16] Other differences between a decree in absence and a decree by default are that the former may be pronounced only against a defender, while the latter may be pronounced against any party to a cause; and that while a defender may be reponed against a decree in absence by the sheriff,[17] a party who seeks to be reponed against a decree by default must appeal.[18]

When decree by default may be pronounced

14.04 A decree by default may be pronounced (a) if any production or part of process has not been lodged or intimated within the time required by or order of the sheriff; (b) if an order has not been implemented within the time specified by the sheriff; or (c) if a party fails to appear or be represented at a diet.[19] If none of the parties appears the sheriff may dismiss the action.[20] The object of the rule (at least so far as it applies to default by one party) is to prevent delay in the progress of litigation due to

---

[8] 1907 Act, s. 3(h); *Hardy v. Robinson*, 1985 S.L.T. (Sh. Ct.) 40.
[9] para. 14.02.
[10] OCR, r. 16.1(b),(c).
[11] OCR, r. 16.1(a) referring to OCR, r. 33.37. See para. 14.14.
[12] *Millar v. Chapelside Chemical Co.* (1887) 3 Sh.Ct.Rep. 83; *Reilly Glen & Co. v. Beaton*, 1964 S.L.T. (Sh. Ct.) 73; Fyfe, p. 155; Dobie, p. 139. OCR, rr. 7.2 (applying to all cases other than those where the sheriff may not grant decree without evidence) and 33.28 (applying to certain family actions) in effect define what is meant by an undefended cause. What is a defended cause may be inferred from these rules.
[13] OCR, r. 16.2(1)(a). In the Court of Session by contrast, it is a decree *in absence* which is granted before defences are lodged, even though appearance has been entered: RCS, r. 19.1(2)(b); Maxwell, p. 248.
[14] *Esso Petroleum Co. v. Law*, 1956 S.C. 33.
[15] *Forrest v. Dunlop* (1875) 3 R. 15; paras 8.18, 8.19.
[16] para. 7.18.
[17] OCR, r. 8.1; see paras 7.23 *et seq.*
[18] See paras 14.11 to 14.14.
[19] OCR, r. 16.2(1).
[20] OCR, r. 16.2(3).

indolence or inadvertence[21] or deliberate disregard of duty by parties or their solicitors, and the basis of the decree is some failure in duty in the circumstances defined by the rule.[22] In any circumstances other than those defined, decree by default cannot be pronounced in terms of the rule, notwithstanding that a party may have unreasonably delayed in the conduct of his part in the litigation.[23]

Lodging of production

Where the sheriff has ordered production of a document by a party,[24] decree by default in respect of failure to lodge it within the time required may be warranted where it is a document on which the whole case of the party's opponent rests. Where, however, it is necessary for only part of his opponent's case, the party may be held as confessing the point which his opponent seeks to prove by the document, or a copy produced by his opponent may be held equivalent to the original.[25] **14.05**

Failure to lodge record

The Court of Session has held that, where pursuers failed to lodge a copy of the record timeously for an options hearing[26] and where there were no competing reasons in the interests of justice for granting relief, dismissal of the action was justified since it was vital that the record should be available in time for the sheriff to prepare for the options hearing.[27] An oversight which leads to a failure to lodge a record timeously may be "excusable" and thus fall within the scope of the general dispensing power[28] but the sheriff may nonetheless be entitled to dismiss the action because he was unable to prepare for the options hearing because of the failure.[29] A failure timeously to lodge a record because a solicitor, left temporarily in charge of a case while the principal solicitor was away on holiday, failed to take note of the date of the options hearing has been held to justify dismissal but not absolvitor.[30] In the same case the sheriff principal observed that the dispensing power should be exercised in such circumstances only if failure to exercise it would result in substantial injustice. If decree by default is to be avoided and the sheriff asked to exercise his dispensing power, it is essential that he be given an explanation for the late lodging of the record as otherwise he has nothing on which to base any exercise of discretion.[31] Failure by a pursuer's solicitor to lodge **14.06**

---

21 *Bainbridge v. Bainbridge* (1879) 6 R. 541 at 542, *per* L.J.-C. Moncrieff.

22 *McCraddie v. Markham*, Sh. Pr. Calver, Glasgow Sh. Ct, Dec. 20, 1961, unreported. The circumstances of *Ravelston Steamship Co. Ltd v. Sieberg Bros*, 1947 S.L.T. (Notes) 12, where decree in respect of a technical default was pronounced against defenders who were the victims of *force majeure*, were highly exceptional.

23 *Purdie v. Kincaid & Co. Ltd*, 1959 S.L.T. (Sh. Ct.) 64.

24 paras 15.47, 15.48.

25 *Caledonian Ry v. Orr* (1855) 17 D. 812; *Strathan v. Steuart* (1870) 9 M. 116.

26 OCR, r. 9.11(2) provides that the pursuer must lodge a certified copy of the record not later than two days before the options hearing.

27 *DTZ Debenham Thorpe v. I. Henderson Transport Services*, 1995 S.C. 282.

28 OCR, r. 2.1(1) provides that a sheriff may relieve a party from the consequences of failure to comply with a provision of the rules "which is shown to be due to mistake, oversight or other excusable cause". See paras 5.93 to 5.97.

29 *Morran v. Glasgow Council of Tenants' Associations*, 1995 S.L.T. (Sh. Ct.) 46. See also *Mahoney v. Officer*, 1995 S.L.T. (Sh. Ct.) 49. *Cf. Burtonport Fishermen's Co-operative v. Sans Unkles*, 1994 S.C.L.R. 844.

30 *Group 4 Total Security v. Jaymarke Developments*, 1995 S.C.L.R. 303.

31 *Welsh v. Thornhome Services*, 1994 S.C.L.R. 1021. See also *Baird & Son v. Nisbet*, 1995 S.C.L.R. 1127.

answers to a defender's counterclaim, to adjust the initial writ and to lodge a copy of the record together with a failure to appear at the options hearing resulted in dismissal of the principal action and decree in favour of the defender in the counterclaim.[32] An action was dismissed in respect of failure timeously to lodge a record even though the pursuer had during the course of the action been granted interim interdict on several occasions.[33] However, where a minute of acceptance of tender was lodged prior to the options hearing a sheriff's decision to dismiss an action because of failure to lodge a copy of the record was reversed on appeal to the Court of Session, the court holding that the sheriff should either have prorogated the time for lodging the record or dispensed completely with it.[34] The fact that an action, if dismissed for failure to lodge a record, may thereafter be time-barred is a factor to which a sheriff should give weight when considering whether the granting of decree by default would be in the interests of justice.[35]

Failure to appear at diet

14.07 Ordinary Cause Rule 16.2 provides that decree by default may be pronounced if one party fails to appear or be represented at a diet, or if none of the parties appears. Where a motion to discharge a proof was refused and the solicitor who moved it then advised the sheriff that he was no longer acting and was allowed to withdraw, his clients were held not to have been represented at the proof.[36] When a record had been timeously lodged but the pursuers were not represented at the options hearing, the sheriff was held to be under no duty to inquire why the pursuers' solicitor had not appeared and to be entitled to dismiss the action.[37] If no party appears at a diet, the decree by default is a decree of dismissal.[38] It is submitted that the meaning of "diet" in the rule is a calling of the case appointed by the sheriff for any step in the procedure at which the appearance or representation of a party is essential.[39] It is at such a stage of procedure that the sheriff has power to grant decree by default at common law if a party fails to appear or be represented.[40] Further, since the basis of a decree by default is failure in duty,[41] a party's failure to appear or be represented on any occasion at which he is not obliged to appear or be represented cannot, it is thought, be a basis for decree by default. If it is intended that a calling other than a diet of proof or debate should be a peremptory diet at which a party is

---

[32] *De Melo v. Bazazi*, 1995 S.L.T. (Sh. Ct.) 57. An appeal to the sheriff principal having been unsuccessful, the pursuer appealed to the Court of Session. The defender did not oppose the appeal and it was allowed with the pursuer being found liable to the defender in the expenses of the cause to date, payment of these expenses being made a condition precedent of further procedure, 1995 S.C.L.R. 1172.

[33] *Baird & Son v. Nisbet*, 1995 S.C.L.R. 1127.

[34] *David Winter & Sons Ltd v. George Craig & Sons Ltd*, 1995 S.C.L.R. 109.

[35] *Price v. Fernando*, 1995 S.C.L.R. 23. An added complication in this case was that the *defender* failed to appear or be represented at the options hearing. Despite this the sheriff refused to exercise the dispensing power in favour of the pursuer. His decision was reversed by the sheriff principal.

[36] *Nortech v. Aeroship Sports*, 1996 S.L.T.(Sh. Ct.) 94.

[37] *Colonial Mutual Group (U.K. Holidays) v. Johnston*, 1995 S.C.L.R. 1165.

[38] OCR, r. 16.2(3).

[39] OCR, r. 9.12(7) specifically provides that an options hearing is a diet for the purposes of r. 16.2. Rule 10.6(4) contains a similar provision in respect of the procedural hearing in additional procedure.

[40] *Bain v. Lawson & Son* (1899) 1 F 576, *per* L.J.-C. Macdonald at 578.

[41] para. 14.04.

bound to appear or to be represented if he wishes to avoid decree in the action being pronounced against him by default, the following procedure should be followed. The sheriff should appoint the party to appear or be represented at that calling under certification, and appoint the opposite party to intimate to him a copy of the interlocutor and a copy of any relevant motion or minute, in order that he may be made aware of the calling and the sanction for failure to appear or to be represented.[42] The circumstances in which decree by default may be pronounced after the withdrawal of a party's solicitor are provided for by Ordinary Cause Rule 24.3.[43] Where a party fails to appear or to be represented at a diet of proof or debate the sheriff may decern against him for payment of such expenses as the sheriff may consider reasonable.[44]

Exercise of discretion

Prorogation

The sheriff may, on cause shown, prorogate the time for lodging any production or part of process, or for giving intimation or for implementing any order,[45] either before or after the time has expired.[46] But since the application of the rule turns upon what the ends of justice require,[47] the sheriff will not exercise this discretionary power unless satisfied that it is in the interests of justice to do so. Thus, where prorogation is sought because defences cannot be, or have not been, lodged timeously, the defender should endeavour to satisfy the sheriff that there is an issue between the parties which should be tried in the interests of justice. Prorogation may be refused if, for example, the lodging of defences would serve no useful purpose[48]; or if there is no prima facie defence[49]; or if it must be assumed from the circumstances disclosed to the sheriff that the defender has failed to put his solicitor in a position to draft defences at the proper time either because he has no defence to state or because it is his intention to delay the proceedings.[50] **14.08**

General considerations

Before granting decree by default the sheriff should take account of the principles on which an appeal court will exercise its discretion to repone a party against a decree by default, which are explained below.[51] Where the default consists in a failure to comply with a provision of the Ordinary Cause Rules, the sheriff may be moved to exercise his **14.09**

---

[42] *McKenzie v. John R. Wyatt (Musical Enterprises) Ltd*, 1974 S.L.T. (Sh. Ct.) 8 at 9, *per* Sh. Pr. A. G. Walker.

[43] See paras 12.27, 12.28.

[44] A.S. (Fees of Solicitors in the Sheriff Court) (Amendment and Further Provisions) 1993, Sched. 1, General Regulations, reg. 5(c).

[45] OCR, r. 16.3.

[46] *Macnab v. Nelson*, 1909 S.C. 1102.

[47] *Hyslop v. Flaherty*, 1933 S.C. 588; *Thorniewood United F.C. Social Club v. Hamilton*, 1982 S.L.T. (Sh. Ct.) 97; *Coatbridge Health Studios Ltd v. Alexander George & Co. Ltd*, 1992 S.L.T. 717.

[48] *Watt v. Watt*, 1978 S.L.T. (Notes) 55 (cross-actions of divorce).

[49] *Scott v. Hawkins*, Sh. Pr. Caplan, Kilmarnock Sh. Ct, Dec 19, 1984, unreported; *Secretary of State for Social Services v. Glen*, Sh. Pr. O'Brien, Linlithgow Sh. Ct, April 18, 1985, unreported.

[50] *Ferguson v. Livingstone*, Sh. Pr. Caplan, Oban Sh. Ct, Jan 10, 1985, unreported.

[51] para. 14.14.

dispensing power.[52] Before granting decree by default in favour of a pursuer, the sheriff should examine the crave of the writ in order to ascertain that decree by default will be an appropriate and intelligible disposal. If there are alternative craves, decree should be granted in terms of the primary crave and, if that is not implemented, the pursuer should move for decree in terms of the alternative crave.[53] In some actions, such as certain actions of division and sale, it may be necessary to remit to a man of skill to report before decree can be pronounced. Before granting decree by default in favour of a defender, the sheriff should consider whether in the event of dismissal the expiry of a period of limitation would prevent the pursuer from raising a further action.[54]

14.10 In all cases it is desirable that the sheriff should consider whether the default is that of the party personally or of his solicitor or of an employee of the party or of his solicitor, and if it is not that of the party personally, whether it is in the interests of justice that the party should suffer by the default to the extent that decree should pass against him. In modern practice a failure caused by a party's solicitor or some other person for whom he is responsible is not generally held against the party to the extent that decree passes against him, but he may be required to meet the expense occasioned by the default.[55] However, a succession of errors by a pursuer's solicitor, when considered along with prejudice suffered by a defender, may displace the court's reluctance to allow a decree by default to stand, even where the pursuer has prima facie a substantial defence to the defender's counterclaim.[56] If the default is solely due to the party's solicitor, the latter may be found personally liable in those expenses.[57] The fact that a default was technically occasioned or contributed to by the party's solicitor will not, however, inhibit the court from pronouncing decree by default if it is not satisfied that the default is truly due to the party's inadvertence rather than to his deliberate employment of dilatory tactics or his total disregard for the need to comply with regular procedure.[58] Finally, in all cases the sheriff should take a full note of the information given and the arguments urged on either side at the hearing, so that he may write a fully informative note in the event of an appeal against his decision.

Appeal

14.11 Since a decree by default with a finding of expenses is a final judgment,[59] an appeal may be taken without the leave of the sheriff; but an interlocutor refusing decree by default is appealable only with leave.[60] An appeal against a decree by default differs from other appeals in that its

---

[52] OCR, r. 2.1(1): see paras 5.93 to 5.97.
[53] *cf.* para. 7.08.
[54] *Price v. Fernando*, 1995 S.C.L.R. 23.
[55] *Graham v. Wylie & Lochhead Ltd*, 2nd Div., Feb. 17, 1949, unreported, cited in *Burke v. C. Alexander & Partners (Transport) Ltd* (1957) 73 Sh.Ct.Rep. 153 at 156–157.
[56] *De Melo v. Bazazi*, 1995 S.L.T. (Sh. Ct.) 57.
[57] See para. 19.23.
[58] *Stewart v. McDaid*, 1987 S.C.L.R. 342.
[59] 1907 Act, s. 3(h); *Hardy v. Robinson*, 1985 S.L.T. (Sh. Ct.) 40; *McChristie v. EMS Promotions*, 1991 S.L.T. 934; *GAS Construction Co. Ltd v. Schrader*, 1992 S.L.T. 528.
[60] 1907 Act, ss. 27, 28.

proper object is to repone the appellant, that is, to restore him to the position in which he was before his default. Interlocutors pronounced prior to the decree cannot, therefore, be submitted to review.[61] It is always a matter in the discretion of the appeal court whether the appellant is to be reponed, and if so, upon what conditions as to expenses or otherwise.[62] If the appeal court allows the appeal it recalls the sheriff's interlocutor, imposes any such conditions, and remits the case to the sheriff to proceed as accords.

The appeal court will not open up as a matter of course a decree which has been allowed to go by default: it is for the appellant to satisfy the court that the decree should be recalled.[63] On the other hand, where decree by default has been pronounced against a defender, the appeal court is most reluctant, in any case in which prima facie there appears to be a proper defence put forward, to allow decree to pass against the defender without investigation of that defence. Even if carelessness on the part of the defender or others for whom he is responsible has delayed the course of the procedure of the action, the court will in such a case always be willing to entertain an application for relief.[64] Similar considerations have been applied where decree by default has been pronounced against a pursuer with a prima facie proper claim.[65] Very often, accordingly, where the appeal court is satisfied that there is a proper issue upon which the defaulting party is entitled to a considered judicial determination, he is reponed on meeting the whole expenses that have been occasioned by the default, including the expenses of the appeal.[66] These considerations, however, are subordinate to the overriding consideration that the court must do what the ends of justice require.[67] The court must do justice not only to the defaulter but to the innocent victim of the default; and where the defaulter's failures in duty transcend what is acceptable to the court and fair to the other party, and matters cannot be mended by an award of expenses, even against the defaulter's solicitors personally where the default has been theirs, the appeal will be refused.[68] A party may be reponed more than once, but only in very special circumstances.[69] **14.12**

---

[61] *Winning v. Napier, Son & Co. Ltd*, 1963 S.C. 293, *per* L.P. Clyde at 298, Lord Guthrie at 299. It is thought that this principle has not been affected by the decision in *McCue v. Scottish Daily Record and Sunday Mail*, 1998 S.C.L.R. 792: see the comment of L.J-C. Cullen at 754A-B.

[62] *Anderson v. Garson* (1875) 3 R. 254; *Winning, supra.*

[63] *Morrison v. Smith* (1876) 4 R. 9, *per* Lord Deas at 11; *Winning, supra.*

[64] *McKelvie v. Scottish Steel Scaffolding Co.*, 1938 S.C. 278, *per* L.P. Normand at 280, Lord Moncrieff at 281; *Thorniewood United F.C. Social Club v. Hamilton*, 1982 S.L.T. (Sh. Ct.) 97; *Differ v. GKN Kwikform Ltd*, 1990 S.L.T. (Sh. Ct.) 49; *McGowan v. Cartner*, 1995 S.C.L.R. 312.

[65] *Eriks Allied Polymer Ltd v. Hydracrat Ltd*, Sh. Pr. Gillies, Hamilton Sh. Ct, Dec. 8, 1982, unreported.

[66] *Hyslop v. Flaherty*, 1933 S.C. 588; *Winning, supra*; *Thorniewood United F.C. Social Club v. Hamilton, supra*; *Eriks Allied Polymer Ltd, supra*; *Coatbridge Health Studios Ltd v. Alexander George & Co. Ltd*, 1992 S.L.T. 717.

[67] *Hyslop*; *Thorniewood United F.C. Social Club, supra.*

[68] *Niven v. Holmes*, 1979 S.L.T. (Sh. Ct.) 15; *Muir v. Milne*, Sh. Pr. Caplan, Paisley Sh. Ct, June 7, 1984, unreported; *Stewart v. McDaid*, 1987 S.C.L.R. 342.

[69] *Mather v. Smith* (1858) 21 D. 24; *Hamilton v. Christie* (1857) 19 D. 712; *Pearson v. McGavin* (1866) 4 M. 754.

14.13 An action of reduction in the Court of Session is not an alternative to the ordinary method of appeal against a decree by default, and is competent only in exceptional circumstances.[70]

Decree by default in family actions

14.14 Decree by default in family actions does not fall within the scope of rule 16.2.[71] Instead it is governed by rule 33.37. The circumstances in which a party in a family action may be in default are almost identical with those for other actions.[72] Thus default is constituted by a failure to lodge a production or part of process,[73] a failure to implement an order of the sheriff within a specified period[74] or a failure to appear or be represented at any diet.[75] The only difference is that rule 33.37(1)(a) refers simply to a failure "to lodge, or intimate the lodging of, any production or part of process" whereas rule 16.2(1)(a) refers to a failure "to lodge, or to intimate the lodging of, any production or part of process within the period required under a provision in these Rules or an order of the sheriff". The reason for the difference between the two rules is obscure and it is submitted that it is immaterial. The powers of the sheriff in the event of default by a defender depend on the type of action. In the case of actions of divorce, separation, declarator of legitimacy, declarator of illegitimacy, declarator of parentage, declarator of non-parentage and declarator of legitimation the sheriff may not grant decree as craved but may allow the action to proceed as undefended.[76] The sheriff has the same limited power in the event of default by a defender in the case of an action under section 11 of the Children (Scotland) Act 1995 (action seeking an order relating to parental responsibilities or rights) except an application for the appointment of a judicial factor under section 11(2)(g) of the 1995 Act or an application for the appointment or removal of a guardian under section 11(2)(h) of the Act.[77] In all other family actions the sheriff has the same power to grant decree as craved as he does in the case of non-family actions under rule 16.2.[78] In the event of default in a family action by a pursuer or any other party making a claim the sheriff may grant absolvitor[79] or dismiss the action or any claim made or any order sought.[80] In all cases the sheriff has power to award expenses.[81] As in the case of non-family actions, if no party appears at a diet the sheriff may dismiss the action.[82] Again, as in non-family actions the sheriff has power to prorogate the time for lodging any production or part of process or for intimating or implementing any order.[83]

---

[70] *Philp v. Reid*, 1927 S.C. 224 (an Outer House case); *Stewart v. Lothians Construction (Edinburgh) Ltd*, 1972 S.L.T. (Notes) 75; *J. & C. Black (Haulage) Ltd v. Alltransport International Group Ltd*, 1980 S.C. 57 (an Outer House case which was not followed in *Kirkwood v. City of Glasgow D.C.*, 1988 S.L.T. 430).

[71] OCR, r. 16.1(a).

[72] OCR, r. 33.37(1).

[73] OCR, r. 33.37(1)(a).

[74] OCR, r. 33.37(1)(b).

[75] OCR, r. 33.37(1)(c). A failure of a party to be personally present at an options hearing in a family action (as is required by r. 33.36) is not a default within the meaning of r. 33.37(1)(c): *Grimes v. Grimes*, 1995 S.C.L.R. 268. As in the case of non-family actions the rules provide that options hearings and procedural hearings are diets for the purposes of decree by default: OCR, rr. 9.12(7), 10.6(4).

[76] OCR, r. 33.37(2)(a), referring to r. 33.1(1)(a)–(g).

[77] OCR, r. 33.37(2)(a), referring to r. 33.1(1)(h).

[78] OCR, r. 33.37(2)(b), referring to r. 33.1(1)(i)–(m).

[79] OCR, r. 33.37(2)(c).

[80] OCR, r. 33.37(2)(d).

[81] OCR, r. 33.37(2)(e).

[82] OCR, r. 33.37(3).

II. Abandonment

As soon as the initial writ is served the action is in dependence, and the pursuer, and when defences are lodged the defender, "become subject to the procedure of the court and neither can escape from its toils until the action is judicially disposed of."[84] If either party wishes to withdraw from the action, it is not merely discourteous but imprudent simply to default, for example by failing to implement an order of court or to appear or be represented at a peremptory diet, since to do so is to invite the consequences of default.[85] The correct practice is to withdraw according to the established forms of procedure and subject to such conditions as to expenses and the like as the sheriff may lawfully impose. A pursuer may initiate his withdrawal by abandonment of the cause, while a defender may initiate his withdrawal by lodging a minute withdrawing his defences and consenting to decree.[86] If a pursuer wishes to depart from part of his claim he should alter his crave and averments accordingly.[87] This section of this chapter is concerned with abandonment by a pursuer. The rules applicable to abandonment in an action where there is a counterclaim have already been discussed.[88] **14.15**

It is a general principle of the adversary system of civil procedure that the jurisdiction of the court must be invoked by a party; and it follows that, in the absence of any special rule to the contrary, such a party may abandon his litigation at any time, subject to such conditions as the court may lawfully impose upon him.[89] A pursuer may abandon an action either at common law (although this is unusual in modern practice) or in terms of rule 23.1 of the Ordinary Cause Rules. He may wish to abandon for a variety of reasons. Having raised the action he may find, for example, that he has no right of action at all, or that he has adopted the wrong form of action, or that he cannot now produce the evidence in support of his claim. In order to determine which is the appropriate mode of abandonment, it is necessary for the pursuer to decide whether he wishes to reserve the right to raise a further action against the defender. If the pursuer is satisfied that he need not do so, he should abandon either at common law or under rule 23.1(1)(a), when the court may grant the defender decree of absolvitor. If, on the other hand, the pursuer considers that he may be entitled to obtain a remedy against the defender in another process, he should abandon in terms of rule 23.1(1)(b), for in that event the court will pronounce decree of dismissal, and will not grant decree of absolvitor unless the pursuer fails to pay the **14.16**

---

83 OCR, r. 33.37(4). See para. 14.08.

84 *Argyllshire Weavers Ltd v. A. Macaulay (Tweeds) Ltd*, 1962 S.C. 388, *per* Lord Hunter at 394, 395.

85 paras 14.02 to 14.14.

86 *Ower v. Crichton* (1902) 10 S.L.T. 279. Such a minute does not, however, bring the action to an end: *Cowie v. Carron Co.*, 1945 S.C. 280; *Auld & Macdonald v. George Wimpey & Co. Ltd*, 1977 S.L.T. (Notes) 23.

87 Before the closing of the record any sum sued for may be amended, and the averments may be adjusted, without the leave of the sheriff (OCR, r. 18.1). Any other alterations of the crave or, after the closing of the record, of the averments may be effected only by amendment with the leave of the sheriff (OCR, r. 18.2): see para. 10.01.

88 paras 12.40, 12.41.

89 *Castlegreen Storage & Distributors Ltd v. Schreiber*, 1982 S.L.T. 269, *per* Lord Murray at 271. On the absence of any discretion in the court to refuse to allow abandonment, see paras 14.18 to 14.27.

defender's expenses.[90] The details of each mode of abandonment are considered in the following paragraphs.

14.17 Whichever mode of abandonment is adopted, the pursuer's solicitor should, in general, obtain a special mandate to abandon.[91] Counsel may abandon without the pursuer's instructions, but normally does not do so.[92]

Abandonment at common law

14.18 The pursuer may give up his action at common law without reservation at any stage of the cause before decree of absolvitor or dismissal is pronounced.[93] He does so by lodging a minute in the following terms: "A for the pursuer stated and hereby states to the court that the pursuer abandons this cause at common law." The minute should not contain any conditions or qualifications.[94] The pursuer is absolutely entitled to abandon: the sheriff has no discretion to refuse to allow him to do so.[95] The sheriff has, however, a full discretion when allowing abandonment to pronounce decree of absolvitor or dismissal and to attach any condition to the decree. The appropriate decree is normally, but not invariably, one of absolvitor, and the pursuer is normally found liable in expenses.[96] Along with the minute should be lodged a motion stating exactly what it is the pursuer wishes the court to do.[97] A pursuer may abandon at common law against one of several defenders.[98]

14.19 While the normal and most satisfactory method of abandonment at common law is by means of a minute, where a second action has been raised the abandonment of the first action may be effected by intimation by minute in the second action[99]; or, where the first action has been served but no order for defences has been made and the defender has incurred no expense, by intimation by letter and averment in the condescendence in the second action.[1] It is also possible for there to be constructive abandonment, as where the pursuer lodges a minute which is not quite accurately framed,[2] or where the pursuer intimates at the bar that he does

---

[90] OCR, r. 23.1(2),(3). *Goldie v. Chrysler Motors Ltd* (1939) 55 Sh.Ct.Rep. 99 at 102–103; *Macinsure Brokers v. McKenzie & Co.*, 1984 S.L.T. (Sh. Ct.) 66.

[91] *Urquhart v. Grigar* (1857) 19 D. 853, *per* L.J.-C. Hope at 855.

[92] *Duncan v. Salmand* (1874) 1 R. 329; *Batchelor v. Pattison and Mackersy* (1876) 3 R. 914, *per* L.J.-C. Inglis at 918; *cf. Brodt v. King*, 1991 S.L.T. 272.

[93] *Goldie v. Chrysler Motors Ltd* (1939) 55 Sh.Ct.Rep. 99 at 102–103; *Hutchison v. Hutchison*, 1962 S.C. 596 at 598; *Walker v. Walker*, 1995 S.C.L.R. 387.

[94] *Grant v. Countess of Seafield*, 1926 S.L.T. 726.

[95] Only one reported instance of refusal of abandonment at common law has been found: *Lauriston v. Lauriston* (1953) 69 Sh.Ct.Rep. 337.

[96] *Bookless Bros v. Gudmundsson*, 1921 S.C. 602; *Grant, supra*; *A v. B*, 1935 S.L.T. 12; *Walker v. Walker*, 1947 S.L.T. (Notes) 8; *Farquhar v. Farquhar*, 1948 S.L.T. (Notes) 25; *Mackie v. Mackie* (1953) 69 Sh.Ct.Rep. 167; *Hutchison, supra*; *Petty v. Harris*, 1977 S.L.T. (Notes) 27; *cf. Haggerty v. Nisbet*, 1933 S.L.T. 188 where the defender was found liable in expenses to the pursuer, having misled the pursuer into raising the action against him.

[97] *Walker v. Walker*, 1995 S.C.L.R. 187.

[98] *Malcolmson v. Sampson* (1927) 44 Sh.Ct.Rep. 88.

[99] *Nelson v. Gordon* (1874) 1 R. 1903.

[1] *Laidlaw v. Smith* (1834) 12 S. 538; *McAuley v. Cowe* (1873) I.R. 307; *Roxburgh v. Commercial Bank of Scotland* (1903) 19 Sh.Ct.Rep. 248.

[2] *Goldie, supra.*

not intend to proceed further in the action and moves the sheriff to assoilzie the defender.[3]

Abandonment under rule 23.2(1)(a)

At any time before decree of absolvitor or dismissal a pursuer may lodge a minute consenting to decree of absolvitor.[4] He does so by lodging a minute in the following terms: "A for the pursuer stated and hereby states to the court that the pursuer abandons the cause and consents to decree of absolvitor in terms of rule 23.2(1)(a) of the Ordinary Cause Rules [with expenses as taxed in favour of the defender]." The minute should be accompanied by a motion which should ask the court to grant decree in terms of the minute.[5] If the minute does not contain an offer to pay the defender's expenses and the defender wishes to have an award of expenses in his favour, he should lodge a notice of opposition to the motion[6] and the sheriff will decide the matter. In practice there is little difference between abandonment at common law and abandonment under rule 23.1(1)(a). Neither is as common in practice as the form of abandonment discussed in the following paragraphs. **14.20**

Abandonment under rule 23.1(1)(b)

Rule

By abandonment under rule 23.1(1)(b) the pursuer obtains the privilege of a decree of dismissal if he abandons on payment of the defender's expenses.[7] The pursuer therefore proceeds by this method when he wishes to reserve his right to raise a fresh action against the defender raising the same question as the action he proposes to abandon. The rule provides that a pursuer may, at any stage of a cause before an interlocutor granting absolvitor or dismissing the cause has been pronounced,[8] abandon the cause by lodging in process a minute to that effect. Thereafter the sheriff may, on payment by the pursuer to the defender and any third party of their expenses, dismiss the cause.[9] If, however, the pursuer fails within 28 days of the date of taxation to pay these expenses, the defender and any third party is entitled to decree of absolvitor, with expenses.[10] **14.21**

Minute

The pursuer initiates the procedure by lodging a minute in these terms: "A for the pursuer stated and hereby states to the court that the pursuer abandons the cause and seeks decree of dismissal in terms of rule 23.1(1)(b) of the Ordinary Cause Rules." The minute should not contain any reservation or qualification.[11] The minute does not require to be **14.22**

---

[3] *Reynolds v. Mackenzie*, Sh. Pr. Caplan, Kilmarnock Sh. Ct, May 30, 1986, unreported. See also *Hare v. Stein* (1882) 9 R. 910.

[4] OCR, r. 23.1(1)(a).

[5] *Walker v. Walker*, 1995 S.C.L.R. 187.

[6] In terms of OCR, r. 15.3.

[7] Abandonment under this rule is competent in an action of multiplepoinding: *Haliburton Manufacturing Services Ltd v. Picts (Construction) Co.*, 1986 S.L.T. (Sh. Ct.) 24.

[8] The pursuer cannot abandon after he obtains decree against the defender: *Lamont & Co. v. Reid* (1925) 42 Sh.Ct.Rep. 262.

[9] OCR, r. 23.1(2).

[10] OCR, r. 21.2(3).

[11] *Adamson, Howie & Co. v. Guild* (1867) 6 M. 347 at 358; *Stewart v. Stewart* (1906) 8 F. 769; *Lauriston v. Lauriston* (1953) 69 Sh.Ct.Rep. 337 at 338.

accepted by the defender, or constitute a contract between the parties[12]: it is a proposal to abandon, which is of no effect, and may be withdrawn, until it is given effect to by the court.[13] The minute should be lodged accompanied by a motion seeking to have the minute received, the defender [and any third party] ordained to make up an account of expenses and to have the account, when lodged, remitted to the auditor of court to tax and report. The motion should be intimated to all other parties in the usual way.[14]

Withdrawal of minute

14.23 The pursuer has an absolute right to withdraw the minute before final decree.[15] He should do so by lodging the appropriate motion. An interlocutor allowing withdrawal is necessary, and the defender may move for absolvitor. That motion will be granted unless the pursuer is able to show that his proceedings have been in bona fide. In that event, the pursuer will be entitled to go on with the case, subject to such conditions as to expenses as the sheriff chooses to lay down.[16] The pursuer is usually ordered to pay all the defender's expenses connected with the proposed abandonment.[17] The defender's solicitor should therefore move for expenses since the date of lodging the minute if he has incurred any expense, such as the expense of having his account audited.[18]

Subsequent procedure

14.24 The motion lodged along with the minute, which will almost certainly be unopposed, is likely to be granted by the sheriff in chambers.[19] He pronounces an interlocutor in which he allows the minute to be received and before pronouncing further appoints the defender to lodge an account of expenses[20] and remits the same when lodged to the auditor of court to tax and to report. The object of remitting the account for taxation is to reduce to a fixed sum the condition which the pursuer has to fulfil in order to get his minute of abandonment given effect to.[21] When the case comes back from the auditor, the sheriff does not decern for payment of the taxed expenses, since it is optional to the pursuer to make payment. The defender's solicitor should therefore formally demand that the pursuer make payment within 28 days of the date of taxation. If the pursuer still seeks decree of dismissal he must, whether payment has been formally

---

[12] *Lee v. Pollock's Trs* (1906) 8 F. 857; *Batchelor v. Reilly*, Sh. Pr. Dick, Glasgow Sh. Ct, Feb. 11, 1981, unreported; *Macinsure Brokers Ltd v. Mackenzie & Co.*, 1984 S.L.T. (Sh. Ct.) 66.

[13] *Cormack v. Waters* (1846) 8 D. 889, *per* Lord Fullerton at 892; *Muir v. Barr* (1849) 11 D. 487, *per* L.P. Hoyle at 493; *Lee, supra; Hepburn & Ross v. Tritonia Ltd*, 1951 S.L.T. (Sh. Ct.) 6; *Batchelor, supra.*

[14] In terms of OCR, r. 15.2(1).

[15] *Lee, Batchelor, supra.*

[16] *Lee, supra.*

[17] *Todd and Higginbotham v. Glasgow Corporation* (1879) 16 S.L.R. 718; *Dalgleish v. Mitchell* (1886) 23 S.L.R. 552.

[18] Lees, *Pleading*, p. 134.

[19] In terms of OCR, r. 15.5(1).

[20] If the pursuer is anxious to raise a fresh action and it is thought that the defender may delay in lodging his account his motion to have the defender ordained to lodge his account of expenses should specify a time-limit, and the sheriff may appoint him to do so within a specified period: Lees, *Interlocutors*, p. 47.

[21] *Lee v. Pollock's Trs* (1906) 8 F. 857; *Batchelor v. Reilly*, Sh. Pr. Dick, Glasgow Sh. Ct, Feb. 11, 1981, unreported.

demanded or not, within the 28 days pay the taxed amount or, if payment cannot be effected, consign it in the hands of the sheriff clerk.[22] He should then lodge the receipt in process, together with a motion for the final interlocutor, which bears that the sheriff, in respect that the expenses due to the defender have been paid (or consigned), allows the pursuer to abandon the cause, dismisses the action, and decerns.[23] Until the sheriff pronounces such an interlocutor, the action cannot be held to be abandoned.[24] A decree of absolvitor pronounced in error does not bar a new action.[25]

If the pursuer does not pay or consign the taxed amount of the defender's expenses within 28 days of the date of taxation, the defender's solicitor should lodge a motion for absolvitor, with expenses. The sheriff may then pronounce an interlocutor in which he approves of the auditor's report and decerns against the pursuer for the taxed amount thereof, assoilzies the defender from the crave of the initial writ, and decerns.[26] However, it may be that the pursuer could seek to invoke the general dispensing power if he could satisfy the sheriff that his failure to pay the expenses within 28 days was "due to mistake, oversight or other excusable cause".[27] **14.25**

Discretion of sheriff

Rule 58 of the Ordinary Cause Rules 1983 and its predecessor in earlier versions of the Ordinary Cause Rules were in broadly similar terms to those of rule 23.1(1)(b), (2) and (3) of the 1993 Rules. Differing views were expressed on the question whether the sheriff had any discretion to refuse to allow the pursuer to abandon the cause in terms of the old rule 58. One view was that the pursuer had no absolute right to abandon upon payment of the defender's expenses, and that the sheriff was entitled to exercise a discretion as to whether or not abandonment should be allowed.[28] On the other hand there are dicta of eminent judges which stated[29] or strongly indicated[30] that the pursuer had an unfettered right to abandon and to obtain decree of dismissal on payment of the defender's taxed expenses. **14.26**

It is submitted that the latter view is to be preferred, not only because it is supported by the weight of those dicta, but also because it is consistent with the principle that in an adversary system of procedure a party who **14.27**

---

22 *Lawson v. Low* (1845) 7 D. 960.

23 Maclaren, p. 446; Lees, *Pleading*, pp. 133–134.

24 *Cormack v. Waters* (1846) 8 D. 889, *per* Lord Fullerton at 892; *Muir v. Barr* (1849) 11 D. 487, *per* L.P. Boyle at 493; *Hepburn & Ross v. Trilonia Ltd*, 1951 S.L.T. (Sh. Ct.) 6.

25 *Shirreff v. Brodie* (1836) 14 S. 825.

26 Maclaren, p. 447.

27 In terms of OCR, r. 2.1(1). *Cobb v. Baker Oil Tools (U.K.) Ltd*, 1984 S.L.T. 232, in which it was held that the sheriff had no discretion to refuse absolvitor, was decided under Ordinary Cause Rules which contained no dispensing power. In *McGregor v. Wimpey Construction Ltd*, 1991 S.C.L.R. 868 the sheriff principal reserved his opinion as to whether the equivalent of r. 2.1(1) under the 1983 OCR could be invoked to overcome the mandatory terms of the then equivalent of r. 23.1(3).

28 Wallace, p. 248; *Cadzow v. White*, 1986 S.L.T. (Sh. Ct.) 21.

29 *Lee v. Pollock's Trs* (1906) 8 F. 857, *per* L.P. Dunedin at 860. See also *Craw v. Malcolm* (1908) 24 Sh.Ct.Rep. 268 at 269; *Goldie v. Chrysler Motors Ltd* (1938) 55 Sh.Ct.Rep. 99 at 102; *Macinsure Brokers Ltd v. Mackenzie & Co.*, 1984 S.L.T. (Sh. Ct.) 66; *Haliburton Manufacturing and Services Ltd v. Picts (Construction) Co. Ltd*, 1986 S.L.T. (Sh. Ct.) 24; Lees, *Pleading*, p. 133; Lewis, pp. 185–186; Dobie, p. 244.

30 *Singer v. Gray Tool Co. (Europe) Ltd*, 1984 S.L.T. 149, *per* L.P. Emslie (giving the opinion of the court) at 150.

invokes the jurisdiction of the court is entitled to abandon his litigation at any time subject to such conditions as the court may lawfully impose upon him.[31] Further, it is thought that if Parliament or the Court of Session had intended to enable the pursuer to abandon only with the leave of the court, it could readily have done so in express terms.[32] The terms of rule 58, however, which were "simple, specific, and susceptible to no confusion or dubiety",[33] did not so provide nor do the terms of rule 23.1 which may be similarly described.

Plurality of parties

14.28 **Pursuers.** Where pursuers sue together, each with a separate crave in respect of his own claim, each may abandon his claim separately.[34]

14.29 **Defenders.** Where a pursuer sues more than one defender, he may abandon as against one of them under rule 23.1, adapting the style of the minute accordingly.[35] He cannot abandon against a defender in respect of whom decree in absence has been taken.[36] In several cases the court has been invited to proceed upon the view that it has a discretion to refuse to permit abandonment against one of several defenders.[37] It has already been submitted that the court has no such discretion.[38] The pursuer of an action of multiplepoinding may abandon the action unless he has parted with the fund *in medio* by consignation or has been discharged.[39]

Expenses

14.30 If the pursuer chooses to avail himself of rule 23.1(1)(b), he must pay the defender's taxed expenses. Since the rule requires that the expenses must be taxed, the sheriff is not empowered to modify them to a specific sum instead of remitting to the auditor.[40] The expenses payable by the pursuer are the taxed expenses which the defender could have recovered from the pursuer under a decree of absolvitor with expenses, had the action not been abandoned,[41] and which remain undisposed of by the court: earlier awards of expenses against the defender are not disturbed.[42] The ordinary rule is that the expenses are taxed as between party and party only, but the

---

[31] para. 14.16.

[32] As in the Court of Session Act 1868, s. 39, which was incorporated in RCS, r. 91A(2) of the 1965 Rules of Court but which does not appear in the current Rules of Court. The present position in the Court of Session is governed by RCS, r. 29.1 which is in terms very similar to those of OCR, r. 23.1.

[33] *Cobb, supra.*

[34] *Todd and Higginbotham v. Glasgow Corporation* (1879) 16 S.L.R. 718; *Buchan v. Thomson*, 1976 S.L.T. 42, *per* Lord Fraser at 44.

[35] *e.g.* "abandons the cause as laid against the second-named defender". See paras 14.20 and 14.22. He may likewise abandon against one defender at common law: *Malcolmson v. Sampson* (1927) 44 Sh.Ct.Rep. 88.

[36] *Lamont & Co. v. Reid* (1925) 42 Sh.Ct.Rep. 262.

[37] *e.g. Hardy v. British Airways Board*, 1983 S.L.T. 45; *Singer v. Gray Tool Co. (Europe) Ltd*, 1984 S.L.T. 149.

[38] para. 14.27.

[39] *Castlegreen Storage & Distributors Ltd v. Schreiber*, 1982 S.L.T. 269; *Haliburton Manufacturing and Services Ltd v. Picts (Construction) Co. Ltd*, 1986 S.L.T. (Sh. Ct.) 24.

[40] *cf. Mica Insulator Co. Ltd v. Bruce Peebles & Co. Ltd*, 1907 S.C. 1293; *Johnston v. Johnston*, 1985 S.L.T. 510, *per* Lord Cowie at 512. However there could be no objection to the parties' agreeing the amount of expenses and thus dispensing with taxation.

[41] *cf. Nobel's Explosives Co. v. British Dominions General Insurance Co.*, 1919 S.C. 455; *Lord Hamilton v. Glasgow Dairy Co.*, 1933 S.C. 18.

[42] *Lord Hamilton, supra; Hayward v. Edinburgh Royal Infirmary*, 1955 S.L.T. (Notes) 69.

sheriff may grant expenses upon a higher scale if he thinks it suitable to do so.[43] Although the sheriff does not decern against the pursuer for payment of the defender's expenses, he may entertain objections to the auditor's report.[44] But since there is no interlocutor dealing with expenses, the pursuer cannot seek relief for the defender's expenses against another defender, for example where he abandons against a defender whom he has sued only because that defender had been in error named and blamed by another defender.[45] Similarly, since no award of expenses is made the sheriff has no jurisdiction to assess the liability for expenses of a pursuer who is legally aided.[46]

III. Settlement

Introduction

General

It is in the public interest that disputes should be settled without recourse to litigation or, where litigation has ensued, with as little expenditure of time and money as possible. In practice, a very considerable proportion of actions are settled before proceeding to judgment; and if that were not so, the courts would be overwhelmed by the volume of work and litigants would be put to inordinate trouble, delay and expense before their actions were disposed of. The law encourages the compromise of disputes by making admissions in the course of negotiations for settlement inadmissible in evidence[47]; and sheriffs often encourage attempts at settlement by granting sists, adjournments or continuations to enable negotiations to be pursued even though the strict terms of the Ordinary Cause Rules may be to some extent stretched in order to achieve this end. But the court has no formal power or duty to initiate or promote the settlement of actions. Parties may settle their differences just as and when they please without the leave or approval of the court, since settlement is a matter with which the court is not concerned.[48] The court may become concerned where settlement has not been satisfactorily achieved, for example where parties are not agreed as to whether settlement has been effected,[49] or as to the construction of the terms of settlement,[50] or as to the effect on expenses of a rejected offer[51] or of the absence of any offer,[52] or where the procedural machinery for settlement has been incorrectly operated. Very often, however, settlement is successfully effected by the parties' advisers. During the progress of a 14.31

[43] *P v. P*, 1940 S.C. 389.

[44] *Buchanan & French Ltd v. Watson* (1910) 26 Sh.Ct.Rep. 246; *Lord Hamilton, supra*, at 19.

[45] *Appleby v. Glasgow Corporation*, 1949 S.L.T. (Sh. Ct.) 72. *Cf. Haggerty v. Nisbet*, 1933 S.L.T. 188 (abandonment at common law).

[46] *Collum v. Glasgow Corporation*, 1964 S.L.T. 199; *Campbell v. Lindsay*, 1967 S.L.T. (Sh. Ct.) 30; *Johnston v. Johnston*, 1985 S.L.T. 510. *Cf. Thompson v. Fairfeld Shipbuilding & Engineering Co.*, 1954 S.C. 354.

[47] Walkers, p. 28, para. 29; Macphail, *Evidence*, paras 18.28, S18.28.

[48] *Gow v. Henry* (1899) 2 F. 48, *per* Lord Trayner at 55.

[49] para. 14.66.

[50] para. 14.68.

[51] para. 14.68.

[52] *e.g. Howitt v. Alexander & Sons*, 1948 S.C. 154, *per* L.P. Cooper at 158 (distinguished in *Morrison v. Barton (No. 2)*, 1994 S.L.T. 685); *Bradie v. National Coal Board*, 1951 S.C. 575 at 578; *Chalmers v. Atlas Steel Foundry and Engineering Co. Ltd*, 1964 S.L.T. (Notes) 98 at 99; *Bond v. British Railways Board*, 1972 S.L.T. (Notes) 48; *Sidlaw Industries Ltd v. Cable Bell Ltd*, 1979 S.L.T. (Notes) 40.

litigation the skilful practitioner keeps under review the development of the parties' cases in the pleadings and the nature of the evidence available in support of either side, and by accurately gauging the relative strengths of the parties' cases is often able to save his client great trouble and expense by judicious and timely compromise.[53] Such compromises seldom require any more than formal notice by the court, but they play a large and essential part in the operation of the court system.

Summary

14.32 The procedural rules relative to settlement, which will be examined in this section, may be briefly summarised as follows. The settlement of an action may be brought about judicially or extrajudicially. A judicial settlement is operated by a judicial offer, known as a tender, and a judicial acceptance, both made by minute in the process. In an action brought against a single defender by a single pursuer,[54] the tender is an explicit, unqualified and unconditional offer by the defender to pay to the pursuer in settlement of the action a specified amount, together with the expenses to date. If the pursuer accepts the tender, the court pronounces decree in terms of the tender and acceptance. If the pursuer does not accept the tender and the action proceeds to judgment, the tender is not brought to the notice of the sheriff until after decree has been pronounced, when it may have far-reaching consequences on expenses. If the pursuer has obtained decree for more than the sum tendered, he is awarded the whole expenses of the action, unless some are withheld for reasons other than the existence of the tender; but if he has obtained decree for the sum tendered or less, he is awarded only expenses to the date when he should have accepted the tender, and the defender is entitled to his expenses thereafter. A tender has therefore been described as "a well tried expedient for controlling unnecessary or vexatious litigation or excessive demands."[55] Where a settlement is brought about extrajudicially, the parties agree the terms of settlement and usually lodge a joint minute stating that the action has been settled extrajudicially and requesting the court to interpone authority to the joint minute and pronounce decree in the terms they have agreed. Counsel may effect a judicial settlement, but not an extrajudicial settlement, without the client's express authority,[56] but a solicitor must in all cases obtain such authority.[57]

Judicial settlement

Tender

14.33 **Nature and form of tender.** A tender is a judicial offer by a party to pay a part of the sum asked for by his adversary after the action is raised.[58] Usually a tender is made by a defender to a pursuer, but where there is a

---

[53] D. Foskett, *The Law and Practice of Compromise* (2nd ed., 1985), foreword by Lord Lane C.J.

[54] The following paragraphs on judicial settlement are primarily concerned with a tender made in an action brought by a single pursuer against a single defender. Tenders in actions brought by more than one pursuer, or against more than one defender, or against a defender and a third party are separately considered in paras 14.54 to 14.62. Where there is a counterclaim, a tender may be made by a pursuer.

[55] *Howitt v. Alexander & Sons*, 1948 S.C. 154, *per* L.P. Cooper at 158.

[56] *Hendry v. Hendry*, 1916 1 S.L.T. 208; 1916 2 S.L.T. 135; *Brodt v. King*, 1991 S.L.T. 272.

[57] *Weir v. Stevenson* (1885) 1 Sh.Ct.Rep. 161.

[58] *Ramsay's Trs v. Souter* (1864) 2 M. 891, *per* L.J.-C. Inglis at 892.

counterclaim, the pursuer may make a tender to the defender, and where the pursuer directs his action against a third party, the latter may make a tender to the pursuer. The following paragraphs describe the usual case of a defender tendering to a pursuer, but the rules examined apply *mutatis mutandis* to these other cases. Tenders in actions where there is a plurality of parties are separately considered later.[59]

A tender may take one of two forms. (1) Where the defender admits that part of the sum sued for is due, the tender may be made on record, by averments admitting the pursuer's claim to a certain extent and tendering the sum admitted to be due. Tenders of this kind are seldom encountered in modern practice. Where the defender admits in his defences that a specific sum is due, he usually does not expressly tender it in his defences. He may lodge a separate minute of tender. The pursuer may accept such a tender, if made, or may move for interim decree for the sum admitted in the defences to be due.[60] If the defender is willing to pay the whole sum asked for by the pursuer, he should lodge a minute consenting to decree, although that will not at once bring the action to an end.[61] **14.34**

(2) The second and more usual form of tender is made when a defender is willing to tender "for the sake of peace".[62] In many circumstances a defender may wish to settle the action although he disputes that any part of the sum claimed is due, or where he accepts that some payment is due to the pursuer which cannot be precisely quantified before decree, for example when the defender has lodged an illiquid counterclaim in answer to a liquid claim by the pursuer,[63] or when the defender in a personal injuries action is prepared to admit liability but parties cannot agree on the *quantum* of damages. This section of the chapter is concerned with tenders which are made in such circumstances for the sake of peace. Such a tender should only be made by a separate minute lodged in process.[64] If it is made on record, it may be deleted.[65] The practice of repeating on record extrajudicial offers made before litiscontestation[66] has been criticised[67] and is thought to be no longer generally followed. If a defender wishes to repeat any such offer, he should state it in a separate minute of tender, and on record meet with a simple denial the pursuer's averment that he has refused or delayed to make payment. **14.35**

Contents of tender. *General rules.* The minute of tender is headed "Minute of Tender / for the Defenders / *in causa* [etc.]" and is usually in the following terms: **14.36**

"A for the defenders stated and hereby states to the court that without admitting liability and under reservation of their whole

---

[59] paras 14.54 to 14.62.

[60] paras 11.81 to 11.83.

[61] *Cowie v. Carron Co.*, 1945 S.C. 280; *Auld & Macdonald v. George Wimpey & Co. Ltd*, 1977 S.L.T. (Notes) 23.

[62] *Ramsay, supra.*

[63] *e.g.* a tender could have been lodged in *Sidlaw Industries Ltd v. Cable Belt Ltd*, 1979 S.L.T. (Notes) 40.

[64] *Ramsay, supra; Smeaton v. Dundee Corporation*, 1941 S.C. 600; *Avery v. Cantilever Shoe Co.*, 1942 S.C. 469.

[65] *Key v. Scottish Chemist Supply Co.*, 1956 S.L.T. (Notes) 43.

[66] *Gunn v. Hunter* (1886) 13 R. 573; *Avery, supra.*

[67] *O'Donnell v. A.M. & G. Robertson*, 1965 S.L.T. (Notes) 155. See also T. J. D. C., "Tenders, Judicial or Other", 1946 S.L.T. (News) 33.

> rights and pleas the defenders tendered and hereby tender to the pursuer the sum of [*stated in words and figures*] sterling together with the taxed expenses of process to the date hereof, in full of the crave [or craves] of the initial writ."

It should be noted that the minute states that the tender is made by the defenders: a style which suggests that the tender is made by the advocate (for example, "A for the defender without prejudice to his rights and pleas tendered and hereby tenders") should be avoided.

14.37 Until recently it was accepted that a tender had to be explicit, unqualified and unconditional.[68] However, in *Ferguson v. McLennan Salmon Co. Ltd*[69] Lord McCluskey suggested that there is no reason why a tender should not, in certain circumstances, be subject to qualification provided that it is in clear and unambiguous terms which it is open to the other party to accept thereby bringing the litigation to an end in whole or in part. It is submitted that there is merit in this suggestion. The statement in the tender that the defender does not admit liability and reserves his rights and pleas is made not as a qualification but so that, if the tender is not accepted, the defender may maintain that he is under no liability and may argue his pleas, and the tender may not be referred to as inferring an admission of liability or a waiver of his pleas.[70] In actions of defamation, a tender must contain a full retraction, which may be prefaced by an explanation or hypothetical apology,[71] but need not contain an offer of damages.[72] In an action with several craves a tender directed only to one of them, with the taxed expenses of process to date so far as incurred in connection with[73] that crave, is unusual, but competent.[74]

14.38 *Expenses.* The tender, in order to be effective, must contain an offer to pay the pursuer's expenses to the date of the tender[75] except, perhaps, where the pursuer has unreasonably failed to intimate a claim before raising the action and the tender is lodged with the defences.[76] The offer of expenses must be unconditional. A style offering "such expenses as the court may award" has been used in the past,[77] but has more recently been criticised on

---

[68] *Bisset v. Anderson* (1847) 10 D. 233 at 234; *Gunn v. Marquis of Breadalbane* (1849) 11 D. 1040 at 1050–1052; *Low v. Spences Ltd* (1895) 3 S.L.T. 170; *Thomson & Co. v. Dailly* (1897) 24 R. 1173. In *Corvi v. Ellis*, 1969 S.C. 312, the conditional nature of the tender was not commented on.

[69] 1990 S.C. 45.

[70] *Grangemouth and Forth Towing Co. Ltd v. Netherlands East Indies Govt*, 1942 S.L.T. 228; Thomson and Middleton, p. 423.

[71] *Faulks v. Park* (1854) 17 D. 247; *Mitchells v. Nicoll* (1890) 17 R. 795; *Sproll v. Walker* (1899) 2 F. 73; *Malcolm v. Moore* (1901) 4 F. 23; *Sturrock v. Deas & Co.*, 1913 1 S.L.T. 60.

[72] *Hunter v. Russell* (1901) 3 F. 596; *Davidson v. Panri*, 1915 1 S.L.T. 273.

[73] Not "applicable to that crave" (as in Dobie, *Styles*, p. 326), since that may be understood to mean that the expenses are to be taxed by reference to the sum sued for: see *Hopkinson Ltd v. Scottish Radio and Sounding Co. Ltd* (1954) 70 Sh.Ct.Rep. 297, and para. 14.38.

[74] *John Hamilton & Co. v. John Fleming & Co. Ltd*, 1918 1 S.L.T. 229; *Hopkinson Ltd*, *supra* (alternative pecuniary crave in action for delivery); *Macleod v. Glen Talla Ltd*, Sh. Pr. Caplan, Kilmarnock Sh. Ct, June 12, 1986, unreported.

[75] *Little v. Burns* (1881) 9 R. 118; *Gunn v. Hunter* (1886) 13 R. 573; *Wick v. Wick* (1898) 1 F. 195; *Addison v. Kellock* (1906) 14 S.L.T. 410.

[76] *Lees v. Gordon*, 1929 S.L.T. 400; *Crombie v. British Transport Commission*, 1961 S.C 108. In *Crombie* the validity of the tender was not challenged. It seems questionable whether an offer of expenses should be required where an extrajudicial offer of the sum tendered has been made before the raising of the action.

[77] *McCulloch v. G. & C. Moore*, 1928 S.N. 114.

the ground that it is conditional on the court making an award.[78] A style offering "such expenses as the court considers proper" ought not to be used, as these words are tautologous and likely to lead to confusion.[79]

It is thought that an offer of "the taxed expenses of process to the date hereof", as in the style in paragraph 14.36, avoids any ambiguity. The words "expenses of process" occurring in a tender prima facie mean the legitimate and proper expenses to which the pursuer would be entitled if he succeeded at the date of the tender.[80] An offer of "the taxed expenses of process to the date hereof" is an offer of expenses up to the date when the tender was lodged,[81] as taxed in terms of the current Act of Sederunt relative to sheriff court fees.[82] Thus, where, as at present, the Act of Sederunt provides that the pursuer's solicitor's account as between party and party shall be taxed by reference to the sum decerned for unless the sheriff otherwise directs,[83] a tender in an ordinary action of an amount below the limit of value for summary causes with the taxed expenses of process to date is a tender of expenses as taxed on the summary cause scale, unless the sheriff otherwise directs.[84] Under the current Act of Sederunt the sheriff when pronouncing decree in terms of a minute of tender and acceptance not only may "otherwise direct" but may direct that expenses shall be subject to modification[85] or may allow a percentage increase of the solicitors' fees.[86] A tender of "expenses of process so far as not otherwise dealt with" includes expenses which have been reserved at an earlier stage of procedure.[87] **14.39**

Interest. A tender is, unless otherwise stated therein, in full satisfaction of the pursuer's claim to interest. If, the tender not having been accepted, the pursuer obtains an award, the court when dealing with expenses may have to consider whether the award is equal to or greater than the amount tendered. In doing so, the court takes account of any interest awarded.[88] In an action of damages the court in considering the amount of an award must take account of the amount of any interest awarded under the Interest on Damages (Scotland) Act 1958, as amended, or such part of that interest as the court considers appropriate.[89] A question may arise **14.40**

---

78 *Anderson v. Thomson*, 1985 S.L.T. (Sh. Ct.) 8.

79 *McKenzie v. H. D. Fraser & Sons*, 1990 S.C. 311 at 321, *per* L.P. Hope giving the opinion of the court, disapproving the forms of tender in *Smith v. British Rail Engineering Ltd*, 1985 S.L.T. 463, *McPherson v. British Railways Board*, 1985 S.L.T. 467 and *Rooney v. F. W. Woolworth plc*, 1990 S.L.T. 257.

80 *Macdonald v. SMT Co.*, 1948 S.C. 529, *per* L.P. Cooper at 531.

81 Even where those expenses have been caused by the pursuer's previous refusal of an extrajudicial offer of the sum tendered: *Burke v. Magistrates of Dunfermline*, 1932 S.N. 68.

82 *Watson v. Speedie Bros Ltd* (1932) 49 Sh.Ct.Rep. 83 at 86, 87; *Murray & Cruden Ltd v. Walker*, 1955 S.L.T. (Sh. Ct.) 9; *T. & R. Aitken v. Cordner*, 1958 S.L.T. (Sh. Ct.) 28; *C.R. Perry Ltd v Connell*, 1981 S.L.T. (Sh. Ct.) 190. *Campbell v. Rossi*, 1975 S.L.T. (Sh. Ct.) 25 must be considered to have been wrongly decided.

83 A.S. (Fees of Solicitors in the Sheriff Court) (Amendment and Further Provisions) 1993, Sched. 1, General Regulations, regs 1 and 2.

84 *C.R. Perry Ltd, supra.*

85 A.S., *supra*, reg. 5(a).

86 *ibid.* reg. 5(b). *Cf. Fleming Bros (Structural Engineers) Ltd v. Ford Motor Co. Ltd*, 1969 S.L.T. (Notes) 54; *Marks & Spencer Ltd v British Gas Corpn*, 1985 S.L.T. 17; *UCB Bank plc v. Dundas & Wilson C.S.*, 1990 S.C. 377.

87 *Cunningham v. Western SMT Co. Ltd* (1945) 61 Sh.Ct.Rep. 99.

88 *Cutlar v. McLeod's Tr.* (1876) 13 S.L.R. 308.

89 Interest on Damages (Scotland) Act 1958, s. 1(1 B), substituted by Interest on Damages (Scotland) Act 1971, s. 1(1); Walker, *Civil Remedies*, pp. 383–384. On interest on damages see paras 21.35, 21.36.

whether it is interest to the date of the tender or interest to the date of decree which should be taken into account.[90] Accordingly, the defender when deciding how much to tender must consider both what award of damages the court is likely to make and how much interest it is likely to award thereon; and the pursuer, when deciding whether to accept a tender, must observe that, unless it states otherwise, it includes interest.

14.41 In cases other than those to which the Interest on Damages (Scotland) Act 1958, as amended, applies, the question whether a tender is in full satisfaction of the pursuer's claim to interest depends on the court's construction of the terms of the tender. A tender "in full of the crave of the initial writ" or "in full satisfaction and settlement of his claim" will be construed as excluding any claim for interest in addition to the sum offered.[91] In actions where the amount of the defender's liability is limited by statute, an explicit reference to interest in the tender has been said to be just as important to its effectiveness as an offer of expenses.[92]

14.42 **Lodging of tender.** It is thought that a tender may be lodged at any time between the raising of the action[93] and final judgment. It should, however, be lodged at a stage when the pursuer will have a reasonable time to make up his mind whether to accept it. He must be given an ample opportunity to consider and weigh the situation: defenders must not be allowed to hustle pursuers into what may be hurried and hasty decisions.[94] The question of what is a reasonable time depends on the circumstances of the particular case, including the whereabouts of the pursuer, whether medical or other expert advice is reasonably required, and the stage which the action has reached: where a proof is imminent, a very much shorter time may be reasonable than where the case is in the process of adjustment.[95] It is usual for the auditor to determine within what time from its date the tender should have been accepted.[96]

14.43 At the same time as he lodges the tender, the defender's solicitor should intimate it to the solicitors for the pursuer[97] and any other parties, usually by sending them copies. Before lodging the tender in process the defender's solicitor should endorse upon it a certificate of intimation.[98] The sheriff clerk endorses the date of lodging on the tender,[99] places it in a sealed envelope, and does not draw it to the attention of the sheriff until he hears parties on expenses after pronouncing decree, if reference to the

---

[90] *Quinn v. Bowie (No. 2)*, 1987 S.L.T. 576; *Peacock v. Sutton*, 1998 G.W.D. 15-766.

[91] *Carmichael v. Caledonian Ry* (1868) 6 M. 671 at 681, 688 (revsd (1870) 8 M.(H.L.) 119); *Riddell v. Lanarkshire and Ayrshire Ry* (1904) 6 F. 432.

[92] The *"Devotion II"*, 1979 S.C. 80 at 91.

[93] *i.e.* not only after the lodging of defences: *Stoddart v. R. J. Macleod Ltd*, 1963 S.L.T. (Notes) 23.

[94] *Wood v. Miller*, 1960 S.C. 86, *per* L.J.-C. Thomson at 98.

[95] *Smeaton v. Dundee Corporation*, 1941 S.C. 600, *per* L.J.-C. Cooper at 604, Lord Jamieson at 507.

[96] See para. 14.48.

[97] OCR, r. 11.6(1).

[98] *cf.* RCS, r. 4.6(2). In the Ordinary Cause Rules there is no specific provision for certifying intimation of a part of process, but r. 11.6(2) (which deals with modes of intimation) refers to OCR, Chap. 5 which provides *inter alia* for intimation and certification thereof.

[99] A "perfect record" must be kept of the date of lodging: *Ramsay's Trs v. Sourer* (1864) 2 M. 891, *per* L.J.-C. Inglis at 892; *Smeaton v. Dundee Corporation, supra, per* Lord Jamieson at 608.

tender at that stage becomes necessary.[1] The minute of tender cannot be borrowed from process by any party.[2]

Withdrawal of tender. A tender may be withdrawn at any time before it is accepted by the lodging in process of a minute of acceptance of tender. The tender is withdrawn by lodging in process a minute of withdrawal, which must be duly intimated forthwith to the solicitors for the other parties. The minute of withdrawal may not be borrowed from process by any party.[3] **14.44**

Lapse of tender. A tender which is made, as most are, without a limit of time being stated within which it must be accepted, may become inoperative by reason of any important change of circumstances, without any formal withdrawal of the tender being made.[4] Whether a tender automatically falls on the death of the pursuer has not been authoritatively decided.[5] **14.45**

Acceptance of tender

Minute of acceptance of tender. Upon receipt of the intimation of the lodging of the tender, the pursuer is allowed a reasonable time to decide whether to accept it,[6] but he should reach a decision without delay. If he decides to accept the tender, his solicitor should obtain his express authority to accept it on his behalf.[7] The solicitor should then lodge in process, and intimate, a minute of acceptance of tender[8] in terms which meet those of the tender, for example: "B for the pursuer stated and hereby states to the court that the pursuer accepted and hereby accepts the tender contained in the minute of tender (no. 24 of process) in full of the crave of the initial writ." The solicitor should lodge along with the minute of acceptance a motion for decree in terms of the minutes of tender and acceptance. In an unusual case it was held by a sheriff that, where the defender claimed that the sum tendered (and accepted by the pursuer) was inaccurate because of a careless clerical error, there was an *ex facie* valid and binding contract between the parties, and the court was bound to grant decree in terms thereof unless and until the agreement was reduced or exception taken in terms of Ordinary Cause Rule 21.3.[9] **14.46**

Decree and expenses. If the defender's solicitor does not wish to seek expenses then he need do nothing when the pursuer's motion for decree is lodged, or he may endorse the motion as being consented to.[10] The **14.47**

---

[1] Sheriffdom of Glasgow and Strathkelvin Practice Notes, para. 1.01, printed in *Parliament House Book*, D-601, (1982) 27 J.L.S. 344 at 345. Although there is no specific provision for dealing with tenders in any other sheriffdom, what is provided here is the practice which is universally followed. See paras 14.49, 14.50.

[2] *ibid.* para. 1.02.

[3] *ibid.* para. 1.02.

[4] *Macrae v. Edinburgh Street Tramways Co.* (1885) 13 R. 265 (intimation of result of judicial reference); *Bright v. Low*, 1940 S.C. 280; *Bond v. British Railways Board*, 1972 S.L.T. (Notes) 47 (judgment by court of first instance); *Somerville v. National Coal Board*, 1963 S.C. 666 (death of pursuer claiming loss of future earnings).

[5] *Somerville, supra*; *Stoddart v. R. J. Macleod*, 1963 S.L.T. (Notes) 23.

[6] See para. 14.42.

[7] *Weir v. Stevenson* (1885) 1 Sh.Ct.Rep. 161.

[8] It is thought to be incorrect to accept a judicial tender by an extrajudicial letter, as in *Penman & Sons v. Crawford* (1903) 20 Sh.Ct.Rep. 123, because the parties "should speak through the process" (*Ramsay's Trs v. Sourer* (1864) 2 M. 891, *per* L.J.-C. Inglis at 892).

[9] *Manor Lifts Ltd v. J. H. Gray (Builders) Ltd*, 1989 S.L.T. (Sh. Ct.) 63. See para. 14.66.

is lodged, or he may endorse the motion as being consented to.[10] The pursuer's motion will then be dealt with as an unopposed motion.[11] However, if the defender's solicitor wishes to make any representation about expenses he should lodge a notice of opposition to the pursuer's motion. If such a notice is lodged the motion will call in court in the normal way.[12] At the hearing of the motion the defender's solicitor should move for expenses from the date of the tender or make any other motion as to expenses which he considers appropriate. If he fails to make such a motion, the sheriff will not make a finding of expenses in the defender's favour.[13] If the minute of tender is invalid, or if the minute of acceptance does not meet it, the sheriff will not grant decree.[14] If, however, the minute of tender is valid and is met by the acceptance, the sheriff will usually pronounce an interlocutor in which, in respect of the minutes of tender and acceptance, he decerns against the defender for payment to the pursuer of the sum tendered in full of the crave of the initial writ, finds the pursuer entitled to expenses down to the date of the tender and the defender entitled to expenses against the pursuer thereafter (except in so far as expenses have already been dealt with), allows accounts of these expenses to be given in and remits the same when lodged to the auditor to tax and to report.

14.48 Although the interlocutor finds the pursuer entitled to expenses against the defender down to "the date of the tender" and the defender entitled to expenses thereafter, it is usually for the auditor to determine the "true date" of the tender, that is, the date by which in the circumstances of the case the tender ought reasonably to have been either accepted or refused.[15] The matter is peculiarly within the province of the auditor,[16] but in an unusual case where all the material facts are before him the sheriff may himself determine the date.[17] The pursuer's expenses down to "the date of the tender" include the expenses of considering the tender,[18] and the remuneration of a curator *ad litem* to a minor, appointed on the motion of the defender.[19] The expenses to which the defender is entitled from "the date of the tender" are those incurred in the natural progress of the case between the date when the tender should reasonably have been accepted and the actual date of acceptance.[20] These expenses do not include expenses thrown away, for example the expenses occasioned by an amendment by the defender,[21] or the expenses of a debate on the defender's preliminary plea in which the defender has been unsuccessful.[22]

---

[10] OCR, r. 15.4.

[11] OCR, r. 15.5(1).

[12] OCR, r. 15.5(5).

[13] *Henderson v. Peeblesshire C.C.*, 1972 S.C. 195.

[14] *Wilson v. Rapp*, 1911 S.C. 1360 at 1363; *Wilkinson v. Richards*, 1967 S.L.T. 270; *Anderson v. Thomson*, 1985 S.L.T. (Sh. Ct.) 8.

[15] *Smeaton v. Dundee Corporation*, 1941 S.C. 600.

[16] *Wood v. Miller*, 1960 S.C. 86 at 97. See also *McLaughlin v. A. A. Stuart & Sons (Glasgow) Ltd*, 1955 S.L.T. (Notes) 2 (date of instruction of counsel for trial).

[17] *Jack v. Black*, 1911 S.C. 691 at 700; *Dougan v. Cruickshank & Co. Ltd*, 1954 S.L.T. (Notes) 73; *Morron v. O'Donnell*, 1979 S.L.T. (Notes) 26.

[18] *Jack, supra*; *McLean v. Galbraith Stores*, 1935 S.C. 165 at 168.

[19] *Campbell v. Alexander & Sons Ltd*, 1934 S.L.T. 52.

[20] *Jack, supra.*

[21] *Jacobs v. Provincial Motor Cab Co. Ltd*, 1910 S.C. 567.

[22] *Dougan, supra.*

Procedure where tender not accepted

Non-disclosure to sheriff. Where the tender is declined, the action pursues its course until decree is pronounced. It is a well-established principle that the tender must not be brought to the notice of the sheriff except at the stage when he is dealing with expenses.[23] The principle refers to the contents of the tender, not to its mere existence: since it forms a distinct step in the process[24] the sheriff may well notice a reference to it in the inventory of process, and no harm will ensue if he does so.[25] At a time when it was the general practice in the sheriff court to issue a final interlocutor which dealt both with the merits of the cause and with expenses, various recommendations were made as to the stage when and means by which the tender should be brought to the notice of the sheriff. One view was that the sheriff should be informed of its existence by the clerk of court and the parties' advocates when he made avizandum[26]; and another, that at the conclusion of the hearing on evidence the defender's advocate should move the sheriff to reserve the question of expenses.[27] A motion such as the latter, however, if not made as a matter of course, would indicate to the sheriff that a tender had been lodged. No doubt such an indication would not affect his mind; but it is submitted that the simplest way to observe the principle is to follow the course recommended elsewhere[28]: as a general rule, the advocates should move the sheriff to reserve the question of expenses, and the sheriff in his interlocutor should do so, dealing only with the merits and appointing the parties to be heard on all questions of expenses at a subsequent diet. If such a course is generally followed, there is no need to advise the sheriff of the existence of the tender when he makes avizandum, and the motion to reserve expenses does not necessarily hint at its existence. 14.49

If the sheriff becomes aware of the contents of the tender at any stage before his interlocutor is issued, he should disclose the fact to the parties. It is not, however, a ground of declinature, and normally need not vitiate any proof taken before the disclosure of the tender.[29] 14.50

Expenses. If the pursuer recovers more than the amount of the tender, he is said to "beat the tender". If he fails to do so, the general rules as to expenses which are discussed below will usually be applied. In considering whether he has done so, the court takes account of any award of interest. Where damages are awarded, the court must take account of the amount of any interest awarded under the Interest on Damages (Scotland) Act 1958, as amended, or such part of that interest as the court considers appropriate.[30] There is a discretion in the court as to the matter of expenses, independent of any question of tender,[31] and the following are only general rules. 14.51

---

[23] *Avery v. Cantilever Shoe Co.*, 1942 S.C. 469, *per* L.P. Normand at 470; Sheriffdom of Glasgow and Strathkelvin Practice Notes, para. 1.01, printed in *Parliament House Book*, D-601; (1982) 27 J.L.S. 344.
[24] *Smeaton v. Dundee Corporation*, 1941 S.C. 600, *per* Lord Jamieson at 608.
[25] *Bryce v. West Lothian D.C.*, 1979 S.L.T. (Sh. Ct.) 50.
[26] *Associated Portland Cement Manufacturers Ltd v. McInally*, 1970 S.L.T. (Sh. Ct.) 9.
[27] *Jack v. Jack*, 1953 S.L.T. (Sh. Ct.) 26; *Bryce*, *supra*.
[28] para. 16.103.
[29] *Ronald McDermid Ltd v. Muir Crawford (Builders) Ltd*, 1978 S.L.T. (Sh. Ct.) 17.
[30] para. 14.40.
[31] *Aitchison v. Steven* (1864) 3 M. 81, *per* L.P. McNeill at 82. For a modern example of the exercise of discretion, see *Peacock v. Sutton*, 1998 G.W.D. 15-766.

14.52 *Where pursuer beats tender*. If the pursuer, though he is awarded less than the sum sued for, recovers more than the amount of the tender, he is entitled to full expenses,[32] unless some are withheld for reasons other than the existence of the tender. He is entitled to the expenses of considering the tender, even if it is a repetition of an extrajudicial offer made before the raising of the action.[33]

14.53 *Where pursuer fails to beat tender*. If the pursuer recovers the exact amount of the tender or a lesser sum, as a general rule he is entitled to expenses down to the date of the tender itself (not to the date when it should have been accepted), and the defender is entitled to expenses thereafter. Special circumstances may, however, justify some other determination.[34] A party wishing to maintain that expenses should run from a later date should raise the question when the finding for expenses is made and before the remit to the auditor takes place.[35] The sheriff may supersede extract of the decree in favour of the pursuer until the expenses found due to the defender have been taxed and decerned for.[36] Where a pursuer who had failed to beat a tender reclaimed and obtained an increased award which was, however, lower than the sum which had been tendered, no expenses were awarded to either party in the Inner House.[37] In a case disputed only on *quantum*[38] the pursuer beat the tender in the Outer House. The defender reclaimed and lodged a substantially higher tender. The reclaiming motion was successful but the sum awarded to the pursuer still exceeded the amount of the defender's latest tender. The court nevertheless found the defender entitled to the expenses of the reclaiming motion. The court commented that it would have been open to the pursuer to make an extrajudicial offer in response to the defender's tender.[39]

Plurality of pursuers

14.54 Where several pursuers sue in one action, each craving a separate award, as in a family claim for damages in respect of the death of a relative, or where actions have been conjoined,[40] a tender whereby the defender seeks to settle all the pursuers' claims must offer to each pursuer a sum which is definitely appropriated to him as in full of the crave relative to his claim, and which he can accept for himself, whether or not the other pursuers make a similar acceptance of the sums respectively appropriated or apportioned to them.[41] It is therefore incompetent to tender one lump sum, leaving it to the pursuers to allocate amongst themselves[42]; or to tender a lump sum to a pursuer who sues both as an individual and as tutor and administrator-at-law of a pupil child[43]; or to

---

[32] *Heriot v. Thomson* (1833) 12 S. 145.

[33] *McMillan v. Central SMT Co.*, 1947 S.L.T. (Notes) 3.

[34] *McLean v. Galbraith Stores*, 1935 S.C. 165; *Associated Portland Cement Manufacturers Ltd v. McInally*, 1970 S.L.T. (Sh. Ct.) 9, *per* Sh. Pr. A. G. Walker at 10.

[35] *McLean, supra*; *Gysin v. Pochin (Joinery) Ltd*, 1970 S.L.T. (Notes) 9.

[36] *Fry v. N.E. Ry* (1882) 10 R. 290; *Bruce v. McLellan*, 1925 S.C. 103; *McKeown v. Palmers Scaffolding (Scotland) Ltd*, 1962 S.L.T. (Notes) 10.

[37] *Bond v. British Railways Board*, 1972 S.L.T. (Notes) 47.

[38] *Morrison v. Barton (No. 2)*, 1994 S.L.T. 685 in which *Bond, supra* was distinguished.

[39] *ibid. per* L.P. Hope (giving the opinion of the court) at 687.

[40] *Boyle v. Olsen*, 1912 S.C. 1235; see also *Wilson v. Rapp*, 1911 S.C. 1360.

[41] *Flanagan v. Dempster Moore & Co. Ltd*, 1928 S.C. 308.

[42] *Flanagan, supra.*

[43] *Wilkinson v. Richards*, 1967 S.L.T. 270.

make a tender of a specific sum to each pursuer, conditional on all the pursuers accepting.[44]

Where the tender is in proper form, it is competent for only certain of the pursuers to accept and obtain decree for the sums respectively tendered to them, while the action proceeds on behalf of the remaining pursuers.[45] Where one of two pursuers is awarded more than the sum tendered to him and the other is awarded the same as or less than the sum tendered to him, the former will be entitled to all proper items of expense particularly referable to his case alone plus one-half of the items of general expense incurred in the action jointly by both pursuers, while the latter will normally be found liable to pay one-half of the defender's taxed expenses subsequent to the date of the tender.[46] In family claims, however, that course is sometimes not followed.[47] **14.55**

Plurality of defenders

Tender by one defender to pursuer. One of several defenders sued jointly and severally may make a tender to the pursuer. If the tender is for the full sum sued for or is, without qualification, in full of the crave of the initial writ, the pursuer by his acceptance is precluded from continuing the action against the other defenders unless he is unable to recover from the tendering defender the whole sum decerned for in terms of the minutes of tender and acceptance.[48] Usually, however, the tender is of an amount which is less than the sum sued for, together with the taxed expenses of process to date "in full of the crave of the initial writ so far as directed against this defender". If the pursuer accepts such a tender he is not precluded from continuing the action against the other defenders.[49] **14.56**

Where the averments of the tendering defender have been such as to make it a matter of prudence for the pursuer to call a second defender, the defender's tender of the expenses of process includes a right to the pursuer to relief from that defender in respect of the expenses awarded against the pursuer in favour of the second defender; and on being so moved in the motion for decree in terms of the minutes of tender and acceptance, the court will include in the interlocutor granting decree a finding that the pursuer is entitled to a right of relief against the tendering defender in respect of the second defender's expenses.[50] In such a case it is usual for the tendering defender to advise the second defender that his expenses will be paid if the tender is accepted. Where, however, the tendering defender's averments contain nothing which expressly or impliedly causes the pursuer as a matter of prudence to call the other defender in, and the pursuer's pleadings do not suggest that his case against the other defender derived from the tendering **14.57**

---

44 *McNeil v. National Coal Board*, 1966 S.C. 72.

45 *e.g. Rankin v. Waddell*, 1949 S.C. 555 at 556.

46 *McFadyen v. St Cuthbert's Co-operative Association* [1951] C.L.Y. 3992; *Barbour v. McGruer*, 1968 S.L.T. (Notes) 52.

47 *McCrae v. Bryson*, 1922 S.L.T. 164 (not reported on this point, 1923 S.C. 896); *Peggie v. Keddie*, 1932 S.C. 721; *McKeown v. Palmers Scaffolding (Scotland) Ltd*, 1962 S.L.T. (Notes) 10.

48 *Arrow Chemicals Ltd v. Guild*, 1978 S.L.T 206.

49 *McNair v. Dunfermline Corporation*, 1953 S.C. 183.

50 *Clegg v. McKirdy & MacMillan*, 1932 S.C. 442, *per* Lord Hunter at 446; *Macdonald v. SMT Co.*, 1948 S.C. 529; *Johnston v. Lithgows Ltd*, 1964 S.L.T. (Notes) 96; *MacLinden v. Colvilles Ltd*, 1967 S.L.T. (Notes) 80.

defender's defences, the pursuer will not be entitled to a right of relief.[51] Where, too, the pursuer has called two defenders although, had he exercised due care in his inquiries, he might have ascertained that his case truly lay against only one of them, he will not be entitled to a right of relief.[52] If the tendering defender wishes to exclude from his tender any liability he might have to relieve the pursuer of the second defender's expenses, he should make that clear in his minute of tender.[53]

14.58 **Separate tenders by each defender to pursuer.** Where each of two defenders sued jointly and severally lodged separate but cumulative tenders of £300 each, and after proof the pursuer obtained a joint and several decree for £450, the defenders were found liable in expenses to the pursuer down to the date of the second tender, upon the view that there was no doubt that the pursuer would have received payment of the sums tendered. It was observed that two independent and cumulative tenders of £300 did not necessarily exceed a joint and several decree for £450, because one of the defenders might be a man of straw.[54]

14.59 **Williamson tender by one defender to other defender or defenders.** Where defenders in an action of damages are sued jointly and severally, one defender may by minute propose to the other or others that he will admit liability to the pursuer on the basis of a contribution by the defenders *inter se*, in certain specified proportions, to any damages and expenses awarded to the pursuer. The minute may be in such terms as the following[55]:

> "A for the first-named defenders stated and hereby states to the court that without prejudice to and under reservation of their whole rights and pleas, the first-named defenders offered and hereby offer to the second-named defenders to admit liability to make reparation to the pursuer jointly and severally with the second-named defenders, but only on the basis that the defenders shall be liable *inter se* to contribute to any damages and expenses awarded to the pursuer in the proportions of three-quarters (3/4) to the first-named defenders and one-quarter (1/4) to the second-named defenders."

14.60 Such a minute has come to be known as a "Williamson tender", from the decision in *Williamson v. McPherson*.[56] It is not, of course, a tender as traditionally defined,[57] and acceptance of it does not lead at once to the settlement of the action, since it is not addressed to the pursuer, although acceptance of it by the other defenders may be followed by a joint minute of tender to the pursuer by all the defenders, which the pursuer may accept.[58] Such a result is not always achieved, however, because, apart from any question of the acceptability of the apportionment proposed, the

---

51 *Mitchell v. Redpath Engineering Ltd*, 1990 S.L.T. 259.

52 *Mackintosh v. Galbraith and Arthur* (1900) 3 F. 66; *Morrison v. Waters & Co.* (1906) 8 F. 867; *McIntyre v. Ellams & Curry*, 1938 S.L.T 413 (pursuer adopting irrelevant case); *Tavendale v. Burgh of Motherwell and Wishaw*, 1962 S.C. 216; *Johnston, supra*; *Mitchell, supra*.

53 *Macdonald, supra*.

54 *Jackson v. Clyde Navigation Trust*, 1961 S.L.T. (Sh. Ct.) 35.

55 The style may, of course, be varied to suit the circumstances of each case. Where, for example, there are three defenders, the offer may be that they should contribute "in equal proportions or in any event so that the first-named defender shall not be liable thus to contribute more than one-third (1/3) of such award."

56 1951 S.C. 438.

57 *Ramsay's Trs v. Souter* (1864) 2 M. 891, *per* L.J.-C. Inglis at 892; para. 14.33.

58 *Morton v. O'Donnell*, 1979 S.L.T. (Notes) 26.

procedure has certain unattractive features. Unless damages have been agreed,[59] a defender to whom a Williamson tender is addressed is asked to accept a specific proportion of a liability of unknown amount which remains to be judicially determined after proof. Even if he accepts, the minute leaves open the issue of quantification and cannot affect the liability for the subsequent expenses incurred in regard to that issue. Let it be assumed that the tender is declined, the pursuer establishes liability and the sheriff finds the tendering defender liable in a smaller proportion than he was prepared to accept in his tender. That defender will escape liability for the expenses which were incurred subsequent to the date of the tender only in so far as these relate to the determination of liability between, or among, the defenders. He will remain liable to contribute, in the proportions fixed by the sheriff, to the whole expenses found due to the pursuer down to the date of the tender and, subsequent to the date of the tender, to the pursuer's expenses *quoad* quantification of the damages.[60]

As in the case of a tender addressed to a pursuer, the question of what is a reasonable time by which a Williamson tender should be accepted or rejected depends on the circumstances of each case.[61] Where it is already clear before it is lodged that the apportionment of liability between, or among, the defenders is a very live issue, and the proof is imminent, a defender should be prepared to make a decision within a very few days.[62] **14.61**

Tender by one defender to pursuer and other defender or defenders. A defender may lodge a minute addressed both to the other defender or defenders and to the pursuer, proposing that the defenders should contribute in specified proportions to a specific sum of damages and the taxed expenses of process to date, for which the pursuer shall be entitled to decree.[63] The consequences of refusal of such a tender do not appear to have been judicially considered in any reported decision. It is thought that the tender may be so framed as to be capable of acceptance by each of the defenders and by the pursuer separately. If a defender declines to accept and is found liable to contribute to the pursuer's award in more than the tendered proportion, the consequences would probably be similar to those following from the refusal of a Williamson tender.[64] If the pursuer declines to accept and is awarded an amount less than the sum tendered, it may be that he would not be found liable in expenses unless all the defenders had accepted the tender.[65] **14.62**

Extrajudicial negotiation and settlement

The parties may, without resorting to formal procedure by minutes of tender and acceptance, settle the action extrajudicially, and record that **14.63**

---

[59] As in *Associated Portland Cement Manufatrurers Ltd v. McInally*, 1970 S.L.T. (Sh. Ct.) 9.
[60] *Williamson, supra.*
[61] *Morton v. O'Donnell*, 1979 S.L.T. (Notes) 26; paras 14.42, 14.47.
[62] *Morton, supra*; and see the concession in *Associated Portland Cement Manufacturers Ltd v. McInally, supra*, at 11.
[63] *Houston v. British Road Services Ltd*, 1967 S.L.T. 329.
[64] para. 14.60.
[65] C. N. McEachran, "The Gentle Art of Tendering", 1969 S.L.T. (News) 53 at 56.

fact in a joint minute[66] or otherwise.[67] Extrajudicial negotiations or settlements usually become matters for judicial scrutiny only where there is a dispute as to whether settlement has been effected,[68] or where the contract embodying the settlement is open to construction,[69] or where in a question as to expenses reference is made to an extrajudicial offer which has been declined.[70]

Joint minute

14.64 When parties settle an action extrajudicially, they usually prepare and lodge a joint minute and ask the court to interpone its authority thereto and grant decree in terms of the arrangement arrived at in the settlement. Once the joint minute is lodged it cannot be withdrawn, except in very special circumstances.[71] The settlement is binding and effective although the court has not interponed authority thereto, and there is no *locus poenitentiae* until authority is interponed.[72] The court will interpone authority and grant decree unless the decree sought is not within the ambit of the craves of the writ and any counterclaim,[73] or unless the circumstances are highly special.[74] In an action raised against several defenders where one defender has settled with the pursuer, it does not appear to be necessary to postpone pronouncing decree in favour of that defender in order not to defeat the other defenders' rights of relief in terms of section 3(2) of the Law Reform (Miscellaneous Provisions) (Scotland) Act 1940.[75] A motion to interpone authority to the joint minute may be lodged and intimated in the normal way.[76] It will either be unopposed or endorsed as consented to.[77] Alternatively a simple oral motion may be made if the case is calling in court in any event.[78–79]

Alternative procedure

14.65 Disclosure of the terms of settlement to the court, and the interposition of the authority of the court, are not essential except where the approval of the court is required, as in certain family proceedings. In general, if the parties have settled the litigation, the settlement is binding although the court has not interponed its authority, for the making of an extrajudicial offer by one party and its acceptance by the other is a contract between them which is binding just like any other contract.[80] The parties may

---

[66] para. 14.64.
[67] para. 14.65.
[68] para. 14.66.
[69] para. 14.67.
[70] para. 14.68.
[71] *Paterson v. Magistrates of St Andrews* (1880) 7 R. 712.
[72] *McAthey v. Patriotic Investment Co. Ltd*, 1910 S.C. 584; *Lothian v. Lothian*, 1965 S.L.T. 368; *Dalzell v. Dalzell*, 1985 S.L.T. 286. *Cf. Robson v. Robson*, 1973 S.L.T. (Notes) 4.
[73] *McAthey, supra.*
[74] *Aberdeen Grit Co. v. Aberdeen Corporation*, 1948 S.L.T. (Notes) 44; *Baird's Exrx v. Wylie*, 1956 S.L.T. (Sh. Ct.) 10 (tenant renouncing statutory protection).
[75] *Singer v. Gray Tool Co. (Europe) Ltd*, 1984 S.L.T. 149. *Cf. Magee & Co. (Belfast) Ltd v. Bracewell Harrison & Coton*, 1981 S.L.T. 107.
[76] OCR, rr. 15.1(1)(b),(2), 15.2.
[77] OCR, rr. 15.4, 15.5(1).
[78–79] OCR, r. 15.1(1)(a).
[80] *Gow v. Henry* (1899) 2 F. 48; *Welsh v. Cousin* (1899) 2 F. 277 (settlement when pursuer ignorant of tender); *Davidson v. Whatmough*, 1930 S.L.T. 536 (supervening bankruptcy of defender).

simply state to the court, either by joint minute or orally at the bar, that the action has been settled, and ask the court to dispose of the action by pronouncing decree, usually of absolvitor or dismissal,[81] with or without an order for expenses. In general, the parties when concurring in asking the court to bring the action to an end must be in agreement about the question of expenses. The court will not adjudicate on a dispute as to expenses where it has no knowledge of the merits of the action, except perhaps upon the basis of a joint minute in which the relevant facts are agreed. In other cases, if agreement on expenses is found impossible, the action must proceed in order that the question of expenses may be decided in ordinary course.[82] Usually, however, common sense prevails and agreement on expenses is reached.

Dispute as to whether settlement effected

Where one party moves the court to dispose of the action on the basis that it has been settled, and the other party denies that settlement has been reached, the first party may be allowed to lodge a minute setting forth the circumstances of the alleged settlement and the other may be allowed to lodge answers.[83] The sheriff may then dispose of the motion on the basis of the admitted facts,[84] or may sist the action to enable the first party if so advised to raise an action of declarator of the alleged agreement to settle.[85] **14.66**

Construction of settlement

Of the various questions which may arise as to the construction of an extrajudicial settlement,[86] it is necessary to notice here only those relative to procedure, which are usually concerned with expenses. Where it is agreed that a party is entitled to expenses as taxed, he is not allowed expenses incurred prior to the raising of the action, but only such expenses as are expenses of process.[87] He is, however, entitled to the expenses which are appropriate to the case.[88] These may include a percentage increase of fees,[89] a motion for which perhaps need not be made at the time when these expenses are awarded.[90] The party's expenses will be taxed in terms of the current Act of Sederunt relative to sheriff court fees. When the court has granted decree for payment of an agreed principal sum together with expenses as taxed, the expenses will under the current rule be taxed by reference to the sum decerned for, unless the sheriff otherwise directs.[91] If there is no decerniture for a principal sum, the expenses will be taxed on the ordinary cause scale.[92] A **14.67**

---

[81] *McAthey v. Patriotic Investment Co. Ltd,* 1910 S.C. 584; *Luxmoore v. Red Deer Commission,* 1979 S.L.T. (Notes) 53.

[82] *Miller v. Campbell's Trs,* 1965 S.L.T. (Notes) 57; *Reynolds v McKenzie,* Sh. Pr. Caplan, Kilmarnock Sh. Ct, May 30, 1986, unreported.

[83] *Manor Lifts Ltd v. J. H. Gray (Builders) Ltd,* 1989 S.L.T. (Sh. Ct.) 63.

[84] *Lawrence v. Knight,* 1972 S.C. 26.

[85] *N.B. Ry v. Bernards Ltd* (1900) 7 S.L.T. 329.

[86] *e.g. Christie v. Fife Coal Co.* (1899) 2 F. 192; *Anderson v. Dick* (1901) 4 F. 68.

[87] *Clyde Nail Co. Ltd v. A.G. Moore & Co. Ltd,* 1949 S.L.T. (Notes) 43.

[88] *Marks & Spencer Ltd v. British Gas Corporation,* 1985 S.L.T. 17; *UCB Bank plc v. Dundas & Wilson, C.S.,* 1990 S.C. 337.

[89] A.S. (Fees of Solicitors in the Sheriff Court) (Amendment and Further Provisions) 1993, Sched. 1, General Regulations, reg. 5(b).

[90] *Marks & Spencer Ltd, supra.*

[91] A.S., *supra,* Sched. 1, General Regulations, reg. 2. See para. 14.39.

[92] *Lothian Hotels v. Ferer,* 1981 S.L.T. (Sh. Ct.) 52.

legally aided party who wishes to reserve his right to move for modification of his liability for the expenses of his opponent should ensure that the joint minute so provides.[93] A reference to "scale charges" in an arrangement for settlement has been held to refer to the fees in the chapter of the Law Society of Scotland's table of fees relative to negotiated settlements,[94] and to exclude outlays.[95]

Rejected extrajudicial offer

14.68 An extrajudicial offer which has been rejected may be taken into consideration when expenses are being awarded, whether the offer was made before the action was raised[96] or during its course.[97] Under an old rule of practice, much appeared to depend on whether an extrajudicial offer made before litiscontestation was repeated on record. If it was so repeated and the pursuer recovered a lesser sum, expenses were awarded against the pursuer, even though no expenses were tendered on record, in view of the reasonable attitude of the defenders throughout.[98] If it was not so repeated and the pursuer recovered a lesser sum, neither party was entitled to expenses.[99] The rule is included in some textbooks,[1] but its soundness has long been doubted[2] and there does not appear to be any reported example of its application in modern practice. It seems inappropriate nowadays, when the practice of referring to extrajudicial offers on record is no longer generally followed and it is not considered to be a function of written pleadings to provide a basis for eventual arguments on questions of expenses.[3] It is thought that the effect of an extrajudicial offer on expenses would now depend on the whole circumstances of the case, and not on whether it was made before or after litiscontestation, or was referred to on record. Sheriff Principal Sir Allan G. Walker held, after an examination of the authorities, that the question which the court will normally have to consider is whether, in all the circumstances, the party to whom the offer was made acted unreasonably in refusing it, and whether as a result of the refusal unnecessary judicial expense was caused. In order to reach a decision on that point, the agreed facts must be put before the court. If necessary, the whole correspondence relative to the negotiations should be lodged, and its accuracy agreed.[4] An extrajudicial offer, like a tender, falls on an important change of circumstances.[5]

Advising court when settlement imminent or effected

14.69 At any stage before debate or proof a party may advise the sheriff that a case is likely to be settled and move the sheriff to continue the case

---

93 *Boughen v. Scott*, 1983 S.L.T. (Sh. Ct.) 94; *Roy, Nicholson, Becker & Day v. Clarke*, 1984 S.L.T. (Sh. Ct.) 16.

94 Now Chap. 10 of the Society's Table of Fees for Conveyancing and General Business.

95 *Staff v. Allan*, 1971 S.L.T. (Notes) 61.

96 *O'Donnell v. A.M. & G. Robertson*, 1965 S.L.T. 155.

97 *Pearce & Co. v. Owners of S.S. "Hans Maersk"*, 1935 S.C. 703.

98 *Gunn v. Hunter* (1886) 13 R. 573; *Mavor & Coulson v. Grierson* (1892) 19 R. 868.

99 *Gunn, supra*; *Critchley v. Campbell* (1884) 11 R. 475.

1 Dobie, p. 150; Wilson, *Debt* (2nd ed.), p. 139.

2 *Miller v. McPhun* (1895) 22 R. 600; *O'Donnell, supra.*

3 *O'Donnell, supra.*

4 *Calder v. Rush*, 1970 S.L.T. (Sh. Ct.) 51.

5 *Lawrence v. Knight*, 1972 S.C. 26; para. 14.45.

simpliciter for the lodging of a joint minute. This may happen at an options hearing. Although the sheriff's powers are, according to the strict letter of the rules, severely limited at such a hearing,[6] it is not uncommon in practice in these circumstances for a case to be continued to a "procedure roll" rather than to be sent to debate, proof before answer or proof.

Where in any action a settlement has been reached, with the result that a proof, debate or appeal will not proceed on a date which has been fixed, it is good practice for the solicitors acting in the case to intimate the position at once by telephone to the sheriff clerk, and to confirm such intimation in writing.[7] **14.70**

IV. Summary Decree

The power to grant a summary decree in favour of a pursuer on the ground that defences do not disclose a defence to an action or part of it was first introduced into the pre-1993 Ordinary Cause Rules in 1992.[8] That power is now to be found in Chapter 17 of the 1993 Rules. **14.71**

A summary decree may be granted in any action other than: (a) a family action within the meaning of rule 33.1(1); (b) an action of multiplepoinding; or (c) an action under the Presumption of Death (Scotland) Act 1977.[9] In an action to which Chapter 17 applies a pursuer may, at any time after a defender has lodged defences, apply by motion for summary decree against that defender on the ground that there is no defence to the action, or part of it, disclosed in the defences.[10] In applying for such a decree the pursuer may move the sheriff (a) to grant decree in terms of all or any of the craves of the writ; (b) to pronounce an interlocutor sustaining or repelling a plea-in-law; or (c) to dispose of the whole or part of the subject-matter of the cause.[11] A motion for summary decree must be intimated by registered post or the first class recorded delivery service to every other party not less than 14 days before the date fixed for the hearing of the motion.[12] **14.72**

On considering a motion the sheriff may (a) if satisfied that there is no defence to the action or to any part of it to which the motion relates, grant the motion for summary decree in whole or in part, as the case may be; or (b) ordain any party, or a partner, director, officer or office-bearer of, any party to produce any relevant document or article, or to lodge an affidavit in support of any assertion of fact made in the pleadings or at the hearing of the motion.[13] Notwithstanding the refusal of all or part of a motion for **14.73**

---

6 OCR, r. 9.12(3).

7 Intimation is required in the Sheriffdom of South Strathclyde, Dumfries and Galloway (Practice note of June 25, 1982, Schedule, para. 3(2), printed in *Parliament House Book*, D-803), and is desiderated in the Sheriffdoms of Glasgow and Strathkelvin (Practice by Solicitors which would Assist the Running of the Sheriff Court at Glasgow, para. 10, printed in *Parliament House Book*, D-803) and North Strathclyde (Practice Note of Oct. 20, 1992, para. 1.16, printed in *Parliament House Book*, D-703).

8 1983 OCR, r. 59A.

9 OCR, r. 17.1.

10 OCR, r. 17.2(1).

11 OCR, r. 17.2(2).

12 OCR, r. 17.2(3).

13 OCR, r. 17.2(4).

summary decree, a subsequent motion may be made where there has been a change of circumstances.[14] Subject to any necessary modifications the foregoing provisions in relation to a motion for summary decree at the instance of a pursuer also apply in relation to a motion by a defender who has lodged a counterclaim[15] and in relation to a motion by a defender or third party who has made a claim against another defender or third party who has lodged defences or answers.[16]

14.74 It has been held that, in determining a motion for summary decree, a court must consider the defence presented as at the date of the motion, and should concentrate on the substance and authenticity of the defence rather than just on the manner in which it is expressed in the defences.[17] In reaching a decision as to whether or not to grant summary decree a court may have regard to matters of evidence, such as an affidavit, and is not bound to exclude such material in the way that would be required in a debate on relevancy.[18] However, where the material facts are not in issue, and the defence is founded solely on a proposition of law, it may be appropriate for the court to consider the legal force and validity of that defence in a way that is not very different from what would be appropriate at a debate.[19]

---

[14] OCR, r. 17.2(5).
[15] OCR, r. 17.3(1).
[16] OCR, r. 17.3(2).
[17] *Frimokar (U.K.) Ltd v. Mobile Technical Plant (International) Ltd*, 1990 S.L.T. 180, 1989 S.C.L.R. 767, *Whiteway Laidlaw Bank Ltd v. Green*, 1993 S.C.L.R. 968.
[18] *Delta Sales & Marketing Ltd v. Nugent*, 1991 S.C.L.R. 461.
[19] *Matthews v. Scottish Legal Aid Board*, 1995 S.C.L.R. 184.

Chapter 15

RECOVERY OF EVIDENCE

This chapter is concerned with the procedural aspects of the preparation of the case for proof. It examines the various procedures which a party may adopt in order to obtain precognitions, oral evidence, documents, real evidence and other information which may be used at the proof. While it is true that only a small proportion of defended actions reach the stage of proof, and that discretion must be exercised in order to avoid unnecessary expense in preparation, each case should be prepared on the basis that it will go to proof. Many cases are won or lost long before the day in court because of the degree of care and diligence which has been bestowed on their preparation, both before and after the commencement of the action. Before the action is raised the party's solicitor should ascertain as clearly as possible the issues of fact and law which are likely to be relevant, and in the light of these should precognosce important potential witnesses and obtain and carefully examine any material documents and other property in his client's possession. He should also consider whether any application should be made to the court under section 1 of the Administration of Justice (Scotland) Act 1972 for orders for the inspection, photographing, preservation, custody or detention of documents or other property[1] or for the disclosure of the identity of witnesses.[2] Once the action is raised, the nature of the preparation required will continue to depend on the issues in the case, which may alter as the pleadings are adjusted and amended. Accordingly, the question of what evidence will be required on the day in court not only should be considered before the drafting of the pleadings, but should be kept under review throughout the progress of the case. Once the action has been raised, the parties' advisers should not overestimate the time at their disposal for preparation for the proof and should bear in mind the fairly tight timetable imposed by the Ordinary Cause Rules. Plans for detailed preparation should be formulated at an early stage, and set in motion at the first appropriate opportunity. During the progress of the proceedings, each party's advisers should continue to assess the strengths and weaknesses of the cases on either side as they may be revealed in the course of preparation, and their bearing on the prospects of success or the advisability of settlement. **15.01**

I. Evidence of Witnesses

Disclosure of identity of witnesses

At common law, one party is not obliged to disclose to the other the identity of any witness unless "the person is, from the circumstances, put forward as representing the person against whom the suit is raised in the **15.02**

---

[1] Any such application before the raising of an action is made by summary application: A.S. (Sheriff Court Summary Application Rules) 1993, r. 30(1). See paras 15.84 to 15.92.

[2] paras 15.03 to 15.06.

matters whereon the question turns."[3] Employers have accordingly been required to disclose the names and addresses of allegedly negligent employees.[4] A pursuer in a personal injuries action may recover a list of witnesses indirectly, if it happens to be contained in a report made to the defender at or about the time of the accident by a responsible employee who was present at the time of the accident.[5] In an ordinary cause proceeding under the standard procedure (but not the additional procedure) each party must, within 14 days after the date of the interlocutor allowing a proof or proof before answer, provide every other party with a list of the witnesses which the first party intends to call.[6] Such lists must include the name, occupation (where known) and address of each intended witness.[7] A party may call a witness whose name is not on his list only with leave of the sheriff unless no other party objects.[8]

15.03 By section l(lA) of the Administration of Justice (Scotland) Act 1972[9] the court is empowered to order any person (not necessarily a party to the action) to disclose such information as he has as to the identity of any persons who appear to the court to be persons who might be witnesses in any existing civil proceedings before the court or in proceedings which appear to the court to be likely to be brought. The power is conferred without prejudice to the existing powers of the court, but subject to section 1(4) of the Act which preserves the law and practice relative to the privilege of witnesses and havers, confidentiality of communications and withholding or non-disclosure of information on the grounds of public interest, and section 47 of the Crown Proceedings Act 1947 which makes provision as to the recovery of documents in the hands of the Crown.[10] An application to the court to exercise the power conferred by section l(lA) may be made at any time before the commencement of proceedings by a person who appears to the court to be likely to be a party to or minuter in proceedings which are likely to be brought; and at any time after the commencement of proceedings by a party to or minuter in the proceedings, or any other person who appears to the court to have an interest to be joined as such party or minuter. The court may exercise the power unless there is special reason why the application should not be granted.[11]

15.04 Before the commencement of proceedings an application is made by summary application.[12] As with all summary applications the procedure is essentially within the discretion of the sheriff.[13] He may order intimation

---

3 *Henderson v. Patrick Thomson Ltd*, 1911 S.C. 246, *per* L.P. Dunedin at 249–250.

4 *Clarke v. Edinburgh and District Tramways Co. Ltd*, 1914 S.C. 775; *McDade v. Glasgow Corporation*, 1966 S.L.T. (Notes) 4; *McGinn v. Meiklejohn Ltd*, 1969 S.L.T. (Notes) 49; *Halloran v. Greater Glasgow Passenger Transport Executive*, 1976 S.L.T. 77.

5 *Macphee v. Glasgow Corporation*, 1915 S.C. 990; *McCulloch v. Glasgow Corporation*, 1918 S.C. 155; *McBride v. Lewis*, 1922 S.L.T. 380 (the word "not" seems to have been omitted from the first sentence of the penultimate paragraph of the opinion). *Cf. Ross v. Glasgow Corporation*, 1919 2 S.L.T. 209. See Macphail, *Evidence*, para. 24–60.

6 OCR, r. 9.14(1). See para. 16.01.

7 OCR, r. 9.14(3).

8 OCR, r. 9.14(2).

9 Inserted by the Law Reform (Miscellaneous Provisions) (Scotland) Act 1985, s. 19.

10 On s. 47 of the Crown Proceedings Act 1947 see paras 4.71 to 4.75.

11 1972 Act, s. 1(2): see para. 15.90.

12 A.S. (Sheriff Court Summary Application Rules) 1993, r. 30(2).

13 *ibid.* r. 32.

to any person who appears to him to have an interest in the application.[14] He may, if necessary, appoint a hearing.[15]

After the commencement of proceedings an application is made by motion with accompanying specification of the matter in respect of which information is sought as to the identity of the person who might be a witness or the defender, intimated to every other party, and where necessary to the Lord Advocate.[16] After hearing parties, the sheriff may either grant or refuse the order sought in whole or in part, or as amended, and subject to such conditions, including caution or other security, as he thinks fit.[17] **15.05**

Where an order is granted, whether before or after the commencement of proceedings, the interlocutor should specify the manner and the time within which it is to be obtempered. The party in whose favour the order is granted should serve a certified copy of the interlocutor on the person to whom it is directed, and should intimate a further copy to any other person to whom intimation of the summary application or the motion has been made unless that person was present when the application was determined. The person to whom the order is directed must obtemper it in the manner and within the time specified.[18] **15.06**

Precognition of witnesses

A precognition is a written statement in intelligible form of the matters which a witness is prepared to give in evidence in the witness-box. The thorough and accurate precognition of witnesses is an essential step in the preparation for the proof. Good precognitions of all the appropriate witnesses will indicate the strengths and weaknesses of a party's case, and will form the basis for the selection of the party's witnesses and the leading of their evidence at the proof. The following paragraphs discuss the obligations of witnesses and their employers in regard to precognitions, the taking of precognitions and the use which may be made of them. **15.07**

Obligations in regard to precognition

The court will not order a witness in a civil case to submit to precognition.[19] Usually, however, it is in a witness's own interest to agree to be precognosced, because if he refuses, his refusal is likely to be founded on as indicating prejudice on his part against the party seeking to precognosce him, and he is likely to be cross-examined to that effect. Similarly, while the court will not compel an employer to allow his employees to be precognosced, in most cases it is in his interest to afford facilities for them to be precognosced, in order to avoid suggestions of partisanship.[20] Employers who refused such facilities have been held liable **15.08**

---

[14] A.S. (Sheriff Court Summary Application Rules) 1993, r. 5.

[15] Sheriff Courts (Scotland) Act 1907, s. 50.

[16] OCR, r. 28.2(2) and (3).

[17] OCR, r. 28.2(4).

[18] The procedures specified in this paragraph were specifically provided in the 1983 Ordinary Cause Rules (r. 84A(8), (9), (10)). The 1993 Ordinary Cause Rules contain no such provisions, nor do the 1993 Summary Application Rules. It is, however, submitted that these procedures simply reflect accepted good practice and should be complied with.

[19] *Henderson v. Patrick Thomson Ltd*, 1911 S.C. 246.

[20] *Henderson, supra.*

in expenses, although successful on the merits.[21] The court does not approve of employers in any way influencing their employees to give or refuse a precognition to the opposite party. The employer is not entitled to prescribe any conditions as to how or in whose presence a precognition is to be taken.[22] The court may order an employer to disclose such information as he has as to the identity of any of his employees, or others, who appear to the court to be persons who might be witnesses.[23] In any event a party's solicitor is entitled to approach the employees directly and invite them to be precognosced, whatever the attitude of the employer.[24] A party has no right to insist that his solicitor be present while a witness is being precognosced by the opposite party.[25]

Taking of precognitions

15.09 It is important that precognitions should be taken at the earliest opportunity, in order to ascertain important facts with accuracy at an early stage and take advantage of the witnesses' recollections before they begin to fade. Indeed, a solicitor should if possible precognosce the prospective key witnesses before advising whether an action should be raised or defended. If he cannot do so then he should certainly do so before the closing of the record. Timeous and accurate precognoscing may save trouble and expense by indicating that the party should modify the case originally contemplated, or even should not risk going to proof but should seek to achieve a settlement.

15.10 Each witness should be precognosced separately and outwith the presence of the other witnesses. The precognition of one witness in the presence of another or others is no longer a ground of exclusion of the witnesses, but it is regarded as highly reprehensible and the court is likely to take an adverse view of the witnesses' credibility.[26]

15.11 The preparation of a satisfactory precognition requires considerable skill and care.[27] Each precognition should be headed with the name of the case; the witness's name, age, occupation, address and telephone number; and the date on which the precognition was taken. It then proceeds to explain, in the first person singular, who the witness is, indicating any relevant qualifications, employment history or experience, and then all the facts relevant to the case so far as these are within his personal knowledge. When interviewing the witness and framing the precognition, the precognoscer should keep the following comments[28] in view:

> "in a precognition you cannot be sure that you are getting what the potential witness has to say in a pure and undefiled form. It is filtered through the mind of another, whose job it is to put what he thinks the witness means into a form suitable for use in judicial proceedings. This process tends to colour the result. Precognoscers as a rule appear to be gifted with a measure of optimism which no amount of disillusionment can damp."

---

21 *Barrie v. Caledonian Ry* (1902) 5 F. 30.
22 *McPhee v. Glasgow Corporation*, 1910 1 S.L.T. 380.
23 Administration of Justice (Scotland) Act 1972, s. 1(1A): see paras 15.03 to 15.06.
24 *Barrie, supra*, at 38; *McPhee, supra*.
25 *McPhee, Henderson, supra*.
26 Macphail, *Evidence*, para. 24.11.
27 See Kearney, pp. 66–70.
28 *Kerr v. H.M. Advocate*, 1958 J.C. 14, *per* L.J.-C. Thomson at 19.

It is therefore of great importance that the precognition should state as accurately as possible just what the witness is and is not prepared to say in court. It should contain exhaustively all the facts of the case so far as the witness knows them, with all the circumstances fully detailed, and with complete accuracy as regards persons, places, dates and figures. It should never state as facts matters on which the witness indicates he is in doubt. It should generally exclude inferences which he has drawn, or hearsay which he has reported, except in so far as the making of the hearsay statement is in itself a fact.[29] It is often necessary for intelligibility that matters of doubt, inference or hearsay should be included in the precognition, but they should not be stated as facts and their nature should be made very clear. Thus, if the witness has drawn an inference of fact the precognition should clearly show that it is a matter of inference. In eliciting information from the witness the precognoscer should avoid leading questions, and should get from him all the points on which he is against the precognoscer's client, as well as those on which he is in the client's favour. It is important to make sure that he will stick to the latter points; some witnesses tell each precognoscer what they think he wants to hear. On vital matters, the precognoscer should ask the witness the same question in different ways, including such questions as a cross-examiner may be expected to ask. **15.12**

The precognition should be expressed in the first person singular and, as far as possible, in the witness's own words: a witness's vigorous, natural use of the Scottish tongue should not be pallidly reduced to stately anglicisms and euphemisms. If he uses technical or other terms which a reader of the precognition may not understand, their meaning should be indicated in brackets. Any misuse by the witness of legal terminology, such as "sale" or "purchase" in relation to a hire-purchase agreement, or "wages" in relation to drawings from a partnership, should be similarly noted, in order to remind or alert the draftsman not to use the witness's own words in the pleadings.[30] It may be necessary in the precognition to arrange his story in logical order, but his own words and phrases should be used. The witness is not normally asked to sign his precognition, and cannot be required to do so. If the precognoscer considers that the witness may be prejudiced, slow or easily confused, or if he has any other doubts about the value of his evidence, he should note his views at the end of the precognition or, if the precognition is to be seen by the witness, on a sheet attached to the file of precognitions. It is thought that it is unobjectionable to send the witness a copy of his precognition and ask him to check it and return it with any proposed corrections. **15.13**

Shortly before the proof, the witnesses of critical importance should be re-precognosced, in order to see what evidence they are now prepared to give in court, especially in the light of any developments on averment of the other party's case.[31] Where counsel has been instructed, the solicitor should carefully follow his advice in the note on the line of evidence[32] as to the further precognition of witnesses and other preparations. **15.14**

---

[29] Primary hearsay evidence is itself now, of course, generally admissible (Civil Evidence (Scotland) Act 1988, s. 2) but direct evidence is always preferable if it is available.

[30] Sheriff Principal Sir Allan G. Walker, "Written Pleadings" (1963) 79 Sc.L.Rev. 161 at pp. 163–164.

[31] Kearney, p. 102.

[32] See para. 12.22.

Use of precognition

15.15 **Refreshment of memory.** There appear to be two views on the question whether a witness should be allowed to read his precognition before he gives evidence. It may be thought, on the one hand, that to allow him to do so is to tutor him. On the other hand, if the object of a judicial inquiry is not to put witnesses through a memory test but to ascertain the truth, that object may be achieved by allowing a witness to refresh his memory of events which occurred years previously from a good precognition taken at a time reasonably close to the events in question. It is submitted that the latter course is unobjectionable.[33]

15.16 **Use of precognitions in court.** Precognitions are private documents, and are inadmissible in evidence. They cannot be recovered by diligence.[34] In court a witness cannot be examined as to whether he has made a statement on precognition different from his evidence in the witness-box.[35] Statements made solely on precognition by a witness who has subsequently died are inadmissible,[36] even though a statement by such a witness made in other circumstances would be admissible. The question whether the statement in question was made on precognition may depend on the circumstances in which it was made, and on a consideration of many decisions. Statements made on precognition are protected by absolute privilege.[37]

Expert witnesses

15.17 When the case has medical or other scientific aspects on which evidence is required, an expert witness or witnesses should be selected with care, having regard to the appositeness of their qualifications and experience, and should as soon as possible be instructed to provide a report or reports. Each expert should be provided with as much information as possible including, where appropriate, a copy of the pleadings and all the relevant productions. He should be told specifically the matters on which his opinion is sought, including the allegations made about these matters by the other side. His report should set out his qualifications and experience, the factual data on which he bases his views, his conclusions, and his reasons for discounting any allegations on scientific matters which have been made or may be made by the other side. The report should contain sufficient information to enable the party's advocate to cross-examine effectively any expert witness called by the other side. If the party's solicitor does not fully understand any aspect of the report, or considers that it should be elaborated or supplemented in any respect, he should not hesitate to write to or, preferably, speak to the expert and question him until he fully understands the import of the expert's evidence. Where counsel is instructed, it is proper and often most useful for the expert to attend a consultation with counsel. Any object forming the foundation of the expert's evidence must be lodged if it is practicable and convenient to do so.[38] Where necessary, evidence should be obtained which links any sample or other material examined by the expert with the other real

---

33 See Macphail, *Evidence*, paras 8.50–8.51.

34 *Ritchie v. Leith Docks Commissioners* (1902) 10 S.L.T. 395; *Anderson v. St Andrew's Ambulance Association*, 1942 S.C. 555 at 557.

35 *Kerr v. H.M. Advocate*, 1958 J.C. 14; Macphail, *Evidence*, paras 19.47–19.49.

36 *Thomson v. Jamieson*, 1986 S.L.T. 72; Walkers, *Evidence*, para. 372; Macphail, *Evidence*, paras 19.29–19.30.

37 *Watson v. McEwan* (1905) 7 F. (H.L.) 109; Macphail, *Evidence*, paras 24.24, S24.24.

38 *McGowan v. Belling & Co. Ltd*, 1983 S.L.T. 77.

evidence in the case. Court procedure for the recovery of documents which the expert may require to consider and for arranging inspections and examinations is considered below.[39]

Evidence on commission

As a rule, the oral evidence in a cause is led before the sheriff by witnesses who attend at the diet of proof at the court house. In certain circumstances, however, a witness's evidence may be taken by means of a commission and diligence. It is by commission and diligence that the court makes the whole or part of the evidence in an action, whether oral or documentary, available to the court for the decision of the case without requiring the attendance of witnesses or havers[40] before the sheriff. The court delegates to a commissioner the duty of taking the depositions of witnesses or havers upon oath or affirmation, and the commissioner thereafter reports to the court. The commission is the judicial warrant to the commissioner so to act; and it is accompanied by a diligence, which is a judicial warrant under which the witnesses and havers are cited to appear before the commissioner and may be compelled to attend.[41] The following paragraphs deal with commission and diligence to examine witnesses. There is no substantial difference in principle or procedure between a commission to take the evidence of witnesses and one for the recovery of documents, but there are specialties in connection with the latter which will be separately considered.[42] As to the former, a commission may be granted (i) to take evidence in danger of being lost, to lie *in retentis* or (ii) to take evidence after proof has been allowed. The circumstances in which a commission may be granted for each of these purposes, and the procedure common to both, will now be discussed. 15.18

Evidence to lie in retentis

Grounds for application. Evidence in danger of being lost may be taken to lie *in retentis*, that is, to be held back or laid aside until the proper time arrives for adducing it.[43] The sheriff may, upon the motion of any party, grant authority to a commissioner to take such evidence.[44] There is no reason why the sheriff should not appoint himself or another sheriff as commissioner, and in some cases it may be appropriate for him to do so. The rule places no restriction on the variety of reasons for the danger of loss of the evidence. The danger usually arises from the witness's extreme old age or dangerous sickness,[45] so that he is in danger of early death, or from the fact that he is obliged to go abroad. As to old age, it is customary to grant a commission when the witness is 70 years of age or over.[46] His age, if challenged, is proved by the production of a birth extract or equivalent document, and his sickness by a medical certificate,[47] the 15.19

---

[39] See paras 15.44 to 15.92.

[40] Havers are possessors of documents, whether parties to the cause or not.

[41] Bell, *Dictionary*, p. 199.

[42] paras 15.50 to 15.83.

[43] Trayner, pp. 274–275. For the history of this practice, see ***Boettcher v. Carron Co.*** (1861) 23 D. 322, *per* Lord Cowan at 325–326.

[44] OCR, r. 28.10(1)(b) and (2).

[45] Expression used in the A.S., July 10, 1839, s. 73.

[46] *Wilson v. Young* (1896) 4 S.L.T. 73.

[47] It is thought that the medical certificate need not bear the words "on soul and conscience": Court of Session Practice Note, June 6, 1968 (*Parliament House Book*, C-2002). Where a medical certificate was challenged a remit was made of consent to a doctor appointed by the court: *Lunn v. Watt*, 1911 2 S.L.T. 479.

documents being produced to the court when the commission is applied for.[48] A commission may be granted where the witness is to go abroad of necessity, whether in performance of a duty, or in the course of his employment[49] or his service with H.M. Forces,[50] or through poverty,[51] or perhaps for reasons of health[52]; but not for reasons of personal convenience, as where he is going abroad on holiday.[53]

15.20 **Application.** A motion to take evidence to lie *in retentis* may be made by any party any time after the commencement of the proceedings by the service of the initial writ.[54] If the emergency justifying the application occurs before the commencement of the proceedings, it is thought that application may be made to the Court of Session to grant a commission under the *nobile officium*.[55] The motion should specify the name and address of at least one proposed commissioner for approval and appointment.[56] It should also specify the name and address of the witness and the reasons for the application.[57] There should be lodged along with the motion any documents necessary to support it, such as birth extracts or medical certificates.

15.21 **Decision.** The grant or refusal of the application is a matter for the discretion of the sheriff. It is thought that the applicant must satisfy him that the evidence is in danger of being lost, and that it is desirable that it should be taken to lie *in retentis*. The sheriff would appear to be entitled to require specification of the matters in regard to which the evidence of the witness is desired. A commission has been refused where other witnesses were available to speak to these matters[58]; and where the witness was in the applicant's employment and he could arrange for the witness's attendance at the proof.[59] There is no absolute rule that a pursuer's evidence cannot be taken to lie *in retentis*: every case must be determined on its own special circumstances.[60] The sisting of a mandatary has been required before evidence to lie *in retentis* was taken from a pursuer resident abroad,[61] and from witnesses required by a defender resident in England.[62]

---

[48] Walkers, *Evidence*, para. 401(a).

[49] *Hansen v. Donaldson* (1873) 1 R. 237; *Galloway Water Power Co. v. Carmichael*, 1937 S.C. 135.

[50] *Grant v. Countess of Seafield*, 1926 S.C. 274 at 279, 280.

[51] *Anderson*, 1912 S.C. 1144.

[52] *Grant, supra*, at 279; *cf. Craig v. Walker*, 1930 S.N. 144.

[53] *Grant, supra*.

[54] In the Court of Session the rule governing the taking of a witness's evidence on commission (RCS, r. 35.11) is specifically stated to apply to "a case depending before the court" (RCS, r. 35.1). Although there is no specific provision to that effect in the OCR it is submitted that such can be implied.

[55] In *Galloway Water Power Co. v. Carmichael*, 1937 S.C. 135, the court granted a commission before commencement of arbitration proceedings: see Walkers, *Evidence*, para. 40(b).

[56] OCR, r. 28.10(2).

[57] Dobie, *Styles*, pp. 332–333.

[58] *Dudgeon v. Forbes* (1832) 10 S. 810.

[59] *Munn v. Macgregor* (1854) 16 D. 385.

[60] *Samson & Co. v. Hough* (1886) 13 R. 1154. See also *Robertson v. Robertson* (1897) 4 S.L.T. 358; *Anderson v. Morrison* (1905) 7 F. 561.

[61] *Hansen v. Donaldson* (1873) 1 R. 237; *Robertson v. Robertson* (1897) 4 S.L.T. 358.

[62] *Sandilands v. Sandilands* (1848) 10 D. 1091. A mandatary may now be required where a party resides, not in England but outside the United Kingdom: see paras 11.67 to 11.69.

Reservation. Evidence *in retentis* is taken under reservation of all pleas competent to the party against whom it is taken, including objections to jurisdiction and other preliminary pleas.[63] Other aspects of the procedure, and the use which may be made of the evidence at the proof, are considered below.[64] 15.22

Commission after proof allowed

Evidence may be taken by commission, in like manner as evidence to lie *in retentis*, of a witness— 15.23

(1) who is resident beyond the jurisdiction of the court; or
(2) who, although resident within the jurisdiction, resides at some place remote from the court; or
(3) who is unable to attend the diet of proof by reason of age, infirmity or sickness.[65]

The reference in rule 28.10(1)(a) to "the diet of proof" appears to indicate that procedure under that rule is appropriate where proof has been allowed. In any event it is not usual to grant a commission to take evidence before the allowance of proof, unless it is merely to lie *in retentis*. Evidence may also be taken on commission on a ground other than those stated above "on special cause shown".[66]

Grounds for application. *Necessity*. It appears that the party moving for the commission must satisfy the sheriff not only that the motion is justified on one or more of the grounds set out in rule 28.10(1), but also that the witness is a necessary witness for that party.[67] The latter ground should be supported by reference to the averments on record: it will not do to say that the averments will be added by amendment after the witness's evidence has been elicited.[68] On the other hand a commission may be refused where the witness is of primary importance for the determination of the issue between the parties, or where the party against whom the witness is to be adduced would be prejudiced by having the evidence taken on commission.[69] 15.24

Residence. It is thought that where the application is based only on the place of residence of the witness, a commission will not usually be granted if he is resident in Scotland[70] and would be able to attend the proof without inordinate trouble and expense, unless his evidence is in short compass or of secondary importance, or his credibility and reliability are unlikely to be serious issues. 15.25

---

[63] *Moreton v. McDonald* (1849) 11 D. 1417; *Laing v. Nixon* (1866) 4 M. 327; *Sheard v. Haldane* (1867) 5 M. 636; Dove Wilson, p. 277; Wallace, p. 289.
[64] paras 15.30 to 15.42.
[65] OCR, r. 28.10(1)(a).
[66] OCR, r. 28.10(1)(c).
[67] *Dudgeon v. Forbes* (1832) 10 S. 810; *Bank of Scotland v. Shakeshaft*, Sh. Pr. O'Brien, Dumbarton Sh. Ct, Dec. 29, 1977, unreported.
[68] *Bank of Scotland, supra.*
[69] *Grant v. Countess of Seafield*, 1926 S.L.T. 213 (sequel to 1926 S.C. 274). See also para. 15.28.
[70] As to the taking of evidence on commission of witnesses furth of Scotland, see paras 15.40 to 15.42.

15.26 *Sickness, age or infirmity*. As in an application to take evidence to lie *in retentis*, the motion should be supported by appropriate documents.[71] If an essential witness is ill prior to the proof, the proper procedure, unless the illness is chronic and there is no near prospect of recovery,[72] is to move for the discharge of the diet and the assigning of a new diet on a date when the witness will be fit to attend, and not to move for a commission. A commission to take the witness's evidence to lie *in retentis* pending his recovery may, however, be granted.[73]

15.27 *Mental illness*. A commission may be granted for the examination of a patient in a mental hospital, with an appropriate proviso or reservation, as that the commissioner should satisfy himself that the patient is mentally fit to be examined[74] or that the examination will not injuriously affect his health,[75] or under reservation of all questions as to the effect of his evidence.[76] The court will not, however, require a witness to submit to medical examination before giving evidence.[77] Where the state of the witness's mind is doubtful, it is for the commissioner to satisfy himself that he is a competent witness, and for the court on his report as to the witness's mental condition to decide whether he has acted rightly.[78] It is thought that the conditions of competency are similar to those for a child: whether the witness appears to be able to understand what he has seen or heard and to give an account of it, and to appreciate the duty to speak the truth[79]; the nature of the matters on which his evidence is sought,[80] and the effect of the examination upon him.[81] It seems unnecessary that he should understand the taking of an oath.[82]

15.28 *Special cause shown*. The granting of a commission to take evidence "on special cause shown" is an innovation introduced in the 1993 Ordinary Cause Rules.[83] The 1983 Rules used the words "other sufficient cause". It is debatable whether the change in terminology is of great significance, and it is suggested that the authorities on "other sufficient cause" would be equally relevant to the concept of "special cause shown". It is, of course, impossible exhaustively to define the circumstances which might amount to "special cause" but the following examples provide some idea of its scope. Thus a commission has been granted where there was reason to believe that delay and inconvenience might be occasioned in obtaining the evidence of the witnesses at the proof[84]; or where the parties agreed that a commission was appropriate[85]; or where there was a prima facie

---

[71] para. 15.20.
[72] *Anderson v. Morrison* (1905) 7 F. 561 (commission to take evidence of pursuer granted).
[73] *Gordon v. Orrok* (1849) 11 D. 1358.
[74] *Riddell v. Riddell* (1890) 18 R. 1.
[75] *Kilpatrick Parish Council v. Row Parish Council*, 1911 2 S.L.T. 32.
[76] *Tosh v. Ogilvy* (1873) 1 R. 254.
[77] *McIntyre v. McIntyre*, 1920 1 S.L.T. 207.
[78] *Riley v. McLaren* (1853) 16 D. 323.
[79] Dickson, para. 1543; *McIntyre v. McIntyre, supra*, at 208 ("capable of understanding an interrogation and giving testimony").
[80] *Buckie v. Kirk* (1907) 15 S.L.T. 98.
[81] *Tosh, Kilpatrick Parish Council, supra*.
[82] *H.M. Advocate v. Skene Black* (1887) 1 White 365. But see *contra*, *McNamara* (1866) Ark. 521, *H.M. Advocate v. Murray* (1866) 5 Irv. 232.
[83] The current Court of Session Rule also makes use of these words: RCS, r. 35.11(1)(c).
[84] *cf.* RCS, r. 35.11.
[85] *Malcolm v. Stewart* (1829) 7 S. 715; Maclaren, p. 1033; Maxwell, p. 272.

case of *penuria testium.*[86] The smallness of the amount at stake might not be sufficient cause where it was of importance that the sheriff should himself see and hear the witness.[87] Where a witness is of great importance, it appears that only strong reasons would amount to sufficient cause for his examination on commission.[88] In certain circumstances, however, even the evidence of a party to a case who was resident abroad has been taken on commission.[89]

Application. The motion for a commission[90] should be lodged at a date early enough to enable the commission to be executed in time for the evidence to be used at the proof if the motion is granted, and to enable the party to do his best to get the witness to be present at the proof if the motion is refused. It may be convenient that a commission for the party leading in the proof should be executed before the proof, and a commission for the other party after it. An application for a commission may be granted in the course of the proof, where it is made in a situation of emergency or sudden illness.[91] Where it is made in circumstances of which the party moving for the commission should have been aware before the commencement of the proof, he may be ordered to meet the expenses thereby occasioned.[92] In all cases the grant or refusal of the commission is within the discretion of the sheriff.[93] The witness is not entitled to appear or to be represented before the sheriff in order to make submissions relative to the motion.[94] **15.29**

Procedure

Interlocutor. If the sheriff grants a motion to take evidence on commission under rule 28.10(1), he pronounces an interlocutor which grants the commission and diligence, nominates the commissioner, specifies the names and addresses of the witnesses, appoints or dispenses with interrogatories, and appoints the depositions and productions to be transmitted to the sheriff clerk with the commissioner's report either before a certain date *or quam primum*. Any suitable person may be appointed as commissioner: usually a solicitor is appointed. There is no reason why a sheriff should not appoint himself or another sheriff as commissioner. The advantage of doing so when it is known which sheriff is to take the proof in the action is obvious. An interlocutor granting or refusing commission and diligence may be appealed against only with leave of the sheriff. **15.30**

Interrogatories. It used to be the case that a commission to take a witness's evidence was conducted on interrogatories unless the sheriff **15.31**

---

[86] *Maltman's Factor v. Cook* (1867) 5 M. 1076; Maclaren, p. 1033; Maxwell, p. 272.

[87] *Mackenzie v. British Linen Co.* (1879) 17 S.L.R. 241 ("special cause").

[88] *Western Ranches Ltd v. Nelson's Trs* (1898) 25 R. 527; *Grant v. Countess of Seafield*, 1926 S.L.T. 213 (sequel to 1926 S.C. 274).

[89] *Samson & Co. v. Hough* (1886) 13 R. 1154 (pursuer); *Henderson v. Henderson*, 1953 S.L.T. 270 (defender); *Morris v. Goldrich*, 1953 S.L.T. (Sh. Ct.) 43 (defender subject to jurisdiction by arrestment). See also para. 15.21.

[90] The motion should specify the name and address of at least one proposed commissioner: OCR, r. 28.10(2).

[91] *Stone v. Aberdeen Marine Insurance Co.* (1849) 11 D. 1041 at 1043 (note); *Campbell v. Henderson*, 1948 S.L.T. (Notes) 71.

[92] *Cecil v. Marchioness of Huntly* (1905) 13 S.L.T. 189. See also *Lyell v. Harthill Thistle Pipe Band* (1905) 21 Sh.Ct.Rep. 294.

[93] *Campbell v. Henderson*, 1948 S.L.T. (Notes) 71.

[94] *Bank of Scotland v. Shakeshaft*, Sh. Pr. O'Brien, Dumbarton Sh. Ct, Dec. 29, 1977, unreported. A haver is in a similar position: see para. 15.60.

dispensed with them.[95] However, the converse is now the case: a commission proceeds without interrogatories unless, on cause shown, the sheriff directs otherwise.[96] A commission without interrogatories is often described as "an open commission". Although commissions with interrogatories are now uncommon[97] the Ordinary Cause Rules contain provisions for them and it is appropriate that these should be examined. Interrogatories are written numbered questions to be put to the witness on behalf of the party obtaining the commission.[98] That party lodges draft interrogatories in process.[99] Any other party may lodge cross-interrogatories.[1] The other party cannot postpone preparation of the cross-interrogatories until the answers to the interrogatories have been lodged.[2] The interrogatories and cross-interrogatories are adjusted by the parties and when that stage has been completed, they are extended and returned to the sheriff clerk for approval by the sheriff and, in the event of any dispute as to their contents, for the sheriff to settle the matter.[3] At the diet at which the commission is executed, the commissioner reads the questions *seriatim* to the witness, and his replies to each question are numbered and recorded. The commissioner may put further questions to the witness and require him to make such additions and explanations as he thinks necessary. It has been observed that interrogatories and cross interrogatories, although satisfactory enough for obtaining certain types of evidence, are a very inadequate and sometimes wholly unsuccessful expedient for testing the evidence of a witness whose credibility and reliability are likely to be serious issues.[4]

15.32 **Procedure before diet.** *Commission with interrogatories.* In the case of a commission which is to proceed on interrogatories the party who obtained the commission must provide the commissioner with a copy of the pleadings (including any adjustments and amendments), the approved interrogatories and any cross-interrogatories and a certified copy of the interlocutor of his appointment.[5] That party must instruct the commissioner's clerk.[6] He is also responsible, in the first instance, for the fee of the commissioner and his clerk.[7] The commissioner, in consultation with the parties, fixes a diet for the execution of the commission.[8] Where the commissioner is not legally qualified in Scotland he should be given particulars of his duties and a skeleton form of report. Before the diet the clerk usually prepares the preamble of the report, narrating the place

---

[95] It may be noted that in the Court of Session there is still effectively a presumption in favour of interrogatories. The RCS, r. 35.11(10) provides that the court may "on the motion of any party and on cause shown dispense with interrogatories".

[96] OCR, r. 28.10(5).

[97] They are perhaps most commonly used, in order to save expense, to take the evidence of witnesses who are abroad. See, *e.g. Dexter & Carpenter v. Waugh & Robertson*, 1925 S.C. 28; *Henderson v. Henderson*, 1953 S.L.T. 270.

[98] Dobie, *Styles*, pp. 250–251.

[99] OCR, r. 28.11(1).

[1] OCR, r. 28.11(2).

[2] *Charteris v. Charteris*, 1967 S.C. 33.

[3] OCR, r. 28.11(3).

[4] *Nicolson v. Maclachlan and Brown*, 1985 S.L.T. 132. See also *Grant v. Countess of Seafield*, 1926 S.C. 274, *per* Lord Anderson at 280; *Barr v. British Transport Commission*, 1963 S.L.T. (Notes) 59; *Muirhead v. H.M. Advocate*, 1983 S.L.T. 545 at 548.

[5] OCR, r. 28.11(4)(a).

[6] OCR, r. 28.11(4)(b).

[7] OCR, r. 28.11(4)(c).

[8] OCR, r. 28.11(5).

and date of the diet, the granting of the warrant and the commissioner's acceptance and the appointment of the clerk.

Commission without interrogatories. Where interrogatories have been dispensed with the party who has moved for the commission must provide the commissioner with a copy of the pleadings (including any adjustments and amendments) and a certified copy of the interlocutor of his appointment.[9] That party (and *not* the commissioner) fixes a diet for the execution of the commission in consultation with the commissioner and every other party.[10] That party also instructs the commissioner's clerk and a shorthand writer.[11] He is responsible, in the first instance, for the fees of the commissioner, his clerk and the shorthand writer.[12] Before the diet the shorthand writer usually prepares the preamble of the report, narrating the place and date of the diet, the granting of the warrant and the commissioner's acceptance, the appointment of the clerk (and shorthand writer), the agreement of the parties to employ a shorthand writer and dispense with the signature of the witnesses to their depositions,[13] and the administration of the oath *de fideli.* **15.33**

Citation of witnesses. A certified copy of the interlocutor granting the commission is the warrant for citing the witnesses.[14] The rule relating to citation of witnesses for a proof applies to the citation of witnesses to attend a commission, with the exception of the provision that a witness is to be cited on a period of notice of seven days.[15] The reason for this is probably to allow for the possibility that a commission to take evidence may have to be arranged at short notice. However, wherever possible a witness for a commission should be given at least seven days' notice. As in the case of witnesses cited to attend a proof witnesses cited to attend a commission are liable to a penalty if they fail without reasonable cause to attend after being duly cited and being paid their travelling expenses if demanded.[16] If a witness fails to attend, letters of second diligence may be granted, and he may be liable for the expenses thereby incurred.[17] The sheriff may also grant warrant for the apprehension of the witness.[18] If the witness is ill or aged, citation may be unnecessary, and the diet may be held by arrangement at the place where the witness is residing or is a patient. **15.34**

Procedure at diet. At the diet, where the evidence is to be recorded in shorthand the commissioner administers the oath *de fideli administratione* to the shorthand writer,[19] who records the evidence by question and **15.35**

---

[9] OCR, r. 28.12(1)(a).
[10] OCR, r. 28.12(1)(b).
[11] OCR, r. 28.12(1)(c).
[12] OCR, r. 28.12(1)(d).
[13] *Laird v. Scott*, 1914 1 S.L.T. 368 at 369.
[14] OCR, r. 28.10(3).
[15] OCR, r. 28.15 applies OCR, r. 29.7 to commissions with the exception of para. 4 thereof (which relates to the period of notice and also prescribes the use of Forms G12 and G13).
[16] OCR, rr. 28.15 and 29.10(2): see paras 16.04 to 16.07.
[17] OCR, rr. 28.15 and 29.9: see paras 16.12 to 16.14, and *Collins v. N.B. Banking Co.* (1851) 13 D. 541, *National Exchange Co. v. Drew & Dick* (1858) 20 D. 837, *per* Lord Deas at 840 (both cases regarding havers).
[18] OCR, rr. 28.15 and 29.10(1): see para. 16.15.
[19] OCR, r. 28.10(4)(a). The customary form of oath is: "I do swear that I will faithfully discharge the duties of clerk and shorthand writer to this commission. So help me God."

answer.[20] The commissioner also dictates the preamble of the report, if it has not already been prepared.[21] The commissioner is present throughout the proceedings[22] and controls the examination of the witnesses much as the sheriff does at a proof.[23] All parties are entitled to be present and represented at the execution of a commission without interrogatories.[24] The following extracts from the recommendations of the Court of Session to commissioners[25] remain of value:

> "[A]s the Commissioners are to act in this matter under the special authority of the Court, it is recommended to them to exercise their own judgment, in the manner of conducting the proof, and particularly to allow no matter to be introduced which is not pertinent to the cause, nor any unnecessary pleading or altercation about the competency of questions, or the admissibility of witnesses, and to check the parties, if they attempt to load the proceedings with unnecessary evidence, or superfluous matter of any kind. It is likewise recommended to them to attend to the rules of evidence, and to give their own deliverances, either *viva voce* or in writing, as they see cause, upon any debate which may occur, it being always understood that their whole proceedings shall be subject to the after consideration of the Court, upon application made by either party; in order to which the Commissioner himself, or those acting for the parties, may take such notes, on a separate paper, as they think proper, for the due information of the Court, but nothing shall enter the report but what the Commissioner himself may think material . . .
>
> That, in the course of taking the depositions, if it shall appear to the Commissioner that any witness is not disposed to tell the truth, or behaves in any unusual manner, it is recommended to him to take a note thereof at the time, by way of assistance to his memory, in case he should be appealed to on that subject, by either of the parties when the proof comes to be advised; or, if he thinks proper, he may annex the same to his report of the proof."

15.36 The commissioner administers the oath or affirmation[26] to each witness. If the examination takes place on interrogatories, the commissioner administers them to the witness, and his answers are taken down in writing. His deposition is then read over to him and signed at the foot of each page by him and by the commissioner, who adds to his signature the word "Commissioner". They should authenticate any marginal addition by writing their forenames at one side of such addition and their surnames at the other.[27] If the witness cannot write, that should be noted in the deposition. If interrogatories have been dispensed with, the witness is examined, cross-examined and re-examined by the parties' advocates, as at a proof.[28] Whether interrogatories have been dispensed with or not, the

---

20 See para. 16.55.
21 See para. 15.33.
22 *Jaffray v. Murray* (1830) 8 S. 667.
23 See para. 16.39.
24 OCR, r. 28.12(2).
25 A.S., March 11, 1800, ss. 4, 7, made perpetual by A.S., June 22, 1809 (see Alexander's *Abridgement*, pp. 117, 119). See also *Lockyer v. Sinclair* (1846) 8 D. 582, interlocutor at 627.
26 OCR, r. 28.10(4)(b), Forms G14 and G15; see paras 16.62 to 16.64.
27 *Elrick v. Elrick*, 1973 S.L.T. (Notes) 68.
28 See paras 16.70 to 16.79.

commissioner may put any questions he considers necessary. It is his duty to give the witness any necessary warnings, as that he need not answer any question the reply to which may be incriminating.[29] He should note the credibility and demeanour of each witness, and may express an opinion upon his credibility for the guidance of the sheriff who has to try the case.[30] In the interlocutor granting the commission he may be specially directed to report on the demeanour and credibility of the witnesses if he sees cause to do so.[31] Objections to the admissibility of evidence are recorded and disposed of in the same way as at a proof.[32] At a commission it is often desirable to repel objections under reservation of all questions of competency and relevancy, leaving it to the sheriff to rule on the objection. If the examination cannot be completed in one day, a short note of adjournment is made and signed by the commissioner and clerk, and on re-assembling a short preamble recites the adjourned diet.

Report of commission. Where a date is fixed by the interlocutor the commission must be reported within the time specified. Failure to report before the day fixed may be held to denote an abandonment of the commission. The time may be prorogated on cause shown, on application to the court before the period expires. The report contains the preamble[33]; the depositions of the witnesses, or the extended shorthand notes of their evidence certified by the shorthand writer; and an inventory of any productions founded on by the witnesses other than those already lodged in process. Such new productions should be initialled and numbered by the commissioner. The commissioner signs the report at the end of the narrative, the extended shorthand notes, and any inventory. The commissioner sends to the sheriff clerk the report of the commission together with any document produced by the witness and an inventory thereof.[34] Not later than the day after he has received the report and other documents the sheriff clerk must intimate receipt of them to all parties to the action.[35] The report must be lodged in process by the party who obtained the commission.[36] Although in the interlocutor granting the commission the evidence may be ordered to be sealed up,[37] it is made available to the parties, who are entitled to make copies.[38] **15.37**

Use of report at proof

If the witness becomes available to attend the proof, the evidence he gave before the commissioner cannot be used as his evidence,[39] but it is available as evidence in so far as it tends to reflect on the witness's **15.38**

---

[29] Dickson, para. 1759; *Roger v. Roger* (1896) 6 S.L.T. 233.

[30] *Ferguson v. Ferguson*, 1936 S.C. 808, *per* L.J.-C. Aitchison at 810.

[31] *Scott v. Scott*, 1913 2 S.L.T. 278.

[32] OCR, r. 29.18(13) applying the other provisions of r. 29.18 (recording of evidence at proof) to the recording of evidence at a commission; paras 16.84 to 16.88.

[33] para. 15.33.

[34] OCR, rr. 28.11(6) (commission with interrogatories: this rule does not actually mention a report as such, only "the executed interrogatories"); 28.12(3) (open commission).

[35] OCR, rr. 28.11(7) (commission with interrogatories); 28.12(4) (open commission).

[36] OCR, rr. 28.11(8) (commission with interrogatories: this rule mentions both the report and the executed interrogatories and cross-interrogatories); 28.12(5) (open commission).

[37] Maclaren, p. 1042. This style of interlocutor appears not to be generally followed in modern sheriff court practice.

[38] The view that the evidence should lie *in retentis* and not be available to the parties until the proof (*Duke of Argyll v. Duchess of Argyll*, 1963 S.L.T. (Notes) 42) has not been adopted: Macphail, *Evidence*, para. 24.49.

[39] OCR, r. 28.13(3).

credibility,[40] whether favourably or unfavourably.[41] If the witness is not available to attend the proof then the evidence taken on commission may be used as the evidence of that witness subject to all questions of relevancy and admissibility,[42] but a party wishing to use the report of the commission as evidence must expressly make it part of his case at the proof,[43] and the notes of evidence should record that he has done so.[44] A party may use the evidence obtained on commission even though it was obtained at the instance of another party.[45] Any party may state an objection to the use of such evidence at the proof, and the sheriff determines the objection.[46] Evidence taken on commission for one diet of proof may be used at a subsequent diet[47] and, at least in certain circumstances, at a proof in a subsequent action arising out of the same circumstances.[48]

Expenses

15.39 The expenses of a commission are usually part of the expenses in the cause. Where, however, the witness is examined at the proof, the expenses of executing the commission may not be allowed, since no party is entitled to throw costs incurred by him in connection with litigation upon his opponent unless he can show that they were incurred upon reasonable necessity for the conduct of the case. Each such case must be considered on its own circumstances, and the matter is one with which the auditor in his discretion is peculiarly fitted to deal.[49] Similarly, expenses may not be allowed where no proof is ultimately allowed.[50] They may, however, be allowed where proof is allowed and a commission to take the evidence of an important witness is returned unexecuted, all reasonable steps to execute it having failed.[51] The commissioner is entitled to a fee. The party who obtained the commission is, in the first instance, responsible for this fee.[52] The solicitor for the party obtaining the commission is personally liable therefor,[53] and should pay it at the time when it is incurred. It has been stated that the commissioner may retain his report until he has received his fee,[54] but that course may not be strictly correct where the interlocutor granting the commission has appointed him to report *quam primum*: it is thought that in such a case the report should be lodged and the fact of non-payment reported to the sheriff, who may in an appropriate case intimate that any decree in favour of the party obtaining the commission will not be extractable until the fee is paid. In the last resort the commissioner may apply to the sheriff, by motion in the process, for

---

[40] *Forrest v. Low's Trs*, 1907 S.C. 1240. In *Webster v. Simpson's Motors*, 1967 S.L.T. 287, the circumstances in which the report came to be used at the proof do not appear from the report.

[41] Civil Evidence (Scotland) Act 1988, s. 3.

[42] OCR, r. 28.13(1).

[43] *Cameron v. Woolfson*, 1918 S.C. 190.

[44] Lewis, p. 140.

[45] OCR, r. 28.13(4).

[46] OCR, r. 28.13(2).

[47] OCR, r. 28.13(1) provides that evidence taken on commission may be used at *any* proof of the cause.

[48] *Hogg v. Frew*, 1951 S.L.T. 397.

[49] *Speirs v. Caledonian Ry*, 1921 S.C. 889; *Webster v. Simpson's Motors*, 1967 S.L.T. 287.

[50] *North of Scotland Bank Ltd v. Mackenzie*, 1925 S.L.T. 352; *Gilchrist v. National Cash Register Co. Ltd*, 1929 S.C. 272. *Cf. Burn-Murdoch's Trs v. Thomson's Trs* (1908) 15 S.L.T. 721 (expenses allowed to defenders where case abandoned).

[51] *Napier v. Leith* (1860) 22 D. 1262.

[52] OCR, rr. 28.11(4)(c) (commission on interrogatories) and 28.12(1)(c) (open commission).

[53] *Watson v. Cowan*, 1913 1 S.L.T. 435.

[54] Fyfe, p. 225; *Encyclopaedia*, iii, para. 1349; Dobie, p. 210.

decree for the amount of his fee and expenses, including the fee of the clerk; or he may raise an action for payment.[55] The sheriff may remit his account to the auditor for taxation.[56]

Evidence of witnesses furth of Scotland

The sheriff court has no power to cite witnesses furth of Scotland to attend a diet in a civil action in the sheriff court,[57] but a party may apply to the court for the witness's evidence to be taken on commission or by letter of request. 15.40

Witnesses in England or Northern Ireland. The sheriff may appoint a commissioner to take the evidence of a witness in England or Northern Ireland, and the attendance of the witness before the commissioner there may be compelled by an order of the High Court, or of the High Court of Justice of Northern Ireland. Such an order may be obtained upon an application to that court made in pursuance of a letter of request issued by the sheriff court.[58] The sheriff court may issue such a letter of request upon consideration of an application made by minute, duly lodged and intimated, and after allowing the other parties to the action to lodge answers and hearing any objections.[59] 15.41

Witnesses furth of the United Kingdom. If the witness resides in a country furth of the United Kingdom, it is advisable to ascertain whether there is an International Convention providing for the taking of evidence in that country for the purpose of civil proceedings in the courts of the United Kingdom. The United Kingdom has made a number of bilateral Conventions with other countries on the subject, while the Hague Convention on the Taking of Evidence Abroad in Civil or Commercial Matters makes provision for the taking of evidence abroad in such matters.[60] It is impossible to list here the countries to which these Conventions apply, or the various procedures which are permitted in each. Any such list would in any event be subject to alteration. It is suggested that the solicitor for a party seeking to take evidence abroad should apply for information to the Foreign and Commonwealth Office. If the witness is in a country with which no Convention exists, an ordinary commission to take evidence before a commissioner appointed by the court may be appropriate where the foreign state does not object to the operation of such commissions within its territory[61] and where the witnesses may be relied upon to attend voluntarily. If such reliance cannot be placed on the witnesses, or if for other reasons an ordinary commission would be inappropriate, the party seeking the witness's evidence may apply by minute to the sheriff for a letter of request addressed to the judge or judges of the foreign tribunal within whose jurisdiction the witness is residing.[62] Along with 15.42

---

[55] *McLachlan v. Flowerdew* (1851) 13 D. 1345; *Menzies v. Baird*, 1912 1 S.L.T. 84; *Watson v. Cowan*, 1913 1 S.L.T. 435.

[56] *Menzies, supra.*

[57] *Lawson v. Swan National Car Rental Ltd*, Sh. Pr. Dick, Glasgow Sh. Ct, Sept. 29, 1985, unreported.

[58] Evidence (Proceedings in Other Jurisdictions) Act 1975, ss. 1–4, as amended.

[59] OCR, r. 28.14(3). See para. 15.42.

[60] See *Practical Handbook on the Operation of the Hague Convention of 18 March 1970 on the Taking of Evidence Abroad in Civil or Commercial Matters* (Hague Conference on Private International Law, 1984).

[61] *Lawson v. Donaldson* (1893) 10 Sh.Ct.Rep. 110.

[62] OCR, r. 28.14.

the minute there must be lodged the proposed letter of request.[63] The minute and letter must be respectively in Forms G16 and G17 in Appendix 1 to the Ordinary Clause Rules.[64] The normal procedure for minutes is followed,[65] and answers may be lodged by any party objecting. Interrogatories and cross-interrogatories may be lodged and adjusted as in the case of a commission in terms of rule 28.11.[66] It is a condition of a letter of request being granted that the solicitor for the applicant, or the applicant himself if he is unrepresented, is personally liable in the first instance for the whole expenses which may become due and payable in respect of the letter of request to the court or tribunal obtaining the evidence and to any witness who may be examined for that purpose.[67] The applicant's solicitor, or the applicant if he is unrepresented, must consign into court such sum as the sheriff thinks fit in respect of these expenses.[68] Unless the court or tribunal to which a letter of request is addressed is in a country or territory where English is an official language or in relation to which the sheriff clerk certifies that no translation is required, the applicant must, before the issue of the letter of request, lodge in process a translation of the letter and any interrogatories and cross-interrogatories into the official language of the country concerned.[69] When the letter of request is issued, it is sent, together with any interrogatories and cross-interrogatories as adjusted and the translations (if any) of the various documents, by the sheriff clerk to the Foreign and Commonwealth Office or to such other person and in such manner as directed by the sheriff.[70]

Evidence by affidavit

15.43 Until the coming into effect of the Civil Evidence (Scotland) Act 1988 affidavit evidence was not generally admissible in any defended action in the sheriff court.[71] Section 2(1) of the 1988 Act provides: "(1) In any civil proceedings . . . a statement made by a person otherwise than in the course of the proof shall be admissible as evidence of any matter contained in the statement of which direct oral evidence by that person would be admissible". The Ordinary Cause Rules provide for an application to be made to the court for the evidence of a witness to be received by way of affidavit evidence.[72] Application is made by motion and the sheriff "may make such order as he thinks fit".[73] There are conflicting decisions on the question whether the court has a discretion to refuse to accept affidavit evidence. In *Ebraham v. Ebraham*[74] Lord Caplan sitting in the Outer House held that the

---

[63] OCR, r. 28.14(3).
[64] *ibid.*
[65] OCR, Chap. 14. See paras 5.56 to 5.71.
[66] OCR, r. 28.14(6).
[67] OCR, r. 28.14(4).
[68] *ibid.*
[69] OCR, r. 28.14(5).
[70] OCR, r. 28.14(6).
[71] In terms of the OCR 1983, r. 72(1) affidavit evidence was admissible in opposed applications for orders under the Matrimonial Homes (Family Protection) (Scotland) Act 1981. The same rule provided that affidavit evidence was also admissible in undefended actions of divorce, separation and declarator of parentage, non-parentage, legitimacy, legitimation or illegitimacy. The present OCR contain similar provisions for affidavit evidence in certain undefended family actions: OCR, r. 33.28.
[72] OCR, r. 29.3(1).
[73] *ibid.*
[74] 1989 S.L.T. 808.

Rule of the Court of Session then in force[75] conferred on a judge a discretion to refuse to admit affidavit evidence where it would be inappropriate to do so because the evidence concerned related to critical matters in the case. In *Smith v. Alexander Baird Ltd*[76] Lord Cameron of Lochbroom, again sitting in the Outer House, while not specifically disagreeing with Lord Caplan, held that affidavit evidence should be admitted even though it related to a matter which was controversial. In *McVinnie v. McVinnie*[77] Sheriff Macphail, looking to the terms of the 1983 Ordinary Cause Rules,[78] held that he had no discretion to refuse to admit affidavit evidence. He gave it as his opinion that this would also be the case under the 1993 Rules. In *Lobban v. Philip*[79] Sheriff Principal Risk declined to follow the decision in *McVinnie*, holding that a sheriff had a discretion to refuse to admit affidavit evidence if he considered it inappropriate to do so. In the most recent case on the matter[80] Lord McFadyen, sitting in the Outer House, approved of and followed Sheriff Macphail's decision in *McVinnie*. It appears, however, that he was not referred to *Lobban*. It is submitted that the views of Sheriff Macphail and Lord Macfadyen are to be preferred and that a sheriff has no discretion to refuse to admit affidavit evidence.[81] If any part of such evidence is of doubtful competency or relevancy it should be admitted under reservation of all such questions.[82]

II. Documentary and Real Evidence

The preservation and recovery of documentary and real evidence should be one of the practitioner's primary considerations from the moment that litigation is contemplated. Writings contemporaneous with the events in issue are often of the highest evidential value, and should be obtained and carefully scrutinised and preserved. It is also of importance to obtain the original and complete versions of all documents of importance. When the originals exist, copies are not in general admissible as evidence in the absence of agreement,[83] unless the party has exhausted his power to recover the originals[84]; and it is unwise to neglect to obtain the originals in the hope that agreement will be reached. Once all the relevant documents have been obtained and examined, responsible practitioners usually agree as many of them as possible, but preparation should always be made on the assumption that all the necessary primary documentary and real evidence will have to be not only lodged but formally proved. Real evidence, like documentary evidence, should be obtained as soon as possible and carefully preserved. If the condition of any machine, vehicle or site is of a transitory nature it should be appropriately recorded, as by photographs, film, plans or experts' reports.[85] 15.44

[75] RCS, r. 108A. The present Court of Session rule (RCS, r. 36.8) is similar in terms to r. 108A and is much more elaborate than OCR, r. 29.3(1).
[76] 1993 S.C.L.R. 563.
[77] 1995 S.L.T. (Sh. Ct.) 81.
[78] 1983 OCR, r. 72A. This rule was in similar terms to those of RCS, r. 108A.
[79] 1995 S.C.L.R. 1104.
[80] *Glasser v. Glasser*, 1997 S.L.T. 456.
[81] See the editor's commentary to *Lobban v. Philip* at 1995 S.C.L.R. 1110.
[82] *McVinnie v. McVinnie*, 1995 S.L.T. (Sh. Ct.) 81, *per* Sheriff Macphail at 85C–D.
[83] See paras 16.24, 16.30.
[84] *Caledonian Ry v. Symington*, 1912 S.C. 1033.
[85] See Kearney, pp. 71–72.

15.45 Where the material documentary and real evidence is already in the possession of the party's solicitor it should simply be preserved, submitted to experts for reports where appropriate, and timeously lodged, unless the court at an earlier stage has ordered it to be produced by one of the methods about to be described. Where such evidence is not in the client's own hands, it is often possible for it to be obtained, or for inspections and other examinations to be carried out, by agreement with the other party or with third parties, without resorting to legal procedure.[86] The remainder of this chapter is concerned with the recovery by legal procedure of documentary and real evidence which is not in the client's own hands. Documents and other materials to which he has a right of ownership or possession may be recovered by him in an action of delivery, which is discussed elsewhere.[87] Documents to which he has no such right, which are not in his hands, and to which he requires access as a party may under certain conditions be recovered by formal procedure in the action in which he is a party, whether they are in the hands of his opponent in the action or in the hands of third parties. Since the opponent may be compelled to produce writings and other materials in his custody upon which the proof of his adversary's averments depends,[88] such recovery forms one of the few exceptions to the adversarial character of our system of procedure. It assists parties and the court to discover the truth, and by doing so it not only helps towards a just determination, but saves expense: a party who recovers timeously a document or other material fatal to his case can save himself and others the vexation, delay and expense of further litigation.[89]

15.46 Where the documents are in the hands of a party to the action, the court may order that party to produce them, either where he has founded on them in his pleadings in terms of rule 21.1(1),[90] or in terms of rule 21.1(2).[91] An alternative method of recovery where the documents required are in the hands of a party, the only method where they are in the hands of third parties, and in practice the usual method whether they are in the hands of a party or of third parties, is recovery by commission and diligence or by a frequently used optional alternative procedure. These procedures may be invoked only after the commencement of the action, and apply only to documents.[92] Both before and after the commencement of the action, however, the court may order the inspection, photography, preservation, custody and detention not only of documents but also of other property (including, where appropriate, land) under section 1 of the Administration of Justice (Scotland) Act 1972. There are special rules and practices relative to entries in bankers' books, original documents in public records, notes of evidence and productions in another process, medical examinations and blood tests. Each of those matters will now be discussed, and finally the effect of irregular recovery will be noticed. The lodging of productions for the proof is considered in a later chapter.[93]

---

[86] Kearney, pp. 74–76.
[87] para. 21.78.
[88] Ersk., IV, i, 52; *Somervell v. Somervell* (1900) 8 S.L.T. 84.
[89] *Air Canada v. Secretary of State for Trade* [1983] 2 A.C. 394, *per* Lord Scarman at pp. 445–446.
[90] See paras 15.47, 15.48.
[91] *ibid.*
[92] *Mactaggart v. MacKillop*, 1938 S.L.T. 559.
[93] paras 16.18 to 16.27.

Compulsory production of documents by order of court

Documents founded on in pleadings

Any document founded on by a party or adopted as incorporated in his **15.47**
pleadings must, so far as in his possession or within his control, be lodged in process by him as a production.[94] If the document concerned is founded on or adopted in the initial writ, it must be lodged at the time when the initial writ is returned.[95] If it is founded on or adopted in a minute, defences, counterclaims or answers, it must be lodged at the time of lodging that part of process.[96] When founded on or adopted in an adjustment to the pleadings it must be lodged at the time when that adjustment is intimated to any other party.[97] These provisions are without prejudice to the power of the sheriff to order any production of any document or to grant a commission and diligence for recovery of it.[98] In the event of a party failing timeously to lodge a document founded on or adopted by him in his pleadings he may be found liable in the expenses of any order for production or recovery of it obtained by any other party.[99] The object of the foregoing provisions appears to be to give to each party an opportunity to see, before the record is closed, the documents founded on in the pleadings of the other parties. The rule is, however, strictly limited to such documents.[1] Accordingly, the documents which a party may be required to produce in terms of the rule are those which form the foundation of his own case, not those which form the foundation of his opponent's case, or which may be required only *in modum probationis*, that is, for the purposes of the proof. Documents required for the latter purpose may be recovered by commission and diligence after the closing of the record.[2]

Ordering of production of documents by sheriff

Under the 1993 Ordinary Cause Rules there is no specific power given **15.48**
to a sheriff to order the production of documents. This was not the case under the 1983 Rules where a power was conferred on the sheriff "to order production of documents at any stage of the cause".[3] There can, however, be no doubt that the sheriff has a residuary power to order production and this is specifically preserved under the 1993 Rules.[4]

Claims for aliment or financial provision

In an action for aliment, or in an action which includes a claim for an **15.49**
order for financial provision or a claim for interim aliment, the court may order either party to provide details of his resources or those relating to a child or incapax on whose behalf he is acting.[5]

---

94 OCR, r. 21.1(1).
95 OCR, r. 21.1(1)(a).
96 OCR, r. 21.1(1)(b).
97 OCR, r. 21.1(1)(c).
98 OCR, r. 21.1(2).
99 OCR, r. 21.2.
1 *Western Bank v. Baird* (1863) 2 M. 127 at 133, 136; *Wright v. Valentine* (1910) 26 Sh.Ct.Rep. 26, 151; *Cameron v. Ferrier* (1913) 29 Sh.Ct.Rep. 125; *Reavis v. Clan Line Steamers*, 1926 S.C. 215; *Thomson v. Watson Ltd* (1943) 61 Sh.Ct.Rep. 67.
2 See paras 15.58, 15.59.
3 1983 OCR, r. 80.
4 OCR, r. 21.1(2) which provides that the rule requiring lodging of a document which is founded on or adopted as incorporated by a party is "without prejudice to any power of the sheriff to order the production of any document".
5 Family Law (Scotland) Act 1985, s. 20.

Recovery of documents by commission and diligence

15.50 The nature of commission and diligence has already been explained.[6] A commission and diligence for the recovery of documents is allowed in order that the court may be put in possession of documentary evidence bearing upon the issues of fact which have to be determined,[7] the documents being made available by order upon the havers, who are the possessors of the documents, whether parties to the cause or not. An application for a commission and diligence to recover documents is made by motion to the sheriff in any action depending before him.[8]

Object of recovery

15.51 A commission and diligence to recover documents under rule 28.2 may be granted at two distinct stages of procedure. Before the record is closed, it may be granted in order to enable a party to make more specific a case which he has already stated, or to answer the averments or calls of his opponent.[9] After the record is closed, it may be granted in order to enable him to recover for the purposes of the proof documents which have a bearing on the averments remitted to proof.[10] In no circumstances, however, will the court at any stage grant a "fishing" diligence[11] for the recovery of documents which a party hopes will disclose material for a case which he has not yet averred on record. A diligence to enable a party to make a proposed amendment more specific has been refused.[12] There is, however, a weakness in this system. After the record is closed, a party may by commission and diligence recover documents ostensibly for the purposes of the proof, which in fact enable him to amend, not only to make his averments on record more specific, but also to make a new case.

Documents which may be recovered

15.52 Although rule 28.2, unlike its predecessor,[13] makes no express reference to relevancy, it is well established that the court will not grant authority for the recovery of any document unless it can be demonstrated that the document has some relevance to the depending case. Where a commission and diligence is sought after the record is closed, the purpose of the recovery is to enable the party to prove his case, and the facts which he is entitled to prove are determined by his averments on record. A commission and diligence will not, therefore, be granted unless the documents will, or at least may, have a bearing on the averments remitted to proof.[14] That is not, however, a complete statement of the test of recoverability,

---

[6] para. 15.18.

[7] *Paterson v. Paterson*, 1919 1 S.L.T. 12. Real evidence is not recoverable by commission and diligence: *Mactaggart v. MacKillop*, 1938 S.L.T. 559.

[8] OCR, rr. 28.1(1), 28.2(1).

[9] See para. 15.58.

[10] See para. 15.59.

[11] "Fishing diligence" is a venerable expression: see, *e.g. Mackintosh v. Macqueen* (1828) 6 S. 784.

[12] *Thomson v. Gordon* (1869) 7 M. 687.

[13] 1983 OCR, r. 78(3) provided that the sheriff could grant commission and diligence for the recovery of such documents "as he shall deem relevant to the cause".

[14] Walkers, p. 319, para. 288, citing *British Publishing Co. Ltd v. Hedderwick & Sons* (1892) 19 R. 1008.

which is difficult to formulate. The Sheriffs Walker[15] discuss the matter in these terms:

> "It is thought that the rule justified by the decisions can be stated most precisely in negative form. A document is not recoverable if it has not been communicated to or by one of the parties and if it can be used only to provide material for the examination in chief or in cross of a witness who is not a party. To state the rule more positively, and at the same time comprehensively, is more difficult, but it is thought that it may be stated thus. Subject to confidentiality and relevancy, a document is recoverable if it is a deed granted by or in favour of a party or his predecessor in title, or a communication sent to, or by or on behalf of, a party, or a written record kept by or on behalf of a party. The distinction between what is and what is not recoverable by diligence has been assimilated to the distinction between documents which, both in the Court of Session and in the sheriff court, must be lodged in process before the proof and those which may be produced for the first time at the proof. Although a document in the second category is not in general recoverable by diligence, a witness who has it in his possession may be cited to bring it with him to the proof."

To the qualifications of confidentiality and relevancy which are prefixed to the learned authors' positive statement of the rule there may be added the privilege of havers against self-incrimination, and the withholding or non-disclosure of information on the grounds of public interest. Documents which may be produced for the first time at the proof, which are referred to in the final sentences of the quotation, are those written by a witness who is not a party and used merely to test the credibility of that witness, or to refresh his memory.[16] The learned authors' work should be consulted for a full discussion of the various grounds on which documents may not be recovered.[17] The following paragraphs merely illustrate the practical operation of the rule by reference to some of its qualifications and some of the categories of documents which are, and are not, recoverable.[18]

Relevance. Relevance as a qualification of recoverability signifies relevance to the facts averred in the pleadings. There is no rule that the documents sought to be recovered should be admissible as evidence.[19] The question of their admissibility may be raised and decided at the proof when a party seeks to adduce them in evidence. Nor may a diligence be refused on the ground that the averments remitted to probation are irrelevant or of doubtful relevancy.[20] An application for the recovery of documents which are not relevant to the case which has been pleaded, but which it is expected will be relevant to the case which it is hoped to make with the assistance of those documents, is known as a "fishing" or **15.53**

---

[15] Walkers, p. 321, para. 289(b).

[16] Walkers, p. 330, para. 300(b).

[17] Walkers, pp. 369–371, para. 345 (incrimination), Chap. 31 (confidentiality).

[18] For a full citation of authority, see Walkers, pp. 318–326.

[19] *Admiralty v. Aberdeen Steam Trawling and Fishing Co. Ltd*, 1909 S.C. 335, *per* L.P. Dunedin at 340, Lord Kinnear at 343; *Wheatley v. Anderson*, 1927 S.C. 133, *per* L.J.-C. Alness at 142; *Black v. Bairds & Dalmellington*, 1939 S.C. 427, *per* L.J.-C. Aitchison at 478–479; *Young v. National Coal Board*, 1957 S.C. 99, *per* Lord Blades at 108; *Johnston v. South of Scotland Electricity Board*, 1968 S.L.T. (Notes) 7.

[20] *Duke of Hamilton's Trs v. Woodside Coal Co.* (1897) 24 R. 294.

speculative diligence,[21] and will be refused.[22] The sheriff is entitled to discriminate between averments which are, and are not, crucial, and to exercise his discretion as to the length to which the recovery of documents should go, notwithstanding that a party's whole averments have been remitted to proof.[23]

15.54 **Confidentiality.** As a general rule, communications passing between a client and his professional legal adviser for professional purposes are irrecoverable on the ground of confidentiality, the privilege of refusing to disclose being that of the client.[24] The general rule is superseded at common law only where fraud or some other illegal act is alleged against a party and where his professional legal adviser has been directly concerned in the carrying out of the transaction which is the subject-matter of inquiry.[25] There is no confidentiality where the existence of the relationship of professional legal adviser and client, or the extent of the adviser's authority, is in issue.[26] A further general rule is that no party can recover from his opponent material which the opponent has made in preparing his own case.[27] Thus, communications to or by a litigant in connection with his investigations into an accident, an alleged breach of contract, a consistorial dispute or other event giving rise to the action are, generally speaking, confidential. By an important exception to that general rule, reports by an employee present at the time of an accident, made to his employer at or about the time of the accident, are not confidential.[28] Another general rule is that private documents will be protected from recovery as far as possible. The court will exercise its discretion to refuse to order a third party to produce private documents containing relevant information if the information has been, or can be, obtained from other sources which do not involve disclosing private information.[29] Communications between husband and wife are not treated as confidential in actions concerned with the conduct of the spouses towards each other.[30]

15.55 **Public interest immunity.** Objection may be taken by a minister of the Crown to the recovery of documents on the ground that recovery would be contrary to the public interest. In considering such an objection the test to be applied is whether the objection is outweighed by the public interest in the administration of justice not being frustrated.[31] This complex branch of the law has already been noticed.[32] Public interest as a ground

---

21 *Fife C.C. v. Thoms* (1898) 25 R. 1097; *Earl of Morton v. Fleming*, 1921 1 S.L.T. 205.

22 See para. 15.51.

23 *Macqueen v. Mackie & Co. Distillers*, 1920 S.C. 544.

24 Walkers, pp. 414–416, para. 393; Macphail, *Evidence*, paras 18.20–18.22.

25 *Micosta SA v. Shetland Islands Council*, 1983 S.L.T. 483 at 485.

26 Walkers, *op.cit.*

27 *Anderson v. St Andrew's Ambulance Association*, 1942 S.C. 555; *Secretary of State for Trade and Industry v. Houston*, 1994 S.C.L.R. 209; *Hepburn v. Scottish Power plc*, 1997 S.C.L.R. 295; Walkers, p. 416, para. 394; Macphail, *Evidence*, para. 18.24.

28 *Young v. National Coal Board*, 1957 S.C. 99; *Marks & Spencer Ltd v. British Gas Corporation*, 1983 S.L.T. 196; *More v. Brown & Root Wimpey Highland Fabricators Ltd*, 1983 S.L.T. 669; *Hepburn*, *supra*; Walkers, pp. 417–418, para. 395(b); Macphail, *Evidence*, paras 18.25–S18.27B.

29 *N.B. Ry v. R. & J. Garroway* (1893) 20 R. 397; *Science Research Council v. Nasse* [1980] A.C. 1028, *per* Lord Fraser of Tullybelton at 1086.

30 Walkers, pp. 379–380, para. 355(b).

31 *Glasgow Corporation v. Central Land Board*, 1956 S.C.(H.L.) 1; *Conway v. Rimmer* [1968] A.C. 910.

32 paras 4.72 to 4.75.

for refusal of recovery has not yet been upheld in Scotland where proponed by a body other than a government department.[33] Objection has often been taken to the recovery of documents in the hands of the criminal authorities.[34] In an ordinary road accident case, however, the police normally supply an abstract of a report and a list of witnesses, and afford facilities for the precognition of the police officers concerned.

Examples of recoverable and irrecoverable documents.[35] Subject to such qualifications as relevancy, confidentiality and public interest immunity, documents of the following classes may be recoverable. **15.56**

(1) Documents which, if their authenticity is presumed or averred, constitute written evidence, such as formally valid writings in terms of the Requirements of Writing (Scotland) Act 1995, and documents which by statute are made evidence, such as the minutes of meetings of a company.[36]

(2) Documents written to or by or on behalf of a party, including his business books and financial records.[37] Income tax receipts are recoverable but not, in general, income tax returns.[38] Where a party founds on a part of a correspondence bearing on an issue raised on record, his opponent is entitled to recover the remainder of it.[39]

(3) In personal injuries actions, the following are normally recoverable: all reports, memoranda and other written communications made, at or about the time of the accident to the pursuer, to the defenders or anyone on their behalf by any employee of the defenders present at the time of the accident; relative to the matters mentioned on record[40]; and the hospital records and wages records relating to the pursuer. Before hospital records can be recovered, the name of the hospital must be mentioned on record,[41] and intimation of the application must be made to the Lord Advocate.[42] The greatest care must be taken in the preservation, copying and return of hospital and other medical records. The drafting of specifications[43] and joint minutes[44] is considered elsewhere. The employers' accident book may be recoverable in special circumstances.[45] If the accident book is kept in terms of statutory provisions, these should be stated in the call.[46]

---

[33] *Higgins v. Burton*, 1968 S.L.T. (Notes) 52; *Strathclyde R.C. v. B*, Sh. Pr. Dick, Glasgow Sh. Ct, Feb. 17, 1984, unreported: see Macphail, *Evidence*, para. S18.54C; *Parks v. Tayside R.C.*, 1989 S.L.T. 345. *Cf. D v. National Society for the Prevention of Cruelty to Children* [1978] A.C. 171, but English authorities in this field have to be treated with some caution: *Parks, supra.*

[34] *e.g. Rogers v. Orr*, 1939 S.C. 492; *McKie v. Western SMT Co.*, 1952 S.C. 206; *Friel v. Chief Constable of Strathclyde*, 1981 S.C. 1; *P. Cannon (Garages) Ltd v. Lord Advocate*, 1983 S.L.T. (Sh. Ct.) 50.

[35] Many examples are given in *Encyclopaedia*, iii, paras 1302–1322, and Walkers, pp. 322–325, paras 289(d), 294.

[36] Companies Act 1985, s. 382(2).

[37] *Gould v. Gould*, 1966 S.C. 88; *Douglas v. Douglas*, 1966 S.L.T. (Notes) 43.

[38] See para. 15.57.

[39] *Stevenson v. Kyle* (1849) 11 D. 1086; *Clavering v. McCunn* (1881) 19 S.L.R. 139. See para. 16.24.

[40] See para. 15.54.

[41] *Gill v. National Coal Board* [1955] C.L.Y. 3497.

[42] para. 15.60.

[43] paras 15.61 to 15.63.

[44] paras 16.28 to 16.30.

[45] *Dobbie v. Forth Ports Authority*, 1974 S.C. 40; *Comer v. James Scott & Co. (Electrical Engineers) Ltd*, 1976 S.L.T. (Notes) 72; *Boyes v. Eaton Yale & Towne Inc.*, 1978 S.L.T. (Notes) 6; *McIntyre v. NCB*, 1978 S.L.T. (Sh. Ct.) 32; *Govan v. National Coal Board*, 1987 S.L.T. 511. See Macphail, *Evidence*, paras 25.13–S25.15.

[46] *Dobbie, supra, per* Lord Kissen at 46.

(4) A factual report of an examination made on behalf of one party which was necessarily destructive of an object whose condition is in issue, made before any claim was made or contemplated, may be recoverable by the other party.[47]

15.57 In addition to the classes of documents already noted as being, in general, irrecoverable, are the following.

(1) Income tax returns. Objection to the recovery of income tax returns is normally taken by the Commissioners of Inland Revenue on the ground of public interest. They contain information which the taxpayer is required by statute to provide.[48] It is in the public interest that he should make a candid and complete disclosure of his income, and to that end he should be able to rely on the Inland Revenue not to use that information for any purpose other than the assessment of his tax liability, and not to pass that information to any other party. The court's power to override the Revenue's objection to production is exercised only in very exceptional cases.[49]

(2) Title deeds. Since title deeds are regarded as the private property of the party whose rights are stated in them, recovery of the opposite party's title deeds is limited to specific documents for a specific purpose.[50] Where the holder of the titles is not a party to the cause, they cannot be recovered[51] unless the rights conferred in them are in dispute.[52] There are special rules as to the production of public records.[53]

Stage at which recovery allowed

15.58 **Before record closed.** Until relatively recently the granting of a commission and diligence before the closing of the record and the allowance of proof was exceptional. This has now changed. "The modern practice has favoured earlier recovery of documents which appear to be necessary for giving specification when such specification is expressly desiderated, more particularly when the documents are already available to all the other parties in the litigation."[54] In practice in the sheriff court it is not uncommon for commission and diligence to be granted prior to an options hearing, especially in reparation cases where a defender desires to recover the pursuer's medical records with a view to assessing the value of the claim. The earlier cases on this subject[55] are accordingly of limited value and should be approached with caution. However, as has already been observed, the court will not grant a "fishing diligence".[56] In an action of

---

[47] *Waddington v. Buchan Poultry Products Ltd*, 1961 S.L.T. 428.

[48] Taxes Management Act 1970, s. 8(1).

[49] *Henderson v. McGown*, 1916 S.C. 821; *Wilson's Exrs v. Bank of England*, 1925 S.L.T. 81; *Milne v. Wakelin*, 1933 S.L.T. 274; *Jenkins v. Glasgow Corporation*, 1934 S.L.T. 53; *Brownlie v. Maitland*, Aberdeen Sh. Ct, Nov. 5, 1985, unreported; cases cited in para. 15.55.

[50] *Richardson v. Fleming* (1867) 5 M. 586; *Earl of Lauderdale v. Scrymgeour Wedderburn* (1905) 7 F. 1045.

[51] *Fisher v. Bontine* (1827) 6 S. 330; *Riggs v. Drummond* (1861) 23 D. 1251.

[52] Thomson and Middleton, p. 374.

[53] paras 15.98, 15.99.

[54] *per* Lord McCluskey in *Gallier v. Lothan Regional Council*, O.H., June 28, 1985, unreported, quoted with approval in *Bank of East Asia Ltd v. Shepherd & Wedderburn W.S.*, 1994 S.C.L.R. 526, *per* Lord Milligan at 527. See also *Moore v. Greater Glasgow Health Board*, 1978 S.C. 123; *Civil Service Building Society v. MacDougall*, 1988 S.L.T. 687; *Graham Builders Merchants Ltd v. Royal Bank of Scotland plc*, 1992 S.C.L.R. 402.

[55] *e.g. Boyle v. Glasgow Royal Infirmary*, 1969 S.C. 72.

[56] paras 15.51, 15.52.

divorce in which the financial provisions are in issue, a diligence is frequently granted before the closing of the record in order to obtain details of the parties' means and resources.[57] The question whether a diligence should be granted before the closing of the record is a matter within the discretion of the sheriff, with which an appeal court will not lightly interfere.[58]

After record closed. Application for a commission and diligence is normally made after the record has been closed, any preliminary pleas have been disposed of, and proof has been allowed.[59] The application should be made in ample time to allow the documents recovered to be timeously lodged not later than 14 days before the date of the proof.[60] The sheriff may, however, allow documents to be lodged late of consent, or on cause shown.[61] Since commission and diligence may be granted "in a case depending before the sheriff"[62] an application may be granted during an adjournment of a proof.[63] Commission and diligence has, however, been refused in the course of a proof where its purpose was to discredit a witness who had given evidence.[64] **15.59**

Procedure

Motion. The application is made by motion.[65] Along with the motion must be lodged a specification of documents.[66] A copy of the specification should be sent to the other parties along with the intimation of the motion.[67] If the motion is made before the options hearing each party must lodge in process, not later than two days before the hearing of the motion, a copy of his pleadings as adjusted.[68] All specifications which include a call for the recovery of documents belonging to or in the possession of the Crown,[69] or for the recovery of the records of a National Health Service hospital,[70] must be intimated to the Lord Advocate before submission to the court.[71] At the hearing of the motion a representative of the Lord Advocate is entitled to be heard.[72] If an objection on the ground of public policy is made and sustained, the call in the specification to which objection has been taken is struck out. Even if intimation is not made, the objection may be taken when the department concerned is **15.60**

---

57 *Douglas v. Douglas*, 1966 S.L.T. (Notes) 43.

58 *MacRae v. British Transport Commission*, 1957 S.C. 195.

59 Thomson and Middleton, pp. 327, 375.

60 OCR, r. 29.11(1).

61 OCR, r. 29.11(2).

62 OCR, r. 28.1(1).

63 *Baroness Gray v. Richardson* (1874) 1 R. 1138.

64 *Scottish Omnibuses Ltd v. Gillies*, Sh. Pr. O'Brien, Dumbarton Sh. Ct, Feb. 1978, unreported.

65 OCR, r. 28.2(1). Dobie, *Styles*, p. 338; Kearney, p. 214. The normal motion procedure under OCR, Chap. 15 is followed. See paras 5.44 to 5.55. When it was impossible to apply to a sheriff court due to industrial action by court staff, an application to the *nobile officium* of the Court of Session was granted: *Manson v. British Gas Corporation*, 1982 S.L.T. 77.

66 OCR, r. 28.2(2). Dobie, *Styles*, p. 524; Kearney, pp. 213–214.

67 OCR, r. 28.2(3)(a).

68 OCR, r. 9.4.

69 *Sheridan v. Peel*, 1907 S.C. 577, *per* L.P. Dunedin at 580; *Henderson v. McCown*, 1916 S.C. 821, *per* L.P. Strathclyde at 825; *Whitehall v. Whitehall*, 1957 S.C. 30, *per* Lord Sorn at 42.

70 *Glacken v. National Coal Board*, 1951 S.C. 82.

71 The Lord Advocate's style and address are given in para. 4.66.

72 OCR, r. 28.2(5).

summoned as a haver before the commissioner,[73] or when the optional procedure is operated.[74] No other haver who is not a party to the action has a locus to appear and oppose the motion.[75] If he is unwilling to produce, he may refuse to produce before the commissioner, and if the matter comes before the court he may appear or be represented before the sheriff and justify his grounds for refusal.[76]

15.61 **Specification of documents.** The specification of documents is a separate step of process, headed: "Specification of Documents / for the recovery of which a Commission and Diligence is sought by the Pursuer [or Defender] / *in causa* [etc.]." It contains a detailed and articulate statement, in numbered paragraphs or "calls", of the documents or classes of documents which are sought to be recovered. The names of the persons who are believed to be in possession of the documents are not stated. Since the object of the application, when made after the closing of the record, is to enable the party to recover documents required *in modum probationis*, that is, for the purposes of the proof, the specification should be drafted with distinct reference to the averments of fact remitted to probation[77] upon which the documents are supposed to have a bearing.[78] The scope of the recovery will be strictly limited to the averments remitted to probation,[79] and a call which is not related to any averment,[80] or is related only to a vague or unspecific averment,[81] will be refused.

15.62 Since the documents which may be properly recovered in different cases are of infinite variety, it is not possible to define for practical purposes the conditions which should regulate the scope and limits of the calls: they must depend materially on the general nature of the case and on the averments of fact which are made and which the documents sought to be recovered are intended to support or establish.[82] It is important to notice, however, that it is necessary to exhaust a diligence to recover an original document before secondary evidence of its contents may be admitted. If a party fails to take the proper steps to recover by commission and diligence a document not in his possession, he will not be allowed to prove it by secondary evidence, although it may be that the document would not have been recovered.[83] A "general call" of an extensive and sweeping character is prima facie of the nature of a fishing or speculative diligence, and may be refused in the absence of special averments indicating the necessity for a wide and comprehensive recovery.[84] Where fraud is in issue, the court

---

[73] *Whitehall, supra.*

[74] *Brownlie v. Maitland*, Aberdeen Sh. Ct, Nov. 5, 1985, unreported. See para. 15.68.

[75] *Harry Sarna Ltd v. Barnett & Co. Sales (Central) Ltd*, 1954 S.L.T. (Sh. Ct.) 105. Note that if the application is not for a commission and diligence to recover documents in normal course but for an order under s. 1 of the Administration of Justice (Scotland) Act 1972, intimation of the motion and specification must be made to the haver (OCR, r. 28.2(3)(b)). In such a case the haver has a locus to appear and oppose the motion. See para. 15.89.

[76] paras 15.75, 15.76.

[77] *Scott, Simpson & Wallis v. Forrest & Turnbull* (1897) 24 R. 877.

[78] *Paterson v. Paterson*, 1919 1 S.L.T. 12; *Wheatley v. Anderson*, 1927 S.C. 133 at 142.

[79] *Rogerson v. Rogerson*, 1964 S.L.T. (Notes) 89.

[80] *Burrows v. Glasgow Corporation*, 1916 1 S.L.T. 420.

[81] *Scott v. Portsoy Harbour Co.* (1900) 8 S.L.T. 38.

[82] *Earl of Morton v. Fleming*, 1921 1 S.L.T. 205 at 209.

[83] *Dowgray v. Gilmour*, 1907 S.C. 715.

[84] *Van Engers, Roeclofs & Co. v. Ellis Hughes* (1898) 6 S.L.T. 90 (granted); *Earl of Lauderdale v. Scrymgeour Wedderburn* (1904) 7 F. 1045 (granted); *Earl of Morton, supra* (granted in part).

generally admits, with more than usual liberality, recovery which may clear up what is likely to be obscure or hidden.[85]

Where it is reasonably expected that documentary evidence relevant to a matter averred is contained in business books or other voluminous records whose contents include entries relating to other matters, it is usual to call for the books kept between two specific dates relative to a date or period mentioned on record, "in order that excerpts may be taken therefrom at the sight of the Commissioner of all entries showing or tending to show" the information relevant to the matter averred. The objects of that practice are to protect private entries or trade secrets from disclosure, and to avoid any inconvenience which the removal of the books might cause to their owner. The books themselves may, however, be required if significance is attached to their appearance, or to the position or surroundings of particular entries.[86] In a personal injuries action, a call for hospital records usually seeks excerpts of all entries showing or tending to show the nature and extent of the injuries from which the pursuer was suffering when he was admitted to the hospital on the date averred on record, his condition while there and his certificate of discharge. In all specifications the final call is normally: "Failing principals, drafts, copies or duplicates of the above or any of them." Under such a call, however, there can be no recovery of drafts, copies or duplicates, except of consent, unless and until reasonable diligence has been exercised in attempting to recover the principals.[87] 15.63

Disposal of motion. If no opposition is intimated to the motion for commission and diligence or it is consented to, it may very well be granted by the sheriff in chambers without the necessity for an appearance by the party whose motion it is.[88] Even if the motion is unopposed or consented to, the sheriff may wish it to be called in court because he is not satisfied that it is justified or considers that it requires some explanation.[89] If the motion is opposed it calls in court in the usual way.[90] Explanations of the purposes for which the documents specified are required may be offered and challenged, and argument presented as to the proper scope of the calls. After hearing parties, the sheriff pronounces an interlocutor granting or refusing the application in whole or in part. Any call which the sheriff refuses is deleted: if he disallows it only in part, it is adjusted. Deletions or adjustments made by the sheriff should be authenticated by the sheriff or the clerk of court. The parties' advocates often reach agreement as to the terms of the calls before or in the course of the hearing, and initial any amendments made. The interlocutor should make clear how any alterations to the specification have taken place, and distinguish between a limited recovery granted of consent, and a refusal in part of the diligence. If, therefore, a call is altered by decision of the sheriff, the interlocutor should state the part allowed and the part refused, and that it was altered at the sight of the court and authenticated by the sheriff or the clerk of court. If it is altered by the party moving for the commission and diligence, the interlocutor should state that it was altered 15.64

---

85 *Wilson's Exrs v. Bank of England*, 1925 S.L.T. 81.
86 Dobie, p. 199.
87 *Caledonian Ry v. Symington*, 1912 S.C. 1033.
88 OCR, r. 15.5(1),(8).
89 OCR, r. 15.5(4).
90 OCR, r. 15.5(5).

at the bar.[91] In addition to granting commission and diligence and approving the specification, with or without modification of its terms, the sheriff either nominates a commissioner to take the oaths and examinations of the havers, to be reported on or before a particular date or *quam primum*,[92] or "finds it unnecessary to appoint a commissioner meantime", the latter course being adopted where the party obtaining the diligence proposes to operate the optional procedure under rule 28.3.[93]

15.65 **Appeal.** An interlocutor granting diligence is not appealable without the leave of the sheriff.[94] A former Court of Session rule that an interlocutor refusing diligence was reclaimable without leave has influenced the view that leave to appeal against such an interlocutor is not required in the sheriff court[95]; but the decision establishing that rule[96] was strongly doubted,[97] and was later superseded by the enactment of a rule of court in the Court of Session that interlocutors allowing or refusing diligence can only be reclaimed with leave.[98] In the sheriff court sheriffs principal on the one hand have followed the decision with obvious reluctance[99] and, on the other, have repudiated it as a guide to sheriff court practice and held that leave is required.[1] A sheriff court rule on the matter has been desiderated.[2] It is thought that the better view is that an appeal against an interlocutor refusing a diligence requires the leave of the sheriff. In any event, in an appeal against an interlocutor granting or refusing a diligence, the appeal court will not readily interfere unless some matter of principle has been transgressed.[3]

15.66 **Optional procedure.** In the majority of cases, the party who has obtained the commission does not execute it in the ordinary way but adopts the optional procedure provided by rule 28.3, which is in terms similar to those of rule 35.3 of the Rules of the Court of Session. At any time before a commission and diligence for the recovery of documents has been executed against a haver, the party who has obtained it may serve on the haver an order in Form G11 requiring him to produce to the sheriff clerk *inter alia* the documents in his possession falling within the specification.[4] The order and a copy of the specification must be served on the haver or his known solicitor.[5]

---

[91] *Thomson & Co. v. Bowater & Sons*, 1918 S.C. 316. On the leave to appeal point this decision has been superseded: see para. 15.65.

[92] As soon as possible, forthwith.

[93] paras 15.66 to 15.71.

[94] The Sheriff Courts (Scotland) Act 1907, ss. 27 and 28 do not mention such interlocutors as being appealable without leave. *Stewart v. Kennedy* (1890) 17 R. 755; *Baikie v. Doull* (1908) 24 Sh.Ct.Rep. 211.

[95] Lewis, p. 312; Dobie, pp. 193–194, 290.

[96] *Thomson & Co. v. Bowater & Sons*, 1918 S.C. 316.

[97] *Galloway v. Galloway*, 1947 S.C. 330.

[98] R.C. 273(c) of the 1948 Rules of Court. This was repeated in r. 164(c) of the 1965 Rules but not in the current 1994 Rules.

[99] *Lund v. Briggs & Sons Ltd*, Sh. Pr. O'Brien, Airdrie Sh. Ct, Mar. 20, 1981, unreported.

[1] *Buchan Supply Stores v. Morgan*, 1954 S.L.T. (Sh. Ct.) 7 (not cited in *Lund, supra*). See also *Dick v. Blairgowrie Town Council* (1910) 27 Sh.Ct.Rep 243; *Mowbray v. Secretary of State for Scotland*, 1992 S.L.T. (Sh. Ct.) 84.

[2] *Lund, supra.*

[3] *Young v. National Coal Board*, 1957 S.C. 99, *per* L.J.-C. Thomson at 106.

[4] OCR, r. 28.3(1).

[5] OCR, r. 28.3(2). Service may be by post (OCR, r. 5.3) or sheriff officer (OCR, r. 5.4).

The party or haver must obtemper the order in the manner and within the time specified therein.[6] No period for production is specified in the rule, but Form G11 states it as within seven days of the service of the order. The party or haver must obtemper the order by producing to the sheriff clerk (1) the order itself, which must be produced intact; (2) a certificate signed and completed in terms of the form appended to Form G11; and (3) all documents in his possession falling within the specification together with an inventory of such documents signed by him as relating to the order and to his certificate. The certificate states: (1) that the documents produced and numbered in the inventory are the whole documents in his possession falling under the specification, or that he has no documents in his possession falling within the specification; and (2) that, to the best of his knowledge and belief, there are in existence other documents falling within the specification, but not in his possession—he describes the documents and states when, where and in whose hands he last saw them; or (3) that he knows of the existence of no documents in the possession of any person, other than himself, which fall within the specification.[7] **15.67**

If the party or haver claims confidentiality for any of the documents produced by him, he must nevertheless produce them, but he should enclose them by themselves in a separate sealed packet marked "Confidential".[8] That packet will not be opened or put in process except by authority of the sheriff obtained on the application of the party serving the order, after opportunity to be heard has been given to the party or haver making production.[9] **15.68**

The party or haver produces the order, certificate and any inventoried documents either by lodging them at the sheriff clerk's office or by sending them to the sheriff clerk by registered post or first class recorded delivery service.[10] Not later than the day after the date on which the sheriff clerk receives these documents he must intimate that fact to every party.[11] Only the party who served the order may uplift any of the documents during the seven days after the date of intimation.[12] Thereafter, the normal borrowing rules apply.[13] Where the party who served the order fails to uplift the delivered documents within seven days after intimation, the sheriff clerk must intimate this failure to every other party.[14] Where no party has uplifted the documents within 14 days after the intimation of failure mentioned in the previous sentence, the sheriff clerk must return the documents to the haver who delivered them.[15] Where any party who has uplifted a document does not wish to lodge it as a production, he must return it to the sheriff clerk who then intimates the return to every other party.[16] If no other party uplifts the document **15.69**

---

[6] OCR, r. 28.3(1).

[7] OCR, Form G11.

[8] OCR, r. 28.8(1). Form G11. The records of a National Health Service venereal diseases clinic may be dealt with in this way, after intimation to the Lord Advocate, the relevant hospital board, the clinic and the other parties.

[9] OCR, r. 28.8(2),(3),(4). See para. 15.101.

[10] OCR, Form G11.

[11] OCR, r. 28.3(3).

[12] OCR, r.28.3(4).

[13] See paras 8.09 to 8.13.

[14] OCR, r. 28.3(5).

[15] OCR, r. 28.3(6).

[16] OCR, r. 28.3(7)(a).

within 14 days of such intimation, the sheriff clerk must return it to the haver.[17]

15.70 If an extract from a book of any description (whether or not the extract is certified) is produced under the order, the sheriff may, on the motion of the party who served the order, order that that party should be allowed to inspect the book and take copies of any entries falling under the specification.[18] In the event of any question of confidentiality arising in relation to a book so ordered to be inspected, the inspection is made and copies taken at the sight of the commissioner appointed in the interlocutor granting commission and diligence.[19] If no commissioner has been appointed the sheriff should be moved to appoint one. Even though a certified extract from a book containing entries falling under a specification has been produced, the sheriff may, on cause shown, order the production of that book (provided that it is not a banker's book or a book of public record).[20]

15.71 If the party who served the order is not satisfied that full compliance has been made with the order, or that adequate reasons for non-compliance have been given, he may execute the commission and diligence in normal form, notwithstanding his adoption in the first instance of the optional procedure.[21] If no commissioner has been appointed, he should move the sheriff to make an appointment.

15.72 **Procedure before diet.** The party seeking to execute a commission and diligence for the recovery of documents must (a) provide the commissioner with a copy of the specification, a copy of the pleadings (including any adjustments and amendments) and a certified copy of the interlocutor of his appointment[22]; (b) instruct the clerk and any shorthand writer considered necessary by the commissioner or any party.[23] The party seeking to execute the commission is responsible for the fees of the commissioner and his clerk and of any shorthand writer.[24] The commissioner, in consultation with the parties, fixes a diet for the execution of the commission.[25] The diet should be intimated to all parties.[26] A citation in Form G13 is served on each haver along with a copy of the specification and, where it is necessary for a proper understanding of the specification, a copy of the pleadings including any adjustments and amendments.[27] Where the haver is a company or firm, a responsible official or agent may be cited. The party citing the haver must lodge a certificate of citation in Form G12.[28] The haver is entitled to demand and be paid in advance by

---

[17] OCR, r. 28.3(7)(b).
[18] OCR, r. 28.3(9).
[19] OCR, r. 28.3(10).
[20] OCR, r. 28.3(11).
[21] OCR, r. 28.3(8).
[22] OCR, r. 28.4(1)(a).
[23] OCR, r. 28.4(1)(b).
[24] OCR, r. 28.4(1)(c).
[25] OCR, r. 28.4(2).
[26] Failure to intimate the diet to a party may render the commission abortive: *Craig v. Craig* (1905) 13 S.L.T. 556.
[27] OCR, r. 28.4(4). Form G 13 is the same form as is used for citation of a witness to a proof. It is capable of adaptation for a haver, but see *Stewart v. Callaghan*, 1996 S.L.T. (Sh. Ct.) 12, especially *per* Sh. Pr. Nicholson at 16J–L. The interlocutor granting commission and diligence is sufficient authority to cite a haver: OCR, r. 29.4(3).
[28] OCR, r. 28.4(4).

the party citing him travelling expenses for attending the diet.[29] He is also entitled to payment by the party citing him for necessary outlays and loss of earnings.[30] A fee may be payable for searching for documents called for,[31] but not for copying documents or for making and copying excerpts unless such copies have been requested by the party citing the haver.[32] The solicitor who cites a haver is personally liable for paying any sums due to him.[33] Where the party citing him is due to pay the haver an account for professional services, the court may appoint the haver to produce the documents under that party's diligence but find that the party cannot make use of them at the proof without paying the haver's account.[34]

Execution of commission. The parties and the haver are entitled to be represented at the execution of the commission by a solicitor or any person having a right of audience before the sheriff.[35] The proceedings commence with the commissioner administering the oath *de fideli administratione* to the clerk and shorthand writer.[36] The commissioner then administers the oath or affirmation to the haver[37] and he is examined by the party who has cited him. The only legitimate purposes of the examination are to trace and recover a document or its copy if it is extant, and to account for its destruction if it has been destroyed. No question which does not tend to one or other of the two ends is regular or competent.[38] The haver may not be examined in any way as to the contents of the documents[39] or as to the merits of the cause,[40] and it is the commissioner's duty to disallow questions tending to that end. The haver must, however, produce and answer questions about documents which may be injurious to his character[41] or to his interests or the interests of those whom he represents[42]; but he need not answer a question if his answer could imply that he has been guilty of a crime.[43] When the party who has cited him has finished his examination, the other party may put any further questions necessary to secure a full and fair production of the documents.[44] The commissioner may reject documents which the specification clearly does not cover, but if he is doubtful whether the specification covers them he should receive them and leave it to the court to rule subsequently on any objection.[45] The commissioner does not entertain objections that a document is inadmissible in evidence or is null in respect that it has been executed without the necessary statutory solemnities or is 15.73

---

29 OCR, Form G13.
30 *ibid.*
31 *Mackinnon v. Guildford* (1894) 2 S.L.T. 309; *Forsyth v. Pringle Taylor & Lamond Lawson* (1906) 14 S.L.T. 658.
32 *Forsyth, supra.*
33 *Bayley v. Middleton*, 1909 1 S.L.T. 493.
34 *Montgomerie v. AB* (1845) 7 D. 553; *Train & McIntyre Ltd v. Forbes*, 1925 S.L.T. 286. *Cf. Mackinnon, supra.*
35 OCR, r. 28.4(5).
36 OCR, r. 28.4(6)(a).
37 OCR, r. 28.4(6)(b). The forms of oaths and affirmations are OCR, Forms 14 and 15 respectively.
38 *Somervell v. Somervell* (1900) 8 S.L.T. 84; Walkers, p. 328, para. 298.
39 *Somervell, supra.*
40 *Dye v. Reid* (1831) 9 S. 342.
41 *Don v. Don* (1848) 10 D. 1046.
42 *Graham v. Sprot* (1847) 9 D. 545.
43 *Livingston v. Murrays* (1830) 9 S. 161.
44 *Dunlop's Trs v. Lord Belhaven* (1852) 14 D. 825; *Thorburn v. Hoby & Co.* (1853) 15 D. 767.
45 Dobie, p. 197.

unstamped or understamped; but he may refer to any apparent nullity in his report.

15.74 The lines which the examination of the haver may take are as follows. He is asked if he has the document. If he answers that he has, and has no objection to delivering it, he hands it over to the commissioner, and that ends the matter. If he says he does not have it, he may be asked whether he ever had it. If he answers in the affirmative, he may be asked what he has done with it. If he has destroyed it, he may be asked when, where, how and why he did so; and if he has handed it to someone else, to whom.[46] The haver is not entitled to refuse production on the ground that the document would not help on the point at issue,[47] but he may refuse to answer or to produce on the ground of confidentiality[48] or self-incrimination or, it would appear, on the ground that the information required has been, or can be, obtained from other sources which do not involve disclosing private information.[49]

15.75 **Disposal of objection.** When confidentiality is claimed for any of the documents produced, they must be enclosed in a separate sealed packet, as described above in connection with the optional procedure,[50] and then dealt with in terms of Ordinary Cause Rule 28.8(2) to (4).[51] The rules give no further guidance on the procedure to be followed when a haver objects to the production of documents. It is thought that where objection is taken on any ground other than confidentiality, it is the commissioner's duty to rule on it. If, however, the matter is one of any complexity or delicacy, it may be preferable for the commissioner to repel the objection under reservation of all questions of competency and relevancy. If the haver then produces the document, it should be sealed up to await the decision of the sheriff, who before ruling on the objection will give the haver an opportunity to be heard on a motion to open the sealed packet lodged by the party who has obtained the diligence and intimated by him to the other parties and to the haver.[52]

15.76 If the haver refuses to produce the document to the commissioner after the latter has repelled his objection, whether under reservation or not, the commissioner has no power to compel him to produce it. There may be two alternative methods of procedure. The first is that the commissioner should adjourn the diet and make an interim report with regard to the refusal to the sheriff, who may hear parties and the haver on the report. The haver is entitled,[53] and may be required,[54] to appear or be represented at the hearing to support his objection. After hearing parties and the haver, the sheriff may fix a further diet at which the haver may again be called on to produce the document to the commissioner,[55] with the

---

[46] *Somervell, supra.*

[47] *Campbell v. Earl of Crawford* (1783) Mor. 3973.

[48] See para. 15.54.

[49] *N.B. Ry v. R. & J. Garroway* (1893) 20 R. 397; *Science Research Council v. Nassé* [1980] A.C. 1028, *per* Lord Fraser of Tullybelton at 1086.

[50] para. 15.68.

[51] See para. 15.101.

[52] *Fife C.C. v. Thoms* (1898) 25 R. 1097; *Train & McIntyre Ltd v. Forbes*, 1925 S.L.T. 286. *Cf.* OCR, r. 28.8(2)–(4).

[53] *Montgomerie v. AB* (1845) 7 D. 553; *Train & McIntyre Ltd, supra. Cf.* OCR, r. 28.8(4).

[54] *Mackinnon v. Guildford* (1894) 2 S.L.T. 309.

[55] *McDonald v. McDonalds* (1881) 8 R. 357.

sanction of punishment by the sheriff for contempt of court if he fails to do so.[56] The alternative and, it is thought, less satisfactory course[57] is to cite the haver to produce the document at the diet of proof. The sheriff may then hear the haver and parties on his objection to production and give a ruling. Any party dissatisfied with the ruling may express immediately his formal dissatisfaction with the ruling and, with leave of the sheriff, appeal to the sheriff principal.[58] It is then the duty of the sheriff principal to dispose of the appeal with the least possible delay,[59] although the sheriff may proceed with the cause as regards points not necessarily dependent on the ruling appealed against.[60] The former course appears to be preferable since it may allow the matter to be settled before the diet of proof.

Taking of excerpts. It is the duty of the haver to search for and produce the books and documents described in the specification and, where the commissioner is not ordered to make excerpts from the books, it is the duty of the commissioner only to receive the books and documents produced by the haver conform to the specification and to interrogate the haver, or to allow him to be interrogated, upon the limited matters set out in paragraphs 15.73 and 15.74. It is not enough for the haver to appear before the commissioner, to depone that he may or may not have documents of which the court has ordered production, and invite the commissioner to find out for himself whether he has or not.[61] Where, however, excerpts from books and documents described in the specification are to be taken at the sight of the commissioner, the haver's only duty is to search for and produce the books or documents, and the party who has obtained the diligence is not bound to accept any excerpts other than those made on the instructions of the commissioner. In practice, the haver often makes the necessary excerpts, but he is not obliged to do so.[62] The books and documents produced by the haver remain in the commissioner's hands; the haver may object to their being examined by parties outwith his presence; and the party who obtained the commission and diligence is not entitled to private access to them in order to make a general search for information.[63] It may be necessary to excerpt more than the particular entry relating to the action if the entry is in any way peculiar, as where it is interlined or apparently entered under a wrong date. Where the appearance of the books presents peculiarities, the commissioner should specially report thereon.[64] **15.77**

The commissioner is not entitled himself to appoint an accountant or other person to assist him,[65] but the court may authorise him to arrange for accountants or other suitably qualified persons to assist him in perusing and considering documents and to excerpt entries under his supervision; to obtain secretarial assistance in making excerpts; and to obtain any necessary advice from a suitably qualified engineer or other person in determining what documents fall within the calls in the **15.78**

---

[56] *National Exchange Co. v. Drew and Dick* (1858) 20 D. 837.
[57] Suggested by Dobie, pp. 197–198.
[58] OCR, r. 29.19(1); see paras 16.89, 16.90.
[59] OCR, r. 29.19(2).
[60] OCR, r. 29.19(4).
[61] *Burgh of Ayr v. British Transport Commission*, 1956 S.L.T. (Sh. Ct.) 3 at 6.
[62] *Forsyth v. Pringle Taylor & Lamond Lowson* (1906) 14 S.L.T. 658.
[63] *Cassils & Co. v. Absalon* (1907) 15 S.L.T. 48.
[64] Fyfe, p. 217; Dobie, p. 199.
[65] *Cassils & Co., supra.*

specification. The court will grant such authority where to do so is in the interests of expeditious preparation for the proof and of the satisfactory administration of justice.[66]

15.79 **Report of commission.** The report of the execution of the commission, any document recovered and an inventory of that document is sent by the commissioner to the sheriff clerk.[67] Not later than the day after the date on which the report and other documents, if any, are received by the sheriff clerk he must intimate to all parties that he has received them.[68] Only the party who obtained the commission may uplift any document recovered during the seven days after the date of intimation.[69] If that party fails to uplift any document within the seven-day period, the sheriff clerk must intimate that failure to every other party.[70] Where no party has uplifted the documents within 14 days after the intimation of failure mentioned in the previous sentence, the sheriff clerk must return the documents to the haver.[71] Where any party who has uplifted any document does not wish to lodge it as a production, he must return it to the sheriff clerk who must intimate the return to every other party.[72] If no other party uplifts the document within 14 days of such intimation, the sheriff clerk must return it to the haver.[73]

15.80 **Second commission.** When the documents recovered indicate the existence of further material relevant to the applicant's averments on record, he may apply to the court for a second commission and diligence to recover such material; but a fishing diligence will be refused.[74]

Use of report at proof

15.81 The documents recovered may be lodged in process by the party who recovered them or, if he does not do so, by the other party. The statement of a haver that he has destroyed a document may be used as evidence at the proof.[75] The documents cannot be used as productions in another process, or for any purposes other than those of the action in which they are produced. After decree has been extracted, the solicitor for the party who recovered the documents should uplift them from the sheriff clerk, giving him a receipt therefor, and return them to the havers.

Expenses

15.82 The expense of the specification and of the execution of the commission will normally be allowed to the successful party, even although no documents have been recovered,[76] or the documents recovered do not

---

[66] *Wm Whiteley Ltd v. Dobson, Molle & Co. Ltd* (1902) 10 S.L.T. 71; *Johannesburg Municipal Council v. Stewart & Co. Ltd*, 1911 1 S.L.T. 359; *Argyllshire Weavers Ltd v. A. Macaulay (Tweeds) Ltd*, 1962 S.L.T. (Notes) 96; *Santa Fe International Corp. v. Napier Shipping SA, 1985 S.L.T. 430.*

[67] OCR, r. 28.4(7).

[68] OCR, r. 28.4(8).

[69] OCR, r. 28.4(9).

[70] OCR, r. 28.4(10).

[71] OCR, r. 28.4(11).

[72] OCR, r. 28.4(12)(a).

[73] OCR, r. 28.4(12)(b).

[74] *Fairlights Assets Co. Ltd v. Wright, Johnston & Mackenzie*, 1948 S.L.T. (Notes) 79.

[75] *Home v. Hardy* (1842) 4 D. 1184; *Falconer v. Stephen* (1849) 11 D. 1338.

[76] *McLeod v. Leslie* (1868) 5 S.L.R. 687.

establish his allegations[77]; but if he recovers documents and does not lodge them as productions, he will not, as a rule, be allowed the expense of the recovery of them.[78]

Documents furth of Scotland

15.83 The procedure for the obtaining of the evidence of witnesses in England, Wales and Northern Ireland[79] is applicable to the recovery of documents there.[80] An order by the High Court in England or Wales or by the High Court of Justice in Northern Ireland does not, however, require a person "(a) to state what documents relevant to the proceedings to which the application for the order relates are or have been in his possession, custody or power; or (b) to produce any documents other than particular documents specified in the order as being documents appearing to the court making the order to be, or to be likely to be, in his possession, custody or power".[81] While it may be that, technically, the only means of recovering documents in England, Wales or Northern Ireland under the Evidence (Proceedings in Other Jurisdictions) Act 1975 is by letter of request procedure, in many cases it will be worth trying to obtain the documents by something similar to the optional procedure[82] as there is every likelihood that a haver outwith Scotland would be prepared voluntarily to provide documents in his possession in terms of a specification of documents sent to him.[83] However, if such an attempt does not succeed a letter of request will be necessary. Such a letter must be in clear and specific terms.[84] So far as recovery of documents from furth of the United Kingdom is concerned, the letter of request procedure is available for that purpose to the same extent as for the taking of the evidence of a witness.[85]

Administration of Justice (Scotland) Act 1972, s. 1

Powers of the court

15.84 By a commission and diligence for the recovery of documents a party may recover only documents, and may do so only after the action has been commenced. By an application under section 1(1) of the Administration of Justice (Scotland) Act 1972, however, he may obtain a variety of orders relative not only to documents but also to other property, and may do so both before and after the commencement of the action.[86] Section 1(1) has been said to be directed towards making as much relevant information as possible available to the parties to litigation at a sufficiently early stage to enable them to prepare their cases properly and to expedite settlements and proofs.[87] The court will not, however, encourage "fishing" or

---

77 *Stirling v. Dunn* (1831) 9 S. 562.

78 *Mackie & Stark v. Cruikshank* (1896) 4 S.L.T. 84.

79 para. 15.41.

80 Evidence (Proceedings in Other Jurisdictions) Act 1975, s. 2(2)(b).

81 *ibid.* s. 2(4). The word "as" in para. (b) appears to be a drafting error: *Re Asbestos Insurance Coverage Cases* [1985] 1 W.L.R. 331, *per* Lord Fraser of Tullybelton at 336.

82 See paras 15.66 to 15.71.

83 *Stewart v. Callaghan*, 1996 S.L.T. (Sh. Ct.) 12.

84 *Stewart, supra.*

85 OCR, r. 28.14(2)(b). See para. 15.42.

86 s. 1(1A), which makes provision for the disclosure of the identity of witnesses, has been discussed in paras 15.03 to 15.06.

87 H.L. Deb., Vol. 329, col. 220, *cit.* I. S. Dickinson, "Petitioning for Disclosure", 1980 S.L.T. (News) 237 at p. 238.

speculative applications, and before making an order must be satisfied that the applicant is already able to state a prima facie case.[88]

15.85 Section 1(1) empowers the Court of Session and the sheriff court to order the inspection, photographing, preservation, custody and detention of documents and other property (including, where appropriate, land) which appear to the court to be property as to which any question may relevantly arise not only in any existing civil proceedings before that court but in civil proceedings which are likely to be brought, and to order the production and recovery of any such property, the taking of samples thereof and the carrying out of any experiment thereon or therewith.[89] The court may exercise the powers mentioned in subsection (l) unless there is special reason why the application should not be granted.[90]

15.86 The provisions of section 1 do not affect the rules of law and practice relating to the privilege of witnesses and havers, confidentiality of communications and withholding or non-disclosure of information on the grounds of public interest.[91] The privilege against self-incrimination cannot, however, be claimed in proceedings under section 1(1) which are likely to be brought (a) for infringement of rights pertaining to any intellectual property or for passing off; (b) to obtain disclosure of information relating to any infringement of such rights or to any passing off; and (c) to prevent any apprehended infringement of such rights or any apprehended passing off.[92] It would appear from the fact that the privilege has been withdrawn in relation to such proceedings that it is intended to be otherwise protected.[93] Section 47 of the Crown Proceedings Act 1947, which makes provision as to the recovery of documents in the hands of the Crown, and which has already been discussed,[94] applies in relation to any application under section 1 in respect of a document or other property as it applied before the commencement of section 1 to an application for commission and diligence for the recovery of a document.[95]

Procedure before commencement of proceedings

15.87 Prior to the commencement of any proceedings, a person who appears to the court to be likely to be a party to or a minuter in proceedings which are likely to be brought may at any time make an application to the court under section 1(1).[96] An application is made by summary application.[97] As with all summary applications the procedure is essentially within the discretion of the sheriff.[98] He may order intimation to any person who

---

[88] paras 15.88, 15.89.

[89] Similar powers have been conferred on superior courts in England and Australia: see the Supreme Court Act 1981, ss. 33, 35; B. C. Cairns, "Discovery and Preservation of Evidence under Inherent Jurisdiction" (1985) 4 C.J.Q. 309.

[90] Administration of Justice (Scotland) Act 1972, s. 1(2). See para. 15.90.

[91] *ibid.* s. 1(4).

[92] Law Reform (Miscellaneous Provisions) (Scotland) Act 1985, s. 15(3)(b) as amended, which in effect overrules observations in *British Phonographic Industry Ltd v. Cohen, Cohen, Kelly, Cohen & Cohen Ltd*, 1983 S.L.T. 137 at 138, 139.

[93] *cf.* G. L. Gretton, 1983 J.B.L. at pp. 504–505.

[94] paras 4.72 to 4.75.

[95] Administration of Justice (Scotland) Act 1972, s. 1(4); *Friel v. Chief Constable of Strathclyde*, 1981 S.C. 1; *P. Cannon (Garages) Ltd v. Lord Advocate*, 1983 S.L.T. (Sh. Ct.) 50.

[96] Administration of Justice (Scotland) Act 1972, s. 1(2)(b).

[97] A.S. (Sheriff Court Summary Application Rules) 1993, r. 30(1).

[98] *ibid.* r. 32.

appears to him to have an interest in the application.[99] He may, if necessary, appoint a hearing.[1] The crave may seek a commission and diligence for the recovery of documents, where that is appropriate. A separate specification of documents would not appear to be necessary where only one or a few documents are sought.[2]

Before the court may grant the order it is necessary for the applicant to show that civil proceedings are likely to be brought, and that in such proceedings questions may relevantly arise as to the documents or other property. In order to do so he must give sufficient information in his averments to enable the court to know what the action is going to be about, and what assistance the documents or other property referred to will give in deciding it.[3] It is not necessary to make full averments of fact which would make an action relevant, or to give an assurance that proceedings will be brought, but the applicant must disclose the nature of the claim he intends to make and show, not only the intention of making it, but also that there is a reasonable basis for making it. A prima facie case must be made out. Ill-founded, irresponsible and speculative allegations based merely on hope would not provide a reasonable basis for an intended claim in subsequent proceedings.[4] The obtaining of a report negativing the proposed ground of liability may cause the court not to be satisfied that proceedings are likely to be brought.[5] It has been observed that the order sought must be necessary for the purpose of enabling the applicant to make more pointed or specific that which is already averred, or to make adequate and specific replies to his opponent's averments[6]; but these tests, particularly the latter, seem difficult to apply where an application is made before the commencement of proceedings. Documents written by third parties cannot be recovered under section 1(1) for the purpose of putting them to witnesses with a view to testing their credibility or refreshing their memories.[7] **15.88**

Procedure after commencement of proceedings

After the proceedings have been commenced, an application under section 1(1) is made by motion.[8] With the motion should be lodged a specification of "the document or other property sought to be inspected, photographed, preserved, taken into custody, detained, produced, recovered, sampled or experimented with or upon, as the case may be".[9] A copy of the specification and the motion must be intimated to every other party, to any third party haver and, where necessary, to the Lord Advocate.[10] After hearing parties, the sheriff may either grant or refuse the order sought, in whole or in part, or as amended, and may order the applicant to find such caution or other security as he thinks fit.[11] The order will be **15.89**

---

[99] A.S. (Sheriff Court Summary Application Rules) 1993, r. 5.

[1] Sheriff Courts (Scotland) Act 1907, s. 50.

[2] *McCann v. Trs of St Andrews Links Trust*, Cupar Sh. Ct, June 3, 1983, unreported.

[3] *Falkingham v. Lothian R.C.*, 1983 S.L.T. (Sh. Ct.) 2; *Yau v. Ogilvie & Co.*, 1985 S.L.T. 91 *Dominion Technology Ltd v. Gardner Cryogenics Ltd (No. 1)*, 1993 S.L.T. 828; *Peason v. Educational Institute of Scotland*, 1998 S.L.T. 189.

[4] *Friel, supra*, at 5–6, citing *Dunning v. United Liverpool Hospitals' Board of Governors* [1973] 1 W.L.R. 586, *per* James L.J. at 593; *Smith, Petr*, 1985 S.L.T. 461; *Parks v. Tayside R.C.*, 1989 S.L.T. 345.

[5] *Connolly v. Edinburgh Northern Hospitals*, 1974 S.L.T. (Notes) 53.

[6] *Thorne v. Strathclyde R.C.*, 1984 S.L.T. 161.

[7] *Micosta SA v. Shetland Islands Council*, 1983 S.L.T. 483.

[8] OCR, r. 28.2(1)(b).

[9] OCR, r. 28.2(2).

[10] OCR, r. 28.2(3).

[11] OCR, r. 28.2(4).

granted only where the applicant shows that it is required in order to enable him to make more specific that which is already averred, or to enable him to make adequate and specific replies to his opponent's averments or calls for further specification.[12]

"Special reason"

15.90 The provision in section 1(2) that the court may exercise the powers mentioned in section 1(1) "unless there is special reason why the application should not be granted" has been construed in two different ways. One view is that the applicant must show cause why the order should be granted, and notwithstanding that he makes out a prima facie case for the granting of the order, there may yet be some special reason for refusing it.[13] The other view which, it is thought, is to be preferred, is that if prima facie it appears to the court that it is in the interests of justice to grant the motion, then the court should do so, unless the defender can demonstrate a special reason why it should not do so.[14]

Form of order

15.91 An order for the production or recovery of a document or other property grants a commission and diligence for the production or recovery of that document or other property.[15] An order for the inspection or photographing of a document or other property, the taking of samples or the carrying out of any experiment thereon or therewith authorises and appoints a specified person to photograph, inspect, take samples of or carry out any experiment on or with any such document or other property as the case may be, subject to such conditions, if any, as the sheriff thinks fit.[16] An order for the preservation, custody and detention of a document or other property grants a commission and diligence for the detention and custody of that document or other property.[17]

Execution of order

15.92 In the case of an order for the production or recovery of a document or other property it is executed exactly as if it were an order for commission and diligence for the recovery of documents, *i.e.* either the optional procedure may be used or a commission may take place.[18] In the case of an order for the inspection or photographing of a document or other property, the taking of samples or the carrying out of any inspection thereon or therewith a certified copy of the interlocutor granting the order is sufficient authority for the person specified to execute the order.[19] The party obtaining the order serves on the haver a copy of the interlocutor, a copy of the specification and, where necessary for a proper understanding of the specification, a copy of the pleadings including any adjustments and

---

[12] *Moore v. Greater Glasgow Health Board*, 1978 S.C. 123; *Thorne v Strathclyde R.C.*, 1984 S.L.T. 161; *Civil Service Building Society v. MacDougall*, 1988 S.L.T. 687.

[13] *Baxter v. Lothian Health Board*, 1976 S.L.T. (Notes) 37.

[14] *McGown v. Erskine*, 1978 S.L.T. (Notes) 4; *Kirkwood & Co. (Fashions) Ltd v. Glasgow D.C.*, Glasgow Sh. Ct, Jan. 12, 1981, unreported; Macphail, *Evidence*, para. 25–05.

[15] OCR, r. 28.5(1).

[16] OCR, r. 28.6(1).

[17] OCR, r. 28.7(1).

[18] OCR, r. 28.5(2). See paras 15.66 to 15.71 (optional procedure) and 15.72 to 15.79 (commission).

[19] OCR, r. 28.6(2).

amendments.[20] In the case of an order for the preservation, custody and detention of a document or other property the party obtaining the order must provide the commissioner with a copy of the specification, a copy of the pleadings as adjusted and amended, and a certified copy of the interlocutor appointing him.[21] That party must serve a copy of the order on the haver,[22] and is responsible for the fees of the commissioner and his clerk.[23] When the commission has been executed the commissioner sends a report of the execution, any document or other property taken by him and an inventory thereof to the sheriff clerk for the further order of the sheriff.[24]

Bankers' books

Entries in bankers' books are frequently included in a specification of documents, and on diligence being granted the bank often supplies certified excerpts which the parties agree to accept as sufficient. It is therefore seldom necessary to resort to the provisions of the Bankers' Books Evidence Act 1879, the object of which is to facilitate the proof of matters recorded in bankers' books and to avoid the expense and trouble of attendance at court by bank officials with their books.[25] The Act provides that in any legal proceeding to which the bank is not a party,[26] a banker or officer of a bank is not compellable to produce any banker's book the contents of which can be proved under the Act, or to appear as a witness to prove the matters, transactions, and accounts therein recorded, unless by order of a judge made for special cause.[27] **15.93**

The Act provides, by section 7, that on the application of any party to a legal proceeding,[28] a court or judge[29] may order that such party be at liberty to inspect and take copies of any entries in a banker's book for any of the purposes of such proceedings. Such an order may be made either with or without summoning the bank or any other party, and must be served on the bank three clear days before it is to be obeyed, unless the court or judge otherwise directs.[30] While it is therefore competent to grant an *ex parte* application without prior intimation to the bank or any other party, it is thought that as a general rule notice of the application should be given to the bank and to the **15.94**

---

20 OCR, r. 28.6(3).
21 OCR, r. 28.7(2)(a).
22 OCR, r. 28.7(2)(c).
23 OCR, r. 28.7(2)(b).
24 OCR, r. 28.7(3).
25 On the origins and purpose of the Act, see *Waterhouse v. Barker* [1924] 2 K.B. 759 at 763, 768–769.
26 Where the bank is a party its books, like those of any other litigant, may be recovered subject to the qualifications already discussed in paras 15.52 to 15.55.
27 Bankers' Books Evidence Act 1879, s. 6. "A judge" means, in Scotland, a Lord Ordinary (1879 Act, s. 10). It may be noted that s. 10 also provides that in England and Wales a judge of the county court is empowered to exercise the powers of a judge with respect to any action in his court. A sheriff is given no such power.
28 "Legal proceeding" includes any civil proceeding: s. 10. The words "in which evidence is or may be given" in s. 10 qualify only "inquiry" and not "civil or criminal proceeding": *Carmichael v. Sexton*, 1986 S.L.T. 16.
29 "The court" means the court before whom a legal proceeding is held or taken: s. 10. An order for inspection under s. 7 may therefore be made by the sheriff, unlike an order under s. 6.
30 As to applications under s. 7 in criminal proceedings, see Macphail, *Evidence*, paras 25.48–S25.48B.

other parties to the action.[31] The court appears to have jurisdiction to order inspection of the accounts of a person who is not a party to the action, but there are no reported cases of such an order in Scotland, and in England the power to make such an order is said to be seldom, if ever, exercised.[32]

15.95 An application under section 7 cannot be used to support a fishing diligence or searching inquiry beyond the ordinary rules applicable to the recovery of documents by commission and diligence.[33] Thus, while an application under section 7 may be granted before the closing of the record,[34] the applicant must show that the documents are required to enable him to make his averments more specific, or to meet a call from his opponent for further specification, or to make adequate reply to his opponent's averments.[35] The question whether to grant an application under section 7, like the question whether to grant a diligence, is one for the discretion of the sheriff.[36] A party to civil proceedings seems entitled to object that the entries tend to incriminate him.[37] As in a commission and diligence, the order should be carefully limited in point of time.[38]

15.96 The expenses of any procedure under the Act are also in the discretion of the sheriff. He may order the expenses or any part thereof to be paid to any party by the bank where they have been occasioned by any default or delay on the part of the bank, and any such order against the bank may be enforced as if the bank was a party to the proceeding.[39]

15.97 In the Act[40] "bank" and "banker" mean an institution authorised under the Banking Act 1987 or a municipal bank within the meaning of that Act; a building society within the meaning of the Building Societies Act 1986; the National Savings Bank; and the Post Office in the exercise of its powers to provide banking services.[41] "Bankers' books" include ledgers, day books, cash books, account books and other records used in the ordinary business of the bank, whether those records are in written form or are kept on microfilm, magnetic tape or any other form of mechanical or electronic data retrieval mechanism.

---

[31] For a form of minute, see Dobie, *Styles*, p. 327. Orders relative to entries in the books of foreign banks, which are kept abroad, should ordinarily be made on notice to the bank, and only in very exceptional circumstances: *Mackinnon v. Donaldson, Lufkin and Jenrette Securities Corpn* [1986] Ch. 482.

[32] Halsbury's *Laws of England* (4th ed., 1973), Vol. 3, para. 126; *R. v. Grossman* (1981) 73 Cr.App. 302

[33] *Blue Sky Holdings Ltd v. Doran*, Sh. Pr. Dick, Glasgow Sh. Ct, Dec. 13, 1982, unreported, considering, *inter alia, Re Bankers' Books Evidence Act 1879, R. v. Bono* (1913) 29 T.L.R. 635 and *Williams v. Summerfield* [1972] 2 Q.B. 513. See also *Waterhouse v. Barker* [1924] 2 K.B. 759.

[34] *Burrows, Petr* (1905) 21 Sh.Ct.Rep. 215; *Blue Sky Holdings Ltd, supra.*

[35] *Blue Sky Holdings Ltd, supra.* See also paras 15.51 to 15.53.

[36] *Blue Sky Holdings Ltd, supra.*

[37] *Waterhouse, supra; cf. Williams, supra.*

[38] *Blue Sky Holdings Ltd, supra; cf. R. v. Marlborough St. Stipendiary Magistrate, ex p. Simpson* (1980) 70 Cr. App. R. 291; *R. v. Grossman, supra.*

[39] Bankers' Books Evidence Act 1879, s. 8.

[40] *ibid.* s. 9, as substituted by Banking Act 1979, Sched. 6, para. 1, and amended by Banking Act 1987, Sched. 6 and Building Societies Act 1986.

[41] An objection by the Postmaster General to production on the ground of confidentiality was overruled in *Forrest v MacGregor*, 1913 1 S.L.T. 372.

Public records

Extracts from public records are generally admissible.[42] If it is necessary to produce an original document, the following special procedure is prescribed. Where any party to a cause desires to obtain from the Keeper of the Registers of Scotland or the Keeper of the Records of Scotland production of the originals of any register or deed under his custody, he must apply by motion[43] to the sheriff before whom the cause depends, after seven days' notice of such application given in writing to the Keeper in charge of the originals.[44] Upon such application the sheriff may by interlocutor certify that it is necessary for the ends of justice that the application should be granted. The party may then make application by letter (enclosing a copy of the interlocutor duly certified by the sheriff clerk or one of his deputes) addressed to the Deputy Principal Clerk of Session, for an order from the Court of Session authorising the Keeper to exhibit the original of any register or deed to the sheriff.[45] The Deputy Principal Clerk of Session submits the application to a Lord Ordinary in Chambers, who, if satisfied, grants a warrant for production or exhibition of the original.[46] A certified copy of the warrant is served on the Keeper.[47] The officer selected attends the court with the record, which must remain in his physical custody unless the order expressly authorises it to be handed over to the court. A fee is payable, being the full value of the work and materials involved and/or the full cost (including travelling expenses) of an officer attending court.[48] The expense of the production or the exhibition of an original register or deed must be met in the first instance by the party who made the application.[49] Since the document is in court only to be exhibited to the sheriff by virtue of the warrant, the sheriff may not sanction any experiments upon it.[50] In practice it is rarely necessary to produce an original document because its attributes are usually sufficiently clear from an extract made by photocopying or a similar facsimile process. An application for an original document in the custody of the Keeper of the Registers of Scotland is very seldom made because such a document is in the Keeper's hands only during the process of registration, and is thereafter returned to the ingiver or transmitted for preservation to the Scottish Record Office. **15.98**

Where any sheriff court record which has been transmitted to the Keeper of the Records of Scotland is required for the purposes of any proceedings in the sheriff court, the Keeper will re-transmit the record to the sheriff clerk on an order by the sheriff. The sheriff clerk must return the record to the Keeper as soon as may be after it has ceased to be required for that purpose.[51] **15.99**

Documents in another process

Where a party requires a document which is already a production in another depending sheriff court process, the party's solicitor may **15.100**

---

[42] Walkers, p. 240, para. 227.
[43] OCR, r. 28.9(1).
[44] OCR, r. 28.9(2).
[45] OCR, r. 28.9(3).
[46] OCR, r. 28.9(4).
[47] OCR, r. 28.9(5).
[48] Fees in the Registers of Scotland Order 1995 (S.I. 1995 No.1945), Sched., Pt XII, Item 3.
[49] OCR, r. 28.9(6).
[50] *cf. Irvine v. Powrie's Trs*, 1915 S.C. 1006.
[51] Public Records (Scotland) Act 1937, s. 2(2).

borrow it if he is also the solicitor for a party in that process. The sheriff, however, unlike the Court of Session,[52] cannot be applied to in order to authorise the production of a process which is depending in any other sheriff court, unless perhaps by means of an application for a commission and diligence designed to procure the recovery of some part of the process from the custody of the sheriff clerk of that court. Such an application would have to be intimated to the Lord Advocate.[53] In theory there may be no reason why a document lodged in one depending process should not be borrowed or recovered and lodged in another, but there may be practical difficulties involved in ensuring that it would be returned for any diet at which it might be required in each process, and that it would be conveniently borrowable by the parties to each process. The sheriff may not grant a commission and diligence for the recovery of a transcript of the shorthand notes of a criminal trial on indictment.[54]

Confidentiality

15.101 The Ordinary Cause Rules provide[55] for the protection of any evidence in respect of which confidentiality is claimed in the proceedings for recovery which have been discussed above, namely the optional procedure,[56] execution of a commission and diligence for the recovery of documents,[57] execution of an order for production or recovery of documents or other property under section 1(1) of the Administration of Justice (Scotland) Act 1972,[58] execution of an order for the preservation, etc., of documents or other property under section 1(1) of the 1972 Act.[59] The rule provides that where confidentiality is claimed for any evidence sought to be recovered, such evidence must, where practicable, be enclosed in a sealed packet.[60] If sealing up the evidence is not practicable it is not to be recovered without the authority of the court. The party who has obtained the commission and diligence may lodge a motion to have a sealed package of evidence opened up or, where sealing has not been practicable, to have the evidence recovered.[61] Such a motion may be lodged by any other party to the cause after the date of intimation by the sheriff clerk (in terms of either rule 28.3(5) or rule 28.4(10)) that the party obtaining the commission has failed to uplift documents.[62] Any party lodging such a motion must as well as intimating the motion to all other parties in the usual way,[63] intimate the motion to the haver by first class recorded delivery post.[64] The person claiming confidentiality is entitled to oppose the motion.[65]

---

[52] RCS 35.10; *Brown v. Glenboig Union Fire Clay Co. Ltd*, 1911 1 S.L.T. 27.
[53] para. 15.60.
[54] *Storrie v. Murray*, 1974 S.L.T. (Sh. Ct.) 45: Macphail, *Evidence*, paras 25.16–S25.18.
[55] OCR, r. 28.8.
[56] paras 15.66 to 15.71.
[57] paras 15.72 to 15.79.
[58] paras 15.91, 15.92.
[59] *ibid.*
[60] OCR, r. 28.8(1).
[61] OCR, r. 28.8(2)(a).
[62] OCR, r. 28.8(2)(b).
[63] In terms of OCR, r. 15.2.
[64] OCR, r. 28.8(3).
[65] OCR, r. 28.8(4).

Medical examinations

In practice medical examinations in personal injuries actions are nearly always arranged by agreement between the parties. The court may, however, ordain the pursuer to submit himself for medical examination by a doctor selected by the defenders.[66] Such an order has been pronounced before the closing of the record.[67] Whether the court may ordain the pursuer to submit to examination elsewhere than in the neighbourhood of his home has not been decided.[68] An order to submit to medical examination may be made, exceptionally, in consistorial causes, where a party's medical condition is in issue.[69] In theory, if a party refuses to obey such an order, it may be enforced by imprisonment,[70] but in practice an inference adverse to him may be drawn from his refusal.[71] It has been recommended that if a pursuer refuses, the action should be sisted, and if a defender refuses, an adverse inference might be drawn.[72] The court will not, however, require a party, upon an allegation by his opponent that the party is mentally incapable, to submit to medical examination before giving evidence.[73] The court has no power to ordain a witness to submit to medical examination; and evidence of the medical condition of a paramour is inadmissible in the absence of her consent to examination on behalf of the pursuer.[74] **15.102**

Blood tests

No one can be compelled to give a sample of blood for the purpose of tests to determine paternity. A person who consents to give a sample should be made fully aware of what the tests might establish. A person who consents to his blood being taken for testing in hospital in the ordinary course of treatment impliedly consents to any use being made of the blood for testing which the hospital authorities consider is necessary, and evidence has been admitted regarding the blood grouping of such samples of blood taken from a person who subsequently died.[75] **15.103**

Section 6 of the Law Reform (Parent and Child) (Scotland) Act 1986[76] applies where, for the purpose of obtaining evidence relating to the determination of parentage in civil proceedings, a sample of blood or other body fluid or body tissue is sought by a party to the proceedings or by a curator *ad litem*.[77] It provides that, where such a sample is sought from a child under the age of 16 years, consent to the taking of the sample may be given by any person having parental responsibilities (within the meaning of section 1(3) of the Children (Scotland) Act 1995) in relation to him or having care and control of him.[78] Where such a sample is sought **15.104**

---

[66] *Junner v. N.B. Ry* (1877) 4 R. 686.

[67] *Smith v. Gow* (1895) 2 S.L.T. 473.

[68] *McDonald v. Western SMT Co.*, 1945 S.C 47.

[69] *AB or D v. CD* (1908) 15 S.L.T. 911; *X v. Y*, 1922 S.L.T. 158. See Clive, pp. 99–100; Walkers, pp. 442–443, para. 418(a).

[70] *Whitehall v. Whitehall*, 1958 S.C. 252, *per* L.J.-C. Thomson at 258.

[71] *Docherty v. McGlynn*, 1983 S.L.T. 645, *per* Lord Cameron at 650.

[72] Scot. Law Com., *Evidence* (Memo. No. 46, 1980), para. M.03.

[73] *McIntyre v. McIntyre*, 1920 1 S.L.T. 207.

[74] *Davidson v. Davidson* (1860) 22 D. 749; *Borthwick v. Borthwick*, 1929 S.L.T. 57; *Mitchell v. Mitchell*, 1954 S.L.T. (Sh. Ct.) 45.

[75] *Docherty v. McGlynn*, 1985 S.L.T. 237.

[76] As amended by Law Reform (Miscellaneous Provision) (Scotland) Act 1990, s. 70(3), Age of Legal Capacity (Scotland) Act 1991, Sched. 1, Children (Scotland) Act 1995, Sched. 4.

[77] 1986 Act, s. 6(1).

[78] *ibid.* s. 6(2).

from any person who is incapable of giving consent, the Court of Session or the sheriff may consent to the taking of the sample where (a) there is no person who is entitled to give such consent, or (b) there is such a person, but it is not reasonably practicable to obtain his consent in the circumstances, or he is unwilling to accept the responsibility of giving or withholding consent.[79] The Court of Session or the sheriff must not, however, consent unless satisfied that the taking of the sample would not be detrimental to the person's health.[80]

III. Effect of Irregular Recovery of Evidence

15.105 It has been said that it is the policy of the law to admit almost all evidence which will throw light on disputed facts and enable justice to be done,[81] and evidence illegally or irregularly obtained has been admitted in a number of cases.[82] But in *Rattray v. Rattray*,[83] the only Inner House case which is cited on the point in modern times, there was no majority in favour of the admissibility of such evidence, and the general question of its admissibility has not since then been judicially considered in the Inner House.[84] It has been proposed that in civil cases, as in criminal cases, the court should be entitled to exclude evidence obtained by illegal or irregular means.[85]

15.106 Documents which are legitimately in a party's possession may be used in evidence although he could not have recovered them by commission and diligence.[86]

---

[79] 1986 Act, s. 6(3).

[80] *ibid*, s. 6(4).

[81] *Rattray v. Rattray* (1897) 25 R. 315, *per* Lord Trayner at 318–319; *Docherty v. McGlynn*, 1985 S.L.T. 237 at 239–240.

[82] *MacNeill v. MacNeill*, 1929 S.L.T. 251; *Turner v. Turner*, 1930 S.L.T. 393; *Watson v. Watson*, 1934 S.C. 374; *MacColl v. MacColl*, 1946 S.L.T. 312; *Duke of Argyll v. Duchess of Argyll*, 1963 S.L.T. (Notes) 42.

[83] (1897) 25 R. 315, discussed in Macphail, *Evidence*, paras 21.08–21.09.

[84] See *Duke of Argyll v. Duchess of Argyll*, 1962 S.C. 140, *per* Lord Guthrie at 152; Macphail, *Evidence*, paras 21.08–S21.15.

[85] Scot. Law Com., *Evidence* (Memo. No. 46, 1980), para. U.06.

[86] *McLeish v. Glasgow Bonding Co. Ltd*, 1965 S.L.T. 39; *Gibson, Petr*, 1984 S.L.T. 61.

CHAPTER 16

THE PROOF

MATTERS PRELIMINARY TO THE DIET OF PROOF

Preparation for the proof

A party's solicitor should have carefully considered the factual and legal basis of his client's case before drafting the initial writ or defences.[1] Further thought and investigation are required while the action is at the stage of adjustment, and the solicitor should always keep in view the nature of the evidence and the arguments which he may require to adduce at the proof. Preparation for the proof always entails the precognition of witnesses and the examination of all documentary or real evidence which may be relevant, and decisions as to which witnesses are to be cited, which documents or objects are to be lodged in court as productions, and what procedural steps should be taken to protect the client's interests before judgment. Under the Ordinary Cause Rules 1993 it is necessary to give careful thought to such matters at an earlier stage than was formerly the case since each party is now required, within 14 days after the date of the interlocutor allowing a proof or proof before answer, to intimate to every other party a list of witnesses, including any skilled witnesses, whom he intends to call to give evidence.[2] That list must include the name, occupation (where known) and address of each intended witness.[3] If a party seeks to call as a witness a person who is not on that list, and if any other party objects to that being done, he must seek leave of the sheriff to call that person as a witness. Leave may be granted on such conditions, if any, as the sheriff thinks fit.[4] Thorough investigation and preparation are invaluable skills which are not always fully cultivated: cases may be lost because a witness has not been traced or has not been fully and accurately precognosced, or a document has not been recovered or lodged, or its significance has not been appreciated. Excellent practical advice about preparation for proof is available in the undernoted work.[5] By contrast this chapter and others are concerned to explain the procedural framework within which the practitioner operates. This section of this chapter explains the rules of procedure relative to preliminary matters which must be considered in all cases in which proof has been allowed. Other incidental procedures which may be invoked prior to proof, including those relative to amendment of pleadings and recovery of evidence, are dealt with in earlier chapters. 16.01

---

[1] See para. 9.12.

[2] OCR, r. 9.14(1).

[3] *ibid.* r. 9.14(3).

[4] *ibid.* r. 9.14(2).

[5] B. Kearney, *An Introduction to Ordinary Civil Procedure in the Sheriff Court* (1982) (hereafter "Kearney").

Citation of witnesses

Whether necessary

16.02 The purpose and effect of a citation is to compel a person's attendance within the precincts of the court.[6] A witness may also be required by his citation to bring with him specified documents[7] but that will be appropriate only in the rare instance of a document which does not require to be lodged as a production in advance of the diet of proof.[8] No person adduced as a witness is excluded by reason of having appeared without citation[9] or on an irregular or invalid citation.[10] If a competent witness, who has knowledge of the circumstances to be inquired into, is present in court, there is no inherent objection to his being compelled to give evidence, whether he is a party or not, if the court decides that that is desirable in the interests of justice with a view to the ascertainment of the facts.[11] But while citation of a witness is not a necessary preliminary to his examination, it is a wise precaution to cite every witness required.[12] Moreover, as has already been noted in the preceding paragraph, difficulties may may be encountered if a particular witness has not been named in the list of witnesses which must be intimated at an early stage in the proceedings.

Warrant for citation

16.03 A copy of an interlocutor certified by the sheriff clerk allowing a proof is sufficient warrant for citation of witnesses.[13] The interlocutor should expressly bear that the diet is for proof.[14] It may specify the sheriff court house, or a specific court room within the sheriff court house, as the place where the proof is to be taken. A Court of Session interlocutor allowing proof is also sufficient warrant for citation of witnesses.[15]

Period of notice

16.04 The witness must be duly cited on a period of notice of at least seven days.[16] In practice, longer notice should be given if possible. As soon as the proof is fixed, a letter should be sent to all witnesses advising them of the date and that a formal citation will follow.[17] In particular, a medical or other expert witness should be told of the date of the proof as soon as it is fixed, so that he may make alternative arrangements relative to his professional commitments: he may be formally cited later.[18] Postal citation should in any event be made in sufficient time to allow for personal citation by sheriff officer in the event of the citation being returned. In order to minimise inconvenience to a busy witness, he may be advised that he need

---

[6] *Watson v. Livingstone* (1902) 5 F. 171 at 176; *McDonnell v. McShane*, 1967 S.L.T. (Sh. Ct.) 61 at 63.

[7] OCR App., Form G.13. The reference to the bringing of documents is primarily applicable to the citation of a haver in procedure for the recovery of documents: see para. 15.76).

[8] See paras 16.18 *et seq.*

[9] Evidence (Scotland) Act 1852, s. 1.

[10] *Watson, supra.*

[11] *McDonnell, supra*, at 63.

[12] Maclaren, p. 557; *McDonnell, supra*, at 64.

[13] OCR, r. 29.7(3).

[14] *Grant v. Grant* (1908) 24 Sh.Ct.Rep. 114 at 118–119.

[15] RCS, r. 36.2(2).

[16] OCR, r. 29.7(4).

[17] Kearney, pp. 105–106.

[18] (1985) 30 J.L.S. 2.

not attend until a certain hour of the day; and where the proof is likely to take more than one day, he should not be required to attend until the day and time when his evidence is likely to be needed. For this purpose the defender's solicitor should ascertain from the pursuer's solicitor how much time the pursuer's case is likely to occupy.[19]

Citation by party litigants

Where a party to a cause is a party litigant, he must (a) not later than four weeks before the diet of proof apply to the sheriff by motion to fix caution in such sum as the sheriff considers reasonable having regard to the number of witnesses he proposes to cite and the period for which they may be required to attend court; and (b) before instructing a sheriff officer to cite a witness, find caution for such expenses as can reasonably be anticipated to be incurred by the witness in answering the citation.[20] A party litigant who does not intend to cite all the witnesses referred to in the foregoing application may apply by motion for variation of the amount of caution.[21] The terms of rule 29.8, coupled with the fact that the Form of citation can be signed only by a sheriff officer or a solicitor (see below), suggest that citation by a sheriff officer is the only competent method of citation available to a party litigant. **16.05**

Travelling expenses

A penalty for failure to attend[22] may be imposed on a witness who has been duly cited and has demanded and been paid his travelling expenses.[23] It is prudent for the party citing the witness not to await a demand for travelling expenses but to tender the travelling expenses along with the citation, and to make any other necessary outlays or arrangements relative to his attendance at court.[24] **16.06**

Penalty

If the witness fails to attend, he may be ordained by the sheriff to forfeit and pay a penalty not exceeding £250, unless a reasonable excuse is offered and sustained, and the sheriff may grant decree for that penalty in favour of the party on whose behalf the witness was cited.[25] Such a penalty is additional to any expenses which may be decerned for against the witness *quoad* a warrant for a second diligence[26] or a warrant to arrest.[27] **16.07**

Form and modes of citation

Witnesses should be cited in terms of Form G.13 as set out in the Appendix to the Ordinary Cause Rules.[28] Any documents they are required to produce should be specified in the form. The form may be signed only by a sheriff officer or a solicitor.[29] The witness is normally **16.08**

---

19 *Kelvin v. Whyte, Thomson & Co.*, 1909 1 S.L.T. 477 at 478.
20 OCR, r. 29.8(1).
21 *ibid.* r. 29.8(2).
22 See para. 16.07.
23 OCR, r. 29.10(2).
24 Kearney, p. 104.
25 OCR, r. 29.10(2).
26 OCR, r. 29.9: see para. 16.12.
27 OCR, r. 29.10(1): see para. 16.15.
28 OCR, r. 29.7(4).
29 OCR, App., Form G.13; *Wilson* (1885) 13 R. 342.

cited postally by recorded delivery first-class service.[30] The period of notice starts to run from the beginning of the day after the date of posting.[31] On the face of the envelope there must be written or printed a notice in the terms specified in rule 5.3(3), indicating that the letter contains a citation to the particular sheriff court and instructing immediate return of the letter to the sheriff clerk if delivery cannot be made at the address shown.[32] The sheriff clerk then intimates the fact to the party who has endeavoured to cite.[33] Citation by sheriff officer is also competent, but fees for such citation are not allowed on taxation unless the sheriff deciding the case is of opinion that it was not expedient in the interests of justice that postal citation should be made.[34]

Certificate of citation

16.09 The certificate of citation, which requires to be lodged after citation has taken place, should be in the terms of Form G.12 as set out in the Appendix to the Ordinary Cause Rules,[35] and may be signed only by a sheriff officer or a solicitor.[36] Where the citation has been postal, any relevant postal receipts must be annexed to the certificate.[37] If the witness fails to answer his citation, the sheriff will not grant second diligence[38] or a warrant for his arrest[39] unless a relevant certificate of citation is produced.

Cancellation of citation

16.10 If, after the citation of the witness, it is decided that his attendance is not required, or that the diet of proof is to be discharged, the solicitor who has cited him should at once inform him that his citation is cancelled. The solicitor must, however, advise him that the cancellation is not to affect any other citation which he may have received from another party in that cause.[40]

Fees and expenses

16.11 Witnesses' fees and travelling and subsistence allowances are fixed by the auditor of court, limits being prescribed for the fees.[41] The auditor's determinations are subject to revision by the sheriff upon objections to his report.[42] Charges in addition to the ordinary witness fees may be allowed in respect of persons certified by the sheriff for remuneration as skilled witnesses.[43] A solicitor who cites a witness is personally liable for his fees and expenses,[44] but he is entitled to be reimbursed by his client or, in most cases where the client is an assisted person, out of the legal aid fund.

---

[30] Citation Amendment (Scotland) Act 1882, s. 6; Recorded Delivery Service Act 1962, s. 1; OCR, r. 29.7.
[31] OCR, r. 5.3(2).
[32] OCR, r. 5.3(3).
[33] Citation Amendment (Scotland) Act 1882, s. 4.
[34] *ibid.* s. 6.
[35] OCR, r. 29.7(4).
[36] OCR, App., Form G.12; *Wilson, supra.*
[37] OCR, r. 5.3(4).
[38] See para. 16.12.
[39] See para. 16.15.
[40] OCR, r. 29.7(6).
[41] A.S. (Fees of Witnesses and Shorthand Writers in the Sheriff Court) 1992 (S.I. 1992 No. 1878): see *Parliament House Book*, A237 *et seq.* See paras 19.59 to 19.66
[42] See paras 19.38 to 19.41.
[43] A. S. 1992, *supra*, Sched. 1, para. 9: see paras. 16.103, 19.61 to 19.66.
[44] OCR, r. 29.7(5); *Fraser v. Stronach* (1885) 23 S.L.R. 76; *Bayley v. Middleton*, 1909 1 S.L.T. 493.

Second diligence and apprehension of witness

The sheriff may grant second diligence to compel the attendance of a witness under pain of arrest and imprisonment until caution can be found for his due attendance.[45] The warrant for a second diligence is effective in any sheriffdom without endorsation, and the expenses thereof may be decerned for against the witness,[46] who is not entitled to expenses.[47] **16.12**

The sheriff may also grant a warrant for the apprehension of a witness who fails to answer a citation.[48] Second diligence may, where the diet is adjourned, be an alternative remedy for such failure and it is the only measure available before the proof where a party has duly cited or attempted to cite a witness and there is reason to believe that he will not attend the court.[49] The sheriff pronounces an interlocutor granting letters of second diligence,[50] which are issued by the sheriff clerk in the name of the sheriff principal and addressed to sheriff officers, requiring them to apprehend the witness and imprison him within a named prison. The usual style of letters of second diligence[51] does not appear to be prescribed by statute or Act of Sederunt, and it is submitted that its terms need not be copied but may with advantage be modernised where appropriate and adapted to the circumstances of the particular case. It is thought that a reference to a penalty of £250 should be substituted for the reference to a penalty of 40 shillings,[52] and that the sheriff should fix a sum in name of caution which should be specified in the warrant and letters.[53] Caution should be related to the person's means and not fixed at an impossible sum.[54] **16.13**

In a criminal case it is open to the sheriff to order the detention of a witness without giving him the opportunity of finding caution if, on the information before him, the sheriff has reasonable grounds for apprehending that there is a real risk of a material witness not obeying his citation to appear in court for the trial.[55] There is no such power in a civil case. Arrest and imprisonment on second diligence are competent only until caution be found. While in a criminal case any person cited must give his attendance as matter of imperative duty, there is no such public duty to appear as a witness regarding a question of private right at the instance of a private party.[56] In a civil case the sheriff should proceed with care before granting a warrant for a second diligence prior to a proof. He must be satisfied that the witness is a material witness; that he has been cited or has frustrated an attempt to cite him, as by refusing his citation[57]; and that there is a real risk of his not appearing. **16.14**

---

45 OCR, r. 29.9(1).

46 OCR, r. 29.9(2).

47 *Mason* (1830) 5 Mur. 129 (note).

48 See para. 16.15.

49 Maclaren, pp. 343, 557.

50 So called to distinguish them from letters of first diligence to cite witnesses and havers: the certified interlocutor which is the warrant for citation (OCR, r. 29.7(3)) is used in place of these: see Maclaren, pp. 343–344.

51 Lewis, pp. 553–554; Dobie, *Styles*, p. 554.

52 See OCR, r. 29.10(2): *cf.* the original r. 71 in the 1907 Act, Sched. 1.

53 *cf.* Criminal Procedure (Scotland) Act 1975, s. 321(5), now repealed (and replaced, in different terms, by Criminal Procedure (Scotland) Act 1995, s. 156 (3), (4)).

54 *Stallworth v. H.M. Advocate*, 1978 S.L.T. 93 at 94.

55 Hume, ii, 375; *Stallworth, supra*; *Gerrard, Petr*, 1984 S.L.T. 108.

56 *Fraser v. Stronach* (1885) 23 S.L.R. 76.

57 *cf. Steedman v. Steedman* (1886) 23 S.L.R. 856.

Warrant to arrest

16.15 Where any witness fails to answer a citation after having been duly cited the sheriff may, upon production of a relevant certificate of citation, grant warrant for the apprehension of the witness and for bringing him to the court, and the expenses thereof may be decerned for against the witness.[58] This rule, which was introduced in 1983, corresponds approximately with the practice of the Court of Session.[59] It is thought that the power to issue such a warrant should be exercised with caution,[60] and that the sheriff should be satisfied not only that the witness has been cited but that his travelling expenses have been tendered to him,[61] that he is a material witness and that the party moving for the warrant has ascertained whether there is any reasonable explanation for his non-attendance. If there is, the diet may be adjourned and he may be cited again.

Witness in custody

16.16 Whether a person in custody should be produced in a civil court is a matter for the discretion of the responsible minister, who may direct that the person be taken to court if satisfied that his attendance is desirable in the interests of justice.[62] Accordingly, where a person detained in a prison or other establishment in the United Kingdom, the Channel Islands or the Isle of Man is a material witness for a party, the party's solicitor should in good time make a written application for his attendance at court by letter to the governor of the establishment, if the person is detained in Scotland, or to the Home Office, if he is detained elsewhere.[63] Since the party may be required to tender the reasonable expenses of the prisoner and his escort,[64] the letter should give the solicitor's undertaking to pay the expenses of production. It should also state the title of the action, the relevant facts, the grounds of the application, that the prisoner's evidence is essential, and the place, date and time at which the prisoner's presence is required. In the case of an untried prisoner, it is necessary to obtain the consent of the procurator fiscal or other prosecutor at whose instance he is detained: the solicitor should obtain the prosecutor's consent before making the application. It is the duty of the Secretary of State or, in practice, of the governor acting under powers delegated to him to consider whether he is satisfied that it is desirable in the interests of justice that the prisoner should attend.[65] If the prisoner is a party litigant, his production may be refused if he has no funds to pay the costs of his production.[66]

---

[58] OCR, r. 29.10(1).

[59] Maclaren, pp. 344–345; Maxwell, p. 305; Green's *Annotated Rules of the Court of Session*, note 36.2.7.

[60] *cf.* Renton and Brown's *Criminal Procedure* (6th ed., 1996), para. 11–22.

[61] See para. 16.06.

[62] Criminal Justice Act 1961, s. 29(1), as amended by Children and Young Persons Act 1963, Sched. 3, para. 50, Children and Young Persons Act 1969, Sched. 5, para. 46, Sched. 6, and Criminal Law Act 1977, Sched. 12.

[63] The address is: The Home Office, Cleland House, Page Street, London SW1P 4LN. In case of urgency an application may be made by telephone.

[64] *Becker v. Home Office* [1972] 2 Q.B. 407. It is understood that where the person is detained in Scotland the question whether expenses will be charged is a matter for the Scottish Home Department.

[65] *R. v. Governor of Brixton Prison, ex. p. Walsh* [1985] A.C. 154.

[66] *R. v. Secretary of State for the Home Department, ex. p. Greenwood, The Times*, Aug. 2, 1986.

Witness furth of Scotland

A witness furth of Scotland cannot be effectively cited to attend a diet in a civil action in the sheriff court.[67] A party may apply to the court for his evidence to be taken on commission or by letter of request.[68] **16.17**

Lodging of productions

Documents founded on in pleadings

Any document founded on by a party, or adopted as incorporated in his pleadings, must, so far as in his possession or within his control, be lodged in process as a production (a) when founded on or adopted in an initial writ, at the time of returning the initial writ under rule 9.3; (b) when founded on or adopted in a minute, defences, counterclaim or answers, at the time of lodging that part of process; and (c) when founded on or adopted in an adjustment to any pleadings, at the time when any such adjustment is intimated to any other party.[69] However, the foregoing is without prejudice to any power of the sheriff to order the production of any document or grant commssion and diligence for recovery of it.[70] If a party fails to lodge a document in the manner, and at the time, just described, he may be found liable in the expenses of any order for production or recovery of it obtained by any other party.[71] **16.18**

Return of parts of process and productions

All parts of process and productions which have been borrowed must be returned before 12.30 p.m. on the day preceding the diet of proof.[72] **16.19**

Productions for proof

All productions which are intended to be used at the proof must be lodged in process not later than 14 days before the diet of proof.[73] They should be accompanied by an inventory entitled "Inventory of Productions for the Pursuer [or Defender]", which is a numbered list of the productions lodged and to which any documentary productions are attached. Each production should itself be numbered with the serial number of the case and the production's number on the inventory. Inventories and productions, like other parts of process, should be presented unbacked and unfolded.[74] In the modern style of process a numbered file or folder is prescribed for pursuer's productions and for defender's productions, with the former being number 5 of process and the latter being number 6 of process. Consequently, the first inventory of productions lodged by a pursuer will be known as number 5/1 of process and, for example, the third document in a second inventory of productions for the pursuer will be number 5/2/3 of process. **16.20**

---

67 *Lawson v. Swan National Car Rental Ltd*, Sh. Pr. Dick, Glasgow Sh. Ct, Sept. 27, 1985, unreported; Macphail, *Evidence*, para. 24.37.

68 See paras 15.40 to 15.42.

69 OCR, r. 21.1(1).

70 OCR, r. 21.1(2).

71 OCR, r. 21.2.

72 OCR, r. 29.13.

73 OCR, r. 29.11(1).

74 OCR, r. 11.1.

Intimation; copy productions

16.21 At the same time as the productions are lodged, intimation of their lodging must be given to the other party or parties[75] by delivering a copy of the inventory and, where practicable, of any documentary productions. Not later than 48 hours before the diet of proof a copy of every production, marked with the appropriate number of process, must be lodged for the use of the sheriff.[76] The productions lodged are borrowable, but must be returned not later than 12.30 p.m. on the date preceding the diet of proof.[77]

Restriction on other productions

16.22 No production other than those timeously lodged may be used or put in evidence at the proof unless by consent of parties or by leave of the sheriff on cause shown, and on such conditions, if any, as to expenses or otherwise as the sheriff thinks fit.[78]

Preparation and copying of documents

16.23 There are no general rules as to the preparation and copying of documents for use in court except those already noticed for the delivery of copies to other parties and the provision of copies for the sheriff.[79] The following recommendations are, however, in accordance with good practice.

(i) Documents should be securely fastened to the inventory, but not in such a way that parts of them cannot be read.

(ii) Each copy should be clearly marked with its identifying number of process. Care should be taken that the copies are legible and that edges and other parts of documents are not omitted. They should not be so stapled or bound that parts of them cannot be read.

(iii) Where many documents have been lodged, in more than one inventory, the parties' solicitors should agree the most efficient way of presenting them to the court. That may be done by preparing one indexed and consecutively paginated dossier of copies of all parties' documents, arranged either in chronological order or in some other way which renders them intelligible.[80] Such an "agreed bundle" makes for ease of reference by the sheriff, the parties' advocates and the witnesses, and avoids unnecessary duplication where documents common to more than one inventory are separately copied.[81] Unless there is a joint minute of admissions,[82] the agreeing of such a bundle does not mean that the contents of the documents are accepted as being true, or that the documents are admissible in evidence. If a party wishes to object to the admissibility of a document and to make legal submissions before the sheriff reads it, it may be omitted from the bundle and

---

75 OCR, r. 11.6(1).

76 OCR, r. 29.12(1).

77 See para. 16.19.

78 OCR, r. 29.11(2).

79 See para. 16.21.

80 It may be convenient to present experts' reports or solicitors' correspondence separately.

81 Unnecessary duplication of documents was criticised in *Murray's Trs v. Wilson's Exrx*, 1945 S.C. 51. See also *Unigate Foods Ltd v. Scottish Milk Marketing Board*, 1975 S.C. (H.L.) 75 at 106.

82 See paras 16.28 *et seq.*

an application made to dispense with the requirement that a copy be lodged for the use of the sheriff. The need for that course can, however, seldom arise.[83]

What should be lodged

The nature of the productions to be lodged obviously depends on the circumstances of the particular case. The following are only a few general rules, which are fully expounded in textbooks on evidence. Secondary or substitutionary evidence is inadmissible when primary or original evidence is, or ought to be, available.[84] Thus an item of real evidence, including any object forming the foundation of expert evidence,[85] must be lodged if it is practicable and convenient to do so.[86] A copy of a document, purporting to be authenticated by a person responsible for making the copy, is, unless the court otherwise directs, deemed a true copy and treated as if it were the document itself.[87] With that exception, principals of documents must be lodged, unless parties agree that copies are to be accepted as principals.[88] If a document is not in a party's possession and could not have been recovered by him in spite of all due exertion, its terms may usually be incidentally proved; but if a document which constitutes a right as opposed to being evidence of a right has been lost or destroyed, its terms can be proved only in an action of proving the tenor in the Court of Session.[89] It is usually incorrect to lodge only part of a document.[90] When the terms of correspondence are relevant, the complete correspondence should be lodged,[91] or as much of it as will preclude any criticism that only a selection of letters has been lodged and some important letter has been deliberately withheld.[92] A document written by a witness and used by him in the witness-box to refresh his memory need not be lodged, but the other side is entitled to see it.[93] Inconvenience will be avoided if any document which requires stamping is duly stamped before it is lodged.[94] **16.24**

Documents used in cross-examination

It is clear that the rules as to the lodging of productions for proof do not apply to a document written by a witness and used merely to test the credibility of that witness: such a document may be produced at the diet, or the witness may be cited to produce it.[95] There is a question whether the provisions apply to other documents used to test credibility. It has been **16.25**

---

[83] See C. Style and C. Hollander, *Documentary Evidence* (1984), pp. 128–130.
[84] Walkers, *Evidence*, p. 243, para. 229.
[85] *McGowan v. Belling & Co. Ltd*, 1983 S.L.T. 77.
[86] *Maciver v. Mackenzie*, 1942 J.C. 51; *MacLeod v. Woodmuir Miners Welfare Society Social Club*, 1961 J.C. 5; Walkers, *Evidence*, p. 445, para. 420.
[87] Civil Evidence (Scotland) Act 1988, s. 6(1).
[88] Walkers, *Evidence*, p. 243, para. 229; *Ribble Paper Mills Ltd v. Clyde Paper Mills Ltd*, 1972 S.L.T. (Notes) 25.
[89] Walkers, *Evidence*, pp. 244–245, para. 230; *Crichton v. Wood*, 1981 S.L.T. (Notes) 66.
[90] *Murray's Trs v. Wilson's Exrx*, 1945 S.C. 51; *Unigate Foods Ltd v. Scottish Milk Marketing Board*, 1975 S.C. (H.L.) 75 at 106.
[91] *Macdonald v. Macdonald*, 1970 S.L.T. (Notes) 71.
[92] *Dingwall v. Dingwall*, 1958 S.L.T. (Notes) 41. The other side may be entitled to recover the remainder of the correspondence: *Stevenson v. Kyle* (1849) 11 D. 1086; *Clavering v. McCunn* (1881) 19 S.L.R. 139.
[93] Walkers, *Evidence*, p. 363, para. 341(b).
[94] *ibid.* Chap. 20.
[95] *Paterson & Sons v. Kit Coffee Co. Ltd* (1908) 16 S.L.T. 180; Walkers, *Evidence*, p. 330, para. 300(b). See also *Irvine v. Irvine* (1857) 19 D. 284.

held in the sheriff court that such documents used in the cross-examination of witnesses other than parties need not be lodged, but if used in the cross-examination of parties must be lodged. The reasons for the distinction are that while it is out of place to require the lodging of documents with a view to the cross-examination of a witness when it is still unknown whether that witness will be adduced, it may easily be anticipated that a party is likely to give evidence; and that the rule is designed to exclude the unfair surprise of a party.[96] It is, however, submitted, with respect, that that distinction is unsound. Surprise may be a legitimate element in cross-examination of a witness as to credit and there is no reason that a party giving evidence should be afforded an advantage denied to other witnesses. The correct view, it is thought, is that documents used in the cross-examination of a witness, whether or not a party, need not be lodged in advance of the cross-examination but, when used in cross-examination, should be exhibited to the court, to the witness and to the other party's advocate, and thereafter lodged.[97]

Medical records[98]

16.26 It is desirable to follow the Court of Session Practice Notes relative to medical records, which are based on the consideration that a doctor's or a hospital's lack of records can seriously impede the continuing treatment of a patient. Where a solicitor receives the records of a party's general practitioner, he should immediately provide the general practitioner with a copy of them, because they should at all times be available to him. If they are received in an envelope marked "Confidential" the solicitor must lodge a motion to have the envelope opened and, if the motion is granted, send a copy of them to the general practitioner without delay.[99] Medical records which have been recovered from a health board must be borrowed from process and returned to the lending authority as soon as it is known that they are no longer required or as soon as the case is concluded. Such records must also be made available to a hospital immediately on request if they are required at any stage for the treatment of the individual concerned.[1] The greatest care should be used in dealing with x-ray plates, especially in guarding them from damage during transmission.[2] In the interests of the protection of confidentiality, all copies of medical records should be returned along with the principals, or arrangements should be made for their confidential disposal, as soon as they are no longer required.[3]

Return of productions

16.27 The productions lodged may be uplifted by the solicitor at the conclusion of the case, after decree has been extracted. Reference has already been made to the need for the prompt return of medical records.[4]

---

[96] *Anderson v. Urban*, Sh. Pr. Dick, Glasgow Sh. Ct, Nov. 11, 1985, unreported.
[97] *Evidence* (Scot. Law Com. Memo. No. 46), para. G.25.
[98] On the recovery of hospital records, see paras 15.56, 15.63.
[99] Practice Note, Dec. 14, 1972: *Parliament House Book*, C2003.
[1] Practice Note, Sept. 15, 1983.
[2] Practice Note, Nov. 15, 1957: *Parliament House Book*, C2002.
[3] (1984) 29 J.L.S. 155 at p. 156.
[4] para. 16.26.

Joint minutes of admissions

Function

Before every proof the parties' solicitors should consider the preparation of a joint minute of admissions in order to avoid the expense and inconvenience of calling witnesses to prove matters which have not been admitted in the pleadings but which, as the proof approaches, are seen to be not, or no longer, in dispute. The joint minute is a form of making judicial admissions, which are conclusive for the purposes of the action in which they are made,[5] the joint minute constituting a contract whereby the parties accept as true the facts stated therein.[6] It does not exclude consideration of admissions made in the closed record or of the terms of documents admitted therein to be genuine[7]; but, unless the contrary appears, it excludes all other or additional evidence upon the matters contained in it, and the construction of statements in it is subject to the decision of the court.[8] The expense of any evidence led on matters covered by the joint minute may be disallowed.[9] Where the evidence of skilled witnesses is led on matters not in issue which in the court's view should have been covered by a joint minute, the court may refuse to certify the witnesses and direct that the fees paid to them are not to be charged against the opposing party.[10] **16.28**

Preparation

The joint minute is headed: "Joint Minute of Admissions / for the Parties / *in causa* / [*etc.*]".[11] The body of the minute should begin. "A for the pursuer and B for the defender concurred in stating to the Court that the parties are agreed as follows:" and setting out the matters admitted in numbered paragraphs.[12] The adjustment of a joint minute is a delicate task.[13] It is normally drafted by the pursuer's solicitor, sent to the other parties' solicitors for revisal, and, once adjusted, signed on behalf of all the parties and lodged in process. Since it is contractual in character, it should not be signed by one solicitor on behalf of another, but only by the solicitor instructed by the party concerned.[14] **16.29**

Examples

In any action a joint minute may be used to agree many facts which are no longer in dispute.[15] The authenticity of uncontroversial documents, including correspondence, photographs and plans, and the sufficiency of copies or extracts of documents as equivalent to the originals, are generally agreed by joint minute. In actions of damages for personal **16.30**

---

[5] Stair, IV, xlv, 5–6; Ersk., IV, ii, 33; *Scottish Marine Insurance Co. v. Turner* (1853) 1 Macq. 334, *per* Lord Truro at 340.

[6] *Carswell & Son v. Finlay* (1887) 24 S.L.R. 643 at 645; *Bowers v. Strathclyde R.C.*, 1981 S.L.T. 122; Lewis, *Evidence*, p. 15; Thomson and Middleton, p. 401.

[7] *Nisbet v. Cairns* (1864) 2 M. 863.

[8] *London and Edinburgh Shipping Co. v. The Admiralty*, 1920 S.C. 309; *Bowers, supra*.

[9] RCS, r. 36.7(3): it is thought that the same rule is applicable in sheriff court proofs.

[10] *Ayton v. National Coal Board*, 1965 S.L.T. (Notes) 24.

[11] See para. 5.57.

[12] Dobie, *Styles*, p. 317.

[13] *London and Edinburgh Shipping Co., supra, per* Lord Dundas at 318.

[14] Thomson and Middleton, p. 401.

[15] *e.g. Johnstone's Exrs v. Harris*, 1977 S.L.T. (Notes) 10 (terms of joint minute not reported in 1977 S.C. 365).

injuries or the death of a relative such minutes are often used to record the parties' agreement as to the contents of medical records, medical reports, marriage, birth and death certificates and the confirmation in favour of the deceased's executor, elements of patrimonial loss and, if necessary, any documents relating thereto such as statements of wages and benefits. The practice of so using joint minutes in such cases has often been commended by the courts.[16] As to hospital records, the minute should expressly cover the facts and opinions stated therein, if these are not in dispute[17]; and similarly an agreement as to a medical report should specify the purpose for which it is agreed, *e.g.* that it is to be held as constituting full proof as to the nature and extent of the injuries sustained by the pursuer and as to his treatment and prognosis,[18] or that it is to be held as the evidence of its author.[19] Where in a personal injuries or death action the total damages payable in the event of liability being established are agreed, the joint minute should state not only the total sum but the figures representing each of its constituent elements: past loss of wages or loss of support, past solatium or loss of society and, where appropriate, future loss of wages or loss of support and future solatium or loss of society. The joint minute may also make provision for interest on each of these elements and should make clear whether or not it does so. If it does not, it remains incumbent on the court to award interest on the constituent elements in terms of the Interest on Damages (Scotland) Act 1971, as amended.[20] As appropriate, a joint minute should also take account of the requirements of the Social Security (Recovery of Benefits) Act 1997. Where two actions raising related issues are to be heard together, a joint minute may be used to record the parties' agreement that the evidence led in each action should so far as competent and relevant be held to be evidence in the other.[21] Joint minutes in family proceedings, whereby custody, access, financial arrangements and other matters may be agreed, are discussed elsewhere.[22]

Notices to admit

16.31 At any time after a proof has been allowed, a party may intimate to any other party a notice calling on him to admit (a) facts specified in the notice relating to an issue averred in the pleadings, (b) that a particular document lodged in process and specified in the notice is an original and properly authenticated document or, as the case may be, a true copy of such a document.[23] Where the party on whom the notice is intimated does not admit the specified fact or challenges the authenticity of the document, he must within 21 days intimate a notice of non-admission.[24] If he fails to do so, he will be deemed to admit the specified fact or document which may then, if otherwise admissible, be used in evidence unless the sheriff, on special cause shown, otherwise directs.[25] Such a deemed admission may,

---

[16] *Bell v. Blackwood, Morton & Sons Ltd*, 1959 S.L.T. (Notes) 54; *Mearns v. British Transport Commission*, 1960 S.L.T. (Notes) 56; *Convery v. Kirkwood*, 1985 S.L.T. 483.

[17] *McHugh v. Leslie*, 1961 S.L.T. (Notes) 65.

[18] *Bell, supra.*

[19] *Convery, supra.*

[20] *cf. Ross v. British Railways Board*, 1972 S.C. 154. On interest on damages, see paras 21.35, 21.36.

[21] *H. & A. Scott Ltd v. J. Mackenzie Stewart & Co. Ltd*, O.H., Aug. 7, 1972, unreported.

[22] See, *e.g.* para. 22.42.

[23] OCR, r. 29.14(1).

[24] OCR, r. 29.14(2).

[25] OCR, r. 29.14(3).

however, be used only in favour of the party by whom the notice was given.[26] It appears therefore that in contrast with the general rule applicable to express admissions on record,[27] it cannot be used by the party deemed to have made the admission where that would be to his advantage; nor can it be used by any other party.

Recording of evidence

Rule

In every defended case the evidence is recorded by a shorthand writer or by tape recording or other mechanical means approved by the sheriff, unless the parties by agreement and with the approval of the sheriff dispense with the recording of evidence.[28] The responsibility for instructing a shorthand writer for the proof lies with the pursuer.[29] If a shorthand writer is not instructed and a mechanical means of recording is not available, the proof cannot competently proceed as in an ordinary cause unless recording of evidence is dispensed with. In that event, it is therefore incorrect for the sheriff to invite parties to lead evidence.[30] **16.32**

Dispensing with the recording of the evidence

In practice, the recording of the evidence is seldom dispensed with. There is no statutory provision that without extended shorthand notes of evidence any appeal will be on law only, but in such a case the sheriff's findings in fact are binding on the appeal court with the result that the appeal is limited to questions of law or to the conclusions which the sheriff drew from his findings in fact.[31] Parties who wish to dispense with the recording of the evidence should apply by motion to the sheriff for his consent, in time for a shorthand writer to be instructed if the sheriff refuses. Instead of moving for consent to the dispensing with the recording of the evidence and otherwise proceeding as in an ordinary cause, the parties may jointly move the sheriff to direct that the cause be treated as a summary cause: the sheriff is then obliged so to direct, and the cause is thereafter treated for all purposes (including appeal) as a summary cause and proceeds accordingly.[32] **16.33**

Instruction and payment of shorthand writer

It is the pursuer's responsibility to instruct a shorthand writer, if required, for the proof.[33] It is wise to do so as soon as the date of the proof is fixed. A firm of shorthand writers may charge a booking fee for booking the proof in their diary, which is returnable in the event of their being informed of the discharge of the diet of proof more than 21 days before the date of the proof, but is usually not returnable if the diet is **16.34**

---

[26] OCR, r. 29.14(6).
[27] *Stewart v. Glasgow Corpn*, 1958 S.C. 28 at 39.
[28] OCR, r. 29.18(1).
[29] OCR, r. 29.15.
[30] *Advance Building and Construction Services Ltd v. Cunningham*, Sh. Pr. Caplan, Kilmarnock Sh. Ct, Apr. 8, 1987, unreported.
[31] *Allardice v. Wallace*, 1957 S.L.T. 225 at 227 and 229; *Scott v. National Coal Board*, 1979 S.L.T. (Sh. Ct.) 38; *Butler v. Bowman*, 1989 S.C.L.R. 770; *Marsh v. Taylor*, 1992 S.L.T. (Sh. Ct.) 28; *McGibbon v. Sanchez*, 1998 G.W.D. 15–736.
[32] 1971 Act, s. 37(1)(a).
[33] OCR, r. 29.15.

discharged thereafter.[34] The shorthand writer is in the first instance paid by the parties equally as in any fee payable where evidence is recorded by mechanical means. Parties' solicitors are personally liable for such fees, and the sheriff may make an order directing payment to be made.[35] It is doubtful whether, in the event of failure to implement such an order before judgment, decree by default may be pronounced against the party whose solicitor has failed to pay.[36] The liability under the order is the solicitor's, not the party's. Decree by default would moreover be competent only if a time for payment had been specified in the order and had expired. The recording of evidence at the proof is further considered below.[37]

Discharge of diet of proof

16.35 The sheriff may discharge the diet of proof on the motion of any or all of the parties, upon such terms as to expenses or otherwise as he thinks just. It is thought that his power to do so arises from the inherent jurisdiction of the court so to regulate its procedure as to do justice between the parties. The decision whether or not to discharge the diet is a matter of discretion which may be reviewed on appeal, although the appeal court will interfere only if the sheriff has misapprehended the material facts and has reached a decision which no reasonable sheriff would have reached.[38] A motion for the discharge of the diet should be made as soon as the necessity for it arises, otherwise it may be granted only on terms as to expenses, or may be refused. The sheriff is not entitled to discharge the diet *ex proprio motu* without a motion to that effect by one of the parties[39] unless, it is thought, the exigencies of the business of the court make the discharge of the diet inevitable irrespective of the parties' desire that it should proceed.

16.36 Each motion for the discharge of a diet of proof must be determined on the facts of the particular case.[40] The sheriff will not necessarily grant a motion which is unopposed: he may refuse it *ex proprio motu.*[41] A joint motion to discharge a diet is, however, normally granted where it is responsibly stated on behalf of all parties that the action has been settled or is virtually certain to be settled, and that it is proposed to lodge a joint minute in appropriate terms. In such a case the sheriff usually discharges the diet and continues the cause to enable the joint minute to be lodged and then disposes of the action in terms of the joint minute.[42]

16.37 Normally, also, if a bona fide medical certificate is produced vouching that a party will be unable to attend court due to ill health, or if a party is unavoidably prevented from attending due to difficulties which were not reasonably foreseeable, the court will accommodate itself to such

---

[34] (1985) 30 J.L.S. 407.

[35] OCR, r. 29.18 (2), (3), (4).

[36] OCR, r. 16.2(1)(b), (2): see paras 14.03 to 14.14; see also, *contra*, 1st ed. of this work, para. 16–32.

[37] para. 16.55.

[38] *Skiponian Ltd v. Barratt Developments (Scotland) Ltd*, 1983 S.L.T. 313.

[39] *Sutherland v. Leith Provident Co-operative Society*, 1964 S.C. 151.

[40] *Skiponian Ltd, supra.*

[41] *Skiponian Ltd, supra*, at 315.

[42] See para. 14.64.

misfortunes and discharge the diet. The court always has regard, however, to the interests of justice in the widest sense. The fact that refusal of the motion may have drastic consequences for the party making it is a matter to be taken into account, but it is not necessarily conclusive[43]; the interests of the other parties, and of other litigants, and the public interest in the due administration of justice, must also be considered. Thus, if a party moves for discharge shortly before the diet only because he belatedly seeks leave to amend his pleadings, the motion will be granted only in highly exceptional circumstances in view of the prejudice which would be caused to the other party by the delay in the final determination of the case and the additional expense occasioned by further precognition of the witnesses.[44] The court must also consider the unfairness to other litigants whose proofs would have to be postponed to make room for the proof which it is sought to discharge,[45] and the need to dispose of litigation in a reasonably rapid and business-like manner.[46]

The Course of the Proof

The role of the sheriff

General. The sheriff controls the conduct of the proceedings at the proof, exercising judicial authority over its progress and over any points at issue which may arise during its course. His duty is to safeguard the public interest in the due administration of justice by ensuring that the litigation is carried on fairly between the parties,[47] and that each party has a full opportunity to present his case according to the practice and procedure of the court. The sheriff's function in controlling the proceedings is less active at the proof than at the earlier stages of the action,[48] since the proof proceeds on the footing that each side, working at arm's length, selects and presents its own evidence. The sheriff cannot make investigations on his own behalf, or call witnesses[49] or interview them in private,[50] but must decide where he thinks the truth lies as between the evidence which the parties have thought it to be in their respective interests to adduce before him. If that evidence is so inconclusive as to leave him uncertain where the truth lies, he must decide the case by applying the rules as to the onus of proof in civil litigation.[51] Within these limits, however, his objective is to attain the ascertainment of the truth and the doing of justice, and not to give scope or encouragement to tactical manoeuvring.[52] **16.38**

---

[43] *Skiponian Ltd, supra,* at 316.

[44] *Dryburgh v. National Coal Board,* 1962 S.C. 485; *Strachan v. Caledonian Fish-selling and Marine Stores Co.,* 1963 S.C. 157; *McGhie v. British Transport Commission,* 1964 S.L.T. (Notes) 56.

[45] *Strachan, supra,* at 161.

[46] *Fairley v. National Coal Board,* 1965 S.L.T. (Notes) 17.

[47] *Thomson v. Glasgow Corporation,* 1962 S.C. (H.L.) 36, *per* L.J.-C. Thomson at 52.

[48] See paras 5.98 to 5.102.

[49] *Thomson, supra.*

[50] *MacDonald v. MacDonald,* 1985 S.L.T. 244; *W v. Sunderland MBC* [1980] 1 W.L.R. 1101.

[51] *Mahon v. Air New Zealand Ltd* [1984] A.C. 808.

[52] *Duke of Argyll v. Duchess of Argyll,* 1962 S.C. 140, *per* L.P. Clyde at 151 (revsd, 1962 S.C. (H.L.) 88); *Lennie v. Lennie,* 1948 S.C. 466, *per* L.J.-C. Thomson at 475 (affd, 1950 S.C. (H.L.) 1).

16.39 **Examination of witnesses**. In pursuit of that objective the sheriff listens to and watches the witnesses and evaluates their evidence. He is entitled to question them himself, but must do so with caution,[53] usually only when it is necessary to clear up any point which has been overlooked or left obscure.[54] If he elicits any new matter, he should give the parties an opportunity to question the witness further thereon.[55] He should not intervene more than is strictly necessary or desirable, but should allow each advocate to conduct his own examination or cross-examination without undue interruption lest its sequence be lost or broken.[56] He may intervene to disallow insulting or annoying questions where that is necessary for the proper protection of the witness and the decent conduct of judicial business.[57] It is thought that in the interests of justice he may properly assist a party litigant, who is at a disadvantage in court, to present his case in an orderly way by helping him to elicit evidence on relevant matters from his witnesses. He must not, however, give the impression that he is not holding the scales of justice quite evenly, and he therefore should not go so far as to undertake the examination or, in particular, the cross-examination of witnesses on behalf of a party litigant, but should remain "aloof and detached from the arena of contention".[58] He must also be careful not to prevent a party litigant from developing his cross-examination on an important issue.[59]

16.40 **Hearing on evidence**. Similarly, when being addressed by the parties' advocates the sheriff will intervene only in order to clarify any matters on which he is in doubt, or to ensure that the details of a complicated set of facts or of a legal submission are clear in his mind. It is for the sheriff

> "to see that the advocates behave themselves seemly and keep to the rules laid down by law; to exclude irrelevancies and discourage repetition; to make sure by wise intervention that he follows the points the advocates are making and can assess their worth, and at the end to make up his mind where the truth lies. If he goes beyond this, he drops the mantle of a judge and assumes the robe of an advocate, and the change does not become him well. Lord Chancellor Bacon spoke right when he said that 'Patience and gravity of hearing is an essential part of justice; and an over-speaking judge is no well-tuned cymbal.' "[60]

16.41 **Death, disability, retiral or removal of sheriff.** In the event of the death, disability, or removal of a sheriff before whom a proof has been taken in whole or in part, application should be made to the sheriff principal for directions as to further procedure.[61] Such an application may also be

---

[53] *Thomson, supra*; *Black v. Black*, 1990 S.L.T. (Sh. Ct.) 42.

[54] *Livingstone v. H.M. Advocate*, May 23, 1974, Crown Office Circular No. 1278, printed in *Tallis v. H.M. Advocate*, 1982 S.C.C.R. 91 at 100 and in Macphail, *Evidence*, para. S8.62B; *Harris v. Harris*, C.A., Apr. 8, 1952, unreported, *per* Birkett L.J., printed in *The Language of the Law* (ed. Louis Blom-Cooper, 1965), p. 317 n.; *Jones v. National Coal Board* [1957] 2 Q.B. 55, *per* Lord Denning M.R. at 63–65.

[55] *McLeod v. H.M. Advocate*, 1939 J.C. 68.

[56] Sir Jack I. H. Jacob, "Practice and Procedure", Halsbury, Vol. 37, para. 510.

[57] *Falconer v. Brown* (1893) 1 Adam 96.

[58] *Harris, supra.*

[59] *Baretdji v. Baretdji*, 1985 S.L.T. 126.

[60] *Jones, supra.* The quotation is from Bacon's *Essays or Counsels Civil and Moral*, no. LVI, "Of Judicature".

[61] *Lumsden v. Lang's Trs*, 1940 S.L.T. (Sh. Ct.) 6. *Cf.* 1996 R.C., r.112. It is thought that the parties cannot competently arrange the matter by joint minute as apparently envisaged in Dobie, *Styles*, p. 322.

necessary where a sheriff who has retired or vacated office otherwise than by removal is not available to complete proceedings which had been pending before him. It appears that of consent of parties the sheriff principal may direct that the case be proceeded with and disposed of by another sheriff upon the notes of the evidence already taken and any further evidence to be led before him.[62] It is undecided whether that course can be followed otherwise than of consent.[63] Alternatively, the sheriff principal may direct that the whole proof be heard before another sheriff *de novo*.[64] If the action is not one of status, the parties may agree that any draft interlocutor left by the sheriff may be treated as his judgment.[65] Where a sheriff before his death had prepared and signed an interlocutor with note annexed which had not been entered in the books of court, the sheriff principal of consent of parties appointed the sheriff clerk to make up and include the interlocutor and note as a step of process, remitted the cause to the roll of another sheriff and authorised and empowered that sheriff to issue and sign an interlocutor giving effect as nearly as may be to the deceased sheriff's interlocutor, reserving to both parties their usual rights of appeal.[66] A sheriff who has retired or who has vacated or ceased to hold office otherwise than by removal, including a sheriff transferred to another court, may continue to deal with and may give judgment in any case begun before him before he ceased to hold office.[67]

The role of the advocates

An advocate, whether counsel or a solicitor, who conducts a proof in the sheriff court owes a duty not only to his client but also to the court, and must conform to the rules and practice of the court in the conduct of the litigation. He is also bound by that unwritten law of his profession which embodies the honourable understanding of the individual members as to their bearing and conduct towards each other.[68] The following dicta are applicable both to counsel and to solicitors. **16.42**

> "Every counsel has a duty to his client fearlessly to raise every issue, advance every argument and ask every question, however distasteful, which he thinks will help his client's case. But, as an officer of the court concerned in the administration of justice, he has an overriding duty to the court, to the standards of his profession, and to the public, which may and often does lead to a conflict with his client's wishes or with what the client thinks are his personal interests. Counsel must not mislead the court, he must not lend himself to casting aspersions on the other party or witnesses for which there is no sufficient basis in the information in his possession, he must not withhold authorities or documents which may tell against his clients but which the law or the standards of his profession require him to produce."[69]

---

62 *Lumsden, supra*; *Ferguson v. Ferguson*, 1936 S.C. 808; *Pearce v. Pearce*, 1945 S.L.T. 17; *Ravelston S.S. Co. v. Sieberg Bros*, 1946 S.C. 349.
63 *Amarnath v. A.J. Drilling Ltd*, 1993 S.C.L.R. 57.
64 *ibid.*
65 *Ferguson, supra.*
66 Sh. Pr. Walker, Glasgow Sh. Ct, Aug. 28, 1968, unreported.
67 Judicial Pensions and Retirement Act 1993, s. 27(1).
68 *Batchelor v. Pattison and Mackersy* (1876) 3 R. 914, *per* L.P. Inglis at 918.
69 *Rondel v. Worsley* [1969] 1 A.C. 191, *per* Lord Reid at 227–228.

> "[A]lthough an advocate must of course give of his best for his client, that is by no means the limit of his duty. His primary obligation is to the fair administration of the law itself. It is part of the tradition of the Bar in this country that no advocate will put forward a contention which he knows to be false, and if he is aware of any previous decision adverse to his case he has a duty to refer the court to it.[70] For the members of the Scots Bar are an essential part of the judicial machine, and under our system the whole process is a co-operative exercise in which the Bench and Bar rely on one another, and literally by their joint efforts are seeking to achieve a fair and just result."[71]

16.43 At the proof, the advocates lead the evidence from the witnesses and test it by cross-examination, their object being to get from the witnesses the best they can. They then present the two conflicting views of the points at issue to the sheriff, their skill depending on knowing what arguments to discard and what facts to stress.[72] Each advocate should conduct the case in such manner as in his discretion he thinks will be most to the advantage of his client, although he must not knowingly deceive or mislead the court and must at all times act with due courtesy to it, using his best endeavours to avoid unnecessary expense and waste of the court's time.[73]

Publicity

16.44 As a general rule the proof is heard in open court.[74]

Preliminary

Calling of case

16.45 The clerk of court calls the case in the courtroom usually upon the sitting of the court at the time specified in the interlocutor assigning the diet of proof or, if there is other business to be disposed of, as soon as possible thereafter.

Attendance of parties and advocates

16.46 When the case is called the parties or their advocates should be in attendance and should take their places at the table of the court, the defender or his advocate sitting on the sheriff's right, and the pursuer or his advocate on the sheriff's left. There is, in general, no rule requiring the attendance of a party who is legally represented and who is not to give evidence but his presence is expedient for the purpose of instructing the conduct of his case and his absence may cause inconvenience if the need for such instructions arises. A solicitor's mandate to appear is, however, to be presumed although his client is absent.[75] It is incompetent to exclude a party from hearing the evidence, but in a case where his credibility on any matter may be in issue it may be prudent for him to withdraw from the courtroom during other evidence on that matter, until he has given his

---

[70] He must cite any relevant decision whether reported or unreported, and any legislative provision, whether it be for or against his contention: *Glebe Sugar Refining Co. v. Greenock Harbour Trs*, 1921 S.C. (H.L.) 72; *Leighton v. Harland & Wolff Ltd*, 1953 S.L.T. (Notes) 34.

[71] Lord Clyde, *Equity and Law* (1964), pp. 16–17.

[72] Lord Clyde, *supra*.

[73] Halsbury (4th ed.), Vol. 37, para. 511.

[74] See paras 5.19 to 5.26.

[75] *Dunlop v. Dunlop*, 1992 S.C.L.R. 989.

own evidence.[76] A representative of a party who is a corporate body or a partnership is not, however, entitled to be present before giving evidence.[77] If his presence is desired, the party's advocate should intimate that fact to the court and to the opposite party, and if the other party consents he is usually allowed to be present. If the other party does not consent, the court has no power to permit the representative's presence. If he is present, without consent, and is later called as a witness, the other party may state an objection to his evidence under section 3 of the Evidence (Scotland) Act 1840.[78]

Rule 16.2, which makes provision for decree by default in all actions other than family actions[79] and actions of multiplepoinding, provides that if one party fails to appear or be represented at a diet, the sheriff may grant decree as craved or decree of absolvitor, or dismiss the cause, as the case may be, with expenses[80]; and if none of the parties appears, the sheriff may dismiss the cause.[81] These rules do not apply where a party appears or, whether or not personally present, is represented by a solicitor, but is not in a position to proceed with his case.[82] A party or solicitor in that position may move for the diet to be discharged or adjourned, and whether such a motion should be granted will depend on the circumstances of the case.[83] If such a motion is not made, or if it is made and refused, the procedure is as follows. **16.47**

(1) If it is the pursuer who is unable to proceed, he should nonetheless be given an opportunity of tendering evidence, and if he fails to do so, decree of absolvitor may be properly granted, not by default, but because the pursuer has failed to prove his case.[84] If the defender has stated a counterclaim, the sheriff may proceed with the proof of the counterclaim, giving the pursuer an opportunity to cross-examine, and to address the court at the hearing on evidence. The sheriff may thereafter grant decree in the defender's favour on the counterclaim to the extent that he has proved it, and make an appropriate award of expenses.[85]

(2) If it is the defender who is unable to proceed with his defence, the pursuer should be put to proof of his claim, and the defender may cross-examine and address the court at the hearing on evidence. The sheriff may thereafter grant decree in favour of the pursuer to the extent that he has proved his claim, and award expenses accordingly.[86]

While rule 16.2 provides that the sheriff may grant decree by default if one party fails to appear or be represented or if none of the parties appears, it will often be prudent, at least in the former case, not to grant decree by default at once, in ignorance of the reason for absence, but to **16.48**

---

[76] *Perman v. Binny's Trs*, 1925 S.L.T. 123; *Fraser v. Smith*, 1937 S.N. 67, and Walkers, para. 175 (pursuer in action of affiliation and aliment).

[77] See Macphail, *Evidence*, para. 3.22.

[78] See para. 16.52.

[79] On decree by default in family actions, see OCR, r. 33.37. See also para. 22.54.

[80] OCR, r. 16.2(1)(c), (2).

[81] OCR, r. 16.2(3).

[82] *Finlay v. Bush*, 1925 S.L.T. (Sh. Ct.) 140; *Jack v. Wardrop*, 1928 S.L.T. (Sh. Ct.) 9; *McLean v. Thomas O'Connor Autos*, 1967 S.L.T. (Sh. Ct.) 41; *Reid v. Russell*, 1971 S.L.T. (Sh. Ct.) 15; *Station Garage v. Masson*, 1978 S.L.T. (Sh. Ct.) 65.

[83] See paras 16.35 to 16.37.

[84] *Reid, supra.*

[85] *cf. Station Garage, supra.*

[86] *Station Garage, supra.*

discharge the diet of proof and appoint an early diet at which the parties are ordained to appear before the sheriff, personally or through their solicitors, to explain or excuse the absence and to show cause why decree by default should not be pronounced. Such a procedure may obviate the possibility of decree by default being pronounced against a party where that would not be in the interests of justice and is generally the preferable course.[87] The procedural history of the case or other special feature may, however, justify the granting of decree by default forthwith[88] and the sheriff's discretion is not to be regarded as fettered by any general rule. Where decree is granted forthwith it may be appropriate to order intimation of the interlocutor granting decree to the absent party and to supersede extract.[89] Decree in terms of rule 16.2 (1) and (2), where one party has failed to appear or be represented, is usually pronounced with expenses against the defaulter: where none of the parties has appeared and decree in terms of rule 16.2(3) is pronounced, the sheriff finds no expenses due to or by either party.[90] A less drastic course than decree by default is provided by the rule that where a party or his solicitor on one side attends any diet of proof or debate and the other is absent or not prepared to proceed the sheriff may decern against the latter party for payment of such expenses as the sheriff may consider reasonable.[91]

Watching brief

16.49 An advocate may be instructed to watch the proceedings on behalf of some interested person who is not a party to the cause. He may not sit at the table of the court or take any part in the proof or address the court on behalf of his client, but he may sit in court unrobed and take a note and report to his client.

Management of witnesses

16.50 **List**. It is good practice for each solicitor to prepare a numbered list of his witnesses in the order in which it is proposed to call them and, before the examination of his witnesses commences, to give copies of the list to the court officer, the clerk of court and the shorthand writer.[92] In the sheriff court, however, there is no obligation to provide such a list, or to call any of the witnesses on it, or not to call any witness who is not on it. On the other hand, a list of witnesses should already be in existence by virtue of the provisions of rule 9.14.[93]

16.51 **Enclosure of witnesses**. The practice of the Court of Session with regard to the enclosure of witnesses[94] is followed, so far as practicable, in the sheriff court. It is the duty of solicitors to see that all witnesses are enclosed under the charge of the court officer in one of the witness-rooms; and no witness may leave the witness-room except with the permission of

---

[87] *Saleem v. Hamilton District Licensing Board*, 1993 S.L.T. 1092; *McGowan v. Carter*, 1995 S.C.L.R. 312.

[88] *Munro and Miller (Pakistan) v. Wyvern Structures Ltd*, 1996 S.L.T. 135.

[89] *ibid.*

[90] Decree by default is further discussed in paras 14.02 to 14.15.

[91] A.S. (Fees of Solicitors in the Sheriff Court) (Amendment and Further Provision) 1993, Sched. 1, General Regulations, reg. 5(c).

[92] Kearney, p. 124. *Cf.* RCS, r. 36.9(2). Such a list is referred to in *McDougall v. James Jones & Sons Ltd*, O.H., Nov. 27, 1970, unreported: see Macphail, *Evidence*, para. 23.14.

[93] See para. 16.01.

[94] RCS, r.36.9.

the clerk of court until called by the court officer to be in readiness for being examined. After a witness has been enclosed by the court officer, no person other than the solicitor for the party citing the witness may have access to him, nor may any person interfere with the court officer in regard to such witness. These rules are enforced by the court officer, who must report to the court if any person, solicitor or other, transgresses them. Only in extreme circumstances, it is thought, would an approach made to a witness in a civil case, after enclosure and prior to or during his examination, be held to be so improper as to require the sheriff to hold that the witness's subsequent evidence was inadmissible.[95]

Witness in court before examination. At common law it is a ground for excluding a witness, other than a skilled witness, that he has been in court during the examination of any of the previous witnesses.[96] The common law is modified in relation to civil proceedings in the Court of Session and the sheriff court by section 3 of the Evidence (Scotland) Act 1840.[97] Section 3 provides that if it is objected that a witness has, without the permission of the court, and without the consent of the party objecting, been present in court during all or any part of the proceedings, it is not imperative on the court to reject the witness, but it is competent for the court, in its discretion, to admit the witness, where it appears to the court that the presence of the witness was not the consequence of culpable negligence or criminal intent and that the witness has not been unduly instructed or influenced by what took place during his presence, or that injustice will not be done by his examination. Objection to the witness may be taken by a party or by the sheriff.[98] It appears to be for the party tendering the witness to satisfy the court that he should be admitted,[99] but there has been no judicial guidance as to whose "culpable negligence" or "criminal intent" is involved, or as to how the court is to be satisfied on the points mentioned in the section. 16.52

Section 3 does not apply to the parties or their advocates, who are entitled to be present during the examination of witnesses,[1] or to any witness who has been in court with the sheriff's permission and the consent of the other party. An expert witness is not allowed to be present in court while other experts are giving evidence, but as a general rule he is allowed to hear the evidence of the witnesses to fact unless objection is taken, or unless he himself is to speak to facts as well as opinion.[2] 16.53

Procedure after examination. Witnesses should be advised by the solicitors citing them not to discuss the case while waiting to give evidence 16.54

---

[95] *cf. Williamson v. H.M. Advocate*, 1979 J.C. 36.

[96] Dickson, para. 1599; *Docherty and Graham v. McLellan*, 1912 S.C.(J.) 102.

[97] s. 3 was repealed so far as relating to criminal proceedings by the Criminal Procedure (Scotland) Act 1975, Sched. 10, Pt. I, and replaced by ss. 140 and 343 of that Act (now Criminal Procedure (Scotland) Act 1995, s. 267). On s. 3 see Macphail, *Evidence*, paras 3.16–3.25.

[98] *Macdonald v. Mackenzie*, 1947 J.C. 169, *per* Lord Mackay at 175, Lord Jamieson at 176–177.

[99] *Macdonald, supra*; *Ryan v. Paterson* (1972) J.C.L 111.

[1] Evidence Act 1686. This Act is repealed, at least in its application to Court of Session proceedings, by A.S. (Rules of Court Amendment) 1986 (S.I. 1986 No. 1937). It is doubtful if the repeal has any further extent and, in any event, the right of parties and their advocates to be present during the hearing of evidence is now an undoubted principle and their competency as witnesses debarred any legislation and practice subsequent to 1986. See Wilkinson, *The Scottish Law of Evidence*, pp. 150, 151.

[2] Macphail, *Evidence*, para. 17.11.

and, after giving evidence, not to disclose the evidence they have given to any person who may subsequently be a witness in the case.[3] A witness who has been examined ought not to be allowed to mix in company with others who are in attendance for examination,[4] since any communication he has with them may affect the weight of their evidence. Normally a witness who has been examined is directed to sit in the courtroom until dismissed by the court officer by order of the sheriff. The sheriff will normally grant an application to dismiss a witness as soon as his examination has been completed, unless he is satisfied that his dismissal at that stage would not be in the interests of justice. If it appears that the witness may be recalled, he should not be dismissed but should be directed to wait in a suitable place outside the courtroom and apart from the other witnesses.

Recording of evidence

16.55 Unless the parties have by agreement and with the sheriff's approval dispensed with the recording of the evidence or the evidence is to be recorded by tape recording or other mechanical means approved by the sheriff, a shorthand writer, who has been instructed by the pursuer and to whom the oath *de fideli administratione* has been administered in connection with the sheriff court service generally,[5] should be present to record the evidence.[6] The shorthand writer records the evidence by question and answer.[7] A transcript of the record of the evidence is made only if the sheriff so directs[8] and should be certified as a faithful record by the shorthand writer or, where the evidence has been recorded by mechanical means, by the person who transcribed the record.[9] It is then lodged in process. The hearing on evidence should not be postponed as a matter of course until the transcript is available.[10] The sheriff may make such alterations to the transcript as appear to him to be necessary after hearing the parties.[11] Previous provisions on the examination of witnesses in this connection[12] have not been re-enacted but it is thought that is still a competent course if one to be used only in exceptional circumstances. The sheriff may take the witnesses' evidence of new if the record is destroyed[13] or is found to be inaccurate[14] or defective or, it is thought, if it is lost or cannot for any good reason be transcribed. If the transcript is lost or destroyed after being lodged in process, an authenticated copy may be substituted under rule 11.5.[15]

Adjourning proof

16.56 A power to adjourn in order to promote the interests of justice is inherent in every court, and must be exercised according to the discretion of the judge.[16] The sheriff's common law power to adjourn is modified by

---

[3] Kearney, pp. 110–111.
[4] McGlashan, p. 243.
[5] OCR, r. 29.18(1)(a).
[6] See paras 16.32 to 16.34. The unauthorised use of a tape recorder is a contempt of court (Contempt of Court Act 1981, s. 9: see para. 5.27).
[7] *i.e.* not in narrative form.
[8] OCR, r. 29.18(6).
[9] OCR, r. 29.18(7).
[10] Grant Report, para. 598.
[11] OCR, r. 29.18(8).
[12] OCR (1983), r. 73(5).
[13] *Yates v. Robertson* (1891) 18 R. 1206.
[14] *Wilson v. MacQueen*, 1925 S.L.T. (Sh. Ct.) 130.
[15] See para. 8.14.
[16] *Bruce v. Linton* (1860) 23 D. 85, *per* L.J.-C. Inglis at 94, Lord Cowan at 95.

rule 29.17, which provides that the proof must be taken so far as possible continuously, but the sheriff may adjourn the diet from time to time. It appears to follow from the requirement that the proof be taken so far as possible continuously that a proof which is considered likely to take more than one day should have been set down for hearing on consecutive days, and if it is not completed by the end of the first day it should if possible be adjourned to the following day, unless it is necessary to adjourn it to a later date in order to do justice between the parties. If adjournment to the following day is not possible or not in the interests of justice, the adjournment should be for as short an interval as the circumstances or the justice of the case will admit of, so that the issues and the evidence already led will remain as fresh as possible in the minds of the sheriff and the advocates.[17] The requirement to take the proof so far as possible continuously also appears to involve that the proof must proceed as a single step in procedure uninterrupted by steps of a different character, any break in continuity being merely a necessary incident of that continuity producing completion of the proof with expedition and fairness to both sides.[18] It is accordingly incompetent, without consent of the parties, to adjourn in the course of the proof in order to hold a diet of debate on a preliminary plea.[19]

Good reasons for adjournment include the inability of a party or a duly cited witness to attend through ill-health or difficulties which were not reasonably foreseeable[20]; the proof taking longer than its allotted time[21]; the sheriff being necessarily employed on other business; and other unavoidable circumstances,[22] including a party being taken by unavoidable surprise by the evidence led.[23] As a general rule, however, a party who has failed to make timeous arrangements for the proof has no right to delay matters by obtaining an adjournment.[24] Since the power to grant or refuse an adjournment implies a power to grant conditionally, the sheriff may grant an adjournment on such conditions as to expenses as he thinks right.[25] The question whether there should be an adjournment between the close of the proof and the hearing on evidence is considered below.[26] **16.57**

Presentation of parties' cases

Once the case has been called and the parties and their advocates are in attendance, the procedure at the proof ordinarily takes the following course, subject to any variations arising from the nature of the case or the directions of the sheriff. The pursuer's advocate intimates to the sheriff for which parties he and the other advocate or advocates appear. After any preliminary matters have been dealt with, such as motions for leave to amend pleadings[27] or to lodge productions late,[28] or the intimation that certain matters have **16.58**

---

[17] *cf. Meiklejohn v. Stevenson* (1870) 8 M. 890. The now repealed provision there considered embodies a salutary practical rule.
[18] *McColl v. Strathclyde R.C.*, 1981 S.L.T. (Notes) 70.
[19] *McColl, supra.*
[20] See *MacColl v. MacColl*, 1946 S.L.T. 312 at 313; para. 16.37.
[21] *McColl v. Strathclyde R.C.*, 1981 S.L.T. (Notes) 70.
[22] *Smith v. Watson*, 1912 S.C. 553 at 554.
[23] Dove Wilson, p. 177.
[24] *MacColl v. MacColl, supra.*
[25] Dove Wilson, p. 177.
[26] para. 16.95.
[27] See para. 10.19.
[28] See paras 16.18 to 16.22.

been agreed by joint minute,[29] the advocate for the pursuer[30] does not make any opening statement or read the record to the sheriff, but calls his first witness. Each witness's evidence is elicited by question and answer, the questions being put to the witness by the parties or their advocates and, to a limited extent, by the sheriff.[31] The witness is subject to interrogation first by the party calling him (examination-in-chief), then by each of the other parties in turn (cross-examination), and again by the party calling him (re-examination). At the conclusion of the evidence of his witnesses, the pursuer's advocate puts in as evidence all documents admitted or put to witnesses, and reports of any evidence taken on commission,[32] and formally closes his proof. The defender's advocate then presents and closes his case in a similar manner. Where there are two or more defenders, the cross-examination by one defender of one of the pursuer's witnesses can be used for or against another defender although the latter does not adopt it as his own cross[33]; and it appears to be generally accepted in modern practice that any evidence given by a witness called by any party is evidence in the cause which is available to, and can be used against, all parties.[34] The defender's proof having been closed, the sheriff hears the advocates on the evidence, either immediately or at an adjourned diet.[35]

Examination of witnesses

16.59 The rules of evidence relative to the competence and compellability of witnesses and the nature and content of the questions which may be put to them are beyond the scope of this book. This section of the present chapter is concerned only to consider briefly such of the general rules as to the examination of witnesses as have a bearing on the course of the proceedings at the proof.

General rules

16.60 A party or his advocate has a discretion to call such competent witnesses as he pleases, in the order that he chooses. It has, however, been said that in an action of declarator of paternity, it is undesirable that the defender should be called as the first witness for the pursuer.[36] It is thought that the sheriff may grant leave for the interposition of a witness for one party in or before the evidence for another party where he is satisfied that to do so would be in the interests of justice, or where the parties consent. Of consent, a party's proof may be closed subject to the later examination of a named witness who for sufficient reason cannot attend, the other party meantime proceeding with his proof.[37] The witnesses must be examined in the presence of the parties or their advocates.[38]

---

[29] See paras 16.28 to 16.30.

[30] The text describes the course of the proof where the party leading in the proof is the pursuer.

[31] As to questioning by the sheriff, see para. 16.39.

[32] If a document is not formally put in as evidence before the party's proof is closed, it is for the discretion of the court where it will be admitted thereafter: *Liquidator of the Universal Stock Exchange Co. Ltd v. Howat* (1891) 19 R. 128; *Cameron v. Woolfson*, 1918 S.C. 190.

[33] *Ayr Road Trs v. Adams* (1883) 11 R. 326.

[34] Walkers, para. 344(a); *cf. Todd v. H.M. Advocate*, 1984 S.L.T. 123.

[35] See paras 16.98 *et seq.*

[36] *Fraser v. Smith*, 1937 S.N. 67; Walkers, para. 175. See, *contra*, *Darroch v. Kerr*, 1909 S.C. 112; Wilkinson and Norrie, *Parent and Child*, pp. 150–151.

[37] Dobie, p. 224.

[38] Evidence Act 1686.

The following rules are considered in subsequent paragraphs. As a general rule, the oath or affirmation is administered to each witness,[39] the examination is conducted in English,[40] and the witness is bound to answer any competent and relevant question put to him.[41] Each witness is examined in chief by the party calling him[42] and is then liable to be cross-examined by each of the other parties[43] and thereafter re-examined by the party calling him.[44] Questions may then be put to him through the court.[45] He may also be questioned at any stage by the sheriff.[46] After he has left the witness-box he may be recalled.[47] One witness may be held as concurring with another.[48] Objections to the questions put to witnesses may be stated, argued and disposed of.[49] In certain circumstances an incidental appeal against the sheriff's ruling on the confidentiality of evidence or production of documents may be taken to the sheriff principal.[50] **16.61**

Oath and affirmation[51]

With certain exceptions, no evidence is admissible in court unless it is given on oath or affirmation[52]; and every person called as a witness is obliged to swear or affirm, and may be punished for contempt if he refuses to do so.[53] The exceptions are these. Children under 12 years of age are admonished to tell the truth: those between 12 and 14 are sworn or admonished at the judge's discretion[54]; and those over 14 are usually sworn. A witness of defective mental capacity is sworn or admonished at the sheriff's discretion.[55] Before exercising his discretion the sheriff must be satisfied that the child or person of defective mental capacity is a competent witness, in respect that he appears to be able to understand what he has seen or heard and to appreciate the duty to speak the truth.[56] The sheriff must satisfy himself by examination of the child and, if need be, of others that the child knows the difference between telling the truth and telling lies and consequently the duty to tell the truth. It is not usually necessary to deal separately with the requirement that the child understands what he is to be asked about, because that is closely bound up with his understanding of the differences between truth and **16.62**

---

39 paras 16.62 to 16.64.
40 paras 16.65 to 16.68.
41 para. 16.69.
42 paras 16.70 to 16.72.
43 paras 16.73 to 16.77.
44 paras 16.78, 16.79.
45 para. 16.80.
46 para. 16.39.
47 paras 16.81, 16.82.
48 para. 16.83.
49 paras 16.84 to 16.88.
50 paras 16.89, 16.90.
51 Walkers, para. 337.
52 *McLaughlin v. Douglas & Kidston* (1863) 4 Irv. 273, *per* L.J.-C. McNeill at 286; *Forbes v. H.M. Advocate*, 1963 J.C. 68.
53 *Tweedie* (1829) Shaw 222; *Bonnar v. Simpson* (1836) 1 Swin. 39; *Wylie v. H.M. Advocate*, 1966 S.L.T. 149; *cf.* Criminal Procedure (Scotland) Act 1995, s. 155(1).
54 *Anderson v. McFarlane* (1899) 1 F.(J.) 36. The discretion is not, however, unfettered. See *Quinn v. Lees*, n. 60).
55 *Black* (1887) 1 White 365, *per* Lord McLaren at 367–368.
56 Dickson, paras 1543, 1550–1554. It appears that a witness of defective mental capacity may be examined under reservation of all questions as to the effect of his evidence: *Tosh v. Ogilvy* (1873) 1 R. 254.

falsehood.[57] It is not an objection to a child giving evidence that he cannot give a spontaneous account. That is a consideration which goes to quality but not to competency.[58] It is thought that if the sheriff concludes that a witness is competent and not in a category in which an admonition to tell the truth is appropriate and that he does not object to being sworn, the sheriff need not inquire into his appreciation of the divine sanction of the oath, but should administer the oath if satisfied that he "has a sufficient appreciation of the solemnity of the occasion and the added responsibility to tell the truth, which is involved in taking an oath, over and above the duty to tell the truth which is an ordinary duty of normal social conduct".[59] In the case of a child between 12 and 14, however, the sheriff should ask him whether he understands the nature of an oath and if he does not he should not be sworn.[60]

16.63 The form and manner of administering the oath is as follows. The form is: "I swear by Almighty God that I will tell the truth, the whole truth and nothing but the truth."[61] The sheriff stands with his right hand uplifted, as does the witness if he is physically capable of doing so,[62] and the sheriff utters each phrase and pauses until the witness audibly repeats it after him. The whole oath must be administered.[63] A Jewish witness usually silently covers his head. If, however, the witness states that the manner of taking the oath is not appropriate to his religious belief, an oath in the manner appropriate to that belief is administered if that is reasonably practicable without inconvenience or delay: otherwise, the witness is permitted or obliged to make his solemn affirmation instead of taking an oath.[64] If an oath is administered in a form and manner other than that prescribed by law, the witness is bound by it if it has been administered in such form and with such ceremonies as he may have declared to be binding.[65] Where an oath has been duly administered and taken, the fact that the person to whom it was administered had, at the time of taking it, no religious belief, does not for any purpose affect the validity of the oath.[66]

16.64 Any person who objects to being sworn is permitted, without inquiry, to make his solemn affirmation instead of taking an oath.[67] The form of affirmation is: "I solemnly, sincerely and truly declare and affirm that I will tell the truth, the whole truth and nothing but the truth."[68] The sheriff administers the affirmation by uttering each phrase and pausing until the witness audibly repeats it after him, but he does not stand and neither he nor the witness raises his right hand.[69] The whole affirmation should be

---

[57] *M. v. Kennedy*, 1993 S.C.L.R. 69 at 76. See also *Rees v. Lowe*, 1989 S.C.C.R. 664; *Kelly v. Docherty*, 1991 S.C.C.R. 312; *P. v. H.M. Advocate*, 1991 S.C.C.R. 933.

[58] *M. v. Kennedy, supra.*

[59] *R. v. Hayes* (1976) 64 Cr.App.R. 194; *R. v. Bellamy* [1986] Crim. L.R. 54; *Black* (1887) 1 White 365. *Cf. Anderson v. McFarlane* (1899) 1 F. (J.) 36.

[60] *Quinn v. Lees*, 1994 S.C.C.R. 159.

[61] OCR, r. 29.16, App., Form G.14.

[62] The practice of raising the hand when taking an oath appears to be ancient: see Genesis, xiv, 22–23.

[63] *McLaughlin v. Douglas & Kidston* (1863) 4 Irv. 273.

[64] Oaths Act 1978, s. 5.

[65] *ibid.* s. 4(1).

[66] *ibid.* s. 4(2).

[67] *ibid.* s. 5(1).

[68] OCR, r. 29.16, App., Form G.15. In the form prescribed by s. 6 (1) of the Oaths Act 1978 the witness's name is included.

[69] The direction to raise the right hand is omitted from the form prescribed for an affirmation where, as in contrast with an oath, it is inappropriate. *Cf.* Walkers, para. 337(b).

administered.[70] A solemn affirmation is of the same force and effect as an oath.[71] The sanction against giving false evidence on oath or affirmation is prosecution for perjury.[72]

Interpreter

16.65 The language of the courts in Scotland is English, and an interpreter may be appointed only for a person who does not understand English[73] or who cannot understand questions or answer them intelligibly due to a defect of hearing or speech.[74] It is for the party citing the witness to instruct an interpreter, and for the court to decide whether an interpreter is necessary.[75] The interpreter is *pro hac vice* an official of the court, and ought to be an independent person.[76] The sheriff administers to him the declaration *de fideli administratione*.

16.66 Except in emergencies, only an interpreter on the register of interpreters maintained by the Scottish Association for the Deaf should be instructed as an interpreter for a deaf witness. As an alternative to an interpreter, a deaf mute may be examined by written question and answer, and a person who is dumb or inarticulate but not deaf may answer in writing. "In every case that mode of examination should be adopted which the education and habits of the witness show to be the best mode of eliciting a distinct statement from him."[77] Normally, however, the examination is conducted through an interpreter.

16.67 Where evidence is given through an interpreter, the advocate's questions ought to be directed to the witness as though there were no interpreter there, in the form of words which would be used to a witness who was going to answer in English, and should not be directed to the interpreter, referring to the witness as "he" or "she"; and the witness's answers ought to be given by the interpreter translating each answer fully and directly as given by the witness.[78] In practice, however, when an interpreter translates an advocate's questions into the language of the witness that practice may not be observed, and rules of evidence may be broken, and unless the advocate or the sheriff knows the language, he is powerless to prevent it.[79]

16.68 Where a party litigant is deaf or does not understand English, it may be sufficient for the court to give him an opportunity to provide an interpreter who would make it possible for him to follow the evidence, and the extent to which the evidence is translated may be within the discretion of the sheriff.[80]

---

[70] Oaths Act 1978, s. 6(1); *McCubbin v. Turnbull* (1850) 12 D. 1123. *Cf. McLaughlin v. Douglas & Kidston* (1863) 4 Irv. 273.

[71] Oaths Act 1978, s. 5(4).

[72] G. H. Gordon, *The Criminal Law of Scotland* (2nd ed., 1978), para. 48–02.

[73] *Taylor v. Haughney*, 1982 S.C.C.R. 360, following *Alexander McRae* (1841) Bell's Notes to Hume, ii, 270. See A. C. Evans, "Use of Gaelic in Court Proceedings", 1982 S.L.T. (News) 286.

[74] See Dickson, para. 1556.

[75] *Furnheim v. Watson*, 1946 S.L.T. 297, *per* L.J.-C. Cooper at 300 (not reported on this point, 1946 J.C. 99).

[76] *Liszewski v. Thomson*, 1942 J.C. 55, *per* Lord Fleming at 58.

[77] Dickson, para. 1556.

[78] *Rukat v. Rukat* [1975] Fam. 63, *per* Megaw L.J. at 69–70.

[79] *Re Trepca Mines Ltd* [1960] 1 W.L.R. 24 at 27.

[80] *In the Estate of Field, decd (No. 2)* [1965] 1 W.L.R. 1336. *Cf. H.M. Advocate v. Olssen*, 1941 J.C. 63; *Liszewski, supra*; *Furnheim, supra, per* L.J.-C. Cooper at 300.

Questions

16.69 A witness is bound to answer any competent and relevant question put to him, and may be punished for contempt of court if he refuses to do so, unless in highly exceptional circumstances the court excuses him from answering a question which is judged unnecessary or not useful.[81] The manner in which the witness is questioned is a matter for the party or his advocate, subject to the sheriff seeing that the witness has fair play, the questioner giving the witness a fair opportunity of answering any charge of unreliability or untruthfulness which may emerge from his evidence,[82] and the sheriff's power to disallow questions which are merely insulting or annoying.[83–84]

Examination-in-chief

16.70 After the witness has taken the oath or made his solemn affirmation, he is examined-in-chief by the party calling him. The object of examination-in-chief is to elicit from the witness evidence in support of that party's case and in anticipation of or reply to his opponent's case; but it is sometimes advisable also to bring out evidence adverse to that party's case in examination-in-chief rather than to leave it to be brought out with greater effect in cross-examination. The examiner begins by identifying the witness to the court. He usually asks him his full name, age, address, occupation and, where appropriate, rank and experience (as in the case of a police officer) or professional qualifications and experience (as in the case of a skilled witness). Where necessary for the administration of justice, as where a witness is reasonably in a state of fear, these personal details, or some of them, may be written down at the discretion of the sheriff. The witness's age may be important information for a court of appeal,[85] and it has been suggested that it is required in order to distinguish him from others, and to inform the judge what were his capacity and maturity of understanding at the time when the events deponed to took place, and at the time when he is examined.[86]

16.71 Leading questions, which are questions which by their form suggest the answer which the questioner desires to receive, are not permitted in examination-in-chief, since it is important that the witness should give his evidence on matters in dispute in his own words. To that general rule there are, however, some exceptions. The witness's personal particulars are elicited by leading questions, unless directly related to the facts in issue; and such questions may also be asked on any matters which are not in dispute, or are no longer in dispute having been established by other evidence, or on matters on which the advocates have agreed that leading questions are permissible. Leading questions on matters in dispute are, however, permitted in examination-in-chief where the witness displays unwillingness or reluctance to give evidence, or hostility to the party calling him. The examiner may then treat the witness as hostile, or unfavourable to his case, and ask leading questions and in effect

---

[81] *Wylie v. H.M. Advocate*, 1966 S.L.T. 149; *H.M. Advocate v. Airs*, 1975 J.C. 64 at 70.
[82] *Avery v. Cantilever Shoe Co.*, 1942 S.C. 469, *per* L.P. Normand at 471.
[83–84] See para. 16.39.
[85] *Meiklejohn v. Stevenson* (1870) 8 M. 890.
[86] G. Tait, *A Treatise on the Law of Evidence in Scotland* (1824), p. 424.

subject him to cross-examination.[87] He may do so without the leave of the court.[88]

The examination-in-chief continues until it is exhausted, without interruption except for objections to evidence, necessary questions by the sheriff, and adjournments.[89] **16.72**

Cross-examination

Immediately after the examination-in-chief has been concluded, the witness is liable to be cross-examined by or on behalf of the other parties to the proceedings. The objects of cross-examination are (1) to weaken or destroy the witness's evidence where his version of the facts is inconsistent with that of the cross-examining party, by challenging his evidence as inaccurate or unreliable; and (2) to elicit or develop evidence favourable to the cross-examining party which the witness has not referred to or has only briefly mentioned.[90] The witness's liability to be cross-examined does not depend on whether he has given evidence adverse to the party cross-examining, and cross-examination is not confined to the subject-matter of the evidence given by the witness in chief, but may extend to all pertinent facts and circumstances.[91] **16.73**

Where several defenders with conflicting interests are separately represented, each witness for the pursuer may be cross-examined in turn by each of the defenders in the order in which they appear in the instance. A witness for the first-named defender may be cross-examined by each of the other defenders in turn and then by the pursuer; and where there are, say, three defenders, a witness for the second-named defender is cross examined by the third-named defender, the first-named defender and the pursuer; and a witness for the third-named defender by the first-named defender, the second-named defender and the pursuer.[92] It is thought that the order may be changed of consent or by direction of the sheriff. **16.74**

Leading questions are permitted in cross-examination; but where the witness appears to be favourable to the cross-examiner it may be more effective to allow him to give his evidence without leading him. The court will not allow questions which are asked only in order to insult or annoy the witness.[93] It is thought that the court may also intervene to protect witnesses by stopping cross-examination which is vexatious or oppressive in other respects, as where it is unduly long or repetitious.[94] Otherwise, the cross-examiner may question the witness with only the same liability to interruption as the examiner-in-chief[95]; but cross-examination should always be as short as is consistent with the proper presentation of the cross-examiner's case. **16.75**

---

[87] Dickson, para. 1773; *Gall v. Gall* (1870) 9 M. 177, *per* L.P. Inglis at 179; *Frank v. H.M. Advocate*, 1938 J.C. 17; *Brennan v. Edinburgh Corporation*, 1962 S.C. 36, *per* Lord Sorn at 42.

[88] *Lowe v. Bristol Motor Omnibus Co.*, 1934 S.C. 1; *Avery v. Cantilever Shoe Co.*, 1942 S.C. 469.

[89] CAS, F, II, 2. It seems that this provision in the Codifying Act of Sederunt 1913 has never been repealed or replacement.

[90] *Hartley v. H.M. Advocate*, 1979 S.L.T. 26, *per* Lord Avonside at 28; Walkers, para. 342.

[91] CAS, F, II, 4.

[92] In *Boyle v. Olsen*, 1912 S.C. 1235, separately represented pursuers were given the right to cross-examine each other's witnesses.

[93] *Falconer v. Brown* (1893) 1 Adam 96.

[94] *Inch v. Inch* (1856) 18 D. 997.

[95] See para. 16.72.

16.76 It has been authoritatively pointed out[96] that if it is intended later to contradict a witness upon a specific and important issue to which that witness has deponed, or to prove some critical fact to which that witness ought to have a chance of tendering an explanation or denial, the point ought normally to be put to the witness in cross-examination. If such cross-examination is omitted, the witness may have to be recalled with the leave of the court,[97] possibly on conditions as to expenses,[98] and in some circumstances the omission may cause fatal damage to the case.[99] Failure to cross-examine a single witness on an essential point does not supersede any necessity for corroboration of his evidence on that point, though of course the need for corroboration now seldom arises in civil practice.[1] Whether failure to cross-examine a witness on any matter implies that the cross-examiner accepts the witness's evidence as credible and reliable on that point appears to depend on the tenor of the cross-examination on other matters and on considerations of fairness.[2] Failure to cross-examine a witness on a material point has been said to preclude the cross-examiner from leading evidence to contradict the witness,[3] but that drastic rule does not appear to be followed in modern practice, no doubt because the court is able to prevent prejudice to the other party by such means as recalling the witness for cross-examination and awarding expenses,[4] or allowing proof in replication,[5] or admitting the evidence subject to comment.[6] Failure to cross-examine on a material point may not prevent the cross-examination of subsequent witnesses on the same point.[7]

16.77 It has been submitted above that documents used in the cross-examination of witnesses as to credit need not be lodged before being used.[8]

Re-examination

16.78 On the conclusion of his cross-examination the witness may be re-examined by the party who examined him in chief. The objects of re-examination are to explain or clarify any answers given in cross-examination which appear to be unfavourable to that party's case, and to restore, if possible, the credibility of a witness who has been attacked in cross-examination. Re-examination is governed by two general rules: leading questions are permitted only to the same extent as they are in examination-in-chief, and for the same reasons[9]; and the re-examination

---

96 *McKenzie v. McKenzie*, 1943 S.C. 108, *per* L.J.-C. Cooper at 109.

97 See paras 16.81, 16.82.

98 *Bishop v. Bryce*, 1910 S.C. 426, *per* L.P. Dunedin at 431.

99 *Keenan v. Scottish Wholesale Co-operative Society Ltd*, 1914 S.C. 959 ("a special case": *McTague v. LNER* [1948] C.L.Y. 4684).

1 *Moore v. Harland & Wolff*, 1937 S.C. 707; *Stewart v. Glasgow Corporation*, 1958 S.C. 28; *Dingwall v. J. Wharton (Shipping) Ltd* [1961] 2 Lloyd's Rep. 213, *per* Lord Keith of Avonholm at 219; *Prangnell-O'Neill v. Lady Skiffington*, 1984 S.L.T. 282. Civil Evidence (Scotland) Act 1988, s.1.

2 *Keenan, supra*; *Jordan v. Court Line*, 1947 S.C 29; *Stewart, supra*; *Walker v. McGruther & Marshall Ltd*, 1982 S.L.T. 345.

3 *Robertson* (1842) 1 Broun 152 at 177; *Stewart, supra, per* L.P. Clyde at 38; Lewis, p. 226.

4 *Bishop v. Bryce*, 1910 S.C. 426, *per* L.P. Dunedin at 431.

5 *Wilson v. Thomas Usher & Son*, 1934 S.C. 322, *per* L.J.-C. Aitchison at 338; see para. 16.91.

6 *Dawson v. Dawson*, 1956 S.L.T. (Notes) 58.

7 *Evidence* (Scot. Law Com. Memo. No. 46), para. G.24.

8 para. 16.25.

9 *Evidence* (Scot. Law Com. Memo. No. 46), para. G.26; *Ireland v. Taylor* [1949] 1 K.B. 300 at 313.

must be strictly confined to such new matter as may have arisen in cross-examination, unless with permission of the sheriff.[10] The purpose of the latter rule is to prevent the proliferation and repetition of issues.[11] Reference may, however, be made to facts not previously referred to, if they are relevant in order to deal with the matters raised in cross-examination. If the sheriff allows re-examination on new matter he usually allows the other party a second cross-examination thereon.[12] It is thought that when considering whether to allow re-examination on new matter the sheriff requires to consider not only the adequacy of the explanation tendered for failure to examine on that matter in chief, but also the extent to which the allowance of such re-examination might prejudice the other party, who will have conducted his cross-examination in the manner and to the extent that the examination-in-chief suggested as the most appropriate in the circumstances. There may be cases in which such prejudice may not be dissipated by a second cross-examination restricted to the new matter.

It appears that a duty to re-examine may in effect be incumbent on a defender's advocate where the pursuer founds on statutory provisions or regulations which impose on the defender a duty to take certain measures "so far as is reasonably practicable". A pursuer, whose advocate may have examined and rejected a particular method as "not reasonably practicable", may yet found successfully on that same method by extracting from the defender's witnesses in cross-examination, without prior notice, an admission that it would have been "possible" to adopt it.[13] It then becomes necessary for the defender's counsel to limit the effect of that admission in re-examination.[14] **16.79**

Questions through the court

Some textbooks state that once the re-examination is closed, any question which a party may wish to ask must be put through the court.[15] It is thought, however, that this practice is sometimes cumbersome and unnecessary,[16] and that in many cases there may be no practical reason why the question should not be put directly to the witness and answered by him, provided that the sheriff and the other parties are given an opportunity to take exception to the question,[17] and any party affected by any new matter elicited is given an opportunity to question the witness further thereon. **16.80**

Recall of witness

By statute the sheriff may, on the motion of either party, permit any witness who has been examined in the course of the proof or jury trial to be recalled.[18] A party may make such a motion at any time up to the closing of his case. It is for the sheriff to grant or refuse the motion and, if **16.81**

---

[10] *Niven v. Tudhope*, 1982 S.C.C.R. 365; CAS, F, II, 2.
[11] P. Murphy and D. Barnard, *Evidence and Advocacy* (1984), p. 137.
[12] Walkers, para. 388(a); *Evidence, supra*, para. G.27.
[13] *Whyte v. Smith Anderson & Co Ltd*, 1974 S.L.T. (Notes) 75.
[14] See Macphail, *Evidence*, para. S8.35A.
[15] Dobie, p. 221; J. H. A. Macdonald, *Criminal Law of Scotland* (5th ed., 1948), p. 299.
[16] *cf. Sandlan v. H.M. Advocate*, 1983 S.L.T. 519, *per* Lord Hunter at 522.
[17] Macphail, *Evidence*, para. 8.35.
[18] Evidence (Scotland) Act 1852, s. 4.

he grants it, to control the taking of additional evidence and keep it within proper limits.[19] The following are examples of circumstances in which such a motion may be granted. Where prejudice might result to a pursuer through the basis of the defender's case not having been properly put in cross-examination, the pursuer's witnesses may be recalled.[20] Witnesses may also be recalled for the purpose of proving that before giving evidence a witness made a statement inconsistent with his testimony.[21]

16.82 It is said that in civil cases, as in criminal cases,[22] the sheriff may recall a witness *ex proprio motu* for the purpose of clearing up ambiguities in his evidence.[23] There appears to be no modern reported example of the exercise of such a power in a civil case, and it is thought that any judicial power to recall a witness whom neither party seeks to recall would be exercised with great caution.

Concurring witness

16.83 In the past it seems to have been a familiar practice, to save time and expense in civil cases[24] in relation to formal evidence or the evidence of skilled witnesses, for parties to agree that one witness led by one party should be held as concurring in chief and in cross with the evidence of a previous witness led by that party. The concurring witness, having heard the evidence of the previous witness, was sworn in the ordinary way and expressed his concurrence, and the notes of evidence bore that he was held as concurring with the previous witness. The procedure appears still to be competent,[25] but to be seldom employed.

Objections to evidence

16.84 **Timeous objection**. A party may object to the admission of evidence, or to any defect in form or irregularity in the procedure at the proof. The objection should be stated whenever the point arises, and the sheriff should thereupon deal with it, either by sustaining or repelling it or by reserving his opinion until he ultimately gives judgment. An objection which may be taken to the admission of evidence may be either an objection to the line of evidence or an objection to a particular question. An objection to the line of evidence is directed to the trend of the evidence, or to the whole evidence which is being led as to some particular matter. An objection to a particular question must be stated before the question is answered. While as a general rule a defender has to meet the case made against him on record and nothing more,[26] a party may be entitled to found on evidence to which no timeous objection has

---

[19] *Todd v. Macdonald*, 1960 J.C. 93, *per* Lord Sorn at 96.

[20] *Wilson v. Thomas Usher & Son*, 1934 S.C. 332, *per* L.J.-C. Aitchison at 338–339.

[21] *Robertson v. Steuart* (1874) 1 R. 532; *Hoey v. Hoey* (1884) 11 R. 578; *Dyet v. National Coal Board*, 1957 S.L.T. (Notes) 18. *Cf. Begg v. Begg* (1887) 14 R. 497.

[22] *McNeilie v. H.M. Advocate*, 1929 J.C. 50; *Davidson v. McFadyean*, 1942 J.C. 95; *Todd, supra*; *Lindie v. H.M. Advocate*, 1974 J.C. 1.

[23] Dickson, para. 1769; Maxwell, p. 306.

[24] The procedure is incompetent in criminal cases: see *Cafferty v. Cheyne*, 1939 J.C. 1; *Black v. Bairds & Dalmellington Ltd*, 1939 S.C. 472 at 477.

[25] It was used in *Davie v. Magistrates of Edinburgh*, 1953 S.C. 34, and it is provided for in the A.S. (Fees of Witnesses and Shorthand Writers in the Sheriff Court) 1992 (S.I. 1992 No. 1878), Sched. 1, Note 8.

[26] *McGrath v. National Coal Board*, H.L., May 4, 1954, unreported, *per* Lord Reid, *cit. Hamilton v. John Brown & Co. (Clydebank) Ltd*, 1969 S.L.T. (Notes) 18.

been taken.[27] It appears that a party may object to evidence elicited by the sheriff.[28]

Ruling. When an advocate raises an objection to a question or to a line of evidence, the sheriff should rule on it at once, and if he does not, the advocate should ask him to do so. The sheriff should hear argument on the objection, normally from the advocate raising the objection, then the opposite advocate, and then the first advocate in reply.[29] He should then rule on the objection, by sustaining it, repelling it, or repelling it under reservation of all questions of competency and relevancy. **16.85**

Where the sheriff sustains an objection to a line of evidence and the advocate for the opposite party has other witnesses ready to speak to the line of evidence objected to, it is competent for him to put the question to each of these witnesses and have it overruled. A less formal and equally competent procedure is that the advocate states formally to the sheriff, before he closes his proof, that named witnesses were prepared to deal with the question overruled, but that he was refraining from putting them in the box out of respect to the sheriff's ruling: then, if there is any doubt about the situation, the sheriff can deal with it in an appropriate manner. Alternatively, if the advocate has examined such a witness upon other matters, he should state at the close of the examination-in-chief that he is prepared to put the question disallowed previously. That procedure ensures that, if the sheriff's ruling is reversed, only those witnesses will be examined who might have been examined if the objection had not been taken.[30] Where the sheriff sustains an objection on the ground that the evidence is not in line with the record, the advocate for the opposite party should at once consider whether he should seek leave to amend his pleadings, and if he decides to do so he should so move forthwith, specifying precisely the terms of the proposed amendment; and the sheriff should at once hear parties and give a ruling on the motion.[31] **16.86**

If the sheriff repels the objection under reservation of all questions of competency and relevancy, which is a very general practice,[32] he allows the evidence to be received under reservation as to its admissibility. Parties may argue the point at the hearing on evidence, and if so, the sheriff disposes of the objection in his interlocutor. **16.87**

Recording of objection and ruling. The record of the evidence must include any objection taken to a question or line of evidence, any submission thereon and the ruling of the court on the objection and submission.[33] The sheriff may, if he considers it necessary or desirable to do so, dictate a short note of the objection and decision. Where the recording of evidence has been dispensed with in terms of rule 29.18(1)[34] **16.88**

---

[27] *McGlone v. British Railways Board*, 1966 S.C. (H.L.) 1; *O'Donnell v. Murdoch McKenzie & Co.*, 1966 S.C. 58 at 60 (revsd, 1967 S.C. (H.L.) 63); *Albacora SRL v. Westcott & Laurence Line*, 1966 S.C. (H.L.) 19; *Brown's Exrx v. N.B. Steel Foundry Ltd*, 1968 S.L.T. 121. See also *Gibson v. British Insulated Callenders' Construction Co. Ltd*, 1973 S.C. (H.L.) 15; Macphail, *Evidence*, para. 8.40.

[28] *McCallum v. Paterson*, 1969 S.C. 85, *per* Lord Guthrie at 92.

[29] CAS, F, II, 3. See para. 16.72, n. 89.

[30] *Hewat v. Edinburgh Corporation*, 1944 S.C. 30, *per* L.P. Normand at 34–35.

[31] On amendment in the course of the proof, see paras 10.19 to 10.21.

[32] *Thomson v. Glasgow Corporation*, 1962 S.C. (H.L.) 36 at 47, 50, 65.

[33] OCR, r. 29.18(5).

[34] See para. 16.33.

the sheriff must take the following steps if called upon to do so. Where objection is taken to the admissibility of evidence on the ground of confidentiality or to the production of a document on any ground, he must note in writing the terms of such objections and his decision thereon. In all other cases he must record, in the note to his interlocutor disposing of the merits of the cause, the terms of any objections and his decision thereon.[35]

16.89 **Incidental appeal**. It is not competent during a proof to submit to review any decision of the sheriff as to the admissibility of evidence or the production of documents, except in the following situations.[36] Where a party to the cause or other person objects to the admissibility of oral or documentary evidence on the ground of confidentiality, or to the production of a document on any ground, he may, if dissatisfied with the ruling of the sheriff on the objection, express immediately his formal dissatisfaction and, with leave of the sheriff, appeal to the sheriff principal.[37] The sheriff principal must dispose of the appeal with the least possible delay.[38] Such an incidental appeal does not remove the cause from the sheriff, who may proceed with the cause as regards points not necessarily dependent upon the ruling appealed against.[39] It is submitted that leave to appeal should be granted only in the most exceptional circumstances.[40]

16.90 The appeal is taken by lodging a note of appeal in the prescribed form.[41] The note should state the grounds of appeal and should contain a request that the sheriff write a note.[42] Where leave to appeal against the ruling is not sought, it is not competent to raise the matter on appeal at a later stage.[43] If an appeal to the sheriff principal is timeously taken, his decision cannot at once be appealed to the Court of Session unless he grants leave to appeal[44]; but a later appeal to the Court of Session will be effectual to submit to review the whole of the interlocutors pronounced in the case, including the sheriff principal's decision.[45] If the sheriff refuses leave to appeal, his interlocutor so doing cannot be appealed,[46] but an appeal should be taken at the first opportunity thereafter, usually when the sheriff's final judgment is pronounced.[47]

Proof in replication

16.91 The party who leads in the proof not only adduces evidence in support of his own case but also by anticipation negatives the case of which he has notice in the pleadings.[48] If, after he has closed his case, matters come out in the other party's evidence which he could not reasonably have

---

[35] OCR, r. 29.18(12).
[36] OCR, r. 29.19(3).
[37] OCR, r. 29.19(1).
[38] OCR, r. 29.19(2).
[39] OCR, r. 29.19(4).
[40] See para. 18.53.
[41] OCR, r. 31.4(1) App., Form A.1.
[42] See para. 5.85.
[43] *Jackson v. McKay*, 1923 S.C. 286; *McDonnell v. McShane*, 1967 S.L.T. (Sh. Ct.) 61. *Cf. McMillan v. Hassan* (1945) 61 Sh.Ct.Rep. 91.
[44] 1907 Act, s. 28(1)(d).
[45] 1907 Act, s. 29.
[46] *Ure v. Ure*, 1947 S.C. 305.
[47] *Boss v. Lyle Shipping Co. Ltd*, 1980 S.L.T. (Sh. Ct.) 65.
[48] *Wilson v. Thomas Usher & Son*, 1934 S.C. 332, *per* L.J.-C. Aitchison at 338.

anticipated, a proof in replication may be granted in the discretion of the sheriff, the interlocutor allowing such proof exactly specifying the particular matters of fact to which it is to be directed.[49]

View

It appears to be competent for the sheriff to inspect any place or thing[50] with respect to which any question arises in the proof. In the absence of modern authoritative guidance on the matter, it is recommended that anything other than a conservative approach to the holding of a view should be adopted with caution. The matter appears to be one for the proper exercise of a judicial discretion. A party cannot require the sheriff to hold a view, or insist that he must not hold a view.[51] He should normally do so, however, only after hearing parties on a motion that he should do so. If he proposes *ex proprio motu* to hold a view, he should advise the parties that he proposes to do so and at least give them an opportunity of being present.[52] An accidental or casual visit to a locus which does not influence his decision is, however, unobjectionable.[53] **16.92**

Views are often held on the parties' joint motion, or on the motion of one party and of consent of the other. Where the parties disagree about whether or not a view should be held, the sheriff should weigh the advantages of holding a view against the disadvantages. Considerations of time and money may point against holding it, whereas considerations of assistance in reaching a proper decision may point in favour of holding it. Inconvenience to the sheriff should be left wholly out of account, if it falls within the bounds of what a litigant is reasonably entitled to expect from a judge.[54] If the sheriff decides to hold a view, he should pronounce an interlocutor appointing the parties or their advocates to meet him at a specified place and time for the purpose of a view of a specified locus or object, and stating on whose initiative the order is made.[55] The clerk of court attends with the sheriff. It is immaterial if, after due intimation, a party fails to attend or to be represented at the view.[56] It has been stated that a view should take place before the sheriff hears the evidence,[57] but in practice views have been held of consent of parties in the course of a proof, and between the close of the proof and the hearing on evidence.[58] The purpose of the view is to enable the sheriff to understand the evidence, not to enable him to criticise or contradict it.[59] **16.93**

---

[49] *Dick & Stevenson v. Mackay* (1880) 7 R. 778, *per* Lord Shand at 791; *Wilson, supra.* See also *Rankine v. Roberts* (1873) 1 R. 225; *Gairdner v. Young* (1874) 2 R. 173; *Kessack v. Kessack* (1899) 1 F. 398.

[50] See Macphail, *Evidence*, para. 25.39, n. 63.

[51] *cf. Tito v. Waddell* [1975] 1 W.L.R. 1303.

[52] *cf. Sutherland v. Prestongrange Coal and Fire-Brick Co. Ltd* (1888) 15 R. 494; *Hope v. Gemmell* (1898) 1 F. 74; *Goold v. Evans* [1951] 2 T.L.R. 1189, *per* Denning L.J. at 1191; *Salsbury v. Woodland* [1970] 1 Q.B. 324.

[53] *Sime v. Linton* (1897) 24 R.(J.) 70.

[54] *cf. Tito, supra.*

[55] See para. 5.79.

[56] Dove Wilson, p. 266.

[57] *Hattie v. Leitch* (1889) 16 R. 1128.

[58] See Macphail, *Evidence, supra.*

[59] *Hattie, supra*; *cf. Tito, supra*; Macphail, *Evidence*, para. 25.31.

Closing of proof

16.94 After the examination of his witnesses is concluded, the party leading in the proof formally closes his proof. Before he does so he should put in as evidence all documents admitted or put to witnesses, and reports of any evidence taken on commission: if he does not, it is for the discretion of the court whether the document will be admitted thereafter.[60] Each of the other parties then leads such evidence as he wishes, and similarly closes his proof. Of consent, a party's proof is sometimes closed subject to future examination of a named witness who, for sufficient reason, cannot attend, the other party meantime proceeding with his proof.[61] The closing of the proof of each party is noted in the shorthand notes. A party's proof may be reopened where justice so requires.[62] The conclusion of the whole proof is recorded in the interlocutor pronounced at the end of the day's proceedings.[63]

16.95 At the close of the proof the sheriff either at once hears parties on the evidence and makes avizandum or, if for any reason he sees fit to postpone the hearing, appoints parties to be heard on the evidence at a specified future diet.[64] In the ordinary case, parties are heard at once, the advocates relying on their own notes and recollection of the evidence. The hearing may, however, be postponed if there is no time for it at the conclusion of the proof; and if the case is complex or the proof is of such a nature that it would be difficult for the sheriff or the advocates to digest it on the spot, it may be in the interest of parties, and conducive to the ends of justice, that an adjournment should take place, and the notes of evidence be extended for the use of the sheriff and the advocates before and at the hearing.[65] The matter is one for the discretion of the sheriff: the hearing should not be postponed as a matter of course until the extended notes are available, not least because the extension of notes of evidence will add substantially to the expenses of the counsel.[66]

Additional proof

After amendment

16.96 Since the sheriff may allow amendment of the pleadings at any time before final judgment,[67] it is possible for amendment to be allowed after the proof has been closed. If the amendment raises a fresh issue of fact, it is implicit in its allowance that additional proof may be necessary.[68] The sheriff may allow such amendment and proof, however, only when it is in the interests of justice to do so; and in many cases to do so would unjustly prejudice the opposite party to an extent which could not be obviated by any conditions attached to the allowance of the amendment.[69]

---

60 *Liquidator of the Universal Stock Exchange Co. Ltd v. Howat* (1891) 19 R. 128; *Cameron v. Woolfson*, 1918 S.C. 190.

61 Dobie, p. 224.

62 *Wilson v. Imrie Engineering Services*, 1993 S.L.T. 235.

63 It is strictly unnecessary for the sheriff to pronounce an interlocutor declaring the proof to be closed, as the proof closes of itself if the diet is not adjourned: Dove Wilson, p. 178, n. 1.

64 OCR, r. 29.20. As to the hearing on evidence, see paras 16.98 to 16.103.

65 *Birrell v. Beveridge* (1868) 6 M. 421; *Smith v. Watson*, 1912 S.C. 553.

66 Grant Report, para. 598.

67 OCR, r. 18.2.

68 *Johnston v. Johnston* (1903) 40 S.L.R. 499.

69 *Thomson v. Glasgow Corporation*, 1962 S.C. (H.L.) 36. See also *McKenzie v. Jones* (1926) 42 Sh.Ct.Rep. 289; *Union Bank of Scotland Ltd v. Fulton*, 1929 S.L.T. (Sh. Ct.) 37.

Otherwise

It appears to be widely accepted that it is incompetent for the sheriff to allow additional proof, apart from additional proof following upon amendment of the record. By statute the sheriff principal may allow further proof when the action is before him on appeal,[70] and the Court of Session has a similar power[71] on appeal. No specific power to allow additional proof is conferred on the sheriff by statute or Act of Sederunt. The Act of Sederunt of July 10, 1839, by virtue of section 83 of which petitions for the allowance of further proof might be presented to the sheriff, fell with the repeal by the 1907 Act of the Sheriff Courts (Scotland) Act 1838.[72] It is generally assumed that the sheriff has no inherent power at common law to allow additional proof,[73] one view being that such power is excluded by the scrupulous attention to detail with which the powers of the sheriff are laid down by the rules.[74] In fact, however, the rules do not provide a comprehensive code of procedure, and many of the sheriff's powers to regulate procedure can only be derived from the inherent jurisdiction of the court.[75] It seems unfortunate that whatever grounds there may be for admitting further evidence should not be considered until after the sheriff has pronounced his decision on a proof which may be incomplete,[76] and there appears to be no reason in principle why the sheriff should not have the power to allow further proof so as to enable him to do complete justice between the parties so long as he is seised with their case.[77] Such a power is vested in the Lord Ordinary in the Court of Session,[78] apparently without the need for statutory authority, and there is no sound reason that it should not also be within the inherent powers of the sheriff. Cases in which the power would be exercised would no doubt be extremely few and would require very strong grounds.[79] But the view that the sheriff has no such power, although often repeated in sheriff court decisions and generally accepted in the textbooks, appears to be wrong in principle. **16.97**

The Hearing on Evidence

Authorities

If possible, before the hearing on evidence the parties' advocates should give to the court officer lists of the authorities to which they propose to refer. In some sheriffdoms the lodging of such a list with the sheriff clerk in advance of the diet of proof is required.[80] Since some **16.98**

---

[70] 1907 Act, s. 27, as amended by the 1913 Act, Sched. 1: see paras 18.81, 18.82.
[71] Court of Session Act 1988, s. 32(3): see para. 18.98.
[72] *Inglis' Trs v. Macpherson*, 1910 S.C. 46.
[73] *McWilliam v. Robertson* (1911) 27 Sh.Ct.Rep. 219; *Hogan v. Cunningham* (1915) 32 Sh.Ct.Rep. 67; *Cook v. Crane*, 1922 S.C. 631 at 633; *McGhee v. Ellingham* (1932) 49 Sh.Ct.Rep. 282; *Grierson v. McGarva* (1934) 50 Sh.Ct.Rep. 88; Wallace, pp. 188–189; Fyfe, p. 240; Lewis, pp. 144–146; Dobie, pp. 225–226.
[74] *Hogan, supra*.
[75] See paras 2.05 to 2.25.
[76] Lewis, p. 146.
[77] *Grierson, supra*.
[78] *Lacy v. Lacy* (1869) 7 M. 369; *Rainsford-Hannay v. Smith*, 1934 S.L.T. 491.
[79] *Cook, supra, per* Lord Hunter at 636; Maclaren, pp. 562–563; Maxwell, p. 308, n. 6.
[80] *e.g.* Lothian and Borders, Act of Court (Consolidation etc.) 1990, No. 1 as amended, Direction 13 (24 hours before the diet); North Strathclyde Act of Court (Consolidation etc.) 1992, Direction 1.12 (two clear working days prior to the diet).

sheriff court libraries are inadequately stocked and few hold English reports, arrangements should be made for copies of the authorities to be available to the sheriff.[81]

Speeches

16.99 The speeches at the hearing on evidence are of great importance because the sheriff relies very much on the assistance of the advocates in arriving at his decision. The party who led in the proof makes the first speech, followed by the other party or parties, normally in the order in which they appear in the instance. It is in the discretion of the sheriff to grant a right of reply to the first speaker.[82] It is appropriate to allow him to notice any new matter and, after a proof before answer, any legal arguments brought forward in the other speech or speeches.

16.100 In each speech[83] the advocate indicates to the sheriff the material facts which he will invite the sheriff to hold as proved, and analyses the evidence with reference to the parties' cases on record with the object of submitting that he has made good his material averments while his opponent has failed to establish his. To that end he commends or criticises the witnesses, suggesting reasons why their evidence should be accepted or rejected, and making submissions as to the weight to be attached to their evidence. If necessary, he seeks rulings on objections which have been made at the proof to evidence which has been led under reservation.[84] He also states, in language as definite and precise as possible, the legal propositions on which he relies. He refers to the parties' averments of legal duty, if any, and to their pleas-in-law, and makes submissions as to the legal consequences which should be drawn from the facts. These matters of law should be fully argued, with citation and examination of any relevant statutory provisions and decisions, whether they are for or against the advocate's contention.[85] At a hearing on evidence after a proof before answer the relevancy of the averments attacked by the preliminary plea may be scrutinised, with the result that the action may be dismissed.[86] In actions of damages for personal injuries, awards in comparable English and Scottish cases may be cited.[87]

16.101 At the conclusion of his speech the advocate moves the sheriff to dispose appropriately of the parties' pleas-in-law, usually by sustaining his own material pleas and repelling those of his opponent. A party seeking to put forward an argument which is not supported by his averments or pleas-in-law must seek leave to amend his pleadings by adding to or altering his averments or, where necessary, by adding an appropriate plea-in-law.[88] The precise terms of the proposed amendment should be stated, and parties heard thereon.

---

[81] For the sheriff's role at the hearing on evidence, see para. 16.40.

[82] Dove Wilson, p. 180; Wallace, p. 190. *Cf.* Court of Session Practice Note, May 14, 1970 (*Parliament House Book*, C2003).

[83] On the structure and content of a speech at a hearing on evidence, see R. G. McEwan, *Pleading in Court* (2nd ed., 1995), pp. 39–40.

[84] See para. 16.87.

[85] See para. 16.42.

[86] See para. 17.12.

[87] *Allan v. Scott*, 1972 S.C. 59.

[88] *Robb v. Logiealmond School Board* (1875) 2 R. 417, *per* L.P. Inglis at 422; *Kelly v. Edmund Nuttall Sons & Co (London) Ltd*, 1965 S.C. 427 at 434.

In the course of his speech the advocate may make concessions on matters of fact or law. Such concessions should be made with care. Concessions on matters of fact are conclusive against the party making them, and may be acted on by the sheriff.[89] The sheriff should carefully note and check with the advocate the terms of any concession, and refer to it in the note appended to his final interlocutor. In some circumstances he should require the concession to be recorded in a minute, such as a minute restricting the sum sued for,[90] or to be reflected in an amendment of the pleadings, for example by the deletion of a plea-in-law, which should be noted in the interlocutor making avizandum. A concession may be withdrawn before the conclusion of the hearing, but its withdrawal may result in an award of expenses against the party on whose behalf it is made if it adds to the expense of the proceedings.[91] A concession of fact may not normally be withdrawn thereafter but a concession on a question of law may be withdrawn on appeal in appropriate circumstances which give rise to no material prejudice to the other party.[92] It is undecided whether a judge is entitled to proceed on a concession of substantive law which is plainly wrong but he is entitled to acquiesce in parties' procedural or evidential arrangements even if they involve some departure from the normal course.[93] **16.102**

At the conclusion of the speech, the following matters should not be overlooked. **16.103**

(1) In an action of damages, the sheriff should be addressed on the question of the interest to be allowed on any damages which may be awarded.[94]

(2) Where witnesses have been present at the proof but have not been called or held as concurring with another witness, a motion should be made that charges for their attendance be allowed. The charges will only be allowed if the sheriff grants the motion at the close of the proof and the names of the witnesses are recorded in the interlocutor.[95]

(3) The sheriff should also be moved to certify for additional remuneration as skilled witnesses any skilled persons whom it has been necessary to employ to make investigations prior to the proof in order to qualify them to give evidence thereat. Charges therefor, and for their attendance at the proof, will be allowed in addition to the ordinary witness fees of such persons at such rate in the discretion of the auditor as is fair and reasonable for each skilled person if the sheriff grants a motion to that effect not later than the time at which he awards expenses and the names of the witnesses are recorded in the interlocutor.[96] It is, however, good practice to make the motion at the hearing on evidence, lest it be later overlooked.[97]

(4) If counsel has been instructed, the sheriff should be moved to certify the cause as suitable for the employment of counsel, or of senior counsel, or of senior and junior counsel, as the case may be.[98]

---

[89] *e.g. Nicolson v. Johnstone* (1872) 11 M. 179; *Minister of Brydekirk v. Minister and Heritors of Hoddam* (1877) 4 R. 798.

[90] *cf. Sinclair v. Mossend Iron Co.* (1854) 17 D. 258.

[91] *Campbell v. Henderson*, 1949 S.C. 172; *Roofcare Ltd v. Gillies*, 1984 S.L.T. (Sh. Ct.) 8.

[92] *e.g. Marshall v. Wm Sharp and Sons*, 1991 S.L.T. 114.

[93] *John Thorburn and Sons v. Border Harvesters Ltd*, 1992 S.L.T. 549.

[94] See paras 21.35, 21.36.

[95] A.S. (Fees of Witnesses and Shorthand Writers in the Sheriff Court) 1992, Sched. 1, Note 8.

[96] *ibid.* Note 9.

[97] For the grounds for certification, see paras 19.62 to 19.65.

[98] See paras 12.24 to 12.26.

(5) Where the result as regards expenses is complex or where a tender has been lodged, the sheriff should be moved to reserve the question of expenses. If that is not done, submissions on expenses made at the hearing on evidence will involve hypothetical arguments based on the various possible disposals of the case; and a tender cannot at that stage be brought to the notice of the sheriff.[99] In such cases the sheriff in his final interlocutor should reserve all questions of expenses and appoint parties to be heard thereon at a subsequent diet. At that stage any tender lodged, which may have a bearing on expenses, may be brought to his notice[1]; and, if the relevant information is available, he may assess the liability of any legally-aided party against whom an award of expenses is made. Unnecessary reservation of expenses may, however, cause delay in the execution of the judgment or in the appeal process as well as additional, if minor, expense.

Conclusion of hearing

16.104 At the conclusion of the hearing on evidence the sheriff either pronounces judgment at once, or "makes avizandum"[2] and takes time to consider the case with a view to pronouncing judgment with the least possible delay.[3] The latter is by far the commoner course, for these reasons. The judgment must be formally set out, with findings in fact and law and a note setting forth the reasons for the decision[4]; the shorthand writer is not obliged to attend the hearing on evidence and record and extend any judgment then delivered, and the parties are not required to meet such expense; and it is unlikely that a sheriff would be subsequently able to reproduce accurately in writing what he had said in the course of an extempore judgement. But in cases involving much personal anxiety for the parties, such as cases concerning the welfare of children, it may be appropriate for the sheriff when making avizandum to announce informally from the bench what the effect of his judgment will be, provided that he is certain of the result and that its disclosure at that stage will not prejudice the rights of parties or, where applicable, the welfare of the child.

---

99 See paras 14.49, 14.50.

1 See paras 14.49, 14.50.

2 *i.e.* "to be considered". Until the final interlocutor is issued the process is said to be "at avizandum".

3 OCR, r. 29.20.

4 OCR, r. 12.2(3): see paras 17.02, 17.03.

Chapter 17

THE JUDGMENT

Delay

17.01 The sheriff is directed to pronounce judgment with the least possible delay after hearing parties.[1] It is sometimes desirable for the sheriff to direct the extension of the shorthand notes and to consider them before pronouncing judgment, but extending the notes may take some weeks and is usually unnecessary in short and straightforward cases. Moreover, extension of notes may add unreasonably to the expenses to be borne by one or more of the parties. Long delays in pronouncing judgment can cause disquiet and suspicion among litigants who lose; and those who win may find that they have been deprived of justice far too long. Such delays should not occur unless there are compelling reasons why they should; and, if there are such reasons, it is prudent for the sheriff to refer to them briefly in the note appended to his interlocutor.[2]

Form of interlocutor

General rules

17.02 The general rules as to the nature, form, correction and effect of interlocutors have already been considered.[3] The following paragraphs deal with the special rules relative to final interlocutors on the merits and other interlocutors pursuant to the leading of evidence. A final interlocutor on the merits is one which, by itself, or taken along with previous interlocutors, disposes of the subject-matter of the cause, notwithstanding that judgment may not have been pronounced on every question raised, and that the expenses found due may not have been modified, taxed or decerned for.[4] Any interlocutor other than a final interlocutor may, in accordance with directions given by the sheriff principal, be written and signed by the sheriff clerk.[5]

17.03 Where, in any cause other than a family action which has proceeded as undefended, evidence has at any stage been led, the sheriff should include in his interlocutor findings in fact and law and append to the interlocutor a note setting out the reasons for his decision.[6] If an interlocutor is not

---

[1] OCR, r. 29.20.

[2] *Rolled Steel Products (Holdings) Ltd v. British Steel Corporation* [1986] Ch. 246, *per* Lawton L.J. at 310.

[3] paras. 5.72 to 5.92.

[4] 1907 Act, s. 3(h). An interlocutor merely holding a defender as confessed is, in the absence of an operative decree, incompetent (*Squire Light and Sound Ltd v. Vidicom Systems Ltd*, 1987 S.C.L.R. 538).

[5] OCR, r. 12.1. The sheriffs principal have not given any directions in terms of the foregoing rule. However, they have prescribed certain classes of motion which may be determined by a sheriff clerk in terms of r. 15.5(2): see para. 5.51.

[6] OCR, r. 12.2(3).

framed in accordance with that rule, an appeal court may remit the case back to the sheriff with a direction to recall it and pronounce another interlocutor in the prescribed form.[7] In special circumstances, however, the court may refrain from doing so.[8] The present rule, in contrast with its predecessor,[9] does not require findings in fact and in law to be stated separately. A sheriff may therefore make a finding, which embraces both fact and law. Such findings are often convenient and even necessary to express a conclusion,[10] but it must be clear what facts material to the cause the sheriff finds to be established and how far his judgment proceeds on the matter of facts so found, or on matter of law.[11] After setting out his findings, the sheriff sustains or repels the material pleas-in-law stated by the parties on record, and disposes of the case by pronouncing or refusing decree in terms of the craves of the initial writ and of any counterclaim. Broadly speaking, the subject-matter of the findings in fact is limited by the parties' averments of fact on record, that of the findings in law or in fact and law by their pleas-in law, that of the decerniture by the craves, and that of the note by the parties' submissions at the hearing on evidence.

Findings in fact

17.04 The interlocutor should be headed with the serial number and name of the case. Having stated the place of sitting of the court and the date in the usual way, the interlocutor normally proceeds, "The Sheriff, having resumed consideration of the proof and whole cause,[12] Finds in fact that . . ."—and thereafter sets out the sheriff's findings in fact. These should be numbered,[13] and expressed in language which is as clear and precise as possible. It is normal to begin by explaining who the parties are, and then to state in a logical order the material facts which are admitted or which the sheriff finds to have been proved or not to have been proved.[14] It is recommended that each finding should be stated in a short sentence, and that findings on different branches of the case should be grouped in sections under appropriate headings where that would assist intelligibility. The old style of running all the findings together into one very long paragraph is unkind to the reader. The traditional reference to the parties as "pursuer" and "defender" instead of "the pursuer" and "the defender" and unnecessary reliance on the expression "the said"[15] should also be avoided.

17.05 The findings in fact should be stated in sufficient detail to explain and justify the decerniture. They should include all the facts material to the

---

[7] *Glasgow Gas-Light Co. v. Glasgow Working Men's Total Abstinence Society* (1866) 4 M. 1041; *Melrose v. Spalding* (1868) 6 M. 952; *Mackay v. Mackenzie* (1894) 21 R. 894; *James Y. Keanie v. Maycrete Sales Ltd*, 1949 S.L.T. (Notes) 28.

[8] *Selby v. Baldry* (1867) 5 S.L.R. 64; *Dawson v. McLean* (1896), unreported, *cit.* Lees, *Interlocutors*, p. 15; *Duke of Norfolk v. Wilson*, 1950 S.L.T. (Notes) 11.

[9] OCR (1983), r. 89(1). Although apparently excluded under this rule, mixed findings in fact and law were often found to be necessary and were made.

[10] See para. 17.08.

[11] *cf.* Court of Session Act 1988, s. 32(4).

[12] Or, where appropriate, "the proof, productions, joint minute of admissions and whole cause."

[13] *Calderwood v. Dundee Magistrates*, 1944 S.C. 24.

[14] A finding that a fact is not proved should be stated in the interlocutor as a finding in fact: *McCaffer v. Allan* (1896) 33 S.L.R. 601; though this requirement is seldom followed in modern practice. If the sheriff's conclusions on fact sufficiently emerge from the facts found to be proved, negative findings may not, however, be necessary.

[15] See para. 9.65.

contentions of either of the parties, even though not material to the point on which the judgment proceeds.[16] These facts may be ascertained by reference to the parties' averments on record of their substantive grounds of pursuit or defence.[17] The sheriff should always express a conclusion on all issues regarding the facts which have been argued before him and which are capable of being raised on appeal. Accordingly, if on the sheriff's view of the case it falls to be decided on one issue and the other questions of fact argued before him are thereby superseded, he should nevertheless state findings on these other matters so that if an appeal court holds that his judgment is incorrect, it will have in the interlocutor all the material facts which it may consider necessary for the correct disposal of the case.[18]

The findings in fact should be based on the oral evidence which the sheriff has heard and on any written or real evidence which he has examined.[19] They should not, however, narrate evidence. If a witness, X, states a fact, and the sheriff accepts his evidence, he should find the fact proved, and should not in any circumstances state as a finding in fact that X stated the fact. An inference of fact which is drawn from other findings in fact may be stated as a finding in fact, the facts from which it is drawn having already been stated. In an action of damages for personal injuries the sum which the sheriff considers to be a reasonable award in name of solatium may be expressed as a finding in fact. **17.06**

The interlocutor should be coherent and self-sufficient if read separately from the note, the function of the note being to explain, not to control or complete, the findings in the interlocutor. The interlocutor should not refer to or incorporate the terms of the note,[20] and it should not be necessary for a reader to refer to the note in order to ascertain the sheriff's finding on any matter of fact or law which has been in issue. **17.07**

Findings in law, and in fact and law

Numbered findings in law follow the findings in fact. Findings which involve both fact and law should be set out separately from the findings in fact and the findings in law, as numbered findings in fact and law, preceded by the words "Finds in fact and law that . . .". A finding in law embodies the sheriff's conclusion, or direction to himself, on a relevant question of law, which should already have been focused in a plea in law. Examples of such findings are: "The defender is not resting owing to the pursuer in the sum sued for." "(1) The defender is bound to make reparation to the pursuer. (2) The damages payable to the pursuer fall to be reduced in terms of the Law Reform (Contributory Negligence) Act 1945."[21] A finding in fact and law normally precedes the findings in law, and embodies the sheriff's application of the findings in law to the facts which he has found, such as: "(1) The accident was caused partly by the **17.08**

---

[16] *cf. Little v. Stevenson & Co.* (1896) 23 R. (H.L.) 12, *per* Lord Herschell at 15 (a recommendation as to Court of Session interlocutors in appeals from the sheriff court).

[17] *cf. Mackay v. Dick & Stevenson* (1881) 8 R. (H.L.) 37.

[18] *Morrow v. Enterprise Sheet Metal Works (Aberdeen) Ltd*, 1986 S.L.T. 697, *per* L.J.-C. Ross at 700.

[19] *James Y. Keanie Ltd, supra.*

[20] *Campbell v. Caledonian Ry* (1852) 14 D. 441; *Glasgow Gas-Light Co., supra; Mackay, supra; McCaffer, supra; Lord Advocate v. Johnston*, 1983 S.L.T. 290 at 291, 293.

[21] *Gardner v. J. Robertson (Canisters) Ltd* (1960) 76 Sh.Ct.Rep. 167 at 169.

fault of the defenders in respect that they failed to take reasonable care for the safety of the pursuer. (2) The accident was also caused partly by the fault of the pursuer in respect that he failed to take reasonable care for his own safety. (3) The proportion of fault attributable to the defenders is nine-tenths and to the pursuer one-tenth."[22] In some cases a finding in fact and law may be alone sufficient, without any subsequent finding in law, such as: "The pursuer has failed to prove that the accident was caused to any extent by fault on the part of the defenders."[23] It is, however, sometimes difficult to achieve a categorisation of findings into findings in fact, findings in fact and law, and findings in law which is generally acceptable.[24] In a finding in law or in fact and law care should be taken to quote accurately the material terms of any statutory provision, since a misquotation may ground an argument on appeal that the judgment is based on an error in law.[25]

Decerniture

17.09 Having ascertained and set out the facts of the case in his findings in fact, having stated the rules of law which are applicable in his findings in law, and having where appropriate applied these rules of law to the facts in findings in fact and law, the sheriff goes on to dispose of the parties' pleas-in-law and to give effect to such pleas as he sustains by pronouncing a decree or specific order which is the result of the application of the law to the facts of the case.

17.10 Pleas-in-law are disposed of by being either sustained or repelled. How any plea-in-law is to be disposed of will be apparent from the findings in law and in fact and law which will have been derived from some or all of the parties' pleas-in-law. It is seldom necessary to dispose of all the pleas-in-law stated on record. Preliminary pleas are only infrequently disposed of after proof on the merits[26]; and if a plea on the merits is disposed of in one way, it is unnecessary to deal with consequential pleas which would have had to be considered only if that plea had been disposed of in another way.

17.11 Having disposed of the pleas-in-law, the sheriff gives effect to those which he has sustained by pronouncing in appropriate terms a decree which disposes of all the craves of the initial writ and of any counterclaim.[27] He may pronounce decree in any of four modes: (1) by granting a decree finally determining the merits of the action in favour of the pursuer in terms of the craves of the writ (a decree of condemnator[28]); (2) by granting a similar decree in favour of the defender (a decree of absolvitor, whereby the defender is assoilzied); (3) by granting decree of dismissal in

---

[22] *Stewart v. Colvilles Ltd* (1963) 79 Sh.Ct.Rep. 64 at 65 (not reported on this point, 1963 S.L.T. (Sh.Ct.) 15).

[23] See also *Cook v. Robertson's Exr* (1959) 75 Sh.Ct.Rep. 161 at 164 (not reported on this point, 1960 S.L.T. (Sh. Ct.) 4).

[24] The distinction between findings in fact and in law was discussed in *Mackay v. Dick & Stevenson* (1881) 8 R. (H.L.) 37; *Shepherd v. Henderson* (1881) 9 R. (H.L.) 1; *Caird v. Sime* (1887) 14 R. (H.L.) 37; *Sutherland v. Glasgow Corporation*, 1951 S.C. (H.L.) 1.

[25] *Lanark C.C. v. Frank Doonin Ltd*, 1974 S.L.T. (Sh. Ct.) 13.

[26] See para. 17.12.

[27] In the text it is assumed that there is no counterclaim. As to counterclaims, see paras 12.29 to 12.41.

[28] An expression now rarely used in practice.

favour of the defender (a rare occurrence after proof[29]), whereby the action as laid is put out of court but a new action is not excluded; or (4) by granting a mixed decree of condemnator and absolvitor or dismissal, whereby the craves are only sustained in part and *quoad ultra*, *i.e.* as regards the remaining craves, the defender is assoilzied or the action is dismissed. A decree of condemnator against one or more defenders, and of absolvitor or dismissal in favour of another or others, is another example of a mixed decree.[30] A decree of condemnator founds a plea of *res judicata* and excludes an action or defence by the defender upon any grounds pleaded in the original action, or which might have been pleaded, but were omitted.[31] A decree of absolvitor will also found a plea of *res judicata* and will exclude a new action on the same grounds, but a new action on different grounds may be raised since the plea of competent and omitted does not apply to pursuers.[32] A decree of dismissal cannot found a plea of *res judicata*, and the pursuer may raise another action with the same craves.[33]

A decree of dismissal may be pronounced after proof only where the proof has been before answer, under reservation of a preliminary plea. It is rare for decree of dismissal to be pronounced after proof before answer, but not incompetent.[34] Where there has been proof before answer in a simple case, however, the sheriff ought in ordinary circumstances to decide the case upon the evidence rather than upon the relevancy or otherwise of a party's averments: if there has been no objection to the admissibility of any of the evidence led, the law should where possible be applied to the reality of the circumstances disclosed at the proof rather than to the words used in a party's averments.[35] If the pursuer has given the defender sufficient notice of his case, as may appear from the facts being almost common ground, or from the withdrawal of a plea to relevancy or from the absence of objections to evidence, it is inappropriate after proof before answer to subject the pursuer's averments to the degree of scrutiny appropriate to a debate on relevancy or on an objection to the admissibility of evidence, with the result of denying to him a remedy which in justice he is entitled to receive.[36] If, on the other hand, the case of which the pursuer has given notice fails, he is not entitled to the advantage of decree of dismissal rather than absolvitor in order to have an opportunity to raise a fresh action on a ground which emerged at the proof but which was not added, or was not allowed to be added, to his pleadings by amendment.[37] Confusion and injustice may result from dismissing an action when the defender is entitled to a decree of absolvitor.[38] **17.12**

---

[29] See para. 17.12.

[30] Mackay, *Manual*, pp. 312–313.

[31] See para. 2.106.

[32] See paras 2.108, 2.113.

[33] See para. 2.106.

[34] *e.g. Coutts v J.M. Piggins Ltd*, 1983 S.L.T. 320.

[35] *O'Connor v. McRobb*, 1975 S.L.T. (Sh. Ct.) 42; *Merchandise Funds Co. Ltd v. Maxwell*, 1978 S.L.T. (Sh. Ct.) 19.

[36] *Gunn v. McAdam & Son*, 1949 S.C. 31, *per* L.P. Cooper at 39–40; *Maitland v. Bingorama Ltd*, 1977 S.L.T. (Sh. Ct.) 58.

[37] *McLinden v. British Steel Corporation*, 1972 S.L.T. (Sh. Ct.) 25; *Merchandise Funds Co. Ltd, supra.*

[38] *Dundee General Hospitals v. Bell's Trs*, 1952 S.C.(H.L.) 78, *per* Lord Normand at 88.

Essentials of decree

17.13 As already explained, the decree must dispose of the whole of the craves of the initial writ and any counterclaim.[39] A decree which is in favour of the pursuer must keep within the craves of the writ: if it goes beyond them, as by giving judgment for a larger sum than that craved, it may be set aside. Where, however, it is competent to crave a specific sum or such other sum as may be found due, as in an action of accounting, decree for a larger sum than the specific sum may be granted.[40] It is therefore desirable, before issuing the interlocutor, to compare it with the craves to see that it deals with all of them and does not go beyond them.

17.14 The decree must be clear and precise. Clerical or incidental errors, and perhaps other errors, may be corrected before extract, or before transmission of the process where an appeal has been taken[41]; but if the decree is past correction the only remedy is the recall of the interlocutor on appeal. The sheriff may not issue a further interlocutor explaining a supposed ambiguity in a prior interlocutor, or supply any deficiency in such an interlocutor by pronouncing a further interlocutor in the same[42] or in a subsequent[43] process.[44] The decree should be so framed that the loser is left in no doubt as to what he is to do or to pay, and the winner should know exactly what he has gained.[45] The use of the formula "decree as craved" may cause doubt, confusion and further expensive procedure; and in actions of interdict the precise terms of the interdict granted must appear *ad longum* in the interlocutor.[46] Similarly, in an action *ad factum praestandum* the decree should plainly specify what is to be done.[47] The interlocutor should not grant decree for payment of sums brought out in some production, or refer to a minute or other pleading or production for a statement of the terms of the decision which is being pronounced, unless it is wholly impracticable to embody the details in the interlocutor, as where a scheme is approved.[48]

17.15 The decree must be so expressed as to leave the sheriff clerk in no doubt as to what he should put into the extract. If the result of the case is not codified in the form of a specific order or orders disposing of the craves, the decree is not in extractable form. It is not necessary for the word "decerns" to be used in the interlocutor in order for it to be extracted.[49] "Decerns" continues to be used in practice, however, as a word of style for two purposes, namely to mark the fact that the interlocutor is final on the subject with which it deals, and as showing that the interlocutor in which it occurs is meant to be and is extractable.[50] Its use avoids any possible

---

[39] para. 17.11.
[40] *Spottiswoode v. Hopkirk* (1853) 16 D. 59.
[41] paras 5.87 to 5.89.
[42] *Agnew's Trs v. Macneel* (1827) 5 S. 309 (N.E. 287).
[43] *Young v. Nith Commissioners* (1880) 7 R. 891.
[44] The interlocutor may, however, be interpreted in a subsequent action: *Marquis of Huntly v. Nicol* (1896) 23 R. 610.
[45] *Middleton v. Leslie* (1892) 19 R. 801, *per* L.P. Robertson at 802; Lees, *Interlocutors*, p. 20.
[46] *Middleton, supra*; see para. 7.15.
[47] *Middleton, supra*; *Marshall v. Callander and Trossachs Hydropathic Co. Ltd* (1896) 24 R. 33, *per* L.P. Robertson at 34.
[48] *McDougall* (1878) 5 R. 1014.
[49] Sheriff Courts (Scotland) Extracts Act 1892, s. 4.
[50] *McLean v. MacBrayne Ltd* (1916) 33 Sh.Ct.Rep. 74.

confusion between what is meant to be a final or operative judgment and an interlocutory order or findings.[51]

Decree for payment

Where a decree for payment is pronounced, the sum awarded should be stated in words and figures. **17.16**

The sheriff may grant decree for payment of a sum of money expressed in a foreign currency. The procedure has already been discussed.[52] **17.17**

Cases of contribution among joint wrongdoers, and cases of contributory negligence, require to be specially dealt with in the interlocutor. Where in any action of damages in respect of loss or damage arising from any wrongful acts or negligent acts or omissions two or more persons are, in pursuance of the judgment of the court, found jointly and severally liable in damages or expenses, they are liable *inter se* to contribute to such damages or expenses in such proportions as the court may deem just.[53] Where a defender has stated a plea-in-law seeking apportionment in terms of the statute, and the sheriff finds the defenders jointly and severally liable in damages to the pursuer, he should decern against the defenders jointly and severally for payment to the pursuer of the sum of damages awarded, and find the proportions in which they are liable *inter se* to contribute to that sum.[54] Where damages are recoverable by virtue of the Law Reform (Contributory Negligence) Act 1945, the sheriff must find and record the total damages which would have been recoverable if the claimant had not been at fault,[55] apportion liability between the defender and the claimant, and decern against the defender for payment to the pursuer of the reduced sum of damages.[56] **17.18**

Although interest runs *ex lege* from the date of the decree or of its affirmation on appeal,[57] failure to decern for it expressly may cause confusion.[58] Parties should have been heard on the question of interest at the hearing on evidence,[59] and it should be specifically awarded. **17.19**

The appropriate form of interlocutor where money has been consigned is considered elsewhere.[60] **17.20**

As a general rule, the sheriff is not empowered to allow payment by instalments of a sum decerned for in an ordinary action. If the debtor requires time to pay, he should move the sheriff to supersede extract. Payment by instalments may, however, be allowed where a time order is **17.21**

---

51 Lewis, p. 208.

52 paras 9.91, 9.92.

53 Law Reform (Miscellaneous Provisions) (Scotland) Act 1940, s. 3(1). See Walker, *Delict* (2nd ed.), pp. 119–123; Walker, *Civil Remedies*, pp. 1243–1244.

54 *e.g. Drew v. Western SMT Co.*, 1947 S.C. 222 at 243; *Kennedy v. Glasgow Corporation* (1959) 70 Sh.Ct.Rep. 239 at 241 (not reported on this point, 1954 S.L.T. (Sh. Ct.) 56).

55 Law Reform (Contributory Negligence) Act 1945, s. 1(2).

56 *e.g. Stewart v. Colvilles Ltd* (1963) 79 Sh.Ct.Rep. 64 at 65–66 (not reported on this point, 1963 S.L.T. (Sh. Ct.) 15).

57 See para. 9.93.

58 *Project Contract Services Ltd v. Fraoli*, 1980 S.C. 261.

59 para. 16.101.

60 para. 11.50.

made under the Consumer Credit Act 1974[61] or a time to pay direction is made under the Debtors (Scotland) Act 1987.[62]

Directions to officers of court

17.22 A court does not pronounce decree against one of its own officers, but only orders him to do what is necessary.[63] When, therefore, it is necessary for the sheriff to order the sheriff clerk, or sheriff officers, to do something,[64] he "grants warrant to" or "appoints" or "directs" them to do so. As officers of the court they are bound to obey his orders. If a sheriff officer were to fail to do so, he and his cautioner would be liable in damages.[65]

Expenses

17.23 It has been recommended above that, except in a case where the result as regards expenses is likely to be straightforward and no tender has been lodged, the sheriff should be moved to reserve the question of expenses.[66] If he does so, the interlocutor will not be a final interlocutor, since in such an interlocutor expenses are found due.[67] If the question of expenses is straightforward, or has been fully argued, the sheriff may find the unsuccessful party liable to the successful party in expenses, or find the successful party entitled to expenses, which is "just the same thing".[68] Unless the expenses are modified at a fixed amount, they must be taxed before decree is granted for them.[69] If there is no modification, the interlocutor therefore runs: "Finds the pursuer [or defender] liable to the defender [or pursuer] in expenses; allows an account thereof to be given in and remits the same, when lodged, to the auditor to tax and to report." The rules relative to expenses are considered elsewhere.[70]

Superseding extract

17.24 Where it is desired to supersede extract for a certain time, that should be done in the decree,[71] because the supersession of extract is virtually a condition made by the judgment and forms part of the decree on the merits.[72] A motion to allow extract to be applied for and issued earlier than provided for in rule 30.4(1) may be disposed of in the interlocutor if parties have been heard thereon at the hearing on evidence, or it may be made after the decree has been pronounced.[73]

---

[61] s. 129. See para. 17.24.

[62] s. 1. A time to pay direction may be made, in cases to which the Act applies, on an application by the defender made at any time before the granting of decree. It cannot be made thereafter (*Watson v. McHugh*, 1992 S.L.T. (Sh. Ct.) 35). Where, however, a charge for payment has been served, arrestment executed or an action of adjudication commenced, application may be made for a time to pay order (s. 5).

[63] *Baird v. Glendinning* (1874) 2 R. 25, *per* L.P. Inglis at 26.

[64] *e.g.* the sheriff clerk may be required to pay over consigned money, or to execute a deed in terms of s. 5A(2) of the 1907 Act: sheriff officers may be required to break open lockfast places.

[65] Graham Stewart, *Diligence*, pp. 806–808; *cf.* Maher and Cusine, *The Law and Practice of Diligence*, para. 12–22.

[66] para. 16.103.

[67] 1907 Act, s. 3(h). See para. 18.37.

[68] *S. S. Fulwood Ltd v. Dumfries Harbour Commissioners*, 1907 S.C. 735, *per* L.P. Dunedin at 737.

[69] OCR, r. 32.1.

[70] Chap. 18.

[71] *e.g. Webster v. Lord Advocate*, 1984 S.L.T. 13.

[72] Dove Wilson, p. 327; Wallace, p. 352; Dobie, pp. 253–254.

[73] OCR, r. 30.4(2), (3).

Note

The only formal direction to the sheriff as to the note is that he must set out in the note the reasons for his decision.[74] But the need for the sheriff to state the reasons for his decision is no mere technicality, nor does it depend mainly on the rules of court. It is an important part of the sheriff's duty in every case, where he gives judgment after a proof, to state the grounds of his decision. The parties are entitled to know his reasons, as are any appellate courts in the event of an appeal.[75] It has already been explained that the note is not part of the interlocutor, and that while it may explain the interlocutor, it cannot control or limit its effect, except in very special circumstances.[76] An interlocutor which is clearly competent cannot be made incompetent by any opinions expressed in the note, and where an interlocutor has allowed a proof before answer, the sheriff who hears the proof before answer is not bound by any opinions expressed in the note to that interlocutor by the sheriff who issued it.[77] **17.25**

It would be presumptuous to propose any formula for the writing of a note. However, it is often helpful, not only to readers without access to the pleadings and interlocutor sheets but also to the sheriff, to begin by summarising the parties' material averments and pleas-in-law and, where appropriate, the procedure in the case prior to the proof. In the earlier part of the note it is usual to explain the basis of the findings in fact. Some matters will have been admitted on record or in a joint minute of admissions, or will not have been disputed at the hearing on evidence, while others will have been the subject of conflicting evidence. Any concessions made in the course of the proof or at the hearing on evidence should be carefully noted, in order to avoid any misunderstanding or dispute which may arise on appeal, especially where the advocates appearing before the appeal court are not those who appeared before the sheriff. **17.26**

It is unnecessary for the sheriff to incorporate in the note a lengthy rehearsal of the evidence led, but where there has been a conflict of evidence on matters material for his decision he must refer to the evidence in sufficient detail to enable him to discharge his duty to make clear to the parties and to any appellate court what evidence he has accepted and rejected, and his reasons for doing so. For that purpose he is obliged to observe and deal with inconsistencies and discrepancies in the evidence led, to record the parties' submissions thereon and to explain his own view of the credibility and reliability of each of the witnesses, his reasons for accepting or rejecting their evidence, and thus the basis of his finding in fact on the matter about which the conflicting evidence has been led.[78] He should also explain and justify inferences of fact made from primary facts.[79] Where corroborative evidence is required, or where parties are in dispute as to whether there is any evidence at all to support a finding on a particular matter, the sheriff should explain what evidence was tendered, **17.27**

---

[74] OCR, r. 12.2(3).

[75] *Lai Wee Lian v. Singapore Bus Service (1978) Ltd* [1984] A.C. 729, *per* Lord Fraser of Tullybelton at 734.

[76] para. 17.07.

[77] paras 5.86, 17.07.

[78] *Shevchuk v. National Coal Board,* 1982 S.L.T. 557 at 560, 565; *Greenline Carriers (Tayside) Ltd v. City of Dundee District Council,* 1991 S.L.T. 673 at 675J.

[79] *Greenline Carriers (Tayside) Ltd v. City of Dundee District Council, supra.*

the parties' submissions thereon, and his reasons for accepting or rejecting it. When rejecting evidence, no judge ever wishes to be compelled to say that he has listened to evidence which is false: he always prefers to say, and give reasons for saying, that he cannot accept the witness's evidence, or that he prefers a contrary version spoken to by another witness.[80] It is, however, essential, where he considers a witness to be unworthy of credit in the sense of imputing to him wilful untruth, that he should say so unambiguously, and give his reasons.[81] Where his determination of any particular question of fact is based on matters which passed before him but cannot be reproduced in the notes of evidence, such as the demeanour of a witness, he should explain such matters in his note. He will frequently find himself compelled to choose between the evidence adduced by each party, though he has no reason for disbelieving either set of witnesses. In such a case his decision may be determined by a balance of the probabilities.[82]

17.28 When he comes to explain his findings in law, or in fact and law, the sheriff normally summarises the arguments presented at the hearing on evidence and mentions all the authorities cited. An omission to record and deal with any matter raised in argument may give rise to a contention on appeal that he has ignored or misunderstood it. It may also be useful for an appeal court to know what arguments and authorities were canvassed before the sheriff. It is generally incorrect to decide any matter raised on record which the parties have declined to argue.[83] It is incorrect to decide any matter in dispute on a ground which has not been explored in evidence or argument.[84] If the sheriff notices a matter which is *pars judicis*, or any other consideration previously unmentioned before him which may have a bearing on his decision, he should give parties an opportunity to be heard thereon.[85]

17.29 Similarly, as a general rule the sheriff should not issue a judgment which is based in any degree on cases which have not been fully canvassed and examined.[86] If after making avizandum the sheriff comes upon possibly relevant authorities not cited in argument which raise a new point or change or modify, even provisionally, the conclusion he has already reached, or resolve his doubts on a point, he should pronounce an interlocutor appointing parties to be heard further, if so advised, and putting the case out for the purpose of enabling parties to intimate whether they desire to be heard further, and if so, of assigning a further diet. The note to the interlocutor should draw attention to the new authorities and explain that parties are being given an opportunity to be heard thereon.[87] While the expense and delay of a further hearing is undesirable, the paramount consideration in such a case must be that of avoiding the injustice of a party's being defeated by authorities which he has had no opportunity of controverting or explaining. If, on the other

---

[80] *Mahon v. Air New Zealand Ltd* [1984] A.C. 808 at 818.
[81] *Jordan v. Court Line Ltd*, 1947 S.C. 29, *per* Lord Moncrieff at 38.
[82] *Duncan v. Wilson*, 1940 S.C. 221, *per* L.P. Normand at 225.
[83] *cf. Mackinnon's Trs v. MacNeill* (1897) 24 R. 981.
[84] *Kay v. Ayrshire and Arran Health Board*, 1986 S.L.T. 435; 1987 S.L.T. 577.
[85] *Bell v. McCurdie*, 1981 S.C. 64 at 67; *Clark v. Watson*, 1982 S.L.T. 450 at 451.
[86] *Lindsay v. Giles* (1844) 6 D. 771, *per* L.J.-C. Hope at 800.
[87] *Bathgate Storage and Distribution Co. Ltd v. Canada Permanent Trust Co. (U.K.) Ltd*, Linlithgow Sh. Ct, June 13, 1984, unreported.

hand, the new authorities do no more than confirm or support the conclusions which the sheriff has already reached on a point that has been fairly argued, a further hearing would not appear to be necessary.[88]

It has been said that the reader of a judgment is entitled to expect lucidity of thought and expression, compression and a power to pursue an argument in a way that relates conclusions to facts and principles that are relevant to them.[89] Judgments are traditionally objective and impersonal in style. "One hint that the judge is enjoying the sound of his own voice, an innocent pleasure enough, or that he is palming off emotion as reason, and authority has flown out of the window."[90] **17.30**

Issue of interlocutor

Where money has been consigned into court under the Sheriff Court Consignations (Scotland) Act 1893, no decree, warrant or order for payment to any person may be granted until there has been lodged with the sheriff clerk a certificate by an authorised officer of the Inland Revenue stating that all taxes or duties payable to the Commissioners of Inland Revenue have been paid or satisfied.[91] In an action of multiple-poinding, however, it is not necessary for the grant of a decree, warrant or order for payment that all of the taxes or duties payable on the estate of a deceased claimant have been paid or satisfied.[92] **17.31**

Once any necessary certificate has been lodged and the interlocutor has been signed, the sheriff clerk must forthwith provide the parties with a copy of the interlocutor and note free of charge.[93] **17.32**

---

[88] *Re Lawrence's Will Trusts* [1972] Ch. 418 at 436–437; *Caldwell v. Sumpters* [1972] Ch. 478 at 490; *Howard E. Perry & Co. Ltd v. British Railways Board* [1980] 1 W.L.R. 1375 at 1385–1386.

[89] Lord Radcliffe in *The Language of the Law* (1965, ed. L. Blom-Cooper), p. xii.

[90] *ibid.* p. xiv. See also B. Dickson, "Judgment Writing", 1983 C.J.Q. 27.

[91] OCR, r. 30.2(1).

[92] OCR, r. 30.2(2).

[93] OCR, r. 12.2(5)(b). The fee "to cover inquiring for cause at avizandum" which continues to be allowed for in the A.S. (Fees of Solicitors in the Sheriff Court) (Amendment and Further Provisions) 1993, Sched. 1, Table of Fees, Chap. II, Pt II, para. 21(a), seems unnecessary. R. 12.2(5)(b) does not apply where the sheriff has pronounced his interlocutor in the presence of the parties (a rare occurrence: see para. 16.104).

CHAPTER 18

APPEALS

MODES OF REVIEW

It is a constitutional principle that every judgment of an inferior court is subject to review, unless such review is excluded by express words or by necessary implication.[1] There are three conventional modes of review of sheriff court interlocutors: appeal, suspension and reduction.[2] This chapter is concerned with appeals in ordinary causes.[3] Suspension and reduction are Court of Session processes, and as modes of review are available only in exceptional circumstances, as briefly explained below.[4] In addition to those three modes of review, an interlocutor may also be reduced by the Court of Session in the exercise of the *nobile officium*.[5] It would seem theoretically possible to apply to the court for review of a sheriff court interlocutor by way of an application for judicial review, in circumstances where it would be appropriate to invoke the supervisory jurisdiction of the court[6]; but in practice that does not yet seem to have been attempted. The details of Court of Session procedure in these various processes is beyond the scope of this book. **18.01**

Appeal

An appeal is an application to a superior court or tribunal to reverse, vary or set aside the judgment, order, determination, decision or award of an inferior court or tribunal in the hierarchy of courts or tribunals on the ground that it was wrongly made, that is that the decision was incompetent or *ultra vires*; that there was lack of jurisdiction; that the sheriff had exercised his discretion in a wholly unreasonable manner; that his decision was wrong in law; or that he had not had material before him to justify the decision which he made: but not that as a matter of justice it requires to be corrected.[7] On the **18.02**

---

[1] *Harper v. Inspector of Rutherglen* (1903) 6 F. 23, *per* Lord Trayner at 25; *Mackay v. Macdonald*, 1928 S.C. 776, *per* L.J.-C. Alness at 781; *Arcari v. Dumbartonshire C.C.*, 1948 S.C. 62, *per* L.P. Cooper at 66. See also *Marr & Sons v. Lindsay* (1881) 8 R. 784, *per* L.P. Inglis at 785; *Jeffray v. Angus*, 1909 S.C. 400, *per* L.J.-C. Macdonald at 402.

[2] *Lamb v. Thompson* (1901) 4 F. 88, *per* Lord Moncreiff at 92.

[3] Appeals in summary causes and small claims will be considered in Vol. 2; in summary applications generally, in Chap. 25; and in particular miscellaneous statutory appeals and applications, in Chap. 26.

[4] paras 18.04, 18.05. Such processes and all interlocutors therein granting suspension or recall or reduction of an interlocutor or order of the sheriff court are intimated to the sheriff clerk of the sheriff court where the interlocutor or order was pronounced (Scottish Court Service Circular No. 2/85).

[5] *Royal Bank of Scotland v. Gillies*, 1987 S.L.T. 54.

[6] RCS, Chap. 58.

[7] *Norris v. Norris*, 1992 S.C.L.R. 395; *McFarlane v. McFarlane*, 1995 S.C.L.R. 794 where the reference to correcting a decision "as a matter of justice" in Halsbury, Vol. 37 para. 677, which appeared in the first edition, was questioned. In *Stroud v. Stroud*, 1993 S.C.L.R. 763, Sh. Pr. Nicholson, Q.C. said: "I am not persuaded that the words which appear to be a direct quotation from Halsbury's *Laws of England* are the best guide to appeal practice in Scotland".

general principle that there should be finality in litigation, appeals should be neither necessary nor desirable, but that principle is overridden not only by the need to recognise the human fallibility of judges, to correct any errors they may make and to produce just results in particular cases, but also by the need to maintain and develop a uniform and coherent system of law. A system of appeals also encourages inferior judges to keep in view their duty to apply the law judicially and to refrain from making arbitrary or unreasonable decisions.

18.03 In ordinary causes an appeal may be taken in certain cases from the sheriff either to the sheriff principal, and thence to the Inner House of the Court of Session; or directly from the sheriff to the Inner House. In either case a further appeal on a question of law may be taken from the Inner House to the House of Lords. The majority of appeals are taken from the sheriff to the sheriff principal, and the unsuccessful party is usually content to accept the sheriff principal's decision. Few appeals go to the Inner House, either on appeal from the sheriff principal or directly from the sheriff. Appeals to the House of Lords in cases commenced in the sheriff court are very rare.[8]

Suspension

18.04 A process of suspension in the Court of Session is a mode of obtaining review of a sheriff court decree.[9] The distinction between suspension of a charge following upon a decree and suspension as a process of review of a decree is that the latter process challenges the decree, while the former merely suspends diligence.[10] Suspension as a process of review is competent only in limited circumstances. Where review by appeal is competent, suspension is excluded as unnecessary and incompetent.[11] And if a party has appealed to the Court of Session and failed, either on the merits or by default, he cannot seek review by suspension.[12] It is also incompetent to suspend a decree of absolvitor[13]; a decree which has been implemented[14]; or a decree in a cause which by reason of its value is within the privative jurisdiction of the sheriff court.[15] Suspension of a decree in absence has in practice been superseded by reponing.[16] Suspension is, however, competent where extract has been issued[17]; or where the period for appeal has expired[18]; or where appeal is excluded but review by suspension is not excluded.[19] Further, a suspension of a decree may be presented where

---

[8] *Donoghue v. Stevenson*, 1932 S.C. (H.L.) 31, is a notable example. A more recent example is *Sanderson v. McManus*, 1997 S.C.L.R. 281.

[9] *Lamb, supra, per* Lord Trayner and Lord Moncreiff at 92.

[10] *Macdonald v. Denoon*, 1928 S.L.T. 439.

[11] Mackay, *Practice*, ii, pp. 482–3.

[12] *Lamb, supra, per* Lord Moncreiff at 92; *Watt Bros & Co. v. Foyn* (1879) 7 R. 126; *Mackenzie v. N.B. Ry* (1879) 17 S.L.R. 129.

[13] *McGregor v. Lord Strathallan* (1862) 24 D. 1006. The reason is that a decree of absolvitor is not a decree on which a charge can proceed, and that suspension, even when used as a method of review, assumes the possibility of a charge (Mackay, *Practice*, ii, p. 484).

[14] Mackay, *Practice*, ii, p. 483.

[15] *Brown & Critchley v. Decorative Art Journals*, 1922 S.C. 192.

[16] Mackay, *Practice*, ii, p. 492.

[17] *Turner v. Gray* (1821) 3 S. 235 (N.E. 165). *Cf. Paul v. Henderson* (1867) 5 M. 1120.

[18] Mackay, *Practice*, ii, p. 483.

[19] *Paul, supra*; *Fletcher v. Davidson* (1874) 2 R. 71; *Campbell's Trs v. O'Neill*, 1911 S.C. 188; *Macdonald, supra*.

the sheriff court, or any other inferior court, has exceeded its powers or jurisdiction,[20] even where the appellate jurisdiction of the Court of Session is excluded.[21] Suspension is not, however, the proper process to set aside a decree on the ground that it was obtained by fraud or on any ground extrinsic of the case presented to the court: the appropriate remedy in such a case is an action of reduction.[22]

Reduction

Sheriff court decrees may in certain circumstances be reviewed in the Court of Session by means of an action of reduction. In general, reduction is not competent where other means of review are prescribed, and either these means have been utilised or the parties have failed to take advantage of them, unless there are exceptional circumstances justifiably excusing a party from failing to utilise them.[23] As to a decree in absence, a defender may be reponed at any time before implement in full of the decree[24]: after implement, the decree may be reduced by an action of reduction.[25] A decree *in foro* may be reviewed by way of reduction if it has been extracted[26] or cannot be extracted.[27] As a general rule, a decree which can be, but has not been, extracted cannot be brought under review by reduction unless in circumstances where there is no other remedy available.[28] A decree may be reduced if a party has been misled by an error or ambiguity in the interlocutor,[29] or by a departure from the ordinary practice of the court,[30] but not on the ground that the decree was obtained through inadvertence.[31] A decree by default may be reduced, but the court may require the pursuer to find caution for the expenses awarded in the sheriff court before the action proceeds to proof.[32] Other grounds of reduction include incompetency[33] and fraud.[34] Reduction as a mode of review of decisions of courts is fully examined in the undernoted work.[35] **18.05**

---

20 *Lindsay v. Barr* (1826) 4 S. 748 (N.E. 756); *Bruce v. Irvine* (1835) 13 S. 437.

21 *Campbell v. Brown* (1829) 3 W. & S. 441; *Miller v. McCallum* (1840) 3 D. 65.

22 *Smith v. Kirkwood* (1897) 24 R. 872; *McCarroll v. McKinstery*, 1923 S.C. 94.

23 *Adair v. Colville & Sons*, 1926 S.C. (H.L.) 51, *per* Viscount Dunedin at 55–56; *Philp v. Reid*, 1927 S.C. 224; *Stewart v. Lothians Construction (Edinburgh) Ltd*, 1972 S.L.T. (Notes) 75; *Mitchell Construction Co. (Scotland) Ltd v. Brands Transport and Demolition Ltd*, 1975 S.L.T. (Notes) 58; *J. & C. Black (Haulage) Ltd v. Alltransport International Group Ltd*, 1980 S.L.T. 154.

24 OCR, r. 8.1. The rule does not apply in actions of divorce or separation. See paras 7.23 *et seq.*

25 *McLachlan v. Rutherford* (1854) 16 D. 937.

26 *Taylor's Trs v. McGavigan* (1896) 23 R. 945; *Mathewson v. Yeaman* (1900) 2 F. 873; but where a decree has been extracted it is not competent to exercise the dispensing power so as to allow an appeal to be marked late: *Alloa Brewery Co. Ltd v. Parker*, 1991 S.C.L.R. 70.

27 *Holmes v. Tassie* (1828) 6 S. 394; *Jack v. Umpherston* (1837) 15 S. 833.

28 *Scoutar v. McLaughlan* (1864) 2 M. 955, *per* L.P. McNeill at 960, 962.

29 *Mathewson, supra.*

30 *Brennan v. Central SMT Co.*, 1947 S.N. 7; *Mitchells Construction Co. (Scotland) Ltd, supra.*

31 *Stewart, supra.*

32 *Campbell v. McCance*, 1929 S.L.T. 26; *McGregar v. Rooney*, O.H., Feb. 5, 1971, unreported.

33 *Macdonald v. Mackessack* (1888) 16 R. 168; *Mackenzie v. Munro* (1894) 22 R. 45.

34 *Smith v. Kirkwood* (1897) 24 R. 872; *Adair v. Colville & Sons*, 1926 S.C.(H.L.) 51, *per* Viscount Dunedin at 56; *Rowe v. Elliot*, 1973 S.L.T. (Notes) 41.

35 Walker, *Civil Remedies*, pp. 171–190.

Appeal to Sheriff Principal

Nature of appeal to sheriff principal

Historical development

18.06 The system of appeal from the sheriff to the sheriff principal is so anomalous in theory, as an appeal from one professional judge to another, that "it is almost self-evident that the system could never have had a deliberate originator".[36] The historical development of the system, before its regulation by statute and Act of Sederunt in the nineteenth century, is somewhat obscure.[37] At common law there was originally no right of appeal from the sheriff (formerly the sheriff-substitute) to the sheriff principal (formerly the sheriff): the sheriff substitute, being the deputy of the sheriff, acted in his name, and his decision was in law the decision of the sheriff. It seems, however, that the sheriff-substitute's decision was not final until the giving out of the extract or official copy to the parties; and before extract the parties could petition the sheriff-substitute to reconsider his decision, by presenting reclaiming petitions to the sheriff-substitute until he prohibited further petitions of the kind. When the sheriff principal was in the sheriffdom at the time of presentation of such a petition, he disposed of it personally; and when he was not, the sheriff-substitute was frequently asked to take the opinion of the sheriff principal before disposing of it. In time, the parties directly craved the opinion of the sheriff principal, and the intervention of the sheriff-substitute was limited to the pronouncing of an interlocutor permitting the appeal. Since the nineteenth century, the practice of appealing from the sheriff-substitute (now the sheriff) to the sheriff principal has been embodied in and regulated by statute and Act of Sederunt.

Advantages

18.07 While it may seem anomalous that an appeal should lie from one professional judge to another, the appeal to the sheriff principal is inexpensive, quick and popular. It is less expensive than an appeal to the Court of Session, since it may be conducted by a solicitor (normally the solicitor who appeared before the sheriff), there is usually no necessity to print or copy papers,[38] and additional travelling expenses may be avoided as the sheriff principal frequently hears the appeal in the court house where the case was heard at first instance. The time taken to dispose of an appeal in the sheriff court is considerably shorter than in the Court of Session. Many more appeals are taken from the sheriff to the sheriff principal than from the sheriff to the Inner House, and few of the appellate decisions of the sheriff principal are further appealed.[39]

Judicial precedent[40]

18.08 Sheriffs principal and sheriffs are bound by decisions of the Inner House of the Court of Session and by decisions of the House of Lords in Scottish appeals and, probably, in English appeals on issues which are

---

[36] A phrase applied by Dove Wilson, p. 3 to the evolution of the sheriff court generally.

[37] See Dove Wilson, pp. 310–311; Wallace, pp. 593–594; *Archer's Trs v. Alexander & Sons* (1910) 27 Sh.Ct.Rep. 11.

[38] But see OCR, r. 31.6. It is not known how frequently sheriffs principal are likely to invoke this rule which came into effect on Nov. 1, 1996.

[39] See the annual Civil Judicial Statistics Scotland.

[40] *Stair Memorial Encyclopaedia*, Vol. 22, paras 296 to 301.

based on legislation applicable in both jurisdictions or which have been decided by an authoritative and binding court to be exactly the same in both jurisdictions.[41] It is thought that where a decision of the Inner House cannot stand with a later decision of the House of Lords in one of the categories of appeals mentioned above, a sheriff principal or sheriff would follow the House of Lords decision. Sheriffs principal are not bound by the decisions of a Lord Ordinary or of one another, although they treat the former as strongly persuasive[42] and may treat the latter as persuasive. Occasionally, however, justifiable differences of view among sheriffs principal as to a matter of procedure may remain unresolved for many years, to the detriment of the development of uniformity in practice.[43] A sheriff principal, although not formally bound by his own decisions or by those of his predecessors in office in his sheriffdom, normally follows any such decision unless satisfied that it was given *per incuriam*.[44] The decisions of a sheriff principal, while he holds office, are normally followed by the sheriffs of his sheriffdom.[45] A sheriff is not, however, bound by the decisions of a Lord Ordinary,[46] or of the sheriff principal of another sheriffdom, or of another sheriff, although he will treat the two former as persuasive and may treat the latter as persuasive. It is submitted that where a sheriff is faced with two or more conflicting decisions in point by sheriffs principal of other sheriffdoms, he should prefer the later decision if it has been reached after full consideration of the earlier decision, except where he is convinced that the later decision was wrong in not following the first, as where some binding or persuasive authority has not been cited in either case.[47]

Change of sheriff principal

Notwithstanding the death, resignation or removal of a sheriff principal, appeals may be taken from the judgment of the sheriff. These appeals are heard by the succeeding sheriff principal when he enters upon office.[48] If the sheriff principal dies while the appeal is at avizandum, the succeeding sheriff principal assigns a diet for rehearing the appeal.[49] **18.09**

Competency

General rules

The competency of appeals from the sheriff to the sheriff principal is primarily regulated by the provisions of section 27 of the 1907 Act, which are examined in detail later in this chapter.[50] Section 27 provides that an **18.10**

---

41 *Dalgleish v. Glasgow Corporation*, 1976 S.C. 32, *per* L.J.-C. Wheatley at 51, 52.

42 T. B. Smith, *Judicial Precedent in Scots Law* (1952), pp. 19, 105.

43 *e.g. Cassidy v. Cassidy*, 1986 S.L.T. (Sh. Ct.) 17, and cases there cited, though the matter in issue in that case has subsequently been resolved in a uniform manner: see *Richardson v. Richardson*, 1991 S.C.L.R. 209.

44 *Wales Dove Bitumatic Ltd v. Plastic Sealant Services Ltd*, 1979 S.L.T. (Sh. Ct.) 41; *Ram v. Yadh*, Sh. Pr. Dick, Glasgow Sh. Ct, Mar. 5, 1982, unreported.

45 Smith, *supra*.

46 For an example of a sheriff declining to follow a decision of a Lord Ordinary, see *Foster v. Craigmillar Laundry Ltd*, 1980 S.L.T. (Sh. Ct.) 100.

47 *Minister of Pensions v. Higham* [1948] 2 K.B. 153 at 155; *Colchester Estates (Cardiff) v. Carlton Industries plc* [1986] Ch. 80.

48 1907 Act, s. 27.

49 *Thames Cleaning Co. Ltd v. British Transport Ship Management (S.) Ltd*, Sh. Pr. O'Brien, Stranraer Sh. Ct, May 12, 1981, unreported.

50 paras 18.32 to 18.54 below.

appeal is competent against all final judgments, against certain specified classes of interlocutors and against interlocutors in respect of which the sheriff grants leave to appeal. The view may be entertained that appeals to the sheriff principal other than those provided for by section 27 are incompetent,[51] but it is submitted that that is incorrect. Section 27 does not expressly exclude other appeals. In that respect it differs significantly both from its predecessor, section 27 of the Sheriff Courts (Scotland) Act 1876, which declared that no other appeals should be competent, and from section 28 of the 1907 Act, which provides that appeals from the sheriff court to the Court of Session are competent only if the interlocutor appealed against is a final judgment or falls within specified classes of interlocutors, or if leave to appeal is granted. Further, nothing in sections 27 or 28 of the 1907 Act affects any right of appeal or exclusion of such right provided by any Act of Parliament in force for the time being,[52] and the 1907 Act itself makes provision for appeals other than those mentioned in section 27, by providing for appeals against interlocutors transferring causes to other sheriff courts,[53] and for incidental appeals in the course of a proof.[54] The only appeals to the sheriff principal in ordinary causes which are expressly excluded by the 1907 Act are appeals against interlocutors or orders recalling, or incidental to the recall of, decrees in absence[55]; appeals against fines for failure to return a process[56]; and appeals during a proof against decisions as to the admissibility of evidence or the production of documents, except as provided by rule 29.19(1).

18.11 It is therefore submitted that it is not necessarily fatal to the competency of an appeal to the sheriff principal in an ordinary cause that the interlocutor appealed against does not fall within any of the classes mentioned in section 27. In particular, the 1907 Act does not wholly exclude resort to the sheriff principal's common-law power to review any interlocutor pronounced by the sheriff. While it seems clear that it is the general policy of the Act to exclude appeals without leave against interlocutors outside the specified classes,[57] that policy is overridden by two surviving principles of the common law. The first, which is derived from the sheriff principal's responsibility at common law for the proper regulation of the conduct of judicial business within his sheriffdom, is that the sheriff principal is possibly entitled to recall incompetent interlocutors pronounced by the sheriff.[58] The second is that where Parliament confers a jurisdiction on a court without prescribing any specific form of process, the presumption is that the ordinary forms of that court are to be observed.[59] Thus, where a statute empowers a sheriff to make a certain order and does not prescribe any specific procedure, the ordinary form in the sheriff court will apply, which is that there should be an appeal from the sheriff to the sheriff principal.[60] It is on this principle that the

---

[51] Lewis, p. 313, appears to read *Mulvey v. Mulvey* (1922) 39 Sh.Ct.Rep. 256 as supporting that view.

[52] 1907 Act, s. 28.

[53] OCR, r. 26.1(8).

[54] OCR, r. 29.19(1).

[55] OCR, r. 8.1(5).

[56] OCR, r. 11.4(2).

[57] 1907 Act, s. 27(F).

[58] *Archer's Trs v. Alexander & Sons* (1910) 27 Sh.Ct.Rep. 11. See para. 18.12.

[59] *Mags of Portobello v. Mags of Edinburgh* (1882) 10 R. 130, *per* L.J.-C. Moncreiff at 137; *Central R.C. v. B*, 1985 S.L.T. 413.

[60] *Swan v. Kirk*, 1932 S.L.T. (Sh. Ct.) 9.

sheriff principal may entertain an appeal against a recall of arrestments by the sheriff.[61] In addition to these principles, there are several rules as to the competency of appeals, not derived from section 27 of the 1907 Act, which are discussed in the following paragraphs.

Other rules

Incompetent interlocutor. Notwithstanding the absence of express statutory provision, an appeal is possibly competent without leave against an interlocutor which is incompetent in the sense that the sheriff had no power or right to pronounce it.[62] However, in *Gupta v. Laurie*[63] the Inner House, albeit without the advantage of full argument or the citation of authority, said that a "Sheriff Principal has no supervisory jurisdiction at common law over judicial decisions of a sheriff. Rights of appeal against decisions of sheriffs are regulated by statute". Moreover, at least one sheriff principal has expressly reserved his opinion as to whether or not there is a common law right of appeal against an incompetent interlocutor.[64] In the case of an appeal in a summary cause it has been held that a sheriff principal has no jurisdiction at common law to correct an incompetent interlocutor.[65] **18.12**

New point. In the civil courts in Scotland there is no general rule that an appeal may not be based on a new point which has not been argued or explored at first instance[66]: the question whether a new point will be entertained on appeal is not one of competency, but of discretion. An appellate court may consider a question of competency which strikes at the whole root of the proceedings whether or not it was argued in the court below.[67] Legal arguments on matters other than competency, which were not canvassed before the sheriff, are frequently adduced before the appeal court; but if a fresh argument cannot properly be advanced without the addition by amendment of an appropriate plea-in-law, the allowance of the amendment is within the discretion of the appeal court, who will have regard to considerations of fairness and prejudice to the other side.[68] Further, the appellate court may regard as unacceptable the introduction of a new point on which it does not have the benefit of the opinion of the judge of first instance[69]; and an appellant who succeeds on an argument **18.13**

---

[61] *Mowat v. Kerr*, 1977 S.L.T. (Sh. Ct.) 62. See para. 11.33.

[62] *Gupta's Trustee v. Gupta*, 1996 S.L.T. 1098 at 1099 where the statement in the text was effectively approved. *Archer's Trs, supra*; *Maxwells (Dundee) Ltd v. Adam*, 1911 2 S.L.T. 149; *Sydie v. A. A. Stuart & Sons (Contractors) Ltd*, 1968 S.L.T. (Sh. Ct.) 93 at 95; *McKenzie v. John R. Wyatt (Musual Enterprises) Ltd*, 1974 S.L.T. (Sh. Ct.) 8; *Mackays v. James Deas and Son Ltd*, 1977 S.L.T. (Sh. Ct.) 10, *Appleyard (Aberdeen) Ltd v. Morrison*, 1979 S.L.T. (Sh. Ct.) 65; *Hardy v. Robinson*, 1985 S.L.T. (Sh. Ct.) 40; *Lord Advocate v. Johnston*, 1983 S.L.T. 290 at 293, 294; *Brown v. British Rail Property Board*, 1983 S.L.T. (Sh. Ct.) 19; *VAG Finance Ltd v. Smith* 1988 S.L.T. (Sh. Ct.) 59; *Gray v. Gray*, 1996 S.C.L.R. 531.

[63] 1994 S.C.L.R. 176 at 177F.

[64] *Ampliflaire Ltd v. The Chisholme Institute*, 1995 S.C.L.R. 11.

[65] *L. Mackinnon & Son v. Coles*, Sh. Pr. Bell, Aberdeen Sh. Ct, Jan. 13, 1984, unreported; *Edinburgh D.C. v. Robbin*, 1994 S.C.L.R. 43.

[66] *Cf.* the practice of the House of Lords in Scottish appeals (*British Oxygen Co. v. South West Scotland Electricity Board*, 1956 S.C. (H.L.) 112, *per* Lord Normand at 120) and generally *Moriarty v. Evans Medical Supplies Ltd* [1958] 1 W.L.R. 66, *per* Lord Denning at 88; *Baker v. R.* [1975] A.C. 774, *per* Lord Diplock at 788; *Glen Henderson Stuggart Ltd v. Henderson*, Sh. Pr. Mowat, Ayr Sh. Ct, May 18, 1992, unreported.

[67] *Wolfson v. Glasgow District Licensing Board*, 1980 S.C. 136 at 138.

[68] para. 10.24; *Glen Henderson Stuggart Ltd v. Henderson, supra.*

[69] *Varney (Scotland) Ltd v. Lanark T.C.*, 1974 S.C. 245, *per* L.J.-C. Wheatley at 249.

advanced for the first time in the appeal court may not be awarded the full expenses of the litigation.[70] The new argument cannot be based on evidence other than that led at first instance, except where the court is willing to consider circumstances which have arisen since the hearing in the court below.[71] In an appeal on a question of expenses[72] the court will not alter the judgment of the sheriff on a point which was not argued before him, on the ground that it must be inferred to have been waived.[73]

18.14 *Concession.* On questions other than expenses a litigant may appeal on the footing that before the appeal court he will withdraw a concession on a point of law which he made before the judge of first instance.[74] The withdrawal of the concession may, however, have a bearing on the question of liability for expenses.[75]

18.15 *Interlocutor pronounced of consent.* It is incompetent to appeal against an interlocutor which bears to have been pronounced of consent, unless the appellant maintains on appeal that the interlocutor is incorrect and no consent was given,[76] or, perhaps, unless the respondent does not object to the competency of the appeal.[77]

18.16 *Interlocutor expressly or by implication not subject to review.* The word "final" may be used in two different senses to describe an interlocutor. An interlocutor may be "final" in the sense that it disposes of the merits of the case, or in the sense that it is not subject to review.[78] It is used in the second sense as meaning that an interlocutor which is expressly or by implication a final interlocutor cannot be submitted to review.[79] Interlocutors which are by implication final include interlocutors which, under the Ordinary Cause Rules, can be appealed against only within a certain time-limit but not thereafter, such as interlocutors against which leave to appeal is required.[80]

18.17 *Procedural interlocutor acted upon.* A further example of an interlocutor which is by implication final in the second sense explained above is one ordering some procedural step, upon which a party has acted or in the

---

[70] *Gubay v. Kington* [1984] 1 W.L.R. 163, *per* Lord Fraser of Tullybelton at 168.

[71] para. 18.113. This is most likely to arise in cases involving children where additional events relevant to a child's welfare may have taken place between a proof before the sheriff and the hearing of an appeal: see, for example, *Sanderson v. McManus*, 1995 S.C.L.R. 903, where the sheriff principal heard additional evidence when the case was on appeal before him. The majority decision of the Inner House, sustaining the sheriff principal's decision, was subsequently upheld by the House of Lords: 1997 S.C.L.R. 281.

[72] para. 18.117.

[73] *Aird v. School Board of Tarbert*, 1907 S.C. 22.

[74] *Pollok School v. Glasgow Town Clerk*, 1946 S.C. 373 at 385, 387; *Mutch v. Robertson*, 1981 S.L.T. 217.

[75] *Roofcare v. Gillies*, 1984 S.L.T. (Sh. Ct.) 8 at 9.

[76] *McLaren v. Ferrier* (1865) 3 M. 833; *Rowe v. Rowe* (1872) 9 S.L.R. 492; *Watson v. Russell* (1894) 21 R. 433; *Whyte v. Whyte* (1895) 23 R. 320; *Paterson v. Kidd's Trs* (1896) 23 R. 737; *Fleming v. Eadie & Son* (1897) 25 R. 3; *Lauder v. National Bank of Scotland*, 1918 1 S.L.T. 43; *Fergusons Tr. v. Reid*, 1931 S.C. 714, *per* L.P. Clyde at 716; *Barton v. Caledon Shipbuilding and Engineering Co. Ltd*, 1947 S.L.T. (Notes) 12. See para. 8.81. In *Jones v. Jones*, 1993 S.C.L.R. 151 the appeal was excluded because the action had been sisted on joint motion after the sheriff had granted leave to appeal.

[77] *Pirrie v. McNeil*, 1922 S.L.T. 160; but see *Barton*, *supra*.

[78] *Ammon v. Tod*, 1912 S.C. 306, *per* L.P. Dunedin at 315.

[79] *Macaskill v. Nicol*, 1943 S.C. 17; but some of the opinions expressed in the foregoing case have recently been disapproved: see para. 18.70.

[80] OCR, r. 31.2(1). See para. 18.45. *Marsh v. Baxendale*, 1994 S.C.L.R. 239.

operation of which he has acquiesced. That party may not be permitted subsequently to challenge that interlocutor,[81] except, perhaps, where at the conclusion of the case the court, in reviewing a final decree, has the whole merits of the case fully before it and "the justice of the case" is appreciable.[82] Where an interlocutor deals in part with the merits of the case, such as an interlocutor repelling a plea to the relevancy of the defences, it is competent not to appeal it individually and at once, but to bring it under review together with a later interlocutor which, taken along with it, disposes of the subject-matter of the cause.[83] Delay in appealing such an interlocutor may, however, have a bearing on the question of liability for expenses.[84]

Opinion in note. A litigant may appeal only against an interlocutor and not against an opinion expressed in the note which is appended thereto or which is written by the sheriff at the appellant's request.[85] **18.18**

Extracted interlocutor. As a general rule, there can be no appeal against an extracted interlocutor,[86] unless the interlocutor or the extract has been improperly and incompetently issued.[87] Even an incomplete extract may bar an appeal.[88] But the extract of a decree for expenses following upon a final judgment which has not been extracted does not exclude an appeal against the final judgment.[89] And where an appeal is competently taken against a final interlocutor, an earlier interlocutor which has been extracted may be brought under review if no appeal against it would have been competent until after the date when it was extracted.[90] Where a motion has been lodged before the sheriff principal to allow an appeal to be marked late, and an extract has been subsequently issued, the sheriff principal if he grants the motion will recall the extract.[91] Thus where the *extract* of the interlocutor is "fatally flawed" the appeal may proceed; but where the *interlocutor* which has been extracted is "fatally flawed" it cannot be successfully challenged under Chapter 31 of the Ordinary Cause Rules 1993.[92] **18.19**

---

[81] *Ferguson's Tr. v. Reid*, 1931 S.C. 714; *Mackaskill, supra*; *Burgh of Ayr v. British Transport Commission*, 1956 S.L.T. (Sh. Ct.) 3; *Marsh v. Baxendale, supra.*

[82] *Macaskill, supra, per* L.J.-C. Cooper at 20, Lord Mackay at 22; *Boyle v. West of Scotland Shipbreaking Co.*, 1963 S.L.T. (Sh. Ct.) 54; *Williamson v. Harris*, 1981 S.L.T. (Sh. Ct.) 57.

[83] *Ferguson's Tr., supra, per* Lord Morison at 718; *Newcastle Building Society v. White*, Sh. Pr. Caplan, Kilmarnock Sh. Ct, May 16, 1985, unreported.

[84] *Newcastle Building Society, supra.*

[85] *Kennedy v. Macrae*, 1946 S.C. 118; *Sydie v. A. A. Stuart (Contractors) Ltd*, 1968 S.L.T. (Sh. Ct.) 93. *Cf. Lord Advocate v. Johnston*, 1983 S.L.T. 290.

[86] OCR, rr. 31.1, 31.2(1); *Tennents v. Romanes* (1881) 8 R. 824, *per* L.P. Inglis at 825; *Walker v. Wotherspoon* (1916) 35 Sh.Ct.Rep. 74; *Alloa Brewery Co. Ltd v. Parker*, 1991 S.C.L.R. 70; *Miro Windows v. Mrugala*, 1992 S.L.T. (Sh. Ct.) 66; *Nortech v. Aeroskip Sports Ltd*, 1996 S.L.T. (Sh. Ct.) 94 (error in designation of defenders in the extract).

[87] *Millar v. Millar*, 1992 S.L.T. (Sh. Ct.) 69; *Noble v. Noble*, 1990 S.L.T. (Sh. Ct.) 15; *Gaunt v. Marco's Leisure Ltd*, 1995 S.C.L.R. 966.

[88] *Hutchison v. Robson* (1930) 47 Sh.Ct.Rep. 109. *Cf. Menzies v. Templeton* (1896) 12 Sh.Ct.Rep. 323.

[89] *Macfarlane v. Thompson* (1884) 12 R. 232.

[90] *Weir v. Tudhope* (1892) 19 R. 858; *Levern (Distributors) Ltd v. St Vincent Credit Co.*, 1966 S.L.T. (Sh.Ct.) 57; *McKenzie v. John R. Wyatt (Musical Enterprises) Ltd*, 1974 S.L.T. (Sh. Ct.) 8 at 10.

[91] *Anderson Brown & Co. Ltd v. Morris*, 1987 S.L.T. (Sh. Ct.) 96. See para. 18.56.

[92] *Wagon Finance Ltd v. O'Lone*, 1995 S.C.L.R. 149.

18.20 *Appeal to other court.* If a case has been appealed to the Court of Session by one party, it cannot be appealed to the sheriff principal by any other party until the pending appeal is disposed of; and, similarly, if it is appealed to the sheriff principal, it cannot at that stage be appealed to the Court of Session,[93] even where the respondent consents.[94] Where a party has appealed to the Court of Session and his appeal is abandoned, or is held to be abandoned in terms of the Rules of Court, the judgment complained of becomes final, and that party cannot appeal against it to the sheriff principal.[95] Similarly, where a party appeals to the sheriff principal and does not insist in his appeal, he cannot appeal to the Court of Session.[96] It may be that where a party has in error appealed to the Court of Session instead of to the sheriff principal, the Court of Session would permit the appeal to be withdrawn of consent.[97] However, where leave to appeal is required, and an appellant has proceeded to appeal without leave, he cannot thereafter return to the sheriff (or sheriff principal) to seek leave.[98]

18.21 *No title to appeal.* An appeal is incompetent if the appellant has no title to insist in it.[99] Where one of a plurality of defenders founds on section 3 of the Law Reform (Miscellaneous Provisions) (Scotland) Act 1940 and places joint fault and apportionment of damages in issue, he is entitled to appeal against an interlocutor whereby another defender is assoilzied or the action so far as laid against another defender is dismissed.[1]

18.22 *Recall of decree in absence.* An interlocutor or order recalling, or incidental to the recall of, a decree in absence, is final and not subject to review.[2]

18.23 *Fine for failure to return process.* An order imposing a fine for failure to return a process, or any part of a process, for any diet at which it is required, is not subject to appeal, but may be recalled by the sheriff who granted it.[3]

18.24 *Remits in family proceedings.* A decision by a sheriff to remit or not to remit to the Court of Session an action for divorce or an action in relation to parental responsibilities or parental rights (within the meaning of sections 1(3) and 2(4) respectively of the Children (Scotland) Act 1995) in relation to a child or the guardianship or adoption of a child is not subject to review.[4]

---

[93] *McArthur v. Boucher* (1887) 15 R. 117.

[94] *Thames Cleaning Co. Ltd v. British Rail Transport Ship Management (Scotland) Ltd*, Sh. Pr. O'Brien, Stranraer Sh. Ct, May 12, 1981, unreported: death of sheriff principal while appeal from sheriff at avizandum—joint motion for leave to appeal sheriff's judgment to Court of Session refused.

[95] 1966 R.C., r. 272; *Clark v. Comrie*, 1910 1 S.L.T. 404.

[96] *Manchester and County Bank v. Moore*, 1909 S.C. 246.

[97] *cf. J. & J. Fraser v. Smith*, 1937 S.C. 667.

[98] *McNeill v. McArthur*, 1997 S.C.L.R. 252; *Sheltered Housing Management Ltd v. Aitken*, 1998 S.C.L.R. 59; but see *McCue v. Scottish Daily Record and Sunday Mail Ltd*, 1998 S.C.L.R. 742.

[99] *McDermott v. Western SMT Co.*, 1937 S.C. 239 is thought to vouch this proposition although it is no longer applicable in the circumstances of that case (*Davidson v. North of Scotland Hydro-Electric Board*, 1954 S.C. 230).

[1] *Davidson, supra.*

[2] OCR, r. 8.1(5). See para. 7.36.

[3] OCR, r. 11.4.

[4] Sheriff Courts (Scotland) Act 1971, s. 37(3)(a) referring to s. 37(2A) as amended by the Children (Scotland) Act 1995, Sched. 4, para. 18(3). See para. 13.61.

Divorce. The position in the case of appeals against a decree of divorce is governed by the rules. Before 1993, in divorce procedure, a party was able to appeal in terms of rule 59B where "reponing note considerations" could be advanced and considered. "By contrast, such considerations are not appropriate in a conventional section 27 appeal, which must proceed solely on the basis of seeking to show some error in the approach or in the decision of the inferior court".[5] But since rule 59B has not been re-enacted in the current (1993) rules, it appears that the only form of appeal in a divorce action (other than a simplified divorce action under rule 13.80(1) for which there is a special provision for appeals under rule 33.81) is the ordinary appeal against a final judgment as provided for in section 27 of the 1907 Act.[6] **18.25**

Rulings on objections at proof. It is not competent during a proof to submit to review any decision of the sheriff as to the admissibility of evidence or the production of documents, other than a ruling on an objection to the admissibility of oral or documentary evidence on the ground of confidentiality or to producing a document on any ground. Special procedure is provided for an appeal against a ruling of the latter kind.[7] **18.26**

Process caption.[8] An order by the sheriff dealing with an application for process caption (which is thought to be seldom, if ever, resorted to in modern practice) is not an interlocutor in the cause, and an appeal against it is incompetent.[9] **18.27**

Judicial reference. It is possible for the parties to a judicial reference to exclude rights of appeal.[10] **18.28**

Act not of judicial character. An appeal is incompetent where the sheriff has not acted in his judicial capacity, for example where he has nominated an arbiter upon an application made other than by judicial procedure.[11] **18.29**

It is *pars judicis* to question the competency of an appeal and invite the parties to make submissions thereon before dismissing the appeal as incompetent.[12] The consent of the parties cannot confer on the appellate **18.30**

---

[5] *Stroud v. Stroud*, 1994 S.L.T. (Sh. Ct.) 7, *per* Sh. Pr. Nicholson at 8H; see also *Norris v. Norris*, 1992 S.L.T. (Sh. Ct.) 51; *Colville v. Colville*, 1985 S.L.T. (Sh. Ct.) 23; and *Hunter v. Hunter*, 1993 S.C.L.R. 785; para. 18.02.

[6] *McFarlane v. McFarlane*, 1995 S.C.L.R. 794.

[7] OCR, r. 29.19. See paras 16.89, 16.90.

[8] A process caption is a summary warrant of incarceration granted on the application of the clerk of court, for the purpose of forcing back a process which has been unduly and contumaciously retained by the party whose receipt stands for it in the court books: Bell, *Dictionary and Digest of the Law of Scotland* (7th ed., 1890), s.v. "Caption, process". See also *Stair Memorial Encyclopaedia*, Vol. 17, para. 1040.

[9] *Broatch v. Pattison* (1898) 1 F. 303. See para. 8.16.

[10] para. 13.40.

[11] *Mags of Glasgow v. Glasgow District Subway Co.* (1893) 21 R. 52. *Cf. Ross v. Ross*, 1920 S.C. 530.

[12] *Shirra v. Robertson* (1873) 11 M. 660; *Duke of Roxburghe* (1875) 2 R. 715; *Governors of Strichen Endowments v. Diverall* (1891) 19 R. 79; *Turner's Trs v. Steel* (1900) 2 F. 363; (1900) 7 S.L.T. 287; *Walker v. Wotherspoon* (1916) 35 Sh.Ct.Rep. 74; *Beattie v. Glasgow Corporation*, 1917 S.C. (H.L.) 22; *Gray v. Gray*, 1968 S.C. 185 at 189; McKenzie v. John R. Wyatt (Musical Enterprises) Ltd, 1974 S.L.T. (Sh. Ct.) 8; *Palombo v. James Jack (Hyndford) Ltd*, 1977 S.L.T. (Sh. Ct.) 95.

court jurisdiction to hear an incompetent appeal.[13] Where an objection to the competency of the appeal is taken by the appellate court and is sustained, the court may hold that no expenses should be allowed to either party.[14]

18.31 Before deciding whether to take or oppose an appeal, a party's legal advisers should consider not only the competency and merits of the appeal, but also the principles on which the appellate court acts when hearing an appeal. In general, it is for the appellant to satisfy the court that the judgment of the sheriff was wrong; and there are certain limitations on the court's power to interfere with the sheriff's findings in fact or assessment of evidence, with his exercise of a discretionary power, with his apportionment of liability, with his assessment of damages or with his awards of expenses. These principles are examined below.[15] Where the proposed appeal is against an interlocutory judgment, a party's advisers should also consider what practical advantage would be gained by a successful appeal: it may be an error to suffer the delay involved in an appeal merely in order to succeed on a procedural issue of minor importance.

Section 27 of the 1907 Act in detail

18.32 *The policy of the Act.* It is the policy of the 1907 Act to refuse appeals from the sheriff to the sheriff principal until final judgment, unless the interlocutor is one of material importance or one which would affect the status quo of parties,[16] and not to permit other appeals unless the leave of the sheriff is specially granted.[17] Section 27 of the Act accordingly provides that subject to the provisions of the Act an appeal to the sheriff principal is competent against (1) all final judgments; (2) specified classes of interlocutors, which in practice are usually of material importance or affect the status quo of parties; and (3) interlocutors against which the sheriff grants leave to appeal. These three categories of interlocutors are examined in the following paragraphs.

18.33 *Final judgments.* An appeal to the sheriff principal is competent, without leave, against all final judgments of the sheriff.[18] The Act defines a final judgment as an interlocutor which by itself, or taken along with previous interlocutors, disposes of the subject-matter of the cause, notwithstanding that judgment may not have been pronounced on every question raised, and that the expenses found due may not have been modified, taxed or decerned for.[19] An interlocutor which is not a final judgment is sometimes described as an interlocutory judgment. The following paragraphs deal with, first, that part of the statutory definition

---

[13] *Singer Manufacturing Co. v. Jessiman* (1881) 8 R. 695; *Burns v. Waddell & Son* (1897) 24 R. 325; *Millom and Askam Hematite Co. v. Simpson* (1897) 14 Sh.Ct.Rep. 206; *City of Edinburgh D.C. v. Robbin*, 1994 S.C.L.R. 43 (subsequent appeal to Court of Session dismissed of consent: 1994 S.C.L.R. 976); *Walker, supra*. See para. 18.48.

[14] *Shirra, supra*; *Ramsay v. Shaw* [1949] C.L.Y. 4626.

[15] paras 18.100 to 18.117. It has been observed that it is not "any part of the function of the appeal court to rescue parties, or more accurately solicitors, from a breakdown in the syndicate system": *Swan v. Blaikie*, 1992 S.C.L.R. 405.

[16] *Jack v. Carmichael* (1894) 10 Sh.Ct.Rep. 242.

[17] *Lawson v. Young* (1891) 7 Sh.Ct.Rep. 319.

[18] 1907 Act, s. 27.

[19] 1907 Act, s. 3(h).

of the term "final judgment" which relates to the subject-matter of the cause, and second, the part relative to expenses.

Disposal of the subject-matter of the cause. It is of the essence of a final judgment, as compared with an interlocutory judgment, that, when read by itself or with earlier interlocutors, it should conclusively decide the issues between the parties as recorded in their craves and pleas, including rights to expenses. It need not involve a judicial consideration of the merits of the issues between the parties, but it must dispose of them.[20] It is unnecessary that judgment should have been pronounced "on every question raised", that is, that all the questions of fact or law in the case should have been decided, provided that the decision, if well founded, renders it unnecessary to decide anything further in order to dispose completely of the case. Thus a decree by default,[21] and an interlocutor sustaining a preliminary plea and either dismissing the action[22] or repelling the defences and granting decree as craved,[23] are final judgments. An interlocutor dealing only with expenses, following on dismissal of an action, may also be a final judgment,[24] and a decision by a sheriff on appeal from the decision of a trustee in bankruptcy proceedings rejecting a claim for ranking has been held to be a final judgment.[25] The subject-matter of the cause is disposed of, even though the cause is continued, if the purpose of the continuation is to await the performance of acts which are merely executorial of the decision already pronounced although further orders of court may be necessary, for example where the interlocutor ordains the execution of works.[26] In a process of competition,[27] an interlocutor disposing of questions as regards certain of the parties only may be competently appealed if it disposes of the whole subject-matter of the competition so far as they are concerned.[28] The fact that only part of an interlocutor with all the characteristics of a final judgment is extracted does not alter its character as a final judgment.[29] **18.34**

There are many examples of interlocutors which have been held not to be final judgments. They include interlocutors refusing a warrant for citation,[30] granting protestation,[31] allowing proof,[32] limiting proof to writ or oath,[33] making findings only,[34] dismissing an action or assoilzieing as **18.35**

---

[20] *W. Jack Baillie Associates v. Kennedy*, 1985 S.L.T. (Sh. Ct.) 53 at 56; and see *DTL Gas Supplies Ltd v. Protan Srl*, 1998 G.W.D. 31.1578.

[21] *Robb v. Eglin* (1877) 14 S.L.R. 473; *Laurence v. Gray* (1908) 25 Sh.Ct.Rep. 19; *Hardy v. Robinson*, 1985 S.L.T. (Sh. Ct.) 40.

[22] *Whyte v. Gerrard* (1861) 24 D. 102.

[23] *Malcolm v. McIntyre* (1877) 5 R. 22; *Turner's Trs v. Steel* (1900) 2 F. 363.

[24] *Gamble v. Unison Scotland*, 1997 S.C.L.R. 803.

[25] *Japan Leasing (Europe) plc v. Weir's Trustee*, 1997 S.C.L.R. 519; but *cf. Smith v. Berry's Tr.*, 1995 S.C.L.R. 1132.

[26] *Malcolm, supra; McEwan v. Sharp* (1899) 1 F. 393; *Turner's Trs, supra. Cf. Governors of Strichen Endowments v. Diverall* (1891) 19 R. 79 (interlocutor ranking claimant in multiplepoinding but no operative decree).

[27] A process where one or more persons are claimants on the same fund: Bell, *Dictionary and Digest of the Law of Scotland* (7th ed., 1890), s.v. "competition".

[28] *Gordon v. Graham* (1874) 1 R. 1081 at 1082; *Duke of Roxburghe* (1875) 2 R. 715; *Glasgow Corporation v. General Accident Fire and Life Assurance Corporation Ltd*, 1914 S.C. 835.

[29] *McKenzie v. John R. Wyatt (Musical Enterprises) Ltd*, 1974 S.L.T. (Sh. Ct.) 8.

[30] *Davidson v. Davidson* (1891) 18 R. 884.

[31] *Robertson v. Black & Watson* (1901) 18 Sh.Ct.Rep. 98.

[32] *Johnston v. Brodie* (1862) 24 D. 973.

[33] *Shirra v. Robertson* (1873) 11 M. 660; *Wilson v. Brakenridge* (1888) 15 R. 587.

[34] *Ranken v. Ranken*, 1971 S.L.T. (Notes) 55.

regards one crave and allowing proof as regards others,[35] and disposing of one crave but not of another.[36] In an action of multiplepoinding, an interlocutor sustaining the competency of the action[37] and an interlocutor ranking a claimant but not granting an operative decree[38] are not appealable as final judgments.[39] The subject-matter of the cause includes the question of liability for expenses,[40] and until that has been disposed of the interlocutor cannot be appealed: this limitation is considered in the following paragraphs.

18.36 *Expenses.* The final part of the statutory definition of a final judgment is that it is an interlocutor which, by itself, or taken along with previous interlocutors, disposes of the subject-matter of the cause notwithstanding "that the expenses found due may not have been modified, taxed or decerned for".[41] For an interlocutor to be a final judgment it is therefore normally[42] essential that it should dispose of the question of expenses, not necessarily by deciding the amount of expenses payable, but by dealing with and determining the question of the liability of one or other of the parties for expenses[43] or finding expenses due to neither party.[44] An interlocutor which deals only with the merits,[45] or with the merits and only part of the expenses,[46] is not a final judgment and cannot be appealed without the leave of the sheriff. Where, in accordance with the practice recommended elsewhere in this book,[47] an interlocutor pronounced after proof or debate disposing of the merits of the cause reserves the question of expenses and appoints parties to be heard thereon on a future date, there is no final judgment until the question of expenses has been disposed of.[48] The final judgment is the interlocutor finding expenses due, and appeal against that interlocutor opens both interlocutors, and other prior interlocutors, to review.[49] An interlocutor dealing only with expenses may be alone submitted to review,[50] but in practice appeals on expenses only are strongly discouraged, and are not entertained unless either there has been an obvious miscarriage of justice, or the expenses have become a great deal more valuable than the merits, or a

---

35 *Brotherston v. Livingston* (1892) 20 R. 1; *Ludlow v. Strang*, 1938 S.C. 551.

36 *Jardine v. Mags of Moffat*, 1907 S.C. 1065.

37 *Gordon v. Graham* (1874) 1 R. 1081; *Macduff v. Macduff* (1893) 9 Sh.Ct.Rep. 243.

38 *Governors of Strichen Endowments, supra.*

39 *Monkman v. Monkman*, 1988 S.L.T. (Sh. Ct.) 37.

40 *Baird v. Barton* (1882) 9 R. 970.

41 1907 Act, s. 3(h).

42 An exceptional case is *Duke of Roxburghe* (1875) 2 R. 715, where the interlocutor was held to be appealable although it made no finding as to expenses; but it is not clear from the report that the question of expenses was considered by the court when reaching a view as to competency; and the case was decided before the passing of the 1907 Act. See also *Meadows Removals v. Berry*, 1992 S.C.L.R. 960.

43 *Burns v. Woddell & Sons* (1897) 24 R. 325, *per* L.P. Robertson at 326.

44 *Baird v. Barton* (1882) 9 R. 970.

45 *Greenock Parochial Board v. Miller and Brown* (1877) 4 R. 737; *Russell v. Allan* (1877) 5 R. 22; *Malcolm v. McIntyre* (1877) 5 R. 22; *Baird v. Barton* (1882) 9 R. 970; *Burns v. Waddell & Sons* (1897) 24 R. 325; *Caledonion Ry v. Glasgow Corporation* (1900) 2 F. 871; *Houstoun v. Gault*, 1925 S.C. 429; *Ludlow v. Strang*, 1938 S.C. 551.

46 *Palombo v. James Jack (Hyndford) Ltd*, 1977 S.L.T. (Sh. Ct.) 95.

47 paras 13.24, 16.103, 17.23.

48 See the cases cited in n. 45.

49 *Bannatine's Trs v. Cunninghame* (1872) 10 M. 317; *Williamson v. Harris*, 1981 S.L.T. (Sh. Ct.) 56.

50 *Fleming v. North of Scotland Banking Co.* (1881) 9 R. 11; *Bowman's Trs v. Scott* (1901) 3 F. 450; *Barrie v. Caledonian Ry* (1902) 5 F. 30.

question of principle is involved.[51] An interlocutor disposing of the merits of the cause and continuing it for executorial purposes is appealable if it disposes of the question of expenses[52]: whether it may be appealed if it disposes of the expenses in the cause so far as already incurred, has not been decided.[53]

If the interlocutor disposes of expenses in the sense explained at the beginning of the foregoing paragraph, it is immaterial that the expenses "may not have been modified, taxed or decerned for".[54] "Modification" means the exact ascertainment of the precise sum that is to be paid. If the sheriff thinks that it is necessary that, before expenses are paid, some further deduction should be made from what may have been made in the taxation of a party's account by the auditor, he makes that deduction before the expenses are finally decerned for.[55] An interlocutor modifying expenses, which follows a prior interlocutor disposing of the merits of the cause and finding expenses due, may be appealed without leave, and the appeal has the effect of submitting the whole previous interlocutors to review.[56] An interlocutor disposing of objections to the auditor's report on a party's account of expenses,[57] or decerning for expenses after a hearing on questions raised in the report,[58] is also appealable without leave. But supplementary or executorial interlocutors fixing the scale of taxation for,[59] or decerning for,[60] expenses already found due are not final judgments in the sense of the statutory definition and may be appealed, not as final judgments,[61] but only with leave[62]; and, it is thought, the appeal does not have the effect of submitting prior interlocutors to review.[63] If, however, the final interlocutor in the case has for any reason become unappealable, such supplementary or executorial interlocutors cannot be appealed against, even with leave,[64] except on the ground of incompetency.[65] **18.37**

Interlocutory judgments appealable without leave

Interdict. An interlocutor granting or refusing interdict, interim or final, may be appealed without leave to the sheriff principal.[66] An interim interdict, although appealed against, is binding till recalled.[67] **18.38**

---

[51] For a full citation of authority, see para. 18.117.

[52] *Malcolm v. McIntyre* (1877) 5 R. 22.

[53] *Caledonian Ry v. Glasgow Corporation* (1900) 2 F. 871.

[54] 1907 Act, s. 3(h).

[55] *Earl of Kintore v. Pirie* (1904) 12 S.L.T. 385, *per* Lord Kinnear at 386.

[56] *Inglis v. National Bank of Scotland*, 1911 S.C. 6.

[57] *Stirling Maxwell's Trs v. Kirkintilloch Police Commissioners* (1883) 11 R. 1; *Craig v. Craig* (1906) 14 S.L.T. 469; Maclaren, *Expenses*, p. 55. *Cf. Mulvey v. Mulvey* (1922) 39 Sh.Ct.Rep. 256; *McKinstery v. Plean Colliery Co. Ltd* (1910) 27 Sh.Ct.Rep. 62; Dobie, p. 292.

[58] *Innes v. McDonald* (1899) 1 F. 380.

[59] *Shaw v. Browne* (1886) 2 Sh.Ct.Rep. 203. *Sed quaere.* It is thought that such an interlocutor disposes of a litigated question upon the matter of expenses, which is included in the subject-matter of the cause: *cf. Baird v. Barton* (1882) 9 R. 970; *Innes, supra.*

[60] *Inglis, supra.*

[61] *Stirling Maxwell's Trs, Inglis, supra*; *Carson v. McDowall* (1908) 24 Sh.Ct.Rep. 324.

[62] *Paterson v. Whitelaw* (1899) 15 Sh.Ct.Rep. 256; *Laurenson v. Gordon* (1901) 18 Sh.Ct.Rep. 319; *Dalton & Co. v. Boyle & Co.* (1909) 26 Sh.Ct.Rep. 53.

[63] *Stirling Maxwell's Trs, Inglis, supra.*

[64] *Tennents v. Romanes* (1881) 8 R. 824; *Thompson & Co. v. King* (1883) 10 R. 469.

[65] *Macgillivray v. Mackintosh* (1891) 19 R. 103. See para. 18.12.

[66] 1907 Act, s. 27(A). See para. 21.93.

[67] 1907 Act, s. 29. See para. 21.92.

18.39 *Interim decree.* An interlocutor granting interim decree for payment of money other than a decree for expenses may be appealed without leave to the sheriff principal.[68] The object of this provision is to bring under review an order whereby a sum of money is placed in a party's hands: it accordingly does not apply to an interim order for consignation,[69] which is an order *ad factum praestandum.*[70] The rules as to the pronouncing and appealing of interim decrees for the payment of money, other than decrees for expenses, are considered elsewhere.[71] In all sheriffdoms it has now been held that an appeal to the sheriff principal against an award of interim aliment is not competent without leave.[72] A decree for the full amount of a counterclaim is not an interim decree for the payment of money.[73] However, an interim order in a family action requiring one party to pay monthly mortgage instalments has been held to be an interim decree for payment of money, and therefore appealable without leave.[74] Warrants to uplift money which are the same in substance and effect as interim decrees for payment of money have been equiparated with such decrees, so as to make appeal against them competent,[75] in cases where the defender had consigned money in a bank to await the orders of court, and the court made an order releasing that money in favour of the pursuer[76]; and where the money which was the subject of the warrant or authority granted was in the hands of an officer of court, and therefore at the disposal of the court.[77] An interlocutory decree for payment of expenses was held to be competently appealed where it was contained in an interlocutor which was otherwise appealable, and at the appeal hearing the appellant confined himself to challenging the decree for expenses.[78] It is submitted, however, that that course should not be permitted, since it is a device to circumvent the exclusion of interlocutory appeals on expenses only which is clearly expressed in section 27(B). In any event appeals on expenses only should as a general rule be severely discouraged.[79]

18.40 *Order* ad factum praestandum. An interlocutor making an order *ad factum praestandum* may be appealed without leave to the sheriff principal.[80] Such orders include an order to make consignation,[81] an interlocutor ordering a party to appear at the bar[82] and an award of interim access to which an order for delivery is attached.[83] Generally, the effect of the interlocutor is suspended until it is adhered to by the appellate court[84] but

---

68 1907 Act, s. 27(h).
69 *Maxton v. Bone* (1886) 13 R. 912.
70 See para. 18.39.
71 On interim decrees generally, see paras 11.81 to 11.85; on interim payment of damages in personal injuries actions, see paras 21.19 to 21.28.
72 The authorities on decrees for interim aliment were reviewed in *Hulme v. Hulme*, 1990 S.L.T. (Sh. Ct.) 25; see also *Richardson v. Richardson*, 1991 S.L.T. (Sh. Ct.) 7; *Rixson v. Rixson*, 1990 S.L.T. (Sh. Ct.) 75.
73 *Palombo v. James Jack (Hyndford) Ltd*, 1977 S.L.T. (Sh. Ct.) 95.
74 *Irving v. Irving*, 1998 S.C.L.R. 373.
75 *Hughes's Trs v. Hughes*, 1925 S.C. 25, *per* L.P. Clyde at 27.
76 *Sinclair v. Baikie* (1884) 11 R. 413.
77 *Baird v Glendinning* (1874) 2 R. 25.
78 *Nelson v. Wilson & Sons* (1912) 29 Sh.Ct.Rep. 90. See para. 18.58.
79 See para. 18.117.
80 1907 Act, s. 27(B).
81 para. 11.46.
82 *Boyd v. Drummond, Robbie & Gibson*, 1995 S.C.L.R. 178.
83 *Thomson v. Thomson*, 1979 S.L.T. (Sh. Ct.) 11 but not an award of interim access without an order for delivery: *Black v. Black*, 1990 S.C.L.R. 817; 1991 S.L.T. (Sh. Ct.) 5.
84 *Marshall v. Callander and Trossachs Hydropathic Co. Ltd* (1896) 24 R. 33.

there are qualifications of that statement under the rules in respect of certain family actions.[85] Other procedural orders, such as an order to find caution for expenses[86] or to sist a mandatary,[87] which are not enforceable by diligence, are not orders *ad factum praestandum*.[88] The two latter orders are appealable only with leave. Actions *ad facta praestanda* are considered elsewhere.[89]

Sist.[90] An interlocutor sisting an action is appealable to the sheriff principal without leave.[91] Any interlocutor which is not a final judgment must be either an interlocutor carrying on the action, or else an interlocutor sisting it. In determining whether or not an interlocutor sists process the court looks at the realities or practical effect of the interlocutor and not at its mere words.[92] Thus, any interlocutor which has the effect of sisting the action falls under this provision, such as an order sisting procedure until caution for expenses has been found,[93] or an order continuing the cause to allow the dispute between the parties to be referred to arbitration.[94] On the other hand an interlocutor recalling or refusing a sist is appealable only with leave of the sheriff.[95] **18.41**

Allowance, refusal or limitation of mode of proof. An interlocutor allowing or refusing or limiting the mode of proof is subject to appeal to the sheriff principal without leave.[96] Where a proof has been allowed, it is the interlocutor allowing it which is subject to appeal, and not any separate interlocutor fixing the diet of proof, or assigning a new diet where the proof has not proceeded on the day originally assigned.[97] If, however, the allowance of proof itself has lapsed, and it is necessary to allow proof of new, the interlocutor reviving the allowance of proof is subject to appeal without leave.[98] Examples of interlocutors refusing proof are those which exclude certain averments from probation, or dismiss an action as regards one of several craves. An interlocutor ordering production of accounts in an action of accounting does not allow proof,[99] and an interlocutor refusing commission and diligence for the recovery of documents does not refuse proof[1] nor does an interlocutor allowing certain evidence to be taken on interrogatories.[2] Interlocutors limiting the mode of proof are those by which a proof at large, or *prout de jure*, is refused and the method of **18.42**

---

[85] OCR, r. 31.9; para. 18.68.
[86] paras 11.52 to 11.66, esp. para. 11.65.
[87] paras 11.67 to 11.80, esp. para. 11.79.
[88] *Jack v. Carmichael* (1894) 10 Sh.Ct.Rep. 242.
[89] paras 21.75 to 21.82.
[90] paras 13.71 to 13.83.
[91] 1907 Act, s. 27(C).
[92] *Watson v. Stewart* (1872) 10 M. 494; *Derber v. J. Smith Stewart & Co. Ltd*, 1957 S.L.T. (Sh. Ct.) 53.
[93] *Horn & Co. Ltd v. Tangyes Ltd* (1906) 8 F. 475.
[94] *Barker v. Steel*, 1951 S.L.T. (Sh. Ct.) 93.
[95] paras 13.81, 13.83.
[96] 1907 Act, s. 27(D).
[97] *Kinnes v. Fleming* (1881) 8 R. 386.
[98] *Murphy v. McKeand* (1866) 4 M. 444; *Kinnes, supra, Sinclair v. McColl* (1894) 10 Sh.Ct.Rep. 144; and see *Eurocopy (Scotland) plc v. British Geological Survey*, 1997 S.C.L.R. 392.
[99] *Lamont v. Dublin and Glasgow Steam Packet Co.*, 1908 S.C. 1017.
[1] *Mowbray v. Secretary of State*, 1992 S.L.T. (Sh. Ct.) 84; 1992 S.C.L.R. 328 where the authorities are considered. See para. 15.65.
[2] *Fagan v. Fagan*, 1991 S.L.T. (Sh. Ct.) 2.

proof is restricted by the allowance formerly of a proof by writ or oath,[3] or a proof *habili modo*.[4]

18.43 *Refusal of reponing note*. An interlocutor refusing a reponing note may be appealed without leave to the sheriff principal.[5] Such appeals are considered elsewhere.[6] On the other hand an interlocutor or order recalling, or incidental to the recall of a decree in absence, is final and not subject to review.[7]

18.44 *Recall of arrestment*. An order recalling an arrestment, which is not listed among the interlocutors appealable without leave in section 27 of the 1907 Act, is nevertheless appealable without leave to the sheriff principal.[8]

Appeal with leave

18.45 *Competency*. Appeal is competent against interlocutors against which the sheriff grants leave to appeal. He may grant leave *ex proprio motu* or on the motion of any party.[9] He may not, of course, grant leave to appeal where appeal is incompetent.[10] The Ordinary Cause Rules expressly mention, as appealable with leave of the sheriff, an interlocutor transferring a cause to another sheriff court[11]; and a ruling, given during a proof, on an objection to the admissibility of oral or documentary evidence on the ground of confidentiality, or to producing documents on any ground.[12] There are many other examples of interlocutors which are appealable only with leave of the sheriff, including interlocutors granting or refusing a motion to allow a minute of amendment to be received, or to grant leave to amend[13]; granting or refusing a commission and diligence[14]; recalling or refusing a sist[15]; ordering a party to find caution for expenses,[16] or to sist a mandatary[17]; refusing to grant decree by default[18]; or fixing the scale of taxation for, or decerning for, expenses already found due.[19]

18.46 An interlocutor which has been appealed against may consist of one part which may be appealed without leave and another part which may be appealed only with leave. In that situation the appellate court can deal

---

[3] Except in relation to proceedings begun before Aug. 1, 1995, any rule of law or enactment whereby the proof of any matter is restricted to proof by writ or by reference to oath ceased to have effect: Requirements of Writing (Scotland) Act 1995, s. 11(1).

[4] paras 8.54 *et seq.*

[5] 1907 Act, s. 27(e).

[6] para. 7.37.

[7] OCR, r. 8.1(5). See para. 7.36.

[8] para. 11.33.

[9] 1907 Act, s. 27(F).

[10] paras 18.15 to 18.29. In addition to matters of fundamental incompetency an appeal will also become incompetent if, leave to appeal being required, a party proceeds to appeal without leave. He cannot thereafter return to seek leave from the court below: *McNeill v. McArthur*, 1997 S.C.L.R. 252; *Sheltered Housing Management Ltd v. Aitken*, 1998 S.C.L.R. 59.

[11] OCR, r. 26.1(8). See para. 11.57.

[12] OCR, r. 29.19(1). See paras 16.89, 16.90.

[13] para. 10.59.

[14] paras 15.30 (evidence of witness), 15.65 (documents); and see n. 1.

[15] paras 13.81, 13.83.

[16] para. 11.65.

[17] para. 11.29.

[18] para. 14.11.

[19] para. 18.37.

with the whole interlocutor regardless of whether or not leave to appeal has been granted: "they are both part of the same interlocutor; it would not be in accord with the ordinary use of the word to say that the sheriff had issued two interlocutors, one dealing with interim interdict and one dealing with interim aliment".[20] Presumably, where the separate parts of the decision of the sheriff have not been incorporated in a single interlocutor but are each preceded by the words "*eo die*" and are separately signed by the sheriff, this difficulty would not arise. Moreover, it may be that this situation will now arise less often since there is an obligation under the rules to state the grounds of appeal.[21]

Procedure. The sheriff may grant leave to appeal either *ex proprio motu* or on the motion of any party.[22] If he is to grant leave *ex proprio motu*, the proper time to do it is in the interlocutor against which he is granting leave to appeal. It is not competent to grant leave to appeal *ex proprio motu* at a later stage.[23] It has been held that where the sheriff made a request for guidance from the appeal court, that in effect amounted to granting leave to appeal.[24] If a party applies for leave to appeal, the application should be made by motion to the sheriff who pronounced the interlocutor, not to the appeal court.[25] The application is competent only if it is made within seven days of the date of the interlocutor against which it is desired to appeal though a sheriff may be entitled to exercise the dispensing power under rule 2.1 so as to allow an application to be heard after the expiry of seven days.[26] If the interlocutor has been extracted following a motion for early extract, the application is incompetent.[27] Where a sheriff has reserved his decision the date of the interlocutor is the date on which it is received by the sheriff clerk.[28] An unsuccessful party who wishes to keep open his right of appeal, and receives intimation of a motion for early extract, should apply for leave before the motion is heard. The sheriff hears parties on the motion for leave to appeal, but it may be unnecessary to have a full hearing where the matter has already been fully argued.[29] Where the sheriff grants leave to appeal, an appeal is competent only if made within seven days of the granting of leave.[30] The form of appeal and subsequent procedure are described below.[31] **18.47**

If the sheriff refuses leave to appeal,[32] or if leave is not timeously applied for,[33] the appellate court cannot supply the want of leave, and an **18.48**

---

[20] *McColl v. McColl*, 1992 S.C.L.R. 187 (following *Nelson v. J. Wilson & Sons* (1912) S.L.R. 90); *Oliver v. Oliver*, 1989 S.L.T. (Sh. Ct.) 2 (exclusion order along with interim interdict); but see *Jones v. Jones*, 1993 S.C.L.R. 151 where it was held that an interlocutor containing an award of interim aliment and a sist pronounced on joint motion could not competently be appealed since the interlocutor could not be divided into separate parts.

[21] OCR, r. 31.4(3); para. 18.56.

[22] 1907 Act, s. 27(F).

[23] *Kearney's Exrs v. John Finlay MacLeod and Parker*, 1965 S.C. 450.

[24] *AB and CD, Petitioners*, 1992 S.L.T. 1064.

[25] Dove Wilson, p. 315.

[26] *Thompson v. Lynn*, 1995 S.C.L.R. 1090.

[27] OCR, r. 31.1.

[28] OCR, r. 12.2(5)(a); see para. 5.75.

[29] *Fagan v. Fagan*, 1991 S.L.T. (Sh. Ct.) 2.

[30] OCR, r. 31.2(2).

[31] paras 18.57 *et seq.*

[32] *Macdonald v. Macdonald* (1956) 72 Sh.Ct.Rep. 171.

[33] *Hamilton v. Hamilton*, 1948 S.L.T. (Notes) 8; *Korner v. Shennan*, 1949 S.L.T. (Notes) 42.

appeal against the interlocutor complained of is incompetent at that stage.[34] The first and proper time at which an appeal may be taken is when an appealable interlocutor is subsequently pronounced.[35] If an appeal is nevertheless taken, the appellate court will consider whether leave to appeal is required, even if no objection is taken to the absence of leave, because the absence of leave, when it is required, renders the appeal incompetent, and the consent of the parties cannot confer on the appellate court jurisdiction to entertain it.[36] However, it has been observed that the cases cited in the footnotes to this paragraph, as they appeared in the first edition, do not support the view that it is incompetent to invite a sheriff to exercise the dispensing power so as to allow a late application for leave to appeal.[37] It is submitted that that observation is correct given the views which were expressed by a Bench of Five Judges in *Grier v. Wimpey Plant and Transport Ltd.*[38]

18.49 *Appeal.* Whenever power is given to a legal authority to grant or refuse leave to appeal, the authority's decision to grant or refuse leave cannot be appealed.[39] Thus, the granting or refusal of leave to appeal is a matter for the sole discretion of the sheriff, and an appeal against his decision is incompetent.[40]

Principles on which leave granted or refused

18.50 *General considerations.* It is the policy of the 1907 Act to discourage incidental appeals unless the leave of the sheriff is specially granted.[41] The object of requiring leave to appeal against judgments other than final judgments or the classes of interlocutors specified in section 27(A) to (E) is thought to be to prevent appeals in cases which "are not worth the appeal"[42] and thus to avoid inconvenience, expense and delay in the progress of litigation by the taking of appeals which are frivolous[43] or devoid of merit, or which are not concerned with questions of material importance. When considering an application for leave the sheriff is not entitled to grant or refuse leave as a matter of course, but is required to exercise his discretion upon his assessment of the circumstances of each particular case.[44] He must consider the interests of all the parties to the litigation,[45] the determining considerations being those which are relevant to convenience, economy and expedition in the course of justice, viewed

---

[34] *Mags of Leith v. Lennon* (1875) 3 R. 152, *per* Lord Ormidale at 153–154, L.J.-C Moncreiff at 155.

[35] *Lawson v. Young* (1891) 7 Sh.Ct.Rep. 319; *Boss v. Lyle Shipping Co. Ltd*, 1980 S.L.T. (Sh. Ct.) 65.

[36] *Beattie v. Glasgow Corporation*, 1917 S.C. (H.L.) 22; *Ross v. Ross*, 1927 S.C. (H.L.) 4; *Palombo v. James Jack (Hyndford) Ltd*, 1977 S.L.T. (Sh. Ct.) 95. See para. 18.29.

[37] *Thompson v. Lynn, supra.*

[38] 1994 S.L.T. 714; 1994 S.C.L.R. 454.

[39] *Mags of Leith, supra*; *Re Housing of the Working Classes Act 1890, ex p. Stevenson* [1892] 1 Q.B. 609, *per* Lord Esher M.R. at 610–611; *Bland v. Chief Supplementary Benefit Officer* [1983] 1 W.L.R. 262 at 266–267.

[40] *Ure v. Ure*, 1947 S.C. 305. *Cf.* RCS, r. 38.5(6).

[41] *Lawson v. Young* (1891) 7 Sh.Ct.Rep. 319.

[42] *Duke of Argyll v. Muir*, 1910 S.C. 96, *per* L.P. Dunedin at 103.

[43] *Edinburgh Northern Tramways Co. v. Mann* (1891) 18 R. 1140, *per* Lord McLaren at 1153.

[44] *Gardner v. Beresford's Trs* (1877) 4 R. 1091, *per* L.P. Inglis at 1092; *Edinburgh Northern Tramways Co., supra, per* L.P. Inglis at 1153. *Cf. Reid v. H.M. Advocate*, 1984 S.L.T. 391.

[45] *Stewart v. Kennedy* (1889) 16 R. 521, *per* L.P. Inglis at 522.

from the standpoint of the parties.[46] The details of these considerations which will weigh with a sheriff, especially as regards economy and expedition, will normally be different from those examined by the Court of Session in relation to leave to appeal to the House of Lords in the undernoted cases; and considerations of economy and expedition will usually differ in weight according as leave is sought to appeal to the sheriff principal or to the Court of Session. When the considerations of convenience, economy and expedition appear to the sheriff to be evenly balanced, he should grant leave to appeal.[47] Among the considerations which may favour granting leave are that the interlocutor complained of, although not in form a final judgment, in effect disposes of the main issue in the cause or brings the action to an end[48]; or that the application for leave is not opposed.[49] A consideration in favour of refusing leave is that the applicant for leave will not be ultimately prejudiced by the refusal.[50]

Exercise of discretion. The principles on which leave to appeal should be granted or refused do not appear to have been further elucidated in the reported decisions. Since the object of requiring leave to appeal is thought to be to exclude appeals which are frivolous or devoid of merit or which are not concerned with questions of material importance,[51] it is submitted that the sheriff may require the appellant to state and explain his proposed grounds of appeal. The sheriff may then have regard to any authoritative pronouncements by the superior courts as to how an appellate court will approach an appeal on the grounds stated.[52] Where it is clear from any such pronouncements that an appeal on the grounds stated will very probably be refused, the sheriff should refuse leave. Thus, where the decision complained of has been on a matter placed within his discretion, such as the allowance or refusal of amendment or of a commission and diligence, or an order to find caution for expenses or to sist a mandatary, it is not appropriate for the sheriff to grant leave unless it is demonstrated to him that there is a statable argument that he has misdirected himself in law, or has left out of account, or taken into account, some factor which he should, or should not, have considered, or has not given due weight to a relevant factor, or that he has reached a result which is manifestly inequitable.[53] **18.51**

Question of law. Where the decision complained of is on a question of law, the sheriff should grant leave to appeal if he is satisfied that there is a substantial and arguable point of law on which the sheriff principal might reasonably and on identifiable grounds take a different view to his own, or if there is a conflict of judicial opinion on some important matter of principle. On the other hand, he should refuse leave if he considers that in the event of a further appeal to the Inner House his own view might be as **18.52**

---

[46] *Duke of Portland v. Wood's Trs*, 1926 S.C. 640, *per* L.P. Clyde at 653; *Beardmore & Co. v. Barry*, 1928 S.C. 366, *per* L.J.-C. Alness at 369; *Fraser v. McNeill*, 1948 S.C. 517 at 525; *Caddies v. Harold Houldsworth & Co. (Wakehead) Ltd*, 1954 S.L.T. (Notes) 3; *Adelphi Hotel (Glasgow) Ltd v. Walker*, 1960 S.C. 182 at 185.

[47] *Duke of Portland, Caddies, supra.*

[48] *Jones v. The Admiralty*, 1956 S.L.T. (Sh. Ct.) 20; *cf. Beattie v. Glasgow Corporation*, 1917 S.C. (H.L.) 22; *Ross v. Ross*, 1927 S.C. (H.L.) 4.

[49] *Beardmore & Co., supra*, at 370–371.

[50] *Adelphi Hotel (Glasgow) Ltd, supra*; *Hope v. Hope* (1956) 72 Sh.Ct.Rep. 244.

[51] para. 18.50.

[52] *cf. Reid v. H.M. Advocate*, 1984 S.L.T. 391.

[53] See para. 18.111.

likely to be affirmed as any different view taken by the sheriff principal. The granting or refusing of leave to appeal is a difficult matter for a sheriff, because he is aware that he is occasionally wrong, or at least that he has had the experience of taking a different view from that of an appellate court, and he may feel that he is not the best judge of the merits of an argument designed to question his decision. It is submitted, however, that it is his duty to consider the proposed grounds of appeal, in order properly to exercise his discretion as regards the granting of leave.

18.53 *Appeal in course of proof.* During a proof the sheriff may grant leave to appeal against a ruling on an objection to the admissibility of oral or documentary evidence on the ground of confidentiality, or to producing a document on any ground. No other decision as to the admissibility of evidence or the production of documents which is made in the course of a proof may be appealed.[54] It is possible, however, that in the course of a proof the sheriff may be required to give other rulings which are appealable with leave, for example, as to the amendment of pleadings or the granting of a commission and diligence. It is submitted that leave to appeal in the course of a proof, whether against rulings on objections to evidence or otherwise, should be refused save in the most exceptional circumstances, because such appeals cause difficulties for the litigants, the sheriff and the sheriff principal. The latter is almost inevitably handicapped by an incomplete appreciation of the whole circumstances, notwithstanding the assistance of the parties' advocates and of any note written by the sheriff, and by the necessity for a speedy determination of the appeal. In an appeal taken other than against a ruling on an objection to evidence, the case is removed from the sheriff and there is inevitable delay until the proof can be resumed, and in all cases the expense of an appeal is incurred.

18.54 *Statement of reasons.* There seems to be no general practice of appending a note to an interlocutor granting or refusing leave to appeal.[55] It is recommended, however, that where leave is granted the sheriff should append to the interlocutor granting leave a note explaining why he conceives an appeal against the interlocutor complained of to be a proper case to be heard by the sheriff principal; and where the reasons for the interlocutor sought to be appealed against are not already expressed in a note appended thereto, he should include a statement of these reasons in the note appended to the interlocutor granting leave. Where leave is refused, it is desirable that the sheriff should orally give parties a sufficient indication of his reasons for refusing leave, notwithstanding that they are not reviewable.

Time for appeal

18.55 *General rules.* An appeal, when competent, must be taken within certain specified times. The time-limits where an application for leave to appeal is required have already been noted.[56] Any other appealable interlocutor may be appealed within 14 days of its date unless it has been extracted following a motion under rule 30.4(2).[57] The date of the interlocutor is the date when it is pronounced in open court or, where the sheriff has reserved

---

[54] OCR, r. 29.19(3).
[55] *Jones v. The Admiralty*, 1956 S.L.T. (Sh. Ct.) 20.
[56] para. 18.47.
[57] OCR, r. 31.1.

his decision, the date on which the interlocutor is received by the sheriff clerk.[58] An unsuccessful party who wishes to keep open his right of appeal, and receives intimation of a motion for early extract, should mark his appeal before the motion is heard. As a general rule, there can be no appeal against an extracted interlocutor,[59] and an appeal which is taken out of time is also incompetent.[60] An appellant will not be allowed to evade a time-limit for appealing by lodging an incompetent motion, appealing or obtaining leave to appeal against its refusal, and using that appeal to challenge the interlocutor against which he wishes to appeal.[61]

Dispensing power. The sheriff principal may, however, allow the appellant to mark his appeal out of time by virtue of the dispensing power in rule 2.1(1) of the Ordinary Cause Rules.[62] An appellant who wishes to apply for the exercise of the dispensing power should lodge a motion before the sheriff principal to allow his appeal to be marked late by virtue of the dispensing power, at the same time as he marks his appeal late.[63] The motion will bar extract until the motion has been refused or the appeal decided. If an extract has been issued after the lodging of the motion, the sheriff principal, if he grants the motion, will recall the extract on the ground that it was issued prematurely.[64] It is at least doubtful whether it would be open to the sheriff principal to recall an extract which had been competently issued and obtained in good faith before the lodging of the motion.[65] The principles on which the dispensing power is exercised have already been considered.[66] It is thought that where the delay in marking the appeal has been short and there is an acceptable excuse for the delay, sheriffs principal are as a general rule reluctant to deprive a bona fide appellant of his right of appeal.[67] On the other hand, where there is a long delay or no acceptable excuse a sheriff principal may take the view that it is in the public interest that the prescribed time-limits should be enforced, since gross failure to observe them causes prejudice not only to the other parties to the cause but also to litigants in other cases and to society generally, whose interest it is that disputes should be disposed of as swiftly as justice allows. **18.56**

Procedure before hearing

Marking of appeal. An appeal to the sheriff principal must be marked by lodging a note of appeal in Form A1.[68] The note must (a) be signed by the appellant or his solicitor, (b) bear the date on which it is signed, (c) where **18.57**

---

[58] OCR, r. 12.2(5)(a). See para. 5.75.

[59] para. 18.19.

[60] *Millom and Askam Hematite Co. v. Simpson* (1897) 14 Sh.Ct.Rep. 206.

[61] *Malone v. Glasgow D.C.*, Sh. Pr. Reid, Glasgow Sh. Ct, Nov. 20, 1979, unreported.

[62] The effect of the new rule 2.1(1) has been considered in *DTZ Debenham Thorpe v. I. Henderson Transport Services*, 1995 S.L.T. 553; 1995 S.C.L.R. 345; *Morran v. Glasgow Council of Tenants*, 1994 S.C.L.R. 1065; *Andrew Welsh Ltd v. Thornhome Services*, 1994 S.C.L.R. 1021; *Mahoney v. Officer*, 1995 S.L.T. (Sh. Ct.) 49; 1994 S.C.L.R. 1059; and see *McChristie v. EMS Promotions Ltd*, 1991 S.L.T. 934; *McGregor v. Wimpey Construction Ltd*, 1991 S.C.L.R. 868; *Crendon Timber Engineering Ltd v. Miller Construction Ltd*, 1996 S.L.T. (Sh. Ct.) 102 (delay caused by misunderstanding of solicitors).

[63] *Hardy v. Robinson*, 1985 S.L.T. (Sh. Ct.) 40.

[64] *Anderson Brown & Co. v. Morris*, 1987 S.L.T. (Sh. Ct.) 96; *Gaunt v. Marco's Leisure*, 1995 S.C.L.R. 966.

[65] The point was left open in *Anderson Brown & Co., supra.*

[66] paras 5.93 to 5.97.

[67] *Anderson Brown & Co. v. Morris*; *Gaunt v. Marco's Leisure, supra*; see also *Eurocopy (Scotland) plc v. British Geological Survey*, 1997 S.C.L.R. 392.

[68] OCR, r. 31.4(1).

the appellant is represented, specify the name and address of the solicitor or other agent who will be acting for him in the appeal, and where a note has not been provided by the sheriff, request that the sheriff write a note setting out his reasons for his decision.[69]

18.58 *Grounds of appeal.* The grounds of appeal in a note of appeal should consist of brief specific numbered propositions stating the grounds on which it is proposed to submit that the appeal should be allowed or as the case may be.[70] It is also helpful to the sheriff principal and the sheriff clerk if the appellant intimates to the sheriff clerk any limitation in the scope of the appeal and, in all cases, the expected duration of the hearing. On marking or lodging a note of appeal, the appellant must send a copy of the note of appeal to every other party.[71] An appellant may (a) amend the grounds of appeal at any time up to 14 days before the date assigned for the hearing of the appeal; and if so must (b) at the same time send or deliver a copy of such amendment to every other party.[72] Where any party wishes to cross-appeal, he must (a) lodge a note of the grounds of appeal in accordance with paragraph (1) of rule 31.4 not less than seven days before the date assigned for the hearing of the appeal; and (b) at the same time send a copy of the note to every other party.[73] On a note of appeal being lodged, the sheriff clerk must note on the interlocutor sheet that the appeal has been marked and the date of the appeal.[74] Any limitation by the appellant as to the scope of the appeal does not qualify the powers of the sheriff principal in dealing with the appeal, or the availability of the appeal to the other parties. If any other party wishes to bring a matter under review, it is unnecessary for him to note a separate appeal[75] but, it is submitted, the provision in section 29 of the 1907 Act must now be read subject to the procedural requirements for a cross-appeal which have just been noted.

18.59 *Request for note.* Following a request for a note the sheriff writes and initials a note setting out the grounds on which he has proceeded. The note is dated, issued to the parties and added to the interlocutor sheets. If the appellant fails to request a note—which now seems unlikely standing the requirements in the rules—and as a result there is undue delay in hearing the appeal, or a diet fixed for a hearing is rendered abortive, his failure may be taken into account in determining liability for payment of the expenses of the appeal.

18.60 *Duties of sheriff clerk.* Where an appeal is marked in terms of rule 31.3 (appeal to Court of Session) or 31.4 (appeal to sheriff principal), the sheriff clerk must transmit the process of the cause (a) in an appeal to the sheriff principal, to him; or (b) in an appeal to the Court of Session, to the Deputy Principal Clerk of Session, within four days.[76] On transmitting the process, the sheriff clerk should (a) send written notice of the appeal to every party; and (b) certify on the interlocutor sheet that

---

[69] OCR, r. 31.4(2).
[70] OCR, r. 31.4(3).
[71] OCR, r. 31.4(4).
[72] OCR, r. 31.4(5).
[73] OCR, r. 31.4(6).
[74] OCR, r. 31.4(7).
[75] See para. 18.71.
[76] OCR, r. 31.5(1); RCS, r. 40.6(1)(b).

he has done so.[77] Failure of the sheriff clerk to give such notice or make such certification does not invalidate the appeal.[78]

Order by sheriff principal. In an appeal to him, the sheriff principal may order the appellant to lodge a record of the pleadings containing all the adjustments made in the cause with (a) a copy of all relevant interlocutors; (b) any other documents lodged in process by any party or produced by order of the sheriff, whether or not pursuant to a commission and diligence for its recovery; and (c) any other document to which reference is intended to be made in the appeal, by any party.[79] The sheriff principal usually pronounces an interlocutor fixing a diet for the hearing of the appeal. The date fixed for the hearing may depend on the appellant's estimate of the duration of the hearing[80] and on the availability of any notes of evidence.[81] The place fixed for the hearing is normally the court house in which the action has proceeded before the sheriff, but considerations of convenience may lead to the hearing being held in another courthouse in the sheriffdom. In an appeal to him, the sheriff principal will normally (a) hear parties at an oral hearing; or may (b) on the motion of the parties, and if he thinks fit, dispose of the appeal without ordering an oral hearing.[82] An oral hearing may, for example, be deemed unnecessary if parties are agreed as to how an appeal should be disposed of. Where an appeal is against a decision made by a sheriff before or at an options hearing or any continuation of it, the sheriff principal may order the sheriff clerk to fix a new date for a hearing under rule 9.12 (options hearing) or may make such other order as he thinks fit.[83] **18.61**

Reclaiming petition and answers. The former provisions dealing with procedure by reclaiming petition have not been reproduced in the current rules. **18.62**

Notes of evidence. Where an appeal is taken against an interlocutor which has been pronounced after proof, established practice requires the appellant to produce timeously the notes of evidence upon which he proposes to found.[84] Normally this will be so only in ordinary actions. However, where in a summary application a party had instructed a shorthand writer and the sheriff administered the oath *de fideli administratione* to her at the commencement of the proof, the sheriff principal held that this was by implication an order that the evidence should be recorded and the appellant was entitled to an appeal on fact as in an ordinary action.[85] In one case the evidence was not recorded, but without the consent of all parties: the appellant in an appeal on the merits, not having sought leave to appeal against the decision not to have the evidence recorded, had to be taken to have waived his right to challenge the proceedings; since there was no record of the evidence, the appeal court was bound by findings in fact and the appeal was limited to questions of **18.63**

---

[77] OCR, r. 31.5(2).
[78] OCR, r. 31.5(3).
[79] OCR, r. 31.6.
[80] para. 18.54.
[81] para. 18.63.
[82] OCR, r. 31.7.
[83] OCR, r. 31.8.
[84] *Leddy v. Rudport Ltd*, Sh. Pr. O'Brien, Duns Sh. Ct, Mar., 1981, unreported.
[85] *G. D. Lang Lanarkshire Mining Co. v. Clarkson*, Sh. Pr. Mowat, Airdrie Sh. Ct, Oct. 9, 1989.

law.[86] Where the appellant had not produced the shorthand notes, it was held that it was not open to the sheriff principal to hold that the sheriff failed to address his mind to the evidence and had not dealt with certain parts of it.[87] Where the appeal is marked before the notes of evidence have been extended and lodged in process, the appellant's solicitor must inform the shorthand writer forthwith that the notes of evidence are required, and ascertain from him the date when they will be available. The appellant's solicitor must thereafter inform the sheriff principal's clerk of the date when the notes of evidence will be available, in order that an appropriate diet may be fixed for the hearing of the appeal. Failure by the appellant or his solicitor to follow this procedure, so that there is undue delay in hearing the appeal, or a diet fixed for a hearing is rendered abortive, may be taken into account in determining liability for payment of the expenses of the appeal.[88] It should not be assumed, however, that a motion to continue the appeal to enable the notes of evidence to be obtained will be granted. An offer to make the notes available to the sheriff principal while the case is at avizandum is likely to be refused on the ground that it is improper for the court to have regard to material which was not before it, and the parties, at the hearing of the appeal.[89]

18.64 *Motions*. The sheriff principal may entertain any motion which is competent in the action. Before the hearing of the appeal, a party may lodge with the sheriff clerk or the clerk to the sheriff principal, and intimate, any motion which he desires the sheriff principal to hear, and indicate whether he wishes the sheriff principal to deal with it at or before the hearing. Motions in the course of an appeal may, for example, include motions to allow amendment of pleadings or motions to ordain a party to find caution for expenses.

18.65 *Abandonment*. After an appeal to the sheriff principal has been marked, the appellant is not entitled to abandon his appeal unless (a) of consent of all other parties, or (b) with leave of the sheriff principal.[90] In a highly exceptional case, for example, where the appellant has inadvertently marked his appeal to the sheriff principal instead of to the Court of Session and an appeal to the Court of Session of new would still be timeous, it appears that the appeal may be withdrawn of consent of all parties.[91] In general, however, after an appeal to the sheriff principal has been marked he must either dispose of the case, by hearing or one of the other modes mentioned above,[92] or allow it to be abandoned in terms of rule 31.11 of the Ordinary Cause Rules.[93] The rules as to abandonment and withdrawal are designed to prevent the defeat of the rule whereby the

---

86 *Marsh v. Taylor*, 1992 S.L.T. (Sh. Ct.) 28; See also para. 18.85.

87 *Anderson v. Harrold*, 1991 S.C.L.R. 135.

88 These general rules of practice are expressed in the Glasgow and Strathkelvin Practice Notes, para. 2.02 (*Parliament House Book*, D601). However, in two sheriffdoms (North Strathclyde and Lothian and Borders) provision is made in Acts of Court whereby, if it appears to an appellant or his solicitor that the ground of appeal is such as not to require the notes of evidence, a motion to dispense with the requirement to produce them may be made to the sheriff principal whose decision on the matter will be final (*Parliament House Book*, D705, D1008).

89 *Leddy*, *supra*.

90 OCR, r. 31.11.

91 *J. & J. Fraser v. Smith*, 1937 S.C. 667. *Cf.* RCS, r. 38.8(1) and (3).

92 para. 18.57.

93 *J. & J. Fraser*, *supra*, *per* Lord Wark at 673.

respondent may avail himself of the appeal.[94] An appellant who abandons is normally liable in the expenses of the appeal, but the sheriff principal has a complete discretion in the matter of awarding expenses.[95] The basis on which an appeal is to be abandoned is often agreed by a joint minute, which must be clear and comprehensive in its terms. The sheriff principal normally pronounces an interlocutor dismissing the appeal in respect that it is not insisted in. A further appeal to the Court of Session is then incompetent. If a party states to the court that he does not insist in his appeal, that is understood to mean that he cannot maintain his case, and to be equivalent to a consent that the appeal be dismissed.[96] Where a party or his solicitor abandons, fails to attend or is not prepared to proceed with any diet of proof, debate, appeal or meeting ordered by the court, the court shall have power to decern against that party for payment of such expenses as it considers reasonable.[97]

Return of process. Any parts of process in an action under appeal should **18.66**
be returned to the sheriff principal's clerk before the hearing. In Glasgow and Strathkelvin it is expected that that will be done not later than 10 a.m. on the day before the diet of hearing.[98] Similar, though not always identical, provision is made in Practice Notes and Acts of Court applicable in other sheriffdoms. Practitioners should be at pains to ascertain the rules which apply in each sheriffdom where they are practising.

Note of authorities. Before the hearing, each of the solicitors for the **18.67**
parties to the action under appeal should lodge with the sheriff clerk a note of all the authorities to which reference is to be made in the course of the argument for the party he represents. In Glasgow and Strathkelvin he is expected to lodge the list with the sheriff principal's clerk not later than 10 a.m. on the day before the diet of hearing.[99] In South Strathclyde, Dumfries and Galloway he is required, not later than two clear working days prior to the day of the diet of hearing, to lodge the list with the sheriff clerk of the court where the hearing of the appeal is to take place, and to send a copy to the sheriff clerk.[1] Similar, though not necessarily identical, provision is made in Practice Notes and Acts of Court applicable in other sheriffdoms. They are all to be found in the *Parliament House Book*.

Effect of appeal

Suspension of operation of decree. In general, when an appeal is taken **18.68**
against an interlocutor, the effect of the appeal is to sist all execution upon the decree until the appeal has been determined by the appellate court.[2] The appeal precludes extract, which is in normal circumstances a prerequisite of diligence.[3] It does not, however, prevent immediate execution of a warrant of sequestration for rent, or of warrants to take inventories, or place effects in custody *ad interim*, or warrants for interim preservation.

---

94 para. 18.71.

95 *cf. McGuire v. Union Cold Storage Co. Ltd*, 1909 S.C. 384.

96 *Manchester and County Bank Ltd v. Moore*, 1909 S.C. 246.

97 A.S. (Fees of Solicitors in the Sheriff Court) (Amendment and Further Provisions) 1993, Sched. 1, General Regulations, reg. 5(c).

98 Glasgow and Strathkelvin Practice Notes, note 11. See this and other Acts of Court and Practice Notes in *Parliament House Book*, Div. D.

99 Glasgow and Strathkelvin Practice Notes, note 12.

1 South Strathclyde, Dumfries and Galloway Practice Note, June 25, 1982.

2 *Macleay v. Macdonald*, 1928 S.C. 776.

3 *Fowler v. Fowler (No. 2)*, 1981 S.L.T. (Notes) 78.

An interim interdict, although appealed against, is binding till recalled.[4] The operation of a sentence of imprisonment for breach of interdict is suspended by an appeal,[5] but the sentence, or any unexpired portion, must be served after the date of dismissal of the appeal.[6] The effect of an interlocutor *ad factum praestandum* is suspended until it is adhered to by the appellate court.[7] However, where an appeal is marked against an interlocutor making an order under section 11 of the Children (Scotland) Act 1995 (court orders relating to parental responsibilities, etc.) or in respect of aliment, the marking of that appeal does not excuse obedience to or implement of that order unless by order of the sheriff, the sheriff principal, or the Court of Session, as the case may be.[8]

18.69 *Powers of sheriff.* In principle, once an appeal has been marked against an interlocutor of an inferior court, that court is *functus officio*, that is, it has discharged its official duty in the cause unless and until the superior court remits the cause back to it.[9] Thus, pending an appeal the sheriff has no power to pronounce further interlocutors except where he is authorised by statute to do so[10] or, perhaps, where in exceptional circumstances not provided for by statute the interests of justice urgently require an order of court in the interval between the marking of the appeal and its transmission to the sheriff principal. In view of the breadth of the statutory authority conferred on the sheriff to pronounce further interlocutors such circumstances are likely to be few. The statutory authority is contained in rule 31.10 of the Ordinary Cause Rules, which confers on the sheriff or sheriff principal from whose decision an appeal has been taken the following powers: (1) to regulate all matters relating to interim possession; (2) to make any order for the preservation of any property to which the action relates or for its sale if perishable; (3) to make provision for the preservation of evidence; or (4) to make any interim order which a due regard to the interests of the parties may require. Under the final branch of the rule the sheriff may make interim orders in respect of aliment[11] or residence of children.[12] Orders under rule 31.10 are written on a separate interlocutor sheet, as the process is no longer with the sheriff.[13] An order under rule 31.10 may be reviewed by (a) the sheriff principal in an appeal to him; or (b) the Court of Session on an appeal to it.[14]

18.70 *Review of prior interlocutors.* An appeal is effectual to submit to review the whole of the interlocutors pronounced in the cause,[15] including an extracted interlocutor which was not appealable before the date of extract.[16] A final judgment on the merits may be reviewed on an appeal

---

[4] 1907 Act, s. 29.
[5] *Macleay, supra.*
[6] *Macleay v. Macdonald,* 1929 S.C. 371.
[7] *Marshall v. Callander and Trossachs Hydropathic Co. Ltd* (1896) 24 R. 33.
[8] OCR, r. 31.9.
[9] *Love v. Montgomerie and Logan,* 1982 S.L.T. (Sh. Ct.) 60 at 63; *Hardy v. Robinson,* 1985 S.L.T. (Sh. Ct.) 40.
[10] *Love v. Montgomerie and Logan, supra.*
[11] *Cunningham v. Cunningham,* 1965 S.C. 78; *A.B. v. C.B.,* 1939 S.L.T. (Sh. Ct.) 11, *sub nom. Emmerson v. Emmerson* (1939) 55 Sh.Ct.Rep. 146.
[12] *Ellis v. Macdonald,* 1980 S.L.T. 11.
[13] *Trainer v. Renfrewshire Upper District Committee,* 1907 S.C. 1117.
[14] OCR, r. 31.10(2)
[15] 1907 Act, s. 29.
[16] *Weir v. Tudhope* (1892) 19 R. 858; *McKenzie v. John R. Wyatt (Musical Enterprises) Ltd,* 1974 S.L.T. (Sh. Ct.) 8 at 10. See para. 18.19.

taken against a subsequent decree for expenses,[17] and an appeal against an interim decree for payment of money brings up for review any previous interlocutor disposing of part of the merits, of which it is the logical sequel.[18] An appeal against a final judgment brings up for review a previous interlocutor which deals in part with the merits of the case, such as an interlocutor repelling a plea to the relevancy of the defences.[19] Formerly, the following interlocutors were not, in general, regarded as being open to review: an interloctor which had been pronounced of consent[20]; or which had become final expressly or by implication[21]; or which had been extracted,[22] or which had not been appealed against within the prescribed time limit, which had become final, and which had been acted upon.[23] Moreover, it has in the past been observed that, in considering an appeal, the appellate court will not be inhibited from determining the competency and effect of the material presented for its consideration by the terms of any interlocutor prior to that under appeal and bearing to have decided these matters; but that if the effect of the earlier interlocutor was to exclude material from the case, and it has become final or has become the basis of subsequent procedure, it will not be open to review.[24] It has also been held that an appellant will not be allowed to evade a time-limit for appealing by lodging an incompetent motion, appealing or obtaining leave to appeal against its refusal, and using that appeal to challenge the earlier interlocutor against which he wishes to appeal.[25] All of the foregoing propositions have recently been overturned, or at least put in doubt, by the decision of a court of five judges in the case of *McCue v. Scottish Daily Record and Sunday Mail Ltd*,[26] which overruled the cases of *Marsh v. Baxendale*[27] and *Mowbray v. D.C. Thomson and Co. Ltd*,[28] and which disapproved of certain *dicta* in *Macaskill v. Nicol*.[29] In *McCue* the court essentially held that an interlocutor in respect of which leave to appeal has been refused can competently be brought under review in an appeal against a final judgment in the case; but at the same time the court took the opportunity to review many of the earlier authorities relating to what, in terms of the sheriff courts, is section 29 of the 1907 Act, and to overrule, or at least question, some of the principles on which that section has been applied in the past. The decision in *McCue* was given quite shortly before this book went to press, and it has therefore not been possible to assess all of its implications. It

---

17 para. 18.36.

18 *Cross & Sons v. Bordes* (1879) 6 R. 934.

19 para. 18.17.

20 para. 18.15.

21 paras 18.16, 18.17; *John Young (Bellshill) Ltd v. Jay*, Sh. Pr. Mowat, Hamilton Sh. Ct, May 21, 1992, unreported: where leave had not been sought to appeal against the prior interlocutor, the sheriff principal refused to review the interlocutor; and in *Law v. Law*, Sh. Pr. Mowat, Hamilton Sh. Ct, May 21, 1992, unreported, said: "I incline to the view that an interlocutor in respect of which leave to appeal has been sought and refused is to be regarded as final, and I therefore doubt whether it can be opened up to review in this appeal".

22 para. 18.19.

23 *MacAskill (or Macaskill) v. Nicol*, 1943 S.C. 17; *Marsh v. Baxendale*, 1994 S.C.L.R. 239; *Mowbray v. D.C. Thomson and Co. Ltd*, 1996 S.L.T. 846; *Mowbray v. Secretary of State for Scotland*, 1998 Civ. Pract. B., 20–11.

24 *Williamson v. Harris*, 1981 S.L.T. (Sh. Ct.) 56.

25 *Malone v. Glasgow D.C.*, Sh. Pr. Reid, Glasgow Sh. Ct, Nov. 20, 1979, unreported.

26 1998 S.C.L.R. 742.

27 1994 S.C.L.R. 239.

28 1996 S.L.T. 846.

29 1943 S.C. 17.

seems likely, however, that it may give rise to some interesting judicial decisions in the future. If a final judgment can no longer be appealed, the earlier interlocutory decisions in the case, which it supersedes, are by necessary implication unappealable, since it would be futile to disturb an earlier interlocutor if the final, operative interlocutor were not affected.[30]

18.71 *Respondent's appeal.* In terms of the 1907 Act an appeal is available to and may be insisted in by all other parties in the cause notwithstanding that they may not have noted separate appeals.[31] The rules as to the abandonment and withdrawal of appeals only of consent or by leave of the sheriff principal[32] are designed to prevent the defeat of this rule. The respondent in the appeal is therefore entitled to avail himself of the appeal to challenge any interlocutor in the cause which may be competently brought under review.[33] He may also wish to contend, for example, that the decision of the sheriff against which the appellant has appealed was wrong in whole or in part; or that it should be varied, either in any event or in the event of the appeal being allowed in whole or in part; or that the decision should be affirmed on other grounds. He may also raise a question of expenses only.[34] Now under the rules, where any party wishes to cross-appeal he has to lodge a note of grounds of appeal under rule 31.4(6),[35] and presumably the provisions of section 29 of the 1907 Act must now be read subject to that rule.

The hearing

18.72 *Steps before hearing.* As regards the steps to be taken before the hearing, and the conduct of the hearing, an appeal is similar to a debate.[36] If a solicitor for any party is no longer prepared to act for his client in the appeal he should, at the same time as he so informs his client, intimate the fact in writing to the solicitors for all the other parties to the appeal and to the sheriff clerk.[37] Although Chapter 24 of the Ordinary Cause Rules is not expressly stated as applying to appeals it is submitted that it does so apply, and should be followed. If a party, or parties, does not wish an appeal hearing to proceed on the appointed day, say because counsel is not to be available on that date, or for some other good reason, a motion should be made forthwith to the sheriff principal for an adjournment of the diet. If the motion is a joint one, and the sheriff principal is satisfied that the reason for seeking an adjournment is acceptable, he may grant it, and sign an interlocutor to that effect, without the necessity of any appearance of parties. However, where a motion to adjourn an appeal hearing is opposed, it will be dealt with under formal motion procedures. If the hearing is to proceed, all parts of process should be returned[38] and any notes of evidence[39] and lists of any authorities[40] lodged. An advocate

---

30 *Scott v. Hawkins*, Sh. Pr. Caplan, Kilmarnock Sh. Ct, Dec. 19, 1984, unreported.
31 1907 Act, s. 29; *Bell v. Andrews* (1885) 12 R. 961.
32 para. 18.63.
33 *J. & J. Fraser v. Smith*, 1937 S.C. 667, *per* L.J.-C. Aitchison at 669.
34 *Bonner's Tr. v. Bonner* (1902) 4 F. 429. As to appeals on questions of expenses, see para. 18.117.
35 See para. 18.58.
36 paras 13.03 to 13.09.
37 OCR, r. 24.1.
38 para. 18.66.
39 para. 18.63.
40 para. 18.66.

will prepare for a hearing in much the same way as for a debate.[41] In an appeal taken after proof, he may require to study in detail not only the pleadings and the judgment appealed against but also the notes of evidence.

Attendance of parties. If the appellant fails to appear or to be represented at the appeal, the sheriff principal may dismiss the appeal in respect that it is not insisted in. If the respondent fails to appear, the appellant must nevertheless be prepared to support his appeal, since in general the onus remains on him to satisfy the court that the judgment of the sheriff was wrong.[42] In one case a party litigant, who failed to have the diet adjourned, declined to address the court in support of his appeal: the sheriff principal refused the appeal with expenses.[43] If the parties are agreed as to the way in which the appeal should be disposed of, they should lodge a joint minute which must set forth in clear and comprehensive terms all the matters, including terms as to expenses, which they desire to be included in the interlocutor which is to follow upon the joint minute. They must, however, be represented when the case calls before the sheriff principal, and if the joint minute is not in the terms described above, each party must be separately represented at the hearing. **18.73**

Speeches. At the hearing,[44] the appellant's advocate speaks first, and begins by giving the sheriff principal a brief description of what the case is about and some indication of its history. He states what the sheriff's decision was, and identifies, by reference to his written grounds of appeal,[45] those parts of the interlocutor which he is challenging, and those which he is prepared to accept. Where the interlocutor has been pronounced after proof, he should identify the relevant parts by reference to the numbered findings in fact, and state which of them he wishes the sheriff principal to vary or recall, and the text of any findings which he wishes the sheriff principal to add.[46] In all cases he should also state precisely the terms of the interlocutor he wishes the sheriff principal to pronounce. He should be prepared to read aloud the relevant parts of the pleadings, of the sheriff's interlocutor and note, and of the notes of evidence, though in most instances the sheriff principal will already have read all, or at least some, of these when preparing for the appeal. For that reason a sheriff principal will normally indicate which documents need not be read to him. **18.74**

At the conclusion of the appellant's speech, the respondent replies unless the sheriff principal finds the propositions in the appellant's speech so untenable that he does not call for a reply. After the respondent's speech, the sheriff principal usually gives the appellant's advocate an **18.75**

---

41 para. 13.04.

42 para. 18.98.

43 *TSB Scotland plc v. Haynes*, Sh. Pr. Nicholson, Edinburgh Sh. Ct, June 28, 1990; see also para. 18.65.

44 See Sir Allan G. Walker, Q.C., "Appeals in the Sheriff Court" (1973) 18 J.L.S. 222; Kearney, Chap. 28.

45 See para. 18.57.

46 Where a sheriff principal is to be invited to make additional findings in fact, or to vary the terms of the sheriff's findings, it is good practice for the sheriff principal to be provided with the text of the proposed findings, or amendments, in written form so as to ensure accuracy, and so as to avoid the delay which would otherwise be occasioned if he had to note them verbatim at dictation speed.

opportunity of a second speech if he wishes it. Where the respondent wishes to take advantage of the appeal[47] he divides his speech into two parts, answering the appellant's arguments in one part, and advancing his own contentions in the other. In that event the appellant's advocate is entitled to a second speech in order to answer the respondent's contentions, and the sheriff principal will almost certainly invite the respondent to reply to the appellant's second speech.

18.76 Where an appeal is taken against the sheriff's disposal of preliminary pleas after debate, and the pleas are not being departed from, the parties must state their contentions on all the preliminary pleas debated before the sheriff, even if the sheriff has not dealt with them in his interlocutor.[48] An appeal court is entitled to hear new argument though it may be reluctant to do so where the argument could, and should, have been advanced at first instance.

18.77 In general, the sheriff principal seeks to avoid a subsequent hearing on expenses if only to avoid the expense and possible inconvenience to parties of such a hearing. Each party should therefore include in his speech his submissions as to expenses, or move the sheriff principal that the question of liability for expenses be heard after he has issued his interlocutor. If parties have not dealt with expenses in their speeches, the sheriff principal usually invites them to make submissions thereon at the conclusion of the hearing.[49]

Powers of sheriff principal

18.78 *General: dispensing power*. The sheriff principal may entertain any motion which is competent in the action, and may do so before[50] or in the course of the hearing. He may be moved, for example, to exercise the dispensing power[51] in relation to the late marking of an appeal[52] or other matters, but he may decline to hear a motion where the rules direct that the sheriff from whose decision the appeal has been taken has power to make any interim order, as in a case where rule 31.10(1) applies.[53]

18.79 *Amendment of pleadings*. A motion frequently made to the sheriff principal on appeal is to allow the amendment of pleadings.[54] Any party lodging a motion, before the hearing of an appeal, for a record to be amended in terms of a minute of amendment and any answers thereto, should at the same time lodge an application for a direction as to further procedure, since the sheriff principal may consider it appropriate to remit the case to the sheriff for further hearing on the amended pleadings.[55] The considerations which may be relevant to the allowance of amendment on appeal[56] and of an amendment which requires the allowance of further proof,[57] are noted elsewhere. The sheriff principal may open the record *ex*

---

[47] para. 18.71.
[48] *Kerr v. Toole* (1948) 66 Sh.Ct.Rep. 116 at 120–121.
[49] On the expenses of the appeal, see paras 18.87 to 18.89.
[50] para. 18.64.
[51] paras 5.98 to 5.102.
[52] para. 18.56.
[53] *Millar v. Millar*, Sh. Pr. Nicholson, Edinburgh Sh. Ct., Mar. 29, 1990, unreported.
[54] *Kerr v. Strathclyde R.C.*, 1968 S.L.T. (Sh. Ct.) 42.
[55] para. 10.23.
[56] para. 10.24.
[57] paras 10.25, 10.26.

proprio motu if it appears to him not to have been properly made up,[58] but it is difficult to imagine in what circumstances he would do so, instead of leaving it to the parties to move to amend.[59]

Fixing of Options Hearing or making further orders following appeal. On determination of an appeal from a decision of the sheriff made before or at an Options Hearing or any continuation of it, the sheriff principal may order the sheriff clerk to fix a new date for a hearing under rule 9.12 (Options Hearing) or may make such other order as he thinks fit.[60] **18.80**

Allowance of further proof. The sheriff principal may allow an amendment of the pleadings which requires the allowance of further proof.[61] It is also competent for him, when the action is before him on appeal on any point, to allow further proof although no amendment is made[62]; or take account of uncontested evidence of a party's actings since the hearing before the sheriff.[63] He is not, however, authorised to allow or to order further proof *ex proprio motu.* If further proof is to be allowed, it must be upon the motion of a party[64] who must define the purpose for which proof is required and who might also be required to name the witnesses whom he proposes to adduce.[65] The party lodges a minute specifying these matters.[66] The sheriff principal may allow the opposite party to lodge answers to the minute, allow a proof of the averments in the minute and answers, and remit to the sheriff to take the proof and either report the same to the sheriff principal for further procedure[67] or of new issue judgment.[68] In the note appended to his interlocutor the sheriff principal refers to the factors which he considers sufficient to warrant the course which he orders.[69] The allowance of proof by such procedure may present practical difficulties. Where the sheriff has already expressed a firm view about certain factual aspects of the case, it might be appropriate for the further evidence to be led before the sheriff principal or another sheriff. Again, the new matters may be so inextricably bound up with the earlier evidence that, ideally, it might be best to have the whole proof heard again; but it appears that the powers of the sheriff principal do not extend to the allowance of proof of new on the whole case.[70] Where, after a debate, a party seeks to amend his pleadings prior to an appeal hearing, the appellate court may allow the amendment but remit the cause to the court below for further debate.[71] **18.81**

---

58 1907 Act, s. 27.
59 para. 10.27.
60 OCR, r. 3.18.
61 para. 10.25.
62 1907 Act, s. 27.
63 *McFarlane v. McFarlane*, Sh. Pr. Mowat, Airdrie Sh. Ct, Sept. 19, 1991, unreported.
64 *Lothian R.C. v. S*, Sh. Pr. Nicholson, Edinburgh Sh. Ct, Feb. 14, 1991, unreported: where both parties, in an appeal against the granting of an order to free a child for adoption, wished to lead further evidence, the sheriff principal treated that as sufficient to allow further evidence without the enrolment of a further motion to that effect.
65 *Hutchison v. Davidson*, 1945 S.C. 395, *per* L.P. Normand at 401.
66 Where a party lodges a minute of amendment containing averments which would require further proof, he should also lodge such a minute.
67 *Cook v. Crane*, 1922 S.C. 631 at 633.
68 *Davidson v. Duncan*, 1981 S.C. 83 at 84. *Cf. Macfarlane v. Raeburn*, 1946 S.C. 67 at 70.
69 *Davidson, supra*, at 86.
70 *Whitehouse v. Strathclyde R.C.*, Sh. Pr. Caplan, Dunoon Sh. Ct, Feb. 18, 1986, unreported.
71 *Wallace v. Scottish Special Housing Association*, 1981 S.L.T. (Notes) 60.

18.82 The statute imposes no limitation on the power conferred on the sheriff principal to allow further proof. It is a discretionary power which he must exercise judicially. He may allow further proof not only in a case of *res noviter veniens ad notitiam*[72] but also where the further evidence is merely that of new witnesses adduced to speak to matters already spoken to; but in all cases he may allow further proof only for good and substantial or sufficient reasons.[73] The sheriff principal must consider whether there was any justification for the failure of the party making the motion to lead the evidence in question at the proof, since it is not on light grounds that further proof will be allowed to a party who has by his own negligence failed to bring forward evidence which might have been available to him.[74] The sheriff principal may nevertheless allow further proof if he is satisfied that without the new evidence there might be a miscarriage of justice; but on the other hand he may consider that such a miscarriage might follow if as a result of the new evidence the other party were to be deprived of success after duly following the rules of practice and procedure, which are designed to secure justice.[75] In some instances new evidence may be allowed in cases involving the welfare of children. If further incidents affecting that question are alleged to have occurred during the period between a proof and an appeal hearing, a sheriff principal is likely to be prepared to hear further evidence relating to such matters.[76] The Inner House will not lightly interfere with the sheriff principal's discretion, but will do so only where he appears to have exercised it unwisely or unreasonably.[77] An appeal court is also entitled to hear new argument in order to do justice between the parties,[78] though it may be reluctant to do so where the argument could, and should, have been advanced at first instance.

Judgment

18.83 *General.* The sheriff principal disposes of the appeal by pronouncing an interlocutor in which he identifies the interlocutor or interlocutors brought under review; makes any necessary findings in fact and law; specifies his decision, which is usually to adhere to, vary or recall these interlocutors; and disposes of questions of expenses. The principles on which he acts in reaching his decision are considered later in this chapter.[79] Where it is appropriate or desirable to do so, he appends to the interlocutor a note setting out the reasons for his decision. It is an important part of any judge's duty to state the reasons for his decision because the parties, and in the

---

[72] paras 2.110, 2.111.

[73] *Cook v. Crane*, 1922 S.C. 631. *Cook* is the leading case on the allowance of additional proof under s. 27 of the 1907 Act. It is thought to be in general unhelpful to refer the reader (as in Lewis, pp. 146, 147 and Dobie, pp. 226–227) to authorities decided under other statutory provisions or to sheriff court decisions prior to, or not citing, *Cook* (*e.g. Iannelli v. Stevenson*, 1977 S.L.T. (Sh. Ct.) 5): *Duggie v. A. Tulloch & Sons Ltd*, 1983 S.L.T. (Sh. Ct.) 66.

[74] *Peline v. L. Sterne & Co. Ltd* (1963) 79 Sh.Ct.Rep. 136 at 142–143; *Trojan Plant Hue Co. Ltd v. Durafencing (Northern) Ltd*, 1974 S.L.T. (Sh. Ct.) 3. *Cf. Coul v. Ayr C.C.*, 1909 S.C. 422, *per* L.P. Dunedin at 424.

[75] *Hawthorn v. Milne*, 1956 S.L.T. (Sh. Ct.) 85, (1956) 72 Sh.Ct.Rep. 323; *Trojan Plant Hire Co. Ltd, supra.*

[76] *Sanderson v. McManus*, 1995 S.C.L.R. 902.

[77] *Cook, supra, per* Lord Ormidale at 634, Lord Hunter at 635; *Davidson v. Duncan*, 1981 S.C. 83 at 86.

[78] *Lawson v. Lawson*, 1996 S.L.T. (Sh. Ct.) 83; and see para. 18.76.

[79] paras 18.100 to 18.117.

event of an appeal the appeal court, are entitled to know what they are.[80] It follows that in many instances it will be necessary for a sheriff principal to append a written note to an interlocutor pronounced after an appeal.

Identification of interlocutors reviewed. In the sheriff principal's interlocutor disposing of the appeal the interlocutors submitted to review are identified by date. Such identification is of importance not only because it may facilitate extract, but also because the appeal is effectual to submit to review the whole of the interlocutors pronounced in the cause[81] and is available to all the other parties in the cause,[82] and it is therefore necessary to make clear the scope of the sheriff principal's judgment. **18.84**

Findings in fact and law. In an appeal against a sheriff's final interlocutor the sheriff principal must set out the findings in fact and in law on which his own interlocutor is founded,[83] if these are different from, or additional to, the findings made by the sheriff. The Court of Session may remit back any case on appeal in which such findings have been omitted, with a direction to pronounce another interlocutor in the prescribed form.[84] If, however, the sheriff principal agrees with the findings of the sheriff, it is sufficient for his interlocutor to state that he adheres to the sheriff's interlocutor.[85] If he disagrees with only some of the sheriff's findings, he may adhere to the sheriff's interlocutor with specified variations consisting of inserted words or substituted findings.[86] If he agrees with the sheriff's findings but considers that additional findings are necessary, he may adhere and add further findings.[87] If, however, the evidence has not been recorded,[88] the sheriff's findings in fact are binding on the sheriff principal, and he cannot make different, or further, findings in fact.[89] Other limitations on his power to review matters of fact are examined later in this chapter.[90] If in any case it appears from the note appended to the sheriff's interlocutor that he has considered matters of fact which are not set out in his findings in fact, the sheriff principal may recall the sheriff's interlocutor and remit the case to the sheriff to add a finding or findings in fact on any matter which appears to have been omitted from his interlocutor.[91] **18.85**

Decision.[92] The various disposals open to the sheriff principal may be summarised as follows. **18.86**

(1) Adherence. If the sheriff principal agrees with the sheriff's interlocutor, he pronounces an interlocutor in which he refuses the appeal and

---

[80] *Lai Wee Lian v. Singapore Bus Service (1978) Ltd* [1984] A.C. 729, *per* Lord Fraser of Tullybelton at 734. There appears to be no valid distinction in this respect between appeal judges and judges of first instance. See n. 79.

[81] para. 18.70.

[82] para. 18.71.

[83] OCR, r. 12.2(3) and (4). "Sheriff" in the Rules includes "sheriff principal" unless the contrary appears: Interpretation Act 1978, ss. 5–21, Sched. 1.

[84] *Campbell v. Caledonian Ry* (1852) 14 D. 141; *Mackay v. Mackenzie* (1894) 21 R. 894; *James E. Keanie Ltd v. Maycrete Sales Ltd*, 1949 S.L.T. (Notes) 25.

[85] *Weems v. Mathieson* (1861) 1 Macq. 215.

[86] *Pitoy v. Steel* (1960) 76 Sh.Ct.Rep.79 at 83; *Peline v. L. Sterne & Co. Ltd* (1963) 79 Sh.Ct.Rep. at 141–142.

[87] *The Glassford v. The City of Edinburgh* (1904) 12 S.L.R. 159.

[88] para. 16.33.

[89] *Allardice v. Wallace*, 1957 S.L.T 225; *McGibbon v. Sanchez*, 1998 G.W.D. 15-736.

[90] paras 18.103 to 18.109.

[91] *Walter Wright & Co. Ltd v. Cowdray*, 1973 S.L.T. (Sh. Ct.) 56.

[92] Lees, *Interlocutors*, pp. 38–43, 49–51.

adheres to the interlocutor complained of. If the latter interlocutor is a decree *ad factum praestandum* ordering performance within a specified period, the period may run from the date of the sheriff principal's interlocutor,[93] or he may fix a new date by which performance is required.

(2) Recall. If the sheriff principal decides to reverse the sheriff's judgment, his interlocutor sustains the appeal, recalls the sheriff's interlocutor and, where necessary, states his own findings in fact and in law.

(3) Adherence in part. If the sheriff principal decides that the appeal should be sustained only in part, he recalls the sheriff's interlocutor in so far as it makes a finding or order with which he disagrees; substitutes, if necessary, a different finding or order; to that extent sustains the appeal; *quoad ultra* refuses it, and adheres to the sheriff's interlocutor.

(4) Variation. If the sheriff principal substantially agrees with the sheriff's interlocutor but considers that it requires to be varied, he refuses the appeal and adheres to the interlocutor with specified variations.

(5) Recall *in hoc statu*. The sheriff principal may recall the sheriff's interlocutor *in hoc statu*[94] if he decides that it should be recalled only on conditions, such as payment of expenses. His interlocutor in such a case recalls the sheriff's *in hoc statu*, specifies the condition and continues the cause to a specified date. He may also recall *in hoc statu* an interlocutor which he holds to have been pronounced prematurely, or which he considers should not be pronounced until some further procedure has taken place.[95]

(6) Remit to the sheriff. The sheriff principal may remit the cause to the sheriff to take further proof[96] or to add findings in fact[97] or to take such further steps in the process as may be necessary in the interests of justice. Where the appeal is taken against an interlocutory judgment, the sheriff principal's interlocutor disposing of the appeal usually concludes by remitting the cause to the sheriff "to proceed as accords", which means, "to proceed as accords with law, justice and procedure".[98]

(7) Dismissal. If the appeal is incompetent[99] or is abandoned,[1] the sheriff principal pronounces an interlocutor dismissing it.

18.87 *Expenses*. The expenses of the appeal are in the discretion of the sheriff principal. His interlocutor usually disposes of them by awarding or reserving them. If his interlocutor is a final judgment and is silent on the subject, it will be interpreted as a refusal to award any expenses, and he will have no power thereafter to make an award.[2] Where the sheriff principal awards expenses he may allow an account of these expenses to be given in, remit it to the auditor, and remit the case to the sheriff. Alternatively, in an interlocutory appeal where there is no special urgency about the recovery of these expenses he may avoid the expense and labour of a multiplicity of taxations by making a finding as to liability for expenses, remitting the case to the sheriff and leaving it to the sheriff to remit the account to the auditor along with the account of expenses

---

93 *Marshall v. Callander and Trossachs Hydropathic Co. Ltd* (1896) 24 R. 33.

94 *i.e.* in the present state of matters (Trayner, p. 262).

95 *Cathcart v. Cathcart* (1899) 1 F. 781; *McMahon v. Matheson* (1899) 1 F. 896.

96 paras. 18.81, 18.82.

97 *Walter Wright & Co. Ltd, supra.*

98 *Macleay v. Macdonald*, 1929 S.C. 371, *per* Lord Ormidale and Lord Hunter at 378.

99 para. 18.30.

1 para. 18.65.

2 *Macdonald v. McEachen* (1880) 7 R. 574. *Cf. Wilson's Trustees v. Wilson's Factor* (1869) 7 M. 457; *Dobbie v. Duncanson* (1872) 10 M. 810 at 816; *Fraser v. Fraser* (1903) 11 S.L.T. 70.

allowed to be given in at the conclusion of the litigation. In either event the sheriff will, if necessary, dispose of any objections to the auditor's report, and will decern for the taxed amount of expenses or, where the unsuccessful party is an assisted person, for such proportion of the taxed amount as he may determine. If both the sheriff and the sheriff principal have found no expenses due to or by either party, it is unnecessary to remit the cause to the sheriff.[3]

Where the appeal is against an interlocutory judgment, the party successful in the appeal may be unsuccessful as regards the remainder of the case. The sheriff principal may therefore dispose of the expenses of the appeal by reserving them or refusing them or finding them due and allowing an account to be given in. On the other hand, if he considers that they should not be dealt with until more is known about the merits of the case, he may authorise the sheriff to dispose of them as expenses in the cause.[4] That course may also be taken of consent of parties.[5] **18.88**

In any appeal, the sheriff principal may modify the expenses to which he finds any party entitled[6]; and where counsel is instructed, he may sanction the employment of counsel in the appeal. If sanction has not been granted by the sheriff he will sanction the employment of counsel before the sheriff only where the applicant for sanction shows, not only that the employment was right, but that there are very good reasons why the motion for sanction was not made to the sheriff.[7] **18.89**

Issue of judgment. Like a sheriff's judgment,[8] a sheriff principal's judgment may be produced and signed when he is furth of his sheriffdom.[9] Copies of an interlocutor with a note appended thereto are provided for the parties free of charge by the sheriff clerk,[10] and any clerical or incidental error may be corrected before extract or before the transmission of a process in which an appeal has been taken.[11] **18.90**

Appeal to Court of Session

Introduction

In ordinary causes an appeal may be taken in certain cases from the sheriff either to the sheriff principal, and thence to the Inner House of the Court of Session, or directly from the sheriff to the Inner House. The question whether in a particular case an appeal to the Court of Session is appropriate requires careful consideration by a party's legal advisers. They should not appeal to the Court of Session unless they are prepared to go through with their appeal, and if they are in doubt as to whether they **18.91**

---

[3] *Cadbury Bros Ltd v. T. Mabon Ltd* (1961) 78 Sh.Ct.Rep. 55 (interlocutor not reported in 1962 S.L.T. (Sh. Ct.) 28).

[4] *McMahon v. Matheson* (1899) 1 F. 896.

[5] *Harkness v. Harkness*, 1962 S.L.T. (Sh. Ct.) 32.

[6] *Elliot v. Erikson*, 1960 S.L.T. (Sh. Ct.) 28.

[7] paras 12.24, 12.26.

[8] OCR, r. 12.2(3) and (4). "Sheriff" in the Rules includes "sheriff principal" unless the contrary appears: Interpretation Act 1978, ss. 5, 23, Sched. 1.

[9] para. 5.75.

[10] para. 17.32.

[11] para. 5.87.

have reasonable grounds on which to appeal, they should take the opinion of counsel with a view to avoiding the inconvenience and expense of an abandoned or unsuccessful appeal.[12] They should also take account of the principles on which appellate courts act.[13]

Competency

18.92 The competency of appeals to the Court of Session is primarily regulated by section 28 of the 1907 Act, which resembles section 27 in that it provides that an appeal is competent against final judgments, against certain specified classes of interlocutors (a more restricted list than that in section 27) and against interlocutors against which the sheriff principal or the sheriff grants leave to appeal. It will become clear that much of the discussion of the provisions of section 27 earlier in this chapter is applicable to the provisions of section 28. Unlike section 27, however, section 28 provides that an appeal is competent only if the judgment appealed against falls within one of these categories. On the other hand, nothing in section 27 or section 28 affects any right of appeal or exclusion of such right provided by any Act of Parliament in force for the time being.[14] Further, the Court of Session has power, in the exercise of its supereminent jurisdiction, to review by way of appeal, suspension[15] or reduction[16] the proceedings of inferior courts and tribunals, including the sheriff court, and may set aside any incompetent or irregular proceedings[17] or any purported exercise of jurisdiction which is beyond the powers of the court or tribunal,[18] and may regulate any failure by the court or tribunal to exercise jurisdiction.[19]

Section 28 of the 1907 Act

18.93 *Value*. Section 28 of the 1907 Act provides that an appeal to the Court of Session is competent against judgments in certain categories, subject to the provisions of the 1907 Act. The principal provision of the Act restricting a party's right of appeal in ordinary causes is section 7, as amended, which states the general rule that all causes not exceeding £1,500 in value exclusive of interest and expenses which are competent in the sheriff court must be brought and followed forth in the sheriff court only, and are not subject to review by the Court of Session except as otherwise provided by statute. This general rule has already been examined.[20]

18.94 *Final judgment*. An appeal to the Court of Session is competent, without leave, against a final judgment of a sheriff principal or sheriff.[21] The statutory definition of "final judgment" has been considered above.[22] In the Court of Session it is read as including an interlocutor disposing of the

---

[12] *McGuire v. Union Cold Storage Co. Ltd*, 1909 S.C. 384, *per* L.J.-C. Macdonald at 385.
[13] paras 18.100 to 18.117.
[14] 1907 Act, s. 28(2).
[15] para. 18.04.
[16] para. 18.05.
[17] *Lord Advocate v. Johnston*, 1983 S.L.T. 290.
[18] *Allen & Sons Billposting Ltd v. Edinburgh Corporation*, 1909 S.C. 70; *Moss' Empires v. Assessor for Glasgow*, 1917 S.C. (H.L.) 1, *per* Lord Kinnear at 6.
[19] *Dalgleish v. Leitch* (1889) 2 White 302; *Penny v. Scott* (1894) 22 R. 5; *Caledonian Ry v. Cochran's Trs* (1897) 24 R. 855.
[20] paras 2.27 to 2.34.
[21] 1907 Act, s. 28(1).
[22] paras 18.33 to 18.37.

competition between the parties in a process of competition.[23] If the question of liability for expenses has not been decided, the interlocutor is not a final one, but the appellant may go back to the sheriff court, obtain a finding as to expenses, and present a fresh appeal.[24]

Interlocutory judgments appealable without leave.[25] An appeal to the Court of Session is competent, without leave, against an interlocutor of the sheriff principal or sheriff which is an interlocutor (a) granting interim decree for payment of money other than a decree for expenses[26] or (b) sisting an action[27]; or (c) refusing a reponing note.[28] This list is less extensive than the list in section 27 of interlocutory judgments of the sheriff which are appealable without leave to the sheriff principal. **18.95**

Interlocutory judgments appealable with leave. Appeal to the Court of Session is competent against interlocutors against which the sheriff principal or sheriff, either *ex proprio motu* or on the motion of any party, grants leave to appeal.[29] The list in section 28 of interlocutors appealable without leave being more restricted than the list in section 27 of interlocutors of the sheriff which are appealable without leave to the sheriff principal, the following are among the interlocutors in respect of which leave is required for an appeal to the Court of Session: interlocutors granting or refusing interdict, interim or final; or making an order *ad factum praestandum*; or allowing or refusing or limiting the mode of proof.[30] Further examples of interlocutors appealable only with leave have already been given.[31] The time-limits and other procedural rules relative to an application for leave to appeal, and the principles on which leave to appeal is granted or refused, have also been examined.[32] As to these principles, it may be added that it is appropriate for the sheriff principal to grant leave where there is a difference between himself and the sheriff which goes to the root of the case.[33] **18.96**

Other rules. The lists of competent and incompetent appeals already given[34] apply to appeals to the Court of Session, and, as in the sheriff court, competency is *pars judicis*.[35] **18.97**

Procedure

The time-limits are the same as for appeals to the sheriff principal.[36] It was formerly thought that where a party has failed to prosecute timeously an appeal to the Court of Session, the court's dispensing power will only **18.98**

---

[23] *Glasgow Corporation v. General Accident Fire and Life Assurance Corporation Ltd*, 1914 S.C. 835. A process of competition is where one or more persons are claimants on the same fund: Bell, *Dictionary and Digest of the Law of Scotland* (7th ed., 1890), s.v. "competition".

[24] *Russell v. Allan* (1877) 5 R. 22; *Malcolm v. McIntyre* (1877) 5 R. 22.

[25] 1907 Act, s. 28(1).

[26] para. 18.39.

[27] para. 18.40.

[28] para. 18.43.

[29] 1907 Act, s. 28(1)(d).

[30] *Hamilton v. Hamilton*, 1948 S.L.T. (Notes) 8.

[31] para. 18.45.

[32] paras 18.50 to 18.54.

[33] *Duke of Argyll v. Muir*, 1910 S.C. 96, *per* L.P. Dunedin at 103.

[34] paras 18.12 to 18.29.

[35] para. 18.30.

[36] para. 18.55; rr. 31.1 and 31.2.

very rarely be employed.[37] However, in *Grier v. Wimpey Plant and Transport Ltd*[38] the view was expressed that the discretion to exercise the dispensing power was too narrowly construed in *Grieve v. Batchelor and Buckling*. An appeal to the Court of Session is marked by writing a note of appeal (a) on the interlocutor sheet or other written record containing the interlocutor appealed against, or (b) where the decision appealed against is not available or the proceedings appealed against are recorded in an official book, on a separate sheet lodged with the sheriff clerk in the following terms: "The pursuer [or defender as the case may be] appeals to the Court of Session."[39] The note of appeal must (a) be signed by the appellant or his solicitor, (b) bear the date on which it was signed, and (c) where the appellant is represented, specify the name and address of the solicitor or other agent who will be acting for him in the appeal.[40] The sheriff clerk must transmit the process of the cause to the Deputy Principal Clerk of Session within the period specified in rule 40.6 of the Rules of the Court of Session, namely four days. On transmitting the process the sheriff clerk must (a) send a written notice of the appeal to every party and (b) certify on the interlocutor sheet that he has done so.[41] Failure of the sheriff clerk to comply with the latter of these duties does not invalidate the appeal,[42] but the Court of Session may give such remedy for any disadvantage or inconvenience thereby occasioned as it thinks fit.[43] The effect of the appeal is the same as that of an appeal to the sheriff principal.[44] Before the Court of Session process in the appeal has been made up and lodged, the court will not entertain applications for interim orders which may be competently made in the sheriff court,[45] but it will intervene where an application is properly made to it to set aside incompetent proceedings as a matter of urgency.[46] The court, after hearing, may remit the case to the sheriff court for a report[47] or for further procedure[48]; or may, if necessary for the ends of justice, allow proof or additional proof to be taken before one of the judges of the Division[49]; or may, and usually does, dispose of the case without any such order. The details of the procedure in the Court of Session are beyond the scope of this book.[50]

Appeal to House of Lords

18.99 The procedure in an appeal to the House of Lords from a decision of the Inner House pronounced in a case on appeal from the sheriff court is also

---

[37] *Grieve v. Batchelor and Buckling*, 1961 S.C. 12.
[38] 1994 S.C.L.R. 454.
[39] OCR, r. 31.3(1).
[40] OCR, r. 31.3(2).
[41] OCR, r. 31.5(1)(b) and (2).
[42] OCR, r. 31.5(3).
[43] RCS, r. 40.6(3).
[44] paras 18.68 to 18.71.
[45] *Cunningham v. Cunningham*, 1965 S.C. 78; *Ellis v. MacDonald*, 1980 S.L.T. 11.
[46] *Macleay v. Macdonald*, 1928 S.C. 776 at 778, 783.
[47] *Whyte v. Whyte* (1895) 23 R. 320 (report as to accuracy of interlocutor).
[48] *e.g.* to pronounce interlocutor in prescribed form: *Campbell v. Caledanian Ry* (1852) 14 D. 441; *Mackay v. Mackenzie* (1894) 21 R. 894; *James Y. Keanie Ltd v. Maycrete Sales Ltd*, 1949 S.L.T. (Notes) 28. *Cf. Duke of Norfolk v. Wilson*, 1950 S.L.T. (Notes) 11.
[49] *Gairdner v. Macarthur*, 1915 S.C. 589 and *Pirie v. Leask*, 1964 S.C. 103 which followed Court of Session Act 1868, s. 72 (which was repealed by Court of Session Act 1988, s. 52 and Sched. 2).
[50] See RCS, Chap. 40; Maxwell, pp. 572–576.

beyond the scope of this book,[51] apart from the following rule which is applicable where proof has been taken in the sheriff court. The Court of Session, in reviewing the judgment proceeding on such proof, distinctly specify in their interlocutor the several facts material to the case which they find to be established by the proof, and express how far their judgment proceeds on the matter of fact so found, or on matter of law, and the several points of law which they mean to decide. The judgment of the court thus pronounced is subject to appeal to the House of Lords only in so far as it depends on or is affected by matter of law: it finally and conclusively fixes the facts specified in the interlocutor,[52] even if further proof has been led in the Court of Session.[53] The purpose of the rule is to prevent appeals to the House of Lords in cases decided after proof except where there is a genuine question of law.[54] The rule is subject to two qualifications. First, the House of Lords may go to the opinions of the judges of the Division to explain any ambiguity there may be in the findings; and secondly, if it appears that what purports to be a finding in law is really a finding in fact, it must be treated as a finding in fact, and vice versa.[55]

Principles upon which Appellate Courts act

Burden on appellant

On an appeal from the sheriff principal or the sheriff, the appellate court, whether it is the Inner House or the sheriff principal, regards the interlocutor complained of as a valid and correct judgment which must remain so until the appellant shows cause why it should be altered. Thus, where the respondent does not appear at the hearing to support the judgment, the court will not on that ground sustain the appeal, but will call on the appellant to show cause why the appeal should be sustained.[56] If the court is not satisfied that the court below was wrong, it will refuse the appeal. **18.100**

Rehearing

Before the Sheriff Courts (Scotland) Act 1876, the rule was that under an appeal no redress could be given, except from the particular interlocutor, or part of an interlocutor, against which it was directed, and that no party could benefit by an appeal except the appellant. Hence appeals, special and general, were in use, and cross-appeals were necessary. The 1876 Act, following the procedure adopted as regards appeals from inferior courts in the Court of Session Act 1868, introduced new rules "to the effect of enabling the sheriff [principal] to do complete justice without hindrance from the terms of any interlocutor in the cause, and without the necessity of any counter appeal."[57] Section 29 of the 1907 Act and rule 31.11 of the Ordinary Cause Rules repeat the substance of **18.101**

---

[51] See Maxwell, pp. 591–605.

[52] In the previous edition the authority given in the text was Court of Session Act 1825, s. 40. That provision was repealed by Court of Session Act 1988, s. 52 and Sched. 2.

[53] *Gairdner v. Macarthur*, 1916 S.C.(H.L.) 130.

[54] *Sutherland v. Glasgow Corporation*, 1951 S.C. (H.L.) 1, *per* Lord Normand at 8.

[55] *Sutherland, supra, per* Lord Reid at 10.

[56] *Alder v. Clark* (1880) 7 R. 1093; *Dunbar v. Macadam* (1884) 11 R. 652; *Aitken v. Robertson* (1877) 8 R. 434 (Registration Appeal Court).

[57] 1876 Act, s. 29 derived from the Court of Session Act 1868, s. 69. See Dove Wilson, pp. 318–319.

section 29 of the 1876 Act, and it remains the object of the current legislation to enable the appellate courts "to do complete justice". Hence an appeal is effectual to submit to review the whole of the interlocutors pronounced in the cause,[58] the appeal is available to and may be insisted in by all other parties,[59] and the appellate courts may allow both amendment of the record[60] and further proof.[61]

18.102 The system introduced in 1876 has been described as a system of appeal by a rehearing.[62] That convenient expression is somewhat misleading, because it does not mean that the appellate court literally "rehears" the case, with the parties starting afresh and the witnesses being heard of new. It means that the appellate court considers the pleadings, productions and other documents which were before the court below, including any notes of evidence, and any additional materials properly before the appellate court itself; hears the submissions of the parties, which may be on any matter relative to any of the interlocutors pronounced in the cause; and reaches its own decision, altering or recalling the interlocutor or interlocutors complained of if, on full consideration, it concludes that the court below was wrong. In appeals against decisions in certain categories, however, there are constraints upon the appellate court's power to interfere with the judgment of the inferior court. Such appeals are considered in the following paragraphs.

Questions of fact or credibility

18.103 Where, in an appeal taken against an interlocutor pronounced by a sheriff or other judge of first instance after proof, the appellate court is invited to review a decision by the judge on an issue of fact, it does so not on the basis that the issue is a "jury point" and that the judge's decision is to be tested in the same way as a jury's verdict, by inquiring whether there was evidence to support it, but on the basis that the reasons which he has stated for his decision require to be scrutinised before the appellant can satisfy the court that the judge was wrong.[63] Where, however, the credibility or reliability of one or more witnesses is in dispute, the appellate court attaches much weight to the conclusion or inference made by the judge with regard to the weight or balance of the evidence of the witnesses, whom he has had the advantage of seeing and hearing, and asks itself whether, not having itself seen and heard the witnesses, it is in a position to come to a clear conclusion that the judge was plainly wrong; and if it cannot be so satisfied, it will not disturb his judgment.[64] That general approach has been developed in the following particular rules which are applicable to the scope of review by the appellate court.

18.104 (1) Where a question of fact has been tried by the judge, and there is no question of misdirection of himself by the judge,[65] an appellate court

---

[58] para. 18.70.

[59] para. 18.71.

[60] RCS, r. 40.19; paras 10.23 to 10.28.

[61] paras 18.81, 18.82 (sheriff principal), 18.98 (Court of Session).

[62] Dove Wilson, p. 319.

[63] *Performing Rights Society v. Rangers F.C. Supporters' Club, Greenock*, 1974 S.C. 49.

[64] *Clarke v. Edinburgh and District Tramways Co.*, 1919 S.C. (H.L.) 35, *per* Lord Shaw of Dunfermline at 37.

[65] If the judge has misdirected himself in law, and by so doing has vitiated his judgment, the appellate court is entitled to review the case by applying the proper law to the established facts: *Forbes v. Forbes*, 1965 S.L.T. 109, per Lord Wheatley at 121.

which is disposed to come to a different conclusion on the printed evidence should not do so unless it is satisfied that any advantage enjoyed by the judge by reason of having seen and heard the witnesses could not be sufficient to explain or justify the judge's conclusion.[66] Thus, where the conclusion reached by the judge is one which was open to him in all the proved relevant circumstances, the appellate court is not entitled to reach a different conclusion by considering some of the relevant circumstances and giving its own emphasis to those which it selects. It should not disturb the judge's conclusion unless it is satisfied that it was one he was not entitled to reach in all the relevant proved circumstances of the case derived from the evidence which he has heard.[67] If, however, the judge's findings in fact would necessarily lead to results which are demonstrably impossible or so improbable that they cannot reasonably be accepted, the appellate court will be justified in reaching the conclusion that the findings are open to challenge.[68]

(2) The appellate court may take the view that, without having seen or heard the witnesses, it is not in a position to come to any satisfactory conclusion on the printed evidence.[69] **18.105**

(3) The appellate court, either because the reasons given by the judge are not satisfactory, or because it unmistakably so appears from the evidence, may be satisfied that he has not taken proper advantage of his having seen and heard the witnesses, and the matter will then become at large for the appellate court.[70] Thus the appellate court may reverse his judgment where he has ignored an important body of evidence without adversely commenting on the credibility of the witnesses[71]; or where it is demonstrated that his assessment of a witness's credibility is plainly wrong, for example where it is inconsistent with other acceptable evidence,[72] or is inconsistent with itself or contains an inherent defect; or where he has misapprehended the meaning or the bearing of a piece of evidence, or the relation of one piece of evidence to another.[73] **18.106**

(4) Where the judge's assessment of the credibility of a witness bears to have been arrived at as a result of the advantage of seeing and hearing the witness, as, for example, where he relies to any extent upon his assessment of the demeanour of the witness or of the manner in which he has given his evidence, a finding based on his assessment of credibility will in most cases be inviolate in an appellate court. But where the finding does not bear to have turned upon the judge's observation or impression of the witness, the appellate court is free to examine for itself his stated reasons for accepting **18.107**

---

[66] *Thomas v. Thomas*, 1947 S.C. (H.L.) 45, *per* Lord Thankerton at 54, Lord Simonds at 60; see also Viscount Simon L.C. at 47–48, Lord Macmillan at 59, Lord du Parcq at 62, 63; *Forbes v. Forbes*, 1965 S.L.T. 109, *per* Lord Wheatley at 120, 121.

[67] *Millars of Falkirk v. Turpie*, 1976 S.L.T. (Notes) 66.

[68] *Islip Pedigree Breeding Centre v. Abercromby*, 1959 S.L.T. 161, *per* Lord Tucker at 175, Lord Keith of Avonholm at 180, Lord Birkett at 181.

[69] *Thomas, per* Lord Thankerton, *supra*; *Forbes, supra*.

[70] *ibid.*

[71] *Jordan v. Court Line Ltd*, 1947 S.C. 29; *Morrison v. J. Kelly and Sons Ltd*, 1970 S.C. 65; *McCusker v. Saveheat Cavity Wall Insulation Ltd*, 1987 S.L.T. 24.

[72] *Morrison, supra, per* Lord Guthrie at 81–82.

[73] *Dunn v. Dunn's Trs*, 1930 S.C. 131, *per* L.P. Clyde at 146; *Duncan v. Wilson*, 1940 S.C. 221, *per* Lord Carmont at 228; *Morrison, supra, per* Lord Cameron at 90–91; *Shevchuk v. National Coal Board*, 1982 S.C. 557. See, however, the comment on *Dunn* in *Thomas, supra, per* Lord Thankerton at 56.

or rejecting the witness's evidence and, if they are unsound or unsatisfactory, to form its own conclusion.[74] Thus, where it is demonstrated that the judge's assessment of the witnesses depends not on anything he saw of them in the witness-box but on speculation or assumptions for which there was no foundation in the evidence, any advantage he enjoyed by reason of having seen and heard the witnesses becomes irrelevant and the matter is at large for the appellate court.[75]

18.108 (5) The foregoing rules are applicable to cases where the credibility or reliability of one or more of the witnesses has been in dispute, and where a decision on these matters has led the judge of first instance to come to his decision on the case as a whole. But in cases where there is no question of the credibility or reliability of any witnesses, and in cases where the point in dispute is the proper inference to be drawn from proved facts, an appellate court is generally in as good a position to evaluate the evidence as the judge, and ought not to shrink from that task, though it ought to give weight to his opinion.[76]

18.109 (6) If the evidence has not been recorded,[77] the judge's findings in fact are not open to review: they are binding on the appellate court, which cannot make different, or further, findings in fact.[78]

Exercise of judicial discretion

18.110 *Function of appellate court.* Where an appeal is taken against a decision involving the exercise of judicial discretion, it is not the function of the appellate court, in the first instance, to interfere with the judge's exercise of his discretion merely upon the ground that the appellate court would have exercised the discretion differently, and to proceed to exercise an independent discretion of its own. The appellate court's function is initially one of appeal only. It may set aside the judge's exercise of his discretion only for certain reasons, which are about to be discussed, and it is only if and after it has reached the conclusion that the judge's exercise of his discretion must be set aside for one or other of those reasons that the appellate court becomes entitled to exercise an independent discretion of its own. The approach of an appellate court to discretionary decisions has been briefly explained in various ways in a number of Scottish decisions,[79] but the most authoritative modern exposition is that by Lord Fraser of Tullybelton in *G v. G (Minors: Custody Appeal)*,[80] which was adopted by the First Division in *Britton v. Central Regional Council*.[81]

---

[74] *Angus v. Glasgow Corporation*, 1977 S.L.T. 206, *per* L.P. Emslie at 213.

[75] *Jordan v. Jordan*, 1983 S.L.T. 539 at 541.

[76] *Benmax v. Austin Motor Co. Ltd* [1955] A.C. 370, *per* Lord Reed at 375, 376; *Islip Pedigree Breeding Centre*, *supra* at 174, 175; *Travnor v. Henderson*, 1972 S.L.T. (Sh. Ct.) 73; *Whitehouse v. Jordan* [1981] 1 W.L.R. 246, *per* Lord Fraser of Tullybelton at 263.

[77] para. 16.30.

[78] *Allardut v. Wallace*, 1957 S.L.T. 225; *McGibbon v. Sanchez*, 1998 G.W.D. 15.736.

[79] *e.g. New Mining and Exploring Syndicate Ltd v. Chalmers & Hunter*, 1909 S.C. 1390 at 1392; *Ross & Coulter v. Inland Revenue*, 1948 S.C. (H.L.) 1 at 16, 29, 35–38; *Woods v. Minister of Pensions*, 1952 S.C. 529 at 533; *Thomson v. Glasgow Corporation*, 1962 S.C. (H.L.) 36 at 66; *Gray v. Gray*, 1968 S.C. 185 at 193–197; *Scottish and Universal Newspapers Ltd v. Smith*, 1982 S.L.T 160 at 163; *Skiponian Ltd v. Barratt Developments (Scotland) Ltd*, 1983 S.L.T. 313 at 314; *Forsyth v. A. F. Stoddart & Co.*, 1985 S.L.T. 51 at 53–56, 57; *Brown v. Brown*, 1985 S.L.T 376 at 379; *Berry, Petitioner*, 1985 S.C.C.R. 106 at 113.

[80] [1985] 1 W.L.R. 647 at 651–653. See also *Hadmor Productions Ltd v. Hamilton* [1983] 1 A.C. 191; *Brown v. Hamilton D.C.*, 1983 S.C. (H.L.) 1, *per* Lord Fraser of Tullybelton at 44.

[81] 1986 S.L.T. 207.

Rationale and general rules. The underlying rationale of the appellate court's restrictive approach to the review of discretionary decisions is that it is of the essence of a judicial discretion that on the same material different minds may reach widely different decisions, any one of which may reasonably be thought to be the best, and any one of which, therefore, a judge may make without being held to be wrong.[82] The appellate court may intervene if it is satisfied that the judge did not exercise his discretion at all[83]; or that in exercising it he misdirected himself in law[84]; or misunderstood or misused the evidence or the material facts before him[85]; or took into account an irrelevant consideration[86]; or failed to take into account some relevant consideration[87]; or if his conclusion is such that, though no erroneous assumption of law or fact can be identified, he must have exercised his discretion wrongly. Expressions which have been judicially employed to describe such a conclusion include: "completely"[88] or "plainly"[89] wrong; "wholly unwarranted"[90]; "manifestly inequitable"[91]; "unreasonable"[92]; and "unjudicial".[93] **18.111**

The balancing exercise. The appellate court may also intervene where, although the judge has not erred in law, misapprehended or misused the facts, considered any irrelevant matter, or left out of account any relevant matter, the court is satisfied that his conclusion is vitiated by an error in weighing the relevant considerations, by giving too little or too much weight to one or more of them. The weighing of the relevant considerations has been called "the balancing exercise". If the court is satisfied that there has been an error in the balancing exercise, or that the judge's conclusion is so plainly wrong that there must have been such an error, the court may interfere. The court may be unable to say that there has been any such error where the judge's conclusion is dependent on or justified by his advantage in his having seen and heard witnesses. But the importance of seeing and hearing witnesses may vary very greatly according to the circumstances of individual cases.[94] **18.112**

Additional materials: change of circumstances. It is thought that the appellate court may set aside the judge's exercise of his discretion where further evidence or additional material has become available which was not before the judge, or where there has been a change of circumstances since the date of his judgment. The appellate court appears to have a general discretionary power to have regard to such matters if justice **18.113**

---

[82] *Bellenden (formerly Satterthwaite) v. Bellenden* [1948] 1 All E.R. 343, *per* Asquith L.J. at 345, *cit. C v. G* [1985] 1 W.L.R. 647 at 651–652.
[83] *Orr Pollock & Co. (Printers) Ltd v. Mulholland,* 1983 S.L.T. 558.
[84] *Woods, Gray, Forsyth, supra.*
[85] *Woods, Skiponian Ltd, supra.*
[86] *Thomson, Gray, Berry, supra.*
[87] *ibid.*
[88] *New Mining and Exploring Syndicate Ltd, supra.*
[89] *Britton, supra.*
[90] *Brown, supra.*
[91] *Gray, supra, per* Lord Guthrie at 193.
[92] *Gray, Scottish and Universal Newspapers Ltd, Skiponian Ltd, Berry, supra.*
[93] *Thomson, supra.*
[94] *Re F (A Minor) (Wardship: Appeal)* [1976] Fam. 238, *per* Bridge L.J. at 266, cit. *G v. G, supra* at 653; and see para. 18.107.

requires it.[95] The court may allow amendment[96] or further proof[97] relative to such matters; in very exceptional circumstances it may allow the introduction of material designed to lead to the alteration of the judge's award in an action of damages for personal injuries[98]; and in an action relating to the residence of, or contact with, a child it may consider material changes in circumstances which have taken place since the decision by the court below.[99] In an application to free a child for adoption, the sheriff principal remitted the cause to the sheriff to consider up-to-date medical reports on the natural mother and to report the matter back to the sheriff principal.[1]

18.114 *Judgment under appeal.* It would be idle, even if it were possible, to list all the decisions of a sheriff involving the exercise of a judicial discretion which may be the subject of appeal. Among the more common examples are decisions relative to procedural matters, including the extension of statutory periods of limitation,[2] the amendment of pleadings,[3] and interim protective and remedial procedures such as interim interdict[4]; decisions in family proceedings as to aliment, custody,[5] periodical allowance[6] and interim orders under the Matrimonial Proceedings (Family Protection) (Scotland) Act 1981[7]; decisions on many other matters where a discretion is conferred by statute[8]; and awards of damages and of expenses. Decisions as to apportionment of liability, and awards of damages or expenses, to which special rules apply, are separately considered below.[9] In all cases where an appeal is or may be taken against a decision involving the exercise of a judicial discretion it is desirable that the sheriff should set out in his note the legal principles or statutory rules upon which he has proceeded; the facts, documents or evidence before him; the factors which he considered to be relevant to his decision; and the weight which he gave to each factor. An omission from the note of any matter canvassed before him may found an argument that he has wrongly ignored it or has misunderstood its importance to such an extent that the exercise of his discretion has led to a wrong result.

Apportionment of liability

18.115 An appellate court should not alter the proportions of liability fixed by the judge who tried the case save in exceptional circumstances[10] or, as it

---

95 *Engineers' and Managers' Association v. Advisory, Conciliation and Arbitration Service* [1980] 1 W.L.R. 302, *per* Lord Scarman at 320–321.

96 para. 10.24.

97 paras 10.25, 18.81, 18.82.

98 *Rieley v. Kingslaw Riding School*, 1975 S.C. 28 at 40–41; *Dalgleish v. Glasgow Corporation*, 1976 S.C. 32.

99 *Zagrodnik v. Zagrodnik*, 1952 S.C. 258; *G v. G, supra*, at 654.

1 *R v. Lothian R.C.*, 1987 S.C.L.R. 362.

2 *Forsyth v. A. F. Stoddart & Co. Ltd*, 1985 S.L.T. 51; *McCluskey v. Sir Robert McAlpine & Sons Ltd*, 1994 S.C.L.R. 650; *Clark v. McLean*, 1994 S.C.L.R. 564.

3 *Thomson v. Glasgow Corporation*, 1962 S.C. (H.L.) 36; *Rutherford v. Virtue*, 1993 S.C.L.R. 886.

4 *Scottish and Universal Newspapers Ltd v. Smith*, 1982 S.L.T. 160.

5 *Britton v. Central R.C.*, 1986 S.L.T. 207; *B v. L*, 1994 S.C.L.R. 835 (I.H.); 1996 S.C.L.R. 856 (H.L.).

6 *Gray v. Gray*, 1968 S.C. 185.

7 *McCafferty v. McCafferty*, 1986 S.L.T. 651.

8 *Woods v. Minister of Pensions*, 1952 S.C. 529.

9 paras 18.115 to 18.117.

10 *Boy Andrew (Owners) v. St Rognvald (Owners)*, 1947 S.C. (H.L.) 70, *per* Viscount Simon at 78.

has been put, "if it appears that he has manifestly and to a substantial degree gone wrong".[11]

Assessment of damages

Although a judge or sheriff exercises a discretion in awarding damages, he is expected to explain the grounds upon which he has proceeded in making an award. An appellate court will interfere with his award if he has made an error in law or applied a wrong principle.[12] In a personal injuries case, where patrimonial loss cannot be calculated with near mathematical certainty, the appellate court will interfere with his award only where his assessment has been reached through the use of wrong facts or the application of wrong principles, or is manifestly unfair.[13] In reviewing an award of *solatium* for pain and suffering, the appellate court gives full weight to the privileged position of the judge who presided at the proof, whose decision may have been influenced by that advantage and by the impressions he formed, and will not interfere with his discretion in the assessment of *solatium* unless the sum awarded is out of all proportion to what the court thinks should have been awarded.[14] The court has regard to the general run of awards and to the upper and lower limits within which, in the court's view, the award should have been made on the facts of the particular case.[15] Similarly, an award of damages for loss of society made under section 1(4) of the Damages (Scotland) Act 1976 will not be set aside unless it is wholly unreasonable.[16] **18.116**

Award of expenses

An appeal may be taken on a question of expenses only,[17] and a respondent may avail himself of an appeal in order to raise a question of expenses.[18] In practice, however, appeals solely on questions of expenses are severely discouraged, and are not entertained unless either there has been an obvious miscarriage of justice,[19] or the expenses have become a great deal more valuable than the merits,[20] or a question of principle is involved.[21] The appellate court will not alter the decision of the **18.117**

---

[11] *Beattie v. Halliday*, Feb. 4, 1982, unreported, *per* L.J.-C. Wheatley, cit. *McCusker v. Saveheat Cavity Wall Insulation Ltd*, 1987 S.L.T. 24.

[12] *Purdie v. William Allan & Sons*, 1949 S.C. 477.

[13] *Blair v. F. J. C. Lilley (Marine) Ltd*, 1981 S.L.T. 90.

[14] *Purdie, supra*; *Butler v. Adam Lynn Ltd*, 1965 S.C. 137, *per* Lord Guthrie at 142. See also *Inglis v. LMS Ry*, 1941 S.C. 551 at 560; *Bowers v. Strathclyde R.C.*, 1981 S.L.T. 122.

[15] *Barker v. Murdoch*, 1979 S.L.T. 145 at 146–147.

[16] *Donald v. Strathclyde PTE*, 1986 S.L.T. 625; *cf. Inglis, supra.*

[17] *Fleming v. North of Scotland Banking Co.* (1881) 9 R. 11, 659; *Bouman's Trs v. Scott* (1901) 3 F. 450; *Barrie v. Caledonian Ry* (1902) 5 F. 30.

[18] *Bonner's Tr. v. Bonner* (1902) 4 F. 429.

[19] *e.g. Fraser & Son Ltd v. Bute Gift Co. Ltd* (1958) 74 Sh.Ct.Rep. 154; *D. Macdonald & Bros Ltd v. Cosmos Decorators Ltd*, 1969 S.L.T. (Sh. Ct.) 9; *Kennedy v. Kennedy*, 1991 S.C.L.R. 443; 1992 S.L.T. (Sh. Ct.) 39.

[20] *Caldwell v. Dykes* (1906) 8 F. 839; *Wyllie v. Fisher*, 1907 S.C. 686; *Garrioch v. Glass*, 1911 S.C. 453; *Adair v. J. C. Docherty & Sons*, 1953 S.L.T. (Sh. Ct.) 58; *Watt & Co. Ltd v. McEwan* (1954) 70 Sh.Ct.Rep. 326; *Charles Rogers & Sons v. G. & H. Mullen*, 1957 S.L.T. 23; *Mason v. Foster Wheeler Power Products Ltd*, 1984 S.L.T. (Sh. Ct.) 5.

[21] *Aird v. School Board of Tarbert*, 1907 S.C. 22; *Jack v. Black*, 1911 S.C. 691; *Brooks & Bohm Ltd v. Kitchencraft Co.*, 1994 S.L.T. 191; *McNeil v. National Coal Board*, 1966 S.C. 72; *Lep Industrial Holdings Ltd v. Adsil Products Ltd*, Sh. Pr. Mowat, Ayr Sh. Ct, Oct. 31, 1991, unreported; *Peacock v. Sutton*, 1998 G.W.D. 15-766.

judge below on a point which was not argued before him.[22] It has been held[23] that it is not competent to appeal against a decision regarding modification[24] of expenses decerned for against a legally aided party; but the soundness of that decision has been doubted.[25]

---

[22] *Aird, supra.*
[23] *Todd v. Todd*, 1966 S.L.T. 50.
[24] Under what is now s. 18(2) of the Legal Aid (Scotland) Act 1986.
[25] *Orttewell v. Gilchrist*, 1998 S.L.T. (Sh. Ct.) 63.

CHAPTER 19

EXPENSES

Vexation, delay and expense, said Jeremy Bentham, are "the burthens inseparably attendant on judicial procedure".[1] It is an important part of the duties of courts and practitioners to avoid vexation, delay and expense as far as possible, but each is to some degree inevitable. As to expense, a party by resorting to litigation requires the performance of a service, which must by some means be paid for. "Expenses" are the charges exigible from a party to a process, as court fees, fees to counsel and solicitors, and other liabilities incurred in the prosecution or defence of the action.[2] Court fees are regulated by statutory instrument.[3] A party may be liable not only for his own expenses but also, by virtue of an award by the court, for certain of the expenses of his opponent. Such liabilities may be avoided or mitigated where the party holds a legal aid certificate. Otherwise, however, a party's legal adviser must always keep in view, as vitally important considerations when a litigation is contemplated or while it is being conducted, the probable incidence of liability for expenses for each step of procedure, and their probable amount. Usually each of these factors is difficult to predict. The expenses of incidental steps of procedure may sometimes be found due as soon as they are taken, but in general questions of the liability for and the amount of the expenses cannot be determined until the conclusion of the case, when the sheriff makes a finding as to expenses and the expenses found due are taxed and decerned for. Since expenses are charged for by each step taken, they increase as the litigation progresses, and do so considerably at the stage of preparation for proof and with each day of the proof. The expenses thus often become part of what is at stake in the case, and sometimes they exceed the sum sued for or awarded. **19.01**

A full consideration of the subjects of expenses and legal aid is beyond the scope of this book. Each is the subject of a separate treatise, to which reference should be made.[4] This chapter summarises the general rules as to the awarding and taxation of expenses, and certain rules relative to solicitors, which are applicable in ordinary actions in which no party is legally aided. Special rules as to liability for expenses relative to reponing, amendment, abandonment, settlement, the instruction of counsel and other incidental steps of procedure; interim measures such as caution for expenses, interim awards of expenses and payment of prior expenses as a condition precedent; liability for expenses in particular actions, and the liability of particular parties regarding expenses, are noted in other chapters dealing with such matters. **19.02**

---

1 Bentham, *Works* (ed. Bowring), Vol. ii, p. 19.

2 Bell's *Dictionary*, *s.v.* "Expenses". "Costs" is an English expression.

3 At the time of writing the relevant order is the Sheriff Court Fees Order 1997 (S.I. 1997 No. 687).

4 Maclaren, *Expenses*; Hastings, *Expenses*; see also *Encyclopaedia*, vi, *s.v.* "Expenses"; *Stair Memorial Encyclopaedia*, paras 1187–1202; Stoddart and Neilson, *Legal Aid.*

I. The Award of Expenses

Discretion of the court

19.03 In an ordinary action the court has an inherent discretionary common law power, which it may exercise in every case that comes before it unless the power is expressly taken away or qualified by statute, to determine whether to make an award of expenses and, if making an award, to determine by whom, on what basis and to what extent expenses are to be paid.[5] Thus any of the parties to an ordinary action may be found to be entitled or liable to any extent in expenses to all or any of the other parties. Since the power to award expenses is inherent in the court,[6] the court may award expenses in a defended action even where they are not craved.[7] Where an action was settled on the eve of the proof by joint minute which contained no reference to expenses, the pursuer was held entitled to the whole expenses of the cause as taxed.[8] It has been doubted whether expenses may be awarded in an undefended action in which they have not been craved.[9] The question appears never to have been decided. It is submitted that expenses may be awarded in such a case, upon the general principle that the defender has put the pursuer to expense in vindicating his rights.[10] Such a course would seem to be justified by the consideration that expenses are always a mere accident of process,[11] and by the authorities vouching the general rule stated at the beginning of this paragraph. Since expenses are in the discretion of the court, appeals on questions of expenses alone are severely discouraged.[12]

Procedure

19.04 Expenses allowed in any cause, whether in absence or *in foro*, unless modified at a fixed amount, must be taxed before decree is granted for payment of them.[13] The court therefore normally deals with the question of liability for expenses in two stages. There is first an interlocutor making a finding of liability for expenses,[14] allowing an account thereof to be given in and remitting the same, when lodged, to the auditor of court to tax and to report; and secondly, after taxation and the disposal of any

---

[5] Maclaren, *Expenses*, p. 3; *Brownlie v. Tennant* (1855) 17 D. 422 at 425; *Ledgerwood v. McKenna* (1868) 7 M. 261; *Rooney v. Cormack* (1895) 23 R. 11; *Thomson v. Edinburgh and District Tramways Co. Ltd* (1901) 3 F. 355.

[6] *Heggie & Co. v. Stark and Selkrig* (1826) 4 S. 510 (N.E. 518); *Ledgerwood, supra*; *Mitchell v. Baird* (1902) 4 F. 809; *Pollich v. Heatley*, 1910 S.C. 469 at 482; *McQuater v. Fergusson*, 1911 S.C. 640 at 646.

[7] *Torrance v. Craufuird* (1822) 1 S. 301 (N.E. 280); *Heggie & Co., supra*; *Scott v. Wilson* (1829) 7 S. 566; *Western Bank v. Buchanan* (1865) 4 M. 97, *per* Lord Deas at 99; *Rooney, supra* (one defender liable in expenses to another: see also *Thomson, supra*); *Cambuslang West Church Committee v. Bryce* (1897) 25 R. 322 (pursuers liable to disclaiming pursuers: see also *Edington v. Dunbar Steam Laundry Co.* (1903) 11 S.L.T. 117); *Warrand v. Watson*, 1907 S.C. 432.

[8] *McWilliam v. McWilliam*, 1990 S.C.L.R. 373. This case, which was decided by a sheriff at first instance, was rather unusual. It is suggested that it should not be regarded as laying down a general principle.

[9] *Heggie & Co., supra, per* Lord Glenlee at 511, 519; Wallace, p. 114; Dobie, p. 310.

[10] para. 19.07.

[11] *Heggie & Co., supra, per* Lord Robertson at 511, 519; *Young v. Nith Commissioners* (1880) 7 R. 891, *per* Lord Young at 897, 898.

[12] para. 18.117.

[13] OCR, r. 32.1.

[14] The usual form is: "Finds the [pursuer or defender] liable to the [defender or pursuer] in expenses" (Lees, *Interlocutors*, pp. 29, 67).

objections to the auditor's report, an interlocutor decerning for payment of the taxed amount of the expenses. Where, however, the first interlocutor both makes a finding of liability for expenses and modifies them to a specific sum,[15] it is appropriate to decern for payment of that sum of expenses in that interlocutor. It is incompetent to decern for payment of expenses once the action has ceased to be in dependence.[16]

While expenses need not be craved in the pleadings, a party seeking an award of expenses must move for it at the appropriate time and in appropriate terms. When a party moves the sheriff to pronounce a final interlocutor, that is, an interlocutor which by itself or taken along with previous interlocutors, will dispose of the subject-matter of the cause,[17] he should also move for expenses, or move that the question of expenses be reserved. If that is done, the sheriff in his final interlocutor will expressly award or reserve expenses, or appoint the parties to be heard thereon. If he takes either of the two latter courses, he may competently deal with expenses thereafter. If, however, the interlocutor is silent on the question of expenses, it will generally be interpreted as a refusal to award any,[18] and the sheriff appears to have no power to make an award subsequently,[19] unless perhaps his omission to deal with them has been an error on his part which may be corrected either in terms of rule 12.2(2)[20] or of consent.[21] Since expenses are merely incidental to a legal process,[22] a separate action for the recovery of the expenses of process is incompetent[23] except in the case of a *dominus litis*.[24] **19.05**

After a proof or debate the sheriff may be asked to reserve the question of expenses although this practice has recently met with disapproval.[25] If the question of expenses *is* reserved, in the subsequent interlocutor embodying his judgment the sheriff normally appoints a hearing on expenses, at which the parties may make motions as to expenses.[26] Motions as to the sanctioning of the employment of counsel in a debate or proof and as to charges relating to skilled witnesses or witnesses not called in the proof are usually made at the end of the debate or at the hearing on evidence[27]; and where the pursuer has failed to beat a tender, any question as to the date **19.06**

---

[15] On modification, see paras 19.09, 19.10.

[16] *Macgillivray v. Mackintosh* (1891) 19 R. 103.

[17] 1907 Act, s. 3(h).

[18] *Wilson's Trs v. Wilson's Factor* (1869) 7 M. 457.

[19] *Dobbie v. Duncanson* (1872) 10 M. 810; *Fraser v. Fraser* (1903) 11 S.L.T. 70; *Jack v. King* (1932) 48 Sh.Ct.Rep. 242; *Campbell v. Campbell*, 1934 S.L.T. 45.

[20] Dove Wilson, p. 184. On OCR, r. 12.2(2), see para. 5.87.

[21] paras 5.88 to 5.90.

[22] *Heggie & Co. v. Stark and Selkrig* (1826) 4 S. 510 (N.E. 518), *per* Lord Robertson at 511, 519; *Young v. Nith Commissioners* (1880) 7 R. 891, *per* Lord Young at 897, 898.

[23] *Young, supra*; *Wood v. Wood's Trs* (1904) 6 F. 640; *Cullen's Exrs v. Kilmarnock Theatre Co.*, 1913 1 S.L.T. 290; 1914 2 S.L.T. 334.

[24] *Kerr v. Employers' Liability Assurance Corp. Ltd* (1899) 2 F. 17; *Harvey v. Glasgow Corporation*, 1915 S.C. 600.

[25] Following the decision in *Dingley v. Chief Constable, Strathclyde Police*, 1997 S.C.L.R. 376 and an amendment to the Rules of Court (A.S. (Rules of the Court of Session Amendment No. 8) (Early Disposal of Reclaiming Motions and Appeals) 1997 (S.I. 1997 No. 2692)) sheriffs principal have requested sheriffs, wherever possible, to ask agents or counsel to address them on expenses on any occasion where the interlocutor following the speech in question will be a final judgment provided that it also deals with the question of liability for expenses (see Sheriff Courts (Scotland) Act 1907, ss. 27 and 28, and the definition of "final judgment" in s. 3(h)).

[26] But see *A.F. Drysdale Ltd v. Menzies*, 1998 G.W.D. 32–1667.

[27] paras 13.23 (debate), 16.03 (proof).

from which expenses should run should be raised at the hearing on expenses and before the remit to the auditor takes place.[28] A party seeking a joint and several decree for expenses should move for it at the time he asks for expenses.[29] A party seeking to avoid liability for expenses should likewise state his contentions at the time when the motion for expenses is heard by the sheriff.[30] It is good practice to make any other special application with regard to expenses at the time when the motion for expenses is made, for that is the time at which the sheriff may fairly be expected to be best acquainted with the nature of the case and the course of proceedings which have taken place.[31] Motions for such matters as taxation on the scale not normally applicable,[32] or the sanctioning of the employment of counsel,[33] have however been granted even after taxation of expenses awarded *simpliciter*. Where in an appeal a party wishes the sheriff principal to affirm a judgment of the sheriff awarding expenses and to award the expenses of the appeal, he should expressly so move; and the sheriff principal, if minded to affirm the sheriff and to award the expenses of the appeal, should expressly award them in his interlocutor.[34]

II. General Rules in Awarding Expenses

General rule

19.07 "An award of expenses according to our law is a matter for the exercise in each case of judicial discretion, designed to achieve substantial justice, and very rarely disturbed on appeal. I gravely doubt whether all the conditions upon which that discretion should be exercised have ever been, or ever will be, successfully imprisoned within the framework of rigid and unalterable rules, and I do not think that it would be desirable that they should be. In Maclaren on Expenses the principle is laid down upon the authority of a number of cases that 'if any party is put to expense in vindicating his rights he is entitled to recover it from the person by whom it was created, unless there is something in his own conduct that gives him the character of an improper litigant in insisting on things which his title does not warrant'."[35]

"The principle upon which the court proceeds in awarding expenses is that the cost of litigation should fall on him who has caused it. The general rule for applying this principle is that costs follow the event, the ratio being that the rights of parties are to be taken to have been all along such as the ultimate decree declares them to be, and that

---

[28] para. 14.53.

[29] *Warrand v. Watson*, 1907 S.C. 432.

[30] *Thomson v. Simons & Co. Ltd* (1943) 60 Sh.Ct.Rep. 106.

[31] *Duncan v. Salmond* (1874) 1 R. 839; *Reid v. North Isles District Committee of Orkney C.C.*, 1912 S.C. 627.

[32] *Merry & Cuninghame v. District Committee of Middle Ward of Lanarkshire*, 1926 S.L.T. (Sh. Ct.) 107; *Murphy v. Muir*, 1927 S.L.T. (Sh. Ct.) 55. *Cf. Grant v. Giffnock Collieries Ltd* (1928) 44 Sh.Ct.Rep. 211; and the different practice of the Court of Session: *Walker v. McNeil*, 1981 S.L.T. (Notes) 21 which has been followed in the sheriff court in *Manders v. Lacon Floors*, 1993 S.C.L.R. 311.

[33] para. 12.24. See also *Colbeck Bros Ltd v. Wallace Todd & Co.* (1923) 39 Sh.Ct.Rep. 315 (special debate fee).

[34] *Macdonald v. McEachan* (1880) 7 R. 574.

[35] *Howitt v. Alexander & Sons*, 1948 S.C. 154, *per* L.P. Cooper at 157, citing Maclaren, *Expenses*, p. 21.

whosoever has resisted the vindication of those rights whether by action or by defence, is prima facie to blame. In some cases, however, the application of the general rule would not carry out the principle, and the court has always, on cause shewn, considered whether the conduct of the successful party, either during the litigation, or in the matters giving rise to the litigation, has not either caused or contributed to bring about the law suit."[36]

In straightforward and uncomplicated cases, accordingly, the successful party is usually entitled to his full expenses as taxed.[37] The rule is often expressed in the phrases "Expenses follow success" or "Expenses follow the result".

Exceptions

There are, however, a number of exceptions to that general rule. The successful party may have his expenses modified or refused; or he may be found liable in expenses. If the sheriff does not follow the usual course of awarding expenses to the successful party, he must have materials upon which he can in the exercise of his discretion judicially pronounce that, in his opinion, the usual rule should not be followed: there must be some ground capable of statement which has rendered a departure from the ordinary rule desirable in the particular case.[38] The exceptions to the rule are noted in the following paragraphs. **19.08**

Modification

The sheriff has a wide and quite general[39] discretionary power to direct that expenses shall be subject to modification,[40] that is, subject to assessment or restriction[41] in such a way that the precise sum to be paid may be exactly ascertained.[42] He may direct modification, in the sense of assessment, in order to save the further expense of remitting the successful party's account to taxation. Modification for that purpose is, however, seldom directed unless of consent: in the absence of consent it is appropriate only where there has been little expenditure, and the sheriff knows what it has been and is in a position to judge as to what part of it should be allowed.[43] He may then modify the successful party's expenses to a fixed sum.[44] Modification or assessment may also be appropriate where a party or his solicitor fails to attend or is not prepared to proceed with any diet of proof, debate, appeal or meeting ordered by the sheriff. In that situation **19.09**

---

36 *Shepherd v. Elliot* (1896) 23 R. 695, *per* L.P. Robertson at 696.

37 *Bond v. British Railways Board*, 1972 S.L.T. (Notes) 47, *per* Lord Wheatley at 47.

38 *Rogers & Son v. Mullen*, 1957 S.L.T. 23, *per* Lord Blades at 25.

39 *Smith v. British Rail Engineering Ltd*, 1985 S.L.T. 463; *McKenzie v. H. D. Fraser & Sons*, 1990 S.C. 311.

40 A.S. (Fees of Solicitors in the Sheriff Court) (Amendment and Further Provisions) 1993, as amended by S.I. 1994 No. 1142 and S.I. 1995 No. 1395 (hereinafter referred to as "1993 A.S."), Sched. 1, General Regulations, reg. 5(a).

41 *Russo's Tr., Petr*, 1981 S.L.T. (Sh. Ct.) 26.

42 *Earl of Kintore v. Pirie* (1904) 12 S.L.T. 385.

43 *Clarke v. McNab* (1888) 15 R. 670.

44 In terms of the Legal Aid (Scotland) Act, s. 18(2) (as amended) the sheriff has power to fix the actual sum payable by a legally aided litigant against whom an award of expenses has been made. This is usually referred to, albeit somewhat inaccurately, as "modification" of the party's expenses. The amount fixed "shall not exceed the amount (if any) which in the opinion of the court . . . is a reasonable one for [the assisted person] to pay, having regard to all the circumstances including the means of all the parties and their conduct in connection with the dispute". There is no appeal against a sheriff's refusal to modify: *Orttewell v. Gilchrist*, 1998 S.L.T. (Sh. Ct.) 63, following *Todd v. Todd*, 1966 S.L.T. 50

the sheriff has a discretionary power to decern against that party for payment of such expenses as he considers reasonable.[45]

19.10 Modification, in the sense of restriction of expenses, may be directed in order to mark the court's dissatisfaction with some aspect of the behaviour of the successful party, either as regards the conduct of the litigation or in the matter which gave rise to it. Such modification may be appropriate where his behaviour towards the other party before the litigation merits disapproval[46]; or where his conduct of the action has been inefficient, as where he has only belatedly taken a valid objection to competency,[47] or irresponsible, as where he has made uncandid[48] or unfounded[49] averments, or has failed to adjust a minute of admissions which would have obviated a long proof.[50] In such cases the sheriff usually finds the successful party entitled to only a proportion of the taxed amount of his expenses,[51] and the modification is applied after taxation and the approval of the auditor's report.[52] Modification or restriction of expenses may also be directed where there has been divided success.[53]

Successful party refused expenses

19.11 The successful party may be refused expenses where his behaviour prior to the raising of the action has been improper,[54] careless or misleading[55]; or where the procedure which he has adopted has been erroneous, irregular or unnecessary, for example where a pursuer has unjustifiably raised an action without prior warning,[56] or where several defenders have needlessly maintained separate defences,[57] or where an unnecessary proof has been led.[58] He may be deprived of part[59] or all of his expenses, or of his expenses from or up to a specified stage of the proceedings. Thus, a successful party who had made misleading averments was refused his expenses at first instance and held entitled to expenses only from the date of the interlocutor which the other party had unsuccessfully appealed.[60] It is incorrect to refuse expenses on the ground that the case is a test case, unless the parties so agree.[61] On taxation, the auditor may disallow the expenses of irregular or unnecessary procedure.[62] Further, notwithstanding that a party has been found entitled to expenses generally, if on

---

[45] 1993 A.S., Sched. 1, General Regulations, reg. 5(c).
[46] *Shepherd v. Elliot* (1896) 23 R. 695.
[47] *Stuart v. Carron Co.*, 1948 S.L.T. (Notes) 43.
[48] *Shepherd, supra.*
[49] *Rigg's Exr v. Urquhart* (1902) 10 S.L.T. 503.
[50] *Bannerman's Trs v. Macqueen* (1896) 3 S.L.T. 301.
[51] *Shepherd, supra.*
[52] *McElroy & Sons v. Tharsis Sulphur and Copper Co.* (1879) 6 R. 1119; *Aitken v. Classen*, 1928 S.C. 628.
[53] para. 19.14.
[54] *Robb v. Logiealmond School Board* (1875) 2 R. 698; *Ewart v. Brown* (1882) 10 R. 163; *Maclennan v. Luth*, 1951 S.L.T. (Sh. Ct.) 103.
[55] *Robinson v. National Bank of Scotland*, 1916 S.C. (H.L.) 154; *Hardnec Flooring Co. v. Forbes*, 1975 S.L.T. (Sh. Ct.) 9; *Cleghorn v. Fairgrieve*, 1982 S.L.T. (Sh. Ct.) 17.
[56] *Cellular Clothing Co. v. Schulberg*, 1952 S.L.T. (Notes) 73.
[57] *McEwan v. Pattison* (1865) 3 M. 779; *Duncan v. Salmond* (1874) 1 R. 839.
[58] *Lord Clinton v. Brown* (1874) 1 R. 1137.
[59] *Pickard v. Reid*, 1953 S.L.T. (Sh. Ct.) 5 (expenses of unnecessary proof); *Ayton v. National Coal Board*, 1965 S.L.T. (Notes) 24 (unnecessary witnesses); *Fennel v. Cameron*, 1968 S.L.T. (Sh. Ct.) 30 (failure to notice decisive point).
[60] *Armour v. Duff & Co.*, 1912 S.C. 120.
[61] *Blythswood Motors Ltd v. Raeside*, 1966 S.L.T. (Sh. Ct.) 13.
[62] 1993 A.S., Sched. 1, General Regulations, reg. 8.

taxation it appears that there is any particular part of the litigation in which he has proved unsuccessful or that any part of the expenses has been occasioned through his own fault, he is not allowed the expense of such part of the proceedings.[63]

Successful party found liable

If a party unnecessarily or unreasonably causes litigation to take place or protracts it when it has been initiated, he may not only forfeit his claim for expenses, even if ultimately successful, but he may be found liable in expenses to the other side.[64] For example, a successful party may be found liable in expenses where he has obstructed the precognition of witnesses,[65] or has failed duly to produce a material document,[66] or has raised an action unnecessarily in view of the reasonable attitude of the defender,[67] or has raised an action for payment without making a previous demand.[68] A successful party may likewise be found liable in part of the other party's expenses, as for example in the expenses of unnecessary procedure,[69] or in the expenses caused by his failure to put forward a successful defence which it was *pars judicis* to notice.[70] **19.12**

Construction of deeds

In an action brought to determine a question involving the construction of a testamentary writing, all parties are usually found entitled to expenses out of the estate regarding which the question arises, upon the principle that the litigation is attributable to the testator's choice of language and not to any improper conduct by the parties.[71] Where, however, the litigation is not attributable to the testator, the expenses may follow the result in accordance with the usual rule.[72] **19.13**

Divided success

Where success is divided, "the result upon the award of expenses has in our practice taken a great many different forms according to the circumstances of each case."[73] Those forms include the following. **19.14**

(1) The expenses of the more successful party may be modified to a specified proportion.[74]

---

[63] 1993 A.S., Sched., General Regulations, reg. 9; see para. 19.55.

[64] *Bond v. British Railways Board*, 1972 S.L.T. (Notes) 47.

[65] *Barrie v. Caledonian Ry* (1902) 5 F. 30.

[66] *Goldie v. Chrysler Motors Ltd* (1938) 55 Sh. Ct.Rep. 99.

[67] *Crombie v. British Transport Commission*, 1961 S.C. 108; *O'Donnell v. A. M. & G. Robertson*, 1965 S.L.T. 155.

[68] *Leith Mags v. Lennon* (1881) 18 S.L.R. 313; *cf. Cellular Clothing Co. v. Schulberg*, 1952 S.L.T. (Notes) 73.

[69] *Sinclair v. Brown Bros* (1882) 10 R. 45; *Lee v. Alexander* (1882) 10 R. 230; *Baker v. Glasgow Corporation*, 1916 S.C. 199; *A/B Karlshamns Oljefabriker v. Monarch Steamship Co.*, 1949 S.C. (H.L.) 1.

[70] *Hamilton v. McLauchlan* (1908) 16 S.L.T. 341.

[71] *Gibson's Trs v. Wilson* (1899) 1 F. 1016; *Wordie's Trs v. Wordie*, 1916 S.C. (H L.) 126; *Lethem v. Evans*, 1918 1 S.L.T. 27; *Barrie v. Barrie's Tr.*, 1933 S.C. 132; *Sinclair v. Royal Bank of Scotland*, 1983 S.L.T. 256.

[72] *Brooks v. Brooks's Trs* (1902) 4 F. 1014 (question as to testator's domicile); *Macculloch v. McCulloch's Trs* (1903) 6 F. (H.L.) 3 (unnecessary appeal); *Dundas' Trs v. Dundas' Trs*, 1912 S.C. 375 (statutory construction); *Bannerman's Trs v. Bannerman*, 1915 S.C. 398 (belated attempt to upset trust administration).

[73] *Howitt v. Alexander & Sons*, 1948 S.C. 154, *per* L.P. Cooper at 158.

[74] *Strang v. Brown & Son* (1882) 19 S.L.R. 890; *Arthur v. Lindsay* (1895) 22 R. 904; *Sidlaw Industries Ltd v. Cable Belt Ltd*, 1979 S.L.T. (Notes) 40.

(2) The more successful party may be given his expenses except those relative to a particular point or stage of procedure where he has been unsuccessful.[75]

(3) Each party may be given expenses upon the points on which each has been successful, where it would be practicable for the auditor to ascertain what portion of the expense is applicable to each point.[76]

(4) Neither party may be awarded expenses.[77] In such a case the interlocutor usually "finds no expenses due to or by either party".[78]

19.15 Where the pursuer in an action of damages is awarded less than the sum sued for, he is nevertheless usually entitled to a general finding of expenses.[79] In personal injury cases there is no rule that there must be some reduction of the expenses awarded to the pursuer in cases where damages have been reduced by reason of contributory negligence. Each case must depend on its own circumstances.[80] Where a pursuer sued for excessive damages and was found 90 per cent to blame for the accident, the defenders were found liable in expenses modified at three-quarters.[81] Where at the conclusion of the proof in an ordinary action the sheriff was addressed by the parties on the question of expenses, but not on the taxation scale which might be applied, expenses were held to be taxable on the summary cause scale since the award was only £637.50.[82]

Reserved expenses

19.16 The sheriff may reserve the question of the expenses of any incidental procedure or discussion, such as amendment[83] or debate.[84] The reservation of the question (unless it is to specific diet) means that it is reserved for the sheriff to decide either until the end of the case when, having disposed of the subject-matter of the cause, he deals with all other questions of expenses or until a motion is lodged seeking to have the sheriff decide the reserved question.[85] Where the reserved expenses are not specially referred to in the interlocutor which ultimately finds expenses due, a general finding of expenses includes the reserved expenses and settles the liability for them in favour of the party to whom the general expenses have been awarded.[86] If, therefore, the unsuccessful party intends to seek an award of the reserved expenses, he should not overlook the question, but should bring it to the notice of the sheriff when the motion for the general expenses of the action is made. The sheriff will not necessarily decide it in accordance with his final award of general expenses. The practice of

---

[75] *Milne Home v. Dunse Police Commissioners* (1882) 9 R. 924; *Sinclair, supra, Lee; supra.*

[76] *Dean v. Walker* (1873) 11 M. 759.

[77] *Fleming v. North of Scotland Banking Co.* (1882) 9 R. 659: *Dalkeith Police Commissioners v. Duke of Buccleuch* (1889) 16 R. 575; *Dean, supra.*

[78] *MV "Andoni" v. MV "St Angus"*, 1945 S.C. 468.

[79] *Craig v. Craig* (1906) 14 S.L.T. 469.

[80] *Howitt, supra; Smith v. LMS Ry*, 1948 S.C. 125; *Lever v. Greenock Motor Services Co.*, 1949 S.C. 88.

[81] *Bradie v. National Coal Board*, 1951 S.C. 576. See also *Woods v. British Steel Corporation*, 1974 S.L.T. (Notes) 24.

[82] *Macdonald v. G. 101 Off Sales Ltd*, 1988 S.C.L.R 448.

[83] para. 10.30.

[84] para. 13.23.

[85] *A.F. Drysdale Ltd v. Menzies*, 1998 G.W.D. 32–1667.

[86] *Macfie v. Blair* (1884) 22 S.L.R. 224; *Gardiners v. Victoria Estates Co. Ltd* (1885) 13 R. 80; *Caledonian Ry v. Chisholm* (1889) 16 R. 622; *Alston & Orr v. Allan*, 1910 S.C. 304; *Williamson v. John Williams (Wishaw) Ltd*, 1971 S.L.T. (Sh. Ct.) 2.

reserving expenses has been strongly discouraged, upon the view that any question of expenses connected with incidental procedure such as amendment or debate ought ordinarily to be dealt with as soon as that procedure is completed, when the circumstances are freshly in the minds of the sheriff and the advocates, and that there is no advantage in delaying a decision until some much later time, when the question may be overlooked, or the circumstances imperfectly remembered.[87] If, when the incidental procedure is completed, the sheriff considers that the question should be governed by the general award of expenses at the conclusion of the case, he should not reserve the question, but should find the expenses to be expenses in the cause.[88]

Expenses in the cause

19.17 The sheriff may find the expenses of any branch of the case, or of any incidental procedure or discussion, to be "expenses in the cause". That means that the expenses are to go, as a matter of right, to the party who in the cause is eventually successful, and who gets a general finding of expenses in his favour at the end.[89]

Percentage increase

19.18 The taxation of accounts is regulated by the table of fees contained in Schedule 1 to the Act of Sederunt (Fees of Solicitors in the Sheriff Court) (Amendment and Further Provision) 1993. In certain circumstances in both ordinary and summary causes[90] the sheriff has a discretionary power to allow a percentage increase of the fees authorised by the table.[91] He may do so upon a motion made not later than seven days after the date of any interlocutor disposing of expenses, by pronouncing a further interlocutor regarding these expenses. A motion made more than seven days after the interlocutor awarding expenses and remitting to the auditor to tax the account is incompetent,[92] as is a motion for an additional fee in respect of procedure before the sheriff made within seven days after an appeal to the sheriff principal has been refused, even though the sheriff principal's interlocutor deals with the expenses of the appeal.[93] The sheriff who allows the increase need not be the sheriff who has heard the case; and an increase may be allowed although the previous interlocutor does not contain a finding for expenses so long as it disposes of them.[94] An increase may be allowed where an interlocutor disposing of expenses is pronounced after settlement of an action, whether by minutes of tender and acceptance or by joint minute.[95] It has been said to be

---

87 *Williamson, supra.* See para. 19.06.

88 para. 19.17.

89 *Glasgow and S.-W. Ry v. Ayr Mags*, 1911 S.C. 298.

90 But not in sequestrations: *Russo's Tr., Petr*, 1981 S.L.T. (Sh. Ct.) 26.

91 1993 A.S., Sched. 1, General Reguatlons, reg. 5(b).

92 *Kontos v. Kontos*, 1990 S.C.L.R 293.

93 *James N. Miller & Sons v. Anderson*, 1991 S.C.L.R. 407. It is submitted that, if the sheriff principal's interlocutor deals with the expenses not only of the appeal but of the whole action, a motion for an increase made within seven days of that interlocutor would be competent.

94 That is the effect of the amendment of the A.S. (Alteration of Sheriff Court Fees) 1971, Sched. 2, para. 7(iv), by the A.S. (Solicitors' Fees) 1985, para. 3(1), which is preserved in the 1993 A.S., Sched. 1, General Regulations, reg. 5(b).

95 *Marks & Spencer v. British Gas Corporation*, 1985 S.L.T. 17; *UCB Bank plc v. Dundas & Wilson C.S.*, 1991 S.L.T. 90. But see also *Goodwin v. Farming Agricultural Finance Ltd*, 1996 S.C.L.R. 545.

inappropriate to allow an increase where taxation is allowed on a "solicitor and client" basis.[96] The auditor should allow the maximum fees authorised by the table and then increase them by the percentage directed by the court.[97]

19.19 The percentage increase is stated to be "to cover the responsibility undertaken by the solicitor in the conduct of the cause".[98] The sheriff is directed to fix the amount of the increase by taking into account the following factors: "(i) the complexity of the cause and the number, difficulty or novelty of the questions raised; (ii) the skill, time and labour, and specialised knowledge and responsibility required, of the solicitor; (iii) the number and importance of any documents prepared or perused; (iv) the place and circumstances of the cause or in which the work of the solicitor in preparation for, and conduct of, the cause has been carried out; (v) the importance of the cause or the subject-matter of it to the client; (vi) the amount or value of money or property involved in the cause; (vii) the steps taken with a view to settling the cause, limiting the matters in dispute or limiting the scope of any hearing."[99]

19.20 As to factor (ii), it may be proper to take account of what has been called "the adrenalin factor" in a case where the solicitor has not only had to work urgently but has had absolutely no margin for error. Further, while the amount of time recorded as having been expended by the solicitor may reflect his labour, it may not reflect the skill, specialised knowledge and responsibility required of him.[1]

> "No professional man, or senior employee of a professional man, stops thinking about the day's problems the minute he lifts his coat and umbrella from the stand and sets out on the journey home. Ideas—often very valuable ideas—occur in the train or car home, or in the bath, or even whilst watching television. Yet nothing is ever put down on a time sheet—or can be put down on a time sheet—adequately to reflect this out of hours devotion of time."[2]

Factor (iii) may be reflected in factor (i) or (ii),[3] and factor (v) in factor (i) or (vi).[4]

Failure to appear or proceed

19.21 Where a party or his solicitor abandons, fails to attend or is not prepared to proceed with any diet of proof, debate, appeal or meeting ordered by the sheriff, the sheriff has a discretionary power to decern against that party for payment of such expenses as the sheriff considers

---

[96] *Banque Indo Suez v. Maritime Co. Overseas Inc.*, 1985 S.L.T. 517; but see J. W. Hastings, "Solicitors' Fees for Complexity, etc.", 1986 S.L.T. (News) 50. For taxation on solicitor and client basis, see paras 19.44 to 19.47.

[97] *Hunter & Son v. Weir*, 1955 S.L.T. (Sh. Ct.) 101.

[98] 1993 A.S., Sched. 1, General Regulations, reg. 5(b).

[99] *ibid. Cf.* the Law Society of Scotland's Table of Fees for Conveyancing and General Business, Chap. 1, para. 4, and the guidelines thereon (*Parliament House Book*, A303, 331–336).

[1] *Treasury Solicitor v. Regester* [1978] 1 W.L.R. 446 at 453.

[2] *Maltby v. D. J. Freeman & Co.* [1978] 1 W.L.R. 431 *per* Walton J, at 435.

[3] *Property and Reversionary Investment Corporation Ltd v. Secretary of State for the Environment* [1975] 1 W.L.R. 1504 at 1510–1511.

[4] *Maltby, supra.*

reasonable.[5] However, where because of an error on the part of the sheriff clerk, parties attended a continued diet of proof at which the sheriff was not available, they were held not to be entitled to recover the expenses of the abortive diet from the Scottish Courts Administration[6] although they were offered and accepted an *ex gratia* payment by the Secretary of State.[7]

III. Rules as to Solicitors

Personal liability for expenses

For fees

A party's solicitor is personally responsible for the payment of court fees.[8] He is also personally liable for the fees and expenses of witnesses and havers whom he cites.[9] When a shorthand writer is employed to record evidence at a proof or commission, he is in the first instance paid, as regards commissions by the party moving for the commission,[10] and as regards proofs by the parties equally[11]; the parties' solicitors are personally liable for his fees, and the sheriff may make an order directing payment to be made.[12] When a commission to take evidence is granted, the solicitor for the party obtaining the commission is personally liable for the fees of the commissioner and his clerk.[13] The solicitor is, however, entitled to be supplied by his client with funds for all these disbursements.[14] When a remit is made by the court to an accountant, engineer, or other reporter regarding matters in the record, the parties' solicitors are not, without special agreement, personally responsible to the reporter for his remuneration, the parties alone being liable therefor.[15] **19.22**

For expenses

A solicitor who conducts legal proceedings without the authority of his client is personally liable to the opposite party in the expenses of process if the client disclaims.[16] A solicitor may be made personally liable for expenses occasioned by his own fault.[17] Thus, a solicitor who makes a mistake in noting the date or time of a proof or debate and fails to appear may be made personally liable for the expenses of the lost diet.[18] A solicitor may also be found personally liable in expenses if he is guilty of an abuse of process, as by raising an action which he knows to be **19.23**

---

[5] 1993 A.S., Sched. 1, General Regulations, reg. 5(c).

[6] *Meekison v. Uniroyal Englebert Tyres Ltd*, 1995 S.L.T. (Sh. Ct.) 63.

[7] (1995) 30 J.L.S. 85.

[8] *AB v. CD* (1843) 6 D. 95; *Stirling Park & Co v. Digby Brown & Co*, 1996 S.L.T. (Sh. Ct.) 17 (fee of sheriff officer carrying out poinding).

[9] OCR, r. 29.7(5) (applied to havers and witnesses at commissions by r. 28.15); paras 16.11 (witnesses), 15.72 (havers).

[10] OCR, r. 28.12(1)(d).

[11] OCR, r. 29.18(2).

[12] OCR, r. 29.18(4).

[13] OCR, rr. 28.11(4)(c) (commission with interrogatories), 28.12(1)(d) (open commission); para. 15.39.

[14] *Bell v. Ogilvie* (1863) 2 M. 336, *per* L.J.-C. Inglis at 340–341.

[15] 1993 A.S., Sched. 1, General Regulations, reg. 10; see para. 13.33.

[16] *Cowan v. Farnie* (1836) 14 S. 634; *Philip v. Gordon* (1848) 11 D. 175. On disclamation, see paras 12.19, 12.20.

[17] *McKechnie v. Halliday* (1856) 18 D. 659.

[18] *Stewart v. Stewart*, 1984 S.L.T. (Sh. Ct.) 58.

unfounded[19] or by insisting in an insubstantial defence without applying his mind to the question whether it could be at least plausibly argued.[20] Other examples of abuse of process are given elsewhere.[21] A solicitor may be ordered to bear personally the expenses of his own client,[22] and where he is conscious of failure in duty he often undertakes to do so.[23] It is thought that before the power to award expenses against a solicitor personally is exercised, he should be given sufficient notice of the complaint against him and sufficient opportunity of answering it[24]; and the power should be exercised with care and discretion, and only in clear cases.[25] Since it is not competent to make an award against counsel personally, a solicitor acting on counsel's advice is not personally liable in expenses.[26]

Right to expenses

Solicitor conducting own case

19.24 A solicitor who conducts his own case and is awarded expenses is entitled to make professional charges for those parts of the case where a solicitor would have been required if the party had not been a solicitor. He is not a party litigant within the meaning of the provisions as to the expenses recoverable by party litigants.[27]

Solicitor acting for client

19.25 **Remuneration from own client.** Where the relationship of solicitor and client is constituted, the client is obliged not only to supply funds for disbursements, but to remunerate the solicitor for his services. That obligation is implied, unless expressly dispensed with.[28] The operation of the rule, and the lien allowed to a solicitor in order to aid him to recover his judicial charges from his client, are examined in the undernoted works.[29]

19.26 **Remuneration from opposite side: agent-disburser.** *General rules.* The sheriff may allow a decree for expenses to be extracted in the name of the solicitor who conducted the case on behalf of the party to whom the expenses are awarded.[30] This rule arises from the privilege which the court may allow to a solicitor to take decree in his own name as agent-disburser[31] for the expenses found due to his client.[32] He may then, if necessary, recover the amount by diligence at his own instance. The privilege is founded upon principle qualified by expediency. The principle

---

[19] *Blyth v. Watson*, 1987 S.L.T. 616.
[20] *Stewart, supra.*
[21] para. 2.19.
[22] *Reilly v. Doocey*, 1951 S.L.T. (Notes) 54; *Kelly v. Fyfe Douglas Co.*, 1965 S.L.T. (Notes) 87.
[23] *Dunlop's Trs v. Farquharson*, 1956 S.L.T. 16; *McLean v. Thomas O'Connor Autos*, 1967 S.L.T. (Sh. Ct.) 41.
[24] *Myers v. Elman* [1940] A.C. 282, *per* Lord Wright at 318.
[25] *Orchard v. South Eastern Electricity Board* [1987] Q.B. 565.
[26] *Reid v. Edinburgh Acoustics Ltd (No. 2)*, 1995 S.L.T. 982 in which the Lord Ordinary observed that it was for consideration whether, as in England, there should be a statutory power to make an award against counsel.
[27] *Macbeth Currie & Co. v. Matthew*, 1985 S.L.T. (Sh. Ct.) 44.
[28] *Bell v. Ogilvie* (1863) 2 M. 336, *per* L.J.-C. Inglis at 340–341; *Batchelor v. Pattison and Mackersy* (1876) 3 R. 914, *per* L.P. Inglis at 918.
[29] Maclaren, *Expenses*, pp. 246–256; Hastings, *Expenses*, pp. 121–122.
[30] OCR, r. 32.2.
[31] So called because he has acted as disburser on behalf of his client.
[32] *Agnew v. Norwest Construction Co.*, 1935 S.C. 771, *per* L.J.-C. Aitchison at 778.

is that there is an implied assignation by the client to the solicitor of his right to such expenses. Considerations of expediency, however, prevent the adverse party from putting forward extrinsic claims of compensation.[33] These considerations are: "that it was by the agent's exertions that the fund in question, so to speak, has been brought into practical existence, and that it would be hard upon the agent, who had necessarily incurred expense in order to do so, if that fund were carried away in reference to old debts, having to do with other transactions which existed between the parties."[34] Apart from extrinsic claims of compensation, however, the solicitor's privilege, which is strictly derivative, can never be higher than the right of the client.[35]

Grounds for refusal. The court may refuse to make an order in favour of **19.27** the solicitor, either *ex proprio motu*[36] or at the instance of the opposite party.[37] An order may be refused where the solicitor has not actually disbursed the expenses.[38] The following grounds of refusal are exceptions to the general rule that compensation on a debt due by the agent-disburser's client is not pleadable by the party against whom the agent-disburser moves for decree. The first of these grounds is that both parties have been each in the same cause given different awards of expenses: in such a case the privilege is barred since the one set of expenses may be set off against the other,[39] even if the awards are made at different times.[40] But where the first of two awards of expenses has been obtained in the name of the agent-disburser, the second may not be set off against the first.[41] And the mere possibility of a later counter-award of expenses in the same case will not prevent decree in the solicitor's name for expenses already awarded.[42] The second ground of refusal is that there are two separate processes between the same parties, relating to the same subject matter.[43] But decree may be granted in name of the agent-disburser if the two actions, though arising between the same parties, are quite separate and distinct,[44] or if in the earlier action a decree has been extracted and has become a judgment debt.[45] Thirdly, decree in name of the agent disburser may be refused where in the same action decree is given for a principal sum in favour of one party and an award of expenses in favour of the other, since the principal sum may be pleaded as a set-off against the award of expenses.[46] These appear to be the only exceptions to the general rule. Accordingly, the claim of the

---

[33] Bell, *Comm.*, ii, 36–37; *Gordon v. Davidson* (1865) 3 M. 938, *per* L.J.-C. Inglis at 939. Admissible claims of compensation are noted in the following paragraph.

[34] *Lochgelly Iron and Coal Co. Ltd v. Sinclair*, 1907 S.C. 442, *per* L.P. Dunedin at 444; *S.S. "Fulwood" Ltd v. Dumfries Harbour Commissioners*, 1907 S.C. 735, *per* L.J.-C. Macdonald at 737.

[35] *Grieve's Trs v. Grieve*, 1907 S.C. 963; *Agnew*, *supra*, *per* L.J.-C. Aitchison at 778, Lord Murray at 787–788.

[36] *Baillie* (1872) 10 M. 414.

[37] *Bloe v. Bloe* (1882) 9 R. 894.

[38] *Rennie & Playfair v. Aitken*, June 8, 1811, F.C.; *Lythgoe v. Banks*, 1933 S.N. 76.

[39] *Stothart v. Johnston's Trs* (1822) 2 Mur. 549; *Warburton v. Hamilton* (1826) 4 S. 631 (N.E. 639).

[40] *Gordon v. Davidson* (1865) 3 M. 938; *Byrne v. Wm Baird & Co.*, 1929 S.C. 624.

[41] *Blasquez v. Scott* (1893) 1 S.L.T. 357.

[42] *Hugh Nelson & Co. v. Glasgow Corporation*, 1908 S.C. 879.

[43] *Jack, Son & Co. v. Laing*, 1929 S.C. 426, *per* L.P. Clyde at 428.

[44] *Strain v. Strain* (1890) 17 R. 566; *Holt v. National Bank of Scotland*, 1927 S.L.T. 664; *Richardson v. Richardson*, 1957 S.L.T. 30.

[45] *Paolo v. Parias* (1897) 24 R. 1030; *Fine v. Edinburgh Life Assurance Co.*, 1909 S.C. 636; *Wm Baird & Co. v. McBride*, 1928 S.N. 31.

[46] *Grieve's Tr. v. Grieve*, 1907 S.C. 963.

agent-disburser to decree for expenses in his own name cannot be elided by compensation operating between the expenses decerned for and any expenses in respect of which the court may have given a right of relief against his client.[47]

19.28 *Procedure.* Since decree for expenses in name of the solicitor as agent-disburser is not a matter of right but a privilege,[48] it is within the discretion of the sheriff.[49] An appeal against his decision is competent only with leave.[50] The motion that decree should go out and be extracted in name of the solicitor as agent-disburser should ordinarily be made at the time when the motion for expenses is heard by the sheriff. Sheriff Dobie stated that the motion should be made when an interlocutor is asked for approving of the auditor's report and decerning for the taxed expenses.[51] In practice, however, where decree has been granted and the account of expenses remitted to the auditor to tax and to report, and no objections to the auditor's report are lodged, the sheriff approves the report and grants decree for the taxed expenses without any further reference to or motion by the parties.[52] The learned author also suggested that prior intimation of the motion should always be given, and a written motion lodged.[53] It has been held, however, that where the motion is made at the hearing of the motion for expenses in the ordinary course of procedure, no prior intimation or written motion is necessary[54] and, indeed, the right to make a motion orally is specifically preserved in the Ordinary Cause Rules.[55] The motion appears to be competent at any time before extract, notwithstanding that decree for expenses has already been given in name of the client.[56] A solicitor may move for decree notwithstanding that he has withdrawn from the case,[57] or that the client has been sequestrated.[58] When a case has been appealed to the Court of Session, expenses in both courts may be decerned for in the name of the sheriff court solicitor, if the Court of Session solicitor consents and there is no opposition.[59]

19.29 *Solicitor's right to be sisted.* A solicitor may be sisted as a party to an action, in order that he may take decree for expenses in his own name, in the following cases: (1) where his client has been found entitled to expenses; (2) where an award of expenses is a legitimate consequence from an interlocutor already pronounced; or (3) where there has been collusion between the parties in order to defeat his claim.[60]

19.30 **Remuneration out of property recovered or preserved: charging order.** Where a solicitor has been employed by a client to pursue or defend any action or proceeding, the court before which the action or proceeding has

---

47 *Jack, Son & Co.* v. *Laing*, 1929 S.C. 426.

48 *Agnew* v. *Norwest Construction Co.*, 1935 S.C. 771, *per* L.J.-C. Aitchison at 778.

49 OCR, r. 32.2.

50 1907 Act, ss. 27(f), 28 (1)(d); *Carson* v. *McDowall* (1908) 24 Sh.Ct.Rep. 324.

51 Dobie, p. 329.

52 *Batchelor* v. *Reilly*, Sh. Pr. Dick, Glasgow Sh.Ct, Feb. 11, 1981, unreported; Kearney, p. 152.

53 Dobie, p. 329; Dobie, *Styles*, p. 333.

54 *Batchelor*, *supra*.

55 OCR, r. 15.1(1)(a).

56 *Brown* v. *Brown*, 1929 S.L.T. (Sh. Ct.) 44.

57 *Holt* v. *National Bank of Scotland*, 1927 S.L.T. 664.

58 *Union Bank of Scotland* v. *Macmillan* (1930) 47 Sh.Ct.Rep. 15.

59 *West* v. *Cow*, 1929 S.C. 783.

60 *McLean* v. *Auchinvole* (1824) 3 S. 190 (N.E. 129); *Cornwall* v. *Walker* (1871) 8 S.L.R. 442; *Ammon* v. *Tod*, 1912 S.C. 306.

been heard or is depending may declare the solicitor entitled, in respect of the taxed expenses of or in reference to the action or proceeding, to a charge upon, and a right to payment out of, any property (of whatsoever nature, tenure or kind it may be) which has been recovered or preserved on behalf of the client by the solicitor in the action or proceeding. The court may make such order for the taxation of, and for the raising and payment of, those expenses out of the property as the court thinks just.[61] Where a declaration has been made in terms of these provisions, any act done or deed granted by the client after the date of the declaration, except an act or deed in favour of a bona fide purchaser or lender, is absolutely void as against the charge or right.[62] An order made under these provisions is known as a charging order, since it charges the property with the expenses. These may be the taxed judicial and extrajudicial expenses incurred by the client to the solicitor.[63]

The granting of a charging order is in the discretion of the court.[64] **19.31**
Before an order may be made, however, the property sought to be charged must have been actually recovered or preserved on the client's behalf by the solicitor.[65] An order enables the solicitor to obtain a preference over other creditors of the client whose debts have arisen outwith the ambit of the particular case, upon the theory that without the solicitor's work the property recovered or preserved by the litigation, so far as not necessary to meet the solicitor's accounts, would not have been available for payment of other debts.[66] Thus, an order may be granted notwithstanding that an arrestment has been used on the fund[67]; or that the client has been sequestrated[68] or has gone into voluntary liquidation.[69] But where the opposite party in the litigation is entitled to set off a debt which has arisen in the same case, such as an award in his favour of certain expenses, against any sums found due by him therein, the application of the charging order will be restricted accordingly.[70]

IV. Taxation of Expenses

Nature of taxation

Unless expenses are modified at a fixed amount,[71] they must be taxed **19.32**
before decree is granted for them.[72] Taxation is the proceeding by which accounts are submitted to a skilled person in order that he may examine them and allow, disallow, add to[73] or reduce the charges therein. Sums

---

[61] Solicitors (Scotland) Act 1980, s. 62(1).
[62] *ibid.* s. 62(2).
[63] *e.g. O'Keele v. Grieve's Trs*, 1917 1 S.L.T. 305.
[64] *Carruthers' Tr. v. Finlay & Wilson* (1897) 24 R. 363.
[65] *Carruthers' Tr., supra*; *Hutchison v. Hutchison's Trs* (1902) 10 S.L.T. 562; *Stenhouse v. Stenhouse's Trs* (1903) 10 S.L.T. 684; *J. Smart & Co. v. Stewart*, 1911 2 S.L.T. 340.
[66] *Philip v. Willson*, 1911 S.C. 1203 *per* Lord Salvese, at 1207.
[67] *Automobile Gas Producer Syndicate Ltd v. Caledonian Ry*, 1909 1 S.L.T. 499.
[68] *Paton v. Paton's Trs* (1905) 13 S.L.T. 96. *Cf. Tait & Co. v. Wallace* (1894) 2 S.L.T. 261 and *Pollock & Son v. Crawford* (1900) 16 Sh.Ct.Rep. 124, where orders were refused, the clients' estates having already been sequestrated.
[69] *Philip, supra.*
[70] *O'Keefe, supra.*
[71] On modification, see paras 19.09, 19.10.
[72] OCR, r. 32.1. In undefended causes taxation is unnecessary where the pursuer's solicitor elects to charge the appropriate inclusive fee and outlays: see para. 7.10.
[73] *Reeve v. Dykes* (1829) 7 S. 632.

which are disallowed or reduced are said to be "taxed off", and those which are allowable are called "judicial expenses". Where taxation is necessary, the court pronounces an interlocutor allowing an account of the expenses awarded to be given in and remitting the same, when lodged, to the auditor of court to tax and to report.[74] After the auditor has taxed the account and submitted his report thereon, objections to his report may be lodged. After disposing of any such objections, the court pronounces a further interlocutor decerning for the taxed amount of the expenses. The following paragraphs consider the details of the procedure, the bases and scales of taxation, and certain of the expenses which are chargeable.

Procedure

Motion as to mode or scale of taxation

19.33 An account of expenses is taxed according to one of three modes or bases, and upon one of two scales. The three modes are: party and party; solicitor and client, client paying; and solicitor and client, third party paying. The two scales are the ordinary cause scale and the summary cause scale. These modes and scales are fully explained later. At present it is necessary to notice that an award of expenses *simpliciter* without any specification of mode or scale implies, as to mode, taxation as between party and party[75] and, as to scale, taxation of the account of a pursuer's solicitor by reference to the sum decerned for.[76] If a party wishes taxation other than as between party and party or on the scale indicated by the sum decerned for, he should make an appropriate motion when the sheriff hears the motion for expenses, and if the motion is granted the mode or scale will be specially mentioned in the subsequent interlocutor. A rule that a motion must be made at that stage has been applied by the Court of Session both in cases originating there[77] and in sheriff court appeals,[78] but there is a question whether in the sheriff court there is any inflexible rule to that effect, or only an approved practice. In the sheriff court, motions for taxation on the scale not normally applicable and other special applications with regard to expenses have been granted after taxation of expenses awarded *simpliciter*,[79] and it has been suggested that by parity of reasoning re-taxation of an account as between solicitor and client is competent even after taxation as between party and party.[80]

19.34 It is submitted that in normal circumstances there can be little justification for the introduction of the disorder and delay involved in a re-taxation, except where the party seeking it has had no sufficient opportunity to consider the appropriate mode or scale of taxation, as where expenses have been awarded without a hearing, or where the final decree does not decern for a sum of money. In the latter case the award of expenses without any direction as to scale may be said to be incomplete since the auditor has no criterion by reference to which he may determine the appropriate scale in a

---

[74] On the auditor, see para. 1.26.

[75] *Fletcher's Trs v. Fletcher* (1888) 15 R. 862; *Mackellar v. Mackellar* (1898) 25 R. 883; *Aberchirder Mags v. Banff District Committee* (1906) 8 F. 571; *McGregor's Trs v. Kimbell*, 1912 S.C. 261; *Walker v. McNeil*, 1981 S.L.T. (Notes) 21.

[76] 1993 A.S., Sched. 1, General Regulations, reg. 2.

[77] Cases cited in n. 73.

[78] *Murray v. Rennie & Angus* (1897) 24 R. 1026; *Mickel v. McCoard*, 1913 S.C. 1036.

[79] para. 19.06.

[80] Walker, *Digest*, p. 90.

party and party taxation. In these exceptional cases it may be open to the sheriff, after taxation, to determine the appropriate mode or scale of taxation and direct taxation of new. It is thought that early sheriff court decisions on this subject[81] should be regarded with caution, since they appear to be influenced by the terms of earlier regulations as to fees and by the formerly general sheriff court practice of awarding expenses after proof or debate without hearing parties thereon.

Remit to auditor

After the court pronounces an interlocutor allowing an account of the expenses awarded to be given in and remitting the same when lodged to the auditor of court to tax and to report, the party in whose favour the expenses have been awarded prepares an account of expenses and lodges it with the sheriff clerk for taxation. It is thought that where in the opinion of another party to the action there is unnecessary delay in lodging the account, it is competent for that party to lodge a motion with a view to moving the court to ordain the party to lodge his account for taxation within such period as the court may deem reasonable. When the account is lodged, the sheriff clerk transmits the account and process to the auditor of court.[82] The auditor then assigns a diet of taxation not earlier than seven days from the date he receives the account, and intimates that diet forthwith to the party who lodged the account.[83] That party must then forthwith send a copy of the account and intimate the date, time and place of the diet of taxation to each of the other parties.[84] Instead of following this procedure the parties may endeavour to agree the amount of the expenses extrajudicially, in order to avoid the expense of a remit. If they are unable to agree, or if they agree under the mistaken impression that the account was a full and proper one, the remit remains available.[85] **19.35**

Diet of taxation

At the diet of taxation each party should be represented by a solicitor or by a person authorised by him, such as an experienced court department accountant. If a party intends to take objection to any charge stated in the account, he should advise the other party of his objection. Where it is proposed to object to many items in an account, it may facilitate the taxation if beforehand a written note of the objections is lodged with the auditor and intimated to the other party. In any event the latter party's solicitor should have available at the diet vouchers of all the items stated in the account, since the auditor may call for them. The auditor disallows charges if the dates and circumstances under which they were incurred are not correctly stated in the account.[86] At the diet, both parties are heard on any question arising on the account. The auditor may himself raise questions and tax off, or on, any sums although not moved to do so. A party desiring to object to any charge states the charges to which he takes objection and explains his reasons. Any judicial decision affecting the objection should be cited. The auditor normally intimates his decision **19.36**

---

[81] Considered in W. J. D., "Fixing the Scale of Taxation" (1942) 58 Sc.L.Rev. 41; Z. W., "The Scale of Taxation" (1945) 61 Sc.L.Rev. 133; and Dobie, pp. 326–328.

[82] OCR, r. 32.3(1). In many courts the sheriff clerk is himself the auditor: see para. 1.26.

[83] OCR, r. 32.3(2).

[84] OCR, r. 32.3(3).

[85] *Burgess v. Stag Garage Ltd*, 1959 S.C. 387.

[86] *Ruby v. W. Alexander & Sons*, 1949 S.C. 642.

upon each objection immediately after hearing parties thereon, but he may reserve consideration of the account. When he takes the latter course, he informs the parties who attended the taxation of his decision.[87] Having considered the account and taxed any sums on or off, the auditor prepares and signs his report on the taxation, which is usually in the form of a docquet on the account, stating the amount of the expenses as taxed. He then re-transmits the process with the account and his report to the sheriff clerk.[88] After his report is issued, the auditor himself has no power to alter it.[89] In cases of difficulty the auditor may issue an interim report or a report reserving a point for the consideration of the sheriff,[90] and the sheriff hears parties on the questions raised in the report at a hearing similar to a hearing on a note of objections to the report.[91]

Approval of report and decree for expenses

19.37 If no note of objections to the auditor's report is lodged within seven days from the date of the taxation of the account, the sheriff may, and generally does, pronounce an interlocutor approving the report and granting decree for the expenses as taxed, without any further reference to or motion by the parties.[92] In rare cases he may supersede extract of the decree for expenses on cause shown. The interlocutor is appealable only with leave.[93] Interest on the expenses generally runs from the date of the interlocutor.[94]

Objections to report

19.38 Any party to a taxation who is dissatisfied with the allowance or disallowance by the auditor in whole or in part of any charge in the account may lodge a note of objections to the account as taxed. Only a party who has attended the diet of taxation is entitled to do so.[95] The note must be lodged within seven days after the date of taxation[96] or, where the auditor has reserved consideration of the account, the date on which he intimates his decision.[97] The note of objections[98] should specify the charges or parts of charges the allowance or disallowance of which is objected to, and should in each case state concisely the nature and grounds of the objection and what the objector proposes should be substituted for the auditor's finding.[99]

Disposal of objections

19.39 The sheriff is directed to dispose of the objections in a summary manner, with or without answers.[1] When the note is lodged he fixes a diet for disposing of the objections, and seldom orders answers. It is

---

[87] OCR, r. 32.3(5).
[88] OCR, r. 32.3(4).
[89] *Williamson v. John Williams (Wishaw) Ltd*, 1971 S.L.T. (Sh. Ct.) 2.
[90] *Carlos Leasing v. Taylor*, 1986 S.L.T. (Sh. Ct.) 53.
[91] paras 19.39 to 19.41.
[92] OCR, r. 32.3(6); *Batchelor v. Reilly*, Sh. Pr. Dick, Glasgow Sh. Ct, Feb. 11, 1981, unreported.
[93] para. 18.37.
[94] Maclaren, *Expenses*, pp. 505–507; Hastings, *Expenses*, p. 124.
[95] OCR, r. 32.4(1).
[96] OCR, r. 32.4(2)(a).
[97] OCR, r. 32.4(2)(b).
[98] Dobie, *Styles*, p. 350.
[99] *Crossan v. Caledonian Ry* (1902) 5 F. 187 at 190.
[1] OCR, r. 32.4(3).

thought that if he deems it necessary he may request the auditor to state by minute the reasons for his decision in relation to the items to which objection is taken in the note.[2] Although there is no provision requiring the objector to send a copy of the note to the other parties and to intimate to them the date and time of the diet, the sheriff may ordain him to do so. In any event, it is in accordance with good practice that the objector should do so.

It is for the objector to persuade the sheriff that his objections are well founded.[3] The court is reluctant to interfere with the auditor's discretion unless in special circumstances,[4] or where some question of principle is involved,[5] or where he has misdirected himself as to the considerations which have regulated the exercise of his discretion,[6] or where he has had no or no reasonably sufficient material before him, or has mis-stated or mistaken or misunderstood the material before him, or has reached a decision which is unreasonable,[7] or perhaps where the matter is not purely one for his discretion: for example, where the objection relates to counsel's fees in a case of considerable complexity and difficulty, the matter may be more appropriately determined by the sheriff who heard the case than by the auditor.[8] **19.40**

Having heard parties, the sheriff may sustain or repel any objections in the note and dispose of the question of the expenses of and incidental to the hearing. If he repels the note, he pronounces an interlocutor repelling the note, approving the report and granting decree for the expenses as taxed. If he sustains the note in whole or in part, he pronounces an interlocutor to that effect and remits to the auditor either to amend his report or to tax the account of new in accordance with such directions as the sheriff may give in his interlocutor.[9] A remit is, however, unnecessary if the auditor in his report has already made an alternative taxation to be effective if the note is sustained[10]; or if the amount for which decree should be granted is clear from the report,[11] or if parties can agree the amount to be added to or deducted from the account.[12] The sheriff may also find any party liable in the expenses of the procedure on the note. Where the note is repelled, the expenses are generally awarded against the objector[13]; but if the objections are partially successful the expenses against him may be modified.[14] Where the auditor has reported a point for the consideration of the sheriff, usually no expenses are found due to or **19.41**

---

[2] *cf.* RCS, r. 42.4(2)(b)(ii).

[3] *Shaw & Shaw v. J. & T. Boyd Ltd*, 1907 S.C. 646.

[4] *Ovens & Sons v. Bo'ness Coal Gas-Light Co.* (1891) 28 S.L.R. 255.

[5] *Thoms v. Thoms' Tr.*, 1907 S.C. 343; *MacBeth Currie & Co. v. Matthew*, 1985 S.L.T. (Sh. Ct.) 44; *Hamilton v. Hamilton*, 1998 S.C.L.R. 773.

[6] *Macnaughton v. Macnaughton*, 1949 S.C. 42; *Elas v. SMT Co.*, 1950 S.C. 570; *Cassidy v. Celtic Football and Athletic Co. Ltd*, 1995 S.C.L.R. 395.

[7] *Wood v. Miller*, 1960 S.C. 86 (distinguished in *Ahmed's Tr. v. Ahmed (No. 1)*, 1993 S.L.T. 390); *Webster v. Simpson's Motors*, 1967 S.L.T. 287; and see the authorities on review of judicial discretion in paras 18.110 to 18.114.

[8] *Dobell, Beckett & Co. v. Neilson* (1905) 12 S.L.T. 747; *D. C. Thomson & Co. v. D'Agostino* (1985) 30 J.L.S. 381.

[9] *MacBeth Currie & Co. v. Matthew*, 1985 S.L.T. (Sh. Ct.) 44.

[10] *Woodward v. Woodward*, 1910 2 S.L.T. 248.

[11] *Clements v. Edinburgh Corporation* (1905) 7 F. 651.

[12] *Storrie v. Mitchell*, 1937 S.L.T. 624.

[13] Maclaren, *Expenses*, p. 427; *Matthew v. Ballingall* (1844) 6 D. 1135.

[14] *Treacher v. Galloway* (1845) 7 D. 1099.

by either party.[15] An interlocutor disposing of objections to the auditor's report, or decerning for expenses after a hearing on questions raised in the report, is appealable without leave.[16]

Payment of account

19.42 The party liable in expenses may be willing to pay the account immediately upon taxation. If so, at the close of the taxation his solicitor should advise the opposing solicitor that on receipt of a note of the amount of the taxed account under deduction of items not yet incurred, the expenses will be paid. If the opposite party agrees, extract may be unnecessary, and if so, the expenses included in the account for extracting the decree and for all matters which have not been incurred are deducted. The opposite party may not agree, however,[17] and may require an extract for some purpose other than enforcing the award of expenses.[18]

Modes of taxation

Party and party

19.43 As already explained, an account of expenses is taxed according to one of three modes or bases: party and party; solicitor and client, client paying; or solicitor and client, third party paying. In practice, by far the commonest mode is taxation as between party and party, and an interlocutor awarding expenses without qualification implies taxation on that basis.[19] In such a taxation only such expenses are allowed as are reasonable for conducting the litigation in a proper manner.[20] As to the scale of such a taxation, the pursuer's solicitor's account is taxed by reference to the sum decerned for, unless the sheriff otherwise directs.[21] Where a taxation is to be as between party and party a solicitor has the option, unless the table of fees otherwise provides, of charging his account on the basis either of the inclusive fees or of the detailed fees in the table, but he cannot make charges partly on the one basis and partly on the other.[22] Where counsel is employed, counsel's fees and fees for the instruction of counsel are allowed only where the sheriff has sanctioned the employment of counsel[23]; and except on cause shown, fees to counsel and solicitor for only two consultations in the course of the case are allowed.[24]

Solicitor and client

19.44 There are two modes of taxation as between solicitor and client: (1) solicitor and client, client paying; and (2) solicitor and client, third party paying, the taxation varying according to whether the account of expenses is charged (1) against the solicitor's own client, or (2) against the opposite side. An award of expenses as between solicitor and client,

---

[15] *Dempster v. Wallace Hunter & Co.* (1834) 12 S. 844.
[16] para. 18.37.
[17] *Glasgow District Subway Co. v. McCallum* (1896) 12 Sh.Ct.Rep. 148.
[18] *Leith Mags v. Gibb* (1882) 19 S.L.R. 399; *Orr v. Smith* (1891) 28 S.L.R. 589; *Rutherglen Parish Council v. Glenbucket Parish Council* (1896) 3 S.L.T. 251.
[19] para. 19.33.
[20] 1993 A.S., Sched. 1, General Regulations, reg. 8.
[21] *ibid.* reg. 2. As to scales of taxation, see paras 19.48 to 19.50.
[22] *ibid.* reg. 7.
[23] *ibid.* reg. 12(a).
[24] *ibid.* reg. 12(b).

without further specification, implies that the taxation is to be on the basis that the client is paying.[25]

Client paying. Where the account is charged against the solicitor's own client, **19.45**

> "the rule is that the client is liable for all expenses reasonably incurred by the agent for the protection of his client's interest in the suit, even although such expenses cannot be recovered from the opposite party. The client is, of course, also liable for any expenses which he has specially authorised; and it is proper and prudent that agents should have their client's authority before incurring expenses of an extraordinary character."[26]

In the 1936 edition of the Rules of the Court of Session a decerniture for expenses between solicitor and client when the client was paying was held to cover "those expenses which are necessary and proper for the interests of the client as well as those authorised by him."[27] A person who in a fiduciary or representative capacity, such as a trustee, judicial factor or liquidator, engages in a reasonable and necessary litigation is entitled to be indemnified out of the estate in respect of expenses reasonably and properly incurred by him; and in such a case, taxation between solicitor and client, client paying, is usually the appropriate basis of taxation.[28] It is also within the discretion of the court in exceptional circumstances to order taxation of expenses as between solicitor and client, client paying.[29] It may so order as a mark of disapproval of a party's unreasonable conduct.[30] But in any taxation as between solicitor and client, client paying, extrajudicial expenses are not chargeable.[31]

Third party paying. Where the account of expenses is charged against the opposite side, the mode of taxation, while "not so generous" as in a taxation between solicitor and client, client paying, "is yet not quite so rigorous as the taxation between party and party."[32] "The taxation of an account as between agent and client to be paid by the unsuccessful party should approach more nearly the taxation of party and party than the taxation of an account between an agent and his own client."[33] Thus, in a taxation as between solicitor and client, third party paying, the auditor may disallow numerous items which would be admissible in a taxation as between solicitor and client, client paying.[34] In the 1936 Rules of the Court of Session a decerniture for expenses as between solicitor and client when a third party or fund was paying was held to cover "those expenses which would be incurred by a prudent man of business without special instructions from the client in the knowledge that the account **19.46**

---

[25] *Milligan v. Tinne's Trs*, 1971 S.L.T. (Notes) 64.
[26] Mackay, *Practice*, ii, 585; Maclaren, *Expenses*, p. 509.
[27] R.C., VII, 10 (A.S., Mar. 18, 1936).
[28] *Miln's Judicial Factor v. Spence's Trs*, 1929 S.L.T. 279; *cf. Sinclair v. Royal Bank of Scotland*, 1983 S.L.T. 256.
[29] *Plasticisers Ltd v. Stewart & Sons (Hacklemakers) Ltd*, 1972 S.C. 268; *Milligan v. Tinne's Trs*, 1971 S.L.T. (Notes) 64.
[30] *British Railways Board v. Ross and Cromarty C.C.*, 1974 S.C. 27; *Walker v. McNeil*, 1981 S.L.T. (Notes) 21.
[31] *Milligan, supra.*
[32] Maclaren, *Expenses*, p. 509.
[33] *ibid.* p. 510, based on a consideration of *Walker v. Waterlow* (1869) 7 M. 751.
[34] *Miln's Judicial Factor, supra.*

would be taxed."[35] These rules are subject to the qualification that the expenses to be charged against an opposite party must be limited to "proper expenses of process".[36] Taxation as between solicitor and client, third party paying, is the appropriate basis of taxation where the taxation of expenses as between solicitor and client is authorised by statute.[37] It is usually the appropriate basis in actions of multiplepoinding where parties are allowed expenses as between agent and client out of the fund *in medio*.[38]

Further distinctions

19.47 There are other differences between party and party and solicitor and client accounts. As explained above, in accounts as between party and party it is not competent to make charges partly on the basis of the inclusive fees in the table of fees and partly on the basis of the detailed fees.[39] In accounts as between solicitor and client, however, it is competent to charge the account partly on the basis of the inclusive fees and partly on the basis of the detailed fees, but if an inclusive fee is charged no work falling thereunder may be charged again as a detailed fee. Further, it is specifically provided that in the taxation of accounts as between party and party only such expenses are allowed as are reasonable for conducting the litigation in a proper manner.[40] No such restriction is imposed on the taxation of accounts as between solicitor and client, but in all accounts, extrajudicial expenses are not chargeable.[41] Any expenses awarded against the party making up the account, such as the expenses of an amendment or debate, should not be included in an account on a party and party basis, but may be included in an account framed as between solicitor and client.

Scales of taxation

19.48 The taxation of accounts in ordinary and summary causes is regulated by the Table of Fees.[42] In the table, Chapters I, II and III specify fees and charges in ordinary causes, and Chapter IV those in summary causes. The latter are reduced in certain actions by a specified percentage unless the sheriff otherwise directs.[43] Taxation in accordance with the three former chapters is said to be on the ordinary cause scale, and taxation in accordance with Chapter IV is referred to as taxation on the appropriate summary cause scale. We have already examined the considerations determining which scale is applicable when a summary cause is treated as an ordinary cause,[44] and when an action is settled, whether judicially by minutes of tender and acceptance[45] or extrajudicially by joint minute.[46]

---

35 R.C., VII, 10, based on Lord McLaren's dictum in *Hood v. Gordon* (1896) 23 R. 675 at 676.
36 1993 A.S., Sched. 1, General Regulations, reg. 6; see para. 19.52.
37 *Hood, supra., per* Lord McLaren at 676.
38 *Park v. Colvilles Ltd*, 1960 S.C. 143 at 153.
39 para. 19.43.
40 1993 A.S., Sched. 1, General Regulations, reg. 8; see para. 19.43.
41 *Milligan v. Tinne's Trs*, 1971 S.L.T. (Notes) 64; paras 19.52, 19.53.
42 1993 A.S, Sched. 1, General Regulations, reg 1.
43 *ibid.* reg. 14(f).
44 para. 13.45.
45 para. 14.39.
46 para. 14.65.

Where in an ordinary cause the court has decerned for payment of a sum of money to a pursuer,[47] the pursuer's solicitor's account as between party and party is taxed by reference to the sum decerned for unless the sheriff otherwise directs.[48] Thus, unless the sheriff otherwise directs, where a decree in an ordinary action is pronounced for payment to the pursuer of a sum within the summary cause limit, the account will be taxed on the appropriate summary cause scale, the auditor deciding what expenses the pursuer would properly have incurred had the action been raised as a summary cause. A party seeking a direction that the account be taxed otherwise should so move the sheriff when he hears the motion for expenses. It has been observed[49] that the wording of the rule implies that in such a case taxation on the ordinary cause scale should be the exception rather than the rule, but whether a given case falls within the exception or not is very much a matter for the discretion of the sheriff; and that in determining the matter the sheriff should consider two questions: (1) whether the pursuer was entitled to raise the action as an ordinary cause in the first instance[50]; and if so (2) whether in the course of the action he should have taken steps to have it treated as a summary cause by concurring in or seeking to secure concurrence in a joint motion to that effect in terms of section 37(1)(a) of the 1971 Act.[51] If the answers are (1) yes and (2) no, the sheriff in his interlocutor awarding expenses directs the auditor to tax the account on the scale appropriate to an ordinary cause. In marginal cases the questions should not be answered by weighing the matter in too fine scales.[52] **19.49**

If in an ordinary cause no sum is decerned for and no direction as to the scale of taxation is given in the interlocutor awarding expenses, the account will be taxed on the ordinary cause scale.[53] A party who claims that it should be taxed on a particular summary cause scale should raise the matter when the motion for expenses is heard.[54] **19.50**

General rules in taxations

The General Regulations

Schedule 1 to the Act of Sederunt (Fees of Solicitors in the Sheriff Court) (Amendment and Further Provisions) 1993 contains General Regulations relative to expenses, including certain rules as to taxation which will be examined in the following paragraphs. It was said of similar General Regulations applicable in Court of Session taxations that they were merely a set of rules given out by the court for the guidance of the auditor, and that while they could not be set aside, "they are not a statute where one must necessarily stick upon the mere letter of what has been **19.51**

---

[47] "Pursuer" includes a plurality of pursuers, so that for the purposes of the rule the sums decerned for are aggregated: *Japp v. Adams*, 1939 S.C. 439.

[48] 1993 A.S., Sched. 1, General Regulations, reg. 2.

[49] *Scott v. Edina Garages Ltd*, Sh. Pr. O'Brien, Edinburgh Sh. Ct, Apr. 2, 1982, unreported.

[50] Perhaps the question should be whether he was justified in so raising the action (*Smith v. British Rail Engineering Ltd*, 1985 S.L.T. 463), or whether it was appropriate for him to do so (*McPherson v. British Railways Board*, 1985 S.L.T. 467).

[51] para. 13.47.

[52] *Smith, supra.*

[53] *McLeod v. Munro* (1930) 47 Sh.Ct.Rep. 21.

[54] *Lothian Hotels v. Ferer*, 1981 S.L.T. (Sh. Ct.) 52; approved, *Rae Associates v. Sneddon*, Sh. Pr. O'Brien, Edinburgh Sh. Ct, Apr. 12, 1983, unreported.

enjoined; they are merely rules for our guidance, of which we are fully entitled to interpret the spirit".[55] It is thought that a similar approach to the interpretation of the sheriff court General Regulations would be permissible only if adopted with extreme caution and in highly exceptional circumstances.[56] As already explained, the Regulations confer on the sheriff discretionary powers to increase or modify the fees in the table of fees.[57]

Pre-litigation expenses

19.52 Regulation 6 of the General Regulations provides that the expenses to be charged against the opposite party must be limited to proper expenses of process, and that no allowance beyond that specified in the table of fees may be made for preliminary investigations, with the following exceptions. Precognitions, plans, analyses, reports and the like, so far as relevant and necessary for proof of the matters in the record between the parties, may be allowed although taken or made before the raising of an action or the preparation of defences, or before proof is allowed, and although the case may not proceed to proof.[58] With these exceptions, any expenses incurred by a party in preparing or formulating a claim or defence before raising an action or lodging defences are not recoverable as judicial expenses since they are not "proper expenses of process".[59] The rule has been relaxed in exceptional circumstances,[60] but in general such expenses are not allowable, nor can they be recovered as damages in a subsequent separate action.[61] Thus, in a party and party account the unsuccessful party is chargeable only with the cost of the conduct of the litigation as a process and not with the cost of obtaining legal advice as to the advisability of raising an action or of lodging defences.[62] "It may be that there is a little hardship in it. There is always a certain amount of hardship in defending yourself against an unjust claim [or, it may be added, in vindicating a just claim]. But, at the same time, any opposite rule would lead to inexplicable confusion."[63]

19.53 Sheriff Dobie stated: "costs incurred prior to the service of a writ are not judicial expenses. A defender can avoid liability for expenses if he satisfies the claim or demand before the initial writ has been served."[64] In a subsequent sheriff court decision the latter sentence was disapproved, and it was held that in principle a creditor who has reasonably incurred expense through his debtor's failure to pay timeously should be entitled to recover that expense from his debtor, if before raising the action he has informed the debtor that he is taking active steps to recover the sum due;

---

[55] *Mica Insulator Co. Ltd v. Bruce Peebles & Co. Ltd*, 1907 S.C. 1293, *per* L.P. Dunedin at 1301.

[56] *Govan v. McKillop*, 1909 S.C. 562.

[57] paras 19.18 to 19.20 (increase); 19.09, 19.10 (modification).

[58] 1993 A.S., Sched. 1, General Regulations, reg. 6.

[59] *Mica Insulator Co. Ltd, supra*; *Clyde Nail Co. Ltd v. A. C. Moore & Co. Ltd*, 1949 S.L.T. (Notes) 43; *Milligan v. Tinne's Trs*, 1971 S.L.T. (Notes) 64.

[60] *Govan v. McKillop*, 1909 S.C. 562.

[61] *McDowall v. Stewart* (1871) 10 M. 193; *Shanks v. Cray*, 1977 S.L.T. (Notes) 26. Insurers may agree extrajudicially to pay the legal expenses of a claimant against their insured if the claim is settled before an action is raised.

[62] *Epps v. Newton*, 1951 S.C. 582.

[63] *Mica Insulator Co. Ltd, supra, per* L.P. Dunedin at 1302.

[64] Dobie, p. 309, citing *Mintons v. Hawley & Co.* (1882) 20 S.L.R. 126, and following Fyfe, p. 329.

and that in an undefended summary cause the creditor is entitled to recover the appropriate inclusive fee.[65] It is thought that that decision is incorrect. It is inconsistent with the terms of regulation 6 and with the decisions cited in the previous paragraph, which were apparently not considered. In any event it seems difficult to understand why a creditor whose debt has been paid before service should be entitled to an inclusive fee which includes the unnecessary expenses not only of service but of obtaining decree and an extract.

Unnecessary expenses

In the taxation of accounts as between party and party, only such expenses are allowed as are reasonable for conducting the litigation in a proper manner.[66] The auditor may disallow all charges for papers, parts of papers or particular procedure or agency which he judges irregular or unnecessary.[67] In all taxations, notwithstanding that a party has been found entitled to expenses generally, if it appears to the auditor that there is any particular part of the litigation in which he has proved unsuccessful, or that any part of the expenses has been occasioned through his own fault, he is not allowed the expense of such parts of the proceedings.[68] **19.54**

The latter rule is inapplicable where expenses are found to be expenses in the cause,[69] or where a pursuer merely fails to recover the full sum sued for.[70] Further, a debate on preliminary pleas is not a "part" of the proceedings within the meaning of the rule. Thus a general award of expenses in favour of a defender carries the expenses of a debate in which he has been unsuccessful, if those expenses have not been awarded to the pursuer.[71] But if a pursuer obtains a general award of expenses in an action in which he has craved a total sum made up of items which are founded on different grounds of action or, it would seem, has craved different sums against different defenders or has sued in different capacities, the litigation may be accordingly divided into "parts", and if he is unsuccessful in one of them, the auditor is entitled to apply the rule.[72] Again the rule is applicable notwithstanding that an award of expenses has been made subject to modification in respect of divided success. The auditor taxes the account as if the award were unqualified, taxing off any expenses clearly distinguishable as connected with a particular part of the litigation in which the party found entitled to expenses has proved unsuccessful, and the modification is applied after taxation.[73] In all cases, however, it is only when it is made abundantly clear that a party has been unsuccessful in a part of the case that the auditor, on that ground, should exercise the power conferred on him by the rule.[74] **19.55**

---

65 *Cadzow Finance Co. Ltd v. Fleming*, 1985 S.L.T. (Sh. Ct.) 37.
66 1993 A.S., Sched. 1, General Regulations, reg. 8; see para. 19.43.
67 *ibid.*
68 *ibid.* reg. 9.
69 *Glasgow and S.-W. Ry v. Ayr Mags*, 1911 S.C. 298.
70 *Nairn Bros v. Robertson*, 1954 S.L.T. (Sh. Ct.) 44.
71 *Earl of Lauderdale v. Wedderburn*, 1911 S.C. 4.
72 *Craig v. Craig* (1906) 14 S.L.T. 469; *Aitken v. Classen*, 1928 S.C. 628; Maclaren, *Expenses*, p. 444.
73 *McElroy & Sons v. Tharsis Sulphur and Copper Co.* (1879) 6 R. 1119; *Arthur v. Lindsay* (1895) 22 R. 904; *Aitken, supra.*
74 *Williamson v. John Williams (Wishaw) Ltd*, 1971 S.L.T. (Sh. Ct.) 2.

Outlays

19.56 In all cases the solicitor's outlays reasonably incurred in the furtherance of the litigation are allowed. These include a charge in respect of posts and sundries of 12 per cent of the taxed amount of the fees.[75]

19.57 Where a party who has been found entitled to expenses has incurred an account to an English solicitor, it is incompetent for a Scottish court to make a finding that the account falls to be taxed between party and party according to English rules. The proper procedure is for the auditor to require the English account to be stated in such a form as to make it clear to him what items of work were in fact done by the English solicitors in order for him to decide which items were admissible in a party and party account. Thereafter the auditor should ascertain what charges for the admitted items were appropriate in accordance with English law and practice, either from his own experience or from any reliable source he considered appropriate, *e.g.* the taxing master.[76] The Scottish solicitor's account should be charged on the basis of the detailed fees in Chapter III of the Table of Fees, in order that the auditor may ascertain whether any work charged by the English solicitor has been charged again by the Scottish solicitor.[77]

Value-added tax

19.58 Where the solicitor's charges are taxable supplies in terms of the Finance Act 1972 and the solicitor is a taxable person within the meaning of that Act, authority is given to make an addition to the fees in the table of such amount as is equivalent to the rate of value-added tax (VAT) at the date of supply, and that additional sum is so described in the solicitor's account.[78] Thus, if the party found entitled to expenses is a taxable person and the legal services have been supplied to him for the purposes of his business, the tax which he pays to his solicitor will be an input tax which he may recover by deducting it from his output tax. Accordingly his account should not include any element of VAT. If, on the other hand, the party is not a taxable person or if the legal services have not been supplied to him for the purposes of his business, he cannot recover the VAT but must bear it personally. In either of the latter cases, accordingly, an amount equivalent to the VAT should be added to the account to be paid by the other party.

Witnesses' fees

19.59 **General.** The rates of fees and the travelling and subsistence allowances payable to witnesses are set out in Schedule 1 to the Act of Sederunt (Fees of Witnesses and Shorthand Writers in the Sheriff Court) 1992,[79] as amended. When a party to a case is examined as a witness, whether in his own favour or at the instance of his adversary, he gives his evidence under the same conditions as any other witness, and if his evidence is necessary[80] he will be entitled to a fee and to travelling and subsistence allowances.[81]

---

75 1993 A.S., Sched. 1, General Regulations, reg. 11.

76 *Wimpey Construction (U.K.) Ltd v. Martin Black & Co (Wire Ropes) Ltd*, 1988 S.C. 264.

77 *Carlos Leasing v. Taylor*, 1986 S.L.T. (Sh. Ct.) 53.

78 1993 A.S., Sched. 1, General Regulations, reg. 13. See Practice Note by the Auditor of the Court of Session, Apr. 14, 1973 (*Parliament House Book*, C2004).

79 S.I. 1992 No. 1878, as amended by S.I. 1995 No. 1024; 1997 Nos 1118 and 1265; and 1998 No. 999.

80 If his evidence is unnecessary the charges will be taxed off under reg. 8 of the General Regulations in a party and party taxation: see para. 19.43.

81 *Dairon v. Dairon* (1900) 3 F. 230.

Witnesses present but not examined. Where a witness is present at a proof but is neither examined nor held as concurring with another witness, charges for his attendance may be allowed provided that a motion to that effect is made at the close of the proof and granted by the court, the name of the witness being recorded in the interlocutor.[82] The purpose of the rule is to enable the successful party to charge against the unsuccessful party the expense of the attendance at the proof of the witnesses so noted. The rule must, however, be applied with caution. It appears to be intended to apply to the normal case in which a witness has been precognosced and cited but it has become unnecessary to call him because the point to which his evidence was directed, though in controversy on record, has ceased to be disputed in the course of the proof, either because of an express admission or because of the failure of the opposing party's advocate to cross-examine witnesses already examined on the point. But where the witness has not been called because the advocate in charge of the case has deemed it unnecessary to add, on a point still in dispute, his evidence to that of other witnesses already called by him, a very exceptional case would require to be made out to justify the noting and allowance of that witness under the rule.[83] But pursuers who were awarded their expenses in relation to two aborted diets of proof were held entitled to the expenses of their witnesses attending these diets even although the court had not been made aware of their presence at the time.[84] This was on the basis that as a proof had not taken place on the dates in question, the provisions of the Act of Sederunt did not apply. If a case is settled on the day of the proof without any evidence being led the court should be moved to allow charges for the attendance of witnesses whose names should be recorded in the interlocutor in the same way as if they were witnesses who had not been called to give evidence at a proof which did proceed. A failure to do this will result in charges for the witnesses being disallowed by the auditor.[85] 19.60

Skilled witnesses. The following rules apply in cases where it is necessary to employ skilled persons to make investigations prior to the proof in order to qualify them to give evidence thereat. Charges for such investigations by a skilled person and for his attendance at the proof are allowed, in addition to the ordinary witness fee of such a person, at such a rate as in the discretion of the auditor is fair and reasonable. Before that may be done, however, a motion must be made to the sheriff for the certification of that person for additional remuneration as a skilled witness. The motion must be granted not later than the time at which expenses are awarded, and the witness's name must be recorded in the interlocutor.[86] These rules are applicable whether the taxation is as between party and party or as between solicitor and client.[87] Before the sheriff may grant a certificate the conditions discussed in the following paragraphs must be fulfilled. 19.61

---

[82] A.S. (Fees of Solicitors and Shorthand Writers in the Sheriff Court) 1992, Sched. 1, para. 8; *Towning & Sons v. Watson & Son*, 1968 S.L.T. (Sh. Ct.) 27.
[83] *Barrie v. SMT Co. Ltd*, 1936 S.L.T. 143.
[84] *B. Lewis (Upholstery) Ltd v. Hewitt*, 1987 S.C.L.R. 580.
[85] *Murray Williamson Builders Ltd v. Sweets Services Ltd*, 1992 S.C.L.R. 555.
[86] A.S. (Fees of Solicitors and Shorthand Writers in the Sheriff Court) 1992, Sched. 1, para. 9.
[87] *Reid v. North Isles District Committee of Orkney C.C.*, 1912 S.C. 627.

19.62 (1) The person in respect of whom certification is sought must be a "skilled person". The question whether a particular person is a skilled person may sometimes be difficult to resolve. There is no rigid rule that he must possess some technical qualification.[88] It is thought that he must, however, possess either a theoretical acquaintance with matters of scientific knowledge, or practical experience of the rules of any trade, manufacture or business with which men of ordinary intelligence are not likely to be familiar.[89]

19.63 (2) The person must have made investigations prior to the proof in order to qualify him to give evidence thereat,[90] and it must have been necessary to employ him to do so. If he speaks to matters already within his knowledge which do not require further investigation by him in order to qualify him to give evidence, certification will not be granted.[91] Thus, in a personal injuries action a medical man who has treated the pursuer in the ordinary course of his professional duties and has not required to make any special examination of him to qualify him to give evidence at the proof cannot be certified as a skilled witness. The court will not certify a witness who in the opinion of the court has been employed unnecessarily,[92] or a witness who is an official or employee of the party seeking certification and has made the investigations in the course of his duties.[93]

19.64 (3) As the 1992 Act of Sederunt (unlike its precedessors) does not provide for the motion for certification being made within a period of time after the issue of the sheriff's judgment following a proof, there can be no doubt that certification of an individual as a "skilled witness" is competent even where a case does not proceed to proof. However, if the case does not proceed to proof it is still essential that the motion for certification is made.[94]

19.65 (4) The 1992 Act of Sederunt does not specify the time when the motion for certification must be made. Instead, it states that it must be *granted* not later than the time at which expenses are awarded.[95] In practice such a motion is usually made orally either at the conclusion of the hearing on evidence or, if the question of expenses has been reserved, at the diet appointed for a hearing thereon. However, there is no reason why a written motion should not be lodged and the usual motion procedure followed[96] provided that the motion can be granted before an award of expenses is made. There is, in theory, no necessity for the motion for certification to be considered by the sheriff who heard the proof but there are obvious practical reasons why this should be done.

19.66 If the sheriff grants a certificate, additional charges are allowable only for prior investigations to qualify the witness to give evidence at the proof, and for his attendance at the proof. Charges cannot be allowed in terms of

---

[88] *Hopes and Lavery v. H.M. Advocate*, 1960 J.C. 104, *per* Lord Sorn at 113–114.
[89] Dickson, paras 397, 398, Macphail, *Evidence*, para. S17.10A.
[90] *Ferguson v. Johnston* (1886) 13 R. 635.
[91] *Lacey v. Russell*, 1966 S.L.T. (Sh. Ct.) 76.
[92] *Ayton v. National Coal Board*, 1965 S.L.T. (Notes) 24; *Lacey, supra.*
[93] *McHarg, Rennie & Lindsay v. Tauber*, 1953 S.L.T. (Sh. Ct.) 10.
[94] *Clark v. Laddaws Ltd*, 1994 S.L.T. 792; *Merrick Homes Ltd v. Duff (No.2)*, 1997 S.L.T. 53.
[95] A.S. (Fees of Solicitors and Shorthand Writers in the Sheriff Court) 1992, Sched. 1, para. 9.
[96] In terms of OCR, Chap. 15.

the rule for meetings, correspondence or documents such as precognitions which are extraneous to such investigations,[97] or for assistance given to the party's legal advisers during the proof or the hearing on evidence, or for investigations made during the proof,[98] or for further attendance at the proof after deponing.[99]

If a skilled person prepares a report in order to enable a party properly to prepare his case and the action does not thereafter proceed to proof, certification of the person as a skilled witness is not appropriate; indeed it is incompetent.[1] The question whether a charge for such a report should be attoned is one for the discretion of the auditor.[2]

---

[97] *Butters Bros & Co. v. British Diatomite Co.* (1906) 23 Sh.Ct.Rep. 6; *Bellshill Hosiery Co. v. Lanark C.C.* (1948) 64 Sh.Ct.Rep. 206.

[98] *Caledonian Ry v. Greenock Corporation*, 1922 S.C. 299.

[99] *Butters Bros & Co., supra.*

[1] *Parratt v. Ceiling Decor Ltd*, 1998 S.C.L.R. 556; *cf. Merrick Homes Ltd, supra.*

[2] 1993 A.S., Sched. 1, General Reguations, reg. 6; *Hamilton v. Hamilton*, 1998 S.C.L.R. 773.

PART IV

ORDINARY CAUSES WITH SPECIAL RULES

Chapter 20

DECLARATORY ACTIONS

Nature and competency

Introduction

A declaratory action is one in which a right is craved to be declared in favour of the pursuer, but nothing is demanded to be paid or performed by the defender.[1] The object of the action is either that the court should declare in the pursuer's favour that some right exists, or that the court should declare to be non-existent what appears to be an existent right. It is incompetent to bring an action to have a fact declared which has no legal consequences for the pursuer, or to seek a judicial opinion on an abstract question of law. The pursuer must have an interest to have declared to be his—some particular right which is not clear or which some other person is challenging, or to have it declared that the defender is not entitled to exercise a certain right claimed by him. The court will only grant a declarator in respect of a live, practical issue having a sufficient degree of reality and immediacy. It does not seem possible to formulate any more specific general rule for determining whether the necessary conditions of competency are met.[2] The nature and scope of the remedy of declarator are fully examined in the undernoted work.[3] 20.01

Sheriff court

Section 5(1) of the 1907 Act provides that the jurisdiction of the sheriff extends to and includes "actions of declarator (except declarators of marriage or nullity of marriage)".[4] The effect of section 5(1) was to add to the forms of procedure available in the sheriff court, but not to confer upon it by implication any new jurisdiction, such as jurisdiction to review administrative decisions of local authorities.[5] An action of declarator is therefore competent in the sheriff court where its subject-matter is a right of any description which falls within the court's jurisdiction. Examples include rights regarding heritage, which may be the subject of a declarator of right of way or of the existence of a trust[6]; or rights regarding contract, as in a 20.02

---

[1] Stair, IV, iii, 47; Ersk., IV, i, 46.

[2] *Gifford v. Traill* (1829) 7 S. 854; *N.B. Ry v. Birrel's Trs*, 1918 S.C. (H.L.) 33, *per* Lord Dunedin at 47; *Beardmore & Co. v. Barry*, 1928 S.C. (H.L.) 47 *per* Viscount Dunedin at 52; *Macnaughton v. Macnaughton's Trs*, 1953 S.C. 387, *per* L.J.-C. Thomson at 392; *Aberdeen Development Co. v. Mackie Ramsay & Taylor*, 1977 S.L.T. 177; *Annandale & Eskdale D.C. v. N.W. Water Authority*, 1978 S.C. 187; *Esso Petroleum Co. Ltd v. Hall Russell & Co. Ltd*, 1988 S.L.T. 874, *per* Lord Jauncey of Tullichettle at 886; *Shaw v. Strathclyde R.C.*, 1988 S.L.T. 313; Anon., "Hypothetical or Practical Questions", 1968 S.L.T. (News) 81.

[3] Walker, *Civil Remedies*, Chap. 8.

[4] 1907 Act, s. 5(1), as amended by Law Reform (Parent and Child) (Scotland) Act 1986, Sched. 2.

[5] *Brown v. Hamilton D.C.*, 1983 S.C. (H.L.) 1, *per* Lord Fraser of Tullybelton at 45.

[6] *e.g. Pickard v. Pickard*, 1963 S.C. 604.

declarator that a particular contract was entered into or was terminated; and actions for declarator of death,[7] or for declarator that a will is holograph of the testator.[8] Declarators of marriage or nullity of marriage, and of freedom and putting to silence, and certain declarators that a person is a British subject, are competent in the Court of Session only,[9] but declarators of parentage, non-parentage, legitimacy, legitimation or illegitimacy may be brought in the sheriff court,[10] as may a declarator that a person may legally marry in Scotland.[11] Actions of proving the tenor, which contain declaratory conclusions but are not regarded as actions of declarator,[12] are also privative to the Court of Session; but the terms of a document may in certain circumstances be proved incidentally in the course of a depending action in the sheriff court.[13] An action which is in form a declarator but in substance a reduction is incompetent in the sheriff court.[14] An application to rectify a defectively expressed document, which has much in common with an action of declarator but which is not so styled, is competent in the sheriff court.[15]

Defenders

20.03 All proper contradictors, that is, all parties interested in denying the pursuer's claim, must be called as defenders, so that the decree shall constitute *res judicata* as regards the right in question.[16] Where the legitimacy or parentage of a child is in issue, intimation to the child may be required.[17] Declaratory actions against the Crown have already been discussed.[18]

Crave

20.04 A declaratory crave may be, and usually is, supplemented by a crave for an operative decree such as interdict or damages. If the title upon which an operative decree, of whatsoever kind, is asked requires investigation or proof before it can be satisfactorily made out, it may be expedient to precede the crave for the operative decree by a declaratory crave in order to bring out clearly the issue on which the decision depends.[19] An action which craves only a declarator and no other remedy (usually called a "bare" declarator) is competent provided that the declarator would determine a live practical question.[20]

---

[7] paras 20.06 to 20.18.
[8] paras 20.19 to 20.22.
[9] para. 2.39.
[10] para. 2.64, 22.02.
[11] *Bliersbach v. MacEwen*, 1959 S.C. 43.
[12] *Dunbar & Co. v. Scottish County Investment Co.*, 1920 S.C. 210.
[13] para. 2.43.
[14] *Cornhill Insurance Co. Ltd v. Fraser Owen & Co. Ltd* (1936) 53 Sh.Ct.Rep. 168.
[15] Law Reform (Miscellaneous Provisions) (Scotland) Act 1985, s. 8(9).
[16] *Fleming v. McLagan* (1879) 6 R. 588; *Allgemeine Deutsche Credit Anstalt v. Scottish Amicable Life Assurance Society*, 1908 S.C. 33; *Gillespie v. Riddell*, 1908 S.C. 629 (affd 1909 S.C. (H.L.) 3); *Smith v. McColl's Trs*, 1910 S.C. 1121.
[17] OCR, rr. 33.1 and 33.15; *Soutar v. Kilroe*, 1994 S.C.L.R. 757 (Sh. Ct).
[18] para. 4.57.
[19] *Duke of Argyll v. Campbeltown Coal Co.*, 1924 S.C. 844; *Scott v. Scott*, 1958 S.L.T. (Sh. Ct.) 40.
[20] *Beardmore & Co. v. Barry*, 1928 S.C. (H.L.) 47, *per* Viscount Dunedin at 52; *Macnaughton v. Macnaughton's Trs*, 1953 S.C. 387; *Kelly v. Cornhill Insurance Co.*, 1964 S.C. (H.L.) 46; *Unigate Foods Ltd v. Scottish Milk Marketing Board*, 1975 S.C. (H.L.) 75, *per* Lord Fraser of Tullybelton at 110–111; *McLean v. Marwhirn Developments Ltd*, 1976 S.L.T. (Notes) 47; *Shaw v. Strathclyde R.C.*, *supra*.

An action for declarator is incompetent unless the declarator sought is precise and unambiguous in its terms.[21] **20.05**

Declarator of death

Introduction

Under the Presumption of Death (Scotland) Act 1977 an action of declarator of the death of a missing person may be raised either where the missing person is thought to have died or where he has not been known to be alive for a period of at least seven years.[22] The grounds on which the sheriff court has jurisdiction in such an action have already been explained.[23] **20.06**

Initial writ

The action may be brought by any person having an interest, including the Lord Advocate for the public interest.[24] The missing person should be called as a defender.[25] The initial writ should include a crave for a warrant for intimation to the persons specified in the next paragraph, naming and designing them and stating the capacity in which intimation is to be made.[26] **20.07**

Service

The pursuer must serve a copy initial writ on the following persons, where they have not already been called as defenders[27]: (1) the husband or wife of the missing person; (2) any child including an illegitimate or adopted child of the missing person, or if the missing person has no children, the nearest known relative of that person; (3) any person, including insurers, who as far as the pursuer is aware has any interest in the action; and (4) the Lord Advocate.[28] The sheriff may on the motion of the pursuer dispense with service on any of these persons except the Lord Advocate.[29] The pursuer may move the sheriff, on cause shown, to shorten or extend the period of notice in terms of rule 3.6(2). In the Court of Session the usual period of notice in such an action is 21 days.[30] **20.08**

Advertisement

The sheriff must order advertisement in such form as he thinks fit, and must call for information about the survival or death of the missing person.[31] Since advertisement is obligatory, irrespective of whether defences are lodged indicating knowledge of the present whereabouts of the missing person, it is thought that the order for advertisement may most conveniently be made at the same time as the warrant for service and **20.09**

---

[21] *Rothfield v. N.B. Ry*, 1920 S.C. 805; *Couper v. McGuiness* (1948) 64 Sh.Ct.Rep. 249; *Aberdeen Development Co. v. Mackie Ramsay & Taylor*, 1977 S.L.T. 177.

[22] Presumption of Death (Scotland) Act 1977 (hereafter the "1977 Act"), s. 1(1).

[23] para. 2.65.

[24] 1977 Act, ss. 1(1) and 17.

[25] OCR, rr. 37.2(1) and 5.6(1)(a); *cf. Horak v. Lord Advocate*, 1984 S.L.T. 201.

[26] OCR, r. 37.2(3).

[27] *Horak, supra.*

[28] A.S. (Presumption of Death) 1978 (S.I. 1978 No. 162), para. 2(1); the form of crave and notice of intimation are prescribed by OCR, r. 37.2(3) and (4).

[29] A.S. (Presumption of Death) 1978, para. 2(2); OCR, r. 37.2(5).

[30] RCS, r. 50.2(2).

[31] A.S. (Presumption of Death) 1978, para. 2(3).

intimation is granted, on a written motion by the pursuer which specifies the newspapers or other publications in which it is proposed that advertisement would in all the circumstances be appropriate. Where no minute is lodged indicating knowledge of the whereabouts of the missing person, the sheriff may, at any time before the determination of the action, make such order for further advertisement as he thinks fit.[32]

Defences: minutes

20.10 Any of the persons upon or to whom service or intimation has been made may lodge defences.[33] Any person having an interest, including the Lord Advocate for the public interest, may lodge a minute seeking the making by the court of any determination or appointment[34] not sought by the pursuer.[35]

Remit to the Court of Session

20.11 At any stage of the proceedings the sheriff may remit the action to the Court of Session, either of his own accord or on the application of any party to the action. He must remit if so directed by the Court of Session. The Court of Session may give such a direction on the application of any party to the action. The remit is made where the sheriff or, as the case may be, the Court of Session considers a remit desirable because of the importance or complexity of the matters at issue.[36]

Proof

20.12 Irrespective of whether any defences or minutes are lodged, the sheriff must hear proof. The standard of proof is the balance of probabilities.[37] Where no minute has been lodged, and after such further advertisement as may have been ordered, the pursuer applies to the sheriff by motion for an order for proof.[38] Proof is by affidavit evidence unless the sheriff otherwise directs.[39] Any person, including the Secretary of State for Social Services, who possesses information relating to the survival or death of the missing person, and who is aware that an action of declarator has been raised, has a duty to disclose that information by means of a written communication to the sheriff clerk, subject to the rules of law and practice relating to the privilege of witnesses and havers, confidentiality of communications and withholding or non-disclosure of information on the grounds of public interest.[40] A statement purporting to be an instrument made or issued by or on behalf of any Minister of the Crown and disclosing to the court facts relating to the action is sufficient evidence of those facts.[41] Similarly, a decree or judgment of a court furth of Scotland which is analogous to a decree of declarator under the 1977

---

[32] OCR, r. 37.3.

[33] *Horak*, *supra*.

[34] See para. 20.13

[35] 1977 Act, s. 1(5); the form of such a minute and the mode of intimation are prescribed by OCR, r. 37.2(6) and (7).

[36] 1977 Act, s. 1(6). *Cf.* the criterion of "the importance or difficulty of the cause" in the 1971 Act, s. 37(1)(b): see paras 13.58, 13.59.

[37] 1977 Act, s. 2(1).

[38] OCR, r. 37.4(1).

[39] OCR, r. 37.4(2).

[40] 1977 Act, s. 9(1) and (2).

[41] *ibid.* s. 9(3).

Act is sufficient evidence of the facts declared therein.[42] The reporting of the action by the media is not restricted by the Judicial Proceedings (Regulation of Reports) Act 1926.[43]

Decree

Contents of interlocutor. If, having heard proof, the sheriff is satisfied on a balance of probabilities that the missing person has died, he grants decree of declarator accordingly and includes in the decree a finding as to the date and time of death. If, however, it is uncertain when, within any period of time, the missing person died, the sheriff must find that he died at the end of that period.[44] If the sheriff is satisfied that the missing person has not been known to be alive for a period of at least seven years, he must find that he died at the end of the day occurring seven years after the date on which he was last known to be alive and grant decree accordingly.[45] In granting decree the sheriff has power to deal with the following matters. He may determine the domicile of the missing person at the date of his death.[46] He may determine any question relating to any interest in property which arises as a consequence of the death.[47] He may appoint a judicial factor on the estate of the missing person notwithstanding what the value of the estate may be.[48] The Act of Sederunt (Judicial Factors Rules) 1992 applies to an application for the appointment of a judicial factor under the 1977 Act.[49] **20.13**

Effect of decree. The decree takes effect on the expiry of the time for appeal or, where an appeal has been taken, when the appeal is withdrawn or refused. Subject to the provisions of the 1977 Act as to the recall or variation of decrees,[50] the decree is conclusive of the matters contained in it and is effective against any person and for all purposes including the dissolution of a marriage to which the missing person is a party and the acquisition of rights to or in property belonging to any person. A declarator that a missing person has died seven years after he was last known to be alive does not, however, determine a substantive question which is properly referable to a foreign law otherwise than in accordance with that law. If the missing person was alive at the declared date of death, that fact does not invalidate the dissolution of his marriage, but it leaves unaffected his responsibility or that of any other person for the commission of any crime or offence.[51] **20.14**

Intimation to Registrar General. Where decree has been granted, the sheriff clerk must notify the prescribed particulars[52] to the Registrar General of Births, Deaths and Marriages for Scotland. He does so on the expiration of the time for appeal or, where an appeal has been taken, **20.15**

---

42 1977 Act, s. 10.
43 *ibid.* s. 14.
44 *ibid.* s. 2(1)(a).
45 *ibid.* s. 2(1)(b).
46 *ibid.* s. 2(2)(a).
47 *ibid.* s. 2(2)(b).
48 *ibid.* s. 2(2)(c).
49 OCR, r. 37.6(1).
50 para. 20.18.
51 1977 Act, s. 3.
52 The particulars are prescribed by the Registration of Presumed Deaths (Prescription of Particulars) (Scotland) Regulations 1978 (S.I. 1978 No. 160).

on the conclusion of any appellate proceedings.[53] Where an appeal has been taken or a remit made to the Court of Session this duty devolves on the appropriate clerk of that court.

20.16 **Insurance.** Where decree has been granted, the trustee administering the estate of the missing person or any other trust under which property devolves upon or is transmitted to any person by reason of the missing person's death is required, unless the court otherwise directs, to effect a policy of insurance against any claim which may arise if the decree is varied or recalled on an application made within five years of its date.[54]

Direction that value of certain rights irrecoverable

20.17 Where decree has been granted, the sheriff may then or at any time thereafter make an order directing that the value of any rights to or in any property acquired as a result of the decree shall not be recoverable by virtue of an order made on variation or recall of the decree. Such an order may be made on the application of any person whom the missing person would have had a non-contractual duty to aliment, or of the trustee mentioned in the preceding paragraph. The sheriff may make the order subject to such conditions, if any, as he sees fit.[55] It is thought that the application should be made by minute in the original process.

Recall or variation of decree

20.18 The decree may be varied or recalled on the application of any person having an interest. The application may be made any any time,[56] but no further order as to property rights may be made if the application is made more than five years after the date of the decree.[57] The application should be made by way of minute in the original process.[58] On the lodging of such a minute the sheriff makes an order for service upon the missing person, where his whereabouts have become known, for intimation to those persons mentioned in rule 37.2(3) and for the lodging of answers within such time as he thinks fit.[59] The rules as to remit to the Court of Session,[60] disclosure of information[61] and intimation of particulars to the Registrar General[62] apply to an application for a variation order as they do to an action of declarator. By a variation order the court may make any determination or appointment referred to in section 2 of the 1977 Act.[63] Further any person having an interest may, where an application for a variation order has been sought, apply to the court for the making of any determination or appointment referred to in section 2 of the 1977 Act which has not been sought by the person making the application for the variation order.[64] Where such a person wishes to seek such a determination or appointment he must include the appropriate crave in his

---

53 1977 Act, s. 12.
54 *ibid.* ss. 6(1) and 17.
55 *ibid.* s. 7.
56 *ibid.* s. 4(1).
57 *ibid.* s. 5(4).
58 OCR, r. 57.5(1).
59 OCR, r. 37.5(2).
60 1977 Act, s. 4(4).
61 *ibid.* s. 12; para. 20.12.
62 *ibid.* s. 12; para. 20.15.
63 *ibid.* s. 4(2); see para. 20.13.
64 *ibid.* s. 4(3).

answers,[65] send copies of the answers by registered or recorded delivery post to the minuter and to all other persons on whom service or intimation of the minute was ordered and lodge in process the appropriate evidence of posting.[66] Where the application for the variation order has been made to the court within the period of five years beginning with the date of the decree, the court when making the variation order must make such further order, if any, in relation to any rights to or in any property acquired as a result of the decree as it considers fair and reasonable in all the circumstances of the case. Such a further order must not affect any income accruing between the date of the decree and the date of the order.[67] In making such a further order the court must, so far as practicable in the circumstances, have regard to the considerations set out in section 5(3).[68] Where estate duty or inheritance tax falls to be repaid as a result of a variation order having been pronounced, the court may order the duty or tax to be repaid to the person entitled to receive repayment.[69]

Declarator that will holograph

An action for declarator that a testamentary writing of a deceased person is holograph of that person proceeds as an ordinary action, subject to the following provisions of the Act of Sederunt of July 19, 1935.[70] Since the coming into force of the Requirements of Writing (Scotland) Act 1995 it would appear that only the authenticity of the testator's signature is likely to be relevant.[71] The writ is served on the persons who by virtue of the Succession (Scotland) Act 1964 are entitled to succeed to the heritable property of the deceased on intestacy, and on such other interested persons as the sheriff may direct.[72] **20.19**

The sheriff may accept affidavits as evidence that the writing and signature of the testamentary writing is in the proper handwriting of the deceased. There must be at least two affidavits by persons who depone that they are well acquainted with his handwriting and signature. They may so depone notwithstanding that they have a patrimonial interest in the deceased's estate.[73] The affidavits may be endorsed on the testamentary writing or on an extract thereof, or may be contained in separate documents which refer to the writing or extract *in gremio*. They may be taken before a magistrate, commissioner for oaths, justice of the peace or notary public, not being the pursuer's solicitor or one of his partners or employees, or before any commissioner whom the sheriff may appoint.[74] **20.20**

Where in the opinion of the sheriff the affidavits are insufficient to **20.21**

---

[65] OCR, r. 37.5(3).

[66] OCR, r. 37.5(4).

[67] 1977 Act, s. 5(2) and (4).

[68] See the annotations to s. 5 of the 1977 Act by H. McN. Henderson in *Scottish Current Law Statutes*.

[69] 1977 Act, s. 8, read with Finance Act 1986, s.100.

[70] A.S. (S.R. & O. 1935 No. 756), para. 1(4).

[71] Requirements of Writing (Scotland) Act 1995, ss. 2(1) and 11(3)(b)(ii).

[72] A.S. (S.R. & O. 1935 No. 756), para. 1(1), read with Succession (Scotland) Act 1964, Sched. 2, para. 1, as amended by Law Reform (Miscellaneous Provisions) (Scotland) Act 1968, Sched. 3.

[73] *ibid.* para. 1(2); *quaere* whether the requirement of two or more affidavits is affected by the Civil Evidence (Scotland) Act 1988, s. 1(1).

[74] *ibid.* 1(3). On the formalities relative to affidavits, see Walker and Walker, *Evidence*, para. 409; Macphail, *Evidence*, para. S10.03A.

enable the question at issue to be disposed of, or further evidence is required, the sheriff may direct the party lodging the affidavits to lodge a further affidavit or affidavits, or may appoint that party to prove the relevant facts by the ordinary rules of evidence.[75]

20.22 A holograph will has been set up incidentally, without a declarator, in an action in which it was founded on.[76] It is submitted that it would usually be expedient to include a declaratory crave in such an action.[77]

---

[75] A.S. July 19, 1935, para. 1(2).
[76] *McPherson v. Cameron's Exr*, 1942 S.L.T. (Sh. Ct.) 26.
[77] para. 20.04.

CHAPTER 21

PETITORY ACTIONS

"Petitory actions are so called, not because something is sought to be awarded by the judge (for in that sense all actions must be petitory), but because some demand is made upon the defender, in consequence either of a right of property or credit in the pursuer."[1] In Part III of this book we considered the procedure in an ordinary petitory action for payment of money to which no special procedural rules are applicable. In this chapter we notice various categories of petitory action in which particular rules or practices must be followed. They include: (1) certain actions for payment of money—actions of count, reckoning and payment; actions of damages for personal injuries or death; actions of furthcoming; actions of multiplepoinding; and actions for payment of a solicitor's account; (2) actions *ad factum praestandum*; and (3) actions of interdict. Certain actions connected with heritable subjects, which may be classified as petitory actions, are considered in Chapter 23. **21.01**

ACTIONS FOR PAYMENT OF MONEY

Action of count, reckoning and payment

Competency

In an action of count, reckoning and payment (sometimes less accurately termed an action of accounting) the pursuer craves production by the defender of an account and payment of the sum found due to the pursuer; and failing the defender's appearance or production, payment of a specified sum. The conditions in which such an action is competent are not entirely clear. The traditional explanation is that the action is "founded upon the relation of principal and agent, in which the principal, whether he be a partner, beneficiary, landlord, or other principal, demands an account of his agent's intromissions, whether he be a co-partner, guardian, factor, or other agent, with the estate of the principal."[2] In *Coxall v. Stewart*,[3] however, Lord Maxwell criticised that statement and observed: **21.02**

> "Where assets belonging to one person come into the possession of another and where the person to whom the assets belong has, broadly speaking, a right to recover those assets or their value from the possessor, but where the nature of the property, or the rights and obligations of the possessor, or both are such that the intromissions of the possessor may affect the precise extent or value of

---

[1] Ersk., IV, i, 47.

[2] Maclaren, p. 654; *Unigate Foods Ltd v. Scottish Milk Marketing Board*, 1975 S.C. (H.L.) 75, *per* Lord Stott (Ordinary) at 77–78.

[3] 1976 S.L.T. 275 at 276.

> the owner's claim against him, at least in some cases our law provides the remedy of an action of count, reckoning and payment. For example the remedy is clearly provided where the possessor's possession arises from a contract of agency. I can see neither logic nor equity in granting this remedy in a case where the possession is derived from a legal relationship entitling the possessor to possess, but withholding it where possession has been taken without right or title of any kind."

In a later case his Lordship commented that the precise scope of an action of count, reckoning and payment was not very clear and its procedure was perhaps unduly cumbersome for modern conditions.[4] The nature of the action is examined in the undernoted work.[5]

Procedure

21.03 The procedure in actions of count, reckoning and payment in the sheriff court was in some measure regulated by paragraphs 87 to 90 of the Act of Sederunt of July 10, 1839, which fell with the repeal of the Sheriff Courts (Scotland) Act 1838 by the 1907 Act.[6] There are no special provisions for such actions in the 1907 Act or in the Ordinary Cause Rules.[7] In fact actions of count, reckoning and payment do not fall very happily into the scheme of the Ordinary Cause Rules and may perhaps be looked on as *sui generis*. Callings in court of such actions to decide further procedure[8] may be in the "procedure roll" or whatever other roll the court has for dealing with miscellaneous procedural matters.[9] The subsequent paragraphs of this section attempt only to describe the current practice of the court. The progress of the action ought usually to fall into two separate and clearly defined sections: (1) a decision on the liability of the defender to account to the pursuer; and (2) when that matter has been admitted or decided, a decision on any points in dispute on the figures in the accounts produced.

21.04 **Initial writ.** *Crave.* In the initial writ the pursuer normally craves production by the defender of a full account of his intromissions, and payment of a specified sum or such other sum as may appear to be the true balance due by the defender with interest thereon from the date of citation; and in the event of the defender failing to appear or failing to produce such an account, payment of the specified sum. The account craved is usually an account down to the date of citation, and in that event interest is allowable only from that date.[10] If the pursuer seeks an account down to the date of the decree to be pronounced in the action, that should be specifically craved.[11] A crave for arrestment on the dependence is competent, without supporting averments.[12] The sum stated in the alternative crave may be, but need not be, the maximum which can be found

---

[4] *Cunninghame-Jardine v. Cunninghame-Jardine's Trs*, 1979 S.L.T. 298 at 299; see also *Coxall, supra*, at 278; *Ritchie v. EFT Industrial Ltd*, 1997 S.C.L.R. 955.

[5] Walker, *Civil Remedies*, Chap. 17.

[6] *Inglis's Trs v. Macpherson*, 1910 S.C. 46.

[7] Paradoxically, there is special provision for actions of count, reckoning and payment in the summary cause rules: SCR, rr. 65–67. See Vol. 2 of this work.

[8] See para. 21.11.

[9] See para. 5.41.

[10] *Wallace v. Henderson* (1875) 2 R. 999 at 1001.

[11] *Wauchope v. N.B. Ry* (1860) 23 D. 191 at 201.

[12] para. 11.11.

due on an accounting.[13] The object of the alternative crave is to enable the pursuer to take decree for a definite sum in the event of the defender failing to lodge a notice of intention to defend, or defending and failing to produce an account. If an accounting takes place, decree will be granted for whatever sum is disclosed to be due, even if it is larger than the sum stated.[14]

Condescendence. The condescendence should deal only with the defender's liability to account, averring the relationship between the parties whereby the pursuer is entitled to an accounting, and that he has requested the defender to account and the defender has refused to do so. The appropriate stage for raising matters relating to the basis of the claim and to its quantification is after production of the accounts. It has been observed that if the pursuer has already received accounts and is in as good a position to formulate his claim as he could be after a formal lodging of the accounts, the initial writ should state the basis in law and amount of his claim.[15] It is respectfully submitted that in the sheriff court such a course may be appropriate only where it is clear that the facts at issue will be simple and few in number. In other cases it may be preferable to preserve the distinction between the two stages of procedure referred to above: if the second stage becomes combined and confused with the first in the initial writ, the pleadings may become very difficult to understand.[16] **21.05**

Plea-in-law. The exact form of the plea will depend on the circumstances giving rise to the action. The premises should state the relationship between the parties and the conclusion should state that the pursuer is entitled to an accounting from the defender. An example would be "The defender having acted as agent for the pursuer, the pursuer is entitled to an accounting from the defender in respect of his intromissions." **21.06**

Undefended action. If no notice of intention to defend is lodged, no order for the lodging of accounts will be made and decree in absence may be granted for the sum specified in the alternative crave. **21.07**

Procedure after defences lodged. *Liability to account disputed*. If defences are lodged in which liability to account is not admitted, the action proceeds like any other action,[17] and the sheriff decides the question of liability to account after debate, proof or proof before answer. If he decides that there is no liability to account, the action comes to an end with the defender being assoilzied. **21.08**

Liability to account admitted or established. If liability to account is admitted in the defences or is established by the decision of the sheriff, the defender is ordered to produce an account within a specified period, the pursuer is allowed to lodge objections thereto and the defender to lodge answers to the objections within further specified periods. The interlocutor allowing objections and answers should appoint the case to call on the procedure roll[18] in order that a period for adjustment may be fixed. If accounts are lodged with the defences, it may still be appropriate **21.09**

---

[13] *Coxall, supra.*
[14] *Spottiswoode v. Hopkirk* (1853) 16 D. 59.
[15] *Donald v. Hodgart's Trs* (1893) 21 R. 246; *Cunninghame-Jardine, supra.*
[16] W. J. D., "Procedure in Actions of Accounting" (1950) 66 S.L.R. 276.
[17] See Chap. 8.
[18] See para. 21.03.

to make an order for production of accounts and to hold the accounts already lodged to be the accounts called for under the order.[19] The defender should be given an opportunity to produce an account of his intromissions even though he cannot produce documents such as books, vouchers and receipts.[20] If it is admitted or apparent that after an accounting a sum will be due, the sheriff may order the defender to consign a specified sum.[21] Once accounts have been lodged, it is incompetent to grant decree by default for the sum craved failing production of the accounts.[22] In the usual case where the accounts lodged by a defender have been prepared not by him but by a third party such as an auditor, the defender as well as the pursuer is entitled to challenge the accounts.[23]

21.10 *Form of objections and answers.* The objections and answers should be in the form of statements of facts with pleas-in-law annexed. While pleas-in-law are probably not essential, they are desirable as focusing each point.[24] In the objections and answers the parties may join issue on any question arising from the accounts.[25] Objections are not a vehicle for general criticisms of the defender's intromissions. Their usual purpose is to show that the balance brought out in the accounts as due to the pursuer ought to be larger, either because the defender has taken credit for some amount to which he was not entitled or because he has failed to debit himself with some amount as he ought to have done. Each objection should deal with a particular item and must be supported by relevant averments.[26]

> "The form in which the objections are stated will vary with the nature of the objections themselves. If they consist of unconnected criticisms of various items in the accounts, the most convenient course may be to state each objection as a separate item under its date and keep the whole in chronological order. On the other hand, if one or more objections of a general nature will affect numerous items in the accounts it may be more convenient to state these objections and specify, or detail, under each head the different items which are affected. The primary consideration is to state precisely what is objected to, and to set out the objections in such a way that the items in question can be readily traced in the accounts."[27]

21.11 *Disposal of objections.* As has already been mentioned,[28] once the objections and answers have been lodged the case should call in court so that a period for adjustment may be allowed. The length of this period may be agreed by the parties but, at the end of the day, it is a matter for the sheriff's discretion. Either party may move the sheriff to extend the adjustment period originally allowed. The interlocutor allowing adjustment should appoint the case to call in court again at the end of the adjustment period in order that further procedure may be determined. At

---

19 *Encyclopaedia*, i, para. 103.
20 *Smith v. Barclay*, 1962 S.C. 1.
21 paras 11.43 to 11.51.
22 *Neill v. Neill* [1948] C.L.Y. 4887.
23 *Wylie v. Corrigan*, 1998 G.W.D. 34-1731.
24 *e.g. Clarke v. Clarke's Trs*, 1925 S.C. 693 at 698, 699; *Guthrie v. McKimmie's Tr.*, 1952 S.L.T. (Sh. Ct.) 49.
25 *Polland v. Sturrock's Exrs*, 1952 S.C. 535, *per* L.J.-C. Thomson at 545; *Holiday v. Kirkpatrick's Trs*, 1985 S.L.T. 197.
26 *Guthrie, supra.*
27 W. J .D., "Procedure in Actions of Accounting" (1950) 66 S.L.R. 276 at 278–279.
28 para. 21.09.

this calling the record is closed on the objections and answers. This calling may be compared with an options hearing[29] but as there is no provision for it in the Ordinary Cause Rules, the requirement of lodging a note of the basis of any preliminary plea[30] does not apply. Nevertheless the solicitor appearing for a party who has stated a preliminary plea should be prepared to explain to the sheriff why it justifies a debate if that is what he seeks. The issues in the objections and answers may be disposed of by debate, proof or proof before answer, or by a remit to an accountant. Such a remit may take place at any stage and may be convenient where a material part of the objections consists of matters of pure accountancy such as involve investigations into the books, or the method of stating the accounts, or the production and examination of vouchers.[31] A remit may be made notwithstanding the opposition of either party.[32] The interlocutor making the remit should make it clear that either party is entitled to object to the terms of the report on the remit. When the issues are finally disposed of the decree is not restricted by the sum stated in the crave but may be pronounced for any greater or smaller sum that may be found due.[33] If a contingent tax liability is outstanding, the court may order the defender to lodge the sum in the hands of the sheriff clerk pending the final ascertainment of the liability.[34]

Actions of damages for personal injuries or death

Actions of damages for personal injuries or for the death of a relative follow the general rules of procedure in petitory actions, subject to the qualifications noted in the following paragraphs. The limitation rules which are applicable to such actions have already been noticed,[35] as have the rules and practices as to the contents of the written pleadings,[36] the recovery of documents including accident reports, hospital records and wages records,[37] and the matters to be dealt with at the hearing on evidence.[38] **21.12**

Crave

In both categories of action the amount of damages which may ultimately be decerned for cannot be predicted with accuracy, principally because the sum awarded in name of *solatium* or loss of society is within the discretion of the court. It is advisable to state as the sum sued for an amount somewhat greater than the pleader's own estimate of the probable award, in order to take account of the discretionary element in the assessment of damages and the rule that while decree for less than the sum sued for may be granted, decree for more cannot be obtained.[39] While the sum sued for may be altered without the leave of the court prior to the closing of the record,[40] it may be altered thereafter only with leave, which **21.13**

---

[29] In terms of OCR, r. 9.12. See paras 8.36 *et seq.*
[30] OCR, r. 22.1.
[31] W. J. D., *supra.*
[32] *Carron Co. v. Stainton's Trs* (1857) 19 D. 932; *Western Bank v. Baird's Trs* (1866) 4 M. 1071 at 1083.
[33] para. 21.04.
[34] *Dunlop v. Dunlop*, 1959 S.L.T. (Notes) 5.
[35] paras 2.114 to 2.119.
[36] paras 9.30, 9.33, 9.34, 9.102.
[37] para. 15.56.
[38] paras 16.100 to 16.103.
[39] *McTaggart v. McDouall* (1867) 5 M. 534.
[40] OCR, r. 18.1.

in certain circumstances may not be granted.[41] Where several pursuers sue in one action, the crave must specify a separate sum of damages for each of them. A party suing on behalf of children must crave a separate sum for each child.[42] It is unnecessary to crave interest from a date earlier than the date of decree,[43] although it is customary to do so.[44]

Intimation and sist of pursuers in death actions

21.14 The following rules apply to any action in which, following the death of any person from personal injuries, damages are claimed either by the executor of the deceased in respect of the relevant injuries, or by any relative of the deceased in respect of the death of the deceased.[45] The rules are designed to avoid a multiplicity of actions.[46] In such an action the pursuer must specify in the initial writ (a) that there are no "connected persons",[47] or (b) that there are connected persons, being the persons specified in the crave for intimation, or (c) that there are connected persons in respect of whom intimation should be dispensed with on the ground either that their names or whereabouts are not known to and cannot reasonably be ascertained by the pursuer, or that such persons are unlikely to be awarded more than £200 each.[48] Where the pursuer avers the existence of connected persons he must include in the initial writ a crave for warrant to intimate to any person who is believed to have title to sue the defender in an action in respect of the death of the deceased or the personal injuries from which the deceased died.[49] Warrant for intimation having been granted, the pursuer must intimate the action to every connected person by serving on him a copy of the initial writ to which is attached a notice of intimation in Form D1 as set out in Appendix 1 to the Rules.[50] Form D1 advises the person concerned that he may be entitled to enter the action as an additional pursuer and that, if he wishes to do so, he may apply to be sisted as such within 14 days after the expiry of a specified number of days from a specified date, which will be the date of service if service is by sheriff officer or the day after posting if service is postal.[51]

21.15 Where the pursuer avers that there are connected persons in respect of whom intimation should be dispensed with, the initial writ must contain a crave for an order to dispense with intimation.[52] In deciding whether or not to dispense with intimation the sheriff must have regard to (a) the desirability of avoiding a multiplicity of actions, and (b) the expense, inconvenience or difficulty likely to be involved in taking steps to ascertain

---

[41] See Chap. 10.
[42] *Gray v. Caledonian Ry*, 1912 S.C. 339.
[43] *Orr v. Metcalfe*, 1973 S.C. 57.
[44] For interest, see paras 21.35, 21.36.
[45] OCR, r. 36.1(1). The term "relative" has the meaning assigned to it in Sched. 1 to the Damages (Scotland) Act 1976: r. 36.1(2).
[46] See *Report on Section 5 of the Damages (Scotland) Act 1976* (Scot. Law Com. No. 64) and the subsequently enacted s. 14 of the Administration of Justice Act 1982.
[47] "Connected person" means a person, not being a party to the action, who has title to sue the defender in respect of the personal injuries from which the deceased died or in respect of his death: OCR, r. 36.1(2).
[48] OCR, r. 36.2.
[49] OCR, r. 36.3(1).
[50] OCR, r. 36.3(2).
[51] OCR, r. 5.3(2).
[52] OCR, r. 36.4(1).

the name or whereabouts of the connected person.[53] If the sheriff is not satisfied that intimation should be dispensed with he may (a) order intimation to a connected person whose name and whereabouts are known, (b) order the pursuer to take such further steps as he may specify in the interlocutor to ascertain the name or whereabouts of any connected person, and (c) order advertisement in such manner, place and at such times as he may specify in the interlocutor.[54]

Where the name or whereabouts of a person, in respect of whom the sheriff has dispensed with intimation, subsequently becomes known to the pursuer, the latter must apply to the sheriff by motion for a warrant for intimation to such a person, and matters then proceed as if warrant to intimate had been granted at the commencement of the action.[55] **21.16**

A connected person to whom intimation has been made may apply by minute craving leave to be sisted as an additional pursuer to the action.[56] The minute must crave leave to adopt the existing grounds of action and to amend the craves, condescendence and pleas-in-law.[57] The minute should be intimated to all parties to the action, and answers may be lodged by any party wishing to do so within 14 days from the date of intimation.[58] It is suggested that answers would be appropriate only if the title to sue of the connected person were being challenged or if the triennium[59] had expired before he lodged his minute and the defender sought therefore to argue that his claim was time-barred. If answers are lodged the normal procedure for an opposed minute[60] is followed with a hearing being fixed at which evidence may, if the sheriff considers it appropriate, be led. The interlocutor fixing the hearing should specify whether the sheriff will hear evidence.[61] If no answers are lodged the minute is granted and effect given to the crave therein with the consequence that the connected person becomes an additional pursuer in the action. The normal procedure following the granting of a minute to allow a person to be sisted as a party to an action[62] does not apply in the case of a connected person applying to become an additional pursuer.[63] Instead the action simply proceeds from whatever point it has already reached. **21.17**

Where a connected person who has received intimation does not apply to be sisted as an additional pursuer but subsequently raises a further action against the same defender in respect of the same injuries or death, he cannot be awarded the expenses of the subsequent action except on cause shown.[64] **21.18**

---

[53] OCR, r. 36.4(2).
[54] OCR, r. 36.4(3).
[55] OCR, r. 36.5.
[56] OCR, r. 36.6(1).
[57] OCR, r. 36.6(2).
[58] OCR, r. 36.6(3).
[59] In terms of the Prescription and Limitation (Scotland) Act 1973, s. 17.
[60] OCR, rr. 14.10, 14.11.
[61] OCR, r. 14.10(2).
[62] In terms of OCR, r. 14.13, which in effect provides that the procedure recommences with the fixing of a new period of adjustment and an options hearing.
[63] OCR, r. 36.6(4).
[64] OCR, r. 36.7.

Interim payment of damages

21.19 **Actions to which applicable.** Rules 36.8, 36.9 and 36.10 of the Ordinary Cause Rules make provision for orders for interim payment of damages in "an action of damages for personal injuries or the death of a person in consequence of personal injuries".[65] An "action of damages for personal injuries" does not include an action against a solicitor based on his failure timeously to raise an action of damages for personal injuries.[66] The rules are expressed in terms of payment by a defender to a pursuer, but the provisions of rule 36.9 apply *mutatis mutandis* to a counterclaim for damages for personal injury made by a defender.[67] The sheriff cannot make an order unless he is satisfied that the defender concerned is either (a) a person who is insured in respect of the pursuer's claim, or (b) a public authority, or (c) a person whose means and resources are such as to enable him to make an interim payment.[68] The fact that defences are lodged in a defender's name by the Motor Insurers' Bureau does not place that defender in category (a) or (c),[69] but a defender to whose insurers a provisional liquidator has been appointed still falls within category (a).[70]

21.20 **Motion.** The pursuer may apply for an order by motion at any time after the lodging of defences.[71] The motion must be intimated to every other party on a period of notice of 14 days.[72] The motion seeks an order that the defender or, where there are two or more defenders, any one or more of the defenders, make an interim payment of damages of a specified amount.[73]

21.21 **Conditions for making order.** After hearing parties on the motion the sheriff may, if he thinks fit, make an order if he is "satisfied" that either (a) the defender has admitted liability in the pursuer's action,[74] or (b) if the action proceeded to proof, the pursuer would succeed in the action on the question of liability without any substantial finding of contributory negligence on his part or on the part of any person in respect of whose injury or death the pursuer's claim arises, and would obtain decree for damages against any defender.[75] So far as head (b) is concerned, the test of satisfaction is whether it is practically certain that the pursuer would succeed on the question of liability, or whether he would almost certainly do so, this requiring something less than absolute certainty but more than probability or even high probability.[76] If the sheriff is so satisfied he may order an interim payment to be made to the pursuer "of such amount as

[65] OCR, r. 36.8(1). "Personal injuries" includes any disease or impairment of a person's physical or mental condition: r. 36.8(2).

[66] *Mackenzie v. Digby Brown & Co.*, 1992 S.C.L.R. 339.

[67] OCR, r. 36.9(8). It is submitted that r. 36.10 must be similarly applicable.

[68] OCR, r. 36.9(5).

[69] *Martin v. McKinsley*, 1980 S.L.T. (Notes) 15. See also *Ferguson v. McGrandles*, 1992 S.C.L.R. 735.

[70] *Walker v. Dunn*, 1995 S.C.L.R. 588.

[71] OCR, r. 36.9(1).

[72] OCR, r. 36.9(2).

[73] OCR, r. 36.9(1).

[74] If liability is admitted, the fact that the defender pleads that the pursuer was guilty of contributory negligence is immaterial: *Kay v. G.P. Inveresk Corporation*, 1988 S.C.L.R. 422.

[75] OCR, r. 36.9(3).

[76] *Cowie v. Atlantic Drilling Co. Ltd*, 1995 S.C.L.R. 335, approving on this point *Douglas's Curator Bonis v. Douglas*, 1974 S.L.T. (Notes) 67; *Nelson v. Duraplex Industries Ltd*, 1975 S.L.T. (Notes) 31; *Reid v. Plant Welding Equipment Ltd*, 1980 S.L.T. (Notes) 7.

[he] thinks fit, not exceeding a reasonable proportion of the damages which, in the opinion of the sheriff, are likely to be recovered by the pursuer".[77] Thus, in order to succeed in a motion for an interim payment in a case where liability is not admitted, the pursuer must satisfy the sheriff: (1) that if the action proceeded to proof he would succeed on the question of liability and would obtain damages against the defender; (2) that he would succeed on the question of liability without any substantial finding of contributory negligence; and (3) that the sum specified in the motion does not exceed a reasonable proportion of the damages which he is likely to recover.

Liability. As to the first of those matters, the sheriff must be of opinion that the pursuer would almost or practically certainly succeed on the question of liability at least to some extent.[78] A relevant conviction under road traffic[79] or industrial safety[80] legislation may assist him to reach that opinion. Conversely, he may be unable to do so if the defender in his pleadings denies or does not admit material averments by the pursuer[81] or states a plea to relevancy,[82] unless it is clear that such pleading is no more than formal in character, or the plea is directed against only certain averments.[83] It appears that in considering whether the pursuer would succeed on the question of liability the sheriff may not consider any documents other than the pleadings and any documents properly incorporated therein.[84] On the other hand it may be necessary to consider other documents and *ex parte* statements when determining the amount of any award[85] or the question whether the defender is a party against whom an award may be made in terms of rule 36.9(5).[86] **21.22**

Contributory negligence. The interpretation of the word "substantial" in the expression "any substantial finding of contributory negligence" gave rise to conflicting decisions in the Outer House of the Court of Session. One view was that it had to be construed as "of substance" in the sense of not being *de minimis*.[87] The broader view was that it meant "of considerable amount",[88] or a finding which would have a material effect on the damages awarded.[89] This difficulty has now been resolved. In *Cowie v. Atlantic Drilling Co. Ltd*[90] the Inner House gave approval to the broader approach, holding that "substantial" meant something of real significance to the point at issue, *i.e.* the assessment of the extent of the defender's liability to the pursuer in damages, and did not mean something which was merely not *de minimis*. The Inner House also held that a court is not **21.23**

---

[77] OCR, r. 36.9(3).
[78] *Cowie, Nelson, Reid, supra.*
[79] *Reid, supra*; *McNicol v. Buko Ltd*, 1986 S.L.T. 12; *Herron v. Kennon*, 1986 S.L.T. 260.
[80] *Nelson, supra*; *Curran v. HAT Painters (Scotland) Ltd*, 1987 S.L.T. 98.
[81] *Reid v. J. Smart & Co. Ltd*, 1981 S.L.T. (Notes) 20; *McCann v. Miller Insulation and Engineering Ltd*, 1986 S.L.T. 147.
[82] *Herron, supra.*
[83] *Moodie v. Maclean*, 1981 S.L.T. (Notes) 53.
[84] *McCann, supra.* But see *Calder v. Simpson*, 1994 S.L.T. (Sh. Ct.) 32 where the sheriff principal reserved his opinion on this matter.
[85] See paras 21.25, 21.26.
[86] See para. 21.19.
[87] *Nelson v. Duraple Industries Ltd*, 1975 S.L.T. (Notes) 31; *Noble v. Noble*, 1979 S.L.T. (Notes) 77; *Herron v. Kennon*, 1984 S.L.T. 260.
[88] *Reid v. Planet Welding Equipment Ltd*, 1980 S.L.T. (Notes) 7.
[89] *Duguid v. Wilh. Wilhelmsen Enterprises Ltd A/S*, 1988 S.L.T. 118.
[90] 1995 S.C.L.R. 335. See also *Calder v. Simpson*, 1994 S.L.T. (Sh. Ct.) 32.

required to resolve the issue by reaching any clear view in terms of a fraction or a percentage about the maximum extent to which a pursuer is likely to be held to have been to blame for the accident. All that is necessary is a broad assessment of the matter in order to ensure that an award of interim damages is not made in a case where a finding of contributory negligence is likely to have a material effect on the court's evaluation of the amount which the pursuer is likely to recover as damages. Prior to the decision in *Cowie* it had been suggested that a finding of contributory negligence which would almost certainly not exceed one-quarter, or at most one-third, could not properly be described as substantial,[91] but the value of that suggestion must now be in doubt. In some cases, of course, it may not be possible to form any view as to the likely degree of any finding of contributory negligence.[92]

21.24 *Two or more defenders*. Where there are two or more defenders, the sheriff, before ordering any one of them to make an interim payment, need not be "satisfied" that the pursuer would succeed against that particular defender. The sheriff must first determine whether the pursuer is almost certain to succeed in the action and obtain decree against any of the defenders. If he is so satisfied, he then determines in the exercise of his discretion which defender is to pay the interim damages. If the pursuer does not ultimately succeed in establishing liability against that defender, the sheriff may order the pursuer to repay to that defender the amount of the interim damages.[93] Where there are two defenders and it is clear that the pursuer will succeed against one or both of them but it is not clear that both will be found liable, or, if both are found liable, how liability would be apportioned between them, it may be appropriate to find the pursuer entitled to an interim award against the defenders jointly and severally.[94]

21.25 **Hearing and order.** If the conditions discussed above are satisfied, the sheriff may order any defender in respect of whom they are satisfied, to make an interim payment to the pursuer of such amount as the sheriff thinks fit, not exceeding a reasonable proportion of the damages which, in the opinion of the sheriff, are likely to be recovered by the pursuer.[95] It has been said that there should be no detailed *ex parte* statements or close scrutiny of documents produced by each side, and no concluded view on the medical aspects of the case; but the court may make a rough estimate of the total sum of damages which is likely to be awarded and award a sum which will alleviate or mitigate the sufferings or hardships of the pursuer as a result of the injuries during the interim period until the case is finally decided, always within the framework of the estimated total and of all the circumstances of the case.[96]

21.26 It is respectfully submitted, however, that it is not inappropriate to take account of uncontradicted *ex parte* statements or unchallenged

---

[91] *Reid v. Planet Welding, supra.*

[92] *Herron, supra.*

[93] *Walker v. Infabco Diving Services Ltd*, 1983 S.L.T. 633; *McCann v. Miller Insulation and Engineering Ltd*, 1986 S.L.T. 147. See para. 21.28.

[94] *Walker, supra*; *McNicol v. Buko Ltd*, 1986 S.L.T. 12. But see *Herbertson v. Ascosmit Co. Ltd*, 1992 S.L.T. 1115.

[95] OCR, r. 36.9(3).

[96] *Littlejohn v. Clancy*, 1974 S.L.T. (Notes) 68; *Boyle v. Rennies of Dunfermline*, 1975 S.L.T. (Notes) 13; *Noble v. Noble*, 1979 S.L.T. (Notes) 75; *Hancock's Curator Bonis v. Ellis*, 1980 S.L.T. (Notes) 27.

documents. In recently reported cases the court has considered facts admitted at the bar,[97] photographs,[98] medical reports[99] and statements of benefits.[1] It is further submitted that while it would be relevant to have regard to the sufferings or hardships referred to as having a bearing upon the measure of damages likely to be awarded, the amount of the interim award does not otherwise depend on any such sufferings or hardships and it is not the purpose of the rule to help or relieve them.[2] While it is necessary for the sheriff to form a view as to the amount of the damages likely to be awarded, he should not disclose it because of its provisional nature and its possible effect on any negotiations for settlement.[3] The sheriff may properly have regard to loss which will be suffered after the date of the hearing of the motion where it can be seen that a final award of damages is likely to include a quantifiable element for loss occurring in or attributable to a period after that date.[4] In other cases it may be appropriate to proceed only on the basis of what the pursuer appears to have suffered to date.[5] The amount stated in any tender does not have a bearing on the amount of the interim payment.[6]

The interim payment may be ordered to be paid in a lump sum or otherwise as the sheriff may deem appropriate.[7] Subject to the terms of Part IV of Chapter 36 of the Ordinary Cause Rules (which relates to the management of damages payable to persons under legal disability)[8] any interim payment must be made to the pursuer unless the sheriff otherwise directs.[9] Notwithstanding the grant or refusal of a motion for an interim payment, a subsequent motion may be made where there has been a change of circumstances.[10] **21.27**

Final orders. Where a defender has made an interim payment in terms of rule 36.9 the sheriff may, when granting final decree, make such order with respect to the interim payment as he thinks fit to give effect to the defender's final liability to the pursuer.[11] It is thought that such an order may require the payment of interest.[12] In particular, the sheriff may order that the pursuer repay to the defender any sum by which the interim payment exceeds the amount which that defender is liable to pay to the pursuer.[13] He may likewise order that any other defender or a third party make payment of any part of the interim payment which the defender who made it is entitled to recover from that other defender or third party by **21.28**

---

97 *Walker v. Infabco Diving Services Ltd*, 1983 S.L.T. 633, *per* Lord Kincraig at 634.
98 *Stone v. Mountford*, 1995 S.L.T. 1279; *Cleland v. Campbell*, 1998 S.L.T. 642.
99 *McNicol v. Buko Ltd*, 1986 S.L.T. 12.
1 *Curran v. HAT Painters (Scotland) Ltd*, 1987 S.L.T. 98.
2 *McNicol, supra*; *Curran, supra.*
3 *McNicol, supra.*
4 *Moodie v. Maclean*, 1981 S.L.T. (Notes) 53; *Nisbet v. Marley Roof Tile Co. Ltd*, 1988 S.C.L.R. 56.
5 *Reid v. Planet Welding Equipment Ltd*, 1980 S.L.T. (Notes) 7; *Hancock's Curator Bonis v. Ellis*, 1980 S.L.T. (Notes) 27; *Curran, supra.*
6 *Boyle v. Rennies of Dunfermline*, 1975 S.L.T. (Notes) 13.
7 OCR, r. 36.9(4).
8 See paras 21.37 to 21.42.
9 OCR, r. 36.9(7).
10 OCR, r. 36.9(6).
11 OCR, r. 36.10.
12 *Walker v. Infabco Diving Services Ltd*, 1983 S.L.T. 633, *per* Lord Ross at 641. *Cf.*, however, Lord Stott at 638, Lord Cowie at 642.
13 OCR, r. 36.10(a).

way of contribution or indemnity or in respect of any remedy or relief relating to, or connected with, the pursuer's claim.[14] An interim award is likely to affect interest on the final sum awarded.[15]

Provisional damages

21.29 Section 12 of the Administration of Justice Act 1982 empowers the court to make a provisional award of damages in a personal injuries action[16] where there is a risk that in the future the pursuer[17] will, as a result of the accident, develop some serious disease or suffer some serious deterioration in his condition. The power may be exercised in any action of damages for personal injuries in which there is proved or admitted to be a risk that at some definite or indefinite time in the future the pursuer will, as a result of the act or omission which gave rise to the cause of the action, develop some serious disease or suffer some serious deterioration in his physical or mental condition.[18] Further, the responsible person must have been, at the time of the act or omission giving rise to the cause of action, (i) a public authority or public corporation, or (ii) insured or otherwise indemnified in respect of the claim.[19]

21.30 In such an action it is for the pursuer to elect whether to be content that the judgment of the court after the proof should finally quantify and dispose of his claim in the usual way, or to apply only for provisional damages at that stage and make an application for a further award of damages later. If he chooses the latter course, a crave in appropriate terms should be included in the initial writ.[20] The condescendence must include averments (1) that there is a risk that, at some definite or indefinite time in the future, the pursuer will, as a result of the act or omission which gave rise to the cause of action, develop some serious disease or suffer some serious deterioration of his physical or mental condition; and (2) that the defender was, at the time of the act or omission which gave rise to the cause of action, a public authority, public corporation or insured or otherwise indemnified in respect of the claim.[21] The writ must also contain a plea-in-law appropriate to the claim for provisional damages. At the proof evidence should be led as to the existence of a risk of the kind referred to in section 12(1)(a). At the hearing on evidence the sheriff should be moved to make a finding that there is such a risk, to award damages assessed on the assumption that the pursuer will not develop the disease or suffer the deterioration in his condition, and to order that he may apply for a further award of damages if he develops the disease or suffers the deterioration in his condition. In his interlocutor after the proof the sheriff may make such a finding, assess damages on that assumption and award them to the pursuer, and order that he may apply for such a further award. If he considers it appropriate he may also order that an application for a further award may be made only within a

---

[14] OCR, r. 36.10(b). See *Mitchell v. HAT Contracting Services Ltd (No. 3)*, 1993 S.L.T. 1196.

[15] *Redman v. McRae*, 1991 S.L.T. 785; *Jarvie v. Sharp*, 1992 S.L.T. 350; *Bhatia v. Tribax Ltd*, 1994 S.L.T. 1201.

[16] "Personal injuries" includes any disease or any impairment of a person's physical or mental condition: Administration of Justice Act 1982, s. 13(1).

[17] s. 12 uses the expression "the injured person".

[18] 1982 Act, s. 12(1)(a).

[19] *ibid.* s. 12(1)(b). The categories of defenders may be altered by statutory instrument: s. 12(6).

[20] OCR, r. 36.12(a). For a style, see *Potter v. McCulloch*, 1987 S.L.T. 308.

[21] OCR, r. 36.12(b).

specified period.[22] It seems clear that the sheriff's powers are discretionary.[23] It may be, for example, that he would be entitled to decline to exercise them if he were to be satisfied that to do so would cause serious prejudice to the defender.

An application for a further award is made by minute in the original process.[24] The minute must include a crave for further damages, averments in the statement of facts supporting that crave, and appropriate pleas-in-law.[25] When lodging the minute the pursuer must apply by motion for warrant to serve the minute on every other party and, where such other party is insured or otherwise indemnified, his insurer or indemnifier, if known to the pursuer.[26] Any party, insurer or indemnifier on whom the minute is served may lodge answers within 28 days after the date of service on him.[27] Where answers are lodged the sheriff may, on the motion of any party, make such further order as to procedure as he thinks fit.[28] In most cases it will be appropriate to allow a period for adjustment of the minute and answers and to order a proof. In order to succeed in his claim for further damages the pursuer must satisfy the sheriff that as a result of the act or omission which gave rise to the cause of the action he has developed some serious disease or suffered some serious deterioration in his physical or mental condition. If the sheriff is so satisfied, he may award further damages.[29] It appears that in assessing these damages he will require to consider the factors which the court took into account when making the original award.[30] 21.31

Section 12 does not affect the power of the court to award expenses, or its duty "under any enactment or rule of law to reduce or limit the total damages which would have been recoverable apart from any such duty."[31] Accordingly, any statutory limitation on the amount of damages which may be awarded in particular circumstances[32] remains unaffected, as does the court's power to reduce damages in respect of contributory negligence.[33] 21.32

Social security benefits

The extent to which a decree in an action of damages for personal injuries should have regard to social security benefits paid to the pursuer has varied over the years.[34] The matter is now governed by the Social 21.33

---

[22] 1982 Act, s. 12(2), (4). Before so ordering he may require an acceptable assessment of the period within which the development or deterioration may occur: *Potter, supra, per* Lord Weir at 310.

[23] *Potter, supra, per* Lord Weir at 310. For examples of recent cases where the question of provisional damages has been considered see *Robertson v. British Bakeries Ltd*, 1991 S.C.L.R. 450; *McMenemy v. Argyll Stores Ltd*, 1992 S.C.L.R. 971; *Bonar v. Trafalgar House Offshore Fabrication Ltd*, 1996 S.C.L.R. 340.

[24] OCR, r. 36.13(1).

[25] *ibid.*

[26] OCR, r. 36.13(2).

[27] OCR, r. 36.13(3).

[28] OCR, r. 36.13(4).

[29] 1982 Act, s. 12(3).

[30] *Potter, supra, per* Lord Weir at 311.

[31] 1982 Act, s. 12(5).

[32] *e.g.* Merchant Shipping Act 1894, s. 503, as amended by the Merchant Shipping (Liability of Shipowners and Others) Act 1958, s. 2 and the Merchant Shipping Acts 1981, s. 1 and 1984, s. 12.

[33] Law Reform (Contributory Negligence) Act 1945, s. 1.

[34] For a brief historical summary see *Mitchell v. Laing*, 1998 S.L.T. 203, *per* L.P. Rodger at 205–206.

Security (Recovery of Benefits) Act 1997. The basic provision is that the court is prohibited from taking into account the amount of benefits received when deciding the level of compensation due.[35] However, the amount actually received by the pursuer may be subject to deduction of certain benefits received by him,[36] for which the defender accounts to the Department of Social Security.[37] With a view to enabling assessment of what benefits should be taken into account, section 15 of the Act provides that where a court makes an order for compensation, unless the order is made with the consent of both parties, the court must specify the amount of compensation payment which is attributable to each of the various heads of compensation listed in Column 1 of Schedule 2. These heads are (1) compensation for earnings lost during the relevant period,[38] (2) compensation for cost of care incurred during the relevant period, and (3) compensation for loss of mobility during the relevant period. It should be noted that *solatium* is not one of the heads of compensation which requires to be specified. Even though the Act provides for specification of the amounts of compensation under the various heads only in actions where decree is not granted of consent, the defender still has an obligation to account to the Department of Social Security for benefits received by the pursuer in actions which have been settled. It is therefore highly desirable that in such actions the joint minute should set out the items which the court would have had to list in terms of section 15.

21.34 In the Court of Session a practice note has been issued providing that in all cases to which the 1997 Act applies, parties seeking decree (except where that decree is sought of consent, for instance as the result of a joint minute) should lodge in process a schedule of damages stating the amount of any compensation which is claimed in respect of the relevant period under any of the headings in Column 1 of Schedule 2. It is further provided that for the avoidance of doubt the requirement applies not only to final decrees but to decrees in absence, decrees by default, summary decrees, interim decrees and decrees for provisional damages.[39] At the time of writing practice notes in similar terms have been issued in the Sheriffdoms of Tayside, Central and Fife,[40] South Strathclyde, Dumfries and Galloway,[41] Glasgow and Strathkelvin,[42] North Strathclyde,[43] and Lothian and Borders.[43a] It is expected that similar practice notes will be issued in the two remaining sheriffdoms in due course.

Interest on damages

21.35 Section 1(1) of the Interest on Damages (Scotland) Act 1958, as substituted by section 1 of the 1971 Act of the same name, provides that where the court pronounces an interlocutor decerning for payment of a

---

[35] Social Security (Recovery of Benefits) Act 1997, s. 17.

[36] "Listed benefits" as specified in Column 2 of Sched. 2 to the 1997 Act.

[37] 1997 Act, s. 6.

[38] "Relevant period" is defined in detail in s. 3 of the Act. In general terms it means a period of five years (or to the date when the final compensation payment is made, if earlier) beginning with the date of the accident causing the injury or, in the case of disease, on the first date a listed benefit was claimed.

[39] Court of Session Practice Note, No. 3 of 1997.

[40] See 1998 S.L.T. (News) 52.

[41] See 1998 S.L.T. (News) 74.

[42] See 1998 S.L.T. (News) 83.

[43] See 1998 S.L.T. (News) 107.

[43a] See 1998 S.L.T. (News) 214.

sum of money as damages, the interlocutor may include decree for payment of interest, at such rate or rates as may be specified in the interlocutor, on the whole or any part of that sum for the whole or any part of the period between the date when the right of action arose and the date of the interlocutor. Section 1(1A), also substituted by the 1971 Act, provides that when decerning for payment of a sum which consists of or includes damages or *solatium* in respect of personal injuries sustained by the pursuer or any other person, the court must exercise the power conferred by section 1(1) so as to include in that sum interest on those damages and on that *solatium* or on such part of each as the court considers appropriate, unless the court is satisfied that there are reasons special to the case why no interest should be given in respect thereof.[44] Section 1(1A) applies to damages claimed both in personal injuries actions and in death actions.[45]

Interest may therefore be awarded on those parts of each element of the award of damages which are applicable to the period from the date of the accident to the date of the interlocutor. The sheriff accordingly decerns for payment of a sum of damages, assessed in accordance with accepted principles, together with an additional sum derived from interest at specified rates, for specified periods ending with the date of the interlocutor, on those parts of the total sum which should bear interest. Damages therefore consist of the addition of the two sums, and on the resulting sum interest runs from the date of decree until payment.[46] In practice, interest is often awarded on past loss of wages or past loss of support at about one-half of the judicial rate (or of the average rate, if it has changed) from the date of the accident to the date of decree, while interest on past *solatium* or loss of society may be awarded at a higher proportion of the judicial rate.[47] Delay by a pursuer may have an effect on an award of interest.[48] The question of interest may also be affected by the fact that an interim award of damages has been made.[49] Another factor capable of affecting interest is the legislation concerning the relationship between damages and social security benefits.[50] Since, however, the court is required to adopt a selective and discriminating approach to the awarding of interest,[51] there can be no fixed rules on the matter.[52] The sheriff's exercise of his discretion is subject to review.[53] It is incompetent to apply to the sheriff for an award **21.36**

---

44 Interest on Damages (Scotland) Act 1958, s. 1, substituted by the Interest on Damages (Scotland) Act 1971, s. 1.

45 *Smith v. Middleton*, 1972 S.C. 30 at 35.

46 *Smith, supra*; *Mouland v. Ferguson*, 1979 S.L.T. (Notes) 85.

47 *e.g. Prentice v. Chalmers*, 1985 S.L.T. 168.

48 *Buchan v. J. Marr (Aberdeen) Ltd*, 1987 S.C.L.R. 96; *Bogan's Curator Bonis v. Graham*, 1992 S.C.L.R. 920. But see *Boots the Chemists Ltd v. G.A. Estates Ltd*, 1993 S.L.T. 136 (not a case involving personal injuries); *Bhatia v. Tribax Ltd*, 1994 S.L.T. 1201; *Purryag v. Greater Glasgow Health Board*, 1996 S.L.T. 794.

49 *Redman v. McRae*, 1991 S.L.T. 785; *Jarvie v. Sharp*, 1992 S.L.T. 350; *Bhatia v. Tribax Ltd*, 1994 S.L.T. 1201.

50 At the time of writing the relevant legislation is the Social Security (Recovery of Benefits) Act 1997. See paras 21.33, 21.34. For recent cases dealing with the question of interest as affected by the provisions of the 1997 Act, see *Wisely v. John Fulton (Plumbers) Ltd*, 1998 S.L.T. 1026, approving; *Spence v. Wilson*, 1998 S.L.T. 688.

51 *Smith, supra.*

52 See Walker, *Civil Remedies*, pp. 378–383.

53 *Macrae v. Reed & Mallik Ltd*, 1961 S.C. 68; *Ross v. British Railways Board*, 1972 S.L.T. 174; *Prentice, supra.*

of interest under section 1 after he has pronounced his interlocutor awarding damages.[54]

Damages payable to person under legal disability other than a child

21.37 In terms of rule 36.14 of the Ordinary Cause Rules, where, in an action of damages, a sum becomes payable, by virtue of a decree or an extra-judicial settlement, to or for the benefit of a person under a legal disability who is aged 18 years or over, the sheriff must make such order regarding the payment and management of that sum as he thinks fit.[55] There is an apparent *casus omissus* in respect of persons under legal disability who are aged 16 or 17 years as such persons are not covered either by rule 36.14 or by the Children (Scotland) Act 1995, s. 13.[56] An order under rule 36.14 is made on the granting of decree for payment or of absolvitor.[57] The Ordinary Cause Rules provide for four possible orders which the sheriff may make,[58] but it is suggested that he is not confined to these four.[59]

21.38 **Judicial factor.** First, the sheriff may appoint a judicial factor to apply, invest or otherwise deal with the money for the benefit of the person under legal disability.[60] It is of course possible that a judicial factor may already have been appointed in the form of a curator *bonis* and that he was the pursuer in the action in which the damages were awarded. According to a strict reading of rule 36.14 the fact that decree had been granted in favour of a curator *bonis* would not absolve the sheriff from making an order, but it is submitted that such an order would be quite unnecessary in such a case.

21.39 **Trustee.** Secondly, the sheriff may order the money to be paid to either the Accountant of Court or the guardian of the person under legal disability as trustee, to be applied, invested or otherwise dealt with and administered under the directions of the sheriff for the benefit of that person.[61] An application for directions may be made by minute in the process of the cause to which the application relates by any person having an interest.[62]

21.40 **Payment to sheriff clerk.** Thirdly, the sheriff may order the money to be paid to the sheriff clerk of the sheriff court district in which the person under legal disability resides, to be applied, invested or otherwise dealt with and administered, under the direction of the sheriff of that district.[63] Where the sheriff so orders the sheriff clerk must accept custody of that money.[64] His receipt in Form D2 of Appendix 1 to the Ordinary Cause Rules is a sufficient discharge in respect of any amount paid to him.[65] An application for directions may be made by minute in the process of the cause to which the application relates by any person having an interest.[66]

---

54 *Handren v. Scottish Construction Co. Ltd*, 1967 S.L.T. (Notes) 21.
55 OCR, r. 36.14(1).
56 This section covers only children under the age of 16 years. See para. 21.43.
57 OCR, r. 36.14(2).
58 OCR, r. 36.15.
59 *cf.* Children (Scotland) Act, s. 13(1), (2). See para. 21.43.
60 OCR, r. 36.15(a).
61 OCR, r. 36.15(b).
62 OCR, r. 36.16(2).
63 OCR, r. 36.15(c).
64 OCR, r. 36.17(2).
65 OCR, r. 36.17(1).
66 OCR, r. 36.16(2).

Money paid to the sheriff clerk may be paid out, applied, invested or otherwise dealt with by him only after such intimation, service and enquiry as the sheriff may order.[67] Any money invested by the sheriff clerk may be invested only in a manner in which trustees are authorised to invest by virtue of the Trustee Investments Act 1961.[68]

Direct payment. Finally, the sheriff may order the money to be paid directly to the person under legal disability.[69] **21.41**

Where the sheriff has made an order under rule 36.14, any person having an interest may apply by minute in the process of the cause to which the application relates for any other order.[70] **21.42**

Damages payable to child

The rules concerning damages payable to or for the benefit of a child are very similar to those that have just been described in respect of other persons under legal disability, but in the case of children the rules are contained in an Act of Parliament rather than in the Ordinary Cause Rules. Section 13 of the Children (Scotland) Act 1995 provides that where in any court proceedings a sum of money becomes payable to, or for the benefit of, a child under the age of sixteen years,[71] the court may make such order relating to the payment and management of the sum for the benefit of the child as it thinks fit.[72] It goes on to provide that, without prejudice to the generality of the foregoing, the court may (a) appoint a judicial factor to invest, apply or otherwise deal with the money for the benefit of the child concerned, (b) order the money to be paid to the sheriff clerk or the Accountant of Court, or to a parent or guardian of the child, to be invested, applied or otherwise dealt with, under directions of the court, for the benefit of the child, or (c) order the money to be paid directly to the child.[73] Where payment is made to a person in accordance with an order under the foregoing provisions, a receipt given by that person is a sufficient discharge of the obligation to make payment.[74] Where a court has made an order in terms of section 13, an application by a person for an order for the administration of the child's property in terms of section 11(1)(d) of the 1995 Act may be made in the process of the action in which the section 13 order was made.[75] The comments made in the preceding paragraphs about payments to persons under legal disability other than children apply equally, *mutatis mutandis*, to payments to children, and are not repeated here. **21.43**

Judgment

Comments have already been made on the form of the sheriff's interlocutor where damages are awarded and it is necessary to take account of **21.44**

---

[67] OCR, r. 36.17(3).
[68] OCR, r. 36.17(4).
[69] OCR, r. 36.15(d).
[70] OCR, r. 36.16(1).
[71] A child of or over the age of 16 is presumed to have full legal capacity: Age of Legal Capacity (Scotland) Act 1991, s. 1(1)(b). There appears to be a *casus omissus* in respect of persons under legal disability aged 16 or 17. See para. 21.37.
[72] Children (Scotland) Act 1995, s. 13(1).
[73] *ibid.* s. 13(2).
[74] *ibid.* s. 13(3).
[75] OCR, r. 33.95.

contributory negligence, or contribution among joint wrongdoers,[76] or provisional damages,[77] or interest on damages.[78] Where the sheriff assoilzies the defender after proof, he should in the note appended to his interlocutor state, with reasons, the amount of damages he would have awarded if the pursuer had been successful.

Action of furthcoming

Nature of action

21.45 An action of furthcoming is the process whereby a creditor who has arrested in the hands of a third party money or moveables belonging to his debtor has the arrested subjects effectually transferred to himself in or towards satisfaction of his debt. The decree adjudges to the pursuer as much of the fund attached as may pay his debt, or if the subject is corporeal it authorises a sale and payment out of the proceeds.[79] In practice an action of furthcoming is seldom necessary since the debtor, to avoid the expense of such an action, usually grants a mandate authorising the arrestee to release the subjects to the creditor.[80] The nature of the action and the competent defences are fully explained in the undernoted work.[81]

Jurisdiction

21.46 The jurisdiction of the sheriff court in an action of furthcoming is regulated by the terms of Schedule 8 to the Civil Jurisdiction and Judgments Act 1982. The effect of rules 1 and 2(9) of Schedule 8 is that in proceedings which are brought to assert, declare or determine proprietary or possessory rights, or rights of security, in or over moveable property, or to obtain authority to dispose of moveable property, a person may be sued either in the courts for the place where he is domiciled or in the courts for the place where the property is situated. Since two parties are called as defenders in an action of furthcoming,[82] the action may be brought in the sheriff court for the place where either of them is domiciled.[83]

Raising of action

21.47 No special procedural rules are prescribed for ordinary actions of furthcoming. In the Summary Cause Rules there is a provision that the expenses of an action of furthcoming including the expenses of the arrestment are deemed to be part of the arrestor's claim.[84] There is no such provision in an ordinary cause, and therefore the expenses of the action should be craved against the common debtor personally and against the arrestee in the event of his appearing and opposing.

21.48 When a pursuer who has arrested on the dependence has obtained decree, he may raise an action of furthcoming based on the arrestment on the dependence: it is unnecessary for him to use an arrestment in

---

[76] para. 17.18.
[77] paras 21.29 to 21.32.
[78] paras 21.35, 21.36.
[79] See para. 11.24.
[80] See para. 11.10.
[81] Graham Stewart, Chap. 11.
[82] See para. 21.49.
[83] Civil Jurisdiction and Judgments Act 1982, Sched. 8, r. 2(15)(a).
[84] SCR, r. 64.

execution.[85] The action should be brought before the arrestment prescribes.[86] Where more than one arrestment has been served on the arrestee, and there is accordingly a competition of arrestments, the appropriate action is a multiplepoinding.[87]

The pursuer in the action of furthcoming is the creditor and the defenders are (first) the arrestee and (second) the debtor. It is usual to add at the end of the designation of each in the instance the words "Arrestee" and "Common Debtor" or "Principal Debtor" respectively. Where the arrestment has been loosed on caution, the cautioner is called as an additional defender.[88] The crave must be so framed as to be applicable to the specific subjects arrested.[89] Thus, where money has been arrested, the crave is for payment. Where moveables have been arrested, the crave may be for warrant for sale.[90] Where shares have been arrested, the pursuer may crave their sale or transfer, with authority to the sheriff clerk to execute transfers or similar documents and an order on a company or similar body to accept them so executed.[91] Where money has been arrested under a life policy, the crave is for surrender or sale.[92] If funds arrested are subject to a contingency, the crave should be appropriately qualified.[93] Where the common debtor has been a partner in the arrestees' firm but has retired from it and the obligation attached is the duty of the firm to count and reckon with him and pay him any sum found due to him, the craves ought to be those of an action of count, reckoning and payment adjusted so that the count and reckoning should be with the pursuer and the payment of any sum due be made to him.[94] **21.49**

Expenses

The expenses which the pursuer may recover out of the arrested fund include the expenses decerned for in the decree on which the action proceeds, and the expenses of an arrestment in execution if such was necessary,[95] but not the expenses of an arrestment on the dependence.[96] Where warrant to sell is necessary, the pursuer is entitled to recover the expenses of sale out of the proceeds. As already explained, the expenses of the action of furthcoming itself cannot be recovered from the arrested fund.[97] **21.50**

Competing claims

If decree in absence passes, the arrestee may be reponed.[98] It has been said in several books of practice that any person who has an interest in the **21.51**

---

[85] See para. 11.25.

[86] For the rules as to prescription of arrestments, see para. 11.25.

[87] Bell, *Prin.*, para. 2283; *Paterson & Son v. McInnes* (1950) 66 Sh.Ct.Rep. 226; *e.g. Abbey National Building Society v. Strang*, 1981 S.L.T. (Sh. Ct.) 4. See para. 21.51.

[88] Bell, *Comm.*, ii, 67; Lewis, p. 237; Dobie, p. 275. *Cf.* Graham Stewart, pp. 241–242.

[89] *Lucas's Trs v. Campbell and Scott* (1894) 21 R. 1096. See Green's *Litigation Styles*, A2031–A2033.

[90] Green's *Litigation Styles*, A2031.

[91] *Valentine v. Grangemouth Coal Co.* (1897) 5 S.L.T. 47; *Roney v. Tarakan Petroleum Oil Syndicate*, 1910 1 S.L.T. 272; *Stenhouse London Ltd v. Allwright*, 1972 S.C. 209 at 210, 213.

[92] *Bankhardt's Tr. v. Scottish Amicable Society* (1871) 9 M. 443; *Clark v. Scottish Amicable Society*, 1922 S.L.T. (Sh. Ct.) 88; Green's *Litigation Styles*, A2033.

[93] *Learmonts v. Shearer* (1866) 4 M. 540 at 542; *Jameson v. Sharp* (1887) 14 R. 643 at 648.

[94] *Green v. Miller's Debt Recovery Services*, 1954 S.L.T. (Sh. Ct.) 26.

[95] See para. 11.25.

[96] See paras 11.10, 11.25.

[97] See para. 21.47.

[98] *Fraser v. Savings Investment Trust* (1912) 28 Sh.Ct.Rep. 224.

arrested fund may appear and state defences, and a competition between claimants may be dealt with in the furthcoming process.[99] It is submitted that the better view, expressed by Sheriff Bryden in *Paterson & Son v. McInnes,*[1] is that in an action of furthcoming the court cannot pronounce orders outside the bounds of the crave of the writ and accordingly cannot give effect to other claims except in the sense that, and to the extent to which, they might negative the pursuer's claim. It may be that in some cases it might be expedient or even necessary to allow a competing claimant to come into an action of furthcoming in order to decide whether or not the pursuer's claim is valid, but in general where there are competing claims the appropriate remedy is an action of multiplepoinding.[2] If the sheriff is satisfied that there are competing claims he may grant a motion that the furthcoming be sisted pending the raising of an action of multiplepoinding.[3]

Action of multiplepoinding

Nature and competency

21.52 An action of multiplepoinding is appropriate where any number of parties have claims on a fund or property which is held by another party. The object of the action is to have it decided which of the claimants is entitled to the fund or property, or in what proportions it is to be divided among them, and to enable the holder of the fund or property to part with it in a legally authorised manner. The subject of the action is known as the fund *in medio*. The nature of the action and the circumstances in which it is competent are fully examined in the undernoted work.[4]

Jurisdiction

21.53 The jurisdiction of the sheriff court in an action of multiplepoinding is regulated by the terms of Schedule 8 to the Civil Jurisdiction and Judgments Act 1982. Rule 2(9) of Schedule 8 is concerned with "proceedings which are brought to assert, declare or determine proprietary or possessory rights, or rights of security, in or over moveable property, or to obtain authority to dispose of moveable property". These terms are wide enough to include actions of multiplepoinding.[5] The rule provides that in such proceedings the courts for the place where the property is situated have jurisdiction. As already explained, rule 2(9) is applicable in relation to a defender domiciled in any part of the United Kingdom or in a state other than a Contracting State, but not in relation to a defender domiciled in another Contracting State.[6] If, however, any one of the defenders is domiciled in the sheriffdom the court will have jurisdiction even if another defender is domiciled in a Contracting State.[7] Moreover, where the action is concerned with rights *in rem* in, or tenancies of, immoveable property it may be brought in the sheriff court of the place where the property is situated, which, together with the Court of Session, has exclusive jurisdiction.[8]

---

[99] Mackay, *Manual*, p. 381; Graham Stewart, p. 239; Lewis, p. 236; Dobie, p. 276.
[1] (1950) 66 Sh.Ct.Rep. 226.
[2] Bell, *Prin.*, s. 2283; Wallace, p. 380. *Cf. Walker v. United Creameries Ltd*, 1928 S.L.T. (Sh. Ct.) 21.
[3] *Ross v. Brunton* (1914) 30 Sh.Ct.Rep. 141.
[4] Walker, *Civil Remedies*, Chap. 72.
[5] Anton and Beaumont., para. 10.42(2).
[6] See para. 3.103.
[7] Civil Jurisdiction and Judgments Act 1982, Sched. 8, rr. 1, 2(15)(a): see para. 3.38.
[8] *ibid.*, r. 4(1)(a): see para. 3.24.

Procedure

The procedure in actions of multiplepoinding is very much *sui generis*, and many of the rules governing other ordinary causes do not apply.[9] **21.54**

Initial writ. The action may be raised by any party holding, or having an interest in or claim on, the fund *in medio* in his own name.[10] The pursuer should call as defenders all persons so far as known to him who have an interest in the fund *in medio*.[11] If the pursuer is not himself the holder of the fund *in medio*, the holder should be called as a defender.[12] Where heirs and beneficiaries are not known, the Lord Advocate should be called as representing the Crown as *ultimus haeres*. The crave may be for distribution of the fund *in medio* (which is specifically described) among the claimants found entitled thereto and exoneration of the holder of the fund.[13] The condescendence should specify the grounds on which each defender is called and state facts sufficient to explain and justify the raising of the action. Guidance has already been given as to the pleading of the critical provisions of documents.[14] If the pursuer is the holder of the fund *in medio* he must condescend in detail on the fund in the condescendence.[15] **21.55**

Service and advertisement. The writ is served on all defenders, including, if the pursuer is not the holder of the fund *in medio*, the holder of the fund. The warrant of citation is in Form M1 in Appendix 1 to the Ordinary Cause Rules.[16] Citation is in Form M2 which must have appended to it a notice of appearance in Form M4. A holder who is not the pursuer must, before the expiry of the period of notice (a) lodge in process a condescendence of the fund stating any claim or lien which he may profess to have on the fund together with a list of all persons known to him as having an interest in the fund, and (b) intimate a copy of the condescendence and list to all other parties.[17] The sheriff may make an order for advertisement of the action in such newspapers as he thinks fit.[18] At any time during the progress of the action, either *ex proprio motu* or on the motion of any party, the sheriff may order further service on any person or advertisement.[19] The implementation of an order for advertisement is demonstrated by lodging in process copies of the newspapers in which the advertisements appear.[20] **21.56**

Notice of appearance. A party may wish to enter the process in order to lodge (1) defences to challenge the jurisdiction of the court or the **21.57**

---

[9] OCR, r. 35.2 lists the rules which do not apply. They are rr. 9.1 (notice of intention to defend), 9.2 (fixing date of options hearing), 9.4 (lodging of pleadings before options hearing), 9.8 (adjustment of pleadings), 9.9 (effect of sist on adjustment), 9.10 (open record), 9.11 (record for options hearing), 9.12 (options hearing), 9.15 (applications for time to pay directions), and the whole of Chap. 10 (additional procedure).

[10] OCR, r. 35.3(1).

[11] OCR, r. 35.3(2)(a).

[12] OCR, r. 35.3(2)(b).

[13] Green's *Litigation Styles*, J5. See also J1003, J1007.

[14] para. 9.67.

[15] OCR, r. 35.4(1).

[16] OCR, r. 35.5.

[17] OCR, r. 35.4(2).

[18] OCR, r. 35.7. Advertisement or display on the walls of court is in any event obligatory where a defender's address is unknown to the pursuer: OCR, r. 5.6(1): see paras 6.33 to 6.35.

[19] OCR, r. 35.16.

[20] *cf.* OCR, r. 5.6(4).

competency of the action, (2) objections to the condescendence of the fund *in medio*, or (3) a claim on the fund *in medio*, or any combination of these. If so he must lodge, before the expiry of the appropriate period of notice, a notice of appearance in Form M4 of Appendix 1 to the Rules.[21] He must specify in the notice the purpose of his intended appearance.[22] The notice is signed by the party or his solicitor. It is improper for parties with conflicting interests to be represented by the same solicitors.[23] If no notice of appearance is lodged it may be appropriate for the sheriff to order advertisement, or further advertisement, of the action.[24]

21.58 **Fixing first hearing.** Where a notice of appearance or a condescendence on the fund and list under rule 35.4(2)(a)[25] has been lodged, the sheriff clerk fixes a date and time for the first hearing, which date must be the first suitable court day occurring not sooner than four weeks after the expiry of the period of notice.[26] He must forthwith intimate that date to each party,[27] and prepare and sign an interlocutor recording the date of the first hearing.[28]

21.59 **Hearings.** All hearings in multiplepoindings must be conducted with a view to securing the expeditious progress of the case by ascertaining from parties the matters in dispute.[29] The parties must provide the sheriff with sufficient information to enable him so to conduct the hearing.[30] These provisions are similar to the rules for the conduct of options hearings and procedural hearings in other ordinary causes.[31]

21.60 **First hearing.** At the first hearing the sheriff fixes a period within which defences, objections or claims must be lodged and appoints a date for a second hearing.[32] If a list has been lodged under rule 35.4(2)(a)[33] and that list contains the name of any person who is not a party to the action, the sheriff must order (a) that the initial writ be amended to add that person as a defender, (b) service of the pleadings (by which must surely be meant "the initial writ") on that person with a citation in Form M6, and (c) intimation to that person of the condescendence of the fund *in medio* lodged by the holder who is not pursuer.[34] If a person to whom service has been made as just described lodges a notice of appearance, the sheriff clerk must intimate to him the date of the next hearing.[35]

21.61 **Lodging of defences, etc.** Defences, objections and claims must be lodged with the sheriff clerk in a single document under separate headings.[36] Where a party wishes to state defences to the competency of the

---

[21] OCR, r. 35.8.
[22] OCR, App. 1, Form M4.
[23] *Dunlop's Trs v. Farquharson*, 1956 S.L.T. 16.
[24] OCR, rr. 35.7, 35.16; see para. 21.56.
[25] See para. 21.56.
[26] OCR, r. 35.9(a).
[27] OCR, r. 35.9(b). Intimation is in Form M5 of App. 1.
[28] OCR, r. 35.9(c).
[29] OCR, r. 35.10(1).
[30] OCR, r. 35.10(2).
[31] *cf.* OCR, rr 9.12(1), (2) and 10.6(1), (2). See paras 8.36 *et seq.*
[32] OCR, r. 35.10(3).
[33] See para. 21.56.
[34] OCR, r. 35.10(4).
[35] OCR, r. 35.10(5). Intimation is in form M5.
[36] OCR, r. 35.11(1).

action, he lodges defences in conventional form, with any objections or claim by the defender following the pleas-in-law under separate headings. Where a party does not wish to lodge defences to the competency of the action, but to lodge objections, his writ is headed: "OBJECTIONS/for/ A.B. [*designed*]/to/Condescendence of the fund *in medio*/in/Action of Multiplepoinding/[*names and designations of parties as in the instance*]." Objections, headed "Objections", are specifically stated in numbered paragraphs and have appended appropriate pleas-in-law. If a claim alone is lodged, it is headed: "CONDESCENDENCE AND CLAIM/ for/A.B. [*designed*], Claimant/in/Action of Multiplepoinding [*etc., as above*]." A claim consists of a condescendence, claim and pleas-in-law. The condescendence is headed "Condescendence" and sets out in numbered paragraphs the facts on which the claimant bases his claim. If appropriate, any specified averments in the initial writ may be adopted and held as repeated. The claim is headed "Claim", and sets out specifically what is claimed.[37] A claim may be appended under a separate heading. In a riding claim, lodged by the creditor of a claimant and dependent on that claimant's claim, the claimant is described as a riding claimant. Each claimant must lodge with his claim any documents founded on in his claim, so far as they are within his custody or power.[38]

Preliminary pleas. There are provisions about preliminary pleas in the Ordinary Cause Rules applying to multiplepoindings which are similar to those for other ordinary causes.[39] A party intending to insist on a preliminary plea must, not later than three days before any hearing to determine further procedure following the lodging of defences, objections or claims, lodge with the sheriff clerk a note of the basis of the plea.[40] If a party fails timeously to lodge such a note he is deemed no longer to be insisting on his preliminary plea, and it will be repelled.[41] If a note is properly lodged the sheriff, after considering it and having heard parties, will fix a debate if he is satisfied that there is a preliminary matter of law which justifies a debate.[42] **21.62**

Disposal of defences. The procedural scheme in the Ordinary Cause Rules sets out separate and consecutive procedural stages by which any defences, objections and claims may be successively disposed of. Unless the sheriff otherwise directs, defences challenging the jurisdiction of the court or the competency of the action must be disposed of before any further procedure in the action.[43] Accordingly, at the hearing after defences have been lodged the sheriff may order the initial writ and defences to be adjusted. He thereafter closes the record on the initial writ and defences as adjusted, and regulates further procedure,[44] usually by appointing parties to debate. If he sustains the objections to jurisdiction or the competency of the action, the case will come to an end. If he repels them, he will fix a new hearing at which future procedure will be determined. **21.63**

---

37 This is an essential part of the writ: *Connell v. Ferguson* (1861) 23 D. 683, *per* Lord Neaves at 686.

38 OCR, r. 35.11(2).

39 *cf.* OCR, r. 22.1. See para. 8.48.

40 OCR, r. 35.14(1).

41 OCR, r. 35.14(2).

42 OCR, r. 35.14(3).

43 OCR, r. 35.12(2).

44 OCR, r. 35.12(1).

21.64 **Disposal of objections to fund *in medio*.** Where objections to the fund *in medio* have been lodged the sheriff may, after disposing of any defences, order the condescendence of the fund and objections to be adjusted. He thereafter closes the record thereon and regulates further procedure.[45] In most cases he will order a debate or proof and will thereafter dispose of the objections and fix a further hearing. The interlocutor disposing of the objections is appealable without leave.[46]

21.65 **Approval of condescendence, etc.** The course of procedure described in the two following paragraphs applies to all multiplepoindings irrespective of whether any defences, objections or claims have been lodged, provided that any defences or objections which *have* been lodged have been disposed of. It cannot, however, proceed until the expiry of the period for lodging defences or objections, or of the period for lodging a notice of appearance stated in any advertisement that has been ordered, or until any defences or objections have been disposed of. If no defences or objections have been lodged, or if they have been lodged and disposed of, the following procedure may take place.

21.66 (1) The sheriff, without order for intimation to any party, may on the motion of the holder of the fund approve the condescendence of the fund.[47]

(2) He may likewise find the holder liable only in once and single payment.[48] Such a finding is a judicial determination that the action is competent. The motion in respect of these two matters may be made at any earlier hearing on objections, so that the interlocutor disposing of the objections may also approve the condescendence and find the holder liable in once and single payment.

(3) At any time after the condescendence of the fund *in medio* has been approved, the sheriff may order the whole or any part of the fund to be sold and the proceeds of sale to be consigned into court.[49] The current Ordinary Cause Rules, unlike their immediate predecessors,[50] make no specific provision for consignation or deposit in the sheriff clerk's hands of the fund *in medio* itself where no sale takes place. The reason for this omission is obscure. It is submitted that consignation is still the appropriate step to take even if there is no sale. Problems may arise where the fund consists of or includes a bulky or valuable object which the parties do not wish to be sold. Normally the only means by which the sheriff clerk can keep such objects securely is by storing them commercially at a cost which would materially reduce the value of the fund. In such cases the court may ask the holder of the object to retain it or, if that is impracticable, may ask the parties to agree an arrangement for its safe keeping.

(4) In the ordinary case, after consignation or deposit of the fund with the sheriff clerk, the holder of the fund *in medio* may apply for his exoneration and discharge.[51] This provision makes it all the more difficult to understand why the current Rules provide for consignation only in the event of sale of the fund *in medio*.

---

[45] OCR, r. 35.13(1).

[46] *Walker's Tr. v. Walker* (1878) 5 R. 678; *Harris School Board v. Davidson* (1881) 9 R. 371.

[47] OCR, r. 35.13(2).

[48] *ibid.*

[49] OCR, r. 35.15(1). As to procedure where the fund *in medio* consists of or includes a heritable security, see *Currie's Trs v. Bothwell*, 1954 S.L.T. (Sh. Ct.) 87.

[50] 1983 OCR, r. 123(1).

[51] OCR, r. 35.15(2).

(5) The sheriff may allow the holder of the fund *in medio*, on his exoneration and discharge, his expenses out of the fund as a first charge thereon.[52]

In practice, these stages are normally combined in a single interlocutor, whereby the sheriff: (1) holds the fund *in medio* to be correctly stated in the initial writ or other pleading at the sum therein specified; (2) finds the holder liable only in once and single payment; (3) finds the holder entitled to payment of his expenses out of the fund *in medio* and allows an account thereof to be given in and remits the same, when lodged, to the auditor of court to tax and to report; (4) ordains the holder to lodge the fund *in medio*, under deduction of his taxed expenses, in the hands of the sheriff clerk; and (5) upon consignation being made exoners and discharges him of the fund *in medio* and of his whole actings and intromissions therewith. These steps having been taken, the holder of the fund retires from the process. Where the holder of the fund is to retain possession of an object in the circumstances described in paragraph 21.66(3), he cannot at this stage be exonered and discharged but may wish to be saved the expense of further involvement in the litigation. This may be achieved by holding the fund correctly stated, finding the holder liable only in once and single delivery, finding him entitled to expenses and having these taxed and approved. Thereafter the holder takes no further part in the proceedings and the final interlocutor ranks and prefers, ordains delivery on payment of the holder's expenses and on delivery being made exoners and discharges him on a receipt for such delivery. **21.67**

Disposal of claims. *No competition.* After the approval of the condescendence of the fund, if it appears that there is only one claim, or that there is no conflict between or among the parties who have lodged claims, the sheriff may rank and prefer the claimant or claimants and grant decree in terms of the ranking.[53] If he does so, he directs the sheriff clerk to make payment out of the consigned fund on the lodging of any necessary clearance certificate and to require receipts. The rule that payment must not be made until any necessary clearance certificate has been lodged[54] must be strictly observed.[55] The only exception to this rule, which applies only in the case of a multiplepoinding, is that decree may be granted even though all the taxes or duties payable on the estate of a deceased claimant have not been paid or satisfied.[56] The sheriff also determines questions of expenses.[57] In order to avoid any error or delay in the implementation of the decree, it is essential that an interlocutor disposing of a multiplepoinding should be clearly expressed. Any joint minute should likewise precisely specify the steps which the court is asked to take when pronouncing decree. In particular it is necessary: (1) to ensure that the total fund is disposed of, and that provision is made for such matters as the assignation of life policies or the delivery of goods; (2) wherever possible, to specify the payments to be made in precise figures or in specific fractions of the total, rather than by reference to any formula; (3) to deal clearly and specifically with any accrued interest; and (4) to take account of and deal with expenses. **21.68**

---

[52] OCR, r. 35.15(3).
[53] OCR, r. 35.17(1).
[54] OCR, r. 30.2(1). See paras 11.51, 17.31.
[55] *Simpson's Trs v. Fox*, 1954 S.L.T. (Notes) 12.
[56] OCR, r. 30.2(2).
[57] para. 21.71.

21.69 *Competition.* Where there is competition among the claimants, the sheriff may order the claims to be adjusted and thereafter close the record thereon and regulate further procedure.[58] As at any earlier closings of the record, the case may be heard by debate,[59] or by proof if there is any dispute as to fact. The interlocutor disposing of the competition ranks and prefers the successful claimant or claimants and repels the claims of the unsuccessful. If it deals with expenses it may be appealed without leave by an unsuccessful claimant.[60] An order for payment may be made in the same interlocutor, or may be delayed. In the latter case the interlocutor may make findings in fact and in law determining the principles on which the division of the fund is to proceed, and grant leave to appeal.[61] The sheriff may remit to a reporter to prepare a scheme of division and report,[62] but in practice it is rarely necessary to do so. Such a scheme shows the amounts which the decree of ranking and preference determines to be payable to each of the successful claimants. The expenses of such a remit, when approved by the sheriff, must be made a charge upon the fund to be deducted before division.[63]

21.70 **Decree.** Reference has already been made to the need for clarity and comprehensiveness in the interlocutor and to the rule as to a clearance certificate.[64] The interlocutor ordering payment or transference of the fund *in medio* to the successful claimants secures the holder of the fund, after payment or transference, against any further claims at the instance of any person,[65] and constitutes *res judicata* as against all the parties in the process.[66] The only remedy of a person who has not appeared in the process is by way of reduction: if he was called as a defender, he must show a necessary cause of absence.[67]

21.71 **Expenses.** While there are no fixed rules as to expenses in a multiplepoinding, it is thought that the general rules may be stated as follows.[68] The holder of the fund is found entitled to expenses out of the fund *in medio*,[69] taxed as between solicitor and client, client paying.[70] Where the competition arises out of questions involving the construction of a deed, the claimants' expenses are allowed out of the fund.[71] The expenses of litigation as to the amount of the fund may follow the result,[72] but in exceptional circumstances that course may be departed from and an unsuccessful party who can to some extent justify his position may have

---

[58] OCR, r. 35.17(2).

[59] Provided that a note of the basis of the preliminary plea has been lodged in conformity with OCR, r. 35.14. See para. 21.62.

[60] *Glasgow Corporation v. General Accident Fire and Life Assurance Corporation Ltd*, 1914 S.C. 835.

[61] *cf. Gowans' Trs v. Gowans* (1889) 27 S.L.R. 210.

[62] OCR, r. 35.18(1).

[63] OCR, r. 35.18(2).

[64] para. 21.68.

[65] Stair, IV, xvi, 3; Ersk., IV, iii, 23.

[66] *McCaig v. Maitland* (1887) 14 R. 295; *Elder's Trs v. Elder* (1895) 22 R. 505.

[67] Decrees in Absence Act 1584, c. 10.

[68] See Maclaren, *Expenses*, pp. 285–292; *Stair Memorial Encyclopaedia*, para. 1199.

[69] *Hepburn's Trs v. Rex* (1894) 21 R. 1024.

[70] para. 19.45.

[71] *Costine's Trs v. Costine* (1878) 5. R. 782; and see para. 19.13.

[72] *Hume's Trs v. Ralston's Trs* (1834) 12 S. 727; *Allan v. Fleming* (1845) 7 D. 908; *Bannerman's Trs v. Bannerman*, 1915 S.C. 398; *Grant's Trs v. McDonald*, 1939 S.C. 448.

his expenses allowed out of the fund.[73] On the other hand a party who has raised an incompetent multiplepoinding,[74] or who has rendered the action necessary by maintaining an unreasonable claim,[75] may be found liable in expenses.

Action for payment of solicitor's account

21.72 An action by a solicitor against his client for payment of his business account proceeds in ordinary form, but decree will not be granted without the account being taxed. Thus, even where the action is undefended, the sheriff remits the account to the auditor of court to tax and to report. This rule is applicable in both ordinary and summary causes, and to all solicitors' business accounts, not only to accounts in judicial processes.[76] It even applies to small claims.[77] The only exception to this rule is if the solicitor and client have reached an agreement in writing as to the solicitor's fees for the work done, in which case it is incompetent for the court to remit the account for taxation.[78]

21.73 The rule was first expressed in the Act of Sederunt of February 6, 1806, by which the first office of Auditor of Court was established in the Court of Session. It was repeated in later enactments of the rules of the Court of Session[79] and is now to be found set out in terms in rule 42.7(1)(b). The rule has long been observed in most sheriff courts.[80] It is perhaps best regarded as exemplifying the close control which the courts maintain over their officers in their relations with the lay public: another example is the supervision of curators and factors appointed by the court. It is closely linked with the rule that a client's right to have a business account taxed can only be foreclosed by the most express waiver. The reason for the latter rule is that "the law is extremely jealous of any settlements of accounts between an agent and his client, as the parties do not meet upon equal terms."[81] That rationale is applicable to all actions in the Scottish courts for payment of a solicitor's business account.[82] The remit to the auditor is a remit of a ministerial character for the necessary purpose of informing the court as to the regularity of the account.[83]

21.74 In the Court of Session the rule is applied without any qualification.[84] Lewis and Dobie state, without reference to authority, that taxation may

---

[73] *Clydesdale Bank Ltd v. McColl* (1941) 59 Sh.Ct.Rep. 159.

[74] *Mackenzie's Trs v. Sutherland* (1895) 22 R. 233.

[75] *Pollard v. Galloway and Nivison* (1881) 9 R. 21, *per* Lord Young at 24.

[76] *W. & A. S. Bruce v. Evans*, 1986 S.L.T. (Sh. Ct.) 20.

[77] *Lyall & Wood v. Thomson*, 1993 S.L.T. (Sh. Ct.) 21.

[78] Solicitors (Scotland) Act 1980, s. 61A(1) (inserted by the Law Reform (Miscellaneous Provisions) (Scotland) Act 1990, s. 36(3)).

[79] It appeared in the CAS, K, I, 2(c) and subsequent editions of the Rules of Court.

[80] *R. J. Docherty & Co. v. Horne*, 1967 S.L.T. (Sh. Ct.) 27; Lewis, pp. 105, 106; Dobie, pp. 130, 338.

[81] G. R. (later L.J.-C.) Thomson, "Expenses", *Encyclopaedia*, vi, para. 1347, *cit. McLaren v. Manson* (1857) 20 D. 218, *per* Lord Deas at 222. See also *Cockburn v. Clark* (1885) 12 R. 707 at 709.

[82] *Obiter dicta* in *Alex. Morison & Co. v. McCulloch*, 1984 S.L.T. (Sh. Ct.) 88, are inconsistent with the authorities cited in the preceding footnotes. See *Lyall & Wood*, *supra*.

[83] Mackay, *Manual*, p. 276.

[84] *Guthrie v. McEachern* (1826) 5 S. 135 (N.E. 124), where the Lord Ordinary modified a small account without a remit, appears to be the only reported case of failure to comply with the A.S: Mackay, *Practice*, ii, 601.

be dispensed with of consent[85]; and it has been said that an admission of liability to pay the sum sued for, made in correspondence or in a summary cause on a defender's form of response, would suffice.[86] It is submitted, however, that consistency in the approach of the courts to the whole subject of the settlement of solicitors' accounts must be maintained: accordingly only a conscious waiver of the defender's right to a taxation, expressed in explicit terms, can entitle the sheriff to dispense with taxation[87]; and any document proffered as an admission of liability must make it clear that the defender is aware of his right to a taxation and has waived it. In the Sheriffdom of South Strathclyde, Dumfries and Galloway, Act of Court 1982 No. 4 provides that it shall not be necessary for solicitors suing for the recovery of professional fees to have their accounts taxed by the auditor of court before decree, except when the account is challenged by the defender. It is submitted that since this act of court appears to be contrary to settled law and practice it might be challenged as *ultra vires* of the sheriff principal.[88]

Actions *Ad Factum Praestandum*

Nature of remedy

21.75 An action *ad factum praestandum* is brought to enforce the performance by the defender of an act other than the payment of money.[89] It must be brought as a summary cause unless there is craved in addition, or as an alternative, to a decree *ad factum praestandum*, a decree for payment of money exceeding £1,500 in amount (exclusive of interest and expenses).[90] An order *ad factum praestandum* may in certain circumstances be made in a family action, for example an order for delivery of a child. An action containing a crave for such an order would, of course, contain other craves relating to the child concerned and would be raised as an ordinary action and not as a summary cause. An action *ad factum praestandum* is competent against a limited company.[91] The sheriff court does not have jurisdiction to enforce the performance by a local authority of its statutory duty,[92] as this falls within the scope of judicial review which is within the exclusive jurisdiction of the Court of Session.[93] The nature of the remedy and the circumstances in which it is competent are fully considered in the undernoted works.[94]

---

85 Lewis, pp. 105–106; Dobie, p. 338.

86 *W. & A. S. Bruce, supra.*

87 *McLaren v. Manson, supra, per* Lord Deas at 222; *Cockburn v. Clark* (1885) 12 R. 707, *per* Lord Young at 709.

88 See para. 1.39.

89 *White & Carter (Councils) Ltd v. McGregor*, 1962 S.C. (H.L.) 1, *per* Lord Morton of Henryton at 16. An action at the seller's instance for implement of a contract of sale by payment of the price, with payment of damages as an alternative, is, however, competent: *R. S. Leigh & Co. v. Berger & Co.*, 1958 S.L.T. (Sh. Ct.) 21; *Bosco Design Services Ltd v. Plastic Sealant Services Ltd*, 1979 S.C. 189.

90 1971 Act, s. 35(1)(c). The sum of £1,500 is the present upper limit for a summary cause. The amount may be varied by Order in Council: 1971 Act, s. 41(1).

91 *Postel Properties Ltd v. Miller & Santhouse plc*, 1992 S.C.L.R. 799.

92 *Brown v. Hamilton D.C.*, 1983 S.C. (H.L.) 1.

93 For a discussion of the scope of judicial review see *West v. Secretary of State for Scotland*, 1992 S.C. 385.

Crave

Need for precision

The crave *ad factum praestandum* must be framed in unambiguous terms which plainly specify exactly what is to be done,[95] because the court will not pronounce a decree *ad factum praestandum* except in terms of such precision as will leave the defender in no doubt as to the exact obligation which he must perform.[96] 21.76

Alternative crave

It is usually desirable to add an alternative crave for damages lest compliance with the crave *ad factum praestandum* becomes impossible during the dependence of the action, or lest the court in its discretion decides to refuse decree *ad factum praestandum*.[97] If there is no alternative or additional crave for payment of over £1,500 the action must be brought as a summary cause.[98] The inclusion of an alternative crave for damages does not bar the pursuer from insisting in his crave *ad factum praestandum*.[99] Accordingly the defender is not entitled to evade the granting of decree in terms of the primary crave by consenting to decree in terms of the alternative crave.[1] If decree in terms of the primary crave is pronounced but not obtempered by the defender, the pursuer may move for decree in terms of the alternative crave. Upon the grant of that decree the pursuer is personally barred from enforcing the decree in terms of the primary crave.[2] It is competent to add an alternative crave by amendment.[3] 21.77

Crave for delivery

When the pursuer seeks delivery, he may crave both delivery and a warrant to officers of court to search and take possession of the articles specified in the crave.[4] A warrant to search for moveables must be restricted to the premises occupied by or in the tenancy of the defender.[5] Where the parties to a contract have agreed on the precise method by which the moveables should be repossessed in the event of the defender's failure to implement the contract, a crave for delivery is incompetent.[6] In certain circumstances a crave directed against two or more defenders for a joint and several decree of delivery may be competent.[7] 21.78

---

[94] Burn-Murdoch, Chap. 6; Walker, *Civil Remedies*, Chap. 13.

[95] *Robertson v. Cockburn* (1875) 3 R. 21, *per* L.J.-C. Moncreiff at 23; *Middleton v. Leslie* (1892) 19 R. 801, *per* L.P. Robertson at 802; *Marshall v. Callander and Trossachs Hydropathic Co. Ltd* (1896) 24 R., 33 *per* L.P. Robertson at 34.

[96] *Fleming & Ferguson v. Paisley Mags*, 1948 S.C. 547, *per* L.P. Cooper at 558; *Munro v. Liquidator of Balnagown Estates*, 1949 S.C. 49, *per* L.P. Cooper at 55.

[97] *Summerlee Iron Co. Ltd v. Caledonian Ry*, 1911 S.C. 458. As to the court's discretion to refuse decree, see para. 21.80.

[98] para. 21.75.

[99] *McKellar v. Dallas's Ltd*, 1928 S.C. 503.

[1] *Mackay v. Campbell*, 1967 S.C.(H.L.) 153.

[2] *Bosco Design Services Ltd v. Plastic Sealant Services Ltd*, 1979 S.C. 189.

[3] *Summerlee Iron Co. Ltd, supra*; *Lyle v. Smith*, 1954 S.L.T. (Sh. Ct.) 11.

[4] *Merchants Facilities (Glasgow) Ltd v. Keenan*, 1967 S.L.T. (Sh. Ct.) 65.

[5] *North Central Wagon & Finance Co. Ltd v. McGiffen*, 1958 S.L.T. (Sh. Ct.) 62; *Boyd v. Drummond, Robbie & Gibson*, 1995 S.C.L.R. 178.

[6] *Bruce Bros (Glasgow) Ltd v. McVittie* (1943) 60 Sh.Ct.Rep. 20; *Bell Bros (H.P.) Ltd v. Hamilton* (1945) 62 Sh.Ct.Rep. 31.

[7] *Sinclair v. Gardner* (1915) 32 Sh.Ct.Rep. 211; *Young's Exrx v. Armour*, 1957 S.L.T. (Sh. Ct.) 42.

Interim order

21.79 An interim order *ad factum praestandum* is in general competent.[8] Such an order may be made in appropriate circumstances in an action by a seller for implement of a contract of sale.[9] It has been held that in an action in which interim interdict has been refused, an interim order *ad factum praestandum* should be refused if sought for the same purpose as the interim interdict.[10] An interim order *ad factum praestandum* may be appealed without leave to the sheriff principal and with leave to the Court of Session.[11] An interlocutor ordering a defender to appear at the bar to explain a failure to obey a court order is an order *ad factum praestandum* and may therefore be appealed to the sheriff principal without leave.[12]

Decree

21.80 As already observed, the terms of the decree must specify precisely what is to be done[13] and the time within which it is to be done.[14] The interlocutor should not order performance "forthwith" except where a single act is to be performed which is instantly completed, such as the delivery of a writ.[15] In other cases the interlocutor should specify a date[16] which allows a reasonable time for performance.[17] If no time is specified, the charge will require performance within seven days.[18] Where the action relates to heritable property and the defender is under an obligation to the pursuer to execute a deed relating thereto but he cannot be found or refuses or is unable or otherwise fails to execute the deed, the sheriff may, on application by the pursuer, make an order dispensing with the execution of the deed by the defender and directing the sheriff clerk to execute the deed.[19] The court has a discretion to refuse decree *ad factum praestandum* where in ordinary circumstances the pursuer would be entitled to it as a matter of course. The circumstances in which that discretion may be exercised include cases where performance is impossible, or enforcement of the decree would be impossible or would cause exceptional hardship. The topic is beyond the scope of this book and is fully examined in the undernoted works.[20] If the defender considers that there are grounds on which the court should exercise its discretion, he should state averments and a plea relative to these grounds in his defences.[21]

---

[8] An interlocutor ordering consignation is such an order: *Mackenzie v. Balerno Paper Mill Co.* (1883) 10 R. 1147; *Menzies v. Templeton* (1896) 12 Sh.Ct.Rep. 323.

[9] *George Hotel (Glasgow) Ltd v. Prestwick Hotels Ltd*, 1961 S.L.T. (Sh. Ct.) 61; *Scottish Flavour Ltd v. Watson*, 1982 S.L.T. 78.

[10] *Lindfai v. Stivens*, 1967 S.L.T. (Sh. Ct.) 84.

[11] 1907 Act, ss. 27(b), 28(1)(d): see para. 18.40.

[12] *Boyd v. Drummond, Robbie & Gibson*, 1995 S.C.L.R. 178.

[13] para. 21.76.

[14] *Macdonald v. Mackessack* (1888) 16 R. 168.

[15] *Middleton v. Leslie* (1892) 19 R. 801.

[16] *Munro v. Liquidator of Balnagown Estates Co.*, 1949 S.C. 49, *per* L.P. Cooper at 55.

[17] *Pollock v. N.B. Ry* (1901) 3 F. 727, *per* Lord Trayner at 739.

[18] *McLintock v. Prinzen & Van Glabbeek* (1902) 4 F. 948 referring to the Sheriff Courts (Scotland) Act 1892, s. 4 and Sched., Form 12.

[19] 1907 Act, s. 5A, inserted by the Law Reform (Miscellaneous Provisions) (Scotland) Act 1985, s. 17. The application is by motion if the action is still before the sheriff (s. 5A(2)(a)) and by summary application if decree has already been granted (s. 5A(2)(b)).

[20] Gloag, pp. 657, 661; Walker, *Civil Remedies*, p. 280. See also *Macleod v. Alexander Sutherland Ltd*, 1977 S.L.T. (Notes) 44.

[21] *Salaried Staff London Loan Co. Ltd v. Swears and Wells Ltd*, 1985 S.L.T. 326: *e.g. Mackay v. Campbell*, 1966 S.C. 237 at 242–243 (affd 1967 S.C. (H.L.) 53).

Enforcement of decree

No person may be apprehended or imprisoned on account of his failure to comply with a decree *ad factum praestandum* except in accordance with the provisions of section 1 of the Law Reform (Miscellaneous Provisions) (Scotland) Act 1940. The person in right of the decree (referred to in section 1 as "the applicant") makes an application to the court by which the decree was granted.[22] The application may be made by minute[23] in the original process after a charge has expired without implement of the decree. It is suggested that intimation of the minute to the person against whom the decree was granted ("the respondent") should appoint him to attend a hearing.[24] At that hearing the sheriff determines what further procedure should take place.[25] It is for the applicant to satisfy the court that the respondent is wilfully refusing to comply with the decree.[26] The court, if so satisfied, may grant warrant for the imprisonment of the respondent for any period not exceeding six months.[27] Imprisonment does not operate to extinguish the obligation imposed by the decree, and the applicant is not liable to aliment the respondent while he is in prison.[28] Where the court is satisfied that the respondent has complied, or is no longer wilfully refusing to comply, with the decree, the court must order his immediate liberation. It is the duty of the applicant, as soon as he is satisfied that the decree has been complied with, forthwith to inform the sheriff clerk of such compliance.[29] **21.81**

On an application under section 1(1) the court may, in lieu of granting warrant for imprisonment, recall the decree and make an order for the payment by the respondent to the applicant of a specified sum, or make such other order as appears to the court to be just and equitable in the circumstances.[30] Where the decree is for delivery of corporeal moveables, the court may grant a warrant to officers of court to search any premises in the occupation of the respondent or of such other person as may be named in the warrant, and to take possession of and deliver to the applicant any such moveables which may be found in such premises.[31] Such a warrant is deemed to include authority to open shut and lockfast places for the purpose of carrying the warrant into lawful execution.[32] **21.82**

Actions of Interdict

Nature of remedy: jurisdiction

"Interdict is a remedy, by decree of court, either against a wrong in course of being done, or against an apprehended violation of a party's rights, to be awarded only on evidence of the wrong, or on reasonable **21.83**

---

[22] Law Reform (Miscellaneous Provisions) (Scotland) Act 1940, s. 1(1)(i).
[23] Minute procedure is governed by OCR, Chap. 14. See paras 5.56 *et seq.*
[24] OCR, r. 14.3(2)(c).
[25] OCR, r. 14.11(2).
[26] Dobie, p. 286.
[27] 1940 Act, s. 1(1)(i).
[28] *ibid.* s 1(1)(iii), (iv).
[29] *ibid.* s 1(1)(ii).
[30] *ibid.* s. 1(2); *Ford v. Bell Chandler*, 1977 S.L.T. (Sh. Ct.) 90.
[31] 1940 Act, s. 1(2).
[32] *ibid.* s. 1(3).

grounds of apprehension that such violation is intended."[33] It is fully considered in the undernoted works.[34] In proceedings for interdict the defender may be sued either in the sheriff court for the place where he is domiciled, or in the sheriff court for the place where it is alleged that the wrong is being or is likely to be committed.[35]

Crave

21.84 The crave for interdict may stand alone[36] or may be combined with others, such as craves for declarator or damages. The terms of the crave for interdict must be directed to the illegal actings complained of and the method or methods required to prevent their recurrence, and should be so precise and clear that the defender is left in no doubt what he is forbidden to do.[37] The crave should not beg the question as, for example, by referring to "the property of the pursuer" when there may be a dispute as to what exactly *is* the property of the pursuer. In such a situation a crave for declarator would be necessary. If interim interdict is sought, it must be specially craved and averments made to justify its being granted.[38]

Interim interdict

21.85 Where interim interdict has been craved, with supporting averments, it may be granted before or after service of the writ. The following paragraphs consider restrictions on the grant of interim interdict, the procedure where it is applied for, the conditions on which it may be granted and the scope for appeal.

Restrictions on grant of interim interdict

21.86 **Caveat.** Anyone who is apprehensive that an action of interdict may be raised against him and interim interdict applied for *ex parte* in his absence, may lodge a caveat with the sheriff clerk.[39] A caveat is a written request for notice in the event of such an application being made. The form is now prescribed in the Ordinary Cause Rules.[40] It requests that in the event of an application being made for the order concerned before the lodging of a notice of intention to defend, intimation be made to the caveator before any order is pronounced. It is signed by the caveator or his solicitor. Provision is made in the form for telephone and fax numbers to be stated at which the caveator or his solicitor may be contacted and also for the caveator to state how he or his solicitor may be contacted outwith normal business hours. A fee is paid to the sheriff clerk.[41] Where a caveat has been lodged, no order in respect of which the caveat was lodged may be pronounced unless the sheriff is satisfied that all reasonable steps have been taken to afford the caveator an opportunity of being heard, and the sheriff may continue a hearing on such an order until he is satisfied that such steps have been taken.[42]

---

[33] *Hay's Trs v. Young* (1877) 4 R. 398, *per* Lord Ormidale at 401; *Inverurie Mags v. Sorrie*, 1956 S.C. 175.

[34] Burn-Murdoch on *Interdict*, a classic work of great practical value; Walker, *Civil Remedies*, Chap. 11; Scott Robinson, *The Law of Interdict* (2nd ed., 1994).

[35] Civil Jurisdiction and Judgments Act 1982, Sched. 8, rr. 1, 2(10); see para. 3.104.

[36] *Exchange Telegraph Co. v. White*, 1961 S.L.T. 104.

[37] *Kelso School Board v. Hunter* (1874) 2 R. 228, *per* Lord Deas at 232, Lord Ardmillan at 235; *Murdoch v. Murdoch*, 1973 S.L.T. (Notes) 73; *Webster v. Lord Advocate*, 1985 S.L.T. 361.

[38] Burn-Murdoch, p. 450; Dobie, p. 507.

[39] OCR, rr. 4.1(a), 4.2(1).

[40] OCR, r. 4.2(1), App. 1, Form G2.

[41] Sheriff Court Fees Order 1997, Sched. 1, para. 16. At the time of writing this fee is £17.

[42] OCR, r. 4.2(3).

A caveat remains in force for a period of one year from the date on which it was lodged.[43] On its expiry it may be renewed for a further period of one year and yearly thereafter.[44] A fee is payable on renewal in the same way as when the caveat is first lodged.[45] 21.87

Trade Union and Labour Relations (Consolidation) Act 1992, s. 221(1). Where an application for an interdict is made to the sheriff in the absence of the party against whom the interdict is sought or any representative of his and that party claims, or in the opinion of the sheriff would be likely to claim, that he acted in contemplation or furtherance of a trade dispute, the sheriff must not grant the interdict unless he is satisfied that all steps which in the circumstances were reasonable have been taken with a view to securing that notice of the application and an opportunity of being heard with respect to the application have been given to that party.[46] 21.88

Hearing on interim interdict

Where interim interdict is sought before service, the pursuer's solicitor appears before the sheriff in chambers and moves for a warrant of citation and interim interdict. The sheriff may grant interim interdict if no caveat has been lodged and if he is satisfied prima facie[47] as to the court's jurisdiction, the pursuer's title to sue, the cogency of his case and the urgency of the matter as disclosed by the averments in the initial writ and the *ex parte* statement by the pursuer's solicitor. The interim interdict may be limited in time as, for example, to the date of a further hearing, or it may be "until further orders of court". Whether the sheriff grants or refuses interim interdict, he grants a warrant of citation. He may fix an early diet for hearing parties on the crave for interim interdict. However, if interim interdict has been granted at the first hearing, the value of fixing such an early diet may be doubted, as it is open to the defender at any time to lodge a motion for recall of the interim interdict. If at the first hearing before the sheriff the crave for interim interdict is amended, the interlocutor pronounced should set out *ad longum* the effect of the amendment and the initial writ itself should, of course, be amended. Where the sheriff grants interim interdict, the order should be formally intimated to the defender at once, but it may come into operation against him if in fact he is sufficiently aware of its terms and extent notwithstanding the absence of due intimation.[48] At any further hearing the sheriff, after hearing parties, may grant interim interdict where that was refused at the first hearing, or refuse it, or, where interim interdict was granted at the first hearing, continue or recall it, with or without conditions. 21.89

Sheriff Dobie observed that if interim interdict was granted with the warrant for service, or before the expiry of the *induciae* (*i.e.* the period of notice), and nothing was done to bring the action into court, the whole process, and also the interdict, apparently fell in a year and a day after the 21.90

---

43 OCR, r. 4.2(2).

44 *ibid.*

45 Sheriff Court Fees Order 1997, Sched. 1, para. 16. At the time of writing this fee is £17.

46 Trade Union and Labour Relations (Consolidation) Act 1992, s. 221(1). See *Scotsman Publications Ltd v. SOGAT*, 1986 S.L.T. 646.

47 *Deane v. Lothian R.C.*, 1986 S.L.T. 22; *Reed Stenhouse (U.K.) Ltd v. Brodie*, 1986 S.L.T. 354.

48 *Robertson v. McDonald* (1829) 7 S. 272; *Clark v. Stirling* (1839) 1 D. 955; *Matheson v. Fraser*, 1911 2 S.L.T. 493; *Neville v. Neville*, 1924 S.L.T. (Sh. Ct.) 43.

*inducia*e expired.[49] In the first edition it was suggested that the interim interdict might fall sooner if the action were not tabled.[50] Be that as it may, it is submitted that, with the disappearance of tabling and protestation, Sheriff Dobie's observation is correct.

21.91 At a hearing on interim interdict at which both parties are represented, the discussion is likely to be dominated by the questions whether there is a case to try and, if there is, where the balance of convenience lies.[51] While the court will not subject unadjusted pleadings to detailed scrutiny,[52] it is in use to have regard to the relative strength of the cases put forward in averment and argument by each party as one of the many factors that may go to make up the balance of convenience.[53] In some courts it is considered appropriate to have regard to affidavit evidence when considering whether to grant interim interdict. While there is no express provision in the Ordinary Cause Rules rendering this competent in actions other than family actions,[54] there is equally no provision declaring it incompetent. It may be that in some instances affidavit evidence may assist the making of a decision on a motion for interim interdict.[55] The considerations for and against interim interdict are thoroughly analysed in the undernoted work.[56]

21.92 Interim interdict may be granted upon conditions, for example as to caution or consignation,[57] or may be granted or refused upon an undertaking.[58] While the validity of the undertaking rests on its being given to the court,[59] its terms should be recorded in a minute or in the sheriff's interlocutor so as to avoid any later dispute as to what was undertaken.[60] Breach of the undertaking may be punished as a contempt of court.[61] If interim interdict is granted, the sheriff may direct that its operation be temporarily suspended.[62] Unless restricted in time, it subsists until recalled,[63] or until the action is finally disposed of by the court.[64]

Appeal

21.93 An interlocutor granting or refusing interim interdict may be appealed without leave to the sheriff principal or with leave to the Court of

---

[49] Dobie, p. 508, citing *Home-Drummond v. Norman* (1902) 19 Sh.Ct.Rep. 16.

[50] 1st ed., para. 21-79.

[51] *e.g. Nicoll v. Blott*, 1986 S.L.T. 677.

[52] *Scottish and Universal Newspapers Ltd v. Smith*, 1982 S.L.T. 161; *Group 4 Total Security Ltd v. Ferrier*, 1985 S.L.T. 287.

[53] *NWL Ltd v. Woods* [1979] 1 W.L.R. 1294, *per* Lord Fraser of Tullybelton at 1310.

[54] OCR, r. 33.27 (which applies to all family actions) provides that a sheriff may accept affidavit evidence "at any hearing for an order or interim order".

[55] So far as ordinary causes other than family actions are concerned, OCR, r. 29.3(1) provides that a party may apply by motion for the evidence of a witness to be received by way of affidavit, but this is in the context of a proof. However, *cf.* OCR, r. 17.2(4)(b)(ii) which provides for the lodging of an affidavit in an application for summary decree.

[56] Burn-Murdoch, Chap. 4.

[57] Burn-Murdoch, pp. 140–146.

[58] *e.g. Wm Grant and Sons Ltd v. Wm Cadenhead Ltd*, 1985 S.L.T. 291.

[59] *Graham v. Robert Younger Ltd*, 1955 J.C. 28. (The appeal procedure in this case was incorrect: see *Cordiner, Petitioner*, 1973 J.C. 16; *McIver v. McIver*, 1996 S.C.L.R. 225.)

[60] Burn-Murdoch, pp. 144, 146; *Graham, supra*; *Scotsman Publications Ltd v. SOGAT*, 1986 S.L.T. 646.

[61] *Graham, supra.*

[62] *Phonographic Performance Ltd v. McKenzie*, 1982 S.L.T. 272.

[63] *Home-Drummond v. McLachlan*, 1908 S.C. 12; *Reid v. Mitchell* (1899) 16 Sh.Ct.Rep. 61 (authorities reviewed by Sheriff Ae. J.G. Mackay).

[64] *Clippens Oil Co. v. Edinburgh and District Water Trs* (1906) 8 F. 731, *per* L.P. Dunedin at 749 (affd 1907 S.C. (H.L.) 9).

Session.[65] An interlocutor reserving the question of interim interdict until defences are lodged[66] may be appealed only with leave. If an interim interdict has been granted only until the date of a hearing[67] and at that hearing the interim interdict is "recalled" (which means in effect that it is not granted of new), the recall may be appealed against without leave of the sheriff on the basis that it is not truly a recall but rather a refusal.[68] On the same basis if, at such a hearing, the interim interdict was "continued" (that is to say granted of new), the continuation could be appealed against without leave. However, if interim interdict has been granted "until further orders of court"[69] and the sheriff is then made to recall it, his decision, whether to recall or to refuse to do so, is appealable only with leave.[70] Where an appeal is marked against an interim interdict, the interdict remains binding until recalled.[71] After an appeal has been taken, any motion for recall before the hearing of the appeal should be made to the sheriff and not to the appellate court.[72] When reviewing the discretion of the sheriff in determining where the balance of convenience lies, the appeal court is slow to interfere with his discretion unless he has misunderstood or misapplied the law or has reached an unreasonable conclusion on the facts.[73] The appeal court may recall or restrict any interdict granted by the sheriff.[74]

Decree in action of interdict

Where decree of interdict is pronounced, the expression "Decree as craved" must not be used, but the precise terms of the interdict must be stated *ad longum* in the interlocutor.[75] The terms of the interdict must be no wider than are necessary to curb the illegal actings complained of, and so precise and clear that the person interdicted is left in no doubt what he is forbidden to do.[76] **21.94**

The sheriff may make an informative remit to a person of skill in order to ascertain detailed matters of fact,[77] or the nature of the operations sought to be interdicted[78]; or to determine the effectiveness of proposed remedial measures[79] or the terms in which interdict should be granted[80]; or to see that such steps as may be ordered are carried out.[81] **21.95**

---

65 1907 Act, ss. 27(A), 28(1)(d).

66 *Gauldie v. Arbroath Mags*, 1936 S.C. 861.

67 See para. 21.89.

68 *ASA International Ltd v. Nelson*, 1998 G.W.D. 35-1775.

69 See para. 21.89.

70 1907 Act, ss. 27(f), 28(1)(d). *Cf.* RCS, r. 38. 3(4)(e) which provides specifically that leave is not required to reclaim against an interlocutor "granting, refuting, refusing or refusing to recall" interim interdict.

71 1907 Act, s. 29.

72 OCR, r. 31.10(d); *Trainer v. Renfrewshire Upper District Committee*, 1907 S.C. 1117. See para. 18.69.

73 *Scottish and Universal Newspapers Ltd v. Smith, supra* at 163; and see paras 18.110 to 18.114.

74 *Fergusan v. Tennant*, 1978 S.C. (H.L.) 19; *Webster v. Lord Advocate*, 1985 S.L.T. 361.

75 *Nelson v. Dowden*, Sh. Pr. Dick, Glasgow Sh. Ct, Oct. 20, 1981, unreported.

76 *Murdoch v. Murdoch*, 1973 S.L.T. (Notes) 13; *Webster v. Lord Advocate*, 1985 S.L.T. 361.

77 *Nisbet v. Mitchell-Innes* (1880) 7 R. 575.

78 *Montrose Mags v. Birnie* (1829) 8 S. 108; *Scott v. Scott* (1839) 1 D. 1176.

79 *Dodd v. Hilson* (1874) 1 R. 527.

80 *Earl of Kintore v. Pirie & Sons* (1906) 8 F. 1058; affd (1906) 8 F. (H.L.) 16.

81 *Leonard v. Lindsay & Benzie* (1886) 13 R. 958; *McEwan v. Steedman & McAlister*, 1913 S.C. 761.

Breach of interdict

Initial writ

21.96 When a defender fails to obtemper an interdict, interim or final, the pursuer may take proceedings against him for breach of interdict.[82] This is a separate action which is commenced by initial writ.[83] It is a form of action *sui generis* but, it is submitted, clearly falls into the category of summary application.[84] It requires the concurrence, but not the presence in court, of the procurator fiscal.[85] In the instance the words "(with the concurrence of the Procurator Fiscal)" appear after the name and designation of the pursuer, and the procurator fiscal endorses an appropriate docquet on the principal initial writ below the signature of the pleas-in-law. In the past, the form of the docquet was "I concur", signed by the procurator fiscal.[86] The style used in *Gribben v. Gribben*[87] was: "I do not intend to intervene and to that extent I concur in the foregoing writ." The latter style has been criticised on the ground of ambiguity,[88] but it continues to be followed. The writ craves the court to ordain the defender to appear personally to answer for the breach of interdict, and on the charge being admitted or proved to sentence him to a fine or imprisonment. The writ may be amended.[89]

Hearing

21.97 If the defender fails to appear the pursuer may state that he does not insist on his being summoned, and it is competent thereupon to proceed and to fine him in his absence.[90] Since, however, a complaint of breach of interdict is a serious matter, being a complaint of disobedience of a competent order of court which constitutes contempt of court,[91] it is generally in the public interest that the defender should be present. The diet may be adjourned and, if strictly necessary, a warrant immediately granted for his apprehension. In the first instance, however, it is usually preferable to ordain the defender to appear at the adjourned diet under certification that if he does not appear a warrant for his apprehension will be issued, and to appoint intimation of the interlocutor to be made to him personally.[92]

---

[82] On breach of interdict see Burn-Murdoch, Chaps 27, 28; Walker, *Civil Remedies*, pp. 242–243; Scott Robinson, *The Law of Interdict*, Chap. 16.

[83] For styles see Burn-Murdoch, p. 505; Lewis, p. 492; Dobie, *Styles*, p. 249.

[84] *McIver v. McIver*, 1996 S.C.L.R. 225. Although the court did not specifically hold that an action for breach of interdict was a summary application, it is submitted that that may reasonably be inferred from the court's decision. Procedure is therefore governed by the A.S. (Sheriff Court Summary Application Rules) 1993. See Chap. 25.

[85] *Gribben v. Gribben*, 1976 S.L.T. 266.

[86] Burn-Murdoch, p. 506, Lewis, p. 492.

[87] Not reported on this point, 1976 S.L.T. 266.

[88] *Tough v. Tough*, Aberdeen Sh. Ct, Nov. 22, 1978, unreported.

[89] *Dunlop Pneumatic Tyre Co. Ltd v. Rose* (1901) 3 F. 635. The description of the proceedings there and in other cases as "quasi-criminal" has been disapproved: *Gribben, supra*, but continues to be used: *Forbes v. Forbes*, 1993 S.C.L.R. 348. See also *McIver v. McIver*, 1996 S.C.L.R. 225.

[90] *Anderson v. Connacher* (1850) 13 D. 405, *per* L.P. Boyle at 407; *Walker v. Junor* (1903) 5 F. 1035; *Stark's Trs v. Duncan* (1906) 8 F. 429.

[91] *Gribben, supra.*

[92] *Duke of Atholl v. Robertson* (1872) 10 M. 298; *Welsbach Incandescent Gas Co. v. McMann* (1901) 4 F. 395.

In all cases it must be established[93] that the interdict was in operation at the time of the alleged breach, was directed against the person now charged with breach and had been actually or presumptively brought to his knowledge[94]; and that the conduct complained of amounted to breach of the interdict upon a true construction of its terms. If any of these matters, or the conduct complained of, is not admitted, an early diet of proof should be fixed, with or without defences. Both the interdict and the alleged breach must be proved.[95] The standard of proof is proof beyond reasonable doubt.[96] However, the evidence of only one witness is sufficient.[97] It may be that the defender is a competent and compellable witness.[98] In his interlocutor the sheriff should specify the facts which he finds proved, for the information of the parties and any appeal court. **21.98**

Penalty

A penalty for the breach is specifically craved, but the penalty is in the sheriff's discretion, subject to the following limitations imposed by section 15 of the Contempt of Court Act 1981. The maximum penalty is three months' imprisonment or a fine of level 4 on the standard scale[99] or both. Any sentence of imprisonment must be for a fixed term. The restrictions imposed in summary criminal proceedings on the detention of young offenders and on the disposal of persons suffering from mental disorder apply in relation to "persons found guilty of contempt of court", an expression which includes persons admitted or proved to be in breach of interdict.[1] It is implicit in this provision that there is no restriction on imprisoning an adult contemnor notwithstanding the fact that he has never previously been imprisoned.[2] The penalty may be an admonition, or a fine with a period of imprisonment as an alternative, or imprisonment.[3] Imprisonment for breach of interdict appears to be rare in modern sheriff court practice. Appeals have often been taken to the Court of Session, but an appeal to the sheriff principal is competent as proceedings for breach of interdict are "civil proceedings" within the meaning of section 3(d) of the Sheriff Courts (Scotland) Act 1907.[4] The operation of any sentence is automatically suspended upon the marking of a competent appeal. Accordingly, if a sentence of imprisonment has been imposed, interim liberation should be granted.[5] **21.99**

---

[93] Burn-Murdoch, Chap. 27.

[94] *Anderson v. Moncrieff*, 1966 S.L.T. (Sh. Ct.) 28.

[95] *Home-Drummond v. Douglas* (1904) 20 Sh.Ct.Rep. 87.

[96] *Gribben, supra.*

[97] *Byrne v. Ross*, 1992 S.C.L.R. 898 under reference to the Civil Evidence (Scotland) Act 1988, s. 1(1).

[98] *Christie Miller v. Bain* (1879) 6 R. 1215, where the question was whether the party could competently give evidence on his own behalf.

[99] For the standard scale see Criminal Procedure (Scotland) Act 1995, s. 225.

[1] Contempt of Court Act 1981, s. 15(2), (3), as amended by the Criminal Justice Act 1982, Sched. 7 and Criminal Procedure (Consequential Provisions) (Scotland) Act 1995, Sched. 4; *Gribben, supra.*

[2] *cf.* Criminal Procedure (Scotland) Act 1995, s. 204.

[3] *Boswell's Trs v. Pearson* (1886) 24 S.L.R. 32; *Mackenzie v. Coulthart* (1889) 16 R. 1127; *Johnson v. Grant*, 1923 S.C. 789.

[4] *McIver v. McIver*, 1996 S.C.L.R. 225 disapproving *Forbes v. Forbes*, 1994 S.L.T. 16.

[5] *Macleay v. Macdonald*, 1928 S.C. 776, 1929 S.C. 371.

Chapter 22

FAMILY PROCEEDINGS

Introduction

Since the publication of the first edition of this work, law and practice relating to family proceedings have undergone many significant changes. The Ordinary Cause Rules 1993 now contain a complete, and lengthy, chapter relating to what are there described as "family actions"; and the Children (Scotland) Act 1995 has introduced major new provisions in relation to the welfare of children, many of which are reflected in Chapter 33 of the Ordinary Cause Rules. Part I of this chapter will deal with the provisions for family actions under the 1993 Rules; Part II will mention certain other provisions, mainly under the 1995 Act, relating to children; and Part III will deal with some other matters which fall generally under the heading of "family proceedings". **22.01**

I. Family Actions

Chapter 33 of the Ordinary Cause Rules 1993 contains detailed rules governing procedure in what are therein described as "family actions". Rule 33.1(1) defines such actions as follows: **22.02**

"(a) an action of divorce;
(b) an action of separation;
(c) an action of declarator of legitimacy;
(d) an action of declarator of illegitimacy;
(e) an action of declarator of parentage;
(f) an action of declarator of non-parentage;
(g) an action of declarator of legitimation;
(h) an action or application for, or in respect of, an order under section 11 of the Children (Scotland) Act 1995 (court orders relating to parental responsibilities etc.) except—
  (i) an application for the appointment of a judicial factor mentioned in section 11(2)(g) of the Act of 1995 to which Part I of the Act of Sederunt (Judicial Factors Rules) 1992 applies; and
  (ii) an application for the appointment or removal of a person as a guardian mentioned in section 11(2)(h) of the Act of 1995 to which paragraph 4 of the Act of Sederunt (Family Proceedings in the Sheriff Court) 1996 applies;
(i) an action of affiliation and aliment;
(j) an action of, or application for or in respect of, aliment;
(k) an action or application for financial provision after a divorce or annulment in an overseas country within the meaning of Part IV of the Matrimonial and Family Proceedings Act 1984;
(l) an action or application for an order under [the Matrimonial Homes (Family Protection) (Scotland) Act 1981];

(m) an application for the variation or recall of an order mentioned in section 8(1) of the Law Reform (Miscellaneous Provisions) (Scotland) Act 1966."

This part of this chapter provides a guide to the rules and practices which govern procedure in such actions and applications in the sheriff court.

General Provisions

Jurisdiction

22.03 The sheriff court has concurrent jurisdiction with the Court of Session in family actions. Jurisdiction in the sheriff court is governed partly by section 8 of the Domicile and Matrimonial Proceedings Act 1973 (as respects actions of divorce and separation), partly by Chapter III of the Family Law Act 1986 (as respects certain matters concerning children), and partly by other statutory provisions. The relevant rules are fully explained elsewhere in this work.[1] An action which has been raised may be transferred to another sheriff court or remitted to the Court of Session. The rules as to sisting proceedings to prevent conflict of jurisdiction are noted below.[2]

22.04 Certain actions of divorce may be brought under a simplified procedure which is considered later in this chapter.[3] The following paragraphs are concerned with the procedure in a family action which is brought as an ordinary cause. In such an action the procedure is the same as in an ordinary petitory action except that the special rules considered below are applicable.

Commencement of the action

Initial writ

22.05 The initial writ must be drafted in accordance with the general rules applicable in petitory actions. A crave for divorce may be combined with craves for other orders discussed later in this chapter. The craving of warrants for intimation is also considered below. A crave for expenses may be included in any divorce action in which it is thought that the discretion of the court to award expenses may be properly exercised in favour of the pursuer.

22.06 The condescendence must comply with the general rules applicable in petitory actions. Rule 33.2 requires that, in the action of divorce or separation, there should be an article specifying whether to the knowledge of the pursuer any proceedings are continuing in Scotland or in any other country which are in respect of the marriage to which the initial writ relates or are capable of affecting its validity or subsistence.[4] Where such proceedings are continuing, the article must further specify: (1) the court, tribunal or authority before which the proceedings have been commenced; (2) the date of commencement; (3) the names of the parties; (4) the date or expected date of any proof (or its equivalent) in the proceedings; and

---

[1] See paras 2.56 *et seq.*
[2] See paras 22.27 *et seq.*
[3] See paras 22.83 to 22.91.
[4] OCR, r. 33.2(2)(a).

(5) such other facts as may be relevant to the question of whether or not the action before the sheriff should be sisted under Schedule 3 to the Domicile and Matrimonial Proceedings Act 1973.[5] It is further provided that where such proceedings are continuing, and the action before the sheriff is defended, and the initial writ either does not give the required particulars or is incomplete or incorrect in that respect any defences or minute lodged by any person must include that statement and, where appropriate, further or correct particulars.[6]

The duty to furnish particulars subsists while the action is pending and proof in it has not begun.[7] Neither the taking of evidence on commission nor a separate proof relating to any preliminary plea is regarded as part of the proof in the action.[8] In general, the rules as to mandatory and discretionary sists apply only until the beginning of the proof; but, if at any time thereafter the court is satisfied that a party has failed to furnish the required particulars, it may impose a discretionary sist. No action in respect of any such failure is, however, competent.[9] **22.07**

In terms of rule 33.3, where a party to a family action makes an application therein for an order under section 11 of the 1995 Act, there are certain matters which have to be included in the pleadings. **22.08**

(1) Where the action is one of divorce or separation, there must be an averment of any known proceedings in Scotland or elsewhere, whether concluded or not, relating to the child in respect of whom the order is sought.[10]

(2) In any other family action, in addition to the above there must be averments giving particulars of any known proceedings continuing in Scotland or elsewhere relating to the marriage of the parents of the child.[11] Where such other proceedings are continuing, or have taken place, and the averments of the applicant for the order either do not contain particulars of other proceedings, or such particulars are incomplete or incorrect, any defences or minute lodged by any party must contain such particulars, or such further or correct particulars as are known.[12]

In a family action, where the identity or address of a person in respect of whom a warrant for intimation[13] requires to be applied for is not known and cannot reasonably be ascertained, the party required to apply for the warrant must aver that fact, and also what steps have been taken to ascertain the identity or address.[14] **22.09**

In a family action in which an order for aliment or periodical allowance is sought, or is sought to be varied or recalled, by any party, that party's **22.10**

---

[5] OCR, r. 33.2(2)(b).

[6] OCR, r. 33.2(3).

[7] Domicile and Matrimonial Proceedings Act 1973, Sched. 3, para. 7.

[8] *ibid.* para. 4(a).

[9] *ibid.* para. 9(4).

[10] OCR, r. 33.3(1)(a).

[11] OCR, r. 33.3(1)(b); for this purpose "child" includes a child of the family within the meaning assigned in section 42(4) of the Family Law Act 1986 (OCR, r. 33.3(3)): that subsection defines "child of the family" as meaning "any child who has been treated by both parties as a child of their family, except a child who has been placed with those parties as foster parents by a local authority or a voluntary organisation".

[12] OCR, r. 33.3(2).

[13] See para. 22.15.

[14] OCR, r. 33.4. The following notes refer to OCR unless otherwise indicated.

pleadings must contain an averment stating whether, and if so when and by whom, a maintenance order within the meaning of section 106 of the Debtors (Scotland) Act 1987 has been granted in favour of, or against, that party or any other person in respect of whom the order is sought.[15]

22.11 Where a family action includes a crave relating to aliment in relation to a child, and section 8(6), (7), (8), or (10) of the Child Support Act 1991 (top up maintenance orders) applies, there must be included averments stating, where appropriate, that a maintenance assessment under section 11 of the 1991 Act is in force, the date thereof, the amount and frequency of periodical payments so fixed and the grounds on which the sheriff retains jurisdiction under the section referred to above. Further, unless the sheriff on cause shown directs otherwise, the writ must be accompanied by any document issued by the Secretary of State to the party intimating the making of the maintenance assessment.[16]

22.12 Where a family action includes a crave relating to aliment in relation to a child, but section 8(6), (7), (8) or (10) of the Child Support Act 1991 does not apply, there must be included averments stating: (a) that the habitual residence of the absent parent, person with care or qualifying child, within the meaning of section 3 of the 1991 Act, is furth of the United Kingdom; (b) that the child is not a child within the meaning of section 55 of the 1991 Act; or (c) in a case where the action was lodged for warranting before April 7, 1997, the grounds on which the sheriff retains jurisdiction.[17]

22.13 In an action for declarator of non-parentage or illegitimacy the initial writ must contain an article of condescendence stating whether the pursuer has previously been alleged to be the parent in an application for a maintenance assessment under section 4, 6 or 7 of the 1991 Act and, where such an allegation has been made, the Secretary of State must be named as a defender in the action.[18]

22.14 In a family action involving parties in respect of whom a decision has been made in any application, review or appeal under the 1991 Act relating to any child of those parties, there must be an averment stating that such a decision was made and giving details thereof; and, unless the sheriff on cause shown directs otherwise, the action must be accompanied by any document issued by the Secretary of State to the parties intimating that decision.[19]

Warrants and forms for intimation

22.15 In family actions warrants for intimation must be craved in the initial writ in the following circumstances.

(a) Where the address of the defender is not known to the pursuer and cannot reasonably be ascertained, intimation must be made to every child of the marriage who has reached the age of 16 years and to one of the next-of-kin of the defender who has reached that age, unless the address of such a person is not known and cannot reasonably be ascertained. A notice of

---

[15] r. 33.5.
[16] r. 33.6(2).
[17] r. 33.6(3).
[18] r. 33.6(4).
[19] r. 33.6(5).

intimation in Form F1 must be attached to the copy of the initial writ intimated.[20]

(b) Where the pursuer alleges that the defender has committed adultery with another person, intimation must be made to that person unless (i) that person is not named in the initial writ and, if the adultery is relied upon for showing irretrievable breakdown of the marriage (and not for some other reason such as an aspect of behaviour), there is an averment that that person's identity is not known to the pursuer and cannot reasonably be ascertained, or (ii) the pursuer alleges that the defender has been guilty of rape upon or incest with that named person. A notice of intimation in Form F2 must be attached to the copy of the initial writ intimated to any such person.[21]

(c) Where the defender is a person suffering from mental disorder, intimation must be made to the same parties as where the defender's whereabouts are unknown (see (a) above), unless the address of any such person is not known and cannot reasonably be ascertained; and to the *curator bonis* of the defender, if one has been appointed. A notice of intimation in Form F3 must be attached to the copy of the initial writ intimated to any such person.[22]

(d) Where the action relates to a marriage entered into under a law which permits polygamy, it one of the decrees specified in section 2(2) of the Matrimonial Proceedings (Polygamous Marriages) Act 1972 is sought, and either party to the marriage has any additional spouse, intimation must be made to such additional spouse. A notice of intimation in Form F4 must be attached to the copy of the initial writ intimated to any such person.[23]

(e) Where, in an action of divorce or separation, the sheriff may make a section 11 order in respect of a child: (i) who is in the care of a local authority, intimation must be made to that authority; (ii) who is a child of one party to the marriage, has been accepted as a child of the family by the other party to the marriage, and who is liable to be maintained by a third party, to that third party; or (iii) in respect of whom a third party in fact exercises care and control, to that third party. A notice of intimation in Form F5 must be attached to the copy of the initial writ intimated to the local authority mentioned in (i) above, and to the copy of the initial writ intimated to the third party mentioned in (ii) above. A notice of intimation in Form F6 must be attached to the copy of the initial writ intimated to the third party mentioned in (iii) above.[24]

(f) Where in an action the pursuer craves a section 11 order, intimation must be made to any parent or guardian of the child who is not a party to the action. A notice of intimation in Form F7 must be attached to the copy of the writ intimated to any such parent or guardian.[25]

(g) Where in an action the pursuer craves a residence order in respect of a child, and is not the parent of the child, but is resident in Scotland when the initial writ is lodged, intimation must be made to the local authority within the area where the pursuer resides. A notice of intimation in Form F8 must be attached to the initial writ intimated to that authority.[26]

---

[20] r. 33.7(1)(a).
[21] r. 33.7(1)(b).
[22] r. 33.7(1)(c).
[23] r. 33.7(1)(d).
[24] r. 33.7(1)(e).
[25] r. 33.7(1)(f).
[26] r. 33.7(1)(g).

However, this provision does not apply to an action brought by a father who is not, and has not been, married to the mother of a child, even though that father does not have parental rights.

(h) In any action which includes a crave for a section 11 order intimation must be made to the child to whom such an order would relate if not already a party to the action. Such notice of intimation should be in Form F9.[27] However, where a pursuer considers that such intimation to a child is inappropriate he must include in the initial writ a crave to dispense with intimation and averments setting out the reasons why intimation is inappropriate. The sheriff may then dispense with intimation or make such other order as he thinks fit.[28]

(i) Where in an action the pursuer makes an application for an order for transfer of property under section 8(1)(aa) of the Family Law (Scotland) Act 1985, and the consent of any third party is necessary by virtue of any obligation, enactment or rule of law, or the property in question is subject to a security, intimation must be made to the third party or creditor. A notice of intimation in Form F10 must be attached to the copy of the initial writ intimated to any such third party or creditor.[29]

(j) Where in any action the pursuer makes an application for an order under section 18 of the 1985 Act relating to avoidance transactions, intimation must be made to any third party in whose favour the transfer of, or transaction involving, the property was or is to be made, and to any other person having an interest in such a transfer or transaction. A notice of intimation in Form F38 must be attached to the copy of the initial writ intimated to any such third party or other person.[30]

(k) Where in any action the pursuer makes application for an order under the Matrimonial Homes (Family Protection) (Scotland) Act 1981, (i) if the pursuer is a non-entitled partner and the entitled partner has a spouse, intimation must be made to that spouse, or (ii) where the application is under sections 2(1)(e), 2(4)(a), 3(1), 3(2), 4, 7, 13 or 18 of that Act, and the entitled spouse or entitled partner is a tenant or occupies the matrimonial home by permission of a third party, intimation must be made to the landlord or third party. A notice of intimation in Form F39 must be attached to the copy of the initial writ intimated to any such spouse, landlord or third party.[31]

(l) Where in any action the pursuer makes an application for an order under section 8(1)(ba) of the Family Law (Scotland) Act 1985 (for a pension lump sum), intimation must be made to the trustees or managers of the pension scheme in question. A notice of intimation in Form F12A must be attached to the copy of the initial writ intimated to any such trustees or managers.[32]

(m) Where in any action the pursuer craves a residence order in respect of a child and is neither a parent of that child nor resident in Scotland when the initial writ is lodged for warranting, he must include a crave for an order for intimation in Form F8 to such local authority as the sheriff thinks fit.[33] This requirement, although located in a different part of rule 33.7, appears to be the counterpart of the requirement noted at

---

27 r. 33.7(1)(h).
28 r. 33.7(7); and see para. 22.23.
29 r. 33.7(1)(i).
30 r. 33.7(1)(j).
31 r. 33.7(1)(k).
32 r. 33.7(1)(l).
33 r. 33.7(4).

(g) above, and deals with the case where a pursuer is *not* resident in Scotland at the time when proceedings are commenced.

The foregoing intimations are to be on a period of notice of 21 days unless the sheriff orders otherwise, but the sheriff may not order a period of less than two days.[34] Where the address of a person on whom intimation is required is not known and cannot reasonably be ascertained, the pursuer should include in the initial writ a crave seeking that intimation be dispensed with. The sheriff may grant that crave or make such other order as he thinks fit.[35] Where the identity or address of a person to whom intimation of a family action is required becomes known during the course of the action, a motion for warrant to intimate, or to dispense with intimation, should be lodged at once by the party who would have been required to insert a warrant for intimation to that person.[36] 22.16

Where in any family action the pursuer alleges an improper association (that is to say sodomy, incest or any homosexual relationship) between the defender and another named person, the pursuer must, immediately after the expiry of the period of notice, lodge a motion for an order for intimation to that person or to dispense with such intimation. The sheriff may then make such order for intimation as he thinks fit, or he may dispense with intimation; and in the latter event he may order that the name of the person should be deleted from the condescendence of the initial writ. If intimation is ordered a copy of the initial writ, accompanied by intimation in Form F13, should be intimated to the named person.[37] 22.17

Documents to be produced

Unless the sheriff otherwise directs, in an action of divorce a warrant for citation will not be granted without there being produced with the initial writ an extract of the relevant entry in the register of marriages or an equivalent document. In an action which includes a crave for a section 11 order, a warrant for citation will not be granted without there being produced an extract of the relevant entry in the register of births or an equivalent document.[38] An abbreviated birth certificate is not acceptable. The sheriff may "otherwise direct" where, for example, interim orders are urgently required. 22.18

Citation

The general rules as to citation are applicable in the case of family actions, and the warrant for citation in such actions should be in Form F14.[39] However, it should be noted that, except where the address of a person is not known, citation of a defender should be in Form F15, which should be attached to a copy of the initial writ and warrant of citation. It should have 22.19

---

[34] r. 33.7(3). This rule applies in terms to the various intimations required under paragraph (1) of rule 33.7 (set out in para. 22.15(a) to (l)), and does not in terms apply to intimation as required by rule 33.7(4) (set out in para. 22.15(m)). However, it is submitted that the same periods of notice should apply to intimation under that rule as well.

[35] r. 33.7(5).

[36] r. 33.7(6).

[37] r. 33.8.

[38] r. 33.9.

[39] r. 33.10.

appended to it a notice of intention to defend in Form F26.[40] The certificate of citation to be attached to the initial writ must be in Form F16.[41]

Execution of service on, or intimation to, a local authority

22.20 Where a residence order is sought by a non-parent who is resident in Scotland, or by a pursuer who is not resident in Scotland, and a local authority is named as a defender in an initial writ at the time it is lodged, service thereof must be executed within seven days after the date of granting of the warrant of citation,[42] and a notice in Form F8 must be attached to the copy of the initial writ served on that local authority.[43] In any family action, however, the sheriff may, if he thinks fit, order intimation to a local authority; and any such intimation should also be in Form F8.[44] Where intimation to (as opposed to service on) a local authority requires to be made in any of the circumstances described in this paragraph, that intimation must be given within seven days after the date on which a warrant for citation, or an order for intimation, has been granted.[45]

Service in cases of mental disorder of defender

22.21 Where the defender suffers or appears to suffer from mental disorder and is resident in a hospital or similar institution, citation must be executed by registered post or the first class recorded delivery service addressed to the medical officer in charge of the hospital or institution.[46] The following should be included: a copy of the initial writ; a citation in Form F15; any notice required in terms of rule 33.14(1)[47]; a request to the medical officer in Form F17 asking him to deliver these documents to the defender and to explain their contents to him unless such delivery and explanation would be dangerous to the defender's health or mental condition; a form of certificate in Form F18 in which the medical officer may certify either that he has delivered and explained the initial writ, citation and any notice or form of consent personally to the defender, or that such delivery or explanation would be dangerous to the health or mental condition of the defender; and a stamped addressed envelope for return of that certificate to the pursuer or his solicitor if he has one.[48] Thereafter the medical officer should return the certificate in Form F18 duly completed to the pursuer or his solicitor, when it should be attached to the certificate of citation.[49] Where the certificate bears that the writ has not been delivered to the defender, the sheriff may, at any time before decree, order such further medical enquiry or further service or intimation as he thinks fit.[50]

---

40 r. 33.11(1). For notices of intention to defend, see para. 22.52.
41 r. 33.11(2).
42 r. 33.12(1).
43 r. 33.12(2).
44 r. 33.12(3).
45 r. 33.12(4). At first sight this provision appears to be at odds, at least in part, with the requirements of OCR, r. 33.7(3) (see *supra*, n. 34). However, it is submitted that the distinction is that OCR, r. 33.12(4) applies only in cases where a local authority is named as a defender in an initial writ or where a sheriff *ex proprio motu* determines that intimation to a local authority should be made.
46 r. 33.13(1).
47 See para. 22.22.
48 OCR, r. 33.13(1).
49 r. 33.13(2) and (3).
50 r. 33.13(4).

Notices in certain actions of divorce or separation

Where a divorce action is based on two years' non-cohabitation, and the defender's consent to decree, there must be sent with the initial writ a notice in Form F19 and a notice of consent in Form F20. Where the action is one of separation on that ground the appropriate forms are F21 and F22.[51] Where a divorce action is based on five years' non-cohabitation there must be sent with the initial writ a notice in Form F23. Where the action is one of separation on that ground the appropriate form is F24.[52] The certificate of citation must state which notice or form has been attached to the initial writ.[53] **22.22**

Orders for intimation

In any family action the sheriff has a general power either *ex proprio motu* or if so moved to order intimation to be made on such person as he thinks fit. Alternatively, he may postpone intimation if he thinks fit, or dispense with it if he considers that such dispensation is appropriate.[54] Further, and without prejudice to the foregoing, when the sheriff is considering whether to make a section 11 order by virtue of section 12 of the Children (Scotland) Act 1995,[55] he must order intimation in Form F9 to any child to whom the order would relate unless intimation has already been given, or he considers that the child is not of sufficient age or maturity to express his views.[56] A child of 12 years of age or more is presumed to be of sufficient age or maturity for that purpose.[57] There is no presumption, however, that a younger child is not. Where a party makes a crave or averment in a family action which, had it been made in an initial writ, would have required a warrant for intimation under rule 33.7,[58] that party must include in his writ a crave for a warrant for intimation or to dispense with such intimation. Rule 33.7, as necessarily modified, applies in the case of such a crave.[59] **22.23**

Appointment of curators *ad litem* to defenders

Where it appears to the sheriff, in an action of divorce or separation, that the defender is suffering from a mental disorder within the meaning of the Mental Health (Scotland) Act 1984 he must appoint a curator *ad litem* to the defender.[60] In a case where two years' non-cohabitation with consent is relied upon, the sheriff must also make an order for intimation of the ground of the action to the Mental Welfare Commission for Scotland, and he must include in such an order a requirement that the Commission send to the sheriff clerk a report indicating whether in its **22.24**

---

[51] r. 33.14(1)(a).

[52] r. 33.14(1)(b).

[53] r. 33.14(2).

[54] r. 33.15(1).

[55] The 1995 Act, s. 12(1), provides that, in any action for divorce, judicial separation, or declarator of nullity of marriage, if there is a child of the family under 16 years of age when the question first arises, the court must consider, *inter alia*, whether to make a section 11 order in respect of that child. The practical effect of this provision, when read with OCR, r. 33.15(2), is that intimation must be considered in any family action of the sort mentioned in s. 12(1) where there is a child under 16 years of age: *cf.* OCR, r. 33.7(1)(h) and para. 22.15.

[56] OCR, r. 33.15(2).

[57] Children (Scotland) Act 1995, s. 11(10).

[58] See para. 22.15.

[59] OCR, r. 33.15(3). The following notes refer to OCR unless otherwise indicated.

[60] r. 33.16(1) and (2); and see para. 22.21.

opinion the defender is capable of deciding whether or not to give consent to the granting of decree.[61]

22.25 Within seven days of the appointment of a curator *ad litem* the pursuer must send to him: (a) a copy of the initial writ and any defences, including adjustments and amendments, lodged, and (b) a copy of any notice in Form G5 sent to him by the sheriff clerk.[62] Once the report from the Commission has been received, the sheriff clerk is required to lodge it in process and to intimate that this has been done to the pursuer, to the defender's solicitor, if known, and to the curator *ad litem*.[63] Thereafter, within 14 days of the lodging of the report, or within 21 days after his appointment if no report is required, the curator must lodge in process, as appropriate, either a notice of intention to defend, defences, a minute adopting defences already lodged or a minute stating that the curator does not intend to lodge defences.[64] Notwithstanding that a curator has lodged a minute stating that he does not intend to lodge defences, he may appear at any stage of the action to protect the interests of the defender.[65] If at any time it appears to a curator *ad litem* that the defender is not suffering from a mental disorder, he may report that fact to the court and seek his own discharge.[66]

22.26 The pursuer is responsible in the first instance for payment of the fees and outlays of the curator *ad litem* incurred during the period from his appointment until: (a) he lodges a minute stating that he does not intend to lodge defences; (b) he decides to instruct the lodging of defences or of a minute adopting defences already lodged; or (c) being satisfied after investigation that the defender is not suffering from mental disorder, he is discharged.[67]

Sists

22.27 The duty of the parties to furnish particulars of concurrent proceedings has been noted above.[68] The related provisions as to mandatory and discretionary sists in order to avoid conflicts of jurisdiction are contained in Schedule 3 to the Domicile and Matrimonial Proceedings Act 1973. Nothing in Schedule 3 prejudices any other power of the court to sist an action.[69] Any application for a sist or the recall of sist must be made by written motion.[70]

Mandatory sist

22.28 The court must sist the action if, before the beginning of the proof, it appears to the court on the application of a party to the marriage that the following conditions are satisfied: (a) that in respect of the same marriage proceedings for divorce or nullity of marriage are continuing in a related jurisdiction[71]; and (b) that the parties to the marriage have resided

---

[61] r. 33.16(2).
[62] r. 33.16(3).
[63] r. 33.16(4).
[64] r. 33.16(5) and (6).
[65] r. 33.16(7).
[66] r. 33.16(8).
[67] r. 33.16(9).
[68] para. 22.06.
[69] Domicile and Matrimonial Proceedings Act 1973 (hereafter the "1973 Act"), s. 11.
[70] OCR, r. 33.17.
[71] "Related jurisdiction" means England and Wales, Northern Ireland, Jersey, Guernsey (including Alderney and Sark) and the Isle of Man: 1973 Act, Sched. 3, para. 3(2).

together after the marriage was contracted; and (c) that the place where they resided together when the action in the court concerned was begun or, if they did not then reside together, where they last resided together before the date on which the action was begun, is in that jurisdiction; and (d) that either of the parties was habitually resident[72] in that jurisdiction throughout the year ending with the date on which they last resided together before the date on which that action was begun.[73]

Discretionary sist

The court may, if it thinks fit, sist the action if, before the beginning of the proof, it appears to the court: (a) that any other proceedings in respect of the marriage in question or capable of affecting its validity are continuing in another jurisdiction,[74] and (b) that the balance of fairness, including convenience, as between the parties to the marriage is such that it is appropriate for those other proceedings to be disposed of before further steps are taken in the action before the court.[75] In considering the balance of fairness and convenience, the court must have regard to all factors appearing to be relevant, including the convenience of witnesses and any delay or expense which may result from the proceedings being sisted, or not being sisted.[76] **22.29**

Recall of sist

On the application of a party to the action the court may, if it thinks fit, recall a mandatory or discretionary sist if it appears to the court that the other proceedings by reference to which the action was sisted are sisted or concluded, or that a party to those other proceedings has delayed unreasonably in prosecuting those proceedings.[77] Where a mandatory sist has been thus recalled, no further mandatory sist may be ordered.[78] **22.30**

Effect of sist on interim orders

The general rules as to the effect of a sist on interim orders are as follows. Where an action of divorce is sisted in pursuance of Schedule 3 by reference to proceedings in a related jurisdiction for divorce, separation or declarator of nullity of marriage, the court no longer has power to make interim orders relating to aliment or children.[79] Where any such order has been made, it ceases to have effect three months after the sist comes into operation, unless the sist or the relevant order (*i.e.* an interim order relating to aliment or children) has previously been recalled.[80] These rules do not, however, apply where the court considers that as a matter of necessity and urgency it is necessary to make a relevant order or to extend, or further extend, the duration of an order already made. If, however, in the other proceedings an order providing for any of four specified matters is in force when the sist comes into operation, or any such order **22.31**

---

[72] On "habitually resident", see para. 2.59.
[73] 1973 Act, Sched 3, para. 8.
[74] "Another jurisdiction" means any country outside Scotland: 1973 Act, Sched. 3, para. 3(1).
[75] 1973 Act, Sched. 3, para. 9(1).
[76] *ibid.* para. 9(2): see *Mitchell & Mitchell*, 1992 S.C.L.R. 252.
[77] *ibid.* para. 10(1).
[78] *ibid.* para. 10(2).
[79] *ibid.* para. 11(1), (2)(a), as amended by Children (Scotland) Act 1995, Sched. 4, para. 20(3)(a).
[80] *ibid.* para. 11(2)(b).

subsequently comes into force, that order supersedes any order providing for any of these matters in the Scottish proceedings, and the Scottish court cannot make any further order dealing with the same matter. The four matters are: (1) periodical payments for a spouse of the marriage in question; (2) periodical payments for a child; (3) arrangements to be made as to with whom a child is to live; (4) contact with a child, and any other matter relating to parental responsibilities.[81] These rules do not affect the power of the Scottish court (a) to vary or recall a relevant order in so far as the order is for the time being in force; or (b) to enforce a relevant order as respects any period when it is or was in force; or (c) to make a relevant order in connection with an action which was, but is no longer, sisted.[82]

Notices of consent to divorce or separation

22.32 Where, in an action of divorce or separation based on no cohabitation for two years with consent of the defender to decree, the defender wishes to consent to the grant of decree, he must do so by giving notice in writing in Form F20 (divorce) or Form F22 (separation) to the sheriff clerk. The evidence of one witness is sufficient for the purpose of establishing that the signature on a notice is that of the defender.[83] In any such action, where the writ contains an averment that the defender consents to the granting of decree, the defender may give notice by letter sent to the sheriff clerk stating that he has not so consented or that he withdraws any consent already given.[84] Thereafter the sheriff clerk must intimate this to the pursuer, who then may, within 14 days after the date of the intimation, and if no other ground for divorce is averred in the initial writ, lodge a motion for the action to be sisted.[85] If no such motion is lodged the action will be deemed to have been abandoned and will be dismissed.[86] Further, if a motion to sist has been granted, and the sist is not recalled or renewed within six months from the date of the interlocutor granting the sist, the action will be deemed to have been abandoned and will be dismissed.[87]

Procedure in Respect of Children

General

22.33 In a family action, in relation to any matter affecting a child, where the child has either returned to the court Form F9, or has otherwise indicated to the court a wish to express views on a matter affecting him, the sheriff must not grant any order unless an opportunity has been given for the views of the child to be obtained or heard.[88] Once such a wish has been indicated by a child, the sheriff must order such steps to be taken as he considers appropriate to ascertain the views of the child.[89] In practice this may mean seeing the child personally, or instructing a suitable person to speak to the child and to report thereon to the sheriff. The sheriff must not

---

[81] 1973 Act, Sched. 3, para. 11(3), as amended by Children (Scotland) Act 1995, Sched. 4, para. 20(3)(b).
[82] *ibid.* para. 11(4).
[83] OCR, r. 33.18(1) and (2). The following notes refer to OCR unless otherwise indicated.
[84] r. 33.18(3).
[85] r. 33.18(4) and (5).
[86] r. 33.18(6).
[87] r. 33.18(7).
[88] r. 33.19(1).
[89] r. 33.19(2).

grant any order in a family action, in relation to any matter affecting a child who has indicated his wish to express his views, unless due weight has been given by him to the views so expressed, having appropriate regard to the age and maturity of the child.[90]

Recording the views of the child

22.34 Whether the child expresses a view on a matter affecting him personally to the sheriff, or to a person appointed by the sheriff, or in writing, the sheriff, or the appointed person, must record those views in writing; and thereafter the sheriff may direct that such views, and any written views, given by the child, should: (a) be sealed in an envelope marked "Views of the child—confidential"; (b) be kept in the court process, without being recorded in the inventory of process; (c) be available to a sheriff only; (d) not be opened by any person other than a sheriff; and (e) not form a borrowable part of the process.[91]

Appointment of a local authority or a reporter to report on a child

22.35 At any stage of a family action the sheriff may order a report from a local authority,[92] or from another person (referred to here and in the Ordinary Cause Rules as a "reporter") as to the circumstances of a child and on proposed arrangements for that child's care and upbringing. When this is done, the sheriff must direct that the party who sought the appointment or, where the court made the appointment of its own motion the pursuer or minuter, should instruct the local authority or reporter, and be responsible in the first instance for the fees or outlays incurred by them.[93] The same party must within seven days after the date of the appointment intimate the name and address of the local authority or reporter to any local authority to which intimation of the family action has been made.[94] Once the report has been completed, the person making it must send it, with a copy for each party, to the sheriff clerk, who must then send a copy to each party.[95] Where a report has been ordered, an application for a section 11 order in respect of the child in question must not be determined until the report has been lodged.[96]

Referral to family mediation

22.36 In any family action in which an order in relation to parental responsibilities or parental rights is in issue, the sheriff may, at any stage of the action, if he considers it appropriate to do so, refer that issue to a mediator accredited to a specified family mediation organisation.[97]

Child welfare hearing

22.37 In certain circumstances the sheriff clerk must fix a child welfare hearing on the first suitable court date occurring not sooner than

---

[90] r. 33.19(3).
[91] r. 33.20.
[92] In terms of s. 11(1) of the Matrimonial Proceedings (Children) Act 1958.
[93] OCR, r. 33.21(1), (2).
[94] r. 33.21(3).
[95] r. 33.21(4), (5).
[96] r. 33.21(6).
[97] r. 33.22. Information as to what occurred during family mediation is generally not admissible as evidence in any civil proceedings: Civil Evidence (Family Mediation) (Scotland) Act 1995, s. 1.

21 days after the lodging of a notice of intention to defend,[98] unless the sheriff directs that the hearing should be held on an earlier date. These circumstances are: (a) where a notice of intention to defend has been lodged in a family action in which the pursuer seeks a section 11 order, and the defender wishes to oppose that or seeks the same order as that craved by the pursuer; (b) where, on the lodging of a notice of intention to defend, the defender seeks a section 11 order which is not craved by the pursuer; or (c) in any other circumstances in which the sheriff considers that a child welfare hearing should be fixed and makes an order to that effect, either at his own instance or on the motion of a party.[99]

22.38 On fixing the date for a child welfare hearing, the sheriff clerk must intimate that date to the parties in Form F51.[1] The fact that such a date has been fixed does not affect the right of a party to make any other application to the court, whether by motion or otherwise.[2] The hearing may be held in private, and it is thought that this will normally be the sheriff's decision. All parties, including a child who has indicated a wish to attend, must be personally present unless excused on cause shown, and they are under a duty to provide the sheriff with sufficient information to enable him to conduct the child welfare hearing properly. The purpose of the hearing is to allow the sheriff to seek to secure the expeditious resolution of disputes in relation to the child by ascertaining from the parties what are the matters in dispute, and by obtaining any information relevant thereto. In order that this may be done, the sheriff is given very wide powers. In particular he may order such steps to be taken, or make such order, if any, or order further procedure, all as he thinks fit.[3] In some cases it may even be appropriate for the sheriff to treat the child welfare hearing as a diet at which the action may be disposed of after, or without, hearing evidence.[4]

Applications for orders to disclose the whereabouts of children

22.39 An application for an order to disclose the whereabouts of a child[5] must be made by a motion. Where a sheriff makes such an order he may order the person against whom the order is made to appear before him personally, or to lodge an affidavit.[6]

Applications in relation to the removal of children

22.40 Applications for leave to remove a child from the care and possession of the applicant for a residence order,[7] or for interdict or interim interdict prohibiting removal of a child from the jurisdiction,[8] must be made, if by a party to the action, by motion, and otherwise by minute.[9] An application of the foregoing kind for interdict or interim interdict need not be served or intimated.[10] An application in an action depending before the sheriff

---

98 See para. 22.52.
99 OCR, r. 33.22A(1).
1 r. 33.22A(2).
2 r. 33.22A(3).
3 r. 33.22A(4)–(6).
4 *Hartnett v. Hartnett*, 1997 S.C.L.R. 525; *Morgan v. Morgan*, 1998 S.C.L.R. 681.
5 Such orders are provided for by s. 33(1) of the Family Law Act 1986.
6 OCR, r. 33.23.
7 Under the Children Act 1975, s. 51(1).
8 Under the Family Law Act 1986, s. 35(3).
9 OCR, r. 33.24(1).
10 OCR, r. 33.24(2).

for declarator that removal of a child from the United Kingdom was unlawful[11] must be made, if by a party, in the initial writ, defences or minute as the case may be, or by motion. If the application is by any other person, it must be made by minute. After final decree, application must be made by minute in the process of the action to which the application relates.[12]

Intimation to local authority before supervised contact order

Where the sheriff, at his own instance or on the motion of a party, is considering making a contact order, or an interim contact order, subject to supervision by the social work department of a local authority, he must ordain the party moving for the order to intimate to the chief executive of that local authority (unless it is already a party to the action and represented at the particular hearing): (a) the terms of any relevant motion; (b) the intention of the sheriff to order that the contact order should be supervised by the social work department of that local authority; and (c) that the local authority should, within such period as the sheriff has determined, notify the sheriff clerk whether it intends to make representations to the sheriff, and, where it intends to do so in writing, to do so within that period.[13] It is to be noted, however, that rule 33.25 may be somewhat anomalous since there no longer appears to be any statutory authority for the supervision of contact by a local authority. **22.41**

Joint minutes

Where any parties have reached an agreement in relation to a section 11 order, aliment for a child, or an order for financial provision, a joint minute may be entered into expressing that agreement. Subject to the requirement that no order is to be made before the views of the child have been expressed,[14] the sheriff may grant decree in terms of the joint minute in respect of any matter in relation to which he could otherwise make an order whether or not there is a crave for that particular decree.[15] Once a joint minute has been entered into it is unlikely that the court will permit a party, who has changed his mind, to withdraw from the terms of the minute.[16] **22.42**

Evidence by affidavit

The sheriff may accept evidence by affidavit at any hearing for an order or interim order.[17] An affidavit need not be solely by a party to the action, and in practice affidavits should be available to the court in support of any contentious motion or application. It has to be said, however, that the practical value of affidavits may sometimes be doubted since, as often happens, they may present tendentious and mutually inconsistent accounts of events. **22.43**

---

[11] Under the Child Abduction and Custody Act 1985, s. 23(2).
[12] OCR, r. 33.24(3).
[13] OCR, r. 33.25.
[14] See para. 22.33.
[15] OCR, r. 33.26.
[16] *Anderson v. Anderson*, 1989 S.C.L.R. 475; *Horton v. Horton*, 1992 S.C.L.R. 197.
[17] OCR, r. 33.27; and see para. 22.47.

UNDEFENDED FAMILY ACTIONS

General

22.44 Chapter 7 of the Ordinary Cause Rules 1993[18] does not apply to undefended actions in which the sheriff may not grant decree without evidence.[19] It thus does not apply to actions of divorce as well as to certain other family actions.[20] An action of divorce may be undefended in whole or in part. An action which has been defended may at any stage proceed as undefended if the court so directs—for example, where defences have been withdrawn, where parties have agreed ancillary matters, or where the defender's solicitor has withdrawn from acting for lack of instructions and the defender, after due intimation,[21] has failed to appear or be represented.

Consent to decree

22.45 There are special rules relative to actions founded on two years' non-cohabitation and the defender's consent to decree. In practice the defender usually signs Form F20 or Form F22 and returns it to the sheriff clerk. The evidence of one witness is sufficient for establishing that the signature is that of the defender, and this is usually provided in the pursuer's affidavit. These matters have already been noted above.[22]

Evidence in certain undefended family actions

22.46 Unless the sheriff otherwise directs (and it is always open to the sheriff to insist on oral evidence), evidence must be given by affidavits in certain classes of undefended family actions. These are: (a) all family actions in which no notice of intention to defend has been lodged, other than a family action (i) for a section 11 order or for aliment, (ii) of affiliation and aliment, (iii) for financial provision after an overseas divorce or annulment within the meaning of Part IV of the Matrimonial and Family Proceedings Act 1984, and (iv) for an order under the Matrimonial Homes (Family Protection) (Scotland) Act 1981; (b) a family action in which a curator *ad litem* has been appointed under rule 33.16[23] where he has lodged a minute intimating that he does not intend to lodge defences; (c) any family action which proceeds at any stage as undefended where the sheriff so directs; and (d) a family action which is undefended on the merits notwithstanding that the action is defended on ancillary matters, and the sheriff has directed that evidence on the merits may be by way of affidavit.[24] Unless the sheriff otherwise directs, evidence relating to the welfare of a child must be given by affidavit with at least one affidavit being emitted by a person other than a parent or party to the action.[25] Where evidence is being given by a duly qualified medical practitioner a written statement bearing to be his professional opinion, which has been signed by him and lodged in process, will be admissible in place of parole evidence by him.[26]

---

[18] See para. 7.01.
[19] OCR, r. 7.1.
[20] See para. 22.46.
[21] OCR, Chap. 24.
[22] para. 22.32.
[23] paras 22.24 *et seq.*
[24] OCR, r. 33.28(1), (2).
[25] OCR, r. 33.28(3).
[26] OCR, r. 33.28(4).

Affidavits

"Affidavit" includes an affirmation and a statutory or other declaration; and an affidavit is treated as admissible if it is duly sworn or affirmed before a notary public or any other competent authority.[27] The affidavit should be signed by the witness and the notary at the foot of each page.[28] In adultery cases an affidavit by a defender or alleged paramour need not refer to any warning against self-incrimination.[29] An affidavit relating to jurisdiction or the welfare of a child should be prepared and signed after the raising of an action; but an affidavit relating to the merits of an action may bear an earlier date.[30] Notes on the form and contents of affidavits have been issued by the sheriff principal of each sheriffdom.[31] **22.47**

Procedure for decree

Where it is intended, in an action of a kind mentioned in paragraph 22.46 to submit evidence only by means of affidavits, the pursuer must lodge them along with any other necessary documents and productions such as a notice of consent, a medical report, a photograph, an extract conviction, or a joint minute, in addition to extracts of the marriage certificate and any birth certificates. He must also endorse a minute in Form F27 on the initial writ, although in practice the minute is often a separate document. Form F27 also provides that the documents founded on must be listed in a schedule. Once this has been done the sheriff may at any time, without requiring the appearance of parties, grant decree in terms of the motion for decree, or remit the cause for such further procedure, if any, including proof by parole evidence, as he thinks fit.[32] Upon the expiry of 14 days after the grant of decree, the sheriff clerk must issue an extract decree to the pursuer and defender.[33] If the sheriff is not prepared to grant decree, the action may be dismissed but this would not normally be done without the pursuer's solicitor being given the opportunity to be heard. In practice the pursuer is usually given an opportunity to cure any defect in the evidence by means of lodging additional affidavits. If this is done, the schedule to the minute for decree should be amended to take account of the new evidence. A decree pronounced in an action of divorce in which no notice of intention to defend has been lodged is a decree in absence, even though it is pronounced after proof.[34] **22.48**

Procedure in undefended family actions for a section 11 order

Where no notice of intention to defend has been lodged in a family action for a section 11 order, any proceedings in the cause must be dealt with by the sheriff in chambers. Decree in such a case may be pronounced after such inquiry as the sheriff thinks fit.[35] In practice the sheriff may ask **22.49**

---

[27] OCR, r. 1.2(2); and see A.S. (Child Care and Maintenance Rules 1997) (S.I. 1997 No. 291), r. 1.3.

[28] *Macalister v. Macalister*, 1978 S.L.T. (Notes) 78.

[29] It is thought that *Sinclair v. Sinclair*, 1986 S.L.T. (Sh. Ct.) 54 is to be preferred to *Cooper v. Cooper*, 1987 S.L.T. (Sh. Ct.) 37.

[30] *McInnes v. McInnes*, 1990 S.C.L.R. 327.

[31] These are to be found in the *Parliament House Book*, Div. D.

[32] OCR, r. 33.29.

[33] OCR, r. 33.30.

[34] *Paterson v. Paterson*, 1958 S.C. 141.

[35] OCR, r. 33.31.

for affidavits or a report from a local authority; or he may be satisfied if the pursuer's solicitor is able to assure him about the welfare of the child by his having carried out a home visit or the like.

Supplementary provisions

22.50 It is not necessary to record the evidence in any proof in a family action which is not defended.[36] Other than rule 15.1(1), which applies to the lodging of motions, Chapter 15 of the Ordinary Cause Rules 1993, which deals with motions, does not apply to a family action in which no notice of intention to defend has been lodged, nor to one in so far as it proceeds as undefended.[37]

DEFENDED FAMILY ACTIONS

Introduction

22.51 The defender in a family action may defend both on the merits and on any ancillary matters, or on either of the foregoing. In practice, few actions of divorce or separation are defended on the merits, most disputes being concerned with financial matters or with issues relating to the residence of, or contact with, a child or children. In addition to parties to whom intimation of the proceedings has been made[38] the Lord Advocate, by statute, is entitled to enter appearance as a party and to lead such proof and to maintain such pleas as he may consider warranted by the circumstances of the case. Expenses are not claimable by or against the Lord Advocate in such cases.[39] In practice these provisions are seldom invoked.

Notice of intention to defend and defences

22.52 Certain procedures must be followed where a defender in a family action seeks: (a) to oppose any crave in the initial writ; (b) to make a claim for aliment, an order for financial provision (within the meaning of section 8(3) of the Family Law (Scotland) Act 1985), or a section 11 order; (c) an order setting aside or varying an agreement as to financial provision (under section 16(1)(b) or (3) of the 1985 Act), an order relating to avoidance transactions (under section 18 of the 1985 Act), or an order under the Matrimonial Homes (Family Protection) (Scotland) Act 1981; or (d) to challenge the jurisdiction of the court.[40] In all such cases the defender must lodge a notice of intention to defend in Form F26 (which makes provision for the defender to state what he is asking the court to do) before the expiry of the period of notice, and make any claim or order of the kind just described in his defences. If a defender is seeking an order rather than just opposing an order craved by the pursuer, his defences should set out craves, averments (in the answers to the condescendence) in support of those craves, and appropriate pleas-in-law.[41] Where a defender intends to make an application for a section 11 order which, had it been

---

[36] OCR, r. 33.32.
[37] OCR, r. 33.33.
[38] See para. 22.15.
[39] Conjugal Rights (Scotland) Amendment Act 1861, s. 8.
[40] OCR, r. 33.34(1).
[41] OCR, r. 33.34(2).

made in an initial writ, would have required a warrant for intimation under rule 33.7,[42] he must, in his notice of intention to defend, include a crave for a warrant for intimation or to dispense with such intimation. In such cases rule 33.7 applies with any necessary modifications.[43] Notwithstanding abandonment by a pursuer, the court may allow a defender to pursue an order or claim sought in his defences. In that event the proceedings in relation to that order or claim will continue in dependence as if they were a separate cause.[44]

Attendance at options hearing

All parties must, except on cause shown, personally attend the options hearing.[45] However, a failure by a party to attend the options hearing in person is not a default within the meaning of rule 33.37.[46] **22.53**

Decree by default

In a family action in which the defender has lodged a notice of intention to defend, a party will be in default where that party fails: (a) to lodge or intimate the lodging of any production or part of process; (b) to implement any order of the sheriff within a specified period; or (c) to appear or be represented at any diet.[47] Where a party is in default the sheriff may take certain steps. If the action is one mentioned in paragraphs (a) to (h) of rule 33.1(1)[48] the sheriff may allow the cause to proceed as undefended. If the action is one mentioned in paragraphs (i) to (m) of that rule, the sheriff may grant decree as craved. In any case, the sheriff may grant decree of absolvitor, dismiss the action or any claim made or order sought, and award expenses.[49] In a family action the sheriff may, on cause shown, prorogate the time for lodging any production or part of process, or for intimating or implementing any order.[50] If no party appears at a diet in a family action, the sheriff may dismiss the action.[51] **22.54**

The general rules as to reponing[52] do not apply in those family actions where evidence must be adduced before decree will be granted.[53] Under the Rules which were in force prior to the Ordinary Cause Rules 1993 provision was made[54] to allow a defender who had not lodged a notice of intention to defend or defences to apply to the sheriff for an order allowing him to appear and be heard at a proof, to lodge defences, or to appeal within 14 days of a decree of divorce or separation. However, that provision has not been reproduced in the 1993 Rules; and it has been held that the consequence of that omission is that, where decree has been granted in favour of a pursuer in an action which has proceeded as undefended, a defender will be able to appeal against that decision only on **22.55**

---

[42] See para. 22.15.
[43] OCR, r. 33.34(3).
[44] OCR, r. 33.35.
[45] OCR, r. 33.36.
[46] *Grimes v. Grimes*, 1995 S.C.L.R. 268. For decree by default, see para. 22.54.
[47] OCR, r. 33.37(1); but see *Grimes, supra.*
[48] See para. 22.02.
[49] OCR, r. 33.37(2).
[50] OCR, r. 33.37(4).
[51] OCR, r. 33.37(3).
[52] OCR, Chap. 8.
[53] OCR, r. 8.1(1)(a).
[54] Rule 59B.

a ground appropriate to any appeal against a judgment after proof, that is to say that the sheriff had erred in law, had misunderstood the evidence, or so on. In such an appeal it will not be open to a defender to rely on what have been called "reponing note considerations".[55]

APPLICATIONS AND ORDERS

22.56 Parts IV to X of Chapter 33 of the Ordinary Cause Rules 1993 make detailed provision as to the manner in which certain applications are to be made and certain orders sought. In some circumstances this requires a crave in the initial writ or defences; in some circumstances it requires a separate minute; and in some circumstances it requires a motion. The following paragraphs offer guidance as to the appropriate form of procedure in various circumstances.

Applications and orders relating to children in actions of divorce or separation

22.57 In an action of divorce or separation an application for a section 11 order, or for an order for aliment for a child, must be made by a crave in the initial writ or defences or, where the application is made by a person other than the pursuer or defender, by a minute in the action.[56] Where such an action is depending before the court, and a party applies for, or for variation of, an order for interim aliment for a child under the age of 18, or an interim residence or contact order, that application must be made by motion.[57]

22.58 An application after final decree in an action of divorce or separation for, or for the variation or recall of, a section 11 order or an order for aliment for a child must be made by minute in the process of the action to which the application relates.[58] Where such a minute has been lodged any party may apply by motion for any interim order which may be made pending the determination of the application.[59]

22.59 Where an order for aliment has been made in an action of divorce or separation in favour of a person under the age of 18, and where an obligation of aliment is owed to that person under section 1 of the Family Law (Scotland) Act 1985, that person may, after attaining the age of 18, seek an order for aliment against the person in the action against whom the earlier order for aliment was made. Any such application must be by minute in the process of the action.[60] An application for interim aliment pending the determination of the foregoing application must be made by motion.[61] Where a decree has been pronounced in an application by a person who has attained the age of 18 as just described, any application for variation or recall of that decree must be made by minute in the process of the action to which the application relates.[62]

---

[55] *McFarlane v. McFarlane*, 1995 S.C.L.R. 794, following *Stroud v. Stroud*, 1993 S.C.L.R. 763.

[56] OCR, rr. 33.38, 33.39. The following notes refer to OCR unless otherwise indicated.

[57] r. 33.43. The rule does not specify that the residence or contact order is interim, but this must be the case if the action is only in dependence.

[58] rr. 33.44(1) (s. 11 order), 33.45(1) (aliment).

[59] rr. 33.44(2) (s. 11 order), 33.45(2) (aliment).

[60] r. 33.46(1).

[61] r. 33.46(2).

[62] r. 33.46(3).

Orders relating to financial provision

Special rules apply in actions of divorce to applications for orders: (a) for financial provision (within the meaning of section 8(3) of the Family Law (Scotland) Act 1985); (b) to set aside or vary an agreement as to financial provision (under section 16(1)(b) or (3) of the 1985 Act); (c) relating to avoidance transactions (under section 18 of the 1985 Act); and (d) relating to the transfer or vesting of a tenancy (under section 13 of the Matrimonial Homes (Family Protection) (Scotland) Act 1981). Any such application must be made by a crave in the initial writ or defences in the action or, where the application is made by a person other than the pursuer or defender, by minute in that action.[63] **22.60**

In an action of divorce which is depending before the sheriff the pursuer, notwithstanding that the defender has applied for an order for financial provision, or that there is an application for an order for financial provision in the initial writ or defences, may apply by motion for an incidental order. "Incidental order" in this context has the meaning assigned by section 14(2) of the Family Law (Scotland) Act 1985.[64] The sheriff is not bound to determine such a motion if he considers that the application should properly be by a crave in the initial writ or defences.[65] In a divorce action depending before the sheriff an application under section 14(4) of the 1985 Act for the variation or recall of an incidental order should be made by minute in the process of the action to which the application relates.[66] **22.61**

An application in a divorce action for, or for the variation or recall of, an order for interim aliment for the pursuer or defender must be made by motion.[67] **22.62**

If, after final decree in an action of divorce, an application is made for periodical allowance, payment of a capital sum or transfer of property, variation of the date or method of payment of a capital sum or of the date of transfer of property, or the variation, recall, backdating or conversion of periodical allowance (all under provisions in the Family Law (Scotland) Act 1985), any such application must be made by minute in the process of the action to which the application relates. The same applies in the case of an application after the grant or refusal of an application for an incidental order or for the variation or recall of an incidental order.[68] Where a minute is lodged in any of the circumstances just described, any party may lodge a motion for any interim order which may be made pending the determination of the application.[69] Application by way of minute is also required where the application is for the recall or variation of an order in respect of a pension lump sum, or is for the variation of an order in respect of a pension lump sum to substitute trustees or managers.[70] **22.63**

---

63 rr. 33.47, 33.48.
64 r. 33.47(2).
65 r. 33.49(1).
66 r. 33.49(2).
67 r. 33.50.
68 r. 33.51(1).
69 r. 33.51(2).
70 r. 33.51(3).

22.64 An application, made after final decree in a divorce action, for an order setting aside or varying an agreement as to financial provision must be made by minute in the process of the action to which the application relates.[71]

Applications relating to avoidance transactions

22.65 An application for an order relating to avoidance transactions (under section 18 of the Family Law (Scotland) Act 1985) by a party to a family action must be made by including in the initial writ, defences or minute appropriate craves, averments and pleas-in-law.[72] Such an application, after final decree in an action, must be made by minute in the process of the action to which the action relates.[73]

Financial provision after overseas divorce or annulment

22.66 An application under section 28 of the Matrimonial and Family Proceedings Act 1984 for an order for financial provision after a divorce or annulment in an overseas country[74] must be made by initial writ.[75] An application in such an action, which is made before final decree, for an order for (a) transfer of tenancy of a matrimonial home, (b) interim periodical allowance, or (c) variation or recall of an incidental order, must be made by motion.[76] However, an application made after final decree for (a) variation of the date or method of payment of a capital sum, or the date of transfer of property, (b) variation, recall, backdating or conversion of periodical allowance, or (c) variation or recall of an incidental order, must be made by minute in the process of the action to which the application relates.[77] Where such a minute has been lodged any party may apply by motion for an interim order pending the determination of the application.[78]

22.67 An application in an action for recall or variation of an order in respect of a pension lump sum, or for variation of an order in respect of a pension lump sum to substitute trustees or managers, must be made by minute in the process of the action to which the application relates.[79]

Actions of aliment

22.68 In Chapter 33 of the Ordinary Cause Rules 1993 an "action of aliment" means a claim for aliment under section 2(1) of the Family Law (Scotland) Act 1985.[80]

22.69 Where a motion for decree in absence under Chapter 7 of the 1993 Rules (undefended causes) is lodged in an action of aliment, the pursuer must, on lodging the motion, lodge all documentary evidence of the means

---

[71] r. 33.52(a).
[72] r. 33.53(1).
[73] rr. 33.52(b), 33.53(2).
[74] See definition of "overseas country" in Matrimonial and Family Proceedings Act 1984, s. 30(1).
[75] OCR, r. 33.55(1).
[76] r. 33.55(2).
[77] r. 33.55(3).
[78] r. 33.55(5).
[79] r. 33.55(4).
[80] r. 33.56.

of the parties available to him in support of the amount of aliment sought.[81] If the sheriff requires the appearance of parties, the sheriff clerk must fix a hearing for that purpose.[82] Although the foregoing sentence reflects the wording of the rule in question, it is to be observed that, in the situation with which the rule is dealing, there will in effect be only one party in the action. It is therefore to be doubted if a sheriff will ever require the appearance of an absent defender.

An application for, or for variation of, an order for interim aliment in a depending action of aliment must be made by motion.[83] **22.70**

An application after final decree for the variation or recall of an order for aliment in an action of aliment must be made by minute in the process of the action to which the application relates.[84] Where an order for aliment has been made in favour of a person under the age of 18, and where an obligation of aliment is owed to that person under section 1 of the Family Law (Scotland) Act 1985, that person may, after attaining the age of 18, seek an order for aliment against the person in the action against whom the earlier order for aliment was made. Any such application must be by minute in the process of that action.[85] An application for interim aliment pending the determination of any of these applications must be made by motion.[86] Where a decree has been pronounced in respect of any of these applications an application for variation or recall of such a decree must be made by minute in the process of the action to which the application relates.[87] **22.71**

Generally, an application for variation or termination of an agreement on aliment (under section 7(2) of the Family Law (Scotland) Act 1985) must be made by summary application.[88] However, in a family action in which a crave for aliment may be made, such an application must be made by a crave in the initial writ or defences.[89] **22.72**

Applications for orders under section 11 of the Children (Scotland) Act 1995

Part IX of Chapter 33 of the Ordinary Cause Rules 1993 makes various provisions in respect of applications for section 11 orders in family actions other than actions of divorce or separation.[90] They are as follows. **22.73**

Subject to any other provision in Chapter 33 of the Ordinary Cause Rules an application for a section 11 order must be made (a) by an action for a section 11 order; (b) by a crave in the initial writ or defences in any other family action to which Part IX applies; or (c) where the application is made by a person other than a party to an action, by minute in that action.[91] **22.74**

---

[81] r. 33.57(1). Although the rule uses the word "motion", an application for decree in absence under Chap. 7 of the Rules should in fact be made by minute: OCR, r. 7.2(12).
[82] r. 33.57(2).
[83] r. 33.58(1).
[84] r. 33.58(2).
[85] r. 33.58(3).
[86] r. 33.58(4).
[87] r. 33.58(5) The provisions of OCR, r. 33.58 appear to replicate the terms of r. 33.46 (see para. 22.59). The reason for this is not clear.
[88] r. 33.59(1).
[89] r. 33.59(2).
[90] r. 33.60.
[91] r. 33.61.

22.75 In an action for a section 11 order the pursuer must call as a defender (a) the parents or other parent of the child in respect of whom the order is sought; (b) any guardian of the child; (c) any person who has treated the child as a child of his family; (d) any person who in fact exercises care or control in respect of the child; and (e) in any case where there is no person falling under (a) to (d) above, the Lord Advocate.[92]

22.76 Where an action to which Part IX applies is depending before the sheriff, an application for, or for the variation or recall of, an order for an interim residence order or an interim contact order must be made by motion when at the instance of a party to the action, and by minute when at the instance of a person who is not a party to the action.[93] An application after final decree for variation or recall of a section 11 order must be made by minute in the process of the action to which the application relates.[94] However, where such a minute has been lodged, any party may apply by motion for an interim order pending the determination of the application.[95]

Applications for an order under the Matrimonial Homes (Family Protection) (Scotland) Act 1981

22.77 Subject to any other provision in Chapter 33 of the Ordinary Cause Rules 1993 an application for an order under the 1981 Act must be made: (a) by an action for such an order; (b) by a crave in the initial writ or defences in any other family action; or (c) where the application is made by a person other than a party to an action, by a minute in that action.[96] However, an application to dispense with the consent of a non-entitled spouse to a dealing (under section 7(1) of the Act) or an application in relation to poinding (under section 11 of the Act) must be made by way of summary application.[97]

22.78 The applicant for an order under the 1981 Act must call as a defender: (a) where he is seeking the order as a spouse, the other spouse; (b) where he is a third party making an application under section 7(1) (dispensing with the consent of a non-entitled spouse to a dealing) or under section 8(1) (payment from non-entitled spouse in respect of a loan), both spouses; and (c) where the application is made under section 18 (occupancy rights of cohabiting couples), or is one to which that section applies, the other partner.[98]

22.79 Applications under certain provisions of the 1981 Act must be made by motion in the process of the depending action to which the application relates. These provisions are: (a) section 3(4) (interim order for regulation of rights of occupancy, etc.); (b) section 4(6) (interim order suspending occupancy rights); (c) section 7(1) (dispensing with consent of non-entitled spouse to a dealing); (d) section 15(1) (order attaching power of arrest), if made after application for matrimonial interdict; and (e) the proviso to section 18(1) (extension of period of occupancy rights).[99] Intimation of

---

[92] r. 33.62.
[93] r. 33.63.
[94] r. 33.65.
[95] *ibid.*
[96] r. 33.67(1).
[97] r. 33.67(2).
[98] r. 33.68.
[99] r. 33.69(1).

any of the foregoing motions[1] must be given: (a) to the other spouse or partner; (b) where the motion is under (a), (b) or (e) above, and the entitled spouse or partner is a tenant or occupier of the matrimonial home by the permission of a third party, to the landlord or third party; and (c) to any other person to whom intimation of the application was or is to be made by virtue of rule 33.7(1)(k) (warrant for intimation to certain persons in actions for orders under the 1981 Act) or rule 33.15 (order for intimation by sheriff).[2]

Application by minute is required in the case of applications for an order under (a) section 5 of the 1981 Act (variation and recall of orders regulating occupancy rights and of exclusion order) or (b) section 15(2) and (5) of the Act (variation and recall of matrimonial interdict and power of arrest).[3] A minute of the foregoing kind must be intimated: (a) to the other spouse or partner; (b) where the entitled spouse or partner is a tenant or occupies the matrimonial home by the permission of a third party, to the landlord or third party; and (c) to any other person to whom intimation of the application was or is to be made by virtue of rule 33.7(1)(k) or rule 33.15.[4] **22.80**

Unless the sheriff otherwise directs, the sist of an action by virtue of section 7(4) of the 1981 Act (where action raised by non-entitled spouse to enforce occupancy rights) will apply only to such part of the action as relates to the enforcement of occupancy rights by a non-entitled spouse.[5] This provision would appear to result in the highly unusual situation of an action being sisted in respect of one matter but not being sisted in respect of others. **22.81**

Where an applicant is required to comply with section 15(4) or (5) of the 1981 Act (delivery of documents to chief constable, where power of arrest attached to a matrimonial interdict is granted, varied or recalled), he must, after such compliance, lodge in process a certificate of delivery in Form F30.[6] Where a matrimonial interdict to which a power of arrest has been attached ceases to have effect by reason of a decree of divorce being pronounced by the sheriff, the pursuer must send a copy of the interlocutor granting decree to the chief constable of the police area in which the matrimonial home is situated, and, if the applicant spouse resides in another police area, to the chief constable of that other area. Thereafter the pursuer must lodge in process a certificate of delivery in Form F30.[7] **22.82**

Simplified Divorce Applications

Where certain conditions are satisfied it is possible to apply for divorce by a simplified procedure. These conditions are: (a) the ground for divorce must be either that of no cohabitation for two years, with the consent of the defender to decree, or that of no cohabitation for five years; (b) in the **22.83**

---

1 In terms of OCR, r. 15.2.
2 r. 33.69(2); and see para. 22.15.
3 r. 33.70(1).
4 r. 33.70(2).
5 r. 33.71.
6 r. 33.72(1).
7 r. 33.72(2).

former case, the other party must consent to decree of divorce being granted; (c) no other proceedings should be pending in any court which could have the effect of bringing the marriage to an end; (d) there are no children of the marriage under the age of 16 years; (e) neither party to the marriage is applying for an order for financial provision on divorce; and (f) neither party to the marriage suffers from mental disorder.[8] If an application for divorce ceases to satisfy any of the foregoing requirements at any time before final decree it will be deemed to be abandoned and will be dismissed.[9] In the paragraphs which follow "simplified divorce application" means an application of the kind described above.

22.84 A simplified divorce application, in which the ground founded on is no cohabitation for two years with the consent of the defender, should be in Form F31. However, that application will only be of effect if it is signed by the applicant and the form of consent in Part 2 of Form F31 is signed by the party to the marriage giving consent.[10] An application in which the ground founded on is no cohabitation for five years should be in Form F33, and it will only be of effect if it is signed by the applicant.[11] The applicant should send a simplified divorce application to the sheriff clerk along with (a) an extract or certified copy of the marriage certificate and (b) the appropriate fee.[12]

22.85 Except in certain circumstances where an address is not known[13] it is the duty of the sheriff clerk to cite any person or intimate any document in connection with a simplified divorce application. The form of citation in a two years' non-cohabitation case is Form F34, and in a five years' case it is Form F35.[14] The sheriff clerk must arrange for the required citation or intimation to be made: (a) by registered post or the first class recorded delivery service in accordance with rule 5.3; (b) on payment of an additional fee, by a sheriff officer in accordance with rule 5.4(1) and (2); or (c) where necessary, in accordance with rule 5.5, which governs service on persons furth of Scotland.[15]

22.86 In a simplified divorce application in which the ground for divorce is no cohabitation for five years, if the address of the other party to the marriage is not known and cannot reasonably be ascertained, citation must be executed by displaying a copy of the application and a notice in Form F36 on the walls of court on a period of notice of 21 days. In addition, intimation must be made to every child of the marriage between the parties who has reached the age of 16, and to one of the next-of-kin of the other party to the marriage who has reached that age unless the address of that person is not known and cannot reasonably be ascertained.[16] Intimation to a child or to a next-of-kin must be given by intimating a copy of the application and a notice of intimation in Form F37.[17] The Ordinary Cause Rules 1993 do not appear to

---

[8] r. 33.73(1).
[9] r. 33.73(2).
[10] r. 33.74(1). The second party must sign the form of consent after the applicant has signed the application.
[11] r. 33.74(2).
[12] r. 33.75.
[13] See para. 22.86.
[14] OCR, r. 33.76(1)–(3).
[15] r. 33.76(4).
[16] r. 33.77(1).
[17] r. 33.77(2).

make any express provision for citation where a defender's address is unknown in cases where the ground of divorce is no cohabitation for two years. Presumably the reason for that is that an application on that ground must be accompanied by a form of consent signed by the defender, which cannot be provided when the defender's address is unknown.

Any person on whom service or intimation of a simplified divorce application has been made may give notice that he challenges the jurisdiction of the court or opposes the grant of decree of divorce, and give the reasons therefor. That notice may be given by a letter sent to the sheriff clerk.[18] Where such opposition is made the sheriff must dismiss the application for divorce unless he is satisfied that the reasons given for the opposition are frivolous; and the sheriff clerk must intimate the sheriff's decision to the applicant and to the respondent.[19] The sending of a letter of opposition does not imply acceptance of the jurisdiction of the court.[20] **22.87**

Parole evidence is not to be given in a simplified divorce application.[21] The applicant signs an affidavit deponing to the fact that what is stated in the application is true. In the case of an application based on two years' non-cohabitation with consent, this affidavit must be signed after the second party has signed the form of consent. **22.88**

The sheriff may grant decree in terms of the simplified divorce application on the expiry of the period of notice if the application has been properly served. However, when an application has been served in a country to which the Hague Convention on the Service Abroad of Judicial and Extrajudicial Documents in Civil or Commercial Matters, dated November 15, 1965, applies, decree must not be granted until it is established to the satisfaction of the sheriff that the requirements of Article 15 of that Convention have been complied with.[22] Where decree of divorce has been granted the sheriff clerk, not sooner than 14 days after the granting of the decree, must issue to each party to the marriage an extract of the decree of divorce in Form F38.[23] **22.89**

An appeal against an interlocutor granting decree of divorce under the simplified divorce procedure may be made, within 14 days after the date of decree, by sending a letter to the court giving reasons for the appeal.[24] The pre-1993 Rules contained a rule in similar terms.[25] The rule itself does not suggest what might amount to sufficient "reasons" for an appeal, nor does it indicate whether any such appeal is to be heard by the sheriff principal or by the sheriff who pronounced the interlocutor granting decree of divorce. It is submitted that an appeal in such a case should be heard by the sheriff principal, though in that event an appeal by means of a letter would be inconsistent with the requirements of rule 31.4 which requires that an appeal to the sheriff principal should be marked by the lodging of a **22.90**

---

[18] r. 33.78(1).
[19] r. 33.78(2), (3).
[20] r. 33.78(4).
[21] r. 33.79.
[22] r. 33.80(1). See para. 3.56.
[23] r. 33.80(2).
[24] r. 33.81.
[25] r. 142 of the pre-1993 Rules.

note of appeal in a Form specified in the Rules. As to the "reasons" for an appeal against an interlocutor granting decree of divorce under the simplified procedure the few cases which have been reported[26] reveal a difference of opinion among the sheriffs principal concerned.

22.91 Any application to the court after decree of divorce has been granted in a simplified divorce application, which could have been made if it had been made in an ordinary action of divorce, must be made by minute.[27] It is difficult to conceive what such an application might be.

VARIATION OF COURT OF SESSION DECREES

22.92 Section 8 of the Law Reform (Miscellaneous Provisions) (Scotland) Act 1966 provides that a sheriff may vary or recall certain orders pronounced by the Court of Session. An application for any such variation or recall must be made by initial writ which must be accompanied by a copy of the interlocutor, certified by a clerk of the Court of Session, which it is sought to vary.[28] Before the initial writ is lodged with the sheriff clerk, a copy of it, certified by the pursuer or his solicitor, must be lodged with, or sent by first class recorded delivery post to, the Deputy Principal Clerk of Session to be lodged in the process of the cause in the Court of Session in which the original order was made; and the pursuer or his solicitor must attach a certificate to the initial writ stating that that has been done.[29] On cause shown, the sheriff may prorogate the time for lodging the copy of the interlocutor certified by a clerk of the Court of Session.[30]

22.93 Where a notice of intention to defend is lodged, and no request has been made for a remit of the application to the Court of Session,[31] the pursuer must, within 14 days after the date of the lodging of the notice of intention to defend, or within such other period as the sheriff may order, lodge in process the following documents (or copies) from the process in the Court of Session in which the original order was made, namely: (a) the pleadings; (b) the interlocutor sheets; (c) any opinion of the court; and (d) any productions on which he seeks to found.[32] The sheriff may, on the joint motion of parties made at any time after the lodging of the foregoing documents: (a) dispense with proof; (b) whether defences have been lodged or not, hear the parties; and (c) thereafter, grant decree or otherwise dispose of the cause as he thinks fit.[33] The foregoing procedures, as set out in the Rules, are somewhat confusing since they appear to suggest some sort of summary application, and envisage that the sheriff may proceed without defences and without hearing evidence. At the same time reference is made to a notice of intention to defend, which is incompatible with a summary application. Probably the best explanation is that applications for variation of Court of Session decrees are to be regarded as *sui generis*.

---

[26] *Colville v. Colville*, 1988 S.L.T. (Sh. Ct.) 23; *Norris v. Norris*, 1992 S.C.L.R. 395; *Hunter v. Hunter*, 1993 S.C.L.R. 785.

[27] OCR, r. 33.82. The following notes refer to OCR unless otherwise indicated.

[28] r. 33.84(1), (2).

[29] r. 33.84(3), (4).

[30] r. 33.84(5).

[31] See para. 22.94.

[32] r. 33.85(1).

[33] r. 33.85(2).

Where decree has been granted, or the cause has otherwise been disposed of, the sheriff clerk must transmit to the Court of Session the sheriff court process and the documents from the Court of Session process which have been lodged in the sheriff court process. However, he must do that only (a) after the period for marking an appeal has elapsed without an appeal being marked, or (b) after the determination of the cause on any appeal.[34] A sheriff court process transmitted in the manner just described will then form part of the process of the cause in the Court of Session in which the original order was made.[35] **22.94**

Section 8(3) of the Law Reform (Miscellaneous Provisions) (Scotland) Act 1966 provides that, where a party has applied to the sheriff for variation or recall of an order made in the Court of Session, any other party to the action may, not later than the first calling of the application in court, request that it be remitted to the Court of Session. A request for such a remit must be made by motion.[36] Where any such motion is made, the sheriff must order that the cause be remitted to the Court of Session; and within four days after the date of such order the sheriff clerk must transmit the whole sheriff court process to the Court of Session.[37] A cause so remitted to the Court of Session will form part of the process of the cause in the Court of Session in which the original order was made.[38] **22.95**

CHILD SUPPORT ACT 1991

The Ordinary Cause Rules 1993 contain certain provisions in relation to the Child Support Act 1991. In those Rules "child" has the meaning assigned in section 55 of the 1991 Act, and "maintenance assessment" has the meaning assigned in section 54.[39] **22.96**

Where the Secretary of State is named as a defender in an action for declarator of non-parentage or illegitimacy, and the Secretary of State does not defend the action, no expenses may be awarded against the Secretary of State.[40] **22.97**

When the sheriff clerk receives notification that a maintenance assessment has been made, cancelled or has ceased to have effect so as to affect an order of a kind prescribed[41] for the purposes of section 10 of the 1991 Act, he must endorse on the interlocutor sheet relating to that order a certificate in Form F39 or F40 as appropriate.[42] **22.98**

Where an order relating to aliment is affected by a maintenance assessment, any extract of that order issued by the sheriff clerk must be endorsed with a certificate in the following terms: **22.99**

---

[34] r. 33.86(1).
[35] r. 33.86(2).
[36] r. 33.87(1)
[37] r. 33.87(2).
[38] r. 33.87(3).
[39] r. 33.88.
[40] r. 33.89.
[41] In terms of s. 10(5) of the 1991 Act "prescribed" means prescribed by rules made under that Act.
[42] r. 33.90.

> "A maintenance assessment having been made under the Child Support Act 1991 on [*insert date*], this order, in so far as it relates to the making or securing of periodical payments to or for the benefit of [*insert name(s) of child/children*], ceases to have effect from [*insert date 2 days after the date on which the maintenance assessment was made*]."[43]

Where an order relating to aliment has ceased to have effect on the making of a maintenance assessment, and that maintenance assessment is later cancelled or ceases to have effect, any extract of that order issued by the sheriff clerk must be endorsed also with a certificate in the following terms:

> "The jurisdiction of the child support officer under the Child Support Act 1991 having terminated on [*insert date*], this order, in so far as it relates to [*insert name(s) of child/children*], again shall have effect as from [*insert date of termination of child support officer's jurisdiction*]."[44]

Referrals to Principal Reporter

22.100 Section 54 of the Children (Scotland) Act 1995 provides that, where in certain family proceedings a court considers that one or more of certain of the conditions referred to in section 52(2) of the Act are satisfied with respect to a child, it may refer the matter to the principal reporter. Where such a matter is referred by the sheriff the interlocutor making the reference must be intimated forthwith by the sheriff clerk to the principal reporter; and that intimation must specify which of the conditions in section 52(2) of the 1995 Act appears to the sheriff to have been satisfied.[45]

22.101 Where a matter has been referred by the sheriff to the principal reporter, the principal reporter will make such investigation as he thinks appropriate, and if he reaches the view that compulsory measures of supervision are necessary, he will arrange a children's hearing under section 69 of the 1995 Act.[46] He must then intimate to the court which referred the matter to him (a) the decision to arrange a children's hearing; (b) where there is no appeal made against the decision of that children's hearing once the period for appeal has expired, the outcome of the children's hearing; and (c) where such an appeal has been made, that an appeal has been made and, once determined, the outcome of that appeal.[47] Where the principal reporter decides not to arrange a children's hearing he must intimate that decision to the court which referred the matter to him.[48]

---

[43] r. 33.91(1).
[44] r. 33.91(2).
[45] rr. 33.92, 33.93.
[46] 1995 Act, s. 54(3). This subsection also provides that the case is to proceed before the hearing as if a ground of referral had been established in accordance with s. 68 of the Act. That section provides for a proof being held before a sheriff in the event of the ground not being accepted, or a child being too young to understand.
[47] OCR, r. 33.94(1).
[48] r. 33.94(2).

Management of Money Payable to Children

Where the sheriff has made an order under section 13 of the Children (Scotland) Act 1995, which relates to awards of damages to children, an application by a person for an order by virtue of section 11(1)(d) of that Act, relating to administration of a child's property, may be made in the process of the cause in which the order under section 13 was made.[49] 22.102

II. Other Proceedings in Relation to Children

The Children (Scotland) Act 1995 substantially rewrote the law relating to children, and introduced many new principles and procedures. Enlarging on what went before, the Act provides in relation to several matters that, in considering whether or not to make an order in relation to a child, the court must regard the welfare of the child concerned as its paramount consideration and must not make any order unless it considers that it would be better for the child that the order be made than that none should be made at all.[50] The Act also provides in several places that consideration must, so far as practicable, be given to the views of a child before any decision is taken which affects him or her.[51] 22.103

Many of the provisions of the 1995 Act necessitated amendment of the Ordinary Cause Rules 1993, and the effect of those amendments has already been taken into account in what has been said in Part I of this chapter. However, the Act also deals with many other substantive matters affecting the sheriff courts; and special procedures for many of those matters are provided in the Act of Sederunt (Child Care and Maintenance Rules) 1997.[52] Those matters include: adoption; parental responsibilities orders; orders relating to human fertilisation and embryology; proceedings, including appeals, in relation to children's hearings; child assessment orders; child protection orders; exclusion orders; and the mutual enforcement of maintenance and other orders. With the exception of adoption, which is dealt with in a later chapter in this book,[53] these other matters are outwith the scope of this work.[54] 22.104

III. Other Family Proceedings

The first edition of this work described in some detail the provisions of the Family Law (Scotland) Act 1985 relating to financial provision on divorce, and the provisions of the Matrimonial Homes (Family Protection) (Scotland) Act 1981 relating to the various orders available under that Act. Many of the procedural rules relating to such matters are now incorporated in Chapter 33 of the Ordinary Cause Rules, and have been 22.105

---

[49] r. 33.95.
[50] See, *e.g.* 1995 Act, s. 11(7)(a).
[51] *ibid.* s. 11(7)(b) is an example of this.
[52] S.I. 1997 No. 291.
[53] Chap. 28.
[54] They are, however, dealt with in whole or in part in the following works: Norrie (ed.), *Scottish Family Law Legislation*; Nichols (ed.), *Scottish Family Law Service*; Clive, *Husband and Wife* (4th ed.); Wilkinson and Norrie, *Parent and Child* (2nd ed., forthcoming). See also paras 26.61 *et seq.*

noted in Part I of this chapter. So far as substantive law is concerned, that is dealt with comprehensively in the undernoted work[55] and accordingly it is no longer dealt with in this chapter.

22.106 However, some further notice requires to be taken of certain procedures under the 1981 Act. Prior to the coming into force of the Ordinary Cause Rules 1993[56] procedures under that Act were provided for by the Act of Sederunt (Applications under the Matrimonial Homes (Family Protection) (Scotland) Act 1981) 1982[57]; but most of that Act of Sederunt was revoked in relation to causes commenced on or after January 1, 1994 because by then most of its provisions had been incorporated, with such modifications as appeared necessary, in the new Ordinary Cause Rules. Consequently, the 1982 Act of Sederunt, in its entirety, now applies only to causes commenced prior to the foregoing date.

22.107 There are, however, two provisions in the Act of Sederunt which have been saved, and which therefore continue to apply in respect of causes commenced after January 1, 1994; and they are to be found in paragraph 7 (apart from the proviso) and in paragraph 8. Paragraph 7 deals with applications for an order under section 7 of the 1981 Act. That section relates to applications for an order dispensing with the consent of a non-entitled spouse to a dealing or proposed dealing.[58] Any such application must be made by initial writ under the Sheriff Courts (Scotland) Acts 1907 and 1913, and will be dealt with as a summary application as defined in those Acts.[59] The same procedural requirement applies, by virtue of paragraph 8 of the Act of Sederunt, in the case of an application under section 11 of the 1981 Act. That section allows for certain applications where a poinding has been executed of furniture and plenishings of which the debtor's spouse has the possession or use by virtue of an order under section 3(3) or (4) of the 1981 Act.

---

[55] Clive, *Husband and Wife* (4th ed.), esp. Chaps 15 and 24.

[56] On Jan. 1, 1994.

[57] S.I. 1982 No. 1432.

[58] "Dealing" is defined in s. 6(2) of the 1981 Act as including the grant of a heritable security, but as not including a conveyance under s. 80 of the Lands Clauses Consolidation (Scotland) Act 1845.

[59] The rules governing summary applications are now to be found in the Sheriff Court Summary Application Rules 1993 (S.I. 1993 No. 3240): see Chap. 25.

Chapter 23

ACTIONS CONNECTED WITH HERITABLE SUBJECTS

Jurisdiction

Section 5(4) of the 1907 Act confers on the sheriff court jurisdiction in **23.01** "actions relating to questions of heritable right or title (except actions of adjudication save in so far as now competent and actions of reduction) including all actions of declarator of irritancy and removing, whether at the instance of a superior against a vassal or of a landlord against a tenant." The exception as to actions of adjudication refers to adjudications *contra haereditatem jacentem*, which are competent in the sheriff court but are now unknown in practice.[1] In Schedule 8 to the Civil Jurisdiction and Judgments Act 1982, rule 4(1)(a) provides that in proceedings which have as their object rights *in rem* in, or tenancies of, immoveable property, the courts for the place where the property is situated have exclusive jurisdiction. Such proceedings may accordingly be brought in the Court of Session or, where otherwise competent in the sheriff court, in the sheriff court of the place where the property is situated.[2]

Recovery of possession of heritable property

Summary causes

Actions for the recovery of possession of heritable property form the **23.02** largest category of actions connected with heritable subjects which are brought in the sheriff court. The majority of such actions are raised as summary causes by virtue of the terms of section 35(1)(c) of the 1971 Act whereby summary cause procedure must be used for "actions *ad factum praestandum* and actions for the recovery of possession of heritable or moveable property, other than actions in which there is claimed in addition, or as an alternative, to a decree *ad factum praestandum* or for such recovery, as the case may be, a decree for payment of money exceeding £1,500 in amount (exclusive of interest and expenses)."[3] The foregoing rule is, however, restricted by a number of statutory provisions, and by certain other limitations. They are all examined in the following paragraphs.

Heritable Securities (Scotland) Act 1894, s. 5

Recovery in the expression "actions for the recovery of possession of **23.03** heritable property" has been literally construed as extending only to an action by a proprietor or tenant of subjects seeking to recover possession

---

[1] See para. 2.40.
[2] See para. 3.24.
[3] The procedure in summary cause actions for the recovery of possession of heritable property is fully explained in Vol. 2 of this work.

from an occupier. It was accordingly held that it did not cover an action by a creditor in a heritable security seeking to enter into possession of the subjects disponed in security. The consequence in that case was that an application under section 5 of the Heritable Securities (Scotland) Act 1894 was held to have been properly brought by way of summary application.[4] In other courts, however, such applications proceed as ordinary actions.[5]

Conveyancing and Feudal Reform (Scotland) Act 1970, Pt II

23.04 Any application or counter-application to the court under Part II of the Conveyancing and Feudal Reform (Scotland) Act 1970 was originally directed by that Act to be by way of summary application.[6] However, rule 107A of the Ordinary Cause Rules 1983 provided (by virtue of an amendment made in 1990) that such an application should be brought as an ordinary cause where any other remedy was craved, and as a summary application where no other remedy was craved. The current 1993 Rules provide[7] that an application or counter-application under the 1970 Act is to be made by initial writ where any other remedy is craved, and where the application is brought under section 18(2) (declarator that obligations under contract performed), section 20(3) (application by creditor for warrant to let security subjects), section 22(1) (objections to notice of default), section 22(3) (counter-application for remedies under the Act), section 24(1) (application by a creditor for warrant to exercise remedies on default), or section 28(1) (decree of foreclosure). An interlocutor of the sheriff disposing of any of the foregoing applications or counter-applications is final and not subject to appeal except as to a question of title or any other remedy granted.[8]

Land Tenure Reform (Scotland) Act 1974, s. 9

23.05 An action of removing under section 9 of the Land Tenure Reform (Scotland) Act 1974 is directed by that Act to proceed as an ordinary cause,[9] with the following specialties. The court is entitled to sist extract of the decree to enable any facts to be established which would constitute a defence and, if satisfied that any such facts are established, may vary or rescind the decree.[10] Notwithstanding the general provisions as to the finality of a decree in absence, a decree granted in an action brought under section 9 becomes, in a question with third parties who have acted onerously and in good faith in reliance on the records, final and not subject to challenge when an extract is recorded in the Register of Sasines.[11]

---

[4] *Prestwick Investment Trust v. Jones*, 1981 S.L.T. (Sh. Ct.) 55.

[5] See paras 23.30 *et seq.*

[6] Conveyancing and Feudal Reform (Scotland) Act 1970, s. 29(2).

[7] OCR, r. 34.10(1).

[8] OCR, r. 34.10(2); *Scott v. Hawkins*, Sh. Pr. Caplan, Kilmarnock Sh. Ct, Dec. 19, 1984, unreported: interlocutor refusing to allow answers to be received late and granting decree as craved held unappealable.

[9] s. 9(6).

[10] *ibid.*

[11] s. 9(7). It is to be noted that the 1974 Act, s. 9(7) still refers to the Rules of Court of 1965 and to the Ordinary Cause Rules as they existed prior to 1983. However, it may be taken that the statutory provision still applies in the context of the current rules.

Housing (Scotland) Act 1987, s. 47

An action for recovery of possession under section 47 of the Housing (Scotland) Act 1987 is directed by that Act to proceed by way of summary cause.[12] **23.06**

Extraordinary removings

Extraordinary removings, based on an irritancy at common law, or on section 20 of the Agricultural Holdings (Scotland) Act 1991 which provides for the removal of a tenant of agricultural subjects who is six months in arrears with his rent,[13] proceed as ordinary actions. **23.07**

Composite actions

Difficulties have arisen where a pursuer has sought to combine in one initial writ a crave for a remedy which by statute is allocated to a particular form of process, such as a summary cause or summary application, and an additional or alternative crave for a further remedy which is incompetent in that form of process. None of the proposals for resolving these difficulties appears to be entirely satisfactory. Differing views have been expressed as to the procedure to be followed where a pursuer seeks both to recover the possession of heritable property and to obtain a further remedy other than a decree for payment of £1,500 or less, such as damages exceeding £1,500, or interdict against resumption of occupation. In one case it was held that an ordinary action for ejection and interdict was incompetent. The sheriff accepted that the action would also have been incompetent if raised as a summary cause. He indicated that the pursuer's appropriate course would have been to raise two separate processes: an action for recovery of possession by way of a summary cause, and a separate action for interdict by way of an ordinary cause, with the possibility that the additional expense thus entailed might be minimised by remitting the summary cause to the ordinary roll and conjoining it with the interdict action.[14] In another case, where the pursuer raised an ordinary action craving (1) declarator of irritancy and (2) removing, the latter crave was held to be incompetent and it was observed that the action should have been raised as a summary cause and remitted to the ordinary roll.[15] **23.08**

It seems difficult to reconcile these decisions with the usual practice of the court in dealing with extraordinary removings,[16] which contain craves for declarator of irritancy and for removing. Such actions are regularly brought without objection as ordinary causes, and are competent, though rare, in the Court of Session.[17] A superior seeking to obtain possession by irritating the feu can proceed either by action in the Court of Session or by ordinary action in the sheriff court.[18] The problem arises from the **23.09**

---

[12] s. 47(1).

[13] s. 20(1).

[14] *Disblair Estates Ltd v. Jackson*, Aberdeen Sh. Ct, Nov. 23, 1982, unreported.

[15] *Gerber v. Greggs Bakeries Ltd*, Sh. Pr. O'Brien, Hamilton Sh. Ct, Oct. 18, 1981, unreported. The declaratory crave would appear to be incompetent in a summary cause.

[16] para. 23.07.

[17] If brought in the Court of Session, the ejection is left to be carried out in the sheriff court: *Campbell's Trs v. O'Neill*, 1911 S.C. 188, *per* L.P. Dunedin at 197.

[18] The procedure is provided by OCR, r. 34.5, and explained by Halliday, *Conveyancing* (2nd ed.), Vol. 2, para. 32–125.

inclusion in section 35(1)(c) of the single exception as to a pecuniary crave which exceeds the summary cause limit. It is submitted that that exception was specified only because such a crave would be beyond the scope of summary cause procedure as specified in section 35(1)(a), and that the object of its inclusion was to make it clear that it is competent to raise as a summary cause an action craving recovery of possession with an additional or alternative pecuniary crave within the summary cause limit. Its inclusion does not necessarily imply that it is incompetent to bring an ordinary action with a crave for recovery of possession and other craves beyond the scope of summary cause procedure, and there appears to be no useful purpose to be served by reading section 35(1)(c) in that way. Rules as to forms of procedure are not ends in themselves, but are intended to secure the attainment of justice between the parties consistently with the public interest.[19] It is submitted that the interpretation of section 35(1)(c) which is proposed above would not infringe either the interests of parties or the public interest, and is to be preferred to an interpretation which requires multiplication or complexity in procedure.

23.10 Similar problems arose in the past if a pursuer sought to combine a crave under Part II of the Conveyancing and Feudal Reform (Scotland) Act 1970 with other craves which were inappropriate in a summary application as then required under that statute. However, the Ordinary Cause Rules now make the position clear in that regard.[20]

Intimation to security holders

23.11 In an ordinary action relating to heritable property it is not necessary to call as a defender any person by reason only of any interest he may have as the holder of a heritable security over the heritable property.[21] However, intimation of such an action must be made to the holder of such a heritable security where the action relates to any heritable right or title and, in any other case, if the sheriff so orders.[22]

1907 Act

23.12 Provision as to removings is made by sections 34 to 38A of the 1907 Act and rules 34.5 to 34.9 of the Ordinary Cause Rules. Sections 34 and 35 provide for summary diligence against tenants, section 34 being concerned with the registration and extract, six weeks after the date of the last ish, of a probative lease of lands exceeding two acres specifying a term of endurance, while section 35 deals with the operation of a letter of removal. The provisions of these two sections have been described as "so drastic and their operation so fraught with hazard to any who seek to invoke them that they are seldom if ever used."[23] Rules 34.5 to 34.9 contain provisions as to notices,[24] as does section 38A. Where decree for the

---

[19] *Union Bank of Australia v. Harrison Jones & Devlin Ltd* (1910) 11 C.L.R. 492, *per* Griffith C.J. at 504; *Imperial Tobacco Ltd v. Att.-Gen.* [1979] Q.B. 555, *per* Ormrod L.J. at 582 (revd [1981] A.C. 718).

[20] See para. 23.04.

[21] OCR, r. 3.2(1).

[22] OCR, r. 3.2(2).

[23] Law Reform Committee for Scotland, Report (Cmnd 114, 1957), cit. A. G. M. Duncan, Research Paper on Actions of Ejection and Removing (Scot. Law Com., 1984), para. 7.2.

[24] See Paton and Cameron, pp. 266–279. References in this work are to the pre-1993 Rules; but the relevant rules are relatively unchanged in OCR 1993, and accordingly the passages are still of assistance.

recovery of possession is granted in a summary cause, it has the same force and effect as a decree of removing, or a decree of ejection, or a summary warrant of ejection, or a warrant for summary ejection in common form, or a decree pronounced in a summary application for removing, in terms of sections 36, 37 and 38 respectively.[25]

Caution for violent profits

In any defended action of removing the sheriff may order the defender to find caution for violent profits,[26] which are a form of penal damages for unlawful retention of possession.[27] The motion may be made as soon as defences are lodged.[28] No order will be made if it appears that the defender has an instantly verifiable defence to the action.[29] If it is intended that decree should be granted at once in the event of caution not being found, the interlocutor should not only state the time within which caution is to be found but certify that if the interlocutor is not obtempered decree will be pronounced in terms of the crave for removing. An interlocutor ordering caution is appealable only with leave.[30] **23.13**

Sequestration for rent

Nature of action

The object of an action of sequestration for rent is to enforce a landlord's right of hypothec over moveables brought by his tenant on to the premises let. It is of two kinds: sequestration in payment is used when the term of payment has passed with the rent unpaid, and sequestration in security is used when the term of payment has not come. In practice, both are usually sought in the same action. The nature of the action and the circumstances in which it is competent are explained in the undernoted works.[31] In practice, sequestrations for rent are brought only in the sheriff court.[32] Where the rent in respect of which sequestration is asked does not exceed £1,500, the action is brought as a summary cause.[33] **23.14**

Initial writ

The action must be commenced within three months of the last term of payment.[34] The initial writ usually craves warrant to sequestrate in security of rent to become due and for payment of rent due and unpaid.[35] It also craves warrant to sell and for payment to the pursuer from the proceeds, decree against the defender for any balance due, an order to replenish the subjects if insufficient effects are left on the subjects after sale and, failing replenishment, warrant to eject the defender and authority to **23.15**

---

[25] SCR, r. 69.

[26] OCR, r. 34.5(2). He cannot so order if the action is undefended: *Blythswood Friendly Society v. O'Leary*, 1966 S.L.T. (Sh. Ct.) 64.

[27] See Paton and Cameron, pp. 279–283; Walker, *Civil Remedies*, pp. 770–773.

[28] Rule 34.5(2), and its predecessor, OCR 1983, r. 103(3), modify the Ejection Caution Act 1594 (c. 27), considered in *Middleton v. Booth*, 1986 S.L.T. 450, by conferring a discretion on the court.

[29] *Milne v. Darroch* (1937) 53 Sh.Ct.Rep. 3; *Middleton, supra.*

[30] *Jack v. Carmichael* (1894) 10 Sh. Ct.Rep. 242; *Buchanan v. Dickson*, 1935 S.L.T. (Sh. Ct.) 20.

[31] Graham Stewart, Chap. 23; Walker, *Civil Remedies*, Chap. 19; Paton and Cameron, Chap. 13.

[32] *Duncan v. Lodijensky* (1904) 6 F. 408: see para. 2.35.

[33] 1971 Act, s. 35(1)(b): see Vol. 2 of this work.

[34] Walker, *Civil Remedies*, p. 317.

[35] See Dobie, Styles, pp. 466–471.

the pursuer to relet the premises. It may also crave authority to bring back effects which have been illegally removed from the premises.[36] Along with the initial writ, warrant, and citation, there must be served on the defender a notice in Form H1.[37]

First deliverance

23.16 Unless a caveat has been lodged, in the first deliverance on the initial writ the sheriff may sequestrate the effects of the tenant and grant warrant to inventory and secure them.[38] All warrants to sequestrate, inventory, sell, eject or relet include authority to open shut and lockfast places for the purpose of carrying the warrant into execution.[39] Such warrants must be signed by the sheriff personally.[40]

Inventory

23.17 The warrant in the first deliverance is passed to a sheriff officer for execution. He proceeds to the premises and in the presence of one witness makes an inventory of the articles subject to the hypothec, irrespective of their value in relation to the sum due.[41] He need not appraise their value.[42] The officer leaves a copy of the inventory with a tenant or inmate of the premises and returns to the court the execution of the inventory signed by himself and the witness. The inventory is conclusive evidence of what has been sequestrated: anything not specified in it is not sequestrated.[43]

Warrant to carry back

23.18 The power to sequestrate extends only to effects on the premises. Where goods have been removed before sequestration, the landlord may apply for a warrant to have them brought back to the premises to be inventoried. The warrant may be craved in the initial writ, or in a separate minute,[44] or in a minute endorsed on the writ. Whatever the form of the application, it specifies the articles removed, how they were removed and where they are. Exceptionally, the application may be granted *de plano* for good cause, but normally intimation is ordered to the tenant and to any third party concerned and an opportunity for a hearing given before the warrant is signed.[45] The articles must still be subject to the hypothec.[46]

Care of effects

23.19 The sheriff may at any stage of an action for sequestration and sale appoint a fit person to take charge of the sequestrated effects, or may require the tenant to find caution that they will be made available.[47] He may grant a warrant to sell perishable articles.[48]

---

36 See para. 23.19.
37 OCR, r. 34.1(2).
38 OCR, r. 34.2(1).
39 OCR, r. 34.2(2).
40 OCR, r. 5.1(2)(a).
41 *Marquis of Breadalbane v. Toberonochy Slate Quarry Co.* (1916) 33 Sh.Ct.Rep. 154.
42 *Lochgilphead T.C. v. McIntyre* (1940) 59 Sh.Ct.Rep. 179.
43 *Horsburgh v. Morton* (1825) 3 S. 596 (N.E. 409).
44 Dobie, Styles, p. 473.
45 *Johnston v. Young* (1890) 18 R. (J.) 6; *Gray v. Weir* (1891) 19 R. 25; *McLaughlan v. Reilly* (1892) 20 R. 41; *Jack v. Black*, 1911 S.C. 691 at 696–697; *Shearer v. Nicoll*, 1935 S.L.T. 313.
46 *Thomson v. Barclay* (1883) 10 R. 694; *Sawers v. Kinnair* (1897) 25 R. 45; *McQueen v. Armstrong* (1908) 24 Sh.Ct.Rep. 377; *Henderson v. Huzzard* (1934) 50 Sh.Ct.Rep. 300.
47 OCR, r. 34.4.
48 Dobie, *Styles*, p. 475.

Courses open to tenant

If the tenant opposes sequestration, he may lodge a caveat before sequestration is granted.[49] After sequestration is granted, but not before,[50] he may consign the sum sued for, or find caution therefor, and move for recall of the sequestration. If the sequestration is recalled and decree ultimately granted, payment of the rent and expenses may be given out of the consigned money[51]: where it is recalled on caution, decree for the rent and expenses may be enforced against the cautioner as well as the tenant.[52] Instead of finding caution or consigning the rent the tenant may lodge a notice of intention to defend, after which the proceedings follow the course of a defended ordinary cause. **23.20**

Decree

Once the term of payment of the rent has passed without payment, caution or consignation, and any defence has been repelled, the sheriff on the pursuer's motion[53] grants warrant to sell so much of the sequestrated effects as will satisfy the rent, interest and expenses. He may order them to be sold by a sheriff officer or other named person.[54] When a sale follows it must be reported within 14 days.[55] The pursuer must lodge with the sheriff clerk the roup rolls or certified copies of them and a state of debt.[56] The proceeds of sale are normally ordered to be consigned. If the subjects have been displenished and a balance of rent remains due or rent is to become due at future terms, the pursuer may lodge a minute craving replenishment or caution and, failing that, warrant to eject and relet,[57] where these remedies have not been craved in the initial writ. The auditor taxes the accounts, the sheriff approves the sale, the debt and expenses are paid to the pursuer and the balance is paid to the defender. Where any balance remains due, the sheriff grants decree against the defender therefor either in the interlocutor approving the report of sale or in a separate interlocutor.[58] The decree may be extracted in common form.[59] **23.21**

Registration

All sequestrations for rent may be entered in a register of sequestrations for rent kept by the sheriff clerk.[60] However, the keeping of such a register is not obligatory, and the relevant particulars may be entered in the act book or other suitable register kept by him.[61] **23.22**

Breach of sequestration

The tenant is entitled to use the sequestrated effects, but if he removes, sells or otherwise interferes with them he is liable to punishment for breach of sequestration. In the event of a breach of sequestration the landlord **23.23**

---

49 Dobie, *Styles*, p. 67.
50 *Alexander v. Campbell's Trs* (1903) 5 F. 634.
51 Dove Wilson, p. 489; Wallace, p. 531.
52 *Clark v. Duncan* (1833) 12 S. 158.
53 Dobie, *Styles*, p. 473.
54 OCR, r. 34.3(1).
55 OCR, r. 34.3(2). For a report of sale see Dobie, *Styles*, p. 473.
56 *ibid.*
57 Dobie, *Styles*, p. 474.
58 OCR, r. 34.3(3).
59 OCR, r. 34.1(1).
60 Hypothec Amendment (Scotland) Act 1867, s. 7.
61 A.S., Feb. 3, 1933, para. 2.

may lodge a summary application craving the court to ordain the defender to appear personally and to restore the articles or to find caution for or consign the rent. The application also craves the imposition of a fine on the defender and, failing payment of the fine, imprisonment. The concurrence of the procurator fiscal is accordingly necessary, as in a breach of interdict, and the proceedings follow a similar course. If the defender fails to appear, wilful breach of sequestration is presumed, and decree and warrant of imprisonment may follow. If, however, he appears and shows that any breach of the sequestration was not wilful, no penalty will be imposed.[62] Where a third party has intromitted with the goods in breach of the sequestration a minute for a warrant to carry back may suffice.[63]

Third party

23.24 Where a third party's effects have been included in the sequestration, he is entitled to intervene in the process.[64] He may lodge a minute craving that he be allowed to compear in the cause, specifying the articles he claims and asking that as regards these the sequestration should be recalled. According to old authority the minute should include a condescendence of the facts on which his claim is founded and a note of pleas-in-law.[65] It is therefore thought that the minute, and the procedure to follow thereon, should comply with the provisions of Chapter 14, rather than Chapter 13, of the Ordinary Cause Rules.[66] If warrant of sale has been granted, the third party may ask the judge of the roup not to put up his effects until the other articles have been sold,[67] or he may raise an action of interdict.[68]

Sequestration for feuduty

23.25 A superior has a hypothec for feuduties similar, but preferable, to that of a landlord for rent, which he may make good in an action of sequestration for feuduty.[69] In practice, however, he is more likely to proceed by way of a poinding of the ground.

Poinding of the ground

23.26 By the action of poinding the ground a creditor whose debt is heritably secured attaches moveable effects which are on the subjects so as to make them available for the satisfaction of his debt.[70]

23.27 The action is directed against the vassal or proprietor, or, where there are tenants in the subjects, against him and the tenants. The crave is for warrant to poind and distrain the moveable goods and effects, for payment of the debt and for warrant to inventory and secure.[71] The

---

[62] *Laing v. Harper* (1829) 7 S. 335; *Kippen v. Oppenheim* (1846) 8 D. 957.
[63] See Dobie, *Styles*, p. 471.
[64] *Lindsay v. Earl of Wemyss* (1872) 10 M. 708; *McIntosh v. Potts* (1905) 7 F. 765; *Hoare v. Mackay* (1905) 13 S.L.T. 588.
[65] Dobie, *Styles*, p. 474.
[66] *Ryan v. Little*, 1910 S.C. 219; *Boni v. McIver* (1933) 49 Sh.Ct.Rep. 191.
[67] *McIntosh*, *supra*.
[68] *Jack v. Waddell's Trs*, 1918 S.C. 73.
[69] Walker, *Civil Remedies*, p. 322; *Yuille v. Lawrie* (1823) 2 S. 155 (N.E. 140); *Anderson's Trs v. Donaldson & Co. Ltd*, 1908 S.C. 38.
[70] See Graham Stewart, Chap. 24 and Walker, *Civil Remedies*, Chap. 20, for an explanation of the circumstances in which the action is competent.
[71] Dobie, *Styles*, pp. 372–374.

procedure differs from that in an ordinary action in the following respects. A warrant to cite and to inventory the effects is granted upon presentation of the writ and is signed by the sheriff. Since service of the writ creates a nexus on the effects,[72] which is an important factor in questions of competition of diligence, the writ should be served by a sheriff officer. He executes the warrant to inventory but does not value the effects. The decree takes the form of a warrant to poind. Unless there is a decerniture for expenses, no charge is necessary. After poinding, a warrant of sale is obtained and executed as in the case of effects poinded under an ordinary decree.

Maills and duties

An action for maills and duties is the proceeding by which a heritable creditor, who has a right in security over the rents due from the tenants of the subjects over which his security extends, may enter into possession of the subjects and uplift the rents.[73] The pursuer is the creditor, and the defender the debtor, in the heritable security. Under the optional procedure provided by the Heritable Securities (Scotland) Act 1894, which is followed in practice, the tenants are not called as defenders but receive notice of the action in a prescribed form, which has the effect of interpelling them from making payment of their rents to the defender.[74] On intimation, by registered letter or first class recorded delivery service, of the decree by notice in a further prescribed form, the tenants are obliged to make payment of the rents to the creditor.[75] **23.28**

Heritable Securities (Scotland) Act 1894

Under the Heritable Securities (Scotland) Act 1894 a heritable creditor may make various applications to the sheriff of the sheriffdom in which the security subjects, or part of them, are situated.[76] The Act also provides that any person interested may take proceedings to interpel[77] the creditor from entering into possession of the subjects or collecting the rents thereof.[78] The following are the applications which may be made under the Act by the creditor. **23.29**

Ejection of proprietor

A proprietor who is in personal occupation of the subjects and has made default in the punctual payment of interest, or in due payment of the principal after formal requisition, is deemed to be an occupant without title. The creditor may take proceedings to eject him in all respects in the same way as if he were such an occupant.[79] The provisions of the 1907 Act and the Ordinary Cause Rules as to removings do not apply to such proceedings, and the creditor is not entitled to require the proprietor to find caution for violent profits before defending the action.[80] It appears to **23.30**

---

[72] *Lyons v. Anderson* (1880) 8 R. 24.

[73] Graham Stewart, Chap. 25; Walker, *Civil Remedies*, Chap. 21; Dobie, *Styles*, pp. 310–312.

[74] Heritable Securities (Scotland) Act 1894 (hereafter the "1894 Act"), s. 3, Sched. B.

[75] *ibid.* Sched. C.

[76] s. 15, read with the 1971 Act, Sched. 1, para. 1.

[77] *i.e.* prohibit.

[78] s. 4.

[79] s. 5.

[80] *Inglis' Trs v. Macpherson*, 1910 S.C. 46; *Douglas v. Frew* (1910) 26 Sh.Ct.Rep. 355; *Henderson v. Nelson* (1913) 29 Sh.Ct.Rep. 233.

have been generally assumed that the proceedings should take the form of an ordinary action.[81] It has been held in one sheriff court, however, that they should take the form of a summary application.[82] A practitioner who proposes to raise such proceedings should therefore inquire as to the practice of the particular sheriff court in which they are to be brought.

Leasing security subjects

23.31 A heritable creditor in possession may at his own hand grant leases of the security subjects or part thereof for a period not exceeding seven years.[83] He may apply to the sheriff for a warrant to lease them for a period exceeding seven years and not exceeding 21 years for heritable property in general and 31 years for minerals.[84] The writ sets forth the name of the proposed tenant or tenants and the duration and conditions of the proposed lease.[85] It is served on the proprietor and on the other heritable creditors, if any. After such intimation and inquiry as he thinks proper, and if he is satisfied that a lease for a longer period than seven years is expedient for the beneficial occupation of the lands, the sheriff may approve of the proposed lease on the terms and conditions proposed, or on such other terms and conditions as may appear to him expedient.[86] The sheriff may remit to a conveyancer to inquire and report, whether the defender appears or not. The Act contains special provisions as to appeals and expenses, which are considered below.[87]

Forfeiture of right of redemption

23.32 A creditor who has exposed the security subjects at a price not exceeding the sum due to him and to any prior or *pari passu* creditors (exclusive of the expenses attending the exposure or prior exposures), and has failed to find a purchaser, may apply to the sheriff for decree finding that the debtor has forfeited his right of redemption and that the creditor is vested in the lands as absolute proprietor. The application may be made only in respect of the whole subjects contained in the bond or bonds held by the pursuer.[88] The writ craves declarator of forfeiture of the right of redemption, and that the heritable creditor is vested in the subjects as absolute proprietor at the price at which they were last exposed, and warrant to record the decree in the Register of Sasines.[89] The writ is served on the proprietor and on the other creditors, if any. The action is generally undefended. After such intimation and inquiry as he may think fit, which usually includes a remit to a conveyancer to report on the regularity of the proceedings, the sheriff may grant the application and issue decree in terms of Schedule D appended to the Act, which contains a description of the subjects and is recorded in the Register of Sasines.[90] The effect of the decree is to extinguish the debtor's right of redemption and to give the creditor a right to the lands in the same manner and to the same effect as if

---

[81] *Inglis' Trs, Douglas, Henderson, supra*; *Mountstar Metal Corporation Ltd v. Cameron*, 1987 S.L.T. (Sh. Ct.) 106; Fyfe, p. 574; Dobie, p. 595.
[82] *Prestwick Investment Trust v. Jones*, 1981 S.L.T. 55. See para. 23.03.
[83] 1894 Act, s. 6.
[84] *ibid.* s. 7.
[85] Dobie, *Styles*, p. 183.
[86] 1894 Act, s. 7.
[87] paras 23.34, 23.35.
[88] *Webb's Exrs v. Reid* (1906) 14 S.L.T. 323.
[89] Dobie, *Styles*, p. 181.
[90] 1894 Act, s. 8.

the disposition in security had been an irredeemable disposition as from the date of the decree. After registration the lands are disencumbered of all securities and diligences posterior to the creditor's security.[91] Instead of granting decree the sheriff may appoint the subjects to be re-exposed for sale at a price to be fixed by him, in which event the creditor may bid for and purchase the lands. If the creditor becomes the purchaser, the sheriff may issue a decree in the terms already referred to, or the creditor may grant a disposition to himself as if he had been a stranger.[92] The provisions of the Act as to appeals and expenses in such applications are noted below.[93]

Sale by pari passu *security holder*

A heritable creditor who ranks *pari passu* with another and cannot obtain the other's consent to a sale, may apply to the sheriff for warrant to sell, calling the other creditor as a defender.[94] The sheriff hears parties and makes such inquiry as he thinks fit, usually by remitting to a reporter. If in the sheriff's opinion it is reasonable and expedient that a sale should take place, he may order a sale, fixing the price in case of difference of opinion, and authorise both or either of the parties or some other person to carry through the sale. Upon payment or consignation of the price, the sheriff may authorise such persons to grant a conveyance and disencumber the lands of the securities in the same way and to the same effect as if the creditors were carrying through the sale by agreement, and to fix the times and conditions of sale according to the law and practice relating to premonition and advertisement. The expenses of and connected with the sale are payable preferably out of the price or proceeds of sale, and the balance is paid to the creditors according to their rights and preferences.[95] The Act makes provision as to appeals and expenses.[96] **23.33**

Appeals and expenses

In the case of each of the applications considered in the three preceding paragraphs the Act provides that the interlocutor of the sheriff who pronounces any order or decree is final, and not subject to review, except (1) as to questions of title and (2) where the principal sum due under the heritable security exceeds £1,000.[97] There is accordingly no general right of appeal to the sheriff principal from an interlocutor which does not fall within the exceptional provision.[98] Appeal to the sheriff principal has, however, been allowed where the order appealed against was challenged as incompetent,[99] and where a question of title was decided by prior interlocutors which were open to review.[1] While an appeal against an incompetent interlocutor may be competent,[2] it seems at least doubtful **23.34**

[91] 1894 Act, s. 8; see also s. 9.
[92] *ibid.*; *Lusk v. Tait* (1899) 15 Sh.Ct.Rep. 249.
[93] paras 23.33, 23.34.
[94] 1894 Act, s. 11. See Dobie, *Styles*, p. 182.
[95] *ibid.*
[96] paras 23.33, 23.34.
[97] 1894 Act, s. 12(1).
[98] *Webb's Exrs v. Reid* (1906) 14 S.L.T. 325 is thought to be wrongly decided on this point: see *Nicholson v. Murray* (1927) 43 Sh.Ct.Rep. 108 and the discussion of finality clauses in paras 25.32 to 25.35.
[99] *Lyon's Trs v. Smith*, 1922 S.L.T. (Sh. Ct.) 42.
[1] *Lyon's Trs, supra.*
[2] para. 18.12.

whether an appeal against an unappealable interlocutor may be taken in order to challenge an earlier interlocutor.[3]

23.35 The Act further provides that in the case of each of those three applications the sheriff may award expenses, or may direct that the expenses be treated as part of the expenses of the sale.[4] The latter direction is inappropriate in an application for power to lease the security subjects.

Notice calling up bond

23.36 Section 16 of the 1894 Act provides that when the creditor wishes to make a formal demand for payment of his debt but (1) the debtor has died and the name and address of his heir cannot be ascertained, or (2) the creditor cannot ascertain the debtor's address or whether he is still alive, or (3) the creditor cannot ascertain the address of the person entitled to receive intimation of the demand, the creditor may apply to the sheriff for a warrant for edictal intimation.[5] These provisions, however, are superseded to the extent that where the debtor is a person deceased who has left no heirs or whose heirs are unknown, the notice provided for in the Conveyancing (Scotland) Act 1924 should be given to the Lord Advocate.[6]

Actions of division

General rules

23.37 The 1907 Act provides that the jurisdiction of the sheriff court extends to and includes "actions of division of commonty and of division or of division and sale of common property, in which cases the Act of 1695 concerning the division of commonties shall be read and construed as if it conferred jurisdiction upon the sheriff court in the same manner as upon the Court of Session."[7] Commonty is a species of common property now almost extinct, and there appears to be no reported example of a successful action of division of commonty in recent times.[8] Actions of division or division and sale, however, are frequently encountered in practice. The object of such an action is either to have the subjects physically divided or, if division is impracticable or inexpedient, to have them judicially sold and the proceeds divided in the proportions to which each proprietor is entitled.[9] An action of division or division and sale may be taken as of right by any person having title and interest to do so, and it cannot therefore be described as an equitable remedy.[10] However, considerations of equity may properly be taken into account in determining the method of division and sale and the distribution of proceeds of sale.[11]

---

[3] *cf. Malone v. Glasgow D.C.*, Sh. Pr. Reid, Glasgow Sh. Ct, Nov. 20, 1979, unreported. See para. 18.70.

[4] 1894 Act, s. 12(2).

[5] *ibid.* s. 16; Dobie, *Styles*, p. 184.

[6] Conveyancing (Scotland) Act 1924, ss. 33, 34.

[7] 1907 Act, s. 5(3).

[8] See *Macandrew v. Crerar*, 1929 S.C. 699; Walker, *Civil Remedies*, pp. 1231–1232; Dobie, *Styles*, p. 87.

[9] *Brook v. Hamilton* (1852) 19 D. 701; Walker, *Civil Remedies*, pp. 1229–1230. The action is more accurately described as "an action of sale and division": *Frizell v. Thomson* (1860) 22 D. 1176; *Campbells v. Murray*, 1972 S.L.T. 249.

[10] *Upper Crathes Fishings Ltd v. Barclay*, 1991 S.C.L.R. 151; *Burrows v. Burrows*, 1996 S.L.T. 1313.

[11] *Ralston v. Jackson*, 1994 S.L.T. 771. See also *Johnston v. Robson*, 1995 S.L.T. (Sh. Ct.) 26.

Equitable considerations may also determine whether an action of division and sale should be sisted to await the outcome of other proceedings or should proceed at once.[12]

The action may be brought by any one or more of the joint owners, or joint tenants in a long lease.[13] It may also be brought by a person with a vested right in the property, even though that person is not a heritable proprietor.[14] All the other joint owners or joint tenants should be called as defenders.[15] The crave begins with a crave for declarator that the pursuer is entitled to insist in the action, and proceeds as the circumstances of the case require. The pursuer is entitled to have the subjects divided or, if not divisible, to have them sold.[16] If division is thought to be practicable and expedient the crave may ask for a remit to a surveyor to report. Otherwise it may seek warrant to sell the subjects and divide the proceeds.[17] The pursuer need not aver any justification for raising the action.[18] **23.38**

After the disposal of any preliminary pleas, or before answer, the court, unless parties are agreed, remits to a person of skill. Where division is craved, he reports whether the subjects are divisible. If division is not craved or if he reports that it is impracticable, he suggests the upset price and any special conditions or other matters which require to be considered in view of a public sale. The parties may be heard upon the report, but the reporter's views are usually accepted as conclusive on the matters referred.[19] If the court holds division to be expedient, the parties execute the necessary conveyances, either voluntarily or under decree.[20] **23.39**

If sale is decided on, the sheriff approves the report and may order the subjects to be sold at the sight of the sheriff clerk or other suitable person, under articles of roup drawn up by the reporter and approved by the sheriff, or adjusted at the sight of the sheriff clerk, and upon such advertisement or otherwise as the sheriff may order. The articles of roup may include a clause authorising the parties to bid.[21] A sale by private bargain is often to be preferred to a sale by public roup, and may be permitted subject to a minimum price being fixed by an independent valuator.[22] However, there is no presumption in favour of a private sale.[23] **23.40**

When the sale is carried through,[24] it is reported to and approved by the sheriff and the price is consigned in court. If any question arises as to the division of the fund, the sheriff hears parties thereon. Decree is pronounced disposing of the fund among the parties according to their respective rights and interests. The disposition to the purchaser is usually **23.41**

---

[12] *Rae v. Rae*, 1991 S.L.T. 454.

[13] *Robertson's Tr. v. Roberts*, 1982 S.L.T. 22.

[14] *Johnston v. MacFarlane*, 1987 S.C.L.R. 104.

[15] *Campbell* (1893) 1 S.L.T. 157.

[16] *Morrison v. Kirk*, 1912 S.C. 44.

[17] Dobie, *Styles*, p. 85; Lewis, p. 509.

[18] *Frizell, supra.*

[19] *Thom v. McBeth* (1875) 3 R. 161; but see *Williams v. Cleveland and Highland Holdings Ltd*, 1993 S.L.T. 398.

[20] The extract decree may be recorded: Conveyancing (Scotland) Act 1874, s. 35.

[21] *Thom, supra*; *Vincent v. Anderson* (1919) 36 Sh.Ct.Rep. 182.

[22] *Campbell, supra.*

[23] *The Miller Group Ltd v. Tasker*, 1993 S.L.T. 207.

[24] As to the procedure at and after a sale by public roup, see *Goudie v. Goudie* (1903) 11 S.L.T. 27.

adjusted at the sight of the sheriff clerk. If any of the parties refuses to sign, the sheriff may, on motion, direct the sheriff clerk to do so.[25] The account of the pursuer's solicitor in carrying out the sale may be directed to be taxed as between solicitor and client.[26]

Matrimonial Homes (Family Protection) (Scotland) Act 1981, s. 19

23.42 Section 19 of the Matrimonial Homes (Family Protection) (Scotland) Act 1981 provides that where a spouse brings an action for the division and sale of a matrimonial home which the spouses own in common, the court, after having regard to all the circumstances of the case, may refuse to grant decree in that action or may postpone the granting of decree for such period as it may consider reasonable in the circumstances or may grant decree subject to such conditions as it may prescribe.[27] "All the circumstances of the case" include: (1) the conduct of the spouses in relation to each other and otherwise; (2) the respective needs and financial resources of the spouses; (3) the needs of any child of the family; (4) the extent (if any) to which the matrimonial home is used in connection with a trade, business or profession of either spouse; (5) whether the spouse bringing the action offers or has offered to make available to the other spouse any suitable alternative accommodation.[28] The latter provision contemplates an offer of specific accommodation: "there must be a concrete opportunity offered which would enable the other spouse to move into reasonable accommodation."[29] The court may postpone the granting of decree until after the divorce of the parties,[30] or may sist the action of division and sale until divorce proceedings have been concluded.[31]

23.43 The object of the Act is to establish occupancy rights in the matrimonial home and to protect against undue disturbance of such rights. The restriction on the right to division and sale which is imposed by section 19 is intended to protect the occupancy rights of the defending spouse.[32] An action of division and sale is not a "dealing" in respect of which the court may dispense with the consent of the other spouse by virtue of section 7(1) of the Act.[33] Where a non-entitled spouse in occupation of the matrimonial home refuses to consent to a "dealing", his or her occupancy rights can only be defeated if the entitled spouse satisfies the court that his or her consent should be dispensed with. The Act cannot have intended that the occupancy rights of a spouse with a joint interest in the matrimonial home should have a lesser degree of protection than those of a non-entitled spouse. Accordingly, the reasonableness of displacing the defending spouse should be taken into account in reaching a decision under section 19. Further, just as in an application under section 7(1) it is for the applicant to show that consent should be dispensed with, it is for the pursuer spouse in an action of division and sale to satisfy the sheriff that in all the circumstances decree should be granted.[34]

---

[25] 1907 Act, s. 5A, inserted by the Law Reform (Miscellaneous Provisions) (Scotland) Act 1985, s. 17.

[26] *Reidford v. Liston*, 1931 S.L.T. 418.

[27] Matrimonial Homes (Family Protection) (Scotland) Act 1981, s. 19.

[28] *ibid.* ss. 3(3)(a)–(d), 19.

[29] *Hall v. Hall*, 1987 S.L.T. (Sh. Ct.) 15; *Milne v. Milne*, 1994 S.C.L.R. 437.

[30] *Crow v. Crow*, 1986 S.L.T. 270.

[31] *Rae v. Rae*, 1991 S.L.T. 454.

[32] *Hall, supra*; *Milne, supra.*

[33] *Dunsmore v. Dunsmore*, 1986 S.L.T. (Sh. Ct.) 9.

[34] *Hall, supra*; *Milne, supra.*

March fences

The March Dykes Act 1661 provides for the erection and repair of march fences. A proprietor of lands may by an application to the sheriff compel a conterminous proprietor to bear with him half the expense of erecting, repairing or reconstructing the march dyke or fence between their lands.[35] The action may be brought in the Court of Session, but is usually brought in the sheriff court.[36] The Act is applied only to lands exceeding five or six acres in extent,[37] and where advantage, not necessarily equal, will accrue to both estates.[38] The conterminous proprietor cannot be found liable unless he has consented to the work or has been made a party to proceedings under the Act[39]: accordingly, in the absence of consent the action should be raised before the work is commenced.[40] The application will be refused if in the circumstances the pursuer's demand is oppressive or unfair.[41] It is in the discretion of the sheriff to decide whether an old fence should be repaired or rebuilt.[42] He may remit to a man of skill to report on the nature of any necessary work. If further inquiry is necessary, a proof is not incompetent but the more expedient course is to make a second remit to the reporter.[43] **23.44**

The March Dykes Act 1669 provides that where the marches are crooked and unequal or unfit for a dyke or ditch, a proprietor intending to enclose by a dyke or ditch on the march may require the sheriff to visit the marches and adjudge parts of each heritor's ground to the other so as may be least to the prejudice of either party, and to adjust compensation to whichever of them is prejudiced thereby.[44] Substantial portions of land may be thereby exchanged.[45] As in an action under the 1661 Act, the application will be refused if unfairness or oppression would result, for example where the expense necessary would be out of all proportion to the benefit to be derived.[46] **23.45**

No special procedural rules apply to proceedings under the March Dykes Acts, except that in an application under the 1669 Act the sheriff is obliged to visit and inspect the ground personally.[47] He may, however, obtain such assistance from persons of skill as he may think expedient[48]; and the conclusion at which he may thus arrive after careful examination will not lightly be disturbed by a higher court.[49] Procedure under the 1661 Act is by way of summary cause where the application is for payment of a sum within the summary cause pecuniary limit.[50] **23.46**

---

[35] March Dykes Act 1661 (c. 41); *Paterson v. MacDonald* (1880) 7 R. 958, *per* L.P. Inglis at 960; Walker, *Civil Remedies*, pp. 1232–1233; Dobie, *Styles*, pp. 313–314.

[36] *Pollock v. Ewing* (1869) 7 M. 815; *Paterson, supra.*

[37] *Penman v. Douglas* (1739) Mor. 10481.

[38] *Blackburn v. Head* (1904) 11 S.L.T. 521; *Secker v. Cameron*, 1914 S.C. 354.

[39] *Ord v. Wright* (1738) Mor. 10479.

[40] *Duncan v. Ramsay* (1906) 23 Sh.Ct.Rep. 181; *McKenna v. Wain*, Sh. Pr. Gillies, Ayr Sh. Ct, July 27, 1983, unreported.

[41] *Secker, supra.*

[42] *Paterson, supra.*

[43] *Steel v. Steel* (1898) 25 R. 715.

[44] March Dykes Act 1669 (c. 17); Dobie, *Styles*, p. 312.

[45] *Earl of Kintore v. Earl of Kintore's Trs* (1886) 13 R. 997.

[46] *Lord Advocate v. Sinclair* (1872) 10 M. 137.

[47] *ibid.*

[48] *ibid.*

[49] *Earl of Kintore, supra.*

[50] *e.g. McKenna, supra.*

CHAPTER 24

MISCELLANEOUS ACTIONS

1. Exhibition: Transumpt[1]

The object of an action of exhibition is to permit the inspection of documents by a pursuer who can show sufficient title and interest.[2] It is thought that it would be resorted to in modern practice only where the pursuer could not competently sue for delivery of the documents, or recover them by commission and diligence, or obtain an order for their inspection under section 1 of the Administration of Justice (Scotland) Act 1972.[3] When the documents are to be produced in an action of exhibition, they are ordained to be exhibited in the hands of the sheriff clerk. An action of transumpt is an action of exhibition with a crave for a judicial copy of the documents exhibited. It will not be allowed where the same result could be appropriately obtained in any other way.[4] **24.01**

2. Lawburrows

In an application for lawburrows the pursuer craves the court to ordain the defender to find caution to keep the law by refraining from harming the person or property of the pursuer or his family, tenants or employees. The remedy is founded on the Lawburrows Acts of 1429, 1581 and 1597,[5] but the procedure is regulated by section 6 of the Civil Imprisonment (Scotland) Act 1882. It is arguable that the district court also has jurisdiction,[6] but for practical purposes the application may be brought only in the sheriff court. **24.02**

In the initial writ the pursuer craves the court to ordain the defender to find caution that the pursuer shall not be molested or troubled by the defender, on pain of imprisonment.[7] A crave for lawburrows cannot be combined with a crave for interdict.[8] The pursuer must aver that he apprehends harm to the person or property of himself, or of his family, tenants or employees.[9] Upon the application being presented, the sheriff must immediately order the writ to be served on the defender and grant warrant to both parties to cite witnesses to a diet of proof.[10] Failure to **24.03**

---

[1] See Walker, *Civil Remedies*, p. 1245.
[2] *Whyte v. Kilmarnock District Committee of Ayr C.C.*, 1912 2 S.L.T. 15.
[3] See paras 15.84 to 15.92.
[4] *Selkirk v. Service* (1880) R. 29.
[5] Lawburrows Acts 1429, 1581, 1597.
[6] Civil Imprisonment (Scotland) Act 1882, s. 6(2); District Courts (Scotland) Act 1975, s. 3(1); Criminal Procedure (Scotland) Act 1995, s. 7(1).
[7] *e.g. Morrow v. Neil*, 1975 S.L.T. (Sh. Ct.) 65; *Porteous v. Rutherford*, 1980 S.L.T. (Sh. Ct.) 129.
[8] *Kerr v. Alexander*, Sh. Pr. O'Brien, Edinburgh Sh. Ct, July 14, 1978, unreported.
[9] *Morrow, supra*; *Porteous, supra*.
[10] Civil Imprisonment (Scotland) Act 1882, s. 6(2).

grant warrant to cite witnesses at the same time as the order for service is made does not, however, render the proceedings incompetent.[11] There is no order for defences.[12]

24.04 At the proof, the pursuer must establish that he reasonably apprehends the harm complained of in the writ.[13] The standard of proof is the normal civil standard of proof on the balance of probabilities.[14] The evidence of one credible witness, who may be a party, is sufficient.[15] The application is disposed of summarily, under the provisions as to summary criminal procedure, without any shorthand record of the evidence being kept. Expenses may be awarded against either party if and as it shall seem just.[16] If the pursuer establishes his case, the sheriff may order caution to be found and further order that the defender shall, failing his finding caution, be imprisoned for a period not exceeding six months.[17] Alternatively, the sheriff may order the defender to grant within a specified period his own bond without caution for duly implementing the terms of the order, and further order such imprisonment in the event of his failure to do so.[18] The decree cannot be reviewed by suspension, and any appeal is by way of stated case to the High Court of Justiciary, as in summary criminal procedure.[19]

24.05 If, caution or a bond having been found or granted, the defender does any harm of the kind specified, the pursuer may raise against him and his cautioner, if any, a civil action for contravention of lawburrows. Such an action requires the concurrence of the procurator fiscal and craves forfeiture of the caution.[20] If the action is successful, the caution is divided equally between the Crown and the pursuer. The action is not exclusive of any other remedy competent for the wrong in question, such as an action of damages for assault; and the public prosecutor may bring criminal proceedings.[21]

3. Maritime causes

24.06 The grounds of jurisdiction of the sheriff court in maritime causes, and examples of such causes, have already been noted.[22] In the sheriff court maritime causes which are brought as ordinary actions have no procedural peculiarities. There are, however, special procedural rules as to the arrestment of ships.[23] A ship may only be arrested if she is within the jurisdiction of the court and is either in harbour or at anchor in a roadstead.[24] Whether jurisdiction can be established by arrestment of a ship *ad fundandam jurisdictionem* is uncertain.[25] A warrant for arrestment

---

[11] *Morton v. Liddle*, 1996 J.C. 194.

[12] Civil Imprisonment (Scotland) Act 1882, s. 6(3).

[13] *Morrow, supra*; *MacLeod v. MacLeod*, 1928 S.L.T. (Sh. Ct.) 27; *Cooney v. Kirkpatrick*, 1990 G.W.D. 5–285; *Morton, supra*.

[14] *ibid.*

[15] 1882 Act, s. 6(4); and see *Morrow, supra*.

[16] *ibid.* s. 6(3).

[17] *ibid.* s. 6(6).

[18] *ibid.* s. 6(7).

[19] *Mackenzie v. Maclennan*, 1916 S.C. 617; *Cooney, supra*.

[20] *Robertson v. Ross* (1873) 11 M. 910.

[21] *Morrow, supra* at 66.

[22] paras 2.73 to 2.74. See Walker, *Civil Remedies*, chap. 63.

[23] *Mill v. Fildes*, 1982 S.L.T. 147.

[24] *Borjesson v. Carlberg* (1878) 5 R. (H.L.) 215; *JWA Upham Ltd v. Torode*, 1982 S.C. 5.

[25] *Ladgroup Ltd v. Euroeast Lines SA*, 1997 S.L.T. 916.

on the dependence does not have effect as authority for the detention of the ship unless the action is for the enforcement of a claim to which section 47 of the Administration of Justice Act 1956 applies and either the ship is the ship with which the action is concerned or all the shares in the ship are owned by the defender.[26] Where dismantling is desired as a means of preventing the ship from leaving the jurisdiction, the crave should include a crave for warrant to dismantle. Such a warrant should be signed by the sheriff.[27] If the vessel is at anchor in a roadstead a warrant may be granted to bring it into a safe harbour where it may be safely dismantled.[28] Arrestments on cargo may be recalled on the application of the time charterers or owners of the vessel.[29] A person who is not a party to the action is not, however, entitled to seek recall of the arrestment of the vessel even where he claims to be the true owner thereof.[30] If the vessel sails in breach of the arrestment the defender may be required to find caution or to consign as a condition of insisting in his defence.[31] The arrestment may be followed up by the sale of the vessel upon a warrant to sell obtained either by a separate action, in which all the owners of the vessel, so far as known, should be called as defenders, or by motion in the original process.[32] The cargo owners may be ordained to discharge the cargo in order to enable the sale to proceed.[33]

4. Rectification

Both the Court of Session and the sheriff court have power to order the rectification of defectively expressed contractual or unilateral documents.[34] Before ordering rectification of a contractual document, the court has to be satisfied that (1) there is a document to be rectified; (2) the document was intended to express or give effect to an already existing agreement arrived at between two or more parties; (3) there was when the document was executed such a pre-existing agreement—whether or not enforceable; (4) that agreement itself embodied and was an expression of one or more intentions common to the parties; (5) the intentions were actual as distinct from deemed intentions; and (6) the agreement itself was reached at a definite point in time (*cf.* "the date when it was made").[35] The pursuer must identify the alleged error and specify the terms of the agreement which the parties truly intended.[36] "Defective expression" has been held to include defects in the mode of execution of a document and misidentification or misdescription of a party to an agreement.[37] In considering an application for rectification the court is entitled to have **24.07**

---

[26] Administration of Justice Act 1956, s. 47; *The "Aifanourios"*, 1980 S.C. 346; *Gatoil International Inc. v. Arkwright-Boston Manufacturers Mutual Insurance Co.*, 1985 S.C. (H.L.) 1; *Wm Batey & Co. (Exports) Ltd v. Kent*, 1987 S.L.T. 557.

[27] OCR, r. 5.1(2)(a).

[28] *Turner v. Galway* (1882) 19 S.L.R. 892; *JWA Upham Ltd, supra.*

[29] *Svenska Petroleum AB v. HOR Ltd*, 1982 S.L.T. 343; *West Cumberland Farmers Ltd v. Director of Agriculture of Sri Lanka*, 1985 S.L.T. 296.

[30] *Tait v. Main*, 1989 S.L.T. (Sh. Ct.) 81; paras 11.31.

[31] *Meron v. Umland* (1896) 3 S.L.T. 286.

[32] *Banque Indo Suez v. Maritime Co. Overseas Inc.*, 1985 S.L.T. 117.

[33] *Banque Indo Suez, supra.*

[34] Law Reform (Miscellaneous Provisions) (Scotland) Act 1985 (the "1985 Act"), s. 8(1), (9). Testamentary writings are excluded; s. 8(6).

[35] *Shaw v. Wm Grant (Minerals) Ltd*, 1989 S.L.T. 121.

[36] *Huewind Ltd v. Clydesdale Bank plc*, 1996 S.L.T. 369.

[37] *Bank of Scotland v. Graham's Trustee*, 1992 S.C. 79; *Bank of Scotland v. Brunswick Developments (1987) Ltd*, 1995 S.C. 272.

regard to all relevant evidence, whether written or oral, and thus may examine all relevant evidence extrinsic to the document.[38] The standard of proof is the balance of probabilities.[39] Notice of the application should be served on all parties whose interests may be affected by the proposed rectification, although it appears that the Act does not make such intimation mandatory.[40] Where an application is made for rectification of a document relating to land, and authority for service or intimation has been granted, it is competent to register a notice of the application in the Register of Inhibitions and Adjudications. The land is rendered litigious as from the date of registration of the notice.[41] In ordering rectification the court may, at its own instance or on an application made to it, order the rectification of any similar contractual or unilateral document which is defectively expressed by reason of the defect in the original document.[42] A document ordered to be rectified has effect as if it had always been so rectified[43]; and where a document recorded in the General Register of Sasines is ordered to be rectified and the order is likewise recorded, the document is treated as having been always so recorded as rectified.[44]

24.08 The exercise of these powers is subject to the provisions made for the protection of the interests of a third party who has acted or refrained from acting in reliance on the terms of the document or on the title sheet of an interest in land registered in the Land Register of Scotland being an interest to which the document relates, with the result that his position has been affected to a material extent. The court orders rectification only where it is satisfied that the third party has consented to the proposed rectification or that the rectification would not adversely affect his interests to a material extent.[45] To enable the court to assess the interests of all relevant third parties it is empowered to require the production of information by the Keeper of the Registers of Scotland regarding persons who have asked him to supply details with regard to a title sheet of an interest in land which may be the subject of rectification as a result of rectification of a document. Any expense thereby incurred by the Keeper must be borne by the applicant for the order.[46] For the purpose of protecting a third party's interests the court may postpone the date on which the order for rectification becomes effective.[47] Where a third party is unaware, before the making of the order, that the application has been made, he may apply to the Court of Session for reduction of the order or for an order on the applicant for rectification to pay to the third party such compensation as it thinks fit in respect of his reliance on the terms of the document or on the title sheet.[48] The third party's application to the Court of Session must, however, be made before the expiry of five years after the making of the rectifying order, or before the expiry of

---

[38] 1985 Act, s. 8(2); *McClymont v. McCubbin*, 1994 S.C. 573; *Huewind Ltd v. Clydesdale Bank plc*, 1995 S.L.T. 392 at 402 (revsd on another point: 1996 S.L.T. 369).

[39] *Rehman v. Ahmad*, 1993 S.L.T. 741.

[40] See 1985 Act, s. 9(7), and para. 24.8; *McClymont v. McCubbin*, *supra*, *per* Lord Murray at 581.

[41] *ibid.* s. 8(7), (8).

[42] *ibid.* s. 8(3).

[43] *ibid.* s. 8(4).

[44] *ibid.* s. 8(5).

[45] *ibid.* s. 9(1), (2).

[46] *ibid.* s. 9(6).

[47] *ibid.* s. 9(4), (5).

[48] *ibid.* s. 9(7).

two years after the making of that order first came to the notice of the third party, whichever is the earlier.[49] All these provisions for the protection of the interests of third parties do not apply to a person who knew or ought to have known that the document or title sheet was inaccurately expressed, or whose reliance on its terms was otherwise unreasonable.[50]

5. Action of relief

An action of relief "is generally applicable where the pursuer and the defender were under a common obligation, which ought first to have been performed by the defender, and which, by his neglect, was cast upon the pursuer, so that the pursuer, having been sued, was forced to pay damages, together with the costs of his adversary and his own costs in the suit."[51] It is not, however, necessary in every case that the pursuer should have been sued. At common law the obligation of relief is based upon recompense. Accordingly, an action of relief may be pursued by one co-obligant against another where the former has paid the whole of a joint debt, even where the payment was voluntary rather than in terms of a court decree.[52] The action can only be maintained in cases which are "founded on some special obligation of warrandice or mandate, cautionary or conjunct obligation, or the like."[53] Examples of actions of relief are given in the undernoted works.[54] Reference has already been made to rights of relief in the contexts of third party procedure[55] and of contribution among joint wrongdoers in terms of section 3 of the Law Reform (Miscellaneous Provisions) (Scotland) Act 1940.[56] **24.09**

From a procedural standpoint the principal rules are related to the duty of intimation by a party entitled to relief,[57] and the extinctive prescription of two years which is applicable to obligations to make contributions between wrongdoers.[58] As to the former, where a party (the primary obligant) receives intimation of a claim in respect of which he is entitled to relief, he must intimate the claim to the party who is under obligation to relieve him (the ultimate obligant); and where an action is raised against the primary obligant, he must likewise intimate the action. He should settle neither the claim[59] nor the action[60] without giving notice to the ultimate obligant. The reason for these rules is that as relief is an equitable remedy, parties ought to know precisely where they stand[61]; and the ultimate obligant is entitled to have an opportunity of defending the claim or compromising it.[62] On **24.10**

---

[49] 1985 Act, s. 9(8).

[50] *ibid.* s. 9(3).

[51] *Caledonian Ry v. Colt* (1860) 3 Macq. 833; *British Railways Board v. Ross & Cromarty C.C.*, 1974 S.C. 27 at 36–37.

[52] *Moss v. Penman*, 1994 S.C. 41.

[53] See n. 51.

[54] *Encyclopaedia*, xii, s.v. "Relief"; Walker, *Civil Remedies*, pp. 557–559, 1241–1244; Dobie, *Styles*, pp. 407–413.

[55] paras 12.45 to 12.48.

[56] para. 4.49.

[57] *Encyclopaedia*, xii, para. 960.

[58] Prescription and Limitation (Scotland) Act 1973, s. 8A, inserted by Prescription and Limitation (Scotland) Act 1984, s. 1.

[59] *Clarke v. Scott* (1896) 23 R. 442.

[60] *Gardiner v. Main* (1894) 22 R. 100.

[61] *National Coal Board v. Thomson*, 1959 S.C. 353, *per* L.J.-C. Thomson at 365; *Central SMT Co. v. Cloudsley*, 1974 S.L.T. (Sh. Ct.) 70 at 72.

[62] *Dorman Long & Co. v. Harrower* (1899) 1 F. 1109, *per* Lord Kinnear at 1115; *Alexander v. Perth C.C.* (1939) 56 Sh.Ct.Rep 20 at 26–28.

receiving notice of the claim, the ultimate obligant should either pay the claim or direct the line of defence. If he does neither, the primary obligant is entitled to defend the action and to charge him with the expenses, which are in such a case covered by the right of relief. The primary obligant should intimate to the ultimate obligant the nature of the defence he proposes to state, thereby precluding the ultimate obligant from arguing, when called upon to pay the expenses, that the defence has not been properly pleaded.[63] The primary obligant need not bring an action of relief until his liability is either admitted or established,[64] but he should do so before the expiry of the prescriptive period.

6. Suspension of diligence

Nature and competency

24.11 The object of suspension is to stay or arrest some act or proceeding complained of, and to retain matters in their present position until the rights of parties can be determined by a final judgment.[65] In the Court of Session the procedure may be invoked for two main purposes: either to stay the use of legal diligence, or to review certain decrees.[66] In the sheriff court, however, suspension is competent only for the former purpose, and only to the extent permitted by section 5(5) of the 1907 Act read with the Act of Sederunt (Summary Suspension) 1993.[67] Section 5(5) provides that the jurisdiction of the sheriff includes "suspension of charges or threatened charges upon the decrees of court granted by the sheriff or upon decrees of registration proceeding upon bonds, bills, contracts or other obligations registered in the books of the sheriff court, the Books of Council and Session, or any others competent."[68] Paragraph 2 of the Act of Sederunt provides that where a charge for payment has been executed on any decree to which section 5(5) of the Sheriff Courts (Scotland) Act 1907 applies, the person so charged may apply to the sheriff in the sheriff court having jurisdiction over him for suspension of such charge and diligence. It is thought, however, that since the coming into force of the Debtors (Scotland) Act 1987 a party threatened with diligence will, in many cases, prefer to seek a time to pay order[69] or an order for recall of poinding[70] or to oppose the granting of a warrant for the sale of poinded articles[71] rather than to apply for suspension since the statutory procedures provide for diligence to be stopped at various stages upon grounds which would not necesarily justify suspension.

24.12 It appears that the jurisdiction of the sheriff court extends only to the suspension of a charge or threatened charge on a decree for payment of a sum of money. Section 5(5) as originally enacted ended with the words: "where the debt inclusive of interest and expenses does not exceed £50." The deletion of those words by the Law Reform (Miscellaneous

---

[63] *Leith Harbour and Docks Commissioners v. N.B. Ry* (1904) 12 S.L.T. 192.
[64] *Duncan's Trs v. Stiven* (1897) 24 R. 880.
[65] Mackay, *Manual*, p. 420.
[66] For a full analysis of the remedy see Graham Stewart, Chap. 40; Burn-Murdoch, Chap. 7; Walker, *Civil Remedies*, Chap. 10.
[67] S.I. 1993 No. 3128.
[68] 1907 Act, s. 5(5), as amended by Law Reform (Miscellaneous Provisions) (Scotland) Act 1980.
[69] Debtors (Scotland) Act 1987, s. 6.
[70] *ibid.* s. 24.
[71] *ibid.* s. 30.

Provisions) (Scotland) Act 1980 was intended only to implement the recommendation of the Grant Committee that the financial limit should be abolished,[72] and does not radically alter the previous law by conferring on the sheriff court jurisdiction to suspend charges or threatened charges on other decrees, such as decrees *ad factum praestandum*. Paragraph 2 of the Act of Sederunt makes it clear that any issued charge which it is sought to suspend must be one for the payment of money. Suspension cannot competently be invoked in the sheriff court to review the merits of a decree.[73] It is, however, competent where the suspender contends that he has implemented the decree upon which the charge proceeds.[74] It has been held to be competent in a suspension to inquire into allegations of fraud in relation to a deed which was the basis of a decree of registration,[75] but it seems anomalous that issues appropriate to an action of reduction should be disposed of in a summary application in the sheriff court. In order to determine whether the sheriff court has privative jurisdiction in a suspension by virtue of the value rule,[76] it is necessary to take account of any expenses decerned for in the decree,[77] but matters extrinsic to the subject of the action cannot be considered.[78] The Court of Session may, however, suspend a charge or threatened charge which is not warranted by the decree on which it purports to proceed, whatever the value of the cause.[79]

Jurisdiction

Paragraph 2 of the Act of Sederunt provides that where a charge has **24.13** been executed the person charged may apply for suspension to the sheriff in the sheriff court having jurisdiction over him.[80] It is thought that the rule does not make it incompetent for him to apply in the sheriff court having jurisdiction over the holder of the decree. Where the charge is only threatened, the suspender should apply to the latter court.

Procedure

The procedure is by way of summary application.[81] In the initial writ **24.14** craves for interdict and interim interdict are often added to the crave for suspension, for example where a poinding has been executed or a warrant for sale of the poinded goods granted.[82] It is usual to grant interim interdict[83] because in most cases the pursuer's object in raising the action would be defeated if diligence were to be executed. In exceptional cases,

---

72 Grant Report, para. 159.

73 *Blandford v. Corsock Church of Scotland*, 1950 S.L.T. (Sh. Ct.) 37; *Lamont v. Hall*, 1964 S.L.T. (Sh. Ct.) 25.

74 *Brown v. Brown*, 1971 S.C. 22.

75 *Maclachlan v. Glasgow*, 1925 S.L.T. (Sh. Ct.) 77.

76 paras 2.26 to 2.34; *Bryson v. Belhaven Engineering and Motors Ltd* (1908) 15 S.L.T. 1043.

77 *Aitchison v. McDonald*, 1911 S.C. 174; *Lamont, supra.*

78 *Brown & Critchley v. Decorative Art Journals Co.*, 1922 S.C. 192.

79 *Aitchison, supra.*

80 S.I. 1993 No. 3128, para. 2.

81 The Act of Sederunt is entitled "Summary Suspension", the heading of para. 2 is "Summary application for suspension of charge", and para. 3(1) directs the sheriff to "proceed to dispose of the cause in a summary manner". Procedure in summary applications is regulated by the Sheriff Court Summary Application Rules 1993 (S.I. 1993 No. 3240) and is discussed in Chap. 26.

82 Graham Stewart, pp. 757–759; Scott Robinson, p. 39.

83 Graham Stewart, p. 759; Burn-Murdoch, p. 198.

however, for example where valuable goods are likely to deteriorate in the event of delay, the balance of convenience may not favour the postponement of diligence.[84]

24.15 A caveat may be lodged against the suspension of a charge.[85] In that event the first step is to order a hearing, as in cases where a caveat against an interim interdict has been lodged.[86] In other cases the sheriff first considers whether to make an order for caution or consignation. Where the application relates to a threatened charge, such an order appears to be within his discretion. Where, however, it relates to a charge which has been executed, paragraph 3(1) of the Act of Sederunt requires that sufficient caution be found in the hands of the sheriff clerk for the sum charged for with interest thereon, and expenses, and a further sum to be fixed by the sheriff in respect of expenses to be incurred in the suspension process. It has been held that the sheriff has a discretion to fix such sum as he judges to be reasonable, which may be a lesser sum than the aggregate of those amounts,[87] but it seems clear that that view is not warranted by the plain terms of the rule then in force or the present rule. On caution being found, the sheriff may sist diligence, order intimation and answers, and proceed to dispose of the cause in a summary manner.[88] The sheriff appears to have a discretion as to the sisting of diligence at that stage. It is thought that where an *ex parte* application to sist diligence is made, the sheriff should appoint an early hearing thereon, however he disposes of the application.[89] A sist prohibits poinding,[90] but not arrestment or inhibition.[91] If objections are taken to the competency or regularity of suspension proceedings, the judgment of the sheriff on such objections may be appealed to the sheriff principal, whose judgment thereon is final.[92] That rule does not refer to appeals on the merits, but to objections to the suspension as a form of process.[93] Otherwise, the usual rules as to rights of appeal are applicable.[94]

---

[84] *Gillespie v. Cochran Dickie & Mackenzie*, Sh. Pr. Caplan, Paisley Sh. Ct, Feb. 13, 1985, unreported.

[85] Dobie, *Styles*, p. 68.

[86] See paras 21.86, 21.87.

[87] *Maclachlan v. Glasgow*, 1925 S.L.T. (Sh. Ct.) 77.

[88] S.I. 1993 No. 3128, para. 3(1). For a style of interlocutor see *Summerlee Iron Co. Ltd v. Duff*, 1920 S.C. 291.

[89] *cf.* procedure on an *ex parte* application for interim interdict: para. 21.89.

[90] *Keltie v. Wilson* (1828) 7 S. 208.

[91] *Miller v. Wilson* (1749) Mor. 15148; *Henderson v. Smith* (1750) Mor. 6563; *Clyne v. Murray* (1831) 9 S. 338.

[92] S.I. 1993 No. 3128, para. 4.

[93] *Wilsons and Clyde Coal Co. v. Cairnduff*, 1911 S.C. 647.

[94] para 25.29.

PART V

MISCELLANEOUS POWERS AND DUTIES

CHAPTER 25

SUMMARY APPLICATIONS

Definition

Both at common law and under statute the sheriff has jurisdiction to dispose of a great variety of business in a summary manner, that is, as expeditiously as the administration of justice will allow[1]: without delay and with as little form as possible, avoiding any unnecessary multiplication of procedural steps and dealing with procedure so as to meet the justice of the case.[2] The appropriate form of process for such matters is the summary application. The expression "summary application" means and includes, first, all applications of a summary nature brought under the common law jurisdiction of the sheriff and, secondly, all applications, whether by appeal or otherwise, brought under any Act of Parliament which provides, or, according to any practice in the sheriff court which allows, that the application shall be disposed of in a summary manner, but which does not more particularly define in what form it shall be heard, tried and determined.[3] Procedure by summary application may be directed by act of sederunt. Where a statute allows proceedings to be brought in the sheriff court but the form which they should take is not directed either by the statute or by act of sederunt, they will proceed by way of summary application if they can be classified as being of a kind which, according to the practice of the sheriff court, is disposed of in a summary manner.[4] All summary applications, unless the procedure is otherwise provided by statute or Act of Sederunt, are conducted under the Sheriff Court Summary Application Rules 1993.[5] A distinction must be made between summary applications and informal applications to the sheriff to perform a variety of administrative duties which do not form part of the business of the court,[6] such as the appointment of members of local valuation panels by the sheriff principal.[7] 25.01

In this chapter we give some examples of summary applications brought under the sheriff's common law jurisdiction, notice briefly some of the issues raised by certain applications brought under statute and consider the jurisdiction of the sheriff's civil court in summary applications and the procedure which is generally followed in such applications. Examples of applications brought under statute will be found in the following chapter, which deals with the miscellaneous statutory powers and duties of the sheriff. 25.02

---

1 *Hutcheon v. Hamilton District Licensing Board*, 1978 S.L.T. (Sh.Ct.) 44.
2 *O'Donnell v. Wilson*, 1910 S.C. 799.
3 1907 Act, s. 3(p).
4 *Muir v. Glasgow Corporation*, 1955 S.L.T. (Sh.Ct.) 23; *Director General of Fair Trading v. Boswell*, 1979 S.L.T. (Sh.Ct.) 9.
5 Act of Sederunt (Sheriff Court Summary Application Rules) 1993 (S.I. 1993 No. 3240).
6 *Glasgow Mags v. Glasgow District Subway* (1893) 21 R. 52.
7 Local Government (Scotland) Act 1994, s. 29(2).

Common law applications

25.03 It is hardly possible to compile a list of the many applications of a summary nature which are brought under the common law jurisdiction of the sheriff. They include applications to the sheriff to perform, under his common law powers as judge ordinary of the bounds, miscellaneous duties which cannot be performed appropriately by any other authority. Many such applications are made in circumstances of emergency and are of a nature which suggests that they must be disposed of summarily. If a solicitor is in doubt as to whether to proceed by way of summary application or to raise an ordinary or summary cause, he might consult the sheriff clerk,[8] although it should be remembered that the ultimate responsibility for ensuring that the correct procedure is followed remains that of the solicitor.

25.04 Summary common law applications of an emergency nature include applications for the making of orders relative to property which are required urgently, such as orders as to the management of a farm neglected[9] or deserted[10] by the tenant and warrants to sell goods which are perishable or which have been rejected[11] or have not been uplifted,[12] to sell stray cattle,[13] to seal repositories[14] and to carry back sequestrated effects[15]; and applications for warrants to disinter bodies[16] or to make post-mortem examinations.[17] It is also appropriate to proceed by summary application in order to obtain a warrant to cite witnesses and havers in an arbitration[18] or before a presbytery.[19]

25.05 An application for a warrant to disinter[20] may be taken as an example.[21] It is usually presented by a relative of the deceased[22] or by those responsible for the maintenance of the burial ground.[23] Any relatives who are not applicants are either called as defenders or, more usually, sign letters of consent which are lodged with the application. A certificate from the cemetery authority as to the feasibility of the disinterment is also lodged. If these documents are lodged, the application is often granted without further inquiry. Expenses have been

---

[8] Lees, *Pleading*, p. 159.

[9] *Brock v. Buchanan* (1851) 13 D. 1069.

[10] *Gibson v. Clark* (1895) 23 R. 294.

[11] Dobie, p. 101; Dobie, *Styles*, p. 463.

[12] Dobie, p. 101; Dobie, *Styles*, pp. 413, 461–463; Lewis, pp. 544–545.

[13] Dobie, p. 101; Dobie, *Styles*, p. 464.

[14] Dobie, p. 101; Dobie, *Styles*, pp. 157–158.

[15] Dobie, p. 101; Dobie, *Styles*, pp. 473–474; Lewis, pp. 262, 512.

[16] See para. 25.05. Authority to disinter may also be obtained from the Court of Session: *Mitchell* (1893) 20 R. 902.

[17] Dobie, p. 101.

[18] *Blaikie v. Aberdeen Ry* (1852) 14 D. 590, *per* Lord Rutherfurd at 591; *Presbytery of Lews v. Fraser* (1874) 1 R. 888, *per* Lord Ardmillan at 894; Dobie, *Styles*, pp. 41–42. Such a warrant may also be granted in the Outer House: *Harvey v. Gibsons* (1826) 4 S. 809 (n.e. 816); Ersk., IV, iii, 31, n. 183 (Ivory's ed.); Bell, *Arbitration*, pp. 349–350; Guild, *Arbitration*, p. 61; Hunter, *The Law of Arbitration in Scotland*, paras. 13.33, 13.36–13.38.

[19] *Presbytery of Lews, supra*; Dobie, *Styles*, p. 553; Lewis, p. 541.

[20] *Mitchell, supra*; *Stair Memorial Encyclopaedia*, paras 534–536.

[21] For forms of application, see *Encyclopaedia of Styles*, ii, 260–263; Dobie, *Styles*, pp. 133–135; Lewis, pp. 542–543.

[22] *Black v. McCallum* (1924) 40 Sh.Ct.Rep. 108.

[23] *Sister Jarlath, Petr*, 1980 S.L.T. (Sh.Ct.) 72; *West Lothian D.C.*, Linlithgow Sh.Ct., Sept. 20, 1985, unreported.

awarded in opposed applications,[24] but it seems doubtful whether expenses in such applications should be awarded as a general rule.[25]

Statutory applications

25.06 The great majority of summary applications are brought under particular statutes or acts of sederunt. By such means the sheriff is required to discharge a multiplicity of functions, some of which are not strictly comparable either to his ordinary civil jurisdiction or to his criminal jurisdiction but are imposed upon him, as local judge, in the public interest.[26] Many examples of such applications are given in the next chapter. There are two general problems which often arise when such an application is under consideration, due to the terms of the statute under which the application is presented. First, where the statute provides for an appeal to the sheriff against an act or decision of an administrative body, such as a local authority, it may not specify the scope of the appeal and the powers of the sheriff to interfere with the act or decision. Secondly, many statutes, whether providing for such appeals or for other applications, fail to state explicitly whether there is to be any appeal from the sheriff's decision and afford no guidance as to the nature and scope of any appeal: they do not specify whether it might lie from the sheriff to the sheriff principal or from the sheriff court to the Court of Session, or whether it is to be on fact or law, or on both fact and law. The second problem is discussed later in this chapter.[27] We discuss the first in the following paragraphs.

25.07 The first problem has been examined fully in the undernoted papers.[28] Upon a consideration of the great variety of statutory provisions relative to appeals to the sheriff from acts or decisions of administrative bodies, the writer classifies the provisions into three broad categories: (a) those in which the sheriff's powers of review are not precisely defined; (b) those where Parliament has specified certain states of fact which the sheriff must find to exist before he can uphold the decision under challenge[29]; and (c) those where Parliament has narrowed the grounds of review by restricting them principally to areas of jurisdictional or other legal error, to the exclusion of review of merits or policy.[30]

25.08 The majority of the provisions empowering the sheriff to entertain appeals from the acts or decisions of administrative bodies fall into category (a), so that in such appeals the terms of the statute do not give the sheriff any indication of the approach he should adopt or the tests he should apply in disposing of the appeal. The most recent authoritative guidance on the matter is provided by *Glasgow Corporation v. Glasgow Churches Council*,[31] from which it appears that the sheriff's function in

---

24 *McGruer* (1898) 15 Sh.Ct.Rep. 38; *Black, supra.*

25 See paras 25.46 and 25.47.

26 *Glasgow Corporation v. Glasgow Churches Council*, 1944 S.C. 97, *per* L.P. Cooper at 125–126; *Arcari v. Dumbartonshire C.C.*, 1948 S.C. 62; *Campbell v. Herron*, 1948 J.C. 127, *per* L.J.-C. Thomson at 130.

27 paras 25.36 to 25.45.

28 C.M.G. Himsworth, "Scottish Local Authorities and the Sheriff", 1984 J.R. 63, and "Administrative Appeals to the Sheriff" (unpublished). The latter article is commended to the attention of sheriffs and practitioners.

29 *e.g.* Education (Scotland) Act 1980, s. 28F(5) (inserted by the Education (Scotland) Act 1981, s. 1); Mental Health (Scotland) Act 1984, ss. 33(4), 50(5).

30 *e.g.* Licensing (Scotland) Act 1976, s. 39(4).

31 1944 S.C. 97. See also *General Billposting Co. Ltd v. Glasgow Corporation* (1939) 55 Sh.Ct.Rep. 104.

such cases may extend beyond purely legal issues and include a consideration of the merits and factual basis of the decision under challenge. There are, however, dicta in other cases which indicate that in a statutory application to the sheriff in his administrative capacity relative to a decision of a local authority or other administrative body the sheriff is not entitled to interfere unless he is satisfied that that body has not reasonably exercised the discretion conferred on it by the statute, but has acted in a capricious or arbitrary manner.[32] That test is somewhat similar to the principles laid down in *Associated Provincial Picture Houses Ltd v. Wednesbury Corporation*[33] and *Wordie Property Co. Ltd v. Secretary of State for Scotland*[34] concerning the review of the exercise of discretionary powers, which have already been considered elsewhere.[35] These principles do not appear to have been declared explicitly and authoritatively to be applicable in an appeal to the sheriff where the scope of the appeal is not restricted by the terms of the statute, but it is thought that it is possible that they might now be held to be applicable.[36]

25.09 It is also possible that, in cases to which the dicta as to unreasonable exercise of discretion are not directly applicable, the scope of the appeal is not confined by these principles and the sheriff is entitled to explore the merits of the decision. There are, however, many dicta which indicate that when considering the merits the sheriff should pay due regard to the competence or expertise of the authority in arriving at its decision.[37] In more recent times the weight to be attached to the authority's decision has been particularly emphasised in dicta by sheriffs principal[38] and in courts of high authority in England.[39] On the other hand "there are many, many reported cases in which sheriffs have made decisions clearly based on 'merits' following the hearing of evidence and/or site inspections where there has been no reference at all to deference to local authority expertise".[40]

25.10 The recent statutory instrument[41] regulating appeals against abatement notices in statutory nuisance cases[42] specifies in great detail the grounds

---

[32] *Allen & Sons Billposting Ltd. v. Edinburgh Corporation*, 1909 S.C. 70, *per* Lord Low at 76; *Kaye v. Hunter*, 1958 S.C. 208, *per* L.P. Clyde at 211 (but see *Rodenhurst v. Chief Constable, Grampian Police*, 1992 S.C. 1 in which *Kaye* was overruled). See also *Small & Co. v. Dundee Police Commissioners.* (1884) 12 R. 123; *Campbeltown Building Co. v. Campbeltown Commissioners* (1894) 10 Sh.Ct.Rep. 16; *Glen v. Dumbarton Commissioners* (1897) 13 Sh.Ct.Rep. 244 at 248; *Port Glasgow Property Investment Co. v. Port Glasgow Mags* (1909) 25 Sh.Ct.Rep. 86; *Aberdeen Cemetery Co. v. Clapperton* (1918) 35 Sh.Ct.Rep. 102; *Butler v. Glasgow Corporation* (1930) 47 Sh.Ct.Rep. 72.

[33] [1948] 1 K.B. 223.

[34] 1984 S.L.T. 345.

[35] paras 18.10 to 18.12.

[36] *Rank Leisure Services Ltd v. Motherwell and Wishaw Burgh Licensing Court*, 1976 S.L.T. (Sh.Ct.) 70.

[37] *e.g. Rothesay Town Council, Petrs* (1898) 14 Sh.Ct.Rep. 189; *Gray v. Coupar Angus Town Council* (1905) 21 Sh.Ct.Rep. 214; *Biggar Town Council, Petrs* (1912) 28 Sh.Ct.Rep. 348.

[38] *e.g. Bruce v. Chief Constable of Edinburgh*, 1962 S.L.T. (Sh.Ct.) 9 (*cf. Giulianotti v. Arbroath Licensing Authority*, 1962 S.L.T. (Sh.Ct.) 18); *Prise v. Aberdeen Licensing Court*, 1974 S.L.T. (Sh.Ct.) 48; *Rank Leisure Services Ltd v. Motherwell and Wishaw Burgh Licensing Court*, 1976 S.L.T. (Sh.Ct.) 70; *Classic Cinema Ltd v. Motherwell D.C.*, 1977 S.L.T. (Sh.Ct.) 69. See also *Carvana v. Glasgow Corporation*, 1976 S.L.T. (Sh.Ct.) 3.

[39] *e.g. Stepney B.C. v. Joffe* [1949] 1 K.B. 599; *Sagnata Investments Ltd v. Norwich Corporation* [1971] 2 Q.B. 614.

[40] C.M.G. Himsworth, "Scottish Local Authorities and the Sheriff", 1984 J.R. 63; *e.g. Central R.C. v. Barbour European Ltd*, 1982 S.L.T. (Sh.Ct.) 49.

[41] Statutory Nuisance (Appeals) (Scotland) Regulations 1996 (S.I. 1996 No. 1076).

[42] Under the Environmental Protection Act 1990, s. 80(3).

and scope of appeal.[43] It is expressly provided by a recent amendment to the Firearms Act 1968[44] that appeals are to be determined on the merits (and not by way of review)[45] and that the sheriff hearing an appeal may consider any evidence or other matter whether or not it was available when the decision of the chief officer of police was taken.[46]

Few decisions by a sheriff in such cases are reviewed by the Inner House, principally, no doubt, because his decision is often declared by the relevant statute to be final. Consequently, the question of the proper scope of the sheriff's powers of review in cases where they are not precisely defined by the statute under which the appeal is presented does not appear to have been fully explored by the Court of Session in recent years. The present writer respectfully submits that an approach which might now be favoured could be on the following lines. The sheriff should not interfere with the decision under challenge unless he is satisfied either that it contravenes the *Wednesbury* principles or that, upon a consideration of its merits, it is plainly wrong. He should exercise his powers to interfere upon a consideration of the merits only when he is satisfied that the decision is wrong, not merely because he is not satisfied that it is right; he should pay due regard to the competence of the authority in arriving at its decision; and, in particular, the decision of a duly constituted and elected local authority ought not lightly to be reversed, especially where it involves matters of fact which were before the authority, or matters of local opinion and knowledge, or elements of local or social policy.[47] The nature of the procedure before the authority may be relevant. If there are any formal checks or safeguards against the authority's making an unreasonable decision, its decision should not be set aside except on very clear grounds.[48] Whether, when considering the merits, the sheriff may take account of evidence or material which was not before the authority, or of a change of circumstances since the date of its decision,[49] may depend on a proper construction of the relevant statutory provisions. If the appeal to the sheriff is to be regarded as an extension of the original decision-making function of the authority, such matters may be considered: if, on the other hand, the appeal is to be regarded simply as a process for enabling that decision to be reviewed, they may not.[50] **25.11**

Jurisdiction

Since a summary application is a civil proceeding competent in the sheriff court it is an action[51] to which the general statutory provisions as to jurisdiction[52] apply, so far as appropriate. It is thought[53] that a defender **25.12**

---

[43] See para. 26.345.
[44] c. 27; amended by the Firearms (Amendment) Act 1997, s. 41.
[45] Firearms Act 1968, s. 44(2).
[46] *ibid.* s. 44(3).
[47] *Bruce*; *Prise*; *Rank Leisure Services Ltd*; *Carvana*; *Stepney Borough Council*; *Sagnata Investment Ltd, supra.*
[48] *Classic Cinema Ltd, supra.*
[49] para. 18.113; *Carvana, supra.*
[50] *R. v. Immigration Appeal Tribunal, ex p. Weerasuriya* [1983] 1 All E.R. 195 at 201; *R. v. Immigration Appeal Tribunal, ex p. Kotecha* [1983] 1 W.L.R. 487 at 493.
[51] 1907 Act, s. 3(d).
[52] 1907 Act, ss. 4, 6. S. 6 applies only in so far as jurisdiction is not determined by the Civil Jurisdiction and Judgments Act 1982, Sched. 8.
[53] Dobie, p. 103.

in a summary application may prorogate the jurisdiction of the court[54]; indeed, rule 4(3) of the Summary Application Rules acknowledges this by implication. An enactment which makes provision for a statutory application may specify the court in which it must be brought[55] but, in any event, there is provision for the remit, on cause shown, of a summary application to another sheriff court,[56] even where a plea of no jurisdiction has been sustained.[57]

Procedure

The judge

25.13 The majority of summary applications, whether at common law or under statute, are disposed of by the sheriff. A summary application brought at common law may be disposed of by either the sheriff principal[58] or the sheriff, and the normal rights of appeal are competent. A statutory appeal or application may also be disposed of by either judge, unless the statute under which it is presented otherwise provides, either expressly or by clear implication[59]: but whether there is a right of appeal depends on the terms of the relevant enactment and the nature of the decision.[60] In any event the application, whether brought at common law or under statute, first calls before the sheriff, and where it is thought appropriate that it should be disposed of by the sheriff principal, that takes place by arrangement. In many courts there are general arrangements, approved by the sheriff principal, for the disposal of various classes of summary applications.

General rules

25.14 The procedure in summary applications is subject to to section 50 of the 1907 Act and the Sheriff Court Summary Application Rules 1993.[61] The following paragraphs are concerned only with the general rules and practices in summary applications. In appeals and applications under particular enactments special procedural rules may be prescribed by the relevant statute or act of sederunt. Reference is made to such rules in the following chapter under the headings of the appropriate statutes. If no act of sederunt has been made under the relevant statute, the application may nevertheless fall within the statutory definition of "summary application"[62] and thus be subject to the general rules and practices of the court in such applications.[63]

25.15 The principal statutory provision of general application is section 50 of the 1907 Act, whereby in summary applications where a hearing is necessary the sheriff is directed to appoint the application to be heard at a diet to be fixed by him, and at that or any subsequent diet, without record of evidence unless he orders a record, to dispose of the matter

---

54 1907 Act, s. 6(j).
55 *e.g.* Children (Scotland) Act 1995, s. 80(2).
56 Sheriff Court Summary Application Rules (hereafter referred to as "SAR"), r. 21.
57 *ibid.* r. 21 (3).
58 *e.g. Sister Jarlath, Petr*, 1980 S.L.T. (Sh.Ct.) 72.
59 *Fleming v. Dickson* (1862) 1 M. 188.
60 See paras 25.36 to 25.45.
61 A.S. (Sheriff Court Summary Application Rules) 1993 (S.I. 1993 No. 3240).
62 1907 Act, s. 3(p); see para. 25.01.
63 *Muir v. Glasgow Corporation*, 1955 S.L.T. (Sh.Ct.) 23; *Director-General of Fair Trading v. Boswell*, 1979 S.L.T. (Sh.Ct.) 9.

summarily and give his judgment in writing. Wherever in any Act of Parliament an application is directed to be heard, tried and determined summarily or in the manner provided by section 52 of the Sheriff Courts (Scotland) Act 1876,[64] such direction is to be read and construed as if it referred to section 50 of the 1907 Act. Nothing contained in the 1907 Act affects any right of appeal provided by any Act of Parliament under which a summary application is brought.[65]

Rule 32 of the Summary Application Rules permits the sheriff to make such order as he thinks fit for the progress of a summary application in so far as it is not inconsistent with section 50. It is submitted that this power is wide enough to enable the sheriff to deal with any apparent *lacunae* in any statutory provision. Moreover, he has power to order intimation to any person who appears to him to have an interest in the application.[66] Unless the sheriff otherwise directs, any motion relating to a summary application is to be made in accordance with, and regulated by, Chapter 15 of the Ordinary Cause Rules 1993.[67] **25.16**

Time-limits

Time-limits are prescribed for all summary applications. Where the statutory enactment under which the application is presented prescribes a time within which the application must be made, it must be made within that time. The Summary Application Rules[68] provide that if no time is so prescribed, the application must be lodged with the sheriff clerk not later than 21 days after the date on which the decision, order, scheme, determination, refusal or other act complained of was intimated to the pursuer[69]; but the sheriff, on special cause shown, may in his discretion hear an application notwithstanding that it was not lodged within the 21-day period.[70] He has no discretion under the Summary Application Rules to hear an application lodged later than the time prescribed by any statutory enactment under which the appeal is presented,[71] nor has he any discretion at common law to dispense with any time-limit prescribed by statute which is mandatory rather than directory in character, except perhaps with consent of parties.[72] It may be that he has a discretion at common law to disregard failure to comply with a time-limit provision which is only directory and regulative of procedure, provided that no substantial prejudice has been caused to the opposite party, and the lateness of the application is due to exceptional circumstances of such a nature that it would be grossly unfair to enforce the time-limit strictly.[73] **25.17**

---

[64] s. 50 of the 1907 Act is derived from s. 52 of the 1876 Act, which was repealed by the 1907 Act.

[65] 1907 Act, s. 50.

[66] SAR, r. 5.

[67] *ibid.* r. 31. For OCR, Chap. 15, see paras 5.44 *et seq.*

[68] SAR, r. 6.

[69] *ibid.* r. 6(2).

[70] *ibid.* r. 6(3).

[71] Such a discretion may, however, be conferred by that enactment, *e.g.* Licensing (Scotland) Act 1976, s. 39(3); *H. D. Wines (Inverness) Ltd v. Inverness District Licensing Board*, 1981 S.C. 318.

[72] *Allen & Sons Billposting Ltd v. Edinburgh Corporation*, 1909 S.C. 70, *per* Lord Low at p. 75; *T v. Secretary of State for Scotland*, 1987 S.C.L.R. 65, considering *National Commercial Bank of Scotland v. Assessor for Fife*, 1963 S.C. 197; and *Sinclair v. Lothian R.C.*, 1981 S.L.T. (Sh.Ct.) 13.

[73] *National Commercial Bank of Scotland, supra.*

The possession of such a discretionary power would appear to be particularly appropriate where the sheriff's decision on the merits of an application is final. If, an application having been timeously lodged, it becomes necessary to lodge a further application out of time in order to bring in an additional respondent, the latter application may be regarded as truly a continuation of the former and hence timeous.[74]

Initial writ

25.18 The application is commenced by an initial writ,[75] framed in accordance with rule 4[76] and Form 1 of the Summary Application Rules 1993,[77] unless otherwise provided by statutory enactment.[78] In any statutory appeal or application it is necessary for the title and section of the statute or statutory instrument under which it is brought to be stated in the heading of the writ.[79] The 1993 Rules make it clear that whatever the nature of the summary application the applicant is to be designed "pursuer" and the respondent "defender".[80] A party carrying on business under a trading or descriptive name may be designed in the instance of the initial writ by such name alone.[81]

Citation and service

25.19 A warrant for citation, intimation or arrestment on the dependence may be signed by the sheriff or sheriff clerk.[82] The periods of notice are normally the same as those provided by rules 3.6(1)(a) and (b) of the Ordinary Cause Rules (21 days if the defender resides or has a place of business in Europe, otherwise 42 days), but if a shorter period of notice is to be given the sheriff, not the sheriff clerk, must sign the warrant.[83] If the sheriff clerk, for any reason, refuses to sign a warrant which he is entitled to sign, the party presenting the summary application may apply to the sheriff for the warrant.[84] Unless a time to pay direction may be applied for by the defender the warrant to cite should be in Form 2 of the Appendix to the Summary Application Rules.[85] The citation itself is in Form 3.[86] If the defender is entitled to apply for a time to pay direction the warrant to cite should be in Form 4.[87] In such a case the citation is in Form 6[88] and there must be served on the defender a notice in Form 5.[89] In all cases the certificate of citation is in Form 7.[90] The remaining rules governing

---

[74] *Edinburgh Corporation v. Kirkcudbright Education Authority*, 1954 S.L.T. (Sh.Ct.) 39.

[75] On the initial writ, see paras. 9.74 to 9.104.

[76] The provisions of SAR, r. 4 are almost identical with those of OCR, r. 3.1. The only differences are that SAR, r. 4(2) provides that the initial writ should not be folded and SAR, r. 4(8) (for which there is no equivalent in OCR, r. 3.1) provides that the initial writ must include averments about those persons who appear to the pursuer to have an interest in the application and in respect of whom a warrant for citation is sought.

[77] A.S. (Sheriff Court Summary Application Rules) 1993 (S.I. 1993 No. 3240).

[78] SAR, r. 4.

[79] *ibid.* App., Form 1; *Hutcheon v. Hamilton District Licensing Board*, 1978 S.L.T. (Sh.Ct.) 44.

[80] SAR, r. 4(1) and App., Form 1.

[81] *ibid.* r. 14. This is in identical terms to OCR, r. 5.7. See para. 6.43.

[82] SAR, r. 7(1).

[83] *ibid.* r. 7(2).

[84] *ibid.* r. 7(3).

[85] *ibid.* r. 7(4)(a).

[86] *ibid.* r. 7(4)(b).

[87] *ibid.* r. 7(5).

[88] *ibid.* r. 7(7)

[89] *ibid.* r. 7(6). Form 5 is identical to OCR, App. 1, Form O3. See paras 7.03 *et seq.*

[90] SAR, r. 7(8).

citation are identical to the equivalent rules in the Ordinary Cause Rules.[91] If, by an error in the choice of the form of warrant of citation, the application is served and begins its procedural progress under ordinary cause procedure, the sheriff may subsequently transfer the case to the summary applications roll.[92] If the defender fails to take timeous objection to the form of process, the error may be held to be of no consequence.[93] It has been observed that once a defender has compeared and parties are in court it does not matter that the inappropriate form of warrant was used, if no prejudice has resulted.[94] A party who appears to answer a summary application is not entitled to state any objection to the regularity of the execution of citation, service or intimation on him, and his appearance remedies any defect in such citation, service or intimation.[95] This does not, however, bar a party from pleading that the court has no jurisdiction.[96] It is possible to lodge a caveat in respect of an expected summary application.[97] The provisions thereanent in the Summary Application Rules are identical *mutatis mutandis* to those in the Ordinary Cause Rules.[98]

First calling

Absence of writ or parties. The warrant of citation specifies the date and time when the defender is appointed to "answer", that is, to appear or be represented, within the sheriff court house. The form of citation, Form 3, includes a note in ordinary language to the effect that if the defender does nothing in answer to the writ the court may regard him as admitting the claim and the pursuer may obtain decree against him in his absence. Usually the date specified is that of an ordinary court day. In some courts there may be a "summary applications roll". In other courts the case may call in the "procedure roll".[99] If when the case calls, the writ has not been returned or the pursuer is neither present nor represented, the application should normally not be dismissed but should be dropped from the roll.[1] The pursuer may thereafter lodge a motion to enrol the cause for further procedure and of new to grant warrant to cite the defender. When that motion is heard, the defender may move for dismissal, while the pursuer may move the sheriff to grant his motion. It is thought that dismissal will rarely be appropriate, unless the application has become time-barred. If the writ has been duly served and returned and the pursuer is present or represented while the defender is not, the pursuer may move for decree and the sheriff, having considered the application, may either grant that **25.20**

---

[91] *ibid.* rr. 7(9), (10) and (11) and 10, 11, 12 and 13 are identical to OCR, rr. 5.2(4), (5) and (6) and 5.3, 5.4, 5.5 and 5.6 respectively. See paras 6.14 *et seq.*

[92] *Thirtle v. Copin* (1912) 29 Sh.Ct.Rep. 13 at 20–21; *Borthwick v. Bank of Scotland*, 1985 S.L.T. (Sh.Ct.) 49. See also *United Creameries Co. v. Boyd & Co.*, 1912 S.C. 617 (where there is considerable confusion between "summary cause" and "summary application"); *Muir & Weir v. Petrie* (1910) 27 Sh.Ct.Rep. 151; *Purves v. Graham*, 1924 S.C. 477. *Cf. Tennent Caledonian Breweries Ltd v. Gearty*, 1980 S.L.T. (Sh.Ct.) 71, and see para. 13.50.

[93] *Comrie v. Gow & Sons* (1931) 47 Sh.Ct.Rep. 159; *Cormack v. Crown Estate Commrs*, 1983 S.L.T. 179.

[94] *Macgregor v. McKinnon* (1915) 32 Sh.Ct.Rep. 3 at 8.

[95] SAR, r. 17(1).

[96] *ibid.* r. 17(2).

[97] *ibid.* rr. 8 and 9.

[98] *ibid.* r. 9 is equivalent to OCR, r. 4.2. See paras 21.86 and 21.87.

[99] See paras 5.41, 5.42.

[1] This procedure was approved in *Saleem v. Hamilton District Licensing Board*, 1993 S.L.T. 1092.

motion or appoint such further procedure as he may deem appropriate. As a general rule, a summary application which is an appeal cannot be sustained by default.[2]

Transfer to another sheriff court

25.21 A summary application, like an ordinary cause, may be transferred to another sheriff court in terms of rule 21.[3]

Procedure where no hearing necessary

25.22 If the sheriff considers that no hearing is necessary, he deals with the application on a perusal of its terms.[4] It is said that in the majority of summary applications at common law the usual form of judgment is simply "Grants warrant as craved".[5] It is recommended, however, that such a style should be avoided unless the crave is in simple and unambiguous terms or any obscurity has been dealt with by adjustment and, if necessary, reservice.[6]

Procedure before hearing

25.23 If a hearing is necessary, the sheriff appoints the application to be heard at a diet, which he fixes.[7] The nature of the procedure prior to and at the hearing is in the discretion of the sheriff,[8] unless particular procedural steps are required by any statute or act of sederunt under which the application or appeal is presented. Except in very simple cases where there is no need for answers,[9] it is usual for the sheriff, at the first calling of the application, to order the defender to lodge defences or answers within a specified time and to allow parties to adjust the initial writ and answers up to a reasonable time prior to the hearing.[10] In such cases the pursuer is usually ordained to lodge a record of the pleadings as adjusted no later than a specified time prior to the hearing. Only if such an order is made is a party entitled to the expenses of making up a record. It is suggested that an appropriate period for adjustment would normally be up to 14 days prior to the hearing and that the record should be lodged not later than seven days prior thereto. It is understood that in some courts the warrant to cite in a summary application includes an order to the defender, if so advised, to lodge answers prior to the first calling of the case. This is no doubt by analogy with the procedure for minutes under rule 14.3(2) of the Ordinary Cause Rules. [11] However, it is submitted that, although this procedure has certain attractions, there is no authority for it. The form of warrant to cite

---

[2] *Muir v. Glasgow Corporation*, 1955 S.L.T. (Sh.Ct.) 23; *Ladbrokes the Bookmakers v. Hamilton D.C.*, 1977 S.L.T. (Sh.Ct.) 86; *Charles B. Watson (Scotland) Ltd. v. Glasgow District Licensing Board*, 1980 S.L.T. (Sh.Ct.) 37; and see paras 18.73, 18.100; *Saleem, supra.*

[3] *cf.* OCR 1993, r. 26.1, which is *mutatis mutandis* in terms identical to those of SAR, r. 21.

[4] Lees, *Interlocutors*, p. 38.

[5] Dobie, p. 102.

[6] para. 7.15.

[7] 1907 Act, s. 50.

[8] para. 25.01.

[9] *Kirkpatrick v. Maxwelltown Town Council*, 1912 S.C. 288.

[10] The statement in *Hutcheon v. Hamilton District Licensing Board*, 1978 S.L.T. (Sh.Ct.) 44 at 46 to the effect that there is no need so to provide since adjustment may take place at any time in a summary application is thought to be due to confusion with the former summary cause procedure.

[11] See para. 5.59.

in a summary application is clearly laid down in the Summary Application Rules[12] and it makes no provision for ordering answers.

At the first calling the sheriff should, if possible, ascertain from parties whether the hearing is to take the form of a debate or a proof, and his interlocutor should specify which it is to be. If it is not possible at the first calling for parties to be definite as to the form of hearing, the sheriff should fix a preliminary hearing some time prior to the hearing proper in order that the form of the latter may be determined. In that event the period for adjustment and the date of lodging a record will be related to the preliminary hearing rather than to the hearing proper. Any proof should be restricted to the averments made by parties in the pleadings.[13] A commission and diligence for the recovery of documents may be granted.[14] It has been said that if it appears that the cause cannot be tried appropriately or conveniently in a summary form, the sheriff may transfer it to the ordinary cause roll.[15] It seems at best doubtful whether in a statutory application it is competent for the sheriff formally to depart from procedure by way of summary application where that has been prescribed by enactment. In any event it is submitted that, whatever may previously have been the position, such a transfer would not now be competent as there are two separate bodies of rules for ordinary causes and summary applications respectively with no provision for a remit from one procedure to the other. There is, of course, no reason why a sheriff, in the exercise of the very wide powers which he has to determine procedure in a summary application,[16] should not direct that it should proceed along the same lines as an ordinary cause if he deems that appropriate. **25.24**

Record of evidence

At the hearing, no record of the evidence is made unless the sheriff so orders.[17] Accordingly, if there is to be a proof, the sheriff should decide beforehand whether to make such an order and, if he decides to do so, pronounce an interlocutor to that effect and have it intimated to the pursuer by the sheriff clerk in time for a shorthand writer to be instructed. It has been remarked that a summary application relative to assumption of parental rights (now a parental responsibilities order) is sufficiently important to justify such an order.[18] Further, where there is a right of appeal on a question of fact the evidence should generally be recorded in shorthand.[19] If the evidence is not recorded, the sheriff's findings in fact will not be open to review,[20] and any appeal will lie only on questions of law.[21] **25.25**

---

[12] SAR, r. 7(4)(a), (5); App., Forms 2, 4.

[13] *Rank Leisure Services Ltd v. Motherwell and Wishaw Burgh Licensing Court*, 1976 S.L.T. (Sh.Ct.) 70, *per* Sh. Pr. Reid at 73.

[14] *Strathclyde R.C. v. B*, Sh. Pr. Dick, Glasgow Sh.Ct., Feb. 17, 1984, unreported. SAR, r. 32 which empowers the sheriff to "make such order as he thinks fit for the progress of a summary application" is wide enough to cover such a procedure.

[15] *United Creameries Co. v. Boyd & Co.*, 1912 S.C. 617.

[16] 1907 Act, s. 50; SAR, r. 32.

[17] 1907 Act, s. 50.

[18] *Lothian R.C. v. S*, 1986 S.L.T. (Sh.Ct.) 37, *per* Sh. Pr. O'Brien at 42.

[19] *Director-General of Fair Trading v. Boswell*, 1979 S.L.T. (Sh.Ct.) 9.

[20] *Sinclair v. Spence* (1883) 10 R. 1077; and see para. 16.33.

[21] *United Creameries Co. v. Boyd & Co.*, 1912 S.C. 617 at 623. *cf. Hartnett v. Hartnett*, 1997 S.C.C.R. 525

Hearing

25.26 The sheriff is directed to dispose of the matter at the hearing "summarily".[22] The hearing is, however, a proceeding in a judicial process, in which it is necessary to observe the rules of evidence and any relevant principles of civil litigation, for example as to the recovery of documents,[23] as well as the rules of natural justice. While in principle the court administers justice in public, certain applications may be heard behind closed doors in the exceptional circumstances recognised by the common law[24] or in accordance with a justifiable practice of the court, and some statutory applications are prescribed to be so heard.[25] The hearing may be adjourned to a subsequent diet.[26] Since the sheriff is required to give his judgment in writing[27] he must make *avizandum* at the conclusion of the hearing but, as in an ordinary action, it may in some circumstances be appropriate for him to announce informally from the Bench what the effect of his judgment will be.[28]

Judgment

25.27 The direction that the sheriff must dispose of the matter summarily and give his judgment in writing[29] implies that he must issue his written judgment with the least possible delay.[30] The form of the judgment is in the discretion of the sheriff.[31] There is no formal requirement that the interlocutor should contain findings in fact and in law, or should be accompanied by a note.[32] It is recommended, however, that where the application is contested or where there is a right of appeal a note of the grounds of judgment should be appended to the interlocutor and, where evidence has been led, there should be findings in fact and in law,[33] since the parties and any appeal court are entitled to know the reasons for the sheriff's decision and, where evidence has been challenged or contradicted, the conclusions which he has drawn from the evidence.[34] Where no evidence has been led it is neither necessary nor desirable to include in the interlocutor findings in fact culled from the pleadings.[35]

25.28 In all cases the interlocutor should specify which plea is sustained as the ground of judgment.[36] Where the interlocutor disposes of an application which seeks an order in terms of a statutory provision, care should be taken to use the words of the statute without paraphrase or misquotation, since any deviation therefrom may create doubt as to the effect of the

---

22 1907 Act, s. 50.

23 *Strathclyde R.C. v. B*, Sh. Pr. Dick, Glasgow Sh.Ct., Feb. 17, 1984, unreported.

24 paras 5.19, 5.21 to 5.23.

25 *e.g.* Education (Scotland) Act 1980, s. 28F(3)(c) (inserted by Education (Scotland) Act 1981, s. 1); Children (Scotland) Act 1995, s. 93(5) which provides for all proceedings, including appeals, to be heard in chambers.

26 1907 Act, s. 50.

27 *ibid.*

28 para. 16.104.

29 1907 Act, s. 50.

30 As is expressly provided by OCR, r. 29.20.

31 *Lothian R.C. v. A*, Sh.Pr. O'Brien, Edinburgh Sh.Ct., July 13, 1979, unreported.

32 As is expressly provided by OCR, r. 12.2(3).

33 *Strathclyde R.C. v. T*, 1984 S.L.T. (Sh.Ct.) 18.

34 *Lai Wee Lian v. Singapore Bus Service (1978) Ltd* [1984] A.C. 729, *per* Lord Fraser of Tullybelton at 734.

35 Lees, *Interlocutors*, p. 5.

36 *ibid.* SAR, App., Form 1 expressly provides for the statement of pleas-in-law.

interlocutor and may lead to an appeal on the ground of error in law.[37] If the interlocutor enforces a statutory direction that something should be done "forthwith" which will necessarily take some time to do, it should not use the word "forthwith" but should either simply order the thing to be done, which will be understood as requiring it to be done within the days of charge, or, preferably, order it to be done within a specified time,[38] which should be a reasonable time.[39]

Appeals

Common law applications

Where a summary application is brought under the common law jurisdiction of the sheriff, an appeal to the sheriff principal against the sheriff's final judgment or other interlocutors appears to be competent by virtue of section 27 of the 1907 Act.[40] Similarly, it seems competent to take an appeal to the Court of Session against a final judgment or other interlocutor of the sheriff principal or sheriff by virtue of section 28 of the 1907 Act,[41] subject to the value rule.[42] Appeals against decisions in common law applications are thought to be encountered very rarely in practice. No doubt for that reason, no time-limit or form for appeals against such decisions is prescribed. Although the Ordinary Cause Rules as to appeals do not extend to summary applications, it is suggested that, in the absence of any obvious alternative, it would be advisable to follow the form prescribed for appeals in ordinary causes.[43] It has been held that if an application has been brought and has continued as an ordinary action, an appeal will lie as in an ordinary cause.[44] Whether the same view would be taken today is perhaps open to question.[45] **25.29**

Statutory applications

Introduction. Where a summary application is brought in terms of a particular statute, the statute sometimes either prescribes the extent to which an appeal will be available from the decision of the sheriff or expressly provides that his decision is to be final. Such provisions apply only to cases founded on and falling within the precise terms of the statute.[46] Many statutes do not make any express provision on the matter, and the question of whether an appeal is competent depends upon the construction of the statute and a consideration of the character of the jurisdiction which it confers upon the sheriff. It has often been observed that it is difficult to discover any systematic policy or pattern in the choice of statutory provisions relative to appeals in statutory applications, and much time and expense would be saved if enactments **25.30**

---

[37] *Lanark C.C. v. Frank Doonin Ltd*, 1974 S.L.T. (Sh.Ct.) 13; Lees, *Interlocutors*, p. 22.

[38] Lees, *Interlocutors*, p. 24.

[39] *Middleton v. Leslie* (1892) 19 R. 801; *Pollock v. N.B. Ry* (1901) 3 F. 727, *per* Lord Trayner at 739.

[40] *Arcari v. Dumbartonshire C.C.*, 1948 S.C. 62, *per* L.P. Cooper at 68; *McCallum*, 1925 S.L.T. (Sh.Ct.) 56. *Cf. Black v. McCallum* (1924) 41 Sh.Ct.Rep. 108.

[41] *Arcari, supra*. On s. 28 see paras 18.93 to 18.96.

[42] paras 2.27 to 2.34, 18.93.

[43] OCR, r. 31.4.

[44] *Ross v. Ross*, 1920 S.C. 530.

[45] See para 25.24.

[46] *e.g. Galashiels Provident Building Society v. Newlands* (1893) 20 R. 821; *Mackenzie v. Cameron* (1894) 21 R. 427; *Roxburgh Lunacy Board v. Selkirk Parish Council* (1902) 4 F. 468; *Stirling Parish Council v. Dunblane Parish Council*, 1912 S.C. 316.

making provision for summary applications were to state explicitly whether there is to be an appeal and, if so, to define its nature and scope by specifying whether it is to be from the sheriff to the sheriff principal or from the sheriff court to the Court of Session, and whether on fact or on law.[47]

25.31 **Mode of appeal prescribed**. Some enactments make specific provision for an appeal against a decision of the sheriff in a summary application by giving a right of appeal and laying down the method of review. Where that is done, all other conventional modes of appeal are excluded by necessary implication.[48] For example, it may be provided that there is an appeal from the sheriff to the sheriff principal, whose decision is final[49]; or that there is an appeal on a point of law from the decision of the sheriff to the Court of Session[50]; or that the sheriff may, or must, state a case for the opinion of the Court of Session on a question of law.[51] In the two latter cases an open appeal on the merits from the sheriff to the Court of Session is incompetent,[52] nor does any appeal lie from the sheriff to the sheriff principal, either on the merits or on questions of expenses.[53]

25.32 **Finality clause**. Some enactments provide that the decision of the sheriff is to be final.[54] Such provisions are often referred to as "finality clauses". In such provisions, as in others, "sheriff" includes "sheriff principal" unless the contrary appears.[55] In *Leitch v. Scottish Legal Burial Society*[56] there are dicta to the effect that an appeal is competent from a judgment of the sheriff on the merits to the sheriff principal, and the question whether that is correct has been said to be "vexed and doubtful".[57] In modern times, however, the question appears to have been seldom discussed, and it now seems to be generally accepted that unless the provisions of the statute otherwise provide, the merits of a statutory application may be disposed of by either judge but not by both.[58] The sheriff principal may of course dispose of the merits of an application after preliminary procedural orders have been pronounced by the sheriff.

25.33 The effect of the finality clause is that the decision of either the sheriff principal or the sheriff on the merits is final: no appeal on the merits lies

---

47 *Fleming v. Dickson* (1862) 1 M. 188, *per* Lord Neaves at 195–196; *Neill's Tr. v. Macfarlane's Trs*, 1952 S.C. 356, *per* L.P. Cooper at 359; *Ingle's Tr. v. Ingle*, 1996 S.L.T. 26; *East Kilbride D.C. v. King*, 1996 S.L.T. 30, *per* L.P. Hope at 33; W. J. D., "Appeals in Statutory Jurisdictions" (1946) 62 Sc.L.Rev. 77; Dobie, p. 533; Grant Report, paras 787–792, rec. 374.

48 *Lanark C.C. v. Airdrie Mags* (1906) 8 F. 802; *Dodds v. Ayr C.C.*, 1954 S.C. 86.

49 Railway Clauses Consolidation (Scotland) Act 1845, s. 150; *Main v. Lanarkshire and Dumbartonshire Ry* (1893) 21 R. 323. On finality clauses, see paras 25.32 to 25.35.

50 Licensing (Scotland) Act 1976, s. 39(8).

51 Building (Scotland) Act 1959, s. 16(3).

52 *Dodds, supra.*

53 *Waddell v. Dumfries and Galloway R.C.*, 1979 S.L.T. (Sh.Ct.) 45; *Troc Sales Ltd v. Kirkcaldy District Licensing Board*, 1982 S.L.T. (Sh.Ct.) 77.

54 *e.g.* Slaughter of Animals (Scotland) Act 1980, s. 15(4); Education (Scotland) Act 1980, s. 28F(9) (inserted by Education (Scotland) Act 1981, s. 1). His decision may be final as to certain questions: Conveyancing and Feudal Reform (Scotland) Act 1970, s. 29(3).

55 Interpretation Act 1978, s. 5, Sched. 1.

56 (1879) 9 M. 40, *per* Lord Cowan at 42; L.J.-C. Moncrieff at 42–43.

57 *Ladbrokes the Bookmakers v. Hamilton D.C.*, 1977 S.L.T. (Sh.Ct.) 86, *per* Sh. Pr. Reid at 87.

58 *Bone v. School Board of Sorn* (1886) 13 R. 768; *Strichen Parish Council v. Goodwillie*, 1908 S.C. 835; *Allen & Sons Billposting Ltd v. Edinburgh Corporation*, 1909 S.C. 70; *Arcari v. Dumbartonshire C.C.*, 1948 S.C. 62, *per* L.P. Cooper at 67; *Troc Sales Ltd v. Kirkcaldy District Licensing Board*, 1982 S.L.T. (Sh.Ct.) 77.

from the sheriff to the sheriff principal, or from either to the Court of Session. But a decision by either judge, other than a decision on the merits, is not final. Thus an appeal is competent if the issue relates to the regularity of the procedure before the sheriff, or his power to make the order against which the appeal is taken, or where the interlocutor appealed against is procedural in character.[59] An appeal will accordingly lie from a decision on a procedural matter,[60] such as an interlocutor which dismisses an application[61] or repels preliminary pleas[62] or allows a proof.[63] Similarly, an appeal is competent where the sheriff has refused to exercise his jurisdiction[64]; or where an interlocutor purports to dispose of the merits of the application but in truth the jurisdiction conferred by the statute has not been exercised, for example where an application is granted or refused in a party's absence without inquiry into the merits.[65]

Where the sheriff principal sustains a competent appeal from the sheriff, he may either remit the application to the sheriff to proceed as accords or take up the application and dispose of its merits himself. Though the latter course is competent,[66] it is thought to be seldom followed in modern practice unless it will clearly save time and expense.[67] It may not be followed if it is thought that an appeal on the merits may lie from the sheriff to the sheriff principal.[68] **25.34**

A finality clause which expressly excludes appeal from the sheriff does not oust the jurisdiction of the Court of Session to exercise a supervisory control over the proceedings in the sheriff court.[69] The court exercises such control by declaring a decision to be null or invalid, or by reducing the decision, or by suspension.[70] Notwithstanding the finality clause, the court may intervene by such means if there has been "some clear excess of jurisdiction".[71] Dicta to the effect that a decision of a sheriff which is impugned on the ground that it was pronounced in excess of his jurisdiction may be brought before the Court of Session for review, not only by such **25.35**

---

59 *Chief Constable of Strathclyde v. Hamilton and District Bookmakers' Club*, 1977 S.L.T. (Sh.Ct.) 78.

60 *Rank Leisure Services Ltd v. Motherwell and Wishaw Burgh Licensing Court*, 1976 S.L.T. (Sh.Ct.) 70.

61 *Leitch v. Scottish Legal Burial Society* (1870) 9 M. 40; *Roxburgh C.C. v. Dalrymple's Trs* (1894) 21 R. 1063; *Heddle v. Leith Mags* (1898) 25 R. 801.

62 *Lamont v. Strathclyde R.C.*, Sh. Pr. Caplan, Campbeltown Sh.Ct., Aug. 1, 1986, unreported.

63 *Leitch, supra*; *Bone v. School Board of Sorn* (1886) 13 R. 768. A decision on the question of the expenses of the application has been held not to be appealable: *Waddell v. Dumfries and Galloway R.C.*, 1979 S.L.T. (Sh.Ct.) 45.

64 *Penny v. Scott* (1894) 22 R. 5; *Leggat v. Burgh of Barrhead* (1902) 19 Sh.Ct.Rep. 7 at 11.

65 *Ladbrokes the Bookmakers v. Hamilton D.C.*, 1977 S.L.T. (Sh.Ct.) 86; *Edinburgh North Constituency Association S.N.P. Club v. Thomas H. Peck Ltd*, 1978 S.L.T. (Sh.Ct.) 76.

66 *Fleming v. Dickson* (1862) 1 M. 188; *Bone v. School Board of Sorn* (1886) 13 R. 768; *Roxburgh C.C. v. Dalrymple's Trs* (1894) 21 R. 1063; *cf. Allen & Sons Billposting Ltd v. Edinburgh Corporation*, 1909 S.C. 70.

67 *Charles Watson (Scotland) Ltd v. Glasgow District Licensing Board*, 1980 S.L.T. (Sh.Ct.) 37 (*sed quaere* whether the appeal from the sheriff should not have been taken to the Court of Session: see Licensing (Scotland) Act 1976, s. 39(8)).

68 *Ladbrokes the Bookmakers, supra.*

69 For the supervisory jurisdiction of the Court of Session generally, see *West v. Secretary of State for Scotland*, 1992 S.C. 385.

70 *Brown v. Hamilton D.C.*, 1983 S.C. (H.L.) 1, *per* Lord Fraser of Tullybelton at 42; and see paras 18.02 to 18.05.

71 *Bone, supra, per* L.P. Inglis at 771; *Moss' Empires v. Assessor for Glasgow*, 1917 S.C. (H.L.) 1, *per* Lord Kinnear at 6.

means but also by way of appeal,[72] have been seriously questioned.[73] An excess of jurisdiction may occur not only where the sheriff was not entitled to enter on the inquiry in question but also where, although he was so entitled, he has done or failed to do something in the course of the inquiry which is of such a nature that his decision is a nullity. For example, he may have acted in bad faith or in breach of the requirements of natural justice, or made a decision which he had no power to make, or decided a question which was not remitted to him, or left out of account, or taken into account, some factor which he should or should not have considered.[74]

25.36 **No prescribed right of appeal**. By virtue of sections 27 and 28 of the 1907 Act there is the same scope for appeal in a summary application as in an ordinary action,[75] but these sections do not affect any right of appeal or exclusion of such right provided by any Act of Parliament.[76] Thus, where the statute under which the appeal is presented neither provides a right of appeal nor contains a finality clause, it is necessary to examine its terms and the character of the jurisdiction which it confers upon the sheriff in order to ascertain whether the rights of appeal provided by sections 27 and 28 are excluded by clear or necessary implication.[77] The many statutes under which summary applications are presented require the sheriff to discharge a wide variety of functions which are more administrative or ministerial than judicial in character, and in order to determine whether appeal from his decision is excluded a distinction is drawn between applications to him in his administrative capacity and in his judicial capacity: while he is final in the former, his decision is subject to review in the latter[78]:

> "Many decisions show how difficult it often is to decide whether a given determination by a sheriff is truly a judicial determination of a court, issuing in a judgment within the familiar framework of our system of practice and subject to ordinary methods of review, or whether on the other hand the sheriff is merely discharging a special and particular function confined to him alone. In every case the answer must be found in the provisions of the statute in question."[79]

In the following paragraphs reference is made to certain principles and tests which may assist in the discovery of the answer in a particular case, but no single principle or test is necessarily conclusive: the answer always lies in the terms of the relevant statute.

Principles

New jurisdiction

25.37 "The guiding principle was stated by Lord Trayner in *Harper v. Inspector of Rutherglen*[80] in these words: 'Every judgment of an

---

[72] *Allen & Sons Billposting Ltd, supra.*

[73] *Arcari v. Dumbartonshire C.C.*, 1948 S.C. 62, *per* L.P. Cooper at 69.

[74] *Anisminic Ltd v. Foreign Compensation Commission* [1969] 2 A.C. 147; *Watt v. Lord Advocate*, 1979 S.C. 120, *per* L.P. Emslie at 130; *Brown, supra.*

[75] *Kerr v. Annandale Steamship Co.*, 1927 S.L.T. (Sh.Ct.) 31; *Arcari, supra, per* L.P. Cooper at 68; *Rodenhurst v. Chief Constable of Grampian Police*, 1992 S.C. 1; *MacIver v. MacIver*, 1996 S.C.C.R. 225.

[76] 1907 Act, s. 28(2).

[77] *Arcari, supra*; *Kaye v. Hunter*, 1958 S.C. 208, *per* L.P. Clyde at 210; *Rodenhurst, supra.*

[78] *Kaye, supra*; *Rodenhurst, supra.*

[79] *Arcari, supra, per* L.P. Cooper at 66.

[80] (1903) 6 F. 23 at 25.

inferior court is subject to review, unless such review is excluded expressly or by necessary implication.'[81] It was formulated more fully by Lord President Inglis in *Marr & Sons v. Lindsay*[82] in the statement that 'the general rule is that the right of appeal from an inferior to a superior court cannot be taken away except by express words. That is a rule which may be said to be subject to some qualification, because, if the jurisdiction exercised by the sheriff is a jurisdiction which is specially given to him by statute, and in which this Court has not previously had jurisdiction, it may be much more easily implied that the sheriff's jurisdiction is not only privative, but final, and not subject to review.' "[83]

The latter consideration has also been expressed thus: "that where a new and special jurisdiction is given to any court the exercise of it must be regulated entirely by the conditions of the statute under which it is conferred, and that in the general case remedies which might have been competent in an ordinary civil process are not to be presumed or inferred to be given by the particular statute."[84] The consideration that the jurisdiction is new may not, however, be conclusive.[85]

Established jurisdiction

If, on the other hand: 25.38

"a well-known and recognised jurisdiction is invoked by the Legislature for the purpose of carrying out a series of provisions which are important for the public without any specific form of process being prescribed, the presumption is that the ordinary forms of that court are to be observed in carrying out the provision, and, indeed, generally that the court has been adopted and chosen and selected because it is seen to be advisable that the ordinary rules of such court and the forms of its procedure shall be applied to give effect to the provisions of the legislative Act."[86]

This principle has been invoked to justify the competency of appeals from decisions of the sheriff relative to the assumption of parental rights by a local authority.[87] The principle has been held to be inapplicable, however, in decisions holding appeals under section 29(4) of the Mental Health (Scotland) Act 1984 to be incompetent, on the ground that that provision confers a special jurisdiction for administrative ends which is no more than an extension of pre-existing statutory powers in the field of mental health legislation which are exclusive to the sheriff.[88]

---

[81] The principle applies only to judgments and not to the grant or refusal of a warrant in the exercise of a statutory discretion: *Strain v. Strain* (1886) 13 R. 1029.

[82] (1881) 8 R. 784 at 785.

[83] *Arcari, supra, per* L.P. Cooper at 66.

[84] *Portobello Mags v. Edinburgh Mags* (1882) 10 R. 130, *per* L.J.-C. Moncreiff at 137.

[85] *Arcari, supra, per* L.P. Cooper at 67–68.

[86] *Portobello Mags, supra, per* L.J.-C. Moncreiff at 137.

[87] Social Work (Scotland) Act 1968, s. 16 (now replaced by Children (Scotland) Act 1995, s. 86); *Central R.C. v. B*, 1985 S.L.T. 413. It has also supported appeals relative to the recall of arrestments: *Irvine v. Gow* (1910) 26 Sh.Ct.Rep. 174; *Swan v. Kirk*, 1932 S.L.T. (Sh.Ct.) 9; *Mowat v. Kerr*, 1977 S.L.T. (Sh.Ct.) 62.

[88] *T v. Secretary of State for Scotland*, 1987 S.C.L.R. 65; *Ferns v. Ravenscraig Hospital Management Committee*, 1988 S.C. 158.

Tests

Is there a true lis?

25.39 "There is no single criterion which can be regarded as the conclusive test of whether it is the administrative or judicial capacity of the sheriff which is being invoked. It is, consequently, misleading to search for precise analogies from other statutes, for each one must be considered on its own terms. But from the decisions on this matter one broad distinction seems to me to emerge, which may not be conclusive in all cases, but may well determine the issue in many. It is this. If what is appealed to the sheriff is in a real sense a true *lis* between the parties, so that the sheriff has to pronounce a judgment between the respective claimants, then the appeal involves invoking the sheriff in his judicial capacity and his decision is subject to review by this Court–see the case of *Arcari*[89] and the opinion of the Lord President at the top of p. 68. If, on the other hand, the sheriff has not really to decide a question of law between the parties, and has not to review the determination appealed to him in the sense of weighing the considerations for and against, and deciding which way the balance inclines, but if he is only entitled to interfere with what has been done provided he is satisfied that a discretion conferred by the statute has not been reasonably exercised, then the appeal to him is in his administrative capacity—see the opinion of Lord Low in the *Allen & Sons Billposting* case,[90] at p. 76. For in this latter type of case the appeal is given by the statute, not primarily to determine a legal issue which has arisen between two contestants, but to provide machinery to protect the ordinary citizen from a capricious or arbitrary exercise of a discretion conferred on an official or on a public authority."[91]

How the proceedings originate

25.40 A further test, which may not be conclusive, is whether the proceedings originate in a manner which indicates that the sheriff is to act in his administrative capacity.[92] If, for example, the proceedings "do not originate (as in the ordinary 'action' or 'cause') in a formal demand by a litigant for a remedy from the sheriff court, but in a notice embodying a decision by the local authority, and, when the sheriff first appears, he is exercising what is in substance an appellate and not an original jurisdiction",[93] that may indicate that his decision is not subject to review. "Where a right of appeal to the sheriff is given from the act or decision of some outside body—such as a local authority, a licensing body or the like—and nothing is said as to review of the decision of the sheriff, the presumption is that while such an appeal can be dealt with by either the sheriff-substitute or the sheriff, the decision of either is intended to be final."[94]

---

[89] 1948 S.C. 62.

[90] 1909 S.C. 70.

[91] *Kaye v. Hunter*, 1958 S.C. 208, *per* L.P. Clyde at 211 (but note that the decision in *Kaye* was overruled in *Rodenhurst v. Chief Constable, Grampian Police*, 1992 S.C. 1). See also *Rossshire C.C. v. Macrae-Gilstrap*, 1930 S.C. 808, *per* L.P. Clyde at 811.

[92] *Allen & Sons Billposting Ltd v. Edinburgh Corporation*, 1909 S.C. 70, *per* Lord Low at 75.

[93] *Arcari, supra, per* L.P. Cooper at 67.

[94] Dobie, p. 535; approved in *Hopkin v. Ayr Local Taxation Officer*, 1964 S.L.T. (Sh.Ct.) 60; *T v. Secretary of State for Scotland*, 1987 S.C.L.R. 65.

Description of the tribunal

The language chosen to describe the tribunal invoked by the statute may be of significance. If that tribunal is "the sheriff court", that may indicate that the sheriff is to exercise his ordinary jurisdiction, subject to ordinary methods of review.[95] Where the tribunal is "the sheriff", which includes "the sheriff principal" unless the contrary appears,[96] there may be no room for an appeal unless there are grounds from the terms of the statute for the conclusion that "sheriff" means "sheriff court" as distinct from the individual judge.[97] Some statutory provisions invoke the jurisdiction not of "the sheriff" but of "a sheriff"; and while the expression "the sheriff" may be apt to signify in certain cases "the sheriff's court acting within its ordinary process", the expression "a sheriff" may seem apt only if the power is to be vested in an individual judge.[98] **25.41**

Nature of procedure

The statute may prescribe that the procedure is to be by way of summary application. As we have noted, however, that is not conclusive since appeal may be excluded by clear or necessary implication.[99] Thus, where the function conferred on the sheriff is in all respects clearly ministerial or administrative, the choice of summary application procedure will not be regarded as conclusive on the question of review.[1] **25.42**

Powers conferred

The statute may confer certain powers on the sheriff in terms which indicate that he is to act in his administrative capacity. Where it provides that the sheriff is to have the like jurisdiction and the like powers "as if he were acting in the exercise of his civil jurisdiction",[2] it is clear that the sheriff is to exercise a special and particular function and not the normal jurisdiction of the sheriff court.[3] Where the Act empowers the sheriff to deal with expenses the same inference may be drawn, since if the sheriff were exercising his ordinary jurisdiction he would have an inherent power to deal with expenses[4]; but the conferring of power to deal with expenses may not necessarily indicate that review of his decision is excluded.[5] **25.43**

Record of evidence

If the sheriff is not obliged by the terms of the statutory provisions to keep a record of the evidence, that may indicate that appeal is excluded: "that is just one of the characteristics of summary proceedings in which there is no appeal, because a court of appeal on the merits cannot possibly **25.44**

---

[95] *Portobello Mags v. Edinburgh Mags* (1882) 10 R. 130; *Neill's Trs v. Macfarlane's Trs*, 1952 S.C. 356; *Director-General of Fair Trading v. Boswell*, 1979 S.L.T. (Sh.Ct.) 9.
[96] Interpretation Act 1978, s. 5, Sched. 1.
[97] *Allen & Sons Billposting Ltd v. Edinburgh Corporation*, 1909 S.C. 70, *per* Lord Low at 75; *Rossshire C.C. v. Macrae-Gilstrap*, 1930 S.C. 808, *per* Lord Sands at p. 812; *Arcari, supra*, *per* L.P. Cooper at 67–68.
[98] *T, supra*; *Ferns v. Ravenscraig Hospital Management Committee*, 1988 S.C. 158.
[99] *Arcari, supra, per* L.P. Cooper at 68.
[1] *T, supra.*
[2] Mental Health (Scotland) Act 1984, ss. 21(5), 40(6).
[3] *Ferns, supra.*
[4] *Allen & Sons Billposting Ltd, supra.*
[5] *Arcari, supra, per* L.P. Cooper at 67–68.

exercise its function unless it has some record of the evidence on which the judge of first instance proceeded."[6]

Other statutory provisions

25.45 It may or may not be helpful to examine other provisions of the statute under which the application is presented, or the provisions of another statute dealing with a similar subject,[7] in order to ascertain whether any clear or necessary implication of the exclusion of a right of appeal may be discovered. In some Acts provision is made for a variety of applications, with special provisions as to appeal in some but not in others,[8] or for appeal against the grant, but not against the refusal, of an application.[9] The absence of express exclusion of appeal in applications other than that under consideration may not be significant if it is thought to be obvious for other reasons that the sheriff's jurisdiction in those cases must be conclusive.[10] Some provisions may be derived from earlier legislation on the same subject, and the former practice as to appeal under the earlier provisions may be significant. The history of the legislation may make it clear that throughout the functions required of the sheriff have been administrative or ministerial rather than judicial.[11] It would be of the greatest assistance to the citizen in Scotland, his legal advisers and to sheriffs and Senators of the College of Justice if parliamentary draftsmen were to adopt precise formulae on these matters.

Expenses

25.46 Where the statute or act of sederunt under which an application is presented empowers the sheriff to deal with expenses, he may do so in accordance with the general rules as to the awarding of expenses,[12] subject to any special provision in the enactment.[13] Where the enactment makes no provision as to expenses but the application is made to the sheriff in his judicial capacity, he has an inherent power to dispose of questions of expenses.[14] Where the application raises novel questions of difficulty or importance the sheriff may decide not to exercise his statutory[15] or inherent[16] power and make no award; but in a case involving only the straightforward application of settled rules he may consider an award appropriate.[17] As in ordinary and summary causes, expenses may be modified.[18]

---

[6] *Allen & Sons Billposting Ltd, supra, per* Lord Low at 75–76.

[7] *Neill's Tr. v. Macfarlane's Trs*, 1952 S.C. 356.

[8] *e.g. Arcari, supra, per* L.P. Cooper at 68.

[9] *Harper v. Inspector of Rutherglen* (1903) 6 F. 23.

[10] *Ferns, supra.*

[11] *T, supra.*

[12] Chap. 19.

[13] *e.g.* if he is empowered to award expenses against only one party, he may not award them against another party: *X Insurance Co. v. A and B*, 1936 S.C. 225.

[14] *McQuater v. Ferguson*, 1911 S.C. 640; *Society of Accountants in Edinburgh v. Lord Advocate*, 1924 S.L.T. 194; *Society of Accountants in Edinburgh v. Scottish Health Board*, 1924 S.L.T. 199; *Steele v. Lanarkshire Middle Ward District Committee*, 1928 S.L.T. (Sh.Ct.) 20. The distinction between the judicial and administrative capacities of the sheriff has already been considered: paras 25.36 to 25.45.

[15] *Muir v. Chief Constable of Edinburgh*, 1961 S.L.T. (Sh.Ct.) 41.

[16] *Society of Accountants in Edinburgh v. Lord Advocate, supra.*

[17] *Troc Sales Ltd v. Kirkcaldy District Licensing Board*, 1982 S.L.T. (Sh.Ct.) 77.

[18] *Duncan v. Dundee Licensing Authority*, 1962 S.L.T. (Sh.Ct.) 15.

If the application is made to the sheriff in his administrative capacity, expenses are not normally awarded, and if the question is raised the usual course is to find no expenses due to or by either party.[19] Expenses may, however, be awarded where the application, or the opposition thereto, is vexatious,[20] or where special circumstances exist,[21] such as "very special circumstances of litigious pugnacity".[22] Where an application is brought or opposed in the public interest, or the case of the party against whom an award is sought has been confined within reasonable limits, so that he cannot fairly be described as a "contentious litigant", expenses are not normally awarded.[23] **25.47**

---

[19] *McLean v. Renfrew Mags* (1930) 47 Sh.Ct.Rep. 42; *Tobermory Mags v. Capaldi*, 1938 S.L.T. (Sh.Ct.) 38, *Classic Cinema Ltd v. Motherwell D.C.*, 1977 S.L.T. (Sh.Ct.) 69.

[20] *Dumbartonshire C.C. v. Clydebank Commissioners* (1901) 4 F. 111; *Liddall v. Ballingry Parish Council*, 1908 S.C. 1082.

[21] *Butler v. Glasgow Corporation* (1930) 47 Sh.Ct.Rep. 72.

[22] *Lornie v. Perthshire Highland District Committee* (1909) 25 Sh.Ct.Rep. 124 at 128–129.

[23] *Liddall, supra, per* Lord McLaren at 1090, *per* Lord Dundas at 1092.

Chapter 26

MISCELLANEOUS STATUTORY POWERS AND DUTIES

There are very many statutes which confer on the sheriff court jurisdiction to discharge a wide variety of functions, including the hearing of appeals against administrative decisions of local or other authorities, the granting of search warrants and powers of entry, the appointment of arbiters and other matters. This chapter attempts to bring together a large number of these statutory provisions, grouped in chronological order under headings according to their subject-matter. It is not claimed that the list of provisions under each heading is exhaustive; and the method of grouping the provisions under headings is adopted only for convenience and has no other significance. **26.01**

I. Agriculture

Crofters Common Grazing Regulation Act 1891[1]

The sheriff is empowered to make an order remedying a breach of regulations as to the number of stock which a crofter may put on a common grazing.[2] The crofters' committee, any two interested crofters or the landlord may apply to the sheriff, who also has power to award expenses.[3] This application would appear to exclude other remedies.[4] Where the application is in respect of excessive stock the crave of the writ should be for an order to remove, failing which for warrant to sell.[5] **26.02**

Agriculture (Safety, Health and Welfare Provisions) Act 1956[6]

An appeal lies to the sheriff against a notice of the Health and Safety Executive[7] requiring the provision of sanitary and washing facilities.[8] Notice of the appeal must be given to the sheriff within 21 days of service of the notice, and the decision of the sheriff is final and binding.[9] **26.03**

Agricultural Marketing Act 1958[10]

The Act makes provision for the regulation of the marketing of products by the producers themselves. Boards are established to administer schemes approved by the Secretary of State; the boards have a duty to **26.04**

---

[1] 54 & 55 Vict. c. 41 ("the 1891 Act").
[2] *ibid.* s. 5.
[3] *ibid.*
[4] See *McMillan v. MacPhee* (1914) 30 Sh.Ct.Rep. 342.
[5] See Dobie, p. 549; Dobie, *Styles*, pp. 413, 414.
[6] 4 & 5 Eliz. 2, c. 49 ("the 1956 Act").
[7] Substituted by the Health and Safety (Enforcing Authority) Regulations 1977 (S.I. 1977 No. 746), Sched. 2.
[8] 1956 Act, s. 3(5), applied to Scotland by ss. 25(1), (3).
[9] *ibid.*
[10] 6 & 7 Eliz. 2, c. 47 ("the 1958 Act").

register certain contracts within 14 days of receiving an application for registration.[11] A person aggrieved by the omission of the board to do so may appeal to the sheriff within 21 days of the 14 days time-limit elapsing.[12] The sheriff to whom the aggrieved party may appeal is the sheriff within whose jurisdiction any party to the contract has dwelt or carried on business at any time during the period within which the appeal may be brought.[13] However, at any time before the appeal proceedings commence, the board and all parties to the contract may agree that the appeal should be heard by the Court of Session.[14] The Court of Session, on the application of the board or any party to the contract, may require an appeal to the sheriff to be remitted to the Court of Session.[15]

Agriculture Act 1967[16]

26.05 Under this Act, establishing the Meat and Livestock Commission, the Commission may hold such inquiries as they require properly to discharge any of their functions.[17] The Commission may by notice in writing require any person to attend to give evidence on any of the matters specified in the notice or to produce all documents in his possession or control which relate to any such matters.[18] Within 14 days of service of such notice the person served may appeal in writing to the sheriff on the ground that any evidence or document required by the Commission under the notice is not reasonably required for the exercise of the Commission's functions under the Act.[19] The operation of the notice is suspended pending the appeal,[20] and the sheriff may make such order as he thinks fit.[21]

Agricultural Holdings (Scotland) Act 1991[22]

26.06 On the termination of a lease of an agricultural holding a tenant may be required to leave the stock of sheep to be taken over by the landlord or an incoming tenant at a price to be fixed by an arbiter. This is known as a "sheep stock valuation".[23] If the arbiter fails to state certain particulars in his award[24] it may be set aside by the sheriff.[25] It is not open to the arbiter to seek to amend his award once application to the sheriff has been made.[26] The arbiter may, and must if so directed by the sheriff on application of either party, state a case for the opinion of the sheriff on any question of law arising in the course of any arbitration as to valuation of sheep stock.[27] The decision of the sheriff is final unless appealed to the Court of Session by either party and there is no further appeal.[28]

---

[11] 1958 Act, s. 18(1).
[12] *ibid.* s. 18(2).
[13] *ibid.* s. 18(5), applied to Scotland by s. 18(7).
[14] *ibid.* s. 18(5)(a).
[15] *ibid.* s. 18(5)(b).
[16] c. 22 ("the 1967 Act").
[17] *ibid.* s. 21(1).
[18] *ibid.* s. 21(2).
[19] *ibid.* s. 21(4), applied to Scotland by s. 21(12).
[20] *ibid.* s. 21(4)(a).
[21] *ibid.* s. 21(4)(b).
[22] c. 55 ("the 1991 Act").
[23] 1991 Act, s. 68(1).
[24] See ***Paynter v. Rutherford***, 1940 S.L.T. (Sh.Ct.) 18.
[25] 1991 Act, s. 68(4). See ***Bell v. Simpson***, 1965 S.L.T. (Sh.Ct.) 9.
[26] See *Duke of Argyll v. MacArthur* (1941) 59 Sh.Ct.Rep. 91.
[27] 1991 Act, s. 69 (1).
[28] *ibid.* s. 69(2).

At any time during the duration of a lease of an agricultural holding the landlord or tenant may require the making of a record as to the condition of the holding and any fixed equipment thereon.[29] The expenses of and incidental to the making of such a record are subject to taxation by the auditor of the sheriff court and the taxation is subject to review by the sheriff.[30] **26.07**

Where the landlord or tenant of an agricultural holding is a minor, or of unsound mind, the sheriff may appoint a guardian for the purposes of the Act; he may also recall an appointment and make another if necessary.[31] **26.08**

Unless express provision to the contrary is made by the 1991 Act, differences between landlords and tenants of agricultural holdings are to be settled by arbitration, except for a question or difference as to liability for rent.[32] Arbitration is to be by a single arbiter in accordance with the provisions of Schedule 7.[33] The expenses of and incidental to the arbitration are in the discretion of the arbiter but they are subject to taxation by the auditor of the sheriff court and that taxation may be reviewed by the sheriff.[34] The sheriff may sanction the appointment of an arbiter's clerk or other assistant where the parties do not consent.[35] The arbiter may apply to the sheriff for such an appointment, and the application should be disposed of quickly, with any necessary explanations being given by the parties orally.[36] **26.09**

On the application of either party, the sheriff is empowered to direct the arbiter to state a case for the opinion of the sheriff on any question of law arising in the arbitration[37]; the arbiter himself may state questions of law for the opinion of the sheriff.[38] It is competent to apply for a stated case under the Act only during the arbitration; once the arbiter has made a final award, there can be no such application.[39] If an arbiter is required by the sheriff to state a case he must state the question of law as contained in the sheriff's direction to him.[40] A second stated case has been refused on a matter acquiesced in when the first case was stated.[41] The application to the sheriff to require the arbiter to state a case should be served upon the other party to the arbitration, as well as upon the arbiter.[42] The opinion of the sheriff on any case stated is final unless appeal is taken timeously by either party to the Court of Session[43]; there is no further appeal.[44] **26.10**

---

[29] 1991 Act, s. 8(1).

[30] *ibid.* s. 8(8). For the purposes of the 1991 Act, the sheriff to whom application is to be made seems to be the sheriff having jurisdiction where the holding is situated: see *Shanks v. Nisbet* (1900) 16 Sh.Ct.Rep. 316.

[31] *ibid.* s. 77. See Dobie, *Styles*, p. 23.

[32] *ibid.* s. 60. See *Exven Ltd v. Lumsden*, 1982 S.L.T. (Sh.Ct.) 105.

[33] *ibid.* s. 61.

[34] *ibid.* Sched. 7, para. 17.

[35] *ibid.* Sched. 7, para. 19.

[36] See *Henderson* (1933) 50 Sh.Ct.Rep. 17; Dobie, *Styles*, p. 21.

[37] 1991 Act, Sched. 7, para. 20. See Dobie, *Styles*, p. 21.

[38] *ibid.* See *Turner v. Wilson*, 1954 S.L.T. 131.

[39] See *Hendry v. Fordyce* (1952) 69 Sh.Ct.Rep. 191; *Johnson v. Gill*, 1978 S.C. 74 (*re* determination of proceedings).

[40] See *Williamson v. Stewart* (1910) 27 Sh.Ct.Rep. 240.

[41] See *Earl of Galloway v. McClelland* (1917) 33 Sh.Ct.Rep. 351.

[42] See Dobie, p. 551.

[43] 1991 Act, Sched. 7, para. 21. *Jack v. King* (1932) 48 Sh.Ct.Rep. 242.

[44] *ibid.* Paras 20 and 21 do not apply where the arbiter has been appointed by the Secretary of State or the Land Court (Sched. 7, para. 22).

26.11 The sheriff may remove an arbiter who has misconducted himself[45]; he may also set aside the arbiter's award for the same reason,[46] or if the arbitration or award has been improperly procured.[47] It is competent to combine an application for removal with one for setting aside the award.[48] The remedy is that of setting aside the award, not of reduction.[49] The application may be at the instance of either party, or both, and, if at the instance of one party, the other as well as the arbiter will be called as defender.[50] Misconduct is not defined in the Act, but refusal by the arbiter to accept or act upon the opinion of the sheriff upon a point of law submitted to him,[51] and the issue of an award seven days later than the time allowed by statute,[52] are instances where the arbiter was found to have misconducted himself.[53]

26.12 The remuneration of the arbiter, in default of agreement, is to be fixed by the auditor of the sheriff court, subject to an appeal to the sheriff.[54]

26.13 Where any jurisdiction committed by the Act to the sheriff court is exercised by the sheriff, no appeal lies to the sheriff principal.[55] The only appeal from the sheriff is by way of stated case to the Court of Session.[56]

II. Animals

Dogs Act 1871[57]

26.14 Any court of summary jurisdiction, including the sheriff,[58] may order that a dangerous dog which is not kept under proper control be kept under proper control by the owner or be destroyed.[59] The owner may appeal against an order that the dog be destroyed as if it were a conviction.[60] By virtue of the Dogs Act 1906 these provisions also apply to a dog which is proved to have injured cattle or chased sheep. Should the owner fail to comply with an order issued by the sheriff he is liable to a penalty for every day on which he so fails.[61] Two quite separate steps are prescribed by the 1871 Act: an administrative order and a criminal complaint.[62]

---

[45] 1991 Act, para. 23; Dobie, *Styles*, p. 22.

[46] *ibid.* para. 24; Dobie, *Styles*, p. 23.

[47] *ibid.*

[48] See Dobie, *Styles*, p. 23; *Sim v. McConnell* (1936) 52 Sh.Ct.Rep. 324; *Dundas v. Hogg*, 1937 S.L.T. (Sh.Ct.) 1.

[49] See *Paynter v. Rutherford*, 1940 S.L.T. (Sh.Ct.) 18.

[50] See Dobie, *Styles*, pp. 22, 23.

[51] See *Mitchell-Gill v. Buchanan*, 1921 S.C. 390, *per* L.P. Clyde at 395.

[52] *Halliday v. Semple* (1959) 75 Sh.Ct.Rep. 188.

[53] See *Adams v. Great North of Scotland Ry* (1890) 18 R. (H.L.), 1 *per* Lord Watson at 8; *Arbuthnott v. Williamson* (1909) 25 Sh.Ct.Rep. 255.

[54] 1991 Act, s. 63(3)(b).

[55] *ibid.* s. 67. In terms of the Sheriff Courts (Scotland) Act 1971 (c. 58), s. 4, and the Interpretation Act 1978 (c. 30), Sched. 1, either the sheriff or the sheriff principal is entitled to exercise the jurisdiction.

[56] *Cathcart v. Board of Agriculture*, 1915 S.C. 166.

[57] 34 & 35 Vict. c. 56 ("the 1871 Act").

[58] *ibid.* s. 2 specifies "any court of summary jurisdiction".

[59] *ibid.* s. 2, as amended; see also Dogs Act 1906 (6 Edw. 7, c. 32), s. 1(4).

[60] *ibid.* s. 2, as amended.

[61] *ibid.*; see also Dogs Act 1906, s. 1(4).

[62] *Haldane v. Allan*, 1956 S.L.T. 325; see also *R. v. Dunmow Justices, ex p. Anderson* [1964] 1 W.L.R. 1039.

Protection of Animals (Scotland) Act 1912[63]

On the conviction of a person of an offence of cruelty towards an animal[64] the sheriff may order the destruction of the animal.[65] Unless the owner assents to such an order it may not be made without the evidence of a registered veterinary surgeon.[66] The expenses of destroying the animal may be ordered by the sheriff to be paid by the owner; such expenses are recoverable summarily as a civil debt.[67] **26.15**

The sheriff has the power to deprive a person of the ownership of the animal if he is convicted of cruelty towards it.[68] Before such an order is made the sheriff must be satisfied on the evidence available that the animal would be exposed to further cruelty if it continued to be owned by the present owner.[69] **26.16**

A person who is convicted of a second or subsequent offence of cruelty to an animal under the 1912 Act may be disqualified for such period as the court thinks fit for having custody of any animal or any animal of a kind specified in the order.[70] A disqualified person may, after twelve months from the date of the order imposing disqualification, apply to the sheriff who imposed it, who may remove it.[71] **26.16a**

In any proceedings under the Act the sheriff may cite anyone to produce the animal concerned if this is possible without further cruelty to it[72]; such citation may be issued only after reasonable notice has been given to any person against whom proceedings have been instituted and who is not the owner of the animal.[73] **26.17**

Performing Animals (Regulation) Act 1925[74]

Where it is proved to the satisfaction of a sheriff[75] on a complaint by a constable or an officer of a local authority[76] that the training or exhibition of any performing animal has been accompanied by cruelty he may make an order prohibiting, or imposing conditions on, the training or exhibition.[77] **26.18**

Pet Animals Act 1951[78]

Any person aggrieved by the refusal of a local authority[79] to grant a licence for keeping a pet shop, or by a condition in the grant of such **26.19**

---

63 2 & 3 Geo. 5, c. 14 ("the 1912 Act").
64 Within the meaning of the 1912 Act, s. 13.
65 1912 Act, s. 2, which applies if it would be cruel to keep the animal alive.
66 *ibid.*
67 *ibid.*
68 *ibid.* s. 3.
69 *ibid.*
70 Protection of Animals (Amendment) Act 1954 (2 & 3 Eliz. 2, c.40), s. 1(1)
71 *ibid.* s. 1(3).
72 1912 Act, s. 12(1).
73 *ibid.*
74 15 & 16 Geo. 5, c. 38 ("the 1925 Act").
75 *ibid.* s. 6(b).
76 *ibid.* s. 6(a), as amended by Local Government etc. (Scotland) Act 1994 (c. 39), s. 180(1) and Sched. 13, para. 13.
77 1925 Act, s. 2(1).
78 14 & 15 Geo. 6, c. 35 ("the 1951 Act").
79 *ibid.* s. 7(3), as amended by Local Government etc. (Scotland) Act 1994 (c. 39), s.180 (1) and Sched. 13, para. 36.

a licence, may appeal to the sheriff[80] having jurisdiction in the place where the premises are situated, who may give directions as to the issue of a licence.[81]

Animal Boarding Establishments Act 1963[82]

26.20 A licence is required for keeping a boarding establishment for animals.[83] Any person aggrieved by the refusal of a local authority[84] to grant such a licence or by any condition subject to which it is granted may appeal to the sheriff[85] who may give directions as to the issue of a licence.[86]

26.21 If a person is convicted of any offence under this Act or the Protection of Animals (Scotland) Act 1912,[87] or the Pet Animals Act 1951,[88] the court by which he is convicted may, by order, cancel any licence held under this Act and disqualify him from holding such a licence.[89] The disqualified person may appeal to the High Court of Justiciary against either order, the operation of which may be suspended pending the appeal.[90]

Breeding of Dogs Act 1973[91]

26.22 A licence is required for keeping a breeding or rearing establishment for dogs.[92] Any person aggrieved by the refusal of a local authority[93] to grant such a licence or by any condition subject to which it is granted may appeal to the sheriff[94] who may give such directions as to the issue of the licence as he thinks proper.[95]

Guard Dogs Act 1975[96]

26.23 An applicant for a guard dog kennel licence, or a licence holder, may appeal to the sheriff against the refusal of a local authority[97] to grant a licence, or against the conditions to which the licence is subject, or against the authority's refusal to vary the conditions, or against the revocation of a licence.[98] The sheriff may, if he thinks fit, give directions to the local

---

[80] 1951 Act, s. 1(4) and (8).
[81] *ibid.* s. 1(4).
[82] c. 43 ("the 1963 Act").
[83] 1963 Act, s. 1(1).
[84] *ibid.* s. 5(2), as amended by Local Government etc. (Scotland) Act 1994 (c. 39), s. 180(1) and Sched. 13, para. 61.
[85] *ibid.* s. 1(4) and (9).
[86] *ibid.* s. 1(4).
[87] See paras 26.15 to 27.17.
[88] See para. 26.19.
[89] 1963 Act, s. 3(3), extended by Breeding of Dogs Act 1973 (c. 60), s. 3(3) to apply to convictions under the provisions of that Act, and also by Guard Dogs Act 1975 (c. 50), s. 3(4).
[90] 1963 Act, s. 3(4).
[91] c. 60 ("the 1973 Act").
[92] *ibid.* s. 1(1).
[93] *ibid.* s. 5(2), as amended by Local Government etc. (Scotland) Act 1994 (c. 39), s. 180(1) and Sched. 13, para. 91.
[94] 1973 Act, s. 1(5) and (10).
[95] *ibid.* s. 1(5); see *supra*, n. 88.
[96] c. 50 ("the 1975 Act").
[97] *ibid.* s. 7, as amended by Local Government etc. (Scotland) Act 1994 (c. 39), s. 180(1) and Sched. 13, para. 101.
[98] *ibid.* ss. 3(1), 4(1).

authority with respect to this licence or the conditions, and the authority must comply with them.[99]

Dangerous Wild Animals Act 1976[1]

Similarly, an applicant or licence holder may appeal to the sheriff[2] against the local authority's refusal, or conditions, or refusal to vary conditions, or revocation of a licence for keeping dangerous wild animals.[3] **26.24**

Slaughter of Animals (Scotland) Act 1980[4]

A person aggrieved by the local authority's decision to refuse, cancel or vary any registration as a private slaughterhouse[5] may appeal to the sheriff within one month of the date on which notice of the decision is served upon the person desiring to appeal.[6] The appeal is to be disposed of in a summary manner.[7] **26.25**

A person aggrieved by the refusal of the local authority to grant a licence as a slaughterman or knacker or by the revocation or suspension of such a licence may appeal to the sheriff within one month of intimation of such refusal, revocation or suspension. The sheriff's decision is final.[8] **26.26**

The sheriff may issue warrants authorising entry into premises by local authority officers for the purposes of the Act.[9] **26.27**

Animal Health Act 1981[10]

Where the local authority make an order under the Act (a consolidating measure dealing with many aspects of animal health and welfare) and compliance therewith is refused or delayed, the local authority may inform the procurator fiscal who may apply to the sheriff for a warrant to carry the order into effect. The warrant may be executed by the officers of the court in common form.[11] **26.28**

Zoo Licensing Act 1981[12]

A person aggrieved by the refusal of a local authority to grant a licence for a zoo, by any condition attached to a licence, by any variation or cancellation of a condition or by the revocation of a licence, may appeal within 21 days by summary application to the sheriff.[13] The sheriff may, without prejudice to any other power which he may have, confirm, vary or reverse the decision of the local authority and award such expenses as he thinks fit.[14] The decision of the sheriff is final.[15] **26.29**

---

99 1975 Act, s. 4(2); see n. 89.
1 c. 38 ("the 1976 Act").
2 *ibid.* s. 2(8).
3 *ibid.* s. 2(1).
4 c. 13 ("the 1980 Act").
5 *ibid.* ss. 4, 22.
6 *ibid.* s. 5(5).
7 *ibid.*
8 *ibid.* s. 15(4), as amended by Animal Health Act 1981 (c. 22), Sched. 5.
9 1980 Act, s. 13.
10 c. 22.
11 *ibid.* s. 92(3).
12 c. 37 ("the 1981 Act").
13 *ibid.* s. 18(1)(b).
14 *ibid.* s. 18(4).
15 *ibid.* s. 18(6).

Deer (Scotland) Act 1996[16]

26.30 The sheriff may grant warrant authorising any constable to enter any premises, or vehicle, if he is satisfied by information on oath that there is reasonable ground for suspecting that an offence under the Act has been committed.[17]

26.31 By virtue of an Order[18] made under the predecessor of the 1996 Act[19] an application for the grant or renewal of a venison dealer's licence is to be made to a council,[20] A person to whom a council has refused to grant or renew a licence may appeal to the sheriff.[21] The provisions for such an appeal are in terms broadly similar to those under the Licensing (Scotland) Act 1976.[22] An appeal lies from the sheriff's decision to the Court of Session on a point of law.[23]

III. Arbitration

Arbitration (Scotland) Act 1894[24]

26.32 The sheriff court has concurrent jurisdiction with the Court of Session in relation to the appointment of an arbiter or an oversman, except that where the arbiter appointed is or must be a Senator of the College of Justice, the Inner House of the Court of Session has exclusive jurisdiction under the Act.[25] The sheriff to whom application for an appointment is to be made is "any sheriff having jurisdiction".[26] The sheriff may appoint an arbiter or oversman under the Act on the application of either party to the agreement to refer to arbitration in any of three circumstances: (1) where the agreement is to refer to a single arbiter and there is a failure to concur in the nomination[27]; or (2) where the agreement is to refer to two arbiters and one of the parties refuses to nominate an arbiter[28]; or (3) where arbiters fail to agree in the nomination of an oversman.[29] The sheriff has no power to appoint an arbiter or oversman under the Act in other than these three specified circumstances.[30]

---

[16] c. 58 ("the 1996 Act").
[17] *ibid.* s. 27(2).
[18] Licensing of Venison Dealers (Application Procedures, etc.) (Scotland) Order 1984 (S.I. 1984 No. 922).
[19] Deer (Scotland) Act 1959 (c. 40), s. 25A(2), inserted by Deer (Amendment) (Scotland) Act 1982 (c. 19), s. 11.
[20] As constituted under the Local Government etc. (Scotland) Act 1994 (c. 39), s. 2 (1996 Act, s. 33(8)).
[21] S.I. 1984 No. 922, para. 4.
[22] c. 66, s. 39.
[23] S.I. 1984 No. 922, para. 4(11).
[24] 57 & 58 Vict. c. 13 ("the 1894 Act").
[25] *ibid.* s. 6, as amended by Law Reform (Miscellaneous Provisions) (Scotland) Act 1980, s. 17.
[26] *ibid.* s. 6. Rule 2(13) of Sched. 8 to the Civil Jurisdiction and Judgments Act 1982, which provides that the Court of Session has jurisdiction in proceedings concerning an arbitration which is conducted in Scotland or in which the procedure is governed by Scots law, applies to judicial proceedings in the course of, or following upon, arbitration proceedings.
[27] *ibid.* s. 2; see *Cowie v. Kiddie* (1897) 5 S.L.T. (Sh.Ct.) 331; *British Westinghouse v. Provost of Aberdeen* (1906) 14 S.L.T. 391; Dobie, *Styles*, p. 40.
[28] *ibid.* s. 3; see *McKechnie's Trs v. Meiklam's Trs,* 1909 2 S.L.T. 266, 340; *Highgate & Co. v. British Oil and Guano Co. Ltd,* 1914 2 S.L.T. 241; Dobie, *Styles*, p. 40.
[29] *ibid.* s. 4; see *Glasgow Parish Council v. United Collieries Trs* (1907) 15 S.L.T. 232; Dobie, *Styles*, p. 40.
[30] See *Bryson & Manson v. Picken* (1895) 12 Sh.CtRep. 26; *Twibill v. Niven & Co.* (1897) 12 Sh.Ct.Rep. 313; *McMillan & Son v. Rowan & Co.* (1903) 5 F. 317.

The application for appointment is in the form of a summary application. It is submitted that older authorities stating that an application which raised a difficult question should be raised as an ordinary action[31] are inconsistent with modern practice.[32] There is a right of appeal.[33] Expenses are normally awarded in contested cases.[34]

In many other statutes listed in this chapter, provision is made for the appointment of an arbiter or oversman by a sheriff.[35]

Law Reform (Miscellaneous Provisions) (Scotland) Act 1990[36]

This Act introduces the Model Law of Arbitration to Scotland.[37] Any request or application which may be made to the sheriff under the Model Law is to be made by summary application, unless proceedings involving the same arbitration and parties are already pending before the sheriff, when a note is prescribed.[38] **26.33**

IV. Armed Forces

Reserve and Auxiliary Forces (Protection of Civil Interests) Act 1951[39]

If a landlord's right to recover possession of a dwelling-house matures while a serviceman is on a short period of training, the landlord must apply to the sheriff for leave to recover possession.[40] Application must be made within 14 days from the ending of the training period.[41] **26.34**

Where the termination of the tenancy of premises leased by a serviceman for business or professional purposes would take effect during or shortly after military service, the serviceman may apply to the sheriff for a renewal of the tenancy.[42] The sheriff is empowered to renew the tenancy on such terms as he thinks reasonable.[43] **26.35**

V. Aviation

Civil Aviation Act 1982[44]

The Act makes provision for regulations to be made concerning, amongst other things, the refusal, variation, suspension or revocation of licences for persons who make available accommodation on planes.[45] **26.36**

---

[31] See *United Creameries v. Boyd & Co.*, 1912 S.C. 617; *Ross v. Ross*, 1920 S.C. 530; *Alison v. Blenkhorn* (1907) 23 Sh.Ct.Rep. 208; *Thom & Sons v. Burrell* (1929) 45 Sh.Ct.Rep. 187; *Glasgow Mags. v. Glasgow District Subway Co.* (1893) 21 R. 52.

[32] See Chap. 25 for a description of modern practice.

[33] See paras 25.29 *et seq* for rights of appeal in summary applications.

[34] Dobie, p. 554.

[35] The 1894 Act is excluded by Agricultural Holdings (Scotland) Act 1991 (c. 55), s. 61(1).

[36] c. 40. ("the 1990 Act").

[37] 1990 Act, s. 66, Sched. 7.

[38] A.S. (Proceedings in the Sheriff Court under the Model Law on International Commercial Arbitration) 1991 (S.I. 1991 No. 2214), para. 2.

[39] 14 & 15 Geo. 6, c. 65 ("the 1951 Act"), amended by Agricultural Holdings (Scotland) Act 1991 (c. 55), s. 88(1) and Sched. 11, paras 2–4.

[40] 1951 Act, s. 25.

[41] *ibid.*

[42] *ibid.* s. 38.

[43] *ibid.* s. 39.

[44] c. 16 ("the 1982 Act").

[45] *ibid.* s. 71, and Civil Aviation (Air Travel Organisers' Licensing) Regulations 1995 (S.I. 1995 No. 1054), reg. 11(2)(a), (5).

The Civil Aviation Authority must refuse to grant a licence if it is not satisfied that the applicant is a fit person to make available accommodation,[46] and may do so if it is not satisfied that the applicant has sufficient resources to discharge his obligations under the licence.[47] Similar provisions exist as to the revocation, suspension or variation of licences.[48] An appeal lies to the sheriff against the Civil Aviation Authority's decision that the person is not a fit person to hold a licence.[49] The sheriff may, and must on the application of any party to the appeal, appoint one or more assessors: any objection to a proposed assessor may be stated by any party to the appeal and must be disposed of by the sheriff.[50] There is an appeal on a point of law from the decision of the sheriff to the Court of Session.[51]

Air Navigation (No. 2) Order 1995[52]

26.37 An appeal lies to the sheriff from any decision of the Civil Aviation Authority[53] that a person is not a fit person to hold a licence to act as an aircraft maintenance engineer, member of the flight crew of an aircraft, air traffic controller, student air traffic controller or aerodrome flight information service officer.[54] The sheriff may if he thinks fit, and shall on the application of any parties, appoint one or more persons of skill and experience to act as assessor.[55] Any assessor must be appointed from a list of persons approved for the purpose by the sheriff principal.[56] The sheriff is bound to make a note of any question submitted by him to such assessor and of the answer thereto.[57] An appeal lies on a point of law from any decision of the sheriff to the Court of Session.[58]

VI. Betting, Gaming and Lotteries

Betting, Gaming and Lotteries Act 1963[59]

26.38 The licensing board[60] is responsible for the grant or renewal of a bookmaker's permit,[61] the registration of pool promoters[62] and the grant or renewal of betting office licences and betting agency permits.[63] Where an appropriate authority (*i.e.* a licensing board)[64] refuses an application for the grant or renewal of a bookmaker's permit, betting agency permit or betting office licence the authority must notify the applicant forthwith,

---

46 S.I. 1995 No. 1054, reg. 6(2)(a).
47 *ibid.* reg. 6(2)(b).
48 *ibid.* reg. 7.
49 *ibid.* reg. 11(1), (2)(a).
50 *ibid.* reg. 11(5)(a).
51 *ibid.* reg. 11(5)(d).
52 S.I. 1995 No. 1970.
53 *ibid.* para. 118(1): definition of "authority".
54 *ibid.* para. 117(1), (3)(a).
55 *ibid.* para. 117(6)(a).
56 *ibid.* para. 117(6)(b).
57 *ibid.* para. 117(6)(c).
58 *ibid.* para. 117(6)(d).
59 c. 2 ("the 1963 Act").
60 *ibid.* Sched. 1, para. 1(b), as amended by Licensing (Scotland) Act 1976 (c. 66), s. 133(1).
61 *ibid.* s. 2.
62 *ibid.* s. 4.
63 *ibid.* s. 9.
64 *ibid.* Sched. 1, para. 1(b), as amended by Licensing (Scotland) Act 1976, s. 133(1).

and the applicant may appeal to the sheriff having jurisdiction in the authority's area.[65] The appeal is by summary application,[66] and must be made within 14 days after such notice of the authority's decision has been served.[67] The licensing board is entitled to be a party to an appeal to the sheriff.[68]

The sheriff may uphold an appeal only if he considers that the licensing board erred in law, based its decision on any incorrect material fact, acted contrary to natural justice or exercised its discretion in an unreasonable manner.[69] The sheriff may reverse or modify the decision of the licensing board,[70] or may remit the case to the board with certain recommendations.[71] The sheriff may include such order as to the expenses of the appeal as he thinks proper.[72] An appeal lies to the Court of Session on any point of law within 28 days of the decision of the sheriff.[73] There is no appeal to the sheriff principal from the decision of a sheriff; the applicant may appeal to the sheriff or to the sheriff principal, but not to both.[74] **26.39**

An appeal lies to the sheriff against the forfeiture or cancellation of a bookmaker's permit: in this instance, the sheriff's decision is final.[75] The provisions of the undernoted Act of Sederunt apply.[76] The sheriff may make such order as to expenses as he thinks proper.[77] There is similar provision for an appeal against the forfeiture or cancellation of a betting office licence,[78] and here too the sheriff's decision is final.[79] **26.40**

Where the registration of any person as a pools promoter is refused or revoked, the person aggrieved may appeal by summary application[80] to the sheriff, whose decision is final and may include an order as to expenses.[81] The same procedure applies with regard to a council's revocation of a track betting licence.[82] **26.41**

---

[65] 1963 Act, Sched. 1. para. 24, as applied by Licensing (Scotland) Act 1976, s. 133(4).
[66] A.S. (Betting and Gaming Appeals) 1978 (S.I. 1978 No. 229), para. 3.
[67] *ibid.* para. 4.
[68] See *Joe Coral (Racing) Ltd v. Hamilton D.C.*, 1981 S.C. 285.
[69] Licensing (Scotland) Act 1976 ("the 1976 Act"), ss. 39(4), 133(4); *Ladbroke Racing (Strathclyde) Ltd. v. Cunninghame District Licensing Court*, 1978 S.L.T. (Sh.Ct) 50.
[70] *ibid.* ss. 39(6)(b), 133(4).
[71] *ibid.* ss. 39(6)(a), 39(7), 133(4).
[72] *ibid.* s. 133(4).
[73] *ibid.* ss. 39(8), 133(4); see *Charles Watson (Scotland) Ltd v. Glasgow District Licensing Board*, 1980 S.L.T. (Sh.Ct) 37, in which the s. 39(8) opportunity was not taken.
[74] See *Troc Sales v. Kirkcaldy District Licensing Board*, 1982 S.L.T. (Sh.Ct) 77; but see comments on 1976 Act in "Intoxicating Liquor" at paras 26.252 to 26.256.
[75] 1963 Act, Sched. 1, para. 28(1).
[76] A.S. (Betting and Gaming Appeals) 1978 (S.I. 1978 No. 229); see 1963 Act, Sched. 1, para. 28(2).
[77] 1963 Act, Sched. 1, para 28(2).
[78] *ibid.* paras 28A, 28D, inserted by Deregulation (Betting Licensing) Order 1997 (S.I. 1997, No. 947), para 5.
[79] *ibid.* para 28D(2).
[80] A.S. (Betting, Gaming and Lotteries Acts Appeals) 1965 (S.I. 1965 No. 1168), para. 4.
[81] 1963 Act, Sched. 2, para. 7, as amended by Local Government etc. (Scotland) Act 1994, Sched. 13, para. 59(3). The registering authority is now a council constituted under the 1994 Act, s. 2.
[82] *ibid.* Sched. 3, para. 13(3), as amended by Local Government etc. (Scotland) Act 1994, Sched. 13, para. 59(4). The registering authority is now a council constituted under the 1994 Act, s. 2.

26.42 If the sheriff is satisfied on oath that there are reasonable grounds to suspect that an offence under the Act is being, has been or is about to be committed he may issue a warrant authorising a constable to enter and search the premises and persons thereon.[83]

Gaming Act 1968[84]

(1) Gaming licences

26.43 An applicant for a gaming licence may appeal to the sheriff against a licensing board's refusal to grant or renew a gaming licence or imposition of restrictions.[85] The Gaming Board[86] may appeal to the sheriff against a decision by the licensing board granting or renewing a gaming licence and against the restrictions subject to which the licence is granted or renewed.[87] All such appeals are governed by certain provisions of the Licensing (Scotland) Act 1976[88] which are discussed more fully later in this chapter.[89] An appeal must be made within 14 days of notice being given of the decision of the licensing board,[90] and must be disposed of as a summary application.[91] The sheriff may include such order as to expenses as he thinks proper,[92] and may reverse the licensing board's decision or remit back to the licensing board.[93] An appeal lies to the Court of Session within 28 days of the sheriff's decision.[94]

26.44 The provisions noted in the above paragraph also apply to the transfer of gaming licences with the exception of an appeal against restrictions or conditions imposed on the granting of a licence.[95] Appeals to the sheriff also lie against the decision of the licensing board to cancel[96] or to refuse to cancel a gaming licence.[97]

(2) Registration of clubs and miners' welfare institutes

26.45 Part II and Schedule 4 of the Gaming Act 1968 provide a code for registration for gaming other than by means of machines.[98] In respect of premises within his jurisdiction the sheriff is the authority responsible for the registration of clubs and miners' welfare institutes under Part II and for the renewal and cancellation of such registration.[99] The Act specifies grounds upon which the sheriff must refuse to register a club or renew its registration,[1] and the restriction which he may impose on registration or renewal of

---

[83] 1963 Act, s. 51.
[84] c. 65 ("the 1968 Act").
[85] *ibid.* Sched. 2, para. 33(1).
[86] *ibid.* s. 52(1), defining "the board".
[87] *ibid.* s. 11 and Sched. 2, para. 34(1).
[88] 1976 Act, s. 39(4), (6), (7), (8), as applied by s. 133(4).
[89] See paras 26.252 to 26.256.
[90] A.S. (Betting and Gaming Appeals) 1978 (S.I. 1978 No. 229), 5, 6.
[91] *ibid.* paras. 3; in *Rank Leisure Services v. Motherwell and Wishaw Licensing Court*, 1976 S.L.T. (Sh.Ct) 70, it was said that the only restrictions on the sheriff's discretion to direct such proceedings are that the matter should be summarily disposed of and the judgment given in writing.
[92] 1976 Act, s. 39(1).
[93] *ibid.* s. 39(6), (7).
[94] *ibid.* s. 39(8).
[95] 1968 Act, Sched. 2, para. 61.
[96] *ibid.* Sched. 2, para. 45; A.S. (Betting and Gaming Appeals) 1978, para. 5.
[97] 1968 Act, Sched. 2, para. 47(1); A.S. (Betting and Gaming Appeals) 1978, para. 6.
[98] 1968 Act, ss. 9, 11(2), Sched. 4.
[99] *ibid.* Sched. 4, para. 1(1).
[1] *ibid.* Sched. 4, paras 9–12.

registration.[2] The determination of the sheriff on an application under Part II is final, and may include such order as to expenses as he thinks proper.[3]

Registration for gaming in clubs and miners' welfare institutes by means of machines is dealt with under Part III of the Act. The provisions are similar to those in the above paragraph, the sheriff being the authority for such registration.[4] His decision is final and may include such order as to expenses as he thinks proper.[5] **26.46**

(3) Machines for amusement purposes

Where the licensing board refuses to grant or renew a permit for such machines, or grants or renews it subject to a condition, the applicant may appeal to the sheriff.[6] The permit in question relates to the use of machines for entertainment purposes other than at commercial entertainments.[7] The appeal provisions of the Licensing (Scotland) Act 1976 apply to appeals under this section.[8] Thus, an appeal lies to the Court of Session on a point of law from the sheriff's decision within 28 days.[9] **26.47**

Lotteries and Amusements Act 1976[10]

(1) Societies' lotteries

Where the registration of any society for the purposes of a society's lottery[11] is refused or revoked by a registration authority,[12] the society may appeal to the sheriff, whose decision is final and may include such order as to expenses as the sheriff thinks proper.[13] **26.48**

(2) Amusements with prizes

An appeal lies against the refusal of a council[14] to grant or renew a permit for the commercial provision of amusements with prizes, or granting or renewing it subject to a condition.[15] The sheriff must not allow the appeal if he is satisfied that it was the duty of the appropriate authority to refuse.[16] The appeals provisions of the Licensing (Scotland) Act 1976 apply in so far as they concern the power of the sheriff to revoke, vary or remit the decision of the licensing authority; the restrictions placed upon when he may uphold the appeal; and the provision of an appeal from his decision to the Court of Session.[17] **26.49**

---

[2] 1968 Act, Sched. 4, paras. 13, 18.

[3] *ibid.* Sched. 4, para. 21.

[4] *ibid.* Sched. 8, paras. 1, 3 (applying certain provisions of Sched. 7, which relates to England and Wales) to Scotland.

[5] *ibid.* Sched. 8, para. 4.

[6] *ibid.* Sched. 9, para. 15; A.S. (Betting and Gaming Appeals) 1978, para. 8(1)(b), (c).

[7] *ibid.* s. 34(1).

[8] 1976 Act, s. 39(4), (6)–(8), as applied by s. 133(4).

[9] *ibid.* s. 39(8).

[10] c. 32.

[11] Lotteries and Amusements Act 1976, s. 5.

[12] A council constituted under Local Government etc. (Scotland) Act 1994 (c. 39), s. 2; Lotteries and Amusements Act 1976, s. 23(1) as amended by 1994 Act, Sched. 13, para. 104(2).

[13] Lotteries and Amusements Act 1976, Sched. 1, para. 6.

[14] *ibid.* Sched. 3, paras 1(1)(d), 1(2)(c), as amended by Local Government etc. (Scotland) Act 1994, Sched. 13, para. 104(4).

[15] *ibid.* Sched. 3, para. 12.

[16] *ibid.* Sched. 3, paras 6, 13.

[17] Licensing (Scotland) Act 1976, ss. 39(4), (6), (7), (8) and 133(4), as amended by Law Reform (Miscellaneous Provisions) (Scotland) Act 1985 (c. 73), s. 52; see *Aitken v. Motherwell and Wishaw Licensing Court*, 1971 S.L.T. (Sh.Ct.) 25.

VII. Building

Building (Scotland) Act 1959[18]

26.50 An appeal may be taken to the sheriff by a person aggrieved by any of the following[19]: (1) any decision of a local authority refusing to grant a warrant for construction or demolition of a building or for change of use of the building[20]; (2) any decision of a local authority under section 6(5) of the 1959 Act refusing to extend a period relating to a building intended to have a limited life[21]; (3) any decision of a local authority refusing to issue a certificate of completion[22]; (4) any order made by a local authority under section 10(1B) or 13(2) of the 1959 Act requiring the execution of operations[23]; (5) any order by a local authority under section 11 of the 1959 Act requiring that a building conform to any provision of the building standards regulations[24]; (6) any charging order made under Schedule 6 to the 1959 Act.[25] Notice of the appeal must be given within 21 days after the date of the decision or the making of an order.[26] The decision of the sheriff is final, but the sheriff may at any stage of the proceedings, and must if so directed by the Court of Session, state a case on any question of law for the opinion of the Court of Session.[27] The direction from the Court of Session may be before or after the conclusion of the proceedings.[28] No appeal lies to the sheriff principal on the question of expenses.[29]

26.51 The appeal provisions of section 16[30] also apply to an application to the sheriff under section 17[31] by a person who alleges that all or part of the expenses incurred in complying with certain requirements[32] ought to be borne by another person. The sheriff may make what he considers to be an equitable order on such an application.[33]

26.52 The sheriff may grant warrant authorising a master of works or other authorised person to enter and inspect premises on behalf of the local authority.[34]

---

[18] 7 and 8 Eliz. 2, c. 24 ("the 1959 Act").

[19] *ibid.* s. 16(1), as amended by Building (Scotland) Act 1970 (c. 38) ("the 1970 Act"), Sched. 1, Pt I, para. 5(a); Local Government etc. (Scotland) Act 1994 (c. 39), Sched. 13, para. 52.

[20] 1959 Act, s. 16(1)(a); see also s. 6B (2)(a), inserted by the 1970 Act, s. 4, which restricts the right of appeal.

[21] 1959 Act, s. 16(1)(b); see also s. 6B(2)(b), which restricts the right of appeal.

[22] *ibid.* s. 16(1)(c).

[23] *ibid.* s. 16(1)(d), (f). Section 10(1B) was inserted by the 1970 Act, Sched. 1, Pt 1, para. 3(b). For an example of an appeal against an order under s. 13(2), see *MDW Developments v. Kilmarnock and Loudoun D.C.*, Kilmarnock Sh. Ct, July 5, 1986, unreported.

[24] 1959 Act, s. 16(1)(e).

[25] *ibid.* s. 16(1)(g); see *Howard v. Hamilton D.C.*, 1985 S.L.T. (Sh.Ct.) 42.

[26] 1959 Act, s. 16(1).

[27] *ibid.* s. 16(3).

[28] *ibid.*

[29] *Waddell v. Dumfries & Galloway R.C.*, 1979 S.L.T. (Sh.Ct.) 45.

[30] 1959 Act, ss. 16(3).

[31] *ibid.* s. 17(6), (7).

[32] Under s. 10 (buildings constructed without warrant or in contravention of conditions of warrant), s. 11 (power of local authority to require buildings to conform to building standards regulations) or s. 13 (action in respect of dangerous buildings).

[33] 1959 Act, s. 17(6).

[34] *ibid.* s. 18(4), (9).

VIII. Building Societies

Building Societies Act 1986[35]

This Act repeals and replaces the Building Societies Act of 1962[36] and establishes the Building Societies Commission. 26.53

The Commission may require a building society to change its name if it believes it to be misleading.[37] The building society may apply to the sheriff court to have the direction set aside if the principal office of the society is situated in Scotland[38]: the application lies to the sheriff having jurisdiction where the principal office is situated.[39] The application is to be brought within three weeks of the direction,[40] and the sheriff may set the direction aside or confirm it, placing a time limit upon compliance.[41]

The sheriff may wind up a building society where the amount standing to the credit of shares in the society as shown by the latest balance sheet does not exceed £120,000.[42] In such circumstances the sheriff court has concurrent jurisdiction with the Court of Session, but the Court of Session may remit to the sheriff court any petition presented to the Court of Session or require that the sheriff court remit a petition presented there to the Court of Session or to another sheriff court.[43] If the winding up proceeds in the sheriff court, the sheriff may submit a stated case for the opinion of the Court of Session on any question of law arising in the winding up.[44] 26.54

IX. Burial and Cremation

Burial Grounds (Scotland) Act 1855[45]

Two members of a council[46] or 10 ratepayers or persons liable to pay council tax within the parish or two householders residing within one hundred yards of any burial ground or proposed burial ground may present a petition to the sheriff having jurisdiction in the place where the burial ground is or is to be situated, stating that the ground is or would be dangerous to health or offensive or contrary to decency.[47] The sheriff must hold an advertised hearing and if the allegations are established must pronounce an interlocutor to such effect and transmit a copy of it to the Secretary of State.[48] The sheriff's interlocutor is not in itself an operative judgment: the Secretary of State may arrange for an Order in Council which 26.55

---

35 c. 53 ("the 1986 Act").
36 *ibid.* Sched. 19, Pt I, which also repeals Building Societies Act 1874, ss. 1, 4, 32.
37 *ibid.* s. 108.
38 *ibid.* s. 119(1).
39 *ibid.*
40 *ibid.* s. 108(3).
41 *ibid.*
42 *ibid.* s. 90, Sched. 15, paras 1, 2 and 15; Insolvency Act 1986, s. 120(3).
43 Insolvency Act 1986, s. 120(3)(a), (b).
44 *ibid.* s. 120(3)(c).
45 c. 68 ("the 1855 Act").
46 As defined in Local Government etc. (Scotland) Act 1994 (c. 39), s. 2.
47 1855 Act, s. 4, as amended by Local Government (Scotland) Act 1895 (58 & 59 Vict. c. 52), ss. 21, 22; Public Health (Scotland) Act 1897 (60 & 61 Vict. c. 38), s. 146(2); Local Government Scotland) Act 1929 (19 & 20 Geo. 5, c. 25), ss. 1(1), 2(1)(e); Local Government (Scotland) Act 1973, s. 169(1); S.I. 1952 No. 1334; Local Government etc. (Scotland) Act 1994, Sched. 13, para. 3(2); see Dobie, *Styles*, p. 63.
48 *ibid.*

closes the existing burial ground or prevents the provision of a new one.[49] Before pronouncing an interlocutor the sheriff may order an inquiry, visit the ground or otherwise inform himself.[50] The application may be made to either the sheriff or the sheriff principal.[51] The decision of either is not open to review, nor may it be set aside by reason of defect of form or procedure.[52]

26.56 When the Secretary of State has closed a burial ground by Order in Council, the local burial authority must provide one in its place. If this is not done within six months of the Order, the sheriff, after application[53] by summary petition from certain parties, may make inquiry and designate and set apart land for the purpose of providing a burial ground.[54] At the hearing, of which 10 days' notice must be given to landowners, the sheriff is directed to make such inquiry as he thinks proper. Evidence must be recorded in some cases.[55] The sheriff makes no award of expenses in such applications as he acts in an administrative capacity.[56] There is provision for an appeal to the Court of Session within 14 days of the judgment of the sheriff or sheriff principal,[57] but there is no appeal from the decision of the sheriff to the sheriff principal.[58]

26.57 The local authority may sell the exclusive right of burial in a local authority cemetery, as well as the right to construct any burial chapel or vault and to erect monuments or gravestones, after obtaining the sanction of the sheriff.[59] The local authority applies to the sheriff, who may, after such intimation as is necessary, hear parties and take evidence. The decision of the sheriff is final.[60]

X. Children and Young Persons

Foster Children (Scotland) Act 1984[61]

26.58 Any person aggrieved may appeal to the sheriff against a requirement or prohibition imposed with regard to keeping foster children.[62] The appeal must be brought within 14 days of notification of the requirement or prohibition.[63] The sheriff may vary the requirement or allow more time for compliance with it.[64] If an absolute prohibition has been imposed, the sheriff may substitute for it a qualified prohibition.[65]

---

49 1855 Act, s. 5.

50 *Ayr Town Council, Petr* (1891) 7 Sh.Ct.Rep. 196; *Dunblane and Lecropt Parish Council, Petr* (1923) 40 Sh.Ct.Rep. 3.

51 *Fleming v. Dickson* (1862) 1 M. 188; *Strichen Parish Council v. Goodwillie*, 1908 S.C. 835.

52 1855 Act, s. 32; *Strichen Parish Council, supra.*

53 See Dobie, *Styles*, p. 63.

54 1855 Act, s. 10.

55 *ibid.*; *Dornoch Parish Council* (1929) 46 Sh.Ct.Rep. 33; *Aberdeen C.C. v. Roger* (1936) 53 Sh.Ct.Rep. 171.

56 *Liddall v. Ballingry Parish Council*, 1908 S.C. 1082.

57 1855 Act, s. 10. See *Kilmarnock and Loudoun D.C. v. Young*, 1993 S.L.T. 505.

58 *Strichen Parish Council, supra.*

59 1855 Act, s. 18, as amended by Burial Grounds (Scotland) Amendment Act 1886 (49 & 50 Vict. c. 21); applied by Church of Scotland (Property and Endowments) Act 1925 (15 & 16 Geo. 5, c. 33), s. 32.

60 *ibid.* s. 32.

61 c. 56 ("the 1984 Act").

62 *ibid.* ss. 9, 10, 11(1).

63 *ibid.*

64 *ibid.* s. 11(2)(a).

65 *ibid.* s. 11(2)(b).

Section 12 of the Act provides that if the sheriff is satisfied, on the complaint of a local authority, that a foster child is being kept or about to be received by a person who is unfit to have his care[66] or in other unsuitable circumstances[67] the sheriff may make an order for his removal to a place of safety pending the making of other arrangements. The power to make such an order is exercisable by a justice of the peace on the application of a person authorised to visit the foster child.[68] An order under section 12, if made on the ground that a prohibition in respect of premises has been contravened, may require the removal of all foster children kept in the premises.[69]

Children Act 1989[70]

The Act provides for the registration by a council of child minders.[71] Any person aggrieved by the council's decision, *inter alia,* to refuse an application for registration, or cancellation thereof, or refusing consent, may appeal by summary application within 21 days to the sheriff.[72] **26.59**

Child Support Act 1991[73]

The Secretary of State may apply to the sheriff for a liability order[74] by summary application.[75] A person aggrieved by the making of a deduction from earnings order, or by its terms, or where there is a dispute as to whether payments constitute earnings, may appeal to the sheriff[76] by summary application.[77] **26.60**

Children (Scotland) Act 1995[78]

(1) Appeal from children's hearing to sheriff

This chapter deals only with Part II of the Act; Parts I and III are to be found in the undernoted chapters.[79] **26.61**

In all proceedings under Part II, apart from an application for a child protection order under section 57[80] the sheriff must consider whether it is necessary to appoint a safe-guarder.[81]

A child or a relevant person[82] may within three weeks of a decision of a children's hearing appeal to the sheriff against that decision,[83] and where **26.62**

---

66 1984 Act, s. 12(1)(a).
67 *ibid.* s. 12(1)(b).
68 *ibid.* s. 12(2).
69 *ibid.* s. 12(3).
70 c. 41 ("the 1989 Act").
71 *ibid.* s. 71.
72 *ibid.* s. 77(6), (10).
73 c. 48 ("the 1991 Act").
74 *ibid.* s. 33(2).
75 A.S. (Child Support Rules) 1993 (S.I. 1993 No. 920), r. 2(1).
76 1991 Act, s. 32(5).
77 A.S. 1993, r. 5.
78 c. 36 ("the 1995 Act").
79 See Chap. 22 (family proceedings) and Chap. 28 (adoption).
80 See paras 26.70 to 26.73.
81 A.S. (Child Care and Maintenance Rules) 1997 (S.I. 1997 No. 291) ("A.S. 1997, rr. 3.6–3.10.
82 As defined in 1995 Act, s. 93(2)(b).
83 *ibid.* s. 51(1)(a). There is no appeal under this section against the decision of a children's hearing to continue a child protection order: 1995 Act, s. 51(15)(b). Decisions of a hearing which are merely procedural steps towards the making of a dispositive decision are not appealable; *H. v. McGregor*, 1973 S.C. 95; *Sloan v. B*, 1991 S.L.T. 530 at 595. See Norrie, *Annotated Children (Scotland) Act 1995*, pp. 36–88 and 36–89

such an appeal is made it must be heard by the sheriff[84] in chambers.[85] The sheriff in such an appeal may hear evidence.[86]

(2) Appeal from sheriff

26.63 An appeal against the sheriff's decision in an appeal lies on a point of law as in respect of any irregularity in the conduct of the case by stated case to the sheriff principal.[87] Appeal lies to the Court of Session from any decision of the sheriff, and with leave of the sheriff principal from any decision of the sheriff principal.[88] The decision of the Court of Session is final.[89] The sheriff principal or the Court of Session must remit to the sheriff for disposal with such directions as they may give.[90]

(3) Application to sheriff for funding

26.64 Where either the child or a relevant person or both do not accept the grounds of referral by the Principal Reporter to a children's hearing or accept the grounds in part the hearing may direct the Reporter to make an application to the sheriff for a finding as to whether such grounds as are not accepted are established.[91] Such an application must be heard by the sheriff within 28 days of its being lodged,[92] but may be adjourned.[93] The child and the relevant person may be represented before the sheriff by a person other than a legally qualified person.[94] If, in the course of the hearing of an application, the child and the relevant person accept any ground, the sheriff must dispense with hearing evidence and deem the ground to be established.[95]

26.65 If a children's hearing is satisfied that a child does not understand or is incapable of understanding an explanation of the ground for referral, it may either discharge the referral or direct the Principal Reporter to apply to the sheriff for a find in the same way as described in the previous paragraph.[96] If in the course of the hearing of the application before the sheriff the relevant person accepts any ground, the sheriff may if it appears reasonable to do so dispense with hearing evidence and deem the ground to be established.[97]

26.66 When the sheriff decides that none of the grounds of referral is established he must dismiss the application, discharge the referral and recall, discharge or cancel any warrant or direction relating to the child.[98] Where the sheriff finds any of the grounds of referral established he must remit the case to the Principal Reporter to make arrangements for a children's hearing, and may issue an order that the child be kept in a place

---

[84] 1995 Act, s. 51(1)(b). The rules of procedure in such appeals are contained in A.S. 1997, Chap. 3, Pt VIII.
[85] 1995 Act, s. 93(5).
[86] *ibid.* s. 51(3).
[87] *ibid.* s. 51(11)(a)(i).
[88] *ibid.* s. 51(11)(b).
[89] *ibid.*
[90] *ibid.* s. 51(14).
[91] *ibid.* s. 65(7). The rules relating to applications under this section are contained in A.S. 1997, Chap. 3, Pt VII.
[92] 1995 Act, s. 68(2).
[93] A.S. 1997, r. 3.49.
[94] 1995 Act, s. 68(4).
[95] *ibid.* s. 68(8)(a).
[96] *ibid.* s. 65(9).
[97] *ibid.* s. 68(8)(b).
[98] *ibid.* s. 68(9).

of safety until the hearing.[99] The sheriff sits in chambers to decide such applications.[1]

(4) Place of safety warrant

Where a children's hearing is unable to dispose of a case and certain conditions are satisfied,[2] they may grant a warrant to keep a child in a place of safety.[3] A warrant granted by a children's hearing may last for 22 days.[4] It may be continued by the hearing[5] but the total period a child may be detained under such a warrant cannot exceed 66 days.[6] The Principal Reporter may apply to the sheriff for a warrant so to keep the child after the children's hearing warrant has expired.[7] Such warrant may only be granted on cause shown and must specify the date on which it will expire.[8] **26.67**

(5) Fresh evidence

A child (or a relevant person) in respect of whom the sheriff has found that a ground of referral has been established may make an application claiming that fresh evidence exists and applying for review of the finding.[9] Such evidence must be evidence which the sheriff did not consider, evidence the existence or significance of which might have materially affected the determination of the original application, such evidence as is likely to be credible and reliable and evidence which would have been admissible.[10] There must be a reasonable explanation of the failure to lead the evidence on the original application.[11] Where the sheriff is not satisfied that any of the claims made in the application is established he must dismiss the application.[12] Where the sheriff is satisfied that the claims made in the application are established, he must consider the evidence, and if satisfied that none of the grounds in the original application is established, he must allow the application, and discharge the referral.[13] If the sheriff is satisfied that any of the grounds in the original application *is* established, he may proceed in accordance with section 68(10) of the Act.[14] **26.68**

(6) Child assessment order

On the application of a local authority the sheriff may grant a child assessment order if he is satisfied that the local authority has reasonable cause to suspect that the child is being so treated, or neglected, that he is suffering, or is likely to suffer, significant harm; that an assessment is required to establish whether there is reasonable cause to believe that the child is so treated or neglected; and that such assessment is unlikely to be carried out without the order.[15] **26.69**

---

99 1995 Act, s. 68(10).
1 *ibid.* s. 93(5).
2 The conditions are contained in 1995 Act, s. 66(2).
3 *ibid.* s. 66(1).
4 *ibid.* s. 66(3)(a).
5 *ibid.* s. 66(5).
6 *ibid.* s. 66(8).
7 *ibid.* s. 67(1). The rules relating to warrants are contained in A.S. 1997, Chap. 3, Pt VI.
8 *ibid.* s. 67(2).
9 *ibid.* s. 85(1), (2). The rules relating to applications are contained in A.S. 1997, Chap. 3, Pt X.
10 *ibid.* s. 85(3)(a), (b).
11 *ibid.* s. 85(3)(c).
12 *ibid.* s. 85(5).
13 *ibid.* s. 85(6)(a).
14 *ibid.* s. 85(6)(b). See para. 26.66
15 *ibid.* s. 55. The rules relating to assessment orders are contained in A.S. 1997, Chap. 3, Pt III.

(7) Child protection order

26.70 Where the sheriff, on application by any person, is satisfied that there are reasonable grounds to believe that a child is being so treated or neglected that he is suffering significant harm or will suffer such harm if he is not removed to and kept in a place of safety, or if he does not remain in the place where he is then being accommodated, and an order is necessary to protect the child from such harm or further harm, the sheriff may make a child protection order.[16] On the application by a local authority the sheriff may make such an order if he is satisfied that they have reasonable grounds to suspect that a child is being or will be so treated or neglected that he is suffering or will suffer significant harm, that the local authority are making or causing to be made enquiries to allow them to decide whether they should take any action to safeguard the welfare of the child, and that those enquiries are being frustrated by access to the child being unreasonably denied, the local authority having reasonable cause to believe that such access is required as a matter of urgency.[17] There is no appeal against a sheriff's decision on an application for a child protection order.[18]

26.71 The sheriff in making a child protection order may give directions as to parental responsibilities and contact.[19]

26.72 Once a child protection order has been made and implemented a children's hearing must be arranged to determine whether the order should continue.[20] If the hearing is satisfied that the conditions for the making of the order are established it may continue the order and any direction made by the sheriff.[21] If a hearing does not continue the order it ceases to have effect.[22] There is no appeal to the sheriff from a decision of a children's hearing to continue a child protection order.[23]

26.73 An application may be made to the sheriff[24] to set aside or vary a child protection order or any direction of the sheriff[25] or continuation of such a direction by a children's hearing.[26]

(8) Parental responsibilities order

26.74 On the application of a local authority the sheriff may make a parental responsibilities order, transferring the appropriate parental rights and responsibilities relating to a child to them.[27] Before making such an order the sheriff must be satisfied that each relevant person[28] agrees unconditionally or is a person who (i) is not known, cannot be found or is incapable of giving agreement, (ii) is withholding agreement unreasonably, (iii) has

---

[16] 1995 Act, s. 57(1).

[17] *ibid.* s. 57(2). The rules relating to child protection orders are contained in A.S. 1997, Chap. 3, Pt IV.

[18] *ibid.* s. 51(15)(a).

[19] *ibid.* s. 58.

[20] *ibid.* s. 59(2).

[21] *ibid.* s. 59(4).

[22] *ibid.* s. 60(6)(a).

[23] *ibid.* s. 51(15)(b).

[24] *ibid.* s. 60(7). The disposals available to the sheriff are provided in s. 60(12) and (13).

[25] Made under 1995 Act, s. 58. See para. 26.71.

[26] *ibid.*, s. 59(4). See para. 26.72.

[27] 1995 Act, s. 86. The procedure is analogous to that in adoption and freeing for adoption. The rules relating to parental responsibilites orders are contained in A.S. 1997, Chap. 2, Pt V.

[28] As defined in 1995 Act, s. 86(4).

persistently failed without reasonable excuse to fulfill parental responsibilities in relation to the child, or (iv) has seriously ill-treated the child whose reintegration into the same household as that person is unlikely because of the serious ill-treatment or for other reasons.[29] The sheriff must appoint a curator *ad litem*[30] and a reporting officer.[31] The sheriff may in such an order impose such conditions as he considers appropriate and he may vary or discharge such an order on the application of the local authority, the child, or any person who was a relevant person, or any other person claiming an interest.[32] On an application by the child, the authority; or by any person with an interest, the sheriff may make such an order as to contact as he considers appropriate[33] and may vary or discharge this order.[34]

(9) Exclusion order

Where on an application by a local authority the sheriff is satisfied that a child is suffering, or is likely to suffer, significant harm as a result of any conduct of a named person, he may make an exclusion order excluding that person from the child's family home.[35] The making of the order must be necessary for the protection of the child and must better safeguard the child's welfare than the removal of the child from the family home.[36] There must also be a person capable of taking responsibility for the provision of appropriate care for the child.[37] The sheriff may make an interim order.[38] The application must be made to a sheriff of the sheriffdom within which the family home is situated.[39] **26.75**

In making an exclusion order the sheriff may: (a) grant a warrant for the summary ejection of the named person from the home; (b) grant an interdict prohibiting the named person from entering the home without the express permission of the local authority; (c) grant an interdict prohibiting him from removing specified objects from the home; (d) grant an interdict prohibiting him from entering or remaining in a specified area in the vicinity of the home; (e) grant an interdict prohibiting the taking by the named person of any step of a kind specified in the interdict in relation to the child; (f) make an order regulating contact between the named person and the child.[40] **26.76**

On an application by the named person or the local authority the sheriff may make the exclusion order, or any remedy granted along with it, subject to such terms and conditions as he considers appropriate.[41] The sheriff may attach a power of arrest to any interdict granted.[42] The procedure following on a breach of interdict is the same curious mixture of civil and criminal, involving police, procurator fiscal and sheriff as a court of summary criminal jurisdiction, as is to be found in relation to

---

29 1995 Act, s. 86(2).
30 *ibid.* s. 87(4)(a); A.S. 1997, r. 2.39.
31 *ibid.* s. 87(4)(b); A.S. 1997, r. 2.39.
32 *ibid.* s. 86(5).
33 *ibid.* s. 88(3).
34 *ibid.* s. 88(5).
35 *ibid.* s. 76. The rules relating to exclusion orders are contained in A.S. 1997, Chap. 3, Pt V.
36 *ibid.* s. 76(2)(b).
37 *ibid.* s. 76(2)(c).
38 *ibid.* s. 76(4).
39 *ibid.* s. 80(2).
40 *ibid.* s. 77(2), (3).
41 *ibid.* s. 77(7).
42 *ibid.* s. 78(1).

matrimonial interdicts.[43] The sheriff may vary or recall an exclusion order and any warrant, interdict, order or direction.[44]

(10) Representation

26.77 In most proceedings under Part II of the 1995 Act any party may be represented by an advocate or solicitor or other representative authorised by the party.[45] Such other representative must throughout the proceedings satisfy the sheriff that he is a suitable person to represent the party and that he is authorised to do so.[46]

(11) Expenses

26.78 No expenses may be awarded in any proceedings under Part II with the exception of proceedings for a parental responsibilities order,[47] and proceedings are to be conducted summarily.[48]

(12) Guardian

26.79 The sheriff is given power, *inter alia*, to appoint or remove a person as guardian of a child.[49] Except where the appointment or removal is sought in the crave of a family action, the procedure is by summary application.[50]

XI. Church of Scotland

Church of Scotland Courts Act 1863[51]

26.80 When the minister of any parish is suffering from mental disorder the sheriff may grant a certificate to such effect after due investigation.[52]

Fish Teinds (Scotland) Act 1864[53]

26.81 This Act makes provision for the commutation or redemption of fish teinds which are the vicarage teinds on fish payable to the minister of any parish in Scotland and forming part of his stipend.[54] The minister, presbytery and persons liable in fish teinds may enter into an agreement for the commutation of the teinds and the substitution of a capital sum.[55]

Ten persons[56] liable in fish teinds may petition the sheriff to call a meeting

---

[43] 1995 Act, s. 78(6)–(14), as amended by Criminal Procedure (Consequential Provisions) (Scotland) Act 1995 (c. 40), Sched. 4, para. 97(7). For matrimonial interdicts, see Matrimonial Homes (Family Protection) (Scotland) Act 1981 (c. 59), ss. 14–17.

[44] 1995 Act, s. 79(3).

[45] *ibid.* s. 91(4), A.S. 1997, r. 3.21. This rule does not apply to parental responsibilities orders as they are covered by Chap. 2 of A.S. 1997 and not Chap. 3.

[46] A.S. 1997, r. 3.21(2).

[47] *ibid.* r. 3.19. For parental responsibilities orders, see n. 45.

[48] *ibid.* r. 3.20. Although this rule does not cover parental responsibilities orders (see n. 45) there can be no doubt that an application for such an order would also be a summary application.

[49] 1995 Act, s. 11(2)(h).

[50] A.S. (Family Proceedings in the Sheriff Court) 1996 (S.I. 1996 No. 2167), para. 4.

[51] 26 & 27 Vict., c. 47 ("the 1863 Act").

[52] *ibid.* s. 2, as amended.

[53] 27 & 28 Vict., c. 33 ("the 1864 Act").

[54] *ibid.* s. 2.

[55] *ibid.* s. 4.

[56] Less than 10 persons may petition if the parish has less than 10 persons liable; 1864 Act, s. 4.

of all persons resident in the parish who are liable in fish teinds.[57] Within eight days of the presentation of the petition the sheriff must order the parish minister or the collector of fish teinds to make up a roll of the persons liable in fish teinds.[58] The roll is advertised and revised,[59] and on its completion the sheriff summons a meeting of those on the roll.[60] At the meeting the fish teinds payable may be commuted under the provisions of the Act.[61]

Ecclesiastical Buildings and Glebes (Scotland) Act 1868[62]

Heritors or a parish minister, if dissatisfied with the determinations of presbyteries in regard to churches, manses, glebes and so on, may remove the proceedings by appeal to the sheriff.[63] The Act provides detailed information as to how such appeals proceed.[64] The sheriff's decision is to be final unless an appeal is taken to a Lord Ordinary of the Court of Session.[65] **26.82**

Church of Scotland (Property and Endowments) Act 1925[66]

The computation of a standardised sum from fluctuating victual stipends is governed by certain provisions of this Act.[67] The minister, presbytery or any heritor may apply to the sheriff to fix the average value of the victual.[68] After such intimation and inquiry as the sheriff thinks fit he shall intimate the fixed value to the Clerk of Teinds.[69] **26.83**

The same parties may apply to the sheriff to give such instruction to the Clerk of Teinds as he may deem necessary or proper if there is any special method of calculation of the stipend in any particular parish.[70] This application must be made before the expiry of six months after the date of standardisation of the stipend and the sheriff shall intimate it to such persons as he deems necessary.[71] The decision of the sheriff is final unless appealed to the Inner House of the Court of Session.[72] **26.84**

The parish minister or any heritor may apply to the sheriff to appoint a valuer for the purpose of fixing the annual agricultural value of lands, the teinds of which have not been valued.[73] The sheriff may also be asked to appoint an arbiter failing agreement between the General Trustees and the local authority on the purchase of a burgh church.[74] The application may be made by either party.[75] **26.85**

---

57 1864 Act, s. 5.
58 *ibid.* s. 6.
59 *ibid.*
60 *ibid.* s. 7.
61 *ibid.*
62 31 & 32 Vict. c. 96 ("the 1868 Act").
63 *ibid.* s. 3, as amended by Church of Scotland (Property and Endowments) Act 1925 (15 & 16 Geo. 5, c. 33), s. 7.
64 1868 Act, ss. 4–15.
65 *ibid.* ss. 14, 16–20.
66 15 & 16 Geo. 5, c. 33 ("the 1925 Act").
67 *ibid.* ss. 2(1)(b), 2(2) and Sched. IIB.
68 *ibid.* s. 2(1)(b), Sched. IIB.
69 *ibid.*
70 *ibid.* s. 2(2).
71 *ibid.*
72 *ibid.* See *Kilmarnock and Loudoun D.C. v. Young*, 1993 S.L.T. 505, *per* L. P. Hope at 507–508 and RCS, Chap. 41.
73 *ibid.* s. 16, Sched. VI, para. 1. See *Glasgow University Court v. Lord Advocate*, 1961 S.C. 246.
74 *ibid.* s. 22(2)(h), as amended by Local Government (Scotland) Act 1973, Sched. 27, para. 63(a).
75 *ibid.*

26.86 In respect of the transfer of rights in parish churches and manses any heritor or the General Trustees may apply to the sheriff to grant a certificate that all obligations incumbent on heritors in connection with a church or manse have been fulfilled.[76] A statutory form of certificate is provided.[77] In the case of certain churches, the presbytery or General Trustees may apply to the sheriff to find and declare that the case ought to be dealt with by the Scottish Ecclesiastical Commissioners.[78] In an application under section 28, if a question arises as to whether or not the church or manse in question is the church or manse of a parish, it is to be determined by the sheriff in a summary manner and his decision is final.[79]

26.87 Where a debtor under a bond and disposition in security, bond of annual rent or other heritable security whereby payment of an annual sum is secured over land in favour of the minister of a *quoad sacra* parish, sells a portion of the subjects he is entitled to allocate a proportion of the annual sum on the land sold. Failing agreement between the debtor and the creditor, the debtor may apply to the sheriff to fix such allocation.[80]

Church of Scotland (Property and Endowments) (Amendment) Act 1933[81]

26.88 If a church or manse is sold for any other than ecclesiastical purposes and there is no agreement between the superior and the General Trustees or other vassal as to feuduty for the site, the sheriff may appoint an arbiter to determine it.[82] Before disposing of the ground on which a church or manse has been erected, the General Trustees can give a heritor an opportunity to purchase or feu the ground; if no agreement is reached as to the price or feuduty and as to the arbiter to be appointed to decide it, the sheriff may appoint an arbiter on the application of either party.[83]

XII. Coast Protection and Flooding

Coast Protection Act 1949[84]

26.89 A coast protection authority may serve a notice on the owner or occupier of land to recover from him the cost of maintenance and repair of works carried out by them on his land. Within 21 days of the service of the notice the owner or occupier may apply to the sheriff upon any of four specified grounds and the sheriff may relieve the owner or occupier of all or part of the cost of the maintenance works.[85] In applications under this section the sheriff is acting in a judicial capacity and thus has power to award expenses.[86]

---

[76] 1925 Act, s. 28(2). See *Seafield Trs v. General Trs of Church of Scotland*, 1928 S.L.T. (Sh.Ct.) 18.

[77] *ibid.* Sched. XI.

[78] *ibid.* s. 28(4), as amended by Local Government (Scotland) Act 1973, Sched. 27, para. 65.

[79] *ibid.* s. 28(5). This section is probably spent.

[80] *ibid.* s. 35(1).

[81] 23 & 24 Geo. 5, c. 44 ("the 1933 Act").

[82] *ibid.* s. 9(2).

[83] *ibid.* s. 9(3).

[84] 12 & 13 Geo. 6, c. 74 ("the 1949 Act").

[85] *ibid.* s. 13(3), (9)(a).

[86] *Dunbar v. Edinburgh Corporation*, 1961 S.L.T. (Sh.Ct.) 45 (*Earl of Morton's Trs v. Fife C.C.* (1952) 68 Sh.Ct.Rep. 97 not followed).

The sheriff may grant a warrant to any authorised person to enter on lands for purposes connected with coast protection.[87] **26.90**

Flood Prevention (Scotland) Act 1961[88]

In certain circumstances the sheriff may authorise persons to enter on lands for the purposes of the Act.[89] **26.91**

XIII. Compulsory Acquisition

Lands Clauses Consolidation (Scotland) Act 1845[90]

(1) Capital certificate

The sheriff[91] may grant a certificate that the whole capital of a public undertaking has been subscribed by the promoters, making the compulsory acquisition of land competent.[92] The certificate will be granted on the application of the promoters of the undertaking on the production of such evidence as the sheriff thinks proper and sufficient.[93] **26.92**

(2) Assessment of compensation

The sheriff must determine the amount of compensation in any case of the purchase of land by agreement where the compensation claimed does not exceed £50,[94] unless the parties agree to refer to arbitration.[95] Either party[96] may apply[97] to the sheriff of the district where the lands are situated, and the decision of the sheriff is final.[98] The proceedings are summary, the sheriff must give his decision in writing and expenses are awarded at his discretion.[99] **26.93**

Where the compensation claimed exceeds £50 the amount due is to be fixed by a jury sitting with a sheriff, unless the parties have agreed to settle the question by arbitration.[1] Detailed provision is made in the Act in respect of such proceedings,[2] which are to be conducted in like manner as criminal trials.[3] The amount assessed by the jury is decerned for by the sheriff, whose decision is not subject to review, though it may be set aside by reduction.[4]

---

[87] 1949 Act, s. 25(4).

[88] 9 & 10 Eliz. 2, c. 41 ("the 1961 Act").

[89] *ibid.* s. 8(3).

[90] 8 & 9 Vict., c. 19 ("the 1845 Act"), as applied by Acquisition of Land (Authorisation Procedures) (Scotland) Act 1947 (10 & 11 Geo. 6, c. 42), Sched. 2.

[91] Presumably the sheriff of the district where the promoters carry on business and where the share register is kept; see Dobie, p. 607.

[92] 1845 Act, ss. 15, 16. For a style of an application see Lees, *Sheriff Court Styles* (4th ed.), p. 255.

[93] *ibid.*

[94] *ibid.* s. 21.

[95] *ibid.* ss. 23–35.

[96] *ibid.* s. 22.

[97] For style see Lees, *op. cit.*, p. 255.

[98] 1845 Act, s. 22.

[99] *ibid.* s. 22.

[1] *ibid.* ss. 35, 36; for styles see Lees, *op. cit.*, p. 256.

[2] *ibid.* ss. 36–52. See *Lang v. Glasgow Court House Commissioners* (1871) 9 M. 768; also *Houstoun Local Authority v. McPhedran* (1890) 6 Sh.Ct.Rep. 267.

[3] *ibid.* s. 42.

[4] See *City of Glasgow Union Ry. v. Hunter* (1870) 8 M. (H.L.) 156.

(3) Absent owner

26.94 Where lands are taken other than by agreement the sheriff may appoint a valuator to determine the amount of compensation.[5-6] This appointment is made on the summary application of the promoters and the sheriff must first be satisfied that the party is absent or cannot be found.[7] The expenses are borne by the promoters.[8]

(4) Miscellaneous

26.95 In the case of two valuators failing to agree about the purchase price or compensation for any lands where the claimant is under a disability, the sheriff may appoint a third valuator on the application of either party.[9] The sheriff may authorise persons acquiring any land to enter before paying the price of compensation provided they make a deposit by way of security.[10] A valuator appointed by the sheriff determines the sum to be deposited.[11] In the case of common property, a valuator appointed by the sheriff determines the compensation for the extinction of rights in such lands.[12] Applications to recover a penalty for unlawful entry are made to the sheriff[13] as are applications to obtain entry for the promoters[14] or to ascertain compensation for yearly tenants.[15] Applications for all of the above, except for recovery of penalties, are made by initial writ.[16] If written pleadings have been allowed, a record made up and evidence taken, an appeal lies to the sheriff principal[17] within seven days.

Manoeuvres Act 1958[18]

26.96 An arbiter appointed by a sheriff (on the application of either party) may determine disputes between services, authorities and aggrieved persons regarding compensation for damage or interference due to military manoeuvres.[19]

XIV. Conveyancing and Registration of Writs

Heritable Securities (Scotland) Act 1894[20]

26.97 Applications are to be made to the sheriff of the sheriffdom where the security subjects lie,[21] irrespective of their value.[22]

5-6 1845 Act, ss. 56, 57, as amended by Lands Tribunal Act 1949 (12 & 13 Geo. 6, c. 42), s. 1(6), (8)(a); for style see Lees, *op. cit.*, p. 259.
7 *ibid.* s. 57.
8 *ibid.* s. 60.
9 *ibid.* s. 9.
10 *ibid.* s. 84. See *Birrell Ltd. v. Edinburgh D.C.*, 1982 S.L.T. 111.
11 *ibid.*
12 *ibid.* s. 97, as amended by Lands Tribunal Act 1949 (13 & 14 Geo. 6, c. 42), s. 1(6), (8)(a).
13 *ibid.* s. 87; but see *Dennison v. Paisley Ry* (1899) 16 Sh.Ct.Rep. 17.
14 *ibid.* s. 89.
15 *ibid.* s. 114; as modified by Agriculture (Miscellaneous Provisions) Act 1968 (c. 34), s. 14(3), Sched. 4, paras 4, 5. See *Glasgow District Subway Co. v. Albin & Son* (1895) 23 R. 81.
16 See Lees, *op. cit.* (4th ed.), pp. 260–265.
17 1845 Act, s. 139; *Bridge of Allan Water Co. v. Alexander* (1868) 6 M. 321.
18 7 & 8 Eliz. 2, c. 7 ("the 1958 Act").
19 *ibid.* s. 7(4).
20 57 & 58 Vict., c. 44 ("the 1894 Act").
21 *ibid.* s. 15.
22 *ibid.*

(1) Ejection of proprietor

A 1981 case would suggest that the power to eject a proprietor in personal occupancy of the security subjects[23] may be exercised by way of a summary application,[24] but this seems doubtful.[25] 26.98

(2) Leasing security subjects

A heritable creditor in possession of lands disponed in security may apply to the sheriff for warrant to lease the lands for more than seven years but not for a period exceeding 21 years in the case of heritable property in general or 31 years for minerals.[26] The procedure is discussed in Chapter 23.[27] 26.99

(3) Realising security subjects

A heritable creditor who has exposed the security subjects for sale at a price not exceeding the amount due under the security and has failed to find a purchaser may apply to the sheriff for declarator to the effect that the debtor has forfeited his right in the subjects and that they have vested in the creditor.[28] The proceedings are competent only in respect of the whole of the security subjects.[29] The procedure is discussed in Chapter 23.[30] 26.100

(4) Pari passu security

A heritable creditor holding a *pari passu* security, who wishes to sell the lands conveyed by the security but is unable to obtain the consent of his fellow bondholder, may apply to the sheriff for warrant to sell the security subjects. The procedure is discussed in Chapter 23.[31] 26.101

(5) Notice

Provision is made for notice, including a warrant for edictal intimation, where the debtor in a heritable security has died and the heir cannot be ascertained, or where the creditor cannot ascertain the debtor. The relevant provisions are noted in Chapter 23.[32] 26.102

Sheriff Courts (Scotland) Act 1907[33]

The sheriff is empowered to make an order dispensing with the execution of a deed relating to heritable property by the grantor and directing the sheriff clerk to execute the deed.[34] This applies when the grantor of the deed cannot be found, refuses or is unable to execute the deed, or has 26.103

---

23 1894 Act, s. 5.

24 *Prestwick Investment Trust v. Jones*, 1981 S.L.T. (Sh.Ct.) 55.

25 See paras 23.03, 23.09; Dobie, pp. 595, 596.

26 1894 Act, ss. 6, 7.

27 See paras 23.29 *et seq.*

28 1894 Act, s. 8, Sched. D; amended and repealed in part by Conveyancing and Feudal Reform (Scotland) Act 1970 (c. 35), s. 39(1); Lees, *op. cit.* p. 208.

29 *Webb's Exrs v. Reid* (1906) 14 S.L.T. 323.

30 See paras 23.31, 23.34, 23.35.

31 1894 Act, s. 11; see paras 23.33 to 23.35.

32 See para. 23.36.

33 7 Edw. 7, c. 51 ("the 1907 Act").

34 *ibid.* s. 5A, inserted by Law Reform (Miscellaneous Provisions) (Scotland) Act 1985 (c. 73), s. 17.

failed to execute the deed for any other reason. The order of the sheriff may be granted on application by the grantee made either in an action relating to the heritable property, or by way of summary application where an order is necessary to implement a decree of a sheriff relating to the property.[35]

Conveyancing (Scotland) Act 1924[36]

26.104 A creditor infeft in a ground annual which is in arrears for two consecutive years may apply to the sheriff[37] for adjudication of the subjects.[38] The action of adjudication is raised against the proprietor of the subjects from which the ground annual is payable, and any other persons interested therein whose rights are postponed to the pursuer's.[39]

Conveyancing and Feudal Reform (Scotland) Act 1970[40]

26.105 For the purpose of all applications under Part II of the Act the court is the sheriff court having jurisdiction over any part of the security subjects, of whatever value.[41] Any application is to be by means of summary application and the decision of the sheriff is final, except as to a question of title.[42] The sheriff may therefore: (1) on the application of a debtor in a standard security or the proprietor of the security subjects, in a case other than where the security was granted in respect of an obligation to pay money, grant declarator that the obligations have been performed[43]; (2) on the application of a creditor in a standard security, grant warrant for the lease of the security subjects for a period not exceeding seven years[44]; (3) on the application of a person on whom a notice of default has been served, hear parties and order the notice to be upheld, or set aside in whole or in part, or otherwise varied[45]; (4) on the counter-application of a respondent in an application under (3), grant such remedies as he thinks proper[46]; (5) on the application of a creditor, grant warrant to exercise remedies on default[47]; and (6) on the application of a creditor for a decree of foreclosure, after such intimation and inquiry as he thinks fit, appoint the security subjects to be re-exposed for sale or grant decree of foreclosure.[48]

Land Registration (Scotland) Act 1979[49]

26.106 If a sheriff orders him to do so, the Keeper of the Registers of Scotland must rectify any inaccuracy in the Land Register of Scotland.[50]

---

[35] 1907 Act, s. 5A.

[36] 14 & 15 Geo. 5, c. 27 ("the 1924 Act"), as amended by Civil Jurisdiction and Judgments Act 1982 (c. 27), Sched. 14.

[37] Or, in certain circumstances, the Court of Session: 1924 Act, s. 23(6).

[38] 1924 Act, s. 23(5), Sched. K, form No. 8.

[39] *ibid.* s. 23(5).

[40] c. 35 ("the 1970 Act").

[41] *ibid.* s. 29(1).

[42] *ibid.* ss. 29(2), (3).

[43] *ibid.* s. 18(2)(b), as amended by Redemption of Standard Securities (Scotland) Act 1971 (c.45), s. 1(d).

[44] *ibid.* s. 20(3), (4).

[45] *ibid.* s. 22(1), (2).

[46] *ibid.* s. 22(3).

[47] *ibid.* s. 24.

[48] *ibid.* s. 28.

[49] c. 33 ("the 1979 Act").

[50] *ibid.* s. 9(1), (4), as amended by Matrimonial Homes (Family Protection) (Scotland) Act 1981 (c. 59), s. 6(4).

If a landlord fails to convey his interest to his tenant-at-will[51] under the provisions of the Act,[52] or if he is unknown or cannot be found, the tenant-at-will may apply to the sheriff for an order dispensing with the execution by the landlord of the conveyance to the tenant-at-will and directing the sheriff clerk to execute the conveyance.[53] On making such an order the sheriff may order that the applicant consign certain sums in court.[54] On the application of any party the sheriff may order the investment, payment or distribution of such consigned sums.[55]

Where a landlord has failed to renew a long lease the sheriff may, on summary application by the tenant, direct the sheriff clerk to execute a renewal.[56] Similar provisions apply as to consignation of certain sums in court.[57]

Requirements of Writing (Scotland) Act 1995[58]

Applications under sections 4(1) (certification that document subscribed by granter) and 4(2) (certification of date or place of subscription) and 5(6) (certification of alteration) may be made by summary application to the sheriff, or in the course of other proceedings.[59] **26.107**

XV. Criminal Law

Riotous Assemblies (Scotland) Act 1822[60]

A person injured by damage to a building caused by acts of an unlawful, riotous or tumultuous assembly of persons, is entitled to recover full compensation from the council[61] within whose area the loss or injury was sustained. This is done by summary application to the sheriff.[62] **26.108**

Public Order Act 1986[63]

The sheriff may issue a warrant authorising the entry and search of premises in order to discover unlawfully possessed racially inflammatory material.[64] **26.109**

---

51 Defined in 1979 Act, s. 20(8).

52 *ibid.* s. 20(6).

53 *ibid.* s. 21(3).

54 *ibid.*

55 *ibid.* s. 21(5).

56 *ibid.* s. 22A(1), inserted by Law Reform (Miscellaneous Provisions) (Scotland) Act 1985, s. 2.

57 *ibid.* 22A(2), (8), (9).

58 c. 57 ("the 1995 Act").

59 1995 Act, s. 4(1), (2), (4)–(6); A.S. (Requirements of Writing) 1996 (S.I. 1996 No. 1534), which does not apply to summary applications (para. 3(2)).

60 3 Geo. 4, c. 33, ("the 1822 Act").

61 As defined in Local Government etc. (Scotland) Act 1994 (c. 39), s. 2.

62 1822 Act, s. 10; see *D'Arpino v. Glasgow Town Council* (1935) 51 Sh.Ct.Rep. 228; see correspondence in (1981) 26 J.L.S. 345.

63 c. 64 ("the 1986 Act").

64 *ibid.* s. 24(2).

Proceeds of Crime (Scotland) Act 1995[65]

26.110 The sheriff, "exercising his civil jurisdiction",[66] may order compensation[67] to be paid on a summary application[68] in relation to a confiscation order. The prosecutor may apply by summary application[69] for a restraint order[70] to a sheriff "exercising his civil jurisdiction."[71] Variation or recall of restraint orders is made by note in the process.[72] Where a sheriff has granted a restraint order he may interdict a person not subject to that order from dealing with property affected by it.[73] Application may be by summary application, or note in the original process if a restraint order has been made.[74] The prosecutor may apply to the sheriff by summary application or, if a restraint order has already been applied for, by note in the original process, for arrestment of moveable property affected by a restraint order.[75] The sheriff may on summary application, or following a note in the original process if a restraint order has been made, appoint an administrator in relation to property affected by a restraint order.[76] Appeal to the Court of Session is competent against refusal, variation or recall, or refusal to vary or recall a restraint order.[77]

XVI. Customs and Excise

Criminal Justice (International Co-operation) Act 1990[78]

26.111 A customs officer or constable may seize and detain any cash, being imported into or exported from the United Kingdom, if he has reasonable grounds for suspecting a connection with drug trafficking.[79] Such cash may not be detained for more than 48 hours unless its continued detention is authorised by the sheriff on a summary application by the procurator fiscal.[80] Application may be made for release of the cash,[81] or for its forfeiture.[82] In either case the application is by summary application if it is made prior to the making of an application for an extension order under section 25(2), or by minute in the orginal process if made after such an application.[83]

Value Added Tax Act 1994[84]

26.112 If a sheriff is satisfied on information on oath that there is reasonable ground for suspecting that an offence under the Act is being, has been or is

---

65 c. 43 ("the 1995 Act").
66 *ibid.* s. 17(7).
67 *ibid.* s. 17(1).
68 A.S. (Proceeds of Crime Rules) 1996 (S.I. 1996 No. 2446) ("A.S. 1996"), r. 2.
69 *ibid.* r. 3(1).
70 1995 Act, s. 28(1).
71 *ibid.* s. 28(7).
72 A.S. 1996, r. 4.
73 1995 Act, s. 28(8).
74 A.S. 1996, r. 5.
75 1995 Act, s. 33; A.S. 1996, r. 6(1).
76 *ibid.* Sched. 1, para. 1, A.S. 1996, r. 8(1).
77 *ibid.* s. 31(5), A.S. 1996, r. 7.
78 c. 5 ("the 1990 Act").
79 *ibid.* s. 25(1).
80 *ibid.* s. 25(2), (4). A.S. (Applications under Pt III of the Criminal Justice (International Co-operation) Act 1990) 1992 (S.I. 1992 No. 1007), para. 2.
81 *ibid.* s. 25(5).
82 *ibid.* s. 26.
83 A.S. 1992, paras 3, 4.
84 c. 23 ("the 1994 Act").

about to be committed on any premises he may issue a warrant authorising an authorised person[85] to enter those premises and search them and any person found there.[86]

XVII. Education

Education (Scotland) Act 1980[87]

(1) Placing requests

The education authority is under a duty[88] to place any child in a school which the child's parent desires the child to attend unless the education authority is satisfied that one or more specified[89] grounds of refusal so to place the child exist. If the education authority refuse a parent's placing request, they are to inform him of his right to appeal to an appeal committee.[90] Where the appeal committee decides to confirm the decision of the education authority they must inform[91] the parent of his right to appeal to a sheriff having jurisdiction where the specified school is situated.[92] The education authority may be a party to such an appeal, but the appeal committee may not.[93] The appeal is by way of summary application[94] lodged with the sheriff clerk within 28 days from the date of receiving the appeal committee's decision,[95] but on good cause shown the sheriff may hear an appeal out of time.[96] The appeal is heard in chambers,[97] and is, in effect, "a complete re-hearing of the case".[98] The sheriff may confirm the education authority's decision if he is satisfied that one or more of the specified grounds of refusal exists or exist,[99] and that in all the circumstances it would be appropriate to do so.[1] Otherwise he must refuse to confirm the decision, and require the education authority to give effect to the placing request.[2] **26.113**

---

85 1994 Act, s. 91(1).

86 *ibid.* Sched. 11, para. 10(3).

87 c. 44 ("the 1980 Act"); see F. Doran, "School Attendances and Exclusions" (1980) 44 SCOLAG 66; C. M. G. Himsworth, "School Attendance Orders and the Sheriff" (1980) 25 J.L.S. 450, and "Scottish Local Authorities and the Sheriff", 1984 J.R. 63 at 64, 65, 74; A. L. Seager, "Parental Choice of School", 1982 S.L.T. (News) 29; M. B. Wise, "Sheriff Court Decisions, etc." (1985) 30 J.L.S. 439 and correspondence thereon: (1986) 31 J.L.S. 11, 104.

88 Duty imposed by s. 28A(1) of 1980 Act; ss. 28A to 28H were inserted by the Education (Scotland) Act 1981 (c. 58) ("the 1981 Act"), s. 1(1); see *Black v. Strathclyde R.C.*, Kilmarnock Sh. Ct, Aug. 27, 1982, unreported.

89 1980 Act, s. 28A(3).

90 *ibid.* ss. 28A(4), 28C, 28D, 28E.

91 *ibid.* s. 28E(3).

92 *ibid.* s. 28F(1).

93 *ibid.* s. 28F(2).

94 *ibid.* s. 28F(3)(a).

95 *ibid.* s. 28F(3)(b).

96 *ibid.* s. 28F(4).

97 *ibid.* s. 28F(3)(c).

98 *Coates v. Lothian R.C.*, Linlithgow Sh. Ct, Jan. 3, 1986, unreported.

99 1980 Act, s. 28F(5)(a); see *AK v. Strathclyde R.C.*, Glasgow Sh. Ct, Aug. 16, 1982, unreported; *Black, supra; Thompson v. Strathclyde R.C.*, Glasgow Sh. Ct, Aug. 5, 1983, unreported, which dealt with under-age placing requests, as did *Coates, supra*; *McKerron v. Highland R.C.*, Inverness Sh. Ct, Sept. 2, 1983, unreported, which discusses the powers of the sheriff on appeal.

1 *ibid.* s. 28F(5)(b); see *MY v. Strathclyde R.C.*, Glasgow Sh. Ct, Aug. 16, 1982, unreported; *Thompson, supra*; *Coates, supra*.

2 *ibid.* s. 28F(5).

The grounds of refusal have been interpreted very restrictively in successive appeals.[3]

Where the judgment of the sheriff on an appeal is inconsistent with any decision of the education authority refusing a placing request in respect of another child at the same stage of education and whose parents made a placing request at the same time as that under appeal, the education authority must review their refusal.[4]

The sheriff may make such order as to expenses as he thinks proper.[5] The Act provides that the sheriff's decision is final.[6] The finality of the sheriff's decision is noticed in the undernoted judgment,[7] where the relevant authorities are examined.

(2) Exclusion orders

26.114 Where an education authority decides to exclude a pupil from a school, the pupil[8] or his parent may refer the decision to an appeal committee.[9] If the appeal committee uphold the decision of the education authority, the pupil or parent may appeal to the sheriff having jurisdiction where the school from which the pupil has been excluded is situated.[10] The sheriff may confirm or annul the decision of the education authority; if he decides to confirm it, he may modify any conditions included in it.[11]

(3) Attendance orders

26.115 A person aggrieved by a school attendance order made by an education authority may appeal to the sheriff within 14 days after a copy is served on him.[12] It has been held that where an appeal was lodged 17 days after receiving the attendance order, it was still competent because the delay was not due to the fault of the appellant and had not prejudiced the respondents.[13] The sheriff may confirm, vary or annul the order and his decision is final.[14] A similar right of appeal is given to a person aggrieved by the refusal of, or the failure to deal with, an application for the amendment or revocation of an attendance order.[15] The appeal is to be brought within 14 days of service of a notice by the education authority[16] or within

---

[3] *Kennedy v. Strathclyde R.C.*, Glasgow Sh. Ct, Aug. 9, 1982, unreported; *AK, supra*, approved on appeal in *AK v. Strathclyde R.C.*, Sh. Pr. Dick, Glasgow Sh. Ct, Sept. 6, 1982, unreported; *MY, supra*; *Duggan v. Strathclyde R.C.*, Glasgow Sh. Ct., Aug. 17, 1983, unreported. For further comment, see *Wise, supra*; contrast *Kent v. Glasgow Corporation*, 1974 S.L.T. (Sh.Ct.) 44.

[4] 1980 Act, s. 28F(6).

[5] *ibid.* s. 28F(8).

[6] *ibid.* s. 28F(9).

[7] *AB v. Strathclyde R.C.*, Sh. Pr. Dick, Glasgow Sh. Ct, Sept. 6, 1982, unreported; but see *Boyne v. Grampian R.C.*, Aberdeen Sh. Ct, Apr. 14, 1983, unreported.

[8] Where the pupil is a young person: 1980 Act, s. 28H(1). A "young person" is a person over school age who has not attained the age of 18 years: 1980 Act, s. 135(1).

[9] 1980 Act, s. 28H(1)–(3).

[10] *ibid.* s. 28H(6); s. 28F(2)–(4), (8) and (9) apply.

[11] *ibid.* s. 28H(7).

[12] *ibid.* s. 38(5); *Fraser v. Linlithgow Education Authority* (1923) 39 Sh.Ct.Rep. 262; *Birnie v. Aberdeen Education Authority*, 1937 S.L.T. (Sh.Ct.) 30; *McLennan v. Moray and Nairn Joint C.C.*, 1955 S.L.T. (Sh.Ct.) 14.

[13] *Sinclair v. Lothian R.C.*, 1981 S.L.T. (Sh.Ct.) 13, based on the predecessor of s. 38 of the 1980 Act; but see para. 25.17.

[14] 1980 Act, s. 38(5). See *Bannon v. Dunbarton C.C.* (1934) 50 Sh.Ct.Rep. 301; disapproved in *Huckstep v. Dunfermline District Education Sub-Committee*, 1954 S.L.T (Sh.Ct.) 109.

[15] *ibid.* s. 39(4).

[16] *ibid.* s. 39(3), applying s. 38(5).

one month of the failure of the authority to deal with an application by the parent.[17] This right of appeal also applies to court-imposed attendance orders.[18]

(4) Special educational needs

An appeal lies against an appeal committee's decision, on a reference by a parent or young person, as to which nominated school a recorded[19] child or young person is to be sent.[20] Where the sheriff considers that he cannot deal with the appeal without having the decision of the Secretary of State on certain matters he may, on the motion of a party to the appeal, refer any questions to the Secretary of State,[21] but not if the appeal committee have already done so.[22] The sheriff must decide the appeal in the light of any reference made to the Secretary of State, either by the sheriff himself or by the appeal committee.[23] **26.116**

XVIII. Elections

Representation of the People Act 1983[24]

(1) Registration appeals

An appeal may be made to the sheriff against any of the following: (a) the decision of a registration officer on any claim for registration or objection to a person's registration on the register of voters[25]; (b) the decision of a registration officer disallowing a person's application to vote by proxy or by post as an elector[26]; (c) any decision of the registration officer to make or not to make an alteration in the register as published.[27] **26.117**

There is an appeal on law from the decision of the sheriff to a court of three judges of the Court of Session.[28]

(2) Election expenses

Claims for election expenses not sent to the election agent within 21 days after the declaration of the election result are barred.[29] However, on the application of the claimant candidate or election agent, the sheriff **26.118**

---

[17] 1980 Act, s. 39(4).

[18] *ibid.* s. 44(2).

[19] *i.e.* a child or young person with pronounced, specific or complex special educational needs which are such as to require continuing review: 1980 Act, s. 60(2) as amended by the 1981 Act, s. 4(1), Sched. 8.

[20] 1980 Act, s. 65(1),(2); the provisions of s. 28F(2)–(8) and (9) apply; compare *Donnan v. Glasgow Corporation*, 1970 S.L.T. (Sh.Ct.) 30.

[21] *ibid.* s. 65(3).

[22] *ibid.* s. 65(5).

[23] *ibid.* s. 65(8).

[24] c. 2 ("the 1983 Act"); see J. B. Stewart, "A Survey of Electoral Registration Cases", 1980 S.L.T. (News) 250.

[25] 1983 Act, ss. 56(1)(a), 57; see Representation of the People (Scotland) Regulations 1986 (S.I. 1986 No. 1111), reg. 42.

[26] *ibid.* ss. 56(1)(b), 57, as amended by Representation of the People Act 1985 (c. 50), Sched. 2, para. 1; see *Moore v. Electoral Registration Officer*, 1980 S.L.T. (Sh.Ct.) 39.

[27] *ibid.* s. 56(1)(d).

[28] *ibid.* s. 57(1)(b), (2).

[29] *ibid.* s. 78(1), as amended by Representation of the People Act 1985 (c. 50), Sched. 4, para. 26; s. 204(3).

may grant leave for payment of the expenses after the 21–day period.[30] In the case of a local government election the application must be made to the sheriff court, but it may be made to the Court of Session in the case of other elections.[31] Provision is made for an appeal to the Court of Session from the sheriff's decision.[32]

A claimant may bring an action for a disputed claim in respect of election expenses in the sheriff court.[33] Any payment made by the candidate or agent in pursuance of the decree is not illegal.[34]

The sheriff may, on the application of the candidate or his election agent, grant relief from his or their failure as to a return or declaration in respect of election expenses.[35] Where such an application is made, the Lord Advocate must be notified in order that he, or a representative, may attend the hearing and make representations at it.[36] An appeal lies to the Court of Session from the decision of the sheriff.[37]

(3) Local elections

26.119 A petition questioning the election of councillors may be presented to the sheriff principal by four or more persons who voted as electors or who had a right so to vote,[38] or by a person alleging to have been a candidate.[39] If the election was in respect of a local authority whose area is situated within more than one sheriffdom, the petition is to the sheriffs principal of the sheriffdoms in which the area of the authority is situated.[40] Where the sheriffs principal are unable to reach a unanimous decision they must state a case for the Court of Session, which may pronounce any deliverance which it would have been competent for the sheriffs principal to make.[41]

The sheriff principal may grant relief against certain acts or omissions which would, apart from the section providing for relief, be illegal practices.[42] The person making the application must notify the Lord Advocate in order that he or his representative may attend the hearing and make representations.[43]

XIX. Employment

Factories Act 1961[44]

26.120 If by reason of the terms of an agreement or lease between the owner and occupier of factory premises, the owner or occupier is prevented from carrying out structural alterations to comply with the safety provisions of

---

30 1983 Act, ss. 78(4), 204(3).
31 *ibid.* s. 78(7), 204(3); see *Caddell*, 1936 S.L.T. (Sh.Ct.) 7.
32 *ibid.* ss. 78(4), 204(3).
33 *ibid.* ss. 79(2), 204(3).
34 Not in contravention of ss. 73(1), 78(2) of the 1983 Act.
35 1983 Act, ss. 86(1), 204(3).
36 *ibid.* s. 86(1A), inserted by Representation of the People Act 1985 (c. 50), Sched. 4, para. 30(a); s. 204(3).
37 *ibid.* ss. 86(11), 204(3).
38 *ibid.* s. 128(1), (3)(b).
39 *ibid.*
40 *ibid.*
41 *ibid.* s. 134(1)(b); see also s. 146(1), (5).
42 *ibid.* s. 167.
43 *ibid.* s. 167(1A), inserted by Representation of the People Act 1985 (c. 50), Sched. 4, para. 56; see s. 204(5).
44 9 & 10 Eliz. 2, c. 34 ("the 1961 Act").

the Act, he may apply to the sheriff, who may set aside or modify the terms of the agreement.[45] The owner or occupier may also apply to the sheriff for an order in respect of the expenses and apportionment of expenses of structural alterations required under the safety provisions of the Act.[46] The sheriff will have regard to the terms of any contract between the parties and may, at the request of either party, determine the lease.[47]

Offices, Shops and Railway Premises Act 1963[48]

A person aggrieved by the refusal of a local authority to grant or extend an exemption from requirements issued for improving working conditions, or by a notice of intention to withdraw such an exemption, may appeal to the sheriff within 21 days of the refusal or service of notice.[49] The sheriff may order the authority to grant or extend the exemption, or to cancel the notice of intention to withdraw the exemption.[50] **26.121**

A person who is prevented by the terms of an agreement or lease from carrying out structural work to comply with the Act may apply to the sheriff, who may make an order setting aside or modifying any terms of the agreement or lease as he considers just and equitable.[51] Any person having an interest in the premises who has incurred expense in carrying out structural alterations in order to comply with the Act may apply to the sheriff for an order giving directions with respect to the persons by whom the expense is to be borne and in what proportion.[52] If necessary, the sheriff may modify terms of the lease or agreement relating to rent payable, as he thinks equitable in the circumstances of the case.[53] **26.122**

Trade Union and Labour Relations (Consolidation) Act 1992[54]

The Act provides for restrictions on the application of union funds for certain political purposes. If any trade union member alleges that he is aggrieved by a breach of any such restriction, he may complain to the Certification Officer, who must make such an order for remedying the breach as he thinks just.[55] On any such order being recorded in the sheriff court, it may be enforced as if it had been an order of the sheriff court.[56] **26.123**

XX. Energy

Energy Conservation Act 1981[57]

Disputed questions as to the right to, or the amount of, any compensation for the loss of an appliance seized by an enforcement officer are **26.124**

---

45 1961 Act, s. 169.
46 *ibid.* s. 170.
47 *ibid.* s. 169.
48 c. 41 ("the 1963 Act").
49 *ibid.* s. 46(11).
50 *ibid.*
51 *ibid.* s. 71(1), (3); repealed in part by Offices, Shops and Railway Premises Act 1963, etc. (Repeals) Regulations 1976 (S.I. 1976 No. 2005), Sched, reg. 2.
52 *ibid.* s. 71(2), (3).
53 *ibid.*
54 c. 52 ("the 1992 Act").
55 *ibid.* s. 82(2), (3).
56 *ibid.* s. 82(9).
57 c. 17 ("the 1981 Act").

determined by arbitration: in Scotland, arbitration by a single arbiter appointed, failing agreement between the parties, by a sheriff.[58]

XXI. Enforcement of Decrees

Civil Imprisonment (Scotland) Act 1882[59]

26.125 On a summary application by a creditor in a decree for aliment the sheriff may commit a wilfully defaulting debtor to prison for up to six weeks.[60] Unpaid periodical allowance is not an alimentary debt.[61] That default is wilful is presumed unless rebutted.[62]

Law Reform (Miscellaneous Provisions) (Scotland) Act 1940[63]

26.126 A person in right of a decree *ad factum praestandum* may apply to the court which granted the decree; if satisfied that the failure to obtemper the decree is wilful the sheriff may grant warrant for imprisonment for up to six months.[64] In lieu of granting warrant to imprison, he may recall the decree on which the application proceeds and make an order for payment of a specified sum by the respondent to the applicant, or may make such other order as appears to be just and equitable.[65]

Debtors (Scotland) Act 1987[66]

(1) Time to pay direction

26.127 The sheriff, on application by a defender or a pursuer in a counterclaim, may on granting decree for payment of any principal sum of money, direct payment by instalments, *i.e.* grant a time to pay direction.[67] The sheriff may on application by the debtor or creditor vary or recall the direction.[68]

(2) Time to pay order

26.128 Where a charge for payment has been served under a decree, or other document of debt, or an arrestment has been executed, or an action for adjudication for debt has been commenced, the sheriff may on application by the debtor grant an order for payment by instalments, or by a lump sum after a period, *i.e.* grant a time to pay order.[69] The sheriff may on application by the debtor or creditor recall a time to pay order or recall a poinding or arrestment or restrict the arrestment.[70]

---

[58] 1981 Act, s. 24(2).
[59] 45 & 46 Vict., c. 42 ("the 1882 Act").
[60] *ibid.* s. 4; *Brunt v. Brunt*, 1954 S.L.T. (Sh.Ct.) 74; *Cassells v. Cassells*, 1955 S.L.T. (Sh.Ct.) 41.
[61] *White v. White*, 1984 S.L.T. (Sh.Ct.) 30.
[62] *McWilliams v. McWilliams*, 1963 S.C. 259. See also *Gray v. Gray*, 1993 S.C.L.R. 580.
[63] 3 & 4 Geo. 6, c. 42 ("the 1940 Act").
[64] *ibid.* s. 1(1)(i). The procedure is described in detail in paras 21.81, 21.82.
[65] *ibid.* s. 1(2); see *Ford v. Bell Chandler*, 1977 S.L.T. (Sh.Ct.) 90.
[66] c. 18. ("the 1987 Act").
[67] *ibid.* ss. 1, 15.
[68] *ibid.* s. 3.
[69] *ibid.* ss. 5, 15.
[70] *ibid.* s. 10.

(3) Poindings

After a poinding has been executed the sheriff may on the application of the creditor, the officer of court or the debtor, make an order for (a) the security of any of the poinded articles or (b) for the disposal of perishable articles.[71] The sheriff's decision for the immediate disposal of articles is not subject to appeal.[72] **26.129**

The sheriff may on an application made within 14 days after the date of execution of a poinding by the debtor or any person in possession of a poinded article make an order releasing an article from the poinding if it appears that its continued inclusion would be unduly harsh.[73] If the sheriff makes such an order he may on the application of the creditor authorise the poinding of other articles belonging to the debtor on the same premises.[74] **26.130**

The sheriff may *ex proprio motu* or on the application of the debtor at any time before the sale of poinded articles make an order that the poinding is invalid or has ceased to have effect.[75] On the application of the debtor at any time before application is made for a warrant of sale the sheriff may recall a poinding on certain grounds specified in the Act.[76] **26.131**

Where a caravan, houseboat or other moveable structure which is the only or principal residence of the debtor has been poinded, the sheriff, on application by the debtor before the grant of warrant of sale, may order that for such period as he may specify no further steps shall be taken in the poinding.[77] **26.132**

A poinding normally ceases to have effect on the expiry of one year,[78] but on application by the creditor or an officer of court on his behalf the period may be extended.[79] The application must be made before the expiry of the one year period and before an application has been made for a warrant of sale.[80] The decision of the sheriff on this matter is not subject to appeal.[81] **26.133**

The debtor or the person in possession of poinded articles may move them to another location, if the creditor or an officer of court on his behalf consents in writing, or the sheriff on the debtor's or possessor's application has authorised their removal.[82] **26.134**

Where articles have been removed otherwise than in conformity with the preceding provisions the sheriff may on an application by the creditor make an order requiring the person in possession to restore them; and may **26.135**

---

71 1987 Act, s. 21(1). A.S. (Proceedings in the Sheriff Court under the Debtors (Scotland) Act 1987) 1988 (S.I. 1988 No. 2013) ("A.S. 1988"), para. 12.
72 *ibid.* s. 21(1)(b).
73 *ibid.* s. 23(1).
74 *ibid.* s. 23(2).
75 *ibid.* s. 24(1).
76 *ibid.* s. 24(3).
77 *ibid.* s. 26.
78 *ibid.* s. 27(1).
79 *ibid.* s. 27(2).
80 *ibid.*
81 *ibid.* s. 27(4).
82 *ibid.* s. 28(1).

if such order is not complied with grant warrant to officers of court to search for the articles, and to return them.[83] Where articles are removed through the fault of the debtor the sheriff may on an application by the creditor or an officer of court on his behalf authorise the poinding of other articles belonging to the debtor in the same premises.[84]

26.136 Where poinded articles have been destroyed or damaged the sheriff may on an application by the creditor or an officer of court on his behalf authorise the poinding of other articles belonging to the debtor in the same premises where the debtor has been at fault,[85] and in any case authorise the revaluation of any damaged article.[86]

26.137 Where a third party, knowing that an article has been poinded, wilfully damages or destroys it, or removes it from premises in breach of a poinding, and it is damaged, destroyed, lost or stolen or it is acquired from him by another person without knowledge of the poinding and for value, the sheriff may order the third party to consign a sum equal to its value or diminution in value until the completion of the sale, or until the poinding ceases to have effect.[87]

26.138 A creditor is not entitled to sell poinded articles unless on an application by him the sheriff has granted a warrant of sale.[88] The sheriff may on certain grounds *ex proprio motu* or on the debtor's application refuse a warrant.[89] The sheriff may on an application by the creditor or an officer of court on his behalf grant a variation of the warrant of sale.[90] The sheriff may on certain grounds refuse to grant such an application either *ex proprio motu* or on the debtor's application.[91]

26.139 If an officer of court reports a sale late, or wilfully refuses or delays to make a report, the sheriff may make an order for expenses against him,[92] and also may report the matter to the Court of Session or the sheriff principal.[93]

26.140 Where on an application made to him by a third party before the warrant sale the sheriff is satisfied that a poinded article belongs to this third party, he must make an order releasing it from the poinding.[94] If, on an application by a third party before the warrant sale, the sheriff is satisfied that the article is owned in common by the debtor and the third party, and either the third party undertakes to pay to the officer of court a sum equal to the value of the debtor's interest, or the sheriff is satisfied that the continued poinding or sale of the article would be unduly harsh to the third party, the sheriff must make an order releasing the article from the poinding.[95]

---

83 1987 Act, s. 28(4).
84 *ibid.* s. 28(6).
85 *ibid.* s. 29(2)(a).
86 *ibid.* s. 29(2)(b).
87 *ibid.* s. 29(3), (4).
88 *ibid.* s. 30(1).
89 *ibid.* s. 30(2).
90 *ibid.* s. 35(1).
91 *ibid.* s. 35(2), (3).
92 *ibid.* s. 39(3).
93 *ibid.* s. 79(1)(b).
94 *ibid.* s. 40(2).
95 *ibid.* s. 41(3).

Where an application has been made under various provisions of the 1987 Act[96] it is not competent to grant a warrant of sale (a) while the application is pending, or (b) where the application has been disposed of by the sheriff: (i) during the period during which leave to appeal may be made, (ii) where an application for leave to appeal is made, the period until leave has been refused or the application abandoned, (iii) where leave has been granted, the period during which an appeal may be made, or (iv) when an appeal has been made, the period until the matter has been finally determined or the appeal abandoned.[97] **26.141**

The sheriff may on an application by the creditor conjoin poindings.[98] His decision is not subject to appeal.[99] **26.142**

The liability as between debtor and creditor for expenses incurred in serving a charge and in the process of poinding and warrant sale is set out in Schedule 1. **26.143**

(4) Diligence against earnings

Part III of the Act replaces the diligence of arrestment and action of furthcoming in the case of earnings by earnings arrestment, current maintenance arrestment, and a conjoined arrestment order.[1] **26.144**

If the sheriff is satisfied that an earnings arrestment is invalid or has ceased to have effect, he must, on the application of the debtor, or the person on whom the earnings arrestment schedule was served, make an order declaring that to be the case.[2] Such an order is not subject to appeal.[3] **26.145**

The sheriff, on an application by the debtor, the creditor or the employer, may make an order determining any dispute as to the operation of an earnings arrestment.[4] **26.146**

Similar provisions apply to current maintenance arrestments.[5] **26.147**

Where there is an earnings arrestment or a current maintenance arrestment in force a qualified creditor in respect of a separate debt may apply to the sheriff who must make a conjoined arrestment order.[6] A decision of a sheriff making a conjoined arrestment order is not subject to appeal.[7] Where an employer fails to comply with a conjoined arrestment order, the sheriff clerk may apply to the sheriff, who may grant warrant for diligence against the employer for recovery of the sums which appear to the sheriff to be due.[8] **26.148**

---

[96] The provisions are listed in 1987 Act, s. 42(3).
[97] 1987 Act, s. 42(1), (4).
[98] *ibid.* s. 43(1).
[99] *ibid.* s. 43(5).
[1] *ibid.* s. 46.
[2] *ibid.* s. 50(1).
[3] *ibid.* s. 50(2).
[4] *ibid.* s. 50(3).
[5] *ibid.* s. 55.
[6] *ibid.* s. 60.
[7] *ibid.* s. 60(8).
[8] *ibid.* s. 60(9).

26.149 A creditor may apply to the sheriff for an order that the debtor's employer give him information about existing arrestments.[9] Where a conjoined arrestment order is in effect, the sheriff, on an application made by a creditor whose debt is not being enforced by the order and who, but for the order would be entitled to enforce his debt by an earnings arrestment or a current maintenance arrestment, must make an order varying the conjoined arrestment order so that the creditor's debt is included among the debts enforced by the conjoined arrestment order.[10] Such a decision is not subject to appeal.[11]

26.150 On an application by the debtor, a creditor, the employer or the sheriff clerk, the sheriff may make an order determining any dispute as to the operation of a conjoined assessment order.[12]

26.151 The sheriff must make an order recalling a conjoined assessment order if he is satisfied that the order is invalid, that all the ordinary debts being enforced by the order have been paid or otherwise extinguished or have ceased to be enforceable by diligence and that all obligations to pay current maintenance being so enforced have ceased or have ceased to be enforceable by diligence, or that the debtor's estate has been sequestrated, or on the application for recall of all the creditors whose debts are being enforced by the conjoined arrestment order.[13]

(5) Appeals

26.152 An appeal may be made against any decision of the sheriff under the Act, except where that is expressly forbidden, but only on a question of law and with leave of the sheriff.[14] Since it is provided that the appeal provision in summary causes is not to apply, the appeal is an ordinary appeal.[15] An appeal must be made within 14 days of the grant of leave.[16]

(6) Summary warrants

26.153 Provision is made in the Act[17] for recovery of arrears of rates, of tax, of car tax and of value added tax, by summary warrant, authorising the recovery by poinding and sale in accordance with Schedule 5 to the Act, an earnings arrestment, and an arrestment and action of furthcoming or sale.

(7) Representation

26.154 A party to any proceedings arising solely under the Debtors (Scotland) Act 1987 is entitled to be represented by a person other than a solicitor or an advocate provided that the sheriff is satisfied that such person is a suitable representative and is duly authorised to represent

---

[9] 1987 Act, s. 62(4).
[10] *ibid.* s. 62(5).
[11] *ibid.* s. 62(9).
[12] *ibid.* s. 65.
[13] *ibid.* s. 66, A.S. 1988, paras 62(3), 64.
[14] *ibid.* s. 103(1). The provisions for applying for leave to appeal are contained in A.S. 1988, para. 72.
[15] *ibid.* s. 103(1).
[16] *ibid.* s. 103(2).
[17] *ibid.* Sched. 4.

that party.[18] This exception to the general rule as to representation does not apply to an appeal to the sheriff principal.[19]

XXII. ENTERTAINMENT

Theatres Act 1968[20]

A person aggrieved may appeal to the sheriff against the licensing authority's refusal to grant, renew or transfer a licence for the public performance of plays, refusal to vary the terms, conditions and restrictions of such a licence, imposition of such terms on the grant of a licence, or revocation of a licence.[21] The appeal must be made to the sheriff within whose jurisdiction the premises are situated; and he may make such order as thinks fit.[22] **26.155**

A sheriff may grant warrant authorising entry into premises by police officers or authorised officers of the licensing authority.[23] **26.156**

Safety of Sports Grounds Act 1975[24]

The Secretary of State may designate as a sports ground requiring a safety certificate any sports ground which in his opinion can accommodate at least 10,000 spectators.[25] The local authority[26] may issue safety certificates, with or without conditions attached, to qualified persons.[27] An appeal by any interested party lies by summary application to the sheriff[28] against the decision of the local authority that a person is not a qualified person, or against terms and conditions included in the grant of a licence.[29] **26.157**

If the local authority is of opinion that the risk to the spectators at a stadium is so serious that their admission ought to be prohibited or restricted until steps have been taken to reduce the risk to a reasonable level, they may serve a prohibition notice.[30] Any person aggrieved[31] by the notice may appeal to the sheriff by summary application.[32] Any person aggrieved by the notice, the local authority, the chief officer of police, and the building authority may appeal, notwithstanding that they were not parties to the proceedings on the application.[33] **26.158**

---

[18] 1987 Act, s. 97, OCR, r. 1.3(1).
[19] OCR, r. 1.3(2).
[20] c. 54 ("the 1968 Act").
[21] *ibid.* s. 14(1). The licensing authority is a council as constituted under s. 2 of Local Government (Scotland) Act 1994 (c. 39): 1968 Act, s. 18(1), as amended.
[22] *ibid.* s. 14(1).
[23] *ibid.* s. 15.
[24] c. 52 ("the 1975 Act"), as amended by Fire Safety and Safety of Places of Sport Act 1987 (c. 27), s. 19(1), Sched. 2; extended by Safety of Sports Grounds (Designation) (Scotland) Order 1986 (S.I. 1986 No. 1243).
[25] 1975 Act, s. 1; see also n. 24.
[26] *ibid.* s. 17 (as amended). The local authority is a council as constituted under s. 2 of Local Government (Scotland) Act 1994 (c. 39).
[27] *ibid.* ss. 2, 3(1).
[28] *ibid.* s. 5 as amended by s. 22 of Fire Safety and Safety of Places of Sport Act 1987 (c. 27), ss. 22, 49, Sched. 5, para. 6.
[29] *ibid.*
[30] *ibid.* s. 10(1), (3), as substituted by s. 23 of the Fire Safety and Safety of Places of Sport Act 1987.
[31] *ibid.* s. 10A(1), (9).
[32] *ibid.* s. 10A(9).
[33] *ibid.* s. 10A(8).

Cinemas Act 1985[34]

26.159 Any person aggrieved by a local authority's refusal of, refusal to renew or revocation of a licence to use a building as a cinema may appeal to the sheriff.[35]

Fire Safety and Safety of Places of Sport Act 1987[36]

26.160 Under section 26 of the Act a local authority has the duty to determine whether any stand at a non-designated sports ground requires a safety certificate and to issue safety certificates subject to such terms and conditions as they consider necessary or expedient.[37] Any person served with a notice of determination that a stand is a regulated stand, or that that person does not qualify for the issue of a safety certificate, may appeal to the sheriff by summary application.[38] An applicant for a special safety certificate may so appeal against a refusal.[39] Any interested party may so appeal against the contents of a safety certificate or the refusal of the local authority to amend or replace it.[40]

XXIII. Environment

Caravan Sites and Control of Development Act 1960[41]

26.161 Any person aggrieved by any condition[42] subject to which a site licence is granted may appeal to the sheriff having jurisdiction in the place where the land is situated.[43] The appeal must be made within 28 days of the issue of the licence.[44] If the sheriff is satisfied that the condition is unduly burdensome, he may vary or cancel the condition.[45]

The holder of a site licence, if aggrieved by the local authority's variation of, or refusal to vary, conditions attached to the licence, may appeal to the sheriff within 28 days of notification of the alteration or refusal.[46] If the sheriff allows the appeal, he may give the local authority such directions as may be necessary to give effect to his decision.[47]

On either of the above applications under the Act the sheriff's decision is final and binding.[48] However, the sheriff may at any stage of the proceedings, and must, if so directed by the Court of Session, state a case for the decision of the Court of Session on any question of law arising in

---

34 c. 13 ("the 1985 Act").
35 *ibid.* s. 16(1).
36 c. 27 ("the 1987 Act").
37 *ibid.* ss. 26–29.
38 *ibid.* s. 30(1), (2), (7).
39 *ibid.* s. 30(3).
40 *ibid.* s. 30(4).
41 8 & 9 Eliz. 2, c. 62 ("the 1960 Act").
42 Other than a condition under s. 5(3): 1960 Act, s. 7(1).
43 1960 Act, ss. 7(1), 32(1)(c).
44 *ibid.* s. 7(1).
45 *ibid.*; see *Clyde Caravans (Langbank) Ltd v. Renfrew C.C.*, 1962 S.L.T. (Sh.Ct). 20 at 22; *Haslam v. Kirkcudbright C.C.*, 1962 S.L.T. (Sh.Ct.) 47; *McLellan v. Kirkcudbright C.C.*, 1962 S.L.T. (Sh.Ct.) 43; see also *Owen Cooper Estates v. Lexden and Winstree RDC* (1964) 63 L.G.R. 66.
46 *ibid.* ss. 8(2), (4), 32(1)(c); see *Llanfyllin RDC v. Holland* (1964) 62 L.G.R. 459.
47 *ibid.* s. 8(2).
48 *ibid.* s. 32(2)(b).

connection with the appeal.[49] An appeal lies with leave to the House of Lords from the decision of the Court of Session.[50]

The sheriff may grant warrant authorising authorised officers of the local authority to enter on land used as a caravan site.[51] **26.162**

Caravan Sites Act 1968[52]

If in proceedings by the owner[53] of a protected site[54] the sheriff makes an eviction order he may suspend the enforcement of the order for up to 12 months, on such terms as he thinks reasonable.[55] Where the sheriff makes such an order he must make no order for expenses unless there are special reasons for doing so.[56] The sheriff may vary the order from time to time on the application of either party.[57] In considering how to exercise his powers under the Act the sheriff is directed to have regard to all the circumstances and also to certain specified issues.[58] **26.163**

Control of Pollution Act 1974[59]

(1) Household waste

A collection authority[60] may, by a notice served[61] on the occupier of any premises, require him to place household waste for collection in receptacles which are of a kind and number reasonably specified in the notice. The occupier may appeal to the sheriff against the notice on the ground that any requirement specified in the notice is unreasonable or on the ground that the receptacles in which household waste is placed for collection are adequate.[62] The notice is of no effect pending the determination of the appeal,[63] and the court must either quash or modify the notice or dismiss the appeal.[64] **26.164**

(2) Commercial or industrial waste

The collection authority may serve a notice upon the occupier of the premises requiring him to provide receptacles for the storage of waste which they consider would otherwise cause a nuisance or be detrimental to the locality.[65] A person upon whom such a notice has been served may appeal to the sheriff with 21 days on the grounds that any requirement **26.165**

---

49 1960 Act, s. 32(2); see *Turner v. Garstang RDC* (1965) 64 L.G.R. 28.
50 *ibid.* s. 32(2)
51 *ibid.* ss. 26(2), 32(1)(i).
52 c. 52 ("the 1968 Act"), as extended to Scotland by Mobile Homes Act 1975 (c. 49), s.8, Sched., Pt I, para. 1..
53 *ibid.* s. 1(3).
54 *ibid.* s. 1(2).
55 *ibid.* ss. 4(1), (2), 5, substituted for Scotland by Mobile Homes Act 1975 (c. 49), Sched., Pt II, para. 2.
56 *ibid.* s. 4(5).
57 *ibid.* s. 4(3).
58 *ibid.* s. 4(4).
59 c. 40 ("the 1974 Act").
60 Defined in 1974 Act, s. 30(2) and apparently not amended by Local Government etc. (Scotland) Act 1994 (c. 39), Sched. 13.
61 1974 Act, s. 13(1), (2), as amended by Local Government, Planning and Land Act 1980 (c. 65) ("the 1980 Act"), Sched. 2, para. 10(1).
62 *ibid.* s. 13(3), as amended by 1980 Act, Sched. 2, para. 10(2)(a); s. 106(6).
63 *ibid.* s. 13(3)(a).
64 *ibid.* s. 13(3)(b).
65 *ibid.* s. 13(5), substituted by 1980 Act, Sched. 2, para. 10(3).

specified in the notice is unreasonable or that the waste is not likely to cause a nuisance or be detrimental to the locality.[66]

(3) Controlled waste

26.166 If any controlled waste[67] is deposited on any land in contravention of the Act[68] the disposal authority may serve a notice on the occupier of the land requiring him either to remove the waste or take specified steps to eliminate or reduce the consequences of the deposit.[69] A person who receives such a notice may appeal to the sheriff within 21 days, and the sheriff may quash or modify the notice or dismiss the appeal.[70]

(4) Noise

26.167 The local authority is empowered to serve notices in respect of noise amounting to a nuisance.[71] A person served with a notice to abate or prohibit such noise or requiring works for such purposes, may appeal to the sheriff within 21 days from the service of the notice.[72] Detailed provisions for such an appeal are made by Order.[73] If the local authority consider the notice to be an inadequate remedy they may take proceedings before the sheriff for the purpose of securing abatement, prohibition or restriction of noise nuisance.[74]

26.168 A person aggrieved by noise nuisance may make a summary application to the sheriff who may order either or both of the following: (i) the abatement of the nuisance and execution of works for that purpose; (ii) the prohibition of the recurrence of the nuisance and the execution of works for that purpose.[75] Failure without reasonable excuse to comply with any such order is an offence.[76]

26.169 To control the noise on construction sites the local authority may serve a notice[77] imposing requirements as to the way in which works are to be carried out. A person served with such a notice may appeal to the sheriff within 21 days from the service of the notice.[78]

26.170 A person who intends to carry out construction works may apply to the local authority for a prior consent.[79] If a local authority does not give its consent within 28 days of receiving the application, or does grant it but

---

66 1974 Act, s. 13(6), as amended by 1980 Act, Sched. 2, para. 10(4); s. 106(6).

67 Defined as "household, industrial and commercial waste or any such waste": 1974 Act, s. 30(1).

68 1974 Act, s. 3(1).

69 *ibid.* s. 16(1).

70 *ibid.* ss. 16(2), 106(6).

71 *ibid.* s. 58(1): see *Strathclyde R.C. v. Tudhope*, 1983 S.L.T. 22.

72 1974 Act, ss. 58(3), 106(6); see *A. Lambert Flat Management v. Lomas* [1981] 1 W.L.R. 898 at 902, 903, 906, 907; *Meri Mate Ltd v. City of Dundee D.C.*, 1994 S.C.L.R. 960.

73 See Control of Noise (Appeals) (Scotland) Regulations 1983 (S.I. 1983 No. 1455), regs 4, 10; *Wycombe D.C. v. Jeffways & Pilot Coaches* (1983) 81 L.G.R. 662.

74 1974 Act, ss. 58(8), 106(6); see *Hammersmith LBC v. Magnum Automated Forecourts Ltd* [1978] 1 W.L.R. 50.

75 *ibid.* ss. 59(1), (2)(a), (2)(h), (7)(a), 106(6).

76 *ibid.* s. 59(4).

77 *ibid.* s. 60(2).

78 *ibid.* ss. 60(7), 106(6); S.I. 1983 No. 1455, regs. 5, 10.

79 *ibid.* s. 61(1), (4).

with conditions or qualifications attached, the applicant may appeal to the sheriff within 21 days from the end of that period.[80]

A local authority may designate all or any part of its area a noise abatement zone.[81] A noise abatement order specifies the classes of premises to which it applies.[82] On convicting any person of exceeding the level of noise permitted the sheriff may, if satisfied that an offence is likely to recur, make an order requiring the execution of works necessary to prevent it continuing or recurring,[83] or may direct the local authority to execute the works.[84] The local authority may serve a "noise reduction notice" under the Act[85] and any person upon whom such a notice is served may appeal to the sheriff within three months.[86] This section also applies to buildings constructed within a noise abatement zone after the passing of a noise abatement order.[87] **26.171**

In entertaining any appeal under Part III of the Act the sheriff must have regard to any duty imposed by law on the appellant which concerns the activities in the course of which the noise is emitted.[88] A sheriff is not disqualified from acting by reason of his being liable in common with other ratepayers to contribute to or benefit from any rate or fund of the local authority.[89] An appeal against any decision of the sheriff in pursuance of this Act, other than a decision made in criminal proceedings, lies only to the Court of Session at the instance of any party to the proceedings.[90] **26.172**

The sheriff may issue a warrant to authorise an officer of a relevant authority[91] to enter upon any land or vessel for the purpose of performing any functions conferred upon the authority by the Act.[92] **26.173**

Mobile Homes Act 1983[93]

Where a person ("the occupier") is entitled under an agreement to station a mobile home[94] on a protected site[95] and occupy it as his only or main residence, the owner of the site must within three months of the making of the agreement give to the occupier a written statement of specified particulars.[96] If the owner fails to comply with that duty, the occupier may apply for an order requiring him so to comply.[97] The **26.174**

---

80 1974 Act, ss. 61(6), 106(6); S.I. 1983 No. 1455, reg. 6.
81 *ibid.* s. 63(1), as amended by 1980 Act, Sched. 2, para. 14(a).
82 *ibid.* s. 63(2).
83 *ibid.* ss. 65(6), 106(6).
84 *ibid.* ss. 65(7), 106(6).
85 *ibid.* s. 66(1).
86 *ibid.* ss. 66(7), 106(6); S.I. 1983 No. 1455, regs. 7, 10.
87 *ibid.* s. 67(5).
88 *ibid.* ss. 70(4), 106(6).
89 *ibid.* s. 87(6).
90 *ibid.* s. 85(2).
91 *ibid.* s. 98, as amended by Local Government etc. (Scotland) Act 1994 (c. 39), Sched. 13, para. 95(8).
92 *ibid.* s. 91(1), (5)(b).
93 c. 34 ("the 1983 Act").
94 "Mobile home" has the same meaning as "caravan" in Pt I of Caravan Sites and Control of Development Act 1960 (c.62), as amended by Caravan Sites Act 1968 (c.52): 1983 Act, s. 5(1).
95 1983 Act, s. 5(1); *Balthasar v. Mullane* (1985) 84 L.G.R. 55.
96 *ibid.* s. 1(1), (2).
97 *ibid.* s. 1(5).

application may be made to the sheriff having jurisdiction where the protected site is situated or, where the parties have so agreed, an arbiter.[98] On the application of either party made within six months of the giving of the statement, the sheriff or arbiter may order that there shall be implied in the agreement terms concerning the matters mentioned in Part II of Schedule 1 to the Act.[99] Further, the court or arbiter may, on the application of either party made within the same period of six months, by order vary or delete any express term of the agreement.[1] On any of the foregoing applications[2] the sheriff or arbiter is directed to make such provisions as he considers just and equitable in the circumstances.[3]

26.175 The sheriff or arbiter has jurisdiction to determine any question arising under the Act or any agreement to which it applies, and to entertain any proceedings brought under the Act or any such agreement.[4]

XXIV. Fire Services

Fire Services Act 1947[5]

26.176 Under the Firemen's Pension Scheme the sheriff hears appeals on entitlement.[6] In these appeals the sheriff is specifically required not to reopen decisions on certain medical questions,[7] whilst otherwise authorising such order as appears to be just.[8]

26.177 The sheriff may grant warrant authorising members of the fire brigade to enter premises to obtain information required for fire fighting purposes.[9]

Fire Precautions Act 1971[10]

26.178 The Act makes provision for the protection of persons from fire risks. The fire authority may issue a notice[11] making a fire certificate compulsory for the use of certain premises as a dwelling; and any person upon whom the notice is served may appeal to the sheriff.[12] A person aggrieved by a refusal to grant, conditional grant of, or refusal to cancel or amend a fire certificate by the fire authority,[13] or by any direction in respect of, or threatened cancellation or amendment of a fire certificate for altered premises or premises on which it is proposed to keep explosive or

---

98 1983 Act, s. 5(1).

99 *ibid.* s. 2(2); *Faulkner v. Love* [1977] Q.B. 937; *Taylor v. Calvert* [1978] 1 W.L.R. 899; *Grant v. Allen* [1980] 1 All E.R. 720.

1 *ibid.* s. 2(3).

2 Such applications cannot be made until the written statement is served.

3 1983 Act, s. 2(4).

4 *ibid.* ss. 4, 5(1).

5 10 & 11 Geo. 6, c. 41 ("the 1947 Act").

6 *ibid.* s. 26(2)(h); Firemen's Pension Scheme Order 1973 (S.I. 1973 No. 966) ("1973 Order"), para. 68(1).

7 1973 Order, para. 68(3)(b).

8 *ibid.* para. 68(2).

9 1947 Act, s. 1(2), as substituted for Scotland by s. 36(14).

10 c. 40 ("the 1971 Act").

11 *ibid.* s. 3.

12 *ibid.* ss. 4(1), 43(1).

13 *ibid.* ss. 5, 9(1), (2), 43(1); *McGovern v. Central R.C.*, 1982 S.L.T. (Sh.Ct.) 110.

flammable material[14] may appeal[15] to the sheriff within 21 days from the relevant date.[16] The sheriff may make such order as he thinks fit.[17]

In respect of certain premises[18] the fire authority may serve on the occupier a prohibition notice if the authority is of opinion that the use of the premises involves or will involve a serious risk to persons on the premises in case of fire.[19] A person on whom a prohibition notice has been served may appeal to the sheriff within 21 days.[20] The sheriff may either cancel the notice or affirm it with or without modifications.[21] **26.179**

A person prevented by the terms of a lease from carrying out any structural or other alteration required by a notice or regulation under the Act may apply to the sheriff who may set aside or modify any terms or conditions of the lease as he considers just and equitable.[22] A person alleging that the whole or part of any expense incurred in complying with a notice should be borne by another person, may apply to the sheriff, who may give directions as to expenses and proportions.[23] The sheriff may also provide for modification of rent.[24] **26.180**

Fire Certificates (Special Premises) Regulations 1976[25]

A fire certificate issued by the Health and Safety Executive is required in respect of certain premises.[26] A person who is aggrieved by the refusal of, conditional grant of or refusal to vary such a certificate may appeal to the sheriff within whose jurisdiction the premises are situated.[27] The appeal must be made within 21 days of the relevant date,[28] and the sheriff may make such order as he thinks fit.[29] **26.181**

A person prevented by the terms of a lease from carrying out any structural or other alteration required by the Regulations,[30] or who has carried out such alterations and believes that the expense incurred should be wholly or partially met by another person[31] may apply to the sheriff. The sheriff may modify the terms of the lease, give directions with respect to the expense and modify the rent payable as he considers just and equitable.[32] **26.182**

---

14 1971 Act, s. 8(4)–(7), (9).
15 *ibid.* s. 9(1), 43(1).
16 *ibid.* s. 9(2).
17 *ibid.* ss. 9(1), 43(1).
18 Premises falling within any of the classes of use mentioned in 1971 Act, s. 1(2) or to which s. 2 applies: 1971 Act, s. 10(1), as amended by Fire Safety and Safety of Places of Sport Act 1987 (c. 27), ss. 9(1), 49(2), Sched. 5, para. 4.
19 1971 Act, s. 10(2), as amended.
20 *ibid.* ss. 10A(1) (as amended), 93(1).
21 *ibid.* s. 10A(2).
22 *ibid.* s. 28(2), (5), as amended by Rent Act 1977 (c. 42), Sched. 23, para. 49(a).
23 *ibid.* s. 28(3), (5).
24 *ibid.*
25 S.I. 1976 No. 2003.
26 Specified in S.I. 1976 No. 2003, Sched. 1, Pt 1, as amended by Ionising Radiations Regulations 1985 (S.I. 1985 No. 1333), Sched. 10, Pt II; see also S.I. 1976 No. 2003, reg. 16.
27 S.I. 1976 No. 2003, reg. 12(1), (4).
28 *ibid.* reg. 12(1), (2), (4).
29 *ibid.* reg. 12(1), (4).
30 *ibid.* reg. 14(1), (3).
31 *ibid.* reg. 14(2), (3).
32 *ibid.* reg. 14(1)–(3).

XXV. Firearms

Firearms Act 1968[33]

26.183 Under this Act any person aggrieved by any of the following decisions may appeal to the sheriff[34]: (1) the refusal of a chief officer of police to grant or renew a firearm certificate[35]; (2) the refusal of a chief officer of police to vary a firearm certificate[36]; (3) the revocation of a firearm certificate[37]; (4) partial revocation of a firearm certificate[38]; (5) revocation of a shotgun certificate[39]; (6) the refusal of a chief officer of police to register a person as a firearms dealer[40]; (7) the imposition or variation of, or the refusal to vary or revoke, any condition of a firearms dealer's registration[41]; (8) the refusal of a chief officer of police to register a firearms dealer's place of business[42]; or (9) the removal from the register of a firearms dealer's name.[43]

All of the above appeals are to be by way of summary application.[44] The appeal is to be determined on the merits (and not by way of review).[45] The sheriff hearing an appeal may consider any evidence or other matter whether or not it was available when the decision of the chief officer was taken.[46] The appeal must be made within 21 days of receipt of notice of the decision[47] and on hearing the appeal the sheriff may either dismiss the appeal or give the chief officer of police such directions as he thinks fit as respects the certificate or the register which is the subject of the appeal.[48] The decision of the sheriff on appeal may be appealed only on a point of law.[49]

26.184 The Act places a general prohibition on the possession of firearms by certain classes of person convicted of criminal offences. Such persons may apply to the sheriff for the removal of the prohibition.[50] Application is made to the sheriff within whose jurisdiction the applicant resides,[51] and not less than 21 days notice must be given to the chief officer of

---

33 c. 27 ("the 1968 Act").

34 *ibid.* s. 44(1), as substituted by Firearms (Amendment) Act 1997 (c. 5) ("the 1997 Act"), s. 41.

35 *ibid.* s. 28A(6), inserted by 1997 Act, Sched. 2, para. 4; *Todd v. Neilans*, 1940 S.L.T. (Sh.Ct.) 12; *Anderson v. Neilans*, 1940 S.L.T. (Sh.Ct.) 13; *Hughson v. Lerwick Police*, 1956 S.L.T. (Sh.Ct.) 18; *Pinkerton v. Chief Constable of Strathclyde Police*, Kilmarnock Sh. Ct, Oct. 11, 1976, unreported.

36 *ibid.* s. 29(2).

37 *ibid.* s. 30A(6) as substituted by 1997 Act, s. 40; see *R. v. Acton Crown Court, ex p. Varney* [1984] Crim.L.R. 638; *Miller v. Chief Constable of Strathclyde Police*, Kilmarnock Sh. Ct., Jan. 27, 1978, unreported, which approved *Jarvis v. Chief Constable of Strathclyde*, 1976 S.L.T. (Sh.Ct.) 66, to the effect that the chief constable need not hear the appellant prior to revoking a certificate.

38 *ibid.* s. 30B(3), as substituted by 1997 Act, s. 40.

39 *ibid.* s. 30C(2), as substituted by 1997 Act, s. 40.

40 *ibid.* s. 34(5).

41 *ibid.* s. 36(3).

42 *ibid.* s. 37(3).

43 *ibid.* s. 38(7).

44 *ibid.* s. 44(1), as substituted by 1997 Act, s. 41 and Sched. 5, Pt III.

45 *ibid.* s. 44(2), as substituted by 1997 Act, s. 41.

46 *ibid.* s. 44(3), as substituted by 1997 Act, s. 41..

47 *ibid.* Sched. 5, Pt III, para. 2, as substituted by 1997 Act, s. 41.

48 *ibid.* para. 3.

49 *ibid.* para. 4.

50 *ibid.* s. 21(6).

51 *ibid.* Sched. 3, Pt II, para. 8.

police.[52] The application is to be made by initial writ,[53] and disposed of as a summary application.[54]

The chief constable may apply to the sheriff for an order for the destruction or disposal of firearms or ammunition seized and detained by the police.[55] 26.185

XXVI. FISHERIES

Salmon Fisheries (Scotland) Act 1868[56]

A sheriff may upon an information on oath that there is probable cause to suspect any breach of the Act by warrant under his hand empower any water bailiff, constable, or watcher to enter premises and seize material and illegally taken salmon.[57] 26.186

Sea Fisheries (Scotland) Amendment Act 1885[58]

If an offence under the Sea Fisheries Acts[59] is committed it is competent for an injured person to give notice in writing to the sheriff clerk and to the offender that at the trial of the offence the sheriff will be called upon to consider and dispose of the question of damages.[60] At the close of the trial the sheriff is to consider the question of damages and grant decree as in an ordinary action.[61] If a fishery officer's report is produced[62] no additional evidence is to be heard unless the sheriff considers it to be necessary.[63] Evidence will not be recorded and there is no provision for appeal. The offender's liability for damages flows from his conviction and the only way to avoid liability would thus be to have the conviction upset.[64] This remedy is an alternative to actions at common law.[65] 26.187

British Fishing Boats Act 1983[66]

A sheriff may grant a warrant authorising a British sea-fishery officer, with or without constables, to enter and search premises to determine whether a suspected offence has been committed.[67] 26.188

---

52 1968 Act, para. 9.
53 S.I. 1970 No. 1984, reg. 1.
54 *ibid.*
55 1968 Act. s. 52(4).
56 31 & 32 Vict., c. 123 ("the 1868 Act").
57 *ibid.* s. 26, as amended by Sheriff Courts (Scotland) Act 1971, (c. 58), s. 4.
58 48 & 49 Vict., c. 70 ("the 1885 Act").
59 *ibid.* s. 8. "Sea Fisheries Acts" means the 1885 Act and Sea Fisheries Act 1968: 1885 Act, s.1, as amended by Sea Fisheries Act 1968 (c. 77), Sched. 1, para. 24. Offences under ss. 5–10 of the Sea Fisheries Act 1968, or s. 2 of the Fishery Limits Act 1976 (c. 86), are not included (proviso inserted by 1968 Act, Sched. 1, para. 29).
60 *ibid.* s. 8.
61 *ibid.*
62 *ibid.* s. 7, as amended by 1968 Act, Sched. 1, para 28.
63 *ibid.* s. 8.
64 See Dobie, pp. 665, 666.
65 *Macleod v. Dobson* (1899) 16 Sh.Ct.Rep. 33; *Ferrier v. Coull* (1906) 22 Sh.Ct.Rep. 263.
66 c. 8 ("the 1983 Act").
67 *ibid.* s. 3.

Salmon Act 1986[68]

26.189 A person whose request to a salmon fishing board to add or remove a name in the roll of proprietors and values[69] has not been met, may apply to the sheriff by summary application, and he may order the board to add or remove that name.[70]

XXVII. Food

Food and Environment Protection Act 1985[71]

26.190 A sheriff may issue a warrant authorising an officer to enter a dwelling for the purpose of performing his functions under the Act.[72]

Food Safety Act 1990[73]

26.191 Any person who is aggrieved by: (a) a decision of an authorised officer of an enforcement authority to serve an improvement notice; (b) a decision of an enforcement authority to refuse to issue a certificate under sections 11 or 12; or (c) a decision of such authority to refuse, cancel, suspend, or revoke a licence required under Part II of the Act, is entitled to appeal to the sheriff[74] by summary application.[75] On an appeal against an improvement notice the sheriff may either cancel or affirm the notice, and if he affirms it he may do so either in its original form or with such modifications as he may in the circumstances think fit.[76]

Meat Products (Hygiene) Regulations 1994[77]

26.192 Any person who is aggrieved by the refusal or revocation of an approval or by a special hygiene direction may appeal to the sheriff.[78]

The provisions of section 37(3) to (6) of the 1990 Act apply to such appeals.[79]

Dairy Products (Hygiene) (Scotland) Regulations 1995[80]

26.193 A food authority may revoke[81] a licence granted in respect of any production holding[82] (*i.e.*, for, *inter alia*, producing raw milk) or an approval of a dairy establishment.[83] Without prejudice to the right of appeal under section 37 of the Food Safety Act 1990 any person aggrieved by the revocation of an approval may appeal to the sheriff.[84] The provisions of section 37(4) to (6) of the 1990 Act apply to such appeals.[85]

---

[68] c. 62 ("the 1986 Act").
[69] To be maintained in terms of 1986 Act, s. 11(9).
[70] 1986 Act, s. 11(10).
[71] c. 48 ("the 1985 Act").
[72] *ibid.* Sched. 2, para. 7(1)–(3).
[73] c. 16 ("the 1990 Act").
[74] *ibid.* s. 37(1).
[75] *ibid.* s. 37(4).
[76] *ibid.* s. 39(1).
[77] S.I. 1994 No. 3082.
[78] *ibid.* reg. 7(1).
[79] *ibid.* reg. 7(2).
[80] S.I. 1995 No. 1372.
[81] *ibid.* reg. 8(1).
[82] *ibid.* reg. 4.
[83] *ibid.* reg. 6.
[84] *ibid.* reg. 8(4).
[85] *ibid.* reg. 8(5).

Minced Meat and Meat Preparations (Hygiene) Regulations 1995[86]

Any person who is aggrieved by the refusal or revocation of an approval (of premises for the production of minced meat or meat preparations intended for consignment or sale for consignment to a relevant EEA State for human consumption) may appeal to the sheriff.[87] The provisions of section 37(3)–(6) of the 1990 Act apply to such appeals.[88] **26.194**

Dairy Produce Quotas Regulations 1997[89]

Where apportionments and prospective apportionments in respect of holdings in Scotland are to be carried out by arbitration,[90] the arbiter may at any stage of the proceedings, and shall, if so directed by the sheriff (which direction may be given on the application of any party) state a case for the opinion of the sheriff on any questions of law arising in the course of the arbitration.[91] The opinion of the sheriff on any case is final.[92] The sheriff may sanction payment of remuneration and expenses to the arbiter's clerk,[93] and may remove an arbiter if he has misconducted himself.[94] The sheriff may set aside the award if an arbiter has misconducted himself or an arbitration or award has been improperly procured.[95] **26.195**

XXVIII. Friendly and Other Societies

Industrial Assurance Act 1923[96]

Disputes between a collecting society or an industrial assurance company and an aggrieved member or person assured may be referred to the sheriff court on application by the aggrieved member or person assured.[97] **26.196**

Industrial and Provident Societies Act 1965[98]

The moneys payable to a society from its members are recoverable before the sheriff within whose jurisdiction the society's registered office is situated[99] or within whose jurisdiction the member resides.[1] **26.197**

A society may apply to the sheriff in respect of the neglect or refusal of an officer or servant of the society to account.[2] The sheriff's order is final and conclusive.[3] **26.198**

---

[86] S.I. 1995 No. 3205.
[87] *ibid.* reg. 6(1).
[88] *ibid.* reg. 6(2).
[89] S.I. 1997 No. 733.
[90] *ibid.* Sched. 3, para. 1(1).
[91] *ibid.* para. 20.
[92] *ibid.*
[93] *ibid.* para. 19.
[94] *ibid.* para. 21.
[95] *ibid.* para. 22.
[96] 13 & 14 Geo. 5, c. 8 ("the 1923 Act").
[97] *ibid.* s. 32(1).
[98] c. 12 ("the 1965 Act").
[99] *ibid.* s. 22; *Glasgow Working Men's Building Society v. Kirkwood* (1888) 4 Sh.Ct.Rep. 165.
[1] *ibid.* s. 22.
[2] *ibid.* s. 42(3)(b), (4).
[3] *ibid.*

26.199 A registered society may be wound up by the sheriff.[4] The provisions of the Insolvency Act 1986 apply, and the registrar may petition for a winding up,[5] as may any member or other person interested in or having claim on the funds of the society.[6]

26.200 The sheriff may determine a dispute in a registered society if both parties to the dispute consent or the rules of the society contain no directions as to disputes.[7]

26.201 Any decision of a dispute reached in accordance with the rules of the society may be enforced by application to the sheriff,[8] as may the decision of the registrar.[9] Any dispute directed by the rules of the society to be referred to justices, a justice of the peace court, or a court of summary jurisdiction, is to be determined by a sheriff.[10] Where the rules contain no direction as to disputes, or where no decision is made within 40 days after an application has been made to the society for a reference under its rules, any party to the dispute may apply to the sheriff, who may hear and determine the dispute.[11] Either party may ask the sheriff to state a case on a question of law arising in the dispute for the opinion of the Court of Session.[12] The sheriff is not bound to state a case. This restricted right of appeal seems to apply when the dispute is determined by the sheriff, and not on an application to enforce an award.[13] There is a right of appeal from the sheriff to the sheriff principal.[14] Where a dispute is not within the terms of the Act the sheriff may have a common law jurisdiction.[15]

Friendly Societies Act 1974[16]

26.202 The sheriff may enforce payment of money due by members of registered cattle insurance societies and other specially authorised societies.[17]

26.203 Where any person has possession of any property of a registered society and fails to deliver it on request, the sheriff may order him to deliver it[18]; failing delivery, the person is liable on summary conviction to two months' imprisonment.[19] If the sheriff is satisfied that the person has applied money belonging to the society for unauthorised purposes, he may order him to repay the money[20]; and such an order is enforceable as an

---

[4] 1965 Act, s. 55(a)(ii), as amended by Insolvency Act 1986 (c. 45), Sched. 14.
[5] *ibid.* s. 56.
[6] *ibid.* s. 58(6)(a).
[7] *ibid.* s. 60(2), as substituted by Friendly Societies Act 1992 (c. 40), s. 83.
[8] *ibid.* s. 60(3)(b), (7)(a).
[9] *ibid.*
[10] *ibid.* s. 60(7)(b)(i); Dobie, *Styles*, p. 163.
[11] *ibid.* s. 60(7)(b)(ii).
[12] *ibid.* s. 60(9); *Smith v. Scottish Legal Life Assurance Society*, 1912 S.C. 611.
[13] Dobie, p. 592; *Glasgow District of Order of Foresters v. Stevenson* (1899) 2 F. 14; *Collins v. Barrowfield United Oddfellows*, 1915 S.C. 190.
[14] Dobie, p. 592; *First Edinburgh Starr-Bowkett Building Society v. Munro* (1883) 11 R. 5; *Glasgow Corporation v. Mickel*, 1922 S.C. 228; *Greig v. City of Glasgow Friendly Society*, 1939 S.L.T. (Sh.Ct.) 31.
[15] Dobie, p. 592; *Galashiels Provident Building Society v. Newlands* (1893) 20 R. 821; *McGowan v. City of Glasgow Friendly Society*, 1913 S.C. 991; *Gow v. Portobello Co-operative Society* (1926) 43 Sh.Ct.Rep. 127; *Todd v. Kelso Co-operative Society*, 1953 S.L.T. (Sh.Ct.) 2.
[16] c. 46 ("the 1974 Act").
[17] *ibid.* s. 22.
[18] *ibid.* s.99(3).
[19] *ibid.*
[20] *ibid.* s. 99(4).

order for the payment of money recoverable summarily as a civil debt.[21] Orders made under section 99(3) and (4) of the Act may be appealed against as if they were orders made on conviction of the person to whom the order is directed.[22]

A dispute arising out of loans of surplus funds to societies of different descriptions may be brought before the sheriff, unless before the proceedings commence an application has been made for a reference under the rules of the borrower.[23] Where a special resolution has been passed for the amalgamation of a registered friendly society any person who claims to be entitled to receive a benefit from the society and is dissatisfied with the provision made for satisfying his claim, may apply to the sheriff within three months of the passing of the special resolution.[24] **26.204**

Credit Unions Act 1979[25]

Credit unions may be registered as industrial and provident societies under the Industrial and Provident Societies Act 1965.[26] Thus, they come within the aforementioned provisions. **26.205**

Friendly Societies Act 1992[27]

Section 80 of the Act provides for settlement of disputes between members, societies, branches or offices, by arbitration.[28] An award in such an arbitration is final and is enforceable as if it were an extract registered decree arbitral hearing a warrant for execution issued by the sheriff.[29] The parties to such a dispute may agree that it shall be decided by the sheriff,[30] and if an application for resolution of a dispute in accordance with the rules is made and not determined within 40 days either party may apply to the sheriff for determination of the dispute.[31] Certain disputes about loans between societies or branches are made subject to the provisions of section 80,[32] but it is provided that the sheriff may determine such a dispute, whether or not he would apart from subsection 4 have jurisdiction to entertain it.[33] **26.206**

XXIX. Harbours, Docks and Piers

Harbours, Docks and Piers Clauses Act 1847[34]

The sheriff may correct errors or omissions in plans and issue a certificate as to the corrections.[35] A certificate issued by a sheriff is **26.207**

---

[21] 1974 Act, s. 99(4).
[22] *ibid.* s. 99(5).
[23] *ibid.* s. 80(2)(b).
[24] *ibid.* s. 83(8).
[25] c. 34 ("the 1977 Act").
[26] *ibid.* s. 1(1).
[27] c. 40 ("the 1992 Act").
[28] *ibid.* s. 80(1).
[29] *ibid.* s. 80(3).
[30] *ibid.* s. 80(5).
[31] *ibid.* s. 80(6).
[32] *ibid.* s. 82(1).
[33] *ibid.* s. 82(4).
[34] 10 & 11 Vict. c. 27 ("the 1847 Act"), as amended by Sheriff Courts (Scotland) Act 1971, s. 4, Sched. 1, para. 1.
[35] *ibid.* s. 7.

conclusive evidence that a harbour, dock or pier is completed and fit for the reception of vessels.[36]

26.208 If a dispute arises concerning the rates due or charges occasioned by distress or arrestment under the Act the sheriff may ascertain the rates due or charges of arrestment, and may also award expenses.[37] If the expenses are not paid on demand the sheriff must issue a warrant for poinding and sale.[38] A harbour master may remove an unserviceable vessel[39] at the expense of the owner; such expenses may be recovered summarily before the sheriff.[40] If payment has not been made seven days after the award by the sheriff, the harbour master may arrest and sell, and the sheriff must grant warrant therefor.[41]

26.209 The sheriff may appoint special constables within the harbour limits.[42] If no manner of confirming byelaws made under the Act is prescribed the sheriff may allow or disallow them.[43]

26.210 The recovery of damages not specially provided for and the determination of any other matter referred to the sheriff is to be dealt with under the appropriate clauses of the Railways Clauses Consolidation (Scotland) Act 1845.[44]

Harbours, Piers and Ferries (Scotland) Act 1937[45]

26.211 A grant may be made to a local or harbour authority to carry out certain marine work. If the Secretary of State serves a notice requiring certain work to be done and the authority considers it to be an unnecessary or unreasonable requirement, an application may be made to the sheriff who may cancel or modify the requirement.[46] The decision of the sheriff or sheriff principal is final.[47]

Docks and Harbours Act 1966[48]

26.212 Any person who by reason of the terms of a lease is prevented from carrying out works required under a welfare amenity scheme may apply to the sheriff who may by order set aside or modify the terms of the lease as he considers just and equitable.[49] On an application made by a person with an interest in certain premises, the sheriff may make an order for payment by some other person of a contribution towards the expense incurred by the applicant, or for a modification of the rent, as he considers just and equitable in the circumstances of the case.[50]

---

[36] 1847 Act, s. 26.
[37] *ibid.* s. 46.
[38] *ibid.*
[39] *Peterhead Harbours Trs v. Chalmers*, 1984 S.L.T. 130.
[40] 1847 Act, s. 57, as amended by Debtor (Scotland) Act 1987 (c. 18), Sched. 6, para. 4; see Hovercraft (Application of Enactments) Order 1972 (S.I. 1972 No. 971), art. 8(2)(a).
[41] *ibid.* s. 57, as amended.
[42] *ibid.* ss. 79, 80, 94.
[43] *ibid.* s. 85.
[44] *ibid.* s. 92.
[45] 1 Edw. 8 & 1 Geo. 6, c. 28 ("the 1937 Act").
[46] *ibid.* s. 15(2).
[47] Dobie, p. 537.
[48] c. 28 ("the 1966 Act").
[49] *ibid.* s. 34(1), (4).
[50] *ibid.* s. 34(2), (4).

XXX. Hire Purchase and Consumer Credit

Consumer Credit Act 1974[51]

Where a sheriff[52] finds a credit bargain extortionate[53] he may re-open the credit agreement in order to do justice between the parties.[54] This power is similar to the court's power under the Moneylenders Acts of 1900 and 1927[55] in respect of harsh and unconscionable transactions by moneylenders, but is more far-reaching. The Act defines extortionate credit bargains.[56] An extortionate credit agreement may be re-opened on the application of the debtor or any surety.[57] The application is made to the sheriff having jurisdiction in the district in which the applicant resides or carries on business.[58] The sheriff may also re-open the agreement at the instance of the debtor or surety in any proceedings to which the debtor and creditor are parties, or at the instance of the debtor or surety in other proceedings, in any court where the amount paid or payable under the agreement is relevant.[59] In re-opening the agreement the sheriff has extensive powers.[60] **26.213**

The Act also makes provision for the granting by the sheriff of enforcement orders,[61] time orders,[62] protection orders,[63] and financial relief in hire purchase cases.[64] Conditions may be imposed in any order, and its operation may be suspended.[65] **26.214**

XXXI. Housing

Housing (Scotland) Act 1987[66]

Part III

Secure tenancies are created by the Act.[67] The landlord of a secure tenancy may raise proceedings for recovery of possession of the house by way of summary cause in the sheriff court of the district in which it is situated.[68] **26.215**

The landlord of a house let under a secure tenancy may terminate the tenancy and recover possession by service of a notice if he has reasonable **26.216**

---

51 c. 39 ("the 1974 Act").
52 *ibid.* s. 189(1): definition of "court".
53 *Mills v. Wood, The Times*, Mar. 24, 1984.
54 1974 Act, s. 137(1).
55 See Dobie, pp. 627–630.
56 1974 Act, s. 138; *A. Ketley v. Scott* [1981] I.C.R. 241; *Davies v. Directloans Ltd* [1986] 1 W.L.R. 823.
57 *ibid.* s. 139(1)(a).
58 *ibid.* s. 139(6).
59 *ibid.* s. 139(1)(b), (c).
60 *ibid.* s. 139(2).
61 *ibid.* ss. 127, 128, 189(1).
62 *ibid.* ss. 129, 130, 189(1).
63 *ibid.* ss. 131, 189(1).
64 *ibid.* ss. 132–134, 189(1).
65 *ibid.* ss. 135, 136, 189(1).
66 c. 26 ("the 1987 Act").
67 *ibid.* ss. 44–46.
68 *ibid.* ss. 47(1), 48; Secure Tenancies (Proceedings for Possession) (Scotland) Order 1980 (S.I. 1980 No. 389).

grounds for believing that the house is unoccupied and the tenant does not intend to occupy it as his home.[69] A tenant who is aggrieved by such termination may raise proceedings by summary application within six months,[70] and the sheriff may order that the tenancy shall continue or order the landlord to make other suitable accommodation available to the tenant.[71]

26.217 The landlord and the tenant may raise proceedings by summary application if either wishes certain variations to the terms or condition of a secure tenancy.[72]

26.218 If a tenant of a secure tenancy wishes to carry out work, and the landlord refuses to agree or imposes conditions, the aggrieved tenant may raise a summary application and the sheriff is bound to order the landlord to consent or withdraw the condition unless it appears to him that the refusal or condition is reasonable.[73]

Part IV

26.219 Where a local authority make an improvement order in relation to a sub-standard house, any person aggrieved may appeal against the order.[74]

26.220 Where a local authority make an order prohibiting the occupation of houses in a housing action area,[75] and the owner or person having control of such a house has applied to the local authority to make the order, and this has been refused in relation to that house, he may appeal to the sheriff within 21 days of the refusal[76] by summary application.[77]

26.221 Where the owner of a house has received certain notice of a final resolution relative to a housing action area, and is willing that it be demolished, but cannot obtain vacant possession by agreement of the tenant, he may apply to the sheriff by summary application for an order for possession.[78]

26.222 Nothing in the Rent (Scotland) Act 1984[79] restricting the power of a court to make an order for possession of a dwelling-house applies to any application to the sheriff under Part IV of the 1987 Act.[80]

26.223 The Act makes provision for the obligation of the lessor to keep in repair houses let on short leases.[81]

26.224 The sheriff may, on the application of either party to a lease, by order made with the consent of the other party concerned, authorise the

---

69 1987 Act, ss. 49, 50.
70 *ibid.* s. 51(1).
71 *ibid.* s. 51(2).
72 *ibid.* s. 54(3), (4).
73 *ibid.* s. 57, Sched. 5, paras 5, 6.
74 *ibid.* ss. 88(1), (6), 129.
75 *ibid.* s. 97.
76 *ibid.* s. 97(5), (6).
77 *ibid.* s. 102: s. 103(1) of the Rent (Scotland) Act 1984 applies.
78 *ibid.* ss. 99(1), (3), 102.
79 (c. 58).
80 1987 Act, s. 103.
81 *ibid.* s. 113, Sched. 10, para. 3.

inclusion in the lease, or in any agreement collateral to the lease, of provisions excluding or modifying the provisions of paragraph 3 of Schedule 10 with respect to the repairing obligations of the parties, if it appears to him that it is reasonable to do so.[82] Such application is by summary application and the decision of the sheriff thereon is final.[83]

Part V

Part V of the Act relates to the repair of houses. Where a local authority are satisfied that any house is in a serious state of disrepair they may serve upon the owner a repair notice, and if the notice is not complied with execute the repairs themselves.[84] Any person aggrieved by a repair notice, a demand for the recovery of expenses incurred by the local authority in executing such works an order made by a local authority with respect to any such expenses, may appeal to the sheriff within 21 days.[85] **26.225**

If a tenant or his agent has incurred expense in complying with a repair notice, or in paying the expenditure of a local authority which has carried out the works, the tenant or the landlord may apply to the sheriff to determine what, if any, part of the expenditure is payable by the landlord to the tenant.[86] Any such application is made by summary application and the sheriff's decision is final.[87] **26.226**

Part VI

A local authority may make a closing order prohibiting the use of a house for human habitation,[88] and may make a demolition order.[89] The local authority may make, on an application by the owner of the house, an order revoking a closing order or demolition order.[90] A local authority may determine to purchase a house subject to a closing order or a demolition order.[91] A local authority may by resolution require demolition of an obstructive building.[92] Any person aggrieved by such orders, resolution or determination may appeal to the sheriff within 21 days.[93] **26.227**

Part VIII

If it appears to a local authority that a house which is let in lodgings, or occupied by members of more than one family, is in an unsatisfactory state in consequence of failure to maintain proper standards of management, the authority may direct by order that prescribed standards of management should apply, and serve a copy of the order on the owner and lessees of the house.[94] These persons may appeal to the sheriff within 14 days on the **26.228**

---

82 1987 Act, Sched. 10, para. 5(1).
83 *ibid.* s. 324(1).
84 *ibid.* ss. 108(1), 109.
85 *ibid.* s. 111(1).
86 *ibid.* ss. 110, 324.
87 *ibid.* s. 324(5).
88 *ibid.* s. 114(1).
89 *ibid.* s. 115.
90 *ibid.* s. 116.
91 *ibid.* s. 121(1), (3).
92 *ibid.* s. 125.
93 *ibid.* s. 129.
94 *ibid.* s. 157.

ground that the making of the order was unnecessary.[95] On an application by any of these persons the local authority may revoke the order.[96] If the local authority refuse to revoke or fail to notify the applicant within 42 days of their decision, the applicant may appeal to the sheriff.[97]

26.229 A local authority may serve upon the person managing a house in a defective condition, a notice specifying works which are required to make good the neglect causing the defect and requiring the person to execute those works.[98] A local authority may serve a notice requiring compliance with standards, and specifying works to be executed.[99] A local authority may serve a notice requiring provision of means of escape from fire.[1] Any person on whom such notices have been served, or who is an owner or lessee of the house, or who holds a standard security over the house, may appeal to the sheriff within 21 days on specified grounds.[2]

26.230 A local authority may give directions to prevent or reduce overcrowding.[3] Any person having an interest in the house may apply to the local authority to revoke or vary any such direction.[4] If the local authority refuse the application, or fail to notify the applicant of their decision within 42 days, the applicant may appeal to the sheriff,[5] and the sheriff may revoke the direction or vary it in any manner in which it might have been varied by the local authority.[6]

26.231 A sheriff may grant warrant authorising a person employed by, or acting on the instructions of, a health authority, to enter premises for the purposes of Part VIII[7] of the Act.[8] A sheriff may give consent to the execution of works under Part VIII if it appears to him that any other person having an estate or interest in the premises has unreasonably refused to give consent to the works.[9]

26.232 Any person having an estate or interest in a house to which a control order[10] relates may appeal to the sheriff against the control order not later than six weeks after service of the order.[11] The grounds of appeal are specified.[12]

26.233 Any person may apply to the local authority to revoke a control order.[13] If the local authority refuse the application or do not within

---

[95] 1987 Act, s. 158.
[96] *ibid.* s. 157(5).
[97] *ibid.* s. 158(4).
[98] *ibid.* s. 160.
[99] *ibid.* s. 161.
[1] *ibid.* s. 162.
[2] *ibid.* s. 163(1), (2).
[3] *ibid.* ss. 166, 167.
[4] *ibid.* s. 169(1).
[5] *ibid.* s. 170(1).
[6] *ibid.* s. 170(2).
[7] Pt VIII of the 1987 Act deals with houses in multiple occupation.
[8] 1987 Act, s. 173.
[9] *ibid.* s. 174.
[10] An order to protect the safety, welfare or health of persons living in a house in multiple occupation: 1987 Act, s. 178(1).
[11] 1987 Act, s. 186(1).
[12] *ibid.* s. 186(3).
[13] *ibid.* s. 188(4).

42 days inform the applicant of their decision, the applicant may appeal to the sheriff, who may revoke the order.[14] No further appeal may be brought by any person, except with leave of the sheriff, in respect of the same control order, until the expiry of six months from the determination of the former appeal.[15]

A control order vests in the local authority any furniture in the house.[16] If the local authority's right to possession of any such furniture is a right exercisable against more than one person interested in the furniture, any such person may apply to the sheriff for an adjustment of the rights and liabilities of those persons as regards the furniture, and the sheriff may make such an order as he thinks just and equitable.[17] **26.234**

Either the lessor or the lessee, under any lease of premises subject to a control order, may apply to the sheriff for an order determining the lease, or for its variation, either unconditionally or subject to such conditions as the sheriff may think fair and equitable to impose.[18] **26.235**

When a local authority has made a control order it must prepare a management scheme.[19] Any person having an estate or interest in the house may appeal to the sheriff against the scheme on all or any of specified grounds.[20] The sheriff may, as he thinks fit, confirm or vary the scheme.[21] Proceedings on an appeal against a scheme are, so far as practicable, to be combined with proceedings on any appeal against the control order to which the scheme relates.[22] Either the local authority or any person having an estate or interest in the house to which the scheme relates may at any time apply to the sheriff for a review of the estimate of the surpluses on revenue account in the scheme.[23] **26.236**

For the purposes of Part VIII the withdrawal of an appeal is deemed the final determination of the appeal, having the like effect as a decision dismissing the appeal.[24] **26.237**

Part XIV

Part XIV of the Act makes provision for various sorts of financial assistance for owners of defective housing previously purchased from a local authority. A sheriff of the sheriff court district within which the defective dwelling is situated has jurisdiction: (a) to determine any question arising under Part XIV; (b) to entertain any proceedings brought in connection with performance or discharge of any obligations so arising, including proceedings brought for the recovery of damages or compensation in the event of the obligations not being performed.[25] **26.238**

---

14 1987 Act, Sched. 11, para. 5(1).
15 *ibid.*
16 *ibid.* s. 181(1).
17 *ibid.* s. 181(4).
18 *ibid.* s. 185.
19 *ibid.* s. 184.
20 *ibid.* Sched. 11, para. 3(1).
21 *ibid.* para. 3(2).
22 *ibid.* para. 3(4).
23 *ibid.* para. 4.
24 *ibid.* s. 190(4).
25 *ibid.* s. 299(1).

26.239 Where a local authority offer to re-purchase a property under sections 275 to 276, the person to whom the offer is made may request the authority to strike out or vary a term or condition.[26] A person aggrieved by the refusal of the authority to strike out or vary a term or condition may apply by way of summary application to the sheriff, and the sheriff may, as he thinks fit, uphold the term or condition or strike it out or vary it.[27]

Part XV

26.240 Part XV of the Act relates to compensation payments. Section 309 applies where a house is purchased at a restricted value in pursuance of a compulsory purchase order made by virtue of sections 88, 120 or 121, or paragraph 5 of Schedule 8, or in pursuance of an order under paragraph 2(1) of Schedule 2 to the Land Compensation (Scotland) Act 1963, or has been vacated in pursuance of a demolition order or a closing order, and on the date of the making of the compulsory purchase order or other order the house is occupied in whole or part as a private dwelling by a person who holds an interest in the house, being an interest subject to a heritable security or charge, or is a party to an agreement to purchase the house by instalments.[28] Any party to the heritable security, charge or agreement may apply to the sheriff who, after giving other parties the opportunity of being heard, may, if he thinks fit, make an order: (a) in the case of a house which has been purchased compulsorily, discharging or modifying any outstanding liabilities of the person having an interest in the house, being liabilities arising by virtue of any bond or other obligation with respect to the debt secured by the heritable security or charge, or by virtue of the agreement; or (b) in the case of a house vacated in pursuance of a demolition order, or closing order, discharging or modifying the terms of the heritable security, charge or agreement, and in either case, either unconditionally or subject to such terms and conditions, including conditions with respect to the payment of money, as the sheriff may think just.[29]

Part XVI

26.241 Where in respect of any premises that are leased (a) a closing order, a demolition order or a resolution passed under section 125[30] has become operative, and (b) the lease is not determined, the landlord, the tenant, or any other person deriving right under the lease may apply to the sheriff within whose jurisdiction the premises are situated for an order determining the lease.[31] The sheriff may, if he thinks fit, order that the lease shall be determined either unconditionally or subject to such terms and conditions (including conditions with respect to the payment of money by any party to the proceedings to any other party thereto by way of compensation or damages or otherwise) as he may think it just and equitable to impose.[32]

26.242 The superior of any lands and heritages may apply to the sheriff for an order entitling him to enter on those lands and heritages to execute works

---

[26] 1987 Act, Sched. 20, para. 4.
[27] *ibid.* Sched. 20, para. 5.
[28] *ibid.* s. 309(1).
[29] *ibid.* ss. 309(2).
[30] For demolition of an obstructive building.
[31] 1987 Act, s. 322(1).
[32] *ibid.* s. 322(2).

(including demolition works),[33] if a notice requiring the execution of works, or a closing order, or a notice or resolution requiring the demolition of a building under Part VI of the Act is not being complied with, and the interests of the superior are thereby prejudiced.[34] The sheriff may make the order if he thinks it just to do so.[35]

In any appeal under the Act the sheriff may before considering the appeal require the appellant to deposit such sum to cover the expenses of the appeal as may be prescribed by rules of court.[36] In deciding any appeal under the Act the sheriff may make such order as he thinks just.[37] His order is final.[38] The sheriff may at any stage of the proceedings on an appeal under the Act state a case to the Court of Session on any question of law that arises; and must do so if directed by the Court of Session.[39] **26.243**

Housing (Scotland) Act 1988[40]

The Act creates assured tenancies[41] and short assured tenancies.[42] **26.244**

Schedule 5 sets out the grounds on which the sheriff must, and may, order possession.[43] **26.245**

Where a tenant has a right to shared accommodation[44] the landlord may apply to the sheriff, who may make such order as he thinks fit either (a) terminating the right of the tenant to use the whole or any part of the shared accommodation other than living accommodation, or (b) modifying his right to use the whole or any part of the shared accommodation.[45] **26.246**

Where a sheriff makes an order for possession of a house let on an assured tenancy on Ground 6 or Ground 9 of Schedule 5,[46] the sum payable by the landlord to the tenant for reasonable expenses of removal is to be determined by the sheriff, failing agreement.[47] **26.247**

No diligence may be done in respect of the rent of any house let on an assured tenancy except with leave of the sheriff.[48] **26.248**

It is the duty of the landlord under an assured tenancy to draw up and give to the tenant a document stating the terms of the tenancy.[49] On summary application by a tenant under an assured tenancy, the sheriff must by order (a) where it appears to him that the landlord has failed to draw up a document which fairly reflects the existing terms of the tenancy, **26.249**

---

33 1987 Act, s. 323(1).
34 *ibid.* s. 323(2)(a), (b).
35 *ibid.* s. 323(2)(c).
36 *ibid.* s. 324(3).
37 *ibid.* s. 324(4).
38 *ibid.* s. 324(5).
39 *ibid.* s. 324(7).
40 c. 43 ("the 1988 Act").
41 *ibid.* s. 12.
42 *ibid.* s. 32.
43 Under 1988 Act, ss. 18 and 19.
44 *ibid.* under s. 14.
45 1988 Act, s. 21.
46 *ibid.* s. 22(1).
47 *ibid.* s. 22(2).
48 *ibid.* s. 29.
49 *ibid.* s. 30(1).

draw up such a document, or adjust accordingly the terms of such document as there is; and (b) in any case declare that the document (as originally drawn up, or where the sheriff has drawn it up or adjusted it, as so drawn up or adjusted), fairly reflects the terms of the assured tenancy.[50]

XXXII. Income, Corporation and Capital Gains Taxes

Taxes Management Act 1970[51]

26.250 The sheriff may issue a warrant authorising an officer of the Commissioners of Inland Revenue to enter and search premises.[52] The officer may seize and remove things which he reasonably believes may be required as evidence for the purposes of proceeding under the Act.[53]

26.251 The sheriff upon a certificate by the collector that tax is due and unpaid must grant a summary warrant for recovery of the amount remaining due and unpaid.[54] The procedure for executing summary warrants is set out in the Debtors (Scotland) Act 1987, Sched. 5.[55]

XXXIII. Intoxicating Liquor

Licensing (Scotland) Act 1976[56]

26.252 An appeal to the sheriff is competent by virtue of the following provisions of Part II of the Act: (1) an applicant for the grant or provisional grant of a new licence or for the renewal or permanent transfer of a licence may appeal against a refusal of a licensing board to grant, renew or transfer the licence[57]; (2) any competent objector to such an application may appeal against the decision of the licensing board to grant, renew or transfer the licence[58]; (3) any person entitled to appeal against the grant or refusal of a licence may appeal against a decision of a licensing board to attach or not to attach a condition to the licence[59]; (4) a person to whom a licence has been transferred on a temporary basis may appeal against the board's refusal to confirm the transfer[60]; (5) The holder of a licence may appeal against any condition attached to the licence in terms of section 18A(1)[61]; (6) an applicant for the provisional

---

50 1988 Act, s. 30(2).

51 c. 9 ("the 1970 Act").

52 *ibid.* s. 20(1), 20D(l)(b), as substituted by Finance Act 1976 (c. 40), Sched. 6 and amended by Finance Act 1989 (c. 26), s. 146.

53 *ibid.* s. 20C(3) as substituted and ammended.

54 Debtors (Scotland) Act 1987 (c. 18), s. 74 and Sched. 4, substituting s. 63 in the 1990 Act for Scotland.

55 See para. 26.153.

56 c. 66 ("the 1976 Act"). For a detailed exposition of licensing law, see Cummins, *Licensing Law in Scotland* (1993) and *Parliament House Book*, Div. E.

57 *ibid.* s. 17(4); see *Wolfson v. Glasgow District Licensing Board*, 1981 S.L.T. 17, in which is was held that the grant of a restricted licence constituted a refusal for the purpose of an appeal.

58 *ibid.* s. 17(5).

59 *ibid.* s. 17(6); see ss. 38 (power of board to create byelaws), 101 (restrictions on sale or supply of liquor in premises subject to an entertainments licence).

60 *ibid.* s. 25(4C).

61 *ibid.* s. 18A(6), inserted by Licensing (Amendment) (Scotland) 1996 (c.36), s. 1. S. 18A applies to events such as discos where there will be music and dancing and offences in relation to controlled drugs may be committed: s. 18A(3).

grant of a licence or for such a grant to be declared final may appeal against the decision of the licensing board to refuse to affirm a provisional grant or to declare the provisional grant final[62]; (7) a licence-holder may appeal against an order of the licensing board suspending his licence on receipt of a complaint, and against the period of suspension[63]; (8) if licensed premises are reconstructed or extended or altered without the consent of the board, the board may complain to the sheriff, who may by order declare the licence to be forfeited or order that the premises be restored to their original condition[64]; (9) a licence-holder may appeal against a closure order or the refusal of the licensing board to cancel a closure order[65]; (10) a licence-holder may appeal against a suspension order made following the licence-holder's default in complying with an order requiring structural alteration on renewal of a licence, and may also appeal against the refusal of the licensing board to cancel a suspension order.[66]

Part III of the Act makes provision for the licensing of seamen's canteens. An appeal may be taken by the applicant or licence-holder on the occurrence of any of the following: (1) the refusal of a licensing board to grant, renew or transfer a licence[67]; (2) on an application for the grant of a licence, the specification by the board of types of liquor which may be sold under the licence and which were not the types applied for[68]; (3) on an application for renewal of a licence, the refusal of a licensing board to change the types of liquor which may be sold under the licence[69]; (4) where the licensing board requires modification in the rules proposed to be made as to the persons entitled to use the canteen, or refuses to allow a variation of the rules[70]; (5) where the licensing board orders structural alterations to the canteen when renewing the licence.[71] **26.253**

Part V of the Act makes provision for the permitted hours in licensed premises and registered clubs. An applicant may appeal against the decision of a licensing board to refuse an application for Sunday opening.[72] Any competent objector who appeared at the hearing of an application for Sunday opening may appeal to the sheriff against a decision of the licensing board to grant the application.[73] A licence-holder or a registered club may appeal against the decision of a licensing board to make a restriction order, or against the period specified in the order, or a refusal to revoke the order.[74] It should be noted that there is no appeal against a licensing board's refusal of an application for extended hours.[75] **26.254**

The appeals procedure for the above Part II, Part III and Part V appeals is prescribed by section 39 of the Act and rules made **26.255**

---

62 1976 Act, s. 26(10); see s. 26(2), (4).
63 *ibid.* s. 31(8); see ***Basra v. Cunningham District Licensing Board***, 1995 S.L.T. 1013.
64 *ibid.* s. 35(4).
65 *ibid.* s. 32(1), (7).
66 *ibid.* s. 36(1), (4), (8).
67 *ibid.* s. 44(a).
68 *ibid.* s. 44(b).
69 *ibid.* s. 44(c).
70 *ibid.* s. 44(d).
71 *ibid.* s. 44(e).
72 *ibid.* s. 53, Sched. 4, paras 2, 7, 9.
73 *ibid.* Sched. 4, para. 10.
74 *ibid.* s. 65(8).
75 ***Sloan v. North East Fife District Licensing Board***, 1978 S.L.T. (Sh.Ct.) 62, but judicial review may be possible.

thereunder.[76] Appeal is to the sheriff.[77] It must be made by initial writ and is disposed of as a summary application.[78] At the same time as the initial writ is lodged with the sheriff clerk the appellant must serve a copy either (i) on all other parties who appeared at the hearing before the board if he was the applicant,[79] or (ii) on the applicant, if the appellant was an objector[80]; and a copy must always be served on the clerk of the licensing board.[81] The licensing board may competently be joined as a party to an appeal.[82] A time limit of 14 days is imposed for lodging the appeal to the sheriff[83]; however, on good cause being shown the sheriff may hear an appeal notwithstanding that it was lodged outwith the time-limit.[84] No such discretion exists where requests for reasons are made out of time.[85]

The appeal is to be dealt with as a summary application.[86] The Act provides that the sheriff may uphold an appeal only if he considers that the licensing board in arriving at its decision: (1) erred in law[87]; (2) based its decision on any incorrect material fact[88]; (3) acted contrary to natural justice[89]; or (4) exercised its discretion in an unreasonable manner.[90] These provisions deliberately exclude an appeal on the merits.[91] In considering an appeal under section 39 the sheriff may hear evidence by or on behalf of any party to the appeal[92]; a sheriff who has heard evidence under this provision may be better informed than a licensing board which reached a decision without calling evidence.[93]

---

[76] A.S. (Appeals under the Licensing (Scotland) Act 1976) 1977 (S.I. 1977 No. 1622), as amended by A.S. (Appeals under the Licensing (Scotland) Act 1976) (Amendment) 1979 (S.I. 1979 No. 1520). ("A.S. 1977").

[77] 1976 Act, s. 39(1).

[78] A.S. 1977, para 2.

[79] *ibid.* para. 3(b); see *S. W. Murphy Ltd v. Alloa Town Council*, 1971 S.L.T. (Sh.Ct.) 20; *Grierson v. Greenock Licensing Court*, 1969 S.L.T. (Sh.Ct.) 33.

[80] A.S. 1977, para. 3(c).

[81] *ibid.* para. 3(a).

[82] 1976 Act, s. 39(2A) (inserted by Law Reform (Miscellaneous Provisions) (Scotland) Act 1990 (c. 40), (Sched. 8, para 11(2)).

[83] *ibid.* s. 39(2); see *Crolla v. Edinburgh District Licensing Board*, 1983 S.L.T. (Sh.Ct) 11.

[84] *ibid.* s. 39(3); see *H.D. Wines (Inverness) Ltd v. Inverness District Licensing Board*, 1981 S.C. 318 where an appeal to the Court of Session was allowed.

[85] *ibid.* s. 39(2); *Bourtreehill Baptist Church v. Cunningham District Licensing Board*, Kilmarnock Sh. Ct, Dec. 15, 1977, unreported; *H.D. Wines (Inverness) Ltd, supra.*

[86] A. S. 1977, para. 2; see the observations in *Hutcheon v. Hamilton District Licensing Board*, 1978 S.L.T. (Sh.Ct.) 44, on the convenient and expeditious disposal of appeals.

[87] 1976 Act, s. 39(4)(a).

[88] *ibid.* s. 39(4)(b).

[89] *ibid.* s. 39(4)(c).

[90] *ibid.* s. 39(4)(d); see *MacIntyre v. Elie and Earlsferry Town Council*, 1967 S.L.T. (Sh.Ct.) 78; *MacGregor v. Berwickshire C.C.*, 1967 S.L.T. (Sh.Ct.) 13; *Mecca Ltd. v. Edinburgh Corporation*, 1967 S.L.T. (Sh.Ct.) 43; *Keith v. Dunfermline Town Council*, 1968 S.L.T. (Sh.Ct.) 51; *Atherlay v. Lanark C.C.*, 1968 S.L.T. (Sh.Ct.) 71; *Pattullo v. Dundee Corporation*, 1969 S.L.T. (Sh.Ct.) 31; *Aitken v. Motherwell and Wishaw Licensing Court*, 1971 S.L.T. (Sh.Ct.), 25; *R. W. Cairns Ltd v. Busby East Church Kirk Session*, 1985 S.L.T. 493; *Chung v. Wigtown District Licensing Board*, 1993 S.L.T. 1118; *Latif v. Motherwell District Licensing Board*, 1994 S.L.T. (Notes) 414.

[91] See Second Report of the Guest Committee on Scottish Licensing Law, Cmnd. 2021 (1963), discussed in the Grant Report, paras 266, 267. The Second Report of the Guest Committee, subsequently endorsed by the Clayson Committee on Scottish Licensing Law, Cmnd. 5354 (1973), proposed the basis upon which licensing appeals to the sheriff should be decided under the new system (see Guest, paras 102–105; Clayson, paras 6.12, 6.13).

[92] 1976 Act, s. 39(5), as amended by Law Reform (Miscellaneous Provisions) (Scotland) Act 1990 (c.40), Sched. 8, para. 11(3).

[93] *Martin v. Ellis*, 1978 S.L.T. (Sh.Ct.) 38.

On upholding an appeal under this section the sheriff may either remit the case with the reason for his decision to the licensing board for reconsideration of its decision, or reverse or modify the licensing board's decision.[94] In such an appeal the sheriff is acting in a judicial rather than an administrative capacity.[95] An appeal to the Court of Session (other than an appeal relating to a registered club under Part VII of the Act) may be taken by either party on a point of law and must be made within 28 days of the decision of the sheriff.[96] If the appeal is heard by the sheriff there is no appeal to the sheriff principal[97] under the Act.

Part VII of the Act makes provision for the registration of clubs. The requisite certificate of registration is granted, refused, renewed or cancelled by the sheriff, not by the licensing board.[98] The decision of the sheriff is final.[99] It may, however, be subject to judicial review. **26.256**

A registered club may apply to the sheriff for an order providing that during the winter period the permitted hours in the club on Sundays may be 12.30 p.m. to 2 p.m. and 4 p.m. to 9 p.m. instead of those provided by section 53 of the Act (12.30 to 2.30 and 6.30 to 11 p.m.).[1] The sheriff must make the order provided that he is satisfied that certain conditions are satisfied.[2] The conditions relate to the fact that the club is an athletics or sports club, playing outdoor games and that the normal permitted hours would not be suitable for the supply of liquor in the club's premises to persons participating in the sport or game.[3] **2.256A**

XXXIV. Land Drainage

Land Drainage (Scotland) Act 1930[4]

Where an owner or occupier of agricultural land has served a notice on the owner or occupier of adjoining land requiring him to maintain or join in maintaining the banks and cleansing channels of water courses and this notice is not complied with within two months, he may apply to the sheriff for warrant authorising the works to be carried out.[5] The other party will be called as defender and the sheriff may summon a person of skill and experience in matters relating to drainage to sit with him and act as an **26.257**

---

[94] 1976 Act, s. 39(6)(*a*), (7); *Dingwall v. Cunninghame D.C.*, Kilmarnock Sh. Ct, Jan. 26, 1978, unreported; *Haddow v. Glasgow District Licensing Board*, 1983 S.L.T. (Sh.Ct.) 5; *Coppola v. Midlothian District Licensing Board*, 1983 S.L.T. (Sh.Ct.) 95; *Botterills of Blantyre v. Hamilton District Licensing Board*, 1986 S.L.T. 14.

[95] *Martin v. Ellis*, 1978 S.L.T. (Sh.Ct.) 38. *Botterills of Blantyre v. Hamilton District Licensing Board*, 1986 S.L.T. 14; *Loosefoot Entertainment Ltd v. Glasgow District Licensing Board*, 1991 S.L.T. 843; 1990 S.C.L.R. 584.

[96] 1976 Act, s. 39(8); see *Sutherland v. Edinburgh District Licensing Board*, 1984 S.L.T. 241.

[97] *Troc Sales v. Kirkcaldy District Licensing Board, supra*; note however, *Charles Watson (Scotland) Ltd v. Glasgow District Licensing Board*, 1980 S.L.T. (Sh.Ct.) 37, where there was an "appeal" to the sheriff principal when the sheriff had not considered the merits of the original appeal. The correctness of this decision is doubtful.

[98] See 1976 Act, ss. 104, 105, 108–110; an application cannot be granted subject to conditions: *Strathclyde R.C v. 85 Sound Club*, Kilmarnock Sh. Ct, May 25, 1983, unreported.

[99] 1976 Act, s. 117(2); *cf* s. 39(8). See *Stephen v. Woodend Bowling Club*, 1994 S.L.T.(Sh.Ct) 9.

[1] *ibid.* s. 56(1)

[2] *ibid.*

[3] *ibid.* s. 56(2).

[4] 20 & 21 Geo. 5, c. 20 ("the 1930 Act").

[5] *ibid.* s. 1(1), (2).

assessor, or may remit to such a person to examine and report on any matter involved.[6] The sheriff may ordain the defender to carry out the operations within a specified time and, in the event of failure, may grant warrant authorising another person to enter on the lands and carry out the operations.[7] The sheriff may, and must if either party so applies, direct that the operations be carried out under the supervision of a person of skill.[8] Before granting such an order the sheriff must be satisfied that the applicant's land is in danger of injury, that the defender is being unreasonable, and that the cost of the operations may reasonably be borne by the parties.[9] If the sheriff thinks the cost of the operations unreasonable he may direct intimation of the application and his decision to the Secretary of State, as well as any relevant reports, plans, maps or documents.[10] On granting an application, the sheriff is empowered to make directions as to the costs of carrying out of operations.[11] The remuneration of the skilled person acting as assessor or reporter must, unless the sheriff directs otherwise, be treated as expenses in the application,[12] which the sheriff may award to or against any party in the application.[13]

26.258 Similar provision is made for an application by an owner or occupier of agricultural land for a warrant authorising him to form underground main drains through adjoining land.[14] The sheriff may grant such a warrant if he is satisfied that the refusal of the owner of the adjoining land is unreasonable.[15] The sheriff is empowered to make inquiry,[16] and also to direct that the work be carried out under the supervision of a person of skill.[17] A warrant issued by the sheriff must provide for payment of compensation for any loss or damage caused by the operations and for the maintenance or renewal of the drains.[18] The sheriff may award expenses to or against any party.[19]

The determination of the sheriff is not subject to appeal.[20]

XXXV. Land Tenure

Entail Improvement Act 1770[21]

26.259 A proprietor of an entailed estate who intends to spend money on improvements to the estate must give three months' notice of his intention to the heir of entail, and must lodge a copy of this notice with the sheriff court of the district where the lands are situated.[22] After having completed

---

[6] 1930 Act, s. 1(3).
[7] *ibid.* s. 1(4).
[8] *ibid.*
[9] *ibid.*
[10] *ibid.* s. 1(5), as amended by Reorganisation of Offices (Scotland) Act 1939 (c. 20), s. 1(6).
[11] *ibid.* s. 1(6).
[12] *ibid.* s. 1(7).
[13] *ibid.* s. 2(4).
[14] *ibid.* s. 2(1).
[15] *ibid.* s. 2(2).
[16] *ibid.*
[17] *ibid.*
[18] *ibid.* s. 2(3)(i), (ii).
[19] *ibid.* s. 2(4).
[20] See Dobie, pp. 537, 612.
[21] 10 Geo. 3, c. 51, ("the 1770 Act").
[22] *ibid.* s. 11.

the improvements, the heir of entail may bring an action of declarator in the sheriff court or the Court of Session, and the sheriff may pronounce decree to the effect that part of the sum spent on improvements shall become a charge on succeeding heirs.[23]

On an application made by the proprietor of the entailed estate the sheriff may authorise him to exchange part of the entailed estate for part of another entailed estate.[24] **26.260**

Entail Sites Act 1840[25]

Heirs of entail may grant feus or leases of portions of the estates for sites of churches, schools, burial grounds, and related purposes. Application must be made to the sheriff, who may refuse the application if he deems it to be injurious to future heirs.[26] Detailed provision is made in respect of the making of such an application.[27] **26.261**

Entail Amendment (Scotland) Act 1868[28]

An heir in possession of an entailed estate may grant feus and building leases on application to the sheriff, who makes the necessary procedural directions as set out in the Act.[29] **26.262**

Entail (Scotland) Act 1882[30]

Applications for authority to charge for improvement expenditure and to grant leases may be made to the sheriff.[31] The procedure for such applications is to be that provided for applications under the 1868 Act.[32] There is a right of appeal to the Court of Session, but not from the decision of the sheriff to the sheriff principal.[33] **26.263**

Entail (Scotland) Act 1914[34]

Under this Act the sheriff may authorisc an hcir of cntail in possession to grant a feu although the nearest heir of entail is subject to a legal incapacity or refuses his consent.[35] **26.264**

XXXVI. Landlord and Tenant

Registration of Leases (Scotland) Act 1857[36]

A creditor in right of an assignation in security transferred by translation of a lease may apply to the sheriff for warrant to enter into possession **26.265**

---

23 1770 Act, s. 26.
24 *ibid.* s. 33. as extended by Entail Amendment (Scotland) Act 1868(c. 84), s. 14.
25 3 & 4 Vict. c. 48 ("the 1840 Act").
26 *ibid.* ss. 1, 3.
27 *ibid.* s. 3.
28 31 & 32 Vict. c. 84 ("the 1868 Act").
29 *ibid.*, ss. 3, 4.
30 45 & 46 Vict. c. 53 ("the 1882 Act").
31 *ibid.* ss. 5, 6, 11.
32 *ibid.* ss. 3–6.
33 *ibid.* ss. 5, 6, 11.
34 4 & 5 Geo. 5, c. 43 ("the 1914 Act").
35 *ibid.* s. 4(a).
36 20 & 21 Vict. c. 26 ("the 1857 Act").

of the subjects leased.[37] Such warrant, if granted, is sufficient title for the creditor to enter into possession.[38]

Tenancy of Shops (Scotland) Act 1949[39]

26.266 Where a landlord gives or has given to a tenant of a shop a notice of termination of the tenancy, and the tenant is unable to obtain renewal of the tenancy on terms which are satisfactory to him, he may apply to the sheriff for a renewal of the tenancy.[40] The application takes the form of a summary cause.[41] The sheriff may renew the tenancy for up to one year on such terms and conditions as he thinks reasonable and thereafter the parties will be deemed to have entered into a new lease of the premises.[42] The Act sets out the grounds on which the sheriff will dismiss an application.[43] If the sheriff is satisfied that it will not be possible to dispose finally of the application before the notice of termination takes effect, he may make an interim order authorising the tenant to continue in occupation of the premises for a period not exceeding three months, on such terms and conditions as he thinks fit.[44]

Land Registration (Scotland) Act 1979[45]

26.267 Where a landlord has failed to renew a long lease in implement of an obligation in or under it the sheriff may, on summary application by the tenant, make an order directing the sheriff clerk to execute a renewal of the lease instead of the landlord.[46]

Rent (Scotland) Act 1984[47]

(1) Preliminary

26.268 Most public sector tenancies are exempted from protection under the Act as they do not come within the statutory definition of protected tenancies.[48] Such tenancies fall within the scope of the Housing (Scotland) Act 1987.[49]

The 1984 Act provides for the ascertainment of the rateable value of a dwelling-house.[50] Any question as to the proper apportionment of the rateable value is to be determined by the sheriff whose decision is final.[51] Application must be made to the sheriff by way of summary application.[52]

---

[37] 1857 Act, s. 6.

[38] *ibid.*

[39] 12 & 13 Geo. 6, c. 25 ("the 1949 Act").

[40] *ibid.* s. 1(1); see *Scottish Gas Board v. Kerr's Trs*, 1956 S.L.T. (Sh.Ct.) 69.

[41] *ibid.* s. 1(7), as substituted by Sheriff Courts (Scotland) Act 1971 (c. 58), s. 47(2), Sched. 1, para. 3.

[42] *ibid.* s. 1(2).

[43] *ibid.* s. 1(3).

[44] *ibid.* s. 1(5).

[45] c. 33 ("the 1979 Act").

[46] *ibid.*, s. 22A, inserted by Law Reform (Miscellaneous Provisions) (Scotland) Act 1985 (c. 7), s. 2.

[47] c. 58 ("the 1984 Act").

[48] *ibid.* s. 5, as amended by Housing (Consequential Provisions) Act 1985 (c. 71), Sched. 2, para. 59; Housing (Scotland) Act 1988 (c. 43), s. 47(11); Local Government (Scotland) Act 1994 (c. 39), Sched. 13, para 137(2).

[49] c. 26. See paras 26.215 to 26.243.

[50] 1984 Act, s. 7(1).

[51] *ibid.* s. 7(2).

[52] *ibid.* s. 103(1), (2), as amended by Housing (Scotland) Act 1988 (c. 43), Sched. 9, para. 4.

The sheriff will take into account whether the tenant is sharing part of the accommodation,[53] and in doing so must consider only the comparative size, accessibility, aspect and other advantages of the accommodation in comparison with those of the other parts of the premises in which it is comprised.[54]

(2) Security of tenure

The sheriff will not grant a landlord an order for possession of a dwelling-house which is subject to a protected[55] or statutory[56] tenancy unless he considers it reasonable to do so.[57] The sheriff must also be satisfied that suitable alternative accommodation is available for the tenant,[58] or that the application falls within one or more of several grounds specified in the Act.[59] However, if the landlord has a right to recover possession at common law, the sheriff must order possession if the circumstances of the case are as specified in any of the cases in Part II of Schedule 2 to the Act.[60] **26.269**

In claims for possession of a dwelling-house the sheriff may adjourn the proceedings as he thinks fit, except where the landlord has a right to recover possession under Part II of Schedule 2.[61] He may also sist or suspend the execution of the order for possession or postpone the date of possession.[62]

Where a landlord has obtained an order for possession of a dwelling house either on the ground that he needed it as a residence for a full-time servant of his,[63] or that he or a member of his family required to occupy the dwelling-house as a residence,[64] and the order has been obtained by misrepresentation or concealment, the sheriff may order the landlord to pay compensation to the former tenant,[65] even if the possession order was made with the consent of the tenant.[66]

An occupier under a tenancy of a dwelling which is not a protected tenancy may not be evicted without a court order.[67] The landlord will generally apply to the sheriff for a warrant authorising the ejection of an occupier who refuses to leave the premises.[68] Special provision is made with respect to farm workers and their families occupying "tied" houses; the sheriff may suspend the execution of an order for possession[69] after giving due consideration to specified circumstances.[70] The provisions of **26.270**

---

[53] 1984 Act, s. 97(1)(a), (2).

[54] *Bainbridge v. Congdon* [1925] 2 K.B. 261; *Beck v. Newhold* [1952] 2 All E.R. 412, *per* Somervell L.J. at 415.

[55] Defined in 1984 Act, ss. 1 and 2.

[56] Defined in 1984 Act, s. 3, as amended by Housing (Scotland) Act 1988 (c. 43), s. 46(1).

[57] 1984 Act, s. 11(1); see *Barclay v. Hannah*, 1947 S.C. 245, *per* L.P. Cooper at 248; *Cresswell v. Hodgson* [1951] 2 K.B. 92, *per* Denning L.J. at 97.

[58] *ibid.* s. 11(1)(a).

[59] *ibid.* s. 11(1)(b); Sched. 2, Pt I.

[60] *ibid.* s. 11(2); Sched. 2, Pt II.

[61] *ibid.* s. 12(1), (5).

[62] *ibid.* s. 12(2); see *Mills v. Allen* [1953] 2 Q.B. 341; *Sherrin v. Brand* [1956] 1 Q.B. 403.

[63] *ibid.* Sched. 2, Pt 1, case 7.

[64] *ibid.*, case 8.

[65] 1984 Act, s. 21.

[66] See *Thorne v. Smith* [1947] K.B. 307.

[67] *ibid.* ss. 23(1) as amended by Housing (Scotland) Act 1988 (c. 43), s. 39(1), (2).

[68] See notes to 1984 Act, s. 23 in *Scottish Current Law Statutes.*

[69] 1984 Act, s. 24(3); see notes to 1984 Act, s. 24 in *Scottish Current Law Statutes.*

[70] *ibid.* s. 24(6).

sections 23 and 29 do not apply to certain tenancies, such as tenancies where the tenant is sharing accommodation with the landlord and the premises are the landlord's only or principal home.[71] Any application to the sheriff under Part III of the Act[72] must be by way of summary cause.[73]

(3) Rent

26.271 Where no rent is registered under Part V of the Act,[74] any question whether, or by what amount, the recoverable rent of a regulated tenancy of a dwelling-house is increased or decreased is to be determined by the sheriff failing agreement between the landlord and tenant.[75] The sheriff may also vary an agreement as to the recoverable rent.[76] An application for such a determination or revocation is a summary application.[77]

Summary application[78] may be made to the sheriff for the amendment of a notice of increase in rent of a regulated tenancy.[79] The sheriff may amend the notice by correcting any error or supplying any omission which would have rendered the notice invalid,[80] and any amendment may be made on such terms and conditions as to arrears of rent or otherwise as appear to the sheriff to be just and reasonable.[80a] The sheriff will not amend the notice unless he is satisfied that the error or omission is due to a *bona fide* mistake by the landlord.[81]

Where in any proceedings the recoverable rent of a regulated tenancy[82] is determined by the sheriff, on the application of the tenant the sheriff may call for the production of the rent book or any similar document and direct the sheriff clerk to correct entries therein which purport to show the tenant as being in arrears in respect of a sum which the sheriff has determined to be irrecoverable.[83]

The sheriff has jurisdiction to determine any question as to the rent limit for dwelling-houses let by housing associations, either in the course of any proceedings relating to a dwelling-house or on summary application by the landlord or tenant.[84]

(4) Part VII contracts

26.272 Where a section 7 apportionment[85] is required in respect of rateable lands and heritages, the rent assessment committee has jurisdiction to make such an apportionment unless the lessor insists on an apportionment by the sheriff.[86] The lessor must bring proceedings in the sheriff court within two weeks of requiring an apportionment.[87]

---

[71] 1984 Act, s. 23A as inserted by Housing (Scotland) Act 1988 (c. 43), s. 90.
[72] Pt III includes ss. 23 and 24.
[73] 1984 Act, s. 27.
[74] Rents of "regulated" (*i.e.*, protected or statutory—see s. 8) tenancies should be registered: s. 45(2).
[75] 1984 Act, ss. 29(4), 31(2).
[76] *ibid.* s. 31(2).
[77] *ibid.* s. 103(1), (2), as amended by Housing (Scotland) Act 1988 (c. 43), Sched. 9, para. 4.
[78] *ibid.*
[79] *ibid.* s. 32(4), 103(1), (2), as amended. For "regulated tenancy" see s. 8.
[80] *ibid.* s. 32(4).
[80a] *ibid.* s. 32(5).
[81] *ibid.* s. 32(4).
[82] Defined in 1984 Act, s. 8.
[83] 1984 Act, s. 39.
[84] *ibid.* ss. 60(3), 103(1).
[85] See para. 26.268.
[86] 1984 Act, s. 77.
[87] *ibid.*

(5) Excessive prices for furniture

The sheriff may issue a warrant authorising the local authority to enter a dwelling-house and inspect the furniture for the purposes of detecting an offence under section 87(1) of the Act.[88] **26.273**

(6) Heritable securities

On the summary application[89] of the debtor in a heritable security to which Part IX of the Act applies[90] the sheriff may relieve the debtor of severe financial hardship.[91] The debtor must apply to the sheriff within 21 days, or such longer time as the sheriff may allow, after the occurrence of one of three specific events.[92] If the sheriff is satisfied that unless relief were given the debtor would suffer severe financial hardship he may, by order, limit the rate of interest, extend the time for the repayment of the principal money, vary the terms of the security in any other manner, or impose a limitation or condition on the exercise of any right or remedy in respect of the security.[93] Where the sheriff makes an order under this section he may vary or revoke it by a subsequent order.[94] **26.274**

(7) Tenant sharing accommodation

Where a tenant shares accommodation with a person other than the landlord, the landlord may apply to the sheriff for an order terminating or modifying the right of a tenant to use the shared accommodation, other than living accommodation, or modifying his right to use any part of the shared accommodation.[95] The sheriff may vary the persons or increase the number of persons entitled to use the accommodation as he thinks just.[96] **26.275**

Any question arising under the section in respect of increases of rent or the transfer of burdens or liabilities previously borne by the landlord is to be determined by the sheriff on the application of the landlord or tenant.[97] The decision of the sheriff is final and conclusive.[98]

(8) Miscellaneous

A landlord of a statutory tenancy may apply to the sheriff for an order enabling him to enter and do improvement works on a dwelling-house if the tenant is unwilling to give his consent to the works.[99] This provision applies when an application for a grant has been approved with respect to the improvement works.[1] **26.276**

At any stage before the grant of a warrant sale in an action of sequestration for payment, or in security, of rent of any dwelling-house let on a protected tenancy or subject to a statutory tenancy, the sheriff

---

88 1984 Act, s. 87(5).
89 *ibid.* s. 103(1).
90 Part IX applies to heritable securities created before December 8, 1965 which are regulated securities as defined in s. 92: 1984 Act, s. 91.
91 1984 Act, s. 93(1), (6).
92 *ibid.* s. 93(1).
93 *ibid.* s. 93(2).
94 *ibid.* s. 93(5).
95 *ibid.* s. 97(8).
96 *ibid.*
97 *ibid.* s. 97(3), (9).
98 *ibid.* s. 97(9).
99 *ibid.* s. 106(1).
1 *ibid.*

may sist the proceedings or adjourn them for such period or periods as he thinks fit, in order to enable the tenant to pay the rent in such manner as the sheriff may determine (whether by instalments or otherwise).[2]

In default of agreement, the sheriff is empowered to decide who is to be the statutory tenant by succession on the death of a tenant.[3]

(9) Jurisdiction

26.277 The sheriff has jurisdiction to determine any question as to the application of the Act, either in the course of any proceedings relating to a dwelling-house or on an application made for the purpose by the landlord or tenant.[4] The sheriff has jurisdiction to deal with any claim or proceedings under the Act which falls to be dealt with by a court unless the jurisdiction of the Court of Session is stipulated.[5] If a person takes proceedings in the Court of Session which he could have taken before the sheriff he is not entitled to recover any expenses.[6]

The Court of Session may, by Act of Sederunt, give effect to the provisions of the Act, and provide for the conduct in private of any proceedings, the remission of any fees, and for any question being referred by consent of the parties for final determination by the sheriff sitting as an arbiter or by an arbiter appointed by the sheriff.[7]

XXXVII. Lawyers and Notaries

Solicitors (Scotland) Act 1980[8]

26.278 In the course of proceedings before the Scottish Solicitors' Discipline Tribunal the complainer or respondent may petition the sheriff who, on being satisfied that it would be proper to compel the giving of evidence by any witness or the production of documents by any haver, may: (1) grant warrant to cite witnesses and havers and grant letters of second diligence; (2) grant warrant for recovery of documents; and (3) appoint commissioners to take the evidence of witnesses, to examine havers and to receive exhibits and productions.[9] The sheriff to be petitioned is the sheriff having jurisdiction in any place where the respondent carries on business.[10]

XXXVIII. Legal Aid

Legal Aid (Scotland) Act 1986[11]

26.279 The sheriff may, without inquiring into means, grant legal aid to a child or relevant person[12] in an appeal to the sheriff under section 51 of the

---

[2] 1984 Act, s. 110, as amended by Debtors (Scotland) Act (c. 18), Sched. 6, para. 26.

[3] *ibid.* s. 103(1), Sched. 1, para. 7.

[4] *ibid.* s. 102(1); see *Wilson v. Cumming*, 1970 S.L.T. (Sh.Ct.) 44; *Elder v. Manson*, 1964 S.L.T. (Land Ct.) 15.

[5] *ibid.* s. 102(2); see s. 25(2) as to actions of removing, and s. 93(6) as to heritable securities.

[6] *ibid.* s. 102(3).

[7] *ibid.* s. 104.

[8] c. 46 ("the 1980 Act").

[9] *ibid.* Sched. 4, Pt II, para. 12.

[10] *ibid.*

[11] c. 47 ("the 1986 Act").

[12] As defined in Children (Scotland) Act 1995 (c. 36), s. 93(2)(b): 1986 Act, s. 29(12), as substituted by Children (Scotland) Act 1995, s. 92.

Children (Scotland) Act 1995 against a decision of a children's hearing to grant a warrant.[13] He may grant legal aid in certain other cases if satisfied (a) that it is in the interests of the child that legal aid should be made available and (b) after consideration of the financial circumstances of the child and any relevant person, that the expenses of the case could not be met without undue hardship to the child or the relevant person or the dependents of any of them.[14] The cases to which this provision applies are: (a) proceedings before the sheriff on an application for a child protection order or child assessment order or for variation or recall of such an order[15]; an appeal to the sheriff under section 51 of the 1995 Act against a decision of a children's hearing other than a decision to grant a warrant[16]; (c) an application for a finding whether grounds of referral to a children's hearing have been established or for a review of such a finding.[17]

XXXIX. Local Government

National Assistance Act 1948[18]

If a person is suffering from a grave chronic disease or is aged, infirm or physically incapacitated or living in unsanitary conditions, and is unable to devote to himself and is not receiving proper care and attention, the district medical officer may issue a certificate to the local authority requiring the removal of such a person from the premises in which he is residing.[19] On receiving such a certificate the local authority may apply to the sheriff[20] who may, if satisfied on oral evidence of the allegations in the certificate, and that it is expedient to do so, order the removal of the person to a suitable hospital or other place and his detention and maintenance therein.[21] If it is shown by the applicant that the manager of the hospital or other place agrees to accommodate the person in need of care and assistance, the manager need not be heard in the proceedings.[22] An order made by the sheriff may be varied by a further order to change the place of care,[23] and no order authorising detention may prescribe detention for a period greater than three months.[24] The sheriff may, however, authorise an extension of the order for a further three months if he thinks it to be necessary.[25] **26.280**

Local Government (Omnibus Shelters and Queue Barriers) (Scotland) Act 1958[26]

Any questions with respect to the provision of omnibus shelters by the roads authority which is required by the Act to be determined by **26.281**

---

[13] 1986 Act, s. 29(2)(b)(i), (3), as substituted.
[14] *ibid.* s. 29(4).
[15] *ibid.* s. 29(2)(a), (4).
[16] *ibid.* s. 29(2)(b)(ii), (4).
[17] *ibid.* s. 29(2)(c), (4).
[18] 11 & 12 Geo. 6, c. 29 ("the 1948 Act").
[19] *ibid.* s. 47(1), (2), (12), as amended by National Health Service (Scotland) Act 1972 (c. 58), Sched. 6, para. 83; Local Government etc. (Scotland) Act 1994 (c. 39), Sched. 13, para. 31(3).
[20] *ibid.* ss. 47(2), 65(c).
[21] *ibid.* s. 47(3).
[22] National Assistance (Amendment) Act 1951 (c. 57), s. 1(2).
[23] 1948 Act, s. 47(5).
[24] *ibid.* s. 47(4).
[25] *ibid.*
[26] 6 & 7 Eliz. 2, c. 50 ("the 1958 Act").

arbitration is to be determined by a single arbiter agreed upon by the parties or, failing their agreement, appointed by the sheriff on the application of any party to the question.[27]

Social Work (Scotland) Act 1968[28]

(1) Registration of certain residential and other establishments

26.282 Part IV of the Act provides *inter alia* for the registration of establishments whose function is to provide persons with such personal care or support as may be required for the purposes of the 1968 Act or the Children (Scotland) Act 1995.[29] The requirement for registration does not apply to an establishment controlled or managed by a Government department or by a local authority.[30] Any person aggrieved by the refusal of a local authority or of the Secretary of State to register any establishment for the purposes of the Act, or by the cancellation of such registration, may appeal to a tribunal within 21 days of the notice of refusal or cancellation.[31] The tribunal is to consist of a sheriff principal or, if he is unable to act, a person qualified for appointment as a sheriff principal nominated by the Lord President of the Court of Session, and two other members appointed from a panel[32] by the Secretary of State.[33]

(2) Contributions

26.283 When a child is being looked after by a local authority or is subject to a supervision requirement made by a children's hearing (a "maintainable child"),[34] the local authority may apply to any court of summary jurisdiction having jurisdiction where a contributor[35] is residing to make a contribution order for weekly contributions.[36] The contribution order may be revoked or varied, and is enforceable in the same way as a decree for aliment.[37] Where a decree for aliment of a maintainable child is in force, the local authority may apply to any court of summary jurisdiction for an order for payments under the decree to be made to the local authority.[38] If a child is removed from the care of any person by virtue of a supervision requirement and that person is entitled under a trust to receive money for the maintenance of the child, the local authority may apply to any court of summary jurisdiction for an order ordaining that all or part of any such sums be paid to the local authority and applied for the benefit of the child.[39]

---

[27] 1958 Act, s. 6, as amended by Roads (Scotland) Act 1984 (c. 54), s. 49, Sched. 9, para. 48.

[28] c. 49 (the "1968 Act").

[29] *ibid.* s. 61(1), (2), as substituted by Children (Scotland) Act 1995 (c. 36), s. 34(2).

[30] *ibid.* s. 61(1A), as substituted by Registered Establishments (Scotland) Act 1987 (c. 40), s. 1(1) and amended by National Health Service and Community Care Act 1990 (c. 19), Sched. 9, para. 10.

[31] *ibid.* s. 64(4).

[32] *ibid.* Sched. 5, para. 1.

[33] *ibid.* Sched. 5 paras 4, 7; see Registration of Establishments (Appeal Tribunal) (Scotland) Rules 1983 (S.I. 1983 No. 71).

[34] *ibid.* s. 78(1) as amended by Children (Scotland) Act 1995 (c. 36), s. 105(4) and Sched. 4, para. 15(17).

[35] As defined in 1968 Act, s. 78(3).

[36] 1968 Act, s. 80(1), as amended by Children (Scotland) Act 1995 (c. 36), s. 105(4) and Sched. 4, para. 15(20).

[37] *ibid.* s. 80(6).

[38] *ibid.* s. 81(2), as amended by Law Reform (Parent and Child) (Scotland) Act 1986 (c. 9), Sched. 1, para. 9 and Sched. 2.

[39] *ibid.* s. 83(1).

Local Government (Scotland) Act 1973[40]

(1) Disqualification for membership of local authority

Any opposing candidate for election as a member of a local authority may institute proceedings before the sheriff principal on the ground that another candidate is disqualified for nomination as a candidate.[41] A local authority, or four or more local government electors, may institute proceedings before the sheriff principal against a person who acted or claims to be entitled to act as a member of the local authority while disqualified.[42] Neither of the above proceedings may be instituted after the alleged disqualification has ceased to exist.[43] If it is proved that the person concerned has acted as a member of the local authority while disqualified for so acting the sheriff principal may: (a) make a declaration to that effect and declare that the office is vacant; (b) grant interdict against the person so acting; and (c) order the person to pay the local authority a sum not exceeding £100.[44] In such proceedings the sheriff principal has the same powers and privileges as a judge on the trial of a parliamentary election petition.[45] **26.284**

(2) Disposal of land

Where a local authority desire to dispose of land forming part of the common good and a question arises as to their right to do so, the authority may apply to the sheriff (or to the Court of Session) who may authorise the disposal subject to such conditions as he thinks fit.[46] This "wide and unfettered discretion" is to be exercised where the land "has the quality of inalienability or where it appears that it might have that quality."[47] The sheriff may impose a condition requiring the provision of land to be used in substitution for the land proposed to be disposed of.[48] **26.285**

Where an heir of entail disposes of land not exceeding 20 acres to a local authority for the purpose of public recreation, and the persons in right of heritable securities or other charges affecting the land refuse to consent to such disposal, the heir of entail may apply to the sheriff for a finding that adequate security is afforded by the other lands comprised in the heritable securities or charges. Such a finding has the effect of disburdening the land of the heritable securities or charges. The application must be duly intimated to the persons refusing to consent, who are entitled to appear and object.[49]

(3) Byelaws

Unless the Secretary of State otherwise directs, an inquiry into local authority byelaws made under the Act or under the Civic Government (Scotland) Act 1982 is held by the sheriff.[50] **26.286**

---

40 c. 65 ("the 1973 Act").
41 *ibid.* s. 32(1).
42 *ibid.* s. 32(2).
43 *ibid.* s. 32(3).
44 *ibid.* s. 32(4), (5).
45 *ibid.* s. 32(6).
46 *ibid.* s. 75(2).
47 *East Lothian D.C. v. National Coal Board*, 1982 S.L.T. 460, *per* Lord Maxwell at 469.
48 1973 Act, s. 75(3).
49 *ibid.* s. 76.
50 *ibid.* s. 202(9), as amended by Civic Government (Scotland) Act 1982 (c. 45), s. 110(1), (2)(b).

(4) Miscellaneous

26.287 Cases of difficulty arising out of the carrying into effect of the Act may be referred to the sheriff under sections 231 and 232 of the Act.

Civic Government (Scotland) Act 1982[51]

(1) Licensing

26.288 For the administration of licensing in relation to the activities mentioned in the following paragraph, section 2[52] of the Act establishes a licensing authority for each local authority within whose area the activity is or is to be carried on, the licencing authority being the local authority itself.[53]

A licensing authority must consider an application for the grant or renewal of a licence within three months and reach a final decision within six months of receiving the application,[54] but on summary application by the authority the sheriff may extend the six-month time limit as he thinks fit.[55] If a licensing authority fail to reach a final conclusion within the time allowed under the Act or by the sheriff, the licence applied for is deemed to be granted or renewed unconditionally for one year.[56]

26.289 A person aggrieved by the refusal of a licensing authority to grant or renew any of the following licences may appeal to the sheriff under Schedule 1 to the Act: (a) a taxi licence or private hire car licence[57]; (b) a taxi driver's licence or a private hire car owner's licence[58]; (c) a second hand dealer's licence[59]; (d) a metal dealer's licence[60]; (e) an itinerant metal dealer's licence[61]; (f) a boat hire licence[62]; (g) a street trader's licence[63]; (h) a market operator's licence, required for carrying on a private market[64]; (i) a public entertainment licence[65]; (j) an indoor sports entertainment licence[66]; (k) a late hours catering licence[67]; (l) a window cleaner's licence[68]; and (m) a licence for a house in multiple occupation.[69]

26.290 Appeals with respect to all such applications are governed by the provisions of paragraph 18 of Schedule 1 to the 1982 Act. A person who may require a licensing authority to give him reasons for their

---

51 c. 45 ("the 1982 Act").

52 As amended by Local Government etc. (Scotland) Act 1994 (c. 39) ("1994 Act"), s. 181(1) and Sched. 13, para. 129(2).

53 1982 Act, s. 2(2), as amended.

54 *ibid.* s. 3(1).

55 *ibid.* s. 3(2), (3).

56 *ibid.* s. 3(4).

57 *ibid.* s. 10.

58 *ibid.* s. 13.

59 *ibid.* s. 24.

60 *ibid.* s. 28.

61 *ibid.* s. 32.

62 *ibid.* s. 38.

63 *ibid.* s. 39; see *Seath v. Glasgow D.C.*, 1985 S.L.T. 407.

64 *ibid.* s. 40.

65 *ibid.* s. 41.

66 *ibid.* s. 41A, inserted by Fire Safety and Safety of Places of Sport Act 1987 (c. 27), s. 44(1).

67 *ibid.* s. 42.

68 *ibid.* s. 43; see *Ross v. Edinburgh D.C.*, 1977 S.L.T. (Sh.Ct.) 39.

69 Civic Government (Scotland) Act 1982 (Licensing of Houses in Multiple Occupation) Order 1991 (S.I. 1991 No. 1253), made under 1982 Act, s. 44.

decision may appeal to the sheriff against that decision[70] and may only appeal if he has already taken any opportunity afforded to him to state his case to the authority.[71] It is specifically provided that the licensing authority may be a party to such an appeal.[72] The appeal must be made by summary application and lodged with the sheriff clerk within 28 days from the decision appealed against[73]; however, on good cause being shown, the sheriff may hear an appeal out of time.[74] Where a licensing authority has not given reasons for their decision the sheriff may require the authority to give reasons.[75] The sheriff is entitled to uphold an appeal only on the same grounds as those set out for other licensing appeals by virtue of the Licensing (Scotland) Act 1976: that the licensing authority (a) erred in law; (b) based their decision on any incorrect material fact; (c) acted contrary to natural justice; or (d) exercised their discretion in an unreasonable manner.[76] The sheriff is entitled to hear evidence with respect to any of the above grounds of appeal.[77] On upholding the appeal, the sheriff may remit the case with his reasons to the licensing authority for their reconsideration or reverse or modify the authority's decision.[78] The sheriff is empowered to make an order as to expenses,[79] and any party to the appeal may appeal on a point of law from the sheriff's decision to the Court of Session within 28 days.[80]

A refusal to grant or renew a licence for a sex shop or a revocation of the licence may be appealed to the sheriff on the same grounds as those noted in the previous paragraph.[81] The only difference in the appeal provisions is that a person may not appeal if his application has been refused on one of two specified grounds.[82] **26.291**

(2) Public processions

If a local authority makes an order prohibiting a procession or imposing conditions on the holding of it,[83] a person who falls to be treated as having given notice of the proposal to hold the procession may appeal to the sheriff.[84] The appeal is by way of summary application lodged with the sheriff clerk within 14 days after the order was received by the appellant.[85] On good cause being shown, the sheriff may hear the appeal out of time.[86] The provisions as to when the sheriff may uphold an appeal, his ability to hear evidence and award expenses, and the provisions of an **26.292**

---

70 1982 Act, Sched 1, para. 18(1).
71 *ibid.* para. 18(2).
72 *ibid.* para. 18(3).
73 *ibid.* para. 18(4).
74 *ibid.* para. 18(5).
75 *ibid.* para. 18(6).
76 *ibid.* para. 18(7).
77 *ibid.* para. 18(8).
78 *ibid.* para. 18(9).
79 *ibid.* para. 18(11).
80 *ibid.* para. 18(12).
81 *ibid.* s. 45, Sched. 2, para. 24.
82 *ibid.* Sched. 2, para. 24(2)(b). The grounds are those under Sched. 2, para. 9(5)(c) and (d).
83 *ibid.* s. 63(1), as amended by Public Order Act 1986 (c. 64), Sched. 2, para. 1(3) and by Local Government etc. (Scotland) Act 1994 (c. 39), Sched. 13, para. 129(5), (6).
84 *ibid.* s. 64(1); see *Loyal Orange Lodge No. 493 v. Roxburgh D.C.*, 1980 S.C. 141; note provisions of s. 66, which provides that ss. 62 to 65 are subject to the Public Order Act 1936 (c. 6).
85 *ibid.* s. 64(2).
86 *ibid.* s. 64(3).

appeal to the Court of Session are the same as with respect to the appeals discussed above.[87] However, the sheriff must either remit the case back to the authority, or dismiss it; his only other option is to vary the order when he considers that there is insufficient time to remit the case.[88] Before remitting or dismissing the case the sheriff must be satisfied that all reasonable steps have been taken to secure that notice of the appeal and an opportunity of being heard have been given to the authority.[89]

(3) Lost property

26.293 Certain persons[90] may appeal to the sheriff against any decision of the chief constable made in relation to lost property.[91] The appeal is by summary application within 21 days of the decision appealed against,[92] but the sheriff may hear an appeal out of time on good cause being shown.[93] On upholding the appeal the sheriff may remit the case to the chief constable or reverse or vary the decision of the chief constable.[94]

(4) Property in possession of persons taken into police custody

26.294 Any person taken into police custody may appeal to the sheriff against the decision of the chief constable in relation to property in the person's possession when he was taken into custody.[95] The same procedure applies as in respect of lost property appeals.[96]

(5) Buildings and other miscellaneous works

26.295 A person may appeal against any requirement served by the local authority under Part VIII of the Act,[97] or in respect of the amount of any expenses or interest claimed from him or charged against him under Part VIII of the Act.[98] The owner of land or premises may appeal against any expenses or interest claimed or deducted in respect of works executed by the tenant or other occupier.[99] Appeal is by summary application, within 14 days.[1] The sheriff may order that the requirement shall be of no effect, or modify the requirement, and make an order as to expenses or interest.[2] Either party may appeal on a point of law from the sheriff's decision to the Court of Session within 14 days[3]; there is no further appeal.[4]

26.296 If the tenant or other occupier of land or premises prevents the owner from executing any work he is required to do by notice served by a local

---

87 1982 Act, s. 64(4), (5), (8), (9).
88 *ibid.* s. 64(6).
89 *ibid.* s. 64(7).
90 *ibid.* s. 76(2).
91 *ibid.* s. 76(1).
92 *ibid.* s. 76(3).
93 *ibid.* s. 76(4).
94 *ibid.* s. 76(5).
95 *ibid.* s. 84.
96 *ibid.*
97 As in relation to repair of defects (s. 87), lighting (s. 91), painting (s. 92), open spaces (s. 95), statues and monuments (s. 96).
98 1982 Act, s. 106(1).
99 *ibid.* s. 106(2).
1 *ibid.* s. 106(3).
2 *ibid.* s. 106(4).
3 *ibid.* s. 106(5).
4 *ibid.* s. 106(6).

authority under Part VIII the owner may apply to the sheriff, who may authorise entry for the purpose of executing the work.[5]

(6) Charitable collections

The organiser of a collection[6] may appeal within 14 days by summary application to the sheriff against the decision of a local authority refusing or withdrawing permission for a collection, or imposing a condition on the grant of such permission, or varying any condition imposed.[7] In upholding an appeal the sheriff may remit the case to the authority or reverse or alter the decision.[8] **26.297**

(7) Warrants

The sheriff may issue a warrant authorising entry to and search of unlicensed premises.[9] He may also issue a warrant authorising entry to and search of sex shops.[10] On summary application by the owner of part of a building who requires the consent of any other person for the installation of pipes through a neighbouring property and has not been able to obtain such consent, the sheriff may grant warrant authorising the necessary installation subject to such conditions as he sees fit, and may award expenses.[11] There is an appeal to the Court of Session from the decision of the sheriff.[12] The sheriff may issue a warrant authorising a person entitled to entry to land or premises under Part VIII of the Act but who has been prevented from entering to enter, if need be by force.[13] **26.298**

XL. MEDICAL AND RELATED PROFESSIONS

Nurses (Scotland) Act 1951[14]

A licence is required authorising a person to carry on an agency for the supply of nurses on any premises in the area of any licensing authority.[15] An applicant aggrieved by the refusal of, revocation of, or conditions imposed upon a grant of such a licence by the health board may appeal within 21 days to the sheriff, who may make such order as he thinks just.[16] These provisions do not apply to an agency for the supply of nurses carried on in connection with a hospital maintained or controlled by a Government department, local authority, or body constituted by special Act of Parliament or incorporated by Royal Charter.[17] **26.299**

---

[5] 1982 Act, s. 104.
[6] Defined in *ibid.* s. 119(16).
[7] 1982 Act, s. 119(9).
[8] *ibid.* s. 119(10).
[9] *ibid.* s. 6(1).
[10] *ibid.* Sched. 2, para. 21(1).
[11] *ibid.* s. 88(1)–(3).
[12] *ibid.* s. 88(4).
[13] *ibid.* s. 102(1).
[14] 14 & 15 Geo. 6, c. 55 ("the 1951 Act").
[15] *ibid.* s. 28(1). The licensing authority is the Health Board: 1951 Act, s. 32, as amended by National Health Service (Scotland) Act 1978 (c. 58), Sched. 6, para. 90.
[16] *ibid.* s. 28(4).
[17] *ibid.* s. 31(1).

XLI. Medicines, Poisons and Drugs

Poisons Act 1972[18]

26.300 Every local authority must keep a list of persons entitled to sell non-medicinal poisons.[19] The local authority may refuse to enter in, or may remove from, the list the name of any person whom they consider to be unfit to be on the list.[20] Any person aggrieved by such a refusal or removal may appeal to the sheriff within whose jurisdiction the appellant's place of business is situate.[21]

XLII. Mental Health

Mental Health (Scotland) Act 1984[22]

(1) Admission to hospital

26.301 A person suffering from mental disorder of a nature or degree which makes it appropriate for him to receive medical treatment in a hospital[23] and it is necessary for the health or safety of that person or for the protection of other persons that he should receive such treament and it cannot be provided unless he is detained,[24] may be admitted to and detained in a hospital on the sheriff's approval of an application for admission.[25] An application may be made by the patient's nearest relative or a mental health officer,[26] and must be founded on and accompanied by two medical recommendations.[27] An application must be submitted within seven days of the last date on which the patient was examined for the purposes of any medical recommendation accompanying the application.[28] The sheriff to whom the application should be submitted is the sheriff of the sheriffdom within which the patient resides or, where the patient is a resident patient in a hospital, within which the hospital is situated.[29] On receiving an application the sheriff must appoint a hearing, and the sheriff clerk must serve upon the patient a copy of the application (excluding the medical recommendations) together with a notice informing the patient of the date of the hearing and of his right to attend or have a person appear on his behalf.[30] The sheriff may appoint the hearing of an application to take place in a hospital or other place, if he thinks this to be appropriate in all the circumstances.[31] The sheriff may make such inquiries and hear such persons as he thinks fit[32] (but must make his decision within five days of submission of the application[33]) and may

---

18 c. 66 ("the 1972 Act").
19 *ibid.* s. 5(1).
20 *ibid.* s. 5(3).
21 *ibid.* s. 5(4), (6)(a).
22 c. 36 ("the 1984 Act").
23 *ibid.* s. 17(1)(a).
24 *ibid.* s. 17(1)(b).
25 *ibid.* s. 18(1).
26 *ibid.* s. 19(1).
27 *ibid.* s. 18(2), (3).
28 *ibid.* s. 21(1), as amended by Law Reform (Miscellaneous Provisions) (Scotland) Act 1985 (c. 73) ("the 1985 Act"), s. 51.
29 *ibid.* s. 21(1)(a), (b).
30 A.S. (Mental Health Rules) 1996 (S.I. 1996 No. 2149) ("A.S. 1996"), r. 2(1), Sched., Form 1.
31 *ibid.* r. 2(2).
32 1984 Act, s. 21(2)(a), as amended by 1985 Act, s. 51.
33 *ibid.* s. 21(3A), inserted by Mental Health (Detention) (Scotland) Act 1991 (c. 47) ("the 1991 Act"), s. 2.

conduct the proceedings in private, where the patient or applicant desires or the sheriff thinks fit.[34] In the exercise of his functions in respect of applications for admission, the sheriff has the like jurisdiction and powers with regard to summoning and examining witnesses, administration of oaths and awarding expenses as if he were acting in the exercise of his civil jurisdiction.[35] The sheriff is under a statutory duty to give the patient an opportunity to be heard, either in person or by means of a representative.[36] Where the person who is the subject of the application has indicated that he wishes to be represented but has not nominated a representative, the sheriff may appoint a solicitor to take instructions from him.[37] Where an application for admission is approved by the sheriff the application is sufficient authority for the removal of the patient to hospital.[38] The sheriff is empowered to approve the amendment of an incorrect application or of an incorrect medical recommendation in certain circumstances.[39]

Short-term detention[40] follows an admission to hospital under an emergency recommendation.[41] If the authority for the patient's detention is renewed beyond the period of emergency admission, the patient may appeal to the sheriff to order his discharge,[42] and the sheriff may order his discharge if satisfied that it is either not appropriate or not necessary that he be detained.[43] In certain circumstances the 28 days' short term detention may be extended by three days if a relevant medical practitioner lodges with the sheriff clerk a medical report.[44] A patient so detained may appeal to the sheriff to order his discharge.[45] **26.302**

Any patient admitted to hospital following an application to the sheriff for admission may normally be detained for no more than six months.[46] However, the period of detention may be extended.[47] Where the period has been extended the patient may appeal to the sheriff,[48] and the sheriff may order his discharge if satisfied that it is either not appropriate or not necessary that he be detained.[49] The sheriff may also order the discharge of a patient on an appeal made by the patient's nearest relative.[50] Each of the above appeals must be made by summary application to the sheriff,[51] who must order the discharge of the patient if he finds certain states of fact.[52] As in proceedings in relation to applications for admission, the sheriff is under a duty to give the patient, or his representative, an opportunity to be heard.[53] **26.303**

---

34 1984 Act, s. 21(4).
35 *ibid.* s. 21(5).
36 *ibid.* s. 113.
37 A.S. 1996, r. 6.
38 1984 Act, s. 22(1).
39 *ibid.* s. 23.
40 *ibid.* s. 26 which permits detention for up to 28 days.
41 *ibid.* s. 24 which permits detention for 72 hours.
42 *ibid.* s. 26(6).
43 *ibid.* s. 33(2), (4).
44 *ibid.* s. 26A(1), (2), inserted by 1991 Act, s. 1.
45 *ibid.* ss. 26A(7), 33(2), (4).
46 *ibid.* s. 30(1)
47 *ibid.* s. 30(2)
48 *ibid.* s. 30(6).
49 *ibid.* s. 33(2), (4).
50 *ibid.* ss. 33(2), (4), 34(2).
51 *ibid.* s. 35(2).
52 *ibid.* s. 33(2), (4).
53 *ibid.* s. 113.

26.304 The patient or his nearest relative may appeal to the sheriff within 28 days of the date of the transfer of the patient to a state hospital.[54] The appeal is made by summary application to the sheriff,[55] who must give the patient or his representative an opportunity of being heard.[56] The appeal is made to the sheriff having jurisdiction in the sheriffdom within which the hospital from which the patient was transferred is situated.[57] The sheriff must order the return of the patient to that hospital unless he is satisfied that the patient requires special security because of his dangerous, violent or criminal propensities.[58] Appeal is made to the sheriff or to the sheriff principal, but there is no appeal from the decision of the sheriff to the sheriff principal.[59] The sheriff is acting in an administrative capacity rather than a judicial capacity.[60]

(2) Community care order

26.305 The responsible medical officer may apply to the sheriff for a community care order. Such an order provides that the patient shall, instead of continuing to be liable to be detained in hospital, be subject to conditions which will ensure that he receives medical treatment and after-care services.[61] There is provision for variation by the sheriff of conditions in the community care order, and for the patient to object.[62] While the order is in force and has been renewed the patient may appeal by summary application to the sheriff for its revocation.[63]

(3) Curator ad litem

26.306 In an application for a hospital order under section 21, for a community care order under section 35A or a guardianship order under section 40 the sheriff may appoint a curator *ad litem*[64] and may appoint a solicitor to take instructions from a person who is the subject of the application, and has indicated that he wishes to be represented.[65] It is submitted that the sheriff also has power at common law to appoint a curator *ad litem.*

(4) Reception into guardianship

26.307 The procedure for the reception of patients into guardianship runs parallel to, but is distinct from, that for admission into hospital.[66] An appeal may be made to the sheriff against the extension of a period of guardianship[67] or against the refusal of the local authority to comply with

---

54 1984 Act, s. 29(4).
55 *ibid.*
56 *ibid.* s. 113.
57 *ibid.* s. 29(4).
58 *ibid.*
59 *Ferns v. Management Committee of Ravenscraig Hospital*, 1987 S.L.T (Sh.Ct.) 76; *T v. Secretary of State for Scotland*, 1987 S.C.L.R. 65. Both cases are recommended for their discussion of the background to and purpose of the 1984 Act.
60 *ibid.*
61 1984 Act, s. 35A, as inserted by Mental Health (Patients in the Community) Act 1995 (c. 52), s. 4.
62 *ibid.* s. 35D; A.S. 1996, rr. 9, 10.
63 *ibid.* s. 35F; A.S. 1996, r. 11.
64 A.S. 1996, r. 5.
65 *ibid.* r. 6.
66 1984 Act, ss. 36–42; s. 40, as amended by 1985 Act, s. 51; A.S. 1996, rr. 2, 3, 5, 6 and 7 apply to applications for guardianship.
67 *ibid.* s. 47(6). The period of guardianship is normally six months, but it may be extended in much the same way as the period of detention in hospital.

an order for the discharge of the patient made by his nearest relative.[68] Appeal is made by way of summary application to a sheriff of the sheriffdom within which the patient is resident at the time of the appeal.[69] The sheriff must order that the patient be discharged if he is satisfied either that the patient is not suffering from mental disorder of a nature or degree which warrants his remaining under guardianship or that it is not necessary in the interests of the welfare of the patient that he should remain under guardianship.[70] It should be noted by way of contrast that in the case of appeals against the detention of a patient in hospital, the second ground for release is that it is not necessary for the health or safety of the patient or for the protection of other persons that he receive treatment in hospital.[71]

A patient subject to the guardianship of any person may be transferred to the guardianship of another person with the consent of his guardian; if the guardian refuses such consent, the sheriff's approval is necessary.[72] **26.308**

(5) Acting nearest relative

The sheriff may appoint an acting nearest relative for the purposes of the Act.[73] An application to be so appointed may be made by any relative of the patient, any other person with whom the patient is residing, or a mental health officer,[74] on certain specified grounds.[75] The sheriff must decide whether the applicant is a proper person to act as the patient's nearest relative and whether he is willing to act as such.[76] An order appointing an applicant to act as the patient's nearest relative may be discharged upon an application to the sheriff by the person so appointed or by the patient's nearest relative,[77] or may be varied on the application of the person appointed as the patient's nearest relative or of a mental health officer.[78] **26.309**

(6) Restricted patients

A restricted patient, *i.e.* a person sentenced by a court in criminal proceedings to a hospital order,[79] subject to a restriction order or a restriction direction, may appeal to the sheriff by way of summary application.[80] Where an appeal is made by a restricted patient subject to a restriction order,[81] the sheriff may order the absolute[82] or conditional[83] discharge of the patient. He may defer a direction for the conditional discharge of a patient until such arrangements as appear to **26.310**

---

[68] 1984 Act, s. 51(2).
[69] *ibid.* s. 52(2).
[70] *ibid.* s. 50(5).
[71] *ibid.* s. 33(3)(b).
[72] *ibid.* s. 45(1).
[73] *ibid.* s. 56(1).
[74] *ibid.* s. 56(2).
[75] *ibid.* s. 56(3).
[76] *ibid.* s. 56(1).
[77] *ibid.* s. 57(1).
[78] *ibid.* s. 57(2).
[79] See Criminal Procedure (Scotland) Act 1995 (c. 46), ss. 58, 59.
[80] 1984 Act, s. 63(1), (2).
[81] See *A, Appellant*, Lanark Sh. Ct, Jan. 24, 1985, unreported.
[82] 1984 Act, s. 64(1), (3).
[83] *ibid.* s. 64(2), (4)–(7).

him to be necessary have been made.[84] Any condition imposed by the sheriff or by the Secretary of State may be varied by the Secretary of State.[85]

26.311 Where an appeal is made by a restricted patient subject to a restriction direction, the sheriff may notify the Secretary of State that the patient is entitled to be absolutely or conditionally discharged.[86]

26.312 Where a restricted patient is conditionally discharged and is then recalled to hospital by a warrant issued by the Secretary of State he may appeal to the sheriff within one month of his return to hospital.[87] He may also appeal against his conditional discharge within the second year from the date of his conditional discharge and thereafter in any subsequent period of two years.[88] In either case the sheriff may order the appellant's absolute discharge.[89]

(7) Transfer to hospital or guardianship of prisoners

26.313 If the Secretary of State believes that the grounds upon which a Part V application for admission[90] may be made are satisfied in the case of a person in custody while awaiting trial or sentence he may apply for an order that the person be removed to and detained in a hospital.[91] The sheriff may make a transfer order if he is satisfied by reports from two medical practitioners.[92] The order ceases to have effect after 14 days unless the person is received into the hospital within that period.[93]

26.314 The Secretary of State is empowered to make a transfer direction in respect of a person serving a prison sentence[94] if he is satisfied by reports from two medical practitioners that the grounds are satisfied upon which a Part V application for admission may be made.[95] A transfer direction has the same effect as a hospital order made under the Criminal Proceedure (Scotland) Act 1995.[96] Where a transfer direction is made the prisoner may appeal to the sheriff within one month of his transfer and the sheriff must cancel the direction unless he is satisfied that the grounds for a Part V application for admission are satisfied.[97]

XLIII. Mines and Minerals

Mines and Quarries (Tips) Act 1969[98]

26.315 If an owner of a disused tip receives a notice from the local authority requiring him to carry out remedial operations he may apply to the

---

[84] 1984 Act, s. 64(7).
[85] *ibid.* s. 64(5); see also s. 68.
[86] *ibid.* s. 65(1).
[87] *ibid.* s. 66(1).
[88] *ibid.* s. 66(2).
[89] *ibid.* s. 66(3).
[90] *i.e.* in terms of 1984 Act, s. 21.
[91] 1984 Act, s. 70(1).
[92] *ibid.*
[93] *ibid.* s. 70(2).
[94] *ibid.* s. 71(2).
[95] *ibid.* s. 71(1).
[96] *ibid.* ss. 71(4), 125(1), as amended by Criminal Procedure (Consequential Provisions) (Scotland) Act 1995 (c. 40), Sched. 4, para. 50(10).
[97] *ibid.* s. 71(5).
[98] c. 10 ("the 1969 Act").

sheriff for an order varying or cancelling the notice.[99] The application, like any other application under the Act, is to be by way of summary application.[1] If the owner carries out work on the tip as a result of the notice and the notice is subsequently cancelled, he may apply to the sheriff for an order directing the local authority to reimburse him for the whole or part of his expenditure.[2] In deciding whether to do so the sheriff must have regard to all the circumstances of the case and, in particular, to the grounds on which the notice was cancelled, whether a further notice is envisaged or whether the local authority intends to carry out the remedial operations.[3] On the application of an owner of a disused tip the sheriff may order other persons to contribute to the cost of the remedial work.[4] It should be noted that the tip must be unstable and not merely unsafe.[5]

Any question as to compensation for damage or disturbance in relation to work on a tip is to be determined by the sheriff.[6] A contributory may apply to the sheriff to vary a demand for payment for work done under section 21 of the Act[7] and may also apply for the variation or cancellation of a demand issued by the local authority in respect of expenses incurred in carrying out work on its own tip.[8] Where the local authority has issued a demand in respect of expenses incurred by them in carrying out remedial operations the owner or contributory may apply to the sheriff for an order varying or cancelling the demand on certain grounds.[9] **26.316**

The sheriff may grant warrant authorising the local authority to enter on lands for the purposes of the Act.[10] **26.317**

Coal Mining Subsidence Act 1991[11]

The 1991 Act tranfers most of the sheriff's former functions to the Lands Tribunal.[12] An application may be made to the sheriff where agreement of two or more persons is required and one refuses to agree.[13] If the occupier of any premises refuses to afford the British Coal Corporation facilities to enter upon, inspect, and execute works, the sheriff, on summary application made to him, may confer such powers as appear to him to be necessary.[14] **26.318**

---

99 1969 Act, s. 15(1).
1 *ibid.* s. 35(a).
2 *ibid.* s. 16(4).
3 *ibid.* s. 16(5).
4 *ibid.* s. 19.
5 *Lanark C.C. v. Frank Doonin Ltd*, 1974 S.L.T. (Sh.Ct.) 13.
6 1969 Act, s. 20(5).
7 *ibid.* s. 22(1).
8 *ibid.* Sched. 2, para. 6(4); see also s. 24(2), (4).
9 *ibid.* s. 24.
10 *ibid.* ss. 13(2), (7), 18(2), (7).
11 c. 45 ("the 1991 Act").
12 *ibid.* s. 40.
13 *ibid.* s. 41; A.S. (Coal Mining Subsidence Act 1991) 1992 (S.I. 1992 No. 798)("A.S. 1992").
14 *ibid.* s. 42(1); A.S. 1992, para. 3.

XLIV. Partnerships and Business Names

Partnership Act 1890[15]

26.319 On an application made by a partner the sheriff may dissolve a partnership in six specified situations.[16] Any partner or his representatives may apply to the sheriff to wind up the business and affairs of the firm on the termination of the partnership.[17] The sheriff does not have power to appoint a judicial factor to the partnership estate.[18] On the premature dissolution of a partnership the sheriff may order the repayment of all or part of a premium paid by a partner on entering into the partnership, having regard to the partnership contract and the duration of the partnership.[19] In certain cases the sheriff may award to a person ceasing to be a partner, or to his representatives, a share in profits made after dissolution.[20]

XLV. Posts and Telecommunications

Telecommunications Act 1984[21]

26.320 Where an operator who is authorised to run a telecommunication system requires the agreement of a person for the purpose of executing works or before obstructing access, and such agreement has not been given within 28 days of the service of a notice requiring it, the operator may apply to the sheriff for an order conferring the required rights and dispensing with the need for agreement.[22] Pending the determination of such an application, the sheriff may, on the application of the operator, confer upon him such temporary rights as are reasonably necessary to secure the maintenance and repair of the operator's system.[23] Where the sheriff dispenses with the requisite agreement he may make such financial arrangements as he thinks appropriate,[24] and may order the payment into court of such sum as he thinks fit.[25]

A potential subscriber may issue a notice to an operator requiring him to obtain the necessary agreement from any person.[26] The operator may apply to the sheriff to set aside the notice on the ground that certain conditions are not satisfied or that the operator does not intend to afford the potential subscriber access to his system.[27] The potential subscriber may make an application to have the requisite consent dispensed with,[28] and the sheriff may give such directions as he thinks fit.[29]

---

15 53 & 54 Vict. c. 39 ("the 1890 Act").

16 *ibid.* ss. 35, 45; see *Duthie v. Milne* 1946 S.L.T. (Sh.Ct.) 14; *Roxburgh v. Dinardo*, 1981 S.L.T. 291.

17 *ibid.* s. 39.

18 *Pollock v. Campbell*, 1962 S.L.T. (Sh.Ct.) 89.

19 1890 Act, s. 40.

20 *ibid.* s. 42(1); see *Pathirana v. Pathirana* [1967] 1 A.C. 233; *Meagher v. Meagher* [1961] I.R. 96.

21 c. 12 ("the 1984 Act").

22 *ibid.* Sched. 2, paras 1(1), 5.

23 *ibid.* paras 1(1), 6(2).

24 *ibid.* paras 1(1), 7.

25 *ibid.* paras 1(1), 7(5).

26 *ibid.* paras 1(1), 8(1).

27 *ibid.* paras 1(1), 8(2).

28 *ibid.* paras 1(1), 8(3).

29 *ibid.* paras 1(1), 8(4).

The person with control of any relevant land may give notice requiring the operator to alter apparatus crossing a linear obstacle such as a railway, tramway or canal.[30] Where the operator issues a counter-notice stating his intention not to comply with the notice the person with control of the land may apply to the sheriff for an order requiring the alteration of any telecommunication apparatus to which the notice relates.[31] The sheriff must not make an order unless he considers it necessary, having regard to the principle that no person should unreasonably be denied access to a telecommunication system.[32] An order under this paragraph may be on such terms and conditions as the sheriff thinks fit and may contain such directions as the sheriff thinks necessary for resolving any difference between the parties and for protecting their respective interests.[33] **26.321**

Where an operator has installed apparatus three or more metres above the ground[34] the occupier or owner of the land over or on which the apparatus has been installed or of any land the enjoyment of which is prejudiced by the apparatus may give the operator notice of objection in respect of the apparatus.[35] At any time between two and four months after giving such notice the person may apply to the sheriff to have the objection upheld.[36] Having due regard to all the circumstances,[37] the sheriff may direct the alteration of the apparatus or the installation of alternative apparatus.[38]

The sheriff may confirm a notice given by the operator to the occupier of land requiring a tree to be lopped if it obstructs or interferes with the working of any telecommunication apparatus.[39] A person who suffers loss or damage in consequence of the lopping of the tree may apply to the sheriff who may order the payment of compensation.[40]

A person may serve a notice on an operator requiring him to alter certain telecommunication apparatus to enable the person to carry out improvements on the land.[41] If the operator gives a counter-notice within 28 days, the person may apply to the sheriff, who may make an order requiring the alteration to be made.[42] The sheriff may also make various orders requiring the removal of apparatus from land.[43]

XLVI. Public Finance and Economic Control

Government Annuities Act 1929[44]

If payment of a sum of money alleged to be due under a savings bank insurance is refused by the National Debt Commissioners, the person entitled may, rather than proceeding by arbitration under the Act, take proceedings before the sheriff, whose decision is final and conclusive.[45] **26.322**

---

30 1984 Act, paras 1(1), 14(1).
31 *ibid.* paras 1(1), 14(3).
32 *ibid.* paras 1(1), 14(4).
33 *ibid.* paras 1(1), 14(5).
34 *ibid.* paras 1(1), 17(1).
35 *ibid.* paras 1(1), 17(2).
36 *ibid.* paras 1(1), 17(5).
37 *ibid.* para. 17(8).
38 *ibid.* para. 17(9).
39 *ibid.* para. 19(2).
40 *ibid.* para. 19(5).
41 *ibid.* para. 20(1).
42 *ibid.* para. 20(3).
43 *ibid.* para. 21.
44 19 & 20 Geo. 5, c. 29 ("the 1929 Act").
45 *ibid.* s. 48(1), (3).

26.323 The Commissioners may recover in the sheriff court a fraudulently received savings bank annuity or insurance.[46]

XLVII. Public Health

Public Health (Scotland) Act 1897[47]

(1) Procedure

26.324 All applications to enforce the provisions of the Act are to be brought by way of summary application and commenced by initial writ, which may refer to the sections of the Act without narrating them.[48] In practice, service of the writ is usually effected in the customary manner.[49] The sheriff may appoint answers to be lodged, ordain parties to appear, remit for a report on the premises and act upon it or order a proof giving decree within three days.[50] He may also award and modify expenses.[51] No decree or order, or any other proceeding, matter, or thing done in execution of the Act is to be subject to review in any way whatsoever.[52] The sheriff is not disqualified from dealing with the application if he is a member of the local authority concerned in the application.[53]

(2) Offensive trades

26.325 Byelaws made by a local authority may give power to the sheriff by summary order to deprive a person, either temporarily or permanently, of the right to carry out an offensive trade[54] as a punishment for breaking the byelaw.[55] An appeal lies to the Court of Session[56] but there is no appeal from the decision of the sheriff to the sheriff principal.

(3) Infectious diseases

26.326 On the summary application of a local authority the sheriff may order the removal to hospital of an infected person without proper lodging or may order the removal from the accommodation of all persons not in attendance upon the infected person.[57] The sheriff may also order the transfer of an infected person to another hospital.[58]

On the application of a local authority the sheriff may order that an infected person be detained in hospital to prevent the spread of his disease.[59] The sheriff may order his transfer to another hospital.[60]

---

[46] 1929 Act, s. 61(1).

[47] 60 & 61 Vict. c. 38 ("the 1897 Act").

[48] 1897 Act, s. 154.

[49] *McDougall v. Duke of Argyll* (1864) 3 M. 248; *Waddell v. Stirling C.C.* (1942) 59 Sh.Ct.Rep. 78; Dobie, p. 645.

[50] 1897 Act, s. 154.

[51] *ibid.*

[52] *ibid.* s. 157.

[53] *ibid.* s. 158, repealed in part by Local Government (Scotland) Act 1973, Sched. 27.

[54] *ibid.* s. 32(4).

[55] *ibid.*

[56] *ibid.* s. 156; see also *Kilmarnock and Loudoun D.C. v. Young*, 1993 S.L.T. 505.

[57] *ibid.* s. 54(1), as amended and in part repealed by National Health Service (Scotland) Acts 1947 (c. 27), Sched. 11, Pt I and 1972 (c. 58), Sched. 6, para. 50, and Local Government (Scotland) Act, 1973 (c. 65), Sched. 27; see *Local Authority of Aberdeen* (1893) 1 S.L.T. 210.

[58] *ibid.* s. 54(3), inserted by 1947 Act (c. 27), Sched. 11, Pt I; s. 54(3) repealed in part by 1973 Act (c. 65), Sched. 27.

[59] *ibid.* s. 55(1), inserted by 1947 Act (c. 27), Sched. 11, Pt I; s. 55(1) repealed in part by 1973 Act (c. 65), Sched. 27.

[60] *ibid.* s. 55(3), inserted by 1947 Act (c. 27), Sched. 11, Pt I; s. 55(3) repealed in part by 1973 Act (c. 65), Sched. 27.

On a certificate signed by a medical practitioner the sheriff may direct that the body of a person who died of an infectious disease be removed at the cost of the local authority to a mortuary and buried.[61] The local authority may recover the expense in a summary manner from any person legally liable to pay the expense of such a burial.[62]

(4) Miscellaneous

If an open ditch or watercourse lying near to or forming a boundary between the districts of two local authorities is offensive, either local authority may present a summary application to the sheriff of the other district to order the cleansing of the ditch or the execution of such works as are necessary.[63] The sheriff may make such order as may seem reasonable.[64] **26.327**

The local authority may apply to the sheriff for a warrant for the removal of residents for the purpose of disinfecting a building.[65] Compensation for any unnecessary damage caused in disinfection is to be recovered summarily.[66]

In certain circumstances the sheriff has power to close an underground dwelling or cellar temporarily or permanently.[67]

The local authority may make a summary application to the sheriff for authority to remove an unsuitable common lodging house from the register, temporarily or permanently.[68] The local authority may also remove a common lodging house from the register because of a refusal by the keeper of the common lodging house to provide an extra water supply for the house,[69] and any person interested may appeal to the sheriff.[70]

Full compensation is payable to all persons suffering damage by the exercise of any of the powers of the Act except when otherwise specifically provided. The sheriff may ascertain compensation by summary application where the sum claimed does not exceed £50.[71] The decision of the sheriff may be appealed to the sheriff principal, but if the application is heard at first instance by the sheriff principal, there is no appeal.[72]

An owner of premises may apply to the sheriff for an order requiring the occupier to permit execution of required works, providing that such works appear to the sheriff to be necessary for the purpose of obeying or carrying into effect the provisions of the Act.[73]

---

[61] 1897 Act, s. 69(1), amended by 1972 Act (c. 58), Sched. 6, para. 55; s. 69(1) repealed in part by National Assistance Act 1948 (c. 29), Sched. 7, Pt III and 1973 Act (c. 65), Sched. 27.

[62] *ibid.* s. 69(2).

[63] *ibid.* s. 41, as amended by Radioactive Substances Act 1960 (c. 34), s. 9, Sched. 1, Pt. II, para. 13; *Brown v. Kirkcudbright Mags* (1905) 8 F. 77.

[64] *ibid.* s. 41, as amended.

[65] *ibid.* s. 47(4), amended by 1972 Act (c. 58), Sched. 6, para. 45 and 1973 Act (c. 65), Sched. 27.

[66] *ibid.* s. 47(5).

[67] *ibid.* s. 76.

[68] *ibid.* s. 90, as amended by 1973 Act (c. 65), Sched. 27, Pt I, para. 2.

[69] *ibid.* s. 94, as amended by 1973 Act (c. 65), Sched. 27, Pt I, para. 2.

[70] *ibid.*

[71] *ibid.* s. 164, as amended by Sheriff Courts (Scotland) Act 1971, s. 4; see *Sinclair v. Spence* (1883) 10 R. 1077; *Thomson v. Broughty Ferry Commissioners* (1898) 6 S.L.T. 202; *Cessford v. Millport Commissioners.* (1899) 15 Sh.Ct.Rep. 362; *Craig v. Lorn District Committee of Argyll C.C.* (1911) 28 Sh.Ct.Rep. 14; *Oatman v. Buckhaven Mags.* (1914) 30 Sh.Ct.Rep. 258; *Blyth v. Edinburgh Mags.* (1905) 13 S.L.T. 459.

[72] *ibid.* s. 164.

[73] *ibid.* s. 162; repealed in part by 1973 Act (c. 65), Sched. 27.

(5) Proceedings against local authority

26.328 If any nuisance exists in premises possessed or managed by a local authority or if an authority fails or neglects to perform any duty under the Act, ten ratepayers[74] or the procurator fiscal may give written notice to the local authority of matters in which such neglect exists. If the local authority fail to act, a summary petition may be made to the sheriff who may make such decree as in his judgment is required to enforce the removal or remedy of the nuisance, or to compel execution of the provisions of the Act.[75] If the Secretary of State is satisfied that the local authority have made default in doing their duty, the procurator fiscal may, with the approval of the Lord Advocate, institute proceedings against them.[76] These follow the same procedure as all other summary applications under the Act.[77]

Celluloid and Cinematograph Film Act 1922[78]

26.329 An appeal may be made to the sheriff by any person aggrieved by refusal of or the conditions attached to the grant of any sanction of the local authority for storing raw celluloid or celluloid film.[79] The appeal must be brought within seven days, and not less than 24 hours' notice of the appeal and the grounds of appeal must be given to the local authority.[80] The sheriff is authorised to make such order as he thinks just.[81]

26.330 The sheriff may set aside or modify the terms of any agreement which prevents the occupier of premises from carrying out structural alterations to enable him to comply with the provisions of the Act.[82] The occupier may apply to the sheriff when he is unable to obtain the consent of a person whose consent is necessary in terms of the agreement.[83] Where the occupier alleges that all or part of the expenses of requisite alterations should be borne by the owner, he may apply to the sheriff who may apportion the expenses, or may determine the lease.[84]

Prevention of Damage by Pests Act 1949[85]

26.331 If the occupier of land prevents the owner from carrying out work required by a notice issued under the provisions of the Act, the owner may apply to the sheriff who may order the occupier to permit the work.[86] A person aggrieved may appeal to the sheriff against a local authority's notice for destroying rats and mice and for keeping the land free from them.[87]

---

74 As defined in 1897 Act, s. 3, as amended by Local Government (Finance) Act 1992 (c. 14), Sched. 13, para. 2.
75 1897 Act, s. 146, repealed in part by 1973 Act (c. 65), Sched. 27; see *McGourlich v. Renfrew D.C.* (1982) 73 SCOLAG 58.
76 1897 Act, s. 148.
77 See para. 26.324.
78 12 & 13 Geo. 5, c. 35 ("the 1922 Act").
79 *ibid.* ss. 1(3), 10.
80 *ibid.*
81 *ibid.*
82 *ibid.* ss. 8(1), 10.
83 *ibid.*
84 *ibid.* ss. 8(2), 10.
85 12, 13 & 14 Geo. 6, c. 55 ("the 1949 Act").
86 *ibid.* s. 4(4), (6); *Perry v. Garner* [1953] 1 Q.B. 335.
87 *ibid.* s. 4(1), (5), (6).

An appeal may be made to the sheriff by any person aggrieved by directions given by the Secretary of State in respect of the carrying out of any structural works or the destruction of any food or containers.[88] The sheriff may quash or amend the directions if he is satisfied that they are invalid or that any requirement is excessive or unreasonable; if the appeal is based on the ground of some informality, defect or error in connection with the directions the sheriff will dismiss the appeal if satisfied that the informality, defect or error was not material.[89] An appeal is to be by way of an application to the sheriff within seven days from the service of directions requiring the destruction of food or a container, or within 21 days from the service of directions requiring the carrying out of structural works.[90] **26.332**

Rag, Flock and Other Filling Materials Act 1951[91]

The purpose of this Act is to ensure the use of clean filling materials in upholstered articles. Where samples are taken from the filling materials in any article, and no conviction follows, compensation is payable.[92] Any dispute as to whether compensation ought to be paid and if so what sum is due is to be determined by the sheriff.[93] **26.333**

Health Services and Public Health Act 1968[94]

The Act makes provision for the compensation of persons who have complied with a request to stop work in order to stop the spread of an infectious disease.[95] Any dispute as to the fact of loss suffered or as to the amount of compensation is to be determined by a single arbiter appointed, failing agreement, by the sheriff.[96] The sheriff, acting *ex parte* if he deems it necessary, may order a person to be medically examined if satisfied on receiving a written certificate by a designated medical officer that there is reason to believe that that person is suffering from an infectious disease and that it is expedient that he be examined.[97] On the same basis he may also order that a group of persons be medically examined.[98] **26.334**

Sewerage (Scotland) Act 1968[99]

If an owner or occupier of land objects to the line of a proposed sewer, the sewerage authority may present a summary application to the sheriff who may grant consent unconditionally or subject to such conditions as he thinks fit, or withhold consent.[1] In such applications the sheriff has an **26.335**

---

[88] 1949 Act, s. 15(1), (5).
[89] *ibid.* s. 15(2), (5).
[90] *ibid.* s. 15(1), (5).
[91] 14 & 15 Geo. 6, c. 63 ("the 1951 Act").
[92] *ibid.* s. 14(1), Sched., para. 3.
[93] *ibid.* Sched., para. 4.
[94] c. 46 ("the 1968 Act").
[95] *ibid.* s. 71(2), as amended by National Health Service (Scotland) Act 1972 (c. 58), Sched. 6, para. 138.
[96] *ibid.*
[97] *ibid.* s. 72(1), as amended by National Health Service (Scotland) Act 1972, Sched. 6, para. 139.
[98] *ibid.* s. 72(2).
[99] c. 47 ("the 1968 Act").
[1] *ibid.* s. 3(2), as amended by Roads (Scotland) Act 1984 (c. 54), Sched. 9, para. 64(2) and Local Government etc. (Scotland) Act 1994 (c. 39), Sched. 13, para. 75(4)(a).

unfettered discretion[2] and his power to withhold consent is not limited to cases of improper exercise of discretion by the sewerage authority.[3] The decision of the sheriff is final.[4]

26.336 If any question arises as to the reasonable practicability of emptying septic tanks, or as to whether tanks receive trade effluent, it is to be summarily determined by the sheriff, whose decision is final.[5]

26.337 The sheriff is empowered summarily to determine any question as to the amount of extra payment to be made to a person constructing a drain or sewer who has been instructed by the sewerage authority to construct it in a certain way.[6] The decision of the sheriff is final.[7]

If an owner or occupier is aggrieved by a notice requiring him to remedy defects in drains and other sewage works he may make summary application to the sheriff who may issue such directions as he thinks fit and whose decision is final.[8]

Any question as to whether the sewerage authority has unreasonably withheld consent to a building to be erected or embankment constructed over, or obstructing access to, a sewer, or as to what conditions should be attached to the consent, may be referred by any person aggrieved by summary application to the sheriff, whose decision is final.[9]

26.338 Any dispute between a sewerage authority and a person making a discharge of trade effluent as to whether it is an existing discharge as defined by the Act is to be determined by the sheriff, against whose determination an appeal lies to the Court of Session.[10]

26.339 Compensation for any damage done by the sewerage authority in breaking open a road in a disputed case, is determined summarily by the sheriff, whose decision is final.[11]

26.340 If on a complaint by the owner of premises it appears to the sheriff that the occupier of the premises is preventing the owner from entering the premises for the purpose of carrying out required or authorised work, he may authorise the owner so to enter.[12]

Environmental Protection Act 1990[13]

26.341 Where a local authority is satisfied that a statutory nuisance[14] exists, or is likely to recur, in the area of the authority, they must serve an abatement

---

[2] *Strathclyde R.C. v. Dales of Dalry Ltd*, Kilmarnock Sh. Ct, Oct. 13, 1981, unreported.

[3] *Central R.C. v. Barbour European Ltd*, 1982 S.L.T. (Sh.Ct.) 49.

[4] 1968 Act, s. 3(2), as amended by Roads (Scotland) Act 1984 (c. 54), Sched. 9, para. 64(2).

[5] *ibid.* s. 10(3), as substituted by Local Government etc. (Scotland) Act 1994 (c. 39), s. 102.

[6] *ibid.* s. 14(5).

[7] *ibid.*

[8] *ibid.* s. 15(2).

[9] *ibid.* s. 21(2), as amended by Local Government etc. (Scotland) Act 1994 (c. 39), Sched. 13, para. 75(18).

[10] *ibid.* s. 33(2).

[11] *ibid.* s. 41, as amended by Roads (Scotland) Act 1984 (c. 54), Sched. 9, para. 64(4).

[12] *ibid.* s. 43.

[13] c. 43 ("the 1990 Act").

[14] *ibid.* s. 79 lists statutory nuisances.

notice.[15] A person served with a notice may, within 21 days, appeal to the sheriff against it.[16] The appeal is by way of summary application.[17] Where an abatement notice has not been complied with the local authority may, whether or not they take proceedings for an offence under section 80(4), abate the nuisance and do whatever may be necessary in execution of the notice.[18] Any expenses reasonably so incurred may be recovered from the author of the nuisance or owner of premises; and the sheriff may apportion expenses between joint authors.[19] If the local authority is of opinion that proceedings for an offence would afford an inadequate remedy they may take proceedings in any court of competent jurisdiction[20] for the purpose of securing the abatement, prohibition or restriction of the nuisance.[21]

The sheriff must, on a summary application by a person aggrieved by a statutory nuisance, if satisfied that the nuisance exists, or although abated, is likely to recur, make an order requiring the defender to abate the nuisance and to execute any necessary works for that purpose, and prohibiting the recurrence of the nuisance, and to execute any works necessary to prevent the recurrence.[22] If the sheriff is satisfied that the nuisance exists and is such as to render premises unfit for human habitation, he may prohibit the use of the premises for human habitation until they are to his satisfaction rendered so fit.[23] Where a person is proceeded against criminally for contravening an order made under section 82(2) the sheriff may, after giving the local authority an opportunity of being heard, direct it to do anything which the convicted person was required to do by the order.[24] If neither the person responsible for the nuisance nor the owner or occupier of the premises can be found, the sheriff may, after giving the local authority an opportunity of being heard, direct it to do anything which he would have ordered that person to do.[25] The sheriff may authorise the local authority by any authorised person to enter premises in connection with statutory nuisances.[26] **26.342**

Clean Air Act 1993[27]

The local authority may, by notice in writing, require the owner or occupier of a dwelling-house to carry out adaptations to the house to avoid contravention of rules with respect to smoke control areas.[28] An appeal may be made to the sheriff by the person required to carry out alterations.[29] The sheriff may grant a warrant to enter land for the purposes of the Act.[30] **26.343**

---

15 1990 Act, s. 80(1).

16 *ibid.* s. 80(3) as amended by Environment Act 1995 (c. 25) ("1995 Act"), s. 107, Sched. 17, para. 3. See para. 26.345.

17 *ibid.* Sched. 3, para. 1A(2), inserted by 1995 Act, s. 107, Sched. 17, para. 7.

18 *ibid.* s. 81(3), as amended by 1995 Act, s. 107. Sched. 17, para 4(b).

19 *ibid.* s. 81(4), as amended by 1995 Act, s. 107, Sched. 17. para 4(c).

20 Which expression includes the sheriff.

21 1990 Act, s. 81(5), as amended by 1995 Act, s. 107, Sched. 17, para 4(d).

22 *ibid.* s. 82(1), (2), as amended by 1995 Act, s. 107, Sched. 17, para 6(a), (b). See *Anderson v. Dundee C.C.*, Dundee Sh.Ct, Oct. 26, 1998, unreported.

23 *ibid.* s. 82(3), as amended by 1995 Act, s. 107, Sched. 17, para. 6(c).

24 *ibid.* s. 82(8), (11), as amended by 1995 Act, s. 107, Sched. 17, para. 6(d).

25 *ibid.* s. 82(13), as amended by 1995 Act, s. 107, Sched. 17, para. 6(f).

26 *ibid.* Sched. 3, para. 2(3), (8), as amended by 1995 Act, s. 107, Sched. 17, para. 7(b).

27 c. 11 ("the 1993 Act").

28 *ibid.* s. 24(1).

29 *ibid.* s. 24(4)(b).

30 *ibid.* ss. 35(1), (2) and 56(3), (4), (6).

26.344 If works are reasonably necessary to enable a building to be used without contravention of the Act the occupier may apply to the sheriff for consent to carry out such works if the occupier is unable to obtain the consent of the owner.[31] The occupier may also apply to the sheriff for an order directing the owner to indemnify the occupier in respect of all or part of the cost.[32]

Statutory Nuisance (Appeals) (Scotland) Regulations 1996[33]

26.345 These regulate appeals under section 80(3) of the 1990 Act against an abatement notice served by a local authority.[34] The grounds on which a person may appeal are (a) that the abatement notice is not justified by section 80 of the Act[35]; (b) that there has been some informality, defect or error in, or in connection with, the abatement notice, or in, or in connection with, any copy of the abatement notice served under section 80A(3)[36]; (c) that the authority have unreasonably refused to accept compliance with alternative requirements, or that the requirements of the abatement notice are otherwise unreasonable in character or extent, or are unnecessary[37]; (d) that the time or if more than one time is specified, any of the times within which the requirements of the abatement notice are to be complied with is not reasonably sufficient for the purpose[38]; (e) where the nuisance falls within section 79(1)(a), (b), (d), (e), (f), (g) or (ga) of the 1990 Act, that the best practicable means were used to prevent, or to counteract the effects of, the nuisance[39]; (f) that in the case of a nuisance under section 79(1)(g) or (ga) of the 1990 Act, the requirements imposed by the abatement notice are more onerous than the requirements for the time being in force in relation to notices served under sections 60, 61, 65, 66 or 67 of the Control of Pollution Act 1974[40]; (g) that in the case of a nuisance under section 79(1)(ga) of the 1990 Act, the requirements of the abatement notice are more onerous than the requirements of any condition of a consent given under the Noise and Statutory Nuisance Act 1993[41]; (h) that the abatement notice should have been served upon some person instead of the appellant[42]; (i) that the abatement notice might lawfully have been served on some person instead of the appellant and that it would have been equitable for it to have been so served[43]; (j) that the abatement notice might lawfully have been served on some person in addition to the appellant and that it would have been equitable for it to have been so served.[44]

26.346 On hearing the appeal the court may (a) quash the abatement notice, (b) vary the abatement notice in favour of the appellant in such manner as it thinks fit; or dismiss the appeal.[45]

---

31 1993 Act, s. 54 (1)(a), (2).
32 *ibid.* s. 54(1)(b), (2).
33 S.I. 1996 No. 1076 ("1996 regulations").
34 *ibid.* reg. 2(1). For appeals under s. 80(3) see para. 26.341.
35 *ibid.* reg. 2(2)(a).
36 *ibid.* reg. 2(2)(b).
37 *ibid.* reg. 2(2)(c).
38 *ibid.* reg. 2(2)(d).
39 *ibid.* reg. 2(2)(e).
40 *ibid.* reg. 2(2)(f).
41 *ibid.* reg. 2(2)(g).
42 *ibid.* reg. 2(2)(h).
43 *ibid.* reg. 2(2)(i).
44 *ibid.* reg. 2(2)(j).
45 *ibid.* reg. 2(5).

XLVIII. Railways, Canals and Pipelines

Railway Clauses Consolidation (Scotland) Act 1845[46]

(1) Procedure

Where any question of damages, charges, expenses, or other matter is referred to the sheriff for determination, he may, upon the application of either party, order the other party to appear at a hearing.[47] At the hearing, the sheriff may examine the parties and their witnesses on oath, and award expenses.[48] Proceedings under the Act are to be by summary application; there are no written pleadings or recording of evidence, unless the sheriff considers that the matter can be better decided with written pleadings and a written record.[49] If there are no written pleadings the sheriff's determination is final and conclusive and not subject to review by suspension or advocation or reduction on any point whatever.[50] If written pleadings have been allowed, a record has been made up, and evidence has been recorded, there is an appeal to the sheriff principal from the final determination of the sheriff; but otherwise there is no right of appeal.[51] **26.347**

(2) Applications under the Act

The provisions of the Lands Clauses Consolidation (Scotland) Act 1845 apply to the taking of lands for the purpose of the construction of a railway.[52] The amount and application of the purchase money and other compensation payable under the Act are to be determined in accordance with the terms of that Act.[53] Thus, in fixing the rent payable for the temporary occupation of lands[54] and assessing compensation to be paid for the temporary occupation of roads,[55] the sheriff is to follow that Act. **26.348**

A railway company must deposit with the sheriff clerk documents and plans relating to the railway undertaking,[56] and this applies in the case of every sheriffdom through which the railway is proposed to pass.[57] A railway company may apply to the sheriff to have errors and omissions in plans corrected.[58] If the railway is to deviate more than a short distance from the plan, authorisation by the sheriff is required.[59] **26.349**

---

46 8 & 9 Vict. c. 33 ("the 1845 Act").

47 *ibid.*, s. 134.

48 *ibid.*

49 *ibid.* s. 147.

50 *ibid.*

51 *ibid.* ss. 3, 150, as amended by Local Government (Scotland) Act 1973 (c. 65), Sched. 27, Pt I, para. 1(3); repealed in part by Statute Law Revision Act 1892 (c. 19); see *Main v. Lanarkshire & Dunbartonshire Ry* (1893) 21 R. 323; *Paisley and Barrhead District Ry v. Coats* (1902) 19 Sh.Ct.Rep. 12.

52 *ibid.* s. 6, as amended by Land Compensation (Scotland) Act 1973 (c. 56), s. 61 extended by Telecommunications Act 1984 (c. 12), Sched. 2, para. 6(1), (4).

53 *ibid.* s. 37.

54 *ibid.* s. 36; see also ss. 32–35.

55 *ibid.* s. 25.

56 *ibid.* s. 8.

57 *ibid.*

58 *ibid.* s. 7, as amended by Local Government (Scotland) Act 1973, Sched. 27, Pt I, para. 1(3); see *Glasgow District Subway Co. v. McCallum* (1896) 12 Sh.Ct.Rep. 148; *Paisley and Barrhead District Ry v. Coats* (1902) 19 Sh.Ct.Rep. 12.

59 *ibid.* s. 11, as amended by Roads (Scotland) Act 1984 (c. 54), Sched. 9, para. 3(3)(a), 3(3)(b), 3(3)(c) and Sched. 11.

26.350 When an owner or occupier of lands receives a notice informing him of the railway company's intention temporarily to possess the land for the purpose of constructing a railway he may object in writing within ten days. Should the company refuse to occupy other lands in lieu of those mentioned in the notice, the owner or occupier may apply to the sheriff who is empowered to decide which adjacent lands may be occupied.[60]

26.351 The railway company may apply to the sheriff for his consent if they wish to carry a railway across a road other than the carriageway of a public road.[61] Notice of an application for a level crossing must be given 14 days before the application is made.[62] On the application of two householders within the district, or of the roads authority, the sheriff may order the railway company to make approaches and fences to roads crossing on the level.[63] Ten days notice of the application must be given to the company.[64] If the company fail to comply with the sheriff's order they are liable to pay a penalty, which the sheriff may order to be applied to the provision of approaches or fences.[65]

26.352 The sheriff may determine any question of damage to roads or repair thereof and may direct that repairs be carried out by the company on whatever terms and conditions seem just.[66] If the damage in question has been done to a turnpike road, the sheriff is to make full allowance for tolls paid by the company.[67] On the application of the roads authority or two householders in the district, and after 10 days notice to the company, the sheriff may order the company to repair bridges, fences or approach gates. If they fail to do so they are liable to pay a penalty.[68]

26.353 The railway company is bound to provide certain accommodation works.[69] Any difference as to the number, type, dimensions or maintenance of these works may be determined by the sheriff, who may appoint a time within which works are to be commenced and executed.[70] If the company fail to commence or fail to proceed diligently to execute the works required within seven days of the date set by the sheriff, the aggrieved party may carry out the works and claim the expense from the company.[71] If there is any dispute as to the repayment of expenses incurred, the sheriff may settle it.[72] Any owner or occupier of lands affected by the railway may make additional accommodation works at his own expense, subject to authorisation by the sheriff.[73]

---

60 1845 Act, ss. 30, 31.
61 *ibid.* s. 39, as amended by Roads (Scotland) Act 1984 (c. 54) ("the 1984 Act"), Sched. 9, para. 3(6)(a), (b)(i), (ii).
62 *ibid.* s. 53, as amended by 1984 Act, Sched. 9, para. 3(17)(a), (b), (c).
63 *ibid.* s. 54, as amended by 1984 Act, Sched. 9, para. 3(18)(a), (b).
64 *ibid.*
65 *ibid.*
66 *ibid.* s. 51, as amended by 1984 Act, Sched. 9, para. 3(15)(a), (b).
67 *ibid.*
68 *ibid.* s. 57, as amended by 1984 Act, Sched. 9, para. 3(21).
69 *ibid.* s. 60.
70 *ibid.* s. 61.
71 *ibid.* s. 62.
72 *ibid.*
73 *ibid.* s. 63.

Regulation of Railways Act 1871[74]

The Board of Trade may direct an inquiry into a railway accident. In more serious cases, the Board may direct that a sheriff hold a formal investigation into the accident, its causes and attendant circumstances.[75] The sheriff is assisted by an inspector or by an assessor or assessors,[76] and the investigation is held in open court in whatever way is considered to be most effectual for ascertaining the causes and circumstances of the accident.[77] The court[78] has the powers of a court of summary jurisdiction when acting as a court in the exercise of its ordinary jurisdiction, and all powers of an inspector under the Act.[79] The court is specifically authorised to enter and inspect any place or building, require the attendance of persons and examine them, require and enforce the production of documents, administer an oath, require the signature of any person examined attesting to the verity of his testimony and allow expenses to certain persons.[80] The investigation concludes with the issuing of a report to the Board of Trade.[81] **26.354**

Railway Rolling Stock Protection Act 1872[82]

Rolling stock in a "work"[83] which is not the property of a tenant is not liable to distress for rent by a landlord.[84] Where it is distrained by the landlord, the sheriff may make a summary order for the restoration of the rolling stock or the payment of its value.[85] The sheriff may make such order as to expenses as he thinks just.[86] An appeal lies to the Court of Session.[87] **26.355**

A landlord may distrain and dispose of a tenant's interest in rolling stock. If any disagreement arises as to the disposal of the tenant's interest, either party may apply to the sheriff for its determination.[88]

Railway Fires Act 1905[89]

A railway company may enter on any land and take whatever steps are necessary to extinguish the spread of a fire started by sparks flying from a train,[90] and may also take any precautions which are reasonably necessary for the purpose of preventing or diminishing the risk of fire in a wooded area.[91] The compensation payable by the company to any person injuriously affected is to be determined by the sheriff.[92] **26.356**

---

74 34 & 35 Vict. c. 78 ("the 1871 Act").
75 *ibid.* ss. 7(1), 16(3), as amended by Sheriff Courts (Scotland) Act 1971 s. 4.
76 *ibid.*
77 *ibid.* s. 7(2).
78 *i.e.* the persons holding the formal investigation.
79 1871 Act, s. 7(3).
80 *ibid.*
81 *ibid.* s. 7(4).
82 35 & 36 Vict., c. 50 ("the 1872 Act").
83 Defined in 1872 Act, s.2.
84 1872 Act, s. 3.
85 *ibid.* ss. 2, 4.
86 *ibid.*
87 *ibid.* s. 6(1).
88 *ibid.* s. 5.
89 5 Edw. 7, c. 11 ("the 1905 Act").
90 *ibid.* s. 2(1).
91 *ibid.* s. 2(2).
92 *ibid.* s. 2(3); see Lands Clauses Consolidation (Scotland) Act 1845 (c. 19), s. 22, noted in para. 26.348.

Pipelines Act 1962[93]

26.357 Any dispute between a roads authority and a person proposing to place a pipeline in the road is to be referred to a single arbiter appointed by the parties or, failing agreement, the sheriff.[94]

Where the Secretary of State executes remedial works to safeguard a pipeline[95] or removes deposits imperilling a pipeline[96] he may recover the expense from the owners of the building[97] or the land[98] in such shares as the sheriff may determine to be just and equitable.[99]

If the Secretary of State is satisfied that the demolition of a building is necessary in order to safeguard a pipeline,[1] a summary application for removal and ejection may be made to the sheriff[2] under the Housing (Scotland) Act 1987.[3]

XLIX. Rating

Rating (Disabled Persons) Act 1978[4]

26.358 An applicant for a rebate of rates, whose application is refused by the rating authority may appeal to the sheriff, who may direct that the rebate is to be granted.[5] If the applicant is granted a rebate by the authority but is nevertheless dissatisfied with the amount of the rebate, he may appeal to the sheriff who may give such direction as he thinks fit.[6] Either appeal is to be commenced by initial writ and disposed of as a summary application.[7] An appeal must be brought within 42 days of the date of the rating authority's decision,[8] and the rating authority is to be the respondent in any appeal.[9] An appeal on any question of law lies from the decision of the sheriff in either appeal.[10]

---

93 10 & 11 Eliz. 2, c. 58 ("the 1962 Act").

94 *ibid.* s. 15(7); as amended by Roads (Scotland) Act 1984 (c. 54) Sched. 9 para. 55(2)(c).

95 *ibid.* s. 29(2), (4); s. 66, as amended by virtue of Minister of Technology Order 1969 (S.I. 1969 No. 1498), arts 2(1), 5(6) and Secretary of State for Trade and Industry Order 1970 (S.I. 1970 No. 1537), arts 2(2), 7(4).

96 *ibid.* s. 31(1), (2), (4); extended by Gas Act 1972 (c. 60), s. 39(2), (3).

97 *ibid.* s. 29(2), (4); s. 66, as amended by virtue of Minister of Technology Order 1969 (S.I. 1969 No. 1498), arts 2(1), 5(6) and Secretary of State for Trade and Industry Order 1970 (S.I. 1970 No. 1537), arts 2(2), 7(4).

98 *ibid.* s. 31(1), (2), (4); extended by Gas Act 1972 (c. 60), s. 39(2), (3).

99 *ibid.* ss. 29(2), (4), 31(1), (2), (4); s. 66, as amended by virtue of Minister of Technology Order 1969 (S.I. 1969 No. 1498), arts 2(1), 5(6) and Secretary of State for Trade and Industry Order 1970 (S.I. 1970 No. 1537), arts 2(2), 7(4).

1 1962 Act, s. 27(3).

2 *ibid.* s. 30, as amended by Housing (Scotland) Act 1987 (c. 26), Sched. 23, para. 9.

3 1987 Act, (c.26), s. 127. See para. 26.227.

4 c. 40 ("the 1978 Act").

5 *ibid.* s. 6(5); *The Royal Blind Asylum and School v. Lothian R.C.*, 1981 S.L.T. (Sh.Ct.) 109.

6 *ibid.* s. 6(5A), inserted by Rating and Valuation (Amendment) (Scotland) Act 1984 (c. 31), s. 5(2)(a).

7 A.S. (Appeals under the Rating (Disabled Persons) Act 1978) 1979 (S.I. 1979 No. 446) ("A.S. 1979"), para. 2, as amended by A.S. (Appeals under the Rating (Disabled Persons) Act 1978) (Amendment) 1985, (S.I. 1985 No. 821).

8 A.S. 1979, para. 4.

9 *ibid.* para. 3.

10 1978 Act, s. 6(6), as amended by 1984 Act (c. 31), s. 5(2)(*b*).

L. Registration of Births, Deaths and Marriages

Registration of Births, Deaths and Marriages (Scotland) Act 1965[11]

If a person fails to comply with a registrar's notice requiring him to attend, give particulars of birth and sign the register, the registrar may make summary application to the sheriff who may grant decree ordaining the person to comply with the notice.[12] Such decree is enforceable in the same manner as a decree *ad factum praestandum*.[13] The sheriff may exercise the same power in relation to particulars of death.[14] **26.359**

On an application made by the father of a child, where the mother is dead or cannot be found, the sheriff may order the Registrar General to record the name and surname of the father by making an appropriate entry in the Register of Corrections.[15] **26.360**

If a child's parents were not married at the time when the child's birth was registered in the register of births but have subsequently married one another, the Registrar General may authorise the re-registration of the child's birth if the sheriff sanctions an application made by both parents, the surviving parent or, if both parents are dead, the child or his representative.[16]

The Registrar General may authorise the correction of any errors by causing an appropriate entry to be made in the Register of Corrections. If he refuses to do so the person who claims that an error has been made may appeal to the sheriff, whose decision is final.[17]

If any person ceasing to hold office as a registrar has failed to deliver up keys, books or documents in his possession, the Registrar General may apply to the sheriff for a warrant authorising a constable to enter and search premises and seize any article found therein.[18] **26.361**

LI. Rights of the Subject

Sex Discrimination Act 1975[19]

The proceedings under the Act described in the five following paragraphs are commenced by initial writ and disposed of as summary applications.[20] If the proceedings are brought before the sheriff at first instance, there may be a right of appeal to the sheriff principal. **26.362**

If a person fails to comply with a notice served on him by the Equal Opportunities Commission, requiring him to provide written or oral information and produce documents for the purpose of a formal inves- **26.363**

---

[11] c. 49 ("the 1965 Act").
[12] *ibid.* s. 16(3).
[13] *ibid.*
[14] *ibid.* s. 25(3).
[15] *ibid.* s. 18(2)(c), as amended by Law Reform (Parent and Child) (Scotland) Act 1986 (c. 9) ("1986 Act"), Sched. 1, para. 8(3)(c).
[16] *ibid.* s. 20(1)(i), (ii), (iii), as amended by 1986 Act, Sched. 1, para. 8(5).
[17] *ibid.* s. 42(5); see Clive, para. 06.011.
[18] *ibid.* s. 10.(3).
[19] c. 65 ("the 1975 Act").
[20] A.S. (Proceedings under the Sex Discrimination Act 1975) 1976 (S.I. 1976 No. 374), para. 3.

tigation, the Commission may apply to the sheriff for an order requiring him to comply with it.[21] The Commission may also apply for such an order if it has reasonable cause to believe that a person intends not to comply with it.[22] The sheriff may grant letters of second diligence to compel the attendance of witnesses and havers.[23]

26.364 A person upon whom a non-discrimination notice is served may appeal within six weeks against any requirement of the notice.[24] If the sheriff considers any requirement of the notice to be unreasonable, he must quash the requirement and direct that the notice shall have effect subject to requirements decided on by the sheriff.[25]

26.365 The Commission may apply to the sheriff for an order restraining a person from doing an unlawful discriminatory act.[26]

26.366 The Commission may apply to the sheriff for a decision whether an alleged contravention of the provisions of the Act in respect of discriminatory advertisements, instructions to discriminate or pressure to discriminate has occurred.[27] The alleged discrimination must have been outwith the field of employment,[28] and the application must be made before the end of a six-month period beginning when the alleged discrimination took place.[29] The Commission may also, or alternatively, apply to the sheriff for an order restraining a person from doing any of the acts referred to.[30] The application must be made within five years beginning when the act was done.[31]

26.367 Any person interested may apply to the sheriff for an order removing or modifying any term of a contract made unenforceable by the Act.[32]

26.368 The sheriff court has exclusive jurisdiction in a claim for damages arising by virtue of the provisions of Part III of the Act.[33] In addition to the service of a copy of the initial writ on the defender a copy should be sent to the Commission.[34] The sheriff may *ex proprio motu*, or on the application of any party, appoint an assessor who shall be a person who the sheriff considers has special qualifications to be of assistance in such a cause, to assist in determining the proceedings.[35]

---

[21] 1975 Act, s. 59(1), (4), (5)(a).
[22] *ibid.*
[23] *ibid.* s. 59(5)(b).
[24] *ibid.* s. 68(1)(b).
[25] *ibid.* s. 68(2), (3).
[26] *ibid.* s. 71(1).
[27] *ibid.* s. 72(2)(a).
[28] *ibid.* s. 72(3)(a), (b).
[29] *ibid.* s. 76(3), as substituted by Race Relations Act 1976 (c. 74), Sched. 4, para. 8(b).
[30] *ibid.* s. 72(2)(b), (4).
[31] *ibid.* s. 76(3), as substituted by Race Relations Act 1976 (c. 74), Sched. 4, para. 8(b).
[32] *ibid.* s. 77(2), (5).
[33] *ibid.* s. 66(1), (2), (8).
[34] *ibid.* s. 66(5A), inserted by Race Relations Act, 1976, Sched. 4, para. 5(2), see A.S. (Proceedings under the Sex Discrimination Act 1975) 1977 (S.I. 1977 No. 973), para. 2; see also 1975 Act, s. 76(2)(b), inserted by 1976 Act, Sched. 4, para. 8(a) for the time-limits within which proceedings must be commenced.
[35] *ibid.* s. 66(7), as amended by Transfer of Functions (Minister for the Civil Service and Treasury) Order 1981 (S.I. 1981 No. 1670), arts. 2(2), 3(5); see A.S. (Proceedings under Sex Discrimination Act, 1975) No. 2, 1976 (S.I. 1976 No. 1851), para. 2; OCR, r. 36.18.

Race Relations Act 1976[36]

Proceedings under the Race Relations Act 1976 are regulated by provisions similar to those of the Sex Discrimination Act 1975. The proceedings are to be commenced by initial writ and disposed of as summary applications[37]; and an appeal from the decision of the sheriff would appear to be competent. **26.369**

The Commission for Racial Equality may apply to the sheriff for an order requiring a person to comply with a notice issued for the purpose of a formal investigation.[38] The sheriff may grant second diligence for compelling the attendance of witnesses and havers.[39] **26.370**

The Commission may also apply for an order restraining a person from acts which may amount to persistent discrimination.[40] The sheriff may grant the order in the terms applied for or in more limited terms.[41] **26.371**

The Commission may apply to the sheriff for a decision whether a contravention of the provisions of the Act in respect of discriminatory practices, discriminatory advertisements or instructions to discriminate has occurred,[42] other than in the field of employment. The application must be made before the end of the period of six months beginning when the act to which it relates was done.[43] The Commission may also apply for an order restraining a person from unlawful acts under the same sections of the Act.[44] The application must be made before the expiry of five years from the unlawful act.[45] **26.372**

A person upon whom a non-discrimination notice has been served may appeal within six weeks against any requirement of the notice which the sheriff may quash and replace.[46] **26.373**

Any person interested may apply to the sheriff to make an order removing or modifying any term of a contract made unenforceable by virtue of the Act.[47] **26.374**

In any proceedings under the Act the sheriff must be assisted by two assessors unless the parties consent that he sit without assessors.[48] **26.375**

The sheriff has exclusive jurisdiction in proceedings for damages brought by virtue of Part III of the Act.[49] A copy of the summons or initial writ in such proceedings must be sent to the Commission.[50] **26.376**

---

36 c. 74 ("the 1976 Act").
37 A.S. (Proceedings under Race Relations Act 1976) 1977 (S.I. 1977 No. 975) ("A.S. 1977"), para. 2.
38 1976 Act, s. 50(4).
39 *ibid.* s. 50(5).
40 *ibid.* s. 62(1).
41 *ibid.*
42 *ibid.* s. 63(2)(a), (3)(b).
43 *ibid.* s. 68(4).
44 *ibid.* s. 63(2)(b), (4).
45 *ibid.* s. 68(4).
46 *ibid.* s. 59(1)(b), (2), (3); see *Commission for Racial Equality v. Amari Plastics Ltd* [1982] Q.B. 1194.
47 *ibid.* s. 72(2), (5); see *Orphanos v. Queen Mary College* [1985] A.C. 761.
48 *ibid.* s. 67(4).
49 *ibid.* s. 57(1), (2)(b).
50 A.S. 1977, para. 3.

Data Protection Act 1984[51]

26.377 On the application of any person who complains that he has requested that a data user supply him with data and the data user has not done so, the sheriff, if he considers it reasonable to do so, may order the data user to supply the data.[52]

If the sheriff is satisfied that data held by a data user of which the applicant is the subject are inaccurate, he may order the rectification or erasure of the data held by the user.[53] The erasure of data may be ordered if the sheriff is satisfied that the data subject has suffered such damage as would entitle him to compensation and that there is a substantial risk of further disclosure without authority.[54]

Access to Health Records Act 1990[55]

26.378 Where the court is satisfied that the holder of a health record has failed to comply with any requirement of the Act, and that the applicant has taken all the prescribed steps[56] to secure compliance, the sheriff may order the holder to comply.[57]

Disability Discrimination Act 1995[58]

26.379 A claim by a person that another person has discriminated against him in a way that is unlawful under Part III of the Act may be made the subject of civil proceedings in the same way as any other claim in reparation for breach of statutory duty.[59] Such a claim may be brought only in a sheriff court,[60] within six months of the act complained of.[61]

26.380 The sheriff may make such order as he thinks fit for modifying any contract or agreement which purports to require anything which contravenes Part III.[62]

LII. Road Traffic

Road Traffic Act 1988[63]

26.381 A person who has submitted himself for a test of competence to drive may apply to the sheriff to determine whether the test was properly conducted in accordance with regulations.[64] Where the test is split into separate parts, this right applies with regard to each part of the test.[65]

---

51 c. 35 ("the 1984 Act").
52 *ibid.* ss. 21(8), 25(1).
53 *ibid.* ss. 24(1), 25(1).
54 *ibid.* ss. 24(3), 25(1).
55 c. 23 ("the 1990 Act").
56 *ibid.* s. 8(1), (2), (5).
57 See the Access to Health Records (Steps to Secure Compliance and Complaints Procedures) (Scotland) Regulations 1991 (S.I. 1991 No. 2295).
58 c. 50 ("the 1995 Act").
59 *ibid.* s. 25(1).
60 *ibid.* s. 25(4), (5).
61 *ibid.* Sched. 3, para. 6.(1).
62 *ibid.* s. 26(1), (3).
63 c. 52 ("the 1988 Act").
64 *ibid.* s. 90(1).
65 *ibid.* s. 90(3).

If the sheriff decides that the test was not conducted in accordance with the regulations he may order that the applicant shall be eligible to submit himself for another test and that any fee paid should be refunded.[66]

A person aggrieved by any of the following may appeal to the sheriff after giving notice to the Secretary of State of his intention: (1) the Secretary of State's refusal to grant, or revocation of, a licence in respect of a motorist suffering from a relevant disability[67]; (2) the Secretary of State's grant of a licence for three years or less in respect of a motorist suffering from a relevant disability[68]; (3) the Secretary of State's revocation of a licence granted in error or requiring to be endorsed[69]; (4) a notice served on a motorist suffering from a disability which is likely to result in danger to the public.[70] **26.382**

The appeal must be made within 21 days of the date of intimation of the decision to the applicant, and will be disposed of as a summary application.[71]

The sheriff may make such order as he thinks fit,[72] and his decision is final and not subject to appeal to the sheriff principal.[73]

A person aggrieved by the Secretary of State's refusal or failure to grant, imposition of any limitation on, suspension or revocation of, or disqualification for holding, a large goods vehicle or passenger-carrying vehicle driver's licence or an LGV Community licence or a PCV Community licence, or by a notice served on him in pursuance of section 115A(1) or 116(4) may appeal to the sheriff, after giving notice of his intention to do so to the Secretary of State and any traffic commissioner to whom the matter was referred.[74] The sheriff may make such order as he thinks fit, and an order so made is binding on the Secretary of State.[75] **26.383**

Road Traffic Offenders Act 1988[76]

A person disqualified for holding or obtaining a driving licence may apply to the court which imposed the disqualification. Having regard to the applicant's character, conduct, the nature of the offence and any other circumstance of the case the sheriff may remove the disqualification by order, or refuse to do so.[77] No application for removal of a disqualification may be made before the expiry of certain periods specified in the Act,[78] and if an application is refused, no further application may be brought until three months after the sheriff's decision.[79] **26.384**

---

66 1988 Act, s. 90(2).
67 *ibid.* ss. 92, 93, 100(1)(a).
68 *ibid.* ss. 99(1)(b), 100(1)(b).
69 *ibid.* s. 99(3), 100(1)(c).
70 *ibid.* ss. 92(5), 99C, 100(1) (inserted by Driving Licences (Community Driving Licence) Regulations 1996 (S.I. 1996, No. 1974)).
71 S.A.R., r. 6(2).
72 1988 Act, s.100(2).
73 *Hopkin v. Ayr Local Taxation Officer*, 1964 S.L.T. (Sh.Ct.) 60.
74 1988 Act, s. 119(1), as substituted by Road Traffic (Driver Licensing and Information Systems) Act 1989 (c. 22), ss. 2(1), 16, Scheds 2, 6.
75 *ibid.*, s. 119(3).
76 c. 53 ("the 1988 Offenders Act").
77 *ibid.* s. 42(1), (2).
78 *ibid.* s. 42(3).
79 *ibid.* s. 42(4).

LIII. Roads and Bridges

Roads (Scotland) Act 1984[80]

26.385 The following appeals lie to the sheriff by way of summary application within 28 days of the event giving rise to the appeal. The decision of the sheriff is final.[81]

(1) An appeal by the requisite number of frontagers against a decision of a local roads authority to add to or delete from the list of public roads.[82]

(2) An appeal against a notice of a local roads authority requiring the making up and maintenance of a private road.[83]

(3) An appeal against a notice of a local roads authority's intention to attach road lighting to buildings.[84]

(4) An appeal against a notice of a local roads authority with respect to dangerous works in, or excavations under, a road.[85] The purpose of the notice may be to end such danger, or to see that it does not arise.[86]

(5) An appeal by a person upon whom a local roads authority has served a notice requiring the construction of a crossing over a verge or a footpath.[87]

(6) An appeal by a person upon whom a local roads authority has served a notice requiring the repair of vaults, tunnels and cellars beneath a road.[88]

(7) An appeal by the owner or occupier of the land concerned against a local roads authority's notice of intention to provide a temporary substitute road during road works.[89]

(8) An appeal by a person aggrieved by the refusal of the local roads authority's consent to the placing of bridges or certain apparatus over, across or along roads, or against conditions attached to such consent.[90]

(9) An appeal by the owner or occupier of land on which a hedge, tree or shrub is growing, against a local roads authority's notice requiring him to carry out work to remove any danger, obstruction or interference caused by the plant,[91] or against a notice requiring him to carry out work to obviate the danger from a hedge, tree, shrub, fence or wall.[92] It should be noted that if the local roads authority consider the latter danger to be imminent, it may dispense with the notice, carry out works and recover any expenses reasonably incurred from the owner or occupier.[93]

(10) A person who considers that he should not be required to pay a local roads authority for expenses incurred in removing a roadside danger,[94] or who objects to a notice requiring him to remove a risk of

---

80 c. 54 ("the 1984 Act").

81 See *Whitson v. Blairgowrie District Committee* (1897) 24 R. 519 at 522, 523.

82 1984 Act, ss. 1(5), (7), 151(1); see *Maclean v. Inverness Trs* (1891) 7 Sh.Ct.Rep. 246; *Roxburgh C.C. v. Dalrymple's Trs* (1894) 21 R. 1063.

83 *ibid.* s. 13(7).

84 *ibid.* s. 35(7).

85 *ibid.* s. 57(6).

86 *ibid.* s. 59(1).

87 *ibid.* s. 63(3).

88 *ibid.* s. 66(3).

89 *ibid.* s. 74(4).

90 *ibid.* s. 90(4).

91 *ibid.* s. 91(1), (9).

92 *ibid.* s. 91(2), (9).

93 *ibid.* s. 91(3).

94 *ibid.* s. 93(1), (6).

injury by executing works in respect of barbed wire, an electric fence, spikes or broken glass[95] may appeal to the sheriff. It should be noted that if a local roads authority are occupiers of land adjoining a road, and there is a roadside danger on that land, any ratepayer or person liable to pay council tax may serve a notice on the authority requiring the removal of the risk of injury, and if the authority fail to comply with the notice the ratepayer or council tax payer may apply to the sheriff who may order the roads authority to carry out whatever steps are necessary.[96]

(11) An appeal by an owner or occupier against a notice served by a local roads authority requiring him to prevent the flow or percolation of substances on to a road.[97]

The sheriff may appoint an arbiter, in default of agreement between the parties, to determine any of the following: (1) a dispute in relation to applications for a private road to become a public road[98]; (2) a question arising in connection with obstruction notices[99]; (3) a dispute arising in connection with the transfer of property or liabilities upon a road becoming or ceasing to be a trunk road[1]; (4) a dispute arising as to transfers of offices and property in connection with lighting and bus shelters.[2] **26.386**

Any dispute as to the vesting of the solum of a stopped-up road may be referred to the sheriff on summary application by any party interested. The decision of the sheriff is final.[3] **26.387**

Where admission to land for the purposes of section 140(1) of the Act has been refused or is expected to be refused, or where land is unoccupied, or in an emergency, the sheriff may grant a warrant authorising entry.[4] **26.388**

The owner of land may apply to the sheriff for an order requiring the occupier to permit works required by the Act to be executed by the owner.[5] **26.389**

Where a roads authority incurs extraordinary expense in repairing roads damaged by heavy vehicles it may recover the expenses from the operators by proceedings before the sheriff.[6] The action is brought against the person by or in consequence of whose order the traffic was conducted.[7] Proceedings must be brought within 12 months of the damage being done or, if the operations are continuous, within six months of completion.[8] **26.390**

---

95 1984 Act, s. 93(2), (6).
96 *ibid.* s. 93(3), (4), as amended by Local Government etc (Scotland) Act 1994 (c. 39), Sched. 13, para. 135(4).
97 *ibid.* s. 99(4).
98 *ibid.* s. 16(3).
99 *ibid.* s. 84(1).
1 *ibid.* s. 112(7).
2 *ibid.* s. 114(5).
3 *ibid.* s. 115(2).
4 *ibid.* s. 140(8), as amended by Coal Industry Act 1987 (c. 3), Sched. 1, para. 46.
5 *ibid.* s. 142.
6 *ibid.* s. 96(4).
7 *Partick Town Council v. Muir & Sons* (1905) 21 Sh.Ct.Rep. 196.
8 1984 Act, s. 96(5); *Deer District Committee v. Shanks and McEwan*, 1911 1 S.L.T. 314; *Arbroath District Committee v. Carnoustie Mags* (1911) 28 Sh.Ct.Rep. 101.

New Roads and Street Works Act 1991[9]

26.391 Any matter which is to be settled by arbitration is to be referred to a single arbiter appointed by agreement, which failing, by the sheriff.[10]

LIV. Shipping

Merchant Shipping Act 1894[11]

26.392 The Act provides that to avoid the detention of ships, goods may be placed in the custody of a warehouseman, and if the shipowner has to wait longer than 90 days for payment of his freight, he may instruct the warehouseman to realise the goods.[12] The warehouseman has authority to sell the goods after giving due notice to the owner,[13] but it is the practice in Scotland to obtain the authority of the sheriff by an *ex parte* summary application for permission to sell.[14]

Merchant Shipping Act 1995[15]

26.393 The Act provides for the holding of inquiries into the fitness and conduct of officers,[16] certificate holders other than officers,[17] and seamen.[18] Where an inquiry has been held under sections 61 or 63 the Secretary of State may order the whole or part of the case to be reheard, by the persons who heard it, by the sheriff, or by the Court of Session.[19] Rules therefor are to be made under section 65. If the inquiry is held by the sheriff under sections 61 and 63 he is to dispose of the inquiry as a summary application and his decision is final.[20]

26.394 Where any accident has occurred the Secretary of State may, whether or not an investigation has been carried out by the Chief Inspector of Marine Accidents, cause a formal investigation into the accident to be held by the sheriff,[21] with the assistance of one or more assessors.[22] The sheriff is to dispose of the formal investigation as a summary application, and his decision is with one exception final.[23] The sheriff may cancel or suspend an officer's certificate, or censure him.[24] The sheriff's decision to cancel or suspend a certificate may be appealed to the Court of Session.[25] The sheriff may make such awards as he thinks just with regard to the expenses of the investigation and of any parties, and with regard to the parties by whom those expenses are to be paid.[26] Such expenses are taxable by the auditor of court.[27]

---

9 c. 22 ("the 1991 Act").
10 *ibid.* s. 158(1).
11 57 & 58 Vict. c. 60 ("the 1894 Act").
12 *ibid.* ss. 494–496.
13 *ibid.* s. 497.
14 See Dobie, p. 623.
15 c. 21 ("the 1995 Act").
16 *ibid.* s. 61.
17 *ibid.* s. 62.
18 *ibid.* s. 63.
19 *ibid.* s. 64.
20 *ibid.* s. 69.
21 *ibid.* s. 268(1) (rules not yet made).
22 *ibid.* s. 268(2).
23 *ibid.* s. 268(4).
24 *ibid.* s. 268(5).
25 *ibid.* s. 269(4)(b).
26 *ibid.* s. 268(8).
27 *ibid.* s. 268(9)(b).

The Secretary of State may order the whole or part of the case to be reheard if new and important evidence which could not be produced at the investigation has been discovered or it appears to him that there are other grounds for suspecting that a miscarriage of justice may have occurred.[28] Such re-hearing may be held by the sheriff.[29] **26.395**

Merchant Shipping (Port State Control) Regulations 1995[30]

Under the regulations certain questions relating to a detention notice are to be decided by arbitration.[31] The sheriff may appoint an arbiter if the parties fail to agree.[32] **26.396**

LV. Social Security and Health Services

Nursing Homes Registration (Scotland) Act 1938[33]

Any person aggrieved by an order refusing an application for registration in respect of a nursing home, or the cancellation of any registration may, within 14 days after the date on which the copy of the order was sent to him, appeal against it to the sheriff, whose decision is final.[34] **26.397**

LVI. Succession

Succession (Scotland) Act 1964[35]

The executor of a deceased person may make summary application to the sheriff to extend the time for disposal of a lease held by the deceased.[36] **26.398**

LVII. Town and Country Planning

Planning (Listed Buildings and Conservation Areas) (Scotland) Act 1997[37]

A person having an interest in a listed building in need of repair, which it is proposed should be acquired compulsorily,[38] may apply to the sheriff for an order prohibiting further proceedings on the compulsory purchase order.[39] If he is satisfied that reasonable steps have been taken to preserve the building the sheriff may so order.[40] An appeal lies to the Court of Session on a point of law only.[41] **26.399**

Where a direction for minimum compensation is made by the planning authority, or where the Secretary of State includes such a direction in a **26.400**

---

28 1995 Act, s. 269(1).
29 *ibid.* s. 269(2).
30 S.I. 1995 No. 3128.
31 *ibid.* reg. 11.
32 *ibid.* reg. 11(a).
33 1 & 2 Geo. 6, c. 73. ("the 1938 Act").
34 *ibid.* s. 3(3).
35 c. 41 ("the 1964 Act").
36 *ibid.* s. 16(1), (3)(b); *Gifford v. Buchanan*, 1983 S.L.T. 613.
37 c. 9 ("the 1997 Act")
38 *ibid.* s. 42(1).
39 *ibid.* s. 42(4).
40 *ibid.* s. 42(5).
41 *ibid.* s. 42(6).

draft compulsory purchase order, any person with an interest in the building may apply to the sheriff for an order that the direction be refused or not included.[42] If the sheriff is satisfied that the building has not been deliberately allowed to fall into disrepair,[43] he may grant the order. An appeal lies to the Court of Session on a point of law.[44] The rights conferred by this provision do not prejudice those conferred in respect of an application for an order prohibiting further proceedings on a compulsory purchase order.[45]

LVIII. Trade

Pedlars Act 1871[46]

26.401 If the chief officer of police refuses to grant a pedlar's certificate, the applicant may appeal to the sheriff.[47]

Methylated Spirits (Sale by Retail) (Scotland) Act 1937[48]

26.402 If a local authority refuse to enter a person's name in, or remove it from, the list of persons authorised to sell methylated spirits or surgical spirit, that person may appeal to the sheriff.[49]

Riding Establishments Act 1964[50]

26.403 Any person aggrieved by the refusal of a local authority to grant a licence to keep a riding establishment, or by any condition subject to which such a licence is proposed to be granted, other than one of the conditions specified in the Act, may appeal to the sheriff.[51]

Fair Trading Act 1973[52]

26.404 Under Part III of the Act the Director-General of Fair Trading is empowered to bring proceedings in the Restrictive Practices Court for an order directing that the respondents refrain from continuing a course of conduct detrimental to consumers or a similar course of conduct.[53] If he is satisfied that the person against whom the proceedings are to be brought is not a body corporate having a share capital exceeding £10,000 and that the proceedings are not likely to involve a question of law or of fact of such general application as to justify its being reserved for the Restrictive Practices Court[54] the Director may bring the proceedings in the sheriff court within whose jurisdiction the business is carried on.[55] This provision applies to proceedings where a course of conduct is detrimental to

---

[42] 1997 Act, s. 45(6).
[43] *ibid.* s. 45(7).
[44] *ibid.* s. 45(8).
[45] *ibid.* s. 45(9).
[46] 34 & 35 Vict. c. 96 ("the 1871 Act").
[47] *ibid.* ss. 3, 15, as amended by Sheriff Courts (Scotland) Act 1971 (c. 58), s. 4(2).
[48] Edw. 8 & 1 Geo. 6, c. 48 ("the 1937 Act").
[49] *ibid.* s. 2(3).
[50] c. 70 ("the 1964" Act).
[51] *ibid.* s. 1(5), (10), as amended by Riding Establishments Act 1970 (c. 32), s. 2(2).
[52] c. 41 ("the 1973 Act").
[53] *ibid.* ss. 34–40.
[54] *ibid.* s. 41(2)(a), (b).
[55] *ibid.* s. 41(3).

consumers[56] and where persons are consenting to or conniving at courses of conduct which are detrimental to the interests of consumers.[57] The Act provides for an appeal on fact or law to the Court of Session[58]; and an appeal to the sheriff principal has been held to be competent, although it is submitted that this decision may not be correct.[59]

Any dispute as to the right to or amount of compensation payable in respect of goods seized under the provisions of the Act is to be determined by an arbiter appointed, failing agreement between the parties, by the sheriff.[60] **26.405**

Consumer Protection Act 1987[61]

Any person having an interest in any goods in respect of which a suspension order is in force may apply to the sheriff by summary application for an order setting aside the suspension notice.[62] Any disputed question as to the right to or amount of any compensation payable under a suspension notice is to be determined by a single arbiter appointed, failing agreement, by the sheriff.[63] **26.406**

LIX. TRUSTS

Trusts (Scotland) Act 1921[64]

On the application of any party having an interest in a trust estate the Court of Session or the sheriff may appoint new trustees to a lapsed trust.[65] The sheriff may grant a warrant to complete title to any heritable property forming part of the trust estate in favour of any trustee so appointed,[66] although such a warrant is not necessary in the case of a trustee appointed by the court.[67] The sheriff may determine all questions of expenses in respect of applications under the Act.[68] **26.407**

A co-trustee or any other person interested in the trust estate may apply to the sheriff or the Court of Session for the removal of a trustee on certain grounds.[69] In cases of insanity, medical certificates similar to those required for the appointment of a guardian will usually suffice[70] but in the case of absence or disappearance a hearing will usually be required.[71] Where incapacity is disputed a remit may be appropriate.[72] **26.408**

---

56 1973 Act, ss. 34(1), 35.
57 *ibid.* s. 38.
58 *ibid.* s. 42(2)(b).
59 *Director-General of Fair Trading v. Boswell*, 1979 S.L.T. (Sh.Ct.) 9, in which it was observed that applications under the Act fell within the definition of a summary application in the Sheriff Courts (Scotland) Act 1907, s. 3(p).
60 1973 Act, s. 32(2).
61 c. 43 ("the 1987 Act").
62 *ibid.* s. 15.
63 *ibid.* s. 14(8).
64 11 & 12 Geo. 5, c. 58 ("the 1921 Act").
65 *ibid.* ss. 22, 24A, 34, as amended by Law Reform (Miscellaneous Provisions) (Scotland) Act 1980, s. 13(a)(ii), (iii), (d); see *Glasgow Lock Hospital, Petrs.*, 1949 S.L.T. (Notes) 26.
66 *ibid.* s. 22.
67 Conveyancing Amendment (Scotland) Act 1938 (c. 24), s. 1.
68 1921 Act, s. 34.
69 *ibid.* ss. 23, 24A, 34; as amended by 1980 Act, (c.55), s. 13(b), (d); see Dobie, *Styles*, p. 543.
70 *Lees* (1893) 1 S.L.T. 42.
71 But note *Dickson's Trs* (1894) 2 S.L.T. 61.
72 *A, Petr* (1898) 6 S.L.T. 149.

26.409 The beneficiary of a lapsed trust may apply to the Court of Session or to the sheriff for authority to complete title to the trust property in his own name.[73]

LX. Water

Reservoirs Act 1975[74]

26.410 A sheriff may authorise a person to enter on land if he considers that there is a reasonable ground for entry on to the land for the purpose for which entry is required, and that entry has been refused or a refusal is apprehended, or the occupier is temporarily absent.[75]

Water (Scotland) Act 1980[76]

26.411 If a local authority is of the opinion that a private supply of water for domestic purposes or for the preparation of food or drink for human consumption, is unfit for human consumption it may apply to the sheriff after giving due notice to any person who owns or has control of the supply.[77] After hearing the parties the sheriff may make an order directing that the supply be closed, or cut off temporarily, or permanently, or that the use of it be restricted to certain purposes.[78] As in any application to the sheriff under the Act, an appeal may be made to the sheriff principal within 21 days of the sheriff's decision and the decision of the sheriff principal is final.[79] If any person fails to carry out the order the council may apply to the sheriff who may authorise the council to do whatever is necessary to give effect to the order.[80]

26.412 The sheriff may grant warrant for an officer of the water authority to enter any premises for purposes connected with the construction of water works.[81] Certain provisions of the Railway Clauses Consolidation (Scotland) Act 1845[82] as to the temporary occupation of lands near a railway during its construction apply to the construction of any reservoir, filter, distribution tank or any works connected therewith.[83]

26.413 The owner of premises may apply to the sheriff on the ground that the occupier is preventing him from carrying out works required by virtue of the Act, and the sheriff may authorise the owner to enter for the purpose of executing works.[84]

---

[73] 1921 Act, ss. 24, 24A, 34; as amended by 1980 Act, *supra*, s. 13(c), (d); *Scott's Trs*, 1957 S.L.T. (Notes) 45.

[74] c. 23 ("the 1975 Act").

[75] *ibid.* s. 17(5), (9).

[76] c. 45 ("the 1980 Act").

[77] *ibid.* s. 27(1) as amended by Local Government etc. (Scotland) Act 1994 (c. 39) Sched. 13, para. 119(17); see *Central R.C. v. Barbour European Ltd*, 1982 S.L.T. (Sh.Ct.) 49, as to the nature of the sheriff's powers under a similar provision in the Sewerage (Scotland) Act 1968, s. 3.

[78] *ibid.* s. 27(1), as amended.

[79] *ibid.* s. 104(1).

[80] *ibid.* s. 27(3), as amended.

[81] *ibid.* s. 38(3).

[82] ss. 25–37; see para. 26.350.

[83] 1980 Act, s. 28(2).

[84] *ibid.* s. 37.

Where an owner or occupier is required to carry out works by virtue of any byelaw made under the Act, the owner or occupier may appeal to the sheriff within 28 days of service of the requirement.[85] If the sheriff decides that the requirement is unreasonable he may modify or disallow it.[86] **26.414**

Natural Heritage (Scotland) Act 1991[87]

The sheriff may grant warrant to a person duly authorised by a river purification board to enter upon land if permission has been refused.[88] **26.415**

LXI. Weights and Measures

Weights and Measures Act 1985[89]

The sheriff may issue a warrant authorising entry into certain premises for the purposes of the Act.[90] **26.416**

---

[85] 1980 Act, s. 71(2).
[86] *ibid.*
[87] c. 28 ("the 1991 Act").
[88] *ibid.* s. 24.
[89] c. 72 ("the 1985 Act").
[90] *ibid.* s. 79(3), (4).

CHAPTER 27

FATAL ACCIDENT INQUIRIES

Introduction

The sheriff has had jurisdiction to inquire into fatal accidents in Scotland for over one hundred years; and so far as concerns sudden deaths, that jurisdiction has persisted for almost as long. At first, it was exercised under the Fatal Accidents Inquiry (Scotland) Act 1895 which related only to inquiries into accidental deaths occurring in the course of an industrial employment or occupation; but later, it was extended by virtue of the Fatal Accidents and Sudden Deaths Inquiry (Scotland) Act 1906 to inquiries into sudden or suspicious deaths. Details of the law and practice relating to inquiries under these statutes are now only of historical interest,[1] but it may be observed that both remained unaltered until their repeal in 1976,[2] in spite of the social and economic upheaval throughout the period, two world wars and a technological revolution affecting all walks of life. **27.01**

Current statutory provisions

The jurisdiction of the sheriff to hold an inquiry is now exercised in accordance with the provisions of the Fatal Accidents and Sudden Deaths Inquiry (Scotland) Act 1976.[3] Related procedural matters are regulated by the Fatal Accidents and Sudden Deaths Inquiry Procedure (Scotland) Rules 1977[4] which were made by the Lord Advocate by virtue of section 7 of the 1976 Act. Together, the Act and the Rules are the repositories of almost all the law in this field. Unlike many other areas of law in which the sheriff exercises a statutory jurisdiction, there is very little case law on the interpretation of the relative provisions, no doubt because in the vast majority of cases the sheriff's findings raise few, if any, points of law and are not made the subject of any mode of appeal.[5] In certain circumstances the holding of an inquiry under the 1976 Act is *mandatory*, subject only to an exception in a case where criminal proceedings have been concluded against any person in respect of the death or any accident from which the death resulted, and the Lord Advocate is satisfied that the circumstances of the death have been sufficiently established in the course of such proceedings[6]; but in certain other circumstances the holding of an inquiry is merely *discretionary*.[7] **27.02**

---

[1] For a short historical survey, see *Stair Memorial Encyclopaedia*, Vol. 17, paras 951–960.
[2] Both statutes were repealed by virtue of the Fatal Accidents and Sudden Deaths Inquiry (Scotland) Act 1976, s. 8(2) and Sched.2.
[3] Hereinafter the "1976 Act".
[4] S.I. 1977 No. 191 (the "1977 Rules").
[5] On review of a determination, see para. 27.22.
[6] 1976 Act, ss. 1(1)(a), 1(2).
[7] *ibid.* s. 1(1)(b).

Mandatory inquiries: deaths at work

27.03 An inquiry under the Act is mandatory where it appears that the death has resulted from an accident occurring in Scotland while the person who has died, being an employee, was in the course of his employment or, being an employer or self-employed person, was engaged in his occupation as such (hereinafter referred to as "deaths at work").[8] Such inquiries normally relate to deaths which have occurred on either the mainland or one of the islands of Scotland; but a death or any accident from which death has resulted is taken to have occurred in Scotland if it has occurred in connection with any activity falling within section 23(2) of the Oil and Gas (Enterprise) Act 1982 in that area, or any part of that area, in respect of which it is provided by Order in Council under section 23(1) of that Act that questions arising out of acts or omissions taking place therein are to be determined in accordance with the law in force in Scotland.[9] This extension of the territorial jurisdiction of the sheriff is important in practical terms in respect of deaths occurring in the off-shore gas and oil industries. The activities listed in section 23(2) of the 1982 Act include *inter alia* those connected with the exploration and exploitation of the natural resources of the seabed, the shore, and the subsoil below certain waters which are carried on from installations of various kinds constructed for those purposes.[10] But, unless the Lord Advocate otherwise directs, the sheriff has no jurisdiction to conduct an inquiry under the 1976 Act where an inquiry into a death takes place under the Gas Act 1965, the Mineral Workings (Offshore Installations) Act 1971, the Health and Safety at Work etc. Act 1974, or the Petroleum and Submarine Pipelines Act 1975.[11] However, if a fatal accident inquiry is held under the 1976 Act into a death which would otherwise form the subject of an inquiry under the Merchant Shipping Act 1995, then no inquiry is competent under the latter statute into a death on or from a ship, or into the death of a crew member.[12]

Mandatory inquiries: deaths in custody

27.04 An inquiry is also mandatory in cases where the person who has died was, at the time of his death, in legal custody.[13] A person is deemed to be in legal custody if he is detained in, or subject to detention in, a prison, remand centre or young offenders institution, all within the meaning of the Prisons (Scotland) Act 1989; or where he is detained in a police station, police cell or other similar place; or where he is being taken either to any of these places to be detained there, or from any such place in which immediately before such taking he was detained.[14] The governor of any custodial institution in which the death of an inmate occurs is under a duty to give immediate notice of the death to the procurator fiscal for the area in which the institution is situated.[15]

---

8 1976 Act, s. 1(1)(a).

9 *ibid.* s. 9.

10 For the full list of the "waters" over which the sheriff has jurisdiction, see Oil and Gas (Enterprise) Act 1982, s. 23(6) (a)–(d): the types of "installations" are listed in s. 23(3)(a)–(d).

11 See Gas Act 1965, s. 17(4); Mineral Workings (Offshore Installations) Act 1971, s. 6(5); Health and Safety at Work etc. Act 1974, s. 14(7); Petroleum and Submarine Pipelines Act 1975, s. 27(5).

12 Merchant Shipping Act 1995, s. 271(6).

13 1976 Act, s. 1(1)(a)(ii).

14 *ibid.* s. 1(4).

15 Prisons (Scotland) Act 1989, s. 34.

Discretionary inquiries

27.05 In cases where the circumstances of the death are not such as to require the holding of an inquiry under the 1976 Act, an inquiry may nonetheless be held where to do so appears to the Lord Advocate to be expedient in the public interest on the ground that the death was sudden, suspicious or unexplained, or has occurred in circumstances such as to give rise to serious public concern.[16] The wide discretion thus given to the Lord Advocate permits the holding of an inquiry in situations such as an unexplained death in hospital, a death where the circumstances suggest a risk to the health or safety of the public (such as a death occurring as a result of food poisoning), a death occurring in a road accident on a bad stretch of road, and a death where medical negligence may have been the cause. In exercising his discretion, the Lord Advocate may take into account a wide variety of factors including the wishes of the relatives of the deceased, whether the circumstances have been fully ventilated in the course of any criminal prosecution, and the time which has elapsed since the death occurred.

The duty to investigate

27.06 It is the procurator fiscal for the district with which the circumstances of the death appear to be most closely concerned who has the duty to investigate those circumstances and to apply to the sheriff for the holding of an inquiry under the Act into those circumstances.[17] That investigation will usually be triggered by the receipt of a report prepared by the police into the fact of a death which has come to their attention, or by a report received directly from some other agency, as, for example, a hospital authority where a sudden death has occurred during a medical procedure thought to be routine. For the purposes of carrying out the investigation the procurator fiscal has statutory warrant to cite witnesses for precognition[18]; and, if a witness, having been cited, either fails to attend without reasonable excuse after receiving reasonable notice to attend for precognition at the time and place fixed, or refuses, when so cited, to give information within his knowledge regarding any matter relevant to the investigation in relation to which such precognition is being taken, the procurator fiscal may apply to the sheriff for an order requiring the witness so to attend or to give information.[19] Failure by a witness to comply with an order by the sheriff in this regard renders him liable to summary punishment.[20]

Application for inquiry

27.07 If the procurator fiscal decides to apply for an inquiry, the application must be made to the sheriff with whose sheriffdom the circumstances of the death appear to be most closely connected, and it must narrate briefly the circumstances of the death so far as known to the procurator fiscal.[21] If it appears that more deaths than one have occurred as a result of the same accident, or in the same or similar circumstances, the application

---

16 1976 Act, s. 1(1)(b).
17 *ibid.* s. 1.
18 *ibid.* s. 2(1).
19 *ibid.* s. 2(2).
20 *ibid.* s. 2(3).
21 *ibid.* s. 1(3).

may relate to both or all such deaths.[22] There then follows a crave in which the sheriff is invited to fix a time and place for the inquiry, to grant warrant to cite witnesses and havers to attend, and to grant warrant to officers of law to take possession of, and hold in safe custody, any necessary productions.[23]

Notification that inquiry is to be held

27.08 The first order of the sheriff is usually formal, and is restricted to granting the crave of the application by the procurator fiscal that an inquiry should be held and a warrant to cite witnesses and havers at the instance of the procurator fiscal or of any other person who may be entitled to appear at the inquiry. In the order the sheriff must fix the date of the inquiry, which must be held as soon thereafter as reasonably practicable.[24] The inquiry may be held in such courthouse or other premises as appear to the sheriff to be appropriate having regard to the apparent circumstances of the death.[25] Normally a convenient courthouse is selected as the venue, but occasionally in cases of great public importance another public building is found to be more suitable. On the making of the first order the procurator fiscal must intimate the holding of the inquiry, and the time and place fixed for it, to the wife or husband or the nearest known relative of the deceased; and, in cases where the inquiry is mandatory because the death occurred at work, intimation must also be given to the employer, if any, of the person whose death is the subject of the inquiry.[26] Certain other classes of person are also entitled to intimation in particular circumstances: in the case of a death occurring at work, intimation must be given to the Health and Safety Commission[27]; in the case of a death in custody, to any minister, government department, or other authority in whose legal custody the deceased was at the time of his death[28]; in the case of a death connected with the exploration or exploitation of the continental shelf (deaths in the oil industry), to the Secretary of State for Employment[29]; and in any case where it is competent for a minister or government department under any statute other than the 1976 Act to cause public inquiry to be made into the circumstances of the death, to such minister or government department.[30] Intimation is given according to a prescribed form not less than 21 days before the date of the inquiry; and the form of intimation given to a surviving spouse, nearest relative, or employer informs such person of his rights in matters of leading evidence and representation at the inquiry.[31] In addition to such necessary intimation, the procurator fiscal must give public notice of the holding of the inquiry, and of the time and place fixed for it. This requires to be done by advertisement in at least two newspapers circulating in the sheriff court district where the inquiry is to be held, not less than 21 days before the date of the inquiry.[32]

---

22 1976 Act, s. 1(3).

23 For the forms of application, see 1977 Rules, r. 3 and Forms 1 and 2 set out in the Schedule thereto.

24 1976 Act, s. 3(1).

25 *ibid.*

26 *ibid.* s. 3(2).

27 *ibid.*; 1977 Rules, r. 4(2).

28 *ibid.*

29 *ibid.*

30 *ibid.*

31 See Form 3 in the Schedule to the 1977 Rules.

32 1977 Rules, r. 4(3); see also Form 4 in the Schedule thereto.

Representation at inquiry

The procurator fiscal must always be represented at an inquiry under the 1976 Act since he has the statutory duty to adduce evidence with regard to the circumstances of the death. Usually he is represented by one of his deputes, but in cases of great importance he sometimes appears personally or, exceptionally, through counsel.[33] The wife, husband or nearest known relative of the deceased is also entitled (but not bound) to appear at the inquiry. In addition, in the case of a death at work, the employer, if any, of the deceased, an inspector appointed under section 19 of the Health and Safety at Work etc. Act 1974, and any other person who the sheriff is satisfied has an interest in the inquiry may appear and adduce evidence at the inquiry.[34] Further, any person entitled to appear at an inquiry may appear on his own behalf or be represented by an advocate or solicitor or, with the leave of the sheriff, by any other person.[35] **27.09**

Legal aid

Since the procedure at an inquiry under the 1976 Act is as nearly as possible that applicable in an ordinary civil cause brought before the sheriff,[36] civil legal aid is available for the representation of an interested party at the inquiry, subject of course to the statutory tests of eligibility being met. As with all civil cases, an applicant must satisfy the Scottish Legal Aid Board that he is financially eligible, that he has a *probabilis causa litigandi* in respect of the proceedings, and that it is reasonable that legal aid should be made available to him.[37] The latter two requirements sometimes give difficulty in practice, and the sheriff may find himself having to deal with a motion to adjourn an inquiry on the ground that legal aid has not been made available to a party who seeks to be represented. In any event parties sometimes cite "delays" in obtaining civil legal aid as a reason for seeking an adjournment. The current view of the Board is that *probabilis causa litigandi* can be established if the applicant demonstrates that he falls within the category of persons entitled to be represented, whether as a relative of the deceased or as a potential defender in any civil action which might follow the inquiry, but that the test of "reasonableness" may not be satisfied unless the applicant can clearly establish why he requires separate representation at the inquiry.[38] So far as concerns the latter, a distinction is made by the Board between deaths which occur in custody and those which do not. In relation to the latter, an applicant is expected to address in his application the question whether he could reasonably expect the procurator fiscal, in fulfilment of his statutory duties, to produce all relevant evidence with regard to the circumstances of the particular death; and an applicant is expected to identify any particular lines of inquiry which he intends pursuing, and which he cannot reasonably expect the procurator fiscal to pursue. But these requirements are not now made of an applicant who seeks to show that it is reasonable to grant legal aid for representation at an inquiry into the death of someone who has died in custody.[39] **27.10**

---

33 1976 Act, s. 4(1); 1977 Rules, r. 7(1).
34 *ibid.* s. 4(2).
35 1977 Rules, r. 7(2).
36 1976 Act, s. 4(7).
37 Legal Aid (Scotland) Act 1986, ss. 14, 15.
38 See Scottish Legal Aid Board, "*The Recorder*", issue 15 (Sept. 1996).
39 *ibid.* issue 19 (Oct. 1997).

Conduct of the inquiry

27.11 The general rule is that a fatal accident inquiry is open to the public.[40] The rules of evidence, the procedure, and the powers of the sheriff to deal with contempt of court and to enforce the attendance of witnesses at the inquiry are, as nearly as possible, those applicable in an ordinary civil cause brought before the sheriff sitting alone.[41] The sheriff may at any time adjourn the inquiry to a time and place specified by him at the time of the adjournment.[42]

Powers of the sheriff

27.12 Although the proceedings before the sheriff are judicial, they are not wholly adversarial in the traditional sense. The sheriff's duties and powers are limited by the terms of the 1976 Act and the Rules made thereunder; and these make it clear that in some respects the sheriff has an active investigative role as well as acting simply as an arbiter of fact and law. Thus, while the sheriff may grant warrant to officers of law to take possession of anything connected with the death being inquired into, and which may be considered necessary to produce at the inquiry, and may do so on the application of the procurator fiscal or other person entitled to appear, he may also take such steps at his own instance.[43] Similarly, he may of his own accord inspect any land, premises, article or other thing the inspection of which he considers to be desirable for the purposes of the inquiry, whether or not the procurator fiscal or any other party exercises his right to apply for the sheriff to do so.[44] Occasionally, the sheriff will consider it helpful to visit the locus of some fatal accident. If he does so, his visit need not take place in the presence of the parties, and it will not violate the normal rule prohibiting the acquisition of information privately. Further, the sheriff has power *ex proprio motu* to summon any person having special knowledge, and being willing to do so, to act as an assessor at the inquiry, again whether or not any party asks him to do so.[45] These rules permit (but do not oblige) the sheriff to take a far more proactive role in the ascertainment of the truth than in many other types of proceeding. Again, the sheriff has power at his own hand to make an order restricting the publicity to be given to the proceedings before him where a person under the age of 17 is in any way involved in the inquiry, whether or not any party applies for such an order.[46] If such an order is granted, any report of the inquiry which is made in a newspaper or other publication, or a sound or television broadcast, must not reveal the name, address or school, or include any particulars calculated to lead to the identification of the young person concerned; and any picture relating to the inquiry which is, or includes, a picture of that person must not be published in any newspaper or other publication or television broadcast.[47] Criminal sanctions apply in the

---

40 1976 Act, s. 4(3).
41 *ibid.* s. 4(7).
42 1977 Rules, r. 9.
43 *ibid.* r. 5.
44 *ibid.* r. 6.
45 1976 Act, s. 4(6). A request by a party to summon an assessor is made by written motion lodged with the sheriff clerk not less than seven days before the date of the inquiry. In all cases, the appointment of an assessor does not affect the admissibility of expert evidence in the inquiry: 1977 Rules, r. 12.
46 1976 Act, s. 4(4).
47 *ibid.*

case of breach of such an order.[48] There is nothing in the 1976 Act which prevents the sheriff who conducts a fatal accident inquiry from hearing a subsequent action of damages arising out of the same accident.[49]

Special evidential and procedural rules

Witnesses and criminal proceedings. The examination of a witness or haver at a fatal accident inquiry is not a bar to criminal proceedings being taken against him.[50] Normally, however, if the circumstances of the death are such as to warrant both a criminal prosecution and the holding of an inquiry, the former is normally held in advance of the latter. **27.13**

Compellability of witnesses. No witness at an inquiry is compellable to answer any question tending to show that he is guilty of any crime or offence.[51] Normally, the sheriff will be able to ascertain in advance of the inquiry whether any related criminal proceedings have been instituted or completed so that he may be on notice that a witness may be entitled to invoke the privilege; but, if there is doubt as to whether a particular witness may be asked questions which need not be answered, the issue may be canvassed with the party adducing the witness before his examination begins.

Written statements. The sheriff has power to admit in place of oral evidence by any person in an inquiry, to the like extent as such oral evidence, a written statement by that person signed by that person and sworn or affirmed to be true by that person before a notary public, commissioner for oaths, or justice of the peace, or before a commissioner appointed by the sheriff for that purpose, provided that *either* all persons who appear or are represented at the inquiry agree to its admission *or* the sheriff considers that its admission will not result in unfairness in the conduct of the inquiry to any person who appears or is represented at it.[52] Sufficient evidence that the statement has been sworn or affirmed to be true may be provided by way of a certificate annexed thereto[53]; and any document or object referred to as a production and identified in a written statement so tendered in evidence is treated as if it had been produced and had been identified in court by the maker of the statement.[54] These provisions are usually utilised in relation to post-mortem reports by pathologists, at least in cases where the cause of death is not disputed. Any written statement which is admitted must be read aloud at the inquiry, unless the sheriff otherwise directs[55]; and normally the sheriff clerk reads out the statement. But where the sheriff directs that a statement or any part of it is not to be read out, he must state the reason for his direction; and, where appropriate, an account must be given orally of what the sheriff has directed not to be read aloud.[56]

---

48 1976 Act,. s. 4(5).
49 *Black v. Scott Lithgow Ltd*, 1990 S.C. 322; 1990 S.L.T. 612.
50 1976 Act, s. 5(1).
51 *ibid.* s. 5(2).
52 1977 Rules, r. 10(1).
53 *ibid.* r. 10(2).
54 *ibid.* r. 10(3).
55 *ibid.*
56 *ibid.*

The decision of the sheriff: making the determination

27.14 At the conclusion of the evidence, and any submissions thereon, the sheriff is obliged to make a decision ("the determination") on the various matters canvassed before him. By virtue of section 6(1) of the 1976 Act the sheriff must set out the following circumstances of the death *so far as they have been established to his satisfaction*:

(a) where and when the death and any accident resulting in the death took place;
(b) the cause or causes of such death and any accident resulting in the death;
(c) the reasonable precautions, if any, whereby the death and any accident resulting in the death might have been avoided;
(d) the defects, if any, in any system of working which contributed to the death or any accident resulting in the death; and
(e) any other facts which are relevant to the circumstances of the death.

A few general points may be made in respect of these provisions before they are examined in more detail. First, the sheriff is *entitled* to be satisfied that any of the above circumstances have been established by evidence, notwithstanding that that evidence is not corroborated.[57] It will be noted that this rule predated the general relaxation of the law on corroboration in civil cases which came with the passing of the Civil Evidence (Scotland) Act 1988.[58] But, as with the provisions of the latter, the rule does not *oblige* the sheriff to find something established in the absence of corroboration. Secondly, it should be stressed at the outset that section 6(1) does not give the sheriff any power to make any explicit findings as to fault, or to apportion blame between any persons who might have contributed to any accident which caused the death. The matter has been put thus:

> "It is plain that the function of the sheriff at a fatal accident inquiry is different from that which he is required to perform at a proof in a civil action to recover damages. His examination and analysis of the evidence is conducted with a view only to setting out in his determination the circumstances to which the subsection refers, in so far as this can be done to his satisfaction. He has before him no record or other written pleading, there is no claim of damages by anyone and there are no grounds of fault upon which his decision is required. The inquiry is normally held within a relatively short time after the accident . . . It provides the first opportunity to canvass matters relating to precautions which might have avoided the death or any defects in any system of working which contributed to it, at a stage when these issues have not been clearly focused by the parties to any future litigation which may arise."[59]

But while these dicta clearly indicate that an inquiry under the 1976 Act is concerned with fact-finding rather than fault-finding, the terms of paragraphs (c) and (d) of section 6(1) do place on the sheriff an obligation to make a determination on the matters mentioned where they have been

---

[57] 1976 Act, s. 6(2). See also *Gallacher (Fatal Accident Inquiry)*, 1993 S.C.L.R. 781, where parts of hospital records were not properly introduced into evidence.
[58] Civil Evidence (Scotland) Act 1988, s. 1(1).
[59] *Black v. Scott Lithgow Ltd*, 1990 S.C. 322 at 327.

established to his satisfaction. The sheriff cannot avoid his statutory responsibility under these paragraphs where the evidence is clear, but he must be very careful not to go beyond their precise terms.[60] Lastly, it will be evident that in some cases it will be impossible on the evidence for the sheriff to make more than a "formal" determination, restricted to the circumstances mentioned in paragraphs (a) and (b) of section 6(1).

The decision of the sheriff: particular issues

(a) "where and when the death and any accident resulting in the death took place"

The evidential foundation for a determination under this heading will normally come from a variety of sources, both direct and circumstantial. Expert evidence is often available; and it is usual to hear (or have in written form) evidence from the pathologist(s) who prepared the post-mortem reports on the deceased. Evidence showing where the deceased was found will invariably be led and this, taken with medical evidence, is often sufficient to satisfy the sheriff on the essential matters under this heading. But difficulty may arise where the deceased has been discovered by chance, after lying undisturbed for some time. In such cases the sheriff may have to estimate the time (and place) of death by reference to the time when the deceased was last seen alive, and the time when his body was discovered, in the light of the medical and other evidence as to its condition and the last known movements of the deceased. It should also be noted that the term "accident" is capable of a very wide interpretation; almost any untoward occurrence can be described as an "accident".[61] But the sheriff is obliged only to make a determination of where and when "any accident resulting in the death" took place and should only do so where he is satisfied that the evidence supports the conclusion that the death resulted from the accident, to whatever extent. **27.15**

(b) "the cause or causes of such death and any accident resulting in the death"

The cause of the death is almost always a matter of medical evidence, which may be quite extensive according to the circumstances. It is commonplace for the evidence of pathologists to be supported by other medical witnesses specialising in particular fields. Where, exceptionally, the body of the deceased has not been recovered and examined by a pathologist (as in some cases of drowning or a major explosion on an oil rig), the necessary evidence may have to be taken from other sources such as eye-witnesses to the event. Even if the body has been recovered, satisfactory evidence may be available from the doctor certifying the death, even if he does not carry out a full post-mortem examination. As for the cause(s) of any accident resulting in the death, again the necessary evidence to support a determination under this heading will usually come from witnesses who saw the accident and who may be able to say how it occurred. These witnesses frequently include those with professional qualifications or expertise in the relative field of human endeavour. **27.16**

---

[60] If the sheriff does so, the relative part of his determination may be susceptible to judicial review: see para. 27.22.

[61] The term "accident" has been defined as "any unintended and unexpected occurrence which produces hurt or loss": *Fenton v. Thorley* [1903] A.C. 443, *per* Lord Lindley at 453. See also Stewart, *Scottish Contemporary Judicial Dictionary*, pp. 2–4.

(c) "the reasonable precautions, if any, whereby the death and any accident resulting in the death might have been avoided"

27.17 As its language makes clear, under this heading it is open to the sheriff only to determine how the death "*might*" have been avoided, not how it "*could*" or "*would*" have been avoided. This is the area of possibility rather than probability and, as such, can be entered rather more readily in a fatal accident inquiry than would be appropriate in other cases within the jurisdictional competence of the sheriff. But speculation must be avoided; as with all the paragraphs of section 6(1) of the 1976 Act, there has to be evidence which *satisfies* the sheriff on the material points.[62]

(d) "the defects, if any, in any system of working which contributed to the death or any accident resulting in the death"

27.18 In this area, the sheriff may find that there is considerable scope for identifying deficiencies in the operation of working practices which contributed to the death. The phrase "system of working" is capable of a wide interpretation, covering many methods and routines. It may include a defective "system" in which the deceased was not engaged at the time of his death, but which nonetheless contributed to it.[63] It is here that the sheriff may have a particularly important role to play in identifying mistakes and in seeking to ensure that they do not recur. But, in so doing, he must be careful (for the reasons already explained) not to stray explicitly into the area of fault-finding unless the evidence clearly points that way.

(e) "any other facts which are relevant to the circumstances of the death"

27.19 Unlike paragraphs (c) and (d) of section 6(1) of the 1976 Act, this paragraph is not couched in the language of causation, nor does it suggest that the sheriff should exercise the wisdom of hindsight. Instead, it is the area of relevance which is important.[64]

Determination must be in writing

27.20 The determination by the sheriff must always be in writing, and it must also be signed by the sheriff.[65] It is good practice to relate each of the findings to the relevant paragraphs of section 6(1) of the 1976 Act. In cases where the sheriff does not feel able to go beyond a "formal" determination restricted to the matters set out in paragraphs (a) and (b), the determination may be very brief. In cases where the sheriff is able to decide the relevant matters without needing time for consideration, it is common for him to rise briefly at the end of the evidence and submissions in order to draft this determination. But other cases may not be capable of a swift resolution.

---

[62] In the course of the Note attached to his determination following the inquiry into the Lockerbie disaster, Sheriff Principal Mowat observed that the sheriff should avoid, as far as possible, any connotation of negligence; any findings should not contain any indication as to whether any person was under a duty either at common law or under statute to take the precaution identified in the finding: see 1991 S.L.T. (News) 225 at 227.

[63] *cf.* 1976 Act, s. 6(1)(c).

[64] The view has been expressed that most findings which go beyond the formal stage of s. 6(1)(a) and (b) can be covered by s. 6(1)(c): see 1991 S.L.T. (News) 225 at 227.

[65] 1977 Rules, r. 11(1).

Delivery and distribution of determination

At the conclusion of the inquiry, the sheriff must, except in certain defined circumstances, read out his determination in public.[66] If the determination is "formal", it is usually delivered on the same day either immediately after the close of the evidence and submissions, or after a brief adjournment to allow the sheriff to collect his thoughts. If, however, the sheriff requires time to prepare his determination, he may take one of two courses: he may fix an adjourned sitting of the inquiry for the purpose of reading out his findings; or, almost invariably, he can elect to give a written decision at a later date after making *avizandum*. In the latter eventuality, he is not required to reconvene the court in order to read out the determination in public.[67] But in such cases the sheriff clerk is obliged to send, free of charge, a copy of the determination to the procurator fiscal and to any person who appeared or was represented at the inquiry; and he must allow any person to inspect a copy of the determination at the sheriff clerk's office free of charge during the period of three months after the date when the determination was made.[68] In cases attracting great public interest the sheriff may wish to ensure that advance copies of the determination are made available to the procurator fiscal and other parties prior to issuing it into the public domain. In that way, persons such as relatives of the deceased may be spared any emotional turmoil arising from learning the sheriff's findings directly from television or other news media. The sheriff clerk is usually able to make the necessary administrative arrangements to prevent this. On the conclusion of every inquiry the sheriff clerk is under a duty to send a copy of the determination to the Lord Advocate. In addition, and if requested to do so, he must also send it to any minister or government department or to the Health and Safety Commission along with a copy of the application for the inquiry, the transcript of the evidence, and any report or documentary production used in the inquiry. Likewise, the procurator fiscal must send to the Registrar of Births, Deaths and Marriages for Scotland the name and last known address of the person who has died, and the date, place and cause of his death.[69] Moreover, any person may, upon payment of a fee to the sheriff clerk, obtain a copy of the sheriff's determination; and any person who has an interest in the inquiry may obtain from the clerk (again on payment of a fee) a copy of the transcript of the evidence, but only on application made within a period of three months after the date when the sheriff's determination was made.[70] The determination of the sheriff is not admissible in evidence, nor can it be founded on in any judicial proceedings, of whatever nature, arising out of the death or out of any accident from which the death resulted.[71] 27.21

Review of the determination

The 1976 Act is entirely silent on the question whether or not the sheriff's determination is susceptible to any scrutiny in an appeal court. As a matter of practice, inquiries of great public importance are often conducted by the sheriff principal, thus precluding any appellate scrutiny 27.22

66 1977 Rules, r. 11(2).
67 *ibid.* r. 11(3).
68 *ibid.*
69 1976 Act, s. 6(4).
70 *ibid.* s. 6(5).
71 *ibid.* s. 6(3).

by him. But the determination of the sheriff may be judicially reviewed in the Court of Session. It has been held, in the absence of argument to the contrary, that judicial review is a competent remedy; but that the only part of a determination which can be reduced is a part that falls within the specific findings listed in section 6(1) of the 1976 Act; and further, that, where the sheriff has not misdirected himself in law or acted beyond his jurisdiction, his determination can be reduced only where he has failed to take into account a matter which should have been taken into account.[72] It is not open by judicial review to challenge any view expressed by the sheriff in regard to the credibility or reliability of a witness on the basis that there is nothing in the evidence to justify that view.[73]

Expenses

27.23 Although the Lord Advocate has power in relation to inquiries under the 1976 Act to make rules as to the payment of fees to solicitors and expenses to witnesses and havers,[74] no specific provisions have ever been made in this respect. In any event, an inquiry is not an adversarial process, and no awards of expenses should be made against or in favour of any compearing party. Indeed, it is thought that to make such an award would be contrary to the public interest, and would be susceptible to decree of reduction by judicial review.[75] Accordingly fees charged for representation by counsel or solicitors fall on the instructing party, or on the legal aid fund if appropriate. There appears to be no reason why an additional fee should not be awarded (on an agent and client basis) in a suitable case to the advisers of a party who is legally represented at an inquiry; in practice, a motion to that effect is sometimes lodged and granted.[76] As for the expenses of witnesses and havers, these are met by the party who cites them.

Service of documents and dispensing power of sheriff

27.24 The 1977 Rules contain provisions relating to the manner of service of notices, citations, interlocutors, warrants and other orders of the sheriff.[77] As with other civil proceedings in the sheriff court, the sheriff has a discretion to relieve any person from the consequences of any failure to comply with any of the provisions of the 1977 Rules if the failure resulted from mistake, oversight or any cause other than wilful non-observance, all on such terms and conditions as appear to him to be just. The sheriff may make such order as appears to him to be just regarding extension of time, lodging or amendment of papers or otherwise, so as to enable the inquiry to proceed as if such failure had not happened.[78]

---

[72] *Lothian R.C. v. Lord Advocate*, 1993 S.L.T. 1132; 1993 S.C.L.R. 565.

[73] *Smith v. Lord Advocate*, 1995 S.L.T. 379 at 380.

[74] 1976 Act, s. 7(1)(h).

[75] See *The Herald*, June 27, 1997 for a news report of a case in which decree of reduction was granted in respect of a finding of liability for expenses.

[76] This is only likely to be encountered in a case where one of the parties to an inquiry is in receipt of legal aid: see the Civil Legal Aid (Fees) Regulations 1989 (S.I 1989 No. 119), reg. 5(4).

[77] 1977 Rules, r. 16.

[78] *ibid.* r. 17.

CHAPTER 28

ADOPTION

I. PROCEEDINGS RELATING TO ADOPTION

Nature of proceedings

Adoption is the process by which parental responsibilities and parental rights in respect of a child are irrevocably transferred from biological parents to adopters and the child acquires a new legal status as the child of the adopters. The process was introduced to Scots law by the Adoption of Children (Scotland) Act 1930 and is now governed by the Adoption (Scotland) Act 1978, as amended by the Children (Scotland) Act 1995.[1] Adoption proceedings are *sui generis*[2] and in many respects quite unlike any other form of action. The court has wide discretionary powers to investigate and verify at its own hand all relevant facts. The proceedings are to some extent administrative and the strict rules of evidence do not apply.[3] Rules of procedure should be flexibly interpreted to give full effect to the policy that the need to safeguard and promote the welfare of the child is the paramount consideration.[4] The present rules of procedure are to be found in Chapter 2 of the Child Care and Maintenance Rules 1997.[5] **28.01**

Adoptions fall into two broad categories, with different procedures in each case. The first involves the placement of children for adoption by adoption agencies and the second category covers those cases in which the placement has not been made by an adoption agency. In all cases the parent or guardian of the child must agree to the adoption, or agreement must be dispensed with on grounds specified in the Act.[6] Where a local authority wishes to place a child for adoption, without the agreement of the child's parent or guardian, it must generally make an application to the court for an order declaring the child free for adoption[7] to determine whether, in principle, adoption is the appropriate course. Freeing for adoption is the procedure which involves a determination in principle whether a child should be adopted before there is any transfer of parental responsibilities and parental rights to adopters. **28.02**

Applicable law

An understanding of the substantive law of adoption is necessary to a sound grasp of procedure. A full description of the law of adoption is **28.03**

---

[1] All references to the 1978 Act in this chapter are to the Act as amended by the 1995 Act.
[2] *J and J v. C's Tutor*, 1948 S.C. 636, *per* L.P Cooper at 642.
[3] *T, Petr*, 1997 S.L.T. 724, *per* L.P Hope at 730L.
[4] Adoption (Scotland) Act 1978, s. 6; *AB and CD, Petrs*, 1992 S.L.T. 1064 at 1069I–L; *B v. C*, 1996 S.L.T. 1370 at 1376C–D.
[5] S.I. 1997 No. 291.
[6] 1978 Act, s. 16.
[7] *ibid.* s. 18.

beyond the remit of this work, but available elsewhere.[8] Accordingly the following paragraphs do no more than give an outline of that substantive law.

Statute

28.04 Adoption is a creature of statute, and regulated by the Adoption (Scotland) Act 1978. Issues arising in adoption law are generally questions of interpretation and application of the 1978 Act. Substantive changes to adoption law effected by the Children (Scotland) Act 1995 came into force on April 1, 1997. The 1995 Act affects all proceedings commenced on or after that date.[9] The criteria for decisions in adoption proceedings are amended by the 1995 Act,[10] as are the grounds for dispensing with the agreement of a parent or guardian to adoption.[11]

Case law

28.05 Most adoption cases are decided in the sheriff court. The first reported appeal in which it was held that the welfare of the child was a factor to be taken into account was in 1963,[12] since when there have been a series of cases which assist in understanding adoption. Much of the existing case law relating to adoption will continue to be relevant, despite the amendments introduced by the Children (Scotland) Act 1995. However, where the issue relates to the criteria for adoption, or dispensation with agreement to adoption, previous case law must be applied with caution, having regard to the changes introduced.

28.06 Scottish and English adoption law have developed in parallel. For many years the law in both jurisdictions was in most material respects identical. It has been recognised that the courts in the two jurisdictions should seek to arrive at the same construction of statutory provisions applicable in both,[13] and reference to English case law is appropriate where this does not conflict with Scottish authorities.[14] Care must, however, be exercised as there are some conflicts, the most outstanding example of which is the approach to be taken when considering whether to dispense with a parent's agreement to adoption. Scottish courts consider first whether there exists a ground for dispensation in terms of section 16(2) of the 1978 Act and then apply the tests of section 6.[15] English courts, at least when deciding the issue of whether a parent is unreasonably withholding agreement to adoption, consider welfare first, and then look to see whether a ground is present.[16] Further, the amendments to the Scottish law of adoption effected by the Children (Scotland) Act 1995 have introduced significant differences between the adoption laws of the two jurisdictions, particularly relating to criteria for adoption and dispensation with parental agreement.

---

[8] See McNeill, *Adoption of Children in Scotland* (3rd ed.); Nichols (ed.) *Scottish Family Law Service*; Wilkinson and Norrie, *Parent and Child.*

[9] The Children (Scotland) Act 1995 (Commencement No. 3) (Amendment and Transitional Provisions) Order 1997 (S.I. 1997 No. 744), para. 5.

[10] See paras 28.08 to 28.11.

[11] See para. 28.34.

[12] *AB and CB v. X's Curator*, 1963 S.C. 124.

[13] *ibid.* at 135.

[14] *B v. C*, 1996 S.L.T. 1370 at 1374L–1375A.

[15] *Lothian R.C. v. A*, 1992 S.L.T. 858 at 862D–863D.

[16] *Re D (A Minor) (Adoption: Parental Agreement)* [1990] F.C.R. 615.

Rules of procedure

Special rules of procedure apply to adoptions. The Child Care and Maintenance Rules 1997[17] came into force on April 1, 1997 and apply to all proceedings commenced on or after that date.[18] The sheriff has a wide discretion in relation to the conduct of applications in order to achieve a decision which serves the welfare of the child.[19] Sheriffs may in their discretion follow the pattern of procedure in the Ordinary Cause Rules, where these do not conflict with the rules special to adoption.[20] **28.07**

Criteria in proceedings

Adoption is an extreme measure and the court should not make an adoption order or an order declaring a child free for adoption unless it considers that it would be better for the child that it should do so than that it should not.[21] The Adoption (Scotland) Act 1978, section 6, sets out principles to be applied in all decisions relating to adoption. These principles must be applied in the substantive decisions to be made by the court. They also guide decisions relating to the procedure to be followed in reaching a final decision.[22] In reaching any decision relating to adoption of a child the court must have regard to all the circumstances, but three factors are singled out for particular consideration. **28.08**

Welfare of child paramount

The court must regard the need to safeguard and promote the welfare of the child throughout life as the paramount consideration.[23] The welfare of the child is thus the overriding factor. Care must be taken in applying case law in relation to adoption as, until April 1, 1997,[24] the child's welfare was the first but not the paramount consideration in adoption proceedings. The test to be applied now recognises that adoption effects a lifelong change in legal relationships. Thus the welfare of the child throughout life, not just childhood, must be considered. **28.09**

Views of child

The court must have regard so far as practicable to the views of the child, if the child wishes to express views, taking account of the child's age and maturity.[25] A child of 12 or more is presumed to be of sufficient age and maturity to form a view, but this does not mean that children under 12 may not have views which require to be taken into account.[26] This provision gives effect to Article 12 of the United Nations Convention on the Rights of the Child[27] which commits states who are party to the **28.10**

---

17 S.I. 1997 No. 291, hereinafter referred to as "CCMR".

18 CCMR, r. 1.4(2). The Act of Sederunt (Adoption of Children) 1984 (S.I. 1984 No. 1013) continues to apply to all proceedings pending on Apr. 1, 1997.

19 *J and J v. C's Tutor*, 1948 S.C. 636; *AB and CD, Petrs*, 1992 S.L.T. 1064; *B v. C*, 1996 S.L.T. 1370; *T, Petr*, 1997 S.L.T. 724.

20 *Lothian R.C. v. A*, 1992 S.L.T. 858 at 865L.

21 1978 Act, s. 24(3).

22 See *AB and CD, Petrs*, 1992 S.L.T. 1064.

23 1978 Act, s. 6(1)(a).

24 The date on which Part II of the Children (Scotland) Act 1995, amending the Adoption (Scotland) Act 1978, was brought into force.

25 1978 Act, s. 6(1)(b)(i).

26 *ibid.* s. 6(2).

27 Ratified by the United Kingdom on Dec. 16, 1991.

Convention to assuring to a child who is capable of forming views the right to express those views freely in all matters affecting the child, and in particular to providing the child with the opportunity to be heard in any judicial or administrative proceedings affecting the child. It may be impracticable to ascertain the views of very young children or children suffering from significant handicap, although their wishes and feelings about their situation may be apparent and should be taken into consideration by the court. Difficulties may arise where a child is unaware that there are proceedings pending and the court will then require to determine whether in the circumstances of the case the child should be told about the action and invited to express a view, or that it is impracticable to seek the views of the child.[28]

Religion, race, culture and language

28.11 The court is also required so far as practicable to have regard to the child's religious persuasion, racial origin and cultural and linguistic background.[29] The section refers to the religious persuasion of the child, rather than that of his parent. A parent's wishes in relation to the religious upbringing of the child should be taken into consideration before a child is placed for adoption in those cases where an adoption agency is involved.[30] A young child may have no religious persuasion, although an older child may have decided views about the religion of his or her parents or prospective adopters. The section does have implications when the court is considering an adoption of children of a different racial and cultural background, and there will be an onus on the applicants to show how they propose to deal with these matters. In one case white Scottish applicants were required by the court as a condition of adoption to use their best endeavours to secure that the child adopted was made aware of his black identity and brought up with a knowledge of his ethnic origins and traditions.[31] These considerations will feature in future adoptions of this nature.

Placement by adoption agencies

28.12 Adoption agencies are either local authorities[32] or voluntary organisations approved by the Secretary of State to act as adoption societies.[33] The activities of both are directed by the Adoption Agencies (Scotland) Regulations 1996.[34] Adoption agencies are charged with making decisions about whether a particular child should be placed for adoption; whether prospective adopters would be suitable adoptive parents; and whether a particular prospective adopter would be a suitable adoptive parent for a particular child.[35] The regulations prescribe the information which must be obtained about children, their birth families and about

---

[28] See *C, Petr*, 1993 S.C.L.R. 14.

[29] 1978 Act, s. 6(1)(b)(ii).

[30] *ibid.* s. 7. In relation to adoption agencies, see para. 28.12.

[31] *AH and PH Petrs*, 1997 Fam.L.R. 84.

[32] A local authority for this purpose is a council constituted under s. 2 of the Local Government etc. (Scotland) Act 1994. In some cases (1978 Act, ss. 13, 22, 28, 30, 31, 35(1) and 45) the definition includes an English council. The term "adoption agency" sometimes (1978 Act, ss. 11,13, 18–23 and 27) includes adoption agencies in England and Northern Ireland. See 1978 Act, s. 65(1).

[33] 1978 Act, ss. 1 and 3.

[34] S.I. 1996 No. 3266 (the "1996 Regulations").

[35] 1996 Regulations, regs 8–12.

adopters.[36] The decisions to be taken by the agency must be discussed by an adoption panel. The panel must consist of not less than six persons and is required to include a medical and a legal adviser and at least one man and one woman.[37] The panel makes recommendations which are then considered by the agency before reaching a decision.

If an adoption agency decides that adoption is in the best interests of a child, it may decide that the child should be placed for adoption, or, if the agency is a local authority, that an application should be made that the child should be declared free for adoption. In either case it must within seven days notify the parents and any guardian of the child of the proposed plan for the child, and give information about the legal process involved.[38] If the parent or guardian agrees with the agency decision then he or she should sign and return a certificate stating that this is the case.[39] The certificate is not formal consent to adoption. It is an indication of agreement with the plan for the child, and so by implication that consent to adoption is likely to be given in due course. Provided the certificate is signed and returned within 28 days the adoption agency may proceed to implement the proposed plan for the child.[40] If the parent or guardian indicates they do not agree with the plan, or the certificate is not returned within 28 days, the agency is required to proceed on the basis that there is no agreement to the plan and consent to adoption is unlikely to be forthcoming.[41] If a parent or guardian cannot be contacted, and 28 days have elapsed after reasonable efforts have been made to make contact, the agency must proceed on the basis that there is no agreement.[42] **28.13**

In cases where the parent or guardian has not agreed to the proposal for the child, an adoption agency which is a local authority is obliged to seek an order declaring the child free for adoption,[43] unless an application for an adoption order has already been made. Strict timescales apply, but these vary depending on whether or not the child is subject to a supervision requirement. If there is no supervision requirement the freeing or adoption proceedings must be commenced within 28 days of the receipt of the parent or guardian's certificate to the effect that there is no consent to the plan for the child.[44] In cases where there is no response from the parent the 28 days for raising proceedings runs from the expiry of the time when the certificate should have been returned.[45] **28.14**

Where the child is subject to a supervision requirement and the local authority propose that arrangements for adoption should be made, the children's hearing requires to be consulted.[46] If the local authority decides that the child's parent or guardian is unlikely to agree to the arrangements it must within seven days of that decision notify the principal reporter[47] **28.15**

---

[36] 1996 Regulations, Sched. 2.
[37] *ibid.* reg. 7(4), (5).
[38] *ibid.* regs 12(8), 14, Scheds 4, 5.
[39] *ibid.* regs 14(1)(d) and (e), 15, Sched. 6, 7.
[40] *ibid.* reg. 15(1).
[41] *ibid.* reg. 15(2).
[42] *ibid.*
[43] *ibid.* regs 17, 18; 1978 Act, s. 9(3A).
[44] 1996 Regulations, reg. 17(2).
[45] *ibid.*
[46] 1995 Act, s. 73(4) and (5).
[47] 1996 Regulations, reg. 18(2).

The local authority may reach such a decision on the basis that the parent returns a certificate stating disagreement with the plan for adoption, or where no certificate of agreement is received within 28 days.[48] The principal reporter must arrange a children's hearing within 21 days of such notification.[49] The hearing will consider the proposal at a review of the supervision requirement, and within seven days of the review will supply their advice on the proposal to the local authority.[50] If the advice of the hearing is in favour of adoption the authority must commence freeing proceedings within 28 days from receipt of the hearing's report.[51] If the advice of the hearing is not in favour of adoption the authority must within 28 days review its decision on the matter and come to a further decision taking into account the hearing's report and any further recommendations from the adoption panel.[52] If the authority then decides that adoption is still in the best interests of the child, it must commence freeing proceedings within the same 28-day period as if the hearing's advice had been in favour.[53] None of these provisions applies if an application for an adoption order has already been made.[54]

28.16 No sanction is prescribed for failure to comply with these timescales. Failure to comply with similar regulations and timescales in the past has not vitiated later proceedings.[55] If a local authority which fails to comply with the time-limits prescribed in the regulations is required to recommence the whole procedure of decision making before it may make an application, this will defeat the object of the regulations which is to ensure that decisions about adoption are taken and acted upon with reasonable expedition.

28.17 Where the adoption agency is not a local authority, but an approved adoption society, the regulations simply require that, in cases where a parent does not return the certificate agreeing with the plan for the child, the agency take such steps as it considers appropriate and in the interests of the child as soon as reasonably practicable.[56] An approved adoption society cannot make an application for an order declaring a child free for adoption.[57] Where the child concerned is subject to a supervision requirement, it must refer the case to the principal reporter for the children's hearing to review the matter and to prepare a report in relation to the proposed adoption.[58]

Non-agency placements

28.18 Only an adoption agency may make arrangements for the adoption of a child, or may place a child for adoption, unless the proposed adopter is a relative[59] of the child. It is a criminal offence for any other person to undertake such activities or to receive a child placed in contravention of

---

48 1996 Regulations, reg. 15(2). See para 28.13.
49 Children's Hearings (Scotland) Rules 1996 (S.I. 1996 No. 3261), r. 22(8).
50 *ibid.* r. 22(7).
51 1996 Regulations, reg. 18(3).
52 *ibid.* reg. 18(4).
53 *ibid.* reg. 18(5).
54 *ibid.* reg. 18(6).
55 *Re T (a minor) (adoption: validity of order)* [1986] 2 F.L.R. 31; *Dumfries and Galloway R.C. v. M*, 1990 S.C. 31.
56 1996 Regulations, reg. 16.
57 1978 Act, s. 18(1).
58 *ibid.* s. 22A.
59 "Relative" is defined in 1978 Act, s. 65(1); see para. 28.30.

this provision.[60] While such activity will render a person liable to prosecution, it will not prevent the adoption of a child who has been illegally placed if the conditions for adoption are otherwise satisfied and, in particular, the child's welfare would be best served by an adoption order.[61] An illegally placed child will usually require to be supervised by the local authority as a private foster child pending the grant of an adoption order.[62]

The majority of non-agency adoptions are in families where a child is cared for by a parent and step-parent.[63] Some are adoptions by another relative. There are also adoptions by foster parents who have been looking after a child on behalf of the local authority and desire to adopt the child, without being approved as adopters under the procedures mentioned above. **28.19**

In all non-agency placements the local authority for the area in which the adopter has his or her home must be given notice of the intention to apply for an adoption order.[64] No adoption order can be made for a period of three months from the date of the notice.[65] This is to give the local authority opportunity to investigate and submit a report to the court. The notice may be given before the proceedings are instituted, and this will usually be desirable in order to ascertain the local authority's position, and to prevent delay when proceedings are commenced. **28.20**

Children subject to supervision requirements

Where a child is subject to a supervision requirement made by the children's hearing, the child may be required to reside at any place specified in the requirement and to comply with conditions imposed by the hearing.[66] The hearing may facilitate an adoption by requiring the child to reside with persons who are potential adopters, and this does not constitute "making arrangements" for adoption and thus an offence in terms of section 11(3) of the 1978 Act.[67] It has, however, been observed that the hearing should not otherwise take any step to facilitate adoption, and that any decision about adoption was beyond the hearing's remit, and so should not be discussed by the hearing.[68] The Children (Scotland) Act 1995 now requires a hearing to consider the child's welfare throughout childhood when reaching any decision with respect to the child.[69] A hearing must therefore consider long-term proposals for the child, including any question of adoption. **28.21**

The 1995 Act has also introduced a formal link between the hearing and the court making a decision relating to adoption. All proposed agency placements and applications relevant to children who are subject to **28.22**

---

60 1978 Act, s. 11.

61 *D and D v. F* (1993) 17 Adoption & Fostering 3-57 and (on appeal) 1994 S.C.L.R. 417. See also 1993 Fam. L.B. 4-5 and 1994 Fam.L.B. 9-7.

62 Foster Children (Scotland) Act 1984, ss.1, 3.

63 See paras 28.52, 28.53.

64 1978 Act, s. 22(1).

65 *ibid.*

66 1995 Act, s. 70.

67 1978 Act, s. 65(3).

68 *A v. Children's Hearing for Tayside Region*, 1987 S.L.T. (Sh. Ct.) 126; *M v. Children's Hearing for Strathclyde Region*, 1988 S.C.L.R. 592; *D v. Strathclyde R. C.*, 1991 S.C.L.R. 185 (Notes).

69 1995 Act, s. 16(1).

supervision requirements must be brought to the attention of the principal reporter by the local authority or approved adoption agency concerned.[70] In the case of all non-agency adoptions notice must be given to the appropriate local authority of the intention to apply for an adoption order.[71] Where, as a result of such notification, the local authority becomes aware that an application to adopt has been or is about to be made in respect of a child who is subject to a supervision order, they must refer the case to the principal reporter.[72] The principal reporter is then bound to arrange for the child's supervision requirement to be reviewed by a hearing.[73] The proposed plan for the child must be discussed by the hearing, which is required to draw up a report providing advice for any court which is subsequently required to come to a decision in relation to the child.[74]

28.23 The principal reporter is obliged, within seven days following the determination of the children's hearing, to send a copy of the hearing's report to the court, the local authority, or the approved adoption society, as the case may be, the child, any relevant person[75] and any safeguarder appointed to safeguard the interests of the child in the children's hearing.[76] In the case of an agency plan for adoption, no proceedings will have been commenced, and so the report cannot immediately be supplied to the court, but the agency is obliged to provide the court with the report when proceedings do commence.[77] The situation is slightly more difficult in the case of a non-agency adoption where proceedings have not been commenced, as there is no person who has an obligation to lodge the report after the petition has been lodged. The existence of a report should, however, be brought to the court's attention by the reporting officer who is charged with ascertaining whether the child is subject to a supervision requirement.[78] The local authority will also be aware of the report. Although it is not one of the matters expressly required to be mentioned in the local authority's own report, it would be appropriate for the referral to the children's hearing to be explained. Where the sheriff receives a report prepared by the children's hearing he or she is obliged to consider the report received before making any adoption order or order declaring the child free for adoption.[79]

Parents, guardians and relatives

Parents

28.24 The term "parent" arises frequently in relation to adoption. It is defined in the 1978 Act[80] as meaning, irrespective of whether or not they are, or have been, married to each other, the mother of a child, where she has

---

[70] 1995 Act, s. 73(4)(c)(ii); 1978 Act, s. 22A(1). See para. 28.15.
[71] 1978 Act, s. 22(1).
[72] 1995 Act, s. 73(5).
[73] *ibid.* s. 73(8)(a)(i).
[74] *ibid.* s. 73(13).
[75] For definition of "relevant person", see 1995 Act, s. 93(2). The definition includes persons who are parents or guardians for the purposes of adoption.
[76] Children's Hearing (Scotland) Rules 1996, r. 22(7).
[77] 1996 Regulations, reg. 22(2).
[78] CCMR, r. 2.26(1)(e). See para. 28.77.
[79] 1995 Act, s. 73(14); CCMR, rr. 2.11(5) and 2.28(7). It is possible that there will be a series of reports from the hearing, as referrals must be made and a review arranged when the local authority make a decision that a child should be placed for adoption (or freed for adoption) and when an application for adoption is pending or about to be made (1995 Act, s. 73(4)(c)(ii), 1978 Act, s. 22A(1)).
[80] 1978 Act, s. 65(1).

parental responsibilities or parental rights; the father where he has such responsibilities or rights; and both parents where both have responsibilities or rights. The reference to having parental responsibilities or parental rights is to be construed as a reference to having any of those rights or responsibilities.[81] Thus a mother or father who has one or more responsibilities or rights, but has lost, or never had, any others remains a parent for the purposes of adoption.

A mother will usually be a parent for the purposes of adoption as she has parental responsibilities and rights by operation of law.[82] She will not be a parent if she has been deprived of all parental responsibilities or rights. She may lose all such responsibilities and rights if the child is already adopted or declared free for adoption[83]; if a parental order is made under section 30(9) of the Human Fertilisation and Embryology Act 1990; or if the court deprives her of all responsibilities and rights under section 11(2)(a) of the Children (Scotland) Act 1995. She will not, however, cease to be a parent for the purposes of adoption if a parental responsibilities order is made transferring rights and responsibilities to the local authority under section 86 of the 1995 Act.[84] The father of a child who was married to the mother at the time of conception or subsequently is also a parent by operation of law,[85] unless he has similarly lost all parental responsibilities and rights. **28.25**

An unmarried father will have parental responsibilities or rights only where he has entered into an agreement in terms of the Children (Scotland) Act 1995, section 4, or when he has been given responsibilities or rights by an order of the court under section 11 of that Act. The relevant responsibilities or rights are those set out in sections 1(1) and 2(1) of the 1995 Act. They include the responsibility to safeguard and promote the child's health development and welfare; the right to have the child living with him or otherwise to regulate the child's residence; the responsibility and right to provide direction and guidance, to maintain personal relations and direct contact, and to act as the child's legal representative. These responsibilities and rights may be imposed or given by the court under section 11 of the Children (Scotland) Act 1995. However, it is submitted that a person with a responsibility or right which is in substance one of the matters mentioned in section 1(1) or 2(1) of the 1995 Act should be treated as a parent. Thus an unmarried father with an award of access made under section 3 of the Law Reform (Parent and Child) (Scotland) Act 1986 (which was repealed by the 1995 Act) will be a parent for the purposes of adoption. **28.26**

In cases where the identity of the father is unclear the traditional principle *pater est quem nuptiae demonstrant* applies, and the mother's husband is presumed to be the father of the child, unless there is evidence to demonstrate that this is not the case. **28.27**

---

81 1995 Act, s. 103(1). "Parental rights" and "parental responsibilities" in this context have the meanings respectively given by ss. 1(3) and 2(4) of the 1995 Act (1978 Act, s. 65(1)).

82 1995 Act, s. 3(1)(a).

83 1978 Act, ss. 12(3) and 18(5).

84 1995 Act, s. 86(3)(a). An assumption of parental rights under the Social Work (Scotland) Act 1968, s. 16 takes effect as a parental responsibilities order and is treated in the same way: 1995 Act, Sched. 3, para. 3.

85 1995 Act, s. 3(1)(b).

28.28 A parent under the age of 16 will generally lack capacity to give a consent having legal effect,[86] but is not prevented from exercising parental rights in relation to his or her child.[87] It is submitted that such a person may therefore give agreement to the adoption of a child. In special circumstances, such as where a parent is *incapax* due to mental illness, a curator *ad litem* may be appointed for the parent.[88] However, a curator for the parent will not be necessary merely because the parent is under the age of 16. A young person of that age may be able to resort to his or her own parent for direction and guidance in such matters.[89] The young person is likely to be capable of instructing a solicitor to advise and represent him or her.[90] A curator *ad litem* will however be desirable where a young person's interests require to be represented, but the curator cannot give agreement to adoption on behalf of the parent.[91]

Guardian

28.29 A guardian of a child is a person appointed by deed or will, or by order of the court to be the guardian of the child.[92] The appointment may have taken effect on the death of a parent, who has acted under section 7 of the 1995 Act, in order to provide a substitute parent. Alternatively the appointment may have been made by the court under section 11(2)(h) of that Act.[93]

Relative

28.30 The term "relative" in relation to a child is defined in section 65(1) of the 1978 Act. It includes a grandparent, brother, sister, uncle or aunt, whether of the full blood or half-blood or by affinity. It also includes a father who was not married to the child's mother at the time of conception or subsequently even though he has no parental responsibilities or parental rights. A relative may trace relationship to the child through an unmarried father.[94] Thus, for example, the sister of an unmarried father will be the relative of the child, and the sister's husband will be a relative by affinity. A mother's aunt will not, however, be a relative, as she is great-aunt to the child, and so not within the statutory list.[95]

Agreement to adoption

28.31 No child may be adopted unless each parent or guardian agrees to an adoption order being made, or agreement is dispensed with by the court.[96] Agreement may be dealt with in the course of a petition for an adoption order. Alternatively it may be dealt with in advance of adoption proceedings, when an application is made for an order declaring a child free for

---

[86] Age of Legal Capacity (Scotland) Act 1991, s. 1(1).

[87] *ibid.* s. 1(3)(g).

[88] *Strathclyde R.C., Petrs*, 1996 S.C.L.R. 109.

[89] See *AB and CB v. X's Curator*, 1963 S.C. 124 at 137. It is not clear whether Lord President Clyde assumes that, where a parent is a minor, the minor's parent will deal with the issue of consent, or simply advise the minor. The Age of Legal Capacity (Scotland) Act 1991 suggests that under the present law a young parent may give the required consent.

[90] Age of Legal Capacity (Scotland) Act 1991, s. 2(4A).

[91] Incapacity to give agreement to adoption is however a ground for dispensation of consent: 1978 Act, s. 16(2)(a).

[92] 1978 Act, s. 65(1).

[93] Appointments which took effect before Nov. 1, 1996 under s. 4 of the Law Reform (Parent and Child) (Scotland) Act 1986 (repealed by the 1995 Act) would have the same effect.

[94] 1978 Act, s. 65(1).

[95] *Re C (minors) (wardship: adoption)* [1989] 1 F.L.R. 222.

[96] 1978 Act, s. 16(1).

adoption.[97] A parent or guardian does not require to know the identity of the persons proposing to adopt the child in order to give agreement to adoption. The agreement must, however, be given freely and with full understanding of what is involved.[98] This means that the parent or guardian must comprehend that the effect of an adoption order will be to extinguish his or her parental responsibilities and rights, and vest parental responsibilities and rights in the adopters. Agreement must be unconditional.[99] A mother cannot give effective agreement to the adoption of her child until six weeks or more have elapsed since the child's birth.[1]

No agreement to adoption is required from a father with no parental responsibilities or rights.[2] It has been held that such a father should not be approached in relation to consent to adoption.[3] Where, however, a child's father has taken an active role in the life of the child, he may have information relevant to the welfare of the child, and be in a position to assist the court in reaching an appropriate decision. The court may hear from such a father in the course of adoption proceedings.[4] **28.32**

Agreement to adoption must be distinguished from agreement to the child being placed for adoption or to an application being made for the child to be freed for adoption. A parent or guardian whose child is being considered for adoption by an adoption agency will be asked to complete a certificate stating whether or not they agree to the agency's plan for the child.[5] Indication of agreement allows the agency to place the child, or commence freeing proceedings, on the basis that the parent is likely to agree to adoption, but the parent is not thereby formally committed to agreeing to adoption. Agreement to adoption will be dealt with formally in the course of adoption or freeing proceedings. **28.33**

If a parent or guardian does not give agreement to adoption the court may be asked to dispense with agreement. Section 16(2) of the 1978 Act provides four grounds upon which agreement may be dispensed with. These are that the parent or guardian: **28.34**

(a) is not known, cannot be found or is incapable of giving agreement;
(b) is withholding agreement unreasonably;
(c) has persistently failed without reasonable cause, to fulfil one or other of the following parental responsibilities in relation to the child—
  (i) the responsibility to safeguard and promote the child's health, development and welfare; or
  (ii) if the child is not living with him, the responsibility to maintain personal relations and direct contact with the child on a regular basis;
(d) has seriously ill-treated the child, whose reintegration into the same household as the parent or guardian is, because of the serious ill-treatment or for other reasons, unlikely.

---

[97] 1978 Act, s. 18(1). For a full description of applications for freeing, see paras 28.135 *et seq.*
[98] *ibid.* s. 16(1)(b)(1).
[99] *ibid.*
[1] 1978 Act, s. 16(4).
[2] *A v. B*, 1955 S.C. 378; *A and B v. C*, 1987 S.C.L.R. 514.
[3] *A and B v. C, supra.*
[4] See para. 28.90.
[5] See para. 28.13.

It is for the petitioner to establish the existence of one or more of these grounds.

28.35 A court asked to consider whether agreement to adoption should be dispensed with is required to approach the matter in two stages. First the sheriff should decide whether, as a matter of fact, one or more of the four grounds for dispensation with agreement is established. Secondly the sheriff will be required to exercise discretion in deciding whether the parent's agreement should be dispensed with, having regard to the criteria set out in section 6 of the 1978 Act.[6]

Authorised courts

28.36 The sheriff court is authorised to make an adoption order, or an order declaring a child free for adoption, or any other order under the Adoption (Scotland) Act 1978, if, at the time when the application is made, the child concerned is within the sheriffdom.[7] The child does not have to reside within the sheriff court district in which the action is commenced. The sheriff has discretion to deal with an application relating to a child from another district within the sheriffdom.[8] It is not, however, possible in an application relating to adoption to prorogate the jurisdiction of a court in another sheriffdom, as section 56 of the 1978 Act makes express provision as to which court is authorised in respect of such actions.

28.37 The Court of Session has jurisdiction in respect of a child resident anywhere in Scotland, and exclusive jurisdiction in relation to children who are not in Great Britain when the application is made.[9] The Court of Session also has exclusive jurisdiction in relation to adoptions which take place under the Hague Convention of 1965.[10]

28.38 The sheriff has power, of his own accord, to remit any action relating to adoption of a child to the Court of Session.[11] An application for an order declaring a child free for adoption falls within this description. A sheriff's decision to remit, or not to remit, to the Court of Session may not be appealed.[12] An adoption or freeing application commenced in the Court of Session may be remitted to the sheriff court where the Court of Session considers that the nature of the action makes this course appropriate.[13] While there is nothing intrinsic to an action relating to adoption or freeing making either court a more suitable forum, there may be another action relating to the child in that court which makes it the more appropriate forum.[14]

28.39 The jurisdiction of the court is further qualified in the case of adoption and freeing applications by matters such as the age of the child, the length

---

[6] *Lothian R.C. v. A*, 1992 S.L.T. 858 at 862D–863D.

[7] 1978 Act, s. 56(1) and (2).

[8] McNeill, paras 2.05, 2.06; by analogy with the sheriff's discretion to grant warrant to cite a defender resident in another district: Dobie, *Sheriff Court Practice*, pp. 52–53; *Tait v. Johnston* (1891) 18 R. 606; *Davidson v. Davidson* (1891) 18 R. 884.

[9] 1978 Act, s. 56(3).

[10] *ibid.* s. 56(4). Hague Convention adoptions are governed by the 1978 Act, s. 17. Only the U.K., Austria and Switzerland are signatories. The procedure is rarely used.

[11] Sheriff Courts (Scotland) Act 1971, s. 37(2A). Such a remit was made in *T, Petr*, 1997 S.L.T. 724.

[12] *ibid.* s. 37(3)(a).

[13] Law Reform (Miscellaneous Provisions) (Scotland) Act 1985, s. 14.

[14] See, *e.g. AB and CD, Petrs*, 1992 S.L.T. 1064; *Tayside R.C., Petrs*, 1987 G.W.D. 9-262.

of time the child has lived with prospective adopters, and the domicile or residence of the applicants.[15]

Timetables for proceedings

28.40 In proceedings relating to adoption there are generally important issues which require to be resolved as soon as possible. The court has a responsibility to ensure that applications are dealt with expeditiously, and parties' representatives should exercise reasonable economy and restraint in the presentation of the case in order to assist in its efficient progress.[16] In those cases in which the court is required to determine whether a parent's agreement to adoption should be dispensed with, the court must draw up a timetable for the case.[17] The timetable should specify the periods within which certain steps must be taken in relation to the proceedings. The court must also give such directions as it considers appropriate for the purpose of ensuring, so far as reasonably practicable, that the timetable is adhered to. It may be apparent from the petition for adoption or freeing, or from an agency or local authority report to the court[18] that such an issue arises, or a parent may indicate to the court that agreement previously given is withdrawn. In any such case the timetable must be drawn up forthwith.[19] The court itself should assume responsibility for management of the case to ensure there is no unnecessary delay.[20]

Privacy

28.41 All proceedings relating to adoption are heard and determined in private.[21] There is no definition of what is meant by the term "in private". Adoption proceedings are intended to be confidential, and, provided this purpose is respected, the sheriff has a discretion in relation to the persons who may be present. Any person whose presence advances the enquiry may be admitted.[22] Persons who have applied for an order relating to parental responsibilities or parental rights in other proceedings, and so have interests to be considered before an adoption order is made, may be parties to the adoption process.[23] The court may hear from an *amicus curiae* in the exceptional cases in which such a person is instructed.[24]

II. Adoption Applications

28.42 An adoption order is an order vesting the parental responsibilities and parental rights in relation to a child in the adopters, made on their application by an authorised court.[25] The order affects parental responsibilities and rights only so far as they relate to the period after the making of the order.[26] From the date of the order the parental responsibilities and

---

15 See paras 28.43 to 28.50, 28.136 to 28.139.

16 *Lothian R.C. v. A*, 1992 S.L.T. 858 at 861D–862D. See also *Strathclyde R.C. v. F*, 1995 G.W.D. 33-1677.

17 1978 Act, s. 25A.

18 See paras 28.64 to 28.66.

19 CCMR, r. 2.4.

20 *Strathclyde R.C. v. F*, 1995 G.W.D. 33-1677.

21 1978 Act, s. 57.

22 *Strathclyde R.C., Petrs*, 1996 S.C.L.R. 109.

23 *AB and CD, Petrs*, 1992 S.L.T. 1064.

24 See *T, Petr*, 1997 S.L.T. 724 at 736E–H.

25 1978 Act, s. 12(1).

26 *ibid.* s. 12(2).

rights of a person who was previously a parent or guardian of the child are extinguished,[27] save in the special case of a step-parent adoptions where the spouse of the adopter may retain parental responsibilities and rights.[28]

Children who may be adopted

28.43 A child may be adopted after attaining the age of 19 weeks where the child was placed with the applicants by an adoption agency or where the application for adoption is made by the parent, step-parent or a relative of the child.[29] The child must have had his home with the applicants or one of them for at least the preceding 13 weeks.[30] In any other case the child must be at least 12 months old and have had his home with the applicants or one of them during the preceding 12 months.[31] A child who is physically absent from the home, because in hospital, or at boarding school, may still have his home with the applicants if that is his or her principal residence.[32] However, the court must be satisfied that there has been sufficient opportunity for the adoption agency, or in the case of a non-agency placement the local authority, to see the child in the home environment with the applicants, or in the case of a married couple both applicants together.[33] A child whose home is overseas may not be adopted in Scotland, even if physically present in the sheriffdom at the date of commencement of proceedings, unless placed by an adoption agency. This is because in a non-agency placement there must be sufficient opportunity for the local authority within whose area the home is to see the child in the home environment. If the home in question does not lie within a local authority area, then this condition cannot be met.[34]

28.44 A child for the purposes of adoption proceedings is a person under the age of 18 years.[35] However, where adoption proceedings are commenced before a person's eighteenth birthday, the adoption may proceed despite that person attaining the age of 18 before the order is made.[36] An adoption order may not, however, be made in relation to a child who is or has been married.[37] A child of 12 years or over must give consent before an adoption order may be made, unless consent is dispensed with on the ground that the child is incapable of giving consent.[38] It is no bar to adoption that a child has been previously adopted.[39] A child of any nationality or domicile may be adopted in Scotland.[40]

Persons who may adopt

28.45 An application for adoption may be made by a single person, or by a married couple. More than one person may not apply to adopt together

---

[27] 1978 Act, s. 12(3).
[28] *ibid.* s. 12(3A). See also s. 39(1)(b).
[29] *ibid.* s. 13(1).
[30] *ibid.*
[31] 1978 Act, s. 13(2).
[32] See, *e.g. A, Petrs*, 1953 S.L.T. (Sh. Ct.) 45; *G, Petr*, 1955 S.L.T. (Sh. Ct.) 27; *cf. M, Petr*, 1953 S.C. 277, *sub nom. S, Petr*, 1953 S.L.T. 220.
[33] 1978 Act, s. 13(3).
[34] *Re Y (Minors) (Adoption Jurisdiction)* [1985] Fam. 136.
[35] See definition in 1978 Act, s. 65(1).
[36] 1978 Act, s. 12(1).
[37] *ibid.* s. 12(5).
[38] *ibid.* s. 12(8).
[39] *ibid.* s. 12(7).
[40] But the Home Office should be advised of an application to adopt a child who does not have British nationality, as adoption by a British citizen will confer citizenship on the child.

unless they are married.[41] Where a cohabiting couple are looking after a child, one of the two may adopt. Both cannot, but an order relating to parental responsibilities and rights may be made in respect of the member of the couple who does not adopt.[42] The sheriff has power to make such an order in the adoption proceedings.[43]

A person is not disqualified from adopting by cohabitation with a person of the opposite, or the same, sex.[44] Save for the special case of a step-parent adoption,[45] a married person who does not petition together with his or her spouse is disqualified unless the court is satisfied that the spouse cannot be found; or that the spouses live separate and apart and the separation is likely to be permanent; or that the spouse is unable to make an application due to ill-health, which may be physical or mental.[46] **28.46**

A child's mother or father may in certain circumstances apply to adopt her or his own child.[47] This formerly had the effect of removing the disadvantages of "illegitimacy", but is now rarely used. The court cannot make an adoption order on the application of a mother or father alone unless the other parent is dead or cannot be found, or where by virtue of the Human Fertilisation and Embryology Act 1990 there is no other parent.[48] Alternatively such an order might be made where there is some other reason to justify the exclusion of the other parent.[49] An example of such a reason might be the commission of serious crime by that parent. The court which makes an adoption order in such circumstances must, however, record the reason justifying the exclusion of the other parent.[50] An adoption order made on the application of one parent may be revoked if the parents subsequently marry,[51] although in the event of such a marriage the child will be rendered the legitimate child of both parents without any further steps being taken.[52] **28.47**

An applicant for an adoption order must be at least 21 years of age[53] (save in the case of step-parent adoption where the natural parent must be at least 18 years of age and the other spouse at least 21).[54] There is no statutory upper age limit for an adopter, although the age of an adopter is a relevant issue when considering whether an adoption order is likely to safeguard and promote the welfare of the child throughout life.[55] **28.48**

A person may not usually apply for an adoption order where he or she has made a previous application for adoption of the same child and the application has been refused. The court is, however, permitted to consider a further application for adoption where the court which refused the **28.49**

---

41 1978 Act, s. 14(1), (1A) and (1B).
42 *Re AB (Adoption: Joint Residence)* [1996] 1 F.L.R. 27.
43 1995 Act, s. 11(1) and (3). See para. 28.11.
44 *T, Petr*, 1997 S.L.T. 724.
45 1978 Act, s. 15(1)(aa); see para. 28.52.
46 *ibid.* s. 15(1)(b).
47 *ibid.* s. 15(3).
48 *ibid.* s. 15(3)(a).
49 *ibid.* s. 15(3)(b).
50 *ibid.*
51 *ibid.* s. 46(1). See paras 28.183 to 28.184.
52 *ibid.* s. 39(2).
53 *ibid.* ss. 14(1A) and 15(1).
54 *ibid.* s. 14(1B). See para. 28.53.
55 *ibid.* s. 6(1)(a). See paras. 28.79 to 28.84 in relation to duties of curator *ad litem*.

previous application directed that another application might be made, or where there has been a change in circumstances, or there are other reasons which mean that it is proper to proceed with the application.[56]

28.50 A person wishing to adopt a child in the sheriff court must either be domiciled in the United Kingdom, the Channel Islands or the Isle of Man, or have been habitually resident in any of these places for the period of one year ending with the date of the application.[57] In the case of a married couple, one of the two must be domiciled in such a place, or both must have been habitually resident for the year preceding the application.[58] Domicile in this context is the common law concept involving either a domicile of origin or a domicile of choice.[59] It is not the concept now found in the Civil Jurisdiction and Judgments Act 1982. The difficulties involved in establishing domicile have been ameliorated by the introduction of habitual residence as a qualification to adopt.[60]

Adoption by person domiciled outwith the United Kingdom

28.51 Where a person is not domiciled in any part of the United Kingdom, he may apply for an order under section 49 of the Adoption (Scotland) Act 1978 which will allow the child to be adopted under the law or within the country in which that person is domiciled. Such an order transfers parental responsibilities and parental rights to the proposed adopter.[61] Only under the authority of an order under section 49 or its equivalent granted by a court in England, Wales or Northern Ireland may a child who is a British subject or a citizen of the Republic of Ireland be removed out of Great Britain to any place outside the United Kingdom, the Channel Islands or the Isle of Man with a view to the adoption of that child by any person other than a parent, guardian or relative of the child.[62] Most of the provisions relating to adoption orders apply to a section 49 order.[63] An adoption agency may make a placement for the purpose of such an adoption, although the child must be 32 weeks old and have had a home with the applicants for at least 26 weeks before an order may be made.[64] In the case of non-agency placements the usual requirements that the child be at least 12 months of age and have lived with the applicants for the preceding 12 months apply.[65]

Step-parent adoption

28.52 Special provisions apply to cases where a step-parent desires to assume parental responsibilities and parental rights by adoption in relation to the child of his or her spouse. Where a person is married to the child's natural parent, and that parent has parental responsibilities and rights in respect of the child, the step-parent alone may make an application for an adoption order.[66] Such an order will confer parental responsibilities and

---

56 1978 Act, s. 24(1).
57 *ibid.* s. 15(2)(a) and (c).
58 *ibid.* s. 14(2)(a) and (c).
59 See Anton with Beaumont, *Private International Law* (2nd ed.), pp. 124–144.
60 By 1995 Act, Sched. 2, paras 8 and 9.
61 1978 Act, s. 49(1).
62 *ibid.* s. 50.
63 *ibid.* s. 49(2).
64 *ibid.* as read with s. 13(1).
65 *ibid.* s. 13(2). See para. 28.43.
66 *ibid.* s. 15(1)(aa).

rights on the applicant, but will not affect the responsibilities and rights of the spouse. The child will be treated as the legitimate child of the marriage between the adopter and the natural parent to whom the adopter is married and not the child of any other person.[67]

Alternatively the child may be adopted by the parent and step-parent together, and become the adopted child of both. Until April 1, 1997 this was the only course available in such circumstances, and it was not popular. However, if the procedure is used, and provided that the step-parent is over the age of 21, the natural parent need only have attained the age of 18.[68] **28.53**

Steps before lodging petition

Appointment of reporting officer

The sheriff may appoint a reporting officer prior to the lodging of an adoption petition.[69] This is an exceptional step, as a reporting officer is usually appointed after the petition for adoption has been lodged.[70] The purpose of an early appointment is to allow a parent or guardian to give formal agreement to a proposed adoption before the proceedings have commenced. This might be necessary where a parent or guardian is about to leave the country, or is seriously ill and anxious to give agreement to adoption. It should, however, be noted that a mother cannot give effective agreement to adoption unless at least six weeks have elapsed from the date of the child's birth.[71] An application for the early appointment of a reporting officer should be made by letter addressed to the sheriff clerk at the court at which it is proposed to commence the proceedings. The letter must specify the reasons for the appointment. It does not require to be intimated to any other person.[72] **28.54**

Protection of identity of petitioner

A petitioner who wishes to prevent his or her identity being disclosed to the person whose agreement to adoption is required may apply to the sheriff clerk for a serial number to be assigned for all purposes connected with the petition.[73] This step must be taken before the petition is presented. The sheriff clerk assigns a number and enters a note of the number opposite the name of the applicant in the register of serial numbers.[74] The contents of the register are confidential and may not be disclosed to any person other than the sheriff.[75] The form of agreement to adoption does not then contain the name or designation of the petitioner, but refers to the petitioner by means of the serial number, specifying the date on which the number was assigned.[76] **28.55**

This procedure is adequate to protect the identity of an applicant if the adoption is not opposed, but where there is opposition the parties will **28.56**

---

[67] 1978 Act, s. 39(1)(b).
[68] *ibid.* s. 14(1B). (The age was changed by the Children Act 1989, Sched.10, para.33, and not by the 1995 Act.)
[69] *ibid.* s. 58(3); CCMR, r. 2.25(4) and (5).
[70] See para. 28.63.
[71] 1978 Act, s. 16(4).
[72] CCMR, r. 2.25(5).
[73] *ibid.* r. 2.24(1).
[74] *ibid.* r. 2.24(2).
[75] *ibid.* r. 2.24(3).
[76] *ibid.* r. 2.24(4).

have access to all documents lodged in process, including reports.[77] For this reason in a case allocated a serial number every document lodged should be edited to exclude the name and designation of the petitioner.

Lodging the adoption petition

The petition

28.57 An application for an adoption order is made by petition in Form 11 of Schedule 1 to the court rules.[78] An application for an order under section 49(1) of the 1978 Act allowing a child to be adopted abroad[79] is made in Form 12,[80] but otherwise proceeds in a similar manner. No special form is prescribed for a step-parent adoption. Where an application is made on behalf of a step-parent who wishes to assume parental responsibilities and rights together with the child's natural parent the application[81] should state that this is the case. To achieve this there should be inserted in the crave at the commencement of the form, after the reference to adoption order, the words "by virtue of section 15(1)(aa) of the Adoption (Scotland) Act 1978". The same amendment should be made in the final crave. At the paragraph identifying the petitioner's spouse there should be added the words "who will retain parental responsibilities and parental rights in respect of the child".

28.58 The standard form for an adoption petition does not refer to habitual residence for one year as an alternative to domicile as qualification to apply for an adoption order[82] and will require amendment in cases where habitual residence is relied upon. The form refers to a child's tutor or curator, although these offices were abolished by the Age of Legal Capacity (Scotland) Act 1991, and the form should be amended to refer simply to the child's guardian(s).

28.59 The applicant may require to crave that the parent's or guardian's agreement to adoption should be dispensed with. The ground or grounds upon which dispensation is sought should be stated in the crave of the petition. The ground or grounds should be stated with reference to the specific provision of subsection 16(2) of the 1978 Act which is being founded on.[83] If an order has been made freeing the child for adoption this must be indicated. It must be stated whether the placement was made by an adoption agency, which must be identified, or notice has been given to a named local authority. The final crave of the petition allows the applicant to seek forenames for the child which may differ from those which the child was given at birth. While the printed form seeks that the child be given the surname of the adopter, and this will accord in most cases with the wishes of the applicant, there is no statutory requirement that the child take the surname of the applicant and a different surname could be specified.

---

[77] CCMR, r. 2.30.

[78] *ibid.* r. 2.21(1). Printed forms are available from the sheriff clerk: AD7 for an application by two person and AD8 for one applicant. Form 11 contains several errors, as mentioned in the following paragraphs. It is unfortunate that more care was not taken in its preparation.

[79] See para. 28.51.

[80] CCMR, r. 2.21(1).

[81] See para. 28.52.

[82] See para. 28.50.

[83] See *X v. Y*, 1994 S.C.L.R. 775.

28.60 The form of petition contains a list of documents which may be lodged with the petition. However, the list in the form conflicts with the court rules[84] in relation to the documents which require to be lodged. It is submitted that only the documents mentioned in the rule should be lodged, and the form of petition should be amended accordingly.

28.61 Where proceedings are instituted in respect of two or more children from the same family a separate form of petition should be used in respect of each child. A different decision could be reached in each case. If an adoption order is made the process will require to be sealed up,[85] but the process is not sealed if an order is refused. On attaining the age of 16 every adopted person is entitled to see his or her own adoption process[86]; but a child is not entitled to see the process which relates to another child, even a child adopted at the same time. Each child should therefore have a separate petition and a separate process. A separate process does not, however, mean that there requires to be a separate proof.[87]

28.62 An adoption petition is an application to the court. It is not served on anyone. A potential respondent will usually first hear of the petition when contacted by the reporting officer appointed by the court.[88] The only formal document to be served is notice of the first adoption hearing.[89]

Documents to be lodged

28.63 The rules[90] provide that the documents to be lodged with each petition are as follows.

(a) An extract of the entry in the Register of Births relating to the child should be lodged.

(b) Where the application is made by a married couple, an extract of the entry in the Register of Marriages relating to their marriage should be lodged. While not specified in the rule, the court will require to see the applicant's marriage extract in an application by a step-parent who wishes to share responsibilities and rights with a spouse.

(c) In the case of a child not placed for adoption by an adoption agency, the applicant must produce three copies of a medical report showing the physical and mental health of the child (including any special needs) and his or her emotional, behavioural and educational development. Such a report covers a wide range of issues and will require a detailed examination of all aspects of the child's health and development. While there is no requirement for the report to be made "on soul and conscience" it is plainly an important document and the court will rely upon the professional qualifications and experience of the medical practitioner who supplies it.

(d) Any report by the local authority required by section 22(2) of the 1978 Act should be lodged. This is the report to be prepared by the authority which receives notice of the intention to apply for an adoption order, and which has made the appropriate investigations.[91]

---

84 CCMR, r. 2.21(2).
85 *ibid.* r. 2.33(1).
86 *ibid.* r. 2.33(2)(a).
87 See para. 28.114.
88 See paras 28.72 to 28.73.
89 CCMR, r. 2.28(3) provides for intimation in Form 7.
90 *ibid.* r. 2.21(2).
91 See paras 28.20, 28.64 to 28.67.

(e) Any report on the suitability of the applicants by the adoption agency which placed the child for adoption should be lodged. Such a report is required by section 23 of the 1978 Act.[92]

(f) Where the child has been declared free for adoption, an extract of the freeing order should be produced.[93]

(g) Any other document founded on by the petitioner in support of the terms of the petition should be lodged. This does not, however, prevent an applicant from lodging documents at a later stage in the proceedings.

The local authority or adoption agency report

28.64 Where a child has been placed for adoption by an adoption agency, the agency must submit to the court a report on the suitability of the applicants and any other matters relevant to the operation of section 6, and it must assist the court in any manner the court may direct.[94] Section 6 specifies the duty of the court to have regard to all the circumstances, taking the need to safeguard and promote the welfare of the child throughout life as the paramount consideration, and also having regard to the child's views and religious persuasion, racial origin and cultural and linguistic background. The Adoption Agencies (Scotland) Regulations 1996 require the agency to report to the court, giving such information on the background and circumstances of the child, his or her family and the persons proposing to adopt as it has been able to discover in accordance with the regulations.[95] Regulation 9 requires detailed enquiries to be made before a child may be placed for adoption. The enquiries must cover, among other matters, the health of the proposed adopters and the child.

28.65 In the case of an application which does not follow an agency placement the applicant must, at least three months before the date of the adoption order, give to the local authority within whose area the child has his or her home notice of his intention to apply for the order.[96] The authority is then obliged to investigate the matter and submit a report to the court.[97] The report must, so far as practicable, cover the suitability of the applicant and any other matters relevant to the operation of section 6.[98] It must also deal with the question of whether the child was placed with the applicant contrary to section 11 of the 1978 Act.[99] A placement is contrary to section 11 where it is made or arranged by a person or body other than an adoption agency and the proposed adopter is not a relative of the child.[1]

28.66 The court rules specify the details to be included in the report of an adoption agency or a local authority. The list of information to be supplied is similar in both cases.[2] It covers matters such as: the family circumstances of the child; an account of the discussions with the parents or guardians of the child, and if appropriate with the child about their

---

92 See paras 28.12, 28.64 to 28.67.
93 See para. 28.165.
94 1978 Act, s. 23.
95 1996 Regulations, reg. 22(1).
96 1978 Act, s. 22(1).
97 *ibid.* s. 22(2).
98 *ibid.* s. 22(3).
99 *ibid.*
1 See para. 28.18.
2 CCMR, r. 2.21(3).

wishes and the alternatives to adoption; information about the petitioners, their household, home and means; considerations arising from the difference in age between the petitioners and child if this is more or less than the normal difference in age between parents and children; and a view on whether adoption is likely to safeguard and promote the welfare of the child throughout life.

Although the court rules provide for these reports to be lodged with the petition,[3] adoption agencies and local authorities often prefer to send their reports direct to the sheriff clerk. If the report is not available to be lodged with the petition the sheriff must pronounce an interlocutor requiring it to be prepared and lodged within four weeks or such other period as the court may allow.[4] It has been held by a sheriff at first instance that the report is not a precondition to an adoption order, and the court may pronounce an order in the absence of such a report, provided there has been sufficient opportunity for the local authority to see the child with the applicant or applicants in the home environment.[5] **28.67**

Curator *ad litem* and reporting officer

Appointment

When a petition for adoption has been lodged,[6] the sheriff must appoint a curator *ad litem* and, unless an order has been made declaring the child free for adoption,[7] a reporting officer. The general duty of a curator *ad litem* is to safeguard the interests of the child.[8] A reporting officer is charged principally with witnessing agreements to adoption.[9] **28.68**

The Children (Scotland) Act 1995 provides for the establishment of a panel of persons to act as curators *ad litem* and reporting officers.[10] The appointment, qualifications and training of such persons and the management and organisation of the panel are to be governed by regulations.[11] The sheriff does not, however, have to appoint a member of the panel. Any suitable person may be appointed to discharge the responsibilities of curator and reporting officer. Only a person employed by any adoption agency placing the child is barred from acting.[12] **28.69**

The sheriff may appoint the same person as curator *ad litem* and reporting officer.[13] It is submitted that the same person should wherever **28.70**

---

3 CCMR, r. 21(2)(d) and (e).
4 *ibid.* r. 2.21(5).
5 *C, Petrs*, 1993 S.C.L.R. 14.
6 CCMR, r. 2.25(1) and (2).
7 Where a child is free for adoption the terms of CCMR, r. 2.25(2) require the appointment of a reporting officer to witness the agreement of the parent or guardian to adoption. Such agreement is in fact completely unnecessary as on the making of the freeing order all parental rights and responsibilities vested in the local authority (1978 Act, s. 18(5)). In consequence no reporting officer should be appointed where there has been a freeing order. This view is reinforced by the terms of CCMR, r. 2.28(2) which do not contemplate the production of any report from a reporting officer when a child has been freed for adoption.
8 1978 Act, s. 58(1)(a); CCMR, r. 2.26(2)(a).
9 *ibid.* s. 58(1)(b).
10 1995 Act, s. 101.
11 Regulations have not yet been made.
12 1978 Act, s. 58(2)(a).
13 *ibid.* s. 58(2); CCMR, r. 2.25(1).

possible be appointed to act in both capacities to save duplication of enquiries and the potential distress this may bring, and to ensure that a fully informed view of what will serve the welfare of the child is given to the court. While the reporting officer is formally charged with discussing the effects of an adoption order with the child's parent,[14] the curator will usually require to form a view about the parent's capacity to care for the child in order to establish whether adoption is likely to safeguard and promote the welfare of the child throughout life. Many of the matters to be investigated are also covered in the adoption agency or local authority report. While such matters merit careful enquiry, and duplication can be justified, investigation by three separate persons may be regarded as unnecessarily intrusive.

28.71 The curator *ad litem* and reporting officer are both obliged to complete their investigations and to report to the sheriff within four weeks from the date of appointment, unless the sheriff allows another period, which might be shorter or longer.[15] The general principle remains that adoption proceedings should be determined with minimum delay. A reporting officer and curator *ad litem* must treat all information obtained in the exercise of his or her duties as confidential and must not disclose any such information to any person unless disclosure is necessary for the proper discharge of duties.[16]

Reporting officer

28.72 A reporting officer has specific duties in terms of the court rules.[17] The reporting officer must witness any agreement executed within the United Kingdom by a parent or guardian to the making of an adoption order. The court rules prescribe a form for this purpose.[18] Where the parent or guardian is not within the United Kingdom it is sufficient evidence of agreement if the usual form of consent is witnessed under one of two alternative provisions.[19] Where the person who executes the form is serving in Her Majesty's Forces, an officer holding commission in any of those forces may witness the signature. In any other case a British diplomatic or consular officer, or any person authorised to administer an oath or affirmation under the law of the place where the consent or agreement is executed, may witness the signature.

28.73 Agreement must be given freely, and with full understanding of what is involved.[20] Whether the form of agreement is witnessed by the reporting officer, or by a person outside the United Kingdom, the reporting officer is responsible for ascertaining that the parent or guardian understands the effect of an adoption order.[21] Where a reporting officer finds that a parent or guardian is incapable of understanding what is involved, this is a matter which should be reported to the court so that the court may consider whether a curator *ad litem* should be appointed for the parent.[22]

---

14 CCMR, r. 2.26(1)(b).
15 *ibid.* r. 2.26(1) and (2).
16 *ibid.* r. 2.30(2).
17 *ibid.* r. 2.26(1).
18 *ibid.* r. 2.23(1) and Form 13 (printed form AD10).
19 *ibid.* r. 2.23(2).
20 1978 Act, s. 16(1)(b)(i).
21 CCMR, r. 2.26(1)(b).
22 See para. 28.28.

28.74 Where a step-parent has applied to adopt the child of a spouse, the spouse who is to retain parental responsibilities and rights must consent to the order which will result in the sharing of those responsibilities and rights with the petitioner, and the form prescribed is varied accordingly.[23]

28.75 In every case where a parent or guardian gives agreement he or she must be advised that agreement may be withdrawn at any time before an order is made, and the reporting officer must confirm that this advice has been given.[24] While the rule specifies that the reporting officer should ascertain that each parent or guardian who is not a petitioner,[25] and whose agreement is required or may be dispensed with, understands the effect of the adoption order sought,[26] this is not a precondition of adoption in cases where the parent or guardian is withholding agreement. In such cases the court is bound to consider whether the agreement may be dispensed with.[27] A reporting officer who is able to find the parent or guardian should ascertain whether alternatives to adoption have been discussed with him or her.

28.76 The reporting officer is charged with ascertaining whether there is any person other than those mentioned in the petition upon whom notice of the petition should be served.[28] The persons mentioned in the petition would normally be the natural father and mother of the child and any guardian.[29] Notice of the petition is not served on any person, but notice is required to be given of the first diet of hearing in relation to the petition, and the reporting officer should consider whether there is any person whose presence would be desirable at that hearing in order to assist the sheriff in the disposal of the case.[30] An unmarried father who is not a parent[31] should not be asked for his agreement to adoption,[32] but he may be a person able to assist the court in consideration of all the circumstances of the case, and in that event the reporting officer should advise that it would be desirable to serve notice of the adoption hearing on him.

28.77 It is also necessary for the reporting officer to ascertain whether the child is subject to a supervision requirement as in such cases the court is required to consider a report from the children's hearing.[33]

28.78 The reporting officer must report in writing on all of the above matters to the sheriff within the four weeks or other period allowed for this purpose.[34]

---

[23] CCMR, r. 2.23(1) and Form 14 (printed form AD17).

[24] *ibid.* r. 2.26(1)(f). Were agreement to be withdrawn, it is, however, likely that the court would be asked to dispense with the parent's agreement, and it may be difficult for the parent to show that the withdrawal of agreement is reasonable: *Re H (infants) (adoption: parental consent)* [1977] 2 All E.R. 339.

[25] See para. 28.52 in relation to step-parent adoption.

[26] CCMR, r. 2.26(1)(b).

[27] *T, Petr*, 1997 S.L.T. 724 at 729H.

[28] CCMR, r. 2.26(1)(d).

[29] See para. 28.59.

[30] See paras 28.90, 2898.

[31] See paras 28.24 to 28.27.

[32] *A and B v. C*, 1987 S.C.L.R. 514.

[33] CCMR, r. 2.26(1)(e). For the duty of the the children's hearing to draw up and the court to consider a report see paras 28.21 to 28.23, 28.92.

[34] *ibid.* r. 2.26(1).

Curator ad litem

28.79 The duties of the curator *ad litem* are more extensive and cover a variety of matters.[35] There is a general duty to safeguard the interests of the child whose adoption is the subject of the petition,[36] but that duty is fulfilled, at least in the first instance, by investigating the matters specified in the court rules and reporting to the court. The curator is not expected to express a view on the law, or to undertake the duties more usually associated with a curator *ad litem* in other types of proceedings.[37] The matters to be covered by the curator's report are set out in the relevant rule of court, but are not organised into any logical or coherent order. As all the matters have to be covered, it is of assistance to the court if the report follows the order of matters in the rule of court, despite the patchwork effect. The general areas to be considered are largely the matters reflected in section 6 of the Adoption (Scotland) Act 1978.

28.80 The curator is charged with ascertaining from the child whether he wishes to express a view and, where the child indicates that he or she does so wish, the curator must ascertain that view and report it to the court.[38] While every other matter investigated by the curator must be included in a written report, the curator may convey the child's views to the sheriff orally.[39] This allows for preservation of confidentiality in appropriate cases.[40] In cases where the child has attained the age of 12 the curator must witness the child's own consent to adoption and lodge this in process.[41] The court rules prescribe a form for the child's consent.[42]

28.81 The curator is obliged to check whether the facts stated in the petition are correct,[43] and to obtain particulars of the petitioner's accommodation, household and means.[44] The general suitability of the petitioner and the child for the relationship created by adoption and any matters which might affect the ability of the petitioner to bring up the child should be considered.[45] The curator is particularly asked to establish the petitioner's religion and the religious persuasion, if any, and racial origin and cultural and linguistic background of the child.[46] If the difference in ages between the petitioner and the child is greater or less than the normal difference between parent and child the considerations which might arise should be assessed.[47] The petitioner's understanding of adoption must be explored together with the reasons why the petitioner wishes to adopt the child.[48]

---

35 CCMR, r. 2.26(2).
36 *ibid.* r. 2.26(2)(a).
37 *T, Petr*, 1997 S.L.T. 724 at 730B–731K.
38 CCMR, r. 2.26(2)(u).
39 *ibid.* r. 2.26(3).
40 See paras 28.86 to 28.87.
41 CCMR, r. 2.26(2)(b).
42 *ibid.* r. 2.23(1) and Form 4. This form refers to the child's signature being witnessed by the reporting officer, although the curator *ad litem* is charged with this task. The reference to reporting officer should accordingly be ignored and the form witnessed by the curator. Printed form AD9 refers correctly to the curator *ad litem*.
43 *ibid.* r. 2.26(2)(c).
44 *ibid.* r. 2.26(2)(d), (e) and (g).
45 *ibid.* r. 2.26(2)(s).
46 *ibid.* r. 2.26(2)(q).
47 *ibid.* r. 2.26(2)(r).
48 *ibid.* r. 2.26(2)(i) and (p).

28.82 The curator must also enquire into the child's history, and in particular when the child's mother ceased to have care and possession of the child and to whom care and possession were transferred.[49] It must be ascertained whether the child has any rights or interests in property and whether the life of the child is insured.[50] If there has been any payment or reward in consideration of adoption this must be mentioned.[51] Such payments are prohibited and making or receiving a payment is usually a criminal offence unless the court which makes the adoption order authorises the payment.[52] An illegal payment does not, however, prevent an adoption order being granted.[53] An approved adoption allowance made by an adoption agency pursuant to a scheme approved by the Secretary of State is not an illegal payment.[54]

28.83 The report by the curator should consider whether it may be in the interests of the welfare of the child that the sheriff make an interim order,[55] or an adoption order subject to particular terms and conditions, or whether the petitioner should be required to make special provision for the child.[56] The curator is expected to reach a view regarding whether adoption is likely to safeguard and promote the welfare of the child throughout life, and whether it would be better for the child that the court should make the order sought than that it should not make the order.[57]

28.84 Great weight is usually given to the report of the curator *ad litem*, who has the opportunity to see parties in an informal way.[58] If the report is overlooked this may in itself be a ground for appeal.[59]

Obtaining the views of the child

28.85 The sheriff is obliged to have regard, so far as practicable, to the views of the child if the child wishes to express a view.[60] The curator *ad litem* is obliged to ascertain from the child whether he or she wishes to express a view, and where the child does wish to express a view to ascertain that view.[61] This is not, however, the only means by which a child may express a view in the course of adoption proceedings. Where the child has indicated a wish to express a view the sheriff may order such procedural steps to be taken as he considers appropriate to ascertain the views of the child.[62] The court must give an opportunity for the views of the child to be obtained or heard before making an order in the adoption proceedings.[63]

---

49 CCMR, r. 2.26(2)(j).
50 *ibid.* r. 2.26(2)(h) and (m).
51 *ibid.* r. 2.26(2)(k).
52 1978 Act, s. 51. See *Adoption Application AA212/86 (adoption: payment)* [1987] 2 F.L.R. 291; *Re A (adoption placement)* [1988] 1 W.L.R. 229; *Re AW (adoption applications)* [1993] 1 F.L.R. 62; *C v. S*, 1996 S.L.T. 1387; *cf. Re C (a minor) (adoption application)* [1993] 1 F.L.R. 87.
53 1978 Act, s. 24(2).
54 *ibid.* s. 51A(3) and the Adoption Allowance (Scotland) Regulations 1996 (S.I. 1996 No. 3257).
55 CCMR, r. 2.26(2)(n). See para. 28.123.
56 *ibid.* r. 2.26(2)(b). See para. 28.120.
57 *ibid.* r. 2.26(2)(l) and (t).
58 *A v. B and C*, 1971 S.C. (H.L.) 129 at 141; *T, Petr*, 1997 S.L.T. 724 at 728B.
59 *Petition of AB and CD to adopt X and Y*, 1990 S.C.L.R. 809 at 811.
60 1978 Act, s. 6(1)(b)(i). See para. 28.10.
61 CCMR, r. 2.26(2)(u).
62 *ibid.* r. 2.27(1)(a).
63 *ibid.* r. 2.27(1)(b).

If the child will not speak to the curator, then another person such as a teacher or a clergyman could be appointed to obtain the views of the child and report these to the court. The child may wish to speak directly to the sheriff. Views could be recorded in writing either by the child, or by a person who sees the child. The sheriff is given no guidance in the rules on how the views of the child might be obtained, but there is no limitation imposed on the court, and the proceedings are investigative in nature.[64]

28.86 The court rules make express provision for the child's views to remain confidential. The curator may convey the views orally to the sheriff, rather than recording these in the report.[65] Whether the child's views are recorded in the curator's report, or in any other document, the sheriff may direct that the written record of the child's views be sealed in an envelope marked "views of the child—confidential", be available to a sheriff only, be not opened by any person other than a sheriff, and shall not form a borrowable part or the process.[66]

28.87 Careful consideration will be necessary before withholding from the parties the views of the child. In reaching any decision relating to adoption the court is bound to weigh the matters mentioned in section 6 of the 1978 Act: paramount consideration should be given to the welfare of the child, and regard had, so far as practicable, to the views of the child, taking account of his or her age and maturity. However, in an English case[67] the House of Lords has stated that the fundamental principle of fairness—that a party is entitled to disclosure of all materials which might be taken into account by the court when reaching a decision—applies with particular force to adoption proceedings. The court should therefore consider whether disclosure of the child's views would involve a real possibility of significant harm to the child. If so, the court should go on to consider whether the overall interests of the child would benefit from non-disclosure, weighing the interests of the child in having the material properly tested against the magnitude of risk that harm would occur and the gravity of the harm if it did occur. If a sheriff is satisfied that disclosure is not in the interests of the child, he or she should as a final step proceed to weigh that consideration against the interest of the parent or other party in having an opportunity to see and respond to the material, taking into account the importance of that material to the issues in the case. There is a tension between the legislation and court rules and the guidance handed down by the House of Lords in the light of the European Convention for the Protection of Human Rights and Fundamental Freedoms.[68] The sheriff is, however, obliged to apply the Scottish legislation and should only resort to the European Convention as a guide where there is ambiguity in the legislation.[69]

Adoption hearing

Notice

28.88 When the reports of the reporting officer and curator *ad litem* are received, the sheriff is obliged to fix a diet of hearing.[70] In the case of a

---

64 See para. 28.01.
65 CCMR, r. 2.26(3).
66 *ibid.* r. 2.27(2).
67 *Re D (minors) (adoption reports: confidentiality)* [1995] 4 All E.R. 385.
68 See especially the case of *McMichael v. UK* (1995) 20 E.H.R.R. 205.
69 See *T, Petr*, 1997 S.L.T. 724 at 733H–734H. But see Human Rights Act 1998.
70 CCMR, r. 2.28(1).

child who is free for adoption it is a matter for the sheriff's discretion whether or not he fixes a hearing on receipt of the curator's report.[71] The petitioner is responsible for intimating the diet to those who require to be involved and a form is prescribed for this purpose.[72] The form gives the place, date and time of the hearing and explains that the court will consider the adoption order, but that the recipient does not need to attend if he or she does not wish to be heard by the court, and that the court may make the order requested if the recipient does not attend. The petitioner must give intimation to every person who can be found and whose agreement to the making of an adoption order is required to be given or dispensed with.[73]

The sheriff has a discretion to ordain the petitioner to serve notice of the date of the hearing in the same form on various other people.[74] Notice may be ordered to be given to any person who has the rights and powers of a parent of the child under section 11 of the Children (Scotland) Act 1995.[75] Section 11 allows the court to make orders relating to parental responsibilities and parental rights. It is assumed that a person entrusted with parental responsibilities would qualify for intimation, in the sheriff's discretion. Where a local authority has secured a parental responsibilities order under section 86 of the 1995 Act, the sheriff may order intimation to the authority.[76] Intimation may also be ordered on any person or body with care of the child or a local authority with care by virtue of section 54 of the Children (Scotland) Act 1995.[77] That is the section which allows the court to refer the case of a child to the principal reporter, who may arrange a children's hearing. It is not clear why children who are subject to supervision requirements for this reason are singled out for intimation to those with their care and the rule is in this respect inept. The sheriff also has discretion to order intimation to any person liable by virtue of any order or agreement to contribute to the maintenance of the child[78] and to the local authority to whom notice of intention to apply for an adoption order was given in a non-agency adoption.[79] Finally, the sheriff has a general discretion to order intimation to any other person or body who in the opinion of the sheriff ought to be served with notice of the hearing.[80] **28.89**

The effect of such intimation is to enable the recipient to appear at the first hearing and make representations about the adoption of the child. This has the further implication that if the case proceeds to a proof that person will be entitled to lead evidence.[81] In effect the person who receives notice of the first hearing and attends the hearing becomes a party to the adoption process. It is not a necessary qualification to becoming a party that a person is the petitioner, or a person whose consent to adoption requires to be given or dispensed with.[82] Where a child is, for example, **28.90**

---

71 CCMR, r. 2.28(2).
72 *ibid.* r. 2.28(3), (4) and Form 7 (printed form AD11).
73 *ibid.* r. 2.28(3)(a).
74 *ibid.* r. 2.28(4).
75 *ibid.* r. 2.28(4)(a).
76 *ibid.*
77 *ibid.*
78 *ibid.* r. 2.28(4)(b).
79 *ibid.* r. 2.28(4)(c).
80 *ibid.* r. 2.28(4)(d).
81 *A and A v. G*, Second Division unreported, Apr. 12, 1994.
82 *AB and CD, Petrs*, 1992 S.L.T. 1064.

subject to competing claims relating to adoption and residence or some other parental responsibility or right, it is likely to be appropriate to give intimation of the adoption hearing to the parties in the other process, so that all matters relevant to the welfare of the child may be brought before the court dealing with the proposed adoption. An unmarried father, who is not required to give agreement before an adoption may proceed, may have information about the welfare of the child which makes it appropriate that he be given notice of the hearing.[83] In one English case the House of Lords considered intimation to the brother of a child with whom she had maintained contact.[84] It is the responsibility of the reporting officer to draw the attention of the court to the existence of any such person, so that the sheriff may consider whether notice should be given.[85]

28.91 Where the child who is the subject of the proceedings is not of British nationality notice of the adoption hearing should be given to the Home Office.[86] Where the real object of adoption proceedings is thought to be the circumvention of immigration controls the Secretary of State may wish to make representations at the hearing.[87]

Hearing

28.92 At the first hearing of the adoption petition, if none of the persons to whom notice has been given appears to be heard, the sheriff may grant the adoption order sought. The court will at that stage have the benefit of the reports by the reporting officer and the curator *ad litem*. It should also have the adoption agency or local authority report, although receipt of this latter report may not be a precondition of adoption.[88] It is, however, a precondition that the sheriff consider the report by the children's hearing in respect of a child subject to a supervision requirement before reaching any decision in relation to the petition for adoption.[89]

28.93 No adoption order may be made unless the child concerned is free for adoption; or each parent or guardian of the child freely and with full understanding agrees unconditionally to the making of an adoption order (whether or not the identity of the applicants is known to the parent or guardian); or the agreement of any parent or guardian who does not agree is dispensed with.[90] The child may be free for adoption by virtue of an order made in Scotland under section 18 of the Adoption (Scotland) Act 1978. He or she may also be free for adoption by virtue of an order made under the equivalent procedure in England and Wales[91] or Northern Ireland.[92] The freeing order should not, of course, have been revoked.[93]

28.94 Where a parent or guardian consents to an adoption order the court will usually have a form of consent witnessed by the reporting officer. In the

---

83 *A and A v. G, supra.*
84 *Re C (a minor) (adoption order: conditions)* [1989] 1 A.C. 1.
85 CCMR, r. 2.26(1)(d). See para. 28.76.
86 *Re W (a minor)* [1985] 3 All E.R. 449; and see 1993 Fam. L.B. 4-5.
87 *e.g. Re H (a minor) (adoption: non-patrial)* [1982] 3 All E.R. 84.
88 *C, Petrs*, 1993 S.C.L.R. 14. See para. 28.67.
89 1995 Act, s. 73(14); CCMR, r. 2.28(7).
90 1978 Act, s. 16(1)(a)(i). See paras 28.31 to 28.35.
91 *ibid.* s. 16(1)(a)(ii).
92 *ibid.* s. 16(1)(a)(iii).
93 See paras 28.185 to 28.193.

case of a parent or guardian outside the United Kingdom consent of a person serving in Her Majesty's Forces witnessed by a commissioned officer, or in any other case by a person authorised to administer an oath, is sufficient evidence. In either case the sheriff may be satisfied that consent is given without any other evidence.[94] In the absence of such evidence, the petitioner may seek to satisfy the sheriff of parental consent by any other available evidence. This may be documentary[95] or oral, although information that a parent is content for the adoption to proceed, and does not intend to oppose the proceedings, is probably insufficient to satisfy the test that the parent "freely and with full understanding of what is involved agrees unconditionally to the making of an adoption order".[96] In such a case, however, the court may treat the withholding of formal consent as unreasonable and dispense with agreement.

Where there is no evidence of parental agreement, no adoption order may be made unless the sheriff is prepared to dispense with the agreement of each parent or guardian. The court may have sufficient information in the reports before it, or from other evidence available at the hearing, to decide that agreement should be dispensed with, and if so it should proceed on that basis.[97] The sheriff has a discretion, which he may exercise at the first hearing, to appoint a curator *ad litem* to a parent or guardian who is *incapax*. Such a course has been approved where a parent suffered from mental illness.[98] **28.95**

If the sheriff is not immediately satisfied that an adoption order may be made, there are various courses open to him. He may order the production of further documents or that oral evidence be led.[99] He may seek further information from the curator *ad litem*.[1] The local authority or adoption agency which has supplied a report to the court may be asked to supply further information.[2] The court has considerable power to order further investigation in an adoption application, and should take appropriate steps to ensure that all necessary enquiries have been made before making a decision on whether to grant or refuse the application.[3] **28.96**

If it appears appropriate to do so, the sheriff may remit the case to the Court of Session.[4] In that court it is open to a Lord Ordinary to report the case to the Inner House for guidance when, for example, there appears to be a conflict of authority on a particular point of law. **28.97**

Where one of the persons to whom notice of the hearing has been given does appear, and wishes to be heard, the sheriff may either there and then hear that person, or order a further diet to be fixed at which he may be heard and evidence led. In straightforward cases, where no issue of substance arises, a sheriff may be persuaded to deal with the adoption **28.98**

---

94 CCMR, r. 2.23. See para. 28.72.

95 Adoption proceedings are civil proceedings, and section 2 of the Civil Evidence (Scotland) Act 1988 applies to permit the admission of hearsay.

96 See *T, Petr*, 1997 S.L.T. 724 at 729G–H.

97 *ibid.*

98 *Strathclyde R.C., Petrs*, 1996 S.C.L.R. 109. See also para. 28.28.

99 CCMR, r. 2.29.

1 *T, Petr, supra*, at 729G–H.

2 1978 Act, s. 23.

3 *J and J v. C's Tutor*, 1948 S.C. 636 at 642; *T, Petr, supra*.

4 Sheriff Courts (Scotland) Act 1971, s. 37(2A). See para. 28.38.

application right away despite the appearance of a party at the first hearing. The party may, for example, have appeared to support the adoption. He or she may not be a person whose agreement to adoption is required and any opposition presented might be obviously fanciful. Where, however, it is apparent that there is an issue relating to the agreement of a parent or guardian, or a question whether the adoption should be granted, the sheriff will usually fix a further diet for the hearing of evidence.

28.99 The first hearing of an adoption petition in a disputed case should be used to establish the area of dispute and the mode and time of enquiry.[5] Parties may accept uncontentious matters of history set out in reports before the court, or may agree to deal with other matters by way of further report or affidavit.[6] The sheriff may consider that the issues in dispute should be focused in written pleadings,[7] but he will no doubt have in mind that that may prolong the proceedings, and he may therefore decide against such a course. It is important that a disputed adoption is determined without delay, and with proper economy and restraint. If a timetable for proceedings has not been set, this will require to be done. It may be necessary for the sheriff to give further directions in relation to the timetable.[8]

Preparation for proof

Pleadings

28.100 There is no requirement for formal pleadings in adoption proceedings. The adoption petition is a formal document, and the printed form usually employed leaves little scope for elaboration of the issues. It will not usually be challenged on the grounds of relevancy. The court is obliged to inquire into the circumstances, unless it is patent that the petition cannot succeed.[9] This is only likely to be the case where, for example, the child or the parties do not satisfy the requirements of the 1978 Act as to age, or some other formal qualification.

28.101 Elaboration of the facts may be found in the reports of the adoption agency or local authority and the curator *ad litem*, but the parties are not responsible for the production of these documents, and they may not therefore represent the matters on which they wish to lead evidence. While those representing the parties are urged to "exercise all reasonable economy and restraint in their presentation of the evidence",[10] this may not be easy where the issues are not properly identified. In appropriate cases the court may give directions designed to clarify the matters in dispute.

28.102 In cases where a parent or guardian is withholding agreement to adoption the form of petition should state the ground or grounds upon which the petitioners are asking the court to dispense with consent.[11] If a

---

[5] *X v. Y*, 1994 S.C.L.R. 775.

[6] See para. 28.112.

[7] See paras 28.100, 28.103.

[8] 1978 Act s. 25A. See para. 28.40.

[9] *Z v. Z*, 1954 S.L.T. (Sh. Ct.) 47. This is, of course, consistent with *J and J v. C's Tutor*, 1948 S.C. 636 and *T, Petr*, 1997 S.L.T. 724.

[10] *Lothian R.C. v. A*, 1992 S.L.T. 858 at 862B.

[11] See *X v. Y*, 1994 S.C.L.R. 775.

parent withholds agreement unexpectedly, the petition may require to be amended to seek dispensation with agreement. The court may direct that the petitioner lodge a statement of the facts to be relied upon.

The rules make no provision for answers. The court may direct that answers be lodged specifying the grounds of opposition.[12] This could be simply in response to the petition, or in response to a statement of facts. Such pleadings have no formal place in adoption proceedings but may assist in focusing the questions for the court. **28.103**

Confidentiality

All documents lodged in process, including the reports of the curator *ad litem* and the reporting officer, are confidential. They are available only to the sheriff, the curator *ad litem*, the reporting officer and the parties. These persons and the sheriff clerk are obliged to treat them as confidential.[13] The documents may not be shown to anyone other than the representatives who must have access to the documents in order to prepare the case. In some courts there is a practice of not allowing copies of reports to be made. This hinders the preparation of the case because it prevents proper access by representatives; and it is submitted that copies should be available to parties and their representatives, although attachment of a notice reminding those concerned of the obligation of confidentiality would be a sensible precaution. **28.104**

Where the sheriff has given a direction that the child's views should remain confidential[14] the parties will not be allowed access to any record of the views of the child. **28.105**

Recovery of documents

In some cases, particularly those where a child has been looked after by a local authority, or has been placed for adoption by an adoption agency, there may be a substantial file of papers relating to the matters in dispute in the possession of the authority or agency. While a case should not be burdened with unnecessary productions, it may be of assistance to parties in the course of preparation to have access to the files relating to the child, his or her family, and the prospective adopters. There may also be medical or educational records relating to the child or parties which are relevant. In such cases a party may lodge a specification of documents and seek commission and diligence for their recovery. Many of the documents in question will be confidential. This does not, however, render them privileged from production, and the sheriff has a discretion to grant commission and diligence when satisfied that the production of the documents sought is necessary for the fair and proper determination of the issues in the case.[15] Parties moving for commission and diligence should be prepared to explain to the sheriff why the documents sought are necessary, given the absence of pleadings. **28.106**

---

12 See *A v. B and C*, 1971 S.C. (H.L.) 129; *W v. C* (1939) Sh.Ct.Rep. 261.
13 CCMR, r. 2.30(1).
14 In terms of CCMR, r. 2.27(2). See paras 28.86, 28.87.
15 *Strathclyde R.C. v. B*, 1997 Fam.L.R. 142.

Medical examinations

28.107 In cases in which the welfare of a child is at issue there has been an increasing trend to seek the advice of experts in child psychology or psychiatry. Such a course was discouraged by the House of Lords in 1971[16] when it was said that medical evidence may be helpful in unusual cases, but that a judge was well able to estimate the probable effect of uprooting a child of tender years and transferring it from adopting parents, with whom it is happy, to its natural parents, of whom it has no recollection. Modern sheriffs may be less confident of their knowledge of child psychology, and modern adoption cases often involve older children whose backgrounds may have been troubled. There is therefore some justification for resort to expert evidence. The court rules now require that information about the physical and mental health of the child and his emotional, behavioural and educational development is placed before the court, either by the petitioner or, in the case of an agency adoption, by the adoption agency.[17]

28.108 Difficulties may, however, arise when there is disagreement between the parties regarding whether the child should be further examined. These difficulties have not been explored in any reported case and there is no guidance available on the subject. A child's parent or guardian may have the responsibility and right to consent to examination, unless the child is of sufficient maturity to deal with this.[18] The persons with whom the child is residing will control access to the child for the purposes of examination. The latter are usually in a position to arrange for the child to be seen by an expert, regardless of any question of formal consent. If one party is able to tender expert evidence of this nature, while the other cannot, an issue of fairness arises.[19] The court does not usually have the power to compel a person other than a party to the action to submit to medical examination,[20] although the High Court in the exercise of its *nobile officium* has compelled a local authority to permit a child victim of an alleged criminal offence to submit to medical examination.[21] If it *is* competent for a sheriff to ordain that a child is examined by one or more experts, then the question of whether he or she should do so is, as is the case with all decisions relating to adoption, governed by the provisions of section 6 of the Adoption (Scotland) Act 1978: the need to safeguard and promote the welfare of the child is the paramount consideration; regard must be had to the child's views; and any religious or cultural implications of an examination should be considered.

Proof

28.109 A proof will take place in adoption proceedings if the sheriff has decided at the first hearing that he wishes oral evidence to be led[22] or where a person entitled to appear wishes to be heard and the sheriff has decided that

---

[16] *A v. B and C*, 1971 S.C. (H.L.) 129 at 142.

[17] CCMR, rr. 2.21(2)(c); 2.21(3)(c).

[18] Age of Legal Capacity (Scotland) Act 1991, s. 2(4).

[19] In cases where one party was able to tender medical evidence that there could not have been adultery because the alleged paramour was *virgo intacta* and the other party could not tender any contrary evidence, the court has excluded the evidence altogether: *Mitchell v. Mitchell*, 1954 S.L.T. (Sh. Ct.) 45; *Davidson v. Davidson* (1860) 22 D. 749; *Borthwick v. Borthwick*, 1928 S.N. 155.

[20] *ibid.*

[21] *K, Petr*, 1986 S.C.C.R. 709.

[22] CCMR, r. 2.29.

evidence should be led.[23] In practice most proofs will take place in order that the sheriff may determine whether the agreement to adoption of a parent or guardian should be dispensed with.[24] The proceedings must be heard in private unless the court otherwise directs.[25] Evidence must be given in the presence of the petitioner or his solicitor.[26]

Parties' representatives should assist the court by giving a carefully considered forecast of the time which the proof is expected to take. Arrangements can then be made for the sheriff to be released from other duties so that he can give priority to the case, without interruption, until it has been completed by the issuing of the final interlocutor. The Inner House has given guidance that such special arrangements are necessary so that the sheriff can maintain the continuity of thought throughout the proceedings which is necessary to a proper disposal of the case. Representatives should exercise all reasonable economy and restraint in their presentation of the evidence and submissions to the court.[27] **28.110**

The principal duty of representatives in adoption proceedings is to identify the issues in dispute, and to lead evidence in relation to those issues. Without the benefit of written pleadings this can be a difficult task, but a lengthy and poorly focused proof will not serve the interests of the parties or the child. In the event of an appeal it may mean that the Inner House will not be able to consider notes of evidence because they are too voluminous to put before the court.[28] **28.111**

Consideration should be given to what matters may be agreed. The history as set out in the reports before the court may not be in dispute. There may be other documents which are capable of being agreed. Evidence may be presented in the form of affidavits. While the Ordinary Cause Rules as to the admission of affidavits do not apply, the Civil Evidence (Scotland) Act 1988, section 2, does apply, and the sheriff may receive evidence in the form of affidavits or other written documents.[29] The strict rules of evidence do not apply in adoption proceedings,[30] and the sheriff may, and indeed should, have regard to the reports before him, whether or not any witness is called to speak to them. **28.112**

The reporting officer and the curator *ad litem* are officers of the court and as such are not usually called to give evidence. Where, however, there is a matter in a report which one of the parties, or the court, wishes to have clarified, there is no reason in principle why the curator should not give evidence, although in practice the consent of the sheriff should be sought before a party cites the reporting officer or curator. **28.113**

Where the court is dealing with different petitions relating to children of the same family, it is not necessary to hold separate proofs. To do so **28.114**

---

23 CCMR, r. 2.28(6).
24 See para. 28.34.
25 1978 Act, s. 57. See para. 28.41.
26 CCMR, r. 2.28(6).
27 *Lothian R.C. v. A*, 1992 S.L.T. 858 at 861J–862C.
28 *ibid.*
29 On one view he has no discretion to refuse such evidence, see *McVinnie v. McVinnie*, 1995 S.L.T. (Sh.Ct.) 81; *Glaser v. Glaser*, 1997 S.L.T. 456.
30 *T, Petr*, 1997 S.L.T. 724 at 730L; *Petition of AB and CD to adopt X and Y*, 1990 S.C.L.R. 809 at 811.

would be uneconomic and potentially unjust as different sheriffs could come to different decisions on the basis of similar evidence. There is precedent for the holding of a single proof,[31] and no reported case of separate proofs. The Inner House has approved a sheriff holding a proof in adoption proceedings and then making orders both in relation to adoption and related proceedings concerning parental responsibilities and rights.[32] Where there is more than one petition or action, interlocutors will require to be pronounced in each, and findings in fact made in relation to each.

28.115 While the Ordinary Cause Rules do not apply to an adoption application, the Inner House have approved the practice of making findings in fact following an adoption proof.[33] It is customary to instruct a shorthand writer in an adoption proof.[34] An adoption is an intrinsically important matter and, without a record of the evidence, findings in fact could not be challenged on appeal.

Orders

Adoption

28.116 Where the conditions of the 1978 Act in relation to the child, the adopters, and the consent of the parent or guardian are satisfied, the sheriff has a discretion as to whether to grant an adoption order. That discretion must be exercised on the basis of the criteria in section 6. In addition the sheriff cannot make an adoption order unless he or she considers that to do so would be better for the child than not to do so.[35]

28.117 Where adoption is granted following an agency placement, the order must specify the name and address of the agency which has taken part in the arrangements for placing the child in the care of the petitioner.[36] This information will be of assistance if the adopted person later wishes to trace details of the adoption and his or her family of origin. An adoption order is not usually extracted. An extract may be issued with the authority of the sheriff who made the order or, in that sheriff's absence, the sheriff principal.[37] Although the rule states that a petition is required before an extract may be issued,[38] an extract has been authorised by the Inner House without a petition where an adoption order contained terms or conditions.[39]

28.118 An adoption order will contain a direction to the Registrar General for Scotland to make an entry recording the adoption in the Adopted Children Register, with the names by which the child is to be known following the adoption.[40] A certified copy of the order is sent by the sheriff clerk to the Registrar General in an envelope marked "Confidential" by

---

31 *R v. O; G v. O; S v. O* (unreported, but referred to by Sheriff P. G. B. McNeill in *Adoption of Children in Scotland*, para. 6.10). See also *AB v. CB*, 1985 S.L.T. 514.

32 *AB and CD, Petrs*, 1992 S.L.T. 1064.

33 *Lothian R.C. v. A*, 1992 S.L.T. 858 at 865L.

34 *X v. Y*, 1994 S.C.L.R. 775.

35 1978 Act, s. 24(3).

36 CCMR, r. 2.32. No form of adoption order is prescribed, but printed form AD13 may be used by the sheriff clerk.

37 *ibid.* r. 2.32(2). See para. 28.196.

38 *ibid.* r. 2.32(3).

39 *B v. C*, 1996 S.L.T. 1370 at 1377 D. In relation to terms and conditions, see para. 28.120.

40 1978 Act, Sched. 1, para. 1.

recorded delivery post or by personal delivery.[41] The applicants will thereafter be able to obtain from the Registrar General an extract of the entry in the Adopted Children Register.

Termination of supervision requirement

When making an adoption order in relation to a child who is subject to a supervision requirement the sheriff may terminate the requirement.[42] The supervision requirement is thereby brought immediately to an end without the need for further review by the children's hearing. The sheriff clerk is obliged to intimate the termination of the requirement to the principal reporter.[43] **28.119**

Terms and conditions

An adoption order may contain such terms and conditions as the court thinks fit.[44] Conditions should only rarely be imposed as they fetter the exercise of parental responsibilities and parental rights with which adopters are entrusted when an adoption order is made.[45] Conditions have been imposed, for example, requiring adopters to use their best endeavours to secure that a child be made aware of his black identity and be brought up with a knowledge of his ethnic origins and traditions.[46] Conditions have also been used to allow continued contact between a child and his biological parents[47] or another member of the child's family,[48] although this should only happen in very exceptional cases as in normal circumstances it is desirable that there be a complete break from the child's natural family on adoption.[49] In such a case the court may issue an extract of the adoption order[50] in order to enable parties to return to the court for further orders relating to contact, if required. Such a condition does not confer any parental right on the person who is able to continue to maintain contact with the child, but it does confer an enforceable right in terms of the order of the court. Any person involved, whether a person benefiting from thc condition, the adopters, or the child, may apply to the court in the adoption process if further consideration of the condition is required.[51] Such an application would probably require an application to the sheriff for the adoption process to be re-opened.[52] **28.120**

Section 11 orders

The sheriff may, in adoption proceedings, make an order in relation to parental responsibilities and rights under section 11 of the Children (Scotland) Act 1995.[53] He or she could, for example, refuse an adoption order but make a residence order pursuant to which the child was to live **28.121**

---

41 CCMR, r. 2.31.
42 1978 Act, s. 12(9).
43 CCMR, r. 2.33(3)(a).
44 1978 Act, s. 12(6).
45 *Re S (a minor) (blood transfusion: adoption order condition)* [1994] 2 F.L.R. 416.
46 *AH and PH, Petrs*, 1997 Fam.L.R. 84.
47 *B v. C*, 1996 S.L.T. 1370 at 1377G–J.
48 *Re C (a minor) (adoption order: conditions)* [1989] A.C. 1.
49 *B v. C, supra.*
50 Extracts are not usually issued. See para. 28.117.
51 *B v. C, supra*, at 1376B–D and 1377D–F.
52 In terms of CCMR, r. 2.33(2)(c). See para. 28.196.
53 1995 Act, s. 11(1) and (3)(b).

with the applicants.[54] This would give parental responsibilities and rights to the applicants, if they did not previously have such rights, without irrevocably depriving the child's parent or guardian of responsibilities and rights. An adoption order could be granted, but parental responsibilities and rights given to a cohabitee of the adopter, in order to secure the child in a family unit.[55] This is consistent with the nature of adoption.

28.122 There is, however, a potential overlap between the sheriff's power to make orders under section 11, and the power to make an adoption order subject to terms and conditions. If the sheriff may make a residence order, he or she may also make a contact order, or other order conferring parental responsibilities or rights upon a natural parent. It may, however, be argued that to do so would be inconsistent with the fundamental nature of adoption, and that had Parliament intended that parents divested of responsibilities and rights by an adoption order could be reinvested with responsibilities or rights at the same time, this would require to be expressly stated.[56] The 1995 Act itself, in section 11, confirms that a parent whose responsibilities and rights have been extinguished on the making of an adoption order is deprived of any future right to apply to the court for an order relating to parental responsibilities or rights. The relationship between section 11 and adoption has yet to be explored.

Interim orders

28.123 In cases where the sheriff has reservations about an adoption order, he or she may consider granting an interim order.[57] This is an order giving parental responsibilities and parental rights to the applicants for a probationary period not exceeding two years. Where the period of the original order is less than two years, it may be extended by a further one, provided the total duration of the probationary period does not exceed two years in all.[58] The court may make the order subject to terms as to aliment and otherwise as it thinks fit.[59] This means that the court has the power to impose conditions when making an interim order. The child's parent or guardian must have agreed to the making of an adoption order, or agreement must have been dispensed with.[60] Where the child was not placed for adoption by an adoption agency, notice of intention to adopt must have been given to the local authority.[61]

Referral to principal reporter

28.124 A sheriff in adoption proceedings may refer the child to the principal reporter, if satisfied that any of the conditions for referral to the children's hearing is fulfilled.[62] The sheriff must specify which condition applies. While there is no express bar on referral in cases where there has been no

---

[54] This power replaces the former power (found in section 53 of the Children Act 1975, repealed by the 1995 Act) to make an order for custody in favour of persons who had applied for adoption.

[55] *Re AB (Adoption: Joint Residence)* [1996] 1 F.L.R. 27.

[56] See *D v. Grampian R.C.*, 1995 S.L.T. 519.

[57] 1978 Act, s. 25(1).

[58] *ibid.* s. 25(2).

[59] *ibid.* s. 25(1).

[60] *ibid.*

[61] *ibid.*

[62] 1995 Act, s. 54(1) and (2).

oral evidence, the sheriff may be reluctant to find that a condition exists without hearing proof. If the sheriff does find that there is a condition for referral, the interlocutor to this effect must be intimated forthwith by the sheriff clerk to the principal reporter.[63] The principal reporter will make such investigation as he thinks appropriate and, if he considers that compulsory measures of supervision are necessary, he will arrange a children's hearing.[64] The condition specified by the court will then be treated as an established ground of referral, without any further referral to the sheriff.[65]

In cases where the sheriff is concerned about a child, but unable on the basis of the information before him to make a formal finding that a condition for referral exists, information about the child may be supplied to the principal reporter for him to investigate in the usual way.[66] **28.125**

Refusal of adoption

Where an adoption order is refused, a child placed for adoption by an adoption agency must be returned to the agency within seven days, or such extended period of up to six weeks as the court may allow.[67] In cases where the child is looked after by the local authority the authority may continue to allow the child to remain with the applicants as foster carers. Where the child is subject to a supervision requirement, his or her residence will be subject to any condition imposed by the children's hearing. **28.126**

When an adoption order has been refused by any British court, the applicants are barred from bringing further adoption proceedings in relation to the child unless the court, on refusing the order, directs that this provision should not apply, or there is a change in circumstances.[68] A court refusing an adoption order should therefore be asked to consider whether the refusal is intended to be final. In unusual cases the court on refusing adoption may wish to leave open the possibility of a future application. **28.127**

Expenses

The sheriff may make such order with regard to expenses as he or she thinks fit, and may modify such expenses or direct them to be taxed on such scale as he or she may determine.[69] The sheriff's discretion extends to the expenses of the reporting officer and curator *ad litem* and any other person who attended a hearing.[70] In practice it is rare for an order for expenses to be made in an adoption application. **28.128**

Where a reporting officer and curator *ad litem* is a member of the panel of reporting officers and curators, the local authority will usually meet expenses and pay a small fee. In cases where the sheriff appoints **28.129**

---

63 CCMR, r. 2.3.
64 1995 Act, s. 54(3).
65 *ibid.*
66 *ibid.* s. 53(2)(b).
67 1978 Act, s. 30(3) and (6).
68 *ibid.* s. 24(1).
69 CCMR, r. 2.2.
70 *ibid.*

a reporting officer or curator who is not a member of the panel, or where the local authority does not, for any reason, meet the fees and expenses of a panel reporting officer or curator, the sheriff should make an order relating to such fees and expenses. It is usual for these to be met by the petitioner, at least in the first instance, subject to any order the sheriff may make as to expenses at the conclusion of the proceedings. An order for expenses may only be made against a party to any proceedings.[71] Therefore the sheriff cannot ordain the local authority to pay the fee, unless the local authority has become a party to the proceedings.

Final procedure

28.130 An adoption order contains a direction to the Registrar General for Scotland to make an entry in the Adopted Children Register.[72] The sheriff clerk sends a certified copy of the order to the Registrar General for Scotland.[73] Extracts of the entry in the Adopted Children Register may be secured in place of an extract entry from the Register of Births. The child's entry of birth is marked "Adopted".[74] A register is maintained in which is recorded the connection between the entry of birth and the entry in the Adopted Children Register.[75] When the adopted person attains the age of 16 he or she may have access to that register.[76] Access may also be given to a local authority or adoption society providing counselling for the adopted person.[77]

28.131 Once the sheriff clerk has communicated the order to the Registrar General, or where an extract adoption order is issued, immediately following the issue of the extract the sheriff clerk must seal up the process in an envelope marked "Confidential".[78] The envelope will remain sealed for 100 years, save for authorised access.[79] The process may be produced to the adopted child, after that child has attained the age of 16 years.[80] The sheriff clerk may unseal the process to ascertain the name of the adoption agency responsible for the placement, on application by an adoption agency with the consent of the adopted person.[81] The sheriff may authorise access to the process, on application by a person setting forth the reason why access is required.[82] A court, or other body, within or outside the United Kingdom, with power to authorise adoption, may petition the sheriff court which granted an adoption order requesting information for the purpose of considering an application for adoption. The petition must specify the precise reasons for which access is required.[83] The Secretary of State may authorise access for the purposes of research intended to improve the

---

[71] *Meekison v. Uniroyal Englebert Tyres Ltd*, 1995 S.L.T. (Sh. Ct.) 63.
[72] 1978 Act, s. 45(1) and Sched. 1, para. 1(1).
[73] *ibid.* Sched. 1, para. 1(7). CCMR, r. 2.31.
[74] *ibid.* Sched. 1, para. 1(5).
[75] *ibid.* s. 45(4).
[76] *ibid.* s. 45(5).
[77] *ibid.*
[78] CCMR, r. 2.33(1).
[79] *ibid.* r. 2.33(2).
[80] *ibid.* r. 2.33(2)(a).
[81] *ibid.* r. 2.33(2)(b).
[82] *ibid.* r. 2.33(2)(c).
[83] *ibid.* r. 2.33(2)(d). This process appears to have been used in *T, Petr*, 1997 S.L.T. 724 (see 734L) to give access for the Inner House to unreported decisions relating to adoption by a homosexual and by a lesbian.

working of adoption law and practice.[84] There is no requirement to seal up the process when an adoption order is refused.

Appeals

There is no express provision for appeals from adoption orders, but such orders are regularly appealed, both to the sheriff principal and to the Court of Session. It is accepted that the general provisions for appeal found in the Sheriff Courts (Scotland) Act 1907 apply to adoption orders. An adoption order is a final interlocutor which may be appealed without leave.[85] Other interlocutors will usually require leave to appeal, although the Inner House has been prepared to entertain an appeal relating to a matter of competency in adoption without leave, rather than allow an order to be made which would be subject to later challenge, thus delaying the determination of the proceedings.[86] **28.132**

In cases involving adoption the appellate court is generally reluctant to interfere with the decision of the sheriff who has seen parties. Unless the sheriff has misdirected himself or herself in law or otherwise gone clearly wrong, an appeal will usually be refused.[87] An appellate court may request a report from the sheriff giving further explanation of the conclusion he or she has reached.[88] Where there has been a misdirection in law, the appeal court may remit the case to the sheriff in order that the sheriff may exercise his or her discretion on the correct basis.[89] A case may also be remitted for further evidence where the sheriff has failed to make sufficient enquiry into the facts.[90] Adoption appeals are unusual in that the appeal court may consider the matter on the basis of the situation at the date of the appeal, and is not necessarily confined to consideration of whether the sheriff erred on the basis of the information presented at the date of the hearing or proof.[91] Thus a case may be remitted for further up-to-date evidence.[92] A sheriff principal may himself be prepared to hear further evidence.[93] Where the sheriff has clearly erred, the appeal court may be prepared to decide the matter anew on the basis of the information available.[94] Where extended shorthand notes are available it may be necessary to adjust the sheriff's findings in fact.[95] The appeal court may itself apply the correct criteria to the appropriate findings in fact, and could come to the conclusion that the final decision reached by the sheriff should not be disturbed,[96] or may allow the appeal. **28.133**

The effect of the marking of an appeal is usually to suspend the operation of the order appealed.[97] Some doubt is cast on this principle **28.134**

---

84 CCMR, r. 2.33(2)(e). See para. 28.196.

85 1907 Act, ss. 27 and 28(1).

86 *AB v. CD, Petrs*, 1992 S.L.T. 1064.

87 *A v. B and C*, 1971 S.C. (H.L.) 129, *per* Lord Reid at 141 and *per* Lord Simon of Glaisdale at 147; *Re D (an infant)* [1977] A.C. 602, *per* Lord Simon of Glaisdale at 637.

88 *A and B v. C*, 1977 S.C. 27.

89 *AB and CB v. X's Curator*, 1963 S.C. 124.

90 See, *e.g. C v. D*, 1968 S.L.T. (Sh. Ct.) 39.

91 See *A v. B and C*, 1971 S.C. (H.L.) 129 at 143 and 147–148.

92 *R. v. Lothian R.C.*, 1987 S.C.L.R. 362; *Strathclyde R.C. v. A*, First Division Jan. 29, 1993, unreported.

93 *Sanderson v. McManus*, 1995 S.C.L.R. 902, although this was not an adoption case.

94 See *T, Petr*, 1997 S.L.T. 724.

95 *P v. Lothian R. C.*, 1989 S.L.T. 739; *Central R.C. v. M*, 1991 S.C.L.R. 300.

96 See, *e.g. P v. Lothian R. C., supra.*

97 *Macleay v. Macdonald*, 1928 S.L.T. 463; *Kennedy v. M*, 1993 S.L.T. 717.

in the case of an adoption order by the provisions of paragraph 4(3) in Schedule 1 to the Adoption (Scotland) Act 1978, which provide for an appeal court to direct the Registrar General to cancel any entry in the Adopted Children Register in the event of a successful appeal against an adoption order. It is, however, submitted that this paragraph is intended to provide for the possibility that a direction to the Registrar General has been dispatched by the sheriff clerk and acted upon before the marking of an appeal, and not an indication of an intention on the part of Parliament that an adoption order should change a child's status pending appeal. It would be entirely unsatisfactory for the child's legal position to change following the sheriff's order, only to revert after a successful appeal. The difficulties arising would be particularly acute in relation to matters such as succession. It is submitted that a better view of the law is that the normal rule relating to the effect of taking an appeal applies, and there is no change of the child's status until the appeal has been determined.

III. Freeing for Adoption

28.135 An order declaring a child free for adoption in terms of section 18 of the Adoption (Scotland) Act 1978 has the effect that the child may thereafter be adopted without any issue arising as to the agreement of the child's parent or guardian.[98] The procedure was introduced on September 1, 1984.[99] The original intention was to allow single mothers to relinquish their babies without having to wait for the child to be settled into a new family. The procedure has been more frequently used by local authorities in difficult and contentious cases to resolve the question of parental agreement to adoption in advance of handing responsibility for the child to prospective adopters. Since April 1, 1997 local authorities have been obliged to make an application under section 18 in cases where a parent or guardian is opposed to adoption.[1] When a freeing order is made, parental responsibilities and rights in relation to the child are transferred to the local authority.[2]

Children who may be freed for adoption

28.136 A freeing order may be made in respect of a person under the age of 18.[3] Where the child is 12 or over he or she must consent to the making of a freeing order, unless the court is satisfied that the child is incapable of giving consent.[4]

28.137 Before an application is made to free a child for adoption, the parent or guardian of the child will have been asked for agreement to the proposal that the child be placed for adoption or freed for adoption, in terms of the Adoption Agencies (Scotland) Regulations 1996.[5] In cases where the child's parent or guardian does not agree with the proposed application to free the child for adoption, a freeing application is incompetent unless

---

98 1978 Act, s. 16(1)(a).
99 Adoption (Scotland) Act 1978 Commencement Order 1984 (S.I. 1984 No. 1050).
1 See para. 28.14.
2 1978 Act, s. 18(5).
3 See definition of "child" in 1978 Act, s. 65(1).
4 1978 Act, s. 18(8).
5 regs 14 and 15. See para. 28.13.

the child is being looked after by the local authority.[6] There are several categories of children looked after by the local authority, and these are listed in section 17(6) of the Children (Scotland) Act 1995. The child may be provided with accommodation by the authority in terms of section 25 of the 1995 Act. There may be a supervision requirement in respect of the child made by the children's hearing. A child is looked after when there is an order made, or authorisation or warrant under Chapters 2, 3 or 4 of Part II of the 1995 Act which has the effect that the local authority has responsibilities as respects the child. This may be, for example, a child protection order, or a warrant issued by the children's hearing authorising the child to be kept in a place of safety, although it is unlikely that there will be an application to free when the child is subject only to short-term measures of this nature. The provision does, however, also cover the case where a parental responsibilities order has been made under section 86 of the 1995 Act. Such an order transfers parental responsibilities and rights to the local authority. Finally, a child may be looked after if there is an order made by a court in England and Wales or Northern Ireland, which is similar in nature to an order under Part II of the Children (Scotland) Act 1995, or similar to a supervision requirement, and is recognised as such in regulations, for the purposes of freeing.[7] The local authority seeking a freeing order must prove that the child falls within one of these categories.

When the court is asked to dispense with the agreement to adoption of **28.138** the parent or guardian, the child must have been placed for adoption, or it must be likely that the child will be placed for adoption.[8] Placement for adoption is formal placement pursuant to the Adoption Agencies (Scotland) Regulations 1996. The regulations do not prohibit placement while an application to free a child is pending. However, agencies may refrain from making a placement while freeing proceedings are pending. In such cases they should be prepared to explain to the court the steps they propose to take to find a placement for the child, and the prospects of success. It is for the local authority to prove that the child has been placed or is likely to be placed for adoption.

Applicants for freeing order

Only a local authority may make an application for an order that a child **28.139** be declared free for adoption.[9] Approved adoption societies lost the power to make such an application when Part II of the Children (Scotland) Act 1995 was implemented on April 1, 1997.[10] Although parental responsibilities and parental rights pass to the local authority on the making of a freeing order,[11] such an order is designed to be a temporary expedient pending the adoption of the child.[12]

---

[6] 1978 Act, s. 18(2). The section refers to the child being "in the care of the adoption agency", but this must be taken as a reference to the child being looked after by the local authority in terms of s. 17(6) of the 1995 Act; 1978 Act, s. 65(6).

[7] 1995 Act, s. 33(1).

[8] 1978 Act, s. 18(3).

[9] *ibid.* s. 18(1).

[10] 1995 Act, s. 98 and Sched. 2, para. 11(a).

[11] 1978 Act, s. 18(5).

[12] See 1996 Regulations, reg. 21 which requires an agency to review the case of a child who has not been placed for adoption within six months of freeing. See also provisions for information to former parents and revocation of freeing order, paras. 28.185 to 28.191.

Parental consent and agreement in freeing applications

28.140 There are two different consents relevant to an application to free a child for adoption. The first is consent to the local authority making an application for a freeing order.[13] The second is agreement to the ultimate adoption of the child.[14]

28.141 The court requires to know whether a freeing application is made with the consent of the parent or guardian, because in the absence of such consent the local authority must prove that the child is being "looked after" by the authority[15] and the authority must also apply for dispensation with agreement to adoption. Further, the local authority cannot make use of the freeing procedure where a parent agrees to adoption but does not consent to adoption being achieved by means of an application for an order declaring the child free for adoption.[16] A parent may wish to entrust the child directly to adopters rather than allow the local authority to take over parental responsibility, and thus distance the parent from the final adoption process.

28.142 The local authority should, before starting proceedings, ask a parent or guardian for consent to its proposal to seek a freeing order, or place a child for adoption, under the regulations which apply to adoption agencies.[17] Difficulties arise where the parent or guardian consents to the making of an application to free a child for adoption. He or she will have completed a certificate to this effect in terms of the regulations. However, the court rules provide yet another form of consent to the application.[18] The latter, if duly executed, is sufficient evidence of consent to the application.[19] Due execution requires that the reporting officer witness the form. A reporting officer is not usually appointed until after the proceedings commence, although there is provision for an earlier appointment.[20] Consent to the application will usually require to be taken before the application commences. The form of petition provides for consent to the application, where available, to be lodged with the application.[21] Local authorities thus have the choice of relying on the certificate of consent provided under the adoption agencies regulations, and they will then have to satisfy the court that the consent was duly given; or asking for a reporting officer to be appointed before the proceedings begin, in order to secure a form of consent witnessed by the reporting officer.

28.143 In the event that the authority relies on its own certificate, the reporting officer is still required to present the parent or guardian with the form prescribed in the court rules and to witness any consent.[22] This raises the possibility of a change of heart on the part of a parent. Alternatively, a parent may not see the point of completing another form and may decline

---

13 1978 Act, s. 18(2)(a).
14 *ibid.* s. 18(1)(a).
15 *ibid.* ss. 18(2)(b) and 65(6). See para. 28.137.
16 *ibid.* s. 18(2).
17 1996 Regulations, regs 14 and 15.
18 CCMR, Form 3 (printed form AD 15).
19 *ibid.* r. 2.6(1).
20 *ibid.* r. 2.7(3). See para. 28.147.
21 *ibid.* Form 1 (*cf.* printed form AD); see para. 28.147.
22 *ibid.* r. 2.8(1)(a).

to do so. It is submitted that, where a parent has agreed to the making of the application, and then withdraws support after proceedings have commenced, this does not change the fact that the application was made with consent. The court's form is thus at best otiose and at worst confusing. If a parent does experience a change of heart, the application cannot in any case be granted unless the parent agrees to adoption, or consent is dispensed with.

In the course of the application the court must be satisfied that the parent or guardian agrees to the making of an adoption order, or that agreement may be dispensed with on one of the usual four grounds.[23] The parent is not asked to agree to the freeing order being made.[24] He or she is asked to give advance agreement to the ultimate adoption of the child, at a point where the identity of the adopters is not finally settled. The reporting officer's chief function is to witness this agreement.[25] A form of agreement duly witnessed by the reporting officer is sufficient evidence of agreement to adoption.[26] Where a parent or guardian is outwith the United Kingdom the rules provide for the agreement of a person serving in Her Majesty's Forces to be witnessed by an officer, and in other cases the agreement may be witnessed by a British consular officer, or a person authorised by the law of the country in which the form is executed to administer an oath. Such a form duly executed is sufficient evidence of the agreement.[27] Agreement may, however, be withdrawn at any time before an order is pronounced declaring the child free for adoption. 28.144

A parent or guardian whose child is subject to an application for a freeing order must also be given the opportunity to make a declaration that he or she prefers not to be involved in future questions concerning the adoption of the child.[28] Where the parent does wish to make such a declaration it requires to be witnessed in the manner described in the preceding paragraph.[29] 28.145

The unmarried father

In applications for freeing special provisions apply to the father of a child who is not, and has not been, married to the child's mother, and who does not have any parental responsibilities or parental rights. Such a father will not have responsibilities or rights unless he has entered into an agreement with the child's mother under section 4 of the 1995 Act, or has been given responsibilities or rights by order of the court. Where he has responsibilities or rights by either of these means, his agreement to adoption will be required, or must be dispensed with, before a freeing order may be granted. Where he has no responsibilities or rights the court must be satisfied that he has no intention of applying for an order under section 11 of the 1995 Act, or that, if he did apply, it is likely that his application would be refused. The court must also be satisfied that he has no intention of entering into an agreement under section 4, or that no 28.146

---

[23] 1978 Act, s. 18(1). See para. 28.34.

[24] The form prescribed in Sched. 7 to the Adoption Agencies (Scotland) Regulations 1996 is in error when it advises parents that the court will seek agreement to the making of a freeing order.

[25] 1978 Act, s. 58(1)(b). See para. 28.153.

[26] CCMR, r. 2.6(1) and Form 2 (printed Form AD2).

[27] *ibid.* r. 2.6(2).

[28] 1978 Act, s. 18(6).

[29] CCMR, r. 2.10. See para. 28.185.

section 4 agreement is likely to be made. Unless the court is satisfied that the unmarried father is unlikely to acquire responsibilities or rights by either of these means, it cannot make an order declaring the child free for adoption.[30] The reporting officer is charged with investigating and reporting to the court in relation to the position of a father who is not married to the mother.[31] The reporting officer should also report to the court if he or she considers that such a father should be given the opportunity to make representations by receiving notice of the first hearing of the petition.[32] A person claiming to be the father of the child, but who is not the child's guardian and in respect of whom no order relating to parental responsibilities has been made should, in any event, receive notice of the first hearing.[33]

Steps before lodging petition

Appointment of reporting officer

28.147 The sheriff may, on cause shown, appoint a reporting officer prior to the lodging of the petition for an order declaring a child free for adoption.[34] Such an appointment would be appropriate where a parent or guardian wished to give formal agreement to adoption of the child, but might not be available to do so after the commencement of the proceedings. It might be appropriate where the local authority is not itself looking after the child and a parent is vacillating about whether to give consent to the application being made.[35] The application for an early appointment of a reporting officer should be made by letter addressed to the sheriff clerk.[36] The letter should set out the reasons for the appointment. It does not require to be intimated to any other person.

Withholding child's address

28.148 Where the address of the child is not known to the child's parents or guardian, the local authority may consider that the address should remain confidential. In such a case the authority should before lodging the petition apply to the sheriff clerk for a serial number to be assigned.[37] The sheriff clerk has no discretion to refuse a request for a serial number. The express purpose of the number is to prevent the address of the child being disclosed to any person whose agreement or consent to the application or to the adoption is required. Where a serial number is allocated the child's address should be omitted from all documents lodged in process. Such documents should instead bear the serial number so that the sheriff clerk may, if necessary, refer to the address.

Freeing petition and report

28.149 An application for an order declaring a child free for adoption is made by petition in the form prescribed by the rules of court.[38] Where contemporaneous applications are made in relation to two or more children

---

30 1978 Act, s. 18(7).
31 CCMR, r. 2.8(l)(k).
32 *ibid.* r. 2.8(1)(e).
33 *ibid.* r. 2.11(2)(b).
34 *ibid.* r. 2.7(3).
35 See para. 28.141.
36 CCMR, r. 2.7(4).
37 *ibid.* r. 2.5(3).
38 *ibid.* r. 2.5(1) and Form 1 (printed form AD1).

from the same family, separate forms of petition should be used and separate processes should be made up.[39] The form of petition is very brief, simply giving details of the applicants, the child, and any grounds for dispensation with agreement to adoption. It refers to consent of the parent or guardian to the making of the application, which may be lodged with the petition,[40] and the consent of the child.[41] The latter cannot in fact be produced with the petition as it will be secured by the curator *ad litem* who is appointed only after the petition has been lodged. Documents founded on by the petitioner should also be lodged with the petition,[42] although it is submitted that the court may allow further documents to be lodged at a later stage if these are necessary to the proper consideration of all the circumstances relating to the child.[43] The two documents which must be lodged at the same time as the petition are the child's birth certificate, and a report from adoption agency.[44]

The substantive details in relation to the application will be contained in the report which accompanies the petition. The court rules set out the information which must be included in the report.[45] This includes how the needs of the child came to the notice of the local authority making the application, the family circumstances of the child, and a description of the child's physical and mental health and his or her emotional, behavioural and educational development. The authority must give an account of discussions with the parents or guardians and, if appropriate, with the child, about their wishes and the alternatives to adoption.[46] If parents or guardians cannot be found the authority must give an account of the search for them. Details of the position of relatives or persons likely to be involved with the child with respect to the proposed adoption should be supplied. The circumstances of any reputed father[47] should be reported on. The court must be told what arrangements are to be made for the child after the grant of the order sought and the likelihood of placement for adoption and a petition for adoption in the near future. The authority must report on whether the parent has been given an opportunity to make a declaration that he or she prefers not to be involved in future questions concerning the child. However, because a declaration should be witnessed by the reporting officer the opportunity will not arise until the reporting officer has been appointed.[48] The agency is also required to state its intentions about giving progress reports to former parents after a freeing order is made.[49] **28.150**

---

[39] The justification for separate petitions and processes is the same as for adoption: see para. 28.61.

[40] Form AD1 differs from the form of petition in the court rules because it refers confusingly to the consent of the mother and father generally without distinguishing the two different forms of consent or agreement.

[41] See paras. 28.136, 28.156.

[42] CCMr, r. 2.5(2)(c).

[43] 1978 Act, s. 6.

[44] CCMR, r, 2.5(2)(a) and (b).

[45] *ibid.* r. 2.5(2)(b).

[46] See 1978 Act, s. 6A.

[47] The 1978 Act refers to a person who has no parental responsibilities or rights but claims to be the father. It is unfortunate that this terminology is not followed in CCMR, r. 2.5(2)(x). The terminology of the Act is used in CCMR, r. 2.8(1)(k).

[48] CCMR, r. 2.10. See paras 28.145, 28.155, 28.172 to 28.174.

[49] In terms of the 1978 Act, s. 19(2) and (3). The 1978 Act used to refer to a "former parent". The court rule has not been amended to conform. The local authority have duties in relation to progress reports; see paras 28.172, 28.185.

28.151 Neither the petition nor the report is served on any person. They are lodged in court, and may at a later stage be examined by persons who become parties to the process.[50]

Curator *ad litem* and reporting officer

28.152 When a petition for freeing is lodged the sheriff must appoint both a reporting officer and a curator *ad litem*.[51] This may be a person or persons from the panel of persons nominated to act in these capacities, or another person at the sheriff's discretion.[52] The same person may be appointed to fulfil both functions[53] and it is submitted that this is generally desirable.[54] No person employed by the local authority making the application may be appointed.[55] Reports of the curator *ad litem* and reporting officer must be submitted within four weeks of appointment, unless the sheriff allows a shorter or longer period.[56] The contents of these reports are important considerations in the case, and require to be given express attention by the court when reaching a decision relating to a freeing order.[57] A reporting officer and curator must treat all information obtained in the exercise of their duties as confidential, and should not disclose any such information unless disclosure is necessary for the proper discharge of their duties.[58]

28.153 The reporting officer is generally charged with matters relating to parental consent and agreement.[59] He or she should witness any consent to the making of the application and agreement to adoption given by any parent or guardian in the United Kingdom.[60] Where a parent or guardian is outside the United Kingdom the form of consent may be witnessed by a commissioned officer in the case of a person serving in Her Majesty's Forces, and in any other case by a person authorised to administer an oath in the country in which the form is signed.[61]

28.154 Although a parent or guardian may already have supplied the applicant with formal consent to the making of the application, completion of the form prescribed in the court rules, duly witnessed, has the benefit of being sufficient evidence of consent.[62] Agreement to adoption is central to the proceedings, and the reporting officer must ascertain that the parent or guardian understands that the effect of an adoption order would be to extinguish his parental responsibilities and rights.[63] In fact an order declaring a child free for adoption has this effect, as parental responsibilities and rights pass to the local authority and a parent loses title to make any application to the court relating to the child.[64] The reporting officer

---

[50] See para. 28.163.
[51] CCMR, r. 2.7(1).
[52] *ibid.* r. 2.7(2).
[53] *ibid.* r. 2.7(1).
[54] See para. 28.70.
[55] 1978 Act, s. 58(2)(b).
[56] CCMR, r. 2.8(1) and (2).
[57] *Central R. C. v. M*, 1991 S.C.L.R. 300; see also *A v. B and C*, 1971 S.C. (H.L.) 129 at 141; *T, Petr*, 1997 S.L.T. 724 at 728B; *Petition of AB and CD to adopt X and Y*, 1990 S.C.L.R. 809 at 811.
[58] CCMR, r. 2.12(2).
[59] *ibid.* r. 2.8(1).
[60] See paras 28.140 to 28.144 .
[61] CCMR, r. 2.6.
[62] *ibid.*
[63] CCMR, r. 2.8(1)(c).
[64] 1978 Act, s. 18(5); 1995 Act, s. 11(1), (3)(a) and (4)(b).

must confirm that the parent or guardian understands the implications of freeing.[65] It must be explained that the agreement to adoption may be withdrawn at any time before the freeing order is made.[66] Where the child's father is not married to the mother the reporting officer is required to investigate the position of any person claiming to be the father of the child.[67] The reporting officer must ascertain whether alternatives to adoption have been discussed with the parent or guardian,[68] whether there is any person other than a parent or guardian upon whom notice of the petition[69] should be served,[70] and whether the child is subject to a supervision requirement.[71]

A parent whose child is freed for adoption may prefer not to be involved in any future question concerning the eventual adoption of the child, and there is provision for that parent to make a declaration that this is the case.[72] The reporting officer must confirm that opportunity has been given to make such a declaration, and if the parent does desire to make the declaration should provide the parent with the appropriate form for signature, and should witness the declaration.[73] The consequences of signing the form should be explained.[74] These are connected with receipt of progress reports and with the potential to make an application for revocation of the freeing order, if the child is not placed for adoption within one year of the order being granted,[75] and this too should be explained.[76] **28.155**

The curator *ad litem* must safeguard the interests of the child and ensure that consideration has been given to the interests of the child for the purposes of section 6 of the 1978 Act.[77] Section 6 requires consideration not only of the child's welfare throughout life, but also of any views the child wishes to express and the child's religious persuasion, racial origin and cultural and linguistic background.[78] The curator must ascertain whether the child wishes to express a view and where the child indicates he does so wish, should ascertain that view.[79] The child's views may be conveyed orally to the sheriff.[80] The curator must also witness the consent of any child of or over the age of 12 to the freeing order.[81] The curator is asked to ascertain whether the facts stated in the petition are correct, except where investigation of such facts falls within the duties of the reporting officer.[82] The petition is, however, brief, stating little more than **28.156**

---

65 CCMR, r. 2.8(1)(g).
66 *ibid.* r. 2.8(1)(h).
67 CCMR, r. 2.8(1)(k). See para. 28.146.
68 *ibid.* r. 2.8(1)(d).
69 *i.e.* of the first hearing in relation to the petition, see para. 28.158; the considerations are similar to adoption, see para. 28.76, save in relation to an unmarried father, see para. 28.146.
70 CCMR, r. 2.8(1)(e).
71 *ibid.* r. 2.8(1)(f). See para. 28.23.
72 1978 Act, s. 18(6).
73 CCMR, r. 2.10(1) and Form 5 (printed form AD3).
74 *ibid.* r. 2.10(2).
75 1978 Act, ss. 19 and 20. See paras 28.172, 28.185 to 28.191.
76 CCMR, rr. 2.8(2)(a).
77 *ibid.* r. 2.8(2)(a).
78 See para. 28.11.
79 CCMR, r. 2.8(2)(d).
80 *ibid.* r. 2.8(3).
81 *ibid.* rr. 2.6 and 2.8(2)(c).
82 *ibid.* r. 2.8(2)(b).

the date of birth of the child and whether dispensation with parental agreement to adoption is sought. The facts are set out in the accompanying report, and it is submitted that the curator should address whether the facts in the report are correct. While the reporting officer is required to ascertain the parents' understanding of issues connected with the application, the curator is bound to make enquiries relating to the parents in order to address whether freeing the child for adoption would safeguard and promote the welfare of the child.[83] The curator's report should indicate whether in the opinion of the curator it would be better for the child that the court should make the freeing order than that it should not make the order.[84] The curator is also required to report on the current circumstances of the child.[85]

Obtaining the views of the child

28.157 Where a child has indicated that he or she wishes to express a view in relation to the freeing application the sheriff should not make any order until opportunity has been given for the child's views to be obtained or heard.[86] The court may order such procedural steps as are considered appropriate to ascertain the views of the child,[87] and any written record of the child's views may be sealed in an envelope marked "Views of the child—confidential" and made available only to a sheriff.[88] The procedure in respect of the child's views is identical to the procedure which prevails in relation to an adoption application.[89]

Hearing

28.158 When the reports of the reporting officer and the curator *ad litem* have been received by the court, the sheriff must *ex proprio motu* order a diet of hearing to be fixed.[90] The petitioning authority is responsible for giving notice of the diet of hearing in the form prescribed to each parent or guardian whose consent or agreement to the application or to the adoption is required to be given or dispensed with.[91] Where the child's father is not married to the mother, intimation of the hearing should also be given to any person claiming to be the father who is not otherwise entitled to notice on the basis that he is the child's guardian or that an order relating to parental responsibilities has been granted.[92] Notice is only required when the whereabouts of the person concerned are known to the petitioner, although a local authority should take all reasonable steps to ascertain the person's whereabouts, and be prepared to explain to the court the steps taken. The sheriff is given no express discretion to direct that the hearing be intimated to any other person, although the reporting officer will have reported whether there are other persons upon whom notice should be served.[93] Given the special nature of proceedings relating to adoption, and the necessity for the court to consider all the circum-

---

83 CCMR, r. 2.8(2)(e).
84 1978 Act, s. 24(3); CCMR, r. 2.8(2)(f).
85 CCMR, r. 2.8(2)(g).
86 *ibid.* r. 2.9(1)(b).
87 *ibid.* r. 2.9(1)(a).
88 *ibid.* r. 2.9(2).
89 See paras 28.85 to 28.87.
90 CCMR, r. 2.11(1).
91 *ibid.* r. 2.11(2)(a) and Form 7 (printed form AD11).
92 *ibid.* r. 2.11(2)(b).
93 *ibid.* r. 2.8(1)(e).

stances relating to the child,[94] it is submitted that the sheriff has an implied power to order the making of intimation to others, such as persons with a competing claim relating to parental responsibilities and rights.[95] Where a person receives such a notice and appears at the hearing, he or she becomes a party to the proceedings and may lead evidence and make representations at any subsequent proof.[96]

When the hearing ordered by the court takes place, and if no person entitled to appear attends, the sheriff may make the order sought on the basis of the information before him.[97] The sheriff should, however, ensure that the various statutory requirements are met. These are: **28.159**

(1) each parent or guardian freely and with full understanding of what is involved agrees generally and unconditionally to the making of an adoption order; or that his agreement to the making of an adoption order should be dispensed with[98];
(2) where the child's parent has not consented to the application, that the child is being looked after by the applicant and that dispensation with the parent's agreement to adoption has been sought[99];
(3) if agreement to the making of an adoption order is to be dispensed with, that the child has been, or is likely to be, placed for adoption[1];
(4) that each parent or guardian has been given the opportunity of making a declaration that he prefers not to be involved in future questions regarding the adoption of the child[2];
(5) where the child's father has not been married to the child's mother and has no parental responsibilities or rights, that he has no intention of seeking such responsibilities or rights, or is unlikely to acquire them[3];
(6) that the report of the children's hearing in respect of any child subject to a supervision requirement has been considered[4];
(7) that the making of the order would be better for the child than that no order should be made.[5]

The statutory provisions are not clear in relation to the extent to which the sheriff has a discretion to make or refuse a freeing order. Section 18(1) requires the sheriff to make an order if a parent agrees to adoption or where the sheriff is satisfied that that agreement should be dispensed with. However, section 18(8) restricts the foregoing to the extent that, where the child is aged 12 or over, the child's consent must also be obtained unless dispensed with on the ground that the child is incapable of giving consent. A sheriff plainly has a discretion in relation to the question of dispensation with agreement.[6] He or she may defer a decision while procedural matters **28.160**

---

[94] 1978 Act, s. 6.
[95] *AB and CD, Petrs*, 1992 S.L.T. 1064 at 1069A.
[96] CCMR, r. 2.11(4). As for adoption, see para. 28.90.
[97] *ibid.* r. 2.11(3).
[98] 1978 Act, s. 18(1). See paras 28.31 to 28.34, 28.153, 28.154.
[99] *ibid.* s. 18(2).
[1] *ibid.* s. 18(3).
[2] *ibid.* s. 18(6). Any declaration made must be recorded by sheriff clerk in the Adoption Register: CCMR, r. 2.13; see para. 28.172.
[3] 1978 Act, s. 18(7). See para. 28.146.
[4] 1995 Act, s. 75(14); CCMR, r. 2.11(5).
[5] 1978 Act, s. 24(3).
[6] *Lothian R.C. v. A*, 1992 S.L.T. 858.

are dealt with, such as giving a parent the opportunity to make a declaration, or ensuring that the children's hearing report is read. The difficulty arises where all necessary consents are given or dispensed with but the court, having regard to section 6, does not consider that the welfare of the child would be served by a freeing order. There is then a conflict between the duty of the court to grant the order and its duty to refrain from making any order unless it would be better for the child than no order. The duty in terms of section 24(3) to refrain from making an order must be exercised with regard to the welfare of the child as the paramount consideration. It is consistent with section 6(1)(a) of the Act which requires the court in reaching any decision relating to the adoption of a child to regard the need to safeguard and promote the child's welfare as the paramount consideration. Looking at the 1978 Act as a whole it is submitted that the better view is that a sheriff does ultimately have a discretion whether or not to make a freeing order. A further problem arises where all the requirements of the statute are met, but the sheriff cannot be satisfied that an unmarried father is not likely to secure parental responsibilities. The sheriff may defer a decision to give the father an opportunity to seek responsibilities, but that would introduce an unwelcome delay. If the sheriff is not ultimately satisfied that the conditions in section 18(7) are satisfied he cannot grant an order declaring the child free for adoption However, a failure to deal with the declaration as to future involvement mentioned in section 18(6) is rather easier to remedy. If this has been overlooked, the reporting officer may be asked to see the parent or guardian in question, and the sheriff may then deal with the matter provided that this is done before any order declaring the child free for adoption is made.[7]

28.161 Where a person to whom notice of the hearing has been given appears and wishes to be heard, the sheriff may hear him there and then, or may order a further diet to be fixed at which that person may be heard.[8] When ordering a further diet the sheriff should establish the area of dispute and should determine the mode and time of inquiry.[9] The court rules contemplate that any second diet may be a proof at which evidence will be led.[10]

Preparation and proof

28.162 Freeing proceedings are commenced by a brief petition, and details of the authority's case will be found in the report which accompanies the petition. There is no requirement for written pleadings, but the court may give directions for answers to be lodged, or other steps to be taken, in order to clarify the issues in dispute.[11]

28.163 All documents lodged in process, including the reports of the curator *ad litem* and the reporting officer, are confidential and may be made available only to the sheriff, the curator and reporting officer, and the parties.[12] The provisions relating to confidentiality are identical to the provisions which prevail in adoption applications.[13] In the course of preparation for proof it may be desired to recover documents, or to seek

---

[7] See para. 28.155.
[8] CCMR, r. 2.11(4).
[9] See para. 28.99.
[10] CCMR, r. 2.11(4).
[11] See para. 28.103.
[12] CCMR, r. 2.12(1).
[13] See paras 28.104, 28.105.

medical examination of the child in much the same way as in an adoption application.[14]

A proof will usually take place in a freeing application when the sheriff is required to decide whether a parent's agreement to adoption may be dispensed with.[15] Evidence must be heard in the presence of the authority's solicitor.[16] The considerations relating to procedure at proof in a freeing application are identical to those in adoption proceedings.[17] The sheriff must have regard to the statutory requirements mentioned above.[18] 28.164

Order

If a freeing application is granted the appropriate order will in terms declare the child free for adoption. An order which bears simply to grant the prayer of the petition is inadequate. It is unnecessary to specify the basis upon which the order was pronounced.[19] The order itself need not therefore state whether parental agreement is dispensed with, or on what grounds parental agreement is dispensed with, although in a contested case the sheriff should make findings in fact and write a note explaining the basis for the decision.[20] 28.165

There is no power to insert any terms or conditions in an order declaring a child free for adoption, although it has been suggested that a court granting a freeing order might indicate that this might be a consideration in any future adoption proccedings.[21] A sheriff should be slow to refuse a freeing order on the basis that direct adoption proceedings, in which a condition could be considered, would be more appropriate given that local authorities are constrained to make freeing applications in disputed cases.[22] There may be potential for the sheriff to make an order relating to parental responsibilities and rights in proceedings relating to freeing for adoption as in adoption proceedings.[23] 28.166

Where the child is subject to a supervision requirement and the sheriff is satisfied on making a freeing order that compulsory measures of supervision are no longer necessary, he or she may determine that the requirement forthwith ceases to have effect.[24] If, however, a sheriff is satisfied from the evidence before him that any of the conditions for referral to the children's hearing are present he may refer the child to the principal reporter.[25] The procedure is the same as that which applies in adoption 28.167

---

[14] See paras 28.107, 28.108.

[15] When a parent gives agreement the sheriff is required to grant the freeing order unless he considers that to do so would not promote and safeguard the child's welfare. See para. 28.160.

[16] CCMR, r. 2.11(4). The rule refers to evidence being given in the presence of the "petitioner or his solicitor". The petitioner will always be a local authority. A non-natural person such as a local authority must always be represented by a solicitor (who may in turn instruct counsel). See para. 1.32.

[17] See paras 28.109 to 28.114.

[18] See para. 28.159.

[19] *Lothian R.C. v. A*, 1992 S.L.T. 858 at 866L.

[20] *ibid.* at 865K.

[21] *P v. Lothian R.C.*, 1989 S.L.T. 739 at 745. There may be some difficulty in transmitting this information as the process will be sealed up at the conclusion of the proceedings. See paras 28.170, 28.171 .

[22] See paras 28.14, 28.135.

[23] 1995 Act, s. 11(1) and (3)(b). See paras 28.121, 28.122 .

[24] 1978 Act, s. 18(9).

[25] 1995 Act, s. 54(1) and (2)(c).

proceedings.[26] The sheriff may also give information about the child to the principal reporter, for the reporter to investigate.[27] These powers should rarely be used as in contested cases children will already be looked after by the local authority.[28]

28.168 The sheriff's power with regard to expenses,[29] as in adoption proceedings, is to make such order as he or she thinks fit, to modify such expenses or direct them to be taxed. These include the expenses of the reporting officer and curator *ad litem*. The provisions for the expenses of the reporting officer and curator in freeing applications are identical to those in adoption proceedings.

28.169 While there is no express provision for appeal from an order declaring a child free for adoption, such orders are applicable, in the same way that an adoption order may be appealed.[30]

Final procedure

28.170 Where an order declaring a child free for adoption is granted an extract of the order is required for the purpose of any future adoption application.[31] The sheriff clerk is required to issue an extract automatically after the 14 days, within which an appeal may be marked, have expired.[32] The same rule also requires the issue of an extract 14 days after confirmation of the order, presumably on appeal. In a case where the sheriff has terminated a supervision requirement on making a freeing order, the sheriff clerk must intimate this to the principal reporter.[33] The process in a successful freeing application must be sealed in an envelope marked "Confidential".[34] There is no requirement to seal the process when an order is refused.

28.171 Where the process is sealed up neither the sheriff clerk nor any other person having control of the records may unseal the envelope, nor make it accessible to any person for 100 years after the date of granting of the order, save to certain authorised persons.[35] The person who has been freed for adoption may see the process, once he or she has attained the age of 16 years.[36] The person freed for adoption may authorise the sheriff clerk to open the process, ascertain the name of the agency responsible for the placement for adoption, and supply the name to an adoption agency.[37] This provision is inept in the case of freeing, where the applicant will usually be the agency responsible for any placement made or which is proposed to be made. Any person who can justify access to the process may apply to the sheriff, setting forth the reasons for which access is required.[38] A court, public authority, or administrative board may petition the court which granted a freeing order requesting information from

---

26 1995 Act, s. 54(3). See para. 28.124.
27 *ibid.* s. 53(2)(b). See para. 28.125.
28 1978 Act, s. 18(2). See para. 28.137.
29 CCMR, r. 2.2. See paras 28.128, 28.129.
30 See paras 28.132 to 28.134.
31 See para. 28.63.
32 CCMR, r. 2.14(1)(a).
33 *ibid.* r. 2.14(1)(b). See para. 28.167.
34 *ibid.* r. 2.14(1)(a).
35 *ibid.* r. 2.14(2).
36 *ibid.* r. 2.14(2)(a).
37 *ibid.* r. 2.14(2)(b).
38 *ibid.* r. 2.14(2)(c). See para, 28.196.

the process for the purpose of discharging duties in considering an application for adoption, specifying the reason for the request.[39] Finally the Secretary of State may authorise the release of information from the process to a person carrying out research intended to improve the working of adoption law and practice.[40]

The Adoption Register

The sheriff clerk is required to maintain a register known as "the Adoption Register".[41] This relates solely to freeing proceedings and is a record of whether, after a freeing order has been made, a parent or guardian wishes to be involved in future questions concerning the adoption of the child. Each parent or guardian must be given the opportunity to make a declaration that he or she prefers not to be involved in such questions.[42] The local authority is obliged to give certain information about the child to each parent or guardian who does not make such a declaration.[43] The reporting officer is usually responsible for submitting the completed form of declaration to the sheriff clerk.[44] The sheriff clerk enters any declaration made and submitted to him in the Adoption Register.[45] **28.172**

Where a parent or guardian does not make a declaration at the time of the freeing proceedings, he or she may do so at a later date,[46] by completing the usual form of declaration[47] and sending it to the local authority which secured the freeing order. The authority is obliged to secure the recording of the declaration by the court.[48] **28.173**

Any declaration made can be withdrawn by written notice to the local authority holding parental responsibilities and rights by virtue of the freeing order.[49] The withdrawal may also be notified direct to the court in which case the sheriff clerk will intimate it to the local authority.[50] When a declaration is withdrawn this must be noted in the Adoption Register.[51] **28.174**

IV. Miscellaneous Applications

Application for removal of child pending adoption

There are four sets of circumstances in which leave of the court may be required before a child can be removed from the care of persons who intend to adopt. **28.175**

(1) Where a child has been placed for adoption, with the consent of the parent or guardian, given in terms of the 1996 Regulations,[52] the parent or

---

[39] CCMR, r. 2.14(2)(d).
[40] *ibid.* r. 2.14(2)(e).
[41] CCMR, r. 2.13(1).
[42] 1978 Act, s. 18(6).
[43] *ibid.* s. 19(2) and (3). See para. 28.185.
[44] CCMR, r. 2.10. See para. 28.155.
[45] *ibid.* r. 2.13(2).
[46] 1978 Act, s. 19(4).
[47] CCMR, r. 2.13(3) and Form 5 (printed form AD3).
[48] 1978 Act, s. 19(4)(a).
[49] *ibid.* s. 19(1)(b).
[50] CCMR, r. 2.10(5). This rule prescribes a form for withdrawal of the declaration: Form 6 (printed form AD16).
[51] *ibid.* r. 2.13(2).
[52] See para. 28.13.

guardian cannot then remove the child without the leave of the adoption agency or the court.[53]

(2) If a child has lived with a person for five years or more, and that person intends to adopt the child, leave of the court is required for removal of the child if the removal is against the will of the prospective adopter.[54] This protection extends from the date upon which the prospective adopter gives notice to the local authority within whose area he has his home that he or she intends to apply for an adoption order until the conclusion of the adoption proceedings, provided these are commenced within three months of notice being given.[55] Protection will lapse if there is a delay of more than three months in commencing proceedings and cannot be renewed for 28 days. However, a further notice given 28 days or more after the previous notice expired will renew protection for a further three months.[56] Protection will also revive on commencement of adoption proceedings.[57] Even the local authority looking after the child will require the leave of the court for removal of the child unless the removal is authorised under or by virtue of the provisions relating to the care and protection of children in Chapters 2 and 3 of Part II of the Children (Scotland) Act 1995.[58]

(3) In the case of a child placed by an adoption agency with prospective adopters, the agency is required to give notice in writing to bring the placement to an end.[59] The child must then be returned to the agency within seven days.[60] However, where adoption proceedings have been commenced the agency is prohibited from giving such notice without the leave of the court.[61]

(4) A child may be placed with a foster carer by the local authority responsible for looking after the child.[62] If that foster carer gives notice of intention to adopt to the local authority for the area in which he or she lives[63] the authority responsible for the child may not remove the child except by giving notice in writing.[64] Once adoption proceedings are commenced any such notice requires the leave of the court.[65]

28.176 An application for leave to remove the child, or for leave to give notice in writing for the return of the child, is made by minute in the process of the adoption petition.[66] No form is prescribed, but the minute should set forth the relevant facts and the crave which the minuter wishes to make.[67] On receipt of the minute the sheriff must order a diet of hearing to be fixed

---

53 1978 Act, s. 27.

54 *ibid.* s. 28(1). This provides further that the removal is lawful if it is as a result of the arrest of the child, or under authority conferred by any enactment, such as a condition of a supervision requirement, authorisation or warrant under Part II of the Children (Scotland) Act 1995 (for which specific provision is made by s. 28(4)).

55 1978 Act, s. 28(2)(b).

56 *ibid.* s. 28(6).

57 *ibid.* s. 28(2)(a).

58 *ibid.* s. 28(4).

59 *ibid.* s. 30(3).

60 *ibid.*

61 *ibid.* s. 30(2).

62 Under the 1995 Act, s. 17.

63 In terms of the 1978 Act, s. 22(1).

64 1978 Act, s. 31(1) applying the provisions of s. 30(1) to such a child.

65 These provisions must, of course, operate subject to statutory intervention such as a supervision requirement made by the children's hearing.

66 CCMR, r. 2.36(1).

67 *ibid.* r. 2.36(2).

and ordain the minuter to send notice of the hearing[68] and a copy of the minute by registered post or recorded delivery letter to the petitioner, to the curator *ad litem*, to any person who may have care and possession of the child, and to such other person as the sheriff may deem appropriate.[69]

An application for leave to remove a child may be required before adoption proceedings have commenced. There is no express provision in the sheriff court rules for such an application. It may be possible to deal with such a matter by way of summary application, but the safer and speedier course is to make an application by petition to the Court of Session.[70] **28.177**

Application for return of child pending adoption

If a child has been removed without leave of the court from prospective adopters by a parent or guardian who gave consent to the placement, or has been removed from the care of a prospective adopter with whom he or she has lived for more than five years in circumstances such that leave should have been secured, an application may be made for return of the child.[71] Where there are reasonable grounds to believe that an attempt will be made to remove the child without the necessary leave, the court may by order direct that the child be not removed.[72] **28.178**

The application may be made by the person from whose care and possession the child was or is likely to be removed. Where proceedings are pending in the sheriff court the application is made by minute, and proceeds in exactly the same manner as a minute for leave to remove the child.[73] There is no express provision in the sheriff court rules for an application before adoption proceedings have commenced, and the matter may therefore proceed by way of summary application, or should be dealt with by petition in the Court of Session.[74] **28.179**

The sheriff may be asked to order the return of a child, or to prohibit the removal of a child placed in accordance with, or protected by the terms of, the equivalent legislation in England and Wales or Northern Ireland.[75] **28.180**

Amendment of adoption order

Where there is an error in an adoption order, either the adopter, or the adopted person, may apply for correction of the error.[76] If the adopted person is given a new name within one year of the adoption, whether by baptism or otherwise, either in lieu of or in addition to the name specified in the court's order for entry in the Adopted Children Register, that person or the adopter may seek amendment of the adoption order.[77] If the order wrongly directed that the child's entry of birth be marked **28.181**

---

68 The notice should be in CCMR, Form 15.
69 CCMR, r. 2.36(3).
70 RCS, r. 67.28.
71 1978 Act, s. 29(1).
72 *ibid.* s. 29(2).
73 CCMR, r. 2.36. See para. 28.176.
74 RCS, r. 67.28.
75 1978 Act, s. 29(1) and (2).
76 *ibid.* Sched. 1, para. 4(1).
77 *ibid.* para. 4(1)(a).

"Adopted" or "Readopted", this too may be amended.[78] If the amendment is made the registers will require to be rectified.[79]

28.182 An application for amendment is made by petition to the court which pronounced the adoption order.[80] The sheriff may order intimation of the petition to such persons as to him or her seem appropriate.[81] The sheriff clerk is required to communicate any amendment to the Registrar General.[82]

Revocation of adoption

28.183 Adoptions are generally irrevocable. However, in the rare cases where a child has been adopted in Scotland by one of his or her natural parents, and the parents subsequently marry, "any of the parties concerned" may apply for revocation of the adoption order.[83] It is submitted that this phrase means that either parent or the child may make such an application.

28.184 The application for revocation is by petition[84] to the court which pronounced the adoption order. On the lodging of such a petition the sheriff should order such service as he or she considers appropriate before considering the application.[85]

Revocation of freeing

28.185 Where a child is freed for adoption, a parent or guardian has the choice whether to be involved in future questions concerning the child.[86] He or she may make a declaration of a wish not to be involved. If no such declaration is made, or if any declaration made is withdrawn, the parent remains a "relevant parent".[87] That parent must be given notice within 14 days following the anniversary of the freeing order whether an adoption order has been made in respect of the child, or the child has his home with a person with whom he or she has been placed for adoption.[88] The requirement to give notice at the end of the year does not apply if there has been previous notice of an adoption order.[89] If the year expires without an adoption order being made, then not only must the parent be advised of the position at that point, but thereafter the parent must be advised by notice if an adoption order is made, or the child is placed for adoption, or ceases to be placed with a person with a view to adoption.[90]

28.186 If the child has not been adopted after one year, and does not have a home with a person with whom he or she has been placed for adoption, the

---

[78] 1978 Act, para. 4(1)(b).
[79] *ibid.* para. 4.(2).
[80] CCMR, r. 2.34(1). No form of petition is prescribed. Forms of petition are suggested in McNeill, pp. 240–242.
[81] CCMR, r. 2.34(2).
[82] 1978 Act, Sched. 1, para. 4(2).
[83] *ibid.* s. 46(1).
[84] CCMR, r. 2.35(1). No form of petition is prescribed. A form of petition is suggested in McNeill, p. 242.
[85] CCMR, r. 2.35(2).
[86] 1978 Act, s. 18(6).
[87] *ibid.* s. 19(1).
[88] *ibid.* s. 19(2).
[89] *ibid.*
[90] *ibid.* s. 19(3).

parent may apply to the court for revocation of the freeing order.[91] The local authority may also apply for a revocation provided no adoption order has been made and the child is not placed for adoption, but unlike a relevant parent the authority is not required to wait for one year after the original freeing before making such an application.[92] Where one agency has been substituted for another,[93] the agency holding parental responsibilities and rights at the time of the application should presumably make any such application.

The court rules prescribe that an application for revocation made by a relevant parent should be by minute in the process of the original application.[94] The rules are silent in relation to an application by the local authority, but it is submitted that this too should be by minute, although the form of application will require to be adjusted.[95] The procedure is unusual in the context of adoption as the sheriff must order the applicant to intimate the minute to the petitioner in the original application and to such other person as the sheriff considers appropriate.[96] Where the applicant is the original petitioner it is likely to be appropriate that any relevant parent receive intimation. If the relevant parent is the applicant, and there has been a transfer of parental responsibilities to another adoption agency, it will be appropriate that intimation should be given to the agency holding parental responsibilities and rights. Any person to whom intimation has been made may within 14 days lodge answers to the minute.[97] **28.187**

When a minute for revocation of freeing is lodged the sheriff may appoint a curator *ad litem*.[98] Unlike other adoption proceedings the sheriff has a discretion whether to appoint a curator. If a curator is appointed he or she is required to have regard to the welfare of the child as the paramount duty.[99] The curator must investigate the facts contained in the minute; must investigate the circumstances and care of the child with regard to the promotion of welfare throughout life; and must ascertain from the child whether he or she wishes to express a view; and, where the child does wish to express a view, must ascertain that view.[1] A report in writing should be submitted to the sheriff within four weeks from the curator's appointment unless the sheriff in his or her discretion allows a shorter or longer period.[2] The views of the child may, however, be conveyed to the sheriff orally.[3] **28.188**

If the child has indicated a wish to express views to the sheriff, the sheriff may order such procedural steps as he or she considers appropriate to ascertain the views of the child.[4] An opportunity must be given for the **28.189**

---

[91] 1978 Act, s. 20(1).
[92] *ibid.* s. 20(1A).
[93] *ibid.* s. 21; see para. 28.195.
[94] CCMR, r. 2.15(1) and Form 8 (printed form AD4).
[95] Form 8 refers to more than 12 months passing since the child was freed for adoption, whereas this is not a requirement when the adoption agency makes the application.
[96] CCMR, r. 2.15(2).
[97] *ibid.* r. 2.15(3).
[98] *ibid.* r. 2.16(1).
[99] *ibid.*
[1] *ibid.*
[2] *ibid.*
[3] *ibid.* r. 2.16(2).
[4] *ibid.* r. 2.17(1)(a).

views of the child to be obtained or heard before any order is made.[5] The sheriff may make provision for the child's views to remain confidential.[6]

28.190 Where no answers to the minute are lodged the sheriff has the power to order the relevant adoption agency to submit a report, or he may order a diet of hearing to be fixed, or he may order both of these things.[7] Where answers have been lodged the sheriff is required to order a diet of hearing.[8] The sheriff must determine the application applying the criteria set out in section 6 of the 1978 Act.[9] Where the order declaring the child free for adoption is revoked the sheriff is required to make an order under section 11 of the Children (Scotland) Act 1995 determining on whom are to be imposed the parental responsibilities and to whom are to be given the parental rights in relation to the child.[10]

28.191 If the sheriff dismisses an application for revocation by a relevant parent, that parent cannot make a further application without the leave of the court.[11] A local authority is relieved of the duty to give that parent further information about the child.[12]

Further application for revocation of freeing

28.192 In the event that the parent wishes to make a further application for revocation, he or she must seek the leave of the court.[13] Leave may only be given where there has been a change in circumstances or where there is some other reason why it is proper to allow a further application to be made.[14] The request for leave is made in the form of a further application for revocation.[15]

28.193 Although the 1978 Act appears to contemplate that no further application will be allowed to proceed until leave has been granted, the court rules require intimation of the minute, appointment of a curator *ad litem* and application of the procedure where the child wishes to express a view, as for any other revocation application.[16] The sheriff then has a discretion in relation to any further steps. The court rules prescribe no further procedure. The sheriff may therefore hear the applicant and determine the issue of leave, or order a diet of hearing to be fixed. The provision for leave in such cases was designed to avoid the distress and expense of ill-founded applications. If this objective is to be achieved an application which does not satisfy the test for leave to be granted should be dismissed at the first opportunity, and should not proceed to a further hearing.

Application for leave to place while revocation pending

28.194 Where there is pending before the court an application for revocation of an order declaring a child free for adoption, the adoption agency which

---

[5] CCMR, r. 2.17(1)(b).
[6] *ibid.* r. 2.17(2). In relation to confidentiality of children's views, see paras 28.86, 28.87.
[7] *ibid.* r. 2.18(2).
[8] *ibid.* r. 2.18(1).
[9] See paras. 28.08 to 28.11.
[10] 1978 Act, s. 20(3); CCMR, r. 2.18(3).
[11] *ibid.* s. 20(4)(a) and (5).
[12] *ibid.* s. 20(4)(b) and (5).
[13] *ibid.* s. 20(5).
[14] *ibid.*
[15] CCMR, r. 2.20 and Form 10 (printed form AD6).
[16] *ibid.* applying rr. 2.15(2) and (3), 2.16 and 2.17 to such applications.

has parental rights and duties may not place the child for adoption without the leave of the court.[17] An application for leave should be made by minute in the prescribed form.[18] The minute should be intimated by the applicant to such persons as the sheriff considers appropriate.[19] If leave is granted, the court is still required to determine the application for revocation of the freeing order. The placement of the child will be a circumstances to be weighed in deciding whether the order should be revoked.

Transfer of parental responsibilities and rights between agencies

Where parental responsibilities and parental rights relating to a child are vested in a local authority by virtue of an order declaring a child free for adoption, those responsibilities and rights may be transferred to another adoption agency.[20] Both agencies must apply jointly to the sheriff court for the sheriffdom in which the child resides.[21] The sheriff court rules do not expressly provide for such an application. It is submitted that any such application in the sheriff court should be by way of minute, if made to the court in which the original freeing was granted. In any other case it should be by way of summary application. Alternatively the matter may be dealt with in the Court of Session where there is provision in the court rules.[22] **28.195**

Other applications

There are other applications which may be made in relation to adoption. Some require to be made by petition. These include a request for extract of the adoption order[23] and a request by persons or bodies other than the adopted person (or an agency acting with the consent of the adopted person) for access to the process.[24] Some applications, such as a request to the Secretary of State for information from the process for the purposes of research,[25] may be made by letter. **28.196**

---

17 1978 Act, s. 20(2).

18 CCMR, r. 2.19(1) (printed form AD5).

19 *ibid.* r. 2.19(2).

20 1978 Act, s. 21(1). Whereas there is a transfer the agency to which the responsibilities and rights are transferred is bound to comply with the requirement to give information to the relevant parent in terms of s. 19. See para. 28.125.

21 *ibid.* s. 21(1). The application is not made to the court which made the original freeing order, but to an authorised court in terms of the 1978 Act, s. 56.

22 RCS, r. 67.17. This rule is not entirely satisfactory as it provides for a note, which assumes that the application will be made in the process of the original application.

23 CCMR, r. 2.32(3). See form of petition suggested in McNeill, p. 240.

24 *ibid.* rr. 2.14(2)(c) and (d); 2.33(2)(c) and (d). See form of petition suggested in McNeill, p. 240.

25 *ibid.* rr. 2.14(2)(e); 2.33(2)(e). See suggested form in McNeill, p. 240.

PART VI

ENFORCEMENT OF JUDGMENTS

Chapter 29

ENFORCEMENT OF JUDGMENTS

Introduction

29.01 This chapter deals with the topic of the enforcement of judgments of the sheriff court. The term "judgment" is not an exact term of art in Scots law and the expressions "interlocutor" and "decree" are more frequently used to refer to the court's determination of part or all of an action.[1]

29.02 In Scots law enforcement procedures are part of the law of diligence, an area which also deals with procedures for providing provisional and protective measures prior to or during a court action.[2] It may also be noted that enforcement procedures apply not only to decrees and interlocutors of the court but also to a variety of documents which are deemed to be the equivalent of a decree for enforcement purposes. Examples are documents registered in the books of the court, including judgments of foreign courts, and protested bills of exchange and promissory notes which allow for summary diligence.[3] Another important basis for enforcement are summary warrants granted by a sheriff which are used as a means for the recovery of various taxes and public duties and levies. The procedures for enforcing summary warrants in general follow those used to enforce decrees but are subject to a number of minor variations.[4]

29.03 The type of diligence used to enforce a decree will reflect the nature of the decree itself. This chapter focuses on decrees and interlocutors which decern for payment of a sum of money by one party to another. In respect of such decrees and interlocutors, the most commonly used diligences are common-law arrestments, statutory-based arrestments against earnings, and poinding and sale. Decrees which deal with other issues (e.g. the delivery of children or objects, or the repossession of heritable property) are subject to special diligences. Furthermore, certain types of money payments based on decrees are also subject to some specialised diligence (e.g. the remedy of civil imprisonment to enforce a decree of aliment between spouses) and other forms of debt may be subject to specialised actions for enforcement (e.g. the action of sequestration for rent to give effect to the landlord's hypothec).[5]

---

[1] Chapter 30 of the Ordinary Cause Rules is headed "Decrees, Extracts and Execution". OCR, r. 30.1 states: "In this Chapter 'decree' includes any judgment, deliverance, interlocutor, act, order, finding or authority which may be extracted."

[2] See Chap. 11.

[3] For full discussion, see Maher & Cusine, Chap. 2; Graham [illegible].

[4] S.I. 1988 No. 2013, r. 68, Forms 61 and 62. For discussion see Maher & Cusine, paras 8.07–8.13.

[5] Some of these specialised diligences and actions are dealt with elsewhere in this volume and are not dealt with in this chapter. See paras 23.38 et seq.

CHAPTER 29

ENFORCEMENT OF JUDGMENTS

INTRODUCTION

This chapter deals with the topic of the enforcement of judgments of the sheriff court. The term "judgment" is not an exact term of art in Scots law and the expressions "interlocutor" and "decree" are more frequently used to refer to the court's determination of part or all of an action.[1] **29.01**

In Scots law enforcement procedures are part of the law of diligence, an area which also deals with procedures for providing provisional and protective measures prior to or during a court action.[2] It may also be noted that enforcement procedures apply not only to decrees and interlocutors of the court but also to a variety of documents which are deemed to be the equivalent of a decree for enforcement purposes. Examples are documents registered in the books of the court, including judgments of foreign courts, and protested bills of exchange and promissory notes which allow for summary diligence.[3] Another important basis for enforcement are summary warrants granted by a sheriff which are used as a means for the recovery of various taxes and public duties and levies. The procedures for enforcing summary warrants in general follow those used to enforce decrees but are subject to a number of minor variations.[4] **29.02**

The type of diligence used to enforce a decree will reflect the nature of the decree itself. This chapter focuses on decrees and interlocutors which decern for payment of a sum of money by one party to another. In respect of such decrees and interlocutors, the most commonly used diligences are common law arrestments, statutory-based arrestments against earnings, and poinding and sale. Decrees which deal with other issues (*e.g.* the delivery of children or objects, or the repossession of heritable property) are subject to special diligences. Furthermore, certain types of money payments based on decrees are also subject to some specialised diligences (*e.g.* the remedy of civil imprisonment to enforce a decree of aliment between spouses), and other forms of debt may be subject to specialised actions for enforcement (*e.g.* the action of sequestration for rent to give effect to the landlord's hypothec).[5] **29.03**

---

[1] Chapter 30 of the Ordinary Cause Rules is headed "Decrees, Extracts and Execution". OCR, r. 30.1 states: "In this Chapter, 'decree' includes any judgment, deliverance, interlocutor, act, order, finding or authority which may be extracted."

[2] See Chap. 11.

[3] For full discussion, see Maher & Cusine, Chap. 2; Gretton, paras 120–123.

[4] S.I. 1988 No. 2013, r. 68, Forms 61 and 62. For discussion see Maher & Cusine, paras 8.07–8.12.

[5] Some of these specialised diligences and actions are dealt with elsewhere in this volume and are not dealt with in this chapter. See paras 23.14 *et seq.*

29.04 Parties using diligence should note two sets of statutory provisions which may lessen the effectiveness of the steps they propose to use to recover debts owing to them, namely: (1) under section 64 of the Taxes Management Act 1970, certain diligences used by private creditors may be defeated by claims of the Inland Revenue to recover unpaid tax from the debtor[6]; and (2) the property, including the earnings, of members of the armed forces is exempt from a wide range of diligences. However there also exists a number of statutory schemes which allow for the recovery of various types of debt owing by members of the armed forces.[7]

Extract

Nature and issuing

29.05 For purposes of enforcement, the crucial part of a court judgment is the extract or official copy which acts both as a certificate that a decree exists in the court records,[8] and as the authority for executing the appropriate diligence to give effect to the decree. The normal practice is that as soon as an extract may be issued,[9] the sheriff clerk will on request send an extract to the party (or more usually his agent) entitled to it. No fee is payable in respect of an extract, the using of which is included in the fees payable for the initial writ or summons.[10] An extract is issued by the sheriff clerk, who also signs it.

Form of extract

29.06 The form of extract for various types of sheriff court decrees in ordinary cause actions is set out in Appendix 2 of the Ordinary Cause Rules.[11] Extracts of decrees which are not specifically mentioned in that list have a form modelled on one of those forms with appropriate modifications.[12] In practice decrees in ordinary cause actions are set out on a separate sheet of paper. The forms of extract of decrees in summary cause and small claims actions are set out in an Appendix to the Summary Cause Rules.[13] Normally in summary cause and small claims actions extracts are written on the summons but may also be set out on a separate sheet of paper.[14]

When decrees are extractable

29.07 The first point to be considered in relation to the time when an extract may be issued is whether or not the decree was granted in absence. A decree in absence may be extracted only after a period of 14 days from the date of decree.[15] Where an action has been defended, different rules apply in respect of different levels of sheriff court actions. In an ordinary cause

---

[6] For full discussion, see Maher & Cusine, pp. 232–234; Gretton, para. 129.

[7] For general discussion see "Armed Forces", *Stair Memorial Encyclopaedia*, Vol. 2, paras 766–769.

[8] *Inglis v. McIntyre* (1862) 24 D. 541 at 544.

[9] See OCR, r. 30.4; and see paras 29.07 *et seq.*

[10] Sheriff Court Fees Order 1997, (S.I. 1997 No. 687, para. 4(1).

[11] OCR, r. 30.6(1).

[12] OCR, r. 30.6(2).

[13] SCR, r. 89(2), Forms U1–U14 (applicable to small claims actions: SMCR, App. 3).

[14] SCR, r. 89(2).

[15] OCR, r. 30.4; SCR, r. 89(1) (applicable to small claims actions: SMCR, App. 3). In ordinary cause actions the sheriff has power to order extract of a decree in absence at an earlier date. See para. 29.09.

action, an extract of decree may be obtained once any question of an appeal is no longer an issue for the court. Various situations may be distinguished,[16] namely: (a) where an appeal depends upon leave to appeal and no application has been made, extract is obtainable on expiry of the period for making an application; (b) where leave to appeal has been applied for but refused, extract may be granted at any time thereafter; (c) where an appeal may be marked, extract is obtainable when no appeal is marked within the appropriate period for doing so; and (d) where an appeal is proceeded with, extract is obtainable once the appeal is fully disposed of. Where an appeal is made to the sheriff principal the date of decree to appear in the extract is the date of the sheriff principal's decision.[17]

Where a question of expenses has been reserved when the sheriff pronounced decree, extract of that decree may be issued only after the expiry of 14 days from the date of the subsequent interlocutor which deals with expenses unless the sheriff directs otherwise.[18] **29.08**

A sheriff may grant a motion to allow for earlier extract than those indicated above. This requires (1) cause shown, and (2) the motion for earlier extract having been made in the presence of the parties, or proper intimation having been made to parties not present at the hearing of the motion.[19] **29.09**

In respect of decrees granted in summary cause and small claims actions, extract may be issued only after the lapse of 14 days from the date of granting of decree.[20] Where an appeal has been lodged extract may not be issued until the appeal is disposed of. In summary cause and small claims actions, the sheriff has no power to grant extract earlier than the time provided for by the rules of court.[21] **29.10**

The rules of court on extracting decree do not affect the sheriff's common law power to supersede extract.[22] **29.11**

Extract of decrees for payment in foreign currency

A decree may in certain circumstances be granted for payment of a sum of money in foreign currency or its sterling equivalent.[23] A party requiring extract of a decree in these terms proceeds by way of minute endorsed on or annexed to the initial writ. The minute sets out the rate of exchange between sterling and the foreign currency prevailing at the date the extract is ordered (or within three days of that date) or at the date when the extract is sought. The minute also sets out the sterling equivalent of the principal sum and **29.12**

---

16 OCR, r. 30.4(1)(b).
17 OCR, r. 30.8(1).
18 OCR, r. 30.8(2).
19 OCR, r. 30.4(3).
20 SCR, r. 89(1); SMCR, App. 3.
21 This is subject to the power under SCR, r. 68A in respect of persons in possession of heritable property without right or title. Under this rule the sheriff may shorten or dispense with any time period in the summary cause rules. However, the issue of extract under this provision does not affect the period of appeal, but the lodging of a note of appeal does not act to sist any diligence based on the extract unless the sheriff directs otherwise (SCR, r. 81A).
22 See para. 17.24.
23 See paras 9.91, 9.92.

interest at that rate of exchange.[24] Along with the minute there is also lodged a certificate, which is itself mentioned in the extract, in Form G18 from the Bank of England or another bank authorised under the Banking Act 1987 which certifies the rate of exchange and sterling equivalent.[25] There are no provisions in the summary cause or small claims rules for the granting or extracting of a decree in a foreign currency.

Warrant for execution

29.13 An extract of a decree is in itself warrant for all lawful execution which may follow on it and words to that effect appear in the extract itself.[26] What is the appropriate mode of execution depends on the terms of the decree.[27] Where a decree requires payment of a sum of money, the warrant for execution in the extract has the effect of authorising[28]: (a) in relation to a debt other than one for current maintenance, the serving of a charge on the debtor and, in the event that the debtor fails to pay the sum charged for within the specified time, the execution of an earnings arrestment and of a poinding of the debtor's goods (and if necessary for purposes of the poinding, the opening of shut and lockfast places); (b) in relation to a debt other than one for current maintenance, arrestment other than an arrestment of the debtor's earnings in the hands of his employer; and (c) if the decree consists of or includes a maintenance order as defined by the Debtors (Scotland) Act 1987, a current maintenance arrestment in accordance with Part III of that Act.

ARRESTMENT

Nature of arrestment

29.14 Arrestment is the diligence used against the debtor's moveable property in the hands of a third party.[29] As a diligence in execution of a court decree or its equivalent, arrestment is to be distinguished from arrestment to found jurisdiction and arrestment on the dependence of an action.[30] Furthermore, the appropriate diligence to use against the earnings of a debtor is no longer the common law diligence of arrestment but one of the new statutory-based diligences against earnings established by Part III of the Debtors (Scotland) Act 1987. It may also be noted that special rules apply where the subject of the arrestment is a ship or its cargo.[31]

29.15 Where an arrestment had been made on the dependence of an action and subsequently decree is granted in favour of the arresting creditor, the arrestment is automatically transformed into an arrestment in execution

---

[24] OCR, r. 30.3(1).

[25] OCR, r. 30.3(2), (3).

[26] OCR, r. 30.7; SCR, r. 89(2).

[27] See, for example, SCR, r. 69 (decree for recovery of possession of heritable property); OCR, r. 71 (decree for delivery); SCR, rr. 77–78 (decrees in action of sequestration for rent).

[28] Sheriff Courts (Scotland) Extracts Act 1892, s. 7(1) (as substituted by the Debtors (Scotland) Act 1987, s. 3).

[29] This section deals with common law arrestments. Such arrestments cannot be used where the debtor's property is in the hands of the creditor, unless the creditor holds the property in a different capacity: see Graham Stewart, *The Law of Diligence*, p. 44; *Landcatch Ltd v. Sea Catch plc*, 1993 S.L.T. 451.

[30] For discussion, see paras 3.99 to 3.101 and 11.10 to 11.35.

[31] See at para. 29.28.

and no further service of a schedule of arrestment is required.[32] In contrast to the diligences of poinding and sale, and arrestment against earnings, an arrestment on the dependence of an action or in execution proceeds without a charge having been served on the debtor.

Subjects arrestable

29.16 Arrestment may be used by a creditor against debts owing to the debtor (called in this diligence the common debtor) by a third party (the arrestee) as well as against the common debtor's corporeal moveable property in the hands of a third party. What is crucial for the effectiveness of an arrestment is that at the time when the arrestment is served on the arrestee, the arrestee owes an "obligation to account" for the debt or moveable property to the common debtor.[33] The notion of an obligation to account being the test of arrestability of subjects has for long been stated and, though its application is obvious in many contexts, at times the principle lacks any clear meaning.[34] Indeed, in the classical statement of the principles of the law of diligence it is noted that "it is not, however, every obligation to account which may be arrested under these circumstances, and it is somewhat difficult to state a test for the validity of the arrestment which will be reconcilable with all the decided cases."[35] Accordingly this section is concerned with examining the specific types of property which may or may not be subject to arrestment in execution, and special attention will be given to various practical difficulties which arise in respect of certain types of such property.

Bank accounts

29.17 An account of the debtor held with a bank or building society is a common subject of an arrestment in execution.[36] It was formerly the practice of the Scottish banks that they would inform a creditor using arrestment in execution if the arrestment had attached an account of the common debtor (though the banks would not do so where the arrestment was used on the dependence of an action). More recently this practice has changed and banks do not reveal whether an arrestment, either on the dependence or in execution, has attached any account. This more recent practice is apparently based on the principle of the duty of confidentiality owed by a bank to its customers, though it has been argued that service of a schedule of arrestment on a bank may relieve the bank of a duty of customer confidentiality, at least in certain circumstances.[37]

29.18 Where an account is held in more than one name (often referred to as a joint account, though it is not a type of joint property), an arrestment attaches the entire account even though only one of the account holders is the common debtor.[38] An account which is held by the common debtor on

---

[32] *Abercromby v. Edgar and Crerar*, 1923 S.L.T. 271.

[33] *Shankland v. McGildowny*, 1912 S.C. 857 at 862; *Caldwell v. Hamilton*, 1919 S.C. (H.L.) 100 at 119.

[34] See Gretton, para. 261.

[35] Graham Stewart, *The Law of Diligence*, p. 71.

[36] Formerly accounts held with the National Savings Bank were exempt from arrestment. This prohibition was removed by the Law Reform (Miscellaneous Provisions) (Scotland) Act 1985, s. 49.

[37] L. D. Crerar, *The Law of Banking in Scotland* (1997), pp. 167–168.

[38] *Allan's Exr v. Union Bank of Scotland*, 1909 S.C. 206. The practice is that the rights of the other account holders are determined at a subsequent furthcoming.

behalf of, or in trust for, another party may not be arrested by the creditors of the common debtor except where it is not clear that another party is the true beneficiary of, or has rights to, the funds (*e.g.* where the trust funds have been mixed in with the common debtor's own).[39]

29.19 It has been held in one sheriff court decision that an arrestment served on the head office of a Scottish bank does not attach an account of the common debtor held at an English branch of the bank.[40] However, there may be circumstances in which an arrestment has effect to attach an account held outside Scotland, as where the arrestment was served on the arrestee in Scotland and the common debtor could have demanded payment in Scotland of the funds held in the account.[41]

29.20 There are different views on the proper practice in serving a schedule of arrestment on a bank.[42] Certainly service at the bank's head office will suffice to bring the arrestment into operation as probably will service at any branch. However, the better practice is to serve at the head office and also at any branch where it is thought the common debtor holds an account.[43]

Payments due under contracts

29.21 Fees, commissions and other payments due under a contract may be arrested once the contract has been concluded in the sense that the contracting parties have reached *consensus in idem*, even although the time for payment is not due when the arrestment is served.[44] Parties to a contract may not provide that a payment due under it is not arrestable.[45] Where arrestment is used to attach a payment due by an insurer under a contract of insurance, the arrestment has no effect unless the insurer's liability to make payment has already arisen under the terms of the policy.[46] However, in the case of life assurance the arrestment has effect even when the debtor-assured is still living.[47] Arrestment acts to catch any

---

[39] *Rigby v. Fletcher* (1833) 11 S. 256; *Lindsay v. London and North West Ry* (1860) 22 D. 571; *McAdam v. Martin's Trs* (1872) 11 M. 32; *National Bank v. McQueen* (1881) 18 S.L.R. 683; *Clark v. National Bank of Scotland* (1890) 27 S.L.R. 628; *Union Bank of Scotland v. Mills* (1926) 42 Sh.Ct.Rep. 141; *Royal Bank of Scotland v. Skinner*, 1931 S.L.T. 382.

[40] *Stewart v. Royal Bank of Scotland plc*, 1994 S.L.T. (Sh.Ct.) 27. See also *Ewing v. McLelland* (1860) 33 Sc. J. 1; *J. Verrico & Co. Ltd v. Australian Mutual Provident Society*, 1972 S.L.T. (Sh.Ct.) 57; *Bank of Scotland v. Seitz*, 1990 S.L.T. 584.

[41] *Hopper & Co. v. Walker* (1903) 20 Sh.Ct.Rep. 137; *McNairn v. McNairn*, 1959 S.L.T. (Notes) 35; *O'Brien v. A. Davies & Son Ltd*, 1961 S.L.T. 85; *Brash v. Brash*, 1966 S.C. 56. For further discussion see Maher & Cusine, pp. 116–117; Gretton, para. 260; Scottish Law Commission, *Extra-Territorial Effect of Arrestments and Related Matters*, Discussion Paper No. 90 (1990).

[42] For full discussion see Crerar, *op. cit.*, pp. 168–169.

[43] This is for the reason that where an arrestment is served on a head office, or one of a number of places of business, of a legal person, that person is given a reasonable time to process the arrestment through its various branches and will not be in breach of arrestment if the funds are paid to the debtor during this process: *cf. Laidlaw v. Smith* (1838) 16 S. 376; (1841) 2 Rob. 490.

[44] *Marshall & Nimmo & Co.* (1847) 10 D. 328; *MacLaren v. Preston* (1893) 1 S.L.T. 75; *Park Dobson v. William Taylor & Son*, 1929 S.C. 571; *Royal Bank of Scotland plc v. Law*, 1996 S.L.T. 83.

[45] *Fritz's Agency Ltd v. Moss Empires Ltd* (1922) 38 Sh.Ct.Rep. 124.

[46] *Kerr v. R. & W. Ferguson*, 1931 S.C. 736; *cf. Boland v. White Cross Insurance Association*, 1926 S.C. 1066.

[47] *Strachan v. McDougle* (1835) 13 S. 954; *Bankhardt's Trustees v. Scottish Amicable Assurance Society* (1871) 9 M. 443; *Clark v. Scottish Amicable Assurance Society* (1922) 38 Sh.Ct.Rep. 170.

arrears of rent owing at the time it is served along with the rent owing for the current term of the lease.[48]

Damages

The authorities on whether, or when, a claim for damages may be arrested are far from clear.[49] There is no difficulty in the situation where a court has made an award of damages in favour of the common debtor. Here the right to receive damages may be arrested.[50] Problems arise where arrestment is served at an earlier stage: does the arrestment have effect even if the common debtor has yet to intimate his claim, or when he has intimated the claim but not raised the action, or where he has raised the action which is still proceeding? Authorities on this point are not entirely consistent. General principle suggests that, provided ultimately damages are awarded, arrestment will attach them even if served at some earlier stage. The question is, what is that stage. It is thought that the appropriate moment is when an action has been raised. Accordingly an arrestment served prior to the raising of an action would not be effective to catch any subsequent award of damages. **29.22**

A further difficulty arises where a claim for damages, whether or not an action has been raised, is met by settlement between the parties.[51] The settlement extinguishes the original claim for damages by way of novation and substitutes for it a different debt under the settlement. It would be possible for the arrester to arrest again once the settlement has been reached, and before payment is made under it, but it may be difficult for the creditor to have the precise knowledge which this step requires. An award under the Criminal Injuries Compensation Scheme cannot be arrested in the hands of the Criminal Injuries Compensation Board.[52] **29.23**

Shares

Shares in a company are arrestable by the creditors of the shareholder provided the company is registered in Scotland.[53] An arrestment of shares will also attach the next payment of dividend and any arrears of dividend.[54] Where shares are held by the debtor through a nominee who is the registered shareholder, the arrestment should be served on the nominee not the company.[55] The arrestment is ineffective where the common debtor/shareholder has sold his shares and intimated the sale to the company, even though the sale has not been followed by a change in the register of shareholders.[56] Where a call on shareholders has been made by a company, the amount due on the call is arrestable in the hands of the shareholder by the creditors of the company but uncalled capital is not arrestable.[57] **29.24**

---

[48] *Livingston v. Kinloch* (1795) Mor. 769; *Smith & Kinnear v. Burns* (1847) 9 D. 1344.
[49] For discussion, see Gretton, para. 274.
[50] *Alexander Mather & Son v. John Wilson & Co. Ltd* (1908) 15 S.L.T. 946.
[51] *ibid.* where an action was settled by the defender's insurers.
[52] Criminal Injuries Compensation Act 1995, s. 7.
[53] *Sinclair v. Staples* (1860) 22 D. 600; *American Mortgage Company of Scotland v. Sidway*, 1909 S.C. 500.
[54] Gretton, para. 269.
[55] *Blade Securities Ltd, Petitioners*, 1989 S.L.T. 246.
[56] *Thomson v. Fullerton* (1842) 5 D. 379; *Harvey's Yoker Distillery Ltd v. Singleton* (1901) 8 S.L.T. 294.
[57] *Hill v. College of Glasgow* (1849) 12 D. 46; *Lindsay v. La Martona Rubber Estates Ltd*, 1911 2 S.L.T. 468.

Partnership interest

29.25 The interest of a partner in a partnership may be arrested by his creditors.[58] However, the arrestment cannot be completed by a furthcoming until the partnership is dissolved. A creditor of a partner as an individual cannot arrest in the hands of a person who owes a debt to the partnership itself.[59]

Rights due under trusts and succession

29.26 The right of a beneficiary under a trust is arrestable unless the right is heritable.[60] Where the right is to receive payment of a sum of money, the right is moveable and hence arrestable. Similarly a vested right in succession may be arrested, but not a non-vested *spes successionis*.[61] Where a power exists to restrict or vary payment under a trust, an arrestment will attach the right to the payment, but this is subject to any exercise of the power.[62]

Corporeal moveables

29.27 For corporeal moveables of the common debtor to be subject to an arrestment it is necessary that the goods are in the possession of a third party who has a duty to account for them to the common debtor.[63] Examples include goods of the common debtor held by a banker, custodier, factor, depositary, or solicitor.[64] This test is higher than that required to constitute a right of lien over the goods. Thus goods in the hands of an innkeeper or hotel owner are not subject to arrestment by the creditor of the guest who owns them.[65] Goods in the hands of the police or procurator fiscal are deemed still to be in the possession of their owner and may not be arrested in the hands of those officials.[66] Goods which are exempt from poinding under section 16 of the Debtors (Scotland) Act 1987 are not subject to arrestment.[67] Bills and documents which have no intrinsic mercantile value are not arrestable, nor are bills or negotiable instruments as mere physical objects.[68]

---

58 *Cassells v. Stewart* (1879) 6 R. 936, 956.

59 *Parnell v. Walter* (1889) 16 R. 917.

60 *Learmonts v. Shearer* (1866) 4 M. 540.

61 *Trappes v. Meredith* (1871) 10 M. 38; *Waddell v. Waddell's Tr.*, 1932 S.L.T. 201.

62 *Chamber's Trs v. Smith* (1878) 5 R. (H.L.) 151.

63 Thus goods are not arrestable where the duty to account is owed to someone other than the common debtor: *Young v. Aktiebolaget Ofverums Bank* (1890) 18 R. 163; *Heron v. Winfields Ltd* (1894) 22 R. 182.

64 *Graham v. Macfarlane* (1869) 7 M. 640 (banker); *Inglis v. Robertson & Baxter* (1898) 25 R. (H.L.) 70 (custodier); *Dunlop v. Weir* (1823) 2 S. 167 (factor); *Bridges v. Ewing* (1830) 15 S. 8 (depository); *Telford's Exr v. Blackwood* (1866) 4 M. 369 (solicitor).

65 *Hume v. Baillie* (1852) 14 D. 821; *Hutchison v. Hutchison*, 1912 1 S.L.T. 219. Such creditor may poind goods in the hands of these parties, though the poinding would be subject to any lien that may exist over the goods.

66 *Stuart v. Cowan & Co.* (1883) 10 R. 581; *Jopp v. McHardy* (1890) 2 Guthrie's Sh.Ct.Cas. 145; *Guthrie v. Morren* (1939) 55 Sh.Ct.Rep. 172.

67 Note, however, that goods exempt from poinding under s. 16(2) of the 1987 Act must be situated in a dwelling-house and reasonably required for the use of people resident there. Accordingly the exemption from poinding and arrestment would not apply to the debtor's furniture, etc., stored in a warehouse.

68 *Trowsdale's Tr. v. Forcett Ry* (1870) 9 M. 88; *Millar & Lang v. Poole* (1907) 15 S.L.T. 76. Bills and negotiable instruments as physical objects are considered to be documents of debt. However, the debt embodied in the document is arrestable.

Ships

An important example in practice of a physical object which may be arrested is a ship.[69] Arrestment, not poinding, is the appropriate diligence to use in respect of a ship, even if the vessel is in the possession of her owner.[70] Various limitations exist in respect of the use of arrestment of a ship on the dependence of an action but have no application where arrestment is used in execution of a decree or its equivalent. Arrestment of a ship does not by itself attach cargo, which must be arrested separately. An arrestment of a ship is completed not by an action of furthcoming but by sale. Procedure is by way of motion in the original action.[71] The rules concerning arrestment of a ship do not apply to arrestment of an aircraft.[72] The appropriate diligence to use in respect of an aircraft is either arrestment or poinding depending upon which party (the common debtor or a third party) has possession of the aircraft. **29.28**

Property not subject to arrestment

The diligence of arrestment may be used only against the moveable property of the common debtor which (except in the case of a ship) is not in his possession. As a consequence, heritable property of the common debtor cannot be arrested. Furthermore, property which is not, or is no longer, the common debtor's at the time of service of the arrestment is not caught by the arrestment. A special instance of this principle is property held as joint property, as distinguished from property in which the debtor has common ownership. Joint property in the strict sense cannot be arrested in respect of debts owed by any of the owners as individuals.[73] A debt which is not owed directly by the arrestee to the common debtor is not arrestable, nor are goods the ownership of which has passed from the common debtor.[74] Goods or funds which have been appropriated to a special purpose, and in effect are beyond the debtor's control, may not be arrested provided the appropriation took place prior to the service of the arrestment and was made in good faith.[75] Furthermore, certain types of moveable property of the debtor which would be arrestable in terms of general principle are exempt from arrestment or from diligence generally. They are: **29.29**

(a) Earnings. The common law diligence of arrestment may not be used against the category of earnings of the debtor to which the new statutory

---

[69] For useful discussion see Gretton, paras 322–328. It may be noted that a ship can be arrested on a Sunday: *Nederlandse Scheepshypotheekbank v. Cam Standby Ltd*, 1994 S.C.L.R. 956. *Cf.* RCS, r. 16.13(1).

[70] *Barclay Curle & Co. Ltd v. Sir James Laing & Sons Ltd*, 1908 S.C. 82 at 89.

[71] *Banque Indo Suez v. Maritime Co. Overseas Inc.*, 1985 S.L.T. 117.

[72] *Emerald Airways Ltd v. Nordic Oil Services Ltd*, 1996 S.L.T. 403. However, a seaplane may in some circumstances be treated as a ship for the purposes of the law of diligence.

[73] *Fleming v. Twaddle* (1828) 7 S. 92; *Lucas's Tr. v. Campbell & Scott* (1894) 21 R. 1096; *Lord Ruthven v. Pulford*, 1909 S.C. 951.

[74] *J. & C. Murray v. Wallace Marrs & Co.*, 1914 S.C. 114 (debt owed to arrestee by one of his own debtors not arrestable by creditor of common debtor). See also *Hay v. Dufourcet & Co.* (1880) 7 R. 972 (debt due to a company not arrestable by creditors of a member as individual); *Hope's Tr. v. Hope* (1904) 11 S.L.T. 625 (goods no longer in debtor's ownership not arrestable).

[75] *Mackenzie & Co. v. Finlay* (1868) 7 M. 27; *National Bank of Scotland v. MacQueen* (1881) 18 S.L.R. 683; *British Linen Co. v. Kansas Investment Co.* (1895) 3 S.L.T. 138, 202; *Hughes v. Lord Advocate*, 1993 S.C.L.R. 155.

diligences, introduced by Part III of the Debtors (Scotland) Act 1987, apply.[76]

(b) Alimentary payments. Payments owing to the common debtor for purposes of providing him with aliment and maintenance are not arrestable.[77] However, anything in excess of what is required for alimentary purposes is arrestable, as are arrears of aliment.[78] Where a creditor has supplied the debtor with the necessities for his aliment, that creditor may use arrestment against alimentary payments owing to the common debtor.[79]

(c) Statutory exempt payments; social security benefits and pensions. Where a statute prohibits any "assignation or charge" on any payment of money, the effect is that such a payment cannot be subject to any diligence, including arrestment.[80] Social security benefits and state pensions are generally covered by this prohibition and so cannot be arrested. However, it is not clear whether, once payment has been made, the prohibition on arrestment continues to apply where the payment can still be separately identified as such (*e.g.* in a bank account).[81]

Effect of arrestment

29.30 Arrestment operates by way of preventing the arrestee from paying the arrested debt or handing over the arrested goods to the common debtor. Failure by the arrestee to observe this prohibition will lead to breach of arrestment, for which the arrestee is liable to pay to the creditor the amount of the arrested debt or the value of the arrested property.[82]

29.31 As far as concerns the position of the creditor who uses arrestment, arrestment is an inchoate diligence in the sense that the creditor has no complete right to the arrested subject until or unless there is an action of furthcoming or the more informal method of mandate. Furthermore, a fundamental principle of the law of arrestment is that it affects the arrested subject *tantum et tale*, that is the rights in the subjects which the arrestment protects for the arresting creditor are no greater than the rights in the subjects which the common debtor had at the time of the arrestment. Accordingly the arrested subjects may be affected by the exercise of a power to restrict payment under a trust, provided the existence of this power predated the arrestment (even though its

---

[76] For the definition of earnings to which the new diligences extend, see 1987 Act, s. 73(2) and discussion at para. 29.40 *et seq.* Earnings which do not fall within this statutory definition (*e.g.* fees owed to self-employed persons) are, unless otherwise exempt, open to the diligence of common law arrestment.

[77] *E. Buchan v. His Creditors* (1835) 13 S. 1112; *Lord Ruthven v. Pulford & Sons*, 1909 S.C. 951; *Hughes v. Lord Advocate*, 1993 S.C.L.R. 155.

[78] *Livingstone v. Livingstone* (1886) 14 R. 43; *Cuthbert v. Cuthbert's Trs*, 1908 S.C. 967.

[79] *Waddell v. Waddell* (1836) 15 S. 151; *Lord Ruthven v. Pulford & Sons*, 1909 S.C. 951; *Turnbull & Son v. Scott* (1899) 15 Sh.Ct.Rep. 268. For this purpose a sum owing as aliment under a court decree is not an alimentary debt: Graham Stewart, p. 103; *Officer's Superannuation and Provident Fund v. Cooper*, 1976 S.L.T. (Sh.Ct.) 2.

[80] *Mulvenna v. The Admiralty*, 1926 S.C. 854 at 856.

[81] Gretton (at para. 280) suggests that an alimentary sum remains so as long as it is identifiable as such. The Scottish Law Commission in its *Report on Diligence and Debtor Protection* (Scot. Law Com. No. 95 (1985)), para. 6.285 dismissed the idea that earnings protected from diligence retained their protection once paid into a bank or other account.

[82] Breach of Arrestment Act 1581; *Grant v. Hill* (1792) Mor. 786; *Laidlaw v. Smith* (1838) 16 S. 367, (1841) 2 Rob. 490; *High-Flex (Scotland) Ltd v. Kentallen Mechanical Services Co.*, 1977 S.L.T. (Sh.Ct.) 91; *McSkimming v. Royal Bank of Scotland*, 1996 S.C.L.R. 547.

exercise was subsequent to it).[83] A further example is the right of the arrestee to apply set-off or compensation against the arrested debt.[84]

However, it is clear that an arrestment, even in the absence of a subsequent furthcoming or mandate, provides the arresting creditor with a range of preferences in competition with other diligences and related processes. Priority among arrestments is determined by the date of service of their respective schedules, irrespective of any subsequent furthcoming.[85] Where a debt is subject to both an assignation and arrestment, priority depends on which is the earlier between the service of the schedule of the arrestment and the intimation of the assignation.[86] **29.32**

Where an arrestment is in competition with a poinding, priority depends on the earlier of the date of decree in a subsequent furthcoming and the date of completion of the diligence of poinding and sale.[87] An arrestment not followed by a furthcoming is not an effectually executed diligence in terms of the legislation dealing with floating charges. A floating charge has preference over such an arrestment where the floating charge has been created prior to the arrestment, even though the attachment of the charge is subsequent to the arrestment.[88] The rule is different where the arrestment has preceded the creation of the charge. In that case a subsequent receiver of the company takes the company's property subject to the arrestment.[89] **29.33**

An arrestment will prevail over the subsequent sequestration or liquidation of the common debtor unless it was served within 60 days of the date of the sequestration or liquidation.[90] An arrestment served within this period is in effect cut down by the bankruptcy process though the expenses of the ineffectual arrestment are a preferential debt in that process. Moreover, an arrestment served more than 60 days prior to a bankruptcy process may still be affected by the sequestration or liquidation by operation of the rule that arrestments laid on within 60 days before or four months after the common debtor's apparent insolvency are equalised.[91] The practical effect is that an arrestment served within this equalisation period, and then subject to a bankruptcy process, is ineffective.[92] **29.34**

Where an arrestment is not affected by a sequestration the arrestee hands over the arrested property or funds to the trustee in sequestration who gives effect to the arresting creditor's preference.[93] However, a **29.35**

---

[83] *Chamber's Trs v. Smiths* (1878) 5 R. (H.L.) 151.

[84] *Brodie v. Wilson* (1837) 15 S. 1195; *MacPherson v. Wright* (1885) 12 R. 942; *Lennie v. Mackie & Co.* (1907) 23 Sh. Ct.Rep. 85.

[85] *Wallace v. Scot* (1583) Mor. 807; *Sutie v. Ross* (1705) Mor. 816; *Hertz v. Itzig* (1865) 3 M. 813. However, the preference may be lost by undue delay in following up the arrestment with an action of furthcoming: Graham Stewart, p. 141.

[86] Stair III, I, 43; Graham Stewart, p. 141.

[87] Graham Stewart, p. 365. It is submitted that the diligence of poinding and sale is not complete until the report of the sale has been lodged with the court.

[88] Companies Act 1985, s. 463(1); Insolvency Act 1986, s. 55(3); *Lord Advocate v. Royal Bank of Scotland*, 1977 S.C. 155.

[89] *Iona Hotels Ltd (in receivership), Petrs*, 1991 S.L.T. 11.

[90] Bankruptcy (Scotland) Act 1985, s. 37(4); Insolvency Act 1986, s. 185(1).

[91] *ibid. s. 75(1) and Sched. 7, para. 24.*

[92] *Stewart v. Jarvie*, 1938 S.C. 309.

[93] *Berry v. Taylor*, 1992 S.C.L.R. 910.

different practice applies in respect of liquidation; here the arrestee retains the property or funds until ordered to transfer them under a decree of furthcoming or multiplepoinding.[94]

Ending of arrestment

29.36 As arrestment in execution proceeds on the basis of a decree (or its equivalent) which constitutes a debt, there is less scope for the recall or loosing of the diligence as is the case with arrestment on the dependence of the action.[95] Recall or loosing may be made only where the debt is paid in full (including the expenses of the arrestment) or where, despite the decree, there is some doubt that the debt is or may become due.[96]

29.37 In order to complete an arrestment, and to allow for the transfer of the arrested subjects to the creditor, an action of furthcoming is required. However, in practice this effect is achieved by the more informal practice whereby the common debtor grants a mandate to the arrestee to hand over the arrested property or funds to the creditor. Where the common debtor is called upon, but refuses, to grant a mandate he will normally be liable in the expenses of a subsequent furthcoming.

29.38 An arrestment in execution prescribes after three years from the date of service of the arrestment.[97] The prescription period is interrupted by the raising of an action of furthcoming or multiplepoinding.[98]

Furthcoming

29.39 As noted, to complete fully the diligence of arrestment the arresting creditor has to raise an action of furthcoming, though in practice most arrestments result in the granting of a mandate. Although a furthcoming presupposes a prior existing arrestment, and is really part of the diligence, it proceeds by way of a separate action. Actions of furthcoming are discussed elsewhere in this book.[99]

Arrestment of Earnings

29.40 The common law diligence of arrestment and furthcoming as applied to the earnings of the debtor was abolished by the Debtors (Scotland) Act 1987 and replaced by three new statutory diligences: earnings arrestment,

---

[94] *Commercial Aluminium Windows Ltd v. Cumbernauld Development Corpn*, 1987 S.L.T. (Sh.Ct.) 91.

[95] Although the terms recall and loosing are sometimes used as synonyms, strictly they refer to different processes. Recall has the effect of ending an arrestment, whereas loosing does not entirely extinguish the diligence or the nexus it creates. For full discussion see Scottish Law Commission, *Diligence on the Dependence and Admiralty Arrestments*, Discussion Paper No. 84 (1989), paras 2.246–2.263.

[96] Graham Stewart, pp. 196–198 instances the cases of a decree being under suspension or reduction, where arrestment is founded on a registered mutual contract, and where the debt is future or contingent. An arrestment in execution may be loosed on caution where the arrested subject is owned in common by the debtor and another person.

[97] Debtors (Scotland) Act 1838, s. 22. Special rules apply where the arrestment is used for a contingent or future debt. See *Jamieson v. Sharp* (1887) 14 R. 643.

[98] Any period during which the arrestment is subject to a time to pay order is to be disregarded in calculating the period of prescription: Debtors (Scotland) Act 1838, s. 22(2).

[99] See paras 21.45 to 21.51.

current maintenance arrestment, and conjoined arrestment order.[1] Although the 1987 Act uses the term "arrestment" in the names of these diligences it is clear that each is a new type of diligence, and is not a modified form of the common law diligence.[2] It is important to note that the new diligences apply only in respect of "earnings" as that term is defined in section 73 of the 1987 Act.[3] The common law diligence remains competent, unless otherwise excluded, as against earnings not covered by the statutory definition.

Earnings arrestment

Earnings arrestment is the appropriate diligence to use to recover a debt other than one owing as current maintenance.[4] An earnings arrestment used to recover a debt also recovers interest accrued as at the date of service of the arrestment and the expenses of the diligence. **29.41**

Commencement of earnings arrestment

An earnings arrestment must be preceded by prior service of a charge for payment on the debtor.[5] The period of charge is 14 days if the debtor is in the United Kingdom and otherwise 28 days. Once the days of charge have expired without payment in full an earnings arrestment schedule may be served on the debtor's employer by an officer of court.[6] The employer must be subject to the jurisdiction of the Scottish courts. Service is made by registered or recorded delivery post or where service is not possible by these means by any other competent mode of service.[7] **29.42**

Operation of earnings arrestment

Earnings arrestment operates by requiring the employer of the debtor to make deductions from the debtor's net earnings, and to pay over the sum deducted to the creditor as soon as reasonably practicable.[8] An earnings arrestment comes into effect as soon as it is served on the employer, but he is not required to apply the earnings arrestment until the debtor's next pay seven days after service of the schedule.[9] **29.43**

The earnings arrestment schedule sets out various tables, which correspond to tables in Schedule 2 to the 1987 Act, which provide guidance to the employer in calculating the correct deduction to be made. The employer must first work out the net earnings of the debtor as that term **29.44**

---

[1] 1987 Act, s. 46(1). The common law *beneficium competentiae* has also been abolished in respect of diligence against such earnings: s. 46(2).

[2] *Scobie v. Dumfries & Galloway R.C.*, 1991 S.L.T. (Sh.Ct.) 33; *Slater v. Grampian R.C.*, 1991 S.L.T. (Sh.Ct.) 72.

[3] This includes but is not confined to most forms of payment made to an employee under a contract of employment. See further *Feeney v. United Biscuits*, 1993 S.C.L.R. 965; *GUD Pension Trustee Ltd v. Quinn*, 1994 S.C.L.R. 1105. See also Merchant Shipping Act 1995, s. 34(1)(b) in respect of diligences available against the wages of a seaman.

[4] 1987 Act, s. 46(1)(a). For the definition of current maintenance, see paras 29.50 *et seq*.

[5] Service of a charge for payment is not necessary for an earnings arrestment pursuant to a summary warrant. For further discussion of a charge, see paras 29.67 *et seq*.

[6] 1987 Act, s. 90(1). For form of schedule see A.S. (Proceedings in the Sheriff Court under the Debtors (Scotland) Act 1987) 1988 (S.I. 1988 No. 2013), r. 38, Form 30.

[7] *ibid* s. 70(3), S.I. 1988 No. 2013, r. 66. The officer must also intimate a copy of the schedule to the debtor but failure to make such intimation does not invalidate the diligence: 1987 Act, s. 70(1), (2).

[8] *ibid* s. 47(1).

[9] *ibid.* s. 69(2), (3).

is defined in section 73 of the 1987 Act. From the net earnings the debtor is entitled to receive a certain level of earnings as set out in the tables in Schedule 2 to the 1987 Act for purposes of subsistence. This amount is currently set at £63 per week of net earnings. From the balance left after allowing for the amount representing the debtor's subsistence, a certain level of deduction is to be made by the employer to be paid over to the creditor.[10] The statutory tables provide for the appropriate level of deductions and levels for subsistence in respect of earnings paid at various regular intervals, earnings paid at irregular intervals, and additional forms of payment.

29.45 Where an employer fails to operate an earnings arrestment properly the creditor may recover from him any sums which he should have received under the earnings arrestment. An employer is not bound to operate an earnings arrestment where the schedule wrongly states the name or address of the employee unless (perhaps) the employer can with certainty otherwise identify the employee.[11] Any such claim by the creditor must be made within one year of the date of the employer's failure to make the appropriate deduction or to pay a deducted sum to the creditor.[12] An employer who is required to make a payment for failure to operate an earnings arrestment cannot recover this payment from the debtor.

29.46 An earnings arrestment may be subject to review by application to the sheriff.[13] Application may be made by the debtor or person on whom the schedule of earnings arrestment was served for a declarator that an earnings arrestment is invalid or has ceased to have effect.[14] Where a declarator is granted the sheriff has power to make such consequential orders as are appropriate. Furthermore, an application may be made by the debtor, creditor or employer for the sheriff to determine any dispute arising from the operation of the earnings arrestment.[15] In making a determination the sheriff has power to order payment of sums which should have been paid under the earnings arrestment and repayment of sums wrongfully paid.

Duration of earnings arrestment

29.47 Unless otherwise brought to an end, an earnings arrestment continues in effect until payment in full has been made of the debt it is used to recover. By its very nature earnings arrestment depends upon the debtor being in employment with the employer in whose hands it is served, and an earnings arrestment will also terminate whenever that employer-employee relationship itself ends.

29.48 Where a time to pay order is made in favour of a debtor any earnings arrestment being used against his earnings will be recalled.[16] The granting of an interim time to pay order prevents the service of a schedule of

---

[10] 1987 Act, s. 49.

[11] *Clydesdale Bank plc v. Scottish Midland Co-operative Society Ltd*, 1995 S.C.L.R. 1151.

[12] 1987 Act, ss. 57(1), 69(4).

[13] The appropriate sheriff is one with jurisdiction over the place where the earnings arrestment was executed or, if that is not known, over an established place of business of the employer: 1987 Act, ss. 50, 73(1).

[14] 1987 Act, s. 50(1); S.I. 1988 No. 2013, r. 40, Form 32.

[15] *ibid* s. 50(3); S.I. 1988 No. 2013, Form 33.

[16] *ibid* s. 9(2).

earnings arrestment but does not by itself interrupt the operation of an earnings arrestment currently in force. An earnings arrestment ceases to have effect on the date of the sequestration of the debtor's estate, but deductions under the earnings arrestment made prior to that date may be paid over to the creditor.[17]

In various circumstances where an earnings arrestment comes to an end, especially where the debt has been paid in full, the debtor and employer may not be aware of the relevant facts. Accordingly, whenever the debt is no longer recoverable by the earnings arrestment, the creditor must give written notice to the employer as soon as reasonably practicable.[18] Failure to take this step may render the creditor liable in payment to the debtor.[19] **29.49**

Current maintenance arrestment

Current maintenance arrestment is used as a means of collecting from the debtor's earnings payments owing as maintenance as they fall due. Such a debt is one owing under a type of maintenance order set out in section 106 of the 1987 Act. Accordingly, the diligence of current maintenance arrestment is not used to recover arrears of maintenance, or the expenses involved in the maintenance order, or the current maintenance arrestment. However, a current maintenance arrestment may be used to collect maintenance owing under more than one maintenance order by the same debtor to the same maintenance creditor.[20] **29.50**

Commencement of current maintenance arrestment

No charge for payment needs to be served on the debtor prior to a current maintenance arrestment, but there are two prerequisites which must exist before a current maintenance arrestment schedule can be served on the debtor's employer. These are, first, that the debtor is in default of payment of a sum not less than one instalment of maintenance[21]; and secondly, that the creditor has made intimation on the debtor of the making, registration or confirmation of the maintenance order, followed by a lapse of four weeks.[22] However, these prerequisites do not apply where the creditor has previously used a current maintenance arrestment against the same debtor which has ceased to have effect less than three months earlier,[23] or in certain circumstances as regards enforcement by current maintenance arrestment of various types of non-Scottish maintenance orders.[24] **29.51**

---

[17] 1987 Act, s. 72(2), (4).

[18] *ibid.* s. 57(4); S.I. 1988 No. 2013, r. 50.

[19] This can be for either repayment of any deductions made by the employer and transmitted to the creditor subsequent to the debt being no longer recoverable or for an order from the sheriff for payment of a sum not exceeding twice the amount of any sum wrongfully deducted: 1987 Act, ss. 69(5), 57(6); S.I. 1988 No. 2013, r. 51, Form 41.

[20] 1987 Act, s. 52. Where the creditor is in receipt of income support, payments under a current maintenance arrestment or conjoined arrestment order may be diverted to the Secretary of State: Social Security Administration Act 1992, s. 109.

[21] *ibid.* s. 54(1)(c).

[22] *ibid.* s. 54(1); S.I. 1988 No. 2013, r. 45, Form 37.

[23] *ibid.* s. 54(3). This exception to the need for the prerequisites for the diligence does not apply where the current maintenance arrestment has ceased to have effect because it was recalled under s. 55(2) of the 1987 Act.

[24] *ibid.* s. 54(2).

29.52 A schedule of current maintenance arrestment in prescribed form must be served on the debtor's employer by an officer of court.[25] A copy should also be intimated to the debtor, but failure to take this step does not invalidate the diligence.[26] A current maintenance arrestment takes effect once served on the employer, but he does not need to operate it until the next pay day occurring after seven days from the date of service of the schedule of current maintenance arrestment.[27]

Operation of current maintenance arrestment

29.53 In giving effect to a current maintenance arrestment the employer makes a deduction from the earnings of the debtor on every pay day on which the arrestment is in force. The amount to be deducted is calculated by reference to a daily rate of maintenance due under the maintenance order (the daily rate being specified in the current maintenance arrestment schedule) for each day since the last pay day or in the case of the first deduction since the arrestment came into effect. However, the debtor is entitled to a sum of £9 for each day during the period covered by the deduction.[28] As soon as reasonably practicable the employer must pay to the creditor any sum deducted from the debtor's earnings, and failure to operate a current maintenance arrestment properly, or to hand over deductions made, renders the employer liable to the creditor.[29]

29.54 While a current maintenance arrestment is in effect it may be subject to review by a sheriff. This is done by making an application to the sheriff who has jurisdiction over the place where the arrestment was executed.[30] There are three bases for review of a current maintenance arrestment:

(i) Application may be made by the debtor or person on whom the current maintenance arrestment schedule was served for a declarator that the current maintenance arrestment is invalid or has ceased to have effect.[31] Where a declarator is granted, the sheriff has power to make such consequential orders as are appropriate.

(ii) Application may be made by the debtor for recall of the current maintenance arrestment on the ground that he is unlikely to default again in making payment of maintenance.[32]

(iii) Application may be made by the debtor, creditor or employer for the sheriff to determine any dispute arising from the operation of the current maintenance arrestment.[33] In making a determination the sheriff has power to order payment of sums which should have been paid under the earnings arrestment and repayment of sums wrongfully paid.

Cessation of current maintenance arrestment

29.55 A current maintenance arrestment continues in effect while the debtor remains in employment with the employer unless it has been recalled.[34]

---

[25] 1987 Act, s. 51(2)(a); S.I. 1988 No. 2013, r. 42, Form 34.

[26] *ibid.* s. 70(1), (2).

[27] 1987 Act, s. 69(2), (3).

[28] *ibid.* s. 53(1).

[29] *ibid.* ss. 51(1), 57(1). The rules on the employer's liability are the same as those for failure to operate an earnings arrestment, discussed at para. 29.45.

[30] If that place is not known to the applicant, application is made to the sheriff with jurisdiction over an established place of business of the employer: 1987 Act,. ss. 55, 73(1).

[31] 1987 Act, s. 55(1); S.I. 1988 No. 2013, r. 46, Form 38.

[32] *ibid.* s. 55(2); S.I. 1988 No. 2013, r. 47, Form 39.

[33] *ibid.* s. 55(5), (6), (7); S.I. 1988 No. 2013, r. 48, Form 40.

[34] *ibid.* s. 51(2)(b).

Where the obligation to pay under the maintenance order ceases, or is no longer enforceable in Scotland, the current maintenance arrestment comes to an end.[35] A similar effect arises where the original maintenance order is varied or superseded by a later one but, where the later order is made by a court in Scotland, that court has the power to defer the coming into effect of that order to allow the service of a schedule of a new current maintenance arrestment in respect of it.[36]

The making of an interim or full time to pay order does not affect the operation of a current maintenance arrestment. The rules regarding the effect on a current maintenance arrestment of the apparent insolvency of the debtor or the sequestration of his estate are the same as those which apply to an earnings arrestment.[37] **29.56**

Where the maintenance debt is extinguished or no longer enforceable the creditor must give intimation to the employer as soon as practicable. The creditor may be liable to the debtor in respect of sums wrongfully deducted because of any failure to inform the employer.[38] **29.57**

Conjoined arrestment order

General

Two crucial features of the new diligences against earnings are that they continue until the debt is paid off (or otherwise extinguished) and also allow the debtor-employee a protected level of earnings for purposes of his subsistence. One consequence of these features is that there is little scope for the simultaneous operation of two or more diligences against the same earnings. The 1987 Act makes it a general rule that only one diligence against the same earnings may be in use at any one time. This is subject to one exception, namely that one earnings arrestment and one current maintenance arrestment may be used simultaneously against the earnings of the debtor.[39] In all other circumstances where a creditor is shut out by the general rule, his remedy is to apply for a conjoined arrestment order.[40] **29.58**

Such a creditor must be supplied with information by the employer on the details of the earnings arrestment or current maintenance arrestment currently in force against the debtor's earnings.[41] To be qualified to apply for a conjoined arrestment order the creditor must have taken all steps appropriate for executing an earnings arrestment or current maintenance arrestment against the debtor's earnings.[42] Application for a conjoined arrestment order is made to the sheriff court with jurisdiction over the place where the arrestment currently in force was executed.[43] **29.59**

---

[35] 1987 Act, s. 55(8).

[36] *ibid.* s. 56(1), (2).

[37] See para. 29.48.

[38] 1987 Act, s. 57(4), (6). For discussion, see para. 29.49.

[39] *ibid.* s. 58(1).

[40] The provisions on equalisation of diligences under the Bankruptcy (Scotland) Act 1985, Sched. 7, para. 24 do not apply to diligences against earnings: 1987 Act, s. 67, Sched. 6, para. 28(b).

[41] 1987 Act, s. 59(4), (5).

[42] *ibid.* s. 60(1)(b).

[43] Procedure is governed by S.I. 1988 No. 2013, r. 53, Form 43. Where an earnings arrestment and current maintenance arrestment are both in operation, application for a conjoined arrestment order may be made to the sheriff court for the place where either was executed: 1987 Act, s. 73(1).

Effect and operation of conjoined arrestment order

29.60 Where a conjoined arrestment order is granted a copy must be served on the employer, the debtor, and the creditor or creditors using the existing arrestment or arrestments against the debtor's earnings. The order recalls existing diligences against earnings and requires the employer to make deductions from the earnings on every pay day on which the conjoined arrestment order has effect. The amount to be deducted is governed by section 63 of the 1987 Act, and depends on whether the debts covered by the order (which are specified in the order itself) are non-maintenance debts, current maintenance or a mixture of the two types of debt. The employer is also under a duty to remit each deducted sum to the sheriff clerk who is responsible for distributing the sum to the participating creditors.[44] Disbursement is made in accordance with the rules set out in Schedule 3 to the 1987 Act.[45]

29.61 While a conjoined arrestment order is in effect application may be made to the sheriff by a creditor, debtor, employer, or the sheriff clerk to determine any dispute over its operation. In making any determination the sheriff has power to order payment of sums which should have been paid under the earnings arrestment, and repayment of sums wrongfully paid.[46]

Variation of conjoined arrestment order

29.62 While a conjoined arrestment order is in operation it is not possible to use diligence or a further conjoined arrestment order against the debtor's earnings. A creditor who is qualified to proceed with a diligence against earnings, but is shut out by this rule, may apply to the sheriff for an order to vary the existing conjoined arrestment order to include the debts owing to the applicant within the scope of the order's operation.[47] Application is made to the sheriff court which granted the original conjoined arrestment order.[48] An order making a variation specifies the debt or debts to be recovered by the conjoined arrestment order.

29.63 Where a debt included in a conjoined arrestment order is paid in full or otherwise extinguished, the creditor in question must inform the sheriff clerk of this fact. Failure to do so renders the creditor liable to repay to the sheriff clerk further disbursements received by him.[49] Where a debt is extinguished, or is no longer enforceable, application is made to the sheriff for an order to vary the terms of the conjoined arrestment order to take account of that debt dropping out of the operation of the order.[50] A creditor whose debt is being enforced by a conjoined arrestment order may at any time apply to the sheriff for an order to vary the conjoined arrestment order by excluding his debt from the order's scope.[51]

---

[44] Failure by an employer to comply with his duties under the order renders him liable to make payment to the sheriff clerk of sums which should have been deducted and remitted: s. 60(9), S.I. 1988 No. 2013, r. 55.

[45] 1987 Act, s. 64.

[46] *ibid.* s. 65(1), (2); S.I. 1988 No. 2013, r. 59, Form 54.

[47] *ibid.* s. 62(5); S.I. 1988 No. 2013, r. 57, Form 49.

[48] *ibid.* s. 73(1).

[49] *ibid.* s. 65(5)–(8); S.I. 1988 No. 2013, r. 60, Form 55.

[50] *ibid* s. 66(4); S.I. 1988 No. 2013, r. 63. Application may be made by the debtor, any creditor, the employer or the sheriff clerk.

[51] *ibid.* s. 66(6); S.I. 1988 No. 2013, r. 64.

Cessation of conjoined arrestment order

A conjoined arrestment order remains in effect while the debtor continues in employment with the employer on whom the order was served; but it will cease to have effect if recalled. Application for recall may be made by the debtor, any creditor whose debt is being enforced under the order, any person on whom a copy of the order (or a variation order) has been served, the sheriff clerk, and, where the debtor's estate has been sequestrated, the interim or permanent trustee in sequestration. Furthermore, recall of a conjoined arrestment order may be made on application to the sheriff by all the creditors whose debts are being enforced under the order.[52] Application is made to the sheriff court which granted the conjoined arrestment order.[53] The sheriff must grant recall of the conjoined arrestment order if satisfied (i) that the conjoined arrestment order is invalid; or (ii) that all debts and obligations to pay which the order covers are no longer in effect or enforceable by diligence; or (iii) that the debtor's estate has been sequestrated. In granting recall the sheriff has power to make such consequential orders as are appropriate. **29.64**

Where a time to pay order is made in respect of a debt which is being enforced under a conjoined arrestment order, the sheriff making the time to pay order must vary the conjoined arrestment order to exclude that debt from its scope. If the two orders were made in different sheriff courts, the sheriff making the time to pay order intimates it to the other sheriff court which must then vary the conjoined arrestment order.[54] **29.65**

Poinding and Sale

Poinding and sale is a multi-staged diligence which involves the inventorying and valuation of moveable property of the debtor, and it is completed by the removal of goods for sale, the proceeds of which are applied to pay the debt. The Debtors (Scotland) Act 1987 introduced a number of important reforms of this diligence, and in particular gave debtors various rights to protect their interests. Another significant reform which has affected the practical use of the diligence is that the 1987 Act widened the range of goods exempt from the diligence in poindings held in domestic premises. As a consequence of these changes the diligence continues to be used against both personal and commercial debtors, but as a means of recovering debt it is most effective when used in commercial cases. **29.66**

The charge

The diligence of poinding and sale must be preceded by the service on the debtor of a charge for payment, which is a formal request for payment of the debt with a warning that if the debt is not paid within a specified time diligence may proceed against the debtor.[55] The form of charge is set **29.67**

---

[52] 1987 Act, s. 66(1)(b); S.I. 1988 No. 2013, Form 57.
[53] *ibid.* s. 66(1)(a), (2); S.I. 1988 No. 2013, r. 61, Form 56.
[54] *ibid.* s. 9(2)(b).
[55] A charge for payment is also a prerequisite for the diligence of earnings arrestment. However, diligences proceeding on a summary warrant for recovery of taxes do not require the prior service of a charge on the debtor: 1987 Act, s. 90(1), (2).

out in an Act of Sederunt.[56] It is vital that the charge correctly sets out the required details of the parties concerned, and of the debt in respect of which it is served. However, a charge remains valid if it fails to take account of any payments to account already made, or if it otherwise specifies a sum in excess of what remains due.[57] Any special capacity in which a person is charged should be specified in the charge itself. Normally the designation or capacity of a party in a charge will follow that set out in the extract decree.

29.68 The charge is served by a sheriff officer in the presence of one witness.[58] The modes of service are regulated by the general rules for service of writs and court documents. Special rules exist for service of a charge on a person furth of Scotland, and on a person whose whereabouts are unknown.[59] After service of a charge the sheriff officer returns an "execution" or report, which must accurately set out the details of the charge and its service.[60]

29.69 A charge for payment served on a debtor informs him that, if payment is not made within the specified period of charge, certain diligences (including poinding and sale) may proceed against him. The days of charge are 14 days if the debtor is within the United Kingdom and 28 days if he is outwith the United Kingdom or his whereabouts are unknown.[61] It does not appear to be competent to alter the period of the days of charge. In calculating the expiry of the days of charge the day on which it is served is excluded and a poinding may proceed only on the next competent day following the last day of charge.[62] A charge remains valid for two years from the date of its service on the debtor. A further charge may be served but a creditor cannot recover the expenses of any further charge.[63]

Poinding

Goods which may be poinded

29.70 **General.** The general test for determining whether property may be poinded is that only moveable property of the debtor which is in his possession at the time of the poinding, and which is capable of being sold, is subject to the diligence. However, in respect of non-commercial debtors, many types of property of this nature are exempt from poinding by virtue of the provisions of the Debtors (Scotland) Act 1987.

29.71 It follows from general principle that incorporeal property (including debts) may not be poinded,[64] nor may heritable property (including property

---

56 A.S. (Form of Charge for Payment) 1988 (S.I. 1988 No. 2059).

57 In these circumstances the charge is deemed to be good for the sum which is actually due: *Wilson v. Stronach* (1862) 24 D. 271; *Thiem's Trs v. Collie* (1899) 7 S.L.T. 4; *Haughhead Coal Co. v. Gallocher* (1903) 11 S.L.T. 156; *Dickson v. United Dominions Trust Ltd (No. 2)*, 1983 S.L.T. 502.

58 Debtors (Scotland) Act 1838, s. 32.

59 OCR, rr. 5.5, 5.6.

60 A form of the report of a charge is contained in the Court of Session rules (see RCS, Form 16.15-K) but there is no prescribed form in the sheriff court rules.

61 Debtors (Scotland) Act 1987, s. 90(3).

62 Graham Stewart, p. 338. It is thought that the same rule applies in respect of the diligence of earnings arrestment.

63 Debtors (Scotland) Act 1987, s. 90(5)–(7).

64 Bell, *Comm.*, ii, 59, 60; Bell, *Prin.*, para. 2289; *Mackenzie & Co. v. Finlay* (1868) 7 M. 27.

treated as heritable as being a fixture) be poinded. Moreover, only goods in the possession of the debtor may be poinded, though it must be noted that in this context possession includes not just physical possession but also civil possession (*i.e.* where goods though physically in the hands of a third party are deemed still to be in the possession of the debtor).[65] However, a creditor may poind goods in the creditor's own possession.[66] It is also accepted practice that money in the form of currency may not be poinded as it is incapable of being sold.[67]

Goods in disputed ownership. Section 19(2) of the Debtors (Scotland) Act 1987 lays down a presumption that goods in the possession of the debtor are owned by him unless the officer carrying out a poinding knows or ought to know otherwise. Special procedures apply where a third party claims that goods poinded or about to be poinded belong to that party and not to the debtor.[68] Before starting the poinding the officer has a duty to inquire of any person present as to the ownership of goods which he proposes to include in the poinding.[69] The officer must consider any claim that goods do not belong to the debtor. In practice officers tend to include in a poinding goods whose ownership is disputed unless there is clear evidence to show that the debtor is not the owner or part-owner. Where a claim is made that poinded goods do not belong to the debtor this claim must be noted by the officer in the report of the poinding.[70] Where a third party claims that his goods have been included in a poinding, he may apply for release of those goods from the poinding either to the officer or to the sheriff.[71] Such a person may also be able to interdict the granting of a warrant of sale of his goods or the carrying out of a sale under a warrant of sale already granted.[72] **29.72**

Goods in common ownership. Joint property in the strict sense, that is where two or more persons have an indivisible title to the property, may not be poinded in respect of the debts of any owner as an individual.[73] What is loosely referred to as joint property is often a type of common property, that is where each owner has a separate title to a determinate share of the property. As a matter of principle the share of any one common owner in common property is poindable by that owner's creditors. However, prior to the 1987 Act common property was treated as exempt from poinding. This matter is now regulated by section 41 of the 1987 Act which is to the effect that, where goods are owned in common by a debtor and a third party, the goods are poindable but the third party has **29.73**

---

[65] In *MacIver, Applicant*, 1991 S.C.L.R. 870 it was held that a car parked on the road outside the debtor's house could be poinded.

[66] *Lochhead v. Graham* (1883) 11 R. 201.

[67] Maher & Cusine, para. 7.53. Money in the form of foreign currency may be poinded.

[68] Different rules apply where it is claimed that goods are owned in common by the debtor and another person: see discussion at para. 29.74.

[69] Debtors (Scotland) Act 1987, s. 20(2)(c).

[70] 1987 Act, s. 22(2); S.I. 1988 No. 2013, r. 15, Form 9; *Maxwell v. Controller of Clearing House*, 1923 S.L.T. (Sh.Ct.) 137; *Cameron v. Cuthbertson*, 1924 S.L.T. (Sh.Ct.) 67.

[71] Application may be made at any time after the poinding has been completed and before the sale of the goods under warrant: 1987 Act, s. 40(1) (application to the officer), s. 40(2); S.I. 1988 No. 2013, r. 34(1), (2) (application to the sheriff).

[72] *Jack v. Waddell's Trs*, 1918 S.C. 73; H. Burn-Murdoch, *Interdict in the Law of Scotland*, pp. 188–190.

[73] *Fleming v. Twaddle* (1828) 7 S. 92. The situation is different where the debt is one owed by the joint owners in that capacity.

various rights to protect his interest which derive from his title to the goods.[74]

29.74 Where a co-owner finds that his commonly owned goods have been included in a poinding for the debt of another person, he may apply to the sheriff officer who executed the poinding for redemption of the goods. This is done by paying the whole of the debtor's interest in the goods.[75] A release of commonly owned goods on this particular basis may also be made on application to the sheriff, who also has the power to order their release on the grounds of undue harshness which would be caused to a co-owner by the continued inclusion of the goods in the poinding.[76] Where appropriate, a co-owner may also seek release of the goods from a poinding on the basis that the goods are exempt from poinding under section 16 of the 1987 Act.[77] Where goods in common ownership are not redeemed or released from a poinding, and are subsequently sold under warrant, the co-owner is entitled to receive a share of the sale price which corresponds to his own interest in the goods.[78]

29.75 **Mobile homes.** Where a debtor's only or principal residence is a caravan, houseboat or other moveable structure, the property may be poinded but the debtor may apply to the sheriff for a sist of the poinding to allow time to find alternative accommodation. Application may be made at any time up until the granting of warrant of sale.[79]

Goods exempt from poinding under the Debtors (Scotland) Act 1987

29.76 Various types of goods are exempt from poinding under section 16 of the Debtors (Scotland) Act 1987. This section is a key provision of the reforms of the law on poinding and sale which the 1987 Act introduced, and it seeks to protect the debtor and the members of his household by exempting from the diligence various items which are required for their needs. The goods of a debtor exempt under section 16, are as follows:

(1) Clothing: articles of clothing which are reasonably required for his own use or that of any member of his household are exempt from poinding.[80]

(2) Tools of trade: implements and tools of trade which are reasonably required for use by the debtor or a member of his household in respect of a profession, trade or business are exempt from poinding. However, the exemption extends to such goods only to an aggregate value of £500.[81]

(3) Medical aid and equipment: also exempt are medical aids and equipment reasonably required for use of the debtor or any member of his household.[82]

---

[74] *Kinloch v. Barclays Bank plc*, 1995 S.C.L.R. 975 (household effects in a house occupied by wife of debtor as sole tenant held to be owned in common by debtor and wife by virtue of presumption in section 25 of Family Law (Scotland) Act 1985 and poindable as such).

[75] 1987 Act, s. 41(2), (5).

[76] *ibid.* s. 41(3); S.I. 1988 No. 2013, r. 35. See *McCallum, Applicant*, 1990 S.C.L.R. 399.

[77] *ibid* s. 16(4). See further at para. 29.76.

[78] *ibid.* s. 41(7), (8). Where the goods are not sold at a warrant sale or are sold for less than their appraised value, the co-owner's entitlement is to the appropriate share of the appraised value of the goods.

[79] *ibid.* s. 26. A similar application may be made by another person where a mobile home has been poinded and is the only or principal residence of that person.

[80] *ibid.* s. 16(1)(a).

[81] *ibid.* s. 16(1)(b). This amount may be varied by regulation by the Lord Advocate.

[82] *ibid.* s. 16(1)(c).

(4) Books and educational articles: books and other articles which are reasonably required for the education or training of the debtor or any member of his household are likewise exempt from poinding. The exemption applies only to the first £500 in value of such goods.[83]

(5) Children's toys: toys for the use of any child who is a member of the debtor's household are exempt from poinding.[84] It may be noted that in this case there is no need to show reasonable requirement.

(6) Articles for the upbringing of children: articles reasonably required for the care or upbringing of a child who is a member of the debtor's household are exempt from poinding.[85]

(7) Domestic furniture and plenishings: various items of domestic furniture and plenishings are exempt from poinding if they are in a dwelling-house at the time of the poinding, and are reasonably required for use in the dwelling-house by the person who resides there or any member of his household.[86]

Poinding procedure

A poinding is carried out by a sheriff officer who must be accompanied by one witness.[87] A poinding may not be executed on a Sunday, Christmas Day, New Year's Day or Good Friday and must take place within the hours of 8 a.m. to 8 p.m. (unless extension to these hours has been granted by a sheriff).[88] The sheriff officer has power to open shut and lockfast places in order to conduct a poinding but, where the poinding is to take place in a dwelling-house, the sheriff officer must serve a prior notice if it appears that no one, or only a child under the age of 16 is present.[89] **29.77**

Before valuing the goods to be poinded the sheriff officer must exhibit to any person present the warrant to poind and the execution of the charge. Demand is made for payment from the debtor or anyone authorised to act for him. The officer must also make enquiries of those present as to the ownership of goods which are to be included in the poinding.[90] The poinding as such begins with the valuation of the debtor's goods. The valuation is made by the sheriff officer except where it is necessary to use the services of a professional valuer.[91] Goods are to be valued at the price they would be likely to fetch if sold on the open market.[92] The valuation should proceed on the basis that reasonable steps would be taken to obtain a reasonable price for the goods by an appropriate means of sale.[93] Any unusual basis for valuation must be set out in the poinding schedule and subsequent report of the poinding.[94] Where the **29.78**

---

83 1987 Act, s. 16(1)(d). This amount may be varied by regulation by the Lord Advocate.

84 *ibid.* s. 16(1)(e).

85 *ibid.* s. 16(1)(f).

86 The list of types of article covered by this exemption is set out in s. 16(2) of the 1987 Act. See, *e.g. Irvine v. Strathclyde R.C.*, 1994 S.C.L.R. 388.

87 1987 Act, s. 20(3).

88 *ibid.* s. 17(1),(2).

89 *ibid.* s. 87(2)(a); s. 18(1). The requirement of prior notice may be dispensed with in certain circumstances: *ibid.* s. 18(2).

90 *ibid.* s. 20(2).

91 *ibid.* s. 20(4).

92 *ibid.* s. 20(4).

93 *MacIver, Applicant*, 1991 S.C.L.R. 870.

94 *Lombard North Central Ltd v. Wilson*, Glasgow Sh. Ct, Oct. 7, 1980, unreported (motor vehicles appraised only for their scrap value).

nature of the goods is such that their value is likely to deteriorate because they are perishable or seasonal in nature, application may be made to the sheriff for the immediate sale of the goods.[95] Goods are to be included in a poinding only to the extent required to recover the total sum due if the goods were sold at their appraised value.[96] While a poinding is being conducted another creditor who produces a warrant to poind may demand to be conjoined in the poinding, in which case the officer must complete the poinding to the extent required to recover the debts of both creditors.[97]

29.79 On completion of the poinding the officer and witness sign a schedule which is given to, or left for, the debtor.[98] Where there is danger that the poinded goods may be removed or damaged, application may be made to the sheriff for an order for steps to be taken to ensure the safety of the goods.[99] In certain circumstances the sheriff officer may remove the goods to protect their security in the absence of an order by the sheriff.[1]

29.80 A report of the poinding must be submitted to the sheriff within 14 days of the date of execution of the poinding.[2] The sheriff may refuse to receive a report of poinding on the grounds that it was not submitted in good time, or that it has not been signed by the officer or witness. Where the sheriff refuses to receive a report of poinding the refusal (which has the effect of nullifying the poinding) must be intimated to the debtor (and the person in possession of the goods).[3]

Protection of the debtor

29.81 Various provisions of the Debtors (Scotland) Act 1987 protect the interests of the debtor who is subject to the diligence of poinding and sale.[4] They are as follows:

(1) The debtor has the right to redeem poinded goods by paying their appraised value to the sheriff officer. This right may be exercised within 14 days of the poinding.[5]
(2) Goods which have been included in a poinding may be released on the basis that they were exempt under section 16 of the 1987 Act. A debtor, common owner of the goods, or the party in possession of them may apply to the sheriff within 14 days of the poinding for the release of the goods from the poinding under this ground.[6]

---

95 1987 Act, s. 21(1)(b); S.I. 1988 No. 2013, r. 13.

96 *ibid.* s. 19(1); ***McKinnon v. Hamilton*** (1866) 4 M. 852; ***Hamilton v. Emslie*** (1860) 7 M. 173, 176. For discussion of some of the difficulties arising, see D. I. Nichols, 1989 S.L.T. (News) 386; G. Maher, 1990 S.L.T. (News) 17.

97 1987 Act, s. 21(8), (9).

98 *ibid.* s. 20(6). The form of the schedule is set out in S.I. 1988 No. 2013, Form 5.

99 *ibid.* s. 21(1)(a); S.I. 1988 No. 2013, r. 12(1), Form 6.

1 *ibid.* s. 20(7).

2 The form of report is S.I. 1988 No. 2013, Form 9. A poinding is executed on the date the poinding schedule is delivered to or left for the debtor: 1987 Act, s. 21(7).

3 1987 Act, s. 22(3)–(5).

4 A poinding of goods of an entitled spouse in terms of the Matrimonial Homes (Family Protection) (Scotland) Act 1981 may be challenged in certain circumstances to protect the position of the non-entitled spouse: 1981 Act, s. 11.

5 1987 Act, s. 21(4). See also s. 20(6)(d). The exercise of this right must be mentioned in the report of the poinding or separately reported to the sheriff.

6 *ibid.* s. 16(4); S.I. 1988 No. 2013, r. 8, Form 4.

(3) Within 14 days of the poinding, the debtor or any person in possession of the poinded goods may apply for release of the goods from the poinding on the ground that it would be unduly harsh to continue to include the goods in the poinding, or for the goods to be sold under warrant.[7]

(4) A debtor may apply to the sheriff for recall of the poinding at any time before warrant to sell the poinded goods has been applied for.[8] Recall may be granted if it is established that:
(a) it would be unduly harsh in the circumstances if a warrant for the sale of the poinded goods were to be granted; or
(b) the aggregate appraised values of the goods is substantially below the aggregate of the prices they would be likely to fetch if they were sold on the open market; or
(c) the likely aggregate proceeds of sale on the poinded goods would not exceed the likely expenses of the sale (excluding expenses of the charge and poinding).

(5) At any time prior to goods being sold under warrant a debtor may apply for declarator by the sheriff that a poinding is invalid or has ceased to have effect. The sheriff may also make such a declarator *ex proprio motu*.[9] It is not a ground for declarator of invalidity that goods exempt under section 16 of the 1987 Act have been included in the poinding.[10]

Effect of poinding

Effect on use and removal of goods. A poinding of goods does not affect the right of the debtor or party in possession to use them in the normal way, but this is subject to a general prohibition on the removal of the goods from the premises where the poinding took place.[11] Where poinded goods have been removed without authorisation, the sheriff on application by the creditor may order their return, or that further goods should be poinded.[12] Where poinded goods have been wilfully damaged or destroyed, the matter may be dealt with as a contempt of court.[13] Where the debtor is at fault, the sheriff may authorise a further poinding of goods.[14] Where a third party wilfully damages or destroys goods which he knows are subject to a poinding, he may be ordered to consign a sum equal to their appraised value in court.[15] **29.82**

Poinding and competing rights. Poindings rank *inter se* according to the date of the sale of the goods under warrant: if there is no sale, they rank according to the date of their respective executions.[16] A poinding is cut **29.83**

---

[7] 1987 Act, s. 23(1); S.I. 1988 No. 2013, r. 6, Form 10.
[8] *ibid.* s. 24(3). Procedure is governed by S.I. 1988 No. 2013, r. 17.
[9] *ibid.* s. 24(1); S.I. 1988 No. 2013, r. 17, Form 11.
[10] *ibid.* s. 24(2).
[11] The debtor or person in possession of poinded goods may apply for authorisation from the sheriff to move the goods to another location (1987 Act, s. 28(1); S.I. 1988 No. 2013, r. 20). Alternatively goods may be removed with the written consent of the creditor or officer of court on his behalf (1987 Act, s. 28(1)). Where goods are removed in these circumstances they remain poinded but may be re-poinded in their new location. This procedure allows the removed goods to be subject to a separate poinding procedure, which resolves problems that might arise if goods are moved from a location in one sheriffdom to a location in another.
[12] 1987 Act, s. 28(4), (6).
[13] *ibid.* s. 29(1).
[14] *ibid.* s. 29(2). The sheriff may also authorise the revaluation of damaged goods.
[15] *ibid.* s. 29(4), (5).
[16] Graham Stewart, pp. 365–366.

down if executed within 60 days before the sequestration of the debtor's estate or the liquidation of the debtor, but the expenses of the poinding are a preferred debt against the estate.[17] A poinding executed outwith this 60 days limit provides a preference to the proceeds of the sale where the sale takes place after the debtor's sequestration or liquidation.[18] By analogy with the law on the relationship between an arrestment and a floating charge, it appears that a poinding not followed by a warrant sale, does not confer a preference on the creditor where the floating charge was created prior to the poinding and crystallised prior to a warrant sale, but that a poinding does provide a preference for the creditor if it was executed prior to the creation of the floating charge even if the charge crystallised prior to a warrant sale.[19]

29.84 **Prohibition on second poindings.** The general rule is that, where a poinding has taken place, another poinding in the same premises to enforce the same debt is not competent except in relation to goods subsequently brought on to the premises.[20] It may be noted that this rule is subject to various exceptions.[21]

29.85 **Duration of poinding.** A poinding comes to an end after one year from the date of its execution unless an application is made for warrant to sell the goods or for an extension of the period of the poinding.[22] An application for extension of a poinding may be granted by a sheriff on the ground (1) that, if the poinding is extended the debtor is likely to comply with an agreement to pay off the sums due, or (2) that an extension is necessary to allow the creditor to complete the diligence (in which case the creditor must show that he is not responsible for the circumstances which caused the delay in applying for the warrant of sale).[23] More than one extension may be granted.[24] The period of duration of a poinding is interrupted when an interim or full time to pay order is in effect.[25]

Warrant sale

29.86 **Application for warrant.** To complete the diligence it is necessary to apply for a warrant to sell the goods.[26] Procedure is governed by rule 26 of the Act of Sederunt which allows for objection to be made by the debtor.[27] A hearing will be held to deal with the application if the debtor makes an

---

[17] Bankruptcy (Scotland) Act 1985, s. 37(4); Insolvency Act 1986, s. 185. Note also the possible interaction of these provisions with those on the equalisation effect of apparent insolvency.

[18] *Clark v. Hinde, Milne & Co.* (1884) 12 R. 347; *Bendy Bros Ltd v. M'Alister* (1910) 26 Sh.Ct.Rep. 152. For discussion of this point, see Gretton, para. 238.

[19] See discussion on arrestments at paras 29.32 *et seq*.

[20] 1987 Act, s. 25.

[21] These are set out in the 1987 Act, ss. 9(12); 23(2); 28(1), (2); 28(6); 29(2); 40(5); 41(6).

[22] 1987 Act,. s. 27. For application for warrant to sell poinded goods, see para. 29.86.

[23] *ibid.* s. 27(2). Procedure is governed by S.I. 1988 No. 2013, r. 19.

[24] *ibid.* s. 27(3).

[25] *ibid.* ss. 8(3), 9(9). Interruption also occurs when a poinding is sisted under s. 26 of the 1987 Act (poinding of a mobile home).

[26] If the poinding proceeded under a summary warrant, that summary warrant itself contains a warrant to sell and no further application is necessary.

[27] During the time an application has been made and is being considered and when warrant is granted, the poinding remains in force even after the expiry of the period of one year from its execution. Where an application is refused the poinding remains in force until any issue of appeal against refusal has not been insisted upon or has been finally dealt with: 1987 Act, s. 27(5).

objection or, even if there is no objection, where the sheriff is minded to refuse the application. The sheriff may refuse application for a warrant to sell on the ground that (1) the poinding is invalid or has ceased to have effect[28]; (2) the aggregate of the appraised values of the poinded goods is substantially below the aggregate of the prices they would be likely to fetch if sold on open market; (3) the likely aggregate proceeds of sale of the poinded goods would not exceed the expenses to be incurred in applying for the warrant and in executing its terms; or (4) the granting of the warrant would be unduly harsh in the circumstances.[29]

Content of warrant. The warrant of sale contains the general arrangements for carrying out the sale of poinded goods. These include the location of sale, which will take place in an auction room unless the debtor and all occupiers give consent in writing to its being held in a dwelling-house.[30] A sale may take place in premises other than a dwelling-house or auction room if the occupiers agree or if it is too costly to remove the goods for sale.[31] The warrant also specifies the officer who is to carry out the various steps involved in removing the goods for sale and arranging the sale.[32] The officer has the duty to intimate to the debtor a copy of the warrant and of details for the particular arrangements made for the removal of the goods and sale. The warrant also grants authority to the officer to make more particular arrangements for carrying out the sale. **29.87**

An auctioneer is not specifically appointed in the warrant of sale unless the sale is to take place in premises other than an auction room.[33] The officer may be appointed as auctioneer if the appraised value of the goods is £1,000 or less. The details of the warrant or of the arrangements made thereunder may be varied on application by the creditor or officer.[34] The sheriff may refuse to grant an application for variation only if (1) the poinding is invalid or has ceased to have effect, or (2) the proposed variation is unsuitable. After a warrant of sale has been granted the creditor may cancel the arrangements made for sale in order to give effect to an agreement with the debtor for paying off the debt.[35] The creditor may make a cancellation under this provision on no more than two occasions. **29.88**

The warrant sale. The sale is held as a sale by auction. There does not require to be an upset price nor a reserve price, but any reserve price (which need not be disclosed) cannot be greater than the appraised value of the goods. A bid for the goods may not be made by or on behalf of the **29.89**

---

[28] 1987 Act, s. 30(2). It is not a basis for this ground that the poinding included goods exempt from poinding under section 16 of the 1987 Act: s. 30(5).

[29] The sheriff may apply grounds (1), (2), and (3) *ex proprio motu* or on application by the debtor. Ground (4) may be applied only if the debtor has made an objection on that basis.

[30] 1987 Act, s. 32(1); S.I. 1988 No. 2013, r. 27. The sheriff has power to refuse to grant a warrant where consent has not been given to a sale in a dwelling-house and the likely proceeds of the sale would not exceed those of removing the goods and carrying out the sale: s. 32(2), (3).

[31] *ibid.* s. 32(4), (5).

[32] The warrant confers on the officer warrant to open shut and lockfast places for purposes of executing its terms: s. 31(2)(c).

[33] 1987 Act, s. 31(3).

[34] *ibid.* s. 35(1), (2). Variation on the date of removal of the goods and date of sale may in certain circumstances be varied without application: s. 35(9), (10).

[35] *ibid.* s. 36. The agreement must be reported to the sheriff as soon as is reasonably practicable. While the agreement is in effect the date of sale is extended by six months.

debtor, or by or on behalf of the officer who carried out the poinding or made the arrangements for the sale, but it may be made by the creditor or co-owner of the goods.[36] Where the goods are sold, the debt is reduced by an amount which is the greater of the price received or the appraised value of the goods. Where goods remain unsold, the amount of their appraised value is credited to the debt and the ownership of the goods passes to the creditor.[37] The officer in charge of the sale has the duty of dispersing the proceeds of sale. Any surplus is to be paid to the debtor and is consigned in court if the debtor cannot be found.[38]

29.90 Within 14 days after the sale the officer must submit a report in the prescribed form to the sheriff.[39] The report is remitted to the auditor of court. On receiving the auditor's report, the sheriff makes an order in respect of the balance owing by or to the debtor, which order is intimated to the debtor by the sheriff clerk.[40] The sheriff has power in certain circumstances to modify the balance due or to declare the poinding and sale void.[41]

Inhibition in Execution

29.91 The diligence of inhibition may be used in execution of a sheriff court decree, including decrees in summary cause and small claims actions,[42] but not in execution of a summary warrant.[43] Procedure is by way of petition to the Court of Session for letters of inhibition, the decree being the basis for the granting of the letters.[44]

Adjudication

29.92 Adjudication is a diligence which may be used to enforce a debt constituted by decree (including a deemed decree based on documents registered in the books of court), but not one based on a summary warrant,[45] or a liquid document of debt.[46] Adjudication is used against the debtor's heritable property as well as against moveable property not subject to other diligences (*e.g.* various types of intellectual property). Procedure is by way of an action in the Court of Session.[47]

---

[36] *Shiell v. Guthrie's Trs* (1874) 1 R. 1083; *Wright v. Buchanan*, 1917 S.C. 73; Mock Auctions Act 1961; A.S. (Messengers-at-Arms and Sheriff Officers Rules) 1991 (S.I. 1991 No. 1397), r. 30; 1987 Act, s. 37(5).

[37] 1987 Act, s. 37(6). Special rules apply where goods pass to the creditor after a sale held in premises belonging to the debtor: s. 37(7).

[38] *ibid.* s. 38.

[39] *ibid.* s. 39; S.I. 1988 No. 2013, r. 31, Form 26.

[40] *ibid.* s. 39(5).

[41] *ibid.* s. 39(5); S.I. 1988 No. 2013, r. 32.

[42] G. L. Gretton, *The Law of Inhibition and Adjudication* (2nd ed., 1996), pp. 8–9.

[43] *Commissioners of Customs and Excise, Applicants*, 1992 S.L.T. 11.

[44] For discussion of the procedure for obtaining letters of inhibition on the dependence of a sheriff court action, see paras 11.37, 11.38.

[45] *Commissioners of Customs and Excise, Applicants*, 1992 S.L.T. 11.

[46] 1987 Act, s. 101. Adjudication is competent where the debt is a *debitum fundi*.

[47] See, further, Gretton, *Law of Inhibition and Adjudication*, Chap. 13. The Scottish Law Commission has subjected the existing law of adjudication to critical examination: see Scottish Law Commission, *Adjudication for Debt and Related Matters*, Discussion Paper No. 78 (1988).

INDEX